THE SECOND 50 YEARS

A Reference Manual For Senior Citizens

WALTER J. CHENEY

WILLIAM J. DIEHM

FRANK E. SEELEY

PARAGON HOUSE
NEW YORK

Thank You

To Dotha, a very special person in my life, my friend, wife of 36 years, mother of our two daughters, Marla Jean and Cori Marie, and the one who provides trust, understanding, support, and encouragement. To Bill and Frank for making such important contributions. To my mother, Mary Cheney, now 89, for all those times I forgot to thank her.--Walter J. Cheney

My wife, Ada Carrol Diehm, has been my faithful companion for 50 years. She has been the mother to our six children, keeper of the home, and special nurse for me--sustaining, supporting, and encouraging. Under her inspiration, I have written. So, to her, I dedicate my portion of this book.--William J. Diehm

I want to thank Walter Cheney for the opportunity to put some of my experience and training to work in the preparation of this book. This creative man has helped to open some new doors, including that of computer use, that makes it ever more enjoyable to plan ahead. We hope the reader who finds our book will have the same effect.--Frank E. Seeley

The authors wish to thank all the wonderful people at Paragon House whose efforts and enthusiasm helped make *The Second 50 Years* happen. To the decision makers that saw the potential of this book and committed Paragon's resources: Michael Giampaoli, Director; Ken Stuart, Editor-in-Chief; Tom Miller, Marketing Director; and Leslie Rowe, Sales Manager. A special thanks to PJ Dempsey, Senior Editor, for her recognition of the book's possibilities, the daily consultations, advice, and support; and to assistant editor Christopher O'Connell. To Sara Perrin and Walter Harvey, many thanks for helping with distribution and advertising. To Susan Newman for her magnificent cover design and to the others in the Art Department, Howard Grossman and Susan Olinsky, who contributed in this effort. To all the production and manufacturing people who have such important roles: especially Ed Paige, Carla Sommerstein, Felecia Monroe, and Robert Aronds. Again kudos to Leslie Rowe and all his sales staff, including Sloan Howard of Special Sales.

We must not forget Dr. Michael G. Dempsey for his discerning critique and the excellent work of Mary Dorian, copyeditor; Reg Lansberry, proofreader; and Gail Liss, indexer.

Published in the United States by:
PARAGON HOUSE PUBLISHERS
90 Fifth Avenue
New York, N.Y. 10011

Library of Congress Cataloging-in-Publication Data
Cheney, Walter J., 1926-
    The second 50 years : a reference manual for senior citizens / Walter J. Cheney, William J. Diehm, Frank E. Seeley.--1st ed.
    p.   cm.
    Includes index.
    ISBN 1-55778-531-7 : $21.95
    1. Aged--United States--Handbooks, manuals, etc. 2. Aged--Services for--United States--Handbooks, manuals, etc. 3. Aged--Health and hygiene--United States--Handbooks, manuals, etc. I. Diehm, William J. 1919- II. Seeley, Frank E., 1921- III. Title. IV. Title: Second Fifty Years.
HQ1064.U5C44 1992
305.26'0973--dc20
                                                                                    91-42339
                                                                                    CIP

First edition, 1992
Manufactured in the United States of America

Words from the authors to you

Grow old along with me!
The best is yet to be,
The last of life,
For which the first was made.

Robert Browning

Whether you are retired, or just a beginning senior citizen, you may find that there are, or will be, some major changes in your life. You may also realize that the second 50 years offers the opportunities you have dreamed of for so long. You learn that you now are at the time in your life where "the best is yet to be" and when you can choose what's best for you.

These years offer freedom to pursue interests unhampered by the demands of a job and its day-to-day responsibilities. You can concentrate upon those things that please you. There is no end to the creative and useful activities you can pursue upon retirement. We have many new options to explore like travel, meeting new friends, rounds of golf, fishing, RV trips, a cruise, a chance to enjoy one's hobbies, or just a drive through the country we like best. If we wish, we can go back to school to learn about a special interest, to graduate from high school, or to get that college degree you have always wanted. We can also offer our time, expertise, and experience by volunteering to help those less fortunate and in need. Others, who may miss the work environment, can go back to work in some capacity just to keep active.

Yet retirement can create anxieties--about maintaining a way of life, about financial and personal security, and about physical well-being. These anxieties can prevent you from fully enjoying these years, unless you approach them thoughtfully. We believe that a good understanding of your changing lifestyle, opportunities, and potential physical problems (and what you can do to avoid them) can lead to an increased peace of mind.

As seniors ourselves, we came to realize that problems become less formidable if we educate ourselves on the many conditions we face as we grow older. As we age, the waning life force along with the enemies of life present significantly different physical problems. In addition, many of us will face changes in living arrangements. Often it is traumatic to move from a secure home to a retirement community; it can be even more devastating for some people to be placed in a nursing home. At this time of life, our earning power is usually reduced and we begin to rely on income from Social Security, pensions, investments, or government support by food stamps and welfare. Insurance needs change as employers no longer provide medical coverage; so as older people we need to deal with Medicare, Medigap, Medi-

caid, and long-term care obligations. Add to this list of problems a growing concern for safety and security when we become frail. We also must consider the fraud perpetrated on older persons and abuse of the elderly.

All these factors make it desirable that we be informed in order to adequately face our problems and take advantage of our opportunities. Yet when we reach "Senior Citizen" status the information on many of our concerns is not readily available or it is difficult to find or to understand. When we realized this situation, it created for us the opportunity to offer you information you can use.

In providing this manual, we methodically gathered and sifted data that we felt were important. We digested the data, excluded much of the chaff, and added our own personal knowledge and experience. We, as seniors, approached each subject from a senior citizen's point of view. We were particularly concerned with showing you positive hope in dealing with grim matters. We have written each article with special attention to making it clear, friendly, logical, comprehensive, and highly readable.

As we said, we gathered data from many sources. Some sources we have acknowledged in the articles. Yet the information we offer came from many sources too numerous to mention. We feel it is our obligation to acknowledge that "your government," with all its failings, attempts to provide you with considerable research and information on the many problems that we all face as we grow older. The U.S. House of Representatives Select Committee on Aging needs special mention for their continuous efforts to solve many problems of older persons.

We could use your help!
We anticipate that as the years go by we will update the information and provide revised editions of this work. We would appreciate receiving any information you feel would help our fellow senior citizens and we will include it, if possible, in our revisions. Please send it to:

> Writers Consortium
> c/o Paragon House
> 90 Fifth Avenue
> New York, NY 10011

We hope this manual will help you face retirement with the greatest strength and that you will find happiness and fulfillment in spite of the adversities of life. Our very best to you.

> Walter Cheney
> William Diehm
> Frank Seeley

2 CONTENTS

HEALTH PROBLEMS

Organizations for people over 50

Getting involved!

American Association of Retired Persons (AARP)
601 E. Street, N.W.
Washington, D.C. 20049
(202) 434-2277

The American Association of Retired Persons (AARP) is the largest organization of Americans age 50 and over. AARP was organized in 1958 as a nonprofit corporation for the purpose of promoting the interests of older persons. AARP is a strong legislative advocate for older people on both the state and federal levels and develops local community programs. On the national level AARP representatives are active in representing seniors on many issues including Social Security, Medicare, long-term care, health, housing, age discrimination, elderly abuse, crime prevention, and consumer concerns.

Membership services available include:

* group health insurance program
* Medicare supplement plans
* nonprofit mail-order pharmacies
* auto/homeowners insurance programs
* Amoco Motor club--emergency road service
* travel services--information on escorted tours, hosted cruises, and apartment living abroad
* an investment program from Scudder--no-load mutual funds
* list of service providers and discounts available to members at participating lodging, airlines, sightseeing, and car and RV rental companies
* a Federal Credit Union--CD's, VISA cards

Local community programs include:

* driver education "55 Alive/Mature Driving"--a classroom refresher course for mature drivers
* crime prevention programs that teach preventative measures
* IRS-trained AARP volunteers provide help at tax time
* one-on-one support for newly widowed persons (at 200 locations)
* volunteer talent bank--matches people with appropriate volunteer opportunities
* Medicare/Medicaid assistance in dealing with insurance complexities
* Widowed persons service

Membership: 30 million; 3,700 local chapters nationwide. Publications include: a monthly AARP news *Bulletin;* a bimonthly magazine, *Modern Maturity;* and many free booklets on finances, housing, health, taxes, consumer rights, and more. Membership in AARP is open to those age 50 or older and costs $5 per year.

Older Women's League (OWL)
730 11th Street, N.W. Suite 300
Washington, D.C. 20001
(202) 783-6686

The Older Women's League (OWL) is the first national grassroots membership organization to focus exclusively on women as they age. Founded in 1980, OWL is a non-profit organization that works forcefully to provide mutual support for its members, to achieve economic and social equity, and to improve the image and status of older women. These goals are achieved by working for positive life changes, conducting research, and educating the public and policy makers.

OWL has played a key leadership role in instituting public policy initiatives around pension reform, health insurance continuation, support for spouses of those institutionalized in nursing homes, and in the establishment of "National Family Caregivers Week." Through speak-outs, books, think-tank reports called Gray Papers, research reports, annual Mother's Day campaigns, radio and television appearances, videotapes, and Congressional testimony OWL has expanded the audience of those concerned about the needs of mid-life and older women far beyond the women themselves.

OWL's national agenda:

❶ to protect Social Security
❷ pension reform for women
❸ access to healthcare for all
❹ support for caregivers
❺ access to jobs for older women and fairness in the workplace
❻ challenging budget cuts affecting older women
❼ to promote planning to stay in control to the end of life and to die with dignity

OWL membership benefits:

✿ free subscription to OWL *Observer,* the organization's newspaper
✿ membership discount on all OWL publications, including manuals, tabloids, brochures, and analytical papers, the OWL *Gray Papers*
✿ OWL Powerline, weekly taped messages informing OWL members of what is happening on Capitol Hill
✿ eligibility for five supplemental insurance plans: long-term care, excess major medical, Medicare supplement, hospital indemnity, and group term life
✿ self-sufficiency form, to assess how secure you will be as you age
✿ participation in local and state activities through chapter membership

Membership: 20,000; 120 chapters in 37 states. Membership $20 including $10 national annual fees. For information on local chapters and about OWL publications contact the National OWL office.

> **Friendship improves happiness and abates misery,**
> **by the doubling of our joy and the dividing of our grief.**
> Cicero (106-43 B.C.)

The Gray Panthers
1424 16th Street, N.W.
Washington, D.C. 20036
(202) 387-3111

The Gray Panthers is a social activist organization with members of all ages working to create a society where one can live with dignity from birth to death. The organization was founded in 1970 by Maggie Kuhn when she was 65 years of age along with five friends who were forced to retire.

Over the years, Gray Panthers
* led the successful fight against forced retirement at age 65;
* exposed shocking nursing home abuse that led to convictions and tough new laws;
* helped convince the FDA to monitor and regulate the hearing aid industry for fraudulent practices;
* mobilized hundreds of thousands to fight--and beat--many plans to increase military spending while axing programs such as Medicare and Medicaid.

Besides many other social activities the Gray Panthers are fighting for:
✔ a National Health System and expanded healthcare programs
✔ housing alternatives for those in need
✔ preservation of rent control and prevention of evictions of people over 65
✔ changes in local zoning laws to allow shared living for non-related people--preventing homelessness for thousands
✔ government support for safe and decent housing for all Americans
✔ elimination of ageism, the categorizing and segregating of people according to age, depriving us all of the rich experience of interacting with other generations
✔ preservation of Social Security funds and cost of living adjustments for recipients
✔ greater rights for the disabled
✔ world peace and a better life for people of every age

Membership: 70,000; 120 local networks in 40 states. Publications: *Network* ($15/yr)--a quarterly newspaper, *Healthwatch* ($12/yr)--a bimonthly update on health issues, and *Washington Report* ($12/yr)--a bimonthly summary of Washington-based issues and actions relevant to Gray Panther concerns. For further information write or call the national office. Local groups choose their issues depending upon the needs of the community.

National Council of Senior Citizens (NCSC)
925 15th Street, N.W.
Washington, D.C. 20005
(202) 347-8800

The National Council of Senior Citizens (NCSC) is an advocacy organization, dedicated to the belief that America's elderly, like America's youth, are worthy of the best that this nation can give. NCSC was founded in 1961, born in the struggle for Medicare, its first successful legislative achievement on behalf of seniors. In Washington it works to preserve Social Security, protect Medicare and Medicaid, expand job opportunities for people over 50, and to save senior centers, nutrition programs, and needed services for older Americans.

Membership services available include:

* supplemental Medicare insurance
* in-hospital insurance for people under 65 (group health insurance)
* automobile insurance
* prescription drug service
* senior travel and tour services
* discounts on motels and rental cars

State and local groups work to:

* prevent doctors from charging more than the Medicare-assigned rate
* open up access to nursing homes and demand strict regulation of those homes
* create "lifeline" utility rates for the elderly
* lower prescription drug costs for Medicare patients
* build decent, affordable senior housing
* sponsor local programs that make health care more affordable and accessible to NCSC members
* win senior discounts on buses, subways, and trains
* provide adult care and other supportive services to help older people remain in their own homes

Membership: 4.5 million; 4,800 senior citizen clubs. Provides a monthly newspaper *Senior Citizens News*. Membership in NCSC is open to those 50 or older and costs $12 individual ($16 family) per year.

> **The only way to have a friend**
> **is to be one.**
> Emerson (1803-1883)

National Council on the Aging, Inc. (NCOA)
600 Maryland Avenue, S.W.
Washington, D.C. 20024
(202) 479-1200

The National Council on the Aging, Inc. (NCOA) is the nation's leading resource for professionals serving the aged. Since 1950, NCOA has provided training, information, and technical assistance to those serving America's older men and women. NCOA staff appear before national, state, and local legislative bodies in support of a national long-term care program, enhanced resources for social services, better housing, and improved income and health benefits for older adults.

Professional membership benefits include:

* contact with other professionals in the aging network
* free subscription to *Perspective on Aging*
* access to timely and practical research, publications, and programs
* a strong public policy voice in Washington and across the country
* free subscription to *Current Literature on Aging*

Members have the opportunity to affiliate with any of the following sub-groups that provide specialized newsletters, assistance, legislative advocacy, and ongoing program development:
❶ NAOWES--Nat'l Association of Older Workers Employment Services
❷ NCRA--Nat'l Center on Rural Aging
❸ NIAD--Nat'l Institute on Adult Daycare
❹ NICLC--Nat'l Institute on Community-based Long-term Care
❺ NISC--Nat'l Institute on Senior Centers
❻ NISH--Nat'l Institute on Senior Housing
❼ NVOILA--Nat'l Voluntary Organizations for Independent Living for the Aging
❽ NIHPOA--Nat'l Institute on Health Promotion for Older Adults

Membership is open to those providing service to the aging such as social workers, healthcare professionals, gerontologists, adult care providers, senior housing specialists, volunteers, and others. Any individual may contact the NCOA for information on available resources in your area. Membership--individual $60, full-time retirees, $30 per year.

National Alliance of Senior Citizens, Inc.
2525 Wilson Boulevard
Arlington, VA 22201
(703) 528-4380

The National Alliance of Senior Citizens, Inc. is a non-profit membership organization dedicated to the advancement and preservation of the dignity and rights of working and retired Americans age 45 and over. Goals are accomplished through lobbying in Congress, making sure members' voices are heard on key issues concerning them. NASC conducts polls among the membership to understand their public concerns, and takes these concerns to Congress for action.

NASC accomplishments:
* first to oppose the high-tax, low-benefit Medicare Catastrophic Protection Act
* led the ongoing effort to bring genuine reform to the Social Security program
* leader in gaining repeal of mandatory retirement age
* leading advocate of responsible healthcare reform
* leadership in reform of criminal justice reform

NASC benefits:
* discount prescriptions, vitamins, and minerals
* discounts on car rentals, lodgings, moving expenses
* an automobile club
* best prices on new cars
* travel services
* access to the NASC Classic Visa card
* insured or non-insured membership

Membership: 2 million. Costs: Non-insured--$10 single, $15 couple. Insured membership--inquire. National Alliance of Senior Citizens, 2525 Wilson Boulevard, Arlington, VA 22201; (703) 528-4380. Provides *The Senior Guardian*--an issue-oriented newsletter.

National Association of Retired Federal Employees
1533 New Hampshire Avenue, N.W.
Washington, D.C. 20036-1279
(202) 234-0832

The National Association of Retired Federal Employees (NARFE) is a national membership organization comprised of civilian employees, retirees, survivors, and spouses. By lobbying Congress to protect current federal retirement systems, NARFE ensures the government will attract and retain a competent workforce, and will deliver the retirement benefits earned by its employees now--and into the next century.

Specific objectives include:
* sponsor and support legislation to protect the earned benefits and general welfare of its members;
* oppose legislation that adversely affects member retirement and health benefit programs;
* kindle public recognition and appreciation for government service;
* align with organizations to accomplish similar legislative goals;
* inform members about legislative issues that impact their lives, primarily retirement income and healthcare security;
* strengthen the political influence of current and future federal retirees through NARFE-PAC, a political action committee;
* work in partnership with the Office of Personnel Management to answer questions related to retirement benefits;
* encourage members to contribute to the welfare of their communities.

Benefits of membership include:
* assertive representation on Capitol Hill to protect federal employees' retirement benefits;
* liaison with the Office of Personnel Management to assist annuitants and survivors;
* united network of support with other federal employees and retirees;
* opportunities for leadership, political action, and community service;
* health, life, auto, and home insurance programs;
* NARFE VISA and MasterCard credit card program;
* travel discounts through NARFE-PERKS.

Chapters:
* lobby state and local representatives;
* offer pre-retirement counseling;
* assist members in securing health benefits and annuities;
* staff federal retiree service centers;
* raise funds for medical research;
* elect delegates.

Membership: 500,000; 1,700 chapters, 53 federations of chapters, 10 regions, and governed by an elective leadership. National dues $15 per year. Chapter dues $3-$10. Provides monthly magazine, *Retirement Life,* the prime news source for information on federal income and healthcare security issues.

National Association for Retired Credit Union People
P.O. Box 391
Madison, WI 52701
(608) 238-4286

The National Association for Retired Credit Union People is a non-profit corporation affiliated with the Credit Union National Association, the CUNA Mutual Insurance Group, and your credit union. NARCP was organized in 1978 by retired credit union leaders to help credit union members age 50 or older to better obtain financial services and to extend the benefits of credit union membership to retirees. NARCUP helps you save money on consumer, financial, travel, and insurance services.

NARCUP membership is open to U.S. residents who meet at least one of the following qualifications:

1 Retirees who are or were credit union members (and their spouses), or

2 Individuals who are credit union members and are at least age 50 (and their spouses).

NARCUP benefits or services available:
* Medi Mail--a nationally recognized discount pharmacy
* accident insurance
* Eye Care plan (optional plan)
* hotel and car rental discounts
* NARCUP motoring plan
* emergency cash service
* discounted travel packages and tours plus travel service
* eligible to purchase Medicare supplemental, whole life insurance
* reduced rate on Car/Puter Computerized car pricing

Membership: N/A; Dues: First year $12. Three-year enrollment $23. Provides a quarterly magazine *Prime Times,* a NARCUP *Newsletter* and *Everybody's Money*--credit union money management magazine--extra at $3 per year.

Mature Outlook
6001 N. Clark Street
Chicago, IL 60660-9977
1-800-336-6330

Mature Outlook is an organization sponsored by the country's largest retailer--Sears. It specializes in discounts on products and services in its stores, plus many other benefits for people over 50.

Some of the benefits include:
* mail discount pharmacy
* discounts on eye glasses
* no-fee traveler's checks
* $5,000 accident insurance
* discounts on hotel rooms
* discount on car rentals
* automotive service: coupon book redeemable at Sears Automotive Centers
* discount coupons from Sears-- on regular and sale-price items
* Travel Alert--for domestic and international tours, cruises, and trips (these are last-minute unsold space and cancellations at bargain prices)
* 10 percent meal discount at Holiday Inn restaurants.
* 10 percent discount on membership charge for Allstate Motor Club.

Membership: 1 million plus. Dues: $9.95 includes spouse. Publications include: *Mature Outlook* magazine every other month. *Mature Outlook Newsletter* sent in alternating months.

The Retired Officers Association
201 N. Washington Street
Alexandria, VA 22314-2549
1-800-245-TROA

The Retired Officers Association (TROA) is an independent non-profit, service organization that was founded in 1929. Membership in TROA is open to all men and women who are--or ever have been--commissioned or warrant officers in any component of the seven uniformed services: Army, Navy, Air Force, Marine Corps, Coast Guard, Public Health Service, and National Oceanic and Atmospheric Administration. Widows and widowers of deceased officers and warrant officers qualify for auxiliary membership in the association.

Membership benefits include:
* represents uniformed service personnel on Capitol Hill
* conducts military and career transition seminars
* retirement information, advice, and assistance
* retirement job placement
* low-cost CHAMPUS/Medicare insurance supplements
* survivor assistance
* travel programs
* financial services
* scholarship loans and grants
* other services

Publications include:
* The *Retired Officers Magazine* (monthly), reporting on national defense, military history, second-career opportunities, and legislation affecting the military.
* *Help Your Widow While She's Still Your Wife*--a comprehensive description of military and *VA survivor benefits;* how to apply for them and what to do in an emergency (updated annually).
* Marketing Yourself for a Second Career.
* Reserve Retirement Benefits.
* Survivor Benefits Plan--detailed explanation.
* Taps--a guide to military-oriented burial, including listing of sites and eligibility criteria.

Membership: 370,000; over 410 local chapters. For more information call 1-800-245-TROA or write TROA (Code 04B).

The Canadian Association of Retired Persons
27 Queen Street East, Suite 304
Toronto, Ontario M5C 2M6
(416) 363-CARP

CARP is a national non-profit, non-political association of Canadians over the age of 50, retired or not. CARP has broken down the over-50 population in this manner: 50-64 years is a junior senior; 65-80 years is a prime senior; and 80 and over is a mature senior. CARP is the voice of senior Canadians. They support legislative programs that safeguard interests of seniors, protect their benefits, provide representation, and take action when necessary.

Benefits include:
* Canadian Tire Auto Club membership opportunity
* local and worldwide travel services--cruises with savings
* discounts on hotels
* group insurance for home or auto
* out-of-country and extended healthcare coverage
* optical vision care program at reduced fees
* *CARP News*--newsletter published quarterly
* a CARP TD Visa card
* Home Equity conversion through FirstLine Trust
* CARP Financial workshops
* CARP National Job Bank

Membership: 50,000. Cost: $10 per year or $25 for 3 years including spouse.

International Senior Citizens Association, Inc.
1102 South Crenshaw Boulevard
Los Angeles, CA 90019
(213) 875-6434

ISCA is an international non-profit, non-commercial organization of older persons committed to friendship--social, cultural, economic, and environmental improvement, nuclear disarmament, world peace and a better world for our children, grandchildren, and generations to come. It is a world affairs forum for older persons in affiliation with the United Nations. It is primarily funded by the interest received from two trust funds established by the Borchardts. These funds are supplemented by dues and contributions.

Purposes include:
* to act as a catalyst and forum for the exchange of ideas for mature voices on global issues;
* to establish means of friendly communication among mature people for education and cultural development;
* to enhance the prestige of mature people in world affairs through utilization of their wisdom and experience;
* to cooperate with non-profit and government agencies for the welfare and happiness of mature people throughout the world.

What ISCA offers:
* consulting status--UN--Economic and Social Council
* quarterly newsletter
* biennial Borchardt International Festival
* annual Peace Forum
* grants for world peace and improving the environment
* Marjorie Borchardt Annual Award to outstanding volunteer

Membership: 50,000. Dues: individual $6, organizations $30, new chapter $30, life $100. ISCA is a tax-exempt organization.

Here's help with Medigap or other insurance problems

If you bought or are considering buying a health insurance policy, the company or its agent should answer your questions. If you do not get the service you feel you deserve, discuss the matter with your state insurance department.

Each state has its own laws and regulations governing all types of insurance. The offices listed in these two pages are responsible for enforcing these laws, as well as providing the public with information about insurance.

> For information on private insurance to supplement Medicare, check your state insurance department listed here.

You can also get help with supplemental Medicare insurance by contacting a state agency on aging. These agencies are listed in the assistance for seniors section, pages 24 and 25.

Alabama
Alabama Insurance Department
135 South Union Street
Montgomery, AL 36130-3401
(205) 269-3550

Alaska
Alaska Insurance Department
3601 C Street, Suite 740
Anchorage, AK 99503
(907) 562-3626

American Samoa
American Samoa Insurance Department
Office of the Governor
Pago Pago, AS 96797
011-684/633-4116

Arizona
Arizona Insurance Department
Consumer Affairs & Investigation Division
3030 N. Third Street
Phoenix, AZ 85012
(602) 255-4783

Arkansas
Arkansas Insurance Department
Consumer Service Division
400 University Tower Bldg.
12th and University Streets
Little Rock, AR 72204
(501) 371-1813

California
California Insurance Department
Consumer Services Division
3450 Wilshire Boulevard
Los Angeles, CA 90010
1-800-233-9045

Colorado
Colorado Insurance Division
303 W. Colfax Ave. 5th Floor
Denver, CO 80204
(303) 620-4300

Connecticut
Connecticut Insurance Dept.
165 Capitol Avenue
State Office Building
Hartford, CT 06106
(203) 297-3800

Delaware
Delaware Insurance Department
841 Silver Lake Boulevard
Dover, DE 19901
(302) 736-4251

District of Columbia
613 G Street, N.W., Room 619
P.O. Box 37200
Washington, DC 20001-7200

Florida
Florida Dept. of Insurance
State Capitol
Plaza Level Eleven
Tallahassee, FL 32399-0300
(904) 488-0030
1-800-342-2762 in Florida

Georgia
Georgia Insurance Department
2 Martin L. King, Jr., Drive
Room 716, West Tower
Atlanta, GA 30334
(404) 656-2056

Guam
Guam Insurance Department
855 W. Marine Drive
P.O. Box 2796
Agana, Guam 96910
011-671/477-1040

Hawaii
Hawaii Dept. of Commerce and Consumer Affairs
Insurance Division
P.O. Box 3614
Honolulu, HI 96811
(808) 548-5450

Idaho
Idaho Insurance Department
Public Service Department
500 S. 10th Street
Boise, ID 83720
(208) 334-3102

Illinois
Illinois Insurance Department
320 W. Washington St., 4th Fl.
Springfield, IL 62767
(217) 782-4515

Indiana
Indiana Insurance Department
311 W. Washington Street
Suite 300
Indianapolis, IN 46204
(317) 232-2395

Iowa
Iowa Insurance Division
Lucas State Office Bldg.
E. 12th & Grand St., 6th Fl.
Des Moines, IA 50319
(515) 281-5705

Kansas
Kansas Insurance Department
420 S.W. 9th Street
Topeka, KS 66612
(913) 296-3071

Kentucky
Kentucky Insurance Department
229 West Main Street
P.O. Box 517
Frankfort, KY 40602
(502) 564-3630

Louisiana
Louisiana Insurance Department
P.O. Box 94214
Baton Rouge, LA 70804-9214
(504) 342-5900

Maine
Maine Bureau of Insurance
Consumer Division
State House, Station 34
Augusta, ME 04333
(207) 582-8707

Maryland
Maryland Insurance Department
Complaints & Investigation Unit
501 St. Paul Place
Baltimore, MD 21202-2272
(301) 333-2792

Massachusetts
Massachusetts Ins. Division
Consumer Services Section
280 Friend Street
Boston, MA 02114
(617) 727-7189

Michigan
Michigan Insurance Department
P.O. Box 30220
Lansing, MI 48909
(517) 373-0220

Minnesota
Minnesota Insurance Department
Department of Commerce
133 E. 7th Street
St. Paul, MN 55101
(612) 296-4026

Mississippi
Mississippi Ins. Department
Consumer Assistance Division
P.O. Box 79
Jackson, MS 39205
(601) 359-3569

> Some fraud and deception persist in the Medigap health insurance market. Some duplicate your coverage. Check it out with your state agency.

Missouri
Missouri Division of Insurance
Consumer Services Section
P.O. Box 690
Jefferson City, MO 65102-0690
(314) 751-2640

Montana
Montana Insurance
Department
126 N. Sanders, Mitchell Bldg.
P.O. Box 4009, Room 270
Helena, MT 59604
(406) 444-2040
1-800-332-6148 in Montana

Nebraska
Nebraska Insurance
Department
Terminal Building
941 O Street, Suite 400
Lincoln, NE 68508
(402) 471-2201

Nevada
Nevada Dept. of Commerce
Insurance Division
Consumer Section
1665 Hot Springs Road
Capitol Complex
Carson City, NV 89701
(702) 687-4270

New Hampshire
New Hampshire Ins. Dept.
Life and Health Division
169 Manchester Street
Concord, NH 03301
(603) 271-2261

New Jersey
New Jersey Insurance Dept.
20 W. State Street
Roebling Building
Trenton, NJ 08625
(609) 292-4757

New Mexico
New Mexico Insurance Dept.
P.O. Box 1269
Sante Fe, NM 87504-1269
(505) 827-4500

New York
New York Insurance
Department
160 W. Broadway
New York, NY 10013
(212) 602-0203 NY City
1-800-342-3736 in NY

North Carolina
North Carolina Insurance
Department
Consumer Services
Dobbs Building
P.O. Box 26387
Raleigh, NC 27611
(919) 733-2004

North Dakota
North Dakota Insurance
Department
Capitol Building, 5th Floor
Bismark, ND 58505
(701) 224-2440

Ohio
Ohio Insurance Department
Consumer Services Division
2100 Stella Court
Columbus, OH 43266-0566
(614) 644-2673

Oklahoma
Oklahoma Insurance
Department
P.O. Box 53408
Oklahoma City, OK 73512-3408
(405) 521-2828

Oregon
Oregon Department of
Insurance and Finance
Insurance Division/Consumer
Advocate
21 Labor and Industry Bldg.
Salem, OR 97310
(503) 378-4484

Pennsylvania
Pennsylvania Insurance
Department
1326 Strawberry Square
Harrisburg, PA 17120
(717) 787-2317

Puerto Rico
Puerto Rico Insurance
Department
Fernandez Juncos Station
P.O. Box 8330
Santurce, PR 00910
(809) 722-8686

Rhode Island
Rhode Island Insurance
Division
233 Richmond St., Suite 233
Providence, RI 02903-4233
(401) 277-2223

South Carolina
South Carolina Insurance
Department
Consumer Assistance Section
P.O. Box 100105
Columbia, SC 29202-3105
(803) 737-6140

South Dakota
South Dakota Insurance
Department
Enforcement
910 E. Sioux Avenue
Pierre, SD 57501-3940
(605) 773-3563

Tennessee
Tennessee Department of
Commerce and Insurance
Policyholders Service Section
4th Floor
500 James Robertson Parkway
Nashville, TN 37243-0582
(615) 741-4955
1-800-342-4029 in TN

Texas
Texas Board of Insurance
Complaints Division
1110 San Jacino Blvd.
Austin, TX 78701-1998
(512) 463-6501

Utah
Utah Insurance Department
Consumer Services
3110 State Office Bldg.
Salt Lake City, UT 84114
(801) 530-6400

Vermont
Vermont Department of
Banking and Insurance
Consumer Complaint Division
120 State Street
Montpelier, VT 05602
(802) 828-3301

Virgin Islands
Virgin Islands Insurance
Department
Kongens Grade No. 18
St. Thomas, VI 00802
(809) 774-2991

Virginia
Virginia Insurance
Department
Consumer Services Division
700 Jefferson Building
P.O. Box 1157
Richmond, VA 23209
(804) 786-7691

Washington
Washington Insurance
Department
Insurance Bldg. AQ21
Olympia, WA 98504-0321
(206) 753-7300
1-800-562-6900 in WA

West Virginia
West Virginia Insurance
Department
2019 Washington St. E.
Charleston, WV 25305
(304) 348-3386

Wisconsin
Wisconsin Insurance
Department
Complaints Department
P.O. Box 7873
Madison, WI 53707
(608) 266-0103

Wyoming
Wyoming Insurance
Department
Herschler Building
122 W. 25th Street
Cheyenne, WY 82002
(307) 777-7401

For information about Medicare and Medigap see pages 38 through 50.

Nutrition assistance for those in need

The Federal Food Stamp Program is one of the most direct sources of aid provided to Americans who need help. In a short introductory pamphlet called Program Aid No. 1226, the Food and Nutrition Service of the U.S. Department of Agriculture describes the program as follows:

> The Food Stamp Program provides monthly benefits that help low income households buy the food they need for good health. You may qualify for food stamps if you:
>
> * Work for low wages,
> * Are employed or work part time,
> * Receive welfare or other assistance payments, or
> * Are elderly or disabled and live on a small income.

Under agreement with the U.S. Department of Agriculture, state public assistance agencies run the program through their local offices. The basic rules are the same everywhere.

The Food Stamp Program is a recognition by the government that nutrition is basic. By directing this appropriation to food alone, there is more assurance that assistance is not diverted to less worthy uses. Food stamps represent an obligation of the United States, so that violations of regulations are treated similarly to those involving currency. During 1991 more than 23 million persons were receiving food stamp aid.

THE APPLICATION PROCESS

You can obtain an application for food stamps by visiting the appropriate office in person, by mail, or by telephone. You can file the application immediately. Welfare workers will assist the applicant by explaining the sort of information that is requested in the form. A decision on each case is made within 30 days.

People who are in urgent need may ask for immediate assistance. It is important to tell welfare personnel of that need when you submit your application.

Any person who is applying for public assistance (AFDC) may apply for food stamps at the same time. Individuals who apply for Supplementary Security Income (SSI) may apply for food stamps in the Social Security office.

THE INTERVIEW

Each applicant will have an interview to verify the information in the application. Someone will also assist with the completion of parts that have not been filled in by the applicant. The interviewer may ask for verification of certain information such as the amount earned on the job. Pay stubs are an example of the kind of information that is needed. During the interview, the rules governing food stamps are explained. It is important to be sure that they are understood, and the applicant should ask about anything that is not clear.

These interviews are generally in the welfare office. If a person is unable to come to the office, a member of the family or a friend may represent him/her. If disabled, it is possible to have the interview conducted by telephone, or in the home of the applicant.

ELIGIBILITY RULES

1 Food stamp recipients must be citizens or legal residents of the United States. Immigration documents may be necessary for the latter category of applicants.

2 All adults in the household must submit their Social Security number. Those in the family who are under 18 and are contributing earnings must also provide their Social Security numbers.

3 Able-bodied family members from 18 to 60 must register for work and report to job interviews, and accept suitable work as a condition of eligibility. There are special rules for students.

4 Certain resources are exempted when determining your eligibility for food stamps. For example, your home, household goods, and personal belongings, as well as life insurance, are not counted. Examples of those that do count are stocks and bonds, and land and buildings, other than the home, that produce no income.

5 Income limits are adjusted each year. Wage stubs and grant information from Social Security, Veterans, or unemployment compensation information are needed to establish eligibility.

6 Deductions from income are made for special situations such as high medical costs, age, or disability. Thus, the effect is to allow a higher income when these conditions exist, so that a person or household may still be eligible.

Following the interview, a notice is sent that tells whether or not you qualify for food stamps. If you do, you will be told how long you will receive them before reapplication. If eligible, you will receive your stamps within 30 days of the application date.

USING FOOD STAMPS

Food stamps may be used to purchase only food and plants and seeds to grow food for your household to eat. Prohibited items are alcoholic beverages, tobacco or cigarettes, household supplies such as soap, medicines, food that will be eaten in the store, ready-to-eat hot foods such as barbecued chicken, and pet foods. Stamps must be kept within their cover to be accepted by the store, except for $1 coupons.

It is the responsibility of individuals receiving food stamps to inform the issuing agency about changes in financial circumstances.

People who break food stamp rules may be disqualified from the program, fined, imprisoned, or all three.

FOOD STAMP RETAILERS

There is a very complex set of regulations governing the institutions that are authorized to accept food stamps in lieu of cash payment. For a retailer to be involved in the program a bond is required. An eligible retail establishment is defined as one that has an eligible food sales volume that is more than 50% staple items for home preparation and consumption.

Penalties for retailers who violate food stamp regulations may involve the forfeiture of the bond they have posted, and prosecution for serious cases.

Letter carriers keep a watchful eye on the elderly!

Frequently, the only contact with the outside world that you may have is the daily visit by your mail carrier. If living alone worries you, the Carrier Alert program can offer you the comfort of knowing that someone who visits your home regularly can call for help if you need it. This <u>free service</u> has been developed especially for older adults and the homebound--people who may have difficulty reaching vital services because of an accident or sudden illness.

The Purpose of Carrier Alert is to provide reassurance to participating individuals that a responsible agency will be alerted to check on their well-being when an accumulation of mail might signify the possibility of accident or illness. The National Association of Letter Carriers (NALC) and the United States Postal Service (USPS) have joined together with a variety of social service agencies to provide a community service to those who are the most isolated members of the community. The United Way, the American Red Cross, and the Area Agency on Aging invite you to register for this free service so that your letter carrier can help you if you need it.

Carrier Alert, an all volunteer program, is a natural extension of care that individual letter carriers traditionally have exhibited for their customers not just in the delivery of their mail but in a genuine concern for their well-being. It has been customary for letter carriers to show particular consideration for customers on their routes whose health or advanced age require a little extra special attention.

Delivering mail to the same residences day after day, letter carriers are familiar with customers' habits and often notice any change in routine that may mean a customer is in distress. Though accumulating mail is the most common clue, lights burning in midday, dogs crying to be let in or out of the house, newspapers stacking up in front of the door, drawn draperies or no tracks in the snow--all can signal trouble within.

When carriers note something that might signal illness or accident, they report it to a postal supervisor or another designated individual who in turn contacts the sponsoring local agency. The agency checks on the person, and if something's wrong, it contacts family, police or emergency services.

To implement the program in towns and cities across the country, NALC and USPS have joined forces with a local community service agency. Together they build a resource network that effectively keeps an eye on elderly and disabled patrons registered in the program. The local participating community service agency in each area handles administration, promotion, registration, files, funding, and setting up local procedures. They also work with local police and emergency services to ensure that participants in need are helped quickly.

Here's How Carrier Alert Works

Postal patrons interested in having someone watch out for them register with the sponsoring social service organization. Your local postmaster can give you more details on registration or you can write to NALC.

■ The sponsor notifies the post office of the patron's request, and a letter carrier is authorized to place a Carrier Alert sticker inside the patron's mailbox, indicating participation and alerting all letter carriers to watch your mail for any signs of distress.

■ If your letter carrier finds an accumulation of mail, and you have not covered the sticker to signal that you will be away for a few days, he or she will notify the agency where you are registered or report your name to the postal supervisor who will report it to the agency.

■ The social service agency will then try to contact you by phone. If you cannot be reached, the agency personnel will try to contact a friend or relative whom you have listed as a contact in the event of an emergency.

■ If a friend or relative cannot be reached, the social service agency will send a worker to your home to check on your health and well-being.

Establishing a Carrier Alert Program

Starting a Carrier Alert program in your area is easy. You will find there are four groups whose cooperation is indispensable: local management; the carriers with whom you work; a community service organization to sponsor the program; and the elderly, disabled, or homebound people.

Carrier Alert is designed to serve. Local postmasters are almost always willing and often enthusiastic to help get Carrier Alert underway.

Traditionally organizations such as the United Way's First Call for Help, the American Red Cross, and local Areas on Aging have served as sponsors for Carrier Alert. Some mayors have agreed to have the city sponsor it, pay for printing costs, and have the city police answer calls. Outside the city limits, some sheriff's offices perform the same function. These arrangements work well because the police all have radio cars and can respond quickly.

For a free kit containing a history of the program and guidelines for local implementation, just write to:

Carrier Alert
c/o Assistant Secretary--Treasurer
Halline Overby
National Association of Letter Carriers
100 Indiana Avenue, N.W.
Washington, D.C. 20001

> **If you have a friend, a neighbor, or a relative that could benefit from the Carrier Alert program, invite them to sign up. It might save their life.**

Help available while you remain in your own home

Longevity for older Americans is increasing, thanks to advancement in medical technology and improved healthcare. In 1900, if a person was lucky enough to reach age 65, the odds were that he or she would survive only another 12 years. Today, a 65-year-old can expect to live another 17 years.

Many of us will remain healthy and independent for most of our senior years. But for others, this may not be true. As we grow older, especially once we enter our eighties, the chances increase considerably that we will face health problems or frailty and need assistance with various aspects of daily living.

Many older persons who need some care or help with daily activities do not necessarily need to be placed in a nursing facility. In the past, a nursing home may have been the only option for families who could not adequately provide care to an ill or disabled elderly relative. But today older Americans and their families have a number of alternatives to nursing home care that allow persons in need of medical or other support services to remain in their homes with their family and friends.

Recognizing the growing need for long-term care, many social service agencies and other organizations are now providing a variety of services to help individuals live independently in their homes and communities and preserve their quality of life. Communities throughout the United States have made much progress in developing alternatives to nursing home care. However, not all of the services and programs available in some communities will be found in every other community. A physician often can help decide what alternatives are available and which would be best suited to the personal needs of the individual. The physician can also help define exactly what help is needed in medical and social terms. When appropriately utilized, in-home support and community services are cost-effective alternatives to hospital stays.

What Is Long-Term Care? Why You Need to Know

Simply stated, long-term care refers to a person's need for a wide range of medical, nursing, and social services over a prolonged period of time. This can also be called "chronic" care, as distinct from more intensive medical treatment for a short-term illness, called "acute" care. The need for long-term care can result from chronic illness or disability or from a sudden accident or stroke.

Long-term care does not take place only in a nursing home, nor is it needed only by the elderly. Care might be provided to people of any age at home, in community facilities, or in nursing homes. Relatives, friends and neighbors, and community service workers often provide assistance with the normal activities of daily living such as eating, bathing, and dressing. Or, those who need care could be living in a community for senior citizens that might meet all of their health and social needs--commonly known as a continuing care community.

If an individual requires extensive treatment and round-the-clock supervision for a long time, nursing home admission may be the best option. For many people whose conditions are somewhat less severe, however, a variety of services--perhaps many more than you realize--are available. If you do not have these community and in-home support systems available you may find your only option to be in an institution such as a nursing home.

Social services are as important a part of long-term care as are medical and nursing services, particularly in helping you remain in the community if you need care. They include services provided in one's own home and those provided in a community setting. These services can help people maintain their independence despite chronic illness or disability and preserve their quality of life. Some of the services available include:

In-Home Services

A variety of nursing, medical, and social services can be provided to an individual at home. Most people would prefer to stay at home, if possible, rather than enter an institution. At home, they can live somewhat independently, and be closer to family and friends. Most older people get disoriented in hospitals or unfamiliar settings and do much better with care in the home.

Eligibility--In many states to be eligible for the program a person must meet all of the following requirements:
* must be 65 years of age or older, disabled, or blind;
* unable to live safely at home without help; and
* financially unable to purchase needed services. Persons who receive SSI meet the program's financial requirements. Others may also be eligible but may need to pay a portion of the costs for services.

How to Apply--To apply for in-home supportive services call the county welfare or local area agency on aging. A service worker will come to your home to discuss what help you may need and determine the costs, if any, you may need to pay for the services. The service worker usually conducts a "needs assessment" on the initial home visit. This assessment is based on your medical condition, your living arrangement, and what assistance you may be getting from your family, friends, or available community services.

Home Services Include:

■ **Home Health Care** (Home Health Agency) services are available to care for an elderly or disabled person at home. Not surprisingly, this is the first preference of most older people in comparison to a nursing home. It is the least disruptive option. Registered nurses, therapists, home health aides, and medical social workers provide services that usually include prescribed medical treatments and personal care such as bathing, dressing, and feeding as well as physical, speech, and occupational therapies and medical social services.

In many communities, home nursing services are available. Possible sources include a county public health department, a hospital-based home healthcare service, and private home care nursing agencies. Nursing services can be paid by Medicare or Medicaid on a part-time basis providing the service is prescribed by a physician.

■ **Medical Equipment**--Purchasing or renting medical equipment may become a necessity. Consider your need for equipment and supplies in the event of a disabling illness. In some cases, when ordered by a physician, rental or purchase of medical equipment is covered by Medicare or Medicaid. It is more prudent to assume you will have to rent or purchase the service, supplies, and equipment. Costs can be substantial. Some communities provide medical equipment through local voluntary agencies. In addition to the local area agency on aging, the local health department may provide more information.

■ **Respite Care**--There are ways that a relative can be relieved of caregiving duties for a short period of time. Some communities offer volunteer or paid respite care services that provide short-term temporary care for an impaired older person to relieve the family members who provide daily care to their relative.

■ **Homemaker services**--are available to assist individuals with many of the tasks essential to maintaining a household, from food shopping and preparing meals to light housekeeping and laundry. These services are for the chronically ill or incapacitated and are available from at least two sources:

1 private homemaker agencies--limited services paid on a full-fee basis, and

2 homemaker services provided to persons eligible for welfare benefits.

How to hire and supervise your in-home supportive worker

While your social service worker has the responsibility to assist you in looking for a worker to help, you should make the final choice on who to hire and when to terminate services. The following suggestions can assist you in choosing your worker:

Who are you hiring? It is important that you talk to the worker in person before deciding to hire him or her. You might want to consider the following:

● Have a friend or relative sit in on the interview.
● Ask to see an identification card with a picture of the worker on it. A driver's licence, a Department of Motor Vehicles ID card, an Alien Registration card, or a County Employment ID card are all examples of such cards.
● Write down the worker's name, birth date, address, telephone number, and Social Security account number. Keep this information in a place where you can easily find it as your social service worker will need this information if you hire this person.
● Ask for references from people they have worked for and when and where they last worked. Call and ask what kind of work they performed, and if there were any problems with the worker.
● Ask if the worker lives in the area and how long they have lived there. This will give you a good idea of whether the worker is familiar with the local facilities or if the worker needs a lot of help from you to learn the area. Ask a new worker why he or she moved to this locality.
● Ask if the worker uses alcohol, tobacco, or drugs.
● Look at the worker's appearance. Is the worker neat and clean?

Can the worker do the job? It is not easy to show a worker how to do things all the time, especially when you do not have the energy to explain what it is that has to be done. The following questions or observations may be noted before you hire--get the following information from the worker during your talk.

● **Previous work**--Has the worker done this kind of job before?
● **Knowledge of job duties**--Does the worker know what the job is about? Has the worker attended any job training? Ask direct questions about doing the job. Talk to the worker about what jobs you need done, such as cooking, laundry, cleaning, bathing, and shopping. If you need transportation, be sure to see that the worker has a valid driver's license and insurance policy.
● **Good health**--Make sure the worker does not have physical problems that would keep them from taking good care of you.
● **Working hours**--What hours is the worker able to care for you? Is the worker working any other part-time job?

Shall I hire this worker? Trust your feelings! Making the right choice is not always easy.

● **Ask all the questions you want.** If in doubt about anything, continue to ask more questions of the worker, the social service worker, or the person who told you about the worker.
● Remember to write down things so you do not forget. If anything the worker said sounded odd to you, you can check it out with your social service worker.
● You do not have to hire the first person you interview. You can interview as many people as you wish.

● You can always change your mind-- and hire the worker you want.
● You should pick the worker who takes care of you!
● Call your social service worker immediately, when you hire or fire a worker.

Points to remember once you have hired your worker.

● Do not let your worker mistreat you! It is not okay to be treated badly! If your worker is hitting you, hurting you, ignoring you, screaming and yelling at you, or treating you badly in any way, call your social service worker immediately.
● If your worker is not doing his or her job, call your social service worker.
● If your worker is frequently late, leaves early, or does not report to work, call your social service worker immediately.

DOs and DON'Ts

✔ **DO ask** for a receipt any time your worker shops for you.
✔ **DO call** your adult protective services agency or police department if you feel you are in danger.
✔ **DON'T talk** about how much money you have with the worker. **DON'T talk** about your valuable property items and cash.
✔ **DON'T let** your worker sign your name on their time sheet.
✔ **DON'T sign** your worker's time sheet if you know they have not worked those hours. Call your social service worker.
✔ **DON'T add** your worker's name to your savings, checking, charge accounts, or any other document.
✔ **DON'T add** your worker's name to your SSI, pension, Social Security, or any other check.

In-home and community caring services available

■ **Chore Services**--go beyond homemaking to include more heavy-duty tasks, such as floor and window washing, minor home repairs, yard work, and other types of home maintenance.

■ **Home-delivered Meals**--often called "Meals-on-Wheels," can be delivered five or more days a week to individuals unable to shop and prepare food on their own. These services can provide enhanced nutrition and a sense of security for the homebound.

■ **Companion Services**--whether paid or volunteer, ease loneliness for individuals at home. Their duties range from supervisions to simple companionship.

■ **Telephone Reassurance Services**--are often available through local senior citizens' organizations or volunteer agencies. A volunteer agrees to call an elderly person each day to chat for a while and make sure the person is okay. For someone who is generally healthy, but who lives alone, this service can be a good one. Ensuring personal safety is the main objective of these programs, but these calls also bring personal phone contact to an individual to reduce social isolation.

■ **Emergency Response Systems**--link an individual to a fire department, hospital, or other health facility or social service agency. Simply pressing a button triggers a communicator attached to the telephone that automatically dials the response center.

■ **Home Observation Programs**--sponsored by a number of companies and other concerns are available in many communities to facilitate the health and safety of elderly residents and those who are homebound. Called by a variety of names, this service is provided by letter carriers (see article on Carrier Alert in this manual, page 11), utility workers, and others whose jobs require them to make regular visits to residential areas.

These observers look for unmowed lawns, accumulated mail and newspapers, and other signs that would indicate that a resident is ill or has had an accident, and report their findings to appropriate social service agencies and local authorities.

Community Services

Community services available include:
◆ **Information and Referral**--Most communities have agencies whose primary function is to provide people with information about where to go for the help they may need. If this type of assistance is required, a local area agency on aging can help (see listing in the yellow pages under Senior Citizens' Service Organizations or state listings on pages 24 and 25).

◆ **Emergencies**--Each community has an emergency number to dial in time of crisis. Check the telephone book or call the information operator for this number. It is helpful to post this number on each telephone for quick use in times of crisis.

◆ **Transportation**--There are services that can help in getting around in the community. A number of communities offer door-to-door transportation services for older persons such as vans or mini-buses that accommodate wheelchairs, walkers, and other devices. Transportation may be provided to and from the doctor's office or other medical services; community facilities (like senior centers); banking and other services. Help may also be available in the form of escort services and shopping assistance.

◆ **Adult Day Care Centers**--are for elderly persons who are ambulatory but who need supervision during the day. Their programs vary, but centers generally provide daytime activities, counseling and health assessment, personal care, therapy, a hot noontime meal, various social activities, and some also provide transportation to medical or dental appointments as well as special outings. These centers are especially good for the person who has help at home only in the evenings or whose spouse or family is employed during the day. They allow many older persons to continue to live at home or with their adult children instead of being placed in out-of-home care.

These programs are conducted in a variety of settings, among them multipurpose senior centers, hospitals, nursing homes, churches and synagogues, and mental health centers. Some adult day care centers are freestanding agencies.

The cost of adult day care varies. In some states, public funds pay for adult day care services; in others, participants and their families must pay the cost themselves. Some centers will adjust their fees according to the individual's ability to pay. In most cases, there are minimum age requirements for attending programs on a regular basis.

◆ **Senior Centers**--have been developed throughout most communities in response to the growing number of older citizens. The centers vary in scope of service, size, staffing, and program activities depending on community financial resources and the desire of the participants. Their programs vary in each locale. Many are multipurpose centers offering a wide range of services. These include congregate meals, exercise sessions, health screening, health education, recreational and social activities. Many senior centers offer information and referral services that connect the older person in need to an appropriate community service.

◆ **Support Groups**--Groups have been formed in many communities that provide information and emotional support to older persons and/or their caregivers. These groups frequently focus on special needs such as Alzheimer's disease, terminally ill persons, bereavement, and other serious life situations.

◆ **Social Recreational Activities**--Many communities support group activities for social, physical, religious, and recreational purposes. Senior centers offer a good opportunity for recreation and social involvement with others. There are a number of other groups that focus on special interests such as arts and crafts, education, travel, and other interests.

◆ **Counseling**--Communities often offer guidance and assistance for older persons and families in coping with physical impairments and such problems as substance abuse, financial crisis, bereavement, and elder abuse.

> **Age makes us not childish,**
> **as some say;**
> **it finds us still true children.**
>
> Goethe (1749-1832)

Who provides long-term-care services?

Nearly every community has social service agencies and other organizations that can provide long-term-care services. In addition, community agencies can assist in locating suitable housing for individuals as well as help them handle their personal finances if they are incapable of doing so. Low-income people can receive assistance from community action agencies in gaining access to home-delivered meals, transportation, and other services. Also, counseling is available from community mental health centers. Legal service programs are available to aid people with problems relating to Social Security, Medicare and Medicaid benefits, and other needs calling for legal representation. Some of these agencies that can help include:

Community Agencies--People who need help have a broad spectrum of social organizations to choose from within the community. Some have religious affiliations, such as the Catholic charities or Jewish social service agencies. Others are nonsectarian organizations such as the Visiting Nurses Association. Many community service programs for older Americans and their families are funded by the United Way.

State and Local Government Agencies, for example, the Public Health Department, might be able to provide some home healthcare services, while the Department of Social Services acts as a clearinghouse of information and referrals for a wide range of needs.

Community Hospitals--are yet another resource. Discharge planners at many hospitals coordinate follow-up care, including home care, for patients after their release. Some hospitals operate their own home healthcare and adult day care programs.

Voluntary Health Organizations--Local chapters of national health organizations can help you find services or offer advice with respect to specific health problems. To illustrate, Parkinson's disease patients can turn to a chapter of the American Parkinson Disease Association, if one is available in their community, to receive counseling for themselves and their families.

Consumer-oriented home nursing courses for family caregivers are offered by the American Red Cross chapters. Transportation services for medical needs or shopping also are run by some chapters.

Volunteer Groups--Volunteer services are offered by churches and synagogues, as well as by civic and service organizations. These groups may provide chore and shopping assistance, telephone reassurance, home-delivered meals, and other daily activities.

Self-help Support Groups--Volunteer support groups, such as groups for families of Alzheimer's patients, focus on mutual concerns and sharing of problems for families, caregivers, and those who need care. In a sense, they represent a "caring community within a community," offering peer group comfort and ideas for coping with specific diseases and stressful situations. Indeed, such groups exist for almost every human condition; widows, stroke victims, cancer patients, and family caregivers are just a few of the people who can benefit from mutual aid self-help groups (see article on mutual-help groups pages 17 through 19).

How Do I Find These Services
in my Community?

In general, you can locate these and other aging organizations that provide services by checking the yellow pages of your telephone directory under the headings "Senior Citizens Service Organizations" or "Social Services." Government agency listings may be found in the blue pages.

If you can't find the information you need in your local directory, your state office on aging (see pages 24 and 25) can refer you to local aging resources. Even if your telephone directory includes listings for private organizations that provide services to seniors, it is still a good idea to check with the state office on aging, the Better Business Bureau, or some impartial organization for a rating of the service provided.

Sometimes it is difficult to determine what specific services you or a family member may need. Therefore, you may want to seek the help of a professional who can assess your personal situation and then refer you to the appropriate resources.

Many social service agencies can help sort out your needs and pull together a personalized plan for long-term care. This is called case management. Essentially, a case manager can assess your total needs, identify resources, make all necessary arrangements, and monitor and evaluate the services you receive. Private case management services may also be available in your community. Their fees and extent of services will vary.

Another good source to help you determine your needs and find services is your local area agency on aging. These agencies help individuals remain independent and avoid institutional care, if possible.

Eligibility requirements for specific services vary. Some services may be open to everyone over age 60, while others may be limited to people who are categorized as "frail elderly" or to individuals with low incomes. Agency staff will help you determine your eligibility for a particular service.

Some services subsidized by local, state, or federal government agencies may be offered free or at a low cost. Others may require a full or reduced fee.

Resources

Numerous organizations offer consumer publications or programs on aspects of long-term care at a low cost or free of charge. Contact each organization for specific ordering information.

American Association of Homes for the Aging
1129 20th Street, N.W.
Washington, D.C. 20036
(202) 296-5960

American Association of Retired Persons
Health Advocacy Services
601 E Street, N.W.
Washington, D.C. 20049
(202) 434-2277

American Health Care Association
1200 15th Street, N.W.
Washington, D.C. 20005
(202) 833-2050

National Council of Catholic Women
1312 Massachusetts Avenue N.W.
Washington, D.C. 20005
(202) 638-6050

The National Council on the Aging, Inc.
West Wing 100
600 Maryland Avenue S.W.
Washington, D.C. 20024
(202) 479-1200

Medicaid--medical care for those who cannot afford it

Medicaid is a cooperative program between the federal government and the states to provide medical care for persons who cannot afford it for a variety of reasons. Since this program operates under enabling legislation in each state, the programs vary significantly, even in the name that is used. In California, for example, it is called Medi-Cal. The federal program is administered by the Health Care Financing Administration which also handles the Medicare program. This agency is a part of the Department of Health and Human Services. Medicaid was authorized under Title XIX of the Social Security Act.

ELIGIBILITY

Generally, those receiving cash assistance under the Aid to Families with Dependent Children (AFDC) or Supplementary Social Security Income (SSI) also receive Medicaid. In addition, each state has the option of providing Medicaid benefits to those who cannot afford needed healthcare, but have income above the maximum allowable for public assistance. Each state has considerable flexibility concerning its Medicaid program. Within broad federal guidelines, states determine who will be eligible, what services will be provided, and what limits will be placed on the services.

SERVICES AVAILABLE

Virtually all conventional hospital and outpatient services are available through the Medicaid program. Some categories of eligible people are cared for under the Medicare program. Some examples of services that go beyond Medicare are: dental service, podiatry, routine eye care and glasses, and hearing aids.

Medicaid becomes important for many who have never before sought public assistance for healthcare when they enter a long-term-care facility, such as a nursing home, and have exhausted their private resources. At that point, if one meets the eligibility requirements, the person enters the Medicaid program and further hospitalization is provided. When that happens, the additional services beyond Medicare that are mentioned above also become available to the patient.

All states offer skilled nursing home care, intermediate nursing home care, and home healthcare under Medicaid. Most states also offer occupational therapy, chiropractic care, podiatric care, dental care and dentures, refractions and eye glasses, medical transportation, and prescription drugs.

In addition to the above, some states offer private duty nursing, personal care services, adult day care, emergency response systems, home-delivered meals, and homemaker service.

CARE PROVIDERS

Those individuals and institutions that provide care for Medicaid patients must agree to accept the allocation that is established for that service. Payment is made directly to the care provider by the state agency charged with the administration of the program. In most cases, the recipient of the service pays nothing. However, there are some circumstances where the agency may establish a "cost sharing" arrangement with the patient. Some services are specifically excluded from such arrangements.

MORE ON ELIGIBILITY

As indicated earlier, some categories of public assistance receivers are automatically covered by Medicaid. Others do not need or apply for such coverage until they face what has often been called catastrophic illness. For example, a person who requires prolonged hospitalization and/or surgery due to accident or illness may exhaust his/her private resources and become "medically needy."

Many of the financial eligibility rules become rather complex with respect to different categories of patients asking for coverage. There is a limit to the amount such persons may hold in personal property. Generally, the family residence is exempt and the family automobile is also exempt if it does not exceed value limits. However, more expensive cars are exempt if the subject needs the automobile to get to work or to medical appointments.

A person who receives medical support for maintenance in an institution, such as a nursing home, is expected to contribute his/her community property. A spouse who is not hospitalized is known as a community spouse and is allowed to retain a portion of the couple's combined community property. In other words, a couple of modest means does not need to exhaust the resources of both persons in order to have one person covered by Medicaid. See the article on "Spousal Asset Protection," page 100.

Applicants for Medicaid coverage who exceed the resource limits for eligibility may be allowed to "spend down" the excess funds to pay for medical bills and other necessary expenses. This process occurs quite frequently in the case of elderly applicants.

MEDICAID PROBLEMS

The major problem in the Medicaid program is money. Over time, there has tended to be less money available for Medicaid and prices for medical services have increased. The practical effect of this process is that fewer and fewer medical suppliers are willing to accept Medicaid reimbursement. Thus, the person who had a Medicaid card and eligibility may have solved only half the problem. It is increasingly difficult to find doctors and medical institutions that accept Medicaid payments. For example, a recent report found that only 4% of the physicians in California treat nearly all of the Medi-Cal patients. That is because they receive only half of their usual fees when they treat Medi-Cal patients. The same report found that two-thirds of applicants for Medi-Cal coverage are denied. This was attributed to the complexity of the application process. The California form is eleven pages long and requires an educational level of two years in college to understand.

NURSING HOMES AND MEDICAID

Since the need for nursing home care is one of the most frequent reasons for Medicaid application, some information about these homes is vital. Many nursing homes do not accept Medicaid patients. Some have a mix, but private patients pay much higher rates than the institution receives for their Medicaid patients. Because of these circumstances, it is extremely important patients of limited means who may exhaust their resources after a period of time should select a nursing home that will continue to care for them on Medicaid assignment.

For more specific information on your state's Medicaid assistance, contact your local welfare department. You will find the phone number in the yellow pages.

Self-help--an effective way of dealing with problems.

For many human problems there are no easy answers or easy cures. Even after the best professional help has been obtained, a person may be left with difficulties too great to handle. In this situation, millions of people have found much-needed personal support in mutual-help groups. It is within these groups, whose members share common concerns, that they are offered an important aid to recovery, the understanding and help of others who have gone through similar experiences.

What Is Mutual Help?

Mutual help has been a mainstay of life for as long as families have existed. As social beings, all of us need to be accepted, cared for, and emotionally supported. We also find it satisfying to care for and support those around us.

Within the most natural "mutual-help networks"--made up of our families and friends-- we establish the one-to-one contact so important to our happiness and well-being. We often take this informal support for granted, but it clearly influences our ability to handle distressing events in our lives.

Many of our daily conversations are actually mutual counseling sessions in which we exchange the reassurance and advice that help us deal with routine stresses. In fact, scientists have found that this sort of emotional support can help prevent ill health and promote recovery when an illness or accident does occur.

The supportive relationships we establish with family and friends, however, constitute only some of the interpersonal networks that help sustain us through life. As we develop socially and intellectually, we tend

---

The rule of friendship means there should be mutual sympathy between them, each supplying what the other lacks and trying to benefit the other, always using friendly and sincere words.
Budda (568-488 B.C.)

To give counsel as well as to take it is a feature of true friendship.
Cicero (106-43 B.C.)

---

to associate with others who have similar interests and beliefs. These associations include religious congregations, civic and fraternal organizations, and social clubs: in them, members benefit from a shared identity and a sense of a common purpose. Some groups are aimed primarily at social enjoyment. Others come together to bring about social change. Through combined efforts, the group can often promote or accomplish what the individual cannot. Yet each member's presence and participation adds to the strength of the group.

Why the Need for Mutual-Help Groups?

The twentieth century has produced social changes that affect our traditional patterns of support. Living in a highly mobile society, we may not enjoy the benefits of a permanent community and longstanding stable relationships. People today are apt to live in more than one home and have a series of jobs requiring them to form new relationships in new locations. Their families, once close, are now separated by distance. The emotional and practical support they gave is no longer available and may not be forthcoming from new neighbors and friends. And, perhaps most significantly, divorce is separating millions of families each year.

Despite these changing social patterns, our needs for stability and support remain constant. We are likely to feel a sense of isolation, questioning "What role do I play in such a vast, impersonal world? Where can I find other people like me?" To overcome this sense of isolation, to exercise more control over the quality of their lives, and to get help with serious mental disorders, millions are turning to mutual-help groups.

What Is the Purpose of Mutual-Help Groups?

The estimated half-million mutual-help groups in existence deal with almost every human problem. There are four types of formal groups:

1. the **self-care groups** for those suffering physical and mental illness (there is at least one group for nearly every major disease;

2. the **reform groups** for addiction behaviors (particularly the "anonymous"

groups such as Alcoholics Anonymous, Gamblers Anonymous, and Overeaters Anonymous);

3. **advocacy groups** for certain minorities (handicapped, elderly, mentally ill, etc.);

4. **mutual-help groups** for those who need support in times of crisis. See the article on the Widowed Persons Service, page 243.

In spite of the enormous diversity of the problems they address, all mutual-help groups have the same underlying purpose: to provide emotional support and practical help in dealing with a problem common to all members. There is a special bond among people who share the troubling experience; it begins when one person says to another, "I know just how you feel." Knowing that someone else truly understands one's feelings by virtue of having "been there" brings a sense of relief; one's pain is no longer a burden borne alone. Stepping into the security of such a group can be like coming home for those who have been too long isolated by their painful concerns.

Each mutual-help group provides an atmosphere of acceptance that encourages members to share their sorrows, fears, and frustrations. They can then begin to communicate more openly, view their problems more objectively, and find more effective strategies.

How Do Mutual-Help Groups Operate?

The structure of mutual-help groups and the way they serve their members depends primarily on their goals. Each local group determines its own programs and meeting schedules. Typically, groups hold regular meetings in church halls, public buildings, or other no-rent or low-rent facilities. Many small groups meet in a member's home.

Programs for those meetings can include group discussions, study groups, visiting speakers, and other activities that inform the members and help to build their confidence.

Along with the personal support gained from meeting together, the groups may offer additional services. Newsletters published by both parent organizations and local groups report individual success stories, treatment updates, and other information about the

*He who has a thousand friends
has not a friend to spare.
And he who has an enemy
will meet him everywhere.*

Ali ibn-Abi-Talib (602-661)

group's concerns. Some groups maintain a "hotline" so that those in need will have constant access to information and an understanding listener. Others, particularly those focusing on addictive behavior or emotional disorder, use a "buddy system" so that members can count on one-to-one encouragement between meetings. Some groups, such as those who deal with a rare disease and have only a few members in each part of the country, have a correspondence referral system to put members in touch with one another.

Although some mutual-help groups receive funding from government health agencies and public contributions, many are entirely self-supporting through members' voluntary contributions or minimal dues (average: $10-$15 yearly). Since the groups are run by members for members, there are seldom any professional salaries or overhead costs (although an office administrator or secretary is sometimes necessary). Some groups will even refuse outside contributions on the grounds that it would compromise their independent status.

What Happens at a Mutual-Help Group Meeting?

For the millions currently utilizing and contributing to mutual-help groups, the process began with a tentative exploration, a first meeting. Of course, the prospect of exposing a previously concealed pain may be frightening; thus, many approach their first group meeting with their defenses up. All new members wonder what the group can do for them and what it will ask in return. Experienced members, aware of these mixed emotions, encourage new members to feel relaxed and welcome. A veteran member may begin a conversation and offer literature that outlines the group's purposes. In an atmosphere that is friendly, compassionate, and accepting, new members soon realize that their participation is purely voluntary, with no strings attached. There is an unwritten code of confidentiality within the group, and each member's privacy and dignity is respected. Everyone is given the freedom to draw on the strength of the group as needed and to extend support to others when possible.

Even in the groups that have a series of steps to recovery (such as the "Anonymous" or-

ganizations), members proceed at their own pace, within their own limits. Group disapproval of those who stumble in the march toward recovery is rare because everyone knows how difficult it can be. In fact, mutual-help groups use the knowledge gained from a conflict or crisis as a valuable tool for building better ways to manage such problems in the future.

To those new to a mutual-help group, being with others like themselves, who are successfully getting on with life despite their problems, can be the best encouragement of all. Who are the "others" who provide the positive example that keeps the group together? If they have passed a crisis or gained confidence in coping with their hardship, what further need do they have for shared support? While there are no levels of distinction among the members in a group, there are always those who are stronger, more experienced, more committed to the group's goals and more able to give of themselves. These people often assume leadership roles, continuing to receive comfort and encouragement while helping others. There is a natural tendency among those who have derived benefit from the group to want to perpetuate the cycle of being helped and helping. For those helpers who lead, organize, reach out to others, and bolster the group's morale by their own example, reward comes in seeing the progress of others. Says one group member, "I've been there and know what it's like. I could have been saved 20 years of misery if there had been a group to help me."

What About Professional Help?

Mutual-help groups do not intend to replace physicians, therapists, or other skilled professionals. Rather, the groups function in the belief that many of our physical and mental health needs go beyond the bounds of formal care measures.

Some who have received treatment for an illness have taken only the first step toward recovery; adjusting to a long convalescence becomes the greater challenge. Others must deal with a lifelong handicap or chronic illness. For both, the practical problems of everyday life can be overwhelming. In particular, those who have a mental or emotional illness require the continuing support of others to help them along the

road to recovery. These ongoing problems do not signify a failure on the part of professional caretakers but indicate that there are limits to their ability to serve our needs.

Some mutual-help groups avoid formal professional guidance or consultation, although many have benefitted from the informal help of professionals. Despite the distance maintained between the groups and their professional counterparts, each acknowledges the role of the other: groups typically encourage their members to seek or continue with the professional help they need, and many physicians and other service providers strongly endorse group programs as an appropriate extension of care.

Finding the Mutual-Help Group That You Need

You may already have heard about a mutual-help group that deals with your concerns. There are a number of ways to get more information about groups that may interest you. Some of the larger groups are listed by subject in the phone directory, and the names and phone numbers of many more are available from hospitals and local health and social-service agencies. If you're interested in an organization that does not have a group in your area, the central office will provide information on organizing one.

Directories of mutual-help groups can be found in public libraries, and more comprehensive information and assistance, including how to organize a group, can be found through the organizations listed on page 19 entitled "Self-Help Organizations."

> **The important thing to realize is that mutual-help groups are there for you. They're economical and effective. And they can reassure you that you are not alone: there are others who understand your problem and are eager to share their experience and support with you.**

Organizations that offer support for human problems

Al-Anon Family Group Headquarters
1372 Broadway
New York, NY 10018-0862
(800) 356-9996; (212) 245-3151 in NY
Helps spouses and family members of alcoholics cope with the problems at home through information, group support, and publications. Cooperates with alcoholism treatment programs by support to patients and families.

Alcoholics Anonymous
P.O. Box 459
Grand Central Station
New York, NY 10163
For men and women who share the common problems of alcoholism.

Alzheimer's Disease and Related Disorders Association
70 East Lake Street, Suite 600
Chicago, IL 60601-5997
(800) 621-0379; (800) 572-6037 in IL
Provides practical information on caring for the patient at home and describes community healthcare services that assist caregivers, such as respite care, services for the family of the patient, and long-term residential care. The national office will refer callers to its 188 local chapters.

American Association of Suicidology
2459 South Ash
Denver, CO 80222
For those who have experienced the suicide of someone close.

American Narcolepsy Association
P.O. Box 1187
San Carlos, CA
(415) 591-7979
Provides information and referrals to people with sleep disorders.

The Compassionate Friends
P.O. Box 3696
Oak Brook, IL 60522-3696
(312) 990-0010
For bereaved parents: peer support.

Emotions Anonymous
P.O. Box 4245
St. Paul, MN 55104
(612) 647-9712
For persons with emotional problems: a 12-step program adapted from the AA program.

Nar-Anon Family Groups, Inc.
P.O. Box 2562
Palos Verdes, CA 90274-0119
(213) 547-5800
Patterned on the Al-Anon model, local groups offer education, information, and support for relatives and friends concerned about drug abuse by a family member or friend.

Narcotics Anonymous
P.O. Box 9999
Van Nuys, CA 91409
(818) 780-3951
For narcotic addicts: peer support for recovered addicts.

The National Alliance for the Mentally Ill
2101 Wilson Blvd.
Suite 302
Arlington, VA 22201
(703) 524-7600
For families and friends of seriously mentally ill individuals; provides information, emotional support, and advocacy through local and state affiliates.

National Coalition Against Domestic Violence
P.O. Box 15127
Washington, DC 20003-0127
1-800-333-SAFE
National organization of shelters and support services for battered women and their children.

National Depressive and Manic Depression Association
Merchandise Mart
P.O. Box 3395
Chicago, IL 60654
1-800-248-4344
For depressed persons and their families.

National Mental Health Association
1021 Prince Street
Alexandria, VA 22314-2971
(703) 684-7722
Provides emotional support for families and helps them learn how to help mentally ill family members. Publishes pamphlets on all aspects of mental health and mental illness including aging.

National Stroke Association
300 E. Hampden Avenue
Suite 240
Englewood, CO 80110-2622
(303) 762-9922
Provides an information exchange and support network for stroke victims and their families.

OCD Foundation, Inc.
P.O. Box 9573
New Haven, CT 06535
(203) 772-0565
For sufferers of obsessive-compulsive disorder and their families and friends.

Phobia Society of America
133 Rollins Avenue
Suite 4B
Rockville, MD 20852
(301) 231-9350
For people who suffer from phobia and panic attacks.

Recovery, Inc.
802 North Dearborn Street
Chicago, IL 60610
(312) 337-5661
For former mental patients: peer support.

Widowed Persons Service
601 E Street, N.W.
Washington, D.C. 20049
(202) 434-2260
This is a cooperative service with the American Association of Retired Persons and offers peer support for widows and widowers.

WHERE TO FIND MORE INFORMATION ON SELF-HELP GROUPS

California Self-Help Center
2349 Franz Hall UCLA
405 Hilgard Avenue
Los Angeles, CA 90024-1563
(213) 825-1799
CA 1-800-222-5465
Publishes Self-Help Group Resources Catalog: A guide to Print, Audio, and Visual materials and services for starting and maintaining self-help groups.

The National Mental Health Consumers' Self-Help Clearinghouse
311 South Juniper St., Rm 902
Philadelphia, PA 19107
(215) 735-6367
Provides technical assistance and information and referral services to further the development of consumer-run mental health self-help groups.

National Self-Help Clearinghouse Graduate School and University Center
33 West 42nd Street
New York, NY 10036
(212) 840-1259
Newsletter, free brochure.

Self-Help Clearinghouse
St. Clare's Riverside Medical Center
Denville, NJ 07834
(201) 625-7101
Publishes the Self-Help Source Book, listing 500 national organizations.

Self-Help Center
1600 Dodge Avenue
Suite S-122
Evanston, IL 60201
(312) 328-0470
Publishes in conjunction with the American Hospital Association Directory of National Self-Help/Mutual Aid Resources.

> **A true friend is somebody who can make us do what we can.**
> Emerson (1803-1882)

Here's good news for older Americans!

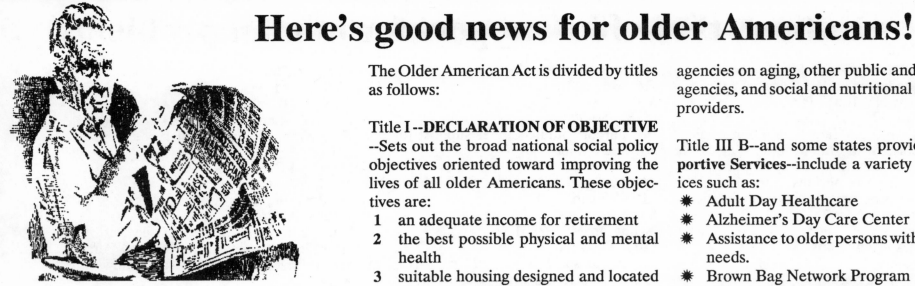

For the past 23 years, millions of senior citizens have benefitted from the services provided by a federal law called the Older Americans Act. The purpose of this Act is to serve those elderly in the greatest social and economic need, giving particular attention to low-income minority individuals and providing services and programs that assist them in maintaining their independence as well as their dignity. In fact, many of the 9 million elderly that the Act serves are able to avoid institutionalization because of the services provided.

The way the system works is as follows:

- ■ Federal government's Older American Act establishes certain programs that must be implemented by the states and the federal government provides the funds (or most of the funds) for these programs.
- ■ Each state establishes a Department of Aging to implement the provisions of the Older American Act and acts as a unifying force for services to seniors. States also legislate to provide additional funds and other entitlement programs for senior citizens.
- ■ Some states establish local Area Agencies on Aging that work with other private nonprofit agencies to implement the desired programs.

NOTE: Some programs are mandated by the federal government and are available in all states. Others can be either state programs or optional federal/state programs. Program services vary somewhat between states. To find out what opportunities are available in your location, contact your area or state agency. Their phone number can be found in the yellow pages of your telephone book under the heading of "Senior Citizens' Service Organizations."

The Older American Act is divided by titles as follows:

Title I--**DECLARATION OF OBJECTIVE** --Sets out the broad national social policy objectives oriented toward improving the lives of all older Americans. These objectives are:

1 an adequate income for retirement
2 the best possible physical and mental health
3 suitable housing designed and located to meet special needs
4 full restorative services for those who require institutional care including a comprehensive array of community-based long-term-care services
5 opportunity for employment without age discrimination
6 retirement in health, honor, and dignity
7 pursuit of civic, cultural, education and training, and recreational opportunities
8 efficient community services with emphasis on maintaining a continuum of care for the vulnerable elderly
9 benefits from research designed to sustain and improve health and happiness
10 freedom for older persons to plan and manage their lives, participate in the planning and operation of services designed for their benefit, and protection against abuse, neglect, and exploitation

Title II--**ADMINISTRATION ON AGING** --Established the Administration on Aging (AoA) within the Department of Health and Human Services (DHHS) to administer the program. Also established the Federal Council on Aging--an advisory body to the president and to Congress.

Title III--**GRANTS FOR STATE AND COMMUNITY PROGRAMS ON AGING**-- Provides grants to state and area agencies on aging to develop supportive and nutrition services, to act as advocates on behalf of programs for older persons, and to coordinate programs for the elderly. The program supports 57 state agencies and 670 area agencies on aging. Funds are distributed on the basis of each state's population aged 60 or over as compared to other states. Title III is intended to form a "network on aging" linking AoA, state, and area

agencies on aging, other public and private agencies, and social and nutritional services providers.

Title III B--and some states provide **Supportive Services**--include a variety of services such as:

- ✳ Adult Day Healthcare
- ✳ Alzheimer's Day Care Center
- ✳ Assistance to older persons with special needs.
- ✳ Brown Bag Network Program
- ✳ Elder abuse prevention activities
- ✳ Foster Grandparent Program
- ✳ Health education and promotion services
- ✳ Health Insurance Counseling and Advocacy Program (HICAP)
- ✳ Information and referral
- ✳ In-home services
- ✳ Legal assistance
- ✳ Linkages
- ✳ Long-term care ombudsman services
- ✳ Outreach activities
- ✳ Respite Care
- ✳ Senior centers
- ✳ Senior discount program
- ✳ Transportation

ADULT DAY HEALTHCARE (ADHC)--is a licenced community-based day program providing a variety of health, therapeutic, and social services designed to serve the specialized needs of those at risk of being placed in a nursing home. The primary objectives are:

- ✔ to restore or maintain optimal capacity for self-care to frail elderly persons and other physically or mentally impaired adults;
- ✔ to delay or prevent inappropriate or personally undesirable institutionalization.

The program stresses partnership with the participant, the family, the physician, and the community in working toward maintaining personal independence. In some situations, individuals already institutionalized may be placed back in the community with ADHC assistance and support services. Participants may attend up to five days a week.

Individual Care Plan--Each ADHC center has a multidisciplinary team of health professionals who conduct a comprehensive

Adult day care--brown bags--help against elder abuse

assessment of each potential participant to determine which ADHC services fulfill the individual's specific health and social needs. This individualized plan of care may include any of the following:

- ❤ medical services by a personal or staff physician emphasizing prevention, treatment, rehabilitation, and continuity of care;
- ❤ nursing services including assistance in bathing, toileting, grooming, administration and monitoring of medication, and nursing care;
- ❤ physical therapy;
- ❤ occupational therapy;
- ❤ speech therapy;
- ❤ transportation to and from center;
- ❤ hot meal and nutritional counseling--at least one meal per day that provides one-third of daily nutritional needs with special diets as required;
- ❤ psychiatric and psychological services;
- ❤ social services--include group or individual discussion of problems, coordination with family or other community agencies, counseling, and referral to available community resources;
- ❤ recreation and social activities;
- ❤ emergency physician, hospital, and ambulance services.

Some centers offer optional services such as podiatry or dentistry. Participation in group activities is encouraged as the social environment itself is therapeutic. By providing intellectual stimulation and emotional satisfaction, group activities lead to a renewed interest in life.

Eligibility and Fees. ADHC centers accept adults who need individualized medical and/or psychological treatment but who are not

Anyone over 60 years of age is entitled to these benefits.

Means tests are prohibited; Voluntary contributions toward the cost of meals are permitted.

"Means test" means the use of older person's income or resource to deny or limit that person's receipt of services.

bedridden. Persons in walkers, wheelchairs, and those who require supervision and help with medications are welcome. Eligibility criteria are:

- ✔ a medical condition that requires treatment or rehabilitative services prescribed by a physician;
- ✔ mental or physical impairments that handicap daily living activities but are not of such a serious nature as to require 24-hour institutional care;
- ✔ reasonable expectation that preventative service will maintain or improve the present level of functioning; and
- ✔ high potential for further deterioration and probable institutionalization if adult day healthcare were not available.

ADHC services are reimbursed by Medi-Cal (in California), Medicaid, or through private payment. Most centers have a sliding fee scale based on private participant's ability to pay.

ALZHEIMER'S DAY CARE CENTER--In California (check with your state AoA) these centers provide services that support the physical and psychosocial needs of patients with Alzheimer's disease or related dementias. Services may vary from center to center but most provide:

- ✳ counseling, information, and referral
- ✳ day care for persons with Alzheimer's disease or related disorders
- ✳ respite care for families who care for these persons at home
- ✳ social and support services to family and caregivers
- ✳ training opportunities for persons caring for these persons
- ✳ public information and training for professionals, caregivers, and family members
- ✳ resource to family support groups
- ✳ recreational and social activities
- ✳ functional assessments

Eligibility--Patients in the moderate to severe stages of Alzheimer's disease and other dementias, whose care needs and behavioral problems make it difficult for them to participate in other care programs, are eligible to participate.

Fees--Participation entails no specific financial eligibility. Those able to share in

Adult Day Care

the cost of care are asked to contribute on a sliding fee scale. However, no one is turned away based upon inability to pay.

BROWN BAG NETWORK PROGRAM--is a California state-funded program that provides surplus and unmarketable edible fruits, vegetables, and other unsold food products to low-income elderly persons. There are no distribution costs. The program serves people 60 years of age and older who are on fixed incomes. Participants often cannot afford to purchase these foods at market prices. Brown Bag volunteers, many of whom are older people, gain a sense of purpose and satisfaction of helping others.

In California, state funds are awarded to selected public and private non-profit organizations that procure (at no purchase cost) surplus food products from farm fields and grocery shelves for distribution to low-income elderly. Priority is given to those in the greatest economic need. The types of food distributed vary depending on the season, weather, and other factors. The food distributed by the program is not intended to meet all of the nutritional needs of older people but helps to supplement their diet.

ELDER ABUSE--States are required to identify abuse, neglect, or exploitation; procedures for receipt of reports of abuse; and referral of complaints to law enforcement, public protection service agencies, or other appropriate agencies. Involuntary or coerced participation in the program by alleged victims, abusers, or their households is prohibited.

Information, Legal Help, Long-term-care Ombudsman

FOSTER GRANDPARENT PROGRAM-- is a state-funded program similar to the Federal ACTION Agency program that provides the opportunity for low-income persons, 60 years or older, to aid children having exceptional or special needs.

Host sites--Volunteers help children in institutions such as mental retardation, mental health, correctional, physically handicapped, acute care hospitals; and in settings such as day care center, pre-school, Head Start, kindergarten, grand and high schools, group shelters, courts, and others.

Requirements--Volunteers must be 60 years of age or older; low-income; available to work 4 hours per day, 5 days a week, for a total of 20 hours per week; and cannot be in the regular work force. Income eligibility is based on the poverty income guidelines of the Department of Health and Human Services. Each volunteer receives 40 hours of orientation training prior to assignment at a host site and 4 hours of in-service training each month thereafter.

Volunteer Benefits--After placement and in return for their services, the volunteers receive the following benefits: a tax-exempt stipend to cover the cost of volunteering; a free meal or meal reimbursement for each day of service; provision site; an annual free physical examination; training (orientation and ongoing); insurance coverage; uniforms when appropriate; and participation in the annual awards/recognition event.

HEALTH INSURANCE COUNSELING AND ADVOCACY PROGRAM (HICAP)-- Assists individuals and families with Medicare problems and other health-related concerns. Trained volunteer counselors provide objective information on Medicare and health insurance. These counselors are available at senior centers, senior nutrition sites, libraries, hospitals, and community centers. Counselors may also visit the homebound individual unable to come to a site. The goals of HICAP are to provide:

* information through community forums about the myths and realities of Medicare and private health insurance;
* counseling and advocacy to assist individuals with health billing claims and insurance;
* legal representation and advice when necessary and appropriate.

HICAP will help an individual file Medicare or other health insurance claims, and will understand his or her insurance and healthcare needs. HICAP serves current and future Medicare beneficiaries and their children, supplemental health insurance subscribers, and those planning for retirement and future health and long-term-care needs. HICAP counseling is confidential and free of charge.

INFORMATION AND REFERRAL SERVICES--Trained staff help link older persons and their families to specific community services.

IN-HOME SERVICES--Assistance with personal care and daily tasks, homemaker and home health aide, visiting and telephone reassurance, chore maintenance, and supportive services for families of elderly victims of Alzheimer's and related diseases.

LEGAL SERVICES--are provided to identify legal problems and legal service needs of older persons. The legal services can help you with a variety of legal problems concerning housing, consumer fraud, elder abuse, Social Security, Supplemental Security Income (SSI), Medicare, Medicaid, age discrimination, pensions, nursing homes, protective services, conservatorships, and other matters. The legal assistance provider:

* must have expertise in specific areas of the law affecting older persons in economic or social need, for example, public benefits, institutionalization, and alternates to institutionalization.
* must have the capacity to provide support to other advocacy efforts, for example, the long-term-care ombudsman program.
* must provide legal assistance in the principal language spoken by clients in areas where a significant number of clients do not speak English.
* must provide effective administration and judicial representation in all areas of the law affecting older persons.
* may not require an older person to disclose information about income or resources as a condition for providing legal assistance.
* may ask about the person's financial circumstances as a part of a process of providing legal advice, counseling, and representation, or for the purpose of identifying additional resources and benefits for which the person may be eligible.

LINKAGES--Provides four levels of services ranging from in-depth information and referral to ongoing case management. Linkages serves elderly and younger functionally impaired adults at risk of institutionalization. Clients do not need to be eligible for Medi-Cal (Medicaid).

LONG-TERM-CARE OMBUDSMAN PROGRAM: Since 1978, the Older Americans Act has mandated all State Units on Aging to establish and operate a long-term-care Ombudsman program. A state-certified ombudsman is a public official who investigates and resolves complaints made by, or on behalf of, older individuals who are residents of long-term-care facilities, nursing homes, and residential care homes. They do not represent the facility.

Complaints may relate to inadequate hygiene; physical abuse; personal items lost, stolen, or used by others; understaffing of the facility; action, inaction, or decisions of

> The senior who needs assistance can contact a legal services project by calling the local Area Agency on Aging listed under the "Senior Citizens' Services Organizations" in the yellow pages of every telephone directory.
>
> Many senior centers provide for regular opportunities to meet with attorneys to discuss their specific problems.

Outreach, companion, transportation, nutrition

long-term-care providers (or their representatives), public agencies, or social service agencies that may adversely affect the health, safety, welfare, or rights of residents.

If you or your loved one is not getting the care they deserve, don't hesitate to contact your ombudsman--it is your right!

Ombudsmen are required to exercise oversight of skilled nursing facilities, intermediate care facilities, board and care homes, and other adult care homes. Ombudsmen are guaranteed access to facilities and must maintain strict rules of confidentiality for clients and complainants. Your ombudsman can be located through your area agency on aging or through your state office of aging (see state offices of aging page 24).

OUTREACH--Seek out persons who may be eligible for assistance under SSI, Medicaid, and Food Stamp programs but are not receiving such assistance.

RESPITE CARE/RESPITE CARE REGISTRIES--Provide information and referral to help caregivers obtain temporary or periodic relief (in-home and out-of-home). The Respite Care program also gathers data on the availability of respite in local communities.

SENIOR COMPANION PROGRAM--is like the Foster Grandparent program except it gives support to adults (instead of children) with special needs, such as the frail homebound elderly in jeopardy of being institutionalized, those physically handicapped, and those who are mentally or neurologically impaired. Requirements and volunteer benefits are the same as the Foster Grandparent program.

Senior companions serve as an integral part of a care plan designed to allow homebound persons to continue independent living. Volunteers serve as peer counselors and advocates, linking their clients to appropriate community services. Special emphasis is on acute care, discharge planning, mental health, and care of the terminally ill.

Host Site Facilities--Senior companions serve in many settings such as private homes, nursing homes, convalescent hospitals, private nonprofit health agencies, day care centers, nutrition sites, multipurpose senior centers, and other facilities that serve seniors.

SENIOR DISCOUNT PROGRAMS--Many states develop a statewide network of community-based discount programs for persons 60 years of age or older. The primary goal is to extend the purchasing power of older consumers by enhancing existing discount programs. Benefits include:

✳ Seniors can stretch their buying power by taking advantage of cash discounts.
✳ Businesses can increase visibility by offering discounts and other special benefits to seniors.

TRANSPORTATION--Local agencies secure escorts and travel vouchers or provide vehicles to assist in transportation of older persons to essential services.

Seniors on Wheels

Three mice died and went to heaven. When they arrived, St. Peter asked them, "What would you like to have up here? You can have anything you want." The mice said, "We would like some roller skates since they never made skates on earth small enough to fit our feet." Later three cats died and went to heaven. When they arrived, St. Peter asked them, "What would you like?" They said they wanted to look around first and did. When they came back St. Peter asked, "Did you find anything you like?" They replied, "We sure like those meals on wheels."

Title III C --**NUTRITIONAL SERVICES**-- A central focal point of the Older American Act for the past 15 years has been the nutrition program. This program has improved the quality of life for millions of seniors through the provision of daily meals in either congregate settings or in the home. The average age of those being served by the congregate program is now 73 and for the home delivered meals program it is nearly 78. Meals must meet nutritional standards by providing a minimum of one-third of the Recommended Dietary Allowance (RDA).

Eligibility--Persons who are 60 years of age or older, and their spouses of any age, may participate in the nutrition program. The following groups are also allowed to receive meals:

✔ people with disabilities under 60 years who reside in housing facilities occupied primarily by the elderly where congregate meals are served;
✔ people with disabilites of any age who reside at home with and accompany older persons are eligible under the Act;
✔ volunteers of any age who provide services during the meal hours.

Home-delivered meals are available to persons who are homebound by reason of illness, disability, or who are otherwise isolated. Spouses of such persons, regardless of age or condition, may also receive home-delivered meals, if according to criteria determined by the area agency receipt of the meal is in the best interest of the homebound older person.

Availability--State agencies establish sites in close proximity to areas where a majority of eligible participants reside, and preferably within walking distance. Particular attention is given to establish sites in multipurpose senior centers, schools, and churches.

Where possible providers arrange for transportation to meal sites and provide outreach efforts to others so the maximum number of eligible individuals may participate. Nutritional providers are required to offer older persons at least one free meal daily, 5 or more days a week. Each meal is to assure a minimum of one-third the daily recommended dietary allowance. Providers are to furnish special menus to meet particular dietary needs of the elderly.

Meals, training and research, and senior employment

Senior Citizens' Centers
A great place to meet
new friends!

CONGREGATE NUTRITIONAL SERVICES provide meals in a group setting. Services also include nutrition education, nutrition counseling (normal and therapeutic nutrition), and opportunities for socialization. Participants are provided an opportunity to contribute to the cost of the meal. Project facilities and operations conform to health and safety standards and provide safe, wholesome, and nutritious meal services.

HOME-DELIVERED MEAL SERVICES are available to people age 60 or older who are homebound by reason of illness, incapacitation, disability, or are otherwise isolated. Because homebound meal recipients are usually older and frailer, screening and referral services are stressed. Some home-delivered meals programs provide their clients with weekend and holiday meals, therapeutic diets, and two-meal-per-day services. In addition, nutrition education and nutrition counseling are available.

Title IV--**TRAINING, RESEARCH, AND DISCRETIONARY PROJECTS AND PROGRAMS:** In recent years the following projects were supported:

- ❤ community-based long-term care
- ❤ adult literacy
- ❤ Alzheimer's disease support services
- ❤ training programs to assist persons employed or preparing for employment in the field of aging
- ❤ studies in the area of healthcare, housing, social services, retirement roles, and the needs of low-income and minority older persons
- ❤ funding to support innovative approaches to provide services under this Act

Title V--**SENIOR COMMUNITY SERVICE EMPLOYMENT PROGRAM (SCSEP)**--is designed to provide funds to subsidize, foster, and promote useful part-time opportunities in community service employment for unemployed, low-income persons 55 years or older and to assist in the transition of enrollees to private or other unsubsidized employment.

Wages--Enrollees are paid no less than federal or state minimum wage or local prevailing rate. Federal funds may be used to compensate participants for a maximum of 1,300 hours of work per year (52 weeks at 25 hours a week), including orientation and training. Participants work an average of 20-25 hours per week.

SCSEP projects are located in all 50 states, the District of Columbia, Puerto Rico, and U.S. territories. These projects place you in part-time jobs in public or nonprofit community agencies including, but not limited to, social services, health, welfare, education, and legal services. The employment projects are sponsored by national contractors and by state and territorial governments. Training is part of the effort. Some of these contractors may include:

- ✳ American Association of Retired Persons
- ✳ Asociacion Nacional Por Personas Mayores
- ✳ Green Thumb, Inc.
- ✳ National Caucus and Center on Black Aged
- ✳ National Council of Senior Citizens
- ✳ National Council of the Aging, Inc.
- ✳ National Pacific/Asian Resource Center on Aging
- ✳ National Urban League
- ✳ United States Department of Agriculture, Forest Service

Eligibility: Persons eligible under the program are those who are 55 years of age or older (and the law requires that priority be given to persons 60 years and older), unemployed, and whose income level is not more than 125 percent of the poverty level guidelines issued by DHHS (in 1990, $6,280 for a one-person household and $8,420 for a two-person household, with higher amounts for Alaska and Hawai. When determining eligibility, non-cash income such as food stamps and compensation received in the form of food or housing, unemployment benefits, and welfare benefits are not counted as income.

Title VI--**GRANTS TO NATIVE AMERICANS** (older Indians and native Hawaiians)--authorizes funds for social and nutritional services awarded directly to tribal organizations.

STATE DEPARTMENTS ON AGING

The offices listed in this section provide information on services, programs, and opportunities for the aging.

Alabama
Commission on Aging
136 Catoma St., 2nd Floor
Montgomery, AL 36130
(205) 242-5743

Alaska
Older Alaskans Commission
P.O. Box C, MS-0209
Juneau, AK 99811
(907) 465-3250

American Samoa
Administration on Aging
Government of American Samoa
Pago Pago, AS 96799
(011-684) 633-1251

Arizona
Aging and Adult Administration
Department of Economic Security
1400 West Washington St.
Phoenix, AZ 85007
(602) 542-4446
1-800-352-3792 in AZ

Arkansas
Division of Aging and Adult Services
Department of Human Services
Main & 7th Streets
Donaghey Bldg., Suite 1428
Little Rock, AR 72201
(501) 682-2441

California
Department of Aging
1600 K Street
Sacramento, CA 95814
(916) 322-5290

Colorado
Aging and Adult Services
Department of Social Services
1575 Sherman St., 10th Floor
Denver, CO 80203-1714
(303) 866-5905

Commonwealth of Northern Mariana Islands
Office of Aging
Civic Center
Saipan, Mariana Islands 96950
(011-670) 234-6011

Connecticut
Department of Aging
175 Main Street
Hartford, CT 06106
(203) 566-3238
1-800-443-9946 in CT

Delaware
Division of Aging
Department of Health and Social Services
1901 N. DuPont Hwy, 2nd Floor
New Castle, DE 19720
(302) 421-6791
1-800-233-9074 in DE

District of Columbia
Office on Aging
1424 K St., N.W., 2nd Floor
Washington, D.C. 20005
(202) 724-5622

Need help?--Call your Area Agency or a State Department

Florida
Aging and Adult Services
Department of Health and Rehabilitation Services
Bldg. 2, Room 328
1317 Winewood Blvd.
Tallahassee, FL 32399-0700
(904) 488-8922
1-800-342-0825 in FL

Georgia
Office of Aging
Department of Human Resouces
Sixth Floor
878 Peachtree St., N.E.
Atlanta, GA 30309
(404) 894-5333

Guam
Division of Senior Citizens
Department of Public Health &
Social Services
P.O. Box 2816
Government of Guam
Agana, Guam 96910
(011-671) 734-2942

Hawaii
Executive Office on Aging
335 Merchant St., Rm. 241
Honolulu, HI 96813
(808) 548-2593

Idaho
Office on Aging
Statehouse, Room 108
Boise, ID 83720
(208) 334-3833

Illinois
Department on Aging
421 East Capital Avenue
Springfield, IL 62701
(217) 785-2870
1-800-252-8966 in IL

Indiana
Aging Division
Department of Human Services
251 N. Illinois St.
P.O. Box 7083
Indianapolis, IN 46207-7083
(317) 232-1139
1-800-545-7763 in IN

Iowa
Department of Elder Affairs
914 Grand Ave., Suite 236
Des Moines, IA 50319
(515) 281-5187
1-800-532-3213 in IA

Kansas
Department on Aging
Docking State Office Bldg. 122-S
915 SW Harrison
Topeka, KS 66612-1500
(913) 296-4986
1-800-432-3535 in KS

Kentucky
Division for Aging Services
275 East Main St., 6th Floor W.
Frankfort, KY 40621
(502) 564-6930

Louisiana
Governor's Office of Elder Affairs
P.O. Box 80374
Baton Rouge, LA 70898-0374
(504) 925-1700

Maine
Bureau of Maine's Elderly
Department of Human Services
Statehouse, Station 11
Augusta, ME 04333
(207) 289-2561

Maryland
Office on Aging
301 W. Preston St.
Baltimore, MD 21201
(301) 225-1102
1-800-338-0153 in MD

Massachusetts
Office of Elder Affairs
38 Chauncy Street
Boston, MA 02111
(617) 727-7750
1-800-882-2003 in MA

Michigan
Office of Services to the Aging
P.O. Box 30026
Lansing, MI 48909
(517) 373-8230

Minnesota
Board on Aging
Human Services Bldg., 4th Floor
444 Lafayette Road
St. Paul, MN 55155-3843
(612) 296-2770
1-800-652-9747 in MN

Mississippi
Division of Aging and Adult Services
421 W. Pascagoula St.
Jackson, MS 39203
(601) 949-2070
1-800-222-7622 in MS

Missouri
Division on Aging
Department of Social Services
2701 W. Main St.
P.O. Box 1337
Jefferson City, MO 65102
(314) 751-3082
1-800-235-5503 in MO

Montana
Department of Family Services
P.O. Box 8005
Helena, MT 59604
(406) 444-5900
1-800-332-2272 in MT

Nebraska
Department on Aging
301 Centennial Mall-South
P.O. Box 95044
Lincoln, NE 68509
(402) 471-2306

Nevada
Division for Aging Services
State Mail Room
Las Vegas, NV 89158
(702) 486-3545

New Hampshire
Division of Elderly & Adult Services
NH Dept. of Health & Human
Services
6 Hazen Drive
Concord, NH 03301
(603) 271-4390
1-800-852-3311 in NH

New Jersey
Division on Aging
Department of Community Affairs
101 S. Broad St., CN 807
Trenton, NJ 08625-0807
(609) 292-0920
1-800-792-8820 in NJ

New Mexico
State Agency on Aging
La Villa Rivera Bldg.
224 E. Palace Ave., 4th Floor
Sante Fe, NM 87501
(505) 827-7640
1-800-432-2080 in NM

New York
Office for the Aging
Agency Building No. 2
Empire State Plaza
Albany, NY 12223-0001
(518) 474-5431
1-800-342-9871 in NY

North Carolina
Division of Aging
Department of Human Resources
Kirby Building
1985 Umstead Drive
Raleigh, NC 27603
(919) 733-3983
1-800-662-7030 in NC

North Dakota
Aging Services Division
Department of Human Services
State Capital Building
Bismark, ND 58505
(701) 224-2577
1-800-472-2622 in ND

Ohio
Department of Aging
50 W. Broad St., 9th Floor
Columbus, OH 43215
(614) 466-5500
1-800-282-1206 in OH

Oklahoma
Special Unit on Aging
Department of Human Services
P.O. Box 25352
Oklahoma City, OK 73125
(405) 521-2327

Oregon
Senior & Disabled Services Division
Department of Human Resources
313 Public Service Building
Salem, OR 97310
(503) 378-4728
1-800-232-3020 in OR

Pennsylvania
Department of Aging
Barto Building
231 State Street
Harrisburg, PA 17101
(717) 783-1550

Puerto Rico
Office of Elderly Affairs
Call Box 50063
Old San Juan Station, PR 00902
(809) 721-0753

Republic of Palau
State Agency on Aging
Department of Social Services
Republic of Palau
Koror, Palau 96940

Rhode Island
Department of Elderly Affairs
160 Pine Street
Providence, RI 02903
(401) 277-2858
1-800-752-8088 in RI

South Carolina
Commission on Aging
400 Arbor Lake Dr., Suite B-500
Columbia, SC 29223
(803) 735-0210
1-800-922-1107

South Dakota
Office of Adult Services and Aging
Richard F. Kneip Bldg.
700 Governors Drive
Pierre, SD 57501-2291
(605) 773-3656

Tennessee
Commission on Aging
706 Church St., Suite 201
Nashville, TN 37219-5573
(615) 741-2056

Texas
Department on Aging
P.O. Box 12786
Capital Station
Austin, TX 78711
(515) 444-2727
1-800-252-9240 in TX

Utah
Division of Aging and Adult Services
120 North, 200 W, Room 4A
P.O. Box 45500
Salt Lake City, UT 84145-0500
(801) 538-3910

Vermont
Office on Aging
103 South Main Street
Waterbury, VT 05676
(802) 241-2400
1-800-642-5119 in VT

Virgin Islands
Department of Human Services
Barbel Plaza South
Charlotte Amalie
St. Thomas, VI 00802
(809) 774-0930

Virginia
Department for the Aging
700 E. Franklin St., 10th Floor
Richmond, VA 23219-2327
(804) 225-2271
1-800-552-4464

Washington
Aging and Adult Services
Administration
Department of Social and
Health Services
Mail Stop OB-44-A
Olympia, WA 98504
(206) 586-3768
1-800-422-3263 in WA

West Virginia
Commission on Aging
State Capital Complex - Holly Grove
1710 Kanawha Boulevard
Charleston, WV 25305
(304) 348-3317
1-800-642-3671 in WV

Wisconsin
Bureau on Aging
Department of Health and
Human Services
1 W. Wilson St., Rm 480
P.O. Box 7851
Madison, WI 53707
(608) 266-2536

Wyoming
Commission on Aging
Hathaway Building, 1st Floor
Cheyenne, WY 82002
(307) 777-7986

> **Area agencies on aging
> are found in the
> yellow pages under
> "Senior Citizens
> Organizations"**

A heavy purse makes a light heart.   English Proverb

When you need medical help you see a doctor. When you need legal help you see a lawyer. If you need help in managing your money matters you may need professional help such as a financial planner. How you manage your money can determine the quality of your life.

Most people can easily educate themselves in money matters through courses and research. Many investments can be acquired at little or no expense without an expert's help. You can keep up-to-date by regularly reading magazines such as: *Money, Changing Times, Consumer Reports,* and *Personal Investor. Sylvia Porter's Retirement Newsletter* and the *No-Load Investment Newspaper* are available by subscription or in most libraries.

Many people produce their own financial plan without using a planner. In some circumstances, depending upon the amount of discretionary funds you have, the most important step may be deciding whether a financial planner is needed at all. Even with a planner it is still important to educate yourself regarding investments so as to be able to evaluate a financial planner's investment recommendations.

Today, nearly a quarter of a million American men and women earn their living as financial planners. If you decide to hire a financial planner, a good one should analyze your finances and recommend how to improve your financial situation. Successful financial planners may have as many different investment strategies as the clients they serve. Make sure the financial planner you choose works on behalf of your interest and needs.

A financial planner should assist you in the following ways:
- ◼ Assess your relevant financial history, such as tax returns, investments, retirement plan, wills, and insurance policies.
- ◼ Review your net-worth statement, examine your debts, and determine if any should be consolidated, paid off from other available funds, or refinanced.
- ◼ Help you decide on a financial plan, based on your personal and financial goals, history, preferences, and psychological investment risk level.
- ◼ Identify financial areas where you may need help, such as building up a retirement income or improving your investment returns, buying or selling an insurance policy, and tax saving suggestions.
- ◼ Write down a financial plan based on your individual situation in language you can understand and discuss it thoroughly with you to make sure you are comfortable with it.
- ◼ Help you implement your financial plan, including referring you to a specialist, such as lawyers or accountants, if necessary.
- ◼ Review your situation and financial plan periodically and suggest changes in your program when needed.

Before you select a financial planner, you may want to ask yourself these questions:

What are my financial goals today and ten years from now?

Before you ask for advice, it is helpful to know where you want that advice to take you. Factors to consider in analyzing your needs include the size of your family, whether you want to go into business for yourself some day, how much money you expect to need in retirement, and what your budget can afford now and in the near future.

What is my personal investment philosophy?

Do you enjoy risky ventures? Do you seek the comfort of solid, blue-chip investments? Or, do you want an investment mix? Be sure to make clear to a financial planner exactly what investment philosophy you are most comfortable with. During retirement many choose as their primary goal the preservation of capital.

Selecting Financial Planners

Finding the professional advisor whose talents and resources best fit your needs may require a real investment of time and effort on your part. But it is an investment that can pay substantial dividends in the long run. Investigating a financial planner holds no foolproof formula, but investors can use many tactics to guard against abuse.

There are several ways you can look for a financial planner who will suit your needs. One place to begin is by contacting one of the major groups representing financial planners, such as the International Association of Financial Planning (IAFP), an association of individuals who work in the financial planning industry, or the Institute of Certified Financial Planners (ICFP), a professional organization of accredited planners. Both can provide you with free information about the financial industry as well as the names of members in your area. See the end of this article for names and addresses.

Recommendations of friends and colleagues who have had investment successes may play a role as you select a financial advisor. You will want to select a firm or individual who has the skills and expertise to meet your specific needs. Be certain that any planner you consider hiring has ample knowledge of taxes, insurance, estate and retirement planning issues, as well as the basics of investment and family budgeting. Check with the Better Business Bureau to determine if any complaints have been lodged against the planner you expect to use.

In a preliminary interview, you may wish to ask any financial planner these questions:

What credentials do you have to practice financial planning?

Financial planners come from a variety of backgrounds and, therefore, may hold a variety of degrees and licenses. There are no state or federal regulations for the financial planning industry. However, some take specialized training in financial planning and earn credentials such as Certified Financial Planner (CFP) or Chartered Financial Consultant (CHFC). Others may hold degrees or registrations such as lawyer (JD), Certified Public Accountant (CPA), or Chartered Life Underwriter (CLU).

Question financial planners carefully about their background and experience. Be wary of individuals who promote various investment items without discussing with you any overall financial planning goal. They may lack the expertise to formulate one.

Are you registered with the federal Securities and Exchange Commission (SEC) or with a state agency?

Anyone who may be giving advice on securities (including tax shelters), use of the

Beware of planners who use high-pressure tactics or promise unusually high rates of return.

stock market, or the value of securities over other types of investments should be registered with the SEC or registered under state laws dealing with investment advisors.

How would you prepare my financial plan?

Financial planners usually prepare financial plans after carefully discussing and analyzing your personal and financial history, your current situation, and your future goals. Some financial planners enter relevant financial information into a computer to generate standard financial plans. This type of plan is often useful, though be certain your unique financial situation is taken into account.

How many companies do you represent?

Someone who represents only one or two companies probably is not a financial planner, but more likely a broker or salesperson. It will be to their advantage to sell you only those products offered by the companies they represent. You may want to seek an advisor who can offer you a wide range of choices to suit your needs.

Who will I deal with on a regular basis?

You will want to work consistently with someone who is completely familiar with your account. Many large firms offer a variety of different financial services. Make sure that such institutions provide a comprehensive and coordinated method of referral among the various "experts" who can advise you about financial plans. Ask how the planner will keep you regularly advised.

How do you keep up with the latest financial developments?

You may want to look for a planner who enrolls in continuing education courses (or, perhaps, teaches in a business school) to keep current on tax and investment strategies. Regular members of the Institute of Certified Financial Planners, for example, are required to complete 30 hours of continuing education every year in order to maintain full membership status.

Will you be involved in implementing the plan you suggest?

Financial planners will develop a plan specifically tailored to your situation and needs.

Some planners also will include provisions for updating your plan to adjust to changes in your life, current economic conditions, and tax laws. Your financial planner also can provide for periodic reviews of your plan to show you the progress that is being made in reaching your goals. You should ask if your planner can provide this type of ongoing service and what those services will cost you.

10 Common Financial Mistakes

Even professional financial planners make mistakes. You should be on the lookout for these common errors:

1. Lack of detailed financial records.
2. Failure to set goals, both short- and long-term.
3. Failure to follow a balanced investment program.
4. Trading or speculating rather than investing.
5. Being too greedy.
6. Failure to recognize that tax shelters have both positive and negative advantages.
7. "Falling in love" with investments.
8. Neglecting an insurance program.
9. Not seeking professional advice when called for.
10. Lack of an up-to-date will and estate plan.

Negotiating Fees

Fee arrangements with a financial planner are quite similar to the payment system for a lawyer. There are a variety of fee options that you should explore to see which serves your interests best. Ask about the following arrangements:

Fee-only Financial Planners--base their charges on gathering your financial data, analyzing it, and recommending a plan of action. Hourly or flat fees are most common. Payment is required whether or not you choose to implement the suggested plan. Many fee-only planners cater to wealthy investors, but you may try this arrangement if you can negotiate a reasonable price.

Commission-only Planners--Some planners charge no fee for service to their client but make their money instead through commissions paid by the marketers of the investment products they sell. For example,

if a client buys insurance on the advice of a financial planner, the planner will not charge the client for that advice but will receive a commission from the insurance company.

Planners who rely only on commissions might be more eager to direct your financial plan toward the purchase of products that provide them with the best commissions. Therefore, you may want to exercise caution in following the advice of a planner who works on commission until you develop a trusting relationship.

Fee and Commission Planners--receive payments from both a sales commission and a fee. If, for example, the planner receives a commission from the company that sells the product you purchase, the fee you are charged may be less.

Written Estimate of Fees and Services-- Make sure you get a written estimate of what services you can expect for what price. Compare this with others and select the package of services that best meets your needs at a reasonable cost.

Complaints About Financial Planners

If you are dissatisfied with the services provided by someone you hired for help with money matters, it is up to you to make your grievance known. If you have kept copies of important agreements between you and your planner, you should have no problem documenting your complaint.

First, discuss your complaint with the planner involved. Many misunderstandings can be resolved at this level. If you are still not satisfied, contact the supervisor or the senior partner, if there is one, in the firm.

If your grievance cannot be resolved at these levels, go the organization or licensing authority that oversees the planner. Two major organizations that respond to complaints from consumers and investigate disputes involving their members are:

1. The International Association of Financial Planners (IAFP) at 2 Concourse Parkway, Suite 800, Atlanta, GA 30328; (800) 241-2148, and

2. The Institute of Certified Financial Planners (ICFP) at 3443 South Galena, Suite 190, Denver, CO 80231-5093; (303) 751-7600.

Protecting the old buggy and you

The revolution in transportation during the lifetimes of some of our oldest citizens is incredible. Equally remarkable is the growth of automobile insurance as an industry. No one could have predicted the industry, much less the chaos and confusion we find it in today.

The reality is that most of us would not think of driving without the protection of adequate insurance. Added to that is the requirement of most states that we carry minimum protection. Complete protection is expensive, no matter where you live, so it is important to understand what protection we truly need and at what levels.

The regulation of the insurance business is in the hands of the state governments. Regulation varies between the states from rigid controls of rates, offerings, and settlement procedures to virtual laissez-faire attitudes toward the business.

TYPES OF COVERAGE

There are six basic areas insured by automobile insurance companies. They are:

❶ **Liability for bodily injury.** This protects you, family members, and persons you allow to drive your vehicle against suit for bodily injury in an accident your car or one you are driving is in, up to the limits set in your policy.

❷ **Liability for property damage.** You are protected from suit for property damage caused by your car or one you are driving. That includes other vehicles, houses, fences, or anything of value. Limits for the various kinds of liability are expressed in three numbers, i.e., 10/30/5. That means that $10,000 is the amount that they would pay to one person injured by your vehicle. They would pay up to $30,000 to all persons injured by your vehicle. They would pay up to $5,000 for all property damage in one accident.

When states require auto insurance it is for liability coverage. Most of them require 25/50/10. Any person who has assets to protect, such as a house, should carry more. Most experts suggest limits of 100/300/50, or even higher. Generally if you wish to go beyond those numbers you will need to purchase an umbrella policy. Many persons get $1,000,000 coverage in this way. Sometimes you can buy single limit liability insurance that provides a lump sum that is available for either bodily injury or property damage.

❸ **Medical payments insurance.** This coverage protects you and members of your family in your car. It protects you and family members in another car. It protects you and family members as pedestrians. It also protects guests who are riding in your car from bodily injury costs. It even provides for funeral expenses.

❹ **Collision insurance.** This coverage pays for damage to your car in the event of any accident, single car or multiple car. This insurance carries a deductible so that minor damage is not reimbursed. The amount of the deductible greatly influences the cost of the premiums. If you buy a new car and borrow money for the purpose, the lender will insist that you carry collision coverage. When the car is older you should consider dropping collision because when the value of the vehicle drops so does the amount you can recover in an accident.

❺ **Comprehensive physical damage insurance.** Almost anything that happens to your car can be compensated by comprehensive insurance. If it is stolen, damaged by a fire, or by a falling tree, etc., you are protected. This coverage also includes a deductible. Again, when your vehicle ages, you should drop this coverage because it is wasteful in terms of what you can collect in damages.

❻ **Uninsured or underinsured motorist insurance.** As insurance costs have increased, more drivers decide to drive without insurance. This may be particularly true in rural areas where there are no transportation alternatives. Many states require that this insurance be included in every policy sold. However, in such cases it is possible to reject that coverage in writing. It is wise to accept it, because the danger of being involved with an uninsured or underinsured motorist seems to become more likely all the time.

NO-FAULT INSURANCE

Many states have adopted what is called no-fault insurance. This system is intended to recognize that persons injured in automobile accidents often need help to cover the cost of their injuries. Therefore, all persons injured are given the money needed to treat their injuries, without regard to fault. In theory, they may not sue for additional damages unless their injuries are extremely serious. Unfortunately, in most states the rules have been so watered down through the influence of trial lawyers that the system does not work. The only state where real success seems to have been achieved in this field is Michigan. Ironically, under this system, in spite of smaller awards, those who are injured get more money than in states where litigation is common.

FINANCIAL RESPONSIBILITY

As we said earlier, regulations vary greatly from state to state concerning mandatory insurance. There are three basic variations:

■ Some states require you have insurance before the fact. This is enforced in different ways. One method is to deny a driver's license if you do not have proof of insurance. Cancellation of

When a fellow says it ain't the money
but the principle of the thing, it's the
money. -- Kin Hubbard

INSURANCE

AUTO INSURANCE 29

your automobile registration is another weapon.

2 Some states require insurance after you have had an accident and a judgment against you.

3 Some require you to prove you can pay certain amounts in the event of an accident. Obviously, the most convenient way to accomplish that is through the purchase of insurance.

INSURANCE RATES

Many factors influence the premiums you are charged for your insurance. Some of them are:

* The coverage you choose from the six categories of protection.
* The cost of your automobile.
* Where you live--urban versus rural.
* The driving record of you and your family members.
* Young drivers at home will cost more.
* Variations between companies.

Keeping costs as low as possible while obtaining adequate protection can be done by attending to the following:

* Accept higher deductibles on collision and comprehensive.
* Drop collision and comprehensive after a vehicle is about five years old.
* Check for changes in circumstances such as a child marrying and moving away.
* Insure all vehicles with the same company to get a multi-car discount.
* Keep your driving under 7,500 miles a year.
* Take advantage of good student discounts.
* Select a car with lower loss insurance experience by checking with your company.
* Compare rates between companies.
* Buy from a company that rewards good driving.

RENTING A CAR

There has been a good deal of confusion about whether it is necessary to purchase damage coverage from the rental company when you rent a car. It can exceed the cost of the rental. Most broad coverage policies will cover you when driving a rental car. However, it is best to check with your agent

to make sure of that coverage. Another way of obtaining such coverage is by using a premium credit card. The extra cost of a "gold" or similar premium card can easily be saved in one rental.

WHAT IF YOU HAVE AN ACCIDENT?

The selection of a policy and the payment of the premiums are all we hope we will have to do with the insurance company. However, the reality is that sooner or later most drivers will file a claim, even if they never have an accident. When that time comes, having a local agent you know personally who has a commitment to service makes all the difference. He or she will help you with your claim or file it for you, tell you what to expect, and go to bat for you with the company.

WHAT TO DO AFTER AN ACCIDENT

✔ If there are injuries, call the paramedics.

✔ Call the police, and if they should not come to the scene, file a police report at the appropriate agency. Some states require that you inform the DMV (Department of Motor Vehicles).

✔ Obtain information from the other driver, including license number of car and driver. Also get the number of his insurance policy and company name, telephone, and any other pertinent data.

✔ Get the names and addresses of witnesses if there are any.

✔ Record what happened while it is still fresh--location, time, directions of travel, weather conditions, traffic sign or signals. If you have a camera, take pictures at the scene.

✔ Make no statement about your liability or how much insurance you carry.

✔ Leave a note with your name, address, and phone number if the accident involves a parked car or other property.

✔ Call your agent at the earliest opportunity.

CLAIMS HANDLING

Companies handle claims in different ways. Some of the larger companies have drive-in claim centers where you can take your car, have the damage assessed, and receive a check for the repair the same day. This

process is handled by adjusters. Other companies use appraisers. They look at the damage and send their estimate to the company and the company later tells you what they will pay on your claim. A third way is for you to take your vehicle to three different repair shops and get estimates. The company then decides which one to accept for your claim.

If you disagree with the decision of the company, you can appeal to them at various levels. You can also involve your state insurance commissioner's office (see state insurance listings pages 8 or 9). They may intervene for you. Finally, if you fail to get satisfaction, you can hire a lawyer and sue. State laws vary also in regard to blame for an accident. Some states have what is called "pure comparative negligence" to determine who was at fault and who should be reimbursed. A second approach is "modified comparative negligence," in which you are reimbursed to the same extent as you are determined not to be responsible for the accident. The third approach is called "contributory negligence" in which you receive no payment if you are even 1% at fault for the accident!

CANCELLATION AND NONRENEWAL

State laws vary about what a company can do if they don't want to have your business any longer. Usually they cannot cancel unless there are unusual circumstances. It is easier for them just to not renew your policy at the anniversary date. You may appeal such decisions to your state insurance commissioner. Usually there are laws that govern when the company can raise your rates because of bad accident or law observance history.

There is one more source of information about insurance that you may turn to. That is the office of the Insurance Information Institute. You can call them at 800-221-4954.

Good driving!

Insurance--and you say you are not a gambler?

Buying insurance is like placing a wager. You bet that something will happen and the company bets it will not. The odds are calculated, not by bookies, but by actuaries who consider every possible relevant factor. That may range from whether you are a smoker to what your driving record is. The amount of the bet the company requires is the premium.

Where this comparison becomes less accurate is that you hope you won't win the bet. So you are buying protection against losses from death, auto accident, or fire, to take the most common examples.

HOW INSURANCE COMPANIES WORK

Insurance companies accept your wager (premium) betting either that the event (fire or accident) won't happen at all or that it won't happen for a significant period of time (death).

The company uses the premiums you and other customers pay to cover the costs of operating the business and invest the rest in order to put the money to work. Thus they hope to meet their business obligations and make a profit as well. So insurance companies are a main source of capital for a variety of uses in our economy. When losses do not exceed expectations and investments do well, the company makes a profit. When a disaster strikes so that there are many claims and the investment program does not do well, the company suffers. They may not only fail to make a profit, they also may not be able to pay the claims. This is the time when insurance companies go broke.

Such business problems occurred in the 1980s when some companies established premiums because the interest rates they were earning soared into the teens. When interest rates fell, the companies were sometimes unable to deliver the protection they had promised.

INSURANCE POLICIES

An insurance policy is a contract between the company and the policy holder. As with other types of businesses, there are specific laws that govern their operation in each state. An insurance commissioner is appointed or elected to oversee the operation and regulations of the companies in that state. They are specifically charged with protecting the interests of the public.

Regulations include such matters as the level of reserves a company is required to maintain, laws governing the cancellation of policies and, sometimes, regulation of rates. The office of the insurance commissioner can also assist individual policy holders who have disputes with companies.

GOOD FAITH AND FAIR DEALING

The law requires that insurance companies operate under a principle that is called "good faith and fair dealing." They are expected to treat the interests of the policy holder on a par with their own interests. Now it is doubtful that any company practices that principle fully; but some do it more than others, and your mission is to find the ones that do.

STOCK COMPANIES VERSUS MUTUAL COMPANIES

There are two basic kinds of insurance companies:

❶ The first is a stock company in which the stock holders own and operate an insurance company for the benefit of the owners. Sometimes their rates will be cheaper, especially for initial policies.

❷ The second type is the mutual insurance company. When you buy a policy, you in effect become a stock holder. The usual benefit from such a company is to receive dividends. You do so when your policy is labeled "participating." Thus, profits from the operation of the business are shared with the policy holders.

CHOOSING YOUR INSURANCE AGENT

When you want to purchase an insurance policy, you have a choice between an agent who works for and represents just one company, or a broker who has the choice of several companies. Both are paid by commissions from the selling company.

The insurance buyer needs to find an agent who is willing to put the interests of the client in a paramount position. You may have to test that attitude by shopping around and finding if what your agent says is true. Going to a broker is no assurance that the policy recommended is best for you. It may simply pay him or her more commission than their other policies.

Will the agent be there for you to answer questions or help you with a claim? Do they seem to know what they are talking about?

The insurance industry has a very high employment turnover rate. If your agent is young and has had a short tenure, there is a fair chance that person may not be around for long. When you are looking for an agent, treat it the same way as you would in looking for a doctor. Ask your friends. Check his/her training. Interview the prospective agent.

SHOPPING FOR INSURANCE

Most of us go to an agency and buy what it offers. The best advice is to shop around for your policy. We don't have any trouble doing that when we look for a car or a washing machine.

When you do check prices with different companies, it is important for you to specify what you are looking for and how much coverage you desire. Give the same information to each company. Otherwise, you may be comparing the basic stripped down model with a fancy one that has many special features.

With certain types of insurance, there is a third choice. Some estate planners and financial advisors can give you advice about what to buy and can actually purchase it for you. It is best to go to fee-based advisors for this service. That eliminates them totally from having a financial interest in which policy you buy.

One other opportunity to purchase insurance is offered through the media. We are besieged with such advertisements. It is best to avoid that sort of purchase unless you are absolutely sure of what you are getting.

ADDITIONAL HELP

Insurance is one of the most complicated parts of our culture. There are publications that evaluate policies that are offered in such profusion. Magazines like *Money* give general tips. From time to time, *Consumer Reports* evaluates various kinds of insurance. They use judging criteria that most of us do not have available. You would do well to check out policies you are considering against their evaluations.

Fate

The wheel goes round and round, and some are up and some are on the down.
And still the wheel goes round.

Josephine Pollare (1843-1892)

Getting the most for your insurance dollar

Even for those born to shop, insurance seldom tops the list of favorite purchases. For less enthusiastic buyers, the thought of calling an agent and sitting through a session of deductibles, exclusions, riders, or other insurance jargon can seem intimidating.

Further, insurance protection is an intangible benefit. You usually don't collect on your investment until tragedy strikes--whether it's property damage, injury, illness or death. Although many consider insurance necessary, it is seldom understood. As a result, consumers often buy insurance without adequate planning or even understanding what the marketplace has to offer.

Although most insurance salespersons are reliable, there are still others who are more interested in their own financial rewards than in your concerns. It is unrealistic to expect otherwise. In order to retain control of the transaction, you must prepare yourself to buy only the insurance you want and need. Here are some tips to help you:

■ Decide what you want to buy. Don't leave this decision to the salesperson.

■ List the points that are important to you such as coverage and price.

■ Find out what insurance products are available to cover the points on your list by reading books and magazines, and by talking to several insurance salespersons.

■ Consider the amount of insurance you will need. For property insurance, replacement cost is a good benchmark. With liability insurance, which covers legal responsibility for specified occurrences, the amount needed is more difficult to determine. Factors influencing the face value of life insurance purchased include survivors' needs, assets, lifestyle, and debts.

■ Determine the price range. The insurance you want may be more expensive than your projection, but you will find significant price variations by comparison shopping. Also, you may be able to achieve your price range by making adjustments in the coverage you buy. Most policies have maximum limits, deductibles, and optional coverages. As these change, so does the price.

Shop Around

■ Prices vary considerably, so it pays to compare several companies' rates. However, keep in mind the axiom "you get what you pay for."

■ For service, if possible, deal with companies, agents, and brokers known to give the level of service that meets your needs. Consult with knowledgeable friends and respected advisors for recommendations.

■ Keep in mind that any salesperson has a financial stake in what you buy. Thus, you may also want to seek advice from someone with no sales commission at stake.

Do Research

■ On benefits--You may not know exactly the different types of insurance available when you begin. For example, life insurance products and their prices vary dramatically.

■ On insurers and salespeople--Purchasing insurance can be complicated. Choose both the insurer and the salesperson with care. Find out how an insurance company or agent has performed in the past. Check with the State Department of Insurance.

> Other sources include:
> Friends and advisors.
> Best's Insurance Reports--check with your library.
> Consumer groups and magazines--check the phone directory and library.
> Better Business Bureau.
> Court records--to see if the person or company has been sued.

■ Carefully research the proposal you receive. If necessary consult your attorney or accountant for legal, financial, and tax advice.

Document and Understand the Transaction

■ Any promises made to you about future costs, benefits, or coverages should be made in writing. Ask the agent to show you where these promises appear in the policy.

■ Obtain copies of everything you sign. Obtain receipts for any payment you make. Never pay in cash. All checks should be made payable to the insurance company, not the agent. Be sure all receipts and checks show the policy number and the name of the insurer receiving payment. Keep receipts in a safe place.

■ When illustrations or proposals are shown to you, request copies so you may study them at home without pressure.

■ Use your list to make sure your important points are covered. Many consumer complaints arise because the buyer did not understand the coverage or limitations of the policy.

■ Keep in mind that only the insurance company has authority to change insurance policies. Be suspicious of any salesperson claiming to have this authority. Get any promise in writing.

Review the Policy As Soon As You Get It

Make sure that the contract is what you ordered. Most policies provide a "free look" period (10 to 30 days after delivery) during which you may cancel for a refund. If substantial time has passed, it may be too late to do anything about it.

Some Final Tips

The purchase of insurance is one of the most important transactions you're involved in. Your financial future, and that of your family, may depend on the policies you buy. Smart shopping takes time and effort. Here are some suggestions to help you effectively use the services of an insurance salesperson:

DO

✔ Do plan your purchase. List points regarding coverage and price that are important to you.

✔ Do shop around comparing products and services.

✔ Do check credentials and qualifications of those with whom you deal.

✔ Do ask friends and neighbors about their experience with insurers and salespeople to compare price, coverage, and service.

✔ Do keep copies of all proposals.

✔ Do make your own decisions. You, not the salesperson, must make the final choice on what you need and can afford.

✔ Do get any promises regarding coverage or policy provisions in writing.

✔ Do get a receipt and keep it for the time the policy is in force.

✔ Do read the policy as soon as you receive it to make sure it is what you ordered.

DON'T

✘ Don't be rushed or hurried by high-pressure sales tactics. Buy only the insurance you want and need!

✘ Don't assume the salesperson knows all about the insurance market. Do your own research.

✘ Don't borrow from a premium finance company unless you understand the terms and conditions.

✘ Don't let the agent keep the policy for you. Keep it yourself.

Protecting one of your largest assets--your home

Everyone needs protection against loss. That is especially true in the case of what is for most of us our largest asset--our home. Insurance for that purpose comes in a confusing variety of forms and variations.

Fortunately, modern home insurance comes in packages that protect us against many hazards. The industry has developed five packages for homeowners, one for renters, and one for condominium owners. An additional policy is available for owners of older homes that could not possibly be replicated without prohibitive cost.

The hazards covered in today's policies vary between packages, but none of them routinely covers flood, earthquake, or war. The package combinations that follow may vary between companies in detail, but they tend to cover the same hazards.

HO-1 BASIC COVERAGE
In the basic coverage several types of losses to both the house and its contents are included. They are:

✘ Smoke
✘ Windstorm and hail
✘ Vandalism and theft
✘ Explosion
✘ Riots and civil commotion
✘ Damage from vehicles and aircraft
✘ Glass breakage
✘ Volcanic eruption

HO-2 BROAD FORM
If you obtain broad coverage additional areas of loss are included:

✘ Damage from weight of snow, ice, or sleet
✘ Surges or short circuits in electricity
✘ Problems resulting from improperly functioning plumbing
✘ Damage from faulty heating or air-conditioning systems
✘ Damage from faulty domestic appliances

HO-3 SPECIAL FORM
This form provides more protection for the structure than HO-1 and HO-2. There is also more coverage for personal belongings.

HO-4 RENTER'S INSURANCE
This policy protects personal property of the tenants and gives liability protection to them. Costs are dependent on location, type of structure, and availability of fire equipment and can run anywhere from approximately $95 for $8,000 to $600 for $35,000 protection per year.

HO-5 COMPREHENSIVE FORM
Not all companies sell this policy. It provides greater protection than the other policies for all hazards except war, flood, and earthquakes.

HO-6 CONDOMINIUM OWNERS POLICY
This protects the interior space of a condominium and its contents. Coverage of the basic structure should be provided by the condominium association. Costs are typically less than HO-4 policies since insurance companies consider the fact that you are an owner of the property.

HO-8 OLDER HOMES POLICY
This policy provides actual cash value of the structure in the case of loss rather than replacement costs.

HOW MUCH COVERAGE?
In the final analysis you determine the level of protection you carry on your house. Therefore, it is important that you understand clearly what it would cost to replace the structure, contents, and whatever outbuildings you may have. There are various local sources, including your insurance dealer, who can tell you building costs in your area. It is also important to be sure that your insurance is tied to the cost of living so that the amount in the policy will keep up with inflation. Beyond that, you should review your coverage regularly to be sure you are adequately covered.

There are two settlement formulas that are used by most companies to determine how a loss will be paid. One is based upon those policies that cover 80% or more of replacement costs. The second formula is for policies that cover less than 80%. Having the higher coverage assures a better payment from the insurance company, especially for partial losses, such as a fire in the kitchen.

OTHER PROTECTION
Several other kinds of protection are included in these insurance packages. Probably the greatest potential monetary loss to any homeowner is from suit for liability. A person who is injured on your property can sue you for several times the cost of your house. Built-in amounts for liability protection range from $25,000 to $100,000. Almost without exception, it is wise to purchase additional protection by the payment of modest additional premiums. You may wish to consider the purchase of an umbrella policy that will protect you in more ways than just injury sustained on your property.

Other examples of included protection are:

✦ Additional living expenses as the result of a loss
✦ Credit card losses
✦ Other damages to your property or other's property
✦ Medical payments for injury to nonfamily members on your property

FLOOD INSURANCE

Private companies may now sell flood insurance that is backed by the Federal Insurance Administration. To qualify to purchase such insurance, the homeowner's property must be located in a community that has agreed to plan and carry out land-use control measures to reduce future flooding. This insurance is in addition to the home insurance packages discussed earlier.

EARTHQUAKE INSURANCE

It is now possible to purchase earthquake insurance from most companies. Typically policies carry a 5% or 10% deductible. In California, for example, and depending upon your location, earthquake policies for frame structures run from approximately $2 to $3.25 per $1,000 whereas masonry structures run from $10 to $15 per thousand.

PERSONAL PROPERTY

Personal property coverage in the insurance packages is generally limited to 50% of the value of the structure. This provision does not protect against loss for cars, aircraft, or pets. There are limits on the value of certain categories of personal property. These limits make it important to take action to provide special protection for things you may collect either as a hobby or as an investment. You can do this through the purchase of a rider or floater specifically to protect those items. Coverage beyond the limits will cost approximately $1 to $1.75 per $100. Typical limits are:

- ✱ Securities, deeds, manuscripts, etc. $1,000.
- ✱ Some boats, trailers, and motors $1,000.
- ✱ Jewelry, watches, furs, semiprecious stones $1,000.
- ✱ Silverware, goldware, pewter $2,500.
- ✱ Guns and firearms $2,500.

What is essential in the protection of your personal property is an inventory. It should describe the item, tell when purchased, and the cost. If it is valuable, it helps to have an appraisal. One way of doing this that is increasingly popular is to walk through the house with a video camera filming the item and adding the information alluded to above. Obviously such inventories, whether written or on tape, should be housed in a safe-deposit vault or some other safe place away from your house.

WHAT TO DO IN CASE OF A LOSS

- ✓ Call the police to make a report.
- ✓ Write down what happened while it is fresh in your mind.
- ✓ Call your agent and report the loss.
- ✓ Fill out the report of loss for the insurance company.
- ✓ Provide them with documents or evidence they request.
- ✓ Request a detailed report if you are dissatisfied with the offer or how they arrived at the total.
- ✓ Ask your attorney to write a letter or call the company.
- ✓ Write a letter with documentation to your agent, the claims manager, or other appropriate official stating your case.
- ✓ Go to mediation or arbitration (cost from $150 to $650).
- ✓ Go to court as a last resort.

INSURANCE RATES

There are many factors that influence what you will actually pay for insurance protection. Obviously the first factor is the plan of coverage you select, and whether you have additional coverage for personal property. Other factors that influence cost are:

- ● The size of your house and the type of construction
- ● The material you have on your roof
- ● How close you are to a fire-hydrant
- ● How far you are from the nearest fire station
- ● The protective devices you may have in your home such as smoke detectors and sprinklers

Another recommendation that is made by insurance experts is to consider the wisdom of accepting a higher deductible. That may mean that you will collect nothing for small losses, but it will do more to hold down your premiums than any other option that is open to you.

A GLOSSARY OF HOME INSURANCE TERMS

- ✱ **Actual Cash Value**--Replacement cost less the depreciated value of the home or property.
- ✱ **Agent**--A person authorized, by and on behalf of an insurer, to sell insurance.
- ✱ **Binder**--A temporary or preliminary agreement that provides coverage until a policy can be written or delivered.
- ✱ **Deductible**--The amount of the loss that the insured has to pay.
- ✱ **Depreciation**--A decrease in value due to age, wear and tear, etc.
- ✱ **Endorsement**--An amendment to the policy that is used to add or delete coverage.
- ✱ **Exclusion**--Certain causes and conditions listed in the policy that are not covered.
- ✱ **Insured**--The policy holder or the person(s) protected in case of a loss or claim.
- ✱ **Insurer**--The insurance company.
- ✱ **Peril**--The cause of a possible loss (i.e., fire, theft, hail).
- ✱ **Policy**--The written contract of insurance.
- ✱ **Premium**--The amount of money that the policyholder agrees to pay for the policy of insurance.
- ✱ **Quote**--An estimate of the cost of insurance, based on information supplied to the insurance company by the applicant.
- ✱ **Replacement Value**--The full cost to repair or replace the damaged property with no deduction for depreciation, subject to policy limits and contract provisions.

WEALTH
Is any income that is at least one hundred dollars more a year than the income of one's wife's sister's husband.

H. L. Mencken (1880-1956)

Life insurance--when you bet your life

When a company insures your life, it is their belief (and hope) that you will die later rather than earlier. Your motivation is to protect your family from financial trauma should the unthinkable happen. One way to decide how much life insurance you need is to figure how much cash and income your dependents would need in the event of your premature death. You should think of life insurance as a source of cash needed for expenses of final illness, paying taxes, mortgages, or other debts. It should provide income for your family's living expenses and other future expenses.

There are three basic types of life insurance policies: whole life insurance, term insurance, and endowment insurance.

WHOLE LIFE INSURANCE

Some advisors believe that term insurance is the only kind you should buy because the other services sold by the companies, such as savings, are better attended to in other ways. However, many people are attracted to the combination of risk protection and savings included in other kinds of policies.

Whole life insurance is also known as straight life or ordinary life. The combination of risk protection and savings that are included in these policies leave something for the policy holder at the end of any given period, unlike term insurance. In the beginning this accumulation is slow. It may be as many as eight years before the cash accumulations equal the total of the premiums that have been paid. Often, all the premiums for the first year of a policy will go to commissions and sales costs.

However, during the early years of the policy the risk costs are low and so a greater portion of the set premium goes into savings. Higher-risk costs as the policy holder grows older are somewhat modified by compounding and dividends if it is a participating policy.

VARIATIONS OF WHOLE LIFE POLICIES AND PAYMENT OPTIONS

You have several choices when you buy a whole life policy:

❶ You can pay annual premiums as long as you live.

❷ You can pay lower premiums initially and they increase as you get older (Modified Whole Life).

❸ You can pay premiums for a set period such as 20 pay life or 30 pay life (Limited Payment Whole Life).

❹ You can make a single payment to buy a paid-up policy (Single Premium Whole Life).

There are also several ways in which you can utilize the cash value accumulation of your policy. It is tax deferred until you begin to withdraw the money. This money may be used:

✳ To borrow against for any purpose. Interest rates are often lower than what prevails in the community.

✳ To pay the premiums on the policy if you want.

✳ To purchase a paid-up policy.

✳ To purchase an annuity with optional payoff arrangements.

✳ To terminate the policy by withdrawing its cash value.

UNIVERSAL LIFE

Universal life is a more flexible policy that allows you to increase or decrease both payments and the amount of coverage. Earnings on the policy are a reflection of the current financial market.

Another variation on this type of contract is called excess interest whole life. It provides that premiums can be reduced or eliminated if business conditions are good enough. Thus the earnings of the policy are applied to the premiums.

VARIABLE LIFE

With this policy you can direct that your premiums go into an equity, money market, or bond fund. If the investment prospers the cash value and the death benefit can increase. If the market fails to perform, the death benefit and cash value may not fall below the original amount. You may buy such a policy with schedules premiums or flexible premiums. Agents who sell this type of policy must be licensed to sell securities and must provide a prospectus before the sale.

ADJUSTABLE LIFE

This policy allows the policy holder to change the face amount, the premiums, and the protection period.

TERM INSURANCE

The purest play in life insurance is term insurance. Payment of the company premium, after acceptance of you as a customer, means they will pay your beneficiary the face amount of the policy if you die within the term of the policy. If you pay the premiums and continue to live, you get nothing at the end of the term. There is no cash accumulation.

This is the sort of insurance employers provide as a fringe benefit. In that case your family is the beneficiary. Sometimes companies protect themselves from the disruption caused by the loss of a vital leader by buying term insurance on top executives. In this case the company is the beneficiary.

A healthy person who is younger enjoys lower premiums than an older person. As the name implies, you buy term insurance for a set period. Each time it is renewed, the premiums grow.

If a person buys term insurance, it is important to get what is called renewable term. Thus, a person who develops a health problem is able to renew his/her policy without health questions or physical examination.

Some term life insurance renewals cannot be made beyond a specified age (such as 65 or 70) and premiums are much higher at older ages.

Another variation is called convertible term. In this case the insured can convert the policy to a cash accumulation type such as whole life. Again, health questions are not required for this change.

ENDOWMENT INSURANCE

Endowment insurance pays a sum of money to you if you live to or if you die before a certain age. It can serve as a vehicle for accumulating retirement funds to be paid as a lump sum or as installments. Keep in mind that tax rules may change. Premiums and cash values are higher than for the same amount of whole life insurance. Thus, endowment insurance gives you the least amount of death benefit for your premium dollar.

ANNUITIES

While life insurance provides money for the beneficiary when the insured dies, an annuity provides money for the insured when the insured lives. Annuities are often purchased for retirement purposes.

Many business firms include group annuities for their employees as fringe benefits, with payment scheduled to begin at an employee's retirement. You may also buy annuities individually, either on an installment plan or with a single payment at the time of retirement. Payment of benefits is also flexible. Some annuities pay a certain sum each month; others pay for a specified period of time, whether one lives or dies.

SPECIAL POLICIES

There are many kinds of special policies that are available for purchase. One of the best known is mortgage insurance to pay off the balance of your loan if you die. Some lenders require this coverage with their loan. Other policies can pay off other obligations such as credit cards in the event of your death.

Remember that when you buy life insurance from a mutual company you can get a participating policy that pays dividends representing your share of the profits. They can add significantly to the cash value of your policy.

It is important not to be lulled by the purchase of a life policy so that you do no other saving or investing. Remember that a policy purchased in 1970 or 1980 has much less real value when you apply inflation to the face value. Make that policy the cornerstone of your financial planning, rather than its sole basis.

LOW-LOAD POLICIES

Today certain companies will sell low-load policies directly to the consumer. This eliminates the high commission involved with most policies and means that your money goes immediately to work for you. You call the company and tell them of your interest in a low load policy. Describe the kind of policy you are looking for and ask for a quotation.

> **Buy an annuity cheap, and make your life interesting to yourself and everybody else that watches the speculation.**
>
> **Charles Dickens**

LIFE INSURANCE FOR PEOPLE WITH HEALTH PROBLEMS

Insurance buyers who have health problems are either refused policies or are accepted at higher premiums. This modified status is called a rating. Companies may have as many as five or six ratings that call for higher premiums depending upon the nature of your health problem. Once they have admitted you to a given rating, the company cannot demote you to a worse one that calls for higher premiums. Such policies are also referred to as rated policies as opposed to the standard policies that are issued to healthy candidates.

APPLYING FOR LIFE INSURANCE

When you are applying for life insurance, it is essential to be accurate in the information you provide the company about your health history. Your correct age is also important, but giving a wrong answer there is less serious than those about your health. If the company finds out about untrue health information within two years, they can cancel the policy. That leaves you in a far worse situation because you have lost two years and have no insurance.

AGENTS

Most people apply for life insurance through an agent who may represent one or more companies.

If you use an agent, choose carefully. One who is an established businessperson in your community, and who maintains a high degree of professional competency and honesty is a wise choice.

After selecting an agent, do not hesitate to bring him or her your insurance problems and questions. Agents earn a commission on your business and should do more than just sell you a policy. They should advise you, answer your questions, and help you update your insurance.

COMPARING POLICIES

The simplest way for the lay person to compare insurance is to ask for similar policy amounts and coverage from several companies. Bring counter offers to the agents with whom you are dealing and ask them to point out how their policies are better or worse. Some states require a disclosure statement to tell you how much protection you get for your dollar on a given policy.

One comparison is called the cost index, and the lower the number the better the policy. Bear in mind that small differences in this index may be overcome by special policy features. Finally, after you do decide, the law gives you another ten days to change your mind and get your money back.

HELP
If you don't think that you have been treated fairly in shopping for insurance or in getting a claim paid, or if you have any problems or questions about your insurance, contact your State Department of Insurance. You can find their address on page 8 or 9.

Catastrophic insurance or a rip-off?

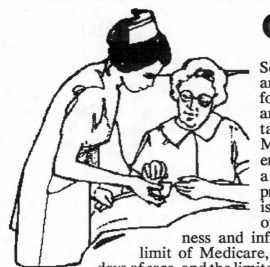

Seniors who are qualified for Medicare and have obtained good Medigap coverage still have a potential problem. That is the problem of chronic illness and infirmity. The limit of Medicare, in terms of days of care, and the limited extensions that most Medigap policies provide, mean that a person who is hospitalized beyond those limits has no coverage. Likewise, the person who becomes infirm but does not need acute care has no coverage.

This is custodial care and it is beyond the ability of most families to provide. Thus nursing home care is required. Studies show that the average term for such care is between two and three years. However, it is not unknown for such patients to remain in custodial care for two and three times that period. If you have no long-term care insurance, you must pay the bill, at least until you have exhausted your resources.

When you exhaust your resources, you become eligible for Medicaid. That program requires very limited resources, but it does pay the cost of nursing home admission and custodial care.

The cost of nursing home care has been subject to the same inflationary factors we have seen in all medical care. Depending upon the location and standards of the institution, yearly costs in 1991 ranged from $20,000 to $30,000. There is every reason to believe that these increases will continue in the future.

Having identified the need and the costly nature of long-term care, we will identify some of the variables that exist in selecting appropriate insurance.

DOLLAR COVERAGE: One of the choices in selecting a LTC policy is the amount of daily cost you choose to buy. For example, you can decide to buy a policy that will cover only a part of the cost of a day's care. Thus a $50 a day policy would leave you to cover the remainder of the cost out of your own pocket. As of 1991 most daily rates are in the area of $80. Companies often specify the maximum total amount that would be paid out under given coverage.

Many policies carry an inflation formula of about 5% to cover the increase of costs from year to year. This is a wise provision to have included in the policy you choose. For example, if you bought an $80 daily coverage plan beginning in 1992 at the age of 65, and you entered a nursing home when you became 70, the daily cost would have risen to about $97.25.

Another choice in LTC insurance is to have a waiting period before the insurance coverage comes into play. This waiting period could be from a few days to several months. Such a choice might be made on the basis that the financial strain would not be felt until you had been in the hospital for the period selected.

The other vital alternative you must choose when buying LTC insurance is the period of coverage. If the average time spent in a nursing home is about three years, you need to decide whether to gamble on less coverage than that or to purchase more. All of these choices have a direct bearing on the premium you will pay. When that period of coverage is exceeded, you are back into the position of having no insurance, and must manage all costs from your own resources. Selecting a life-time care option carries substantially higher premiums than coverage for definite periods.

HEALTH CONSIDERATIONS: All policies have a waiting period for preexisting conditions. They are defined as conditions for which medical advice or treatment was recommended by or received from, a provider of healthcare services, within the defined period preceding the effective date of coverage of the insured person. That is consistent with most health insurance policies of all kinds. It is wise to have a clear understanding of this provision and to be absolutely honest about the existence of such conditions. It is possible that a failure to be candid will result in the cancellation of your coverage just when you need it most.

Don't wait until you have had medical confirmation of a fatal illness before buying insurance. Insurance companies must enforce preexisting-condition regulations to safeguard their clients who share the costs through their premiums. Most insurance companies have specific exclusions for their policies. They are:

❶ Being outside the United States or its possessions.
❷ Being in a Veteran's Administration or federal government institution unless you are charged for the stay.
❸ Needing care as a consequence of war or an act of war.
❹ Needing care as a consequence of an attempt at suicide or an intentionally self-inflicted injury.
❺ Needing care as a consequence of mental, nervous, psychotic, or psychoneurotic deficiencies or disorders without demonstrable organic disease. (Some states prohibit such an exclusion if it is for Alzheimer's disease or a related illness, unless preexisting.)

Insurance coverage for an admission to a nursing home is dependent upon a doctor's certification that you need such care. Some companies used to require hospitalization in an acute care facility for three or more days to qualify for LTC coverage. While that is not common now, it is a feature you should be sure to check when buying coverage.

Another variable affecting premium rates is the age at which you purchase coverage. If you are 60 years old, premiums will be less at your entry into the program than if you are 70.

Because of these variables, it is difficult to make easy comparisons between policies. To give you an idea of the general magnitude of LTC premiums, here are some examples of rates in 1991:

Company	Term of Coverage	Daily Coverage	Yearly Premium
-A-			
Age 69	2 years	$70	$577
69	4 years	$70	$801
-B-			
69	life	$70	$1,519
70	life	$70	$1,691

Several other types of care are available through LTC policies. Some have provisions for skilled nursing care, intermediate care, and home healthcare. You should check to see what these provisions are when you examine the policies you are considering.

At the end of 1991, approximately 1.6 million Americans purchased long-term care insurance. Although the National Association of Insurance Commissioners (NAIC) established standards for this insurance, 24 states still have not developed standards requiring insurers to guarantee policy renewal, and 18 states have not adopted standards disallowing Alzheimer's disease exclusions. Most policies still contain restrictive definitions that potentially limit access to benefits.

Consumers also risk unpredictable premium increases that make it difficult to retain their policies. Yet, if you allow your policy to lapse, you will lose the money you invested in premiums. Some unscrupulous insurance agents will sell you policies when you have Medicaid or policies you don't need.

Before you sign up for this type of insurance get advice from someone who is knowledgeable on this subject. Contact your local Area Agency on Aging office or your state insurance department. For listing of state offices, see pages 8 and 9.

Health Maintenance Organizations--an alternate

An alternative to a Medigap policy from regular insurance carriers is membership in a health maintenance organization (HMO), or a competitive medical plan (CMP). These organizations contract with Medicare to provide services to Medicare recipients who select that type of coverage.

As the name implies, these organizations believe in and stress preventive medicine. With only a few exceptions, neither Medicare nor most insurance plans give more than lip service to prevention. The most obvious example is the refusal of Medicare, and thus most insurance plans, to pay for physical examinations. By contrast, it is not uncommon for HMO's to require regular physicals.

HMO's and similar organizations charge the member regular premiums that may range from $50 to more than $100 per month, and modest coinsurance payments. For example, each visit to a doctor may cost a few dollars as a kind of deductible. Just as with regular Medigap plans, the service you receive varies according to the size of the premium.

Since 1990, most HMO's and CMP's that enrolled Medicare beneficiaries are required by law to provide certain benefits, not available under fee-for-service Medicare, at no additional charge to the member. These include extended hospital and skilled nursing facility stays, expanded home health benefits, respite care, and coverage for certain drugs. In addition, many of these organizations offer such services as dental care, hearing testing and hearing aids, and refractions for eyeglasses.

MEDICARE REQUIREMENTS FOR COVERAGE IN AN HMO:

❶ You must be enrolled in Medicare's medical insurance (Part B) and continue to pay the premiums.
❷ You must live within the area serviced by the HMO or CMP.
❸ You will usually be required to receive all care from the HMO or CMP, except in emergency or urgent situations.
❹ You cannot enroll in an HMO or CMP if you have chronic kidney disease. But if you are a member of an HMO or CMP when you develop chronic kidney disease, the care you need will be provided through the organization.
❺ If you have elected hospice care, you may not enroll in an HMO or CMP as long as the hospice election remains in

effect. However, when you are already a member of an HMO or CMP, you may elect hospice and continue in the organization's plan. In that case you must receive all care related to your terminal illness from the hospice and not the HMO or CMP.

It is important to understand that you are not locked into membership in one of these organizations. If you decide that you prefer fee-for-service Medicare, you can drop the HMO or CMP plan in any month and transfer to regular Medicare at the beginning of the next month. In such a case, be sure that Medicare knows of the change and it would be prudent to arrange for some alternative supplementary insurance before you make the change.

ADVANTAGES OF MEMBERSHIP IN AN HMO OR CMP:

* Preventive medicine.
* Other health services such as dental care and routine eye care.
* Broader coverage generally than most Medigap insurance.
* Less paperwork than conventional insurance.
* Responsibility of an organization for your healthcare as opposed to individual practitioners.

DISADVANTAGES OF MEMBERSHIP IN AN HMO OR CMP:

* You must live near where the service is offered, i.e., clinics and hospitals.
* You have a more limited choice of staff than in a fee-for-service plan.
* There may be greater delays for certain services such as elective surgery.
* You may not be able to get the HMO to perform a service that you desire, such as certain elective surgery.

WHAT TO LOOK FOR WHEN YOU SELECT AN HMO OR CMP:

These organizations range from highly integrated healthcare facilities such as Group Health and Kaiser-Permanente to organizations that are made up of cooperating independent doctors and healthcare services. One example of the latter is the individual practice association (IPA) wherein private doctors treat the patient in their own offices with costs and benefits arranged through membership in the HMO. In addition to the organizational structure of the HMO, you should inquire about the following:

BASIC SERVICES

In addition to regular Medicare-authorized service, will you be able to have physical examinations; eye refractions and glasses; hearing examinations and hearing aids; prescription drugs; dental care; and podiatric care? You should also inquire about the limitations on hospital stays.

EXTENDED SERVICES

How does the HMO provide for emergency care that you may require outside of their facilities? How about treatment while traveling in and out of the United States? If a second opinion is needed about your condition will it be authorized without extra cost, including an outside physician? If an HMO doctor refers you to an outside specialist will the plan pay the cost? For those interested, is chiropractic care provided for? What are the benefits for mental healthcare? How does the HMO manage care for degenerative diseases such as Alzheimer's?

OTHER CARE CONSIDERATIONS

What are the provisions for urgent or emergency care? How long must one wait for an appointment for nonurgent care? Can you change staff doctors with minimum trouble if you are not satisfied? Are most primary-care physicians accepting new patients? Are most specialties represented on the staff and are they board-certified? What does the HMO do to orient new members to its services, procedures, and appeal routine? Does it publish an easily understood and clear members handbook? Are there tours or open houses from time to time when a new or prospective member may become familiar with the facilities? Is there a special effort to clarify Medicare coverage and procedures? Can you get to the HMO easily on public transportation? Is there provision for homebound patients?

OTHER QUALITY CONSIDERATIONS

Can you get in contact with members of the HMO to determine their assessment of the services offered? Does the organization appear to be well run in terms of reception of patients and the providing of information in the offices and over the phone? Is the office clean? Are there comfortable waiting areas and well-equipped examination rooms? Is the staff courteous and helpful? You may have special questions you wish answered that have not been suggested. If so, add them to the list and make an effort to find the answers before you sign up. By the same token, many of the above questions can be applied to any system of healthcare and insurance you may consider.

MEDICARE--an introduction

MEDICARE is a medical insurance program for people 65 and older and certain disabled people. This federally supported insurance helps to pay for a portion of your medical costs. You apply for this insurance through local Social Security offices. Although the program is run by the U.S. Department of Health and Human Services, the actual claim services are handled, under contract, with insurance companies such as Blue Shield or Blue Cross.

MEDIGAP (also called supplemental insurance) is a term used to denote private health insurance you buy to help cover the payment gaps in the insurance offered by Medicare.

MEDICAID is a state sponsored program that provides financial support for low-income people by paying the monthly Medicare premiums. Such persons do not have to pay Medicare deductibles and co-payments. Each state sets its own guidelines for qualification for such assistance. State or local welfare, social service, or public health agencies can tell you about local regulations. Most states require that:
❶ Your annual income level must be at or below the poverty level.
❷ You cannot have access to many financial resources such as bank accounts or stocks and bonds.

MEDICARE

There are two parts to the Medicare insurance:
Part A --Hospital Insurance. It is premium-free if you qualify.
Part B --Medical Insurance. It pays for doctors and other medical services. You pay monthly premiums deducted from your Social Security check.

QUALIFICATIONS FOR HOSPITAL INSURANCE (Part A)
❶ If not disabled you must be at least 65 years old.
❷ You must also be eligible for Social Security or the Railroad Retirement system either as:
✓ a covered worker based on your employment
✓ a dependent of a covered worker (a spouse)
✓ a survivor of a covered worker

❸ If disabled, and under 65 years old, you must have been a disability beneficiary for more than 24 months either under Social Security or the Railroad Retirement Board. Certain government employees and certain members of their families can also get Medicare when they are disabled for more than 29 months.
❹ You also qualify if you receive continuing dialysis for permanent kidney failure or have had a kidney transplant.

Enrollment in Medicare (Part A) is automatic if you apply for or are receiving Social Security payments at age 65. The local Social Security office can answer all questions about eligibility and can take care of the details of such enrollment. If you are 65 or older and do not qualify for Medicare you may purchase Part A coverage. Premiums in 1991 were $175 per month.

QUALIFICATIONS FOR MEDICAL INSURANCE (Part B)
❶ You must be qualified under part A.
❷ You elect to enroll in part B.
❸ You agree to pay the monthly insurance premium. The monthly premium ($31.60 in 1992) ($36.60 in 1993) ($41.10 in 1994) ($46.10 in 1995) is withheld from your retirement allowance (your Social Security check).

DO YOU NEED MORE INSURANCE IF YOU ARE COVERED BY MEDICARE?
Examine the coverage outlined in the pages of Part A and B. In most cases, Medicare pays only part of the costs; you must pay for the remainder. You can purchase insurance that pays for costs that Medicare does not pay. This insurance is called supplemental insurance or medigap--they are both the same thing. In most cases it is wise to carry this additional insurance. However, everyone needs to assess their own medical history and determine which policies are most suited for them.

You may not need additional private health insurance, if:
❶ You are eligible for Medicaid (this is for low-income people).
❷ You qualify through Medicaid for limited financial assistance. Medicaid pays a share of acute care costs for certain low-income elderly and disabled Medicare beneficiaries. If your annual income is below $6,280 for one person ($8,420 for a couple) (1990 limits), and you do not have access to many financial resources, you may qualify for government assistance in paying Medicare monthly premiums and at least some of the Medicare deductibles and co-payments. This may vary by state. If you qualify, this financial assistance is available through your state Medicaid office.
❸ You have Medicare and are enrolled in a prepayment plan, such as a health maintenance organization (HMO) or competitive medical plan (CMP), which has a contract with Medicare as HMO's or CMP's are insurance alternatives.

ADVICE: Whether or not you need health insurance to supplement Medicare is a matter you may want to discuss with someone you know who understands insurance and your financial situation. The best time to do this is before you reach 65. Some state insurance departments (see pages 8 or 9) offer health insurance counselling services.

NOTE: Some states, such as Pennsylvania, Massachusetts, and Rhode Island, prohibit physicians from charging Medicare beneficiaries more than the federal government's "reasonable" rate for a medical service--you would then only be responsible for the 20%. THEREFORE: In these states most insurance policies that provide you with more than the 20% co-payment offer you no additional benefits. New York, after 1991, barred billing patients more than 15% in excess of Medicare-approved rates. In New York, then, you would be responsible for the 20% plus any excess up to 15%.

> **Federal Limits:**
>
> **After 1991, physicians may not charge more than 25 % in excess of the Medicare-approved rate.**

--terms you will need to know

Approved Amount--Charges Medicare determines to be "reasonable."

Assignment--Your doctor or supplier of medical services agrees to accept the amount approved by Medicare as the full amount he expects to be paid. (Participating doctors and suppliers always accept assignment.) With assignment, after you meet the deductible, Medicare pays 80% and you pay 20% of the amount approved.

Benefit Period--A period of time, determined under Medicare, that begins on the day you enter a hospital as an inpatient and ends when you have been out of the hospital or skilled nursing facility for 60 days in a row. During that 60 days you can reenter the hospital without paying a new deductible. There is no limit to the number of benefit periods you may have.

Customary Charge--The midpoint of all the charges your doctor or supplier of medical services made during a previous 12-month period for the same service.

Deductible--You must take care of the first part of your medical bills each year. This yearly share is called the deductible.

EOMB (Explanation of Medicare Benefits)--The form Medicare sends you to show what action was taken on your Medicare claim. You and your doctor will always receive an EOMB in response to any claim filed with Medicare. The EOMB will show: the date of service, type of service billed, procedural number, amount billed, amount approved by Medicare, amount applied to the deductible, and an explanation of the actions taken.

HMO's--Health Maintenance Organizations that contract with Medicare to provide all medical services for its Medicare subscribers. If you use other providers without HMO's permission, you pay the bill except in some emergencies. The physicians work on salary or contract with the HMO's. You can choose your primary-care physician within the HMO. Hospital admission is strictly controlled. Some well-known HMO's are: Kaiser, Group Health Cooperative of Puget Sound, Group Health Association of Washington, DC, the Health Insurance Plan of Greater NY (HIP), and the Harvard Community Health Plan in Boston.

IPA's--These plans contract with doctors who maintain a private practice in addition to seeing HMO members. In these plans, compared to HMO's, your costs may be higher, the benefits may be more limited, or there may be deductibles you may have to pay. Where IPA's are available, you might be able to keep your own doctor--if yours participates in the plan.

Lifetime Reserve Days--The 60 hospital days after the 90th day of hospital stays for which Medicare pays hospital benefits. These days may be used only once in your lifetime. All of the days need not be used in the same benefit period. During these days, Medicare pays only a portion of your hospital costs.

Medicare Eligible Expenses--Healthcare expenses covered by Medicare to the extent allowable and medically necessary under Medicare.

Medigap--Private health insurance designed to supplement Medicare.

Nonparticipating Physician--One who refuses to accept the amount approved by Medicare for a service performed as payment in full. Medicare pays 80% of the amount allowed by Medicare. You or your supplemental insurance must pay 20% of the amount allowed by Medicare and any excess charges above the amount allowed.

Participating Physician--One who accepts the amount allowed by Medicare for a service performed as payment in full. You or your supplemental insurance must pay 20% of the amount allowed by Medicare.

PPO's--With Preferred Provider Organizations, your insurance company makes a deal with a group of physicians and hospitals who agree to hold down costs through price discounts to patients. Enrollment is unnecessary. You are encouraged to use the preferred provider; if you don't, it costs you more money.

Prevailing charge--The amount based upon the customary charges for covered medical services or items. The prevailing charge is the maximum charge Medicare can approve for any item.

Reasonable Charges--amounts approved by the Medicare carrier that will be either the customary charge, the prevailing charge, or the actual charge, whichever is lowest.

Skilled Nursing Facility--A specially qualified facility with the staff and equipment to provide skilled nursing care or rehabilitation services and other related health services.

Surgicenters--Perform a range of surgeries, including many that require general anesthesia on an outpatient or ambulatory basis. They may be a separate center or part of a hospital and are just as safe as one. Typically, all tests are done before the day of the surgery. The day of the surgery you generally come in early in the morning and go home in the late afternoon or early evening. No membership is required and the costs are often less expensive than in a hospital.

Urgicenters, Emergicenters, and Walk-in Medical Offices--Typically care for injuries, acute illnesses, and other emergencies that require little or no follow-up. These centers offer convenience but the doctors on duty often work part-time and continuity of care with one physician may be difficult. No membership or even appointments are required.

CHIROPRACTIC SERVICES AND MEDICARE

Medicare helps pay for only one kind of treatment furnished by a licensed chiropractor: manual manipulation of the spine to correct subluxation that can be demonstrated by X-ray. Medicare medical insurance does not pay for any other diagnostic or therapeutic services, including X-rays, furnished by a chiropractor.

Private insurance may pay other costs, but even though you know Medicare will not pay, you must submit chiropractic bills and then send the EOMB to your insurance company with its denial of coverage.

> Contraceptives should be used on every conceivable occasion.
>
> **Spike Milligan**

Part A--helps pay for some of your hospital expenses

WHAT IS MEDICARE? It is a health insurance program that is sponsored by the federal government and administered by private insurance organizations. These carriers handle the medical insurance claims. The program is divided into two parts:
Part A: Hospital insurance (premium-free)
Part B: Medical insurance (monthly premium deducted from your SS check).

QUALIFICATIONS: To obtain Medicare benefits you must be either:
❶ 65 years old and receiving Social Security, or
❷ Of any age but have permanent kidney failure, or
❸ Have certain disabilities and be under 65.

You are entitled to Medicare because you are entitled to Social Security. If you have Medicare based on your own work record, your protection will continue as long as you live. If you receive Medicare based on your husband's or wife's work record, your protection will end if you and your spouse divorce before your marriage has lasted 10 years.

WHAT IS COVERED UNDER PART A?
❶ Inpatient hospital care
❷ Skilled nursing facility care
❸ Home healthcare
❹ Hospice care

INPATIENT HOSPITAL CARE: See lower chart for services provided. Note: Extra charges for a private room may be paid by Medicare if it is determined to be medically necessary.

SKILLED NURSING FACILITY CARE: Coverage includes semiprivate room, meals, regular nursing service, rehabilitation services, drugs furnished by the facility, medical supplies, and use of appliances such as a wheelchair.

Services not covered include personal convenience items such as a TV or telephone, private nurses, a private room, or custodial nursing home-care services.

HOME HEALTHCARE: If you need part-time skilled healthcare in your home, Medicare can pay for covered services if:
❶ Services are provided by a Medicare "participating" home health agency (a public or private agency specializing in giving skilled nursing care or other therapeutic services, such as physical or speech therapy, in the home).
❷ You are confined to your home.
❸ A doctor determines you need this care and sets it up.
Medicare doesn't pay for full-time nurses, drugs, meals, home services, shopping, etc.

HOSPICE CARE: Medical hospital insurance can help pay for hospice care if:
❶ A doctor certifies that a patient is terminally ill.
❷ A patient chooses hospice care instead of regular Medicare.
❸ Care is provided by a Medicare-certified hospice program (see article on Hospice, page 223).

You may want supplemental insurance. See below what Medicare doesn't pay for. Then see article on Medigap, page 42.

WHAT PART A MEDICARE PAYS: Payments are made on the basis of benefit periods. A benefit period begins the first day you receive Medicare-covered services as an inpatient in a hospital or skilled nursing facility. The benefit period can last from 1 day to 150 days (after 150 days there is no benefit) or more for hospital care and 100 days or more for skilled nursing facility care. Each benefit period ends when you have been out of either facility for 60 days in a row. Medicare pays only partial costs after 60 days (see chart below).

If you enter either facility again after 60 days, a new benefit period begins and benefits start over from scratch. There is no limit to the number of benefit periods you can have.

NOTE: Medicare and private insurance will not pay for most nursing home care. You pay for custodial care and most care in a nursing home.

Reserve days--Every person has a lifetime reserve of 60 days for inpatient hospital care. These days may be used whenever more than 90 days of inpatient hospital care are needed in a benefit period. While reserve days are being used, Part A pays for all covered services except for $314 (1991) a day. Once used, reserve days are used up.

Medicare will help pay for only 190 days of care in a participating psychiatric hospital in your lifetime. Hospital insurance payments are made directly to the organization providing services. You must pay part of the costs (see chart below).

MEDICARE (PART A): HOSPITAL INSURANCE--COVERED SERVICES PER BENEFIT PERIOD *1991

SERVICES PROVIDED	BENEFIT	MEDICARE PAYS	YOU PAY
HOSPITALIZATION Semiprivate room, meals, regular nursing services, operating and recovery room costs, anesthesia services, intensive care, drugs, lab tests, X-rays, and all other medically necessary services and supplies. Not personal convenience items such as TV or telephone, private nurses, or charges for a private room.	First 60 days	All but $628	**$628** (1991) rates
	61st to 90th day	All but $157 a day	**$157 a day (1991)**
	91st to 150th day	All but $314 a day	**$314 a day(1991)**
	Beyond 150 days	Nothing	**All costs**
POST-HOSPITAL SKILLED NURSING FACILITY CARE In a facility approved by Medicare. You must have been in the hospital for at least 3 days and enter the facility within 30 days after hospital discharge.	First 20 days	100% of approved amt.	Nothing
	Additional 80 days	All but $74 a day	**$74 a day**
	Beyond 100 days	Nothing	**All costs**
HOME HEALTHCARE Part-time skilled nursing care and home health aides, physical or speech therapy, and medical supplies and equip.	Visits limited to medically necessary skilled care.	Full cost of services. 80% of appr. amt. for durable medical equip.	Nothing for services. 20% of approved amt. for durable medical equip.
HOSPICE CARE Doctors' and nursing services, medical appliances and supplies including drugs for pain relief, home aide, counseling.	Up to 210 days if doctor certifies need.	All but limited costs for outpatient drugs and inpatient respite care.	Limited cost sharing for outpatient drugs and inpatient respite care.

Part B--helps pay for some medical expenses

WHAT IS MEDICARE (Part B)? When you qualify for Medicare (Part A) hospital insurance you are automatically enrolled in a federal government-sponsored medical insurance program--Medicare (Part B). Of course, you can state that you don't want it but this is not a wise choice. Part B requires a monthly premium that is deducted from your social security check.

WHAT IS COVERED?
❶ Doctors' services
❷ Outpatient hospital treatment
❸ Home healthcare

DOCTORS' SERVICES
Most treatment reimbursed by Medicare must be provided by a physician, either an M.D. or a D.O. In specialized situations that are quite limited they will pay for services of a chiropractor, podiatrist, dentist, or an optometrist. Medicare medical insurance helps pay for these services:

1. Physicians' and surgeons' services no matter where you receive them: at home, in the doctor's office, in a clinic or hospital.
2. Medical and surgical services, including anesthesia.
3. Diagnostic tests and procedures that are part of your treatment.
4. Radiology and pathology services by doctors while you are a hospital inpatient or outpatient.
5. Treatment of mental illness (Medicare covers 50% instead of 80% of approved costs).
6. Other services that are ordinarily furnished in the doctor's office and included in his or her bill, such as:

* X-rays.
* Services of your doctor's office nurse.
* Drugs and biologicals that cannot be self-administered.
* Transfusions of blood and blood components.
* Medical supplies.
* Physical/occupational therapy and speech pathology services.
7. Mammographic screening.
8. Home health visits if you qualify and visits are medically necessary.
9. The only chiropractor treatment covered is manipulation of the spine to correct subluxation that can be demonstrated by X-ray. The chiropractor must be a licensed Medicare-certified one. Medical insurance does not pay for any other diagnostic or therapeutic services including X-rays furnished by a chiropractor.
10. Dental care if it involves surgery, setting fractures, or services that would be covered when provided by a doctor.
11. Optometrist's services. (limited cases)
12. A second opinion if surgery is contemplated.

SERVICES NOT COVERED
1. Routine annual physical examinations and tests directly related to such examinations, except some pap smears.
2. Most routine foot care.
3. Examinations for prescribing and fitting eyeglasses or hearing aids.
4. Immunizations (except pneumococcal vaccinations or immunizations).
5. Cosmetic surgery, unless it is needed because of accidental injury or to improve the function of a malformed part of the body.

OUTPATIENT HOSPITAL SERVICES COVERED: Medicare will help to pay for outpatient services provided by hospitals that might, under other circumstances, be provided by your doctor.

1. Services in an emergency room or outpatient clinic.
2. X-rays and other radiology services billed by the hospital.
3. Medical supplies. (splints, casts, etc.)
4. Blood transfusions furnished to you as an outpatient.
5. Outpatient physical and occupational therapy or speech pathology services if prescribed by your doctor.
6. Comprehensive outpatient rehabilitation facility services if referred by a physician.
7. Diagnostic tests provided by certified independent labs.
8. Portable diagnostic X-ray services in your home if ordered by your doctor.
9. Medically necessary ambulance costs.
10. Durable medical equipment for use in your home ordered by your doctor. (oxygen equipment, wheelchairs, etc.)
11. Prosthetic devices.
12. Mental healthcare in a partial hospitalization psychiatric program, if a physician certifies that inpatient treatment would be required without it.

HOME HEALTHCARE: Medicare will help to pay for a variety of services and supplies for home healthcare such as wheelchairs and oxygen equipment if authorized by a prescription from your doctor. **NOTE:** Part A helps to pay for home health care if you have it. If you only have Part B, then Part B helps to pay for home healthcare.

MEDICARE (PART B): MEDICAL INSURANCE-COVERED SERVICES *1991 RATES

SERVICES PROVIDED	BENEFIT	MEDICARE PAYS	YOU PAY	YOU PAY ALSO
MEDICAL EXPENSE Physicians' services; inpatient and outpatient medical services; diagnostic tests, X-rays, medical supplies (furnished in your doctor's office), physical and speech therapy, ambulance, etc.	Medicare pays for medical services in or out of the hospital.	80% of approved amount (after $100 deductible)	$100 deductible plus 20% of approved amount. Note: If doctor accepts Medicare assignment there are no other charges you pay.	**Any charges above approved amount.** Note: If doctors don't accept Medicare assignment you pay all additional charges.
OUTPATIENT HOSPITAL TREATMENT Covers treatment you receive for diagnosis and treatment, such as care in an emergency room or outpatient clinic of a hospital.	Unlimited if medically necessary care	80% of approved charges (after $100 deductible)	Subject to deductible plus 20% of approved amount (see note above).	**Any charges above approved amount** (see note above).
HOME HEALTHCARE Part-time skilled nursing care and home health aides, physical and speech therapy, medical supplies & equip.	Visits limited to medically skilled care	Full cost of services 80% of approved amt. for durable med. equip. (after $100 deductible)	Nothing for services 20% of approved amt. for durable med. equip. (after $100 deductible)	**Any charges above approved amount** (see note above).
EXAMPLES	**BENEFIT**	**MEDICARE PAYS**	**YOU PAY**	**YOU PAY ALSO**
*Doctor accepts assignment, i.e., charges approved by Medicare.	Actual charge $500	Medicare approves $400 and pays $320 (80%)	20% of $400 = $80 if deductible was paid	Nothing more
Doctor does not accept assignment (is not a participating physician).	Actual charge $500	Medicare approves $400 and pays $320 (80%)	20% of $400 = $80 if deductible was paid	You also pay Dr. $100 ($500-$400)

* You can get names of Medicare participating doctors from your Medical carrier, Social Security offices, Offices of Aging, and hospitals.

Medicare supplemental insurance--called Medigap

Medigap insurance is coverage to pay for medical costs that Medicare does not provide for. There are needs in both Part A and Part B of Medicare for which insurance is available. Let's look at some of the gaps.

GAPS IN PART A

❶ The deductible associated with each benefit period. When you are hospitalized you are billed for the first $628 (1991 rates) of cost. If you reenter the hospital later in the year, that deductible becomes due again if more than 60 days have elapsed since your last hospitalization.

❷ When hospitalized for 60 days, Medicare pays all authorized costs. From the 61st to the 90th days they pay everything except $157 (1991 rates) per day. That would total $4,710 for 30 days.

❸ If your hospital stay exceeds 90 days you are able to use 60 reserve days for one time only. Thus, Medicare pays all costs except $314 (1991 rates) per day. Your costs for those 60 days would be $18,840.

❹ Assuming your hospitalization continued beyond the 150th day, you would be expected to pay all costs. That situation gets into the area of catastrophic health needs.

❺ Some people might also consider that some of the basic limitations of Medicare such as lack of provision for a private room or private duty nurse constitute a gap as well.

GAPS IN PART B

❶ The first gap is the 20% that Medicare deducts from their approved cost when they reimburse the caregiver or the patient.

❷ The next gap is when a doctor or other caregiver will not accept Medicare assignment for services rendered, the patient faces the immediate gap between what Medicare approves for that procedure and what the caregiver charges.

❸ The $100 deductible at the beginning of the year represents a gap that is two to three times that amount in real costs.

❹ Costs of medications not provided by the doctor in his office.

❺ Costs of routine physical examinations and most diagnostic tests associated with such examinations.

❻ Routine eye care for refraction and fitting of glasses is not included, nor is dental or podiatric care or most cosmetic surgery.

> Virtue has never been as respectable as money. -- Mark Twain

PLUGGING THE GAPS

If an individual wished to cover all of the out-of-pocket costs described above, the coverage would cost a fortune. Some of those risks may not even be insurable. However, the insurance picture changes rapidly. For example, coverage for long-time nursing home care was hard to find a few years ago. It now is becoming more widely available, and with better benefits but be cautious (see the article on page 36).

The individual or family needs to decide what risks they wish to leave to chance and which ones they feel they must cover with insurance. This becomes a gamble based upon two basic considerations: costs and health histories of those involved. Most people probably prefer to balance cost and risk with some intermediate program of insurance. If an individual has had many hospital admissions and persistent health problems throughout his or her adult life, not having supplemental insurance would be foolhardy indeed. Insurance programs are increasingly tailored to supplement Medicare coverage, with benefits specifically addressing those gaps alluded to above.

The following two pages provide a means of comparing a few insurance plans. By noting the benefit promised opposite each need, you can determine which insurance plan provides the most protection for you. These comparisons are not to help you decide between these plans, but rather to show you some of the kinds of comparisons you should make when selecting a plan. You will notice the better the coverage the higher the premium costs. Plans and premium costs for these plans are for 1991.

> **It's the law!**
> You have a free-look provision of 30 days after a policy has been delivered to you and if you are not satisfied for any reason you can cancel for a full refund. Remember, the best way to combat the high cost of healthcare is to stay happy, active, and wise!

HERE ARE SOME TIPS IN SELECTING YOUR MEDIGAP POLICY:

1. If you are eligible for Part A Medicare Hospital Insurance, most experts recommend you sign up for Part B Medicare Medical Expense Insurance.

2. Buy only one Medigap (supplemental policy) in addition to Part B.

3. Get a copy of the policy you are planning to buy. Give yourself time to evaluate it before you buy it and make comparisons with the example policies shown on pages 43 and 44.

4. Evaluate your needs without the insurance agent present. Do not make a hasty decision in buying an insurance policy. If you are unclear of your needs and the terms and conditions, do not hesitate to ask for help from a lawyer, physician, friend, relative, or from your local senior citizens' office.

5. If your doctors are not participating members of Medicare consider buying Medigap insurance that pays some of the excess above what is allowable under Medicare. They are called "usual and prevailing" or "usual and customary" charges.

6. If you plan to travel outside the United States consider buying a policy that provides for eligible expenses while you are away.

7. Shop around for a policy that best fits your needs. Do not allow an agent to cause you to "sign up right away."

8. Don't buy a policy if you are eligible for Medicaid. Medicaid takes care of your bills.

9. Ask your insurance company if it offers another plan if your current Medicare supplement does not provide coverage for excess charges.

10. Do not switch policies strictly for price reasons. Premiums can change.

11. Be careful if you plan to switch policies. The new one may leave any pre-existing conditions uninsured for a specified period of time.

12. Understand, fully, the clauses that refer to renewing the policy.

13. Pay by check, money order, or a bank draft payable to the insurance company. Never pay in cash or write a check payable to an insurance agent.

Medigap--examples of insurance policies--1991 rates

SERVICES	BENEFITS	MEDICARE PROVIDES	INSURANCE Plan No. 1	INSURANCE Plan No. 2	INSURANCE Plan No. 3
			Age 65 + $120.00/mo.	Age 65-66 67+ $77.25 $98.50/mo.	Age 65+ $79.50/mo.
Part A Hospitalization. Semiprivate room and board, general nursing and misc. hospital services and supplies. Includes meals, special-care units, drugs, lab tests, diagnostic X-rays, medical supplies, operating and recovery room, anesthesia and rehabilitation service.		You must be 65 $29.90/month (deducted from SS check)			
	First 60 days	All but $628	To $628 each benefit period	To $628 each benefit period	To $628 each benefit period
	61st to 90th day	All but $157 a day	$157 a day	$157 a day	$157 a day
	91st to 150th day	All but $314 a day (2)	$314 a day	$314 a day	$314 a day
	Beyond 150 days	Nothing	All eligible expenses	Total costs (151st to 515th day)	(lifetime 365 days)
Post-hospital Skilled Nursing Care. In facility approved by Medicare, for an admission for which Medicare is providing benefits.	First 20 days	100% of approved amount	-0-	-0-	-0-
	Additional 80 days	All but $74 a day	$74 a day	$74 a day	$74 a day
	Beyond 100 days	Nothing	$157 a day(101 thru 365 days)	Nothing	$74 a day for 265 days
Blood (pints or packed red blood cells)	Blood	All but 1st 3 pints**	1st 3 pints	Nothing	1st 3 pints
Part B Medical Expenses. Physician's services, inpatient and outpatient medical services and supplies, physical and speech therapy, ambulance, etc.	Medicare pays for medical services in or out of hospital.	80% of Medicare-eligible expenses (3)	20% of Medicare-eligible expenses (3) Plus "Usual and Prevailing" expenses not paid by Medicare	20% of Medicare-eligible expenses (3) You pay any excess beyond Medicare-eligible expenses.	100% of actual charges not paid by Medicare for charges of a type covered by Medicare
Part B deductible		You pay $100 deductible once per year.	You pay $100 deductible	Pays $100 deductible	Pays $100 deductible
Extra Benefits (NOT COVERED BY MEDICARE)			You pay $50 deductible	You pay $100 deductible	
Inpatient Private Duty Nursing		No benefit	80% of the "Usual and Prevailing" charges	50% of reasonable charges	$30 per shift, 2 shifts per day for 90 days
Outpatient Prescription Drugs		No benefit	50% of the "Usual and Prevailing" charges $500 max. per year	50% of reasonable charges up to $1,000 per year	
		Helps pay hospital expenses in Canada and Mexico in an emergency or if hospital is closer than one in U.S.*	Emergency care 80% of "reasonable charges" for 60 days (less $50) to $25,000 per trip	Pays the eligible expenses you would have received from Medicare as if you were in U.S. plus all the supplemental, up to 6 mo.	Pays the eligible expenses you would have received from Medicare as if in the U.S. plus all supplemental, up to 6 mo. $50,000 lifetime

1. **Benefit Period**--A period of time, determined under Medicare, that begins on the day you enter a hospital as an inpatient and ends when you have been out of a hospital or a skilled nursing facility for 60 days in a row. There is no limit to the number of benefit periods you can have each year.
2. **Lifetime Reserve Days**--Medicare helps pay for your care in a hospital for up to 90 days in each benefit period. Medicare also provides you with 60 lifetime reserve days that can be used to help pay for costs if you need to stay beyond 90 days. Medicare pays for all but $314 a day during these 60 days. These days may be used only once. All of the days need not be used in the same benefit period.
3. **Medicare Eligible Expenses**--The health-care expenses covered by Medicare to the extent allowable and medically necessary under Medicare.
4. **Reasonable Charge**--The customary charge for a like service or supply in the U.S., as determined by the insurance company.
5. **Usual and Prevailing Charge**--The normal charge made by a provider (doctor, nurse, pharmacist) for the service or supply when there is no insurance, but not more than the range of charges made in the area for a like service or supply. The area and that range are determined by the insurance company.
6. **Usual and Customary Expense**--The same as No. 5.   *Except replacement costs

MEDICARE DOES NOT PAY FOR HOSPITAL OR MEDICAL EXPENSES OUTSIDE OF THE UNITED STATES!
* see exception under Medicare

Medigap examples of insurance policies--1991 rates

SERVICES	BENEFITS	MEDICARE PROVIDES	INSURANCE Plan No. 3	INSURANCE Plan No. 4	INSURANCE Plan No. 5
		You must be 65 $29.90/month (deducted from SS check)	Age 65 + $68.66/mo	Age 65-66 $52.75/mo. 67+ $62.55/mo.	Age 65+ $55.00/mo.
Part A Hospitalization. Semiprivate room and board, general nursing and misc. hospital services and supplies. Includes meals, special-care units, drugs, lab tests, diagnostic X-rays, medical supplies, operating and recovery room, anesthesia and rehabilitation service.	First 60 days	All but $628	To $628 each benefit period	You pay to $628 each period	To $628 each benefit period
	61st to 90th day	All but $157 a day	$157 a day	$157 a day	$157 a day
	91st to 150th day	All but $314 a day (2)	$314 a day (2)	$314 a day (2)	$314 a day (2)
	Beyond 150 days	Nothing	Eligible expenses to 365 days	Total costs (151st to 515th day)	All eligible expenses
Post-hospital Skilled Nursing Care. In facility approved by Medicare, for an admission for which Medicare is providing benefits.	First 20 days	100% of approved amount	-0-	-0-	-0-
	Additional 80 days	All but $74 a day	$74 a day	$74 a day	$74 a day
	Beyond 100 days	Nothing	$74 a day up to 265 days	Nothing	$157 a day (101-365)
Blood (pints or packed red blood cells)	Blood	All but 1st 3 pints**	1st 3 pints	Nothing	1st 3 pints
Part B Medical Expenses. Physician's services, inpatient and outpatient medical services and supplies, physical and speech therapy, ambulance, etc.	Medicare pays for medical services in or out of hospital.	80% of Medicare-eligible expenses (3)	20% of Medicare-eligible expenses (3) Plus up to 180% times what Medicare pays	20% of Medicare-eligible expenses (3) You pay any excess beyond Medicare-eligible expenses.	20% of Medicare-eligible expenses (3) You pay any excess beyond Medicare-eligible expenses.
Part B deductible		You pay $100 deductible once per year.	You pay $100 deductible	Pays $100 deductible	You pay $100 deductible
Extra Benefits (NOT COVERED BY MEDICARE)					
Inpatient Private Duty Nursing		No benefit	$30 per shift, 2 shifts per day for 90 days	No benefit	To $30(RN), $24(LPN) per 8-hr. shift 60 shifts per stay
Outpatient Prescription Drugs		No benefit	No benefit	No benefit	No benefit
Foreign Hospital		Helps pay hospital expenses in Canada and Mexico in an emergency or if hospital is closer than one in U.S.	No benefit	Pays the eligible expenses you would have received from Medicare as if you were in U.S. plus all the supplemental, up to 6 mo.	Emergency care 80% of reasonable charges for 60 days to $25,000 per trip

1. **Benefit Period**--A period of time, determined under Medicare, that begins on the day you enter a hospital as an inpatient and ends when you have been out of a hospital or a skilled nursing facility for 60 days in a row. There is no limit to the number of benefit periods you can have each year.
2. **Lifetime Reserve Days**--Medicare helps pay for your care in a hospital for up to 90 days in each benefit period. Medicare also provides you with 60 lifetime reserve days that can be used to help pay for costs if you need to stay beyond 90 days. Medicare pays for all but $314 a day during these 60 days. These days may be used only once. All of the days need not be used in the same benefit period.
3. **Medicare Eligible Expenses**--The healthcare expenses covered by Medicare to the extent allowable and medically necessary under Medicare.
4. **Reasonable Charge**--The customary charge for a like service or supply in the U.S., as determined by the insurance company.
5. **Usual and Prevailing Charge**--The normal charge made by a provider (doctor, nurse, pharmacist) for the service or supply when there is no insurance, but not more than the range of charges made in the area for a like service or supply. The area and that range are determined by the insurance company.
6. **Usual and Customary Expense**--The same as No. 5.

* Except replacement costs
** Usual and Customary Expense--The same as No. 5.

PLEASE NOTE! Premiums and benefits change from year to year. These examples are provided to show how to compare policies.

Miscellaneous regulations, claims, appeals, time limits

HOME HEALTHCARE: Medicare will pay for services received in your home that are provided by a public or private healthcare agency under the following conditions:

❶ The care you need includes intermittent skilled nursing care, physical therapy, or speech therapy.

❷ You are confined to your home.

❸ You are under the care of a physician who determines you need home healthcare and sets up a home healthcare plan for you.

❹ The home healthcare agency providing the services is participating in Medicare.

HOSPICE CARE: Medicare hospital insurance helps pay hospice care if all of the following conditions are met:

✔ A doctor certifies that a patient is terminally ill.

✔ A patient chooses to receive care from a hospice instead of standard Medicare benefits for the terminal illness.

✔ Care is provided by a Medicare participating hospice program.

Medicare provides hospice care for two 90-day periods and one 30-day period. These periods may be consecutive. A beneficiary may disenroll from the hospice during any benefit period and return to regular Medicare coverage, then later return to hospice care if another benefit period is available. There are no deductibles under hospice treatment. The patient pays a small amount for drugs under coinsurance and for inpatient respite care. Medicare pays for the following services under hospice care: nursing services; doctor's services; drugs, including outpatient drugs for pain relief and symptom management.

FOREIGN HOSPITAL CARE: Medicare does not generally pay for treatment in a hospital outside the United States except:

❶ When you are in the U.S. when an emergency occurs and a Canadian or Mexican hospital is closer than the nearest in the United States that can provide the care you need.

❷ When you live in the U.S. and a Canadian or Mexican hospital is closer to your home than the nearest U.S. hospital that can provide the care you need, regardless of whether or not an emergency exists.

❸ When you are in Canada traveling by the most direct route to or from Alaska and another state and an emergency occurs that requires you be admitted to a Canadian hospital.

When hospital insurance covers your inpatient stay in a Mexican or Canadian hospital, your medical insurance (Part B) can cover any necessary doctor's services and any required use of an ambulance.

CHRISTIAN SCIENCE COVERAGE: Medicare hospital insurance helps to pay for inpatient hospital and skilled nursing facility services you receive in a participating Christian Science sanatorium if it is operated or listed and certified by the First Church of Christ Scientists, in Boston.

> Note: If you are being considered for elective surgery, by law, you are required to be notified if your costs beyond what Medicare pays will exceed $500.

CLAIMS: Carriers handle Medicare insurance claims. The Social Security Administration does not handle claims for Medicare payment. The U.S. Health Care Financing Administration administers Medicare through private insurance organizations called carriers and intermediaries such as Blue Shield, Blue Cross, and Prudential. The Medicare Handbook gives more information about how to contact your carrier or intermediary in your location.

RULES: It's your doctor or medical supplier's responsibility to submit Medicare insurance claims. This rule went into effect September 1, 1990.

✳ If your doctor or medical supplier accepts Medicare's approved amount as payment in full, you'll be billed by the provider only for your portion of that amount--20%.

✳ If they don't, you are responsible for paying the provider's whole bill. Your doctor or medical supplier will submit your claim and Medicare will reimburse you for 80% of the approved amount directly.

You are still responsible for 20% of the Medicare approved amount plus any charges above the approved amount. Of course, you still will need to submit claims to your insurance company.

HMO's or CMP CLAIMS: For your ordinary healthcare all paperwork is handled by the HMO or CMP. However, if you should find it necessary to seek assistance from another supplier, as in an emergency, you should send the resulting bills to your HMO for processing.

It's a good idea to keep a record of your medical insurance claim in case you ever want to inquire about it. Before you send in a claim make a photocopy of it and mark on it the date of submission and to whom you sent it.

If you have Medigap (supplemental insurance), you will need to submit your own claims to recover the 20% of the approved amount and excess charges. Payment will depend upon the type of insurance you have.

TIME LIMITS: Under the law, for Medicare to make payments on your claims, you or your health provider must send in your claims within the time limits given below. You always have at least 15 months to submit claims.

For service you receive between	Submit by
Oct. 1, 1990 and Sept. 30, 1991	Dec. 31, 1992
Oct. 1, 1991 and Sept. 30, 1992	Dec. 31, 1993
Oct. 1, 1992 and Sept. 30, 1993	Dec. 31, 1994
Oct. 1, 1993 and Sept. 30, 1994	Dec. 31, 1995

YOUR RIGHT OF APPEAL: If you disagree with a decision on the amount Medicare pays on a claim or whether services you received are covered by Medicare, you have the right to appeal the decision. The EOMB that you receive from Medicare will tell you of the decision made on the claim. If you do not agree with the explanation of Medicare benefits as provided on your EOMB you may call, write, or visit your carrier and they will tell you the facts used to decide what and how much to approve. If you still do not agree with the decision you need to ask, in writing, for it to be reviewed. It must be done within 6 months of the date of the EOMB. If you want more information on the appeals process read "Your Medicare Handbook."

Such appeals may be made concerning decisions:

❶ By providers of services on your Medicare hospital insurance claims.

❷ By peer review organizations.

❸ By Medicare intermediaries on your hospital insurance claims.

❹ By Medicare carriers on your medical insurance claims.

> If you have questions about how to enroll in Medicare, visit or write any Social Security office, or phone the toll-free number 1-800-234-5772.

Information on your rights and options for healthcare

To many older Americans, Medicare and Medicaid are nightmares of regulations and stipulations. This confusion leaves many seniors unaware of their rights under the federal medical assistance system and vulnerable to illegal schemes by unscrupulous healthcare providers.

Most hospitals are required to give Medicare beneficiaries a brochure explaining their rights of appeal, and most nursing homes and hospitals employ patient advocates or social workers to help beneficiaries.

Federal law protects your rights to affordable, quality healthcare under the Medicare and Medicaid programs. But you should be aware of these laws in order to benefit from their protections. Are you aware of the basic protections that have existed for some time, but that few people use? Are you aware of recent changes in the laws safeguarding your rights? If you don't score 100% on the following test, you might get short-changed on benefits or incur unnecessary expenses:

❑ If you are hospitalized, and a hospital representative informs you that you must check out before you and/or your doctor believes appropriate, are you required to leave the hospital? (**Answer: No!**)

❑ If you disagree with Medicare over the amount of the bill the program will cover can you appeal the decision? (**Answer: Yes!**)

❑ If your doctor does not accept assignment, will the services he or she delivers be covered by Medicare? (**Answer: Yes!**)

❑ If you are eligible for Medicaid but have signed a contract promising to pay a nursing home more than the Medicaid rate in order to be admitted, is this contract a lawful one that can be enforced against you? (**Answer: No!**)

If you didn't know the answers to one or more of these questions, read on. The following information will help you exercise your rights granted to you by law.

Medicare's prospective method of payment to hospitals does not mean you are entitled to less care than before.
In 1984, Medicare's prospective payment system (PPS), using diagnostic-related groups

(DRG's), changed the way hospitals are reimbursed for care, but it was not intended to change the amount of care to which you are entitled.

Under PPS, however, average lengths of stay have been reduced. Patients are more likely to be discharged earlier than before. This is not necessarily a bad thing since it reduces the patient's risk of infection and also has cut some of the excesses out of hospital charges. Yet, in some instances, Senate Special Committee on Aging investigators found that patients were being discharged too early.

The important thing to remember is that your physician still bears final responsibility for deciding when you should leave the hospital and what type of post-hospital care you may require. Nonetheless, the hospital may decide that Medicare will not cover the remainder of your stay. The hospital may ask you to leave. In order to charge you for your care, however, the hospital must provide you with a written notice that Medicare coverage is no longer available. The notice that you receive from the hospital--Hospital "Notice of Noncoverage"--should explain your appeal rights if you feel that you are being discharged too soon.

If you do receive a written notice, urge your doctor to explain to the hospital that you still need to remain in the hospital--because you still need acute-care services, or because you need skilled nursing facility services and an appropriate skilled nursing facility bed is not available, or because your post-hospital care plans are not yet arranged.

If the hospital does not change its mind, and the written notice remains in effect, you can appeal the Medicare denial. Do this as soon as you can and, again, get your doctor's help if at all possible. By noon of the first working day following your receipt of the hospital's Medicare denial notice, request an immediate review of your case by the local Peer Review Organization (PRO), a federally funded organization that oversees the care given to beneficiaries. PRO's are primarily made up of physicians, but they can have representatives from the beneficiary community as well.

The PRO must then review your case within 24 hours. If you wait beyond noon of the next work day following notification by the hospital of the discharge date to contact the

PRO, you are still entitled to a decision within 3 working days. Keep in mind, however, that this means the PRO may not decide your appeal until after the recommended date of Medicare denial. If Medicare payment for the stay is denied, and you remain in the hospital, you may be personally liable for the additional cost.

The law assures your right to appeal a decision by Medicare concerning payment of a health care bill.
Medicare was enacted in 1965 as a health insurance program to protect older Americans from the cost of healthcare. Medicare is comprised of two parts:

✳ **Part A:** Hospital insurance

✳ **Part B:** Supplementary medical insurance (doctor's services, etc.)

If you disagree with how much Medicare has paid for your claim, you have a right to a review of that decision. You do not lose this right to appeal when your doctor accepts assignment of your claim.

Disagreements arise frequently over Part B. Assume, for example, that your Medicare carrier (the insurance company that processes Part B claims) determines Medicare should only pay $50 of a $100 doctor's bill. You feel the decision is unreasonable. Your Medicare carrier must review the original determination if you send a request in writing. Be sure to include all pertinent information no matter how much money is in question.

If you are dissatisfied with the review decision, and the amount of the controversy is $100 or more, you can request that your Medicare carrier company's hearing officer conduct a more formal review called a "fair hearing." This is a legal proceeding but does not require that you be represented by an attorney. However, representation at that stage and at all stages is available.

Even if the amount is less than $100, you can call your Medicare carrier, toll-free, and they must tell you why Medicare paid less than the full amount. They will also tell you what additional information you or your doctor can provide for them to better review your claim.

For amounts of $500 or more, you can also have your claim reviewed by an administrative law judge. If your dispute is not resolved in your favor and involves more than $1,000, you can pursue your case in federal court.

The notice you receive from Medicare (EMB --the explanation of Medicare benefits) that reports the decision made on your claim will also tell you exactly what appeal steps you can take. Don't be reluctant about contacting your carrier when you disagree with the determination.

Be alert! Examine your payment notices regularly. Only 2% to 3% of Medicare patients exercise their right to appeal, despite the fact that over 50% of the appeals result in higher reimbursement awards.

With Medicare's participating physician program, your doctor costs can be reduced.
How? Assume you have met your annual deductible of $100 and your doctor charges $120 for a particular service, but Medicare's reasonable or allowable charge for that service is $100. If your doctor accepts assignment, that means your doctor accepts Medicare's determination of a reasonable charge of the total amount due and will bill you for the 20% coinsurance (or $20) and will bill Medicare for 80% (or $80). If your doctor does not accept assignment, Medicare still pays $80 and you must pay the total amount that Medicare does not cover--in this case $40. In either case, your doctor files all the paperwork for you.

Under Medicare's program, doctors now choose each year to be either "participating" or "nonparticipating" physicians. A participating physician is one who promises to accept assignment on all Medicare claims. In other words, a participating physician charges only the amount Medicare considers reasonable or allowable. Of that amount, Medicare pays 80% and you pay the remaining 20%--and no more!

A nonparticipating physician may still choose to accept or refuse assignment on a claim-by-claim basis. However, fee limits are still in effect. For those who accept assignment, you cannot be charged any more than the fee limit set by Medicare.

If your doctor isn't a participating physician, be sure to ask if he or she will accept assignment for you. If your doctor doesn't accept assignment, you will still receive reimbursement for Medicare, but will likely face higher out-of-pocket expenses. Remember, your greatest savings usually come if your doctor is a participating physician.

How can you find out who is a participating physician? The "Medicare-Participating Physician/Supplier Directory" is available for review in all Social Security offices and State and Area Agencies on Aging and some senior centers. Also, you can request a copy of this directory from your Medicare carrier. Participating doctors may display emblems or certificates showing that they accept assignment on all Medicare claims. Some states now have laws requiring physicians and suppliers to accept assignment from some or all Medicare patients. If you're not sure, just ask your state ombudsman.

As a Medicaid beneficiary, you have certain basic rights to nursing home care. Protect yourself.
The vast majority of nursing facilities (over 13,000) are "certified" for Medicaid residents. That is, the states have inspected these facilities, found them to meet federal standards, and permitted or certified them to admit residents eligible for Medicaid and bill the Medicaid program. If the nursing facility administrator does not make clear whether the facility is certified, call your state Long-Term-Care Ombudsman and ask. (You can get the number from your local area agency on aging from the yellow pages in your phone directory or check with the state area agency on aging see page 24 and 25), or Senior Center.

Federal law does not require these certified nursing facilities to accept a certain number of residents who are eligible for Medicaid nor does it prohibit facilities from denying admission to a Medicaid recipient. However, when a nursing facility does admit a Medicaid resident or one who could become eligible for Medicaid in the future, it may not require that resident to sign away his or her right to seek Medicaid coverage then or at some later point--a so-called "private-pay duration-of-stay" contract. Nor may certified nursing facilities:

* Charge the Medicaid resident, or the resident's family, more than Medicaid pays for covered services.

* Require a cash payment or donation before admitting Medicaid patients.

* Demand additional payment above the Medicaid rate in return for allow-

ing a private-pay patient to stay once he or she becomes eligible for Medicaid.

Each of these practices is a felony under federal law, punishable by a fine of up to $25,000 and a prison term of up to 5 years.

Two examples of illegal practices were illustrated in testimony at a hearing of the Senate Aging Committee. A California woman testified that when her mother became eligible for Medicaid, the nursing home administrator called and told her that unless the family continued to pay the $1,600 monthly private fee themselves for 1 full year, the home wanted her out. That's illegal.

Another witness had to sign an 18-month private-pay duration-of-stay contract to get his 81-year-old mother into a nursing home in New York. He was advised by his lawyer to apply for Medicaid for his mother and to make no further payments himself to the nursing home. His lawyer was right; that's illegal too.

You can protect yourself by knowing what practices are illegal, and by knowing where to get help. Every state, as required by law, has an ombudsman who is empowered to investigate and resolve complaints made by or on behalf of individuals residing in long-term-care facilities, and to monitor the implementation of federal, state, and local laws regarding those facilities.

* The ombudsman can help with problems relating to such things as the right to privacy and dignity, missing possessions, and transfers of residents against their will.

* Any nursing home resident, or a concerned friend or relative, can contact the ombudsman for help.

* The ombudsman has a right to access to the nursing home to investigate problems, and each patient has the right to meet privately with the ombudsman.

* There is no charge for the ombudsman's services.

In order to find the nearest ombudsman, call your state long-term-care ombudsman, the nearest legal services for the elderly office, or your local Senior Center or area agency on aging.

How to prevent Medigap insurance abuse

Fraud and deception persist in the so-called Medigap health insurance market. Medigap health policies are designed to help the elderly bridge gaps in their Medicare coverage. Many older Americans, however, are pressured into buying policies that duplicate each other. Others are misled about what their policies cover or their claims are denied when companies find after-the-fact excuses to rescind coverage.

HERE ARE SOME MEDIGAP ABUSES:

❶ Using advertising and other insurance solicitations that resemble an official notice from Medicare, Social Security, or the federal government.

❷ Using phony consumer and/or senior citizens' organizations as a front to solicit Medigap insurance.

❸ Misrepresenting Medigap insurance policies, such as exaggerating benefits and omitting restrictions on coverage.

❹ Selling multiple, overlapping, and unnecessary insurance policies.

❺ Replacing Medigap policies for the sole purpose of generating new first-year commissions for the agent.

❻ Failing to place insurance or stealing the applicant's premium payment.

❼ Using high-pressure sales tactics.

WHO ARE THE VICTIMS?

Medigap abuse victims are generally senior citizens who unwittingly trust an unscrupulous insurance agent. The unscrupulous agent makes recommendations based on what is profitable to him or her, rather than based on what is in the client's best interest.

Some victims are lonely and isolated. An unethical agent becomes a friend. These seniors are willing victims as they buy insurance policies from the agent solely "to help their friend," and ensure continued visits and friendship.

On the other hand, some victims may buy the policy and write the check just to get rid of the pushy agent who will not leave.

Other victims simply do not understand the complex wording of Medicare and Medigap insurance policies. These individuals are easy marks for the dishonest agent because they don't know that they are being deceived.

Seniors who purchase insurance based on emotion rather than need are also frequently victimized. These seniors are fearful of becoming destitute and dependent on others as a result of uncovered medical expenses. So they buy several policies based on the mistaken belief that if one policy is good, two must be better. Very often these policies provide no more protection than a single comprehensive Medigap policy would.

Finally, there are seniors who basically understand Medicare and their insurance needs. Under normal circumstances, these people would make reasonable insurance purchasing decisions. But they can fall victim when unscrupulous agents either misrepresent the provisions of a policy or simply steal an insurance premium from them.

HOW TO AVOID BECOMING A MEDIGAP ABUSE VICTIM:

1. Know your Medicare benefits. Read carefully the information provided in this book, and if you are already on Medicare, read your "Medicare Handbook" issued to you by Medicare. If you are not on Medicare or if you have misplaced this handbook, get another copy from your Social Security office.

2. Make a list of your health insurance policies (see Form B, page 50).

3. Get complete information on any agent offering you insurance policies (see Form D, page 50).

4. If an agent wants to sell you insurance, show the agent your health insurance policy inventory list. If, after reviewing your policy inventory, the agent still recommends that you buy additional insurance, ask the agent to fill out an agent certification of insurance sale (see Form C, page 50). It asks the agent to explain, in writing, why he or she feels your present coverage is inadequate and how more insurance will benefit you. The agent is not required to sign this form. However, you should decline to do business with an agent who refuses.

5. Before replacing any policy, ask the agent to complete the "Policy Comparison Sheet" (see Form A, page 49).

6. All agents are required to give you an Outline of Coverage summarizing the

benefits, limitations, renewability, and cost of the proposed policy. If the agent refuses to provide the outline, do not deal with him or her.

7. Obtain a "Notice to Applicant Regarding Replacement of Accident and Sickness Insurance" from any agent that proposes to sell you a new policy to replace your existing policy. The agent is required by law to give you this document. This notice gives you important advice to consider before replacing your current policy.

8. When paying the premium to an agent, never pay in cash. Always pay by check and make the check payable to the insurance company, not to the agent.

9. If you are purchasing a Medigap policy or a long-term-care policy, the agent cannot require that you pay more than one month's premium with the application for insurance unless the coverage is effective immediately and then you can be required to pay up to two months' premium.

10. If you do not receive your policy within 45 days from the date you applied for it, immediately contact your State Department of Insurance.

11. If you believe an agent or insurance company has acted improperly, then contact your State Department of Insurance (see addresses, pages 8 and 9).

INSURANCE BUYER'S CHECKLIST

Before you sign any documents or pay any money to an agent, be sure that you have:

❑ Completed your health insurance policy inventory (Form B, page 50).

❑ Received and understood an Outline of Coverage for the proposed policy.

❑ The agent complete the Agent's Identification (Form D, page 50).

❑ A completed Policy Comparison Sheet (Form A, page 49) with the agent's reason for replacing the policy (if that is the case). Make sure you understand it and especially what benefits are paid if the physician is not a Medicare participating physician.

❑ Agent Certification of Insurance Sale (Form C, page 50).

❑ Replacement Notice if you are replacing your current policy with another. The agent is required by law to provide you with it.

Medigap--policy comparison sheet (Form A)

SERVICES	BENEFITS	MEDICARE PROVIDES	EXISTING INSURANCE (If any)	PROPOSED INSURANCE	REPLACEMENT INSURANCE
INSURANCE CARRIER		Medicare			
MONTHLY PREMIUM		$__.__/month from SS check			
Part A Hospitalization. Semiprivate room and board, general nursing and misc. hospital services and supplies. Includes meals, special-care units, drugs, lab tests, diagnostic X-rays, medical supplies, operating and recovery room, anesthesia and rehabilitation service.	First 60 days	All but $____			
	61st to 90th day	All but $____ a day			
	91st to 150th day	All but $____ a day (2)			
	Beyond 150 days	Nothing			
Post-hospital Skilled Nursing Care In facility approved by Medicare, for an admission for which Medicare is providing benefits.	First 20 days	100% of approved amount	-0-	-0-	-0-
	Additional 80 days	All but $____ a day			
	Beyond 100th day	Nothing			
Blood (pints or packed red blood cells)	blood	All but 1st 3 pints			
Part B Medical expenses. Physician's services, inpatient and outpatient medical services and supplies, physical and speech therapy, ambulance, etc.	Medicare pays for medical services in or out of hospital.	80% of Medicare-eligible expenses (3)			
Part B deductible		You pay $____ deductible once per year.			
Extra Benefits (NOT COVERED BY MEDICARE)					
Inpatient Private Duty Nursing		No benefit			
Outpatient Prescription Drugs		No benefit			
Foreign Hospital		Helps pay hospital expenses in Canada and Mexico in an emergency or if hospital is closer than one in U.S.			
Are preexisting conditions covered?			Yes or No. If "yes" the waiting period is ____	Yes or No. If "yes" the waiting period is ____	Yes or No. If "yes" the waiting period is ____
Is the policy guaranteed renewable?			Yes or No.	Yes or No.	Yes or No.
Agent's reason for replacing policy					
Agent's signature					

Agent identification and evaluations--Forms B, C, D

YOUR HEALTH INSURANCE POLICY INVENTORY (FORM B)

Use this form to list each of your current health policies. The information will help you evaluate your present insurance coverage and whether you need additional coverage.

Insurance Company	Policy Number	Type of Policy	Effective Date	Expiration Date	Premium
1.					
2.					
3.					
4.					
5.					

AGENT CERTIFICATION OF INSURANCE SALE (FORM C)

Ask any agent wanting to sell you Medigap insurance to review Form B. If, after reviewing your inventory of existing policies, the agent feels you need additional coverage, ask him or her to complete this form. It will explain why the agent feels your present coverage is inadequate and why more insurance will benefit you. The agent is not required to sign this form, but you may choose not to do business with any agent that refuses.

I, the undersigned agent, hereby certify that I have reviewed and evaluated
_____'s health insurance policy inventory
(enter applicant's name)
consisting of the following policies:

Insurance Company	Policy Number
1.	
2.	
3.	
4.	

Based on my evaluation, I have recommended that _____
(enter applicant's name)
purchase additional insurance as follows:

Insurance Company	Type of Policy	Policy Form Number
1.		
2.		

This additional insurance is necessary for the following reasons: _____
_____
_____

(Agent's signature)

AGENT'S NAME (FORM D)

Use this form to obtain information on any insurance agent who contacts you regarding the purchase of Medigap health insurance. It will assure you that you know who you are dealing with and how you can contact that agent if necessary. The information can also be used to check out the agent with your local Better Business Bureau.

Agent's Name _____

Agent's License No. _____

Agent's Business Address:
_____
_____

Agent's Phone No. _____

Name(s) of Insurance Company or Companies Represented by Agent:
_____
_____
_____

Date 1st contacted by Agent
_____

Date(s) of Subsequent Calls by Agent:
_____
_____

Ten ways to control healthcare costs

1. Seek out participating physicians. Use the toll-free telephone information line at your Medicare insurance carrier. Find out whether your state has a law that requires physicians to accept Medicare assignment and whether you can participate in the state program. Seeing a participating physician will not only keep your out-of-pocket costs down; it may also encourage more doctors to decide to participate in the program next year.

If you see a nonparticipating physician, be aware that he or she can still accept assignment on a claim-by-claim basis--encourage him or her to accept assignment on your claim. Be assertive--discuss fees and payment options with your doctor.

2. Check your bill for possible errors. Surveys reveal that hospital bills frequently contain errors, some of which are quite costly. Protect yourself, your Medicare and Medigap insurers, and your tax and premium dollars by checking for billing errors.

3. Ask for a second opinion if surgery is recommended. A 1983 study by the Inspector General of the Department of Health and Human Services concluded that if Medicaid and Medicare patients would seek second opinions before going ahead with surgery, elective procedures for the Medicaid population would be reduced by 30%, and for the Medicare population by 20%. This would mean a savings to Medicare of almost twice that much.

In addition to asking second opinions, it pays to ask whether the hospital with which your doctor is associated has a medical peer review board. A peer review board will review your physician's recommendations for surgery and help you guard against unnecessary surgery.

4. Take no more drugs than are absolutely necessary. If you take a prescription or over-the-counter drug, you should know exactly what it is and why you are taking it. Ask your doctor why he or she is prescribing it and what he or she hopes the drug will do. Ask what side effects you should watch out for, and how you will know if the drug is working for you. Ask whether you really need the medication, or whether changes in diet, exercise, or sleep habits would solve the problem.

5. Consider generic drugs. Given that generic drugs are often 50% less expensive than their brand name counterparts, it's easy to see the potential for cutting healthcare costs. Ask your physician or pharmacist about using A-rated generic substitutes for prescription drugs.

6. Consider "outpatient" surgery. If an operation is necessary, ask your doctor if "same-day" or "outpatient" surgery is appropriate. When appropriate, outpatient surgery may mean lower out-of-pocket expenses for most patients.

7. Be aware of alternatives to institutional care (that is, hospitals and nursing homes). Alternatives include adult day care, meals on wheels, home health, hospice, life care communities, group homes, respite care, and others. These alternatives are often less expensive, and more personally appropriate, than institutionalization. To find out more about programs in your area, contact your local Area Agency on Aging (see state listing pages 24 and 25), senior center, or home health agency listed in the yellow pages of the phone book.

8. Stay healthy! If preventive measures and healthy lifestyles could eliminate just 5% of our nation's health problems, this would reduce by 30% the problems treated by primary-care physicians.

Think of your doctor, nurse, pharmacist, other healthcare professionals you consult, and yourself as your healthcare team. Of course, you must be the leading member of the team since your doctor and pharmacist depend on you for information about your health. Prepare for discussions by making a list of any symptoms or physical complaints you want to discuss, and a list of all medications you are currently taking. Provide them with complete information so that they can properly prescribe treatment, then follow their prescriptions carefully.

9. Make wise decisions about supplemental insurance. One good, comprehensive Medigap insurance policy can provide additional insurance protection for Medicare Part A and B expenses. As you examine the many different kinds of insurance plans, be careful to understand your coverage to avoid unnecessary duplication and unreasonably high premiums. Shop around, and take

Your best defense is staying well

your time. You can save money and still buy a good plan.

10. Prepare health care decision-making instruments. Durable power of attorney for healthcare decision-making is a good idea (see article, page 109). The ABA's Commission on Legal Problems of the Elderly has a sample kit to be used in considering what you would want in such an instrument. This kit will help you in thinking through the features you will want to discuss with your family and with your attorney. For a free copy, send a postcard requesting "Health Care Powers of Attorney" to: AARP Fulfillment, 601 E. Street, N.W., Washington, D.C. 20049 (Stock #D 13895).

The number of U.S. physicians who have agreed to limit their charges to Medicare patients and Medicare-approved amounts increased in 1989 to 283,475.

The total represents 40.7% of all physicians who bill the federal healthcare program, and is up from the 1988 total of 37.7% of Medicare participating physicians. Moreover, participating physicians account for more than 60% of the total Medicare spending on physicians' services. However, the percentage of participation varies from state to state--from a high of 74% in Alabama to a low of 16% in Idaho.

THE MESSAGE: If you have medical problems and limited income, retire in a state where physicians participate in the Medicare program.

What you should know about healthcare costs

*"Everybody complains about the weather,
but nobody does anything about it."*
- Will Rogers

The same thing can be said for the United States healthcare system. The news often carries stories of skyrocketing costs of doctors' fees, hospital stays, drugs, malpractice suits, and medical insurance. Almost everyone agrees that healthcare costs are rising faster than our ability to pay for them.

As older Americans, those costs not covered by Medicare or Medicaid are rising much more rapidly than our income. We are also at risk as federal and state governments try to rein in their Medicare and Medicaid costs. Each year for the past decade our out-of-pocket costs, such as Medicare premiums, supplemental insurance, and drugs, have been increasing rapidly. In 1991, it was estimated that on average 20% of individual income went for out-of-pocket healthcare, and it is increasing every year.

Reported causes for our healthcare system failure include:
- Our continued delusion that it operates as a competitive, supply-and-demand market system--it doesn't.
- Doctors' fees, hospital charges, drug prices, and other healthcare costs are hidden from the consumer until the bill arrives.
- Fee-for-service physicians frequently provide unneeded care for "revenue enhancement."
- Patients are unable to or do not question quality, need, alternatives, or price of the care.
- The high awards in malpractice suits increase doctors' costs and cause doctors to perform many unneeded tests.
- Consumers with insurance coverage fail to be concerned about costs.
- Greedy pharmaceutical companies charge high prices for drugs.
- Hospitals make wasteful capital expenditures trying to maintain market share by expanding, despite empty beds and duplication of technology within the same hospital (325,000 of the nation's 930,000 hospital beds on average are empty every day).
- Doctors' incomes are high, averaging more than $150,000 per year and increase nearly triple that of inflation each year.
- Contrary to popular belief, doctors (and patients) often don't know which treatments are most effective for patients.

DRUG COSTS

As we grow older, many of us will suffer from chronic illnesses that require long-term use of medications for such conditions as hypertension, heart disease, diabetes, and arthritis. Medications for these and other conditions are presently commanding increases in already outlandishly high drug prices and are an impediment to our healthcare. We, who are 65 or older, use 32% of the prescription drugs sold in the United States at an annual cost of $9 billion. Yet we exercise little influence on the market price of these drugs. In 1991, nearly 20% of an older person's income was used for healthcare, mostly for drugs. It is unfortunate for us that drug prices have increased 149% over a ten-year period--nearly five times the price increase of American-made passenger cars. Drug

makers' prices have easily outpaced inflation and consumer-price indexes, escalating at more than four times the rate of consumer products taken as a whole. One study found prices for drugs sold in the United States average 54% higher than the same drugs sold in Europe.

Many low-income older people are devastated by the high cost of their prescriptions. Of their $1,100 monthly income from Social Security, one couple in Dallas spend more than $600 a month for ten prescription drugs. Although you pay for drugs, what you need is specified by your doctor and you cannot substitute any other product. The brand-name, prescription drug market is not like other competitive markets. An example is the food market, where you can choose from a variety of products to meet your nutritional needs. Food prices are competitive between suppliers and posted prices tell you exactly what each item will cost.

Companies that develop a new brand-name drug patent it. This patent gives the company the exclusive right to manufacture and sell this drug for seven years. During this period of patent protection, there is no head-to-head direct price competition for that particular product. Therefore, the drug company owning the patent can charge "whatever the market will bear," and usually does--making pretax profits of three or four times that of other manufacturing companies. They also obtain patents on copycat drugs that are not "new" in that they make little or no contribution to existing therapies. Drug companies argue the high prices are due to high research costs for a new drug and because they have only seven years to recover these costs. Yet drug companies will not reveal their research or the manufacturing costs.

Generic Drugs

A generic drug is bioequivalent and chemically identical with the original brand-name drug. It can only be made after the patent for the brand-name drug has expired. A generic is sold under a common or "generic" name for that drug, not the brand name. For example, the brand name for one well-known tranquilizer is Valium, but it is also available under the generic name diazepam. Because a number of companies can produce generic drugs, there is competition leading to prices 30% to 50% below that of the counterpart, brand-name drug.

There are more than 200 manufacturers of generic drugs in the United States. Generic drugs are made by divisions of major brand-name drug companies and firms that make only generic drugs. A generic manufacturer must comply with all federal regulations and follow good manufacturing practices in order to market its drugs.

Your doctor and pharmacist have access to a publication from the FDA called "Approved Drug Products with Therapeutic Equivalence Evaluation," more commonly called the "Orange Book." It contains ratings of generic drugs on their suitability to be substituted for the brand-name drug. Caution: For some individuals, even if products contain the same active ingredients, they are not always exactly bioequivalent because of differences in manufacturing or inert ingredients.

SUGGESTION: Publish a "Red Book" for Medicare-approved
amounts for healthcare similar to the "Blue Book" for autos
so we all can learn what the Medicare-approved amounts are.

FINANCIAL MATTERS
MEDICAL COSTS   **53**

The rising cost of healthcare

and what you can do about it

If the drug you are taking, whether a brand-name or generic, seems to be working and you have no unexpected side effects, you shouldn't worry. **However, if you have side effects or think the drug isn't working as well as it should, consult your physician.** Remember, if you have a prescription medicine that you are supposed to take until it is gone, do not stop taking it without checking with your physician or pharmacist.

For the treatment of our illnesses, we are dependent upon our doctors, pharmacists, medical research, and products that this research produces. Doctors assume that their patients want the best and they fear malpractice suits if they recommend anything less; therefore, they often disregard prices when they prescribe drugs. Sometimes doctors prescribe an expensive drug when a cheaper one is better. For example, cardiologists continue to prescribe TPA, a drug that dissolves clots, for $2,000 a dose, though studies have shown that streptokinase, at $200 a dose, serves heart attack patients even better. For some therapies, there are lower-cost drugs on the market, although not identical products to the new drug, which the doctor might choose. Many doctors, unless they themselves are buying drugs, might not be aware of your monthly costs for drugs or your economic situation.

Here are some suggestions to consider:

1 Tell your doctor how high your monthly drug bills are and ask if all prescriptions are needed or if there are alternatives that cost less.

2 If your doctor prescribes a brand-name drug, ask him/her to prescribe generic drugs, if possible. They are about one-half the price of their brand-name counterparts. By law, pharmacists are unable to supply generic drugs if the doctor calls for a brand name.

3 Make sure your doctor writes the prescription so you understand what it means without a decoding expert. By law, pharmacies must give you the price of the prescription before they fill it. Most will do so over the phone if you can accurately tell them the name of the drug, dosage form, and strength. Otherwise, you must show them the prescription.

4 Drug prices (even generic ones) differ widely between pharmacies and different areas in the U.S. A survey by AARP found it commonplace for prices to differ by more than 25% within communities. It discovered that the average price for drugs included in the survey varied as much as 32% between states. Nationally, prices varied by factors of up to 14 to 1, meaning a person might pay $28 in one region and $2 someplace else for the same prescription. NOTE: A store that charges the lowest price for some drugs does not necessarily charge less for all drugs. Shopping around can result in significant savings, especially if you take a drug regularly.

5 If the drugs are beyond your means, tell your doctor. He might provide some free samples given to him by drug companies.

6 Most pharmacies charge a $3 or $4 dispensing fee plus their overhead costs. They have no control over the outlandish price increases by drug companies.

7 Special customer services provided by some pharmacies such as 24-hour service, free delivery, patient profiles, and discounts--frequently advertised as "free"--result in an overall 7% increase in prices. However, some pharmacies provide such services as: checking your prescription drug history records, your allergy and sensitivity information, or drug-drug interactions (which can be potentially life-threatening) and may be worth this added cost.

8 Let your congressmen know you are concerned about healthcare and drug costs. Seniors should demand legislation that:
  * establishes a federal commission that limits the pre-tax profits of pharmaceutical firms from the present 22.6% of sales to 10% or limits the maximum prices of drugs;
  * encourages European drug manufacturers to offer drugs in the United States--meeting the objectives of our open market position;
  * mandates that pharmacies post prices of the most commonly prescribed prescription drugs and generic equivalents on a sign inside every pharmacy readily accessible to customers;
  * requires all pharmacies to post generic equivalents of prescription drugs;
  * eliminates patents for "new molecule copycat drugs" that are similar to an existing drug with an added molecule that make little or no contributions to existing therapies as determined by the FDA; and
  * control the escalating costs of healthcare.

9 Contact your senior citizens' organizations asking them to vigorously lobby for laws needed to control healthcare costs and drug prices.

The United States drug industry is the strongest in the world and its percent of profits are higher than any other industry. Prices they can charge for drugs are not restricted. **Presently you have one option to lower your costs of the drugs you need--compare prices with a vengeance.**

The older worker and age discrimination

Recent years have brought a significant increase in retirement of workers at an earlier age. Although there are almost as many reasons as retirees, there are some trends that contribute to this phenomenon:

1 Retirement has changed from an end-of-the-road experience to the beginning of a new life. Better retirement plans and longer life expectation have contributed to the feeling that retirement is a release from restraint.

2 In many cases retirement incentives have made it possible for older workers to consider retirement long before they had thought it possible.

3 Because of declines in many industries in the United States, many workers have been faced with forced retirement.

4 Many otherwise healthy industries have decided to downsize their work force in order to be more competitive. The result has been either layoffs or the urging of older workers to retire.

5 Since older workers tend to be at the top of their wage categories, it is more cost effective to have them leave employment than for younger persons to do so.

Age Discrimination Law

The original age discrimination law was passed in 1967. It is known as the Age Discrimination in Employment Act (ADEA). Its provisions were to be enforced by the Equal Employment Opportunity Commission (EEOC). In succeeding years virtually all the states have passed similar legislation and have set up means of enforcing its provisions on the state level. Those provisions are that no person or business may do any of the following in regard to a worker who is 40 years of age or older:

■ To fire or refuse to hire a person strictly on the basis of age.
■ To refuse to refer an employment agency client to a prospective employer or a job opening on the basis of age.
■ To state age preferences in help-wanted advertisements.
■ To deny union membership to an individual because of age.

There are other general provisions in the federal law. The law applies to all employers who have 20 or more workers. No employer may require a pre-employment physical, although after selection a physical examination may be required that can eliminate the worker from the position.

Complaints

Any worker who has a complaint under the provisions of the ADEA must go to the local office of the EEOC and present his/her complaint in writing. The burden of proof is on the worker to show that discrimination of some kind took place. In many states the complaint may also be made to the appropriate state agency. Either the EEOC or the state agency should then investigate the claim and make a decision about its merits.

Subsequent meetings between the agency and the worker determine what action is to be taken. The accused employer may fight the case or make an offer of reemployment to the worker.

There is a statute of limitations in such cases. Certain acts must have been taken by the end of two years and certain others by the end of three. This can be a problem for the complainant because the company can stall at each phase of the process so that time slips away and the rights of the person involved may be lost. Congress has been very critical of the administration of the Act by the EEOC. Thousands of cases have expired when the EEOC failed to take timely action. Therefore, it is important for the individual to press his/her case with the EEOC

in order to be sure that his/her rights under the law are fully protected.

Once application for a discrimination ruling has been made it is possible to go to court to protest inadequate action by the agency. If there are any complexities about your case, it may well be wise to hire an attorney who is knowledgeable about EEOC procedures to monitor your case and recommend action. Since the decision in your case can mean much in respect to your future income, it is important not to miss any step in the process.

Waiver of rights

One aspect of the process of early retirement that has been of some concern has been the efforts of employers to get prospective retirees to waive their rights under the provisions of the ADEA. Specifically, they are asked to waive their right to sue under the provisions of the law. Some observers have felt that excessive pressure has been exercised to get workers to sign such agreements. Often workers are not aware of what rights they are surrendering until it is too late.

How Older Workers

Perform

It is important that the individual who is asking to continue employment be well informed about the performance of older workers in the market. There are often efforts to suggest that an older person is not able to do his/her job as well as younger persons. Experience and research have shown that:

✔ Older workers are often more productive than younger ones.
✔ Older workers tend to be steadier--less variable in their productivity than younger workers.
✔ Older workers are often more flexible about assignments.
✔ Attendance, health, safety and turnover of older workers compare favorably with other work groups and are often better.
✔ Older workers tend to be responsible and reliable.

To work or not to work--that is the question!

Senior Employment

More than one person has changed his/her mind about sitting in a rocking chair for the duration of their life after having been retired for a while. That is just one example of why seniors may decide to seek employment after they have formally retired. There are many other reasons to go back to work after retirement:

✱ The individual may need the income to survive decently.

✱ One may wish to pursue an old interest that regular employment has prohibited in the past.

✱ A person may wish to meet new people and establish contacts.

✱ One might wish to develop new interests different from his/her old employment.

✱ An individual might feel that continued employment would keep him/her from aging more quickly than otherwise.

✱ Employment may be a means of making the retirement more comfortable because of the extra income.

Lest you feel that it is not fair for you to possibly take a younger person's job by entering the job market, it is important to understand some demographics and some research data. Our population is aging. In 1987, some 17% of the U.S. was over 64 years of age. Predictions are that by 2030, that group will be some 28% of the population. That means that the younger group must be more productive, and/or more older persons will need to work in order for there not to be a decline in the standard of living. Remember that older workers more than hold their own when compared with other workers. It may well prove to be a combination of increased productivity and more older workers, but something has to give.

Deciding What to Do

It is important to understand that you don't have to decide immediately how you are going to occupy your time after retirement. It is sometimes difficult to be at ease doing nothing after so many years of directed and compulsive activity. Remind yourself that you are retired and needn't feel guilt for

inactivity. You may decide that you want to play golf every day for the rest of your life. On the other hand, you may come to the conclusion that you want to continue being useful to your family and to others by reentering the job market in some fashion. Once you have made that decision, then the next steps are to choose what you want to do.

What Sort of Work?

If you are fortunate enough to be able to select employment without regard to the amount of income, then you can ask, "What would I really like to do?" Are there friends that you have envied because of what they do for a living? Is there some hobby that you have pursued or wanted to pursue that might be used to bring in income? Depending on the answers to these questions there are logical steps.

❑ If you have no special interests as outlined above, you may wish to talk to your old employer. They might just love to have you back for a few hours a week, sharing your expertise with younger workers.

❑ Read the want ads, not just in the newspaper, but in magazines and trade journals. See what kinds of jobs there are out there.

❑ Consider getting new training or more education if there is a field you think you would like to enter.

❑ Get a resume together. You may find it fun to decide what you have to offer to a new employer.

❑ Get information about special programs like Vista or the Peace Corps that cater to older persons who may not have great financial needs.

❑ Investigate job training programs such as the Job Training Partnership Act (JTPA). In this case local agencies have obtained grants that provide training for jobs that are needed in the community.

❑ Go to employment agencies, public and private, to decide if it is worth paying a fee to find the type of employment you would like.

❑ Look into opening your own business if that is something you have always wanted to do. Check out needs, consider a

franchise, talk to other people in that business. Leave nothing to chance when committing your hard-earned savings.

If You Have to Work

If you must work to live because you have been forced into early retirement or have lost your job, do all of the above, and also look into special programs that are offered to persons in your circumstance. Have you been a victim of discrimination? If so, pursue the alternatives discussed in the article on older worker discrimination, page 54. The Job Training Partnership Act has a special program under Title III that is aimed at dislocated workers and their special needs.

There are other special programs that can help, although they do not offer much income. An example is the Senior Community Service Employment Program (SCSEP). Under Title V of the Older Americans Act, it is administered by the Department of Labor. Seniors are paid minimum wage for doing work in the community such as helping with a senior nutrition program. This program is limited to persons 55 or over who do not earn more income than 125% of the poverty level ($6,280 single, $8,420 married--1990 values).

Social Security and Earned Income

You need to remember that if you are retired and drawing a Social Security pension, it may be reduced because of income earned in gainful employment. The amount of the reduction in your pension declines as you grow older so that there is no penalty once you reach 70. Before that, the average deduction in Social Security income is $1 for every $ earned above certain limits (see the article on Social Security, page 58).

Elsewhere in this book you will find discussion of volunteering in a variety of community enterprises. Work of that nature has been known to lead to paid employment. In any case, there are some worthwhile adventures out there that can enrich your life, whether or not you are paid for them. Retirement is an opportunity to take a new run at life. If there is something you have always wanted to try, now's the time.

Hanging on to retirement monies

If you have been able to retire with a nest egg, you probably need to refocus your investment program. It is a time when one needs to be conservative and develop an investment program that in order of importance:

* Will preserve your capital
* Will keep up with inflation
* Will earn income to enhance your retirement and provide security

No two advisors will agree on the exact makeup of a retirement investment strategy. But they all will agree that one should be conservative because you no longer have the potential to earn back money that is lost on bad investments. Here is a sample investment strategy:

30% or more in cash--bank accounts, insured certificates of deposit, insured money market accounts, etc.

40% or more in government-backed securities, either in direct ownership of T-bills or bonds, or a mutual fund that invests in them. The key criterion is "the good faith and credit of the United States."

30% in conservative stocks and bonds or no-load mutual funds that are rated low risk or low volatility. Here, especially, it is essential to diversify investments. Mutual funds are able to provide that diversification far better than most investors can through different stocks.

Mutual Funds A few words about mutual funds is in order. These organizations are investment companies that offer to invest your money through your purchase of their shares with a given strategy in mind. For example, they might limit a fund to blue chip stocks, allowing you to own an interest in a variety of stocks with a modest investment. Other funds attempt to buy undervalued stocks, or only companies that provide a specific service or product such as utilities or biotechnology products. These companies finance their service through the collection of a load or sales fee at purchase or sale and/or a management fee. In most cases the total value of all investments is calculated daily to determine the value of the shares in the fund. The dividends earned by

the fund are credited to the individual accounts as are profits from the sale of securities that have increased in value. Losses are shared in the same way.

Mutual funds may be purchased through a broker, or directly from the fund offices. Generally a broker will charge a commission, even on no-load funds. The advantage of ownership through a broker is that it is generally easier to sell the fund quickly through their offices. Closed-end funds are no longer open to investment and are sold on the stock exchange. Their prices can vary according to the stock market and do not necessarily equal the cash value of the securities they hold.

Many studies have shown that the mutual funds that charge a load are no more profitable than those that do not. In fact, when you subtract a load of from 2% to 8% from your initial investment, you will be earning less because you have less invested. Government regulations now require that funds provide their investors with accurate information about the actual cost of their management services. These charges should total less than 1% per year.

Mutual funds generally require a minimum initial investment with smaller amounts allowed for additions. Many of them waive this limit for IRA's. These minimums can vary from $500 to $50,000.

Mutual fund families (different types of funds offered by the same company) offer some features that can overcome the advantage of buying through a broker cited above. Some of them offer telephone requests for the sale of your shares. All of them offer telephone exchanges between funds. For example, if you determine that you wish to sell your shares in a stock fund, you can ask the company to switch your investment from their stock fund to a money market account or a government bond fund. Many of them will make this switch without charge unless you have made several switches in the previous months. There are a number of fund families available in the market, and some of them specialize in no-load sales.

Tax-free Bonds Depending on the size of your estate and your tax bracket, an important alternative investment is in tax-free bonds. These are exempt from income taxes, and most often are municipal or other local government issues. Their interest rates are lower than other types of bonds, but since they are not taxed, they may be more profitable than investments paying 2% to 3% more. Again, such bonds are

available through mutual funds. Several companies offer funds they call "double tax-free" because they are exempt from both state and federal income taxes. These are generally designed for a specific state but are offered by national companies.

Investment Advice If your estate is sufficiently large, it may be wise to seek a financial advisor and perhaps manager or trustee. These advisors generally manage your investments on a percentage basis. Such an advisor should have appropriate training and experience, as well as certification as a financial consultant. Ask for references and talk to clients who have been with him/her over time. Discuss the philosophy of investment you wish, and retain the power of review over major decisions. With rare exceptions, it is best to avoid dealing with an advisor who earns his fees through commissions. Such an advisor might not recommend you purchase a no-load mutual fund, even though many of the best funds fall into that category. There have been instances where commission advisors have bought and sold items in a portfolio only because they earn commissions for these transactions.

Self-Education An alternative to hiring someone to manage your affairs is to do it yourself. The task of educating yourself so that you can make wise decisions and avoid bad advice is not very difficult. If you wish to invest in individual stocks and bonds entirely, then you do need to study and keep up-to-date on a daily basis. That requires a commitment of time and energy that is significant.

On the other hand, if you wish to be able to make some basic investment decisions about strategy and review them from time to time, it is possible to educate yourself and keep up with only modest expenditures of time. Magazines such as *Money* and *Forbes* are two examples of publications that can help you to find out what trends are afoot and what changes you need to make. Such magazines recommend stocks that are promising and regularly review mutual fund performance. They not only compare earnings, but management costs and changes in investment strategy. There are also specialized publications that carry model portfolios or rate mutual funds.

The important thing is to be able to select investments that will not cause you major and persistent worry. You want to be able to enjoy your retirement, and worry does not promote that end. There is no way one can avoid risk altogether, but you can minimize it and thus enjoy the fruits of your labor more fully.

> **When I was young I thought that money was the most important thing in life; now that I am old I know it is.**
> - Oscar Wilde (1856-1900)

Since Social Security was never intended to provide the sole support of retired workers, additional resources are needed to allow retirement with comfort and dignity. In many cases, private employers have created, as a condition of employment, private pension plans that fulfill this need. The problem has been that in the past, many of these pension benefits did not materialize for the worker when he retired. Companies closed, went broke, were involved in a merger, or the worker was dismissed after years of service, but before retirement.

ERISA
In 1974, Congress passed the Employee Retirement and Income Security Act (ERISA) to remedy some of these inequities. ERISA did not require a private pension, but it did set minimum standards for private pension plans that were established. It made such rules as:

■ When pension funds can be accumulated by a worker.
■ How long you can be away from your job before you have a "break" in service.
■ Establishing the spouse's right to have part of your pension in the event of your death.

REA and TRA
In 1984 the Retirement Equity Act was passed, and in 1986 the Tax Reform Act. Both liberalized the protections that were included in ERISA. Together they established the following principles for private pension plans:

✳ Age and service requirements must not be unreasonable.
✳ A person who works for a specified minimum period will receive some pension at retirement.
✳ The money must be there to pay the benefits when due.
✳ There must be prudent handling of pension funds.
✳ Employees and their beneficiaries must be informed of their rights and entitlement.
✳ Protects the rights of spouses.
✳ By including insurance provisions the benefits of workers are protected in the event of plan termination.
✳ There must be an appeal process.
✳ The worker must be able to exercise his/her rights under the pension plan without harassment or interference.
✳ The worker has the right to sue in federal court if there is a dispute.

VESTING
Vesting is the act of gaining the nonforfeitable right or entitlement to employer-provided pension benefits. This principle is vital because it protects the worker from all sorts of abuses that previously existed. There are two kinds of vesting: cliff and graded. Cliff vesting requires a worker to be employed for a stated period, after which he/she receives full rights to the pension so far earned. With graded vesting the worker earns partial pension rights after a given period (a percentage of his pension). Full rights are earned after additional years of employment. The first reform required cliff vesting after ten years. That changed to five years in 1989. Graded vesting set minimum periods of five and ten years for partial and full vesting. The 1989 reform changed that to three and seven.

Accrued benefits that have been contributed by the employee must be fully and immediately vested. ERISA requires that pension funds must be rigidly protected, and establishes regulations for governance and auditing. There are sanctions for underfunding a pension plan, and protection against plan termination and/or mergers with other companies. A worker is protected from being dropped from employment in order to avoid paying a pension. Any company official who does harass an employee for exercising rights under the pension plan can be subject to a $10,000 fine and one year in prison.

PENSION PAYMENT OPTIONS
At the time of retirement, a choice is made about the way in which the pension will be paid. There are generally several options. The maximum lifetime payment will end at the time of the death of the retiree. Other options will give the spouse a percentage, usually 50%, of the retirement allowance at the time of the death of the worker. Other options might be for a stated period such as ten years, with no more payments after the time is up. Still another option is the lump sum payment.

SURVIVOR RIGHTS
A spouse who has been married to the pension member for ten years has certain rights under ERISA and its subsequent reform acts. Because retired workers often selected the highest paying annuity option, their wives were not protected at the time of their death. **Since research indicates that 85% of surviving spouses over 65 years of age are women, it is critical that the future of the spouse be considered at the time of option selection.** The new law provided that the pension administrators must provide an option that specifies 50% of the workers pension upon his or her death for the surviving spouse. The only exception allowed was when the spouse had signed a different annuity election and it was witnessed by a pension administrator or a notary.

DISPUTES
When a dispute about any matter touching a private pension plan occurs, there are appeals procedures available. The individual should contact the plan administrator and try to work out the problem. If it cannot be resolved in that way, the Pension Benefit Guarantee Corporation (PBGC) may be able to help. Address inquiries to the Pension Benefit Guarantee Corporation, 2020 K Street, Washington, D.C. 20006, Attn: Coverage and Inquiries Branch. Among other groups that provide assistance to elderly persons is the National Senior Citizens Law Center (NSCLC). They have two locations to serve you. One is at 1052 W. 6th Street, Los Angeles, CA 90017. Their telephone is (213) 482-3550. The second office is at 2025 M Street, N.W., Washington D.C. 20036. Telephone (202) 887-5280.

There are several other retirement mechanisms that are authorized for employees.

Simplified Employees Pension
The 1978 Revenue Act authorized employers to set up simple plans to which both employee and employer could contribute. These plans were limited to $7,000 per tax year.

401 K Plans--KEOGH
This plan is governed by the provisions in the tax laws and allows joint contributions to these accounts. These plans allow taxes on this income to be deferred, and employees are allowed to borrow from the funds on deposit. This plan also has a $7,000 limit.

Employee Stock Ownership Plans (ESOP)
ERISA classifies these plans as a variety of pension. These plans have the advantage of involving employees in corporate ownership, thus increasing their stake in the welfare of and profit earned by the company.

Individual Retirement Accounts (IRA)
In 1981 it became possible for a wage earner to save up to $2,000 ($2,500 for couples) and subtract that amount from the gross income. The money was placed in special accounts and drew interest that was not taxed until withdrawn. Workers could begin to withdraw such funds without penalty when they reached 59 1/2 years of age. The Tax Reform Act of 1986 changed the law so that full IRA's are only possible for those who have an adjusted gross income under $25,000, and $40,000 for couples.

> **Money is like a sixth sense-- and you can't make use of the other five without it.**
> - Somerset Maugham (1874-1965)

Social Security--a part of your retirement income

Social Security is a vast social program that was enacted in 1936 and constantly amended and added to since that time. The term covers several major programs that provide:

❶ Retirement income (SS)
❷ Disability income (DI)
❸ Dependent's and survivor's benefits
❹ Supplementary Security Income (SSI)
❺ Medicare

Who is eligible for SS retirement income?

Every person who works in covered employment for a sufficient period and for whom contributions (they are really SS imposed taxes) are made to the system is eligible to receive benefits. Covered employment is any job that is not exempted from the system and includes self-employed persons. Today fewer types of employment are exempt from Social Security than formerly.

How long must one work to be eligible for SS retirement income?

Beginning in 1991, a person must have worked enough to accumulate 40 quarters (ten years) in covered employment. A quarter is a three-month period: January through March, April through June, July through September, and October through December. Originally members of the system were required to actually earn a given minimum in each of those quarters to receive credit. But beginning in 1978, one could earn money in one quarter and have it credited for another quarter if one earned multiples of the minimum amount required at that time. For example, that quarterly minimum was $470

in 1988. If you earned three times that, $1,410, in the first quarter, you would receive credit for three quarters for that year, even if you did not work at all for the other nine months. That quarterly minimum is expected to continue to rise. No person can be credited with more than four quarters in any given year no matter how much they earned in how many jobs.

The amount of earnings that are taxed for Social Security purposes has increased significantly over the years, as has the amount of withholding for contributions to Social Security.

How is your retirement SS allowance determined?

The amount you receive from Social Security depends upon:
❶ How much you earned over the years
❷ How long you worked in covered employment
❸ At what age you retire

The size of your retirement allowance is mainly based upon the amount of your accumulated earnings over your covered working life. A complicated formula is used to calculate the amount of your monthly allowance. If your earnings did not total enough to provide a minimum allowance by using the formula, there is a minimum award that goes to such cases. In 1988 the average benefit check was $513 for an individual. A couple received about $876 per month.

An eligible worker may retire at the age of 62. However, the system is predicated on

retirement at 65, and at that age the allowance is 20% higher than at 62. If you continue working after 65, you will gain approximately 1% per year in your retirement allowance until you are 72. It does not increase after that.

How to determine your approximate SS retirement allowance.

The Social Security Administration will, upon request, provide a history of any worker's earnings and an estimate of his or her future monthly benefits. To obtain the earnings and benefits statement, you can call 1-800-234-5SSA (toll-free), or write to: Consumer Information Center, Dept. 55, Social Security Administration, Pueblo, CO, 81000, or go to any local Social Security office and ask for form SSA-7004. The form will ask you to estimate your current and future earnings, and when you plan to retire. In about a month, you will receive a "Personal Earnings and Benefit Statement" that will give you your Social Security history, showing the amount of covered earnings you earned each year and what you have paid in Social Security taxes. In addition, the report will provide an estimate, in today's dollars, of what you will get each month from Social Security when you retire --at age 62, 65, or 70--based on your earnings to date and your projected future earnings.

It is important to check your earnings every 3 years to be sure they have been properly credited to you. Form 7004 can also be used to request information about your earnings in recent years. Request also a statement of the number of quarters of coverage you have earned. To qualify for retirement benefits, you must have the required number of quarters of coverage. The number of quarters of coverage you need depends on your year of birth.

What are the minimum and maximum benefits you could receive?

Benefits are based on an average of earnings over the years. Don't assume you qualify for maximum benefits even if earnings were high. A worker who turns age 65 in 1990, who worked at the federal minimum

Amounts of payroll earnings subject to SS taxes

Year	Earnings taxed (maximum)	Percent SS taxes	Your SS taxes (maximum)	Employer's SS taxes (max)	Total taxes to SS (max)
1984	$37,800	6.70	$2,533	$2,533	$5,066
1985	$39,600	7.05	$2,792	$2,792	$5,584
1986	$42,000	7.15	$3,003	$3,003	$6,006
1987	$43,000	7.15	$3,075	$3,075	$6,150
1988	$45,000	7.51	$3,380	$3,380	$6,760
1989	$48,000	7.51	$3,605	$3,605	$7,210
1990	$53,100	7.65	$4,062	$4,062	$8,124

Self-employed persons pay the amount listed as Total taxes.

Did you know that our government is spending the Social Security trust fund moneys? When the baby-boomers expect Social Security they are going to find IOU's.

FINANCIAL MATTERS
SOCIAL SECURITY 59

wage would receive a benefit of about $439 a month. If the worker's spouse is also 65, the couple will receive an additional $219 (50 % of the worker's monthly amount) for a total of $658. Currently a worker who retires at age 65 in 1990 who has always earned the maximum amount covered by Social Security will receive a benefit of $975 and a couple will receive $1,462.

Restrictions on SS earnings after retirement

Once you have begun to draw Social Security, you are considered a retiree. You may earn all the income you wish from savings and investments. However, if you continue to work at a salaried position, there are limits on what you can earn without penalty. In 1991 the limit on retirees under 65 is $7,080 per year. From 65 to 70 the limit is $9,720. After 70 there is no penalty. The limits change from year to year, but the general rule is that for every $3 earned by a 65-year-old retiree over this maximum, $1 is deducted from the retirement allowance. For an under-65 retiree, $1 out of every $2 earned over the limit is deducted.

What portion of Social Security will be taxed?

For most people, the answer is none. Most people will not have to pay any taxes on their Social Security benefit. However, beneficiaries whose adjusted gross income, plus one-half of their Social Security benefits, exceeds certain thresholds can have up to one-half of their Social Security benefits subject to the federal income tax. The thresholds are $25,000 for a single individual and $32,000 for couples.

A worksheet contained in the booklet accompanying your 1040 income tax form explains how to compute the amount of your benefits that may be taxable. Also, some states currently include Social Security benefits as subject to their state income tax.

Disability Insurance (DI)

Social Security protects the covered worker against disability from sickness or accident with a consequent inability to earn a living. See article on SS Disability page 60.

Dependent's and Survivor's Benefits

Social Security provides protection for dependents and survivors of members of the system both before and after retirement. The spouse of a covered worker who has minor children will receive an allowance that covers the spouse and children until they are 18. Allowances can continue as long as the children are in school.

The spouse of a retired worker receives an allowance as long as the worker lives, and when death occurs, the spouse receives the allowance of the deceased retiree. Even a divorced spouse who is 62 or over can claim an allowance if the marriage lasted 10 years or more and the divorce took place at least 2 years before. Such a spouse is eligible even if the worker has not retired.

Medicare

When a covered worker and spouse reach 65 they are eligible for coverage under Medicare Hospital Insurance Part A without payment of premiums. They normally elect to enroll in Part B for doctor's care by the payment of premiums withheld from their Social Security retirement allowance. See page 38 for article on Medicare.

How to apply to receive Social Security

Go to your local Social Security office about three months before you are ready to retire. The Social Security Office will tell you what proof is needed for your particular case. If you are missing certain documents, ask if you can bring substitutes.

You will generally be asked to provide the following:

❶ Proof of age (birth certificate).
❷ Social Security card or record of your SS number.
❸ Your W-2 withholding form from the past 2 years or a copy of your last federal tax return and proof of payment. This is necessary to ensure that your record of earnings agree with the Social Security office. In many cases your latest earnings will not have been posted with the Social Security Administration. Unless you provide these

forms, it could be several months before all your earnings are included in calculating your Social Security benefit.
❹ Your marriage certificate, if you are applying for a spouse's benefits.
❺ Proof of military service if you were in the military.
❻ If applying as a dependent or survivor, you need evidence of marriage and the Social Security number of the person under whose work record you are retiring.

Appeals

At every step of every process in Social Security and related programs there are opportunities and procedures for appeal of decisions that are made in your case. If you question a ruling it is important to appeal it promptly in order to safeguard your rights under the law. Information about these appeal processes is available at your local Social Security office.

Additional Information

✳ Social Security benefits and divorce. A divorced spouse age 62 or older (not remarried), is eligible for benefits if the marriage lasted 10 years or more and if the ex is retired and eligible for retirement benefits. If you marry #2 you lose these benefits. If you divorce #2 you can again collect on #1's. If you are married to #2 for 10 years you can receive benefits on #2's but not from both. For more information check this out with your Social Security office.

✳ The Social Security program was never intended to provide the sole support for retirees or their dependents.

✳ In 1983, the Social Security payroll taxes were increased to produce a surplus so as to cover the expanded retirement costs of the post-World War II baby boomers. Under the law, the money must be put in trust funds and these funds used only to pay benefits and the cost of administering the respective programs. Our government is not putting this money in trust as required by law but is issuing the trust fund IOU's and using the funds to offset federal spending.

✳ Cost-of-living adjustments (COLA's) are annual increases in SS and are linked to the Consumer Price Index.

Social Security disability for nonretired workers

The Social Security law has insurance provisions that provide protection for workers who may become disabled before reaching retirement age. As much as 25 % of workers experience accident or illness that makes it impossible to work for a year or longer during their lifetime. Social Security's definition of disability is:

✔ You must have some physical or mental impairment.
✔ The impairment must prevent you from doing any substantial gainful work.
✔ The disability must be expected to last, or has lasted, at least 12 months, or is expected to result in death.

It can be difficult to prove disability to the satisfaction of Social Security authorities. Therefore, it is important to have statements from your doctor or doctors when you apply for disability status. As with every phase of Social Security, there are appeals procedures available to the applicant to obtain reconsideration of a claim.

QUALIFYING FOR SOCIAL SECURITY DISABILITY

The general rule for younger workers is that you must have worked and paid into your Social Security during half the quarters between the age of 21 and the time of your injury or illness. There are tables for workers who have been in the work force longer, ranging from a requirement of 20 quarters for someone disabled at 42 or younger to 40 quarters for someone disabled at 62 or older. At least 20 quarters of that work credit must have been earned in the 10 years before you become disabled.

Although the problem you have may not be on Social Security's list of disabilities, it is possible to prove that you are unable to function in a way that you can successfully earn a living. Social Security interprets "substantial gainful work" to mean that you cannot perform work that pays you $300 a month or more. Of course, the kind of work you do also can affect their decision. A logger who has lost the use of his legs might not be seen in the same way as an accountant with a similar condition.

There are a few special situations that award disability payments without qualifying as above:

■ A widow or widower who is over 50 and had a spouse who was fully qualified before death may receive disability with certain limitations.
■ A qualified person whose vision is less than 20/200 (legally blind) may receive disability benefits even though he or she is still working with earnings up to about $700 a month. There are other special rules for legally blind workers.

DISABILITY PAYMENTS

The amount you receive after you have been awarded disability status depends upon your earnings over time just as if you had retired in the regular way. While you cannot receive more than one disability benefit at a time, you will always get the one that will pay you the most. You may receive disability income from other sources such as industrial insurance or veteran's benefits. Since SSI payments are not considered Social Security, you also may receive them without affecting your disability award.

When you apply for disability status, you may be referred to your state rehabilitation agency. They would study your case to see if their services might be of benefit to you. They might make recommendations for medical help, counseling, or job training. You may refuse to act on these recommendations, but if you fail to cooperate in the study you may be denied disability status.

WHEN DISABILITY PAYMENTS BEGIN

The general rule is that you must wait 5 full months before you will receive your first disability check. If your disability began, and you were unable to work more than 6 months before you applied for disability, you may be eligible for some months of back benefits, up to a limit of 12 months.

MEDICARE AND DISABILITY

Remember that Medicare coverage is available to you after you have been disabled for a total of 24 months. This is true no matter what your age. You would, of course, have to pay hospital deductibles and the premiums for Part B (medical) coverage, just as a retired person does.

If you have received Medicare because of

being disabled, your protection will end if you recover from your disability before you are 65.

If you go to work but are still disabled, your premium-free hospital insurance protection will continue for at least 48 months after you begin working. Your medical insurance will also continue for at least 48 months if you continue to pay the monthly premiums. If you lose your premium-free hospital insurance solely because you are working, you may elect to buy hospital and medical insurance for as long as you remain disabled. The first possible month to buy insurance under this provision was July 1990.

LEAVING DISABILITY STATUS

If your condition improves, it is possible to return to work and your regular status in the Social Security system. In fact, you may enter a trial work period to see if you can manage regular employment again. As long as you are still classified as disabled in terms of your physical condition, you can undertake employment for a total of 9 months during which you would continue to receive your disability payments and any money that you earned. Social Security would evaluate your success and make a determination about your future status. If you are unable to continue to work and your disability remains, you would be able to reenter the disability program.

If you have left disability status and then find that you become disabled again, you may return to your disability status without the 5-month waiting period if it is within 5 years of having left disability. Your new disability status begins with the first full month of your disability.

As with all other aspects of Social Security, your local office is the best place to obtain detailed information about disability programs and qualification.

> I reckon being ill
> as one of the great pleasures
> of life,
> provided one is not too ill
> and is not obliged to work
> till one is better.
>
> - Samuel Butler (1835-1902)

 **SSI**

Supplementary Security Income

SSI stands for Supplementary Security Income. It's a program run by Social Security but it is not the same as Social Security. It is a cooperative program between federal and state governments that seeks to assure that there will be a minimum level of support available for older citizens and persons who are blind or disabled. Therefore, the program is based upon need, not what you have paid into Social Security.

It should be understood that SSI is a program for the very poor. A full Social Security allowance as the sole income will eliminate a person from receiving SSI assistance. Even though the amount of assistance available through SSI is small, it may be a good idea to apply. Naturally, any little bit helps when a person is truly needy, and SSI could qualify you for other assistance you might not otherwise be eligible for. Examples are Medicaid and food stamps. Other examples might be free rehabilitation assistance and home-care programs.

GENERAL ELIGIBILITY

To qualify for SSI you must be aged, or blind, or disabled, have little income, and have limited resources.

* Aged means you are 65 or older.
* Blind means you are either totally blind or have less than 20/200 eyesight.
* Disabled means:
  ❶ You must have some physical or mental impairment.
  ❷ The disability must prevent you from getting employment.
  ❸ The disability must be expected to last, or has lasted, at least 12 months, or is expected to result in death.
* Your income must be below a certain amount.
* Your personal worth must be below a certain amount.
* You must be a U.S. citizen or be in the U.S. legally.
* You must live in the U.S. or the Northern Mariana Islands.

INCOME LIMITS

The amount of income you can have each month while getting SSI depends on where you live and whether you work or not. In some states you can have more income than in others. There are a number of exceptions to these regulations. Certain types of income are not counted toward the established limit. Here are some rules:

■ **IF YOU DON'T WORK:** No matter where you live, you may be able to get SSI if you don't work and your monthly income adds up to less than:
* $406 for one person
* $599 for a couple

■ **IF YOU WORK:** You can have more income each month than if you didn't work. If most of your income is from working, you may be able to get SSI if you make less than:
* $284 a month for one person
* $426 a month for a couple

WHAT COUNTS AS INCOME
✔ Social Security and pension checks
✔ Interest, dividends, or any earnings on investments
✔ Noncash items you receive such as food, clothing, or shelter
✔ Moneys received from work

RESOURCE LIMITATIONS

To get SSI your resources must be below certain amounts. Resources are the things you own. They don't count everything you own in figuring the amount of resources you can have and still get SSI. You may be able to get SSI if the resources counted are no more than:
* $2,000 for one person
* $3,000 for a couple

WHAT IS COUNTED:

■ **Finances**--include cash, bank accounts (checking and savings), stocks, bonds, or any like ownership.
■ **Home**--If you own your home and the land it sits on, it does not count no matter what its value.
■ **Auto**--There is a limit on the value of your car, but if it is needed to get to work or to transport you and/or your spouse for medical treatment, there is no limit on its value.
■ **Personal property**--There is a $2,000 limit on personal property based upon what it could be sold for (some of your personal belongings are not counted).
■ **Life Insurance**--There is a limit on life insurance policies with face value over $1,500.

You may appeal any decision regarding your SSI application and/or allowance. Check with your Social Security office.

HOW MUCH CAN YOU GET FROM SSI?

The federal basic monthly SSI check is the same in all states. Benefits change each year as the cost of living increases. Some states add money to the basic check. The basic monthly check is about:

* $386 for one person
* $579 for a couple

Not everyone gets this exact amount. These allowances may then be increased by supplemental payments from the individual states that can raise totals to over $500 for individuals and over $800 for couples.

These allowances are reduced if you earn more than the limit set for SSI earnings, and are reduced even more by unearned income such as Social Security payments, interest, or rental income. Likewise if you receive in-kind assistance such as housing or board from someone else, your allotment can be reduced.

APPLYING FOR SSI

You apply for SSI at your local Social Security office. You can do it at the same time that you apply for Social Security itself. SSI does require a separate application from Social Security. You must bring with you the following items:

❶ Your Social Security card or number.
❷ Proof of your age such as a birth certificate.
❸ If you own real estate in addition to your home you should bring the latest tax bill or assessment.
❹ Evidence of your current income such as pay stubs.
❺ Registration for your automobile, if you own one.
❻ Evidence of your financial assets such as bank books or stock certificates.
❼ Medical evidence of your condition if you are applying on the basis of blindness or disability.
❽ If you live with your spouse bring evidence of his or her earnings and assets.

SSI allowances are subject to occasional reviews of your current financial status. Moreover, you are expected to promptly report any change in your situation that may affect the allowance you receive.

Taking their cut of your retirement moneys

Federal income taxes continue to be a reality for seniors as they were in younger years. However, there are some special features of the tax laws that have particular application to taxpayers who are 65 or over and/or have disabilities of one kind or another.

The U.S. House of Representatives Select Committee on Aging offers free a brochure each year entitled "Federal Income Tax Guide for Older Americans." It is available from the U.S. Government Printing Office. It is useful because it reminds you of your continuing tax obligations and some of the special benefits for seniors in the tax laws.

Tax Preparation Assistance

It is important to select the right form to make your tax return. By calling 1-800-424-FORM you can get information about which form to use and may also request some of the IRS publications that are especially relevant for seniors. The Tax Guide for Older Americans lists the following publications as being of special interest:

Publication	Title
1	Your Rights As a Taxpayer
17	Your Federal Income Tax
524	Credit for the Elderly or the Disabled
530	Tax Information for Homeowners
553	Highlights of Tax Changes
554	Tax Information for Older Americans
575	Pension and Annuity Income (Including Simplified General Rule)
721	Comprehensive Tax Guide to U.S. Civil Service Retirement Benefits
907	Tax Information for Handicapped and Disabled Individuals
910	Guide to Free Tax Services
915	Social Security Benefits and Equivalent Railroad Retirement Benefits

Tax Counseling for the Elderly--Read the article entitled tax preparers, page 64. You will find information on free tax assistance that is available to help persons 60 or older prepare their tax returns. Also, Voluntary Income Tax Assistance (VITA) is available to assist older, handicapped, and non-English-speaking taxpayers. To find the nearest location for such assistance, call the IRS toll-free number for your area or the general number 1-800-424-1040. Another source for this information and assistance

will be found in your local senior center or call your local office of the Area on Aging.

Tele-tax tapes--The IRS has 140 prerecorded tapes on a variety of topics. If you live near a center that offers this service, you can call and take notes. Look in your local directory under IRS for the number. If you live away from such a center, you may face additional telephone charges for the calls.

Tax Preparers--whether public or private are not held responsible for errors in your return. You are the one who is at risk so you should check your return carefully if someone else does it for you. Be sure you understand the contract you make with the preparer when you request his/her assistance.

Who must file?

The rules for who must file are generally the same for seniors as for others, except that there are some extra exemptions. The criteria for who must file are included in the table below.

What is taxable?

The general answer to the question of what is taxable is everything. But, of course, there are some exceptions. The amount that you paid into a pension fund is exempt. When you retire that amount is stipulated, and you are free to leave it out of your income accounting. Once you have received that amount in pension payments, future payments become taxable. That is also

true of annuities, unless they have been tax sheltered. Such annuities and payouts from IRA deposits are totally taxable. Remember that you must begin withdrawing these funds by the time you are 70-1/2 and face the tax consequences at that time.

On page 59 we have described the tax rules on Social Security pensions. If you exceed the income limits in effect at the time of your retirement, you are taxed at your tax rate on one half of the monies paid to you by the Social Security Administration.

Unemployment compensation is fully taxable as are interest, capital gains, and other profits of labor or investment.

Profit on the Sale of a Home. You can postpone reporting the profit on a sale of a residence by purchasing a new home that is more expensive. However, you may also exempt up to $125,000 of profit from taxation if you are married and one party is over 55 years of age. A single person or a married person filing separately may deduct $62,500. In all cases, you must have lived in the house for at least three (out of the last five) years. This is a one-time thing. If a couple takes this exemption and then divorces, a new marriage will not renew the exemption. In fact, such a person is known in the tax jargon as a "tainted spouse," not eligible for exemption.

Dependents: The reality of life is that growing older does not always mean our dependents always ride off into the sunset of independence. Sometimes they return, or one can even acquire new dependents due to fortune and fate. The IRS has five tests for dependency that must be met for you to be able to declare them on your return. They are:

Income exceeding	Under 65	65 or older
Single	$5,300	$6,100
Married		
Filing a Joint Return--one over 65	$9,500	$10,200
Filing a Joint Return--both over 65	$9,500	$10,850
Married but not living with spouse		$2,050
Married filing separate return		$2,050
Head of Household	$6,800	$7,600
Qualifying Widow(er)	$7,500	$8,150

The art of taxation consists in so plucking the goose as to obtain the largest amount of feathers with the least possible amount of hissing.

- Jean Baptiste Colbert

FINANCIAL MATTERS
TAXES AND SENIORS 63

Relationship: Anyone you claim must be a relative in one of the accepted categories. Relationships established by marriage are not necessarily ended by divorce or death. It may also be a person who is not related but lives as a member of your household all year.

Married Dependent: A dependent of yours who is also married may not file a joint return. However, if neither the dependent nor the dependent's spouse is required to file, they may file to recover taxes that have been withheld, and you may still claim that person as a dependent if the other four tests are met.

Citizen or Resident: The dependent must be an American citizen or a resident alien or a resident of Canada or Mexico. A noncitizen may also be a dependent if he/she is your adopted child and lived with you all year in a foreign country.

Income: Generally the dependent's income must be less than $2,000. Gross income does not include nontaxable income such as welfare benefits or nontaxable Social Security benefits. There are some special rules about dependents who are disabled or full-time students.

Support: The general rule for dependency is that you must provide more than half of the support for the individual you are claiming. It is important that a person who is listed as a dependent knows the regulations concerning when to file a return.

Deductions for Seniors
There are tax consequences that accrue from age that affect the number of deductions you take when you file a return. An additional deduction is granted when you reach age 65. If you are legally blind, you have another deduction available to you. These extra deductions sometimes can make the difference in deciding whether or not to itemize deductions in your return.

As we get older, we will find these special tax breaks for seniors helpful; unfortunately, there are also some negatives that affect senior taxpayers as well.

One example of a tax benefit that is often not available for seniors is the exemption of interest on home mortgages. Of course, this is not a regulation aimed at seniors. However, since the tendency is to pay off mortgages as we age, and a large percentage of seniors have homes paid for, or nearly so, this tax benefit is not something we can generally count on in our advanced years.

By the same token, exemptions associated with younger people such as those from dependent children are not a part of the normal senior household. Of course, we don't want dependent children in our advanced age, but it does mean more taxes for the same income.

Tax on Social Security Benefits
In our discussion of Social Security benefits, we pointed out that when a single person's income reaches $25,000, counting one half of the Social Security allotment toward this total, 50% of that allotment becomes subject to income tax at the rate paid by the senior taxpayer. Thus the marginal tax rate (the rate at which every dollar above a given level is taxed) is applied to those dollars that are part of your Social Security grant. Therefore, the effect of this regulation is that the tax rate can rise from one bracket to another and result in significant additional taxes. Tax forms and instructions, mailed to every taxpayer, have worksheets for the purpose of calculating your possible tax obligation in connection with Social Security income.

Earnings Restrictions
You will recall that there are earnings limits (salary and wages only) on those who continue to work after Social Security retirement. This limit tends to add extra taxes on such individuals, because if you earn beyond the limits your Social Security benefits are reduced. Remember that you can earn any amount in interest income without penalty, but wages or salary earnings will be penalized if they exceed the limitations for that year. This restriction continues until the retiree reaches age 70, after which there is no restriction on earnings.

Fixed Income and Taxes
After you retire, there is a tendency for your income to become static, unless you have many investments. Because of that, price rises and increases in taxes have a devastat-

ing effect on the standard of living enjoyed by the retiree. In most cases, personal preference and home ownership make it difficult or undesirable to move to a different location. But, it does make a difference where you live. According to an article in *Money,* the states with the lowest total taxes are New Hampshire, Florida, Alaska, Texas, and Nevada. The worst states for taxes were Hawaii, Oregon, the District of Columbia, Maryland, and Idaho. This survey dealt with sales, income, property, and death taxes. So it does make a difference where you live, and it may well be worth careful investigation of the current tax situation when you are nearing retirement and have the flexibility of settling in the place of your choice.

Dealing with the IRS:
It is not uncommon for the most careful taxpayer to be confronted by a message from the IRS demanding additional money for one reason or another. Since government agency research has discovered that a high percentage of these demands are in error, it is important to check out their validity carefully before sending additional money. The income tax laws are far too complex for government employees with limited training to make consistently accurate determinations. A *Money* article states five rules it recommends for dealing with the IRS:

1 Never ignore a notice.

2 Respond quickly with the correct information or ask for a clarification.

3 Make simple, sharp responses, including the evidence that proves your point.

4 Be forceful and positive. If you get a second notice, include a copy of your response to the first notice. If you get a third notice, you can appeal to the Problem Resolution Officer (PRO). This ombudsman can help.

5 Get outside help if you need it, especially if it involves interpretation of the tax laws.

The records show that you have a good chance of winning an appeal if you are right and are systematic about dealing with the IRS claim.

Our Constitution is in actual operation; everything appears to promise that it will last; but in this world nothing is certain but death and taxes.

- Letter to M. Leroy (1789)

Do you need help with filing your tax returns?

Many people look for help to avoid over-paying taxes. But even if you have someone to help you, you are still the one responsible for compiling information that translates into money-saving deductions, exemptions, credits, and tax losses. And, no matter who prepares your tax return, the IRS will hold you responsible for its accuracy.

How Much Tax Advice Do I Need?

In general, the more money you make, the more tax help you may need. But if you do not itemize deductions or claim tax credits, then you may not need professional help. If you simply want someone to fill out your tax form for you, you can find someone to do that relatively inexpensively. If, on the other hand, your tax return is complicated, you may want to consider hiring a tax accountant or tax attorney.

How Long Should I Keep My Tax Records?

Most records need only be kept for three years. But a few documents should be kept for seven years or longer, such as sales papers relating to the transfer of valuable property like a home, or bill-of-sale for stocks or bonds that will take more than three years to mature. If you have any questions about how long to keep a record, ask the IRS or your tax preparer.

How to Select a Tax Preparer

There is a wide range of experience, expertise, and expense involved in the tax preparation business. You may want to know about the following options:

Free Tax Assistance--There are at least two programs for persons who do not have many tax problems or a lot of money to spend on tax advice:

1. **Tax Counseling for the Elderly.** This is an IRS-funded program, that sponsors free services to older taxpayers who need help in filing their tax forms. Tax Counseling centers are located in senior centers, libraries, banks, savings and loan institutions, and other central sites in cities and towns around the nation. The staff are trained volunteers. Tax counselors also make housecalls and visits to nursing homes and other locations to help persons unable to travel. Many of the tax counseling centers are organized by the American Association of Retired Persons (AARP) and are called tax-aide centers.

2. **VITA.** This Volunteer Income Tax Assistance program also is sponsored by the IRS. It trains volunteers working in VITA centers around the country. VITA workers provide free tax preparation services, primarily to low-income, elderly, non-English-speaking, or disabled individuals who file simple tax returns.

You can learn more about the VITA or tax counseling programs through your local IRS office.

High-volume Walk-in Tax Services--Big-volume tax service companies (H & R Block is one example) generally charge modest prices for preparing simple tax forms. Such companies hire on a seasonal basis and provide employees with a basic tax training program. The companies keep some offices open all year to answer clients' tax questions. It may be difficult, however, to maintain a year-round relationship with a tax preparer.

Tax Accountants--Depending upon your income and the complexity of your financial status, you may benefit from more sophisticated tax help. Such broad assistance is offered by accountants, certified public accountants (CPAs), and enrolled agents who have passed a written IRS examination. These professionals provide extensive tax-planning services and can be valuable to people in high-income brackets or to taxpayers with complicated tax situations.

Tax Attorneys--Of all the options available for tax preparation, a tax attorney probably will be the most costly. Yet, it may be the best option if you are involved in serious disputes with the IRS. If you believe a tax lawyer is necessary, refer to the article on lawyers, page 104, for suggestions about finding the right one to suit your needs.

How to Hire Tax Help

If you decide you need more help than one of the federally funded tax assistance programs like tax counseling can provide, be prepared to spend some time shopping for the best advice you can get for the money you are willing to spend. Start your search early in the tax year. You can help narrow your selection by posing questions like these:

Are you open all year long or only at tax time?

Tax problems can occur at any time during the year, and so can questions from the IRS. You may want to work with someone who is available all year.

What will you charge to handle my taxes?

You may have to wait until the tax preparer, accountant, or lawyer studies your case to get a workable estimate. But the amount you pay for a tax preparation service should never exceed the value of that service to you--either in terms of refunded taxes or time and tax knowledge required on your part. Be prepared to pay more for tax advice from a CPA or a lawyer than you would from a tax preparer employed by a walk-in tax preparation company.

What is your professional educational background?

Ask the tax preparer about his or her certifications, licenses, and degrees. The tax preparer should be able to explain to you what he or she does to keep up-to-date in the field.

Will you accompany me to the IRS if I am audited? What is the additional cost for this service?

Anyone who prepares your return should be willing to accompany you to an audit. Only certain persons, however, can legally "represent" you before the IRS. Among those who may represent you (and go in your place to meet with an auditor, if you wish) are attorneys, enrolled agents, and others, such as close relatives, whom the IRS allows to assume this role.

Among those the IRS does not permit to represent a taxpayer at an audit include many of the people who work part-time as tax preparers or commercial or walk-in firms. The IRS can provide consumers with information regarding a certain tax preparer's eligibility to represent taxpayers at audits. Those who "accompany" you to an audit can only explain how your tax return was prepared. They cannot act as your legal representative or speak on your behalf.

Will I get a refund?

If you are promised a refund before all your financial records have been reviewed or you are asked to sign a blank tax form, you may not be doing business with a reputable person. You may want to consider looking for another tax preparer.

Will you provide references from people in financial or business situations similar to my own?

Ask the tax preparer for a list of present and former clients and contact them. Find out if they were or are satisfied with the service.

Complaints about Tax Preparers

If your tax preparer is a lawyer, you might want to contact the IRS or look to the article on Legal Help--complaints about lawyers, page 107. If your tax preparer is a certified public accountant, you could contact your state board of certified public accountants. If your accountant is not a CPA, try contacting the IRS. If you hired a commercial firm to do your taxes, you could contact any of the following organizations for help: the IRS, the Better Business Bureau, or your state, county, or city consumer affairs office.

The investor who is looking for absolute security in his investments tends to purchase government securities. They want the "full faith and credit of the United States" behind their nest egg, and the easiest way to do that is to purchase T-bills, bonds, or treasury notes issued by the United States. In the article on retirement investment, page 56, we discussed mutual funds that select only government securities for their investments. The convenience of that sort of investment has the disadvantage of having to pay the costs of fund management. Therefore, some persons prefer to buy these instruments directly, eliminating the middle man.

As noted above, the United States issues three types of marketable securities: bills, notes, and bonds. These securities are direct obligations of the United States. When originally issued, they are sold through an auction process. They are known as marketable securities because after their original issue, they may be bought or sold in the secondary (commercial) market at prevailing market prices through financial institutions, brokers, and dealers in investment securities.

The major distinction between these types of instruments is the length of time the security will be outstanding from the date of issue:

- **Treasury bills** (T-bills) are short-term--one year or less.
- **Notes** are medium-term--from one to ten years.
- **Bonds** are long-term obligations that all run longer than ten years.

In financial reporting they are called long bonds. Another distinction is that T-bills do not bear a stated interest rate as do Treasury notes and bonds. Bills are sold at a discount from par (face value). The difference between the purchase price and the amount paid to the owner at maturity represents the interest earned. The market price for these obligations before the maturity date is determined by the interest rates on bonds in general. In most cases, if bond interest rates rise, the value of the existing bond falls. If interest rates decline, the bill, note, or bond rises in value.

> **Riches exclude only one inconvenience, and that is poverty.**
> Johnson (1709-1784)

Individual Purchase of Government Securities
Individual investors may purchase these government securities through their local branch of the United States Federal Reserve Bank. Most large cities in the U.S. have branches. By writing or calling them you can get all the information needed to open an account, learn dates of issues, obtain forms to make bids on upcoming issues, etc. The minimum investment for T-bills is $10,000 and multiples of $5,000 beyond that minimum. This sort of purchase is called Treasury Direct.

Book Entry Purchase
The treasury no longer issues engraved bonds or notes when a sale is made. Instead, an entry is made in the accounting system maintained by the Treasury or the Federal Reserve Bank. In most cases, book entries are maintained for individuals or institutions that intend to hold the security to maturity. If the individual investor decides to sell or trade the security, it must be transferred to the commercial book entry system so that the selling institution has access to the investment.

New Issues--Treasury Bills
There is an elaborate system of offerings of government securities. Thirteen-week and 26-week T-bills are offered every week. The offering is announced on Tuesday, auctioned the following Monday, and issued on the Thursday following. Fifty-two-week T-bills are offered every four months. Notes and bonds have similar interval offerings. The buyer may make a competitive or noncompetitive bid. The competitive bidder offers a given interest rate stated to two decimals. Noncompetitive bidders agree to pay the price equivalent to the weighted average discount rate of accepted competitive bidders. These bids are called tenders. Most individual purchasers are noncompetitive.

Purchase Procedure
You obtain the information and applications mentioned above. Complete the necessary forms and send in your tender. If competitive, it must be sent after the announcement of the issue, but before the sale. Noncompetitive bidders can send their offers at any time. The payment for the investment must accompany your bid. Personal checks that are certified are accepted. You can pay cash at the Federal Reserve Bank, or make a trade of existing securities. Once your account is established, you can arrange for automatic repurchase of new issues as your old ones mature.

T-Bill Advantage
Many investors prefer to purchase T-bills because of the volatility of interest rates and other market factors in recent times. The short terms of bills tend to allow the investor to take advantage of spikes in interest rates, and to avoid the trap of being stuck with a long-term investment with a low interest rate when the market takes an up-turn. It is also possible to further flatten the interest rate variation by purchasing different term bills over time. One suggested combination of purchases is as follows:

❶ Buy a 52-week bill.
❷ After 13 weeks, buy a 26-week bill.
❸ After 13 weeks, buy a 52-week bill.
❹ After 13 weeks, sell the 26-week bill and buy another 26-week bill.
❺ After 13 weeks, sell the 52-week bill and buy another 26-week bill.
❻ Repeat #4.
❼ Repeat #5.
❽ Repeat #4.
❾ Repeat #5.

Remember that this can be arranged on an automatic renewal basis. This direct purchase process seems very complicated at first. However, once your account is established and regular information about offerings is sent to you, it is less formidable. It does allow the individual to eliminate buying and selling costs. While the rates for government securities are generally less than you earn in equity investments, they do have the virtue of allowing the retired person to sleep at night and still earn interest on his principal.

Remember that you can obtain this information from your closest Federal Reserve Bank office or by writing to The Bureau of the Public Debt, Division of Customer Services, Washington, D.C. 20239-0001

What a Grandparent Is

(a third grade essay)

A grandmother is a lady who has no children of her own, so she likes other people's little girls and boys. A grandfather is a man-grandmother. He goes for walks with boys and they talk about fishing and tractors and like that. Grandmothers don't have to do anything except be there. They're old so they shouldn't play hard or run. It is enough to drive us to the market where the pretend horse is, and have lots of dimes ready. Or if they take us for walks they should slow down past pretty things like leaves and caterpillars. They should never say, "hurry up."

Usually they are fat but not too fat to tie shoes. They wear glasses and funny underwear. They can take their teeth and gums off. It is better if they don't typewrite or play cards except with us. They don't have to be smart--only answer questions like why dogs hate cats, and how come God isn't married? They don't talk babytalk like visitors do because it is hard to understand. Whey they read to us, they don't skip or mind if it is the same story again.

Everybody should try and have one, especially if they don't have television, because grandma's are the only grown-ups who have got the time.

One of the many things that is said about being a parent is that it just happens without regard for your aptitude or skill to raise a child. Being a grandparent is not a great deal different except that you have had no direct participation in the process save siring one of the parents of the grandchild. In this modern world of divorce or birth out of wedlock and the increasing number of adoptions, you can become a grandparent without even a biological connection.

There are few of us who retain much objectivity when grandchildren actually arrive. Whether they carry our genes or not we look at them with very special feelings and begin to want all sorts of things for them from loving care to a college education. While everyone can wear out their welcome our tendency is to want to be with them or have them with us. It is also often the case that because we are further along with our lives we are more free and more able financially to do things for them.

GRANDPARENTS AS PARENTS

We are told that there are three million grandparents raising their children's children in the United States. Obviously, when that happens something is wrong with conventional relationships. That can happen for many reasons, and in most cases, when such unhappy circumstances occur it is a fortunate alternative for the child or children in question to be taken in by grandparents.

Grandparents have always served special nurturing roles in their relationship with their grandchildren. While research increasingly reflects the general value of social support to improved mental and physical health, for a variety of reasons, grandparents are often less available to their grandchildren to fulfill those supportive roles in our society today.

However, literature is full of stories of successful and happy people who were raised by grandparents. Grandparents have always been important in the transmission of cultural lore to the young. American Indians, in particular, seem to allot this task to the grandparent. It is less true in the formal sense in our culture, but it often happens.

THE GRANDPARENT ROLE

In most cases our roles as grandparents are different than those of parents. The majority of people can understand and appreciate those distinctions, but we can all use help to become more skillful as grandparents. Ironically our laws have tended to give no official recognition to the role of grandparent in terms of rights and often in respect to responsibility. Rights advocates point out that some school districts will not allow admission to the local school if the child has not been formally adopted by the grandparent. While that is undoubtedly rare, it illustrates an extreme example of the lack of status of this role in our society. In general, grandparents want to be able to:

● Have mutually satisfying contacts with their grandchildren.

● Pass along family and cultural information and values to give them a sense of continuity and belonging. We want to contribute to the idea of belonging to a family.

● Make special financial contributions, if we are able, that may vary from paying for music lessons to orthodontia. Another popular contribution for those who can afford it is to start a college fund.

● Be there when needed. To reinforce the good things in their immediate family and keep our involvement at an appropriate level. It is essential that our gifts should not spoil the children.

Where to get some help and information

If you are already a grandparent, or that state of being is facing you in the near future, there is help and support out there of several kinds:

❑ First, there are organizations that are concerned about grandparents and grandchildren who are devoted to helping you be a better grandparent.

❑ Second, there are some organizations that offer newsletters that provide a wealth of information on the aspirations and problems of grandparenting.

❑ Third, there are grandparent support groups or self-help groups (sometimes called mutual-help groups) for those facing problems along that line, or, in their absence, assistance in starting a support group yourself in your community.

❑ Fourth, you will find there are other groups devoted to the identification of and the extension of legal rights for grandparents who may be cut off from their grandchildren. These people identify states where these legal rights exist and work for their establishment in the remaining states.

❑ Fifth, there are also college courses in some states such as at Arizona State University in grandparenting. Courses are supported by the American Association of Retired Persons (AARP). Get your local college to offer a course!

❑ Sixth, a body of literature treating the subject is available to those who wish to read about desirable aims and appropriate values for grandparents to attempt to develop.

ORGANIZATIONS AND GRANDPARENTING

Listed below are organizations that are concerned about grandparents and grandchildren. Several of the organizations listed below publish newsletters that can be very helpful to grandparents. All of them need and deserve support. If you wish information please send a self-addressed stamped envelope. They also would appreciate any donation as most of these groups work on limited funds.

Compassionate Friends
(for death of a child)
P.O. Box 3696
Oak Brook, IL 60522
(708) 990-0010

Creative Grandparenting
609 Blackgates Road
Wilmington, DE 19803

Foundation for Grandparenting
P.O. Box 31
Lake Placid, NY 12946

Grandparents Against Immorality and Neglect
Attn: Betty Parbs
720 Kensington Place
Shreveport, LA 71108
(318) 688-4246

Grandparents Anonymous
1924 Beverly
Sylvan Lake, MI 48053
(313) 682-8384

Grandparents Little Dividends
P.O. Box 11143
Shawnee Mission, KS 66207

Grandparents Offering Love and Direction (GOLD)
3851 Centraloma Drives
San Diego, CA 92107
(619) 223-0344

Grandparents as Parents (GAP)
c/o Psychiatric Clinic for Youth
280 Atlantic Avenue
Long Beach, CA 90801
(213) 595-3151

Grandparents Raising Grandchildren
Attn: Barbara Kirkland
P.O. Box 104
Colleyville, TX 76034
(817) 577-0435

Grandparents Raising Grandchildren
Attn: Rose Mancour
P.O. Box 144
Sterling Heights, MI 48311

Grandparents Rights Organization
Suite 600
555 South Woodward Avenue
Birmingham, MI 48009
(313) 646-7191

Grandparents Support Group
Alice Abner, founder
c/o Middlesex City Social Ser.
181 Howe Lane
New Brunswick, NJ 08903

Grandparents Visitation Rights
Lee & Lucile Sumpter
5728 Bayonne Avenue
Hazlett, MI 48840

Second Time Around
c/o Michele Day
Family & Community Service of Delaware County
100 West Front Street
Media, PA 19063
(215) 566-7540

Unwed Parents Anonymous
P.O. Box 44556
Phoenix, AZ 85064
(602) 952-1463

Information about grandparenting organizations

Grandparents or grandparents-to-be can find many helpful sources of information. Periodicals for seniors often carry articles about the role of the grandparent and how to get help. However, the most specifically helpful publications are newsletters from organizations devoted to the problems of grandparents. These organizations are usually happy to send a sample of their newsletter or other literature especially if you send a self-addressed stamped envelope. After looking them over, you can better choose the organization or organizations that will be most helpful.

THE TOO-FAR-AWAY GRANDPARENTS NEWSLETTER

In our present world the likelihood of grandparents and grandchildren living a long way apart is much greater than it used to be. The problem of this distance presents a special challenge to help children understand and appreciate the role of a grandparent.

All of the grandparent organizations devoted to increasing skills deal with the problem of great distance between grandparents and grandchildren. They make suggestions about what works under these circumstances. *The Too-Far Away Grandparents' Newsletter* has as its main concern the improvement of this problem. It is published by Mike Moldeven, P.O. Box 71, Del Mar, CA, 92014-0071; Telephone (619) 259-0762. The newsletter provides many suggestions on how to span the miles and maintain relationships.

THE FOUNDATION FOR GRANDPARENTING

Vital Connections--The Grandparenting Newsletter is published in Lake Placid, New York. The address is: The Foundation for Grandparenting, P.O. Box 31, Lake Placid, NY 12946. The President of the Foundation is Dr. Arthur Kornhaber. He is a child and family psychiatrist and a pioneer in grandparenting issues who has written extensively on the subject. Some examples of articles from their publication are:

* Between Parents and Grandparents
* When Grandparents Die
* A Quick Story-telling How-To
* Visitation, The Trouble Down Under
* Programs: Adopt a Grandparent
* Is It O.K. to Have a Favorite Grandchild?

YOUNG GRANDPARENTS' CLUB

Another organization that is devoted to helping is the Young Grandparents' Club. You may feel you aren't young, but their ideas are useful for all grandparents. Their director, Sunnie Levin, describes their purpose as follows,

> The role of the (Young Grandparents') Club is threefold: relationships, understanding, and activism. The basic element of the Club will be to bring grandparents and grandchildren together in mutual understanding and trust--to establish a strong relationship.

> Secondly, through educational programs the grandparents will develop an understanding of their grandchildren in today's society--what affects them and makes them the way they are, particularly important for those grandparents who are in the role of both parent and grandparent.

> And thirdly, through the Club's educational and workshop programs the grandparents will become activists in affecting the changes in our society which will benefit their grandchildren and their peers.

Their newsletter is entitled *Today's Young Grandparent*. Examples of topics they have covered are:

* Into the World of Make-Believe
* Opening Communications
* Instant Grandparents--Step Grandparenting
* Fun Activities with Your Infant Grandbaby
* Grandma, I Just Love to Read
* Playing the Game (Value of Game Playing with Children)

CREATIVE GRANDPARENTING, INC.

Creative Grandparenting is a nonprofit organization founded by Bob Kasey and located at 609 Blackgates Road, Wilmington, DE 19803. Their purpose is:

> . . .educating, enabling and empowering grandparents and other adults to value and encourage the natural development of children as unique individuals.

In addition to a newsletter, they sponsor forums, workshops, and a resource development series. Examples of the topics in their newsletter are:

* Grandparents' Rights
* Report on the Forum Series
* A Message from the Founder
* "Out of My Mind"--A report on a family newsletter
* Readers Responses
* Baking Magical Bread--A suggested activity

A SPECIAL CONTRIBUTION

In multiple-child families, one of the best things that grandparents can do is to vary the practice of having all the children at once by inviting one child at a time to visit or take part in an activity. Such special treatment for one child at a time can contribute to that child's sense of self.

A variation on this practice would be to include that child's best friend, rather than a sibling.

It goes without saying that this must be done for each of the grandchildren. When this is done, good things can also happen back home with the change in routine.

Learning grandparenting through self-help groups

While there is much organized assistance for grandparents who are experiencing problems or who want to improve their grandparenting skills, we often need something more. That is where the self-help groups that bring together people with common problems can help. Feelings of isolation and desperation can quickly be dispelled when you discover that others have had similar experiences.

AMERICAN SELF-HELP CLEARINGHOUSE

This organization is concerned with the general process of starting and maintaining self-help groups for a great variety of purposes. They are located in The St. Clare's-Riverside Medical Center, Denville, NJ 07834. The groups they engender go through the total range of specific diseases and physical problems. Other groups are directed toward common problems that many of us share such as bereavement, aging, women's concerns, and grandparents' rights. Listed below are a number of the states that have clearinghouses that assist those who wish to start self-help groups.

Arizona--Scottsdale area (602) 840-1029
California--1-800-222-LINK (5465) (in California only)
Connecticut--(203) 789-7645
Illinois--(708) 328-0470
Iowa--1-800-383-4777 (In Iowa only)
Kansas--1-800-445-0116 (In Kansas only)
Massachusetts--(413) 545-2313
Michigan--1-800-752-5858 (In Michigan only)
Minnesota--(612) 224-1133
Missouri--(816) 561-HELP (4357) or (314) 773-1399
Nebraska--(402) 476-9668
New Jersey--1-800-FOR-MASH (367-6274) (NJ only)
New York State--1-800-724-0152 (In NY only)
NY--Long Island--(516) 348-3030
NY--Westchester (914) 347-3620
North Carolina--Mechlenberg area (704) 331-9500
Ohio--Dayton (513) 225-3004
Oregon--Portland area (503) 222-5555
Pennsylvania--Pittsburgh area (412) 261-5363
Pennsylvania--Scranton area (717) 961-1234
Rhode Island--(401) 277-2231
South Carolina--Midlands area (803) 791-9227
Tennessee--Knoxville area (615) 584-6736
Texas--(512) 454-3706
Greater Washington D.C. (703) 536-4100
American Self-Help Clearinghouse (201) 625-7101, TDD 625-9053
National Self-Help Clearinghouse (212) 642-2944

Canadian Offices
Calgary--(403) 262-1117
Halifax--(902) 422-5831
Saskatchewan--(306) 652-7817
Toronto--(416) 487-4512
Vancouver--(604) 731-7781
Winnipeg--(204) 589-5500 or 683-5955

STARTING A SELF-HELP GROUP

Check first to find if one already exists in your area. This can be done by examining announcements of meetings in your local paper or on radio and television. Then try calling the appropriate Self-Help Clearinghouse to see if they have information that will help. They may also have literature available on how to start a group. They sometimes run workshops on the process that can be very helpful. Another part of getting ready would be to attend a meeting or two of some other self-help group in the community, such as one on parenting, in order to get the feel of how such an organization can operate.

HOW TO GET THE WORD OUT

When you think you are ready to try and find others who are interested, write an announcement. Have it duplicated and then post it at the community center, senior center, library, post office, or a grocery store bulletin board. Ask for people who are interested in starting a group as opposed to joining one. The community newspaper is also a resource. They are often happy to publish such notices for the goodwill it brings.

When people respond to your announcement ask them what they are willing to do to help. Have tasks in mind when they call such as acting as co-chairman, greeting people, handling name tags, refreshments, or record keeping. By lining up help before the first meeting you get across the point that this is something people are going to do for themselves.

WHERE TO MEET

There are many possible meeting places in the average community: community centers, senior centers, churches or synagogues, the library, or in members' homes. Find out how often you want to meet. Having a regular day such as the second Tuesday of each month is generally easier to remember. Discuss whether you want to meet in the daytime or the evening and what that decision will mean for attendance.

Publicity for the first meeting can be handled in the same way as your search for interested people. At this point, the editor of the paper may be willing to write a story about the formation of the new group.

THE FIRST MEETING

It is very important to have a gathering that is warm, cordial, and rewarding. An essential part of that is for people to have an opportunity to learn something about each other. Name tags will help. The chairman should draw out each person to find out what interests they have. You may wish to prepare a short questionnaire to discover what topics are good for future meetings. Some organizational details should be handled, such as meeting times and places, and the appointment of a steering committee to plan future meetings in response to the discussion. It is probably a good idea to have some subject content at the first meeting. It might be as simple as the distribution of a reprint about grandparent problems.

And so you are underway! By having a few topics to choose from future meetings may be expedited. Some examples might be:

1. How should grandparents handle discipline when grandchildren are with them?
2. What is the most important role of a grandparent?
3. How can we best enrich the experience of our grandchildren?
4. What are our legal rights for visitation and access to our grandchildren?
5. Where are some good places to take our grandchildren?
6. What can we provide for our grandchildren that their parents are not providing?

As your group develops you will find there will be no end to topics.

Bring in professionals when possible to share their wisdom and their research in the area of childrearing and grandparenting. The local university is a good source. Subscribe to one or more of the newsletters devoted to grandparenting so that their content can be shared.

Every organization has high and low points. Don't be discouraged when a meeting is not as productive as usual. Do your best to make sure that there is some reward for being there. If a speaker is not as good as you hoped, make sure that there is still an opportunity to share and update mutual experiences. When people have a chance to express themselves, they will usually come back for future meetings. Good luck.

On grandparents' rights to visit with grandchildren

Anyone who has the need for information about grandparents' rights or needs information about how to be a better grandparent owes a debt to a number of people across the United States. Some have devoted much time and energy, not to mention money, to the needs of grandparents and grandchildren. Lee and Lucile Sumpter, of Haslett, Michigan, are a prime example. They formed an organization that acts as a clearinghouse for information about serious child abuse and neglect problems in our society. They have answered more than 30,000 requests for information about the rights of grandparents. They call their organization:

Grandparents'-Children's Rights, Inc.
5728 Bayonne Avenue
Haslett, MI 48840

They have been trying to encourage grandparents, who have been denied the right to associate with their grandchildren to form self-help groups that enable the people of their community to support each other through the exchange of information, discussion of their problems, and mutual support for local, state, and national laws that would allow:

■ Any grandparent and/or any member of the child's extended family to petition a court to request reasonable visitation with a grandchild, regardless of the marital status of the parents of the child or the relationship of the grandparent to the person having custody of the child.

■ The formation of a mediation panel consisting of an uneven number of professional members from the social sciences to assist in determining what is in the best interest of the child.

■ The court to issue any necessary orders to enforce the decree if it has been determined that it is in the best interest of the child to do so.

■ Each state to honor the visitation codes of the other states.

The previous pages have the information needed to start and maintain your own support group. You will also find a list of existing self-help support group clearinghouses in the states where they now exist.

The Sumpters recommend that any person who is being denied the right to see their grandchildren should write a brief account of the problem and send copies to their state representative and state senator. They believe that such letters provide legislators with the information they need to convince them to pass uniform state laws concerning these problems. They also believe that many of the children who are being denied the right to see their grandparents are also being physically, mentally, emotionally, or sexually abused. Because of inadequate laws in many of the states, grandparents are unable to obtain help for these children.

They point out that the turmoil in our society during the last forty years has resulted in many persons of childbearing age being inadequate parents. Some of them are mentally ill. Many of the parents who deny visitation rights to the grandparents of their children belong to this segment of society.

More than one half of the fifty states have the actively involved self-help groups alluded to above. Few people make any effort to change the law because they experience the deprivation alone. Participation in the self-help groups helps people to become involved and to focus their energies to change the law where that is needed.

> Information in this article on visitation rights has been furnished and approved for this publication by Lee and Lucile Sumpter.

Existing state laws

I. The following states have laws that provide for reasonable visitation rights for maternal and paternal grandparents:

Connecticut	New York
Georgia	North Dakota
Idaho	Rhode Island
Kansas	South Dakota
Kentucky	Tennessee
Missouri	Texas
Montana	Vermont
New Hampshire	Washington

II. In these states the court has the jurisdiction to grant visitation rights to grandparents or to others when the court deems such visits to be appropriate:

Oregon
South Carolina
Virginia
Wisconsin

III. These states grant visitation rights to grandparents under special circumstances such as the death of a parent, divorce, custody, or step-parent adoption. They are not considered adequate as are the states above.

Alabama*	Massachusetts
Alaska	Michigan*
Arizona	Minnesota*
Arkansas*	Mississippi
California*	Nebraska*
Colorado*	New Jersey
Delaware*	New Mexico
Florida*	Nevada
Guam, Territory of	North Carolina
Hawaii	Ohio*
Illinois*	Oklahoma
Indiana*	Pennsylvania*
Iowa	Utah*
Louisiana	West Virginia*
Maine	Wyoming
Maryland*	

* At this writing, grandparents in these states are lobbying for better laws.

IV. Washington, D.C. has no grandparent visitation law.

In most cases, **grandparents must abide by the laws of the state where their grandchildren reside.**

Grandparent travel and other cultural experiences

One of the special gifts that grandparents can sometimes give to their grandchildren is that of broadening their horizons. This may take a variety of forms and can often be the most simple of experiences. For example, staying in a hotel and riding in an elevator can be enlightening and exciting for children who live in small towns or the country. Eating in a good restaurant can also be a new experience.

Some of these experiences can be almost as exciting for the grandparents as for the children. Think about a first trip to a large zoo or aquarium. Imagine the first experience with live theater or ballet, or the power and beauty of a symphony orchestra, even in this age of television. Climb to the top balcony of the opera house between acts for a marvelous revelation of size and beauty.

Grandparents who are interested in sports can take children to special sporting events they might not otherwise be able to see. Incidentally, this can be a good opportunity to introduce the idea of college and university to children as important parts of their future. A visit to one of the huge domed stadiums for an event will bring back the experience whenever they subsequently see it on television.

Cultural Enrichment

Grandparents often have the leisure and the means to provide experiences that enrich the lives of children. On a continuum, that can range from reading *Treasure Island* aloud to a trip to Europe. Travel, by the way, can be a wonderful way to bring literature and history to life.

Travel has its own continuum. At one extreme could be a hike in the woods or a park. This can be a rich experience if children are taught to be keen observers. Naming birds and trees is a good start. Which side of the tree does the moss grow on and why? How can you tell directions without a compass? How do you read a map (even a simple one) and find where you are on that map?

Travel in the U.S.

Some of the favorite destinations for travel with grandchildren are the East Coast and New England. There is no other part of the nation that offers such rich cultural and historical backgrounds to share with your grandchildren. Washington, D.C., Virginia, Philadelphia, New York, and Boston reinforce many of the things children have learned in school. All of these destinations have museums and other attractions that can add significantly to the trip.

Many other historical sites that have national, state, or local importance are available throughout the United States. Check on them before the trip. Many locations have special publications featuring local attractions that appeal to children. A few dollars spent for such a publication can save time and ensure that you won't miss important experiences.

Natural Wonders

Our country has more than its share of natural wonders set aside in national parks and monuments. Parks like Yosemite and Yellowstone constitute single destinations where you can spend days or weeks. Other parks are not so large so it is often possible to see several of them in the same general region of the country.

Theme Parks

It is not realistic to leave out places like Disneyland or Epcot Center. There are increasing numbers of these theme parks, and children love them. Often they are in locations that have other attractions so you can combine them.

International Travel

Most of us want our grandchildren to grow up as Americans who are comfortable with our role in the world, appreciating the existence of other cultures and other languages that are as worthwhile as our own. There is no better way to accomplish that kind of open mind than by enlightened travel to other countries.

Planning a Trip

"Planning the trip is half the fun," is an old saying that carries much truth. It heightens the anticipation of the trip. It assures that you will go where you want to go and do what you want to do. It prepares you for what you are going to see and assures that you will get the most from the experience. Some children will really enjoy learning a few words of the language of the country you are to visit. Get out the maps. Show how you get from home to your destination. If you are flying to a distant destination, help your child to understand what a great circle route is so that he/she will understand why you fly over the Arctic, for example. Watch for icebergs on the way.

Talk about the history of the country you are to visit. What are some of the famous sights you will see? Who are some famous Americans whose roots were from that country? Have they seen movies that were set in that country or city? This sort of preparation can really pay off in giving maximum enjoyment and benefit.

When to Go

You can take grandchildren traveling any time you can make the arrangement. Many grandparents make a trip a special rite of passage such as when the children reach the age of 12/16. Graduation from some level such as grade eight or high school is another such occasion. That gives them something to look forward to (and to try and outdo siblings in the choices they make).

How to Get There

It is certainly possible to make your own plans and arrangements through your travel agent or travel company. Some companies have tours that are designed for grandparents and grandchildren traveling together. An example is Grandtravel, 6900 Wisconsin Ave. #706, Chevy Chase, MD 20815. AARP also has travel plans including tours for children. Contact AARP Travel Experience, 400 Pinnacle Way, Suite 450, Norcross, GA 30071. Remember that Club Med has special children's programs at some of their locations (see page 200 or ask at your travel agent). There are numerous other agencies that plan for children's travel.

> **IMPORTANT NOTE:**
> **Before taking your grandchildren on an extended trip, be sure to obtain a statement from their parents authorizing you to make medical decisions while they are in your care. This can avoid delay or treatment if they should need medical attention.**

Home is where the heart is

As we get older the phrase "there's no place like home" becomes more and more meaningful for us. It's a place for family and friends to gather, share birthdays, holidays, ball games, TV programs, meals, and experiences. It's a place where we have our own garden, flower beds, lawns, shade trees, bird feeders, neighborhood animals, and all those unfinished projects. The walls gather our favorite pictures, we know which light works and which facet leaks, and where everything is--even with a mess in the garage. It's a place where we can relax, wear old clothes, take off our shoes, and just be ourselves.

If you are like most older Americans, you probably live in your own home. In fact, many of you have probably lived in the same house and neighborhood for a number of years. However, we all need to think about our older years--whether we want to or will be able to stay in our homes, or will it be necessary to move to a smaller house, or retirement communities or continuing care communities. These decisions depend, of course, on the state of our health and the degree to which we are independent.

Housing Considerations

Check off which are important to you?
- ☐ Staying in your present home
- ☐ Living near your family or friends
- ☐ Living near your place of worship
- ☐ Having access to public transportation, stores, and community services
- ☐ Having home maintenance services available
- ☐ Privacy
- ☐ Keeping housing costs to a minimum
- ☐ Having in-home companionship
- ☐ Keeping your pets, your own furnishings, and other personal items
- ☐ Feeling secure in your home and neighborhood

- ☐ Living in a homelike environment
- ☐ Having numerous activities available to you
- ☐ Having a large amount of living space
- ☐ Knowing that healthcare services are readily available

Do you need or anticipate needing assistance with the following:

- ☐ Preparing meals
- ☐ Transportation
- ☐ Light housekeeping
- ☐ Medical care
- ☐ Bathing and personal care
- ☐ Home maintenance
- ☐ Getting around the house
- ☐ Overcoming loneliness or isolation

Financial Considerations

- ☐ What percentage of your income do you currently spend on housing? (A general rule of thumb is that approximately 30% of one's gross income can be spent on housing, including utilities.)
- ☐ Is the amount you presently spend on housing minimal, adequate, or comfortable?
- ☐ What is your anticipated budget for housing over the next 5 years?
- ☐ Do you expect your income to increase or decrease over the next 5 years?
- ☐ Would you consider changing your housing arrangement to adjust to any change in income?
- ☐ Would the arrangement that brought in rental income for an accessory apartment or a house sharer be worth the modification costs?
- ☐ Would the financial benefits of living with others be worth adapting to a new living arrangement?
- ☐ Would you be eligible for an arrangement that offers subsidized rents? (Income limitations vary across the country, so check with your local housing authority).
- ☐ If you need minimal health care services under a physician's care, have you considered the cost difference between home healthcare and moving into a nursing home?
- ☐ What is the possibility of receiving Medicare, Medicaid, or private insurance reimbursement for any of the health care services that you need?

If you plan to stay in your own home, there are a number of factors to consider:
1. Availability of in-home and community services
2. Accident-proofing your home
3. Home improvements
4. Home maintenance requirements
5. Financial options

In-home and Community Services–You may find that regular or even occasional help can make your life easier and more enjoyable. For example, if you need assistance with housework, personal care, nursing, or cooking, you can hire someone to come into your home to help you. If one spouse needs regular attention, in-home care may make it easier for you and your spouse to continue living together. In addition, in-home care may be a less costly alternative than institutional living.

There are a number of sources of information about in-home and community services. See the articles on long-term-care and the Older American Act in the Senior Assistance section, page 12 and page 20.

Accident-proofing--most acccidents occur in the home, especially in bathrooms. Yet, most of us think our homes are safe, secure places. Yet the surprising truth is that each year thousands of older men and women are disabled, sometimes permanently, or even killed by falls that result in broken bones. Many of these accidents could be prevented by making simple changes in the home. Read the articles on home accidents and falls, burns, home security, and home fire safety under the Safety and Security section, pages 176 through 179.

Home Improvements--Older persons tend to be cold and need warmer homes. With the high costs of energy it is necessary to insulate your home. Insulation significantly reduces your utility bills and can make for more comfortable living. Also, weatherize all exterior doors and windows. Put storm windows on homes in very cold climates. Install a bright exterior light to prevent accidents. Install a garage door opener. Install ramps and wider doors where needed if one person needs a wheelchair. See that there are reliable grab bars in the bathrooms. For some, it may be prudent to modify the ground floor as the entire living area to eliminate the hazards of stairs.

The happiest moments of my life
have been the few which I have passed
at home in the bosom of my family.
- Thomas Jefferson 1743

HOUSING
ALTERNATIVE HOUSING   73

Limited home improvement grants and/or loans are available to older persons who meet income eligibility guidelines under a federal block grant program. Funds can be used for roofing, ramps, and insulation. Some federal loans are especially designed to rehabilitate or convert older homes, with low interest rates and favorable terms for adults. See your banker or write to the Federal Department of Housing and Urban Development (HUD) for further information.

Home Maintenance Requirements--Although there are many maintenance steps that need to be taken each year, two serious home maintenance concerns are caulking and landscaping drainage. It can cost $2500 to replace a tub area damaged by poor caulking and $800 for double entry doors that have rotted out. Leaking roofs can do immeasurable damage and most roofs last only 15 or 20 years. Exteriors need painting every 3 or 4 years. Stucco should be resealed once a year, especially on the first 4 feet above ground, where mud and groundwater stain. Of course, the chimney must be cleaned and carpet seams and other defects repaired.

Financial Options--Many retired persons who desire to remain in their own homes have generally reduced incomes and the mortgage is paid off. These persons are said to be "house rich, and cash poor." In the last few years, reverse mortgages are available and offer an opportunity to convert home equity into monthly income. For further details see the articles on home equity conversion plans and reverse mortgages in the Housing section pages 74 and 75.

ALTERNATIVE HOUSING

According to a recent national housing survey, sponsored by the American Association of Retired Persons, rather than rush to sunny retirement communities, most elderly Americans want to live in their current homes as long as possible. Actually, nearly 9 out of 10 people 60 or older would like to stay in their present homes and never move. However, the poll said that many of those queried expect to be forced to move eventually because of financial shortfalls, declining health, or lack of services.

Older persons are reluctant to give up their homes of many years because they're comfortable in the neighborhood and secure that they're near familiar stores and friends. However, the day may come when your circumstances change and you need to alter your living arrangements. You may decide that your house is too large and that you no longer want to be burdened with constant maintenance and costly utility bills. You may find that common household tasks, like shopping and cleaning, are too taxing. Or, if your health begins to fail, you may need regular nursing attention.

It can be traumatic to think about giving up your home, disposing of many treasured belongings, moving into smaller quarters. But time eases the pain, and once settled you can adapt nicely to the new lifestyle.

More than a million retirees moved to the Sunbelt states in the last decade. Each year, more than 150,000 retirees cross state boarders to settle in new places. Thousands move to Mexico. Others seek retirement or life-care communities or many of the numerous options we write about in the following pages.

> Don't act until you have had good advice and have made up your own mind about what kind of living arrangements --and where--will best meet your needs in the years ahead.

Before you choose any new living arrangements, keep in mind the following:

■ **Plan ahead.** Too often, housing decisions are made in response to a crisis. You will have the opportunity to make a wiser decision if you are not under time constraints.

■ **Thoroughly research any prospective change.** For example, before you hire a nurse or an aide to come into your home, carefully check references. Before you move into a home for older persons, visit and talk with its residents. Look beyond the name to learn what services the facility actually provides. "Retirement communities," for example, may differ widely in the services they offer.

■ **Evaluate your finances.** Not surprisingly, you will find that the more services you require, the more it will cost. The cost

differences exist because the level of care and expertise differs substantially between occasional household help and full-time skilled nursing care. Remember that you may be reimbursed for some of your expenses through Medicare, private health insurance, or other sources.

■ **Discuss the options with your family.** A new housing arrangement should be made with the participation and understanding of your family and close friends. Together, try to determine your present needs and try to anticipate what your needs may be in the future. Consider health, finances, comfort, and how much you value your independence and privacy. The housing choice you make is one you may live with for a long time. The decision to change your living arrangement may be a significant event in the life of your entire family.

■ Be realistic about your house's value if you decide to sell in the current market and what you can expect to pay for alternate housing.

Decision Making
Before making your final decision, keep reviewing the following questions:

❑ What could force you to give up your present home?

❑ What would allow you to stay in your present home?

❑ Have you carefully reviewed all the options available to you?

❑ Have you learned enough about the available providers in your community?

❑ Have you talked to other consumers about their experiences?

❑ Have you discussed the options with members of your family? With friends?

❑ Are you confident that the provider you have selected offers services that will meet your needs?

❑ Have you determined the prospective costs and benefits of each housing option?

❑ Is there a waiting period for the housing service you want and, if so, when should you put your name on the waiting list?

> Gerontologists believe that Americans overuse nursing homes. That is, they move in long before they're physically needy or mentally ready, and, by doing so, rob themselves of active years and most, if not all, of their assets.

How to live off your home equity nestegg

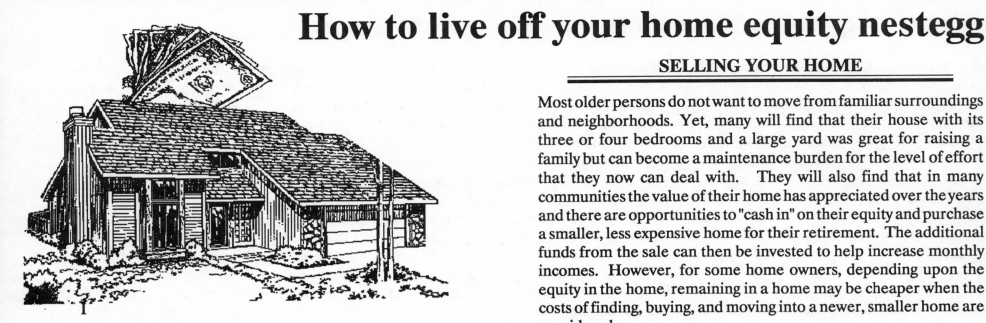

SELLING YOUR HOME

Most older persons do not want to move from familiar surroundings and neighborhoods. Yet, many will find that their house with its three or four bedrooms and a large yard was great for raising a family but can become a maintenance burden for the level of effort that they now can deal with.   They will also find that in many communities the value of their home has appreciated over the years and there are opportunities to "cash in" on their equity and purchase a smaller, less expensive home for their retirement. The additional funds from the sale can then be invested to help increase monthly incomes. However, for some home owners, depending upon the equity in the home, remaining in a home may be cheaper when the costs of finding, buying, and moving into a newer, smaller home are considered.

If you are like many other Americans, when you retire you want to live in your own home. You worked for many years to reduce the mortgage and to achieve that magic state of having your home "free and clear." In fact, over 12.5 million homes are owned by those over 65 years of age and 80% of these homes are owned without an outstanding mortgage. Once that situation is realized, you expect to have the option of living out your years in your own home if other things do not prohibit it.

And if you are like many others that are retired and living in their own home you receive income from social security, possibly a small pension, and interest or dividends on some investments. Yet, taken all together, even with a spouse's earnings combined, inflationary pressures, rising medical costs, home repairs, and other living expenses can become so great that you are barely able to meet the monthly bills.

Fortunately for the majority of older home owners the equity accumulated in the home represents a large asset. However, until recently, to meet monthly financial obligations there were only two ways to get cash from your home: sell it or borrow against it.

HOME EQUITY CONVERSION PLANS

Sometimes older home owners who have a sizable equity in their home and have difficulty meeting monthly living costs are said to be "house rich, and cash poor." If inflation and diminished earnings are causing problems or the ravages of time make repair or remodeling necessary, there are now options for those with a large home equity other than selling the home or borrowing against it. Within the past several years, a few new programs have been developed or proposed to permit older home owners to unlock home equity. The basic types of these home equity conversion plans are:

- ■ Special-Purpose Loans
    - ♦ Deferred payment loan
    - ♦ Property tax relief programs
- ■ Reverse Mortgages
    - ♦ Reverse-term mortgage
    - ♦ Split-term reverse mortgage
    - ♦ Shared appreciation reverse mortgage

In all of these programs, a home equity is converted to cash, either as a monthly payment to you or a lump sum amount. There are elements of both cost and risk in equity conversion that the homeowner should recognize and weigh carefully.

BORROWING AGAINST YOUR HOME

Home Equity Plan--Obtaining a credit line to borrow against the equity in your home has become one of the fastest-growing sources of consumer credit for many people. By using the equity in your home, you may qualify for a sizable amount of credit, available for use when and how you please, at an interest that is relatively low. You put up your home as collateral for the loan, which may put your home at risk if you cannot make the monthly payments. For those who are retired and living on diminished income, payments against this type of loan just add to a greater monthly payout.

Second Mortgage--Another method to obtain cash without selling your home is to take out a second mortgage. Again, you put up your home as collateral for the loan and you receive a lump sum payment and make monthly payback payments. Second mortgages have the benefit of lower interest rates compared to equity credit, but, both demand higher monthly income to meet the payment obligations. Often home owners have monthly incomes too low to qualify for conventional mortgage or equity loans.

SPECIAL-PURPOSE LOANS

Deferred Payment Loans--An example of this type of loan that is not uncommon for aging persons is for remodeling your house in order to make wheelchair access possible. You want to widen doorways, create a bedroom on the ground floor, and change the bathroom. Generally such loans are offered by a government agency or a private nonprofit group. The interest rate is either zero or very low and repayment is required only when you move, sell, or die.

There is usually an income limit attached to such loans. They may not be used for purposes of improving the appearance of the home. Since the repairs or remodeling may well increase its worth, and since the general trend of real estate is to increase in value, it is possible that when the loan comes due upon sale, moving, or death, the change in value may exceed the loan amount plus the interest.

A fellow that owns his own house
is always just coming out of the
hardware store.   Kin Hubbard

HOUSING
HOME EQUITY CONVERSION   75

Property Tax Relief Programs--It is hardly news that property taxes often increase over time. There are many reasons for that, but whatever the reason, those increases can be a problem for persons on limited retirement incomes. When that happens, a property tax relief program may be just what the doctor ordered.

It is important to understand that a property tax relief (also called deferral) program allows you to borrow money from the government to pay your property taxes--it is a loan. It places a lien against the property that must be ultimately satisfied. Accrued interest and principal must be paid when you move, sell, or die. Programs vary widely from place to place. A few states have statewide programs. Most programs require that the borrower be 65 years or over and meet certain income limits.

Some programs charge simple interest for such loans, but some have compound interest. In a simple interest program, it is perfectly possible for the owner's equity to be larger at the end of the program than at the beginning, due to appreciation of the value of the house.

The best way to discover whether such a program is available where you live is to contact your property taxing agency. If it is available, you will be required to complete a loan application. In most of these programs, the home owner never sees the money because it is sent directly to the taxing agency.

REVERSE MORTGAGES

Term Reverse Mortgage (RM's)--The reverse term mortgage is the opposite of a conventional mortgage loan. Reverse mortgages are also known as "rising debt loans" or "reverse annuity mortgages." The loan is paid to the home owner in monthly payments, with the amount determined by the amount of the home equity borrowed against, the interest rate, and the length of the loan. At the end of the first month you owe the advance for that month plus interest of 30 days. The second month you owe for the first and second advance plus the compounded interest for 60 days. Reverse mortgages are available only if the property is free and clear or nearly so. If a small balance is still due then part of the loan is to pay off that balance. The terms of the loans are generally limited to 12 years, and the average is around 7 years.

The value of the house at the time of the mortgage agreement determines the maximum loan amount. Because of the cost to the lender and the potential risk that the home may decline in value, reverse loans are not made for the full amount for which the house might be sold. Also, some lenders believe that home owners with some continuing equity investment in the house will maintain it better. Usually, the loan amount is between 60% and 80% of the appraised value of the property.

At the conclusion of the term, the principal and interest are due and payable. They also become due if the house is sold, you move, or die. At the end of the term, if you are unable to repay the loan you can face foreclosure on the property. This type of mortgage is usually available through a savings and loan or a bank.

Split-Term Reverse Mortgage--Some state housing finance agencies offer the split-term mortgage. In virtually all regards it is the same as the reverse mortgage discussed above. The difference is that at the end of the term you can go on living in the house. Unfortunately there are not many places that offer such loans, but it is certainly to be preferred over the hard and fast term loan. As one might expect, there are income limits for such loans. Age requirements are either 65 or 68, and the maximum of the loan is a set amount, or up to 80% of the value of the property, whichever is less.

As with regular reverse mortgages, a fixed interest rate and compound interest are charged. These programs do tend to have substantially lower interest rates than the regular RM's.

Shared Appreciation Reverse Mortgages--They are available through the American Homestead Mortgage Corporation of Mount Laurel, New Jersey. Under this program, the home owner receives advances each month for as long as the person lives in the house, no matter how much you have received over the life of the loan. The total amount that you can owe at the conclusion of the loan is limited to 94% of the value of the house. That leaves 6% for the selling costs for the survivors. The borrower agrees to share a certain percentage of any possible appreciation in the value of the house. The amount agreed upon influences the total amount of the advances.

The best way to understand this plan is to compare it with a term insurance policy. If you live a short time, then you pay a very high equivalent interest rate. If you live for a long time and receive a large amount of money, the effective interest rate becomes very small.

PREPARING FOR AN EQUITY CONVERSION LOAN

This whole field of equity conversion is a relatively new one. The array of plans changes constantly and tends toward becoming easier and better than it has been before. For example, Congress has passed a law that provides FHA mortgage insurance on reverse mortgages. That makes it safer for lenders to enter the field, so loan plans become more available. One of the best provisions of this new law is that it requires the borrower to be counseled by HUD-approved mortgage counselors. Thus the potential borrower may discover that some other plan is best for him or her.

There are two sources that provide general information about the whole area of equity conversion. For more information, write:

AARP Home Equity Information Center
601 E Street, N.W.
Washington, D.C. 20049

AARP will send you an excellent bulletin entitled "Home-Made Money--a Consumer's Guide to Home Equity Conversion" and a list of FHA-approved lenders.

The National Center for Home Equity Conversion (NCHEC)
1210 E. College, Suite 300
Marshall, MN 56258

NCHEC offers the booklet "A Financial Guide to Reverse Mortgages" for $35.

On selecting the right real estate advisor

If you are selling or buying a home, you may want to consider using a real estate broker. Although you are not required to use a broker, many consumers do. Real estate brokers may be able to provide information about real estate values, financing, and standard sales agreements. The following information may help you decide whether you want to work with one and, if you do, what services and terms you may want to arrange.

You can find real estate brokers through friends, advertisements, and the yellow pages. Both real estate "brokers" and real estate "salespersons" are licensed by the state, but real estate salespersons must be supervised by brokers. The term "broker" here refers to both groups, but keep in mind that you actually may be dealing with the broker's salesperson.

Before selecting a real estate broker to help you sell or buy a home, you first may want to interview brokers from several firms. Ask them to provide you with the names and phone numbers of previous clients, in your neighborhood if possible.

Selling Your Home Through a Broker

If you decide to sell your home with the help of a broker, you will want to ask each broker a wide range of questions dealing with issues of marketing, negotiating fees, and drawing up a "listing contract." Here are some questions and ideas you might want to discuss with a broker:

What sales price would you suggest for my home?

To price a home realistically, you should ask the broker you interview for the recent asking prices and sales prices of comparable homes in comparable neighborhoods. Be wary of a broker whose suggested asking price is substantially out of line with the suggestions of other brokers.

How would you plan to market my home?

Most consumers want their broker to place their home on Multiple Listing Service (MLS). The MLS is a broker information network, often computerized, that publicizes homes for sale. Most brokers rely heavily on the MLS to select homes to show to potential buyers. The MLS also can help you and the broker set a price for your home because it provides current asking and sales prices of homes that are comparable to yours.

In addition to using the MLS, brokers usually advertise a home for sale through the newspaper and by holding open houses. You may wish to ask each broker you interview where and how frequently the broker would advertise your home, how frequently the broker would hold an open house, and what other marketing techniques he or she might use.

You also may wish to ask how each broker would assist a buyer in locating financing. You will want to know which lenders are offering the most attractive financing packages so that you or the broker can suggest them to potential buyers. You also may wish to discuss what seller-financing options you could offer.

How much would you charge me?

You, as the seller, will probably pay a commission to the broker at settlement for finding a buyer for your home. Your own broker, however, may not receive the full commission. Typically, your broker will place your home on the MLS with an offer to split the commission with any other broker who finds the buyer. Many home sales involve two brokers who split the commission paid by the seller.

Are you willing to negotiate a lower commission rate?

Although commission rates may appear to be relatively standard within your community, it is important to remember that commission rates are not set by law, and you may be able to negotiate a lower rate. For example, some brokers may accept a lower commission rate in order to get your business. Other brokers may agree to a lower commission in exchange for performing fewer services for you, such as reducing the number of newspaper advertisements and open houses. Some may agree to a lower rate if they themselves find the buyer for your home and do not need to split the commission with another broker.

You also may be able to negotiate an arrangement where the broker accepts a lower commission if the house is not sold within a certain period of time. For example, you might agree to pay your broker a 6% commission if the broker finds a buyer within 60 days, and a reduced commission if the broker takes longer than that to sell your home. In addition, in order to help finalize a sale, a broker sometimes will reduce his or her commission to narrow the gap between your minimum selling price and the buyer's offer.

What type of "listing contract" will you want me to sign?

You will be asked to discuss and sign a "listing contract" with your broker. This contract includes the terms of sale for your home (such as the asking price), your brokerage arrangements (such as what the broker will do for you and how much you will pay the broker), and the expiration date of the contract. Make sure that the services and terms that are important to you are written into your listing contract.

Generally, if you want your home placed on the MLS, there are two basic kinds of contracts you may enter into with a broker:

1 In an **exclusive right-to-sell contract**, you agree to pay your broker a commission no matter who finds the buyer--even if you find the buyer independently of a broker. This contract is preferred by most brokers.

If you know specific people who may be interested in buying your home, you may want to include a special "reserve clause" in this type of contract. This reserve clause would allow you to sell your property to any specifically named person and would require you to owe either no commission or a reduced commission.

If you are buying a home, the broker you select to help you may owe primary allegiance to the seller rather than you.

HOUSING
REAL ESTATE BROKERS 77

In an exclusive right-to-sell contract, your broker usually benefits regardless of who finds the buyer. However, you still may be able to negotiate a contract that is more favorable to you. For example, you may try to negotiate a lower commission, more extensive advertising, or other special terms and services in return for your agreement to sign an exclusive right-to-sell contract. You should be sure to have the negotiated terms written into the contract.

❷ In an **exclusive agency contract,** you agree to pay your broker a commission if that broker, or any broker, finds the buyer. However, if you locate the buyer yourself, without a broker's help, you owe no commission, or, perhaps a reduced commission. Although there are some restrictions on who may use the MLS and what types of listings will be accepted, you should be able to have your home placed on the MLS under an exclusive agency contract.

Because an exclusive agency contract does not guarantee a broker a commission if the house is sold, some brokers may not be willing to enter into an exclusive agency contract or may not provide you with as much service under this type of contract. But some brokers may agree to your terms without cutting back on services. That is why it is important to shop for a broker who will meet your needs.

What other information will be included in my listing contract?
The asking price for your home will be included in any listing contract you enter into. Carefully set the asking price. If you set the initial asking price too high, you may turn away potential buyers.

During the term of your contract, you may lower your asking price. If, however, you raise the asking price without your broker's consent and then receive an offer at the original asking price, you may owe a commission whether or not you accept the offer. That is because your broker will have fulfilled his or her contractual obligations to find a buyer who is willing to pay the price specified in your contract.

All listing contracts must specify a beginning and ending date. While brokers prefer as much time as possible to locate a buyer, you may wish to limit the contract period to 90 days, for example. You also may want to reserve the right to cancel the contract upon reasonable notice. These options allow you to hire a new broker if, for example, you are dissatisfied with the services you are receiving.

Buying a Home Through a Broker

If you are buying a home, you also may want to talk with several real estate brokers about your housing needs. This will help you determine which broker is best suited to assist you. You especially may want to ask a broker about some of the following issues:

Whom do you legally represent--the home buyer, the home seller, or both of us?
If you are buying a home, you may believe--as many consumers do --that the broker you have chosen legally represents your interests. This may not necessarily be so. Real estate brokers may represent the seller, the buyer, or both. However, according to most Multiple Listing Services, any broker assisting the buyer usually works under the seller's broker and owes primary allegiance to the seller rather than the buyer.

If you want to be sure that the broker represents your interests as a home buyer, it is advisable that you obtain a written agreement or letter from your broker spelling out that relationship.

Whom the broker represents can be important to you. For example, if a broker showing you homes legally represents the seller, he or she is obligated to seek the highest possible price for the seller and thus may not be able to advise you, the home buyer, what approximate lower price the seller may be willing to accept.

If, as a home buyer, you tell a broker the true "top price" you are willing to pay for a home without having an agreement of confidentiality such information might be passed on to the seller without your knowledge or approval. That could result in the seller asking for that higher price and you paying more that you otherwise might have paid. As a home buyer, therefore, you should carefully consider whether you want to disclose confidential information to a broker who has not agreed to represent you.

Will you agree to represent me as a buyer's broker?
Any broker may agree to represent you, as a home buyer, and some brokers are beginning to specialize in legally representing buyers. Having a "buyer's broker" may offer you some advantages. For example, a buyer's broker may be more motivated to spot problems with a home you are considering and may be able to obtain more favorable purchasing terms. Buyer's brokers may or may not charge you a fee. This is because a buyer's broker can legally share in the commission paid by the seller, as long as you (the home buyer), the homeseller, and the seller's broker agree to this. You can try to locate buyer's brokers by asking friends and looking for advertisements in your newspaper and the yellow pages.

Will you offer me any special benefits or discounts?
If you are buying or selling a home, you may want to consider looking for brokers who offer you special benefits. These may include: discounts for home furnishings, home repairs, moving services, rental cars, motels, or air travel; actual cash bonuses; or a promise to buy your home if it is not sold within a certain time period. Of course, in choosing a broker, you will want to consider the broker's abilities, track record, and basic terms, as well as any special benefits.

For Complaints About Real Estate Brokers and Agents
All real estate agents and brokers must be licensed by the state or states where they do business. Complaints can be filed with the state licensing or regulatory agency. This is usually the Real Estate Commission or the Department or Division of Real Estate. (Contact your local consumer protection agency if you need help in contacting the licensing authority.) Complaints about a realtor, a registered title limited to persons who are members of the National Association of Realtors, also may be taken to any of the 1800 local Board of Realtors. These boards have standing grievance committees for handling consumer complaints. Write:

The National Association of Realtors
777 14th St., N.W.
Washington, D.C. 20005
(202) 383-1000

Housing alternatives for seniors

One day you may realize that living alone in your own home is becoming too difficult even with in-home services. Perhaps your health is beginning to fail or daily chores are becoming unmanageable. You may find yourself facing some serious housing decisions.

Supportive housing is available to individuals who, for health, safety, or other reasons, choose not to remain in their own homes. In the past, leaving one's home for these reasons usually meant living with a relative or going into a nursing home. Today, people have a variety of other arrangements to choose from, depending on their physical and mental ability to cope with daily chores. Some arrangements are best suited only for alert, active persons; normally, none are suitable for individuals who are bedridden. Among the major options for a new living arrangement are the following:

■ Congregate Housing, also called
   Sheltered Housing
   Enriched Housing

■ Shared Housing and Home Matching

■ Board and Care Homes, also called
   Adult Care Homes
   Adult Foster Care Homes
   Assisted Living Facilities
   Personal-Care Operations
   Residential Care Facilities
   Shelter Care Homes

■ Independent Living Facilities

■ Other Options
   Boarding Homes/Rooming Houses
   Single Room Occupancy
   Professional Companionship Arrangements
   Caretaker Arrangements
   Commercial Rentals

■ Continuing Care Retirement Communities (CCRCs),
   also called Life-Care Communities

■ Fannie Mae Senior Housing Opportunities (SHO)
   Accessory Apartment
   ECHO Units (Granny Flats)
   Homesharing
   Sale-leaseback

■ Mobile/Manufactured Homes

Congregate Housing

Congregate housing and group living arrangements are available for rental to older persons in many communities. They also are sometimes known as "sheltered" or "enriched housing." While you have your own private living quarters, including a kitchen for light meals and snacks, you routinely eat with others in a central dining facility. Typically, residents of congregate housing are usually expected to take care of personal needs, such as laundry, whereas board and care homes provide laundry. The home may provide housekeeping services, transportation to shopping areas, movies, speakers, and entertainment. If you are infirm or having trouble getting around, this type of arrangement relieves you of major cooking, housekeeping, and shopping responsibilities. Some may even offer health screening, personal care, or other types of assistance.

Congregate housing is distinguished from board and care homes by the presence of professional staff, such as social workers, counselors, or nutritionists, who help administer services and social activities. In some congregate homes, residents organize advisory councils to work with the staff on policies and home management.

The monthly rate for a unit in a congregate arrangement varies greatly. Often the rates are affected by a federal subsidy to help cover a percentage of the rental fee. Today, most congregate housing facilities are sponsored by nonprofit organizations and others are publicly assisted and may range in size from 35 to 300 units. Under a federally funded program, many facilities offer subsidized rent for low-income individuals. Application for a subsidized rental unit is made through the local Housing Authority (get help from the state or local Area Agency on Aging).

If you explore a congregate housing arrangement, visit the facility and talk to some of the residents before signing a contract. The environment, management, and staff of the facility probably will affect your feelings about living there. You should find satisfactory answers to the following questions:

❑ Is there a flat rate for all services or can you pay for only those you use?
❑ How many meals are provided during the week?
❑ Is there a selection of entrees at meals and does the facility accommodate special dietary needs?
❑ Can you prepare food in your own unit?
❑ Is tray service provided in case you cannot get to the central dining room for a particular meal?
❑ What services are provided in addition to meals?
   ✳ Housekeeping? ✳ Transportation? ✳ Social activities?
   ✳ A library? ✳ Physical, occupational, or speech therapy?
   ✳ Counseling? ✳ Daily telephone monitoring?
   ✳ Recreational activities?
   ✳ Are there additional costs for any of these services?
❑ Will living in a congregate facility provide you with sufficient privacy?
❑ Will you enjoy sharing meals with other residents?
❑ Did you feel comfortable with the general atmosphere of the home during your visit?
❑ Are there individual phones in each room, or on each floor or wing?
❑ Are there restrictions on having visitors?
❑ To what extent does the management assume responsibility for the security of your personal belongings?

> Almost any man worth his salt
> would fight to defend his home,
> but no one ever heard of a man
> going to war for his boarding house.
> - Mark Twain

It is not only the services--such as nutritional programs--that make congregate housing appealing. Without requiring you to give up your privacy and independence, congregate housing provides a source of companionship and group involvement. In addition, the facility makes an effort to monitor your health and well-being. You may have an increased sense of security knowing that assistance is available should you need it.

Shared Housing and Home Matching

This is a living arrangement in which two or more unrelated individuals share the common areas of the house or apartment, while maintaining their own private space such as a bedroom. In home matching programs, potential home or apartment sharers are introduced to home or apartment seekers. Shared housing arrangements have three primary benefits:

1. Financial benefits are derived from pooling resources to pay the rent, utilities, and other expenses associated with maintaining a home.
2. A second benefit results from sharing the responsibilities for homemaking chores with others.
3. Social interaction with other residents of the shared house is a third important benefit.

Arrangements for shared housing can be made by individuals or by public or private agencies who, in some cases, provide cleaning, shopping, cooking, and other services for the residents.

Board and Care Homes

They are also known as Adult Care, Sheltered Care, or Residential Care Facilities. Board and care describes a variety of residential facilities that provide room, meals, and supervision, but no nursing care. Some homes offer more extensive services. For an additional fee, you may receive assistance with personal care, such as bathing or grooming. Some provide for social, recreational, and spiritual needs of the residents.

The cost of living in a board and care home varies with the location and the services provided. In some cases, the rent includes all specified services; in others, services can be an additional charge. The average monthly fee varies from $250 to $1,500 a month.

It is important to visit a home before you decide to move in. Look at the private room you may occupy. Ask about the services provided. Learn where or how laundry and heavy chores are done and how charges are determined. Find out if you can arrange a flexible package of services to fit your needs. Before entering into a contract, make your own assessment of services offered so that your expectations will be met. Most important, make sure that all the arranged services and fee provisions are specified in the contract you sign with the facility. Here are some questions you might consider when evaluating a board and care home:

❑ Will living in a board and care home provide you with the independence, privacy, and security that you want?
❑ What services does the board and care home provide, in addition to room, meals, and laundry? Are there additional charges for these services? How often is housekeeping and laundry done? Does laundry service mean personal laundry as well as a linen service?
❑ Is the home accessible to public transportation, your place of worship, and shopping?
❑ Will the board and care home be able to meet your special dietary needs? Is it possible for you to prepare meals and/or snacks on your own?
❑ Can you use your own furnishings? Is there a living room, TV room, or room for social activities? Are pets permitted? Is there just one telephone or can you have a private phone?
❑ Do you have to share a bathroom?
❑ Is there a common area or extra bedroom for guests?
❑ Are there locks on the individual rooms?
❑ Is it possible to avoid climbing stairs, if difficult for you?
❑ Is the home in compliance with state and local standards for fire safety and health?
❑ To what extent does management assume responsibility for the security of your personal belongings?

More than 500,000 elderly, disabled, and mentally ill persons are residents of licensed board and care homes with nearly the same amount in unlicensed homes. A facility is usually licensed by state and local authorities. The vast majority of residential care owners work hard to provide good care but incidents of abuse do occur. If you are considering a board and care home, first find out if it's licensed. Call your local health department or agency that licenses nursing homes and ask what standards licensed homes must meet. Also check with the local long-term-care ombudsman about both licensed and unlicensed homes. Visit the home unannounced, look it over, and talk to residents.

Independent Living Facilities

These represent an offering of complete apartments for sale or rent with services such as housekeeping, meals, transportation, and emergency medical services for a monthly fee that is often more than $900 per month.

Other Options

You also may want to look into some of the shared living alternatives listed below. Remember to check with your local zoning board for any restrictions.

Boarding Homes/Rooming Homes--These accommodations may include a bedroom and sitting room with a shared or private bathroom. Tenants usually eat together.

Single Room Occupancy--These accommodations, with widely varying facilities, are frequently found in converted hotels, schools, and factories. Rooms are rented at a specified price according to a short-term, renewable lease.

Professional Companionship Arrangements--You could offer your services as a companion to someone who wants the help and company of another person in exchange for living accommodations.

Caretaker Arrangements--If you like caring for a home, doing gardening, or babysitting, you may reduce your costs for room and board by performing these tasks for a family with an extra bedroom or apartment in their home.

Commercial Rentals--These rooms are usually leased for longer periods of time than single room occupancies. They often are found in apartments, houses, or auxiliary buildings of large single-family homes.

Medical and physical care for the remainder of your lif

The continuing care retirement community (CCRC) offers an innovative, appealing lifestyle choice for single or married senior adults. Some people put off planning for how they will spend their retirement because they have been frightened by myths about "institutions" or "old folks homes." Continuing care, sometimes called life care, is a lifestyle option for the older person that dispels stereotypes about retirement homes and lessens the fear of becoming dependent on family. The continuing care's supportive community environment allows the older person to attain personal fulfillment and maintain dignity.

These communities combine lifetime housing with a range of services, mainly the promise of medical and nursing care when needed. It is the healthcare dimension that principally distinguishes CCRC's from other types of retirement housing. Although persons must be ambulatory when they move to such communities, if they later become ill and disabled, certain nursing, health, and personal services are provided. Other services may include meals, housekeeping, diverse social activities, and other amenities such as personal grooming services and transportation.

In addition, a nonprofit continuing care retirement community offers the following advantages:
- It replaces fear about the future with physical and financial security.
- It ensures independence and access to healthcare for the rest of your life.
- It offers privacy in your own apartment or cottage, among your own furnishings.
- It frees you from maintenance and even housekeeping chores.
- It creates opportunities to enjoy the companionship of friends and neighbors of similar age.
- It provides an environment that allows each resident to participate in the community's life to whatever degree is desired.

> More than boarding homes or congregate housing, CCRC's represent a lifetime commitment.

Because the continuing care retirement community provides care for life, it necessarily involves a financial investment by the resident. CCRC's are usually more expensive than board-and-care homes or congregate housing. Here are some financial aspects of continuing care:

Fees

Most continuing care retirement communities require the resident to pay a one-time accommodation or entry fee, in addition to monthly payments for services included in the continuing care contract. The entrance fee may range from $20,000 to $175,000. Monthly fees may range from $650 to $2,000 for maintenance, chore services, housekeeping, meals and other personal care serices and these may increase over time.

Determine how the monthly charges are established and under what conditions they may be changed. Typically, monthly charges are related to the changes in operating expenses, but fees may also be adjusted depending upon the services you select.

In exchange for fees, you are assured of housing and services for the rest of your life, regardless of your health. Some continuing care facilities offer full healthcare benefits at no additional charge. Some facilities offer full care, with additional costs after a certain number of days of healthcare per year. Still others charge fees for certain specific medical services.

Learn from the onset what the entrance requirements are. These tend to vary, but new residents must generally meet certain health requirements, be ambulatory, have evidence of financial resources necessary to meet the expected fees, and fall within minimum or maximum age requirements. You should also be prepared to have your name placed on a waiting list, since these accommodations are often in demand.

> Some retirement communities have all the amenities of a continuing care retirement community, but offer healthcare on a pay-as-you-go basis. Such programs may be more suited to your financial circumstances, especially if you do not want to sign a long-term contract.

Contract

Each community will offer you an agreement or contract stating the services to be provided. You will want to review specific provisions for:
- **Living quarters**--size and type, maintenance and housekeeping responsibilities, furnishings, utilities included, etc.
- **Medical care**--doctor and hospital services, nursing care, various therapies, etc.
- **Recreational and educational activities**
- **Meals and special diets**--number of meals per day guaranteed by monthly fee, group or private dining, availability of entree selection, etc.
- **Personal assistance**--help with bathing, dressing, etc.
- **Emergency help**
- **Additional or individualized services**

If you are considering a continuing care retirement community, you would be wise to seek professional, legal, or financial advice before entering into the arrangement. Some continuing care communities may offer a variety of fee structure and contract options. Make sure you understand the contract you sign. Look closely at the conditions, if any, under which the entrance fee is refundable. For example, what portion of the fee will be refunded if you decide to leave the community within a few months of your having moved in? If you die, will a portion of your entrance fee be refunded to your estate? If so, how much?

The contract should establish the basis on which you may be moved from your own residential living unit to a healthcare facility. It should also state what is involved in a transfer back to a residential unit. In many cases, these decisions are made jointly by you or your representative, family members, medical advisors, and the manager. In some states (Wisconsin, for example), a resident requiring more than 7 hours of nursing care a week over an extended period of time is automatically transferred to a medical unit. Even with state guidelines such decisions can be difficult to make.

Continuing care communities are still evolving as a major pattern of supportive housing. Some such communities have suffered economic difficulties due to inflation or the inability to anticipate the effect of the extended lives of residents. However, with the introduction of actuarial and financial advisory services, good management and business practices have become more commonplace. It is advisable to thoroughly investigate the financial integrity of any institution you are considering.

If the facility is new, learn all you can about the sponsors and the management. Ask for a financial statement. Learn the nature of all reserve funding and determine whether prepaid fees will be placed in escrow. Ask the management for biographical information about the owners, sponsors, and board of trustees. Check the management's reputation at the Better Business Bureau. If the facility has been in operation for a number of years, talk to the residents, their families, or local consumer groups.

Locating a Community
Consider visiting several continuing care communities to better assess their suitability to your needs and preferred lifestyle. Many communities welcome prospective residents for brief trial visits so they can experience how daily living might be enjoyed there. Continuing care communities vary in size from about 100 to 500 living units. They serve both individuals and couples. Couples can remain together in the same community setting even though health needs may require one spouse to be transferred to the health care unit. Should one die, the surviving spouse can be assured of uninterrupted care.

How should I choose a CCRC?
Although accreditation is an important consideration in deciding whether to move into a CCRC, it should not be the only criterion in selecting a community. Here are some questions to ask when considering one:
1. What is the policy on entrance fee refunds?
2. Is there a waiting list? If so, how long is it?
3. How large a deposit is required upon application? Is it refundable?
4. Are the healthcare services and the fees charged for these services clearly specified in the contract?
5. What are the CCRC's healthcare obligations? Does it have the staff to meet them?
6. What government standards and regulations are required of the CCRC? Are they being met?
7. What is covered by the CCRC's monthly fee?
8. How are residents informed of the CCRC's financial status?
9. What is the community's mission? How does it go about fulfilling it?

Accreditation
Accreditation provides a seal of approval for continuing care retirement communities that meet exacting requirements and provides consumers with a standard of comparison for evaluating different CCRCs. It means a team of experts has scrutinized the continuing care retirement community and found that it meets national standards for quality care. The accreditation process is rigorous. It involves extensive self-study by the CCRC's staff, board of directors, and residents--all of whom measure the facility against its stated mission and against established standards of excellence in the continuing care field. It includes an on-site evaluation by trained continuing care professionals, and it culminates in a review by a national commission based in Washington, DC.

The Continuing Care Accreditation Commission (CCAC)
The Commission is an independent accrediting commission sponsored by the American Association of Homes for the Aging. Its members include 3,300 nonprofit nursing homes, independent housing facilities, community service agencies, and continuing care retirement communities.

Which facilities get accredited?
A CCRC interested in becoming accredited may apply to the commission. Both not-for-profit and for-profit facilities may apply. However, communities under development are not eligible for accreditation until they have been 90% occupied for at least 1 year. Communities are accredited for 5 years and the accreditation process must be completed again.

How do I know if a CCRC is accredited?
Most accredited facilities feature the CCAC seal on their doors, stationery, and promotional materials. The CCAC maintains a list of currently accredited facilities that is provided free of charge. Write: CCAC, 1129 20th St., N.W., Suite 400, Washington, D.C. 20036-3489. If the community you are interested in is not accredited, you should ask when it plans to apply for accreditation.

Where to write for help
The Continuing Care Retirement Community: A Guide book for Consumers--This guidebook examines all aspects of a variety of contractual arrangements offered by CCRCs. It contains information about payment plans for care, financial conditions of the CCRC, its administration, types of shelter and service, refunds and adjustments in fees, and a checklist of facts you should know before signing a contract. Source: AAHA, 1129 20th St., N.W., Suite 400, Washington, D.C. 20036; (202) 296-5960. Cost $4 Allow 6 weeks for delivery.

National Continuing Care Directory--This book written for consumers provides comprehensive individual descriptions of approximately 400 CCRCs nationwide. It lists fees, types of apartments or cottages, special features, and general and health-related services available at each CCRC. It also geographically locates the facility in relation to a major urban center and describes the physical plant. Source: AARP Books, 1865 Miner Street, Des Plaines, IL 60016. Cost $19.95 (AARP members $14.50).

> Forty is the old age of youth;
> fifty the youth of old age.
> - Victor Hugo (1802-1885)

Federal National Mortgage Association housing option

Not everyone can afford a nursing home and not everyone wants to pack elderly parents off to a retirement village. Long waiting lists and the expense of nursing home care have turned attention toward creative uses of existing housing to accommodate the elderly. You may be able to participate in new alternatives in housing offered by Fannie Mae. These options provide a way for you to modify your current home to accommodate physical limitations or to tap the equity in your home to supplement retirement income.

To qualify for this program at least one person involved in the lending transaction must be at least 62 years old.

As the USA's housing partner, Fannie Mae--more formally known as the Federal National Mortgage Association--has a demonstration program (called Senior Housing Opportunities SHO) to help with the demands for housing that accommodate the special needs and preferences of older Americans. Fannie Mae does not lend money to consumers, but buys mortgages from lenders. But, the lending standards have been relaxed, making mortgages easier to get even for those who no longer have income from a full-time job.

Fannie Mae has come up with five approaches:

1. **Accessory apartment**--apartments included in a single-family home;
2. **ECHO units** (Granny flats)--temporary units built on a family member's property;

Granny Flats

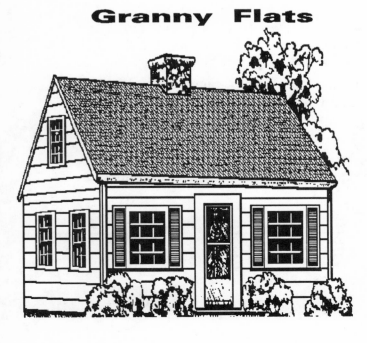

3. **Mobile home**--installed on the property where zoning allows;
4. **Home sharing**--sharing a one- to four-family home by two or more adults; and
5. **Sale-leaseback**--sale of a home to an investor, possibly a relative, who then rents it back to the seller.

All five of these approaches allow you to maintain your independence and privacy. Some, like accessory apartments, offer separate living units with help close at hand. Some, like sale-leasebacks, are designed to supplement your income with income for the equity in the home you currently own.

How Fannie Mae's SHO Program Works

With Fannie Mae's SHO demonstration project, the owner of the primary unit may refinance the home, taking enough cash out of the equity in the home to install an accessory apartment, mobile home, or ECHO. The new mortgage may equal as much as 90% of the value of the home, as long as all of the proceeds are used to construct or install your unit.

Or, perhaps, you or a relative might purchase a home that already contains an accessory apartment. Participants in SHO may borrow up to 95% of the value when they purchase a home containing such a unit. Of course, there may be other ways to finance an accessory apartment, mobile home, or ECHO unit. You might use your own savings to cover construction or installation costs or obtain a second mortgage.

Qualifications for a Mortgage

Typically, your monthly payments for mortgage principal and interest, real estate taxes, and insurance should not exceed 28% of your gross monthly income. These expenses plus other payments for debt, alimony, etc., should not exceed 36% of your gross monthly income.

Your gross monthly income can include part-time work, retirement income, social security, income from notes receivable, interest, and dividends.

Many lenders also give special consideration to regular income that is nontaxable, such as disability retirement payments. These lenders may add your tax savings to your actual income for qualification purposes.

Accessory Apartments

An accessory apartment is a second, completely private living unit installed in the extra space of a single-family residence. Accessory apartments can provide you with additional income, as well as security and the companionship of someone living nearby.

To qualify for Fannie Mae's mortgage assistance for an accessory apartment, the occupant of the principal unit must be a senior or a relative. If the senior owns the principal unit, the boarder need not be a relative. The apartment can be rented for extra income, or used for a tenant who agrees to help out in return for reduction in rent. An adult child can also use this program to build an apartment in his home for an elderly parent.

ECHO Units

ECHO stands for Elderly Cottage Housing Opportunity and is a separate, self-contained, temporary unit built on the lot of an existing home. To qualify for financing on an ECHO unit, at least one occupant of the ECHO unit must have a family relationship with the owner of the principal unit, but the parties need not be parent or child.

Because the homes are both removable and reusable they're generally produced as manufactured homes. The AARP is developing design standards for granny flats. Possible requirements include extra-wide doorways and showers to accommodate wheelchairs, and levers in place of doorknobs to help those with arthritis-stricken hands. Built properly, they have no stairs, are energy efficient, and require no painting or maintenance. Unlike a mobile home or trailer, they have no wheels or undercarriages, typically being placed on pressure-treated piling foundations. When the unit is relocated there is no concrete to remove. Most have about 500 square feet with one bedroom, one bath, full kitchen, and a living room. A few manufacturers in this country are beginning to make ECHO homes that cost about $14,000 to $25,000 (check with Fannie Mae--address is on the next page).

Mobile Home

A home owner can install a mobile home on the property, where zoning allows, to house an elderly relative (see page 84).

Objections

These proposed housing alternatives for seniors are not without problems.

Here are a few you may encounter:

* **Zoning:** The major problem with accessory apartments, granny flats, and other types of second living units is that they often run afoul of local zoning restrictions, and zoning boards are wary of changing the rules. Proposals to legalize single-family conversions have met with strong resistance. But, as the problem of housing for more and more senior citizens becomes acute in communities, some laws are being relaxed. Still, many zoning barriers contribute to the plight of older Americans and block the productive use of much unused space in homes. You may want to encourage your local government to amend zoning laws.

  When trying to change zoning codes, remember that the purpose of zoning is to protect and improve the quality of life and the value of property. Except for accessory apartments, the usual understanding in the zoning variance is that the ECHO or mobile unit will be moved from the premises when the elderly party no longer resides there.

* **Owner-occupant conversion:** Some people express fears that speculators will buy up houses for conversion to rental duplexes. One way to overcome this objection is to limit conversions to owner-occupants, thus keeping out absentee landlords.

* **Neighborhood appearance:** Many opponents worry about absentee landlords, increased traffic, security, and building code violations. Some localities solve this problem by granting permits as special exceptions. This allows neighborhoods to comment on every application and to stop conversions if they have a negative impact.

* **Age limit:** Some communities limit use of "granny flats" to relatives over 62 of the homeowner. In case of death, some localities allow the space to be rented to older persons not necessarily related, but who are over 62 years old.

Home sharing

There are many ways to share a home. You might simply rent an extra bedroom in your home to a boarder. If you're looking for companionship, you might choose another senior for a housemate. If you need help with heavier chores, you could select a younger person who would agree to certain housekeeping tasks in exchange for lower rent. Or, you and a friend may agree to purchase a home together. In another variation, you and one or more other seniors might rent rooms in a home owned by a private or public agency. A senior citizens housing agency can buy a house to be shared by two or more rent-paying older people.

Shared housing is not for everybody, but for those who are amenable it can really enrich lives.

With the SHO's home-sharing demonstration project, you may use income from a boarder to qualify when you apply for a mortgage on a home you are purchasing or refinancing. To protect your interests and Fannie Mae's, however, they generally require that an agency with experience in home-sharing or home matching participate in working out the arrangement.

Caution: Before entering into a home-sharing arrangement, consider what would happen if it didn't work out. What would you do if your housemate needed help in getting around? What if the two of you didn't get along? You will need to check the zoning restrictions. Zoning, for example, may allow two or three unrelated people to live together, but might bar a married couple from living with an unrelated parent and child. SSI or food stamp recipients can risk reductions or loss of benefits if they share housing, because it can have an impact on income. Public opposition can also be a factor.

Sale-leaseback

With a sale-leaseback, you sell your home to an investor, possibly one of your children, and lease it back and you then pay rent. In this way you can enjoy the proceeds from the sale of your home without moving. With Fannie Mae's SHO project, the investor must grant you a lease for at least 5 years, although life tenancy certainly is preferable. The investor may be an individual. Or, it may be a public or nonprofit agency, a partnership, or a corporation with experience in senior housing.

Caution: Be careful before entering into sale-leaseback arrangements. Your adult children may do this deal on favorable terms, but a sophisticated investor might take advantage of you unless you have an experienced lawyer to negotiate terms. You must have a rent control contract, so you can't be forced out of your house by rising rents. Any subsequent buyer must be required to honor your lease. And you need the right to stay in the home for life (see also home equity conversion page 74).

SHO Participating Lenders:
The Prudential Home Mortgage Company
Seniors' Housing Opportunity Program
P.O. Box 59088
Minneapolis, MN 55459
(800) 541-2025

For more information and names of other SHO lenders in your area call or write:
Fannie Mae
P.O. Drawer SHO
3900 Wisconsin Avenue N.W.
Washington, D.C. 20016-2899
(202) 752-7000

> **There are fathers who do not love their children; there is no grandfather who does not adore his grandson.**
>
> - Victor Hugo (1802-1885)

Homes made in factories

In recent years, nearly one-third of all new single-family homes bought have been manufactured homes. The term "manufactured home" was adopted in 1980 by the U.S. Congress to describe a type of house that is constructed in a factory. In the past, manufactured homes were called "mobile homes," a term that many people still use. However, "mobile" is no longer an accurate name because fewer than 5% of such homes are ever moved off the owner's original site.

Advantages
- The cost of a manufactured home is low relative to other alternatives.
- The home is easy to clean and maintain.
- You have instant housing with instant furnishings.
- You can get started with a low down payment--generally 15% to 20% of the purchase price.
- You can obtain both VA and FHA loans--up to $47,000 and terms to 25 years.
- Standards of construction are regulated by the federal government.
- Homes can be moved although special equipment is required to move them.

Mobile Home Parks
The sociability and informality of a mobile/manufactured home park or community attract many older people; in some parks they comprise a large percentage of the resident population. A great number of mobile/manufactured home parks are designed exclusively for older people. Some are within a community, convenient to necessary facilities and services; others have a community center and lively social activity.

Advantages of living in a mobile/manufactured home park include:
- Most offer a variety of social and recreational activities.
- There is little outside yard maintenance, yet you can raise flowers.
- Others with similar interests are close by.
- Neighbors are close in case you need help in an emergency.
- A community may offer a swimming pool, walking and cycling paths, shuffleboard courts, and a clubhouse.
- Some communities may offer their own golf course.
- A quality community may also be a quiet, peaceful, and secure place to live.

Appearance
Manufactured homes are provided in a variety of exterior designs, depending upon taste and your budget. External siding options come in a variety of colors and materials including metal, vinyl, wood, or hardboard. You can also select such outside design features as a bay window, a gable front, or a pitched roof with shingles. Awnings, enclosures around the crawl space, patio covers, decks, and steps are also available.

Warranties
Every manufactured home now offered for sale has a small red and silver seal that certifies that the home has been inspected during construction and meets federal home construction and safety standards. These standards, together with the manufacturers' warranties--for appliances, etc.--serve to protect the home buyer. The National Manufactured Housing Construction and Safety Standards Act also requires that you receive a home owner's manual when you buy your home.

Size, Floor Plans, and Costs
Manufactured homes are available in a variety of floor plans that include living rooms, dining rooms, fully equipped kitchens, one or more bedrooms, family rooms, and utility rooms. Single-section homes are 14 feet wide by as much as 80 feet long. This offers up to 1,200 square feet of living area. Cost: $12,000 to $40,000. Multisection homes are two single units built and towed separately to the site and joined together to make one living unit. A typical model has 24 feet by 60 feet of living area, or 1,440 square feet. Cost: $20,000 to $60,000. Prices vary for both single and multisection homes depending on the geographical construction requirements, the number of appliances, and the furnishings of the home. Of course, in addition to the cost of your home, there are other expenses: Space in parks rents for $75 to $250 a month, and insurance, taxes, and maintenance will boost your monthly outlay.

Placing It in a Rental Community
There are several questions to ask before deciding upon a particular community:
- Is a lease required--for how long?
- What are the charges for utility connections or other services?
- Who is responsible for the installation?
- Who is responsible for ground maintenance, snow removal, refuse collection, street maintenance, and mail?
- What are the community's rules and regulations?
- Are pets prohibited?
- Are there any special requirements or restrictions when you sell your home?

Home Installation
There are a number of steps required to install your home.
1. Site preparation
2. Constructing a foundation
3. Placing utilities
4. Transporting your home
5. Installing your home
6. Leveling and anchoring
7. Interior finishing and exterior enclosure
8. Utilities connection
9. Installation inspection

Site Preparation
If you are having your home installed on your own land, you are responsible for site preparation. Here are some guidelines that must be followed in preparing the site:
- The site must be accessible by the truck transporting your home.
- The site must be as level as possible.
- The precise site area must be cleared of trees, rocks, and other surface debris.
- The soil must be graded and sloped for water runoff.
- If in a fill area, the soil must be compacted so the foundation will not sink.

Disadvantages
The disadvantages of a mobile home may include:
- Rapid depreciation
- Difficult resale in some parts of the country
- Too much togetherness for some
- No formal health plans or services
- If remote from a community, problems of getting good water pressure/supply and garbage disposal
- Not for you if you can't adapt to a smaller space
- Unsuitability for those of advanced age, who may require more safeguards

If you plan on placing your mobile/manufactured home in a planned community, check their CC&R's* FIRST.
***Conditions, covenants and restrictions**

The value of homesteading

One day a neighbor threatened to sue me and take away my house if my dog got loose and bit his child. My dog was a pussycat--no chance of biting anyone; but, the remark about taking my house made me think. Another neighbor asked, "Have you homesteaded your house?" I consulted a lawyer, checked out some books from the library, went to the county courthouse, and "homesteaded my house"; and, here's what I know about it.

To me, the word "homestead" was used to describe certain land laws of the United States that allowed settlers to obtain free federal land. That meaning of "homestead" we are not covering in this article. We are interested in the term "homestead" that means protecting your present home from lawsuits. Various state constitutions give you the right to keep some of the equity in your home if creditors force its sale. Homestead protection often keeps creditors from even trying to force a sale of your home. To get the maximum legal protection, you must file a Declaration of Homestead before a judgment lien is recorded against you.

Since homestead laws change from time to time and there is variation from state to state, an article on homesteading your house must be kept up-to-date and consider where you live. You shouldn't need a lawyer. Here in the state of California, filing a homestead is a simple process:

❑ Pick up a **"Declaration of Homestead"** form at the county courthouse. There are two types: one for individuals and one for you and your spouse if you own the property jointly.

❑ Fill out the Declaration of Homestead form. The questions are simple to answer. Following the words "described as follows" you must copy the legal description from your deed to the property. Include on your homestead declaration everything from your deed that appears to describe your property. If you have trouble finding the deed, you can get a copy of it from the County Recorder.

❑ It must be sworn to and signed in the presence of a Notary Public, who will charge a small amount for notarizing a document. If it is a joint declaration by husband and wife, then both must appear and sign before the notary.

❑ After the homestead declaration is signed and notarized, you can either mail it or take it to the County Recorder for the county in which your property is located. The County Recorder will make a copy of the declaration and enter it into the formal public records of your county. When the document has been recorded, it will be returned to you.

WHEN TO CONSULT A LAWYER

■ If you own a house and are not sure it is your legal residence.

■ If the place you are homesteading is used primarily for business purposes.

■ If you want to homestead a long-term lease.

■ If your home is owned by a corporation rather than by an individual or couple.

■ If a creditor is trying to force the sale of your dwelling, whether or not you have filed a Declaration of Homestead.

AUTOMATIC HOMESTEADS

Even people who don't record a Declaration of Homestead get protection from forced sales under California's "automatic homestead" law. However, it isn't really automatic. If a creditor gets a court judgment against you and tries to force a sale of your home, you must go to court to protect your homestead rights. No one does it for you. In the case of a recorded homestead declaration the creditor must go to court to prove that your homestead is invalid in order to reach the portion of your equity that the homestead protects.

If you are relying on the automatic homestead provisions, you won't be able to sell your dwelling and get your money out of it and into another without first paying off the liens that creditors have filed against you. If you have a declared homestead, however, you may be able to sell your house voluntarily without paying the judgment.

To qualify for automatic homestead protection, you or your spouse must be living in the dwelling when the creditor creates a lien against the property.

HOW MUCH EQUITY IS PROTECTED

The state legislature raises homestead exemption levels fairly regularly. If you have already recorded a Declaration of Homestead, you don't need to file a new one to be entitled to the higher amount. At the present time the protection in California is:

For single people	$30,000
A member of a family unit	$45,000
Over 65 or disabled (or spouse)	$75,000
Over 55 and low income	$75,000

Homestead protection comes from the state constitution, whose writers wanted people to have a degree of security in their homes--not live with the fear that some unexpected debt might cause them to lose it. The legislature raises homestead protection amounts from time to time and we must encourage them to do so. The present rates are inadequate for the present market.

DEBTS NOT COVERED

A homestead will protect your home from being sold to pay off judgments that result from most kinds of debts. However, some are not covered by either an automatic or declared homestead:

◆ **Child Support and Alimony.** The homestead laws do not protect your home against court judgments obtained for back child support or spousal support. The reason for this is the strong social policy in favor of making sure these obligations are met.

◆ **Mortgage (Deed of Trust) and Home Equity Loans.** Mortgage loans and home equity loans and remodeling loans are secured by the property itself. They are exempt from the homestead laws for the obvious reason that no creditor would give you a mortgage or home equity loan in the first place unless they could sell your home if you didn't make your payments.

◆ **Taxes.** The government thinks there is something sacred about the money you owe for taxes. Local and county governments are usually quite slow to move toward forcing a sale of your house and reasonable about helping you out, but watch out for the federal government. The IRS has been known to act rather heartlessly.

◆ **Mechanic's Lien Note.** Someone who works on a house--an architect or plumber, for example--is automatically granted a mechanic's lien against the property to guarantee payment for the work. The liens will have to be paid if the property is sold.

If a judgment creditor tries to force the sale of your home, see a lawyer. You will need individual professional help to have the best chance of keeping your home.

Selecting a nursing home

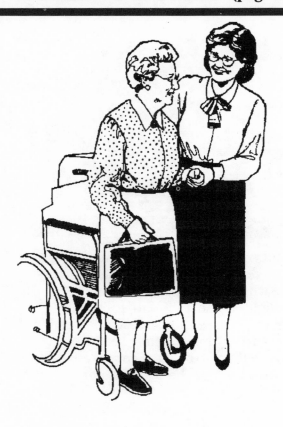

Is there a nursing home in your future? There are currently over one million residents in the more than 19,000 nursing homes in the United States. The nursing home population has been growing, and will continue to grow with the increase in the number of elderly. While only 5% of the elderly population is in a nursing home at any one time, approximately 20% to 30% of all people can expect to spend some time in a nursing home setting.

Before considering placement of a loved one or friend in a nursing home, explore the possibility of using alternate services or programs that permit an older person to receive needed services in his or her own home or other community setting. An increasing number and variety of community-based health and supportive services and specialized living arrangements are being created in communities throughout the country. For some persons, an alternative to institutional care may serve as an effective holding action that will prevent or delay the need for nursing home care. For others, however, nothing can be a substitute for a good nursing home.

The selection of nursing home care for a loved one or friend is often a difficult task. To do the job right, one must be prepared for the time-consuming effort of gathering the many facts needed to help in the decision-making process. Finding the right facility is all-important to a loved one's well-being. The facility selected will be the person's home and community sometimes for the remainder of the person's life. How-

ever, through rehabilitative efforts, nearly one-half of the patients of a proficient nursing home can be discharged to live independently once again.

What Is a Nursing Home?

The term "nursing home" is a widely misused and misunderstood term. The term has been defined as anything from a rest home to an acute care hospital. This is confusing to anyone who needs to know the type of facility to select that will best meet their needs and what the appropriate level of care should be.

Nursing homes are primarily designed to meet the needs of persons convalescing from illness or to provide long-term nursing supervision for persons with chronic medical problems. A nursing home is not a hospital and does not provide the acute care provided in a hospital setting. The goal of nursing home care is to provide care and treatment to restore or maintain the patient's highest level of physical, mental, and social well-being. To help the reader better understand the various levels of care available, included below are definitions of nursing facilities:

◆ A **Skilled Nursing Facility** (SNF) is a facility that is required to provide continuous (24-hour) nursing supervision by registered or licensed vocational nurses. Commonly referred to as "nursing homes" or "convalescent hospitals," these facilities normally care for the incapacitated person in need of long- or short-term care and assistance with many aspects of daily living (walking, bathing, dressing, eating). At a minimum, SNF's provide medical, nursing, dietary, pharmacy, and activity services.

◆ An **Intermediate Care Facility** (ICF) is a facility that is required to provide 8 hours of nursing supervision per day. Because of their physical appearance, these facilities are often confused with the SNF's. Intermediate care, however, is less extensive than skilled nursing care and generally serves patients who are ambulatory and need less supervision and care. Licensed nurses are not always immediately available in an ICF. At a minimum, ICF's provide medical, intermittent nursing, dietary, pharmacy, and activity services.

◆ A **Skilled Nursing Facility for special disabilities** is a facility that provides a "protective" or "security" environment to persons with mental disabilities. Many of these facilities will have "locked" or "security" areas where patients reside for their own protection or the protection of others in the facility. Some SNF's have a designated number of beds for long-term mental patients.

Licensing and Certification

All state governments require that nursing homes be licensed. The licensing requirements establish acceptable practices for care and services. State inspectors visit nursing homes at least once a year to determine their compliance with state standards and their qualifications to receive Medicare and Medicaid reimbursement. Most nursing homes are certified to participate in both the federal Medicare and Medicaid (Medi-Cal in California) programs. Some have been approved to provide both skilled nursing and intermediate care services.

Who Owns and Manages Nursing Homes?

Some nursing homes are operated as non-profit corporations. They are sponsored by religious, charitable, fraternal, and other groups or run by government agencies at the federal, state, or local levels. But many nursing homes are businesses operated for profit. They may be owned by individuals or corporations. Sometimes they are part of a chain of nursing homes.

Final responsibility for the operation of a nursing home lies with its governing body. It is the legal entity licensed by the state to operate the facility. The governing body sets policies, adopts rules, and enforces them for the healthcare and safety of patients. The person in charge of the day-to-day management is called the administrator.

Who Directs Care?

A person in a nursing home must be under the care of a physician. If the person's personal physician will not continue to provide care, a new physician must be chosen. It is the physician's obligation to evaluate a patient's needs and to prescribe a program of medical care for the patient's health and well-being. A nursing home is not free to initiate any form of medical treatment, medication, restraint, special diet, or therapy without the consent of a physician.

Before a person is admitted to a nursing home, a complete physical examination should be completed. The results of this examination will determine whether skilled nursing care or intermediate care is required, the patient's diagnosis, the duration of the illness or need for nursing home care, what treatments are indicated, and the patient's rehabilitation potential.

What About Financing?

Nursing home care is expensive. Although prices vary, the basic charge for a double-bed room in a typical nursing home is in the range of $20,000 to $30,000 a year. Homes in rural areas tend to be slightly less expensive than those in cities. The cost of medications and physician visits are not included in the basic charge. Also, special treatments such as physical, occupational, and speech therapy often add to the cost. There are also possible additional charges for drugs, laundry, haircuts, and extra services.

Three out of four patients are dependent upon government assistance through Medicare and/or Medicaid. Other sources of financial aid might be available to the patient from private health insurance (possibly supplemental Medicare insurance, called Medigap). However, Medicare will partially pay for the first 100 days of skilled nursing home care and nothing for care in an intermediate care nursing facility. Medigap policies typically pay only a portion of the daily costs and then only for a limited number of days. Long-term or catastrophic care insurance is designed to provide benefits for this type of care (see article on long-term-care insurance, page 36).

Eligibility for Medicaid (Medi-Cal in California) is contingent upon the amount of a patient's (and spouse's) income and personal and real property. To receive nursing home services under the Medicaid (Medi-Cal) program, certain medical requirements must also be met. Financial assets accumulated by the patient and spouse could be exhausted through prolonged care in a skilled nursing facility. Therefore, it is extremely important to plan ahead by determining all of the benefits available under Medicare and Medicaid. Medicaid generally pays a daily rate that is significantly lower than private-pay residents. Hence, Medicaid residents are less preferred by nursing homes. Some nursing homes do accept Medicaid residents or retain residents whose personal resources have been depleted and who have become Medicaid recipients.

Federal and state laws are intended to limit discrimination against Medicaid beneficiaries yet they often face discrimination in admissions to nursing homes or the services they receive.

Most states determine Medicaid eligibility using the combined assets and income of a couple. A Medicaid applicant must deplete a spouse's income and assets before receiving coverage. Impoverishment of the spouse of a nursing home resident who is on Medicaid is not uncommon. Consult your state's policies as they relate to spousal assets and income (see spousal asset protection, pages 100 and 101).

Advance Planning

If you think you will need a nursing home at some time in the foreseeable future--for yourself or a relative--it will pay to plan ahead. Many good nursing homes have long waiting lists, and the chances of getting placed in the home of your choice will be greatly enhanced if placement is made on a waiting list prior to the actual time of need. Also, this will give a prospective patient time to get mentally adjusted to the idea of the change.

Unfortunately, the choice of a nursing home is often made in a crisis atmosphere when time is short and minds are troubled. Selecting a home is an important decision--one that deserves foresight and careful clear-headed consideration.

Here are some things you can do in advance that will help you in deciding on a nursing home:

■ Make a point of learning about nursing homes. Watch for articles in newspapers and magazines and for television programs that deal with nursing homes. Also, pick up brochures on the subject from social service agencies, senior centers, or your local health department.

■ Find out what nursing homes are located in your community and learn what you can about them. If you have friends or relatives who are familiar with the homes, ask for their opinions on them. If you know people who live in nursing homes, pay them a visit and gather some firsthand impressions.

■ If your county has published a nursing home guide, you can probably start by making a list of possible homes in your area. Or you may check with the State Department of Health Services' Licensing Field Office and ask to see the latest "Health Facilities Directory." Your local Area on Aging will also be able to help.

■ Each county has an ombudsman program that provides volunteer problem solving for relatives and patients in nursing homes. It may be helpful to contact your local ombudsman office for information about a particular nursing home. The ombudsman program, federally mandated, is designed to provide information to the public about nursing homes in a particular area and to resolve complaints on behalf of the nursing home residents. The ombudsman should be listed in the local government section of your telephone book. Your physician also may be able to suggest some nursing homes you might consider.

Nursing home inspection reports completed by the State Department of Health Services are also available to the public at the field offices. You may wish to review the latest inspection reports for various homes on your list before making actual visits to the facilities. Be sure to check for noncompliance pertaining to patient care, staff adequacy, and facility cleanliness and maintenance.

Selection of a Nursing Home

When you have compiled a list of the places that seem most appropriate, you should make a personal visit to each one. It is best to make an appointment with the administrator and take along a copy of the nursing home checklist on page 102.

When you do visit a home, there are a number of services and other matters that should be observed and evaluated:

❑ **Location**--Consider the home's location. It is not always possible, but it is preferable that the home be convenient for friends, relatives, and your doctor, as well as appealing to you. The home should be reasonably close to a hospital in case of a medical emergency.

What to look for when you select a nursing home

☐ **Facility Size**--A large home may have more activities while a smaller home might be more personal. Decide which is best for your needs. You should also consider the quality--not just the quantity--of the services and activities offered.

☐ **Visiting Hours**--Find out whether the visiting hours are convenient. Often the best arrangement is one that allows visitors to come anytime.

☐ **Financing**--It is very important to check with the facility regarding what services Medicaid (Medi-Cal) or Medicare covers. Make sure you find out what extra costs are involved in addition to the basic daily room rate. Often extra charges are made for professional services beyond basic nursing care (also for things such as television and toiletries). Some homes only provide the bare minimum in the way of services.

☐ **Room Selection**--Find out whether attention is paid to roommate and room selection--two factors that can be very important to your happiness. You do not need to feel committed to your first roommate. If you are dissatisfied, see if you can change. Also, see if you can bring some of your own furniture.

☐ **Bedhold**--Ask if they reserve a bed if you need to be transferred to a hospital. Medicaid will pay for 7 days of bedhold. Medicare and private-pay residents will have to pay for each day the bed is held but not more than the regular daily rate. Sometimes if hospital stay is extended you can make an agreement with the nursing home.

☐ **Medications**--Watch how medications are given to patients. They should only be given by a licensed nurse, physician, or psychiatric technician. The family should consult periodically with the doctor and nursing staff to discuss the kind of medications the patient is receiving. Sometimes the patient's mental attitude or personality changes as a result of certain medications, and it is important that the family be aware of these possible changes. The average nursing home patient takes from four to seven different medications per day, so medication costs are an important economic consideration. The nursing home is not permitted to require you to purchase or rent medical supplies or equipment from a particular pharmacy. If the

home requests that you use a particular pharmacist or vendor, check whether the home had compared the pharmacy's medication prices to those of other pharmacies in the area. The pharmacy you choose is required to comply with reasonable policies and procedures of the home. Many pharmacies deliver free of charge.

☐ **Valuables**--Find out how valuables are protected. Theft is sometimes a problem in nursing homes. If at all possible, you should leave valuable items with friends or relatives.

☐ **Grievance Procedure**--Ask whether patients have some sort of grievance procedure. Find out if there is a patient's council and a way that patients can be involved in decision making.

☐ **Volunteers**--Find out if community volunteers are used at the home. Active community involvement by individuals and groups of volunteers can greatly extend the amount of patient services available and help reduce the isolation and loneliness that many nursing home patients feel.

☐ **Morale**--See how the patients' morale appears to be. Do they have privacy and respect? Do they have access to things like television and radio? Be sure you take into consideration what you are comfortable with when making your selection.

☐ **Food**--Check the food being served. Make a visit at the time of the midday meal which is often the main meal. Ask the other patients about the quality of the food. Is the dining room atmosphere attractive, pleasant, and clean? Does the food look appetizing and nutritious? Is the hot food hot and the cold food cold? Is some food available at times other than mealtimes? Do they supply food for special diets?

Nursing Home Admission Agreements

Once you have made a selection of a nursing home, you will want to review and be sure you thoroughly understand the home's contract or financial agreement. If you have questions, ask a lawyer or the local long-term-care ombudsman in your area (check in phone book). Since this agreement constitutes a legal contract, it is advisable to have a lawyer review the agreement before signing it. Free legal assistance is usually available to senior citizens. You can

find out about this from your Area Agency on Aging (listed in your phone book) or from someone at the Senior Center. **NEVER SIGN A LEGAL DOCUMENT THAT YOU DO NOT UNDERSTAND.**

Your admission papers should include the following items:

✔ The agreement stating the terms and conditions, the daily room rate, and what services are covered by it. States set licensing standards requiring nursing homes to provide a basic set of services (such as nursing and personal care, meals, activities). These are supposed to be covered by the basic rate.

✔ A list of optional services and the charges for them. The facility must provide an itemized bill. Such optional services could include choice of meals, laundry, toiletry items, special trips, etc. If you are a Medicaid recipient, you should receive a special list of optional services (Medicaid pays for laundry and hair trims, for example).

✔ A copy of each Patient's Bill of Rights.

✔ A statement about eligibility for Medicaid.

✔ A statement that the nursing home is or is not Medicare and Medicaid certified.

Illegal Actions

Certified nursing homes may not require Medicaid-eligible persons to make contributions, donations, or gifts as a condition of admission or continued stay in a nursing home. Private-paying individuals do not have this protection. When certified nursing homes sign with the Medicaid program, they agree to accept Medicaid payment as "payment in full." If you become eligible for Medicaid, then the nursing home will receive payment for care and may not discharge the patient on the grounds of "nonpayment." Certified nursing homes may not transfer or discharge you when your private funds have been exhausted and you become eligible for Medicaid unless the home does not participate in the Medicaid or Medicare program. If someone treats you in this manner check with a lawyer or ombudsman.

Resources

While in a nursing home, most problems can be worked out with the nurses, the staff, or the resident council. If they cannot, discuss the problems with family members. Persons who experience problems with nursing homes may obtain assistance from the nursing home ombudsman, a person in your state or local office on aging who is designated to investigate complaints and take corrective action on behalf of nursing home residents. Federal law guarantees your right to seek help from an ombudsman without fear of retaliation.

Making a Smooth Transition

Be prepared to make the transition into a nursing home easy as possible. Such a change may affect the whole family and it will take some time to adjust to the new living arrangements. Some nursing homes have a social worker or nurse specialist who conducts preadmission group sessions for family members. You can make the resident more comfortable by accompanying him or her on moving day, and by helping choose familiar items to bring along--family photos or favorite decorative items to make the room more attractive.

The frequency of visits to the resident is an individual decision, but keep in mind that the presence of family members greatly helps to create a more personal atmosphere in the nursing home. Family visits offer reassurance to the resident that someone still cares. In fact, those residents whose families are involved in their care usually have higher morale and receive better care from the staff. Taking the resident out occasionally is also helpful.

Information Sources

The **Nursing Home Information Service** provides information on nursing homes and alternative community and health services, including a free guide on how to select a nursing home. For more information, write to the National Council of Senior Citizens, Nursing Home Information Service, National Senior Citizens Education and Research Center, Inc., 925 15th Street, N.W., Washington, D.C. 20005, or call (202) 347-8800.

AARP publishes the "Nursing Home Life: A guide for residents and families." AARP interviewed nursing home residents and their families in order to obtain firsthand accounts, experiences, and insights into nursing home life. You can obtain a copy by writing: Health Advocacy Services Program Department, AARP, 601 E Street, N.W., Washington, DC 20049.

Rights of Nursing Home Residents

The federal government has passed laws that establish the rights of nursing home residents. Most states have also passed laws that provide additional protection. You can obtain a copy of the "Nursing Home Residents' Rights," by contacting your area ombudsman. The phone number is located in your phone directory.

Each person admitted to a nursing home has the following rights among others:

❋ To be fully informed, as evidenced by the patient's written acknowledgment prior to or at the time of admission and during the stay, of these rights and all rules and regulations governing patient conduct and responsibilities.

❋ To be fully informed prior to or at the time of admission and during the stay of services available in the facility, and of related charges of these services including any charges not paid by Medicaid or not included in the basic rate per day.

❋ To be fully informed by a physician of his/her medical condition, unless the physician decides that informing the patient is contraindicated, and to be given the opportunity to participate in planning his/her medical treatment and to refuse to participate in experimental research.

❋ To refuse treatment to the extent permitted by law and to be informed of the medical consequences of such refusal.

❋ To be transferred or discharged only for medical reasons or for his/her welfare or that of other patients or for nonpayment for his/her stay (except as prohibited by the Medicaid program); to be given reasonable advance notice to ensure orderly transfer or discharge.

❋ To be encouraged and assisted throughout his/her stay to exercise his/her rights as a patient and as a citizen, and to this end to voice grievances and recommend changes in policies and services to facility staff and/or outside representatives of his/her choice, free from restraint, interference, coercion, discrimination, or reprisal.

❋ To manage his/her personal financial affairs or to be given at least a quarterly accounting of financial transactions made on his/her behalf, should the facility accept his/her written delegation of this responsibility subject to specific record keeping requirements.

❋ To be free from mental and physical abuse, and to be free from chemical and (except in emergencies) physical restraints, except as authorized in writing by a physician for a specified and limited period of time, or when necessary to protect the patient from injury to himself or herself or to others. The use is authorized by a professional staff member identified in the written policies and procedures of the facility as having the authority to do so and promptly reported to the resident's physician by the staff member.

❋ To be assured confidential treatment of his/her personal and medical records, and to approve or refuse to release them to any individual outside the facility except in the case of his/her transfer to another facility or as required by law.

❋ To be treated with consideration, respect, and full recognition of his/her dignity and individuality, including privacy in treatment and care for his/her personal needs.

❋ Not to be required to perform services for the facility that are not included for therapeutic purposes in his/her plan of care.

❋ To associate and communicate privately with persons of his/her choice and to send and receive his/her personal mail unopened unless medically contraindicated.

❋ To meet with and participate in the activities of social, religious, and community groups at his/her discretion unless medically contraindicated.

❋ To retain and use his/her personal clothing and possessions as space permits unless to do so would infringe upon the rights of other patients and unless medically contraindicated.

❋ If married, to be assured of privacy for visits by his/her spouse, and, if both are patients in the facility, to be permitted to share a room unless medically contraindicated.

❋ To have daily visiting hours established.

❋ To have the right to visitation by an ombudsman and the individual's physician at any time, and (with consent of the resident) family, individuals that provide health, social, legal, or other services and others who may wish to visit.

Tips on visiting someone in a nursing home

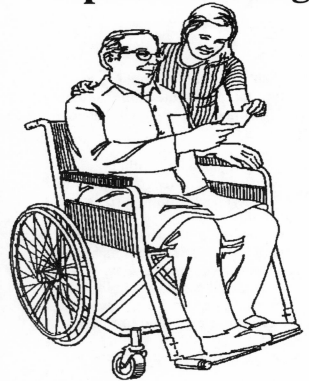

What do you think life would be like if you were living in a nursing home? You might be very conscious of being physically removed from your familiar home and community. You might feel lost, unsure of how you will get along in this new place. You may feel rejected, unloved.

With all of these feelings you might agree experiencing the need for human interaction is important. Ties with old friends and new friends become important in helping you adjust to this new phase of your life.

Hypothetical? No, these are real feelings experienced by real nursing home residents. You, as family member or friend, can help. You may say to yourself, "but I'm uncomfortable visiting a nursing home." People use a variety of reasons for not becoming involved, but ask yourself how well these reasons or excuses hold up.

Excuse #1: **I'm repulsed by what I see in the nursing home.**
This is the reaction of many people, even relatives who have cared for their loved one at home. The problem lies in the concentration or numbers of older people who have suffered some degree of physical or mental disability. Frequently, the sight of so many disabled, dependent, and older individuals is disturbing.

Try to look beyond physical appearances. Think of each of these residents as interesting individuals who have experienced much in life. Each person has a unique personal-

ity that is not dependent upon physical appearance. You may be bothered by those who appear to be confused or disoriented. These people often can be reached simply by gently holding their hands and looking into their eyes. It may take time, but it may work.

Excuse #2: **I'm afraid to go into a nursing home because it reminds me that I may need one some day.**
This response is normal, especially if you are at midlife or beyond. The surest way to overcome this fear is to become familiar with a nursing home and the needs of the residents it serves.

Nursing homes provide support services including medical care, rehabilitation, food, shelter, companionship, recreation, and social activities. These support services help residents function at their highest possible level. This is a positive philosophy.

Inadequate knowledge produces fear, and that fear can be overcome only by more knowledge or information. In this case, knowledge about nursing homes and the residents in them gives one a new perspective on aging.

Excuse #3: **When I visit Mother, she complains the whole time.**
This is a complicated issue. Your relationship is longstanding and you are meeting under stressful conditions. You must listen, evaluate, explain, and limit the time spent on complaints.

Listen. Listen very carefully to the complaint or complaints.

Evaluate. If everything is wrong, then the resident probably is still adjusting to the nursing home. He or she continues to feel alienated and uncomfortable in new surroundings. If there are specific complaints, listen carefully and try to discern the truth. You may want to talk to the appropriate staff on the floor, who may not be aware of the resident's concerns. Often, misunderstandings can be cleared up easily.

Explain. When you have reached a conclusion about a solution for the complaint, be sure the resident understands the explanation. You may have to explain more than once.

Limit. Finally, for the chronic complainer who is never satisfied, set a limit to the complaint time. We all need to vent our feelings and emotions. Then turn to something specific such as letter writing, playing games, looking at old pictures, or visiting another resident.

A resident in a nursing home has few opportunities to make decisions affecting his or her life. For instance, meals are served at specific times, not necessarily when the resident is hungry or used to eating. Fire rules prohibit the resident from arranging the bed in certain ways in the room. Things you take for granted are removed from a resident's control.

Control over one's life is important for positive self-esteem. Visiting is an area over which the resident can maintain control. The following rules of etiquette will enhance the resident's self-esteem and help in retaining control over at least some parts of life.

When to Visit
Telephone ahead and request permission from the resident to visit. Or, when you are visiting, set a time together for the next visit. A resident may feel more energetic or social at certain times of the day. If you establish the time together, the visit will be more successful.

In addition, he or she can look forward to your arranged visit, which extends the pleasure. The resident looks forward to your coming and has the fun of the actual visit. But he or she may decide not to have you visit and you must respect that decision.

Most nursing homes have specified visiting hours. Usually you may visit anytime during a 10-12 hour period. A few homes have no limits on visiting. You must use good judgment and try not to visit when you may interfere with treatments or rest.

If the visiting hours are specified and your schedule does not permit you to visit during those hours, work out an alternative schedule with your family member and the director of nurses, the social worker, or the administrator.

Some homes encourage relatives and friends to join residents at mealtimes. Residents often enjoy having a guest. You should expect to pay a fee for your meal.

One word of caution about visiting is important. There is a tendency to "promise a rose garden" and then be unable to deliver. Do not promise to visit and then not come. That is cruel and the resident feels doubly deserted. If you cannot keep an appointment, call in advance and immediately suggest a substitute time.

When you and your relative are planning your visiting times together, look over your schedule carefully and realistically. Decide how much time you can spend each day, week, or month. Realistic planning avoids disappointment for the resident and feelings of guilt or anger for you.

Who Should Visit?

Anyone who is important to the nursing home resident should visit regularly. Most nursing homes have minimal restrictions. This is not a hospital setting and children should be welcome. Young children rarely react negatively to older or sick individuals. On the other hand, teenagers and older children may need some time to adjust.

If you cannot provide such support, a staff member may be more than willing to support a young adult during the first few visits. The resident is usually the best teacher of all, often putting everyone at ease with a humorous comment.

Preparing a Child for a Visit

The best way to prepare a young child for a visit to a nursing home is to tell him or her everything you can about it. Preparing a child for such a visit should not be rushed or taken lightly. Allow enough time to answer the questions the child has. For example, tell them there will be people with wheelchairs and walkers, and some will be in bed. Instead of living by herself now, grandmother lives with other people who can help take care of her. Nurses are there to take care of the residents. It may even smell different, like a hospital.

Many times, children are afraid of what's behind those doors because you often contribute to the child's fear. Children should feel free to ask any questions about the nursing home. Answer them, because when you don't answer a child's questions, that's

when they think you're trying to hide something from them.

Preparing for the Visit

Once the date and time has been established, you should give some thought to what you will do when you get there. If you plan ahead, you may avoid an unsatisfying visit filled with complaints. Your plans will depend on the mental and physical status of the resident.

If out of bed and alert, the individual might like to go outdoors or to another part of the nursing home. On the other hand, a private visit reminiscing or helping you make some decisions about something in your life may be preferred.

Remember, this is an individual who has lived a long time and whose wisdom is valuable. Read a story together or write letters. Concentrate on the quality of your visit. A visit should be pleasant and a break in a somewhat routine existence.

Conjugal visits are important. Two people who have lived together for years are entitled to private visits without intrusion. For any home that is certified for Medicaid and/or Medicare, the Residents' Bill of Rights protects the right of conjugal visits unless otherwise ordered by a physician. Sometimes staff or administration feel uncomfortable about the subject of conjugal visits. You should approach the subject directly with them. Discussing it in advance will avoid unpleasant problems.

The Visit

When people visit you, they come to the door and knock or ring the doorbell. A resident room in a nursing home is home. Knock before entering and ask permission to enter. If the resident is unable to respond, then announce yourself before walking in.

Greetings usually involve some form of physical contact. You shake hands or hug or kiss. Nursing home residents are removed from family and friends who provide this sense of touch.

Think a moment about what the quality of your life would be if no one ever touched you except to bathe or toilet you. Touching tells us that we are accepted, human and

desirable. Once in the room, make some form of physical contact unless it is absolutely inappropriate.

There are some special instances in which you may think visiting is pointless. Visiting is never pointless. If a resident is comatose, you should continue visiting. No one knows exactly what senses remain in a comatose person; however, we do know that hearing is the last sense to disappear.

Visit, announce yourself, and touch the comatose person as you always have. Then you can sit by the bedside and hold the resident's hand, stroke the forehead, or whatever is comfortable for you. You can even talk quietly since the resident may hear exactly what you are saying.

If a resident is dying, visits are needed more than ever. No one wants to die alone. Continue your pattern of touching. If you are uncomfortable visiting a dying resident, ask the charge nurse, director of nursing, or social worker if you can discuss the matter. They will either help you or find someone who can.

Visits Outside the Nursing Home

We have explored visiting within the nursing home. Many residents are able to leave a home for a meal, a day, a weekend, or a holiday. This assures them they are still part of the family or community. In addition, it may reinforce the benefits the nursing home affords. The difficulty of bathrooms and steps that are not designed for handicapped people may become all too apparent.

If you plan to take a resident out of the home, plan first with the resident. Then decide which of you will tell the staff so they can have medicines and special equipment ready. It is wise to give a week's notice if any special plans have to be made.

Visiting should be pleasant and enjoyable for both family or friend and nursing home resident. Plan ahead, be polite, remember to touch, and above all keep a good sense of humor. We all need to laugh and love.

Myths and realities of living in a nursing home

There are many myths about nursing homes. In the past decade, nursing homes--like all areas of healthcare--have changed radically in terms of staffing, policies and procedures, and the types of care given. Healthcare professionals' goals are to provide both quality of care and quality to residents.

Many people fear the move from their own home to a nursing home. They do not know what to expect at the nursing home. Healthcare professionals understand these concerns, and want residents and their families to know the difference between myths and realistic expectations of life in a nursing home.

Myth #1: A nursing home is like a hospital.
Reality: A nursing home is not a hospital. Many people, especially after recent hospitalization, think of the nursing home as an extension of hospital care. They expect the same kind of intensive care they received in the hospital. A nursing home is different. First, it is a home with nursing care available as needed, 24 hours a day, 7 days a week.

The goals of the nursing home are to:

- ❤ **Rehabilitate** the resident to maximum potential and enable him or her to return to independent living arrangements if possible;

- ❤ **Maintain** that maximum rehabilitation as long as possible within the realities of age and disease;

- ❤ **Delay deterioration** in physical and emotional well-being; and

- ❤ **Support** the resident and family, physically and emotionally, when health declines to the point of death.

Myth #2: All nursing home residents are confused.
Reality: Most people slow down physically as they age. For some this is also true of their mental processes. Many people enter a nursing home because they are considered too forgetful to manage their own care. Often, however, this condition can be reversed with adequate nutrition, exercise, social stimulation, and properly controlled medication. It is realistic to expect a full range of capabilities and personalities among residents in nursing homes. Some will have completely lucid minds in fragile handicapped bodies. Others will have healthy bodies but minds that are no longer functioning normally. Most will fall somewhere between the two extremes.

Myth #3: There is no privacy in a nursing home.
Reality: Because so many nursing home residents need constant supervision, nursing homes are designed so that staff can be aware of residents' whereabouts at all times. However, each resident has the right to privacy. Staff, family members, and visitors are encouraged to observe the common courtesy of knocking before entering a resident's room. The nursing staff, both professionals and nursing assistants, are trained to respect the individual resident's modesty and prevent unnecessary exposure when providing personal care. Family members and residents should expect privacy and remind staff of its importance if they seem to become careless in this area.

Myth #4: Nursing home personnel are not always gentle and caring.
Reality: Some things about working in a nursing home make the job difficult. Lifting and moving adults who are unable to help themselves is physically demanding. Understanding the needs of residents who may be confused or unable to communicate for a variety of reasons is emotionally exhausting. Nursing home staff members care and try hard to do a good job. However, they will have times when, because they are human, they will fail to be their very best selves. Residents and families understanding will help as will their praise for a job well done. Residents have the right to expect good care and the privilege to complain if it is not received.

Myth #5: If I enter a nursing home, I'll never go home.
Reality: The primary goal of the nursing home is to rehabilitate the resident so that he can return to the community. In fact, 30% of all residents are discharged to home-like living arrangements. Those who cannot return permanently to their homes make short visits, health permitting. In some states Medicaid-certified nursing homes are required by law to hold a place for a resident who wants to leave the facility for a few days. You can find out about the law in your state by asking the nursing home administrator or by calling the state Medicaid office. Physicians, families, and staff should truthfully answer the resident's questions about the possibility of going home.

Myth #6: Nursing homes have an unpleasant odor.
Reality: Nursing homes should not smell of urine or feces. At times unpleasant odors may be noticeable; that is true in a private home also. Some residents do lose control of bowel and bladder functions. Many times residents who can regain control are offered retraining programs to correct the problem. For others, proper attention to bathing and changes of clothing eliminate stale odors. The facility that is furnished with materials that do not absorb and retain odors and is kept clean with today's effective cleaning materials should have no noticeable unpleasant smell.

Myth #7: Because nursing home care costs so much, the staff should wait on the residents.
Reality: Some residents feel that because there is a charge for care that the staff should be their servants. In reality, though, if the nursing home is to meet the goals of rehabilitation, maintenance, prevention, and support, the staff must encourage each resident to do as much as possible for himself. Independence is important to self-esteem. To plan and carry out care that promotes self-care, the nursing home staff must have expertise. It is that for which you are paying.

Myth #8: Nursing home residents do not receive adequate care.
Reality: Stories about neglect of nursing home residents make news precisely because they are not typical. It is true that a patient's request for attention is not always immediately answered. There may be an emergency elsewhere in the building that requires the staff's attention. Other residents may be receiving care at the same time so that assigned staff has to delay responding to the request. Repeated incidents should be brought to the attention of the nurse in charge or the administrator.

Myth #9: All residents in nursing homes are female.
Reality: It is true that women outnumber men. In fact, 80% of nursing home residents are female, a situation that reflects the truth that women outlive men. It also means that one of every five residents is a man.

Some married couples enter nursing homes together and share a room. The patient's bill of rights mandates that this be permitted in Medicaid and Medicare institutions.

Reprinted from an American Health Care Association Bulletin.

Myth #10: Families and friends abandon nursing home residents.

Reality: When an elderly person needs more physical care than his family can give, and he or she is admitted to a nursing home, the professionally trained staff takes over a portion of the care. However, the continued social and psychological support of family and friends is essential to the patient's well-being. Many families visit daily. Most nursing homes have liberal visiting hours and are willing to extend those hours in special circumstances. Nursing home staff members are encouraged to make visitors feel welcome and, ideally, relationships between residents and their family and friends continue as they were before the nursing home placement.

Myth #11: The food is terrible in nursing homes.

Reality: Good food is a matter of individual preference. Everyone has certain customary dishes and styles of preparation that no one else can duplicate. In the nursing home some residents are on restricted or special diets as ordered by their physicians and thus have limited food choices. Furthermore, eating similar menus in the same surroundings day after day becomes monotonous. After a while nothing seems appetizing. However, nursing homes employ dieticians to plan menus that are palatable, attractive, and meet the nutritional needs of the individual. Food that is well-prepared and attractively served, warm or cold as appropriate, is the standard for any nursing home. Dietary staff should be available to discuss problems concerning food and should be expected to alter menus within the limits of prescribed diets. Most nursing homes allow family and friends to bring favorite foods to residents from time to time and also give residents an opportunity to do some cooking for themselves.

Myth #12: My possessions will all be lost or stolen in a nursing home.

Reality: In any institutional setting there will be misplaced objects, errors in sorting clothing, and even theft. Before anyone assumes that an item has been stolen, he should consider that a disoriented or forgetful resident may have misplaced it. If other relatives have visited recently, they may have taken the item for laundry or mending.

Many homes recommend that valuable jewelry and large amounts of cash be kept in a central safe to which the resident has access during business hours. All residents should have a drawer, closet, or chest that can be locked. Family members are reminded to label all clothing and personal effects with the resident's name.

Despite all the safeguards thefts may occur. When that happens, administration should be expected to cooperate fully with the family in apprehending the person responsible and notifying proper authorities. A staff person guilty of theft can expect immediate dismissal.

Myth #13: I should be able to bring my own bed into the nursing home.

Reality: Most nursing homes do not allow residents to use their own beds. There are two reasons for this. First, almost all nursing homes have hospital-type beds in all rooms. These beds can be raised or lowered to help the resident get in or out of bed. The head or foot position of the bed can be raised or lowered. This makes providing care easier for both resident and staff. Second, nursing homes must satisfy safety and health regulations that allow only certain kinds of beds in a nursing home. Home mattresses seldom are fireproof, and it is not uncommon to find that the hygienic standards required by law have not been met with home maintenance techniques.

Myth #14: I'll be given medications that will cause me to lose control of my thoughts and actions.

Reality: Every person has the right to know what medications he or she is taking and has the right to refuse any or all of these. Tranquilizers, pain-relieving medications, sleeping pills, and mood changers are all powerful drugs and do have a profound effect on how alert one remains. Properly prescribed, these medications help rather than harm individuals. Staff, residents, and family all have a responsibility to ask for a review of prescriptions by their physician or a pharmacist if they suspect medications are being used improperly.

Myth #15: I'll be physically restrained in the nursing home.

Reality: Restraints (cloth bindings on chairs or beds) may be used in nursing homes only under two conditions:

❶ When an individual is confused and unable to comprehend or remember that by moving about he may harm himself or someone else, and

❷ When a person is unable to maintain his position because of a severe physical handicap such as paralysis. Restraints are used only for a resident's own safety; they are never to be used without a physician's order and then only for the span of time absolutely necessary. People in restraints are checked often. The restraint is then repositioned and the patient moved every hour.

Myth #16: Nursing home care will deplete my savings.

Reality: Nursing home care is expensive. However, it includes a comprehensive set of services under one roof and is far less expensive than the care provided in a hospital. Government programs provide very limited financial help. Medicare assists about 1% of the people admitted to nursing homes, but seldom covers more than a few days' stay. Medicaid is available to low-income people (see spousal asset protection, pages 100 and 101).

Entering a nursing home should be approached with as much thought and preparation as any major life change or any major expense. You should meet the administrator and discuss thoroughly the base price and any extra expenses you can expect to incur. Some homes have extra charges for such services as hand feeding, incontinent care, and personal laundry. Obtain in writing what your basic charge will be, and understand clearly all financial arrangements before signing a contract.

Myth #17: Because I am physically weak and helpless, I have no one to help me get the services I want and need.

Reality: Every state government has a nursing home ombudsman program. Representatives of that program have the authority to help nursing home residents resolve problems that are not of a medical nature. They may resolve complaints with persuasion, or they may encourage legal action if necessary. Information on how to contact the local representative of the ombudsman program is available from the nursing home administrator or his/her number is in the local telephone directory in the government section.

> **It takes a long time to bring excellence to maturity.**
>
> - Publilius Syrus (1st century B.C.)

Activities that help residents' needs in nursing homes

Special programs in nursing homes encompass a wide range of activities and services. Their purposes are:

⁂ To enable residents to react and interact with their environment;

⁂ To help them fight back, to shape their destinies, to find new and satisfying social relationships; and

⁂ To be able to be self-directing and spontaneous.

These programs are planned and carried out by the care team of staff, family, residents, and volunteers working together. The programs should meet the needs of the residents as the resident defines them. In other words, the programs are done with the residents, not for them.

The variety of programs available in any nursing home depends on the health and interests of the residents. The range of activities should meet the needs of all residents, from the disoriented to the wheelchair bound to the ambulatory. Possible programs to meet resident needs are described in this article as activities, religious services, and therapies. While the structure and delivery of programs varies from home to home, their availability is essential to the total nursing home community.

Activities

A broad range of programs is directed by the activities coordinator. A home certified for Medicare and Medicaid must have someone designated as an activities coordinator. The planning and implementation of activities comes from requests by residents, families, staff, and volunteers. The activities are usually posted on a calendar of events that is available to each resident and also posted in large print where a wheelchair-bound resident can easily see it. Examples of a few such activities are:

❤ **Monthly birthday parties** to which all residents are invited. Families and friends may be invited to participate. Volunteers often help to bring residents to the party and join in the fun.

❤ **Celebrations of various holidays,** both secular and religious. Holidays are particularly difficult times for those away from their own homes, families, and friends. Valentine's Day, Halloween, Christmas, Hannukah, Easter, and Memorial Day are a few examples.

❤ **Musical events** can be enjoyed actively or passively depending on the abilities of the residents. Many homes have sing-alongs in which the residents request their favorite songs and sing along with a leader. Again, the involvement of volunteers, families, and friends is crucial to the success of such a program. Sometimes concerts are given by a church or school group or friend of the nursing home. Hopefully, the public is invited to attend, for this allows the residents to provide a source of pleasure to their community.

❤ **Games** foster both one-to-one relationships and group activity. Bingo is a favorite for many, but bridge, chess, and other games for smaller groups usually are available. Volunteers and families often are the ones to stimulate resident interest in a game and they may be able to help arrange suitable opponents. Contests sometimes are run with work games, and tournaments are arranged for bridge or game players.

❤ **Outdoor activities** include gardening, cookouts, or just enjoying time in the sun alone or with a friend. Often the staff does not have the time to take the immobile residents outside. Family and volunteers are relied upon to make this possible.

❤ **Trips and tours** to community events. Some homes have a special resident fund from the sale of arts and crafts made and sold by the residents to finance transportation rentals and ticket purchases. Friends or volunteers may donate to the fund or sometimes the nursing home sets aside money. Transportation can be a problem for those in wheelchairs, but the activities coordinator usually can find volunteer drivers who are taught to cope with the special needs of disabled people. Some communities have special vans that transport residents in wheelchairs. Trips outside the home offer variety and mental stimulation.

❤ **Nursing home newsletter,** especially if published by residents. This is an especially valuable method of expression and uses resident talent that otherwise may lie idle. Poetry, history, birthdays, and resident and staff personality profiles are all topics that can be included.

❤ **Resident discussion groups.** Sometimes a resident is an expert on a particular subject and will be the group leader. Other times a volunteer may offer to lead a discussion group. Topics may include current events, literature, and religion. The residents choose the topics and those interested attend.

❤ **Exercise fun and physical fitness.** Community leaders often volunteer to lead yoga or other exercise sessions. Even wheelchair-bound residents find satisfaction in exercising on a regular basis.

❤ **Books.** Volunteers may run a book service, taking a cart of books to the room of immobile residents. There may be a central library or small bookcases on each floor. Talking books for the blind may be part of the service. Families, friends, and volunteers can buy, bring, and hand out books. Many people help with reading to those unable to see well.

❤ **Coffee or cocktail hours.** Policies vary from home to home, but social hours provide a time of resident interaction. It is a particularly nice time for volunteers, family, and friends to join the residents.

❤ **Arts and crafts programs** separate from occupational therapy frequently are offered by the activities coordinator. A volunteer, resident, or family member may lead this program.

❤ **Religious services.** Every Medicare- and Medicaid-certified nursing home must, by federal regulation, provide the opportunity for residents to attend religious services of their preference. Many nursing homes welcome denominational groups to provide religious services in the home for those who wish to attend. Again, this often provides an opportunity for families and friends to join the resident in worship. The organization of such services is usually handled by the activities coordinator.

Therapies

Reality orientation therapy is a technique used to rehabilitate residents who suffer from moderate or severe disorientation. These people may no longer know who they are, where they are, or what hour, day, or year it is. The technique can be carried out by anyone who comes into contact with the resident. The nursing home offering such a program involves the entire staff, families, and friends in the process. One or two staff members in the home may be responsible for the program. This is a relearning process, individually and through short group sessions, of basic information such as name, place, age, and day. As these facts are learned more facts are added. It is the basis of more advanced remotivation techniques designed to help the resident function better.

Remotivation therapy is under the direction of a trained remotivation coordinator and carried out by her or someone she designates such as an RN, LPN, or nursing assistant. It is for those who are already oriented but who need to take a renewed interest in their surroundings by focusing their attention on simple, objective aspects of daily life.

Regular meetings are important for successful remotivation programs. The meeting site must promote a relaxed atmosphere and be devoid of other distractions. A topic of conversation is introduced by the leader; a short poem or a newspaper item is appropriate. Often, the residents are asked to read part of the poem or story. Next, the topic is developed through the use of a preplanned set of questions. Then the topic is related to each individual experience. Finally, the meeting is brought to a close and plans for the next meeting are made.

Occupational therapy is a service provided by a qualified occupational therapist to evaluate, diagnose, and treat problems that interfere with everyday living skills. Impairments may be due to physical illness, injury, emotional disorders, or the aging process. Therapists and patients together work toward the goals of optimal levels of independent living, prevention of disability, and maintenance of health.

Specific occupational therapy services include education and training to increase independence in activities of daily living such as dressing and eating; to improve eye-motor coordination, sensory integration, concentration and attention span, thought organization, and problem solving; and to correct impaired visual-spatial relationships.

Additional services also seek to prevent muscle atrophy, prevent or minimize deformity, and increase pain tolerance. For instance, someone who has weakness in an arm due to a stroke may benefit from an activity such as sanding wood that strengthens muscles. Or the occupational therapist may make a splint for the hand and arm to prevent the muscles from stretching or contracting.

Volunteer Services

Volunteers provide an important link between the community and the nursing home resident. Many are involved in the activity program because they have special talents and skills to contribute. Many others assist residents who have disabilities, to participate in activities. Friendly volunteer visitors provide one-to-one relationships for residents.

Regardless of their specific roles in the home, volunteers must be recruited, oriented, and supervised to be used effectively. A dedicated group of volunteers from the community is testimony to a concerned nursing home.

Handling Problems in Nursing Homes

As with other living arrangements every day in a nursing home is not always a rose garden. Annoying and upsetting things will happen. A resident may at times feel that he or she is not being treated right.

Complaints may be about such items as: call button not working or out of reach; insufficient staff on duty; medical records are falsified; medications not given or given by an unauthorized person; lack of activities; lack of personal hygiene; dirty linen; inadequate diet; retaliation; snacks unavailable; unsanitary conditions in the hallways, rooms, etc.; patient's funds mishandled, lost, or stolen; violation of patient's rights. This is not an exhaustive list of problems by any means and is only to indicate the range of problems one may encounter in a nursing home.

Often complaints by residents may be vague, such as general complaints as to lack of attention. A friend or relative should elicit more details that may point the way to a serious violation. For example, the complaint about lack of attention may be caused by inadequate staffing, which is a violation of regulations. Despite laws and regulations, insufficient or under-trained staff is a major problem in nursing facilities and often results in inadequate patient attention and care. It is important to be clear about the problem as some investigators will not look for anything that is not specified in the complaint.

Solving Problems

Many residents and family members will not defend themselves when their rights have been violated because they fear retaliation from staff if they complain. While any form of retaliation by staff, either blatant or subtle, is illegal, it does happen on occasion. **Do not let fear stop you or the resident from defending the rights of the resident. Living in fear of being mistreated, receiving poor care, or tolerating neglect or harassment is an unsupportable and unacceptable situation for anyone.**

There are several places where citizens concerned about nursing facilities and residents' problems can turn for help. The important thing is to seek help, because conditions will improve and problems will be solved only if you get involved. The resident should first bring problems, unless they are related to staff, to the attention of the head nurse or the director of nursing in that order. If you are a friend or relative, and not directly exposed to the problem, it may be hard to figure out. It is important then to attempt to gain a clear understanding of what the problem encompasses. Then if you think he or she is not getting a satisfactory response you may obtain help from:

✳ The administrator of the nursing home;
✳ The long-term-care ombudsman program of the State Department of Aging (local telephone numbers are located in the government section of your phone book. The ombudsman's phone number must also be posted in the nursing home);
✳ The Licensing and Certification Division of the State Depart-

Some news reports of nursing home abuses

ment of Health Services (see government section of your phone book);

✳ A "nursing home hot line" or "cool line" (advertized on the consumer information boards of many nursing homes); and

✳ The Attorney General of the State and various district and city attorneys (listed in local telephone directories).

The Administrator

If the administrator of the nursing home is unable to solve your problem--or if you do not want to discuss it with the administrator --you may contact any of the other agencies. If you wish to discuss a problem without other staff present make that clear to the administrator.

The Long-term-care Ombudsman

Federal and state laws provide for an impartial official called an ombudsman to act in your behalf. Your local ombudsman will investigate your complaint and try to help you by acting as your representative or advocate. An ombudsman is a public official and provides his or her services free of charge. They investigate and resolve complaints made by, or on behalf of, older individuals who are residents of long-term-care facilities, nursing homes, and residential care homes. They do not represent the facility. The ombudsman will keep your complaint confidential, unless you wish otherwise.

The State Department of Health Services

If you choose to discuss your problem with an ombudsman, you may still contact your state Department of Health Services or another agency if you wish. The Department of Health Services is responsible for enforcement of the laws and regulations, licensing, and certification. A complaint criticizes the practices, procedures, physical conditions, or quality of care in a nursing facility and asks the state Department of Health Services to determine if a violation exists. A complaint may be made by telephone, personal visit, or letter. A letter provides you with a record and is therefore preferable. Any oral complaint is reduced to writing by the department. There is a right of appeal for the person who made a complaint if he or she is not satisfied with the department's decision.

You have a right to remain anonymous when you file a complaint. However, experience has shown that anonymous complaints seldom contain information specific enough to enable the state agency to perform a thorough investigation. If you will give your name, address, and telephone number, an investigator will be able to contact you if additional information is needed. When the investigation has been completed, you will be notified of the findings.

> There are many caring nurses, nurses aides, social workers, ombudsmen, volunteers, nursing home administrators, and other healthcare professionals. Many work diligently to meet the needs of the residents of nursing homes. We all need to applaud these wonderful people.

Our nursing home coverage must necessarily, because of reality, include some information on abuse in nursing homes. Despite federal legislation to stop nursing home abuse, it still abounds and may be getting worse, according to a federal government report of May 1990. At the end of this article we have listed some positive actions senior citizens can take to correct or at least improve this sad state of affairs.

In a news article in the May 1990 issue of *AARP's Bulletin*, Don McLeod reported that "abuse abounds." The most striking finding in a survey of healthcare professionals is that nearly all respondents indicate abuse is a problem in nursing homes. The abuse comes from a variety of sources, including families and visitors, but most of the perceived abuse was attributed to overworked and undertrained aides and orderlies.

A United Press International news item claimed that there is "shoddy care at nursing homes." It says that "Government inspections showed that nearly one in four nursing homes administers drugs improperly and about the same number did not provide adequate personal hygiene for residents."

A *USA Today* news item dated May 30, 1990 reported that "Nursing homes must clean up their act. Nursing homes are not home, sweet homes. They are places of pain, despair and death. Because they care for those who can no longer care for themselves or be cared for by their families. Because they are often the last stop for loved ones who are dying. But nursing homes should never humiliate patients. They should never mistreat or neglect them. Sadly, they often do. That's the conclusion anyone with a loved one in a nursing home must draw from the 93-volume, 74,000-page, federal report released (May, 1990) on our 15,000 nursing homes and their 1.3 million patients."

The United States Department of Health and Human Services researchers identified seven categories of abuse. Ninety-five percent of those surveyed said they felt that all seven are problems for nursing home residents:

❶ **Physical abuse**--infliction of physical pain or injury.

❷ **Misuse of restraints**--chemical or physical control of a resident beyond physician's order or outside accepted medical practice.

❸ **Verbal/emotional abuse**--infliction of mental or emotional suffering.

❹ **Physical neglect**--disregard for the necessities of daily living.

❺ **Medical neglect**--lack of care for existing medical problems.

❻ **Verbal/emotional neglect**--creating situations harmful to the resident's self-esteem.

❼ **Personal property abuse**--illegal or improper use of a resident's property for personal gain.

Across the USA, the federal report concluded that in nursing homes:

■ 24% improperly administered drugs according to the written orders from the attending physicians (60% in New Jersey);

■ 26% did not provide adequate personal hygiene (67% in the state of Washington);

■ 21% did not follow proper isolation techniques to prevent the spread of infection;

■ 20% did not provide each resident with a urinary catheter with proper routine care;

■ 36% did not follow rules requiring that food be stored, prepared, and served under sanitary conditions (62% in Alabama);

■ 18% failed to provide patients' bathroom needs according to federal standards (33% in Michigan);

■ 12% didn't properly treat bedsores; and

■ 15% didn't provide patients with privacy during treatment and personal care.

USA Today said, "The numbers are abominable." They mean thousands of people whose dignity should be respected are being humiliated, mistreated, and neglected because they've grown old.

Mental Health in Nursing Homes

In hearings by the United States House of Representatives Select Committee on Aging, in August 1989, expert witnesses testified to the seriousness of mental health problems in nursing homes. Some statements include:

■ The rates of psychiatric disorders in nursing homes have been estimated to be at least 50% to 94% of the population; these people are in need of mental health consultation.

■ It is likely that widespread overuse and misuse of psychoactive medications add to the psychological woes of nursing home residents (a news article in SF Chronicle claims 44% of nursing home patients in U.S. are controlled by powerful psychotropic drugs, 70% in California). First, when psychotropic drugs are used inappropriately they may cause depression, agitation, sedation, and confusion. Second, they may mask psychological disease and make depression, anxiety, and confusion difficult to recognize.

Who's Blaming Who?

Healthcare experts, nursing home operators, and federal officials have made statements concerning nursing home problems as follows:

✿ Some tend to view the problems identified by the government researchers as relatively minor incidents overblown by critics. They say the data fail to distinguish between major problems and minor ones that do not affect patient care. At best, the report is an outdated snapshot of a facility. At worst, it leads people to the false conclusion that this guide substitutes for visiting nursing homes during the selection process (this statement is by Paul Willging, executive vice-president of the American Health Care Association). Mr. Willging essentially states that improvements will result only by legal action and by enforcement.

✿ Some say there is a substantial unmet need for trained nursing home staff to care and to cope for mentally disordered geriatric patients, for mental health services, and for funding them.

✿ Faced with heavier levels of care, such as residents with more debilitating diseases, frustrated staff take out more of their stress on the residents. Many believe stress is caused by the difficulties of caring for impaired and dependent residents, who require help in many of the activities of daily living.

✿ Much of the abuse cannot be attacked directly because it is never reported.

✿ Nurses aides who provide most of the care for nursing home residents sometimes have no training.

✿ The federal Health Care Financing Administration, who administers Medicare, has missed every deadline so far set for providing the state with guidelines and regulations.

✿ Only about 20 states have drawn up sanctions to be taken against offending nursing homes short of closing them down, as the law requires.

✿ The nursing facilities lack the capability, particularly in terms of specialized staffing, to manage many of the behaviors that are characteristic of major mental illness.

What You Can Do!

There is a strong need for family involvement in:

◆ the patient's course of treatment;

◆ setting strict standards for rehabilitation; and

◆ providing stronger mechanisms for complaints against negligent facilities.

As a family member or friend of a resident you can:

◆ continue to monitor the nursing home's treatment of their residents, not just for one resident but for others as well;

◆ participate as much as possible in the home's activities to gain firsthand knowledge of what actually goes on;

◆ examine the medication records to see that the resident is not being overmedicated;

◆ periodically review the Health Care Financing Administration's or the State Department of Human Services' report on complaints filed against the nursing home; and

◆ get involved in filing complaints if you find there are real problems and abuses.

As a senior citizen you can:

◆ Get involved in the political process by writing your congressmen, both state and federal, to enact better standards, improved funding for mental services, and improved supervision of nursing homes.

◆ Make your voice heard in the community against records of residents abuse.

> **Never before in the history of the United States have there been so many senior citizens that vote. Senior citizens, wielding the power of the pen, can if they wish put in place means of insuring that abuse in nursing homes is minimized. Not only do you have the power but you also have the responsibility. If you do not take responsibility, abuse will continue.**

> **Old age has a great sense of calm and freedom. When the passions have relaxed their hold and have escaped, not from one master, but from many.**
>
> **- Plato (427?-347? B.C.)**

Glossary--terms used for long-term care

activities director--person who has received a 36-hour training course or has worked a specific time in a social/recreational program. The activities director is responsible for developing, scheduling, and conducting programs to meet the social and diversional needs of residents.

acute care--medical care needed for an illness or injury requiring short-term, intense care and usually hospitalization.

administrator--person licenced to run a nursing home, who has received training in financial, legal, social, and medical aspects of running such an institution.

ambulatory--able to walk about unassisted.

ambulatory with assistance--able to get about with the aid of a cane, crutch, brace, wheelchair, or walker.

analgesic--an agent that alleviates pain without the loss of consciousness.

aphasia--defect or loss of the power of expression by speech.

arteriosclerosis--condition marked by loss of elasticity, thickening, and hardening of the arteries.

bowel and bladder training--program of retaining bowel and bladder functions to minimize or eliminate incontinence.

call bell--button or bell connected to a light in the nurses station; used by residents to summon a nurse or nursing assistant.

catheter--tube passed through the urethra into the bladder to drain urine. Other names are Foley catheter or in-dwelling catheter.

chairbound--unable to get out of a chair without the help of another person; one who is not ambulatory with or without assistance; may also be referred to as a bed-chair patient.

chuks--trade name for bed pad that is soft on one side and waterproof on the other. Used under incontinent persons or under draining areas of the body; disposable.

comatose--pertaining to a state of profound unconsciousness from which the patient cannot be aroused, even by powerful stimulation.

commode--a portable toilet used in a patient's room and emptied by an aide or orderly.

continent--able to control the passage of urine and feces. The opposite is incontinent, or unable to control the passage of urine or feces.

contractures--stiffening of muscles and joints.

custodial care--board, room, and other personal assistance services generally provided on a long-term basis that do not include a medical component. Such services are generally not paid for under private or public health insurance or medical care programs, except as incidental to medical care.

decubitus ulcer--a sore or ulcer caused by a lack of blood circulation to some area of the body. This condition usually results from sitting or lying in one position too long. Other names are bedsore or pressure sore. The treatment includes medication, dressings, and proper positioning.

dehydration--lack of adequate fluid in the body; a crucial factor in the health of people.

dietician--an expert in planning menus and in establishing dietary procedures.

director of nursing--nurse who oversees the nursing supervisors, nurses aides, and orderlies, and who is responsible for nursing procedures and policies.

discharge planner--member of the professional staff of a hospital or nursing home who develops a plan of future care for a patient prior to discharge.

disorientation--loss of one's bearings; loss of sense of familiarity with one's surroundings; loss of place (where one is) and person (who one is).

drainage bag--plastic bag used to collect urine from a catheter.

draw sheet--small sheet covering a rubber plastic sheet on a bed or wheelchair used under an incontinent person.

durable medical equipment--medical and other equipment, including oxygen machines, wheelchairs, and dialysis equipment that can withstand repeated use and is appropriate for use in your home.

edentulous--a condition that occurs when all teeth are missing; toothlessness. If a person has a set of plates and does not use them he/she is classified as edentulous.

functional status--measure of the degree of ability to cope with activities of daily living.

geriatrics--a branch of medicine that deals with the problems and diseases of old age and aging people.

geri-chair--a wheelchair that cannot be self-propelled. It must be pushed by someone.

grab bars--bars or railing placed around the tubs, showers, and toilets to be used to steady oneself.

home healthcare--healthcare services rendered in the home to an individual, e.g., disabled, sick, or convalescent individuals who do not need institutional care. The services may be provided by a visiting nurse association (VNA), home health agency, hospital, or other organized community group, and may be quite specialized or comprehensive (nursing service, speech, physical, occupational and rehabilitation therapy, homemaker services, and social services).

hypertension--medical diagnosis of a condition in which there exists an abnormally high blood pressure measurement.

incontinence--involuntary loss of urine and/or feces.

intermediate nursing care--care that is less intensive in its nursing services than skilled nursing care. Medicaid reimbursement for such services can be provided on behalf of eligible recipients to certified intermediate care facilities.

licensed practical nurse (LPN)--one who has completed one year in a school of nursing or vocational training school. LPNs are in charge of nursing in the absence of a registered nurse, often giving medications and performing treatments. LPNs are licensed by the state.

long-term care--health and personal care services required by the chronically ill, aged, disabled, or retarded in an institution or a home, on a long-term basis. The term often is used more narrowly to refer only to long-term institutional care such as that in nursing homes, homes for the retarded, and mental hospitals. Long-term ambulatory services like home healthcare are seen as alternatives.

long-term-care facilities--range of institutions that provide various levels of care (maintenance and personal or nursing care) to people who are unable to care for themselves and who may have health problems ranging from minimal to very serious. They include free-standing institutions, or identifiable components of other health facilities that provide nursing care and related services, personal care, and residential care.

Long-term-care ombudsman--program under the Older American Act that requires each state to have a statewide watchdog, or ombudsman, over nursing homes and other long-term-care facilities. The state ombudsman investigates and resolves complaints by residents and provides information to the state agency responsible for licensing the facility.

Medicaid (Medi-Cal in California)--medical assistance program that pays certain medical expenses for eligible needy individuals with low incomes. Medicaid will pay for skilled or intermediate nursing care for eligible recipients in appropriately certified facilities.

medical director--physician who formulates and directs policy for medical care in the nursing home.

Medicare--federal health insurance program in which most persons over the age of 65 participate.

N.G. tube (nasal gastric tube)--tube passed through the nose to the stomach for the purpose of feeding (gastric feeding).

nonambulatory--not able to move around by oneself.

nurses aide--employee of the nursing home usually responsible for personal care of the resident (assisting with bathing, feeding, walking, turning in bed, etc.). Nurses aides work under the supervision of a registered nurse or licensed practical nurse. Limited training or experience is required.

occupational therapist--specially trained individual who evaluates the self-care, work, and leisure performance skills of well and disabled clients of all ages; the therapist plans and implements programs and social and interpersonal activities designed to restore, develop, and maintain the client's ability to accomplish satisfactorily those daily living tasks required of his/her specific age and his/her particular occupational role.

patient care plan--written program of care for the patient that is based on the assessment of the individual needs, identified role of each service in meeting those needs, and the supportive measure each service will use to complement each other to accomplish the overall goal of care.

physical therapist--specially trained and licenced individual who uses physical and mechanical means (massage, exercise, water, light, heat) and assertive devices in relieving pain, restoring maximum function, and preventing disability following disease, injury, or loss of a bodily part.

P.R.N.--abbreviation used to indicate that a medication is given or treatment performed only as need arises.

reality orientation--therapeutic sessions designed to reorient confused persons as to time, place, the names of people around them, and their own situation.

registered nurse (R.N.)--graduate nurse who has completed at least two years at an accredited nursing school. RN's are trained in providing skilled nursing care, including the administration of medications and treat-

ment, and are licensed by states.

resident council--organization for nursing home residents. Its function is to improve the quality of life, care, and communication within an institution by providing some measure of control or self-determination by the residents.

restraint--protective device used to prevent a resident from falling out of a chair, e.g., a belt around the waist tied to a wheelchair or a jacket with straps used to prevent a resident from crawling over the side rails of a bed. Wrist restraints are used under unusual circumstances.

sheepskin--natural or synthetic skin that is soft and used to protect bony areas such as elbows, ankles, and coccyx from rubbing against hard surfaces like beds or chairs.

social worker or social service designee--person who provides social service, either as a member of a health team, a social service section of a health facility, or on a consultant basis. Services provided help the patient, family, or others deal with the social needs that affect the well-being of the patient.

speech pathologist (therapist)--specially trained individual who evaluates speech and language problems and performs related research. The speech pathologist plans, directs, and conducts remedial programs designed to restore or improve the communication efficiency of adults with language or speech impairments.

T.P.R.--abbreviation for temperature, pulse, and respiration.

transfer agreement--written agreement to provide for reciprocal transfer of patients/ residents between healthcare facilities.

utilization review--organized plan for evaluating the use of resident services to ensure a high quality of care. The committee in charge of the review consists of members of the nursing home staff and outside physicians.

walker--lightweight frame held in front of a person to give stability in walking. It offers more stability than a cane.

Five strategies you can use to avoid nursing home cost

The greatest threat to older Americans and their families today is the catastrophic cost of long-term care. Nursing home bills run from $25,000 to $50,000 per year and more. Neither Medicare nor private insurance is likely to cover the cost, leaving you on your own. A million Americans every year are forced into destitution to pay long-term-care bills.

A recent report presented to the American Public Health Association by three doctors stated that:

- Almost a third of men turning 65 in 1991 and just over half of women can be expected to use a nursing home sometime before they die.

- About 7 in 10 couples turning 65 in 1991 can expect that at least one of the two will use a nursing home sometime before death.

- Nine out of 10 married couples with four parents turning 65 can expect to have at least one parent use a nursing home.

Medicaid, a cooperative program of the federal and state governments, covers long-term costs, but to qualify for Medicaid funds a person generally must be or become poor by passing an income limitation test. That generally means that one's income must be less than the nursing home costs--unfortunately, an easy test to pass for most older Americans. Once you qualify, you will be able to keep only a small portion of your income, and the rest will go to pay the bills.

To make matters even worse, you must also pass a tough assets limitation test before you receive a cent from Medicaid. Under the test, almost all of your assets, including cash, other liquid assets, or any property you or your spouse could convert to cash, must be turned over to the nursing home.

Married couples with one spouse in a nursing home generally may keep a minimum of $12,000--or one-half of their combined life savings up to a maximum of $60,000--whichever is more. Unmarried nursing home residents may keep only about $2,000, depending on the state. In addition, married couples may keep a home, regardless of its value, as long as one spouse lives there, and a car and personal effects of unlimited value. These exemptions are severely limited for unmarried individuals.

In addition, while there are some state differences, the specific assets you can keep, regardless of your marital status, and still qualify for Medicaid include:

* One wedding and engagement ring;
* Up to $6,000 equity in property essential to support;
* Life insurance with a cash surrender value of up to $1,500 per individual; and
* Burial plots and a fund for burial costs.

You, your parent, or other loved ones need to be resigned to a life of poverty upon entering a nursing home. By taking steps to protect yourself, you can avoid financial disaster. Described briefly are 5 strategies you can use to help protect your assets from the ravaging cost of long-term care.

SOME WORDS OF WARNING:

Don't rush into anything without obtaining as much information as possible. There are other options, one of which may be better suited to your situation.

1 Use your home to shelter assets.

Married nursing home residents may keep their home, regardless of the value, and still get Medicaid assistance. The exemption for a home is available as long as the spouse is living there. As a result, the family home can be a treasure house for savings.

For example, if you have a home with a mortgage, by taking money from your savings accounts or selling some stock to pay off the loan, you can change assets that would be lost to a nursing home into assets that can't be touched. Since you can exclude the entire value of the house, whether its got a large mortgage or no mortgage, you may even decide to use other nonexempt assets to pay it off.

Older Americans can also shelter money in a house by making improvements, such as putting on a new roof or remodeling the kitchen. Again, by placing nonexempt money into a home, individuals can protect assets and enjoy the fruits of their labor while still healthy.

If you or your parents don't own a home but have other financial resources, think about buying one. The same principle will apply to it--assets that could be reached by a nursing home will be unreachable if invested in a house. Since there is no limit on the value of a house that can be protected, you can preserve most or all assets with one simple technique.

If you ever need cash for an emergency, you could take out a mortgage or home equity loan. While a home is certainly not as liquid as cash, the value is still accessible.

2 Purchase household goods.

Like a home, household goods are also protected from nursing home charges. For married couples, these items are safe regardless of their value. If you own a stove or refrigerator that could almost qualify as an antique, buy replacements instead of making do.

In fact, you could use this exemption creatively to hold onto a great deal of assets. For example, oriental rugs or paintings that appreciate in value may be worthwhile investments that add beauty to your surroundings and preserve assets at the same time.

3 Transfer assets to children.

Assets that are not exempt under Medicaid rules may also be transferred to adult children without affecting your eligibility for Medicaid. But there is a time limit. If the transfer is made less than 30 months before you enter a nursing home, Medicaid, for purposes of determining your eligibility, acts as if the transfer never happened.

Let's say that the day you go into a nursing home you transfer all your assets, valued at $100,000, to your son. For 30 months, you will not be eligible for Medicaid, because according to Medicaid rules, you still own all those assets. Using your assets, your son will have to pick up the tab, which may run $60,000 or so. But after 30 months, Medicaid will cover the costs, and the remaining $40,000 will be forever protected. Without making the transfer, you could have lost everything.

4 Transfer assets to a Medicaid trust.

In some cases, giving assets to children may not be desirable. For example, if your children have financial problems, their creditors may seize the funds. Or if a child becomes divorced or dies, his or her spouse may end up with your assets.

Transferring assets to a Medicaid trust may be a better alternative. Medicaid trusts, also called Medicaid Qualifying trusts, work the same way as other trusts. The person setting up the trust, called the trustor, names another person, the trustee, to hold and manage designated property (cash, real estate, personal property) for the trustor's benefit.

Let's say you have $100,000 in certificates of deposit, yielding $10,000 in income per year. You could put the CD's into an irrevocable Medicaid trust, giving you access to the income but not the principal. If you later enter a nursing home, the nursing home could get the $10,000 income, but not the $100,000 principal. Medicaid would pay the difference between the income and the nursing home bill. Upon your death, the $100,000 would be distributed to the people of your choice.

There are some drawbacks to a Medicaid trust. You lose control over all trust assets and must keep them separate from your other property. Transfers to a Medicaid trust generally must be made at least 2-1/2 years before a person enters a nursing home to be safely within the Medicaid rules. And trusts are rarely appropriate for those with assets valued over $600,000, which may be subject to federal estate taxes.

Because of their relative novelty and complications, Medicaid trusts often require the help of someone experienced in such matters. Such experience will not likely come cheap; many lawyers charge $1,500 to $3,000 for the job. You may be able to reduce the cost by preparing the forms yourself and then having an attorney or other expert look them over. But if you take this approach, you must be willing to devote time and work to understand the complexities of Medicaid trusts.

5 Pay children for their help.

If your adult children help you with a variety of chores--driving you to the store, doing your banking, preparing your meals--you can transfer some of your assets by paying them for those services.

This can be a very helpful technique if used carefully. Medicaid personnel are likely to scrutinize payments to children and allow only reasonable payments. You cannot pay a child $2,000 each time a child drives you to the store and expect Medicaid to overlook

it. But if full-time home care costs $40,000 per year in your area, a child providing those services could be fairly paid that much.

Armond D. Budish, an attorney in Cleveland, Ohio, is the author of *Avoiding the Medicaid Trap* (Henry Holt & Co.), from which this article is excerpted. You can order it by sending $25.95 to P.O. Box 24448, Cleveland, OH 44124.

This article is reprinted with permission from the Spring 1990 issue of Nolo News, a quarterly self-help legal newspaper published by NOLO PRESS, 950 Parker Street, Berkeley, CA 94710; (415)549-1976.

Who Pays Nursing Home Bills?

Typically, elderly persons pay the initial costs of nursing homes out of their pockets. But for many, only a few months in a nursing home will exhaust all of their savings. To become eligible for Medicaid, they must "spend down" all their financial resources. Who pays? Here is the breakdown for 1990:

* Personal, family ... 49%
* Medicare ... 2%
* Medicaid ... 43%
* Private insurance ... 1.5%
* VA, state, local public assistance ... 3.9%

What Can We Do?

As senior citizens, we all have a stake in the debate about how to finance long-term care. It's painful to consider a parent in a nursing home and we certainly cannot imagine ourselves in a nursing home or needing constant assistance in our homes. We choose to ignore the issue. It won't happen to our parents. It won't happen to us. Or we prefer to think Medicare will take care of everything.

We can't just ignore the issue as it is everybody's problem. Whether or not we ourselves or a relative ever needs long-term-care services, millions of Americans will. We must help in the search for solutions. Make your voice heard. Write your congressman (see the article on political issues, page 172).

What you should look for

The following is a checklist of points to consider when selecting a nursing home. Refer to it as you talk with staff members and tour a home. It can also help you in comparing three different homes.

NURSING HOME
(Circle Y for yes, N for no.)

	#1	#2	#3
Administration			
1. Does the nursing home have the required current license from the state or letter of approval from a licensing agency?	Y N	Y N	Y N
2. Is the home certified to participate in the Medicare and Medicaid programs?	Y N	Y N	Y N
3. Do staff members show patients genuine interest and affection?	Y N	Y N	Y N
4. Do patients look well cared for and generally content?	Y N	Y N	Y N
5. Are patients allowed to wear their own clothes, decorate their rooms, and keep a few prized possessions on hand?	Y N	Y N	Y N
6. Is there a written statement of patients' rights? Is this statement displayed where it can be seen?	Y N	Y N	Y N
General Physical Considerations:			
Comfort			
1. Is the nursing home clean and orderly?	Y N	Y N	Y N
2. Are toilet and bathing facilities easy for handicapped patients to use?	Y N	Y N	Y N
3. Is the home well lighted?	Y N	Y N	Y N
4. Is the home reasonably free of unpleasant odors?	Y N	Y N	Y N
5. Are rooms well ventilated and kept at a comfortable temperature?	Y N	Y N	Y N
Safety			
1. Are there wheelchair ramps where necessary?	Y N	Y N	Y N
2. Are there grab bars in toilet and bathing facilities?	Y N	Y N	Y N
3. Are there handrails on both sides of the hallways?	Y N	Y N	Y N
4. Is there an automatic sprinkler system and automatic emergency lighting?	Y N	Y N	Y N
5. Are there portable fire extinguishers?	Y N	Y N	Y N
6. Are exit doors unobstructed and unlocked from inside and easily accessible?	Y N	Y N	Y N
7. Are emergency evacuation plans posted in prominent locations?	Y N	Y N	Y N
8. Are there smoke detectors and fire alarms on every floor?	Y N	Y N	Y N
9. Is there a fire station near the home?	Y N	Y N	Y N
Medical, Dental, and Pharmaceutical Services			
1. In case of medical emergencies, is a physician available at all times, either on staff or on call?	Y N	Y N	Y N
2. Does the home have an arrangement with an outside dental service to provide patients with dental care?	Y N	Y N	Y N
3. Are pharmaceutical services supervised by a qualified pharmacist?	Y N	Y N	Y N
4. Does the home have arrangements with a nearby hospital for quick transfer of patients in an emergency?	Y N	Y N	Y N
Nursing Services			
1. Is at least one registered nurse (RN) or licensed practical nurse (LPN) on duty day and night?	Y N	Y N	Y N
2. Are nurse call buttons located at each patient's bed and in toilet and bathing facilities?	Y N	Y N	Y N
Food Services			
1. Is the kitchen clean and reasonably tidy?	Y N	Y N	Y N
2. Are at least three meals served each day?	Y N	Y N	Y N
3. Are patients given enough food?	Y N	Y N	Y N
4. Are special meals prepared for patients on therapeutic or other diets?	Y N	Y N	Y N
5. Do patients who need help receive it, whether in the dining room or in their own rooms?	Y N	Y N	Y N
Rehabilitation Therapy, Social Service, and Patient Activities			
1. Is there a full-time program of physical therapy for patients who need it?	Y N	Y N	Y N
2. Are there special services available to aid patients and their families?	Y N	Y N	Y N
3. Does the nursing home have a varied program of recreational, cultural, and intellectual activities for patients?	Y N	Y N	Y N
4. Are activities offered for patients who are relatively inactive or confined to their rooms?	Y N	Y N	Y N
Patient's Rooms			
1. Is a married couple allowed to share a room?	Y N	Y N	Y N
2. Do all rooms have a window to the outside?	Y N	Y N	Y N
3. Is there a curtain or screen available to provide privacy for each bed whenever necessary?	Y N	Y N	Y N
4. Does each patient have a reading light, a comfortable chair, and a closet and chest of drawers for personal belongings?	Y N	Y N	Y N
Responsibilities			
1. Once a patient is admitted, will the nursing home assume responsibility for taking the patient to medical appointments or other outside community activities?	Y N	Y N	Y N
2. Is the nursing home clear about what responsibilities should be assumed and/or kept by the family?	Y N	Y N	Y N

Reprinted with permission from The American Geriatrics Society, Clinical Report on Aging, Vol. 2, No.5, 1988.

Living the good life in a foreign country

So you are thinking of living in a foreign country! It can be a wonderful experience, but there are many questions you need to settle before you burn all your bridges.

THE EXPATRIATE TRADITION

Living abroad is not a new idea in the United States. Americans have lived in other countries by choice almost from the beginning. Many people have lived in different European locations. Best known have been the artistic and literary personalities who have chosen to live abroad, either because of better opportunities or their preference for the culture.

After both world wars, many of our citizens chose to live and/or study abroad. In the late forties and early fifties, many struggled to survive on the G.I. Bill so that they could be in locations like Paris, London, or Rome. Artists in general found that the opportunities to perform were much greater in Europe.

While there are still rural areas where living can be at reasonable costs, most of the urban settings in Europe have become quite expensive for Americans. Moreover, what may be reasonable this year becomes impossible when the value of the dollar has fallen. Faced with those uncertainties, many persons have looked for and discovered more exotic locations where nature is kind and their dollars go further. We often tend to think of retirement as a permanent vacation, so some look for that kind of setting.

QUESTIONS TO ASK

There are many marvelous places in the world that combine beauty, desirable climate, and an exotic atmosphere. Selecting the right one may be a problem, but which one is academic until some other decisions are made. Any person who considers the possibility of retiring in a foreign country needs to answer some questions before making any decisions. For a couple, these questions have to apply to both people.

1. Am I ready to cut ties at home and live in a foreign country?
2. Am I comfortable in a foreign country when I am there?
3. Do I have the resources to get established and live comfortably away from the United States?
4. Do I have some idea of where I would like to live?

Once those general questions are answered, a whole set of more specific problems needs to be addressed concerning the place to move to:

❑ What is the legal status of an American living there permanently?
❑ How are foreigners treated in respect to taxes?
❑ Is adequate medical care available in that location?
❑ Since Medicare is not available outside the U.S., what provisions for medical care can be made?
❑ Is the government of that country stable, and are living conditions safe?
❑ Can you own property?

PREPARING FOR A LIFE AWAY FROM THE U.S.A.

The most important thing you can do is to go as a tourist to the place you think you want to live and try it out. This has to be for at least several months in order for you to really begin to feel what it would be like to be there permanently. If it is an expatriate colony, get acquainted with the people there. Ask questions and more questions. You can do this from a hotel, but it is even more realistic to sublet a house or apartment to find out what it is like to maintain a household. Do you want servants? Are you comfortable with bargaining for everything if that is the lifestyle of the area? What is it like in the other seasons? What do people do with their time generally? Develop your own set of criteria against which to assess any location you are considering.

MEXICO

The closest location to the United States that combines benign climate with the exotic and reasonable living cost is our neighbor to the south. A few years ago, more than 45,000 Americans were living in Mexico in a variety of locations. The prospective expatriate can choose from modern cities, Colonial towns, spas, beautiful beaches and mountains, just to name a few. For obvious reasons, many people have decided on areas that range in elevation from 2,000 to 5,000 feet.

The largest settlement of Americans seems to be at Lake Chapala. It is the largest lake in Mexico and is only a few miles from Guadalajara. The climate is moderate, and there is a rich cultural tradition in the area. The places in Mexico that have attracted Americans are too numerous to mention here. Setting aside the desirability of living at a higher altitude to enjoy a more moderate climate, many Americans have selected living areas along the Mexican Riviera. Acapulco and Puerto Vallarta are probably the best known.

If you are interested in exploring Mexico as a place to settle, there is now a service to help you do that. Barvi Tours at 11658 Gateway Blvd., Los Angeles, CA 90064, now sponsors tours to several areas settled by Americans. They combine sightseeing with seminars to deal with your questions on what it is like to live there. Their toll-free number is 1-800-824-7102.

SOUTH OF THE MEXICAN BORDER

There are two other places in Central America that have attracted colonies of Americans: Costa Rica and Panama. Costa Rica has been attractive because it is the most democratic and stable country in Latin America. In addition to that, it is beautiful and has a great climate. It is not cheap. Living there will be comparable in cost to living in the United States.

In spite of the fact that the last few years have been politically stormy, Panama has a lot to offer as a retirement haven. Again, people have chosen to settle in highlands that are somewhat removed from population centers. In addition to that, the United States tends to have a continuing interest in Panama, and Americans there have apparently not been bothered by government turmoil.

There are so many handsome and pleasant places in the world that if you start the selection process with no bias, you will have a real problem making a decision.

One book to help you know what is out there is *Retirement Paradises of the World* by Norman D. Ford, Harian Publications, Floral Park, NY 11001. Whatever your decision, don't cut all your ties to home. People and world conditions change, and you may wish to return in the future.

Looking for legal assistance?

The United States has more lawyers per person than any other country. So, if you need one--and many of us do at one time or another--you should be able to find one who will provide the best professional counsel at the fairest price.

When to Look for Legal Advice

Some matters not involving substantial amounts of money or property may be handled without the aid of a lawyer. However, in deciding whether to use a lawyer, you need to make a judgment, based on your own experiences and those of knowledgeable friends or relatives. Some problems where a lawyer should be considered include:

■ Is the matter a complex legal issue or one that is likely to be taken to court?
■ Is a large amount of money, property, or time involved?
■ Does the matter require the filing of complex legal papers, such as complex wills.
■ Is an estate being resolved involving significant amounts of money?
■ Are there serious tax problems?
■ Does the matter involve an accident that caused an injury or death?
■ Is there a divorce being contested?
■ Has significant damage been done to property?
■ Are you planning on home equity conversion?
■ Have you been discriminated against at work because of age?
■ Is guardianship an issue?

Where, besides a lawyer, can I go for help?

Depending upon the situation, you might consider the following alternatives to hiring a lawyer for a specific matter:

❑ Discuss the problem with the people involved and try to work out an acceptable compromise.

❑ Seek the advice of someone who could help mediate the dispute on an informal basis, such as a religious advisor or family counselor.

❑ Consult a good do-it-yourself legal guidebook. To find one, check the selection at your local bookstore or contact: NOLO PRESS, 950 Parker St., Berkeley, CA 94710; (415) 548-5902.

❑ Consider a nonlawyer, independent paralegal to assist you as they may be able to help you use self-help books, kits, and form books. They help you prepare forms (at your direction and decisions) but do not provide legal advice and cannot represent you in case you go into court.

❑ Contact your local or state consumer protection agency.

❑ Consider taking the problem to an impartial third-party organization that will listen to both sides of the dispute and help you reach a resolution. You can find these arbitration or mediation services at places such as your local Better Business Bureau.

❑ Take the matter to Small Claims Court, where claims of from $100 to $5000 can be considered, depending on where you live. Check with your local municipal court for the rules that apply in your area.

❑ If you are 60 years of age or older contact your local area office of aging and request legal assistance.

❑ Hire a general practitioner attorney for one hour and let him or her advise you about alternatives.

You also need to understand--before you hire a paralegal--what they legally can and cannot do. Here are some tips:

✻ They cannot provide legal advice.
✻ They may not legally represent people in court.
✻ They cannot select appropriate forms for their customers.
✻ They can help with routine legal tasks such as typing and filing the paperwork for uncontested divorces, bankruptcies, and wills.
✻ They can recommend self-help books.
✻ They can provide assistance in filling out legal forms since they are familiar with the forms and the rules for filing them.

Where can I go if I cannot afford legal fees, but need a lawyer's help?

If you cannot afford to hire a lawyer at the full fee, there are several legal assistance options. You may want to check your local phone directory to find out which services are available in your community.

Some legal services you may qualify for or should consider include:

1 Legal Aid
2 Legal Assistance for Older Americans
3 Pro Bono Services
4 Mediation
5 Court Appointed Attorney

Legal Aid--The federal government's Legal Services Corporation (LSC) funds offices across the nation (320 centers) to serve persons with incomes below 125% of poverty. Legal aid societies and other public legal assistance programs in your county or city also may be able to help.

To locate a legal aid office look in the telephone book under "legal aid" or call the bar association and ask about sources of free legal help. Legal aid offices generally offer assistance with a variety of legal problems, including those involving landlord-tenant issues, public benefits, credit and utilities disputes, and family law matters such as divorce, adoption, and guardianship cases.

Legal Assistance for Older Americans--The Federal Government's Older American Act (OAA) Title III requires that states provide legal assistance to older Americans. These free legal services, although you need not be poor to qualify for help, are aimed at low-income people over 60. Title III providers generally receive inadequate funding to assist all older persons in need of help. They therefore develop ways to determine which clients to accept. The Act's regulations prohibit use of a "means test" to limit receipt of services, yet mandate that preference be given to serving those in the greatest social or economic need. To resolve this dilemma, legal providers usually establish a case acceptance policy that serves those areas of law that most affect persons in greatest economic or social need (such as public benefits, housing, and healthcare).

Assigned lawyers can help you with a variety of legal problems concerning housing, consumer fraud, elder abuse, Social Security, Supplemental Security Income (SSI), Medicare, Medicaid, age discrimination, pensions, nursing homes, protective services, conservatorship, and other matters (see the article on the Older American Act, page 20 through 25).

State agencies and area agencies are prohibited from requiring a legal assistance provider to reveal information that is protected by the "attorney-client privilege." Your local area agency on aging may be able to assist you or refer you to an appropriate organization.

Pro Bono **Services**--Many older persons have problems outside of a Title III program's priority areas or have incomes above the Legal Services Corporation (LSC) poverty guidelines and thus cannot be served by either. They cannot, however, afford to retain private attorneys to resolve their problems.

Some states have developed innovative resources to provide legal assistance to older persons in this position. One such resource is *pro bono*--from the Latin phrase *pro bono publico* ("for the public good"), which is a term used to describe legal services provided free of charge to someone unable to pay for them. Eighteen states have a state-level *pro bono* coordinator whose goal is to enhance the availability of free legal services to poor persons through volunteer efforts of lawyers, paralegals, and other associated professions (e.g., court reporters). For information in your area contact your local bar association.

Mediation Services--A dispute resolution center (DRC) helps people resolve their disputes out of court. DRC's are sponsored by local judicial systems and funded by private foundations and organizations. Judges, law enforcement officers, bar associations, and legal aid groups refer cases for mediation when appropriate. Most are listed in the yellow pages of your telephone directory.

Mediation is useful in cases involving evictions, zoning changes, consumer issues, neighborhood disputes, and minor misdemeanors, such as vandalism and harassment. The elderly also should consider mediation for problems such as age discrimination and grandparents' visitation rights.

An individual who wants to pursue this type of mediation must first get the other party to agree to the procedure. Then the DRC will appoint a mediator with appropriate skills to help resolve the problem. The mediator may be a retired lawyer, judge, police officer, or other person with law enforcement or specialized experience.

Mediation spares one the expense, confusion, and anxiety of a court trial. To date, forty-six states have local mediation centers, most of which reach an agreement in more than 85% of their cases.

Court-Appointed Attorneys--If you are charged with a crime and cannot afford an attorney to defend you, you should be able to obtain free legal help. Inform the judge in your case that you are unable to afford an attorney, and ask that one be appointed to represent you. A state or local public defender's office can provide you with information.

Other Sources--You also may want to contact the local bar association's referral service, the municipal courthouse, or the district attorney's office for information. If you live near a law school, find out if it has a legal clinic serving the community.

How to Select a Lawyer

Once you decide you need a lawyer, how can you go about finding one to suit your needs? Finding the professional advisor whose talents and resources best fit your needs may require a real investment of time and effort on your part. But it is an investment that can pay substantial dividends in the long run. Here are some suggestions:

■ Begin by asking friends or neighbors about lawyers they have used. Pay special attention to what you hear from people who have had problems like yours that were resolved in a satisfactory way.

■ Contact your state, city, or county bar association and ask for the names and phone numbers of lawyers who handle cases within your area of concern.

■ Check with the Lawyer Referral Service of your state, city, or county bar association, usually listed in the telephone directories. Under a referral service, the lawyer will consult with you for half an hour without charge or for a prescribed and nominal fee, and then render whatever services are requested for an agreed-upon fee or refer you to another lawyer.

■ Check the yellow pages for areas of specialty, hours, and locations. You also may obtain information by looking for lawyer advertisements in newspapers and on the radio or television.

■ If you live near a law school, contact the dean's office, describe the problem, and ask if the school or individual faculty members are able to recommend someone to take your case.

■ Check the *Martindale-Hubbell Law Directory* at your local public library. It

More on evaluating and selecting a legal representative

gives brief biographical sketches of many lawyers and describes the areas of the law in which they practice.

■ Contact a specialist in elder law if the problem involves special needs of older persons such as age discrimination, retirement planning, Medicare, Medicaid, Social Security, planning for healthcare expenses, right to control the extent of medical care, and other issues. For the names of members of the National Academy of Elder Law Attorneys, send a self-addressed stamped envelope to: 1730 East River Road, Suite 107, Tucson, AZ 85718.

Before you hire a lawyer ask these questions:

Will you meet with me to get acquainted before I hire you?

Many lawyers will meet with you once without charge, as long as you make it perfectly clear that you do not expect free advice about the details of your case during the get-acquainted session. Before going to the meeting, write down the questions you want to ask. Bring along any relevant documents so that you can leave copies (not the originals) if you decide to hire the lawyer. You may want to choose a lawyer who talks with you in language you can understand--not "legalese."

What percentage of your practice is devoted to cases like mine?

Some lawyers specialize in a particular type of law, such as family, tax, or criminal law, and they may charge higher fees than general practitioners. On the other hand, they may be able to get the job done faster for you, and so the overall cost may be the same or less. Most general practice lawyers also can handle a variety of legal matters. Ask the lawyer about the results of some recent cases similar to yours, including time spent and fees charged. Finally, ask the lawyer for names and phone numbers of clients you can call for references.

Will you personally work on my case, or will you delegate it to an associate or paralegal assistant?

Some attorneys turn over much of their work to junior associates or paralegal assistants. This can save the client money, but only if assistant services are billed separately from the lawyer's rate and if their work is well-supervised.

Will you keep me notified about the progress of my case?

A lawyer should keep you up-to-date on what is happening with your case, especially if there is a chance the initial estimated fee will increase. You also may want to know whether the lawyer will be easily accessible to you by phone and if calls will be returned.

How long should it take you to complete my case and what, roughly, is it going to cost me?

A lawyer should be willing to openly discuss a time schedule and fees. Get the estimated hours of work and fees in writing.

If something goes wrong between us, will you consent to binding arbitration?

Most state bar associations have arbitration committees that, for a certain charge, will settle disputes that you may have with your lawyer about fees. By agreeing to binding arbitration, both attorney and client agree to present their cases to an outside panel and to abide by its decision in the dispute. Ask whether consumer representatives serve on the arbitration panels and whether the panels will consider disputes other than those over fees. In addition to bar associations, some consumer agencies also offer arbitration services.

Negotiating Fees

Most fees are agreed upon through discussions between client and lawyer. If you cannot afford what the lawyer asks, say so. Fees are negotiable. Shop around until you find a lawyer who is willing to work within your budget. If necessary, you may want to discuss working out a payment plan if you do not think you can afford a lump fee. Here are some questions to ask about fees:

What services do you provide for a flat fee?

Often, you will be able to pay a set fee for straightforward tasks such as composing a deed or will or conducting a title search.

What are your hourly rates?

Depending upon the experience and reputation of the lawyer, you could pay a lawyer from $20 to $300 per hour. If your case is not a fairly simple one for which you can negotiate a single flat fee, the hourly rate you agree to pay the lawyer should be understood at the outset. It is very common for lawyers to charge by the tenth or quarter-hour. This practice can save the client money particularly if your case involves many phone calls. For example, if your lawyer charges by the quarter-hour and you are on the phone for only five minutes, you still will have to pay for a full quarter-hour of the lawyer's time. Since smaller increments may add up to less total cost, clients working with lawyers who work on hourly rates should ask about tenths and quarter-hour charges. Ask your lawyer to put a top limit on the fee you will be charged. Keep a record of the telephone calls you make to your lawyer including the date, time, and length of the call.

Do you require a retainer for your services?

A retainer is similar to a down payment for services to be performed. Be certain you know exactly what services are and are not covered by the retainer. Ask that the retainer be applied to the balance owed. And, you may want to ask the lawyer to agree ahead of time to a refund if the retainer seems to have exceeded the cost of time actually spent on the case.

Do you accept contingency fee arrangements?

If you are under financial pressure or cannot raise enough money to hire a lawyer on an hourly basis, you may want to request a contingency fee arrangement. Under this arrangement, the lawyer collects a percentage of any amount of money you win as a result of the case being decided in your favor. If you do not win the case, the lawyer does not receive a fee. Since you may have to pay court costs, which are different from lawyers' fees, be wary of statements that there will be "no charge" if you do not win.

Ask whether the lawyer computes the contingency fee before or after the expenses for handling the case are disbursed. You may collect more money if expenses, such as court costs or witness fees, are deducted before the contingency fee is computed.

The customary contingency fee is 33% of the settlement or award, although fees range from 25% to 50%. Some lawyers offer a sliding scale in which the percentage changes depending on one or both of these factors: how long it takes to settle the case; and/or how much the award is.

If the sliding scale is based on how long it takes to settle, for example, the lawyer may collect 25% if you settle before trial, 30% if there is a trial, and 40% if there is an appeal. Or, the sliding fee scale may be based on the size of the amount, with the lawyer generally receiving a lower percentage as the amount increases. You should discuss the sliding fee option with your lawyer to negotiate the best price.

Get It In Writing

The best way to protect yourself and avoid misunderstandings is to have the agreement you make with your lawyer put into writing and signed by both parties. A request to put your agreement in writing should be made at the first meeting between you and your lawyer--before your lawyer begins any work on your case. You may want to ask:

Will you put this agreement in writing?

Many lawyers have simple one-page contracts for this purpose, but usually such contracts do not address the client's specific concerns. Ask that all fee arrangements and agreed-upon services be included in your contract. In addition, include in your contract a provision for settling any unforeseen disputes (such as fee disagreements or delays in handling your case) between you and your lawyer. If the lawyer will not put this information in writing, you may want to consider looking for another lawyer.

Will you provide a written estimate of all costs--including expenses--before you begin work on the case?

Among the most important documents required in all dealings is the written estimate. The lawyer should provide one that includes an estimate not only of the fees,

but also of filing and court costs, letters, copying, time on the phone, and other expenses that may be connected with your case.

Will you itemize your bills?

Ask that all billings be itemized and sent to you on a regular basis. If you wish, you may include limitations or a ceiling on costs that cannot be exceeded without your written permission.

For Complaints
About Lawyers

If you are dissatisfied with the services provided by a lawyer you have hired for help in personal, legal, or money matters, it is up to you to make your grievance known. If you have kept copies of important agreements between you and your lawyer, you should have no problem documenting your complaint.

First, discuss the complaint with your lawyer. Many misunderstandings can be resolved at this level. If you still are not satisfied, contact the supervisor or senior partner, if there is one, in the firm. If your grievance cannot be resolved at one of these levels, go to the professional organization or licensing authority that oversees that profession.

All lawyers must be licensed by the state before they can practice in a court of law. Most city, state, and county bar associations have grievance committees to deal with complaints about their members. If you are unable to locate a local bar association, or have questions that deserve the attention of the national bar, contact the American Bar Association at its national headquarters, 750 North Lake Shore Drive, Chicago, IL 60611; (312) 988-5158.

If your complaint is about fees, most state bar associations have arbitration committees to handle this type of problem. If the bar association cannot deal with your problem, your local consumer protection agency may be able to assist you. You also may want to ask the bar association for the name of the special agency or office set up by the state's highest court to deal with client complaints.

Old Lawyer Jokes

A lawyer charged a man $500 for legal services. The man paid him with crisp new $100 bills. After the client left, the lawyer discovered that two bills had stuck together--he'd been overpaid by $100. The ethical dilemma for the lawyer--should he tell his partner?

There is an interesting new novel about two ex-convicts. One of them studies to become a lawyer, and the other one decides to go straight.

The first thing we do, let's kill all the lawyers. Henry IV, Shakespeare, 1600 A.D

As the lawyer slowly came out of anesthetic, he said, "Why are all of the blinds drawn, doctor?" "There's a fire across the street. We didn't want you to think the operation was a failure."

A Brooklyn lawyer, a used car salesman, and a banker were gathered by the coffin containing the body of an old friend. In his grief, one of the three said, "In my family, we have a custom of giving the dead some money, so they'll have something to spend over there." They all agreed that this was appropriate. The banker dropped a $100 bill into the casket, and the car salesman did the same. The lawyer took out the bills and wrote a check for $300.

Two probate lawyers were overheard while discussing a current case: "It's such a splendid estate. What a shame to squander it on the beneficiaries."

Why have scientists begun to use lawyers instead of lab rats for research? Two reasons: First, they are more plentiful than rats, and second, the researchers don't get as attached to them. One problem, though, is that no one has been able to extrapolate the test results to human beings.

Many believe when you get old you need a guardian

Consider what can happen if a sudden illness or accident left you incapacitated--that is, with a medical condition that made it impossible for you to communicate your wishes. Who would make decisions on your behalf? Some people even think just because some older people are eccentric, they are incompetent to manage their affairs. In 33 of our states, an older person can be determined incompetent just due to "advanced age."

Many older Americans with Alzheimer's disease or other mental illnesses may become incapable of handling their own affairs. If this happens to you, doctors may ask the spouse to make minor medical decisions but not life-or-death ones either concerning surgery or terminating life-support systems. It also is unlikely that a financial institution will allow transactions by your relatives in your accounts. Unless you plan in advance and arrange for legal alternatives you may become a ward of a court-ordered guardian where someone else manages your affairs. More than one-half million Americans now get the kind of help they need through court-appointed guardians. Their average age is 80. More than half live in nursing homes.

Guardianship

Adults who have become incapacitated due to severe physical or mental illness often need help from relatives or friends. They may require assistance preparing meals, finding a place to live, getting medical help, paying bills, depositing checks, and managing finances. In order for people to accomplish many of these tasks they require legal authority.

Guardianship (also known as "conservatorship" or "curatorship") is a legal mechanism by which the court declares a person incompetent and appoints a guardian. As a ward of a guardian, people may lose the right to choose where they will live, to drive, to enter into contracts, to marry or divorce, to vote, and even the right to refuse medical treatment. As a ward, the older person is deprived of autonomy and self-determination. The appointed guardian has the broad powers to use the ward's assets on his or her behalf, may not always be the person whom the older person wanted, and may be a total stranger with different values and beliefs.

Guardianship is a very serious matter and should not be taken lightly as the legal rights of a person being supervised can be severely curtailed.

Courts usually look to the spouse, adult child, parent, brother or sister, and then other persons, in that order, as the guardian. The court transfers the responsibility for managing financial affairs, living arrangements, and medical care decisions to the guardian. The guardian is responsible to the court and must account for all transactions made on behalf of the person. Once appointed, the guardian must file periodic reports with the court.

Guardianship laws vary from state to state. In some states, guardianship or conservatorship may go beyond decisions about finances and property to such personal decisions as where the person will live and who will provide any necessary care. In some cases, courts may appoint one person as "guardian of the person" who manages health and personal needs and another "guardian of the estate" who handles money matters.

Guardianship Abuse--Because guardians receive broad authority, there is potential for abuse. Guardians have stolen money or lost it through mismanagement and some have physically abused those they promised to protect. Guardians misusing their powers include relatives, friends, lawyers, and people hired by the courts.

Terminating Guardianship--Once guardianship is set up, it's difficult to end. Critics say judges rarely review a case to see whether guardianship is still appropriate. Even when guardians argue for ending the arrangement, judges are often reluctant to reverse their decisions. But for wards, terminating guardianship can be almost impossible, particularly if their guardian does not agree. In addition, although laws were enacted to provide safeguards to the person who needs help, the conservatorship system is not without flaws.

ALTERNATIVES

Often people who are put under guardianship could manage on their own with a little outside help. There are two legal means that can provide help and not strip a person of most of their rights. These include:
* Power of Attorney
* Durable Power of Attorney

Power of Attorney

This is a legal device that permits one individual (usually a spouse, other relative, or trusted friend) known as the "principal" to give to another person called the "attorney-in-fact" the authority to act on his or her behalf. The person does not have to be an attorney--anyone can act in this capacity. You should have complete trust in the person you select.

The "attorney-in-fact" is authorized to handle banking and real estate, incur expenses, pay bills, and handle a wide variety of legal affairs for a specified period of time. The power of attorney can continue indefinitely during the lifetime of the principal so long as that person is competent and capable of granting power of attorney.

If the principal becomes comatose or mentally incompetent, the Power of Attorney automatically expires just as it would if the principal dies. Therefore, this Power of Attorney may expire just when it is most needed.

Preprinted power of attorney forms can be obtained at stationery stores. You can limit the authorization to certain transactions and if so make sure the document you sign states the limitations clearly. It's best to notarize and record it with the county recorder. A revocation must also be notarized and recorded.

The advances in medical technology that have done so much to produce miraculous cures and recovery from devastating trauma have created a problem. Medicine steadily extends to the elderly the use of drugs, surgery, rehabilitation, and other procedures once thought suitable only for younger patients. Ever-more-aggressive technology means are used to extend the life of the elderly. On the whole, the elderly welcome that development--even as they fear some of its consequences. They want, somehow, that most elusive of all goals: a steadily improving medical technology that will relieve their pain and illness while not leading to overtreatment and to a harmful extension of life. It has become possible to keep people in a vegetative state for almost unlimited periods of time. Moreover, there are sometimes situations in which neither the patient nor the family has the ability to bring such unhappy circumstances to an end.

The vast majority of people would like to avoid such scenarios for themselves and for their loved ones. There are some remedies, but none of them are fool-proof. The problem generally arises when heroic measures have been applied in an emergency situation, placing the patient on life-support systems. Once those systems are in place, it is sometimes very difficult to remove them.

THE FAMILY. When this choice is delegated to the family to make the decision of whether or not to terminate life support, it leaves them in a situation that is very difficult. They have the understandable grief that comes with a critical illness. For them it is like choosing between life and death, even though they are assured that the patient cannot recover, and for all practical purposes, is dead. It is especially hard if the patient has not expressed his/her point of view about such a situation in the past. The advance of technology has made it extremely important that everyone consider this question and make clear their preference.

THE PROFESSION. Dealing with death and suffering on a daily basis does not make it easy for medical people to make decisions about removing life support. They make an effort to be as dispassionate as possible about such situations so that families can make informed decisions. Added to the moral, ethical, and humane considerations,

they also must keep the legal risks in mind. No group is more subject to the risks of litigation than the medical profession and institutions. The medical professional does not want to be accused of pressuring the family for the removal of life support, or to be second-guessed by other medical personnel in a court of law.

The result is that the profession tends to err on the conservative side. That means they tend to resist family efforts to terminate life support unless clear evidence exists that this was the wish of the patient when he/she was in good health. Probably the worst cases are those where the patient has no problems with breathing or heart function, but must be fed through tubes. Thus, the alternative becomes feeding or starving the patient. Even though the patient may be brain-dead, such a decision is very difficult to make.

Right to Refuse Medical Treatment

Under the law--effective November 1991-- patients must receive written information explaining their right to refuse medical treatment. For example, a person checking into a hospital would be told about "advance directives" according to state laws.

Advance Directives--States recognize various forms of "advance directives" that individuals can use to convey their wishes about life support if they become terminally ill or incompetent. These include:

1 Durable Power of Attorney
2 Medical Durable Power of Attorney
3 Healthcare Proxy
4 Living Wills

The law applies to all healthcare providers including: hospitals, hospices, nursing homes, health maintenance organizations, and other healthcare facilities that receive money from Medicare and Medicaid programs. The bill also requires healthcare providers to ensure that living wills are "implemented to the maximum extent permissible under state law." Hospitals and other providers must note on medical records whether patients have legal advance directives on treatment. Providers must have procedures to ensure that they comply with a patient's wishes in

accordance with state law. The law also requires the Department of Health and Human Services to conduct a nationwide campaign to educate people about their legal right to refuse medical treatment.

At present, the law does not require that a patient sign a living will or to name someone whom he/she wishes to act as "surrogate," only that an opportunity to do so be provided. If you are sick or injured, going through the complicated maze of papers required by a nursing home or hospital admissions process, **you might sign such a document without realizing it.** You need to understand that living wills and other advance directives are intended primarily to limit, rather than to request, medical treatment.

Durable Power of Attorney

Because power of attorney is limited by competency of the principal, some states have authorized a special legal device for the principal to express intent concerning the durability of the power of attorney to survive disability or incompetency. A durable power of attorney document contains the words "This power of attorney shall not be affected by subsequent incapacity of the principal" or similar language.

> ## Durable Power of Attorney gives another person the right to make healthcare decisions for you when you are unable to do so.

This legal device is an important alternative to guardianship, conservatorship, or trusteeship. The laws vary from state to state, and since this puts a considerable amount of power in the hands of the attorney-infact, it should be drawn up by an attorney licensed to practice in the state of the client. This device is to compensate for the period of time when an individual becomes incompetent to manage his own affairs appropriately.

Legal means designed to limit heroic life support

Medical Durable Power of Attorney

In some states this is a new use of the durable power of attorney, in which your older relative designates you (or another responsible person) to make medical care decisions. The "durable power of attorney for healthcare decision making" laws allow an individual to appoint someone to make medical decisions, if the individual becomes unable to express wishes and exercise rights on his or her behalf. The medical power can be used even if a person is not terminally ill, but is unable to make his or her own decisions for some other reason. It can be used to avoid unwanted care and to make sure that desired life-sustaining treatment is provided.

Durable powers of attorney are not usually restricted to terminal conditions. You should therefore discuss your convictions regarding all medical treatment, not just terminal care. Decisions about terminal care should reflect your attitude on any medical intervention that in your view cannot acceptably prolong your life but actually prolongs your dying. You should ensure as fully as possible that your agent understands and agrees with your views. Issues one may want to address more specifically include:

- ❏ cardiopulmonary resuscitation
- ❏ mechanical breathing
- ❏ artificial feeding through nasal tubes
- ❏ major elective surgery
- ❏ kidney dialysis
- ❏ chemotherapy
- ❏ invasive diagnostic tests
- ❏ blood transfusions
- ❏ pain medications even if the unintended result would be to hasten death
- ❏ cremation versus burial

Durable power of attorney documents are more flexible than a living will and can be applied to more situations.

Healthcare Proxy

It is another way to designate someone else to act in your stead if you become incompetent. As part of their living will laws, nine states specifically authorize the appointment of a healthcare proxy: Arkansas, Delaware, Florida, Idaho, Louisiana, Texas, Utah, Virginia, and Wyoming.

Living Wills

A living will is a legal document where you put into writing what your preferences are about terminal illness and the use of life-sustaining technology. It is a directive instructing a physician to withhold or discontinue medical treatment from you if you are terminally ill and unable to make decisions. In some states, such a document is called a "directive to physicians." It is a form that allows you to protect yourself by describing the kinds of treatment you don't want and adding any personal instructions. A living will should be a clear expression of your desires, but you should be aware it still needs interpretation.

Terminology in state laws varies but most contain key phrases, each open to broad interpretations. CAUTION: There are no standards for living wills and they can vary from state to state. An example of a living will is shown below.

Such documents must be renewed after a period that is designated by state laws. In general, they should be witnessed by people who know you and notarized to ensure their acceptance. The document can always be revoked.

Having completed such a document, your work is not finished. In the case of the durable power of attorney you appoint an agent, usually your spouse, to make the decisions when you are unable to make them. Your agent must be aware of your wishes and have access to the document. Let everyone know about your decision-- spouse, children, doctor, friends. When a person enters a hospital, a copy should be provided for the patient's chart and personnel informed about your wishes. It simply isn't enough to sign a living will. You have to go out of your way to be sure it's honored.

In spite of everything, your wishes may not be carried out. For example, in an emergency room or on a hospital ward, when a medical emergency occurs, personnel are trained to react quickly and decisively to save the person's life. Thus, heroic measures may be used when you have directed that they not be, and once support systems are in place, they may be difficult to remove.

DIRECTIVE TO PHYSICIANS

Directive made this __th day of ____, 199_.

I,_____, being of sound mind, willfully and voluntarily make known my desire that my life shall not be artificially prolonged pursuant to the following:

1. If the time comes when I can no longer take part in decisions for my own future, this statement and declaration shall stand as the expression of my wishes. I recognize that death is as much a reality as birth, growth, maturity, and old age--it is but a phase in the cycle of life and is the only certainty. I do not fear death as much as I fear the indignity of deterioration, dependence, and hopeless pain. If there is no reasonable expectation of my recovery from physical or mental disability, I wish to be allowed to die and not be kept alive by artificial means or heroic measures, but wish only that drugs be mercifully administered to me for terminal suffering, even if they hasten the moment of my death.

2. I recognize that my wishes place a heavy burden of responsibility upon you, and I therefore make the following declaration with the intention of sharing this responsibility and the decision with you and of mitigating any feelings of guilt that you may have:

DECLARATION

3. If at any time I should have an incurable injury, disease, or illness certified to be a terminal condition by my physician, and where the application of life-sustaining procedures would serve only to artificially prolong the moment of my death and where any physician determines that my death is imminent whether or not life-sustaining procedures are utilized, I direct that such procedures be withheld or withdrawn, and that I be permitted to die naturally.

4. In the absence of my ability to give directions regarding the use of such life-sustaining procedures, it is my intention that this directive shall be honored by my family and physician as the final expression of my legal right to refuse medical or surgical treatment and accept the consequences from such refusal.

5. I have been diagnosed and notified at least 14 days ago as having a terminal condition by Dr. _____, whose address is _____.

6. I understand the full import of this directive and I am emotionally and mentally competent to make this direction.

The arguments against a living will

Traditionally, in the United States, patients received maximum life support without question. Any decision to discontinue this support has been reached by the patient's family or guardian after careful consultation with the patient's physician, acting in the role of consultant to the family and as the patient's chief advocate. Hospitals in general have benefitted financially from the utilization of highly sophisticated life-support technology in the institution's special care units. The hard financial incentives to the physician and hospital were structured in favor of prolonging life in questionable situations. This arrangement no doubt tended to err in favor of life.

Right-to-die (euthanasia) advocates believe that life reaches a point at which it no longer has meaning and that extra-ordinary life-sustaining methods should not be used.

The basic argument against the right-to-die concept is that human existence can never be intrinsically meaningless. Life retains meaning up until the last breath is drawn, and a physician is never entitled to deprive an incurably ill patient of the chance to "die his death." Studies have shown that most older people who have been hospitalized in intensive care units would be willing to undergo the life-sustaining treatment again, even if it would add only one more month to their lives. As one older person remarked, "Toward the end of life, even one month is very meaningful."

Before you write a living will, think carefully about limiting heroic measures to save your life as all living wills have limitations that you should understand. Anti-euthanasia people claim even the name is misleading: Living wills have little to do with living and a lot to do with dying. They claim they are not living wills at all but "death contracts." Some arguments to consider against writing a living will include:

■ **Living wills are written in general language since no one can anticipate all possible circumstances.** This can lead to problems of interpretation. For example, your living will might prohibit "heroic procedures," but does not tell your doctor that you would refuse a respirator while accepting blood transfusions, or vice versa. As new technology develops and yesterday's heroic treatments become routine, the problem is even more complicated.

■ The living will concept assumes that the patient or one that represents them understands the effectiveness and probabilities of success or failure of heroic life-sustaining measures.

■ Medical need, in the context of constant technological innovation, is inherently elastic and open-ended: as a guide to what is actually good for the patient or what physicians are obliged to give them, is a judgement call.

■ The prognosis of terminal illness is always difficult to achieve. This difficulty is part of the problem. In all too many cases, technology is used because it is not known that a patient is dying or in irreversible decline.

The problem is even greater, a recent Office of Technology Assessment (OTA) study concluded, when immediate decisions must be made about initiating treatment. Only for patients who have been fully diagnosed can estimates of survival probability be made. Even then, the probabilities are likely to be insufficient for guiding decision making about withholding or withdrawing treatment for an individual patient.

■ Some proponents of living wills maintain that these documents are necessary for cost and/or population control, and should be mandatory for certain groups including older people. For example, states like Oregon have legislated a "health rationing system" that eliminate procedures that are deemed too costly, ineffective, or rare. Some say the "need" to get rid of the aged has economic roots as the growing population is widely regarded as a threat to the nation's budget.

In America, a number of "logical" proposals have already been made for rationing systems based on age. For instance, in Britain, anyone over age 55 may be denied kidney dialysis. In other words, the older one is, the less he's worth to social policy planners. Obviously, according to many, the older one is, the less effort should be expended toward life support.

Some gerontologists contend there is a growing tendency in medical circles for age-based healthcare rationing. "Death with dignity" may in some cases be a euphemism for extermination.

Studies show that emergency room personnel tend to spend less time and effort to resuscitate elderly heart-attack victims than their younger counterparts.

■ If a physician is employed by an HMO (Health Maintenance Organization), or is a contractor to provide health, his or her own financial reimbursement and even professional position may be directly or indirectly dependent on the financial health of the organization--organizational well-being that potentially will be threatened by the high cost of prolonged sophisticated life-support technology.

Those in the anti-euthanasia movement are not suggesting that we as a society must use heroic, unnecessary, useless, or unduly burdensome measures to prolong life. They are opposed to a healthcare policy based on fiscal restraints rather than the needs of patients and the professional expertise of their physicians and a policy that requires healthcare providers to ensure that living wills are "implemented to the maximum extent permissible under state law." They are opposed to an attitude that sick or hopelessly ill people ought to sacrifice their lives by refusing medical treatment and care in order to make life easier for families or for America's future generations and to help balance the budget.

For more information, call or write to:
International Anti-Euthanasia Task Force (IAETF)
A division of the Human Life Center
University of Steubenville
Steubenville, OH 43952
(612) 542-3120 or (614) 282-9953

Estate planning and probate avoidance for older peopl

A significant number of the things we do today are determined by their tax consequences. Dying is no exception. We have all heard the warnings of attorneys and accountants to have a will prepared and properly witnessed in order to simplify the lives of our loved ones following our death. Not only that, but we are told that if we die without a will (intestate), we throw our families upon the mercy and lassitude of the courts to distribute our estate and see to the welfare of our loved ones.

Estate planning is the process of arranging for your property to go to your family, friends, and organizations, instead of being used to pay probate fees and inheritance taxes. Because your assets and wishes change as you grow older, estate planning isn't something you do once in your life and then forget it; it must be an ongoing process.

When you're young and healthy, all you may need is a simple will and perhaps a life insurance policy. It's probably not worth the trouble to worry about avoiding probate or federal death taxes.

When you are in your fifties or sixties, your concerns begin to change. You probably have more property and want to ensure that the people who inherit it don't have to pay large probate fees or taxes. It's worth spending some time choosing and implementing a sound estate plan that will keep these costs as low as possible. Here are some strategies you may want to pursue.

A Will

No matter what other estate planning methods you use, you'll probably want a will, too. In a will, you can name a "residuary" beneficiary--someone to receive all property that you don't want to make other arrangements for. So if you acquire property shortly before your death, and don't get it transferred to your living trust or other probate-avoidance device, your residuary beneficiary will get it.

You also need to use a will to name an executor--someone to wind up your affairs after your death. And if you want to disinherit a child, who might otherwise be entitled by law to a share of your estate, you must use a will.

Everyone who has any resources at all needs a will. Even if all of your possessions are in joint tenancy with right of survivorship, some institutions will ask for a will when a death occurs. Many lawyers will prepare a simple will for around $100, perhaps in hope that the low price may bring you back to them for other business.

Another way of having a simple will prepared is to join a legal services group that provides consultation and simple procedures for a monthly payment. Most of them include a simple will as one of the free services they provide without additional cost over the monthly payment.

Still another way of writing a will is to purchase a form that is appropriate for your state. Will kits are sold with complete instructions on how to prepare them and appropriate procedures for having them witnessed. Attorneys warn about such documents, but it is hard to tell where their professional opinion may conflict with their interest in having your business. Certainly wills prepared by attorneys are not immune from challenge in the courts. Still another source of assistance is in some of the computer programs that are now available through software companies. Attorneys would again warn you about the lack of individualization in such a method. However, many legal firms are using such programs themselves and they are written in such a way that personal data are requested so that

the will prepared by the software reflects those particular things about the person for whom the will is being written.

For those with access to a computer, Nolo Press offers a software program called *WillMaker*. It makes the job easy, leading you step-by-step in a question and answer format. Once you've gone through the program, you print out the will and sign it in front of witnesses. It comes with a manual providing an overview of probate avoidance and tax planning techniques. It is good in all states but Louisiana. The address of Nolo Press is listed on page 114.

Pay-on-Death Accounts

Pay-on-death accounts are a simple and convenient way to arrange for money you have in bank accounts (and some government securities) to go to someone without probate.

Let's say you want the money in your savings account to go to your son Rob upon your death. All you need to do is put the account in your name, with a notation that you own the account "as trustee for the benefit of Rob Stewart."

Rob won't have any rights to the money in the account while you're alive. But when you die, he will automatically own whatever funds are in the account. No probate will be necessary; the bank will turn over the funds

PROBATE
WHY YOU WANT TO AVOID IT

Probate is a legal process of having a probate court oversee the distribution of deceased person's property and the payment of his debts.

Probate is time-consuming, typically lasting 9 to 18 months. It can also be very expensive. Lawyers' fees can eat up a big chunk of the property you leave, which of course means there's less left for the family members, friends, or organizations you wanted to receive it.

to him when presented with a copy of your death certificate and proper identification.

Pay-on-death accounts are also known as informal bank account trusts, Totten trusts, and bank trust accounts.

Retirement Accounts

Retirement accounts such as IRA's, Keoghs, and 401k plans were not intended to be probate-avoidance devices, but they are routinely used that way.

All you need to do is name a beneficiary to receive any funds still in the account at your death. The beneficiary will get the funds without probate. The only restriction is that to avoid penalties, after age 70 you must withdraw a certain amount from the account every year. The amount is refigured every year, based on your life expectancy.

Gifts

You can save on federal estate tax by reducing the value of your estate if you give away property while you are alive. Estates worth more than $600,000 are subject to estate tax. However, property left to a surviving spouse, charity, or to pay medical bills or tuition is not counted.

As long as you keep your gifts less than $10,000 per recipient per year, you will not be assessed federal gift tax. Even if the gift you make is taxable, the gift tax won't become due until your death, and then only if the amounts you gave away and leave at death total more than $600,000.

Gifts of life insurance on your own life are a particularly good way to transfer a chunky asset but pay a skinny tax. The gift tax is assessed on the cash value of the policy when you give it away, not on the much greater proceeds it eventually pays. To get the estate tax savings, however, you must give the policy away at least three years before your death and scrupulously follow other IRS rules on gifts of insurance policies.

> **He's a Fool that makes his doctor his heir.**
> Franklin (1706-1790)

Joint Tenancy

Joint tenancy is an overrated but sometimes useful probate-avoiding device. It is a way for two or more people to own property together. For estate planning, its most important feature is survivorship: When one joint owner dies, the surviving owners automatically inherit the property. No probate is necessary.

Joint tenancy can work well as a probate-avoidance method for property you acquire with someone else or if you transfer property you already co-own (or are buying) with someone into joint tenancy.

But making someone else a joint tenant of property you own alone, just to avoid probate, is often a bad idea. The new owner could sell his or her half-interest, or the new owner's creditors could go after it. And you may be in trouble if you change your mind and decide you want the property to go to someone else at your death. You've given up your rights to the half-interest the new owner owns.

For people in their seventies or eighties, there is another big disadvantage of adding someone as a joint tenant: The new owner misses out on the potentially huge income tax break.

If you leave property to someone at your death, the property gets a "stepped-up" tax basis. The basis is the amount from which taxable profit is figured if the new owner ever sells the property. Here's the formula: selling price - basis = taxable profit.

When property is transferred at death, the basis goes up to the value of the property at your death. This is good because the higher the tax basis, the lower the taxable profit when the property is sold.

But if you give away property while you're alive, by making someone a joint owner of your property, the tax basis of that half of the property isn't "stepped up" at your death-- it stays what it was when you acquired the property. This means that if the property goes up substantially in value before your death, the owner will owe a big tax when it is eventually sold.

An example shows the difference it can make to wait until death to transfer the property.

Example: The tax basis in Ellen's house is $120,000, the amount she paid for it years ago. She puts her house into joint tenancy with her daughter, which means her daughter already owns half the house before Ellen dies. When Ellen dies, the house is worth $200,000. But only the half that is transferred at death gets a stepped-up tax basis from $60,000 to $100,000. So the new basis is $160,000. If the daughter sells the house later for $230,000, she will owe tax on $70,000.

With a living trust, you can keep control over your property while you are alive, but ensure that it won't have to go through probate upon your death.

If, however, Ellen transfers the house to her daughter at death, her daughter's tax basis will increase to $200,000, its value at Ellen's death. If she sells the house later for $230,000, her taxable profit will be only $30,000.

A Revocable Living Trust

A revocable living trust is a valuable estate planning tool for many older people. With a living trust, you can keep control over your property while you are alive, but ensure that it won't have to go through probate at your death.

You can create a living trust simply by preparing and signing a piece of paper. Once the trust is created, it has the legal capacity to own property, and you can transfer property to it. The person actually in charge of the property owned by the trust is called a trustee.

More on estate planning and probate avoidance

When you create a living trust, normally you make yourself the trustee, so you don't give up any control over the trust property. When you die, the person you've named in the trust to take over as trustee (called the successor trustee) distributes your property to the people you want to get it. It's fine (and common) to name the person who will receive the bulk of your property as the successor trustee.

Successor trustees are designated in the trust documents (such as a son or a daughter), and carry out trust provisions after the death of the survivor spouse, or earlier, if the survivor wishes. Powers of attorney are executed as a part of the trust documents so that this process can be expedited at a time when it may be impossible for an elderly person to hand over such responsibility on his or her own. Again, the trustee is able to act promptly and efficiently after the death of the survivor spouse to distribute the property in accordance with the terms of the trust. Best of all, none of this needs to be taken to a probate court, with all of its attendant costs and delays.

Even when a trust is set up, wills are prepared so that any property left out of the trust for any reason can quickly be transferred into the trust. These documents are sometimes called "Pour-Over Wills." Special provisions may be placed in trusts concerning the distribution of estate property, order of inheritance, and provisions for setting up trusts for beneficiaries who are minors.

A living trust can be created without a lawyer, and can be updated any time. You are always free to change your mind about what property you want in the trust or who you want to get it at your death. But because it does require some paperwork to transfer property to the trust and conduct transactions in the trust's name, some people don't bother with a trust until they are older and more concerned with avoiding probate at their deaths.

For more on estate planning order the book <u>Plan Your Estate: Wills, Probate Avoidance, Trusts and Taxes</u> from Nolo Press.

Revocable Living Trust

Advantages:

1 Avoids probate. Basic probate fees in California run from $6,300 on an estate of $100,000 to $26,300 on $600,000. They can be much higher if there are problems and the average time required to complete the process is two years. Other states vary in costs of probate and court delays.

2 You retain greater control of your estate because changes are easy to make.

3 Property can be distributed immediately without all of the delays associated with probate such as advertising for creditors.

4 Trusts are rarely challenged in court, and are rarely overturned. Wills are often challenged in court and it is not unusual to have challenges upheld. Part of the reason that trusts are difficult to challenge is that by the time someone gets around to it, the property is already distributed to the heirs.

5 The details of your estate remain private because there is no public disclosure.

Disadvantages

1 It is more costly to set up a trust. Costs can vary from about $600 to several thousand. The average is probably close to $1,000. The document can run to many pages.

2 Not every attorney is able to draw up a trust. Very few are expert at the process. One needs a good referral for this purpose. There are estate planning firms that provide the service under the supervision of an attorney. You need to know something of the reputation of the firm before signing an agreement. You need to remember that one of the most lucrative activities of attorneys is in handling probate. Even their minimum fees are set by law.

3 All titled property needs to have changes of title filed with the appropriate company or government agency. The most difficult case is to change the title of real property. Property is listed as "Doe Family Trust." With the exception of real property, there are no particular costs to this process, but it takes time and trouble.

Other Trusts

All kinds of trusts have been developed to save on taxes and let you put various kinds of restrictions on the use of property you leave. Usually, preparing one of these trusts requires the help of an experienced attorney.

Marital A-B Trusts

This kind of trust is common for married people who have children from prior marriages. It provides that when one spouse dies, the survivor gets the use of the deceased spouse's real estate, or the income from other kinds of property, for the rest of his or her life. But when the second spouse dies, the trust property goes to the first spouse's children. This way, the surviving spouse is financially comfortable, but the spouse's children end up inheriting their parent's property.

By leaving property to children instead of the surviving spouse, an A-B trust also offers estate tax savings if a couple has a combined estate worth more than $600,000. If one spouse left all his property to the other without this kind of trust, when the second spouse dies she would have an estate worth more than $600,000, which means it would be subject to the hefty federal estate tax.

Trusts for Incapacitated People

If you want to leave property to someone who is (or may become) incapacitated or has a serious problem such as alcoholism, you need a trust tailored to your situation. It's especially important to structure the trust so that the money available to the beneficiary doesn't jeopardize his or her ability to receive any government benefits that might otherwise be available.

Generation-skipping Trusts

These trusts are for extremely wealthy people who want to pass money to their children and grandchildren and ensure savings on their children's estate taxes. A trust can exempt up to $1 million from estate tax liability.

Portions of this article were written by Mary Randolph. Reprinted with permission from the Spring 1990 issue of <u>Nolo Press</u>, a quarterly self-help legal newspaper published by Nolo Press, 950 Parker Street, Berkeley, CA 94710; (415)549-1976.

Organizing your most important papers

Relatives and friends sometimes must help older people manage their legal, medical, or financial affairs temporarily or even gradually assume these responsibilities. Often the person who provides care has little knowledge of vital information and records. One thing each of us can do for the future is to get our personal, medical, and financial records in order. Afterward, you should then make a trusted friend or relative aware of the location of the records.

These records can be useful and are needed on numerous occasions including: medical, legal, financial, or tax consultations; budgeting income; making investments; dealing with insurance claims; retirement and estate planning; and discharge of your wishes in terms of medical care or burial instructions. If papers are in order, the task is much simpler for all concerned. Although each situation is different, the following suggestions can help most people begin creating this file.

Your filing system doesn't have to be elaborate, but it should be organized. Setting up a record-keeping system is easily done. Office supply stores have a variety of folders and envelopes available that help separate papers into categories. Many people have found colored folders to be helpful. Expandable file folders that hold all your papers in one place can be very useful, especially when you want to take your records with you to a lawyer. Following is a suggested list of record files you might need:

PERSONAL RECORDS
- ☐ legal name and spouse's
- ☐ Social Security number and spouse's
- ☐ legal residence
- ☐ date and place of birth
- ☐ location of **birth certificates, marriage certificate, divorce decrees, naturalization and adoption papers**
- ☐ names and addresses of spouse and children (or location of **death certificates** if any are deceased)
- ☐ **education and military records**
- ☐ list of employers and dates of employment
- ☐ religious affiliation, addresses of church, synagogue, clergy
- ☐ membership in organizations and awards received
- ☐ names and addresses of close friends, relatives, doctors, lawyers, or financial advisors
- ☐ location of **will or trusts** and spouse's (you don't need to disclose contents)
- ☐ **Durable power of attorney, living wills,** requests, preferences, or prearrangements for burial

MEDICAL RECORDS
- ☐ phone numbers--physicians, pharmacists, emergency services, and hospitals
- ☐ health charts for each family member
  - ☐ medical conditions (summary)
  - ☐ allergies
  - ☐ past illnesses (dates)
  - ☐ operations
  - ☐ physicians consulted, reasons, phone numbers, addresses
  - ☐ immunization history
- ☐ Medicare and Medicaid information
- ☐ Medicare EOMB's (explanation of Medicare benefits)

FINANCIAL RECORDS
- ☐ **real estate deeds, mortgages, titles, notes**
- ☐ **Social Security earnings record** and information
- ☐ sources of income, pensions, interest, dividends, etc.
- ☐ investments (**certificates of deposit, stock certificates, bonds, notes, savings bonds**)

- ☐ **insurance policies** or location (life, accident, health, auto, and property), with policy numbers
- ☐ medical expense records
- ☐ bank accounts (checking, savings, credit unions) with **addresses and account numbers**
- ☐ location of safety deposit box and key
- ☐ a listing of the contents or documents in safety deposit box
- ☐ federal, state, and local income tax returns (last 6 years)
- ☐ property tax statements
- ☐ loans you owe and status
- ☐ **automotive title, registration, bills of sale**
- ☐ **business and partnership agreements**
- ☐ liabilities--what is owed, to whom, and when
- ☐ credit cards, charge accounts (**name and numbers**)
- ☐ **location of personal items such as jewelry or family treasures**
- ☐ **personal property inventory**

LONG-TERM CARE
An important consideration in financial planning is the cost of medical services and long-term-care, although there is often no easy or simple way to determine or meet these future needs. It is especially important to know what Medicare does and does not cover (see article on spousal asset protection, page 100).

LIFE-SUSTAINING DOCUMENTS
Caring for an older person or preparing for our own aging can be more successfully managed by making decisions and arrangements before a crisis develops. Three legal documents (power of attorney, durable power of attorney, or a living will) can be helpful in assuming responsibility for another person's affairs (see article on guardians, pages 108 through 111).

Safe-Deposit Boxes
Many people never think of using a safe-deposit box until they have a fire or burglary. Others rent the largest box available from their bank and pack it full of documents, memorabilia, keepsakes, and photographs.

Sizes
The most common size of safe-deposit box is approximately 3"x5"x 21-24". These boxes can often hold most of the documents a single person might accumulate, perhaps even the average couple's valuable papers. However, if you would like to store more than just documents, you might want to consider some of the larger-size boxes. There is often a 3"x10"x 21-24" size--handy if you have some precious, irreplaceable photographs, or larger documents that cannot be folded. The 5"x10"x 21-24"-size box will give you room to stash away prized stamp and coin collections, jewelry, and the like. The largest boxes you'll be likely to find at your bank will be 10"x10"x 21-24". These are often rented by individuals who have various collectibles they want to protect or who travel and do not want to leave valuables at home.

What Should You Keep?
Safe-deposit boxes are ideal for storing the documents **shown in dark lettering on this page.** You might consider keeping the originals of your will or living trust with your attorney, trustee, or executor.

Rules and Regulations
Boxes may be sole rentals, rentals held in joint tenancy, or rentals held by businesses. In the event that the sole renter of a box dies, most banks will hold the contents until deliverable to the properly authorized representative named in the will.

Nutrition guidelines for the second 50 years

The life span of the average American has increased dramatically. Unfortunately, knowledge of the nutritional needs as we age has not kept pace. Most experts agree that nutrition is a factor in the aging process. Age-related changes in body composition and metabolism require seniors to keep a sharp eye on their food choices. Too many seniors are undernourished as a result of:

❶ aging,
❷ eating processed and refined foods that often have lost their nutritional value,
❸ reduced metabolism,
❹ diminished appetite, and
❺ effects of medication.

Metabolic changes, along with decreased physical activity, require obtaining the same amount of nutrients from a lower caloric level. As one gets older the chances of suffering a chronic illness are greater, and health experts believe that poor eating habits contribute to some of those ailments.

WHAT AGING CHANGES HAVE NUTRITIONAL SIGNIFICANCE? First, older people produce less saliva and often have poor dentures. This causes difficulty with very dry foods. An estimated 30% of seniors lose their ability to make stomach acid, and this interferes with the absorption of some nutrients such as vitamin B12 and folic acid. Deficiencies in these nutrients, as well as vitamin B6, can cause neurological changes such as decline in alertness, loss of memory, and numbness of the extremities. The reduction of the natural movement of food and enzyme activity in the gastrointestinal tract, known to be associated with aging, often results in digestive difficulties in dealing with certain foods. Also, this reduction in the natural movement of food through the intestines causes food to remain in the intestines for a longer period of time, producing harder stools and resulting in constipation.

Aging affects certain senses, such as taste, smell, vision, and in turn affects the types of foods that will be chosen. Salty and sweet taste sensations can decline markedly with age, causing some to prefer foods that are richly seasoned. However, certain spicy foods produce gas. Many older persons complain of "heartburn," that often is not caused by increased acidity but by gas production. Others resort to extra salt in order to overcome their gradual loss of taste. Sodium and its role in water retention and high blood pressure may then become a problem.

Due to particular diseases, such as heart disease or osteoporosis, as we age we need less of some minerals (such as sodium to lower blood pressure) and more of others (such as calcium for bone mass). Bones tend to weaken with age; evidence suggests that seniors require at least 1500 milligrams of calcium a day.

Depression and loneliness can further contribute to a disinterest in eating. Many seniors do not have the economical means, knowledge, or willingness to ensure the most nutritious choices in food selection and meal preparation, the result being malnutrition and potential health problems.

Because of changes in the body and decreasing physical activity, older people usually need fewer calories as the rate at which the body uses energy tends to decrease. For some, food intake generally is lower, and the amount of lean body tissue decreases while the amount of body fat increases. Yet others maintain old eating habits not realizing that most people gain weight more easily as they age.

If you have an illness, follow your doctor's advice about your diet.

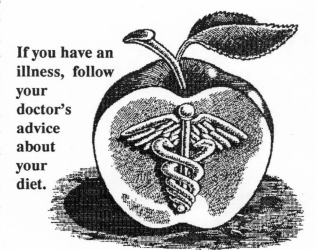

WHAT TO DO? Fortunately, there are nutritional guidelines for seniors that can be derived from conventional wisdom. They are as follows:

❑ Eat a variety of foods from five of the six major food groups (fruits; vegetables; breads and cereals; milk and cheeses; meat, poultry, fish, and dry beans) to obtain all the nutrients needed for good health.
❑ Avoid foods high in cholesterol.
❑ Limit total fat intake to less than 30% of your calories and keep intake of saturated fats to less than 10%.
❑ Increase your intake of dietary fiber (see article on fiber, page 125).
❑ Be selective of foods that cause gas problems (see article on gas, page 305).
❑ Prepare moister or softer foods, or smaller portions, if you have difficulty with dry foods.
❑ Limit the use of salt and sodium compounds.
❑ Increase your calcium intake, especially women (see article on calcium, page 123).
❑ Avoid too much sugar.
❑ Drink at least eight (8 ounce) glasses of water daily (see page 126).
❑ If you drink alcoholic beverages, do so in moderation (see page 332).
❑ Drugs interact adversely with certain nutrients. If in doubt, before you take them, find out.

The guidelines cannot guarantee health and well-being as health depends on many things, including heredity, lifestyle, personality traits, mental health and attitudes, and environment, in addition to one's meals. Food alone cannot make you healthy, but good eating habits based on moderation and variety can keep you healthy and even improve your health. Experts from Health Agencies agree that following these guidelines and eating well-balanced meals support:

✳ Adequate energy to carry out daily tasks.
✳ Good mental health and mental abilities.
✳ Resistance to disease.
✳ Recovery from illness, accident, or surgery.
✳ Medication effectiveness.
✳ Better management of chronic health problems to improve quality of life, mobility, and independence.

at a variety of foods from the food groups

NUTRIENTS--WHAT ARE THEY? A nutrient is a substance that promotes body growth or improvement or repairs the natural waste of the body. You need more than 40 different nutrients for good health. These include:

* energy sources (measured in calories)
  carbohydrates (starches, sugars)
  fats
  proteins
* vitamins
* minerals
* amino acids (from proteins)
* essential fatty acids (from fats and oils)
* water

CARBOHYDRATES include starches, sugars, and dietary fiber. Starches and sugar supply the body with energy. Dietary fiber provides bulk in the diet, which encourages regular elimination of wastes.

FATS provide energy and are carriers of fat-soluble vitamins. Fats also add flavor to foods. Some fats help form cell membranes and hormones.

PROTEINS are the building blocks of the body. They are needed for growth, maintenance, and replacement of body cells. They also form the hormones and enzymes used to regulate body processes. Any extra protein is used to supply energy or is changed into body fat (stored energy).

VITAMINS are organic substances needed by the body in small amounts. They do not supply energy, but they help release energy from carbohydrates, fats, and protein. They also help in other chemical reactions in the body.

MINERALS are also needed in relatively small amounts and do not supply energy. They are used to build strong bones and teeth, and to make hemoglobin in red blood cells. They help maintain body fluids and help in other chemical reactions in the body.

WATER is often called the "forgotten nutrient." It is needed to replace body water lost in urine and sweat. Water helps to transport nutrients, remove wastes, and regulate body temperature.

One way to assure variety and a well-balanced diet is to select daily servings of foods from the first five of the six food groups:

❶ Fruits
❷ Vegetables
❸ Breads and cereals
❹ Milk and cheeses
❺ Meat, poultry, fish, dry beans
❻ Fats, sweets, and alcohol

FRUITS AND VEGETABLES: provide vitamins, minerals, and dietary fiber; some provide starch or protein. Peels and edible seeds are especially rich in fiber. Deep-yellow vegetables are good sources of vitamin A. Dark-green vegetables are a source of vitamin A and C, riboflavin, folic acid, iron, calcium, magnesium, and potassium. Vitamin C is provided by melons, berries, tomatoes, and citrus fruits (oranges, grapefruit, tangerines, lemons). Certain greens--collards, kale, mustard, turnip, and dandelion--provide calcium. Nearly all vegetables and fruits are low in fat, and none contain cholesterol.

BREAD AND CEREAL group: Foods in this group provide starch, thiamin, riboflavin, niacin, iron, magnesium, folacin, fiber, and protein.

WHAT ABOUT CALORIES?
A calorie is not a nutrient. It is a measure of the energy suppled by food when it is used by the body. Our bodies need energy to perform work. The nutrients that supply calories (energy) are carbohydrates, fat, and protein. The alcohol in beer, wine, and liquor also supplies calories but is lacking in essential nutrients.

Most foods contain more than one nutrient. For example, milk provides protein, fats, sugar, riboflavin and other B vitamins, vitamin A, calcium, phosphorus, and other nutrients; meat provides protein, several B vitamins, iron, and zinc in important amounts. No single food supplies all the essential nutrients in the amounts that you need. Milk, for instance, contains very little iron and meat provides little calcium. Thus, you should eat a variety of foods for an adequate diet.

MILK AND CHEESE group: Milk and most milk products are calcium-rich foods. They contribute riboflavin, protein, and vitamins A, B-6, and B-12.

MEAT, POULTRY, FISH, AND BEAN group: It's a good idea to vary your choices in this group. Each food has a distinct nutritional advantage. Red meats are good sources of zinc. Liver and egg yokes are valuable sources of vitamins, but are high in cholesterol. Dry beans, peas, soybeans, and nuts are worthwhile sources of magnesium. All foods of animal origin contain vitamin B-12. Foods of vegetable origin do not.

FATS, SWEETS, AND ALCOHOL: Most foods in this group provide relatively low levels of vitamins, minerals, and protein compared to calories. Vegetable oils generally do supply vitamin E and essential fatty acids.

Ideas
for adding variety to your meals

* Get out of the rut of thinking that certain foods are meant only for certain meals. Try vegetable soup and a tuna fish sandwich on pumpernickel bread at breakfast, or a cheese omelet, bran muffin, vegetable salad, and fresh fruit for dinner.
* Experiment with recipes created especially for one or two people.
* Combine leftover meats and vegetables into one-dish casseroles that can be easily heated for lunch or dinner, or frozen for later use.
* Share pot-luck lunches and dinners with friends or acquaintances on a rotating basis. Not only will it add variety to your diet, but it's also a great way to make new friends.

The six major food groups: some foods they contain

1 Fruits	2 Vegetables		3 Breads & Cereals	4 Milk & Cheeses	5 Meat, Fish, Poultry	6 Fats, Sweets, Alcohol
Citrus, Berries, Mellons Blueberries Cantaloupe Citrus juices Cranberries Grapefruit Kiwi Lemon Orange Raspberries Strawberries Tangerine Watermelon **Other Fruit** Apple Apricot Banana Cherries Dates Figs Fruit juices Grapes Guava Mango Nectarine Papaya Peach Pear Pineapple Plum Prune Raisins	**Dark-green Vegetables** Beet greens Broccoli Chard Chicory Collard greens Dandelion greens Endive Escarole Kale Mustard greens Romaine lettuce Spinach Turnip greens Watercress **Deep Yellow** Carrots Pumpkin Sweet potatoes Winter squash **Starchy Vegetables** Breadfruit Corn Green peas Hominy Lima beans Potatoes Rutabaga Taro	**Other Vegetables** Alfalfa sprouts Artichokes Asparagus Bean sprouts Beets Brussels sprouts Cabbage Cauliflower Celery Chinese cabbage Cucumbers Eggplant Green beans Green peppers Lettuce Mushrooms Okra Onions (mature and green) Radishes Summer squash Tomatoes Turnips Vegetable juices Zucchini **Dry Beans & Peas (legumes)** see column 5 alternates to meat	Brown rice Buckwheat groats Bulgur Corn tortillas Graham crackers Granola Oatmeal Popcorn Pumpernickel bread Ready-to-eat cereals Rye crackers Whole-wheat breads, crackers, pasta, cereals **Enriched** Bagels Biscuits Corn bread Corn muffins Cornmeal Crackers English muffins Farina Grits Rolls & buns Italian bread Macaroni Muffins Noodles Pancakes Pasta Ready-to-eat cereals Rice White bread & rolls	**Low-fat milk products** Buttermilk Low-fat milk (1%, 2%) Low-fat plain yogurt Skim milk **Other Milk Products with More Fat or Sugar** American cheese Cheddar cheese Chocolate milk Flavored yogurt Fruit yogurt Ice cream Processed cheeses Swiss cheese Whole milk	Beef Chicken Fish Ham Lamb Organ meats Pork Shellfish Turkey Veal Luncheon meats Sausage Eggs Nuts and seeds Peanut butter Tofu **Alternates to Meat** **Dry Beans & Peas (legumes)** Black beans Black-eyed peas Chickpeas (garbanzos) Kidney beans Lentils Lima beans (mature) Mung beans Navy beans Pinto beans Split peas	**Fats** Bacon, salt pork Butter Cream (dairy, nondairy) Cream cheese Lard Margarine Mayonnaise Salad dressings Shortening Sour cream Vegetable oil **Sweets** Candy Corn syrup Fruit drinks Gelatin desserts Honey Frosting Jam, jellies Maple syrup Marmalade Molasses Popsicles, ices Sherbets Soft drinks, colas Sugar (white, brown) **Alcohol** Beer Liquor Wine

Suggested Daily Servings

1	2	3	4	5	6
2 to 4 servings	3 to 5 servings (include all types regularly: use dark-green leafy vegetables and dry beans and peas several times a week) (see column 5)	6 to 11 servings (include several servings a day of whole-grain products)	2 servings	2-3 servings-- 5 to 7 ounces lean meat total per day	Avoid too many fats, sweets, and alcoholic beverages.

What Counts as a Serving?

1	2	3	4	5	6
an apple a banana an orange 1/2 grapefruit mellon wedge 3/4 cup juice 1/2 cup berries 1/2 cup cooked or canned fruit	1/2 cup cooked or chopped raw vegetables 1 cup of leafy raw vegetables, such as lettuce or spinach	1 slice of bread 1/2 hamburger bun 1/2 English muffin, a small roll, biscuit, or muffin 3-4 small crackers 1/2 cup cooked cereal, rice, or pasta 1 oz. ready-to-eat cereal	1 cup of milk 8 ounces of yogurt 1-1/2 ounces of natural cheese 2 ounces of processed cheese	1 ounce of lean meat, fish, or poultry 1 egg 1/2 cup cooked dry beans 2 tablespoons of peanut butter or 1 ounce of lean meat	**If you do drink alcoholic beverages, do so in moderation.**

How fats compare

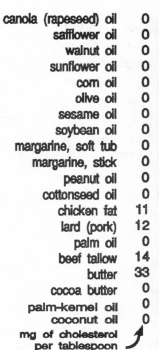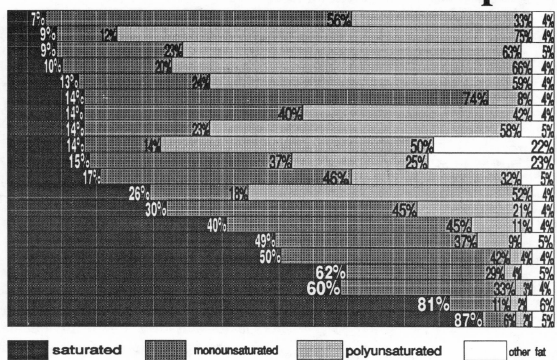

Three nutrients supply calories to your body--carbohydrates, proteins, and fats. Of these foods we eat, fat has the most effect on raising our blood cholesterol and increasing the risk of heart disease. However, it is neither desirable nor realistic to eliminate fat in your diet as fats provide calories, help in the absorption of certain vitamins, contribute to the appealing flavor and aroma of food, and are necessary for normal body functions.

Fats (called lipids) are used by the body for many things. Most fats have a common chemical structure of bead-like strings of up to 20 carbon atoms. The strings are linked together in sets of three by a small molecule called glycerol, so many fats are also called triglycerides. The bead-like strings of carbons have hydrogen atoms attached to them. Chemists classify fats according to this chemical structure. Fats are either saturated or unsaturated. A saturated fat has as many hydrogens as it can hold. Monounsaturated (mono, meaning one) are slightly unsaturated fats since they lack only one pair of hydrogens. Polyunsaturated (poly, meaning many) are fats that are highly unsaturated since they are missing more than one pair of hydrogens.

SATURATED FATS--are fats that are solid at room temperature and found in greatest amounts in foods from animals, such as meat (the marbling and fat along the edges), poultry, whole-milk dairy foods like cream, milk, ice cream, butter, and in some plant products such as palm and coconut oils. Saturated fats tend to raise total blood cholesterol levels.

MONO- AND POLYUNSATURATED FATS--are fats that are found in greatest amounts in foods from plants. These fats are usually liquid at refrigerator temperatures. Monounsaturated fats tend to raise the "good" cholesterol levels (HDL's) without raising total blood cholesterol. Polyunsaturated fats tend to lower total blood cholesterol level, but at the expense of the "good" cholesterol.

HYDROGENATION--is a process used to change unsaturated fats like liquid vegetable oils to a more solid saturated fat. The process improves shelf life but also increases the saturated fat content. Many commercial food products contain hydrogenated vegetable oil, especially commercially baked goods and other processed foods.

TRIGLYCERIDES--are lipids (fat-like substances) carried through the bloodstream to the tissues. The bulk of the body's fat tissue is in the form of triglycerides, stored for later use as energy.

FAT INTAKE--Experts now recommend that no more than 30% of the calories you consume should come from fats and should be evenly distributed (10% each) between saturated, monounsaturated, and polyunsaturated fats. All types of fats supply about 9 calories per gram compared to 4 for carbohydrates and 6 for proteins.

A whopping 60% of most people's fat intake comes from hidden sources in meat, baked goods, and dairy products.

NEWS--Olive oil and canola oil have high percentages of monounsaturated fats. By using these oils some claim it lowers cholesterol, reduces blood pressure, and lowers blood sugar. They say they lower the "bad" LDL and not the "good" HDL. This finding prompted many to switch to these oils for cooking and for salads from polyunsaturated vegetable oils derived from corn, sunflower, safflower seeds, and soybeans.

PERCENTAGES OF FAT IN FOODS

More than 50%	50% to 30%	30% to 10%	Less than 10%
most cuts of beef	whole milk	broiled chicken	tuna in water
pork	french fries	turkey	haddock
fried chicken	ice cream	chicken liver	sole
eggs	whole-milk yogurt	most fish	cod
cheese	most pastry	low-fat cottage cheese	spaghetti
nuts	flank steak	buttermilk	most cereals
tuna packed in oil	2% low-fat milk	skim milk	rice
olives	creamed cottage cheese	low-fat yogurt	potatoes
milk chocolate	pizza	wheat germ	beans (all types)
coleslaw	fish sticks	bread	bean sprouts
peanut butter	macaroni and cheese	pork and beans	fruits
sausage	liver	oatmeal	vegetables

Vitamin supplements--should you take them?

Vitamins and minerals, in small amounts, were found to be needed in the diet for the normal growth and maintenance of all animal life, including that of man. Through extensive tests, nutritionists then established the "recommended daily allowance" required for the average, healthy, normal adult. However, these studies involved younger adults and the needs of the older population have yet to be determined.

Vitamins and Older Persons

Vitamin nutrition of older persons is often caught in a three-way bind:

1   decreased nutritional intake;
2   decreased absorption; and
3   increased need that is caused by decreasing efficiency of some enzyme system with age.

According to health officials, of particular concern to seniors should be the B vitamins. An estimated 30% of seniors lose their ability to make stomach acid, and this interferes with the absorption of vitamin B-12 and folic acid. Studies suggest that deficiencies in these, as well as in vitamin B-6 can cause neurological changes such as a decline in alertness, loss of memory, and numbness of the extremities. B-2, or riboflavin, aids in release of energy from carbohydrates, proteins, and fats. There is also concern that since older persons generally take medications regularly, some medications may cause vitamin deficiencies.

The national theme is: Most people obtain enough vitamins by eating a wide variety of nutritious foods and often do not need a vitamin supplement. Often, people are attracted by advertisements for vitamins that make claims to promote or improve health. Some believe that foods no longer contain the nutrient levels they once did. Others, like Dr. Linus Pauling, believe that higher levels of vitamin C, 10 grams per day, are a powerful tool against colds, flu, cancer, coronary disease, and reduction in age-specific deaths. Nutritional activists contend that ingesting more vitamins A and C is important to reduce the risk of chronic disease, especially cancer and heart disease.

What to Do?

Obviously, our "experts" have established minimum levels of vitamins needed for good health, but they are in disagreement or unsure if higher levels of some vitamins are needed to promote better health. However, most agree that the elderly and sick individuals, whose appetites are depressed, or whose medications may interfere with nutrition, may be deficient in certain vitamins or minerals without supplements, yet "experts" provide no common recommendations. Most contend that a good vitamin/mineral supplement, although not needed, offers an "insurance policy." If one can afford them, they contend that it will do no harm if not taken in excess amounts. Essentially, you make your own decisions or ask advice of one you trust who is knowledgeable about nutrition.

What Are Vitamins?

The many different vitamins required by man were found to be similar because they are made of the same organic elements--carbon, hydrogen, oxygen, and sometimes nitrogen. (Vitamin B-12 also contains cobalt.) They were found to be different because their elementary structures are arranged differently. At first, no one knew what vitamins were chemically, so they were identified by letters. Later, in some cases, what was thought to be one vitamin turned out to be many, and to differentiate numbers were added to the letters; the vitamin B complex is the best example.

When some of these organic compounds were found unnecessary for human needs, they were removed from the list of essential vitamins, which accounts for some of the gaps in the letters and numbers. So now, hoping to minimize confusion, we have only 13 vitamins that are claimed essential.

Anyone who reads a food label or the fine print on the back of a vitamin bottle sees nutritional values compared to RDA's (the Recommended Daily Allowance). These numbers are the nutritional recommended values for 18 essential vitamins and minerals that have been established to "serve as a goal for good nutrition."

Each of the 13 essential vitamins performs one or more specific functions in the body. If any one is missing, a deficiency disease becomes apparent. Vitamins do not provide energy, nor do they construct or build any part of the body. They are specifically needed for transforming foods into energy and body maintenance. Research indicates that getting enough vitamins is essential to life. In contrast, the body has no use for excess vitamins. **High doses of certain vitamins can be dangerous, even fatal.** Add to that the complication that the body can only store some vitamins for only relatively short periods. The fat-soluble vitamins A, D, E, and K are absorbed along with fat from various foods and are stored in the body. The water-soluble vitamins, the B's and C, generally are not stored.

Recommended "Minimums"

People who are interested in nutrition and health should become familiar with the RDA established values. These are the amounts of vitamins, minerals, and proteins believed to be needed by most people each day, to remain healthy, according to the U.S. government. Unfortunately, for those of us in the second 50 years, these "standards" have not been established for older people. Government policy recommends the values needed by the general population.

RDA's are often misunderstood by consumers and are frequently taken for USRDA's--the recommendations found on an increasing number of food labels. Since food labels are too small to include RDA's for all age groups, the FDA sets an average for everyone--the USRDA--which is what appears on a growing number of foods. In addition to this problem, these "standards" for the elderly, especially those with chronic illnesses, are being questioned by a number of nutritionists.

Of course, popping a vitamin or mineral pill should not be viewed as a panacea for a poor diet. Taking excess amounts of one or another nutrient is not a healthy practice.

Extremely sensitive methods of measuring the potency or quantity of vitamins have been developed because they are present in foods in very small amounts. Some vitamins are measured in IU's (international units), which is a measure of biological activity. Other vitamins are expressed by weight in micrograms or milligrams.

To illustrate the small amounts needed by the human body, let's start with an ounce, which is 28.4 grams. A milligram is 1/1000 of a gram, and a microgram is 1/1000 of a milligram. The Recommended Daily Allowance (RDA) of vitamin B_{12} for an adult is 6 micrograms a day. Then, just one ounce of this vitamin could supply the daily needs of 4,724,921 people.

The table below describes the U.S. Recommended Daily Allowance of each vitamin, what it does, and the food sources.

NEWS REPORTS: A study of 333 men who already had evidence of coronary artery disease and had suffered angina (chest pain) showed after six years there were 10 heart attacks among the men who took 50-milligram beta carotene pills every other day. There were 17 heart attacks among the placebo users.

Among men in this group who took both beta carotene (a form of vitamin A common in carrots) and aspirin, there were no heart attacks.

VITAMIN	WHAT IT DOES	FOOD SOURCES
A (retinol) **USRDA 5000 IU	Aids in normal growth, helps to prevent infections, helps form and maintain healthy skin, hair, and mucous membranes. Aids vision in dim light.	Liver,* egg yoke,* cheese, whole milk or butter, fortified margarines, and low-fat milks. (Also: Beta-carotene, which the body converts to vitamin A, is found in deep yellow/orange and dark green vegetables and fruits such as (carrots, broccoli, spinach, sweet potatoes, pumpkin, winter squash, cantaloupe.)
B-1 (thiamine) USRDA 1.5 mg.	Helps carbohydrates release energy. Maintains reserves of energy. Promotes normal function of the nervous system.	Whole-grain and enriched breads and cereals, dried beans and peas, fresh pork.
B-2 (riboflavin) USRDA 1.7 mg.	Helps transform carbohydrates, protein, and fat into energy. Helps to maintain healthy skin and assists in the formation of red blood cells.	Milk, yogurt, cheese, dark-green vegetables, meat, poultry, eggs,* whole-grain and enriched cereals and breads.
B-6 (pyridoxine) USRDA 2.0 mg.	Assists in the formation of neurotransmitters important in brain function and in protein metabolism. Aids in use of amino acids, formation of certain protein, and in the use of fats.	Liver,* meat, poultry, fish, dried beans and peas, nuts, whole-grain breads and cereals, bananas.
B-12 USRDA 6 micrograms	Helps form red blood cells. Helps build genetic material. Aids in nervous system functioning.	Milk, yogurt, cheese, meat, fish, poultry, eggs,* fortified vegetable and grain products.
C (ascorbic acid) USRDA 60 mg.	Needed to form collagen, a substance that holds body cells together including bones, cartilage, muscle, and vascular tissue. Helps maintain capillaries, bones, and teeth. Hastens the healing of wounds and damaged bones. Aids in iron absorption. Helps protect other vitamins from oxidation.	Citrus fruits, berries, melons, dark-green vegetables, tomatoes, green peppers, cabbage, and potatoes.
D (calciferol) USRDA 400 IU	Helps form and maintain bones and teeth. Assists in the absorption and use of calcium and phosphorus.	Egg yoke,* liver,* tuna, salmon, cod liver oil, and fortified milks. (Also made in the skin when it's exposed to sunlight.)
E (tocopherol) USRDA 30 IU	Protects vitamin A and essential fatty acids from oxidation. Prevents cell membrane damage.	Vegetable oils and margarines, nuts, wheat germ, whole-grain breads and cereals, green leafy vegetables.
K (phylioquinone) USRDA none	Helps synthesize substances needed for blood clotting. Helps maintain normal bone metabolism.	Green leafy vegetables, cabbage, cauliflower. (Also made by bacteria in the intestines.)
Biotin	Helps form fatty acids and release energy from carbohydrates.	Organ meats,* eggs,*. (Also made by bacteria in the intestines.)
Folic acid (folacin, folate)	Helps form hemoglobin in red blood cells. Aids in formation of genetic materials.	Dark-green leafy vegetables, whole-grain breads and cereals, dried beans and peas, fruits (especially orange juice).
Niacin USRDA 20 mg	Helps transform carbohydrates, protein, and fat into energy.	Meat, poultry, fish, whole-grain and enriched cereals and breads, nuts, dried beans and peas. (Also can be formed in the body from tryptophan, and amino acids found in proteins.)
Pantothenic acid	Helps form hormones and certain nerve-regulating substances. Helps metabolize carbohydrates, protein, and fat.	Eggs,* meat, organ meats,* whole-grain cereals, dried beans and peas.

* **Liver, eggs, and organ meats are excellent sources of many nutrients, but they are also major sources of cholesterol. Those at risk for heart disease may want to use them in moderation.**

** **USRDA = U.S. Recommended Dietary Allowance. mg = milligrams. IU = International Units.**

Our sea inheritance...minerals we need...how much?

Our need for minerals in our diet, even though in the most tiny amounts, reflects our link with our ancient heritage of the sea. The major salts from seawater in various combinations are the same as the salts in our cells and body fluids. This is why some of the mineral supplements sold today are taken from dry seabeds.

Minerals are inorganic substances. This means they are not formed by living matter and contain no carbon. All organic material contains carbon and once was part of, or was produced by, living plants or animals. We are all familiar with the minerals: sodium, potassium, calcium, magnesium, and many others as well as some combinations. The most common combination is sodium chloride, or ordinary table salt. See the separate articles on calcium, page 123 and salt, page 124.

Minerals used in the body are classified as the major minerals, also called "macrominerals," and trace minerals. Major minerals are calcium, phosphorus, magnesium, potassium, sulfur, chloride, and sodium.

The trace minerals are iron, zinc, copper, iodine, fluoride, chromium, selenium, manganese, and molybdenum. Other trace minerals such as bromide, cadmium, vanadium, tin, nickel, aluminum, and silicon are found in the body but less is known about their usefulness or the amounts required. Authorities feel these latter trace minerals are believed to be received by way of our diet. If there are any disorders associated with these latter trace minerals experts are not aware of them. Lead, mercury, and cadmium are all heavy metals, which can cause severe poisoning and death. Copper can also if used in excess.

Although minerals are of vital importance, they make up only about 4% of the body's weight; all of the trace elements account for only about .01% of total body weight.

Although the role of minerals in body functions is not well understood, it is known that even in tiny amounts they are vital in the delicate balance of body functioning. Too much or too little of a mineral can throw the whole balance off. When this happens

symptoms appear telling something is wrong.

In general, the minerals have the following functions in the body:

1. elements of bone structure;
2. they aid in various metabolic reactions;
3. they help in moving substances across body cell membranes;
4. they assist in the movement of muscles; and
5. they are needed as part of compounds that contain organic matter (vitamins, hormones, certain elements of the blood, and enzymes).

The Federal Drug Administration (FDA) had determined the Recommended Daily Allowance (RDA's) for some of the minerals. In other cases, only government estimates, "Estimated Safe and Adequate Daily Intake," are given because that is the only information currently available.

The table below lists some important minerals, RDA's, what they do, and the food sources containing the mineral.

Mineral *	What It Does	Food Sources
Calcium Women 1200-1500 Men 800 mg/day	Builds bones and teeth and maintains bone strength. Used in muscle contraction, blood clotting, and cell membrane maintenance.	Milk, yogurt, cheese, sardines, canned salmon eaten with bones, dark green leafy vegetables, dried beans and peas, corn tortillas.
Chloride 1.7-5.1 mg/day	Part of hydrochloric acid in gastric juice. Helps regulate blood acidity.	Salt (sodium chloride) added to food in commercial processing, cooking, or eating.
Fluoride 1.5-4.0 mg/day	Helps form strong, decay-resistant teeth. Maintains bone strength.	Fluoridated water, small ocean fish with bones.
Iodine 15 micrograms/day	Part of thyroid hormone. Needed for normal reproduction.	Iodized salt, seafood, seaweed.
Iron 10 mg/day	Needed to form hemoglobin in blood and myoglobin in muscles, which supply oxygen to cells. Part of several enzymes and proteins.	Red meats, liver, kidney, poultry, fish, dark leafy vegetables, dried beans and peas, whole grain products, fortified breads and cereals.
Magnesium Women 300 mg/day Men 350	Helps to build bones, manufacture proteins, release energy from muscle glycogen, regulate body temperature.	Dark green leafy vegetables, nuts and seeds, whole grains, dried beans and peas.
Phosphorus 800 mg/day	Builds bones and teeth. Helps release energy from carbohydrates, proteins, and fats. Used to form genetic material, cell membranes, and many enzymes.	Meat, poultry, fish, eggs, dried beans and peas, milk and milk products.
Potassium 1.8-5.6 mg/day	Helps muscles contract. Maintains fluid and electrolyte balance in cells. Assists in transmission of nerve impulses, release of energy from carbohydrates, proteins, and fats.	Fruits and vegetables, dried beans and peas.
Sodium Salt 1.1-3.3 grams/day safe & adequate	Regulates body fluid volume and blood acidity. Helps in transmission of nerve impulses.	Salt (sodium chloride) added to food in commercial processing, cooking, or eating. Also: milk, meat, fish, poultry, eggs.
Zinc 15 mg/day	Helps form protein, thus assisting in all tissue growth, wound healing, anemia prevention. Part of many enzymes.	Meat, poultry, shellfish, cheese, whole grain cereals, dried beans and peas, nuts, seeds.

* Recommended Daily Allowance (RDA) for those over 50 years of age.

Nutritionists know that using excessive amounts or insufficient amounts of any one mineral is unhealthy.

Calcium--an essential mineral nutrient

Calcium is the most abundant mineral in the body, accounting for about 2% of body weight. This amounts to approximately 1,250 grams (2-3/4 pounds for someone 140 pounds in weight), of which 99% is in the bones and teeth. Calcium is an essential mineral nutrient, although it is not exactly a popular ingredient in the diet typically consumed by adults. Calcium is not only needed to maximize your bone mass but is required for metabolic functions. Your body uses calcium for many of its vital functions and if you don't give it enough calcium for these other purposes, it robs it from the teeth and bones. It has been found that the body first robs the jaw bones, which may account for the prevalence of periodontal disease, particularly among older women.

Bone loss is not always bad. In fact, it is necessary. In the living bone tissue, one type of cell--osteoclasts--breaks down the tissue, and another type--osteoblasts--builds it back up. These two cells work together. The osteoblasts build new bone tissue in response to the bone loss from the osteoclasts. The problem and the cause of osteoporosis occurs when the bone loss begins to exceed the bone gain.

Our bones replace about one-fifth of their total calcium each year, and there is a constant movement of calcium in and out of the bones both for repair and to maintain a constant level of calcium in the blood and other body fluids. To meet these needs, bone experts claim adult women should consume 1200 to 1500 mg (milligrams) of calcium per day. Studies show that the average adult female consumes only a third of the calcium needed to maintain normal bone strength. If calcium intake is not at the higher level, in the first decade after menopause a women could lose 15% of her bone structure. The price being paid by many women for neglect of this vital nutrient is osteoporosis.

Osteoporosis, a debilitating bone disorder, is a virtual epidemic among American women past the age of 60, has its roots in young adulthood, and is caused by insufficient calcium. After menopause, the average American woman loses an inch and a half in height each decade as a result of vertebral collapse. Far more serious, millions of fractures and tens of thousands of deaths occur annually because of osteoporosis. (See the article on osteoporosis, page 320, and hip fractures, page 323.)

Osteoporosis literally means porous bones. It is a weakened condition of the bones that results from a slow, insidious loss of calcium, the mineral that builds strong bones. Weak bones break easily, and the overwhelming majority of fractures that beset older Americans are the result of osteoporosis--bones too weak to withstand the stresses of normal living. The first sign of osteoporosis is usually a broken bone or collapsed vertebra.

SOURCES OF CALCIUM: The best source of calcium is dairy products. One cup of skim milk supplies over 300 milligrams of calcium. Other good sources are yogurt, cheese, ice cream, and leafy green vegetables. Women trying to consume 1,200 milligrams of calcium daily may find it difficult to get all of it from foods and must then turn to supplements.

CALCIUM SUPPLEMENTS: Calcium comes in many forms: calcium carbonate, calcium lactate, calcium phosphate, calcium gluconate, and bone meal. It comes fortified with vitamins and minerals, chewable, swallowable, and in liquid. All forms of calcium are absorbable, but vary widely in cost and the amount of elemental calcium they supply per tablet. Depending on the type you choose your 1,200 milligrams can cost anywhere from a few cents to two dollars per day. Here are some tips:

❶ If you have kidney stones, see a doctor before taking supplements.

❷ Consider the amount of calcium received by your diet and only add your additional needs.

❸ Check the labels. The fine print on a "500-milligram" tablet may reveal only 45 milligrams of elemental calcium. Most products should contain usually 250 to 500 milligrams per pill. The highest level of elemental calcium (40%) is found in calcium carbonate, which is frequently derived from oyster shells. Others are calcium lactate 13% and calcium gluconate 9%.

❹ Calcium products can also contain other additives you don't want in your diet such as sugar, flavoring, and vegetable oils, so check labels carefully.

❺ Avoid compounds fortified with vitamins and minerals. You can easily get all the vitamins and minerals from your diet and these products cost more.

❻ Calcium is calcium so select store brands or generics as they will cost you much less.

❼ Bone meal, oyster shells, and dolomite products are not recommended as they may contain other minerals or contaminates that you may not need.

Foods High in Calcium

Food	Serving size (oz)	Calcium content (mg)
Bean curd (tofu)	4	154
Broccoli	8	136
Buttermilk	8	285
Cheese		
American	1	174
Cheddar	1	204
Low-fat cottage	8	138
Swiss	1	272
Ice cream	8	176
Milk	8	300
Salmon (canned)	3	285
Sardines (with bones)	3	372
Shrimp	8	147
Turnip greens (cooked)	8	267
Yogurt		
Low-fat plain	8	415
Low-fat fruited	8	314
Frozen	8	200

Taking more calcium than you need does no good and any more than twice as much could be harmful.

VITAMIN D: Your body can't absorb or utilize calcium without vitamin D. The recommended daily allowance is 400 I.U., which you can get from a quart of milk, an average multivitamin pill, or 30 to 60 minutes of sunshine. Brief exposure to sunlight each day, which causes the body to manufacture vitamin D, and eating a balanced diet are usually enough to ensure an adequate intake. Too much vitamin D can be harmful.

Salt--the "silent killer"

shake
the
salt habit

Salt is a necessary part of life, not only because it flavors and protects foods. Our bodies need sodium, which is present in salt, because it helps to maintain blood volume and blood pressure, regulate water balance, transmit nerve impulses, and perform other vital functions. It is good for us in limited amounts.

WHAT IS SODIUM?--Sodium is a mineral that occurs naturally in some foods and is added to many foods and beverages. Most of the sodium, about one third, in the American diet comes from table salt (sodium chloride). Salt is 40% sodium and 60% chloride. One teaspoon of salt contains 2 grams of sodium. Average daily sodium intake for adults in the U.S. is 4 to 6 grams--far above the 1.1 to 3.3 grams that is a "safe and adequate amount."

Of course, sodium also occurs in many forms including: baking powder, baking soda, monosodium glutamate, sodium benzoate (a preservative), sodium citrate (used in soft drinks), sodium saccharin (sweetener), sodium phosphate, and sodium propionate (mold inhibitor). Although salt is the major source of sodium in processed foods, many of these other forms of sodium are added as preservatives or for flavor.

HIGH BLOOD PRESSURE--Older people in particular should be cautious about using too much sodium. High sodium intake is associated with high blood pressure (HBP). Having a family history of HBP and being overweight are major factors too. HBP, in turn, can lead to heart disease, stroke, and kidney failure. **Blood pressure rises with age and is much more common in the elderly.** Restricting the amount of sodium in the diet helps lower HBP in many individuals who already have the disease. It also can increase the effectiveness of drug treatment, making lower doses possible.

HOW TO CUT BACK--As people grow older their sensitivity to flavors and smells usually decreases. Because of this, there may be a desire for more salt to combat the flat taste of foods. Cutting down on salt may sound difficult and distasteful. But it doesn't have to be either. Many people have learned to cut down on the salt they use in cooking and at the table. They usually report that after a while they just don't miss the salt flavor. It's generally best to cut back gradually to give the tastebuds time to adjust. Here are some suggestions:

❤ **Use the saltshaker sparingly.** Don't use it until you've tasted your food. If after tasting it, you must salt it, try one shake instead of two.

❤ **Be a label reader.** Look for the amount of sodium in the product. Labels that don't list ingredients by amounts will carry the items in the order of their weight. That is, the first ingredient listed will be the one most used in the product. So if salt comes third on the list, it is the third most-used ingredient. Look for other sodium-containing combinations.

❤ **Look for low-salt, low-sodium, or sodium-reduced products.** These days the low-sodium list runs literally from soup to nuts. Shop carefully. Make sure the reduction in sodium justifies the added cost.

❤ **Limit your use of commercial condiments.** Many are high in sodium such as: onion salt, garlic salt, celery salt, soy sauce, steak sauce, barbecue sauce, catsup, mustard, salad dressings, pickles, chili sauce, and relish.

❤ **Consider making your own condiments, dressings, and sauces** and keep sodium-containing ingredients at a minimum.

❤ **When shopping for lower sodium foods, fresh is usually best.** Fresh fruits, vegetables, meats, and unprocessed grains are generally low in sodium. Items that run higher in sodium include baked goods, most cheeses, lunch meats, seafood, many dry cereals, and some canned or dehydrated soups.

❤ **Plan meals that contain less sodium.** Try new recipes that use less salt and sodium-containing ingredients. Adjust your own recipes by reducing such ingredients a little at a time. Don't be fooled by recipes that have little or no salt but call for soups, bouillon cubes, or condiments that do.

❤ **Cut back on salt used in cooking pasta, rice, noodles, and hot cereals.**

❤ **Experiment with spices and herbs as seasonings.** Use spices and herbs instead of salt. Some alternatives include: garlic and onion powder (not salts), lemon, pepper, finely chopped garlic, fresh grated horseradish, vinegar and oil, powdered mustard, allspice, basil, chives, cloves, curry powder, dill, marjoram, oregano, poppy seeds, rosemary, savory, tarragon, thyme, and turmeric.

❤ **Limit your intake of snacks** such as potato chips, pretzels, corn chips, popcorn, crackers, and nuts.

❤ **When eating out, choose items that are less likely to have large amounts of salt added.** Some restaurants will prepare low-sodium meals if asked to do so.

SALT SUBSTITUTES--Before using a salt substitute, ask your doctor about it. These preparations usually contain potassium. Sodium and potassium work in delicate balance in the body. Salt substitutes can be safely used by most people, but not those with some kidney and other medical conditions.

> **Warning: This book is intended solely to provide you with information. It is not intended to replace the advice of your physician.**

Herbs that can be used instead of salt	
with	**use**
eggs	basil, dill weed (leaves), garlic, parsley
fish	basil, bay leaf (crumbled), French tarragon, lemon, thyme, parsley (options: fennel, sage, savory)
poultry	lovage, marjoram (2 parts), sage (3 parts)
salads	basil, lovage, parsley, French tarragon
tomato sauce	basil (2 parts), bay leaf, marjoram, oregano, parsley (options: celery leaves, cloves)
veggies	basil, parsley, savory
Italian blend	basil, marjoram, oregano, rosemary, sage, savory, thyme cumin, garlic, hot pepper

 Fiber: not just for constipation anymore

Dietary fiber is the stuff that puts the crunch in carrots, the bulk in salads, the chewiness in whole-meal bread, and the thickness in stewed prunes and pea soup. Fiber in the diet can help relieve constipation and promote bowel regularity. It is also considered helpful in controlling the "irritable bowel syndrome," preventing hemorrhoids and diverticular diseases. Other medical researchers and nutritionists believe high-fiber foods may help protect against adult-onset diabetes, cardiovascular disease, and colon cancer. Fiber may also help to lower blood cholesterol levels, reducing the risk of heart attack and stroke.

WHAT IS DIETARY FIBER?--Dietary fiber is that part of fruit, nuts, vegetables, grains, and other plant foods that's not digested or only partially digested by humans. Fiber is a diverse group of chemical compounds--cellulose, hemicelluloses, mucilages, microscopic polysaccharides, pectins, gums, and lignin. All are complex carbohydrates except lignin, a very tough substance found in all plants.

Cellulose, hemicelluloses, and lignin are components of wood as well as edible plants. They are tough, fibrous, and insoluble in water. Pectins (a substance used in jellies) and gums are water-soluble and form gel-like, or viscous, textures. All of the dietary fibers are found in varying combinations and amounts in plant leaves, stems, tubers, roots, flowers, and seeds. Cellulose, the most abundant fiber, forms the basic structural material of cell walls. Cotton is almost pure cellulose, and the outer layers of cereal grains contain large amounts of cellulose.

HOW FIBER WORKS--Aside from a few exceptions (corn being one), most fiber works on a level much more microscopic than the word "roughage" implies. Fiber's effects on the digestive system begins in the mouth. The considerable chewing that may be re-

quired for foods such as salad greens and whole-grain products stimulates saliva flow. This in turn starts the stomach's digestive juices flowing. Once swallowed, fiber contributes to bulk and some swelling of stomach contents as water is absorbed. Soluble forms of fiber such as pectins and gums increase the viscosity, or thickness, of the stomach contents. These effects contribute to a feeling of fullness and also slow down the emptying of the stomach.

Once past the stomach, the insoluble fibers, by increasing the bulk and weight of the food mass, cut down the transit time through the intestines. On the other hand, the increased viscosity resulting from pectin and other soluble fibers slows down the movement. This allows more time for digested food to be absorbed by the body, but the process also has its nutritional drawbacks: Some minerals such as calcium and zinc may be bound by fiber and, as a result, don't get absorbed; and fiber can bind bile acids, which aid in the digestive process.

Cellulose and other insoluble fibers are essentially unchanged as they pass through the intestines, but the pectins and gums are fermented by bacteria in the large intestine, producing gases and some fatty acids. Cellulose and lignin provide stool bulk and water-soluble fibers help relieve constipation by adding softness to stools.

Moderation is the key in adding fiber to your diet. It's better to eat a wide variety of foods rather than just adding a single high-fiber food, such as oat bran. Eating a wide variety of foods will furnish far better nutrition, since different kinds of dietary fiber provide different benefits. **To ensure thorough digestion, be sure to drink plenty of liquids when you eat fiber.**

Nutrition experts also advise against using dietary fiber supplements as they contend natural sources of fiber also contain many other nutrients. However, to minimize constipation while traveling it may be advisable to add packaged fiber to the diet--not as a substitute for eating high fiber foods, but in addition (see the article on constipation and laxatives on page 306).

HOW TO GET FIBER--Most authorities agree that you should get about 20 to 30 grams of dietary fiber a day. They also recommend that you not go overboard in consuming fiber as fiber can bind some minerals (calcium, zinc), preventing absorption and use by the body, and leading to deficiencies in these trace minerals. Here are some sources:

Dietary Fiber Source (for crude fiber multiply by 2.4)	Grams of Fiber
Acorn squash, 1/2 cup	1.7
All-Bran, regular, 1/2 cup	12.7
All-Bran, extra fiber, 1/2 cup	13.0
Apple, 1 medium with skin	2.6
Avocado, 1 medium	4.6
Bagel, oat bran, 1	3.0
Baked beans, 3/4 cup	8.2
Banana, 1 medium	1.4
Beans, green, 1/2 cup	1.1
Blueberries, 1/2 cup	1.8
Bran-Flakes, 3/4 cup	3.0
Bread, wheatberry, 1 slice	2.4
Broccoli, 1/2 cup	2.3
Broccoli spear, 1	4.2
Brussels sprouts, 1/2 cup	3.4
Cabbage, red and white, 1/2 cup	.7
Cauliflower, raw, 1/2 cup	1.4
Carrot, 1 medium	2.3
Celery stalk, 1 medium	.7
Coleslaw, 1/2 cup	.9
Corn, 1/2 cup	3.0
Cracklin' Oat Bran, 1/2 cup	4.0
Fiber-One, 1/2 cup	12.0
Figs, 5	8.6
Grape-Nuts, 1/2 cup	4.0
Lentil soup, 1 cup	3.5
Lettuce, 10 leaves	2.0
Lima beans, 1/2 cup	6.5
Mushrooms, raw, 1/2 cup	.6
Onions, raw, 1/2 cup	.9
Peach, 1 medium	2.8
Pear, 1 medium	5.2
Pizza, 1 slice	1.2
Potato, baked, 1 medium	3.9
Prunes, dried, 3	1.9
Quaker Oats, uncooked, 1/2 cup	4.5
Raisins, 1/4 cup	2.0
Raspberries, 1/2 cup	3.0
Rice, brown, 1/2 cup	1.6
Rice, white, 1/2 cup	.8
Spaghetti, whole wheat, 2 oz. dry	7.2
Spinach, raw, 1/2 cup	.6
Sweet potato, 1 medium	3.9
Triscuit cracker, 4	2.0
Wheat germ, 3 tbs.	3.0
100% Bran, 1/2 cup	8.4

Drink at least 8 glasses of water each day!

Drinking water neither makes a man sick, nor in debt, nor his wife a widow.
- John Neal (1818-1866)

If there is any magic on this Earth, it is contained in each drop of water, and it is with this magic that every living thing is endowed.

Anon.

Water is often called the "forgotten nutrient." Next to air, although it is rarely mentioned as such, water is the most important nutrient of all--vital to health and life itself. We can go without food for almost two months if we start out in good health, but without water we can survive only a few days. Water carries nutrients from the foods we eat, minerals that control the route of the nutrients, oxygen to the body cells, and it helps cool the body through perspiration. It is essential for chemical reactions in digestion and metabolism. It is needed to replace body water and to carry away body wastes in the form of urine, feces, sweat, and exhaled breath. Without enough water, we can become poisoned by our own waste products. It also acts to cushion our tissues and to lubricate our joints.

Solid as we seem, if you are a man, water comprises as much as 60-65% of your body. If you are a woman, your body contains 50-60% water. An average adult contains 45 quarts of water with nearly one-half located in the body cells. Blood is 83% water. Even solid tissue is 75% water and bone is 22%.

How Much Water Do We Use?
An adult loses about 2 to 3 quarts of water or more each day through excretion of body wastes and perspiration. The kidneys must excrete a minimum of 10 ounces a day to rid the body of poisonous waste materials. When the kidneys remove uric acid and urea, the body's waste products, these must be dissolved in water. If we aren't drinking enough water, wastes are not removed as effectively and may build up as kidney stones.

Water contains dissolved salts. The salts regulate the distribution of water within the body. If we drink too little water, dehydration occurs: The salt becomes concentrated, and water is drawn from the cells in an attempt to dilute it. This, in turn, affects the functioning of the kidneys, for regardless of the amount of water taken in, the kidneys must still excrete a minimum of 10 ounces a day to eliminate poisonous waste materials.

Water also is vital for chemical reactions in digestion and metabolism. It carries nutrients and oxygen to the cells through the blood and helps to cool the body through perspiration. Water also lubricates our joints. We even need water to breathe: Our lungs must be moist to take in oxygen and excrete carbon dioxide. It is possible to lose a pint of liquid each day by just exhaling.

The rate at which water is eliminated in each individual varies depending upon body metabolism, physical activity, hot or cold environment, or during illnesses. Under normal circumstances this means putting back some 2-1/2 quarts each day. During illness such as fever, vomiting, and diarrhea, the body can lose 4 quarts of water a day or more.

How Much Do We Take In?
Most people drink about six or eight glasses of liquids each day including water, juices, milk, soft drinks, soup, coffee, and tea. The rest comes from foods that have a high water content, such as fruits and vegetables, which are more than 80% water. Even a slice of bread is one-third water. A portion of our water intake also is derived from metabolic processes within the body when glucose and fat are converted to energy. Yet many people live in a dehydrated state.

Not Enough Water?
If you don't drink enough water to meet bodily needs you could end up with:

* digestive complications
* dry skin and hoarse voice
* decreased organ functions
* water retention problems
* muscle soreness
* joint soreness
* increased toxicity in the body
* poor metabolism of body fat
* excess body fat
* poor muscle tone and size
* persistent constipation

If you are not drinking enough water, your body may retain water to compensate.

Dehydration
Dehydration occurs when one is not getting enough fluids. Nursing homes, for example, are required to provide a clean pitcher of cold water at the bedside of every resident. Several things can go wrong: The fluid is not provided or the resident cannot or does not drink it or needs assistance to do so. **If an older person does not receive enough fluids dehydration can result.** Infection, confusion, and/or bedsores also can result.

Symptoms include: very dry mouth, very dry skin, sunken eyeballs, heavy speech, unexplained confusion, and/or unexplained drowsiness (see hyperthermia--heat stroke, page 427).

How Much Water Should You Drink?
Most experts say you should drink at least eight or ten (8-ounce) glasses of water each day if you weigh 160 pounds. For every 25 pounds you are over this weight drink an extra glass. You need more if you exercise a lot or live in a hot climate. As you increase your fiber intake you also need to drink more water.

Dieting and Water Intake
If you are trying to lose weight and don't drink plenty of water, the body can't metabolize the fat adequately. Retaining fluid also keeps the weight up. It is one of the keys to successful weight loss. Before dieting or before going on an exercise program know the quality of the water you drink.

Types of Bottled Water
Today, partly because of the concern about water pollution and partly because of clever advertising, dozens of kinds of bottled water are available. Some can cost 25 cents a glass. Here are the general types:
✿ Still water--noncarbonated tap water.
✿ Sparkling water--carbonated by dissolving carbon dioxide gas.
✿ Mineral water--water containing dissolved minerals usually drawn from a spring.
✿ Spring water--water that rises naturally to the surface of the earth. Sometimes it is processed before bottling, sometimes not.
✿ Seltzer water--tap water filtered and carbonated (no salts or minerals added).
✿ Club soda--tap water filtered, carbonated, and minerals added. The sodium content may be high, so it is not recommended for people suffering from high blood pressure or heart disease unless it is the no-sodium kind.

Good eating habits equate to better health

Some older people (especially men who live alone) lose interest in eating because they have problems buying and preparing food. A poor diet can result in lack of energy, malnutrition, and bad health. Eating provides pleasure and nourishment. People enjoy the taste, smell, color, and texture of foods. Mealtimes also provide an opportunity to relax and talk with others. Even more important, eating well each day helps you stay active and healthy. By developing a few simple habits, grocery shopping, cooking, and mealtime can be easier and more enjoyable.

PLAN AHEAD--Plan meals in advance and note the ingredients you will need. Keep some canned or frozen fish, meat, fruits, vegetables, dinners, and soups on hand for days when you don't feel like cooking or can't go out. Bread freezes well. Powdered nonfat milk or canned evaporated milk also can be stored easily.

When planning meals, keep in mind that healthful diets contain a wide variety of foods selected from the first five major food groups. Meals should include: (1) fresh fruits; (2) vegetables; (3) whole grain or enriched breads and cereals, rice, and pasta; (4) milk, cheese, and other dairy products; (5) fish, poultry, lean meats, beans, and nuts. Avoid eating too many foods that are high in fat, salt, and sugar.

Plan to divide foods fairly evenly among meals. If one meal must be heartier, midday is usually best. While three meals a day is usual, many people like to eat four or more lighter meals a day. If serving sizes are small, use more servings from each food group every day. Plan for a variety of color, flavor, and texture to add interest to meals; for example, combine bland with tart flavors, mild- with strong-flavored foods, and have something crisp to contrast with softer foods. Use hot and cold foods for variety. Prepare no more than one time-consuming dish in each meal. Plan "leftovers" for another meal.

The grocery list should include both fresh and processed foods. Buy enough fresh fruits and vegetables to last only a few days. They will lose their freshness and some nutrients if stored too long. Meats stay fresh in the refrigerator for varying amounts of time. Ground beef, stew beef, poultry, and fish can be kept safely for only one or two days and should be frozen if kept longer. Roasts, chops, and steaks can be refrigerated three to five days before you use them. Here are some other shopping hints:

❋ Check your supply of staples such as flour, sugar, rice, and cereal.
❋ Choose your store or stores carefully. Stores that offer special services usually charge higher prices.
❋ Buy just what you can use without waste.
❋ Buy foods in season for best quality. Watch for "specials."
❋ Decide which size item is best for you. A large can or package may be cheaper per unit, but it is not a bargain if most of the contents are thrown away.
❋ Consider sharing large packages with a friend.
❋ Frozen vegetables purchased in bags are economical because you can use small amounts at a time.
❋ Remember that cuts of meat high in bone, fat, or gristle are often expensive sources of lean meat, even if they are priced low.
❋ If an item at the meat or fresh produce counter is too large, ask an employee to repackage it.
❋ Read the content labels on packaged and canned foods. The item that is present in the largest amount is listed first, and the ones that follow are present in decreasing amounts. The amount of calories, protein, carbohydrate, fat, and sodium per serving may also be listed (see food labels, page 128).
❋ Check packages for freshness dates.

HOW TO SAVE MONEY--Unit pricing is useful because it lets you know which brand or package size costs less. Plain (generic) label or store brands are usually cheaper than name brands.

Some stores feature "natural," "health foods," and "organic produce." Such foods are considered by some nutritionists no better for you and no "safer" to eat than those found in regular grocery stores and they usually are more expensive.

The federal government provides food stamps to help people with low incomes buy groceries. If you think you may be eligible, read the article on Food Stamps, page 10.

PREPARING FOOD--Here are some things you can do to make meals healthier and easier:
❋ Prepare larger amounts of items you enjoy and refrigerate the leftovers to eat in a day or two.
❋ Divide leftovers into individual servings, write contents (and date) on each package, and freeze for later use.
❋ Try new recipes from newspapers, magazines, and television shows.
❋ Include a variety of colors, textures, and temperatures in your meals.
❋ To avoid excess fat, trim meat before cooking and broil, bake, boil, or pan-fry without added fat instead of frying in fat. Drain off cooked fat whenever possible. If soups and stews are made in advance and refrigerated, the hardened fat on top can be removed before reheating.
❋ To preserve vitamins, don't overcook vegetables to the soft and mushy state. Try eating them raw whenever possible or steam or stir-fry them briefly in a little oil.
❋ Refrigerate leftover cooked foods immediately after meals.

MEALTIME--The traditional three meals at set times each day may not be for everyone. Your eating schedule can be made to suit your own needs. For example, you may want to eat your main meal at noon. Or you may prefer frequent small meals throughout the day.

Meals should be enjoyed in a relaxed manner. An attractive table and music can help make mealtime appealing. Here are some other ideas:
❋ Invite a friend for lunch or dinner. It's more fun to cook for someone else, and the invitation may be returned.
❋ Eat in a different place, such as the living room or outside on the porch.
❋ Join or start a "pot-luck" club where everyone brings a prepared dish.
❋ Check with a local agency on aging to find out if your neighborhood provides free or low-cost meals for older people at a community center, church, or school. These meals offer good food and a chance to be with other people.

NOURISHING SNACKS--Many people enjoy snacks between meals. But some snacks add extra calories or salt to the diet, with few vitamins and minerals. Fruit, vegetable sticks, nuts, yogurt, cheese and crackers, bread, and cereal eaten in moderate amounts are better snack choices than candy, cake, cookies, potato chips, pretzels, and similar high-fat, high-calorie items.

Grocery shopping in the second 50 years

Food labels provide a great deal of information that can help you find out more about what you are getting in the products you buy. Facts found on labels tell not only what the product is, but may also tell what ingredients are in it, the nutrient value of those ingredients, the company responsible for the product, and frequently the date by which it should be sold. Further, labels may give details about substances that a person wishes to avoid, such as fat, sodium, or cholesterol.

The amount of information on food labels varies, but all food labels must contain at least the following:

* the name of the product
* the net contents or net weight, which includes the liquid in canned foods
* the name and place of business of the manufacturer, packer, or distributor.

Here's a rundown on the wealth of other information that may be found on food labels:

LIST OF INGREDIENTS

For most foods, all ingredients must be listed on the label and must be identified by their common or usual names. The ingredient that is present in the largest amount, by weight, must be listed first. Other ingredients follow in descending order according to weight.

Any additives must be listed. If colors and flavors are used, the law permits the use of such general language as "artificial color," "artificial flavor," or "natural flavor." (The only exception to the rule about artificial colors is their use in butter, cheese, and ice cream.) However, the use of the color Yellow No. 5 must be identified specifically in all products because it can cause allergic reactions in some persons.

NUTRITION INFORMATION

Nutrition information is required on a food label when a manufacturer adds a nutrient to it or when a claim is made for the product, such as "now contains fewer calories." Protein and certain vitamins and minerals may be added by the manufacturers to make a food more nutritious or to restore nutrients lost in the processing.

Today more than half the foods on the supermarket shelf are labeled with nutrition information. Many food products don't require nutrition labeling, but the manufacturers include the information anyway, knowing how important nutrition information is to consumers.

Examine the nutrition label. Note that the top part gives the number of calories and the amount of protein, carbohydrates, fat, and sodium--in that order--in a specified serving of the product. Manufacturers also have the option of listing cholesterol, fatty acids, and potassium content. In addition, under the heading "Percentage of Recommended Daily Allowances (U.S. RDAs)," information is provided on the amounts of protein and seven essential vitamins and minerals: vitamin A and C, thiamine, riboflavin, niacin, calcium, and iron. The percentages show how much a serving of the food contributes to the amount recommended per day. Manufacturers may also list any of 12 other nutrients if they contribute at least 2% of the U.S. RDA.

Because many nutrients are present in small amounts, nutrition labels show amounts in grams and milligrams (there are 28.45 grams to an ounce and 1,000 milligrams to a gram).

Sodium content is the latest addition to nutrition labeling. FDA requires sodium listing because sodium intake is associated with high blood pressure in some people. The National Academy of Sciences says that daily sodium consumption of from 1,100 to 3,300 milligrams (1.1 to 3.3 grams) is a safe and adequate amount, but most Americans consume far more than that. The FDA also specified that the terms "low sodium" and "reduced sodium" can be used in labeling products.

New regulations by the FDA are intended to improve labeling of foods to end much of the present "confusion and frustration" among Americans trying to select healthful foods. The new rules require: nutrition labels for all foods except for some spices, flavorings, and foods made by small businesses; listing of nutrients such as saturated fatty acids, total dietary fiber, cholesterol, and calories from fat; and standardizing of serving sizes and descriptive terms such as "low fat" and "high fiber."

STANDARDIZED FOODS

The only foods for which all ingredients may not have to be listed are those for which FDA has adopted "standards of identity." These foods are generally called standardized foods. A standard of identity describes the ingredients the food must contain if it is to be called by a particular common name,

---

Label Example

Nutrition Information Per Serving
Serving size = one-half cup
Servings per container = 12

Calories	190
Protein	2 grams
Carbohydrate	24 grams
Fat	9 grams
Sodium	55 milligrams

Percentage of U.S. Recommended Daily Allowances (U.S. RDA)*

Protein	4
Thiamine	10
Niacin	2

*Contains less than 2% of the U.S. RDA of vitamin A, vitamin C, riboflavin, calcium, and iron.

I'm at the age where food has taken the place of sex in my life. In fact, I've just had a mirror put over my kitchen table.

- Rodney Dangerfield

NUTRITION AND DIET
(page 2 of 4) FOOD LABELS 129

for example, ketchup, mayonnaise, etc. FDA sets standards of identity, quality, and fill-of-containers to protect consumers from being defrauded by cheap substitutes or deceptive packaging. Some 300 standards are in force today, covering a wide array of foods. A standard of identity tells not only what ingredients must be in the food, but also what other ingredients may be added.

Most optional ingredients must be identified on the label, including optional forms of ingredients that are mandatory in these products. Jams, jellies, cheeses, peanut butter, and milk are examples of some standardized foods.

Once a standard is set for a food, other products that resemble it but do not conform to the standard can't be called by the same name. For example, no product resembling peanut butter can be called peanut butter unless it contains 90% peanuts. If a product resembles a standardized food but is not as nutritious, it must be labeled as an imitation. If it's just as nutritious, it doesn't have to be called an imitation but must be given a name that describes it accurately.

Other labeling requirements that are designed to aid consumers concern fruit juices and packages of "helper" products that don't contain all the ingredients necessary to make a dish. Generally, fruit juices can't be called juice unless they're 100% juice. If they're diluted with water or other ingredients, they have to go by the name of "drink" or "beverage." The so-called helper dishes must state clearly on the package what sort of food has to be added, for example, on a chicken casserole "dinner" package the label must clearly state "you must add chicken to complete the recipe."

GRADES

Some food products carry a grade on their labels, such as "U.S. Grade A." The U.S. Department of Agriculture sets grades for meat and poultry. These are based on the quality levels of various characteristics of the product: its taste, texture, and appearance. The grades are not based on nutritional content, although the labels may give information about fat and some other ingredients. The National Marine Fisheries Service grades fish products in a similar manner.

Milk and milk products in most states carry a "Grade A" label. This grade is based on FDA-recommended sanitary standards for producing and processing milk products, which are regulated by the states. The grade is not based on nutritional values. However, FDA has established standards for milk and milk products, some of which require specific levels of vitamin A and others that permit the optional addition of vitamins A and D.

PRODUCT DATING

Many consumers find product dating helpful in shopping for various foods. The dates are designed to give consumers an idea of how long a product will remain wholesome and safe. Of course, handling and storage also may affect the freshness of a food product. With very few exceptions, such dating is not regulated by the FDA, although an expiration date is required on some products.

The terms most often used today with the actual dates are sell date or use by date. Pull date, indicating when the product should be pulled from the store shelf, may also be used in place of use by date. Pack date (indicating the date the product was packed), expiration date, and freshness date are other terms used to indicate the freshness of the product.

CODING DATE

Many companies use code dating on products that have a long "shelf life." This code is usually for the manufacturer's information. The code gives information about where and when the product was packaged, so if a recall should be required the particular product can be quickly identified, tracked down, and withdrawn from the market. For most canned foods, this coding is required by federal regulation.

UNIVERSAL PRODUCT CODE

The Universal Product Code (UPC) is included on most food products. Each product carries a unique code (bar code) that may be used with computerized grocery store checkout equipment, which in turn can provide the store with an automated inventory system. The UPC is not a federal requirement.

SYMBOLS ON FOOD LABELS

The symbol "R" on a label signifies that the trademark used on the label is registered with the U.S. Patent Office. The symbol "C" indicates that any literary and artistic content of the label is protected against infringement under the copyright laws of the United States. The use of the letter "U" inside the letter "O" is authorized by the Union of Orthodox Jewish Congregations of America (Orthodox Union) for use on foods that comply with Jewish dietary laws. The letter "K" inside the letter "O" indicates that the food is Kosher--that is, it complies with Jewish dietary laws and has been processed under the direction of a rabbi.

Recommended Daily Allowance (RDA)

In consulting a label for the nutritive value of a product, U.S. RDAs are the key. FDA has established recommended daily allowances for protein and 19 minerals and vitamins. However, nutrition labeling requires declaration only for protein, five vitamins (vitamins A and C, thiamine, riboflavin, and niacin), and two minerals (calcium and iron). A manufacturer has the option of

---

Food Labels
Weights and Measures

Weight
1 ounce (oz.) = approx. 28 grams (g)
16 ounces = 1 pound (lb)
1 pound = 454 grams
1 kilogram (kg) = 1,000 grams or 2.2 pounds
1 gram = 1,000 milligrams (mg)
1 milligram = 1,000 micrograms (ug)

Volume
1 liter = 1.06 quarts
1 liter = 1,000 milliliters (ml)
1 milliliter = 0.03 fluid ounces
1 gallon = 3.79 liters
1 quart = 0.95 liter
1 cup = 8 fluid ounces
1 tablespoon = 15 milliliters
3 teaspoons = 1 tablespoon
16 tablespoons = 1 cup
4 cups = 1 quart

How to translate the jargon on food labels

listing any or all of the remaining 12 vitamins and minerals. The optional ones are: vitamin D, E, B-6, B-12, folic acid, phosphorus, iodine, magnesium, zinc, copper, biotin, and pantothenic acid. If any of the 19 are added to a food, or a claim is made about any of them, the label must list those nutrients in addition to those required.

The consumer doesn't need to know why a vitamin or mineral is needed. It's just a matter of understanding how to use the percentages. If the label says the product contains 25% of the U.S. RDA for calcium, the consumer knows that a serving of the product will provide about one-fourth of the amount of calcium he or she should try to get in a day.

The recommended daily allowances don't--and can't--take into account the special needs of people who are ill or suffering from other medical disorders that require professionally supervised diets.

FDA allowances on most food labels are based generally on the highest values recommended by the National Academy of Sciences needed for persons 4 and older, especially young adult males. Unfortunately, FDA allowances have not been determined for persons 50 years of age or older. Certainly the roll of calcium and other vitamins and minerals for older persons needs to be addressed. The FDA claims that many normal, healthy people do not necessarily need to consume 100% of the U.S. RDA of a given nutrient each day since the body is able to store nutrients.

> **There are people who strictly deprive themselves of each and every eatable, drinkable, and smokable which has acquired a shady reputation.**
> **They pay this price for health, and health is all they get for it.**
>
> **- Mark Twain**

A Translator's Guide to Food Labels
Here is a glossary of the most commonly misunderstood terms:

Acidulants or acidifiers--Acids that have many uses in foods as flavor-enhancing agents, as preservatives to inhibit the growth of microorganisms, and as antioxidants to prevent discoloration or rancidity. In addition, they may be used to adjust the acidity in some foods.

Anticaking agents--Substances used to prevent powdered or granular foods from absorbing moisture and becoming lumpy. They help products like table salt and powdered sugar flow freely.

Antioxidants--Preservatives that prevent or delay discoloration in foods, such as cut potatoes and sliced apples. They also help keep oils and fats from turning rancid. Some examples are BHA, BHT, and propyl gallate.

Bran--Tough, outer coating of cereal grains (such as wheat, rye, and oats) that is separated in the refining process, but is included in whole-grain products. It may also be added to cereals and other grain products.

Calorie--A unit of measure of the amount of fuel or energy a food provides to the body. Food energy comes from three primary sources: fat, carbohydrates, and protein. (Alcohol also provides calories, but no other nutrients.) The nutrition label on packaged foods includes the number of calories in a specific serving of the product.

Carbohydrate--Sugars and starches that supply energy and help the body use fats efficiently. Carbohydrates are present in varying amounts in many foods. Foods with complex carbohydrates are recommended for a healthful diet--namely, whole-grain breads and cereals and dried peas and beans. Fruits contain mostly simple carbohydrates (sugar) and fiber.

Cholesterol--Fat-like substances found in foods of animal origin (meal, poultry, and dairy products), but not in foods from plants. Cholesterol is essential to body functions. However, the body can make what it needs, so the amount in some people's diets is often excessive, increasing the risk of heart disease.

Emulsifiers--Widely used in food processing, these agents stabilize fat and water mixtures so they will not separate. For example, in mayonnaise, egg yokes act as emulsifiers to keep the oil from separating from the acids (vinegar or lemon juice). Lecithin, derived from soybeans, acts as an emulsifier in such foods as chocolate and margarine.

Fats--A major source of energy, they also play a key role as carrier of fat-soluble vitamins (A, D, E, and K). Fat is a constituent of most foods of plant and animal origin.

Fatty acids--The major components of fat. Fats in food are a mixture of saturated and unsaturated fatty acids. Fats with a high proportion of saturated fatty acids are solid or nearly solid at room temperature and are found in larger amounts in foods of animal origin. Fats with mostly unsaturated fatty acids are liquid at room temperatures and may be monounsaturated or polyunsaturated. Unsaturated fatty acids become more saturated by a process called hydrogenation. Olive oil and peanut oil are especially high in monounsaturated fatty acids. Polyunsaturated fatty acids are found in largest amounts in plant oils, such as safflower, sunflower, corn, soybean, and cottonseed oils.

Fiber--Provides bulk or roughage in the diet. Fiber is derived from such plant sources as cereal grain products, vegetables, fruits, seeds, and nuts. "Dietary fiber" is the amount left after digestion by the body.

Flavor enhancers--Help bring out the natural flavor of foods. Some examples are monosodium glutamate (MSG), disodium guanylate, and disodium inosinate.

Flavors--Naturally occurring and artificial agents used to give more taste to food. Flavoring agents include extracts from spices and herbs, as well as others that are man-made.

Grains--Hard seeds of cereal plants, such as wheat, rice, corn, and rye. Whole grains contain the entire seed of the plant.

> Part of the secret of success in life is to eat what you like and let the food fight it out inside.
>
> - Mark Twain

Humectants--Chemicals such as glycerol, propylene glycol, and sorbitol that are added to foods to help retain moisture, fresh taste, and texture. Often used in candies, shredded coconut, and marshmallows.

Hydrogenated and partially hydrogenated--Labeling terms that describe the process of adding hydrogen to an unsaturated fat to make it saturated; for example, oils may be hydrogenated to various degrees to make them suitable for use in products such as margarine. The more an oil is hydrogenated, the more fatty acids it contains.

Light or lite--Labeling language that suggests a food is lower in calories unless some other meaning is specified or obvious. A "lite" product intended to be useful in reducing body weight or calorie intake must satisfy FDA requirements for low- or reduced-calorie foods and provide full nutrition labeling information. Product labels and nutrition labeling should be checked carefully for calorie, fat, and sodium content. Since 1980, FDA has required food labeled as "low calorie" to contain no more than 40 calories in a serving and no more than 0.4 calories per gram. A "reduced calorie" food must be at least one-third lower in calorie content than the food to which it is compared. Foods naturally low in calories cannot use these terms. Foods labeled as "diet" or "dietetic" products must meet the requirements for low- or reduced-calorie foods or must be clearly described as being useful for a special dietary purpose other than for maintaining or reducing body weight.

Natural--A term that appears on many products, but has little meaning. Such labeling is objectionable, says FDA, when a product contains artificial ingredients, but is described as natural.

Niacin--A water-soluble B vitamin that is important for the health of all body cells. The body needs it to use oxygen to produce energy.

Preservatives--Substances that keep foods from spoiling, becoming rancid, or developing off-color flavors.

Refined flour--Type of flour produced by milling grains to a fine consistency. Refining removes bran, fiber, and some other nutrients. Enriched flour has iron and three B vitamins added to levels required by FDA.

Riboflavin--A water-soluble B vitamin that helps the body obtain energy from food and aids in growth, digestion, and in the proper functioning of the nervous system.

Sequestrants--Chemicals used to bind trace amounts of metal impurities that can cause food to become discolored or rancid. EDTA is an example.

Stabilizers and thickeners--Substances that give foods a smooth, uniform texture. They also protect foods from adverse conditions, such as wide temperature fluctuations and physical shock during distribution. The most common thickening agents are starches (cornstarch and wheat starch) and modified food starches. Other types include carrageenan, locust bean gum, agar-agar, sodium alginate, gelatin, and pectin.

Sugar-free/sugarless--Common table sugar, sucrose, fructose, and corn syrup are among the types of calorie-containing sweeteners found in foods. A food can be labeled sugar-free and still contain calories from sugar alcohols (xylitol, sorbitol, and mannitol), provided the basis for the claim is explained. Saccharin is a nonnutritive sweetener--that is, it has no calories. Aspartame has the same calories as sugar, but is so much sweeter that only small amounts are needed to provide the desired sweetness of the product; hence, its caloric contribution is almost negligible. Acesulfame K, a sweetener approved by FDA in 1988, also is noncaloric as it is not metabolized, or broken down for use by the body.

SODIUM AND CHOLESTEROL CLAIMS

Health concerns about sodium and cholesterol have prompted a number of manufacturers to promote the low levels of those substances in their products. The claims are often made on the product labels. As a result, FDA has provided a set of descriptive terms to use for the claims.

The definitions are provided to ensure uniformity in their use by manufacturers, thus avoiding consumer confusion.

The sodium terms are established while the cholesterol language is still in the proposal stage, awaiting completion of the regulatory process.

Following are the sodium terms:

* *sodium free*--less than 5 milligrams of sodium per serving.
* *very low sodium*--35 milligrams or less per serving.
* *reduced sodium*--for foods in which the usual level of sodium has been reduced by at least 75%.
* *unsalted or no salt added, or some equivalent*--for foods once processed with salt but now produced without it. However, a food so labeled may in fact contain other forms of sodium. (Salt is 40% sodium and is the major source of sodium in the American diet, but at least 70 other sodium compounds are being used in foods today. Sodium is also present naturally in most foods.)

When these terms are used or whenever any sodium claim is made, the number of milligrams in a serving must be declared on the label by itself or as part of the nutritional information.

The proposed cholesterol terms are:

* *cholesterol free*--less than 2 milligrams per serving.
* *low cholesterol*--less than 20 milligrams per serving.
* *cholesterol reduced*--for products reformulated or processed to reduce cholesterol by 75% or more.

Products in which cholesterol is significantly reduced--but not by 75%--could show comparative reductions. For example, "this cake contains 35% less cholesterol than our regular pound cake."

> I went on a diet,
> swore off drinking and heavy eating,
> and in fourteen days
> I lost two weeks.
>
> - Joe E. Lewis

Without food additives, we'd eat like the cavemen

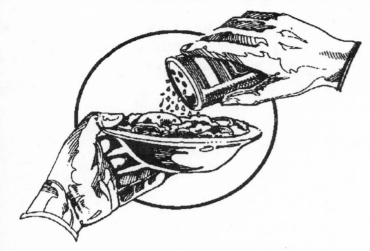

Since the time when the kitchen stove was a campfire outside a cave, people have tinkered with ways to preserve and enhance food. Food was fragile, delicate, prone to rot, and easily injured. Bugs infested it, bacteria invaded it, mold infected it, and the air made it rancid.

Something had to be added to protect food and perhaps make it tastier, too. So the ancient Romans used sulfites to disinfect wine containers and help preserve the wine. Europeans in the 13th and 14th centuries embraced Marco Polo because he brought back spices from the Orient to season their bland diet. Travelers to the New World stored meat in salt to preserve it during their long voyages across the Atlantic Ocean. Later, pioneers in America used saltpeter to preserve their meat.

Food additives are so much a part of the American way of eating today that most of us would find it difficult to put together a meal that did not include them.

Take a typical lunch, for example: sandwich, instant soup, gelatin dessert, and a cola drink. The bread has been fortified with vitamins and also contains an additive to keep it fresh. The margarine has been colored pale yellow--or, if you use salad dressing, it has been made with emulsifiers to keep it from "separating." The luncheon meat contains nitrite; the soup, an additive to keep it from becoming rancid; the gelatin, red coloring to make it pretty. Finally, the cola has coloring, flavoring, sweeteners, and carbonation.

An additive is intentionally used in foods for one or more of these four purposes:

* **To maintain or improve nutritional value.** Many foods are fortified with vitamins and minerals that might otherwise be lacking in a person's diet or that have been destroyed or lost in processing.
* **To maintain freshness.** Foods last as long as they do on the shelf or in the refrigerator because of additives that retard spoilage, preserve natural color and flavor, and keep fats and oils from turning rancid.
* **To make food more appealing.** The most widely used additives are those intended to make food look and taste better. These include coloring agents, natural and synthetic flavors, flavor enhancers such as MSG (monosodium glutamate), and sweeteners.
* **To help in processing or preparation.** A wide variety of compounds are used to give body and texture to foods, evenly distribute particles of one liquid in another, affect cooking or baking results, control acidity or alkalinity, retain moisture, and prevent caking or lumping.

By far the most predominant additives are sugar, salt, and corn syrup. These three, plus citric acid, baking soda, vegetable colors, mustard, and pepper, account for more than 98% by weight of all food additives used in this country.

ADDITIVES FOR NUTRITIONAL PURPOSES

Goiter, rickets, pellagra, beriberi--most Americans have barely heard of these diseases, much less suffered them. Their disappearance in the United States over the past 50 years is in large measure the result of adding essential vitamins and minerals to such everyday foods as milk, flour, cereals, and margarine.

Nutritional fortification began in 1934 when iodine was first added to table salt to prevent goiter, enlargement of the thyroid gland caused by iodine deficiency. Fortification of milk with vitamin D, which began in the 1930s, has helped prevent rickets. Later, it became standard practice to add iron and B vitamins--niacin, thiamine, and riboflavin--

to flour, breads, and cereals to prevent iron deficiency, anemia, pellagra, beriberi, and mental retardation. Today, many additional foods are enriched or fortified with vitamins, minerals, and amino acids.

Consumers can tell which foods are fortified, because all products with nutrients added must be labeled. A misconception among some consumers is that addition of vitamins and minerals always makes the food superior to unfortified foods. In fact, adding nutrients already abundant in the diet provides no extra benefit, because the body uses only what it needs. There also can be too much of a good thing. Excessive amounts of some nutrients, such as vitamins A and D, or of trace elements, such as copper, zinc, molybdenum, and selenium, can be toxic.

Is fortifying food tampering with nature? Some critics say it is. They maintain that nutrients synthesized in the laboratory and added during processing are inferior to those present naturally in foods. Actually, each vitamin, mineral, or amino acid has a specific molecular structure that is the same whatever the origin of the compound. The body cannot distinguish between a vitamin that occurs naturally in a plant or animal product and the same compound created in a laboratory.

ADDITIVES THAT MAINTAIN FRESHNESS

Basically, there are two ways that foods can "go bad." The first, and potentially most serious, is spoilage caused by molds, bacteria, fungi, and yeasts. Bacterial contamination of food can cause distressing digestive disorder, as well as deadly botulism.

Over the years, a number of common substances have been used to protect foods from microbial action. The oldest is salt, probably used before recorded history, to preserve meat and fish. Sugar has long been used in jams and jellies and to help preserve canned and frozen fruits. Today, such chemicals as sodium propionate and potassium sorbate are used to extend the shelf life of breads, cheeses, syrups, cakes, beverages, mayonnaise, and margarine.

He must have had a magnificent build before his stomach went in for a career of its own.

- Margaret Halsey

NUTRITION AND DIET
(page 2 of 4) FOOD ADDITIVES 133

The second, and less serious, way that food can "go bad" is the undesirable change in color and flavor that occurs with the exposure of foods to oxygen. The resulting oxidation is what causes fresh sliced apples or peaches to turn brown or butter to turn rancid after being exposed to air for varying lengths of time.

Preservatives used by the modern food industry perform either or both of two major functions:

1. As **antimicrobial agents**, they keep the food from spoiling.
2. As **antioxidants**, they keep foods from becoming rancid or developing off-colors and flavors.

Antimicrobial agents are added to food formulations to inhibit or prevent the growth of molds, yeasts, and bacteria that spoil foods. Foods high in carbohydrates and protein also are subject to microbial deterioration that can affect flavor. Those with large amounts of carbohydrates also may undergo changes in color instead of developing off-odors or off-tastes. This change in color is sometimes referred to as the "browning effect." Consumers are used to seeing this cosmetic defect in some fresh fruits and produce after they are cut.

Antioxidants are used in a wide variety of food products--particularly the large number that contain fats and oils--to prevent rancidity. Antioxidants slow the development of off-flavor, off-odors, and color changes caused by chemical reactions that take place when foods are exposed to oxygen, moisture, heat, or certain enzymes present in many natural fats. The time it takes for fats and oils to become rancid varies with the particular fat and storage conditions. Unsaturated fats have less resistance than saturated fats to rancidity. Vegetable oils contain more unsaturated fats, but also small amounts of naturally occurring antioxidants such as tocopherols.

Although animal fats are more saturated, they have fewer naturally occurring antioxidant substances. Therefore, animal fats generally require added or higher levels of antioxidants than do vegetable oils.

Antioxidants retard oxidation by scavenging oxygen on the surface of the food. These preservatives are not necessarily exotic chemicals. Vitamins C and E are among the 27 compounds added to foods as antioxidants. Even the lemon juice squeezed on sliced apples to keep them from turning dark is technically an antioxidant.

Since so many foods contain fats and oils susceptible to oxidative and other reactions that cause rancidity and off-odors, the food industry considers it important to inhibit these reactions so as to extend the shelf life of the food products.

ADDITIVES TO MAKE FOOD APPEALING

Some additives are put into foods simply to make them more appealing. Coloring agents, for instance, contribute nothing to nutrition, taste, safety, or ease of processing. And some consumer advocates argue that food is made to look more appetizing at the risk of increasing health hazards.

Today food colors are used in virtually all processed foods. While their use is not restricted, per se, they cannot be used in unnecessary amounts or to cover up unwholesome products. Artificial colors must be listed as ingredients in all foods except butter, ice cream, and cheese. There are 33 colors currently permitted for use in foods. Some 1,700 natural and synthetic substances are used to flavor foods, making flavors the largest single category of food additives.

ADDITIVES USED IN PREPARING AND PROCESSING FOODS

The functions of these additives are many. Some cause baked goods to rise. Others prevent ice crystals from forming in ice cream and keep peanut butter from separating into oily and dry layers. Because of such additives, shredded coconut stays fresh and moist in the can. There are seven major groups of additives that are considered aids in processing and preparation of foods.

❶ *Emulsifiers (Mixers)*--Some liquids don't mix unless there is an emulsifier around.

In salad dressing, for example, oil and vinegar normally separate as soon as mixing stops. When an emulsifier is added, the ingredients stay mixed longer. Many emulsifiers come from natural sources. Lecithin, naturally present in milk, keeps fat and water together. Egg yokes, which also contain lecithin, improve the texture of ice cream and mayonnaise. The mono- and diglycerides come from vegetables or animal tallow and make bread soft, improve the stability of margarine, and prevent the oil and peanuts in peanut butter from separating.

❷ *Stabilizers and Thickeners*--These compounds "improve" the appearance of foods and the way they feel in the mouth by producing a uniform texture. They work by absorbing water. Without stabilizers and thickeners, ice crystals would form in ice cream and other frozen desserts and particles of chocolate would settle out of chocolate milk. Stabilizers also are used to prevent evaporation and deterioration of the volatile flavor oils used in cakes, puddings, and gelatin mixes. Most stabilizers and thickeners are natural carbohydrates. Gelatin, made from animal bones, hooves, and other parts, and pectin, from citrus rind, are used in home and commercial food processing. Extra pectin, for example, is added to thicken jams and jellies.

❸ *pH Control Agents*--These affect the texture, taste, and safety of foods by controlling acidity or alkalinity. Acids, for example, give a tart taste to such foods as soft drinks, sherbets, and cheese spreads. A more important use is to ensure the safety of low-acid canned foods, such as beets. Alkalizers alter the texture and flavor of many foods, including chocolate. After cocoa beans are picked, they are allowed to dry and ferment before they are made into chocolate. During processing, alkalizers are sometimes added to neutralize the acids produced during fermentation and to provide darker, richer color and milder flavor in the finished product.

❹ *Leavening Agents*--Although air and steam help create a light texture in

More than you ever wanted to know about food additive

bread and cake, carbon dioxide is the key to making baked goods rise properly. Without leavening agents that produce or stimulate production of carbon dioxide, we would not have light, soft baked goods.

❺ *Maturing and Bleaching Agents*--are used primarily to get flour ready for baking because natural pigments give freshly milled flour a yellowish color. Flour also lacks the qualities necessary to make a stable, elastic dough. When aged for several months, it gradually whitens and matures to become useful in baking.

❻ *Anti-caking Agents*--Compounds such as calcium silicate, iron ammonium citrate, and silicon dioxide are used to keep table salt, baking powder, confectioner's sugar, and other powdered food ingredients free flowing. By absorbing moisture, these chemicals prevent caking, lumping, and clustering that would make powdered or crystalline products inconvenient to use.

❼ *Humectants*--are substances that retain moisture in shredded coconut, marshmallows, soft candies, and other confections. One of the most common is glycerine. The sweetener sorbitol also is used for this purpose.

Without food additives bread would easily mold, cake wouldn't rise, salt would lump, ice cream would separate into ice crystals, and marshmallows would harden into bite-sized rocks.

PROTECTING THE CONSUMER

Former generations could add just about anything they wanted to food as long as it didn't poison someone. But increasing knowledge about food science and possible long-term harmful effects of food chemicals on health led Congress in 1958 to enact the Food Additive Amendment to the Federal Food, Drug and Cosmetic Act to ensure the safety of the additives. In 1960 the Color Additive Amendments were enacted to make sure colorings used in foods (drugs, medical devices, and cosmetics, as well) were safe.

For purposes of FDA regulations, chemicals added to food--other than pesticides and animal drugs--fall into four categories:

❶ food additives,
❷ generally recognized as safe (GRAS) substances,
❸ prior-sanctioned substances, and
❹ color additives.

These finely drawn legal categories were set up to ensure appropriate safety reviews of food additives. Depending on what category an ingredient falls in, different regulatory requirements apply.

Food additives--The "toughest" category in terms of regulations and safety testing is the food additive category. This covers substances that have no proven track record of safety; scientists just don't know that much about them.

Additives such as the artificial sweetener aspartame and the emulsifying agent polysorbate 60, which is found in salad dressing and other food, were substances that needed to be tested before they could be used because it was not known whether they were safe. Subsequent testing proved them safe.

But what is "safe"? Congress has defined safety as "a reasonable certainty that no harm will result from use of an additive." The FDA evaluations examine whether the additive has any toxic effects, may cause birth defects, interferes with nutrition, or affects individuals with allergies.

When an additive is tested, it is usually fed in large doses over an extended period of time to at least two different animals. These feeding studies, usually done by or for a food company that wants to use or sell the additive, are designed to determine whether the substance causes cancer, birth defects, or other injury to the animals. Cancer is of particular concern. A special provision of the 1958 and 1960 additive amendments, the so-called Delaney clause, states that if an additive is found to cause cancer in humans or animals it may not be added to the food.

The company submits the results of all these tests to the FDA for review. If the FDA review finds that the additive is safe, the agency establishes regulations for how it can be used in food. This commonly includes a 100-fold margin of safety, which means that the substance may be used in food at a level that is no more than 1/100th of the highest level at which it was fed to test animals and did not produce any harmful effects.

GRAS--The second group of substances is known as GRAS, an acronym for substances "generally recognized as safe." This group includes several hundred substances whose use in food is considered safe by experts based either on a history of safe use before 1958 or on published scientific evidence.

Congress established the GRAS category in 1958 because they felt that it was unnecessary to require industry to develop evidence to prove the safety of substances that were already generally regarded as safe by knowledgeable scientists. Included are many spices and herbs, salt, sugar, and vitamins that "logic and common sense," in the words of one expert, tell us are safe to use.

Of the more than two dozen GRAS antimicrobials and antioxidants, FDA has reaffirmed that six may continue to be safely used. These are benzoic acid, methylparaben, propyl gallate, propylparaben, sodium benzoate, and stannous chloride. Of the remainder, FDA has either not finally acted on its published proposals to reaffirm their safety or is still evaluating data before taking final action. The two most widely used antioxidants still being reviewed by the agency are butylated hydroxyanisole (BHA) and its related compound, butylated hydroxytoluene (BHT).

Some of these GRAS substances are:

✳ *Ascorbates and erythorbates*--[ascorbic acid (vitamin C), ascorbyl palmitate, calcium ascorbate, erythorbic acid, sodium ascorbate, sodium erythorbate]. Okayed for use. Used in many foods and beverages, concentrated milk products, meat products, baked goods, candies, fats and oils, gravies, breakfast

Many of us don't know what poor
losers we are until we try dieting.

- Thomas Lamance

NUTRITION AND DIET

(page 4 of 4) **FOOD ADDITIVES** **135**

cereals, and processed fruits and vegetables.

* *Benzoic and sodium benzoate*--Okayed
for use. Used in many products.
* **BHA** *(butylated hydroxyanisole and BHT
butylated hydroxytoluene)*--are approved
antioxidants. Used in breakfast cereals, gum, convenience foods, vegetable
oils, shortening, potato flakes, enriched
rice, potato chips, and candy.
* *Parabens*--Used in many foods for more
than 50 years.
* *Propionic acid*--and its salts. Used for
many years in baked goods and cheeses.
* *Propyl gallate*--Widely used antioxidant
in foods.
* *Sorbic acid*--and its salts. Used in food
for over 30 years.
* *Stannus chloride*--Prevents color changes
and offensive odors in foods.
* *Sulfiting agents*--Used by the food service industry--restaurant salad bars are
a major example--to keep lettuce and
other vegetables fresh and crisp and to
prevent discoloration. Many restaurants
no longer use it.
* *Tocopherols*--Contribute vitamin E to
the diet.

Prior-sanctioned substances--The third category includes ingredients such as the preservative nitrite (used in meat) that had
been sanctioned before the 1958 amendment.

Inclusion in either of the latter two catego-
ries--GRAS and prior-sanctioned--does not
guarantee a substance's safety; sometimes
new evidence shows that "logic and common sense" erred. If new data suggest that
a GRAS or prior-sanctioned substance may
be unsafe, then FDA requires the manufacturer to conduct studies to ascertain the
ingredient's safety. For example, the artificial sweeteners saccharin and cyclamates
are substances that were once included on
the GRAS list but came under fire several
years ago because of new evidence that they
may cause cancer in animals. Based on this
evidence they were removed from the GRAS
list; in fact, cyclamates were banned from
use in food altogether. (Saccharin continues to be used because Congress granted it
a special exemption.)

Color Additives--The Color Additive Amendments subject substances in the fourth cate-
gory--dyes used in foods, drugs, cosmetics,
and medical devices--to premarket testing
similar to that required for the first cate-
gory--food additives. Colors in use when
the amendments were passed were placed
on a provisional approval list pending further investigation to confirm their safety.
Nearly 200 colors were on the provisional
approval list in 1960. Since the passage of
the amendment, several of the colors have
been dropped because manufacturers were
no longer interested in marketing them or
because they were found to be unsafe.

Food additives may also be present in food
packages. Known as indirect additives, they
can end up in the food so FDA requires that
they be evaluated.

REPORTING REACTIONS TO ADDITIVES

Some bodies just don't like certain foods.
And when that happens, the body's reactions can range from headaches or hives to
seizures or death. Food additives have not
been exempt from blame either. With the
introduction of the artificial sweetener
aspartame in soft drinks in 1983, complaints
blaming food additives for allergic reactions soared. To better monitor the effects
of additives and deal with consumer complaints, FDA set up the Adverse Reaction
Monitoring System (ARMS) in early 1985.

FDA officials investigate the complaints,
which are then classified by the severity of
the symptom (headaches, mood changes,
nausea, etc.) and the frequency and consistency of the symptom's association with
eating or drinking a particular product
(whether the symptom occurred more than
once, and how soon it occurred after the
suspect product was eaten).

If you suspect you have had an allergic
reaction to an additive, contact your local
physician for treatment. You or your doctor might want to then contact the nearest
FDA field office (look in the blue pages of
your phone book) to report the reaction.

MSG (MONOSODIUM GLUTAMATE)

The best known flavor enhancer is the amino
acid monosodium glutamate (MSG), widely
used in restaurants and in prepared foods.
Scientists are not sure exactly how it works,
but suspect that it increases the nerve impulses responsible for the perception of
flavors.

MSG is the controversial chemical best
known as the cause of "Chinese restaurant
syndrome" (claims are that relatively large
amounts of MSG are often used in food
served in Chinese-style restaurants), and it
contains a major amino acid that the human
body makes on its own and that can kill
critical brain cells in some people, research
scientists have discovered.

But whether eating large quantities of the
flavor enhancer can cause any damage other
than the brief symptoms of flushing, sweating, dizziness, or headache that many diners
feel after a Chinese dinner is a matter of
continuing debate. According to Dr. Thomas Kearney, a pharmacologist at the poison control center of the University of California, there is no question that even modest amounts of MSG added to food at home
or in a restaurant can cause a variety of
unpleasant symptoms in 15% to 25% of
those who ingest it. But, he says, contrary to
what most people believe, the effect is rarely
if ever an allergic reaction. Annoying effects strike within 10 to 20 minutes after
eating a meal containing even small amounts
of MSG, and they rarely last more than two
or three hours, he says.

> **Life is easier than you think.**
> **All you have to do is this:**
> **accept the impossible,**
> **do without the indispensible,**
> **bear the intolerable, and**
> **be able to smile at everything.**
>
> ❤
>
> **We grow most**
> **when we are down**
> **in the valley**
> **where the fertilizer is.**

Cholesterol--the good, the bad, and the ugly

THE UGLY: How many of your loved ones, friends, or neighbors have had heart attacks or required bypass surgery? In our country, more than 6 million have symptoms of coronary heart disease. Each year an estimated 1.5 million, mostly senior citizens, will suffer heart attacks, resulting in more than 540,000 deaths. It is the number one cause of death in the U.S. Of those who survive the heart attack (40% don't survive the first one) many are "coronary cripples" and missing the good life of retirement. During our earlier years, plaque gradually piled up on our artery linings for most of us due mainly to our American diet. When we've reached 50 or more years, we've had plenty of time to clog up our blood pipelines, choking off blood flow and triggering a heart attack.

THE GOOD: Avoiding coronary disease is in large part still within your control. Physicians and scientists contend that if you stop smoking, control your blood pressure, exercise, keep your weight within 20% of ideal, maintain a low-saturated fat diet, and keep your blood cholesterol level below 200 you can reduce your risk of a heart attack. Test results show if you lower your blood cholesterol from 250 to 200, for example, you'll reduce your risk of a heart attack by 40%.

WHAT IS CHOLESTEROL?--Cholesterol is an odorless, soft, white, waxy substance and is just one of several fats (called lipids) in the blood. Your body needs cholesterol to make essential body substances such as cell walls and hormones. Your liver manufactures it from the foods you eat, not just from foods containing cholesterol. Foods that contain dietary cholesterol and saturated fats contribute to raising blood cholesterol levels. You cannot taste cholesterol or see it in foods.

LIPOPROTEINS--The liver makes packets of cholesterol combined with triglycerides from the foods we eat. Triglycerides, also fat substances, are stored as the body's fat tissue for later use as energy. These two fat-like substances, cholesterol and triglycerides, will not mix with water. Therefore, to carry fat (lipid) in the blood, the body wraps them in protein packets. This combination is called a "lipoprotein."

Very low-density lipoproteins (VLDL's) carry the cholesterol and triglycerides through the bloodstream. After releasing their triglycerides into the body's tissues, the VLDL's are changed to low-density lipoproteins (LDL's) containing a high amount of cholesterol that they deliver to the cells. Excess LDL's, rejected by sated cells and called "bad" cholesterol, become plaque that can build up in artery walls, narrowing your blood pipelines.

High-density lipoprotein (HDL) packets contain a small amount of cholesterol and carry cholesterol away from body cells and tissues to the liver for excretion from the body. These are called "good" cholesterol.

CHOLESTEROL TESTS--To measure your blood cholesterol, a small blood sample is taken and sent to a laboratory or measured using portable testing machines. The amount of cholesterol in the blood is expressed as milligrams per deciliter (mg/dl). A deciliter is about 1/3 of a cup; 280 milligrams is about 1/100th of an ounce.

Most tests measure only your total blood cholesterol level. Recent studies emphasize the need to measure LDL, HDL, and triglycerides as well. Higher HDL levels, in the 70s and 80s, are thought to be protective against heart disease. Even with a total cholesterol level below 200, some think you still can be at risk if your HDL level is below 35.

Medical specialists believe the best indicator of coronary risk is the ratio of total cholesterol divided by the HDL level. For example, a total cholesterol reading of 200 divided by a HDL level of 60 produces a ratio of 3.3. Low-risk vegetarians have a ratio of 2.5. If your ratio is 4.5 or higher it is typical of people who develop coronary heart disease according to the Framingham Heart Study. The average female heart-disease victim comes in at 4.6 to 6.4 and males at 5.4 to 6.1.

Since the average total cholesterol level of men over 50 is above 225 (235 for women), it is important for you to know this total cholesterol/HDL ratio (see chart on cholesterol profile).

CHOLESTEROL PROFILE

TEST	RESULTS	RISK FACTOR	COMMENTS
TOTAL CHOLESTEROL	40 - 200 mg/dl	desirable	Repeat test every 2 years. Monitor your daily intake of saturated fats and cholesterol.
	200 - 239 mg/dl	borderline high	Restrict cholesterol and saturated fats in diet, retest, and take average of readings and retest in 6 months.
	200 - 239 mg/dl	borderline high with risk factors	See a doctor for advice, further analysis, and treatment. Risk factors include: family history of premature heart disease, smoking, diabetes, hypertension, low HDL, and severe obesity.
	240 plus mg/dl	**HIGH RISK**	Definitely see a doctor for further analysis and treatment. (Some studies say this number should be 260 for older persons.)
LDL CHOLESTEROL	66 - 130 mg/dl	acceptable	LDL is the "bad" cholesterol.
	160 plus mg/dl	**HIGH RISK**	
HDL CHOLESTEROL	29 - 77 mg/dl	acceptable	HDL is the "good" cholesterol. Normal 45-50 for men, 50-60 for women.
	low levels	**HIGH RISK**	Too little HDL even with low total cholesterol levels, less than 200 for example, is considered by some a high risk.
TOTAL CHOL/HDL	2.5 ratio	low risk	The average ratio for vegetarians. (Framingham Heart Study)
(CHD RISK RATIO)	3.4		Marathon runners' average ratio.
	4.6 to 6.4		The average female heart-disease victim.
	5.4 to 6.1		The average male heart patient.

The CHD (cholesterol heart disease) ratio is considered by many to be the best indicator of overall risk of heart disease.

Lowering your chances of heart disease

STEPS YOU CAN TAKE--to reduce your chances of coronary heart disease.

* Stop smoking!
* Keep tabs on your blood pressure and cholesterol levels.
* Lose weight if you are overweight.
* Exercise regularly.
* Limit your dietary cholesterol to less than 300 milligrams per day.
* Limit fat intake to less than 30% of your calories with no more than 10% each of saturated, monounsaturated, and polyunsaturated fats.
* Changes in diet to limit intake of foods containing dietary cholesterol and saturated fats. Increase intake of soluble fiber.
* Under special circumstances, your doctor may prescribe cholesterol-lowering drugs.

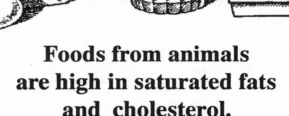

Foods from animals are high in saturated fats and cholesterol.

TESTS--It is important for you to know your cholesterol levels. Have your physician measure your total cholesterol, your LDL, HDL, and triglycerides. Keep a record for yourself to monitor your progress. Repeat the tests every six months if high, less often if low.

KEEP TABS ON YOUR BLOOD PRESSURE--Normal blood pressure and heart rate is:

Age	Blood Pressure		Heart Rate
	systolic	diastolic	beats/min.
At 55	145	95	70-100
At 65	150	95	70-100
At 75	150	100	80-110
At 85	160	100	90-115

LOSE WEIGHT--Limit your calorie intake if you're more than 20% overweight. It will help you have lower LDL and higher HDL levels. Average weight in relationship to your height is:

Men	Over 50	Over 60	Over 70
5 ft. 6 in.	156 lbs.	154 lbs.	140 lbs.
5 ft. 10 in.	176	174	156
6 ft. 2 in	194	194	175
Women			
5 ft. 2 in.	136	136	122
5 ft. 6 in.	152	154	139
5 ft. 10 in.	172	172	155

By 65 most people shrink in height by one inch and decrease in weight by 10%.

DIET--Most of us can decrease our blood cholesterol levels by 10% to 15% by reducing saturated fat and cholesterol in our diet. It may take several weeks to respond to dietary changes. If changes in diet, weight, and exercise do not produce an adequate drop, your physician may prescribe cholesterol-lowering drugs. You should continue the low-fat, low-cholesterol diet even when using these medications. Dieting does not mean you need to go hungry; it just means you must watch more carefully what you eat and the amount you eat.

LIMIT DIETARY CHOLESTEROL--The American Heart Association recommends you limit intake to no more than 300 milligrams per day. Dietary cholesterol is found only in foods of animal origin. One egg contains about 270 milligrams of cholesterol--nearly all in the yoke. Typically, more than 60% of the cholesterol we eat comes from meat, 16% from dairy products, and 7% from soups, gravies, and mixed protein dishes.

LIMIT FAT INTAKE--Limit your total fat intake to less than 30% of your total calories and be evenly divided (10% each) between saturated, monounsaturated, and polyunsaturated.

ALLEVIATE STRESS--Find ways to relax. When you're under stress, it causes a release of fats and cholesterol from your body's stores into the blood. Learn to relax 5 minutes every 30 minutes.

EXERCISE REGULARLY--Walking briskly, swimming, even aerobic dancing, three to five times a week for 30 to 40 minutes continuously, will help control your weight, raise your HDL's, and reduce triglycerides. Exercise usually helps to increase HDL levels, although the reason for this is not understood. Exercise will also help keep your weight in check, and increase your sense of well-being.

Recommended Daily Calorie Intake

		Total	Protein	Total fat	Carbohydrates
Calories/ounce			170	250	112
% of calories			15%	30%	55%
	Age	calories	ounces	ounces	ounces
Men	over 50	2,750	2.4	3.2	13.4
	over 60	2,750	2.4	3.2	13.4
	over 70	2,150	1.9	2.5	10.4
Women	over 50	1,900	1.7	2.2	9.2
	over 60	1,900	1.7	2.2	9.2
	over 70	1,650	1.5	2.0	8.0

Drugs, high fiber, low fat, or fish--you bet your life

Diet, exercise, eliminating smoking, and achieving ideal weight often decreases LDL and increases HDL cholesterol levels. If you have a family history of heart disease or risk factors, your doctor may prescribe a fat-lowering drug along with a restricted diet. There are several fat-lowering drugs on the market.

Cholestyramine and Colestipol bind cholesterol-containing bile within the bowels where it is excreted. The drugs force the liver to make more bile, resulting in lower LDL levels. Adverse effects include constipation, stomach upset, nausea, vomiting, flatulence, diarrhea, or allergic reaction.

Nicotinic acid (Niacin) decreases the liver's production of LDL. Large dosages are used. It is a vitamin B and nonprescription available in most health food stores and pharmacies. It can cause a facial flush, itching, stomach upset, irregular heartbeats, and possibly liver dysfunction. If you use aspirin 20 minutes before taking it and start with a low dose, then gradually build up, side effects are reduced. Ask for your doctor's advice and recommendations.

Probucol combines with LDL in the blood to form a particle more readily removed. Most tolerate it well, but it can cause diarrhea, abdominal pain, or excessive gas.

Lovanstatin blocks the liver's production of cholesterol. It has no noticeable side effects. The manufacturer recommends periodic eye and liver tests because of potential cataracts and liver damage with prolonged use.

Gemfibrozil lowers triglycerides and raises HDL. It is usually not recommended because it has a variety of potentially severe side effects including headaches, diarrhea, blurred vision, and abdominal pain or distress.

THE OAT BRAN CRAZE--Some claim that soluble fiber such as rice bran, corn fiber, and oat bran are effective in lowering cholesterol levels. They claim that 3 ounces of oat bran a day (equal to six cups of cooked oatmeal or about six oat-bran muffins) can lower LDL cholesterol as much as 23%. Such data have caused a rush for oat bran. Soluble fiber is also found in dried beans, bananas, apples, and other fruit (see the article on fiber, page 125).

Others say soluble fiber may not do that itself, but it may help lower cholesterol levels because people ingest the fiber, leaving less room for fat intake and less fat intake lowers cholesterol levels. The diet causes gas, flatulence, cramps, bloating, and diarrhea in 18 out of 20 people--some say you get used to these side effects as they decrease with time. Other reasons for a high-fiber diet include: better digestion, less constipation, and it does a fine job of keeping you "regular" and may help prevent intestinal and colon cancers.

Oat bran, oatmeal, rice bran, and wheat bran are nearly pure fiber. They are as effective as eating dietary fiber. These foods--the same as cholesterol-lowering drugs--must be part of a low-fat diet. Be careful when buying packaged cereals; some, even though high in fiber, contain fat and sugar.

NEWS--Eating fish-oil capsules every day may not lower cholesterol and may increase the "bad" cholesterol--LDL. It is possible that the fish-oil capsule supplements can reduce the blood's clotting ability. It's best just to eat more fish.

A recent study showed a diet of a pound of salmon a day for 40 days reduced LDL and raised HDL levels. The men's blood-clotting time did not go up. Some became allergic to the fish and had to stop the diet.

THE BAD--It's unfortunate, but considerable controversy surrounds the issue of elevated cholesterol levels and the appropriate way to deal with them. Most studies have been done with middle-aged men, few with women, and none with elderly persons. The studies are not conclusive. Therefore, experts disagree on how to handle elevated cholesterol levels in the elderly. The medical profession believes there are many factors that contribute to coronary heart disease. These factors include: genetic causes--a family history of heart disease, poor eating and exercise habits, high total cholesterol levels, high blood pressure, severe obesity, diabetes, smoking, and stress.

But most experts feel that the diet recommended by the American Heart Association is a good basic nutritious diet and one that could be beneficial for the older population. They do not recommend drug treatment for high lipid levels in elderly as readily as they do in the younger population. Conventional wisdom suggests that you follow the steps given on page 137.

The AHA diet book can be purchased in most bookstores. Ask for:
Low-Fat Cholesterol Cookbook
American Heart Association
Scott M. Grundy, M.D., Ph.D.
Editor, Times Books, 1989, $18.95

To be better informed you can write for free educational materials to:

National Cholesterol Education Program
Heart, Lung, and Blood Institute, C-200
Bethesda, MD 20892

National Cholesterol Education
Program Information Center
4733 Bethesda Avenue, Suite 503
Bethesda, MD 20814

The American Heart Association
7320 Greenville Avenue
Dallas, TX 75231

A WORD OF CAUTION--Even though the effectiveness of fat-lowering drugs in reducing mortality from coronary heart disease remains unproven, many doctors recommend their use for high-risk patients. Most of these drugs are prescription drugs and your doctor is familiar with their side effects --and they do have side effects. Before embarking on a program to lower your cholesterol or in using any of these drugs, get your doctor's advice.

CHOLESTEROL-LOWERING DRUGS

Generic Name	Trade Name	Max. Daily Dose	Approx. Cost $/month	
Cholestyramine	Questran	24 gm	$ 40	in bulk
			$150	packaged
Colestipol	Colstid	30 gm	$ 90	in bulk
			$102	packaged
Nicotinic acid	Niacin	4 gm	$ 6	500-mg tablets
			$121	time released
Probucol	Lorelco	1 gm	$ 50	
Gemfibrozil	Lopid	1.2 gm	$ 50	
Lovastatin	Mevacor	80 mg	$175	

Some good old jokes for older folks

The most important thing about life is honesty and sincerity. If you can fake those, you've got it made.   - George Burns, age 93

❀

A fellow came into the bar of a fancy restaurant and began playing the piano. An impressed chap at the bar said to him, "Man, that's great. Now play some Picasso."

❀

Not found in Webster's:
acoustic: what you shoot pool with
bacteria: rear entrance to a cafeteria
gossip: a person with a great sense of rumor
grudge: a place to keep your car
masseurs: people who knead people
polygon: a runaway parrot

❀

Q. What do you call a boomerang that doesn't come back? Answer. A stick.

❀

A burglar came in through the window and when he got inside he heard this voice saying, "Jesus will get you, Jesus will get you." Then he saw this parrot and said, "Shut up." Just then a big bulldog came into the doorway. The parrot shouted, "Sickum Jesus."

❀

Jerry Rand of San Francisco retired after 30 plus years as a Pan Am purser. He became a legend when a bitchy woman passenger, who complained about everything, shouted at him during dinner, "Steward, this potato is BAD!" As the entire first-class cabin watched in silence, Jerry sauntered over, picked up the potato, and spanked it with a spoon, saying, "Bad Potato, bad potato, bad potato!"

❀

Q. Do you know why cowboys roll up the sides of their hats? Answer. So three of them can sit abreast in a pickup.

❀

Whenever one of our authors publishes a book, he always sends a copy to his close friends and relatives. "Usually," he says, "they don't respond, even with a thank you note." However, he has an aunt who lives on a farm in Iowa who wrote him saying, "I love your new book, we use it every day, it's pages are very soft."

❀

A patient confessed to her physician that she had consulted a fortune teller, a faith healer, and a palm reader. "And what foolish advice did they give you?" asked the doctor. Came the wry answer: "They all told me to see you."

God said to Adam, "I'm going to make you a beautiful woman, a companion who will fulfill your life, obey your every command, and serve you night and day." Adam said to God, "How much is this going to cost me?" God said, "An arm and a leg." Adam said, "Sounds pretty steep, what can I get for a rib?"

❀

Tourist: Does it matter which road I take to White River Junction? Vermonter: Not to me, it doesn't.

❀

Psychiatrist: You'll never make any progress until you get over these phobias. Patient: I was afraid you'd say that.

❀

Psychiatrist: Do you find you have trouble making decisions? Patient: Well, yes and no.

❀

When I was a little boy, my father bought me a bat for Christmas. It bit me three times before it flew away.

❀

When asked, "What is a contingent fee?" a lawyer answered, "A contingent fee to a lawyer means, if I don't win your suit, I get nothing. If I do win it, you get nothing."

❀

Then there was this fisherman who saw a sign, "All the worms you want for $1.00." He stopped his car and ordered $2 worth.

❀

When you see a man opening a car door for his wife, you know one of two things: either the car is new or his wife is.

❀

A man was in prison. Every day some convict would yell out a number and everyone would roar with laughter. The man asked his cell-mate, "What is this?" The cell-mate responded, "We have hundreds of jokes numbered, and instead of retelling the joke someone just yells out a number and we all recall the joke and laugh." The man thought, "I'll yell out a number," so he hollered "24"; but no one laughed. "Why didn't they laugh?" he asked his cell-mate. "Some people can tell a joke, and some people can't."

❀

He thought he was a wit, and he was half right.

❀

SMILE: it might rub off on some grouch.

A man's dog died, so he went to the Priest to arrange to have mass. The priest said, "No, Catholics don't do that. Maybe the Baptist minister down the street will have a service." "Father," said the man, "Do you think a $5,000 donation will be enough for the occasion?" Priest: "Man, why didn't you tell me it was a Catholic dog."

❀

Have you seen this ad:
LOST
Dog with 3 legs,
blind in left eye, missing
right ear, tail broken and
recently castrated. Answers
to the name of "Lucky."

❀

Then there was the time the judge was asked to contribute 10 bucks to a lawyer's funeral. "Here's a hundred," he said, "Bury 10 of them."

❀

Crime victim: "Oh, please don't take my wedding ring. It has sentimental value." Robber: "That's OK. I'm a sentimental guy."

❀

Some Jewish boys today don't have the same interest in religion as their fathers. Plotz sent a telegram to his son: DON'T FORGET YOM KIPPUR STARTS TOMORROW. The boy sent a wire back: PUT $200 ON THE NOSE FOR ME.

❀

Little boy to mother: "Why does grandfather read the Bible all the time? Is he preparing for his finals?"

❀

Two golfers were playing on the green past the state mental institution. Suddenly the front door burst open and a beautiful young blonde naked lady ran out, across the lawn, jumped the fence, and streaked across the green into the bushes. She was pursued by two guards in white coats. One guard was carrying a bucket of sand. One golfer said to the other, "What is this all about?" "Well this is a mental institute, that was a patient who took off her clothes, ran away, and is being pursued by the guards." "Yes, I know, but why is one guard carrying a bucket full of sand?" "Oh, he caught her yesterday and must carry a handicap today."

Fitness: a mechanical tune-up for the body

Physical fitness is to the human body what fine-tuning is to an engine. It enables us to perform up to our potential. Fitness can be described as a condition that helps us look, feel, and do our best. More specifically it is: The ability to perform daily tasks vigorously and alertly, with energy left over for enjoying leisure-time activities and meeting emergency demands. It is the ability to endure, to bear up, to withstand stress, to carry on in circumstances where an unfit person could not continue, and it is a major basis for good health and well-being.

Physical fitness involves the performance of the heart, lungs, and muscles. And, since what we do with our bodies also affects what we can do with our minds, fitness influences to some degree qualities such as mental alertness and emotional stability.

THE BASICS--Physical fitness is most easily understood by examining its components or parts. The five ingredients are:

❶ **Cardiorespiratory endurance**--the ability to deliver oxygen and nutrients to tissues, and to remove wastes, over sustained periods of time.

❷ **Muscular strength**--the ability of a muscle to exert force for a brief period of time.

❸ **Muscular endurance**--the ability of a muscle, or a group of muscles, to sustain repeated contractions or to continue to apply force against a fixed object.

❹ **Flexibility**--the ability to move joints and use muscles through their full range of motion. The sit-and-reach test is a good measure of flexibility of the lower back and backs of the upper legs.

❺ **Body composition**--is considered a component of fitness. It refers to the makeup of the body in terms of lean mass (muscle, bone, vital tissue, and organs) and fat mass. An optimal ratio of fat to lean mass is an indication of fitness. The right types of exer-cises will help you decrease body fat and increase or maintain muscle mass.

POTBELLY--For every inch your waistline exceeds the size of your chest, you can deduct two years from your life. That's how funny a potbelly isn't. For all the world to see, a "bay window" is evidence that you are either eating too much, exercising too little, or both. Despite the comic relief afforded by the tummies of some very successful comedians, a loose abdomen is no laughing matter. Why?

Because a weak abdomen can interfere with the proper functioning of the organs inside it. Apart from facilitating movements of the trunk and legs, the stomach muscles provide support and protection for the liver, kidneys, pancreas, and of course the stomach. Abdominal muscles that lose their ability to serve as a kind of natural girdle allow these organs--and the lower spine--more internal movement than they were designed to handle. Digestive disorders can result, as can back problems. An estimated 80% of all lower back pain can be traced to lack of abdominal strength.

Sitting gives stomach muscles little to do, and so they weaken. And because sitting also gives the rest of our bodies little to do, we fatten. The combination is devastating and develops into a vicious circle: As a burgeoning waistline makes movement more difficult, movement becomes less likely. And less movement means fewer calories are burned. And fewer calories burned means more calories stored--around the middle. The force behind the evolution of a potbelly, as you can see, is not one to be taken lightly.

You don't have to be overweight in order to suffer from abdominal prolapse. Excess weight increases one's chances, but a potbelly can develop in anyone who neglects to maintain sufficient abdominal strength and proper posture. Also, osteoporosis can cause potbellies in the slimmest and most fit women.

> **If you feel nauseous
> or faint,
> stop your exercise
> immediately!**

FITNESS ACTIVITIES--More than 30% of Americans age 55 and older say they walk for exercise. Walking is their first choice for fitness activities followed in order by: swimming, fishing, bicycle riding, camping, golf, bowling, exercise equipment, hiking, hunting, aerobics, calisthenics, jogging, and tennis. Women prefer fitness-related activities and men prefer outdoor sports.

AEROBICS--Aerobic means using oxygen. To achieve aerobic conditioning, you must engage in vigorous, sustained exercise at least three times each week. You must raise your pulse rate to a target range and maintain it in that range for the entire time.

> **Before starting an exercise program
> get your doctor's OK!**

MEASURING YOUR HEART RATE--Heart rate is widely accepted as a good method for measuring intensity during aerobic exercises. Exercise that doesn't raise your heart rate to a certain level and keep it there for 20 minutes won't contribute significantly to cardiovascular fitness.

The heart rate you should maintain is called your target heart rate. If you are in good health, you need to set a target zone for the heartbeat, according to your age. Your target zone should be 60% to 75% of your maximum heart rate.

Target Heart Rate Table			
Age	Maximum Heart Rate (beats per minute) (220 minus your age)	Target Zone	
		(60%)	(75%)
50	170	102	127
55	165	99	123
60	160	96	120
65	155	93	116
70	150	90	113

Your maximum heart rate is usually 220 minus your age. However, the above figures are averages and should be used as general guidelines. Take your pulse during your exercise to determine your heart rate: Put the first and second finger of your right hand on the radial artery of the inner wrist of your left hand. Count the number of beats in 30 seconds and multiply by 2 (equals heartbeats per minute). Take your pulse 5 minutes into your exercise, and again just before ending it.

efore you start get the  signal from your doctor

PHYSICAL ACTIVITY--Regular physical activity can help the human body maintain, repair, and improve itself to an amazing degree. And most older people--even those with illnesses or disabilities--can take part in moderate exercise programs. People who exercise regularly may also be less apt to suffer fractures or other accidents. Exercise must become one of those things that you do without question, like bathing and brushing your teeth. Unless you are convinced of the benefits of exercise and the risks of unfitness, you will not succeed. Patience is essential. Don't try too much too soon and don't quit before you have a chance to experience the rewards of improved fitness. You can't gain in a few days or weeks what you have lost in years of sedentary living, but you can get it back if you persevere. And the prize is worth the price.

EXERCISE BENEFITS
* strengthens your heart and lungs
* can lower your blood pressure
* helps protect against the start of adult-onset diabetes
* can strengthen your bones, slowing down the process of osteoporosis
* helps you move about more easily by keeping joints, tendons, and ligaments more flexible
* can help you lose weight (when combined with good eating habits) or maintain ideal weight by burning excess calories and by helping to control your appetite
* improves your appearance and self-confidence
* contributes to good mental health by keeping you socially active
* contributes to sleeping better
* promotes a sense of well-being
* helps to keep you "regular," and improves digestion

> **If exercise could be packed into a pill, it would be the single most widely prescribed, and beneficial, medicine in the nation.**
>
> Robert N. Butler, M.D.
> Director, National Institute on Aging

CHECK YOUR HEALTH--Anyone who has been inactive for many years should never try to do too much too soon. Start by seeing a doctor, especially if you are over 50, if you have a disease or disability, or if you are taking medication. Your doctor can evaluate your physical condition, help you decide which activity will suit you best, and check your progress after the exercise program is underway. Other conditions that indicate a need for medical clearance are:
* high blood pressure
* heart trouble
* family history of early stroke or heart attack
* frequent dizzy spells
* extreme breathlessness after mild exertion
* arthritis or other bone problems
* severe muscular, ligament, or tendon problems
* osteoporosis
* other known or suspected diseases

Those with medical problems may have to avoid some kinds of exercise or adjust their level of activity. Vigorous exercise involves minimum health risks for persons in good health or those following doctor's advice. Far greater risks are presented by habitual inactivity and obesity.

Begin by exercising slowly, especially if you have been inactive. Start with short periods of about 5 to 10 minutes twice a week. Then build up slowly, adding no more than a few minutes each week. If all goes well, as it probably will, slowly increase your exercise periods to 15 to 30 minutes, three or four times a week. Your doctor may advise stretching as well as warm-up and cool-down periods of 5 to 15 minutes to tune up your body before exercise and to help you wind down afterward.

Always pay attention to what your body tells you. If you feel much discomfort, you are trying to do too much. Ease up a bit, or take a break and start again at another time. Although most people will have no problems if they start exercising slowly, be alert to unusual symptoms such as chest pain, breathlessness, joint discomfort, or muscle cramps. **Call your doctor if any of these occur.**

KINDS OF EXERCISE--The most beneficial form of exercise is "aerobic"--exercise that causes the heart and lungs to work at a higher rate continuously to supply oxygen to the muscles. Over time, aerobic exercise increases the efficiency of the cardiovascular system. Some examples of aerobic exercises are: brisk walking, swimming, jogging, bicycling, cross-country skiing, folk dancing. Many older people enjoy these exercises. But there are other possibilities, such as modified aerobic dancing, calisthenics, and yoga. People who have kept in good condition may be able to participate in a wider range of activities. It is very important to tailor your program to fit your own level of ability and special needs. For example, jogging is not for everyone and may be dangerous for those who have unsuspected heart disease or joint problems.

EXERCISE PROGRAMS--It is important to choose an activity you like. Decide whether you want to join a group, exercise with a friend, or exercise alone. If you exercise alone, tell someone of your schedule and plans in case you need assistance. See if you prefer an outdoor or indoor activity, and decide what time of day is best for you. Make your exercise period a routine part of your schedule.

FINDING AN EXERCISE PROGRAM-- Most communities have centers where older people can join exercise classes and other recreational programs. Find out about fitness programs at a local church or synagogue, civic center, community college, park or recreation association, senior citizens' center, or service organization (such as an area agency on aging, see pages 24 and 25).

If you are convinced that regular exercise is not for you, try to stay active in other ways. Activities such as bowling, square dancing, fishing, nature walks, arts and crafts, card and table games, gardening, and community projects will not offer all the benefits of regular, moderate exercise, but they will help you remain actively involved in life, possibly adding years to your own.

Exercise to improve life in the second 50 yea

Second choice in adult exercises!

AEROBICS--The most beneficial forms of exercise are aerobic exercises. Some activities to consider:

✳ **Walking**--Walk briskly, arms swinging vigorously. Walking is inexpensive and requires no special equipment (except for a pair of comfortable shoes).

✳ **Jogging/running**--Wear properly fitted shoes designed for running; whenever possible, run on resilient surfaces such as blacktop or turf, rather than concrete.

✳ **Bicycling**--Wear a helmet and follow the rules of the road.

✳ **Aerobic dancing**--Lively music encourages vigorous group participation, but each person should work in his or her own target heart range. Low-impact aerobics is a particularly good way for beginners and overweight people to start. In fact, many people continue to do only low-impact exercises because they find them more comfortable and because the possibility of injury is reduced.

✳ **Swimming**--Swimming is easy on body joints. Variety comes from using different strokes.

✳ **Cross-country skiing**--An almost total workout for the major limbs of the body, the activity tightens the torso muscles, helps promote lung capacity, and provides excellent aerobic conditioning.

✳ **Fitness equipment**--Most aerobic activities can be done indoors on exercise equipment at home.

WHEN TO EXERCISE--The hour just before the evening meal is a popular time for exercise. The late afternoon workout provides a welcome change of pace at the end of the day and helps dissolve the day's worries and tensions. Another popular time of day to work out is early morning, before the day's main activities begin. Advocates of the early start say it makes them more alert and energetic during the day. Beware--morning stiffness is universal in seniors and can increase the likelihood of injury. If you exercise in the morning, wait a half hour after getting out of bed and, in addition, spend more time in warm-up activity.

Among the factors you should consider in developing your workout schedule are personal preferences, your plans for the day, availability of exercise facilities, and weather.

You should not exercise strenuously during extremely hot, humid weather or within two hours after eating. Heat and/or digestion both make heavy demands on the circulatory system, and in combination with exercise can be an overtaxing double load.

CLOTHING--All exercise clothing should be loose-fitting to permit freedom of movement, and should make you feel comfortable and self-assured. As a general rule, you should wear lighter clothes than temperatures might indicate. Exercise generates great amounts of body heat. Light-colored clothing that reflects the sun's rays is cooler in the summer, and dark clothes are warmer in the winter. When the weather is very cold, it's better to wear several layers of light clothing than one or two heavy layers. The extra layers help trap heat, and it's easier to shed one of them if you become too warm.

In cold weather, and in hot, sunny weather, it's a good idea to wear something on your head. Wool ski caps are recommended for winter wear, and some form of tennis or summer hat that provides shade and can be soaked in water is good for summer. Never wear rubberized or plastic clothing. Such garments interfere with the evaporation of perspiration and can cause body temperature to rise to dangerous levels.

HOW LONG SHOULD I EXERCISE?-- Each exercise session should last from about 25 to 40 minutes and include:

5 min.	warm-up
15-30 min.	exercising in your heart rate target zone (15 to 30 minutes is your goal--begin with a shorter period and build up gradually)
5 min.	cool down
25-40 min.	total

Exercise briskly at least 15-30 minutes three times a week.

Fourth choice in adult exercises!

SELECTION OF AEROBIC EXERCISES

Type I very vigorous, 15 min. 3x week conditions heart and lungs.
Type II moderately vigorous, 30 min. 3x week can condition heart and lungs (if done briskly).
Type III does not condition heart and lungs, but can be enjoyable, improve coordination and muscle tone, and help relieve tension.

Type I	Type II	Type III
cross-country skiing	aerobic exercise	baseball
hiking (uphill)	bicycling	bowling
jogging	calisthenics	football
running in place	downhill skiing	golf (on foot or cart)
stationary cycling	swimming	softball
exercise machines	tennis (singles)	volleyball
	walking (briskly)	

Walking--adults first choice in exercise programs

WALKING--During vigorous walking, the heart beats more rapidly, helping to strengthen the heart muscle. A strong muscle can help lower high blood pressure and reduce the risk of heart attack or stroke. Exercise allows the heart to pump blood more efficiently, improving blood circulation. Walking causes calf muscles to contract, circulating more blood from feet to head. Walking helps the lungs develop a greater capacity, easing breathing and improving the entire respiratory system. It also helps tone muscles in legs, thighs, and abdomen.

Walking is an effective exercise when you walk briskly for at least 20 minutes at a constant clip of 3 to 4 miles per hour. Walking as an exercise can:

❶ relieve tension
❷ provide an effective weight control means
❸ enhance a person's general attitude toward life
❹ keep the body energized
❺ promote physical fitness

CALORIES AND WALKING--Brisk walking burns approximately the same amount of calories per mile as does running. Heavier individuals will burn more calories than lighter persons. For example, a 110-pound person burns about half as many calories as a 216-pound person walking at the same pace for the same distance. Although increasing walking speed does not burn significantly more calories per mile, a more vigorous walking pace will produce more dramatic conditioning effects.

CORRECT WALKING--You may not have thought about it, but there is a correct way to walk. With each step, the body's weight is borne by the foot--from the heel to the base of the big toe. A step starts at the heel, moves to the outside of the foot, then rolls off the big toe. Taking a step is a kind of balancing act, and sometimes it may be off kilter. Look at the heel of your shoe. If it's worn down on one side, your weight is not evenly distributed. That is an indication that just a portion of the heel, instead of your entire heel, is absorbing the pressure when you walk. Over time, this can strain muscles and tendons in your feet and legs.

> **Anyone over 50, overweight, having high blood pressure, respiratory, or cardiovascular problems is advised to consult a physician before starting a walking program.**

Correct posture is always important when you walk. The ideal walking position is to hold your head erect, keeping your back straight, letting your arms swing freely at your sides, and taking long, easy strides.

WALKING PACE--Leisurely strolls do not count as walking exercise. If you are in good health, you need to set a goal for the pace you would like to achieve, but start slowly. Set a target zone for the heartbeat, according to your age. Your target zone should be 60% to 75% of your maximum heart rate (see page 140 for chart). If you are in poor physical condition, a speed of 3 miles per hour for 30 minutes may bring your heart rate into the target zone for your age; if you are in excellent condition, you may have to walk 4 to 5 miles per hour for 30 to 60 minutes to reach your target.

HOW FAR AND HOW FAST?--Don't expect to walk 10 miles the first time out. Start slowly. Walking, like any vigorous exercise, requires moderation until the body has built some stamina. You know you are walking a

Third choice in adult exercises

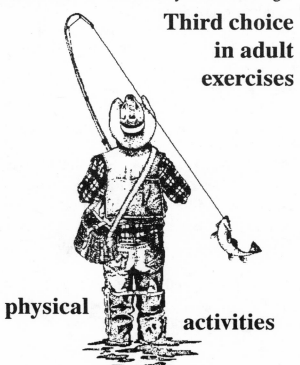

physical **activities**

good clip when you are taking about 120 steps per minute. Begin by walking at a relaxed pace for 10 minutes, working up to 20 minutes every other day at a brisk pace. After you have been walking briskly for 20 minutes three days a week for one month, increase your walking time to 30 minutes. Repeat 30-minute walks four or five times a week.

> **Take the talk test as you walk. If you can't carry on a conversation without becoming breathless, you're going too fast.**

SHOES--A pair of good shoes is the only special equipment required. Any shoes that are comfortable, provide good support, and don't cause blisters or calluses will do. But, whatever shoe you use should have arch supports and should elevate the heel one-half to three-quarters of an inch above the sole of the foot. While walking, wear shoes with uppers made of materials that permit your feet to "breathe." The best shoe materials are leather, canvas, or nylon mesh. Allow one-fourth to one-half inch of space between the longest toe and the tip of the shoe. This will give your feet room to expand while walking. An exercise shoe, just like any other shoe, must be comfortable in the store. Don't try to "break in" an uncomfortable shoe.

Dealing with users, manipulators, and con artists   Wm. J. Di

The word "used" can be one of the most glorious words in the English language. In its proper sense it means we have utilized our talents, property, tools, minds, or selves to further the purposes for which they were made. How the dedicated person longs to be "used" for some magnificent cause. What a privilege it is when someone we love, like parents, husband, wife, siblings, or friends, needs our help. To be honestly "used" by those with whom we have a mutual agreement is one of the goals of life.

However, when we are manipulated with lies, fraud, or force to be "used" for someone's purposes without consideration of our own, then the word "used" can become a horrible connotation of unspeakable evil.

People often tell me how much they hate to be "used" and "manipulated." They bring up how much it hurts to be controlled by insidious unfair means for someone's advantage. They point out the shame they feel when a "user" manipulates them by devious methods to get something for himself without compensation or consideration of their needs.

For a husband and wife to make love and produce a child is to "use" each other for the perpetuation of life. For a man to rape a woman is to "use" her for his own purpose and sometimes ends in death. To be properly "used" through mutual benefit is one of the most satisfying goals of life. To be improperly "used" by someone who takes advantage and manipulates for his own selfish purposes is one of the worst things that can happen to a person.

How to deal with a "user" can be of life-and-death importance because a "user" is often a liar without conscience, a thief without remorse, a person that you trusted who violated your trust.

FIRST

WE MUST TRAIN OUR CHILDREN TO BE CONSCIOUS OF OTHER PE0PLE'S NEEDS AND NOT TO BE "USERS" WHO ONLY THINK OF THEMSELVES.

The above might seem like a surprising thing to say to people who are of retirement age until we remember: "The training of children is a lifetime investment." When older people are receiving the proper respect their children will come to them for advice till the end of their days. I asked my mother for advice and counsel when she was 88 years old and she was my best source of training. I am happy to report that my children are still asking for my counsel. The training of children not to be "users" begins at a very early age and continues through a lifetime.

One of our children was a biter. I will not tell which one. I remember that when our little "biter" would finish drinking at his or her mother's breast, it seemed good to the "biter" to chomp down and hurt mother. My wife asked me, "What shall I do?" My intuitive wisdom responded, "When the baby bites you, thump him/her on the bottom of his/her foot with your finger and withdraw the breast." The advice worked--soon the baby was a proper drinker and not a cruel user.

Some grown-up children will still take nourishment (borrow money) from older parents without a word of thanks, or an intent to pay back, or even a friendly attitude. They are users, and in all love, we must find a way to thump them on the bottom of the foot to remind them that we too are people.

When my wife and I were rearing our children, we taught them not to be "users," when we caught them doing such things as:

- Not sharing toys, but expecting a sibling to share
- Getting each other in trouble
- Being unfair with each other
- Getting their own way by physical violence
- Taking advantage of a younger sibling
- Using emotional force like tears or anger or bullying to get their own way

As our children get older, marry, and make careers and homes for themselves, we find them thoughtful, attentive, loving, and grateful. We taught them not to be users, and it is paying off.

If a 3-year-old child can dominate us to get his/her own way and selfishly "use" us, what chance do we have against the skilled chiselers of this world? Children learn early in life to spot our weaknesses and take advantage of them. My first suggestion: Don't let children, particularly your own, manipulate and use your weaknesses to get their own way. If we can train our children not to be "users" then there will be fewer "users" and it will be easier to handle the others.

However, we could all tell horror stories of children who have taken everything from their parents and have abandoned them. It is never too late to start to improve ourselves and our relationships. If our older children are not treating us fairly, we can remind them of what is right. It is important to remember that we cannot be "con" artists, or users ourselves.

> **Watchfulness is the only guard against cunning. Be intent on his intentions. Many succeed in making others do their own affairs, and unless you possess the key to their motives you may at any moment be forced to take their chestnuts out of the fire to the damage to your own fingers.**
>
> **- Baltasar Gracian (1601-1658)**

We are inclined to believe those
whom we do not know because
they have never deceived us.
- Samuel Johnson 1709

FRAUD
(page 2 of 6) OVERVIEW 145

SECOND

HAVE A PROGRAM TO BECOME AWARE OF AND STRENGTHEN YOUR OWN WEAKNESSES AND VULNERABILITIES.

There is an old saying, "You can't cheat an honest man." Manipulators will "psych-out" a person, discover his moments of dishonesty or other weakness, and use that failing to get what they want. Some of the common weaknesses that manipulators take advantage of:

1 A strong desire to get something for nothing.

Anytime anything is free, look for the hook. Basically, most people must work for a living. We get paid money and we use money to get what we want or need. Sometimes we mutually exchange goods, services, or favors; but note the word 'mutual.' Who likes a bum who constantly asks for something and never gives in return. We worked for our retirement funds and we paid for our Social Security. If we find ourselves in a position of being unfortunate and having to use government or charitable help, then we must remind ourselves, "When we need help, we deserve help." What would this world be like if the fortunate did not have the unfortunate to take care of.

Be instantly suspicious of "something for nothing." A person who offers it usually wants something--much more than you realize. He will often say something like, "You give me $5.00 and I'll give you this knife worth $10.00." That's a good deal, so you get hooked on his bargains. Next time he might say, "You give me $5.00 and I'll give you the Brooklyn Bridge, or something worth much more than $5.00." Since you trust him, you marvel at your good fortune and bite at the bait. Of course, some kind of hook gets lodged in you and in the end you pay and pay and pay.

> The first
> and worst of all frauds
> is to
> cheat oneself.
> - Bailey (1816-1902)

Compulsive gamblers get hooked on attaining something big out of a little investment (something for nothing). Such thinking can become a serious mental illness and give the "user" a point of advantage. Fair is fair, and if you are honest you probably will not try to take advantage of anyone to get something for nothing; and, less probable, you will not let another take advantage of you.

2 An excessive desire to be liked by everyone.

No one can be liked by everyone, not even the movie star, the rich man, the president, or any famous person. It's amazing how many cultured, intelligent people can't stand the thought of not being liked. If manipulators see that you are one of those people who need the approval of everyone, "they gotcha."

Sorry to say, I am prone to this weakness. One time a water-softener salesman came to my door. I told him emphatically, "No, absolutely not, I don't want one of those salt-makers."

A tear appeared in his eye and his face assumed a hurt look: "I'm only trying to make a living, and it is a good product. I thought such an intelligent person as you would at least let me talk about it." He sold me the soft-water system.

Manipulation takes advantage of the other person's weakness. The water-softener salesman did have something to offer, but it was not what I wanted. If you are a person who "can't say no" because you want to please everyone, then you are going to get used.

When we have an excessive desire to be liked by everyone, pleasing people becomes the first and chief thing we do. Our ethics and value system must start with such virtues as fair play, honor, honesty, and kindness. When we put our highest values first, we will have less trouble with manipulators.

3 Fear of emotional tirades and anger.

Some people will do anything to avoid a fight. They either capitulate immediately, or even worse, they out-anger the angry one and so become the manipulators themselves. As I pointed out, little babies often learn to use emotions to get what they want. When babies grow up, unless someone has taught them differently, they continue their successful tirades of making life hell for their loved ones.

For ten years we owned a home at the beach and during that time made considerable improvement to the property. The market had escalated, so we were asking more for the house than what we had paid. A man and his wife tried to purchase our beach home for less than we had paid for it. They were very aggressive. He argued emotionally with our price. She cried and sobbed, trying to made us feel guilty by saying we were depriving them of their dream house. One night he called and informed us that his wife was having a nervous breakdown because we were heartless and wouldn't sell to them. If anything happened to his wife, he was going to sue us for damages. For a month, they never let up in trying to emotionally bully us into selling to them for a loss. We held firm and sold for a fair price, but I will never forget the bruising occasion.

There are some clever parables that sound so true, among them: "In any battle between the emotions and the intellect, the emotions always win." Let me correctly state that parable: "In any battle between the emotions and the intellect, the emotions are inclined to win at first; later on, intelligence will have its way." So when people try to manipulate with their emotions and they win the first round, keep a steady pressure of facts before them. Eventually intelligence wins.

4 Being excessively sympathetic to hard luck stories.

A true hard luck story deserves our attention. Compassionless behavior shuts everyone down, both giver and receiver; but, a sucker falls for every lie and "casts his pearls before swine." We need balanced giving.

When my wife and I go to Los Angeles, we often stop at a convenient rest area. A sad-faced lady carrying an ill-dressed child came up to our car and asked for some money to

O, what a goodly outside
falsehood hath!
- William Shakespeare 1564

help her get to San Francisco (100 miles west). The first time, I weighed the possibilities of what she said and gave her $20. The next time we passed through and stopped, she came up to the car with her story, and I thought, maybe the baby is hungry, so I gave her $10. The third time happened two months later. The same lady, with the same baby, with the same story came up to my car and asked for money to help her get to San Francisco. I figured I was encouraging her life of manipulation. I gave her a word, "I have heard this before. I think you are trying to con me." A person who needs help is one thing; a professional panhandler is another.

5 **Acquiring so much guilt that you allow a "user" to take advantage and you accept it as punishment for your sins.**

In order to keep from being used in this world of clever con artists, people must get their marbles together. When a person knows he has done something wrong and he does not make restitution or get forgiveness, then he will carry a load of guilt. A manipulator can easily use a person who feels like he deserves punishment. The guilty one is a setup for a sharp operator. A manipulator can sense a person's need for punishment and can easily talk him into a bad deal.

If you don't want to be used, it is very important to get yourself forgiven. One of the major purposes of all religion is to offer forgiveness to those who ask. God is a God of love and He forgives. If we are people of love and goodwill, we will forgive ourselves and forgive others. Anyone who holds a grudge against anyone, including himself, is holding a hot potato that will burn, and even when it cools, is not fit to eat.

6 **Becoming so discouraged that you don't care anymore.**

If people don't care what happens, how can they protect themselves against the swindler.

It is not at all uncommon for an older person to get sick and die within a short time after retirement, particularly when he

or she gets down and discouraged and life has lost its meaning. We must keep life meaningful and happy in order to survive. We also must keep "up" in order to protect what belongs to us.

I have a friend who became so depressed when his wife left him that he lost thousands of dollars through bad business deals. He was not able to protect himself against unscrupulous salesmen because his depression led him not to care.

7 **Allowing inferiority to lead you to think that you don't deserve better treatment.**

The Bible accords to the human being the highest praise found in any literature of the world. It says, "So God created man in His own image; in the image of God He created him; male and female He created them." As children of God we deserve the best treatment available as long as we don't get it at someone's expense. Even if we are atheist and do not believe in God, we believe that we are in existence and deserve the best we can get.

A visitor queried an old-time slave owner: "All your slaves walk slumped over with hanging heads and shuffling feet, except that one. He walks with his head high-- what's wrong with him?"

The owner snapped his whip and replied, "He's the son of an African King and he's never been able to forget it." That's us, sons and daughters of the Creator King--let's not forget it.

8 **Having such low self-esteem that you fall for flattery.**

When a manipulator finds out that you don't think highly of yourself, he can put his trade to work. A little flattery here or there and he can do with you as he will.

We can listen to flattery, and even enjoy it, but don't take it too seriously. If we have low self-esteem we are likely to suck it up like a sponge does water. To keep ourselves from vulnerability to flattery we need a program to build self-esteem. I suggest:

Choose to have self-esteem.--The lack of

self-esteem does not come upon a person from outer space but rather from inner space. We are in charge of our inner space; no one can occupy or conquer without our permission. **What difference does it make what other people think.**

Forgiving yourself for past misdeeds.--Don't delay; do it right now. Holding a grudge against yourself is just as bad as holding a grudge against a friend. If you say you can't do it, you are believing a lie; believe the truth--of course you can. Think of the good things that you have done, allow yourself some latitude, make amends if possible, and keep yourself looking at the present and the future--turn away from the past.

Change your ways if you need to.--A rumor runs around saying that personality is chiseled in marble; this is not so--personality is as malleable as soft wax. If a person has some bad habits, he can change if he wants to. A program of self-improvement goes a long way toward building self-esteem.

During World War II, B. F. Skinner programmed some dumb pigeons to guide a missile toward enemy battleships. He did it by rewarding the pigeons for every small improvement toward the larger goals. Set large goals and reward yourself for small improvements--that's the secret to change.

Don't compete with anyone.--No one has ever lived who was exactly like you. No one has your arrangement of genes and chromosomes. No one can duplicate your fingerprints, your voiceprints, or your personality. You are totally unique. You don't have to compete; just do the best you can with what you have. Even a perfect angel can do no more.

> **Falsehood is never so successful as when she baits her hook with truth, and no opinion so fastly misled us as those that are not wholly wrong, as no timepiece so effectively deceives the wearer as those that are sometimes right.**
> - Calton (1780-1832)

The true hypocrite is the one
who ceases to perceive his deceptions,
the one who lies with sincerity.

- André Gide 1869

FRAUD

(page 4 of 6) OVERVIEW 147

Recognize the negative but flow toward the positive.--Of course a lot of negative things happen in this world, but you are not going that way. Emphasize the positive, talk positively, think positively, respond to the positive, ignore the negative as much as possible, and soon your life will be positive, filled with good fortune.

Don't let anyone put you down.--If a person tries to put you down, you can know immediately that he is not under orders from anyone who is good. Good people build up; bad people tear down. Don't accept the judgment of a put-down expert; he does not have that authority. Anyone who points the finger of scorn has three fingers pointed at himself.

Encourage yourself.--What do you do for people who are down and have low self-esteem? You encourage them. Well, do that for yourself. Be your own cheerleader. Encourage yourself. You can talk yourself into being up, being a winner, being a person of value.

A compliment comes from good people. Thank anyone who gives you an honest compliment. Flattery comes from bad people in an attempt to "use" you. Ignore flattery. Dale Carnegie said, "A compliment is from the heart out, flattery is from the teeth out." You can recognize the difference.

Our ability to handle ourselves and cope with difficult people will be greatly increased by curing the above eight weaknesses. It is doubtful if a manipulating user can crash our armor if we have corrected our defects and overcome our failings.

It helps some people to state negative weaknesses in terms of positive strength or virtue:
❤ Find, give, and accept.

> **Distrust**
> **all those who love you extremely**
> **upon a very slight acquaintance**
> **and**
> **without any visible reason.**
>
> - Chesterfield (1694-1773)

❤ Be honest and work for what you get.
❤ Please people, but don't violate your value system.
❤ Let facts and reason rule over emotions.
❤ Be sympathetic, but not a sucker.
❤ Choose to be happy.
❤ Overcome feelings of inferiority.
❤ Develop positive self-esteem.

When a person is strong and has plugged up the chinks in his personal armor, it will be very difficult for a manipulator to use him for his own purposes.

THIRD

EXAMINE AND PERCEIVE THE CHARACTER OF PEOPLE

After strengthening our own weaknesses it is necessary to examine the character of other people. By divine decree, we are not to judge people, but by the same decree we are to be "fruit inspectors." We are to examine the words, deeds, and ideas of other people and compare them to the highest standards of our community. "Fruit inspectors" reject the corrupt behavior (bad fruit) of people and do not participate in it.

Many times people get "fruit inspecting" mixed up with "judging." Judging consists of making the final decision as to the destiny of people--wiping people out. Fruit inspection only wipes out bad behavior--not people. Fruit inspection also consists of deciding whether or not we will associate or participate in that type of behavior. We are to make a decision as to whether or not people, ideas, words, or behavior are to be admitted into our lifestyle.

Judgment decides the fate of another person--only God or the proper authorities can do that. Judgment makes an assumption without proof and comes to a conclusion based on a presumptive conjecture, guess, notion, or opinion, and then passes critical sentence or comes to a verdict on the shabby logic of a faulty theory. Judgment becomes hypocrisy when we condemn a person for doing the same things we do.

Inspection consists of examining, inquiring, probing, scrutinizing, searching, studying, and surveying. Fruit inspection looks a person over to find out who they are, what they do, where they go, and with whom they associate. To assess a person's character we need to know: what are their beliefs and standards, how well do they keep their word, what are their priorities and value systems, what have they done, where have they been, whom have they hurt, or blessed. All these things are within the jurisdiction of a fruit inspector.

When dealing with people we have the right to know about their character. If they are of good character then we will not get hurt or used or manipulated. If they are of bad character, we have a right to know and to protect ourselves against the coming onslaught.

Here are some simple steps to reveal a person's character and personality:

✳ **Consistency.** If you listen carefully you can catch a person speaking inconsistently--another word for lies. Lies are hard to keep track of; the truth is easy. So when we hear a person making claims or proclaiming words that don't make sense, it may be time to start some fruit inspecting.

✳ **Gossiping.** If you hear a person talking about people they know in a negative, gossiping way, you can be fairly certain that you are going to be next on his list. If the gossip is cruel or nasty, probably the gossiper sees other people that way and may be that way himself. People who see too much evil in other people are "evil sniffers"--and the evil is coming from them.

✳ **Treatment.** Notice how people treat people, particularly how they behave toward relatives and loved ones. A con artist often treats susceptible loved ones in a despicable manner. A user often reveals family secrets and tries to show themself as the abused one. One way or another a manipulator who is debased is inclined to debase his family.

✳ **Associates.** The old saying "Birds of a feather, flock together" has some truth. Bad people often pretend to like good

The liar's punishment is not in the
least that he is not believed, but that
he cannot believe anyone else.

- G. B. Shaw (1856-1950)

people in order to use them. We took a con artist into our home in order to help him. As long as he got money from us, he was our friend. When the money started to dry up, he went back to the street.

* **Accomplishments.** Con artists are long on talk and short on accomplishments. They often claim to have graduated from five colleges or more and yet they can't produce a single diploma. It is not insulting to ask to see evidence of accomplishments. A doctor, a teacher, a preacher, or any professional is expected to produce his credentials. If you are going to allow a person to come into a place of unconditional trust, let it be based upon something more than just words.

* **Self-centered.** Very seldom is a con artist actually interested in what anyone else is doing. Sometimes they pretend deep interest, but it is fleeting. Everything revolves around them and their interests, accomplishments, needs and values. They are often highly prejudicial, bigoted, and frequently have an attachment with some extremist group.

* **Rebelliousness.** People who manipulate or use other people have little regard for conventional social ways. Often they are against the government, the schools, the churches, and other normal social ways. They present grandiose ideas that are oversimplistic. The poor corporal longs to show the commander-in-chief how to run things. During World War II, Carole Chessman, the notorious "red-light" bandit, wanted out of jail in order to assassinate Adolf Hitler. But, when he was out of jail, he killed the innocent, not the guilty.

If a person comes into your life and begins to move close to your confidence and trust, you have a right to be a fruit inspector. You can examine the motives, background, and character of anyone who touches you, coming close to your life space. To inquire into the background of an honest man won't hurt him, but a crook does not want you looking into his background. Probing into the char-

acter of a quality person will do no harm; in fact, it will make him or her more prominent. Scrutinizing the credentials of a genuine achiever will be taken as compliment; but, the same action will terrorize a crook. Searching for the right answers will glorify an ethical person; but it is likely to uncover the deceitfulness of slimy moles. To take a survey and study carefully the character of a person who has nothing to hide will make that person great; but to do the same thing to a person who has many shady things to conceal will bring forth embarrassing truth.

Avoid judging, but do become a fruit inspector to keep yourself from being manipulated by the con men of this world.

FOURTH

BE AWARE THAT THERE ARE DANGEROUS PEOPLE IN THIS WORLD

One of the highlights of my career as a psychologist was the three years I spent employed by Terminal Island Federal Penitentiary as a clinical psychologist and therapist for the convicts and inmates. I found that most of the men and women were normal people who had got caught committing a civil crime such as income tax evasion, fraud, or theft--these people were called inmates. When inmates served their time, they learned their lesson and seldom came back to prison.

Twenty-five percent of the people in prison were convicts. Convicts were often incorrigible recidivists, extremely difficult to rehabilitate, and when they left the prison you knew they would be back. The convicts were different from the inmates in that they were professionals, dedicated to a life of

> **Deceivers
> are the most dangerous
> members of society.
> They trifle with the best parts of
> our nature, and violate the most
> sacred obligations.**
>
> **- George Crabbe (1754-1832)**

crime. Convicts seldom admitted their culpability. No matter how heinous their crime, they always blamed the system, not themselves.

In my career at the prison, I learned to deal with both inmate and convict. Dealing with an inmate was like dealing with an average person, but dealing with a convict required some special awareness.

Coping with convicts, sociopaths, and incorrigible evil ones may seem like a superfluous study for older people. However, they represent a small but vicious percent of the population and almost everyone will at some time or another tangle with these impossible people. Perhaps, if you know what you are dealing with, you can avoid getting seriously hurt.

First: Don't be surprised that calloused criminals exist.

Some people have a hard time believing that sociopathic or incorrigible criminals exist. They think ideally everyone can be rehabilitated and no one is hopeless. They ask, "How can we give up on a loved one no matter how far gone he seems to be?" Ideally that is true, but practically there comes a time when we can no longer "give what is holy to the dogs." There are people in this world who have no mercy; we must beware of falling into their hands.

Second: Recognize the symptoms of the convict.

Personality disorders with predominantly sociopathic or asocial or dyssocial manifestations are characterized by disregard for social obligations, lack of feeling for others, and impetuous violence or compassionless unconcern. People with sociopathic personality are often affectively cold and may be abnormally aggressive or irresponsible. Their tolerance to frustration is low; they blame others and offer plausible rationalizations for the behavior that brings them into conflict with society.

The sociopathic personality and the incorrigible criminal seem dedicated to a delinquent lifestyle. They tell lies when the truth would fit better. They are irresponsible, intractable sinners who often act like saints while they secretly laugh at those they are deceiving. Often their value system is completely reversed--for example, they will let their children starve as they give all their money to a prostitute. These recalcitrant people often break the heart of those who love them.

Third: If possible, don't let them get away with bad behavior.

A friend of mine had some company that ran up a $400 telephone bill. He sent them the telephone bill, and when they didn't pay it, he took them to small claims court and got a judgment. He did not nurse anger or take vengeance; he just demanded that these people treat him fairly. To allow people to get away with little crimes encourages them to increase and perpetuate big crimes. If you force dishonest people to do the right thing, in the long run they will be more likely to respect you.

Fourth: Don't be ruled or frightened by violent behavior.

I conducted group therapy for convicts at Terminal Island Federal Penitentiary. One day a bank robber named Jim threw a violent temper tantrum, picked up his chair, and crashed it against the side of the wall. The other convicts became very upset and agitated. Immediately, as group leader, I took charge and decided to remain cool. I sent the convict back to his cell and continued our discussion as if nothing had happened. Later I learned that my unruly convict had lots of clout and if I had let his display of anger disturb me, we could have had a prison riot.

Fifth: Tough love is the order of the day.

We took some teenage foster children into our home and they looted the house, for drugs, I suppose. We put them in juvenile hall and then asked for them back. Our theme was, "Love both gives and demands fair treatment."

In the prison system, convicts would often ask me to break the rules: smuggle mail out, bring contraband in, overlook infractions of rules, etc. I discovered, if you break a rule for a convict, there will be no end to his demands. I tried to show the convicts that I loved them, but I would not join them.

Sixth: If a convict goes too far, you must be prepared to deal firmly with him.

We took a paroled convict into our home who attempted to assault our teenage daugh-

ter. Direct assumption of control and straightforward confrontation is the only way to deal with such people. If they show repentance, then you can reconcile; if not, then you separate. Anger, hate, and hostility have no place even in gross situations. If nothing else works, in a loving, caring, regretful way, you must kick the evil one out of your life and home.

Most people will not work in a prison and so will not find it necessary to deal with an incarcerated convict. **Let me warn you that the world is filled with people who have the potential of criminal behavior. They can be cruel and vicious snakes without conscience.**

On the other hand, the world is full of people who have the potential of being saints saturated with angelic goodness. It is not always easy to detect the difference between an angel and a devil. Go slowly. Both angels and devils eventually reveal themselves. Let your head and your heart

speak, but be wary of your emotions, particularly sensuality. Sensuality means, "Love is blind."

To be lied to, defrauded, manipulated, and forced into a position of being used for the evil purposes of an unconscionable criminal is a horror of horrors. It is our job to be aware that there are some people who are evil convicts and we must not let them take over our life.

People can and do sell themselves out to a devil. When they do you must separate yourself from them or they will take possession of you. Stay away from an evil one. If you find yourself caught by evil, call for help and use all the spiritual force that you can muster. Good loves to conquer evil.

It is very difficult to cope with people who are users, manipulators, and con artists. It will help:

❤ If we can train our children not to be that way;

❤ If we strengthen our own weaknesses;

❤ If we carefully examine the character of people before trusting them; and

❤ If we become aware that some people can be Mother Teresa and others Adolf Hitler.

In the following pages we are sharing with you many of the fraudulent practices perpetrated by unscrupulous persons. Older persons are becoming targets of these con artists since they feel senior citizens are not too sharp, not too savvy, and want to please too readily. There are many out there who are more than willing to take from you everything you have worked for all your life...everything!

A fool and his money are soon parted

In your second 50 years, living out your life with financial security is of major importance, second only to your health. If you are fortunate, you have provided for your retirement so you can live in dignity and with a sense of enjoyment. **It is unfortunate, but many unscrupulous persons will, without the least concern, remove from you any and all of your financial security.** Many make it a specialty to prey on retired persons, the elderly, the handicapped, the widowed, the lonely, the dying, and the relatives of the dying. No one is safe from these predators. Yes, there are obituary and funeral chasers, con artists, swindlers, unscrupulous financial advisors, and unscrupulous attorneys.

INVESTMENT FRAUD--Some estimate that these promoters have an annual take through lying and deceit of $10 billion. **As senior citizens, you're a special target for these swindlers.** They offer you a "once-in-a-lifetime" opportunity to make a lot of money quickly. Swindlers use every trick in the book to gain your trust. They reach you through newspapers, magazines, or television ads. But, three-quarters of all swindlers use the telephone to offer "special bargains" or get-rich-quick schemes.

These telephone pitchmen may perform surgery on your savings from a dingy back office or from a rented plush suite in a bank or savings and loan office. They use persuasive sales pitches that weave together facts and half-truths to deceive you into believing that financial gains will be great and swift with very little risk. They may be glib and fast-talking or so seemingly shy and soft-spoken that you feel almost compelled to force your money on them. Some call a large number of people until they reach you. Others buy lists of senior citizens. They may say they have "inside information, high-level connections," or "will guarantee the investment or buy it back under certain conditions." To add to a sense of urgency, they refer to current events in an attempt to convince you that haste is essential. Or they may say the market is moving so act now.

Typical investments sold by fraudulent operators have included coins, gemstones, oil and gas leases, interests in oil wells, applications for cellular telephone licenses, the sale of precious metals such as gold and silver, or strategic metals such as chromium, used in defense or high-tech industries. They often choose to sell investments you are not well informed about.

REFERRALS--Swindlers will pay fast, large profits to initial investors (from other peoples' investments) knowing they will tell their friends. These friends will tell their friends. Soon, the swindler no longer needs to look for victims.

Money and goods are certainly the best of references.
- Charles Dickens 1864

FINANCIAL PLANNERS--Con artists like fancy titles. For $150 practically anyone can be registered with the SEC (Securities Exchange Commission) as an investment advisor. Confronted with the blizzard of new investment options and tax changes, many people are confused or too busy to manage their financial affairs. Some planners offer you "free" seminars only to sell you dubious products. Some pitch "retirement-planning workshops." Many people go to financial planners on the strength of referrals. Even that is no guarantee of legitimacy. Shady financial planners often establish their "trustworthiness" with early investors, even returning a client's money with interest, if asked. Many impress new investors with phony monthly statements showing strong gains.

There are many reliable financial planners-- you just have to find them. If you do need an advisor check to see that he/she is registered with the SEC, state regulators, and is recommended from others you trust. **Never give them power of attorney.** Be wary of no-risk investment promises with high returns, or deals involving gems, art or condos where the value is difficult to appraise and monitor. Ask questions before you reach for your checkbook.

HOW TO AVOID LOSING YOUR MONEY

- Because it is so difficult to recover money paid to fraudulent sellers, the best thing you can do is refuse to give them your money in the first place.
- If the deal sounds too good, it probably is a scam. Promoters sound so confident about the money they are going to make you they act as if they are doing you a favor.
- Be extremely skeptical about unsolicited phone calls. Ask, "Where did you get my name?" Many swindlers get your name from purchased lists or telephone directories. Don't hesitate to hang up. If a person harasses you call the police.
- Don't be fooled by names. Scam operators imitate or use names of reputable companies.
- If you are promised that the investment is risk-free, a red flag should go up cautioning you against investing with this promoter. Few investments involve little risk.
- The swindler will talk about expectations of large profits to make you eager to invest but not so large you will become overly skeptical.
- Be wary of statements designed to pressure you into buying such as "There isn't time." The last thing a con artist will do is give you time to check him/her out. If in any doubt, do not part with your money.
- Do not be pressured into paying with cash or by money order. Never give your credit card number unless you know the company is reliable and you know precisely to whom you are speaking.
- Invest in business opportunities you know something about. Get all the information you can about the company and check it out. Before you invest with any firm, check the seller's prospectus and risk disclosure statement with someone you trust such as your attorney or banker.
- Request references. Do not accept a list of other investors. You should be referred to a bank or a well-known brokerage firm.
- Avoid investments that seem tied to a religious belief, or with a promoter who tries to capitalize on his connection with your church.

FALSE PROPHETS--Bible-quoting swindlers are out to "fleece the faithful." Religiously-oriented investment swindles have netted con artists over $500 million in the past 5 years. These "born-again" pious frauds play on your religious beliefs to gain your trust and life savings. They pass themselves off as one of your church members to put you, their victim, at ease. Their investments are supposedly associated with your church. When these "divinely inspired" con artists saw the money TV evangelists could raise, they quickly learned to twist Bible verses to bilk believers. The scams include advice about coins, precious metals, real estate, oil drilling, and others.

REAL ESTATE FRAUDS--Each year thousands of Americans, especially those nearing retirement, are "selected" for a free trip to a new land development project--all expenses paid. "Developers" offer a "buy of a lifetime" in "Dreamland Estates." Operators may deal in unimproved land, purported planned communities, or oil and gas leases. Many are completely honest operations. Unhappily, not all the pitches or all the developers are on the level. The pitch varies, but essentially it involves showing a film about the "Dreamland Estates" you can buy into. They tell you it is totally planned with all amenities including golf courses, lakes, sauna baths, horse trails, security, etc. Often this "Dreamland" turns out to be a nightmare for those who invest in it. Your desert home on a half-acre lot turns out to be miles from nowhere. Often the land is too rugged, too damp, too arid, or simply too remote. What is important to these "developers" is raw acreage that they bought cheap and plan to sell high. Most operate within the law and they cleverly hedge their claims so that ambiguous assurances may well seem to be guarantees. In fact, they are not. Before you buy check their credentials with the Better Business Bureau.

> # Never buy property site unseen!

Most vacation programs are highly regarded and run by reliable people. However, some promoters will offer vacations or a timeshare in a campground or a condo. Make sure you really will use it for vacations, because promised rental income or increases in property value may never happen. You should consider the risks and the benefits before signing any contract or a check.

SHADY CAMPSITE SALES--CONGRATULATIONS! If the prize number above matches the winning number, you could win a Buick LeSabre. Even if you don't win the car, you will definitely win one of the following prizes. The letter further states that to claim your prize you must pick it up on a certain day, be married, and have an annual income of at least $25,000. Some prizes include: a stereo set (an inexpensive set of earphones), an electric powerboat (a tiny inflatable raft with a battery-powered motor), a Laz-y-Boy Chair (a canvas beach chair with Laz-y-Boy stamped on the arm), or a 35mm camera (all plastic). Before receiving any "gifts," prize winners must listen to high pressure sales presentations and take a tour of the grounds. When you arrive you're treated like kings; when you refuse to sign you're treated like dirt.

There are reliable campground memberships. Stay at a campground before signing a contract, talk to lifetime members, and check to see that amenities exist. Read the contract! Check with the Better Business Bureau! Don't buy the membership as an investment, buy it because you plan to use it. Walk away from a sales person who is too insistent!

CONDO TIMESHARES--Timeshare con artists use the same techniques and "prizes" as the shady campsite sales swindlers to get you to buy. You buy two weeks in a rundown condo in Fresno for $10,000. The plan is for you to trade two weeks of your condo to someone who wants to vacation in Fresno, so you can spend two weeks in Morocco or the Caribbean. Good luck!

In another con, bogus "resale" firms promise you they can resell your timeshare condo. They ask for a $200 to $500 listing fee up front to defray marketing costs. You're asked that it be put on Visa or Mastercard. As part of the deal you're asked to give the broker the right to use and show the property. What really happens is that the broker takes the listing fee, then rents the timeshare unit to resort travelers. The unit never gets sold and you lose hundreds in fees and rental income. The broker either disappears or says: "We did our best but nobody wanted to buy. For another fee we'll try again."

Other scams offer to sell your timeshare condo through highly publicized auctions. You pay a listing fee in advance. The auction never happens and the broker skips. This con job works well with all types of real estate.

VACATION CERTIFICATES--You're notified that you have won a "free vacation" in the Bahamas or a cruise. Or the offer may include free airfare for one person with the purchase of a second. To receive the vacation certificate, you may be required to attend a sales promotion at a timeshare resort or a membership campground or to purchase a membership in a travel club. "Free" vacations can end up costing hundreds or even thousands of dollars. The second airfare may cost you more than two discounted tickets. Hotel accommodations are arranged through the promoters at inflated prices and many other additional fees.

Some promoters ask for your credit card number to validate the complimentary vacation and then charge fees to your account without your permission. Don't give out your number. Of all vacation certificates sold, only 10% provide actual vacations. If you are told you have won a prize of a vacation certificate, investigate all the conditions carefully.

The "STING!"

Most people, including strangers that we meet can be kind and honest. However, the odds are, sooner or later, you'll be preyed on and lose your part of the millions, maybe billions lost each year to con games. As we grow older we become primary targets for many unscrupulous persons. They prey on the elderly because they believe we are not quite as perceptive or attentive.

DON'T GET HOOKED BY THESE CLASSICS

THE PIGEON DROP--You accidentally meet a very nice person, usually in front of an office building. A second stranger walks by and picks up a sack lying in the street. Excitedly, he tells the two the bag is full of money. A note inside refers to a dope deal, which indicates the owner is not worth locating. One stranger says they had better see a lawyer and says he knows one just inside the building.

The lawyer's advice is to wait 60 to 90 days before dividing the money and each must put up "good faith" money, presumably to prove they are responsible. The strangers volunteer hefty sums, and you the victim, interested in sharing the wealth, will also. All swear to secrecy and accompany you to the bank to get your money. They add your money to the sack and visit the lawyer, who will hold it. One by one they enter the office. You go in last, holding the sack, and when you come out you find the others are gone. Opening the sack you find blank paper-- your "good faith" money is gone. Well-trained con artists can get away with as much as

$25,000 or more in a single drop, usually from retired older women. Don't let it be yours.

THE JAMAICAN SWITCH--After meeting a would-be victim, a stranger says he has just collected an inheritance, usually about $50,000. The stranger says he wants to donate the money to charity but is unfamiliar with the best charities. Would you help? A second stranger approaches and is easily persuaded to help the con artist. You, the victim, are unaware they are working together.

Before the con artist will give up the $50,000, he tells the two they must prove they have money of their own so they won't be tempted to keep the "inheritance." The second stranger eagerly displays "good faith" money, showing maybe $2,000. Then you may find yourself in a backseat of a car going to your bank to get your "good faith" money.

The first con artist claims to be from Africa, then puts the money in a scarf supposedly containing the inheritance money along with yours and that of the second stranger. Then it is "blessed." You are asked to take it home and give it to the charity. When you look in the scarf there is only cut-up paper.

THE BANK EXAMINER--A so-called bank official asks for your help to catch a dishonest teller. Some cons even say, "Our computer's out. Please help us." You are instructed to withdraw $10,000 dollars in cash from your account and bring it home. You are told an official will come to your home, show his police identification, and place your money into a dummy "sting" account. Someone comes to take your money, and several days may pass before you realize you've been had.

THE PYRAMID SCHEME--Someone offers you a painless way to make money. You invest so much cash and you solicit others to do the same, and they solicit others, and so on. Just like a chain letter. When the pyramid crashes, and they always do, you and everyone else loses except a few at the top who never invested.

THE OBITUARY COLUMN STING-- Shortly after the death of a relative, someone delivers to your door a leather-bound

Bible that your deceased relative allegedly ordered (see the movie Paper Moon). Or you get a bill in the mail for an expensive item on which you must make the remaining payments. Con artists use the obituary notices to prey on bereaved families. Don't be conned. You are not responsible for anyone else's purchases. If the claim is legitimate it will be settled by the estate.

THE NEW LOTTERY SCAM--A con artist alters a lottery ticket so that it seems to be worth a few hundred dollars. They offer to sell you the card, saying they need the money immediately and can't wait for the state to send it. They offers to sell it to you for less that its apparent worth.

FALSE CHARITY RACKETS--Some swindlers start their own charity to take advantage of your goodwill. When someone solicits a donation, ask for identification on both the charity and the solicitor. Many con artists use soundalike names of well-known charities. Find out the charity's purposes, how funds are used, and if contributions are tax deductible. If something is not quite right, don't give.

SWEEPSTAKES CONS--Beware of "Official Sweepstakes Winner" mail. It will generally say you have been chosen, or you may have already won a prize of $50,000 or a Buick, etc. Of course, everyone in your block and hundreds of thousands of others have also been "chosen" as Winners. If you read on you learn you will need to buy something. The "bait" are statements like: Official notification, Cash Prize Winner #00000, Nontransferable, **VERIFIED, IMPORTANT, OPEN IMMEDIATELY, OFFICIAL SWEEPSTAKES RULES, EXTRA BONUS** merchandise with your order, **PREAPPROVED BONUS**, First-Class Mail, **RETURN TO** Office of the Chief Controlling Officer, RUSH--Official Sweepstakes' Winner Prize Claim Form, and so on.

The merchandise will be anything from "AUTHENTIC" zirconia, to magazine subscriptions, to cosmetics, or other overpriced items. Some simply just say send money. One just asks for $19.85 for a brand new 35mm camera--a cheapo. The papers are generally legal-looking with envelopes designed to look like official government mail.

Don't get  roped in!

BAIT and SWITCH-- Some unscrupulous stores advertise fabulous but fake bargains just to get you to come in so they can sell you something more expensive. The salesperson may give you any reason: "There aren't any left"; "Customers were dissatisfied with it"; "You can't get delivery for six months." Then the sales-

TELEPHONE SCAMS--The easiest way to reach you is by phone. Of course, thousands of customers buy from legitimate salespeople each year. Yet there are fraudulent sellers that attempt to zero in on your dollars. Offers range from free, prepaid, or special deal on magazine subscriptions to invest-by-phone frauds. **It is easy to buy a list of senior citizens so it is easy for someone to zero in on you.**

Sometimes, instead of an initial phone call, you may receive a postcard that mentions nothing about magazine subscriptions. The postcard may ask you to call about a contest, prize, or sweepstakes entry. If you call, you may be told about the contest prizes but soon the conversation will turn into a sales talk about buying magazine subscriptions. The callers may imply they represent credit card companies or magazine publishers and their purpose in calling is something other than selling magazines. The few dollars a week subscription fee may sound like a bargain until you realize, generally later, that you could be paying hundreds of dollars for subscriptions that you really don't want and that regularly may sell for less.

They may ask to have your address verified so you can be sure to receive a gift or a prize. **They may ask for your credit card number in a ploy to make sure it is current. Never give your credit card number to someone over the phone unless you initiate the call or are familiar with the company. Never give out your bank account number.**

Ask the callers for their name, address, and phone number of the company they represent. Ask them to send a copy of the sales terms of the offer before you agree to buy anything. Read and understand the terms of the sales agreement--what you will be receiving and what it will cost.

Once you agree to buy a magazine subscription over the phone, you cannot simply call the company and cancel your order if you change your mind. They do not honor oral cancellations. They must be in writing and occur within the limited time period. Watch for the arrival of the sales agreement that may come in "junk" mail-type envelopes. Look for the provision that allows you to cancel; generally it is within 3 days of receipt. Sign it and send it back immediately by registered mail.

CREDIT CARD SHARKS--If someone calls and wants to verify that your Visa card number is current because you have won a free gift or vacation, hang up. Don't give details about your credit cards especially your number. Someone who has your number can make purchases to your account. If someone steals your credit card, you are liable for up to $50 of purchases made before reporting a card missing. It is common for a thief to charge the maximum amount before you can report the card as missing.

When you make a purchase using your credit card keep alert. Ask the clerk for all carbons and destroy them. When a card expires, cut it into pieces and throw it away. Keep a list of all major credit cards, their account numbers, and the phone number to call if they are lost or stolen. Keep this in a safe place--not with your cards. If a card is stolen or lost, notify the card company and the police immediately.

CHECK STEALING--Thieves know you receive checks regularly including those from Social Security, a pension fund, a disability fund, the Veterans Administration, bank interest, stock dividends, and holiday gift checks. Your checks could be stolen anywhere from the place of origin to your mailbox. The principal target of check thieves, however, is your mailbox. Most apartment mailboxes are rifled with a screwdriver in seconds. A stolen check may be cashed nearly anywhere using bogus identification. Arrange with the sender to have your checks automatically deposited in your account. Fill out form SF1199 for direct deposit of your Social Security checks. You can get it from a SS office or your bank. Or arrange to have the payee write on the back of the check: valid only if endorsed by [your name] and deposited in [the name of your bank]. Never let a stranger have your checkbook or fill out a check.

person tries to persuade you to buy a high-priced item. Also avoid "unclaimed" or "reprocessed" merchandise sales unless you are certain you are dealing with a reputable company. You may be shown seconds, damaged, or mismatched pieces, then switched to something more expensive.

Watch out for "going out of business" sales. This is another tactic to get you into the store. Be sure the store is really selling out before you buy.

"OFFICIAL" MAIL--How many official-looking letters from official-sounding organizations have you received lately? How many were labeled **"URGENT: IMPORTANT SOCIAL SECURITY AND MEDICARE INFORMATION ENCLOSED," OR "POSTMASTER: TIME-SENSITIVE DOCUMENT ENCLOSED."** Dozens of direct mail fear mongers prey on you as Social Security recipients. The look-alike mailings are intended to confuse you about their origin so you pay for services, such as help in filling out Social Security forms, that the government provides free. Others are after a donation to oppose a new Medicare law, to join a Social Security sweepstakes, to make a real estate deal, or to lobby for you.

These con artists use names like The Federal Social Security Center, Federal Record Service Corp., The Committee to Preserve Social Security, Social Security Protection Bureau, etc. In 1988, Congress made it illegal for private mailings to use words or symbols normally associated with the SSA or The Health Care Financing Association but it hasn't stopped some.

Discard official-looking junk mail once you've checked it out. It attempts to cause you needless worry and tries to make you think that if you fail to contribute you may lose your benefits--don't you believe it. Toss it.

You never get something for nothing

It's a great deal!

BARGAIN REPAIRS--A free inspection turns up the need for repairs that will cost thousands of dollars. A contractor offers you a special half-price chance to have your house reroofed because he has a surplus of material from another project. A salesman has siding that will make you the envy of the neighborhood and only now at this extraordinarily low price, installed free. Don't be conned. Dishonest individuals prey on older persons. Always get three estimates for any major work from reputable firms and check them out with the Better Business Bureau. Don't be pressured into accepting a one-day-only offer. Never pay in advance. Get a written contract and make sure you fully understand it before signing it.

WORK-AT-HOME SCHEMES--There's no "easy way to make money at home" although many ads in newspapers and magazines offer you huge profits working in your home. It is one of the oldest frauds to take advantage of the handicapped or retired persons. Schemes include: home sewing, raising chinchillas, raising rabbits, and clipping news items. These schemes have one thing in common: You must buy something before you begin work. Here are some other common types of fraud:

ENVELOPE STUFFING--For a "small fee" con artists will show you how to earn money stuffing envelopes. You learn that you make money the same way they do by placing similar ads so others can learn how to stuff envelopes. And the game goes on. In a variation of the scheme a company offers to pay 25 to 75 cents per envelope stuffed. You

must buy the company's information on money making plans and place ads at your expense to sucker the next one. In practically all businesses today, envelope stuffing is an automated process. Computer listings and mass mailings eliminate any profit potential for individuals working at home. Each year the post office puts 3,500 of these work-at-home schemes out of business.

ASSEMBLY OR CRAFT WORK--They ask you to invest hundreds of dollars in equipment--a sewing machine, a sign-making machine, materials, or supplies. Then you put in many hours producing goods for the company who promises to buy them. However, after your purchases, your work doesn't meet their quality standards. You have no sales.

Before getting involved you should ask (in writing and get a reply in writing): What are the tasks involved? Is the pay on salary or commission? Who will pay me? When will I get my first check? What is my total cost, including supplies, equipment, and membership or training fees? What will I get for my money? After you get the "right" answers check with the Better Business Bureau in the area where the company is located before you do business with them. Keep a written record of what transpired.

MAIL ORDER BUSINESS--Some con artists claim you can build a profitable mail order business using professional mail order ads with your own catalogs and without investing a cent in inventory. They offer to supply advertisements and do all the shopping for you. They claim they have an amazing new plan for beginners that requires little capital and no previous experience, saying you can pocket cash profits daily. Don't you believe it! Why would anyone want to share this lucrative market?

UNORDERED MERCHANDISE--If you are sent clothing, cookware, linens, or any other merchandise that you did not order, you have a legal right to keep the shipment as a gift. You should send a registered letter stating your intention to keep the shipment as a free gift. It may discourage the seller from sending you repeated bills or dunning notices, or it may help clear up an honest error. If you continue to receive bills or dunning notices, you can use the same approach.

If it was an honest error, write the seller and offer to return the merchandise provided the seller send you the postage within 30 days. Inform the seller that after that time you reserve the right to keep the merchandise.

Protect yourself by reading all the fine print when participating in sweepstakes or ordering goods advertized as "free," "trial," or "unusually low-priced." Make sure you are not joining a club with regular purchases required unless it is your intention.

If you need help in dealing with unordered merchandise problems, contact your local U.S. postal inspector, your local consumer protection office, or the Better Business Bureau.

PROTECTION TIPS

- Don't believe you can get something for nothing. You never get something for nothing.
- Don't give your credit card number to anyone you don't really know. If it sounds like a great deal and they want your number it could be a scam.
- Watch out for "free" gifts, "no-risk" claims, and irresistible bargains.
- Don't act immediately. Ask for information you can check out about their product and its value. If they are genuine they will send it.
- Don't assume all mail is legitimate. Be cautious about official-looking mail.
- Ignore high-pressure sales techniques. Say No! and mean it.
- Never admit the decision will be yours alone. Even if you're widowed or divorced, don't say so. If you appear vulnerable, you could be an easy mark.
- Always comparison shop for price and quality before you buy.
- Read and understand all contracts before signing. If you don't understand it, have someone you trust explain it to you.
- Check with the Better Business Bureau, the police department, or the attorney general's office before you sign contracts for major work.
- Check out all charities before giving. To check, send a postcard to the National Charities Information Bureau, 19 Union Square West, New York, NY 10003.

Quackery--a $25 billion a year ripoff

The Journal of the American Medical Association has estimated that Americans spend some $25 billion a year on quack remedies. They say that the elderly alone spend $10 billion a year on bogus cures. The AMA believes that quacks like to get to desperate people.

An important question is just how to define quackery. The problem is that everything that's ever been new in medicine has been at one time labeled quackery. For example, Sister Kinney was labeled a quack for her polio treatment of body massage and water therapy. Today, her treatment is the order of the day.

I remember the time that my doctor told me cigarette smoking was not bad for your health and that it didn't matter what you ate. Those people who said differently were quacks. Today, of course, cigarettes are out and nutrition is in. We don't go back too far in history to recall that doctors bled patients to rid them of fever.

We must not avoid observing that there is considerable disagreement in modern medicine. Some alternate forms of therapy are too quickly labeled quackery by those who are of a different persuasion. Some medical professionals look askance at things like nutrition, acupuncture, chiropractic, herbs, and visualization as treatments for chronic disease, even though they are valid treatments for some medical problems.

A major problem with quackery is the placebo effect. A typical scientific experiment will divide people into three groups: One group will be given medication for an illness. Another group will be given nothing and a third group will be given a placebo--a sugar pill that looks like the medicine. Surprisingly, a third of the placebo group will have as much benefit as the medicated group. It has been discovered that neutral medicine like a placebo can have a dramatic healing effect. Since we do not understand all the factors that make up therapy, it is wise not to be too opportunistic with the word quackery.

> **Physicians entertain while nature effects a cure.**
> Voltaire

WE NEED TO REMEMBER:

✔ Some of what was considered quackery in the past is now part of accepted practice.

✔ The placebo effect makes some quackery seem to work.

We also need to remember that there is such a thing as "quackery" and there are some general principles that define it.

❶ People who know that their remedies are phoney and peddle them for the single motive of making money are quacks or crooks.

❷ Remedies that are based on unscientific evidence are quackery.

❸ Using cures and treatment that have been scientifically disproved could be labeled quackery. There is a difference between someone's opinion or theory and a scientific fact.

❹ Superstitious cures, old wives tales, witchcraft, and occult mumbo jumbo can be considered quackery.

❺ Cures that work only in the imagination, not in fact, are quackery. For example, I watched a lady loudly proclaim that she had been healed of a hunched back and crooked spine when anyone's eyes could see that it wasn't true.

If you want to venture off the beaten path for treatment, here are some tips to help you avoid medical ripoffs:

✳ Be careful if the word "miracle" or "secret" appear in the treatment. God does work miracles, but seldom do you have to pay for them.

✳ Watch out if someone tells you they are the victim of a conspiracy by the American Medical Association, the FDA, the FBI, or some other government body to keep their product off the market.

✳ Check the person's credentials. Watch out for multiple degrees from strange-sounding or unaccredited institutions or memberships in exotic-sounding organizations. Some people's credentials are self-proclaimed with bogus degrees run off on a printing press.

✳ Use your common sense. If everything you've ever heard says up is up, and someone comes along and says up is

down or black is white, be careful.

✳ Don't buy any treatment that purports to cure everything. There is no one potion that will cure arthritis, multiple sclerosis, diabetes, and warts. Cure-alls end up being cure-nothings.

✳ Watch out for products that are going to "boost" or "enhance" your immune system.

✳ Be careful of people who want to sell you things for both your body and your pets.

✳ Watch out if someone tries to get you to leave your personal physician or tells you not to trust him or her. Medical doctors are people and make mistakes just like anyone else; but down through history the medically educated have the best and most consistent record of healing. On occasions an alternative method of healing will work, but usually the medical doctor has the best reputation for healing because he has earned it.

✳ Beware if they guarantee a cure--no one can do that. After all, no matter whose medicine we use, we all eventually die. Try to avoid the quacks and you will live longer and better.

✳ After all is said and done, use your common sense. And when in doubt, check it out. Remember: If it sounds too good to be true, it probably is.

> **Quackery**
> It can cost you more
> than just your money.
> For quacks, **Old** is Gold.

The FDA's list of top 10 health frauds

A disturbing number of older Americans seem to be entrusting their healthcare to unqualified individuals and are buying unproven--and sometimes dangerous--remedies from them. They have entered--at their own risk--the world of health quackery. Difficult to curtail, health frauds, like crab grass, sprout up here, there, and everywhere.

Quack promoters have learned to stay one step ahead of the law either by moving from state to state or by changing their corporate names. The Food and Drug Administration (FDA) claims they concentrate on the most dangerous abuses, but they say health fraud is bigger than any one organization can deal with. Health fraud is big business in this country. Here is a list of the FDA's top 10 health frauds:

1. Fraudulent Arthritis Products. Arthritis affects some 37 million Americans, 95% of whom are likely to engage in some form of self-treatment even after they have seen a physician.

Copper bracelets, Chinese herbal remedies, large doses of vitamins, and snake or bee venom don't work. Because the symptoms of arthritis go into remission periodically, individuals who try these unproven remedies may associate the remedy with the remission (see article on unproven remedies for arthritis, page 284).

2. Spurious Cancer Clinics. These clinics, many of them in Mexico, promise miracle cures. Treatments use mostly unproven and ineffective substances such as laetrile (derived from apricot kernels) and vitamins and minerals. People who go to these clinics often abandon legitimate cancer treatments. This is particularly tragic because some cancers are curable through legitimate treatment.

3. Bogus AIDS Cures. Victims of incurable diseases are especially vulnerable to the promises of charlatans. AIDS is a prime example. Underground or "guerrilla clinics" offering homemade treatments have sprung up. There is no cure for AIDS yet--proposed treatments such as massive doses of antibiotics, typhus vaccine, or herbal tea made from the bark of Brazilian trees are all unproven.

4. Instant Weight-Loss Schemes. With an estimated 25% of the American population being overweight, quack selling weight-loss gimmicks have a sizable market for their wares.

Unfortunately, there is no quick way to lose weight. Fraudulent weight-loss schemes are usually heralded by full-page newspaper ads promising rapid, dramatic, and easy weight loss or by news ads that look like news stories except that the word "advertisement" is written across the top. Radio and TV ads typically list 800 telephone numbers to facilitate credit card charges and private parcel delivery. This allows the promoters to circumvent the postal service's laws against mail fraud. Some of the latest gimmicks in instant weight-loss plans have included skin patches, herbal capsules, grapefruit diet pills, and Chinese magic weight-loss earrings.

5. Fraudulent Sexual Aids. Products promoted to enhance libido and sexual pleasure are not new. FDA officials recently cracked down on an entrepreneur selling Chinese "Crocodile Penis Pills" purportedly prepared according to a 2,000-year-old formula for rejuvenating male sexual prowess.

FDA says no nonprescription drug ingredients have been proven safe or effective as aphrodisiacs and have acted to ban these products. Over-the-counter (OTC) products that claim to increase the size of a man's penis or cure impotence or "frigidity" don't work.

Serious health risks are associated with the use of such purported aphrodisiacs as cantharides ("Spanish Fly"), a chemical derived from the dried bodies of beetles. Other ingredients of similar OTC products include strychnine (a poison), mandrake and yohimbine (poisonous plants), licorice, zinc, and the herbs anise and fennel.

Although male sex hormones, available by prescription, do influence libido and sexual performance, they have potentially serious side effects and should be used under a physician's supervision. The agency (FDA) advises that people with sexual problems should not attempt to medicate themselves but rather should seek treatment by a medical professional.

6. Quack Baldness Remedies and Other Appearance Modifiers. Entrepreneurs make millions of dollars trying to convince consumers to buy their versions of the fountain of youth, whether it be a remedy to grow hair or prevent its loss, a cream that removes wrinkles, or a device to develop the bust.

Only one prescription product has been approved for growing hair on balding men and women: Rogaine (minoxidil). And this approval is only for a specific type of baldness. FDA has acted to ban the sale of any nonprescription hair cream, lotion, or other external product claiming to grow hair or prevent baldness. None of these products have been shown to be effective.

Clinical studies suggest that one product, Retin-A, may be effective in lessening certain kinds of wrinkles, and some physicians prescribe it for this purpose. This is legitimate because it is approved for treating acne and doctors may thus prescribe it for other uses. However, consumers should be aware that FDA has not evaluated safety and effectiveness data for the drug's use as a wrinkle remover.

7. False Nutritional Schemes. Many Americans whose diets are not nutritionally balanced may be persuaded that some "perfect" food or product will make up for all their nutritional shortcomings. Various food products--such as bee pollen, over-the-counter herbal remedies, and wheat germ capsules--are promoted as sure-fire cures for various diseases. Though usually not harmful, these products have not been proven to be beneficial.

8. Chelation Therapy. Promoters of this therapy claim that an injection or tablet of the amino acid EDTA, taken with vitamins and minerals, cleans out arteries by breaking down arterial plaque (deposits of cholesterol and other lipid materials). Such treatment is supposed to prevent circulatory disease, angina (chest pain), heart attacks, and strokes and is advertised as an "alternative" to heart bypass surgery. Both FDA and the American Heart Association say there is no scientific evidence that chelation therapy works. Nevertheless, patients spend as much as $3,000 to $5,000 for chelation treatments. Not only are they paying for an ineffective treatment, they are also buying a dangerous

Charlatans--they prosper through our ignorance

drug. EDTA can cause kidney failure, bone marrow depression, and convulsions.

9. Unproven Use of Muscle Stimulators. Muscle stimulators are a legitimate medical device approved for certain conditions--to relax muscle spasms, increase blood circulation, prevent blood clots, and rehabilitate muscle function after a stroke. But within the past few years health spas and figure salons have promoted new uses. They claim that muscle stimulators can remove wrinkles, perform face lifts, reduce breast size, and remove cellulite. Some even claim these handy little devices can reduce one's beer belly without the aid of sit-ups! FDA considers promotion of muscle stimulators used for these conditions to be fraudulent.

10. Candidiasis Hyersensitivity. Candida (also known as monilia) is a fungus found naturally in small amounts in the warm moist areas of the body such as the mouth, intestinal tract, and vagina. When the body's resistance is weakened, the fungus can multiply and infect the skin or mucous membranes. More serious infection occurs in individuals whose resistance has been weakened by other illnesses.

However, some promoters assert that approximately 30% of Americans suffer from "candidiasis hypersensitivity," which they say triggers everything from fatigue to constipation, diarrhea, depression and anxiety, impotence, and menstrual problems. To correct the problem, promoters recommend antifungal drugs and vitamins and minerals.

The American Academy of Allergy and Immunology says the existence of such a syndrome has not been proven and the number of symptoms credited to candidiasis hypersensitivity could be due to any number of illnesses.

How to Spot a Quack
After years of doctors' visits and prescription drugs, you've stumbled on an advertisement for what promises to be the perfect cure for your migraine headaches (and, in the bargain, according to the ad, a cure for arthritis, stomachaches, and lack of energy). These claims are boosted by testimony from satisfied users. But remember the rule of thumb for evaluating health claims: If it seems too good to be true, it probably is.

FDA officials and Dr. Stephen Barrett, an author and noted expert on quackery, have analyzed promoter's statements and offer the following "translations" to help you spot the unproven and false claims.

✳ The promoter claims that most doctors are "butchers," that the medical community is against him or her, and that the government will not accept this wonderful discovery. Anyone considering a cure for sterility, cancer, AIDS, or other serious conditions would likely be showered with prizes and grant money and nominated for a Nobel Prize. Legitimate doctors don't conspire to suppress cures for diseases.

✳ The promoter cites testimonials and anecdotes from satisfied customers to support claims. These "satisfied" users may never have had the disease the product is supposed to cure, may be paid spokespersons, or may simply not exist. "Most single episodes of disease simply disappear with the passage of time, and most chronic ailments have symptom-free periods that may be mistaken as evidence of a cure," says Barrett.

✳ The promoter uses a computer-stored questionnaire for diagnosing "nutrient deficiencies." Computers used for such tests are programmed to recommend supplements for virtually everyone, regardless of their symptoms or medical condition.

✳ The promoter claims that the product will make weight loss easy. Beware of this claim. There is no easy way to lose weight--no magic pill, no magic device. Losing weight requires the self-discipline to eat less and exercise more. Any product claims that promise to trim you down and tone you effortlessly are false, says FDA.

✳ The promoter promises quick dramatic cures or claims that the product is based on a "secret formula" available only from this one company. Legitimate scientists share their knowledge so that their peers can review their data. Once a treatment is proven effective, many practitioners in the medical commu-

nity are free to use it--not just one person or company.

✳ The treatment is promoted only in the back of magazines, over the phone, or by mail-order, newspaper ads in the format of news stories or 30-minute commercials in talk show formats. Results of studies on bona fide treatments are reported first in medical journals. If information ads for a treatment appear only via these other means it's probably because the treatment doesn't pass scientific muster.

If you think you've been taken in by a quack treatment, speak out. Complain to the following organizations:

◼ About a product that is mislabeled or misrepresented, or is otherwise harmful: The Food and Drug Administration, Consumer Affairs and Information, 5600 Fishers Lane, HFC-110, Rockville, MD 20857 (or look for the local FDA office listed in the telephone directory under U.S. Department of Health and Human Services); your particular State Attorney General's Office; the Federal Trade Commission, Correspondence Branch, Room 692, Sixth and Pennsylvania Avenues NW, Washington, D.C. 20580; and the newspaper, magazine, or TV or radio station in the ad.

◼ About a quackery product ordered by mail: U.S. Postal Service, Chief Postal Inspector, 475 L'Enfant Plaza, Washington, D.C. 20260 (or check with your local postmaster).

◼ If you want to take legal action against a quack, you can get help from the National Council Against Health Fraud, Contact Michael Botts, P.O. Box 33008, Kansas City, MO 64114; (816) 444-8615. This organization can refer you to an experienced lawyer. The council also offers a registry of expert witnesses, information on defense witnesses, and a list of unproven, fraudulent, and potentially dangerous treatments.

> **The best liar is he who makes the smallest amount of lying go the longest way.**
>
> **- Samuel Butler (1835-1902)**

Creating and maintaining a family history

Everyone who has experienced death in their family has had occasion to regret that one question or another was not asked before that death occurred. When that happens, there is usually nothing that can be done to retrieve information for your own enlightenment and for the benefit of your children and grandchildren. They deserve to know about their past. There is nothing more reassuring for children in today's fragmented families than the sense of belonging and continuity available in a family tree, especially when it is accompanied with anecdotes and information about the lives of their ancestors.

One of the most popular courses being offered at community colleges across the United States is how to develop a family history. You need not be a genealogist to accomplish that task, but genealogy has much to teach us about simple techniques we can use to discover and pass along information about forebears. It is important to remember that a family history is not just the branch that bears the family name. Going back only to your great grandparents gives you eight separate branches, and if you look only at the branch with your family name, you could be missing the very best and most interesting information.

SOURCES OF INFORMATION
We need go no farther than the family living room or bookshelf to discover important information about our families. Get out the family Bible and look for information about births and deaths. Copy the information and distribute it to family members. Add your own current information about marriage, the birth of children, and deaths. There is no reason why this traditional practice should be limited to the past. However, add that current information when you make copies. The more of these copies that are circulated in the family, the better the chance for them to survive for children yet unborn.

PHOTOGRAPHS
Go through the family photographs. On the back of each one you should identify the person(s), the place, and the approximate time of the shot. If there are people you can't identify, keep them handy so that the next time Aunt Sadie visits you, you can show them to her and see if she can help with identification.

RECORDS AND DOCUMENTS
Try to identify and preserve papers and documents that have been handed along from generation to generation. Some, such as a land patent or homestead document, may even be suitable for framing. Records of bills, family business activity, tax statements, and old letters can be rich sources of information that tell much about how our ancestors lived. Information about what prices of labor and commodities were can be fascinating to our children. When we tell our grandchildren that when we were small newspapers cost two cents and milk nine cents, they gain a sense of perspective that they can get in no other way.

ANECDOTES
It is important to do all you can to capture the experiences of older members of the family by interviewing them with a tape recorder. Work out your questions before you interview them so that you will be sure to cover the information adequately. Later on, you can transcribe the interview, if you wish, so that it will be available in written form. Ask them how they lived, how much they earned, how they traveled, how couples met, etc. Try to ascertain where certain relatives were buried, and find out the causes of their deaths. What schools did they attend, and for how long? How did they earn their living?

Remember to ask questions about each phase of their lives: childhood, teen years, and adulthood. Include questions about clothing, school, books read, work, family remembrances, and involvement in events of their time such as a war or the depression.

WRITTEN SOURCES
A common practice in the midwest has been the compilation of county histories. This practice has been expanding so that there are many of these accounts being published throughout the United States. Usually the local historical society has been behind such efforts. They can be excellent sources of information about families who lived there in the past.

There are many federal and state records that can be helpful in tracing an ancestor. The General Services Administration offers two free pamphlets that help to learn how to retrieve information from the National Archives and military service records.

They are "General Information Leaflets" #5 and #7. They are available from the General Services Administration, Washington, D.C. 20408.

The federal census is also a rich source of information about family history. They have been collected every ten years since 1790, although only heads of household were named until 1850. After that there was more detail. There are other federal sources.

Church records are often useful. Many Americans have had to use church records to establish their citizenship for Social Security and passports. They not only recorded births and baptisms, but marriages and deaths.

GENEALOGY
The Mormon Church has been responsible for the collection of vast amounts of information about family histories. There are many repositories of this information. While much of it has been concentrated in Salt Lake City, you can probably find sources closer to you that would enable you to research family lines. If you wish to pursue this study seriously, you would find it useful to take some sort of training course to make your search more effective and efficient. If you are seeking information about one particular branch of the family, you may even find a family genealogy society that has done much of your work for you.

One handy introduction to tracing your family history that you might find useful is *Unpuzzling Your Past* by Emily Anne Croom, Betterway Publications, Inc., P.O. Box 219, Crozet, VA 22932, 2nd Edition 1989, $9.95.

For computer users:
There are a number of computer programs available that help you create your family history and family tree. *My Story* is a program that asks over 400 specific questions that prompt you to provide details of each area of your life. When you're finished, you can print your story. Another program, *Family Tree Maker*, requests information such as name, birthday, birth location, occupation, marriage information, children, and date of death. Both programs are available from Selective Software, 3004 Mission St., Santa Cruz, CA 95060.

Retirement--the beginning of a new life

There are a series of questions you must ask yourself as you begin to plan your retirement. Then as the process develops, you need to ask most of them over and over.

WILL YOU RETIRE TOTALLY AND IRREVOCABLY?--When you leave your job, will it be for good? Does your employer offer an alternative to partial retirement? You need to know how you will feel being totally cut off from the activity that has dominated your life for so long. Would you be interested in some other career, perhaps on a part-time basis? Your answer to these questions should be somewhat dependent on the next major question.

WHAT WILL YOU DO WITH YOUR TIME?--Do you have existing interests that you can pursue? Is there a hobby or a sideline that you have been working on in the past, so that you have a track record of interest and success? Are there new interests that you have been wishing to pursue but have been unable to due to time, location, or opportunity? Would you be interested in volunteer work? Is there an institution or a cause that you have been helping or wanted to work for? Do you like to help adults? Children? Could you teach someone to read? Would you like to help people who are ill or lonely? There are a thousand needs and meeting them can produce genuine satisfaction.

Do you want to travel? Do you wish to buy an RV and wander the country? Do you like cruising? Would you like to be a snowbird-- going south for the winter and north for the summer?

Do you really want to retire? Of course, the choices above do not require that you spend full time on any of them. It is possible to do some of each of these activities.

DO YOU HAVE SUFFICIENT FINANCIAL RESOURCES TO RETIRE?--If you are only a year or two from retirement, it is too late to begin thinking about retirement resources. Years ahead of time you need to make an assessment of your expected needs after retirement in order to know if your pension and savings will support those needs. You need to add up what you can expect from:

❶ Your pension plan
❷ Social Security
❸ Investments and savings
❹ Inheritance
❺ Any remaining work activities

WHERE WILL YOU LIVE?--Should you remain in the family home? If you have previously established a retirement home this question is probably already settled. Selling the family home depends upon such considerations as size, tax consequences, other family proximity, and present value. If your home has multiplied in value, it may be wise to sell it and take advantage of the tax forgiveness for those over 55 years of age. This realized profit might contribute substantially to your retirement nest-egg, even after purchasing a new and better home in a less expensive area.

Retirees who move far away from the areas and people known to them sometimes find that they are unhappy in the new setting. Moving to be near a son or daughter can also be the wrong thing when the younger family is transferred to a new location. On the other hand, many people are stimulated by a new environment and can lead rich and productive lives in a new setting. The relative ease and quickness of travel today makes a thousand miles less forbidding than it once was.

Whatever the inclination, it is wise to test out proposals before making major decisions such as buying a house in a new area. Rent for a while, or stay in other temporary housing while you get the feel of a new location. Find out if your children are going to be comfortable having you near them, if that is the motivation for a move. By doing that, costly mistakes can be avoided.

WHAT SORT OF HEALTHCARE WILL YOU HAVE?--One of the realities of advancing age is an increased demand for healthcare. You need to assess the resources you will have available to you. In picking a location to spend your retirement, the availability of nearby doctors and hospitals may need to be considered.

Will you be eligible for Medicare? If there is a question, you should visit a Social Security office and ask for an evaluation of your status. If a few more quarters will make you eligible, it could be wise to take up new employment of some kind that will contribute to your Social Security record following your retirement from your career position.

Will your company or agency provide health insurance in retirement or contribute to it? Sometimes they will furnish insurance until you become eligible for Medicare. Once you have determined that Medicare will be available, you will need to select a supplementary insurance plan to cover the costs not paid by Medicare.

Failing any of the arrangements above, you will need to inquire about the cost of individual coverage with health insurance. Bear in mind the increasing costs of medical care, and thus of insurance, when you are projecting what it will cost in the future.

WHEN YOU CAN NO LONGER CARE FOR YOURSELF--Most of us can plan on years of active retirement with freedom and mobility adding to the pleasure of the time. However, almost everyone comes to a time when it is no longer possible to live independently. These decisions do not necessarily have to be made before or at retirement, but the question needs to be addressed. Some institutions have long waiting lists, even though they require huge investments in order to buy in, so the decision should not be postponed too long.

There was a time when retirement was seen as the beginning of the end of life. Today, it is more commonly seen as the beginning of a new life. We all know people who have led rich and active lives in retirement. Proper planning and wise decision making can help you to enter this new phase of your life with anticipation and pleasure.

The trick is to live to be 100, very few people die after that

George Burns

Today is a good day to start!

People are born to create. God has given everybody at least some ability to get new ideas, to produce changes, and to bring something new into being. Perhaps your creativity has been squelched, especially during childhood. When you were a child or a youth your teachers or parents may have had objectives set out for you that prevented you from finding an opportunity to do the things you really wanted to do. Later you may have been busy raising a family, making a living, and trying to get ahead. Hence, your creativity never had a chance to develop.

SET A COURSE

There is no end to creative and useful activities that one can pursue upon retirement. Although it is necessary that you set a course, establish objectives, and pursue them, there is no need to approach this "job" of retirement with the same frantic pace that you gave your career or to raising the children. You do not want to develop stress over your retirement program but you do want to establish a meaningful direction to your daily living. Your life must have a purpose and you must be able to see that you are achieving that purpose--even if the pace is leisurely--or you will begin to withdraw and wither away.

LEARN NEW SKILLS

Retirement is not a time to sit on your rocker and wait for death to arrive. It is a time to seek new directions, inspirations, and meanings to your life. Neither age, physical condition, nor finances are reasons to dismiss this opportunity. In fact, the mature years are often one's most productive period. Many people have learned to paint, play musical instruments, or do a variety of things after they have reached their retirement years. Grandma Moses is a notable example, having continued her self-trained "primitive" American painting beyond her hundredth year.

NEW CAREER PERSPECTIVES

Many careers can still be pursued but from a new viewpoint after retirement. As examples, a retired lawyer undertook a lobbying campaign of letter writing and visits with law professors, judges, and others to change a law that he had long thought to be unfair--and gained more recognition than in all the years as a practicing attorney. A retired carpenter developed and patented several new tools. A retired secretary spent years writing a book on the evolution of women as secretaries.

COUNSEL OTHERS

One of the most creative and unique activities that anyone can undertake is to counsel others.

There is probably no time in life that a person is more valuable for the counsel that he or she can offer than in his later years. With maturity and perspective, a person can offer sage advice to young people.

Counseling does not always mean telling people what to do. Many children, teenagers, young parents, and even older people need someone who will listen patiently and advise gently. Obviously there are many opportunities to perform this service informally, but hospitals, social service agencies, and others are always looking for those willing to act as counselors.

THINK ABOUT YOU

Another aspect of retirement is that you can concentrate on those things that please you. No longer must you direct your total activities to those that meet the needs of your boss, provide for your children, or even serve your spouse. Sometimes it is difficult to overcome the feeling that you are being selfish when you spend even a little time doing what you enjoy. It is particularly difficult for women who have spent the majority of their lives serving their family and husband's needs--possibly in addition to a job--to even think about their own desires. That is why it is frequently the woman who has the most difficult time adjusting to retirement as she is unaccustomed to setting her own goals.

MONEY IS NO OBJECT

Finances need not be a deterrent to setting creative retirement goals. Libraries, schools, and colleges provide free or very inexpensive opportunities for study and self-improvement. Senior centers and craft groups are available to help you develop new skills. Most communities have a number of organized recreation programs to help you keep fit, develop new talents, or just meet with others of similar interests.

GET STARTED--TODAY

The most important step in making up your mind to do something is to turn off the TV and get started. Today is a good day to start. It is, after all, the first day of the rest of your life.

Reprinted by permission of Dr. Clyde M. Narramore, Narramore Christian Foundation, Rosemead, CA.

All growth depends upon activity. There is no development physically or intellectually without effort, and effort means work.

- Calvin Coolidge (1872-1933)

Organize a group to help in staying well

Older people now are living longer than any generation in history, but quality of life is desired along with quantity of years. Good health, which is important for maintaining and improving the benefits of a longer life, is everyone's dream. Many older Americans are actively striving to maintain their fitness and well-being, turning that dream into a reality.

We know that adopting good health habits can reduce the risk of illness for people of all ages. Good health habits may also lessen the impact of chronic diseases, thereby preventing health problems from becoming worse and interfering with an older person's active life. In addition, when people focus on staying well, rather than treating disease after it develops, they reduce their reliance on the healthcare system. As knowledgeable consumers, they can work in partnership with their doctors and get more for their healthcare dollars.

The Problem
Learning about good health habits is not easy if you attempt to do so by yourself. Putting them into practice is sometimes even harder.

A Possible Solution
One of the most effective learning environments is in groups that learn from one another and in many cases from a professional. Fortunately, the American Association of Retired Persons (AARP) has a collection of health promotion program ideas available to AARP Health Advocacy Service (HAS) program volunteers and community organizations that are helping older people help themselves to better health.

You can join a group if there is one in your community. If not, you can get together with others and organize a program. There are several benefits for organizing and promoting a program:

❶ You gain knowledge about the health problems in which you are interested.
❷ You are helping others.
❸ You can meet new friends.
❹ You have the satisfaction that you are doing something very worthwhile.

How to Get Started
Write to AARP for a copy of their booklet "Staying Well." It will give you all the information you will need to get started. Look at the programs for topics that might fit your interests and see if the resources necessary are ones to which you have access. Each fully described program lists:

✳ The importance of the subject matter for older adults
✳ The activities involved
✳ What you will need (personnel, facilities/equipment, and materials) and ideas on where to find it
✳ Costs
✳ Occasionally, special tips, other model programs, and other resources (national and local organizations that can provide more educational materials)

You begin your program using these five steps:

❶ Establish a workable committee structure
❷ Working with other community groups
❸ Recruiting volunteers
❹ Publicizing the program
❺ Writing thank-you notes

Programs available from AARP:

✳ Minority Focus of Health Promotion Programs
✳ Activated Patient
✳ Arthritis Self-Help Course
✳ Blood Pressure
✳ Breast Cancer
✳ Colorectal Cancer
✳ Dental Health in the Later Years
✳ Diabetes
✳ Elder Health
✳ Walking, Active, Live and Kicking Seniors
✳ Growing Wiser (Aging)
✳ Over 50 and Fit
✳ Health Fairs
✳ Healthy Life-styles
✳ Have you Heard? (Hearing)
✳ Medication Awareness
✳ Mental Wellness
✳ Nutrition
✳ Osteoporosis
✳ Safety and Injury Prevention
✳ Smoking Cessation
✳ Vision
✳ Women's Health

For AARP information contact:
National Resource Center on Health Promotion and Aging, AARP, 601 E Street, N.W., Washington, D.C. 20049; (202) 434-2277. The NRCHPA is designed to support

the development and implementation of health promotion programs for older adults.

Government Information Source
The National Audiovisual Center (NAC) is the central source for purchasing or renting more than 8,000 federally produced audiovisual programs available to the public. Catalogs and referrals to free loan sources are provided free of charge. Several of the catalogs cover health-related topics, including alcohol and drug abuse, dentistry, emergency medical services, medicine, and nursing. For more information write or call: Information Services, National Audiovisual Center, National Archives and Records Administration, 8700 Edgeworth Drive, Capital Heights, MD 20743-3701; (800) 638-1300.

Other Sources
Modern Talking Pictures, 5000 Park Street N., St. Petersburg, FL 33709; (800)243-6877. Loans free or offers the purchase of hundreds of videos and films on a variety of topics. Request a catalog.

American Heart Association offers free or low-cost materials and information--check with your local affiliate.

American Cancer Society, local chapter. Offers video program on diet and assessing one's diet risks, the nutritional steps that can be taken to reduce the risks of getting various kinds of cancer, tips on food preparation and meal planning for a healthier diet.

> **Learning is kind of a natural food for the mind.**
> - Cicero (106-43 B.C.)

Volunteering--the gift of giving!

The number of Americans over 60 years of age is 42 million-plus and growing. That's a lot of living, a lot of experience. As older persons, we are one of this country's greatest natural resources. We have so much to give and our talent and wisdom are needed at every level of American life. Offering your services helps put this much-needed knowledge and experience back into the community.

America has a proud tradition of neighbor helping neighbor, and today this volunteer spirit is needed more than ever before. If you have finally won the right to pursue relaxation, purpose, and nobility, consider these reasons for volunteering your services:

- ❤ It provides a way to be useful, help others, and do good deeds.
- ❤ The work is enjoyable and makes one feel needed.
- ❤ Volunteerism is good for the heart. It increases your self-esteem and competence as well as lessens stress and depression.
- ❤ Studies show that people who volunteer live longer, healthier, and happier lives.
- ❤ People are so in need of tender loving care that your volunteering efforts will reap appreciation.
- ❤ After a lifetime of needing to take, retirement can be time to give back.
- ❤ Some programs, like the Senior Companion Program, respond to the greatest needs of seniors. Some day you may be in need of this aid.
- ❤ You can help somebody not as healthy or fortunate as you.
- ❤ And of course, you may have your own reasons.

> **Life is a long lesson in humility.**
>
> - John Matthew Barrie (1860-1937)

An impressive 44% of people between the ages of 50 and 74 regularly volunteer, providing services worth more than $110 billion a year. In 1990, Congress authorized $5 million to begin a "Thousand Points of Light Foundation," to encourage volunteerism. It was part of a volunteer bill providing $62 million in the current fiscal year, $105 million in fiscal 1992, and $120 million in fiscal 1993 for national and community service programs.

There are numerous volunteer opportunities for senior citizens. Here is a partial listing:

- ♥ AARP's Volunteer Programs
- ♥ ACTION
  FGP (Foster Grandparents Program)
  RSVP (Retired Senior Volunteer Program)
  SCP (Senior Companion Program)
  VISTA (Volunteers In Service To America)
- ♥ American Cancer Society
- ♥ Area Office on Aging (see Senior Assistance section, page 20)
- ♥ Consumer Watchdogs
- ♥ Chamber of Commerce
- ♥ Fish and Wildlife Service
- ♥ Forest Service Volunteers
- ♥ Hospice
- ♥ Lions Club
- ♥ National Park Service
- ♥ Ombudsmen
- ♥ Peace Corps
- ♥ Red Cross
- ♥ Respite Care
- ♥ Rotary Club
- ♥ SCORE (Service Corps of Retired Executives)
- ♥ United Way
- ♥ Veterans Voluntary Service

> We live in a society that always has depended on volunteers of different kinds--some who can give money, others who give time, and a great many who will freely give their special skills, full-time or part-time. If you look closely you will see that almost anything that really matters to us, anything that embodies our deepest commitment to the way human life should be lived and cared for depends on some form--more often, many forms--of volunteerism.
>
> Margaret Mead and Rhoda Metraud
> "Aspects of the Present"

American Cancer Society

The CanSupport visitor program seeks volunteers who can visit isolated cancer patients in their home and act as friends and companions. Volunteers make themselves available for a cancer patient to:

- ❤ share concerns and listen;
- ❤ find other community resources;
- ❤ help with shopping and errands;
- ❤ give full-time caretaker a break; and
- ❤ read aloud.

A CanSupport visitor is a concerned and caring volunteer who:

- ♥ is selected because of his or her warmth and responsiveness to people who are in need;
- ♥ has experienced cancer personally or through family or friends;
- ♥ completes a special American Cancer Society training program; and
- ♥ will attend regular CanSupport visitor meetings.

The American Cancer Society is also looking for volunteers to drive patients to and from treatments. Many cancer patients have no way to get to treatment. They need your time and your car to help them reach their medical provider. All you do is pick up the patient at home and provide transportation to and from treatment.

To help, contact your local chapter of the American Cancer Society.

Consumer Watchdogs

As an unpaid volunteer, you can work with district and regional commission offices to visit retail stores to make sure that the stores are complying with CPSC safety guidelines. Volunteers identify themselves to the store, check the inventory, and then report their findings back to the CPSC. For more information write: Consumer Deputy Program, Consumer Product Safety Commission, 5401 Westbard Avenue, Washington, D.C. 20207; (202) 492-5788.

Fish And Wildlife Service

Volunteers are needed for banding birds at a wildlife refuge, feeding fish at a fish hatchery, or doing research in a laboratory. For more information write: U.S. Fish and Wildlife Service, 4401 N. Fairfax Drive, Arlington, VA 22203; (703) 343-5333. Or better yet, contact one of the U.S. Fish and Wildlife regional offices for possible volunteer programs in your area.

AARP's volunteer programs

The American Association of Retired Persons has developed a variety of programs, services, and activities that provide help to older Americans and others through volunteers. They welcome new volunteers. Here are brief descriptions of each opportunity:

* **Caregiving**--You would periodically relieve people who take care of seriously ill or disabled friends or relatives.
* **Citizens Representation Program**--ensures that older citizens are represented on public commissions and boards. You would work to increase presence of older citizens on key boards and commissions in your area.
* **Consumer Housing Information Service for Seniors (CHISS)**--You would provide information and answer questions on housing options, reverse mortgages, and housing-related services. Housing Coordinators promote AARP's housing policies at state and local levels.
* **Health Advocacy Services**--provides information on health, fitness, healthcare-consumer issues, and long-term care. You would lead health education programs, conduct health services surveys, and distribute physicians assignment lists.
* **Healthcare Campaign**--promotes better U.S. healthcare, combats rising costs. You would help inform legislators and the public about older persons' healthcare needs.
* **Medicare/Medicaid Assistance Program (MMAP)**--Volunteers help older people understand and file Medicare/Medicaid claims.
* **Mental Health-Social Outreach and Support**--You would help people deal with loneliness and life changes.
* **Minority Affairs Initiative**--provides information and help to improve quality of life for older minorities. If you're a member of a minority group, you can become a Minority Affairs spokesperson, talking to groups about AARP programs and services in your community, via media and at AARP and other organizations' meetings or special events.
* **Retirement Planning**--helps workers prepare for retirement financially, physically, emotionally, and provides assistance to employers setting up programs. You would consult with employers to set up retirement planning programs for their employees, serve as speakers, and provide resources on retirement planning.
* **State Legislative Committees (SLCs)**--volunteer SLCs determine AARP state legislative priorities and with Capital City Task Force (CCTF) volunteers and AARP members they work to promote and enact laws on aging issues, and voice concerns to state lawmakers and government officials. You work with your SLC to voice your concerns to state lawmakers through letters, phone calls, forums, and visits on key legislation.
* **Supplemental Security Income (SSI) Outreach Project**--You would help low-income people in understanding and accessing their right to SSI.
* **Tax-Aide**--Once trained, you would help older persons file income tax returns--January-April.
* **Veterans Administration Voluntary Service**--Volunteers provide support to veterans in VA medical centers and visit veterans.
* **VOTE/AARP**--nonprofit, nonpartisan voter education program that alerts older voters to the issues affecting them. You would receive alerts and issue briefs about pending bills and lead programs for older voters.
* **Widowed Persons Service**--offers support to widows and widowers. If you have been widowed, you can assist newly widowed men and women (see article on WPS, page 243).
* **Women's Financial Information Program**--gives information and help to midlife and older women learning to make educated financial decisions. You would also help organize workshops and counsel women on finances.
* **Women's Initiative**--helps ensure that economic, health, and other important needs of midlife and older women are met. Volunteers act as a Women's Initiative spokesperson and meet with community groups to identify and discuss women's issues.
* **WORKS/AARP**--provides employment planning workshops for those wishing to enter or reenter the job market; not a job placement program. You would facilitate workshops helping job seekers assess their career options and prepare for the job search.
* **55 Alive/Mature Driving**--provides classes to sharpen the skills of older drivers. You would teach driver education classes.

AARP's Volunteer Talent Bank (VTB)

The American Association of Retired Persons (AARP) has developed a computerized referral service to provide a reservoir of talent for AARP's volunteer programs and other national organizations. If you are interested, write to AARP and obtain the proper forms. You will need to complete a questionnaire that includes your personal background, skills, and interests. Your information is then entered into a computer system that can then match your skills, interests, and geographic location with appropriate opportunities. All volunteers are not required to accept the positions offered. The openings can be either with AARP's own volunteer programs or with programs such as the Peace Corps, the Red Cross, SCORE, Girl Scouts, March of Dimes Birth Defect Foundation, U.S. Fish and Wildlife Service, National Park Service, Retired Senior Volunteer Program (RSVP), or other organizations in your community. To register, write: AARP Volunteer Talent Bank, Department NB, 601 E Street, Washington, D.C. 20049.

Code of responsibility for volunteers*

* **Be sure.** Look into your heart and know that you really want to help other people.
* **Be convinced.** Do not offer your services unless you believe in the value of what you are doing.
* **Accept the rules.** Don't criticize what you don't understand. There may be a good reason: Find out why.
* **Speak up.** Ask about things you don't understand. Don't coddle your doubts and frustrations until they drive you away or turn you into a problem worker.

* **Be willing to learn.** Training is essential to any job well done.
* **Welcome supervision.** You will do a better job and enjoy it more if you are doing what is expected of you.
* **Be dependable.** Your word is your bond. Do what you have agreed to do. Don't make promises you can't keep.
* **Be a team player.** Find a place for yourself on the team. The lone operator is pretty much out of place in today's complex community.

* From the USDA Forest Voluntary Service Brochure.

The volunteer programs with ACTION

ACTION is the federal domestic volunteer agency that was established to stimulate and expand voluntary citizen participation through coordination of its efforts with public and private sector organizations. It supports a number of established programs and encourages local volunteer efforts.

ACTION administers three older American volunteer programs: Retired Senior Volunteer Program (RSVP), Senior Companion Program (SCP), and the Foster Grandparent Program (FGP). It also administers a program called VISTA. Contact the nearest state office for specific projects operating in your area (see next page).

Retired Senior Volunteer Program

The Retired Senior Volunteer Program (RSVP) is ACTION's largest program for older volunteers with 752 funded projects and 408,000 volunteers nationally and a budget of $30 million. Volunteers serve on a regular basis throughout the 43,000 communities--in local schools, libraries, courts, daycare centers, crisis centers, hospitals, nursing homes, economic development agencies, and other community service organizations.

Among the services provided are: adult basic education, guardians *ad litem,* tax aid and consultancy services, hospice care, home repair, weatherization, utilities relief, substance abuse counseling, healthcare, home visitation and long-term care, Meals-On-Wheels, telephone reassurance, refugee assistance, and neighborhood watch.

RSVP volunteers also serve disabled veterans and youth through literacy and substance abuse education projects. Volunteers serve without compensation, but may be reimbursed for or provided with transportation and other out-of-pocket expenses. All volunteers are covered with appropriate accident and liability insurance while on assignment.

RSVP volunteers are 60 years of age or older, retired, who work part-time, about 4 hours per week. No restrictions are placed on the volunteer for education, income, experience, ethnic background, or creed.

Senior Companion Program

The Senior Companion Program (SCP) is an ACTION program that provides compassionate peer support to those with exceptional need. Senior Companions help their more frail contemporaries by passing along a positive mental attitude, offering the security of friendship, and helping out wherever they are needed.

Typically, Senior Companions work with adults, often elderly, with mental, emotional, or physical impairments. Some serve in hospital discharge programs or work with the terminally ill; others help those with substance abuse or mental health problems, the homebound elderly living alone, or provide respite care.

Senior Companions help with: shopping, home budgeting, an escort to the doctor's office, exercise and recreational activities, nutritional assistance, health status monitoring, and other personal errands.

Senior Companions must be 60 years or older, physically able to perform 20 hours of service each week, and meet monthly low-income eligibility requirements, which vary from state to state. Companions, in most cases, receive a small stipend to partially offset the cost of volunteering.

Foster Grandparents Program

The Foster Grandparents Program (FGP) is an ACTION program that provides assistance to children with special or exceptional needs, such as those who are mentally retarded, autistic, epileptic, or physically handicapped. Children with special needs also include those who have been abused and neglected, runaway youth, juvenile delinquents, as well as those in need of protective intervention.

Volunteers receive 40 hours of preservice training, plus 4 hours monthly, and are supervised by childcare teams in their assigned agencies. Foster Grandparents help over 72,000 children every day. They are assigned to children on a one-to-one basis during their five-day, 20-hour service week.

Persons 60 years of age or older are eligible to become Foster Grandparents if their income is less than the national poverty level plus the social security supplement or 125% of the poverty level, whichever is higher. Handicapped persons are welcome to serve. In return for sharing their lifetime skills, volunteers receive a modest tax-free allowance to cover the cost of volunteering--transportation, a meal while in service, accident and liability insurance, and an annual physical exam.

Volunteers In Service to America

For 25 years, Volunteers In Service To America (VISTA) has actively worked in low-income areas in the United States by mobilizing people, businesses, and organizations toward community self-reliance. It's a domestic version of the Peace Corps. Volunteers, about one-third of them low-income individuals, live and work among America's poor for one or two years.

ACTION provides a basic subsistence allowance for housing, food, and miscellaneous expenses. More than half the program's resources are focused on alcohol/drug abuse, illiteracy, unemployment, hunger, and homelessness. VISTA volunteers assist with job-training and education programs. They work with nonprofit organizations in tackling poverty-related hunger by setting up or expanding farm production and marketing cooperatives, soliciting surplus food producers, and developing food banks.

VISTA volunteers must be citizens or permanent residents of the U.S. and at least 18 years of age. Twenty-one percent of all volunteers are aged 55 and older. Volunteers remain in the community 24 hours a day, seven days a week.

RETIREMENT

If a child is to keep alive his inborn sense
of wonder, he needs the companionship
of at least one adult who can share it,
rediscovering with him the joy, excitement
and the mystery of the world we live in.
- Rachel Carson

(page 4 of 7) VOLUNTEERISM 165

Alabama
600 Beacon Pkwy. West
Birmingham, AL 35209-3120
(205) 731-1908

Alaska (see Washington)

American Samoa (see Hawaii)

Arizona
522 North Central, Room 205-A
Phoenix, AZ 85004-2190
(602) 379-4825

Arkansas
Fed. Bldg., Room 2506
700 West Capital Street
Little Rock, AR 72201-3291
(501) 378-5234

California
211 Main Street, Room 534
San Francisco, CA 94105-1914
(415) 774-3015
or
Federal Bldg., Room 14218
11000 Wilshire Blvd.
Los Angeles, CA 90024-3671
(213) 575-7421

Colorado/Wyoming
Columbine Bldg., Room 301
1845 Sherman Street
Denver, CO 80203-1167
(303) 866-1070

Connecticut
Abraham Ribicoff Fed. Bldg.
450 Main Street, Room 524
Hartford, CT 06103-3002
(203) 240-3237

Delaware (see Maryland)

District of Columbia (see Virginia)

Florida
3165 McCrory Street, Suite 115
Orlando, FL 32803-3750
(305) 648-6117

Georgia
75 Piedmont Avenue, NE, Suite 412
Atlanta, GA 30303-2587
(404) 331-4646

Guam (see Hawaii)

Hawaii/Guam/American Samoa
Fed. Bldg., P.O. Box 50024
Honolulu, HI 96850-0001
(808) 541-2832

Idaho
Room 344
304 North 8th Street
Boise, ID 83708
(208) 334-1707

Illinois
175 W. Jackson Blvd.
Suite 1207
Chicago, IL 60604
(312) 353-3622

Indiana
46 E. Ohio Street, Room 457
Indianapolis, IN 46204-1922
(317) 226-6724

Iowa
Fed. Bldg., Room 339
210 Walnut
Des Moines, IA 50309-2195
(515)-284-4816

Kansas
Fed. Bldg., Room 248
444 S.E. Quincy
Topeka, KS 66603-3501
(913) 295-2540

Kentucky
Fed. Bldg., Room 372-D
600 Federal Place
Louisville, KY 40202-2230
(502) 582-6384

Louisiana
626 Main Street, Suite 102
Baton Rouge, LA 70801-1910
(504) 389-0471

Maine
Fed. Bldg., Room 305
76 Pearl Street
Portland, ME 04101-4188
(207) 780-3414

Maryland/Delaware
Federal Building
31 Hopkins Plaza, Room 1125
Baltimore, MD 21201-2814
(301) 962-4443

Massachusetts
10 Causeway Street, Room 473
Boston, MA 02222-1039
(617) 565-7015

Michigan
Fed. Bldg., Room 652
231 W. Lafayette Blvd.
Detroit, MI 48226-2799
(313) 226-7848

Minnesota
413 S. 7th Street, Room 2480
Minneapolis, MN 55415
(612) 334-4083

Mississippi
Fed. Bldg., Room 1005-A
100 W. Capital Street
Jackson, MS 39269-1092
(601) 965-5664

Missouri
Fed. Office Building
911 Walnut, Room 1701
Kansas City, MO 64106-2009
(816) 426-5256

Montana
Fed. Office Bldg., Drawer 10051
301 South Park, Room 192
Helena, MT 59626-0101
(406) 449-5404

Nebraska
Fed. Bldg., Room 293
100 Centennial Mall North
Lincoln, NE 68508-3896
(402) 437-5493

Nevada
4600 Kietzke Lane, Suite E-141
Reno, NV 89502-5033
(702) 784-5314

New Hampshire/Vermont
Fed. Post Office and Courthouse
55 Pleasant Street
Concord, NH 03301-3939
(603) 225-1450

New Jersey
402 E. State Street, Room 426
Trenton, NJ 08608-1507
(609) 989-2243

New Mexico
First Interstate Plaza
125 Lincoln Avenue, Suite 214
Santa Fe, NM 87501-2026
(505) 988-6577

New York
U.S. Courthouse and Fed. Bldg.
445 Broadway, Room 103
Albany, NY 12207-2923
(518) 472-3664
or
6 World Trade Center, Room 758
New York, NY 10048-0206
(212) 466-4471

North Carolina
Fed. Bldg., P.O. Century Station
300 Fayetteville Street, Mall, Room 131
Raleigh, NC 27601-1739
(704) 856-4731

North Dakota (see So. Dakota)

Ohio
Fed. Bldg. Room 304A
50 W. Broad Street
Columbus, OH 43215-2888
(614) 469-7441

Oklahoma
200 NW 5th, Suite 912
Oklahoma, OK 73102-6093
(405) 231-5201

Oregon
Federal Bldg., Room 647
511 N.W. Broadway
Portland, OR 97209-3416
(503) 221-2261

Pennsylvania
U.S. Customs House, Room 108
2nd and Chestnut Streets
Philadelphia, PA 19106-2998
(215) 597-3543

Puerto Rico/Virgin Islands
Frederico DeGetau Fed. Office Bldg.
Carlos Chardon Avenue, Suite G49
Hato Rey, PR 00918-2241
(809) 766-5314

Rhode Island
John E. Fogarty Bldg.
2 Exchange Terrace
Providence, RI 02903-2882
(401) 528-5424

South Carolina
Fed. Bldg., Room 872
1835 Assembly Street
Columbia, SC 29201-2430
(803) 765-5771

South Dakota/North Dakota
Fed. Bldg., Room 213
225 S. Pierre Street
Pierre, SD 57501-2452
(605) 224-5996

Tennessee
265 Cumberland Bend Drive
Nashville, TN 37228
(615) 736-5561

Texas
611 East 6th Street, Suite 404
Austin, TX 78701-3747
(512) 482-5671

Utah
U.S. Post Office and Courthouse
350 South Main Street, Room 484
Salt Lake City, UT 84101-2198
(801) 524-5411

Vermont (see New Hampshire)

Virgin Islands (see Puerto Rico)

Virginia/Dist. of Columbia
400 N. 8th Street
P.O. Box 10066
Richmond, VA 23240-1832
(804) 771-2197

Washington/Alaska
Suite 3039, Fed. Office Bldg.
909 First Avenue
Seattle, WA 98174-1103
(206) 442-4975
Alaska (206) 442-1552

West Virginia
603 Morris Street, 2nd Floor
Charleston, WV 25301-1409
(304) 347-5246

Wisconsin
517 East Wisconsin Avenue, Room 601
Milwaukee, WI 53202-4507
(414) 291-1118

Wyoming (see Colorado)

Here is a listing of the
ACTION Program Offices.
Just write to:
Action State Office
and give the address
listed. Or phone.

SCORE

Are you a retired businessman or businesswoman? Would you like to help others that are starting a new business? Are you willing to volunteer your services? Or, if you are starting a business could you use some professional advice free? Here may be the organization for you.

What is SCORE? SCORE:
❶ is the **S**ervice **C**orps **O**f **R**etired **E**xecutives, a volunteer program of the U. S. Small Business Administration (SBA).
❷ is a nonprofit association providing free business counseling.
❸ is brains, ideas, skill, and experience.
❹ is 13,000 retired and active executives in 400 chapters.
❺ is volunteers ready to share their skills.
❻ is counseling on small business problems.
❼ has a background of 25 years of successful counseling.
❽ counseling services are free.

SCORE is comprised of men and women business executives who voluntarily commit their time to share their management and technical expertise with present and prospective owners/managers of small businesses. The collective experience of these volunteers spans the full range of the American enterprise. Begun in 1964, the goal of SCORE is to help American small business to prosper.

SCORE volunteers are members of locally organized, self-administrated chapters in more than 400 locations throughout the United States, Puerto Rico, and the U.S. Virgin Islands. They work in their home communities or nearby to provide management counseling and training to small businesses or to those thinking about going into business. Every effort is made to match a client's need with a counselor experienced in that line of business. Service is provided without charge to the client.

Assistance Offered: Through in-depth counseling and training, owners and managers receive help in identifying basic management problems, determining their cause, and becoming better managers. SCORE counseling also can help successful firms in reviewing their distribution channels, evaluating expansion, modifying their product, and other business challenges. Management counseling is provided to a client either at the place of business or by appointment at an SBA field office or at one of the SCORE offices. An analysis is made of each business and its problems, and a plan is offered to correct the trouble and help the owner through the critical period.

Eligibility for help: Almost any small, independent business not dominant in its field can request assistance. The approach is confidential and person-to-person. A business does not have to have a SBA loan or even be in operation. Prebusiness consultation is an important part of the services offered. To volunteer, contact your SBA office. To find out more, contact any Small Business Administration (SBA) office or look for SCORE in the local telephone directory. National SCORE Office, 1825 Connecticut Ave. N.W., Suite 503, Washington. D.C. 20009; 1-800-368-5855.

United Way

More than 2,300 community-based United Ways throughout America are helping to meet the health and human-care needs of millions of people through a vast network of volunteers and local charities.

Each United Way is autonomous, is governed by a local board of volunteers, and raises funds through a single community-wide campaign. In 1989, United Ways collectively raised $2.98 billion from individuals, corporations, small businesses, and foundations.

United Way is much more than a fund-raiser. United Way volunteers do the following:
✳ Assess current and future community needs.
✳ Bring people and organizations together to address community needs.
✳ Distribute funds where services are most needed.
✳ Recruit and train other volunteers.
✳ Put people in touch with the services they need.
✳ Offer management and technical help to many local charities.

United Ways are among the most efficient charitable organizations, using, on average, only 10.5% of all funds raised for administrative expenses. Volunteer contributions to the United Ways support over 40,000 agencies helping millions of people.

Some of the organizations that United Ways support are local chapters of national agencies. Others are small, one-of-a-kind agencies. United Ways fund programs according to how well these programs can meet local needs--whether those needs are long-standing or new and emerging.

These are some of the human-care services supported by contributions to United Way:
❤ Alcoholism treatment
❤ Community health clinics
❤ Consumer protection
❤ Crime prevention
❤ Drug abuse prevention
❤ Education for adults
❤ Emergency food and shelter
❤ Family counseling
❤ Food banks
❤ Health research
❤ Information and referral services--"First Call for Help"
❤ Job training and placement
❤ Literacy programs
❤ Mental health education
❤ Rehabilitation
❤ Services for the elderly
❤ Services for individuals with disabilities
❤ Services for people with AIDS
❤ Shelter for homeless individuals
❤ Suicide prevention
❤ Transportation for the disabled

United Way--"It brings out the best in all of us." To volunteer, contact your local United Way office. Or contact the National Headquarters: United Way, 701 Fairfax Street, Alexandria, VA 22314-2045; (703) 836-7100.

**Absence of occupation is not rest,
a mind quite vacant is a mind distressed.**
- William Cowper

RETIREMENT
(page 6 of 7) VOLUNTEERISM 167

Become an ombudsman

Thousands of institutionalized elderly have no one to turn to for help in resolving the many problems affecting their lives. How can you help? By becoming a volunteer ombudsman.

What is an Ombudsman?

Ombudsmen are volunteers who respond to complaints on behalf of those living in long-term care facilities that include nursing homes, board and care, and residential care facilities.

What do Ombudsmen Do?

Typically, an ombudsman would work on any of the following cases:

- A nursing home failed to take care of the feet of a diabetic patient who subsequently had to have both legs amputated.
- The elderly wife of a resident had problems understanding the "share of cost" Medicaid arrangement, and her husband was in danger of being discharged against his will.
- A hospital emergency room nurse complained about a patient who was admitted from a residential care home in a fetal position, with contracted arms and legs, and severely dehydrated. She was concerned that the facility was not properly licensed.

Working an average of three to four hours weekly, ombudsmen investigate complaints like these, formulate strategies for dealing with them, and put them into action. Ombudsmen work closely with facility personnel, regulatory and enforcement agencies, family members, and other interested parties.

"I Don't Know That Much About Long-Term-Care Facilities. What Kind of Training Is Provided?"

Ombudsman, Inc., puts all qualified candidates through a free, state-approved (in California--check with your state) training course. It covers various techniques of problem investigation and resolution, use of community services/agencies, patient rights, and an overview of the regulations. An internship is offered where the new ombudsman works alongside an experienced ombudsman to further strengthen skills and build confidence.

What Kind of Person Are They Looking For?

Ombudsmanship is ideally suited to persons with a background in the healthcare and counseling professions. For service in non-medical settings (such as residential care homes), this experience is helpful, but not required. Regardless of your background, you should be able to honestly assess yourself in this manner: I am capable of critical thinking, and am able to sort out facts. I am assertive, yet diplomatic. I am deeply interested in the problems of institutionalized elders, but can remain objective in my work. I am self-directed, responsible, and persevering.

Why Do People Become Ombudsmen?

There are a variety of reasons. Ombudsmen are committed to preserving the civil and human rights of elders in this society. Ombudsmen find it challenging to apply their professional and academic background to this unique service opportunity. Finally, ombudsmen enjoy being part of a very select group of volunteers entrusted with legal authority and responsibilities regarding the care of the elderly.

What Legal Authority Does an Ombudsman Have?

The state of California (and other states are similar) has legislated specific authority and powers to the certified long-term-care ombudsman.

- Volunteers have access to long-term-care facilities to investigate complaints and give advice.
- Facilities may be fined for interfering with the work of a certified long-term-care ombudsman.
- The law provides for the limiting of liability of the ombudsman while he/she is preforming his/her duties, under specific circumstances.
- Certain financial and legal transactions by residents of long-term-care facilities must, to be valid and legal, be witnessed by certified long-term-care ombudsmen.
- The law realizes that ombudsmen, like other professionals, are bound to adhere to the Code of Confidentiality, and such ombudsmen cannot be forced to testify in cases where to do so would violate the patient's right to this confidentiality.

For more information contact your state agency on aging, pages 24 and 25.

Forest Service Volunteers Program

The Volunteers Program welcomes all interested individuals who wish to contribute their time, talents, and knowledge toward improving our nation's natural resources. It is presently operating in offices throughout the country, offering opportunities year-round in various conservation fields. Volunteers in the National Forest double the manpower, 35,000 paid employees vs. 68,000 volunteers. In the 1990s, often referred to as the decade of environmentalism, Forest Service personnel hope that volunteer activity will increase and will include minorities, women, and urban people of various ethnic backgrounds.

The Forest Service actively tries to attract volunteers to help with the following projects: repairing fences, building and maintaining trails, picking up litter, planting trees, building and installing nesting boxes, search and rescue, building and installing picnic tables, reinforcing streambanks, digging latrines, raking and cleaning campgrounds, painting and building signs, answering phones and greeting visitors, sorting, labeling or contributing to photo files, washing and waxing government vehicles, building barrier-free campsites, docks, and trails, and other tasks.

The National Forest System includes 154 National Forests, 17 National Grasslands, and 16 Land Utilization Projects, covering 192 million acres of land located in 44 states, Puerto Rico, and the Virgin Islands. To volunteer, apply to the office in the vicinity where you desire to help out. Otherwise write: VOLUNTEERS, USDA Forest Service, Human Resource Programs, P.O. Box 96090, Washington, D.C. 20090-6090.

You can serve in 65 countries around the world. Host countries want older volunteers because they recognize that you offer experience and maturity. Your lifetime of work and wisdom can be shared with millions of people in developing countries. Your accomplishments in the Peace Corps will endure because your mission will not be to do things for people, but to help people do things for themselves.

By living and working in villages throughout the world, you will offer people firsthand knowledge about Americans. You will return home with an intimate knowledge of other peoples and their cultures. You will learn for yourself that global interdependence is a reality. Despite the hard work, long hours, and personal sacrifice, 9 out of 10 volunteers say they would do it again.

QUALIFICATIONS--There is no upper age limit. You must be a United States citizen, in good health, and have a skill or a trade to share. Volunteers in their 80s have served successfully. Married couples are eligible and encouraged to serve if both qualify and can work. Some assignments require a college or technical school degree or an experience equivalent. Previous knowledge of another language can be helpful but is not always required. Some assignments do require a language other than English.

SELECTION--After sending in your completed application form, you may be invited to enter a training program for a specific assignment. Selection depends upon your successful completion of the training.

THE PEACE CORPS

TRAINING--Training sessions are 8-14 weeks long and most often held in host countries. Your host's expect you to speak the language of the people with whom you will live and work so language instruction is intense during this period. Some technical training in the country of your assignment will help you transfer your skills to the different situations you will encounter. Cross-cultural training will give you an in-depth orientation to the culture and traditions of the people.

WORKING CONDITIONS--Volunteers work for their host country government department, agency, or organization. You will be supervised by and work with host country nationals and subject to local laws. Each country has directors who help you with your project, are responsible for your training, and take care of paperwork.

SAFETY--The Peace Corps places the highest priority on the safety of each volunteer, and constantly scrutinizes the environment of its volunteers. If there is any doubt about your safety, the Peace Corps country staff immediately takes action to evacuate you.

GOOD HEALTH CARE--The Peace Corps focuses on prevention and does everything possible to safeguard your health. Before leaving the U.S. you are given a complete exam, immunizations, preventive medications, and health care training. Every country has a medical officer. They have access to qualified local doctors and medical facilities. Otherwise, you may be treated at U.S. military hospitals or brought back to the U.S. The Federal Employees' Compensation Act covers medical costs for work-related injuries.

FINANCIAL--The Peace Corps provides for your travel. You receive a monthly living allowance for basic living expenses such as housing, food, and incidental expenses. Your housing is modest but comfortable. When you return home you receive a payment of $175 for each month of training and service, $4,200 for a typical 2-year assignment. Most assignments are for 2 years.

VACATIONS--You accrue at the rate of 2 days per month, which can be taken when the work situation permits. Your family may visit you during your assignment, at their expense.

TRAVEL--This is your chance to live, work, and travel in a developing country. You also have the opportunity to visit neighboring countries.

COMMUNICATIONS--You are encouraged to write your family regularly. Airmail takes 5 to 14 days.

FAMILY EMERGENCIES--You will be given leave to travel to the site of the emergency, at government expense, and remain there for 2 weeks.

Job Opportunities

EDUCATION
primary education
physical education
secondary education
library science
special education
secretarial training
industrial arts
teaching English
mathematics
symbolic logic
general science
biology
chemistry
physics
botany

ENGINEERING
water and sanitation engr.
road and structural bldgs.
architecture
urban planning

SKILLED TRADES
cabinetmakers
carpenters
electricians
masons
mechanics
metalworkers
plumbers
welders

AGRICULTURE
crop development
plant protection
soil science
agriculture education
agriculture economics
animal husbandry
community agriculture
farm mechanics
beekeeping
rural youth projects

HOME ECONOMICS AND NUTRITION
nutrition
diet planning
proper food use and storage
commercial handicraft production
vegetable and small animal production
counseling mother and child
school lunch programs
sanitation and health projects

COMMUNITY DEVELOPMENT
improve local craft marketing
upgrade women's self-sufficiency projects
increase employment opportunities in rural areas
small business training
setup income-generating projects

FORESTRY AND FISHING
commercial fishing experience
forestry experience
mechanical training

For further information or for an application, call toll-free 800-424-8580, extension 93, or write:
U.S. Peace Corps
Office of Recruitment
Room P-301
806 Connecticut Avenue, N.W.
Washington, D.C. 20526

senior net

A network of computer using seniors

SeniorNet is a nationwide network of computer users 55 years old and older. It connects its members via a modem and telephone lines. Its purpose is to provide older adults with access to computer technologies and, thereby, enable them to share their wisdom and talents with the rest of society. The organization offers:

■ SeniorNet Online, a telecommunications network for older adults;

■ Computer instructions at local sites throughout the United States and Canada (see listing SeniorNet sites);

■ Help to individuals and organizations who want to establish local SeniorNet sites for computer instruction;

■ Instructional materials to its members who may not be located near an existing site;

■ An annual conference for computer-using seniors.

At each site, there are classes designed to introduce seniors to computer applications. The SeniorNet curriculum includes courses such as:

❑ Instructions on how to operate a computer;

❑ Learning word processing;

❑ Introduction to telecommunications (transmitting messages over phone lines);

❑ Electronic citizenship (a powerful lobbying force on government issues);

❑ Financial management with spreadsheets;

❑ SeniorWriter, a more advanced course in word processing.

Typically, classes are offered for up to two hours once a week for six to eight weeks. Classes are small in size (about 10 participants) and the instruction is "hands on" with the computer.

Network Sites

Presently, there are 38 sites in the United States and Canada located in various schools, community centers, medical clinics, and nursing homes. Many of SeniorNet's 4,000 members do not live near sites but communicate with each other through SeniorNet.

Online, an electronic meeting place accessible through a personal computer and modem. Through the network, seniors send electronic mail, participate in forum discussions, chat in real-time conferences, join special-interest groups, and access information from recipes to health advice.

SeniorNet is a nonprofit organization based at the University of San Francisco. The membership fee of $25 gives a senior two months of hands-on training, a quarterly newletter, the book *Computers for Kids Over 60*, and, at $6.90 per hour (evening and weekend rates--$15 daily), access to an online network. Members pay a one-time fee of $15 to set up a network account.

Sites cost $15,000 to $20,000 to equip. Many groups are supportive of these sites including: American Express, Pacific Telesis Group, Apple Computer, USWEST, Eye Centers, Pacific Bell, the Markle Foundation, Southwestern Bell, and others.

For more information about SeniorNet, contact:

SeniorNet
399 Arguello Boulevard
San Francisco, CA 94118
(415) 750-5030

SeniorNet Sites
As of July, 1991

CALIFORNIA
Bakersfield • • • • • • • • • 805/327-8511
Carmichael • • • • • • • • • • 916/972-1114
Culver City • • • • • • • • • 213/202-5855
El Segundo • • • • • • • • • 213/640-8134
Fullerton • • • • • • • • • • 714/449-7057
Menlo Park • • • • • • • • • 415/326-2025
Newport Beach area • • • • • 714/960-7671
Orinda • • • • • • • • • • • 415/254-5939
Sacramento • • • • • • • • • 916/440-1301
San Diego • • • • • • • • • • 619/237-8814
San Francisco
    downtown branch • • • 415/771-7950
    University of SF • • • • 415/567-7672
    center for the blind
        and visually impaired • • 415/441-1980
    self-help for the elderly • 415/982-9171
Santa Cruz • • • • • • • • • • 408/429-3506

CANADA
Calgary, Alberta • • • • • • • 403/286-6969

COLORADO
Colorado Springs • • • • • • • 719/578-6088

FLORIDA
Ocala • • • • • • • • • • • 904/629-8351
Winter Park • • • • • • • • • 407/647-6366

HAWAII
Honolulu • • • • • • • • • • 808/845-9296
Kahului • • • • • • • • • • • 808/242-1216
Kokua Outpost • • • • • • • • 808/528-4839

ILLINOIS
Peoria • • • • • • • • • • • 309/682-2472

KANSAS
Overland Park • • • • • • • • 913/469-8500
                            Ext. 3424

MASSACHUSETTS
Framingham • • • • • • • • • 508/620-4819

MICHIGAN
Flint • • • • • • • • • • • • 313/232-7111
Rochester • • • • • • • • • • 313/656-1403

NEBRASKA
Omaha • • • • • • • • • • • 402/552-2359

NEVADA
Las Vegas • • • • • • • • • • 702/386-2626

NEW YORK
Valhalla • • • • • • • • • • • 914/285-6793

NORTH DAKOTA
Valley City • • • • • • • • • • 701/845-8222

OKLAHOMA
Oklahoma City • • • • • • • • 405/752-4220

OREGON
Eugene • • • • • • • • • • • 503/345-9441

PENNSYLVANIA
Philadelphia • • • • • • • • • 215/698-7300

TEXAS
Houston • • • • • • • • • • • 713/623-4425
Nacogdoches • • • • • • • • • 409/564-2411
San Antonio • • • • • • • • • 512/224-1684

WASHINGTON
Seattle area, Bellevue • • • • 206/637-1416

WISCONSIN
Appleton • • • • • • • • • • • 414/735-5611

Senior citizens are fast becoming computer whiz kids

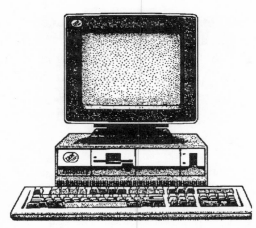

A friend, after he retired, spent four years in Virginia Beach researching and writing his manuscript. He meticulously, with paper and pencil, wrote his creation on hundreds of tablet pages. When he finished a portion he would ask women friends if they would kindly type it for him. Eventually he found someone that would. When he received the typing he would take scissors and paste and make the needed changes. Again he would look to have it retyped. Many times he wanted to make additional changes but the cycle was frustrating for all concerned.

After he finished the first draft, he was advised by publishers that it needed to be completely rewritten. He was discouraged. After many discussions, my wife and I finally convinced our friend to purchase a computer with word processing software. It took nearly a year of persuasion before he finally bought a computer.

Learning a computer was at first baffling to him with all the new jargon to understand. After the first week he threatened to take it back. At one point he was so angry at it he would not even enter the room where it was. However, in less than a month, with very little help and without formal instructions, he learned how to use the computer. He still types everything with one finger but he started writing us a two-page letter nearly once a week. He became enchanted with the writing flexibility it offered. The computer changed his outlook on life. Not only did he do an extensive rewrite, but he produced the pages in "camera-ready" condition for the publisher. He was now in control of his creativity beyond anything he imagined. The computer became not only a challenge but a delight. He purchased his computer when he was 77 years old.

Many people, not just older persons, can easily be afraid to get involved with computers. They are complex systems but they can be easy to use. Unfortunately, many in the computer field make them appear diffi-

cult. Those who write computer manuals are adept at making simple tasks incomprehensible. This has allowed many authors to write computer books that are more readily understood. You can find them in bookstores.

Many of us have learned computer skills from reading manuals and using the computer. It is much easier to learn how to use one if you take computer classes where they provide instructions plus hands-on experience. Many junior colleges offer adult classes at minimal costs. Other groups or organizations such as SeniorNet also provide such courses (see page 169).

If you are just starting out, it's best not to get involved in programming classes, although some find this challenging. Learning to use the computer and programming it are two different undertakings with the latter commanding significant amounts of training. Many people are not familiar with how the engine or transmission of a car works, but can use an auto effectively. This is also true of computers. You don't need to know how to program a computer, or learn a computer language, like BASIC, to use a computer effectively. However, in order to use a computer, you will need to learn some commands that it understands. Today's computer software programs are easy to use since they not only provide you with a "menu" (a choice of options) but they also provide on-line "help" when needed to assist you in making that choice or understanding it.

Those using computers speak of "software" and "hardware." For those engaged in cooking, "recipes" are to "pots and pans" as "software" is to "hardware" in the computer field. Software, also called software programs or just programs, are listings of step-by-step instructions the computer understands. The task can be quite complex but a software program knows how to accomplish it. For example, if you are writing a letter using a software program called a word processor and you want to check for spelling errors, the computer looks up every word in the letter in its dictionary. If it finds a misspelled word it attempts to provide you correct alternates for that word. It can spell-check a letter in a manner of seconds.

Programming or writing complicated software programs such as a word processor can take man-years of work. This word processor I am using to write with probably required 50 man-years of work to write the program and make corrections or revisions. Most people over 50 might prefer to use the software programs already available.

First Things First

If you are thinking about owning a computer, the first question that needs answering is "What will I do with it?" There are hundreds of software programs available that can be fun and useful. Following is a partial listing:

- **Word processing** is generally tops on everyone's list. It is useful for writing personal letters, the book you have always wanted to write, some articles, and letters to the editor or your congressman. Most recent word processing programs provide "spelling checkers" and more sophisticated "grammar checkers." These programs help to make the output appear more intelligent.

- **Games** can be entertaining for you or your grandchildren when they visit-- and there is no end to the number of games available.

- **Finance programs** let you keep track of your income and expenses--nice to have this information organized when income tax time rolls around.

- **Cookbooks** on computers allow you to organize recipes, alter them for the number of servings, give you a shopping list, or let you prepare and print out your own personal recipe books.

- **Willmakers** let you write your own wills and update them easily (see page 112).

- **Music composition programs** make it easy to write musical scores, allowing you to see the notes you compose.

- **Communications programs** (telecommunications) provide a way to keep in touch with friends (one who also has a computer) across the country or to access a data base (an electronic library) or a bulletin board--passing data over the phone line.

- **Database management programs** make it easy to catalog all sorts of information and find it easily--address lists, home inventory, collections (such as books, video tapes, stamps, wines, etc.). There are numerous "canned" database programs that make it easier than learning a database.

We have just talked about software, but you must have both software and hardware for the computer to function. If you intend to purchase a computer you will need to learn some terminology and have an understanding of the hardware that makes up a computer system.

There are five major components needed for a system: the computer assembly; keyboard; disk drives; a monitor; and a printer.

1 **The computer assembly** includes: a computer chip, numerous IC's, read only memory (ROM), random access memories (RAM's) and printed circuit connectors mounted on a printed circuit board called a mother board. The connectors allow the addition of a number of other printed circuit boards to be mounted on and make connection with the mother board. One board, called a controller, that handles the data flow between the computer and the disk drives is essential. Other boards can be purchased and added to enhance functions of a system. The computer assembly also includes an AC-to-DC power supply. Although disk drives are installed in this housing, they are considered separate assemblies.

IBM-type computers are identified as: PC's, XT's, AT's, or PC2's. Apple computers are called: Apple IIc's, IIe's, Macintosh's, etc. Computers are classified and priced by computing speed, meaning how fast they process information. The faster they are the more expensive they are. Price of a computer assembly also is dependent upon the amount of random access memory installed and its speed.

2 **The keyboard** is the device you use to instruct the computer on what you want it to do.

3 **Disk drives** are necessary to read or store software programs or the data you produce. Two types are used: floppy drives and hard drives. All purchased software programs are furnished on flexible (floppies) diskettes. In order for your computer to read them, you need floppy disk drives--a 360K and a 1.2M drive (360,000 bytes or 1,200,000 bytes). Purchased software programs now use thousands of bytes. Hard disk drives provide you with 10 times or more storage capacity than floppies and have faster access times to the data. These drives are needed if you want to keep all your software programs readily available so you don't have to load them each time you want to use them.

4 **Monitors,** monochrome (black and white) or color (EGA, VGA) are offered in various screen sizes and reso-

lutions. Most monitors need a driver (a printed circuit board) that plugs into the mother board. If you plan on installing games a color monitor is essential.

5 **Printers** are available either as: a dot matrix 9 pin or 24 pin (letters are formed by an array of 5x7 dots); ball-type printers (similar to an IBM high-quality typewriter); or a laser printer. Purchase price and print quality is in the same order. Ball-type printers cannot produce graphics and type is fixed to one font unless you change the ball each time for different fonts.

For those interested in communicating with others using your computer a modem is required. Modems (from the terms modulator/demodulator--a means of handling electrical signals) are circuit boards that provide the means to communicate via the telephone lines to other computers. They also require communication software programs to accomplish the task.

The thing to keep in mind is there are self-teaching manuals, home video tapes, and many classes that are offered to help you. In many ways, senior citizens would seem to be perfect candidates for home computing. Most have time on their hands and minds that tend to race ahead of their aging bodies.

Here are just a few examples of what older persons say about their computers:

✳ "Even though I am house-bound most of the time, it gives me the opportunity to make new friends across the country."

✳ "I just want to be able to talk with people my own age."

✳ "I like the social contact outside of just my home."

✳ "There's always someone to talk to, laugh with, and exchange ideas with."

✳ "Since I am a polio victim, I can sit here in front of my computer screen and talk back and forth with so many different people--I think it is marvelous."

✳ "It offers me the opportunity to provide tax assistance for older adults."

✳ "Since I have learned about computers I am now able to relate with my grandchildren and their use of this technology."

✳ "Teleconferencing allows me to debate hot issues like catastrophic healthcare insurance and sometimes we organize congressional lobbying campaigns."

✳ "It provides me a great way to keep my mind active."

✳ "I'm using it to write a book on hotel management."

✳ "I am 85 years old, and had spent two years in bed when I learned about a computer class and signed up. I discovered I wasn't sick, I was just bored to death."

✳ "I bridged the generation gap by organizing an international youth chess tournament."

✳ "I use it in my volunteer work, helping the church publish a newsletter and balance its books."

✳ "I have found the network has been helpful in locating missing relatives as I am writing a genealogy."

✳ "Since I now am widowed, I wake up in the middle of the night and log on for companionship--there is always somebody there."

✳ "I'm writing a book about my doll collection."

✳ "As a numismatist it has allowed me to electronically catalog 65,000 of my rare coins."

✳ "I'm putting out a newsletter about beekeeping."

A Note to Younger Adults:

Older persons can find help or new friends by "turning on"--their computers. If you are wondering what to give your older parents as a gift, perhaps you should consider getting them a computer. Then they would become one of the increasing number of seniors who are using their machines for recreation, intellectual stimulation, research, news, shopping, and perhaps even most important, companionship.

When some fellows decide to retire
nobody knows the difference. - Kin Hubbard

Don't just complain--make your views known

Many important issues facing the United States today need to be addressed by senior citizens. With nearly 60 million age 50 or more, approximately 25% of the population, seniors can make a significant difference in resolving many of these issues by becoming more involved in the political system.

The 100 Senators and 435 Representatives holding seats in Congress represent the public's interest in the nation's legislature. Several senior organizations lobby for you in matters that might directly affect you, such as Social Security and Medicare. However, there are many other issues that you have an obligation, as citizens of a democracy, that may not be adequately represented unless you speak out. One of the best ways to contribute is by communicating with members of Congress.

If you wish to get involved and voice your opinion on an issue, you should make contact with any or all of these groups:

❶ Your own Representatives or Senators,

❷ Members of the Congressional committee that has responsibility or jurisdiction for the issue, and

❸ Members of Congress known for their involvement and interest in the issue.

WAYS TO COMMUNICATE

1 **Meetings**--Attend those of your Representative, Senator, or one of their staff. Most Representatives hold regular local meetings. Check with your newspaper. (Prepare and leave a one-page description of the issue and action you recommend.)

2 **Mail**--Letters are one of the best ways to input your recommendations on an issue. (If possible, state your position on one page.)

3 **Mailgrams or Telegrams**--Use this means if a response is urgent and might have an impact on a pending piece of legislation. (As with letters, most are read by staff members.)

4 **Telephone Calls**--Personal calls generally have more impact but you will, in most cases, be talking to staff unless you arrange otherwise.

5 **Presentations**--You can organize a meeting and invite, through their appointment secretaries, your Representative or Senator to provide a presentation on the issues concerning you.

FOR EFFECTIVE COMMUNICATION

1. Identify the issue clearly. If legislation is pending include the House or Senate bill number. Don't confuse the issue by clouding it with other concerns.

2. State briefly why you are concerned about this issue. Explain how the issue affects you and others. Provide personal experience if appropriate.

3. Contact both Representatives and Senators.

4. If you want action, identify and ask what you want done.

5. If you have an idea you'd like to see turned into legislation, suggest this to your Representative or Senator.

6. If the issue has been discussed in print, be sure to include copies of the news articles or your own correspondence.

7. If your issue hasn't been in the newspapers, it might be useful to attract the news media first.

8. Restrict yourself to one topic at a time.

9. Use your own words. Don't make it appear as a hand-out.

10. See that your communication on an issue gets to the subcommittee before it reaches the House or Senate floor for a vote.

11. Find out the committees or subcommittees on which your Representative or Senators serve. They have more influence over legislation in these jurisdictions.

12. Present the best arguments. Review the opposition's arguments.

13. Communicate with Congress as an individual, not as a self-appointed community spokeperson.

14. If Representatives or Senators support your issue let them know you appreciate their past or present leadership on an issue.

The Bill Status Office can tell you the latest action on any federal legislation. Telephone assistance is free. To obtain a printout that is mailed to your home you should make arrangements through your Representative's or Senator's office. Contact: LEGIS, Office of Legislative Information, House Office Building Annex 2, 3rd and D Streets, S.W., Room 696, Washington, D.C. 20515; (202) 225-1772.

The aide to the Senator or Representative who is the sponsor of a particular bill is the best person to contact next. The Bill Status Office can tell you the sponsor, and the Capitol Hill Switchboard at (202) 225-3121 can transfer you to the appropriate office; then ask to speak to the person in charge of a particular bill. Usually, the aide will offer to send you a copy of the bill, a press announcement, and other background information. Check with the aide to see the likelihood of it becoming law.

Letters should be addressed in the following manner:

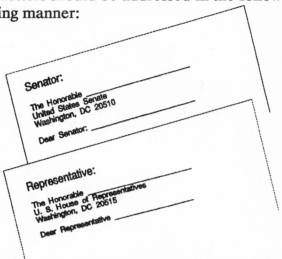

The Bill Status Office can also tell you which committee or subcommittee has jurisdiction over the legislation you are tracking. Contact the committee through the switchboard then ask:

✳ Are hearings expected to be held?

✳ Has the committee chair promised a vote on the measure?

✳ What is the timetable for "markup" and consideration of amendments?

✳ What is the Administration's position on the legislation?

✳ Has the committee filed its report on the bill?

✳ Is there any action or a similar proposal on the other side of the Hill?

You can get free copies of House bills, resolutions, and House committee reports by sending a self-addressed mailing label to the House Document Room, U.S. Capitol, Room H-226, Washington, D.C. 20515; (202) 225-3456. Similarly, you can direct your requests for Senate documents to the Senate Document Room, Hart Senate Bldg., Room B-04, Washington, D.C. 20510; (202) 224-7860.

The Capit0l Hill Switchboard Operator at (202) 224-3121 can also connect you with the Washington office of your Representatives and Senators.

TELL THE PRESIDENT

White House Operators will take messages for the President. You can also write to the Commander-in-Chief and share your views about current issues. The address is:

The President of the United States
of America
White House
1600 Pennsylvania Avenue, N.W.
Washington, D.C. 20500
(202) 456-7639

An adventure of mind, body, and spirit

Elderhostel is an educational program for seniors that began in 1975. It is modeled on the European youth hostel program and Scandinavian folk schools. Marty Knowlton was the founder of Elderhostel. He began with just a few participants. It has grown to 190,000 participants in 1989. They studied in all 50 states, 10 Canadian provinces, and 40 countries overseas. About 1,000 different colleges, universities, and other institutions participated.

COURSES--The typical pattern for an Elderhostel experience is a six-day educational program in some existing institution. Courses are in the liberal arts and sciences. Each school selects the courses it wishes to offer, resulting in an intellectual smorgasbord. Three courses are offered each day for one and one-half hours. A participant is only required to attend one of these courses, but he/she may attend all three. Courses are not for credit and there are no exams, grades, or required homework (except for those in Intensive Studies). No previous knowledge or study is required.

U.S. AND CANADIAN COSTS--A typical six-day program runs around $255. It can be higher, often depending upon location. Canadian programs tend to be higher, for example. The participant is expected to get to U.S. and Canadian locations on his/her own initiative. This figure covers:

❶ Registration

❷ Accommodations

❸ Meals, Sunday evening through Saturday morning

❹ Five days of classes

❺ Extracurricular activities (local arrangements)

RV ELDERHOSTELS--differ from regular Elderhostels as they require hostelers to bring their own housing: recreational vehicle, travel trailer, or tent. Classes are generally held at a nearby host campus. Meals are furnished (in some cases, excluding breakfast) and tuition varies according to services provided. Programs are located in the United States and Canada.

INTERNATIONAL PROGRAMS--More than forty countries are the location for Elderhostel international programs. In these programs costs cover transportation. It is generally possible to extend one's stay in order to spend time touring on one's own.

Most international programs are planned in cooperation with other organizations and institutions. One of these is the Experiment in International Living, which arranges homestays with local people. So you might spend a week at a college or university studying, then a week with a host family, and finally another week at another location studying new subjects. International program fees include:

① International round-trip airfare via regularly scheduled airlines

② All travel and transfers within the foreign country

③ Full room and board, with exceptions

④ Complete academic instruction

⑤ Course-related excursions and admission fees

⑥ Various evening entertainments

⑦ Limited accident, sickness, and baggage insurance

Travel, study and meet new friends
A great combination!

Whereas domestic programs can sometimes make adjustments for people with handicaps or limited mobility, international programs require participants to be in good health in order to take part in active educational and extracurricular experiences. For example, one must be able to carry his/her own baggage and to do a fair amount of walking.

ELIGIBILITY--All persons who are 60 or more years of age and their spouse may register for programs. A person who is 60 or more may bring a companion who is at least 50 or more years of age.

PUBLICATIONS--Catalogs and catalog supplements are published several times a year to everyone on their mailing list. All public libraries and their branches receive these mailings.

REGISTRATION--When you register for a program a deposit is required, and the entire cost must be paid before the program begins. Once an announcement of a program is made, registrations are collected and a lottery assignment system is used to avoid giving an advantage to the person who may receive his/her catalog earlier because of a location advantage. If space remains in a given program, new registrations are accepted.

For more information, write to:

Elderhostel
80 Boylston Street
Suite 400
Boston, MA 02116

Programs have been held in these countries

Argentina	Finland	Lapland
Australia	France	Mexico
Bahamas	Galapagos	Nepal
Bali	Great Britain	New Zealand
Bermuda	Greece	Norway
Brazil	India	Polynesia
Canada	Israel	Spain
Costa Rica	Italy	Turkey
Ecuador	Jamaica	Uruguay
Egypt	Kenya	United States

Writing in the second 50 years
by Wm. J. Diehm

**God wove a web of loveliness
of clouds and stars and birds,
but made not anything at all
so beautiful as words.**
Anna Hempstead Branch (1874-1937)

Writing can start at any age; but during the second 50 years and particularly the time of retirement is the best of times. We are matured, experienced, and knowledgeable. If we are ever going to have something to say, now is the hour. Everyone who retires must absolutely have a hobby to take the place of the missing life work. When I retired, writing saved my life. Here are some comments about the hobby of writing that I developed after writing five books:

Learn to Write by Writing

❑ Write consistently--day in, day out--sick or well--with or without the Muse.

❑ Never wait till you feel like it, just write.

❑ Don't let interruptions break your routine. Even if the house burns down, continue writing.

❑ Fix a minimum number of pages to write each day and do it.

❑ If you get stuck and can't think of anything to say, start putting down words until you get an idea.

❑ Don't make excuses, make writing--a pencil and piece of paper will do it. If necessary, prick your finger and write on the wall in your blood, but write.

Learn to Write by Observing, Reading, Thinking and Experiencing

■ Observe! Look around and see, hear, touch, taste, smell, think, use intuition. Emotionally experience whatever is of interest to you, and then write about it.

■ Read! You positively cannot write unless you read. Go to your library or anyplace you can find a book:

❁ Read everything of interest;
❁ Read a few things that weary you to sleep;
❁ Read some material you can't understand;
❁ Read some writing that nauseates;
❁ Read some writing that any fool could write;
❁ Read something that inspires;
❁ Read some tales of tragedy and woe;
❁ Read some writing that lacks redemption;
❁ Read something that will make you fighting mad; and then,
❁ Read some books that will make you want to change yourself and the whole wide world. If you have a heart, soul, or brain, try to activate them by reading; in fact, if you can, enliven, enrage, and passionately stir yourself to awareness through your reading.

■ Don't say you can't read well; in order to write, you must read. If you can't really read well, then pick up some kindergarten books and read them to a child. Then advance yourself to the first-grade level, reading aloud to anyone who will listen. Continue through the eighth grade and into high school until you reach a level of reading that you can't understand or don't like. Drop back one year and write like crazy at that level.

■ Think! Activate your brains; make them work hard; then use your imagination, your daydreams, and even your night dreams. Blend your awesome cognitive powers with fertile imagination and come up with a brew to make people stew.

■ Experience! Contact all sorts of people; find out about their problems, aspirations, inspirations, perspirations, prejudices, prides, and passions and write about them.

■ Decide! What contributions are you going to make to justify your existence on this planet--write about them.

■ Keep a journal of your life and everyday write down your experiences, no matter how minuscule. Even write down your daydreams, in code, of course.

Learn to write by studying, researching, rethinking, revising, and rewriting, until you are somewhat satisfied.

■ Study the English language until you are a master of its construction unless of course you are going to write in another language.

■ Read books and articles on writing, take courses and seminars in the field, and continue for five years past the time when the experts are asking your opinion about writing.

■ Keep up on what's happening in the world. Make sure you have a good general education with a broad foundation in the liberal arts.

■ Research by reading and studying everything that you can find in the field of your writing subject. You will be surprised how quickly you will collect material that you can use in writing.

■ Rethink, revise, and rewrite until you can't think of any way to say it better. Write as plain and clear as you can. Somebody will be reading your book or article; try to make it easy and fun for them to read.

■ Let the most experienced person you know read your writing for corrections and revisions. Consider each correction carefully as you remember that you are responsible for what you have said. If a publishing company is editing your work, pay close attention to what they say. In my experience the editors are usually right.

> *True ease in writing comes from art, not chance, as those move easiest who have learned to dance.*
> — **Pope (1688-1744)**

Learn to Write by Writing Letters

■ What makes you think you are a writer if you can't keep up on your personal correspondence. Write a letter for every procrastination and every obligation. When you are through, your mind will be clear to write for publication and you will have some friends to buy your works.

■ Never reply to an unreasonable or offensive letter by adopting the same tone. This hurts your case and simply invites more invective. If the letter you received is so offensive that you can't think of a fair, decent way to reply to it, then don't reply.

■ Don't exceedingly regret anything. Few things are more irritating to a letter reader than overstated personal feelings. Let your letters be courteous, friendly, truthful, and sometimes sympathetic. Don't gush or flatter others too much or incriminate yourself.

■ Never write down to your audience. Say what you have to say simply, plainly, and quickly. Treat everyone as your equal. People do not like to be put down; so don't do it.

■ Never be afraid to put factual truth in a letter. Many letters evade questions and issues. While it's not a good idea to gossip or to disclose secrets you will one day regret having revealed, say what you have to say if it's truthful and not designed to hurt or to slander.

■ If your letter is especially important, don't hesitate to use notes and outlines so the letter will be clear, and plain, and not misunderstood. Keep a copy of your correspondence.

■ Letters should be lively, colorful, and loaded with your personality. Writing that constantly generalizes is bad writing--be specific. Shift your word order, vary the sentences, use synonyms, use active verbs, describe your surroundings, and make the reader see and feel what you say.

Learn to Write by Improving Yourself

■ Make a list of your failings and systematically strive to change those things that are holding you back.

■ Make a list of your virtues and studiously strive to capitalize on what you do well.

■ Memorize poetry, clever sayings, jokes, and bits of literature, and on occasions, show off. For men only: Women are very impressed when you can spout a romantic poem with meaning.

■ Be moral, be honest, and be kind. Develop an ethical value system and keep it. A good person can empathize and write well about an evil person or situation; but an evil person knows nothing of goodness, mercy, or fair play--so he or she can't write well about anything worthwhile.

Learn to Write by Motivating Yourself and Being Persistent

■ Learn how to work hard because writing is hard work.

■ Don't quit until you are a rich and famous published author, and then redouble your efforts.

■ Shake yourself awake, cheer yourself on, and write.

■ Do not wait until you feel like writing-- almost no one ever feels like it. Grab yourself by your scruffy neck, kick yourself soundly in your placid butt, slap your recalcitrant face until your sleepy eyes pop open, jab a pencil into your reluctant fist, slap a piece of paper on the messy desk, and yell with frightful anger, *"Write, I command you, Write."*

> *The desire to write grows with writing.*
> — **Erasmus (1466-1536)**

Learn to Write by Submitting Your Manuscript for Sale

■ When you think your work is ready, send it off to a publisher.

■ If you are rejected by one, keep sending it to others until you know exactly why it won't sell. The best unknown writer in all the world will be rejected repeatedly because editors do not even read 5% of the material sent to them.

■ Make an appointment with an editor and go to a publishing house. Try to find out why your material is not selling.

■ Go to writers' conferences and seminars to meet agents, publishers, and editors. Talk to them. Do not worship them--they too are people just like you who pray to God that they can find or write a profitable book to publish.

■ Query, submit, query, submit, submit, submit, and then when you are very tired and discouraged, submit some more.

■ If at last you have tried everything and can't sell your material to a publisher, publish it yourself with as much pride as the author of a number one bestseller. Then, sell it to anyone you meet with the fervor of a religious zealot or an Amway salesperson.

Conclusion

People learn to write by writing, reading, studying, researching, revising, submitting, and starting with something simple like letter writing. People learn to write and become authors by improving themselves, motivating themselves, and by being persistent. The world's biggest handicap to being a published writer is the word "procrastination." I make up many excuses for putting off writing--my favorite, "I'm too busy." What's yours?

Falls and accidents seldom just happen

Accidental injuries become more frequent and serious as we grow older since we become more vulnerable to severe injury and tend to heal slowly. As people age, changes in their vision, hearing, muscle strength, coordination, and reflexes may make them more likely to fall. Older persons are also more likely to have treatable disorders that may affect their balance, including diabetes or conditions of the heart, nervous system, and thyroid. In addition, older persons take more drugs that may cause dizziness or lightheadedness.

Falls are a major health problem among the elderly and are mentioned as a contributing factor in 40% of all admissions to nursing homes. The percentages of people in the community who fall each year are: over the age 65, 30%; over age 89, 40%.

The majority of falls by the elderly generally result in minor injury and are not medically attended. Four to six percent of all falls cause severe injury, such as a fracture, with less than 1% resulting in hip fractures. Yet, each year approximately 250,000 hip fractures of older persons result from falls, and 25,000 of those die of complications. The psychological trauma resulting from falls may be severe and can result in loss of confidence in the ability to perform daily routine, restriction of activity, decreased mobility, and increased dependence.

Preventing Falls and Fractures

Medical researchers established a set of risk factors that contribute to falls. They included prescription drug use, lower body disabilities, degeneration of bone or muscle, and balance abnormalities. They concluded that it is the number of risk factors that predicts falling, not the factors themselves. Over a 1-year period, people with no disabilities had an 8% chance of falling; those with one disability had a 19% chance; those with two, 32%; three 60%; and four, 78%.

Prevention of falls is especially important for people who have osteoporosis, a condition in which bone mass decreases, causing bones to be more fragile and to break easily. Osteoporosis is a major cause of bone fractures in postmenopausal women and older persons in general. Although all bones are affected, fractures of the spine, wrist, and hip are most common. For the person with severe osteoporosis, even a minor fall may cause one or more bones to break.

There are simple steps to take to reduce the likelihood of falling and to make our homes generally safer. Here are some guidelines for preventing falls and fractures.

Everyday Activities

❑ Have your vision and hearing tested regularly and corrected. Even removing ear wax can improve your balance.

❑ Talk to your doctor or pharmacist about the side effects of any drugs you are taking and how they may affect your coordination or balance. Ask them to suggest ways to reduce the possibilities of falling.

❑ Limit your intake of alcohol. Even a little alcohol can further disturb already impaired balance and reflexes.

❑ Use caution in getting up too quickly after eating, lying down, or resting. Low blood pressure may cause dizziness at these times.

❑ Make sure that the nighttime temperature in your home is not lower than 65 degrees F. Prolonged exposure to cold temperatures may cause body temperature to drop, leading to dizziness and falling.

❑ Use a cane, walking stick, or walker to help maintain balance on uneven or unfamiliar ground or if you sometimes feel dizzy. Use special caution in walking outdoors on wet and icy pavement.

❑ Wear supportive, rubber-soled, low-heeled shoes. Avoid wearing only socks or smooth-soled shoes or slippers on stairs or waxed floors. They make it very easy to slip.

❑ Maintain a regular program of exercise. Regular physical activity improves strength and muscle tone, which will help in moving about more easily by keeping joints, tendons, and ligaments more flexible. Many older people enjoy walking, swimming, and other exercise. Mild weight-bearing activities may even reduce the loss of bone from osteoporosis. It is important, however, to check with your doctor or physical therapist to plan a suitable exercise program.

Safety Checklist Your Home

Stairways and steps are dangerous!

❑ Keep all stairways, steps, and walkways free of obstacles and in good repair.

❑ Paint edges of outdoor steps white to see them better at night.

❑ Be sure both sides of stairways have sturdy handrails.

❑ Light all stairways and have switches at the top and bottom.

❑ Make certain all carpet is firmly attached to the steps.

❑ Use nonskid treads or carpet but avoid deep pile or patterned carpet that makes it difficult to see the edge of the steps clearly.

In the Living Quarters

❑ Provide night lights especially in bathrooms and bedrooms.

❑ Get rid of throw rugs.

❑ Repair, remove, or replace worn or torn coverings or nails sticking out from the coverings that could snag your foot or cause you to trip.

❑ Arrange furniture and other objects so they are not obstacles and so outlets are available for lamps and appliances without the use of extension cords.

❑ Keep power cords and decorative items off the floors. Electric cords that run under carpeting may cause a fire. Never stretch cords across walkways.

❑ Use a step stool with a handrail when reaching high shelves. Don't use chairs or other makeshift items.

In the Bathroom

❑ Check grab bars for strength and stability; repair if necessary.

❑ Install and use grab bars on bathroom walls, near the tub and the toilet seat. Attach grab bars through the tile to structural supports in the wall or install bars designed to attach to the sides of the bathtub. If you are not sure how it is done, get someone who is qualified to do it.

❑ Place nonskid mats, strips, or appliques in the bathtub or showers.

❑ If you are unsteady on your feet, use a stool with nonskid tips as a seat while showering or bathing.

**Experience is the name
everyone gives to their mistakes.**

- Oscar Wilde

NEWS ITEM: Hip Pads May Help Elderly When They Fall

The loss of muscle mass that often comes with age also increases the risk of bone fracture by lessening a person's natural protective padding. Researchers at Beth Israel Hospital in Boston believe that padding for the elderly person's brittle hips may help prevent some of the 250,000 annual fractures.

Using impact-absorbing foam, the material used in football and ice hockey, to build lightweight protective padding may offer an answer, the researchers believe. They recommend providing protective padding over the hips for elderly persons who are at high risk of falling and don't have natural padding.

Studies have shown that the impact of a fall from standing height carries 20 times the energy required to break the hip. The severity of injuries among elderly people who fall appears related to how they fall. Elderly people who break their hips fall differently than those who do not. They tend to fall to the side and land directly on their hips, without using an outstretched hand to break the fall according to the report.

Home Safety Activity Program for Crutch Users

Safety
- ☐ Remove all small and medium rugs and hall runners.
- ☐ If you have thresholds between rooms, get close to the edge and step over them.
- ☐ No matter what you sit on or in, all sitting is performed in the same manner in which you were instructed by your medical provider.
- ☐ Restrict all animals (dogs, cats) if they are inclined to be underfoot.
- ☐ As a rule, look where you are going. Look down only if you know or suspect that there is something potentially hazardous on the floor (water, sand, toys, small children).
- ☐ The primary difference between walking on a hard surface and a rug is that when on a rug you must pick up your foot a little higher.
- ☐ The chair you sit on should be sturdy, have arms, and be of sufficient height to allow you to rise with minimum effort.
- ☐ For the first day or so, you should have someone serve as your safety escort. Escorting on stairs is a must until such time as your confidence and smooth performance with crutches no longer require an escort.
- ☐ Whenever you have a handrail on stairs, use it.
- ☐ Check daily to make sure nuts and bolts holding hand pieces and extension tips on your crutches are tight.
- ☐ If crutch tips are used on wet surfaces, tips will be very slippery when used on a smooth linoleum floor.

Activity
- ☐ When you get home from your medical provider, resume as many usual activities as you can safely perform: get dressed, eat at the dining room table, move about frequently but briefly.
- ☐ Watch your foot for swelling or change in color. When one or both occur, elevate your foot on a hassock or stool.
- ☐ Do not restrict those activities you are capable of performing. Introduce yourself slowly to them.
- ☐ Whatever activity you are engaged in, stop at the first sign of fatigue if you can. As you will learn, crutch walking is physically demanding.
- ☐ Use your crutches as instructed. Do not cheat by trying to do without them; your medical provider will tell you when you no longer need them.

Crutch Walking
- ☐ Fix the crutches so that there is ample room for two fingers' width from the arm pit to the top of the crutch pad. Make sure there is a slight bend (30 degrees) at the elbow when the hand grasps the handpiece.
- ☐ Crutches always accompany the affected limb.
- ☐ On level walking, crutches and affected limb advance first. The unaffected leg will follow.
- ☐ Move slowly and use moderate extension to maintain balance.

Stairs Manipulation
- ☐ Good leg always goes up first; affected leg and crutches will follow.
- ☐ When coming downstairs, the crutches and affected leg come down first; good leg follows.
- ☐ If possible, an escort on the stairs should walk behind the patient when going up the stairs and in front when walking down.
- ☐ If a handrail is available, two crutches can be held under one arm and the rail held with the other hand, or the escort should carry the other crutch.

BURNS--are especially disabling when you are older because your body recovers more slowly from such injuries; 70% of all people who die from clothing fires are over 65 years of age. Good practices to follow are:

- ◆ Use light bulbs of the correct wattage in all fixtures. To avoid fire hazard use 60-watt lamp maximum unless otherwise stipulated.
- ◆ Never smoke in bed or when drowsy.
- ◆ Placing or storing noncooking equipment like potholders, dish towels, or plastic utensils on or near the range may result in fires or burns.
- ◆ When cooking, don't wear loosely fitting flammable clothing. Bathrobes, nightgowns, and pajamas can catch fire. Long sleeves are more likely to catch fire and catch on pot handles, overturning pots and causing scalds.
- ◆ Roll back long, loose sleeves or fasten them with elastic bands while you are cooking.
- ◆ Keep a careful watch on cooking oils while heating them. Never turn the burner on high and leave a pan containing oil unattended. Heat oil gradually.
- ◆ Store flammable and combustible items away from range and oven.
- ◆ Remove any towels hanging on oven handles. If towels hang close to a burner, change the location of the towel rack.
- ◆ Set water heater thermostats to a maximum of 120 degrees so the water does not scald the skin. Check the water temperature with a thermometer.
- ◆ Take baths, rather than showers, to reduce the risk of a scald from suddenly changing water temperatures.
- ◆ If a fire starts in a microwave close the door and push the stop button.
- ◆ If a pan containing grease catches fire, cover it with a lid and turn the burner off. Never pour water on grease fires.
- ◆ If a fire starts in an oven turn it off and close the door to suffocate the flames.
- ◆ Use a fire extinguisher on only small self-contained fires.
- ◆ If a fire is big or spreading, get out and call the fire department.
- ◆ Plan emergency exits to use in case of fire.
- ◆ Install one good lock, in place of multiple inexpensive locks, that can be opened from the inside quickly. Many older people trap themselves behind locks that are hard to open during an emergency.
- ◆ If you get burned while cooking, run cool water on the skin immediately until the burning sensation stops. This prevents injury and alleviates some of the pain.

Burns are more serious than they first appear. So, if a burn is severe--charred or blistering-- see a doctor as soon as possible.

Lock up!

How you can have security at home

❏ If you meet a burglar, let him go! Better to lose money or property than your life!

KEY SENSE

❏ Do not hide house keys in mailboxes, planters, or under doormats. Give a duplicate key to a trusted friend or neighbor in case you are locked out.

❏ Do not put any personal identification on key rings.

❏ Leave only your ignition key with service mechanics and parking attendants.

❏ If you lose the keys to your home or move, change the locks immediately.

ANSWERING THE DOOR

❏ Install a peephole or wide-angle viewer in entry doors so you can see who is outside without opening the door. A short chain between the door and the jamb is not a good substitute because it can be broken easily.

❏ Don't open the door to anyone you do not know without first verifying that person's identity.

OUTSIDE

❏ Trim back shrubbery that hides doors and windows.

❏ Cut back tree limbs that could help a thief climb into second-story windows.

❏ Make sure all porches, entrances, and yards are well lighted.

❏ Help keep your neighborhood in good shape. Dark alleys, litter, and run-down areas attract crime.

LOCKS, DOORS AND WINDOWS

❏ Install good deadbolt locks in your doors.

❏ Avoid door locks that can be manipulated by breaking glass or door panels.

❏ Make sure outside doors, including the one between your house and garage, are 1-3/4-inch thick, solid-core wood or metal doors and fit tightly in frames also of solid construction.

❏ Make sure hinges are on the inside. If not, use hinges with nonremovable hinge pins or install a locking pin (in place of a screw) that pins together both halves of the hinge when closed.

❏ Secure sliding glass doors with commercially available locks, with a rigid wooden dowel in the track, or with a nail inserted in a hole drilled in the sliding door frame and projecting into the fixed frame.

❏ Lock double-hung windows by sliding a bolt or nail through a hole drilled at a downward angle in each top corner of the inside sash and partway through the outside sash, or buy window locks.

❏ Consider grills for basement or street-level windows.

ANSWERING THE PHONE

❏ Don't give any information to "wrong number" callers. Ask what number they are dialing.

❏ Check references of any person calling about a survey or credit check before giving information. Offer to call the person back instead of responding immediately.

❏ Hang up immediately on any threatening or embarrassing calls.

❏ If the caller persists, call police and the phone company.

ALARMS--If you keep very valuable possessions in your home or live in an isolated area, consider installing an alarm system. Residential burglar alarms are available from electrical dealers and alarm companies. Be sure you first check the alarm company's references and reliability of the system before you sign up for one. Get several estimates and decide which system is best for you. Check with the police to see if there is an alarm ordinance in your area. Any alarm system should include: a failsafe battery backup; fire sensing capability; readout ability to check the working of the system; and a horn sounding device installed in the attic through a vent.

FOR ADDED PROTECTION

❏ Request a fire and security check of your home from your local fire and police department.

❏ Compile an inventory of your valuables including serial numbers and date of purchase. Use photos or videotapes if possible, and mark each with your social security number using an electric vibrating engraver. Most police departments can help you in obtaining an engraver.

❏ Don't include your address in a classified ad and don't announce plans for a party or vacation in your local newspaper.

❏ Store little-used items like a coin collection or stock certificates in a safe deposit box.

❏ Find an unpredictable place to hide valuable items, like a moveable floorboard.

❏ Take out homeowners' insurance to protect yourself against financial loss from burglary or fire.

GOING AWAY?--Burglars hope to avoid confrontations, so make your home look occupied while you are away! An empty-looking house is a tempting target for them.

❏ Always lock your doors and windows even when leaving for just a minute. About 50% of burglars get in through unlocked doors and windows.

❏ Keep your garage door closed and locked.

❏ Use inexpensive timing devices to turn inside lights and radios on and off at different times when you go out.

❏ Stop deliveries, or arrange for someone to pick up your mail, newspapers, and packages.

❏ Arrange for someone to mow your lawn, shovel snow, or rake leaves.

❏ Hide garbage cans as empty cans tell a burglar you are away.

❏ Turn the bell on your telephone down low so a burglar will not be alerted to your absence by its ringing.

❏ Engrave your valuables with your social security number and post "Operation Identification" stickers in entry doors and windows.

❏ Ask a neighbor to park occasionally in your driveway so it looks like you are home.

❏ Leave your blinds, shades, and curtains in a normal position.

❏ House numbers should be visible day and night from the street. In rural areas a name or number should be displayed on the mailbox. This is important for police, fire, and medical persons responding to a call.

❏ Never put your full name on your mailbox; use initials and last name only.

❏ Don't leave notes showing you aren't home or when you will return.

❏ Ask a neighbor to watch the house while you are away and leave them your vacation address and telephone number so you can be reached in an emergency.

❏ Never enter your house if you see evidence of a burglary.

Accidents with heating equipment are the number one cause of home fires. Most could be prevented. Use only approved heating equipment that is installed and maintained correctly. If you don't understand the installation and operating instructions thoroughly call your local fire department. They will help to point out fire safety problems--it's free. Here are some tips that will help you heat your home without getting burned:

SPACE HEATERS

- ❑ Give space heaters space.
- ❑ Don't place small stoves and heaters where they can be knocked over.
- ❑ Place portable heaters at least 3 feet away from anything that burns--paper, bedding, clothing, furniture, and curtains.
- ❑ Ventilate them according to the manufacturer's instructions. Improper venting is the most frequent cause of carbon monoxide poisoning, and older consumers are at special risks.
- ❑ Turn them off before leaving home or going to bed.
- ❑ Use only the right fuel recommended by the heater manufacturer.
- ❑ Don't refill a heater that runs on liquid fuel, such as kerosene, until the heater has cooled down.
- ❑ Never use substitutes or lower-grade fuels.
- ❑ Never put gasoline in a heater!
- ❑ Make sure the cords on your electric heaters are in good condition.
- ❑ Watch out for frayed or splitting cords or if they overheat when the heater is in operation--you have a fire hazard on your hands. Don't use it until the cord is properly replaced.
- ❑ Use three-prong plugs and outlets or make sure if you use an adapter that the ground wire is attached to the outlet. Never defeat the grounding feature as it prevents electrical shocks.

In case of fire, once you get out, stay out! No possessions are worth your life!

WOOD STOVES AND FIREPLACES

- ❑ Be sure your wood stove is 3 feet away from any wall.
- ❑ Keep combustible materials away from the stove and chimney connectors.
- ❑ Keep your chimney clean and install a spark arrester on top.
- ❑ Don't dump hot ashes into the trash.
- ❑ Never build a fire in a fireplace without a screen.
- ❑ Burn only wood in your fireplace or wood stove.

Note: Some insurance companies will not cover the fire losses if wood stoves are not installed according to local codes.

SMOKE DETECTORS

These devices are inexpensive, sometimes less than $10, and easy to install. Many home fire injuries and deaths are caused by smoke and toxic gases, rather than by the fire itself. Smoke detectors provide you with an early warning and can wake you in the event of a fire. Install detectors on every floor of your home, outside each bedroom, the dining room, furnace room, utility room, and hallways. Don't install the detectors at the top of basement stairs or near windows, doors, hot air registers, or air conditioners. Your local fire department will provide assistance in telling you where it is best to install them if you are not sure. Test detectors once every month and replace the batteries at least once every year. Most detectors take a 9-volt standard battery.

PREPARE JUST IN CASE

- ❑ Have emergency numbers--police, fire, a neighbor--posted near every phone.
- ❑ Purchase fire extinguishers for your home and car (they're also a great housewarming present for friends).
- ❑ Make sure the extinguishers are not stored above the stove or other locations where you couldn't reach it in case of a fire.
- ❑ Work out escape plans in the event of fire or other emergencies for every room of your house.

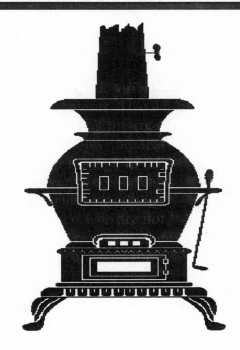

- ❑ Make sure you know how to open windows and that they can open easily.
- ❑ Get your neighborhood watch group to conduct safety tours of elderly neighbors' homes and help fix up their trouble spots.

IN CASE OF FIRE

- ❑ If fire strikes, exit your home immediately. If you think someone may be trapped inside notify the fire department. If you are trapped in smoke, get down on your hands and knees and crawl to the nearest safe way out. Smoke and toxic fumes rise, so cleaner air is near the floor.
- ❑ If your clothes catch on fire, do not run. Stop where you are, drop to the ground, and roll over and over to smother the flames. Once you get out, stay out! No possessions are worth your life!

OTHER FIRE HAZARDS

- ❑ Get rid of all greasy rags stored in the garage.
- ❑ Check for grease buildup around kitchen stoves.
- ❑ See that pot holders are not near the burners.
- ❑ If there are smokers in the house, have ashtrays in every room.
- ❑ Don't smoke in bed.
- ❑ Don't allow anything on top of your electric blanket while in use. Tucking in electric blankets or placing additional coverings on top can cause excessive heat buildup.
- ❑ Don't set electric blankets or heating pads so high that they could burn someone who falls asleep while they are on.

On the mistreatment of the elderly by Wm. J. Diehm

For ten years my wife and I undertook the home care of my mother. She was in her eighties, incontinent, wheelchair-bound, with a fading memory from senility. She had occasional bouts of a paranoid type of mental illness followed by a profound depression and disinterest in life. God bless her, she tried so hard not to be a burden, and we tried so hard to take good care of her--we loved her, and she loved us. I proudly declare that I don't think most families could do what we did. It helped immensely for me to be a psychological specialist in geriatrics and my wife to have some nurses' training.

Sometimes, when mother was suffering from mental illness, she would be physically and verbally abusive. And sometimes we...well, here's an example. Mother wanted so much to get well and go back to work as a real estate agent. Often she would ask me, "Billy, when am I going to get better, so I can go back to work?" I would reply, "Mother can't you just be content with living with us? I don't think it's possible for you to get better and go back to work at your age." What I said, I believed to be true; but, it probably took away hope, and when hope is gone, depression comes to stay. We never gave my mother anything but the best of care, but I now realize that our good care was not necessarily easy on her. Life itself, and the situation of old age, and the ignorance of caregivers often provide a form of mistreatment that is hard to cure.

Mistreatment of older people is nearly as common as child abuse, yet states commonly spend $22.00 per child for protective services and only $2.90 for senior citizens. The House Select Committee on Aging states that "over 1,000,000 older Americans are physically, financially and emotionally abused by their relatives or loved ones annually." The vast majority of cases in all likelihood don't come to the public's attention.

Gradually, life expectancy has increased so that by the year 2000, 18% of our population will be over the age of 65. Right now, more than 2.3 million Americans are over the age of 85. Often the elderly are severely dependent (suffering from Alzheimer's disease, stroke, cardiovascular diseases, and fractures). They are unable to care for their physical, financial, or basic personal needs, and require supervised care, either at home or in an institution.

Caring for a dependent older adult in the home or paying for such care in an institution can run from $19,000 to $35,000 per year or even more, enough to financially cripple many families. With a large and growing aging population--even though it is generally healthy and vigorous--the prevalence of chronic illness, disability, and dependence in old age creates a situation we cannot ignore.

> If you or your loved one is not getting the care they deserve, don't hesitate to contact an Ombudsman--they are there to protect you and help you.

The types of elderly neglect:

■ **Self-neglect,** which consists of the negligent potentially life-threatening actions of a mentally deteriorating older person who lives alone and is unable to care for himself or herself adequately, but who often resists outside help. Self-neglect is not a prosecutable offense, so we do little about this area. Most older people, when left alone and beginning to lose strength, often take very poor care of themselves. It is common for them to skip meals, develop poor body hygiene, cloister themselves, and take little notice of their environment. They can become a hazard to themselves and others. They need caring help and yet they often vigorously refuse it.

■ **Spousal abuse.** Husbands or wives who have been abusive through long marriages are not likely to change their behavior at age 60 or 65 or 85. Spousal abuse that begins in the retirement years often can be traced to mental illness. Again it is very difficult to intervene. A woman who has been assaulted by her husband will often be very protective of him. He may be cruel, but he is all she has. The human spirit can be very loyal even in the face of inhumane treatment. It presents a problem for authorities and care workers when no one will make an accusation.

Most spouse abusers are men. It is often associated with alcohol or drug abuse, unemployment, post-retirement depression, loss of self-esteem, or a long history of such behavior.

■ **Domestic abuse.** Two-thirds of the severely disabled elderly live with and depend upon their families. Large numbers of families are going too far in caring for older people, stripping themselves of economic, social, and emotional resources to do so. Parent caring is becoming a major source of stress in family life. Few families are prepared to provide adequate supervision or personal care without professional help. Many families are very sincere and loyal. They do not want their parents in an institution; yet often, they do not have the resources or the knowledge to care for them. Training courses are needed to provide a family with care knowledge; and home-care providers are needed to help the family in care skills.

■ **Institutional abuse.** I have visited hundreds of care institutions for the elderly around the country, and I have seen very little of what I would call active neglect and physical abuse. However, when it is present, it can be quite awful. I could tell some unbelievable, but true, horror stories. Laws and control systems have not caught up with the rise in older care needs.

Most places are wonderful, but my caution is to investigate well and check often on any home where you place a loved one. Many times older people deteriorate to the point where restraints, psychoactive drugs, and aggressive treatment is required. Then again, institutions have some staff that is non-caring or untrained, or on occasions, actively abusive. It is very important for those who are involved to talk to the superviser and report suspected abusive behavior, even as you recognize that necessary care sometimes seems abusive.

The severity of mistreatment is usually gauged by the extent of harm done to an individual. Stories of criminal assault, rape, forced confinement, torture, homicide, theft, threat, harassment, abandonment, and enforced isolation are common. Emotional and psychological consequences of all forms of mistreatment can be life-threatening. Injuries requiring medical attention, while clearly serious, may be no more painful or life-threatening than intimidation, insults, and exploitation on a continuing basis. Active neglect can be so damaging that it leads the older person to long for death.

The presence or absence of motivation to cause harm to an elderly person is a principal consideration that distinguishes some forms of mistreatment from others. The mistreatment of the elderly takes a number of different forms:

■ **Passive neglect.** The home care of a frail adult is more taxing than most people think. Also the physical, emotional, and financial costs can be enormous, particularly when the dependent older person is bedfast, incontinent, or the victim of a long-term, behavior-changing illness. Most of the time when home care leads to neglect, the family had good intentions. They just didn't realize how demanding around-the-clock care can be. Both family and friends were incapable of meeting the older person's needs, which resulted in needless suffering.

Sometimes passive neglect can be more than inability or ignorance--it can be criminal. Everyone who suspects or sees criminal neglect of a helpless old person bears some responsibility for reporting it. I remember visiting an institution in which a blind old man who had outlived all his relatives cried out for endless hours, "Nurse, I'm lonely." I asked the supervisor why the old man was not attended. She replied, "We can't spend all day holding hands with one resident." It may be true; but I opted for an occasional visit to his bedside and also to put him in a wheelchair and take him to be with some of the other residents. It would give a patient a sense of meaning to hold the hand of another less fortunate person. It was interesting to note that neglect of the older man was not remedied until pressure was brought to bear on the institution.

■ **Psychological abuse.** Often the frustration of meeting the special needs of a deteriorating older adult leads to psychological abuse, which can be the infliction of mental anguish. When caregivers do not understand the older person's condition, often they can be demeaning and resort to name calling. Sometimes the older person is treated as a child, insulted, ignored, frightened, humiliated, intimidated, threatened, and isolated.

Psychological abuse is generally associated with a poor relationship between victim and perpetrator. A caregiver may have negative emotional ties to the elderly or may be financially dependent upon them. The abuse may be made worse by the use of alcohol or drugs or psychological problems of the abuser. When an otherwise self-sufficient older person becomes depressed or isolated, cries frequently, or loses interest in formerly important activities, the cause may be the treatment given by a caregiver.

Today, people have been conditioned to believe that verbal interchanges are none of their business. Words can "break bones" and do even worse. We must not let verbal abuse go unchallenged.

■ **Financial abuse** is the illegal, or unethical exploitation and/or use of funds, property, or other assets belonging to the older person. Often an elderly person can become so ill or frail that he or she is unable to take care of financial resources. When that time comes, the controls of the resources are often passed to a younger member of the family who may or may not have a business head. Often older people can be easily conned and manipulated and financially abused. Many times their money can be misappropriated by family members who had good intentions.

Some institutions seem to think that even after being paid a fair price for services rendered all the resources of their clientele belong to them. Full-care and retirement homes have been very lucrative to some owners--quite a few millionaires have been made by taking care of the elderly. We need more regulations and investigators so that greed does not extend to taking advantage of our elderly.

Full-time care is expensive, but when all the resources of an older person are stolen or used for the benefit of others, that kind of exploitation is called stealing. I have seen some beautiful facilities where the older person was treated with respect and almost reverential care. The Alzheimer's Center in Gig Harbor, Washington, gives wonderful round-the-clock care to very difficult people for $1500.00 per month. The Sharon Guest Home in Tacoma takes warm, compassionate trusting care for the fees supplied by Medicare. If you have good, well-trained, honest management, an institution does not need to be a horror house or a place where you will be stolen from.

■ **Active neglect** is the intentional failure to fulfill a caretaking obligation, including a conscious and willful attempt to inflict physical or emotional stress or injury on the older person. For example: deliberate abandonment, deliberate denial of food or health-related services, depriation of dentures or eyeglasses.

Some people are inclined to paint graphic horror stories of the active physical abuse of the elderly. They make it sound as if the order of the day was institutional and home abuse of the elderly. Not so--horror stories are the exception, not the rule. Not even one horror story is acceptable; but, neither is it acceptable to exaggerate the situation and paint everyone with the same brush.

My beautiful Aunt Agnes spent the last 20 years of her life in a 24-hour care facility. One day I paid a surprise visit and found her in a most despicable condition. My roars of outrage brought care personnel running. They soon convinced me that they could not assign a one-to-one care attendant around-the-clock. My Auntie, in the advanced stages of Alzheimer's, could do a lot of damage to herself, if left alone for just a few minutes. The problem was more complicated than just active physical abuse would indicate. The family arranged to have some volunteers come and spend some time. It is to the credit of her daughter-in-law, Lucy Davidson, that every day she arrived at mealtime to spend a

Why elderly are abused and how it can be stopped

tedious hour feeding her. People do rise to the occasion, if you give them a chance.

■ **Physical abuse** is the infliction of physical pain or injury, or physical coercion (confinement against one's will). Examples: slapping, bruising, sexually molesting, cutting, lacerating, burning, physically restraining, pushing, shoving.

Sick older people can be very frustrating. My mother would often resist taking a bath, not bother to tell us when it was time to use the toilet, insist upon keeping the windows closed and the curtains down on very hot days, and, never want to go anyplace or do anything but sit in a chair shivering from fear, with my wife and I hovering on either side. Occasionally, we would take her for a ride in the car, in spite of her protestations. One day she became so frightened that she tried to jump out of the car. When we pulled to a stop, she left the car and set off down a street that was full of traffic. Obviously, we had to use physical strength to restrain her. We never wanted to force mother to do anything, but we were obligated to try to save her life.

There are times when the elderly drop into a semi-coma stage and try to pull the IV from the arms, or to climb over the bed rail where they would receive a certain fracture. Certain drugs are helpful in quieting emotional disturbance; but again, there is the question of how long do you allow them to remain in the zombie stage.

> There is real live abuse of the elderly and we must do everything we can to stop it; and, there are some problems in taking care of the elderly that must be considered.

The tabloids take an isolated case and exacerbate it to taint the whole industry of elderly care in order to sell papers. I know some dreadful events, but for every one, you can find 100 stories of sacrificial, loving, professional care.

Some Reasons Why the Elderly Are Abused

At Home

❑ The family is not physically, emotionally, or financially capable of arising to the demands of home care.

❑ The family is not adequately trained in necessary skills for caring, for example: cleaning an adult who has little mobility, turning a bed-bound person without causing harm, or even protecting yourself while caring for an adult.

❑ The physical layout of the home can be inappropriate or inadequate for continuous personal care.

❑ Some caregiving households are unstable because of their own problems.

❑ All families suffer from some stress and are fragile. They are not able to cope with any more problems. With an elderly person present, relatively minor problems can reach crisis proportions.

❑ It is a common belief that "all nursing homes are bad"; and that to put our loved ones in a nursing home is to abandon them to a life of abuse. I have found that home care is not necessarily superior or even equal to nursing home care for patients needing high levels of care. Families who avoid placement, while well-meaning, may be intentionally shortchanging their loved ones and themselves.

In an Institution

❑ When a family member is placed in a nursing home and abandoned, that person may get poorer care than the one who has regular visits. No nursing home can afford many complaints about their facilities and care--they will go bankrupt fast.

❑ There are poor adult protection service laws and statutes to deal with mistreatment and to provide help for families.

❑ There are few programs for training professionals in caregiving skills.

❑ Not enough people care what happens.

Some Solutions to the Problems of Elderly Abuse

◆ More publicity is needed about the subject of elder abuse. Greater public awareness can help communities expose mistreatment, establish higher levels of intolerance of abuse, and provide support and assistance to families that need help.

◆ Our legislature needs to be encouraged to make laws and provide supervision to ensure that careproviders don't get greedy and neglectful.

◆ Schools need to be encouraged to establish a department of geriatrics that does research and trains professional caregivers.

◆ People need to be encouraged to make plans for retirement and the possibility of nursing home care. I recommend that more people visit professional care centers; hopefully that will help to upgrade those that need it and encourage those that are doing a commendable job.

◆ We strongly recommend that no institution or home care provider attempt to care for a frail elderly person without some basic caregiving training. Our community colleges could have basic care classes both for home and institutional providers. A large portion of Adult Abuse lies at the door of ignorance.

Offices responsible for adult protective services

Alabama
Department of Pensions and Security
Bureau of Adult Services
64 North Union Street
Montgomery, AL 36130

Alaska
Division of Family and Youth Services
Pouch H-05
Juneau, AK 99811

Arizona
DES Aging and Adult Administration
1400 West Washington
Phoenix, AZ 85007

Arkansas
Adult Protective Services
Donaghey Bldg, Room 1428
Little Rock, AR 72201

California
Department of Social Services
Adult Protective Services
744 P Street
Sacramento, CA 95814

Colorado
State Department of Social Services
Division of Aging and Adult Services
1575 Sherman,
Room 803
Denver, CO 80203

Connecticut
Department on Aging
Department of Human Resources
175 Main Street
Hartford, CT 06106

Delaware
Division on Aging
1901 North DuPont Highway
New Castle, DE 19720

District of Columbia
Adult Protective Services
First and I Sts. S.W.
Room 120
Washington, D.C. 20024

Florida
Aging and Adult Services
1377 Winewood Blvd.
Bldg. 2
Tallahassee, FL 32301

Georgia
Georgia Department of Human Resources
878 Peachtree St. N.E.
Atlanta, GA 30309

Hawaii
Department of Social Services and Housing
P.O. Box 339
Honolulu, HI 96809

Idaho
Division of Welfare
Statehouse
Boise, ID 83720

Illinois
Elder Abuse Demonstration Project
Department on Aging
421 East Capital Avenue
Springfield, IL 62701

Indiana
Commission on Aging & Aged
Graphics Arts Building
215 North Senate Avenue
Indianapolis, IN 46202

Iowa
Bureau of Adult, Children & Family Services
Department of Human Services
Hoover Building, 5th Floor
Des Moines, IA 50319

Kansas
Adult Services Section
State Department of Social Services
Biddle Building, 1st Floor
2700 West 6th Street
Topeka, KS 66006

Kentucky
Commonwealth of Kentucky Cabinet for Human Resources
Department of Social Services
Frankfort, KY 40621

Louisiana
Division of Children, Youth and Family Services
P.O. Box 3318
Baton Rouge, LA 70821

Maine
Maine Department of Human Services
Bureau of Social Services
Division of Adult Services
221 State Street
State House, Station 11
Augusta, ME 04333

Maryland
State Social Services Administration
Adult Protective Services
11 South Street
Baltimore, MD 21212

Massachusetts
Executive Office of Elder Affairs
38 Chauncey Street
Boston, MA 02111

Michigan
Department of Social Services
Bureau of Adult Services
Adult Protective Services Unit

P.O. Box 30337
Lansing, MI 48909

Minnesota
Department of Human Services
Adult Protection
Centennial Office Building
St. Paul, MN 55155

Mississippi
Department of Public Welfare
Social Services Department
P.O. Box 352
Jackson, MS 39205

Missouri
Missouri Division on Aging
P.O. Box 1337
Jefferson City, MO 65102

Nebraska
Division of Social Services
Adult Service Unit
Department of Public Welfare
Lincoln, NE 68509

Nevada
Nevada State Welfare Division
251 Jeanell Drive
Carson City, NV 89710

New Hampshire
Office of Adult and Elderly Services
Division on Human Services
Haven Drive
Concord, NH 03301

New Jersey
Department of Human Services
Division of Youth and Family Services
1 South Montgomery Street
Trenton, NJ 08625

New Mexico
Field Services Bureau
Social Services Division
Human Services Department
P.O. Box 2438
Santa Fe, NM 87503

New York
Department of Social Services
40 North Pearl Street
Albany, NY 12243

North Carolina
Department of Human Resources
Division of Social Services
325 North Salisbury Street
Raleigh, NC 27611

North Dakota
State Office on Aging
State Capital Building
Bismark, ND 58505

Ohio
Bureau of Adult Services
Ohio Department of Public Welfare
Division of Services to Adults and Families
30 East Broad Street
Columbus, OH 43215

Oklahoma
Department of Human Services
Aging Division
Support Services Unit
312 N.E. 28th Street
Oklahoma City, OK 73105

Oregon
Senior Services Division
Program Assistance Section
313 Public Service Building
Salem, OR 97310

Pennsylvania
Department of Public Welfare
P.O. Box 2675
Harrisburg, PA 17105

Rhode Island
Department of Elderly Affairs
79 Washington Street
Providence, RI 02903

South Carolina
Department of Social Services
Adult Protective Services Division
P.O. Box 1520
Columbia, SC 29202

South Dakota
Adult Services and Aging
Department of Social Services
500 North Illinois Avenue
Pierre, SD 57501

Tennessee
Department of Human Services
111 Seventh Avenue North
Nashville, TN 37203

Texas
Department of Human Resources
701 West 51st Street
P.O. Box 2960
Austin, TX 78769

Utah
Division of Aging and Adult Services
150 West North Temple
Room 326
Salt Lake City, UT 84103

Vermont
Department of Health
60 Main Street
Burlington, VT 05401

Virginia
Department of Social Services
8007 Discovery Drive
Richmond, VA 23229

Washington
Department of Social and Health Services
Bureau of Aging, OB-43G
Olympia, WA 98504

West Virginia
Adult Services Program
Division of Social Services
1900 Washington Street, East
Charleston, WV 25305

Wisconsin
Department of Health and Social Services
Division of Community Services
1 West Wilson Street
P.O. Box 7851
Madison, WI 53707

Wyoming
Division of Public Assistance and Social Services
Hathaway Building
Cheyenne, WY 82002

Elder Abuse
In accordance with the Federal Law called the Older American Act, states are required to identify abuse, neglect, or exploitation; and establish procedures for receipt of reports of abuse and referral of complaints to law enforcement, public protection agencies, or other appropriate agencies. Involuntary or coerced participation in the program by alleged victims, abusers, or their household is prohibited.

Check with your state or local Area Agency on Aging (see state listings under the Senior Assistance section, page 24) or the state adult protective offices listed on this page.

To have and to hold...to love and to cherish...

These sentiments reflect the feelings of most people toward marriage, home, and family--but not all. The surprising fact is that a lot of violence, bringing fear and pain, is reported among family members.

For example, about one-quarter of all murders in the United States take place within the family. Surveys of American couples show that 20% to 50% have suffered violence regularly in their marriages. The records indicate that between two and four million incidents of domestic violence occur every single year. Wife abuse is one kind of family violence that probably occurs far more often than most people imagine. The tragedy is that many women suffer this abuse for years without getting help.

What Do We Mean by "Wife Abuse"?

Defining wife abuse or wife battering is not easy. For starters, whom are we thinking of when we use the word "wife"? Actually, any woman who maintains an intimate relationship with a man (her husband, ex-husband, boyfriend, or lover) could become a battered or abused "wife." The words "abused" or "battered" that are used here do not refer to the normal conflict and stress that occur in all close relationships, but rather to the violence that can cause serious injury and death.

In the article,* "Assaults on Women: Rape and Wife-beating," Natalie Jaffe cites a typical description of the kind of physical harm suffered by battered women surveyed in shelters and treatment.

> Most injuries were to the head and neck and, in addition to the bruises, strangle marks, black eyes, and split lips, resulted in eye damage, fractured jaws, broken noses, and permanent hearing loss. Assaults to the trunk of the body were almost as common and produced a broken collarbone, bruised and broken ribs, a fractured tailbone, internal hemorrhaging, and a lacerated liver.

These are serious consequences of serious assaults. Another serious aspect is that once wife beating occurs, it is likely to happen again and again, with violence getting worse over time.

*Public Affairs Pamphlet No. 579. New York: Public Affairs Committee, Inc.

How the Abused Woman Feels

A woman who has been abused over a long period of time is afraid. Not only is she afraid that she, herself, will be seriously hurt, but if she has children, she fears for their safety also. Her feelings of fear link her to all other women, from all classes of society, in similar situations.

Fear might be a woman's first and most immediate feeling during or after a beating, but other negative feelings may surface when she is not in physical danger. The abused woman is apt to develop doubts about herself. She might wonder if she is justified in fearing for her life and calling herself an "abused wife." Most likely, however, a woman who thinks or feels she is being abused, probably is.

Or, she may feel guilty, even though she's done nothing wrong. An abused wife may feel responsible for her husband's violence because in some way she may have provoked him. This has her placing the shame and blame on herself instead of the abuser. The longer she puts up with the abuse and does nothing to avoid or prevent it, the less she likes herself. Along with the feeling of being a failure, both as a woman and in her marriage, may come a real feeling of being trapped and powerless, with no way out.

Why Do Men Abuse Their Wives?

Instances of wife abuse have been on record in the United States since the 1830s, but only every now and then does it arouse public concern. Generally, public opinion supports traditional family relations and male authority.

The battered syndrome is both cause and effect of stereotyped roles and the unequal power relations between men and women. No social class is exempt. Wife abuse occurs in wealthy as well as poor communities--in middle class as well as in working-class families.

Over the years it has been tolerated by those who govern community affairs, the courts, medicine, psychiatry, police, schools, and the church. History shows the helping professions often protected patterns of family authority, unwittingly sanctioning wife abuse rather than condemning it.

Other Factors

Present-day society is one in which violence in the movies, on TV, and in the newspapers is familiar and accepted. Many husbands who abuse their wives have learned that violence, especially against women, is okay. They often were abused themselves as children or saw their mothers abused. The battered wife most likely grew up in a similar environment.

There are other psychological reasons. A wife abuser tends to be filled with anger, resentment, suspicion, and tension. He also, underneath all his aggressive behavior, can be insecure and feel like a loser. He may use violence to give vent to the bad feelings he has about himself or his lot in life. Home is one place he can express those feelings without punishment to himself. If he were angry with his boss and struck him, he would pay the price. But all too often he gets away without penalty when he beats his wife. She becomes the target of his ven-geance, and he gets the satisfaction he's looking for.

What About the Victimized Wife?

If she accepts her husband's traditional male authority, she may be labeled as immature. If she fights back or if she refuses to sleep with him if he's drunk, she might be accused of being hostile, domineering, and masculine. These are complaints of abused women.

Patterns

Familiar patterns of wife abuse often develop in three phases:

❶ the tension-building phase,
❷ the explosion or the actual beating phase, and
❸ the loving phase.

The tension builds over a series of small occurrences such as the wife's request for money, her refusal to do all the household chores without her husband's help, her serving a meal not pleasing to him, or a similar incident. What follows is inevitable. She may become the object of any or all of the following assaults: punching with fists, choking, kicking, knifing, slamming against a wall, throwing to the floor, or shoving down the stairs. Sometimes even threats with a gun have been reported. When the beating is over, the couple moves into the third phase. The batterer feels guilty about what he has done. He is sorry and may become loving toward her. He assures his wife that he will never do anything violent or hurtful to her again. She wants to believe him, hoping that he will change. However, even with professional help, the tension building and the beatings may continue. Some of these men literally beat their wives to death.

Why Do Women Stay?

Women have learned that it may be their own feelings of fear, guilt, or shame that keep them in a relationship that is physically abusive. Often, social and economic pressures compel a woman to stay. Sometimes she stays for lack of somewhere to go for shelter and advice or because she still feels that she loves her husband and that he might change, if only she can "hang in there." Tragically, in most cases, the abuse continues, for in fact her husband's behavior has nothing to do with her actions.

Other reasons for staying with him may seem as compelling. A woman may feel that a divorce is wrong and that she should keep her marriage together at all costs. Perhaps she feels her children need a father. She may be isolated with no outside job and few friends. The friend and relatives she does talk to may give her little support, perhaps because her situation frightens them and they don't want to admit to themselves that such violence could occur. If she confides in a counselor, she may also be encouraged to "save the marriage." And, along with her emotional dependence, she may worry about being able to find a job to support herself and her children. If she has her husband arrested, he may not be able to support her. If she doesn't have him arrested, he may beat her even more severely for trying to leave him. Is there a way out? Most women suffer these attacks for years before they finally find the courage and determination to take steps to keep from being victims of further abuse.

What Can a Battered Woman Do?

The first step for a woman to take is to admit to herself that she is being abused and that she is not being treated fairly. She has the right to feel safe from physical harm, especially in her own home.

This material was written by Lenore Gelg, staff writer, in consultation with the National Institute of Mental Health scientists.

Emergency Action

A woman can do a number of things to protect herself. She can hide extra money, car keys, and important documents somewhere safe so that she can get to them in a hurry. The phone numbers of the police department should be handy. She should have a place to go, such as an emergency shelter, a social service agency, or the home of a trusted friend or relative.

During an actual attack, the woman should defend herself as best she can. As soon as she is able, she should call the police and get their names and badge numbers in case she needs a record of the attack. Most importantly, she should leave the house and take her children with her. She may need medical attention, too, because she might be hurt more severely than she realizes. Having a record of her injuries, including photographs, can protect her legally should she decide to press charges.

Long-Range Plans

A woman needs to talk to people who can help. Good friends can lend support and guidance. Organizations that are devoted to women's concerns and not bound by society's traditions can assist her. They might help her explore options in new ways. Emergency shelters for women, hotlines, women's organizations, social service agencies, community mental health centers, and hospital emergency rooms are all possible sources of support.

The following organizations have information about state contacts and shelters where a battered woman can go for help:

✱ Center for Women Policy Studies
2000 P Street, N.W., #508
Washington, D.C. 20036
(202) 872-1770

✱ National Coalition Against Domestic Violence
1728 N Street, N.W.
Washington, D.C. 20036

Above all, a woman has to determine her own best course of action. Positive measures such as confiding in a relative, talking seriously with a friend, or consulting with a counselor are steps in the right direction. With the help of informal and formal help sources, including individual counseling for the husband as well as herself, a woman may be able to bring an end to the problem.

It has been observed that abused women need to develop better feelings about themselves--that is, change their self-image. In a book, Stopping Wife Abuse, by Jennifer Baker Fleming, the following attitudes are suggested as positive and useful:

❤ I am not to blame for being beaten and abused.
❤ I am not the cause of another's violent behavior.
❤ I do not like it or want it.
❤ I do not have to take it.
❤ I am an important human being.
❤ I am a worthwhile woman.
❤ I deserve to be treated with respect.
❤ I do have power over my own life.
❤ I can use my power to take good care of myself.
❤ I can decide for myself what is best for me.
❤ I can make changes in my life if I want to.
❤ I am not alone; I can ask others to help me.
❤ I am worth working for and changing for.
❤ I deserve to make my own life safe and happy.

Prevention

Since there is no one cause of wife abuse, there is no easy way to prevent it. Until society rejects its tolerance and acceptance of violence for resolving conflict and expressing anger, meaningful changes in family relationships will not occur. Prevention starts with people changing their attitudes toward violence and women. No one deserves to be beaten or physically threatened, no matter what the excuse. It is a crime to beat anyone--a stranger, a friend, or your wife--and the law should be enforced. The tolerance of family violence as a way of life in one generation encourages family violence in another generation. Since the wife abuser didn't learn to deal with anger appropriately as a child, he handles his frustrations through aggression. He needs to know that it's human to feel anger, but inhuman to release those feelings by beating others. By learning to deal with these emotions through acceptable behavior, he can gain respect for himself and others. It's another positive step toward developing mutual respect in the husband/wife relationship where each sees the other as a worthy human being.

Tips for the senior driver

AUTO-RELATED ACCIDENTS--are the most common cause of accidental death among the 65 to 74 age group, and the second most common cause among older persons in general. Today, drivers 65 and older have higher crash rates per mile than all other groups except teenagers. Your ability to drive may be impaired by such age-related changes as: increased sensitivity to glare, poorer adaptation to dark, diminished coordination, slower reaction time, physical changes in your hearing and eyesight, other sensory impairments, and denial of illness that can translate into fender-benders and catastrophes.

But while we're losing our youth, we're still wild about our wheels. As long as our physical and visual capabilities permit, we can continue to drive. Just because you have a driver's license doesn't always mean you are able to or should be driving. For your safety and that of others, as you get older you will need to pay special attention to your limitations. New laws aimed at older drivers are calling for mandatory in-person license renewal, reexamination for degenerative medical conditions, impairment revocation of licenses, and driving restrictions to specified areas. Here are some tips to compensate for your limitations:

CHANGE YOUR DRIVING HABITS--If you're at all uneasy on the road, think about changing how, when, and where you drive. Try driving fewer miles, less often, and more slowly. Plan your trips more carefully by calling ahead. Drive less at night, during rush hours, and in the winter.

CONSIDER A REFRESHER COURSE-- In many communities, organizations offer driver education courses for older people. The 55 Alive/Mature Driving program, created by the American Association of Retired Persons (AARP), is designed to help people over 50 to improve their driving skills and prevent traffic accidents. Two 4-hour classes emphasize safety on the road and promote awareness of the physical changes that occur around the age of 55. Even if you're a good driver, a course can teach you defensive driving habits and ways to protect yourself from others who are not as careful on the road. If you take the course ask your insurance company for a 5% discount--some give it.

WEAR YOUR SEAT BELT--when riding in a car to prevent a crippling injury or death in the event of a crash. Older drivers have fewer accidents per mile driven, but they are more likely to be injured or killed due to more fragile bones and a reduced ability to withstand the trauma of an accident. Safety belts distribute the full force of the impact across the strongest parts of your body, help prevent you from hitting the steering wheel, the windows, or the dash, and help to keep you from being thrown from the vehicle. Avoid excessive slack in the belt and position it over the shoulder, across the chest, and low on the lap. And remember, in 40 states it is not only a good idea to use safety belts, it is the law.

CHECK YOUR EYESIGHT AND HEARING--Physical changes in eyesight and hearing occur as we get older and can affect our driving ability. Over one third of all older persons experience hearing loss that make it more difficult to hear in busy traffic. Many different visual problems can occur such as:

* You may become more sensitive to glare, and adapt more slowly to darkness.
* You may have more difficulty changing focus from distant to near objects and vice versa.
* You may need more light to see well.
* You may be more susceptible to headlight glare and bright sunlight.
* Your reaction time will slow.
* Your ability to see to the side while looking ahead (peripheral awareness) may diminish.
* Your ability to quickly and accurately distinguish colors may diminish. It makes a major difference at a traffic light.
* You may experience a decrease in sharpness of vision under certain lighting conditions.

VISUAL DRIVING TIPS--of importance.
* Have proper glasses for day and night driving (there may be a difference).
* Do not wear sunglasses or tinted lenses for night driving.
* In sunlight, wear good quality sunglasses.
* Avoid driving at dusk or at night.
* Keep glasses clean.
* Avoid frames with wide side (temple) pieces, as they block side vision.
* Get the big picture when driving. Watch the road ahead and check either side for vehicles, children, animals, or hazards. Keep your head and eyes moving. Glance frequently in the rearview mirror and at the instrument panel.
* Keep pace with average traffic flow.
* Choose a car with a clear windshield. A tinted one can reduce the amount of light entering the eye. It is better to have a clear windshield and wear good sunglasses in bright sunlight.
* Keep headlights properly adjusted.
* Keep headlights, taillights, and windshield (both inside and out) clean as well as side windows.

DRUGS AND DRIVING--Many drugs can influence your driving vision. These include prescription cold and sinus remedies, sleeping pills, tranquilizers, sedatives, pain killers, and of course, prescription drugs for any conditions. Even aspirin, when used extensively, can adversely influence vision. Whatever the drug, know its side effects before getting behind the wheel.

ON PUBLIC TRANSPORTATION--If you ride on a bus or street car:
* Remain alert and brace yourself when a bus is slowing down or turning.
* Watch for slippery pavement and other hazards when entering or leaving a vehicle.
* Have fare ready to prevent losing your balance while fumbling for change.
* Do not carry too many packages, and leave one hand free to grasp railings.
* Allow extra time to cross streets, especially in bad weather.
* At night wear light-colored or fluorescent clothing and carry a flashlight.

> **If you be a traveler, have always two bags very full, that is one of patience and the other of money.**
> - John Florio (1553-1625)

Famous quotations--cannon fodder for the sex wars

A woman is as old as she looks before breakfast. - Edgar Watson Howe (probably no longer living)

Nothing upsets a woman more than somebody getting married that she didn't even know had a beau. - Kin Hubbard

A woman does not spend all of her time buying things; she spends part of it taking them back. - Edgar Watson Howe

Not every woman in old slippers can manage to look like Cinderella. - Don Marquis

What passes for woman's intuition is often nothing more than man's transparency. - George Jean Nathan

The whole thing about women is, they lust to be misunderstood. - Will Rogers

As long as a woman can look ten years younger than her own daughter, she is perfectly satisfied. - Oscar Wilde

A woman will doubt everything you say except it be compliments to herself. - Elbert Hubbard

God created man before he created woman, because he didn't want any advice.

Women want mediocre men, and men are working hard to be as mediocre as possible. - Margaret Mead

The ages of woman:
In her infancy...she needs love and care.
In her childhood...she wants fun.
In her twenties...she wants romance.
In her thirties...she wants admiration.
In her forties...she wants sympathy.
In her fifties...she wants cash.

Man has his will, but woman has her way. - Oliver Wendell Holmes, Sr.

Only good girls keep diaries. Bad girls don't have the time. - Tallulah Bankhead

Woman will be the last thing civilized by man. - George Meredith

When you got the personality, you don't need the nudity. - Mae West

At first a woman doesn't want anything but a husband, but just as soon as she gets one, she wants everything else in the world. - Elbert Hubbard

An occasional lucky guess as to what makes a wife tick is the best a man can hope for. Even then no sooner has he learned to cope with the tick than she tocks. - Ogden Nash

Wives are young men's mistresses, companions for middle age, and old men's nurses. - Francis Bacon

A man does not buy his wife a fur coat to keep her warm, but to keep her pleasant. - Sir Seymour Hicks

There's nothing like a good dose of another woman to make a man appreciate his wife. - Clare Booth Luce

To keep your wife happy--First, let her think she is having her way. Second, let her have it.

A perfect wife is one who doesn't expect a perfect husband.

Never eat at a place called Mom's. Never play cards with a man called Doc. And never lie down with a woman who's got more troubles than you. - Nelson Algren

A psychiatrist is a fellow who asks you a lot of expensive questions your wife asks you for nothing. - Joey Adams

The most popular labor-saving device today is still a husband with money. - Joey Adams

Be kind to your mother-in-law but pay for her board at some good hotel. - Josh Billings

A mother takes twenty years to make a man of her boy, and another woman makes a fool out of him in twenty minutes. - Robert Frost (1874)

Even the wisest men make fools of themselves about women, and even the most foolish women are wise about men. - Theodor Reik

He was every other inch a gentleman. - Rebecca West (1892)

Women are as old as they feel--and men are old when they lose their feelings. - Mae West

Happiness? A good cigar, a good meal, a good cigar and a good woman--or a bad woman; it depends on how much happiness you can handle. - George Burns

Disguise our bondage as we will, tis woman, woman, rules us still. - Thomas Moore (1779)

I'm not denyin' the women are foolish: God almighty made em to match the men. - George Eliot (1819)

Man weeps to think that he will die so soon; woman, that she was born so long ago. - H. L. Mencken (1950)

Great men are but life-sized. Most of them, indeed, are rather short. - Max Beerbohm (1872)

If men knew how women pass the time when they are alone, they'd never marry. - O. Henry (1862)

Women like silent men. They think they're listening. - Marcel Achard (1899)

Men look themselves in the mirrors. Women look for themselves. - Elisa Meldicott (1850)

If you never want to see a man again, say, "I love you. I want to marry you. I want to have children"--they leave skid marks. - Rita Rudner (1950)

It has been my experience that folks who have no vices have very few virtues. - Abraham Lincoln

Father told me that if I ever met a lady in a dress like yours, I must look her straight in the eyes. - Prince Charles

Give a man a free hand and he'll run it all over you. - Mae West

It is difficulties that show what men are. - Epictetus (50-138 A.D.)

Maids want nothing but husbands, and when they have them, they want everything. - Shakespeare (1564-1616)

Here are laws and regulations that help protect you

Consumers' rights are protected by federal and state laws and regulations covering many services offered by financial institutions. With the advent of more and more financial institutional failures individuals need to have more knowledge about their rights. This article will help you refer complaints to the proper regulatory agency.

FEDERAL LAWS

Adjustable-Rate Mortgage Loans--are covered by regulations that require, at a minimum, disclosure of the circumstances under which the rate may increase, any limitations on the increase, the effects of the increase, and an example of the payment terms that would result from an increase.

Consumer Leasing Act--requires disclosure of information that helps consumers compare the cost and terms of various leases and the cost and terms of buying on credit versus cash. The Act does not apply to real estate leases or to leases of four months or less.

Credit Practices Rule--prohibits lenders from using certain remedies, such as confessions of judgment; wage assignments; and nonpossessory, nonpurchase money; security interests in household goods. The rule also prohibits lenders from misrepresenting a cosigner's liability and requires that lenders provide cosigners with a notice explaining their credit obligation as a cosigner. It also prohibits pyramiding of late charges.

Electronic Fund Transfer Act--provides consumer protection for all transactions using a debit card or electronic means to debit or credit an account. It also limits a consumer's liability for unauthorized electronic fund transfers.

Equal Credit Opportunity Act--prohibits discrimination against an applicant for credit because of age, sex, marital status, religion, race, color, national origin, or receipt of public assistance. It also prohibits discrimination because of good faith exercise of any right under the federal consumer credit laws. If a consumer has been denied credit, the law requires notification of the denial in writing. The consumer may request, within 60 days, that the reason for denial be provided in writing.

Expedited Funds Availability Act--requires all banks, savings and loan associations, savings banks, and credit unions to make funds deposited into checking, share draft, and NOW accounts available according to specified time schedules and to disclose their available funds policies to their customers. The law does not require an institution to delay the customer's use of deposited funds but instead limits how long any delay must last. The regulation also establishes rules designed to speed the return of unpaid checks.

Fair Credit and Charge Card Disclosure Act--requires new disclosures on credit and charge cards, whether issued by financial institutions, retail stores, or private companies. Information such as APR's, annual fees, and grace periods must be provided in tabular form along with applications and preapproved solicitations for cards. The regulations also require card issuers that impose an annual fee to provide disclosures before annual renewal. Card issuers that offer credit insurance must inform customers of any increase in rate or substantial decrease in coverage should the issuer decide to change insurance providers.

Fair Credit Billing Act--establishes procedures for the prompt correction of errors on open-end credit accounts. It also protects a customer's credit rating while the consumer is settling a dispute.

Fair Credit Reporting Act--establishes procedures for correcting mistakes on a person's credit record and requires that a consumer's record only be provided for legitimate business needs. It also requires that the record be kept confidential. A credit record may be retained 7 years for judgments, liens, suits, and other adverse information except for bankruptcies, which may be retained for 10 years. If a consumer has been denied credit, a cost-free credit report may be requested within 30 days of denial.

Fair Debt Collection Practices Act--is designed to eliminate abusive, deceptive, and unfair debt collection practices. It applies to third-party debt collectors or those who use a name other than their own in collecting consumer debts. Very few commercial banks, savings and loan associations, savings banks, or credit unions are covered by this Act, since they usually collect only their own debts. Complaints concerning debt collection practices should generally be filed with the Federal Trade Commission.

Fair Housing Act--prohibits discrimination on the basis of race, color, sex, religion, handicap, familiar status, or national origin in the financing, sale, or rental of housing.

The Federal Trade Commission Act--requires federal financial regulatory agencies to maintain a consumer affairs division to assist in resolving consumer complaints against institutions they supervise. This assistance is given to help get necessary information to consumers about problems they are having in order to address complaints concerning acts or practices that may be unfair or deceptive.

Home Equity Loan Consumer Protection Act--requires lenders to disclose terms, rates, and conditions (APR's, miscellaneous charges, payment terms, and information about variable rate features) for home equity lines of credit with the applications and before the first transaction under the home equity plan. If the disclosed terms change, the consumer can refuse to open the plan and is entitled to a refund of fees paid in connection with the application. The Act also limits the circumstances under which creditors may terminate or change the terms of a home equity plan after it is opened.

Home Mortgage Disclosure Act (HMDA)--requires certain lending institutions to report annually on their originations of home purchase and home improvement loans as well as applications for such loans. The type of loan, location of the property, race or national origin, sex and income of the applicant or borrower are reported. Institutions are required to make information regarding their lending available to the public and must post a notice of availability in their public lobby. This information can help the public determine how well institutions are serving the housing credit needs of their neighborhoods and communities.

National Flood Insurance Act--is available to any property holder whose local community participates in the national program by adopting and enforcing flood plain management. Federally regulated lenders are required to compel borrowers to purchase flood insurance in certain designated areas. Lenders also must disclose to borrowers if their structure is located in a flood hazard area.

Real Estate Settlement Procedures Act--requires that a consumer be given advance information about the services and costs involved in the closing of a residential mortgage. It also limits the amount that can be collected for mortgage escrow.

Right to Financial Privacy Act--provides that customers of financial institutions have a right to expect that their financial activities will have a reasonable amount of privacy from federal government scrutiny. The Act establishes specific procedures and

A bargain is something you have to find a use for once you buy it.

- Benjamin Franklin

exemptions concerning the release of the financial records of customers and imposes limitations on and requirements of financial institutions prior to the release of such information to the federal government.

Savings and Time Deposits--are covered by regulations that prohibit inaccurate or misleading advertising.

Truth in Lending Act--requires disclosure of the "finance charge" and the "annual percentage rate"--and certain other costs and terms of credit--so that a consumer can compare the price of credit from different sources. It also limits liability on lost or stolen credit cards.

STATE LAWS

Many state laws also provide rights and remedies in consumer financial transactions. Unless a state law conflicts with a particular federal law, the state law usually will apply. Some states have usury laws that establish maximum rates of interest that creditors can charge for loans or credit sales. The maximum interest rates vary from state to state and depend upon the type of credit transaction involved.

COMPLAINT FILING PROCESS

If a consumer has a complaint against a financial institution, the first step is to contact an officer of the institution and attempt to resolve the complaint directly. Financial institutions value their customers and most will be helpful. If the consumer is unable to resolve the complaint directly, the financial institution's regulatory agency may be contacted for assistance.

The agency will usually acknowledge receipt of a complaint letter within a few days. If the letter is referred to another agency, the consumer will be advised of this fact. When the appropriate agency investigates the complaint the financial institution may be given a copy of the complaint letter.

The complaint should be submitted in writing and should include the following:

* Complainant's name, address, phone;
* Institution's name and address;
* Type of account involved in the complaint--checking, savings, or loan--and account numbers, if applicable;
* Description of the complaint, including specific dates and the institution's actions (copies of pertinent information or correspondence are also helpful);
* Date of contact and names of individu-

als contacted at the institution with their responses; and
* Complainant's signature and the date the complaint is being submitted to the regulatory agency.

The regulatory agency will be able to help resolve the complaint if the financial institution has violated a banking law or regulation. They may not be able to help when the consumer is not satisfied with an institution's policy or practices and no law or regulation was violated. Additionally, the regulatory agencies do not resolve factual or most contractual disputes.

The following information will help in determining which agency to contact. Institutions that are **"Federally Insured"** will have a sign prominently displayed saying:

Deposits Federally Insured to $100,000-- Backed by the Full Faith and Credit of the United States Government.

National Bank--The word "National" appears in the bank's name, or the initials N.A. appear after the bank's name. Agency to contact: Comptroller of the Currency.

State-Chartered Bank, Member of the Federal Reserve System--A sign will be prominently displayed on the door of the bank or in the lobby saying "Member, Federal Reserve System." Also a "Federally Insured" sign. Agencies to contact: Federal Reserve Board for federal laws; State Banking Department for state laws.

State Non-Member Bank or State-Chartered Savings Bank, Federally Insured--Institution will have "Federally Insured" sign. Agencies to contact: Federal Deposit Insurance Corporation for federal laws; State Banking Department for state laws.

Federal Savings & Loan Association, Federal Savings Association, or Federal Savings Bank, Federally Insured--Generally, the word "Federal" appears in the name or its name includes initials such as "FA" (for federal savings and loan association) or "FSB" (for federal savings bank). Institution will also have the "Federally Insured" sign. Agency to contact: Office of Thrift Supervision.

State-Chartered Federally Insured Savings Institution--Institution will have the "Federally Insured" sign. Agency to contact: Office of Thrift Supervision.

State-Chartered Banks or Savings Institutions without Federal Deposit Insurance--No "Federally Insured" or other signs mentioned above. Agencies to contact: State

Banking Department for state laws; Federal Trade Commission for federal laws.

Federally Chartered Credit Union--The term "Federal Credit Union" appears in the name of the credit union. Agency to contact: National Credit Union Administration.

State-Chartered, Federally Insured Credit Union--A sign will be displayed by stations or windows where deposits are accepted indicating that deposits are insured by NCUA. The term "Federal Credit Union" does not appear in the name. Agencies to contact: State Agency that regulates credit unions or the Federal Trade Commission.

State-Chartered Credit Unions without Federal Insurance--The term "Federal Credit Union" does not appear in the name. Agencies to contact: State agencies that regulate credit unions or the Federal Trade Commission.

Complaints should be mailed to the appropriate agency with copies of all relevant documents. Original documents or currency should not be sent. Addresses for the federal agencies are:

Board of Governors of the
Federal Reserve System
Division of Consumer & Community
Affairs
20th & Constitution Avenue, N.W.
Washington, D.C. 20551

Federal Deposit Insurance Corporation
Office of Consumer Affairs
550 Seventeenth Street, N.W.
Washington, D.C. 20429

Office of Thrift Supervision
Consumer Affairs
1700 G Street, N.W.
Washington, D.C. 20552

National Credit Union Administration
1776 G Street, N.W.
Washington, D.C. 20456

Office of the Comptroller of the Currency
Consumer Activities Division
490 L'Enfant Plaza, S.W.
Washington, D.C. 20219

Federal Trade Commission
Bureau of Consumer Protection
Office of Credit Practices
Washington, D.C. 20580

Credit and older persons

Securing credit is as important for older Americans as it is for younger ones. Yet, older consumers and particularly older women may find they have special problems with credit.

For example, if you have paid with cash all your life, you may find it difficult to open a credit account, because you have "no credit history." If you now are living on a lower salary or pension, you may find it harder to obtain a loan because you have "insufficient income." Or, if your spouse dies, you may find that creditors try to close credit accounts that you and your spouse once shared.

Under the federal Equal Credit Opportunity Act (ECOA), it is against the law for a creditor to deny you credit or terminate existing credit simply because of your age.

APPLYING FOR CREDIT--used to mean asking a neighborhood banker or tradesperson for a loan. Now, with national credit cards and computerized applications, the day of personal evaluations may be over. Instead, computer evaluations look at, among other things, your income, your past payment records, your credit cards, and your outstanding balances. Paying in cash and in full may be sound financial advice, but will not give you a history on which to get credit.

When you apply for credit or a loan, one major indicator of your ability to repay is your current income. If you are retired or employed part-time, this may be of some concern. But creditors must consider types of income that are likely to be received by older Americans. These include not only a salary from a job, but also income from Social Security, pensions, and other retirement benefits.

In addition, you may want to inform creditors about other assets or sources of income, such as your home, other real estate, savings and checking accounts, money market funds, certificates of deposits, and stocks and bonds.

If you are 62 or over, you have certain other protections when you apply for credit. You cannot be denied credit because of your age

or the fact that you cannot obtain credit-related insurance because of your age. Credit-related insurance pays off the creditor if you should die or become disabled. However, a creditor can consider your age if:
* It favors applicants who are 62 or over.
* It uses your age to determine other aspects of creditworthiness. (For example, a creditor could use your age to see if your income might change because you are at the retirement age.)

CHECK YOUR CREDIT HISTORY--When you apply for credit, a creditor will often check your credit history by contacting a credit bureau. If you want to know what is in your credit file, contact the local credit bureaus that have your file. (Credit bureaus can be found in the yellow pages under the headings "Credit" and "Credit Rating and Reporting Agencies.") They will tell you what information is in your file and may give you a copy of your credit report. Credit bureaus may charge a small fee for this.

You may find that your credit file does not list all of your credit accounts. This is because not all creditors report to credit bureaus. You can request, however, that additional accounts be reported to your file. Credit bureaus, though, may charge a fee for this service.

If you move, request that the credit bureau in your new location transfer your credit file from your previous location. Most credit bureaus are willing to share this information.

If you are a woman, you may find credit information from older accounts shared with your spouse reported only in your husband's name. For these existing accounts, creditors must report the credit history in the name of both husband and wife within 90 days of your written request to do so. Credit information about new accounts should be reported in your name and your spouse's. If it is not, you can write to the creditor and request that the account be reported in both names.

ESTABLISHING A CREDIT HISTORY-- If you are denied a loan or credit card because you have no credit history, you may want to establish one. The best way to do this is to borrow money or use a credit card and make payments regularly. For example, you could apply for a small line of credit from your bank or for a credit card from a local department store. Local creditors that know you usually are more inclined to give you credit.

Of course, you will want to give these creditors your best financial references. Make sure the creditor you open an account with reports your credit history to a credit bureau.

IF A SPOUSE SHOULD DIE--Under ECOA, a creditor cannot automatically close or change the terms of a joint account solely because of the death of your spouse. (A "joint account" is one for which both spouses applied and signed the credit agreement.) In some instances, though, a creditor may ask you to update your application or reapply. This can happen if the initial acceptance was based on all or part of your spouse's income and if the creditor has reason to suspect your income is inadequate to support the credit line.

After you submit a reapplication, the creditor will determine whether to continue to extend you credit or change your credit limits. While your application is being reviewed, the creditor must let you use the account without new restriction. Within 30 days of receiving a completed application, the creditor must give you a written response on your application. If your application is turned down, you must be given specific reasons for denial.

All these protections regarding closing or changing the terms of an account also apply when you retire, reach a certain age, or change your name or marital status.

WHAT KIND OF ACCOUNT DO YOU HAVE?--To ensure that you are protected if a spouse should die, it is important to know what kind of credit accounts you have. For example, there are three basic kinds of credit accounts. They are:

⚙ An **individual account**, where the charge is opened in one person's name and is based only on that person's income and assets.

⚙ A **joint account**, where the charge is opened in two people's names, often a husband and wife, and is based on the income and assets from both or either person, and where both people are contractually liable for any debts because they signed the credit application.

⚙ A **user account**, where two people's names may appear on a charge card, but the account is based on the income and assets of just one of those people, who also is the only one legally responsible for any debts.

> **Only a "joint account"
> gives you the protections
> against closing
> the account
> should your
> spouse die;
> a user account does not!**

If you and your spouse share a credit account, only a joint account gives you the protections against closing the account should your spouse die; a user account does not. If you combine your own and your spouse's financial resources to apply for a credit account, make sure you are opening a joint account and not a user account, where your name simply appears on the credit card.

To find out what kind of account you have, check the application to see if you applied for credit as "joint applicants" or ask your creditor. That way, your credit status would be protected in the event of your spouse's death.

If you are concerned about your credit status if your spouse should die, you may want to try--if you have enough income and assets on your own--to open one or more individual accounts in your own name. Then your credit status would remain unaffected in the event of your spouse's death.

When you are applying for individual credit, you should ask the creditor to consider the credit history of accounts that are reported in your spouse's or former spouse's name only, as well as those that are in your name. The creditor must consider this information if you can show that it reflects on your ability to manage credit. For example, you may be able to show through canceled checks that you made payments on an account, even though it was listed in your spouse's name only.

IF YOU ARE DENIED CREDIT--While the ECOA gives you certain rights, it does not guarantee that you will be granted credit. Creditors are the ones who make that decision. But if you are ever denied credit, first make your request for reasons for denial. It may have been an error or the computer system may not have evaluated all relevant information.

You can always appeal the denial. And, you might be able to negotiate a compromise with the creditor. If, for example, at the age of 70, you apply for a 30-year mortgage, a lender might be concerned about your ability to repay the loan. However, if you applied for a 15-year mortgage, increased your down payment, or did both, you might satisfy the creditor's concerns.

If you believe you have been discriminated against, however, you may want to write to the federal agency that regulates that particular creditor. You should be able to find the name and address of this federal agency in the letter turning down your request for credit.

If you do write, try to remember all the facts including any oral statements or discussions. Keep copies of all documents and submit this information along with a letter of explanation to the appropriate federal agency or, if you wish, to an attorney.

FOR MORE INFORMATION--If you have questions about the Equal Credit Opportunity Act or your credit rights, write: ECOA, Public Reference, Federal Trade Commission, Washington, D.C. 20580. Although the FTC generally does not intervene in individual disputes, the information you provide may indicate a pattern or practice that requires action by the Commission.

SOLVING CREDIT PROBLEMS--If you are having problems getting credit or paying your monthly bills, you may be tempted to turn to businesses that advertise quick and easy solutions to credit problems. Such businesses may offer debt consolidation loans, debt counseling, or debt reorganization plans that are "guaranteed" to stop creditors' collection efforts. Before signing up with such a business, investigate it thoroughly. Check it out with the Better Business Bureau. But do not be misled. There are no instant solutions.

Creditors are reluctant to grant credit to those who have not established a "track record" with other creditors first and most will not extend credit to those with a history of delinquent payments, repossession, judgments, or bankruptcy. The fact is that all legitimate creditors want to know whether you are likely to be a good credit risk. Promises to "repair" or "clean up" a bad credit history can almost never be kept.

A sudden illness or loss of a spouse may make it impossible for you to pay your bills on time. Whatever your situation, if you find that you cannot make your payments, contact your creditors at once. Try to work out a modified payment plan with your creditors that reduces your payments to a more manageable level. If you have paid promptly in the past, they may be willing to work with you. Do not wait until your account is turned over to a debt collector. At that point, the creditor has given up on you.

WHERE TO FIND LOW-COST HELP--
If you need help in dealing with your debts, you may want to contact a Consumer Credit Counseling Service (CCCS). This is a non-profit organization with more than 200 offices located in 44 states. CCCS counselors will try to arrange a repayment plan that is acceptable to you and your creditors. They will also help you set up a realistic budget and plan future expenses. These services are offered at little or no charge to you.

You can find the CCCS office nearest you by contacting:
National Foundation for Consumer Credit
8701 Georgia Avenue, Suite 601
Silver Springs, MD 20910
(301)589-5600

Ordering merchandise by mail

Ordering merchandise by mail can be a convenient way to save time, energy, and sometimes money. It also is a way to buy an article you just cannot find locally. But if your merchandise arrives late or not at all, you need to know your rights.

THE MAIL ORDER MERCHANDISE RULE--The Federal Trade Commission has a rule to protect consumers who shop by mail. According to this rule:

✻ The seller must ship your order when promised.

✻ If no specific shipment or delivery time is promised, the seller must ship your merchandise no later than 30 days after receiving your order.

✻ If the seller is unable to ship your order when promised (or within the 30-day limit), you have a right to cancel your order and get a prompt refund.

HOW THE RULE WORKS--If the promised shipping date or the 30-day period cannot be met, the seller must send you an "option notice." This notice tells you the new shipping date, and gives you the option of either canceling your order and getting a full refund or agreeing to a new shipping date. Instructions on how to cancel your order must be included in this notice. The seller also must provide a free way for you to reply.

If you agree to the delay date given in the first notice, but the seller cannot meet the new shipping date, the seller must send you a second option notice. Your order will be canceled automatically unless you sign your consent on the second notice and return it to the seller.

REFUNDS--If a prepaid order is canceled, the seller must mail your refund within seven business days. If you charged your purchase, the seller must adjust your account within one billing period.

EXCEPTIONS--Some exceptions to this rule are: (1) The rule does not apply to mail order photo-finishing, (2) magazine subscriptions and other serial deliveries (except for the initial shipment), (3) seeds and plants, (4) COD orders, or (5) credit orders where the 30-day shipping requirement applies and your account is not charged before the merchandise is mailed.

PROTECT YOURSELF--Remember that ordering through the mail is different from shopping in a store--you cannot see the product or its labels until after you have received it. If problems arise, you must deal with a distant seller. Whenever you shop by mail, take these precautions:

❶ Read the product description carefully. Make sure the product is what you want--sometimes pictures of products are misleading. Be suspicious of exaggerated product claims or very low prices. When you compare prices be sure to include all shipping and handling charges.

❷ If possible, investigate the seller's claims. Find out if the product will do what the ads say.

❸ If you have any doubts about the company, check with the U.S. Postal Service, your state or local consumer protection agency, or the Better Business Bureau.

❹ Place your order at least 4 weeks before you want the merchandise. Note the promised delivery or shipment date. Order plenty of time before holidays so you will not be disappointed.

❺ Look for the firm's return policy. If it is not stated, ask before you order. For example, does the company pay charges for shipping and return?

❻ Complete the order form as directed. If you leave out information (such as your full address or item details), your order may be delayed or canceled. The delivery time promised in the ad or the 30-day period does not begin until the seller receives a properly completed order.

❼ Keep a complete record of your order including the company's name, address, and telephone number, the price of the items ordered, any handling or other charges, the original ad, the date you mailed (or telephoned) in the order, and the method of payment. Keep copies of canceled checks and/or statements.

❽ Never send cash through the mail. Pay by check, money order, or credit card.

❾ If you order by mail, your order should be shipped within 30 days after the company receives your complete order, unless another period is agreed upon when placing the order or stated in the advertisement. If your order is delayed, a notice of delay should be sent to you within the promised shipping period along with an option to cancel the order.

❿ Whenever your order involves a large amount of money, always check the company and its reputation before buying.

WHAT TO DO IF YOU HAVE A PROBLEM--If you have a complaint against a mail order company, your first step should be to write the company directly and describe the problem. If you cannot resolve your problem, you can:

✻ Call your local or state consumer protection office. They may be able to help you.

✻ Ask for the assistance of the state or local consumer protection agency located nearest the company.

✻ Call your local postmaster. Ask for the name and address of the appropriate postal "Inspector-in-Charge." That person may be able to resolve your dispute.

✻ Contact the book, magazine, or newspaper publisher that carried the advertisement. Publishers often try to resolve problems between their readers and their advertisers.

✻ Contact the Direct Marketing Association. This industry group may be able to help. Their address is: 6 East 43rd St., New York, NY 10017.

HELP SOLVE THE PROBLEM--Send copies of your complaint to the Federal Trade Commission, Washington, D.C. 20580.

900  Numbers

The 900 number is a new twist in telemarketing--where you may pay for the sales pitch, along with the telephone call.

By dialing a 900 telephone number, you can: order products, hear Santa tell a story, vote in an opinion poll, get financial tips, talk to a willing stranger, and more. To do these things, you pay a flat fee for the entire call or for each minute you stay on the phone.

If you know exactly what you are getting and how much you'll be charged, 900 numbers can be a perfectly good way to do business or get information. But, the Federal Trade Commission (FTC) is investigating complaints that some consumers have been charged excessively for 900-number services or have not received the services advertised.

If you are a victim of a 900-number scam, know that the phone company generally won't disconnect your phone because of failure to pay a disputed 900-number charge. In addition, you may be protected under the Fair Debt Collection Practices Act if a 900-number information provider tries to collect for a 900-number charge you dispute.

What You Need to Watch Out For

Long-distance 900 numbers, as well as local "976" and long-distance "700" exchanges, are used in many ways. Your best protection against problems may be to watch out for appeals that:

■ **Fail to disclose any costs upfront.** Some scams entice you to call a 900 number without first telling you how much you will be charged for the call.

■ **Make it difficult to find out total costs.** Some 900-number scams may disclose a cost per minute, but you must listen for many minutes to hear all the information. Other 900 services use announcers who speak so quickly that you need to call back to understand the message. Some computer-generated calls disclose 900-number costs only at the end of long-winded promotions for "free" gifts. With these, people may hang up before realizing there's a charge for dialing the 900 number to get their "free" gift.

■ **Entice you to call for bogus products or services.** Some scams promote 900 numbers for job or housing information.

Once you place--and pay for--the call, you are told that the job or house is already taken. Other scams involve pitches for "gold" credit cards. With these, television, newspaper, or telephone ads promoting the scam may reveal the cost of making the 900 call. Unfortunately, only after you place the call are you told about additional charges and limitations on using the card.

■ **Pitch products or services to children and teenagers.** Some television promotions encourage children to call 900 numbers for "free" gifts or stories. Teenagers may call 900-number "talklines" to chat with other teens, usually at a cost-per-minute charge. Children may take these calls without telling their parents or understanding that the phone calls cost money. Parents have received phone bills for thousands of dollars.

What You Can Do to Protect Yourself

900-number scams are constantly changing. In general, you can protect yourself if you:

✳ *Deal only* with reputable companies. You may see well-known companies or organizations sponsor such 900-number services as opinion surveys or sports information. The costs, usually low, are stated up front. If you are interested in these services and are willing to pay for them, these are usually legitimate 900-number operations to call.

✳ *Know precisely* what the 900 call will cost before you make the call. Companies should state costs up front as flat rates, or if the cost is per minute, the maximum number of minutes for the call. Unfortunately, even with this information, you may still pay to hear sales pitches for bogus products or services.

✳ *Think twice* before calling a 900 number for a "free" gift. You may see television ads or receive postcards or phone calls urging you to call 900 numbers for "free" prizes. Know that you pay for those "free" gifts when you make the 900-number call.

✳ *Don't confuse* 900 numbers with toll-free 800 numbers. You pay for the 900-number call. The company pays for the 800-number call.

✳ *Check* your phone bill carefully for any 900-number charges. This is a largely unregulated industry. Any business can get a 900 number. Make sure any phone charges on your bill for these services are accurate.

What You Can Do If You're Caught in a 900-Number Scam

If you have problems with charges on your phone bill for 900 (or 976 or 700)-number scams, write to your telephone company immediately. You can ask the phone company to delete the charge, although it is not legally obligated to do so. AT&T cannot disconnect your phone for failure to pay. For other carriers, call the carrier or the Federal Communications Commission.

You also can write the phone company for the name of the 900-number company charging you and write to that company to delete the charge. The 900-number company could refuse, however, and have a debt collector contact you. In that event, you can write to the collection agency telling it not to contact you.

Under the law, once the collection agency receives your letter, it cannot contact you again except to say there will be no further contact or that some specific action will be taken (if the debt collector or creditor intends to take such action). Because the debt, if not resolved, can remain on your credit record, you also are legally entitled to have your account of the incident included in your credit report.

In addition, you may want to contact the Federal Trade Commission at 6th and Pennsylvania Avenue, N.W., Washington, D.C. 20580. Complaints about 900-number scams help the FTC in its law enforcement efforts.

Things to consider before you go

BEFORE YOU GO--Learn about the places you plan to visit. Familiarize yourself with local laws and customs in those areas. Consult your library, a travel agent, an airline agent, airline, or the tourist bureaus of the specific countries you plan to visit. You can get good information from: The Traveler's Bookstore, 22 W. 52nd St., New York, NY 10019, or the Book Passage, 57 Post St., Suite 401, San Francisco, CA 94104--ask for a catalog. Keep track as well of what is reported in the news about any recent events in those countries you plan to visit.

The Department of State issues travel advisories cautioning American citizens about travel to specific countries or areas. If you are traveling in an area where there may be some concern about existing conditions, contact the nearest passport agency, your travel agent, or airline, or call 202-647-5225 to learn of any problems.

TRAVEL BROCHURES--Travel is very personal. Once you decide on the trip you want, study all the material contained in travel brochures. It's fun to read trip itineraries and to enjoy all the beautiful photographs, but it's also important to carefully read the details and general information. What about the climate? Off-season rates may be a bargain, but the weather may not be so good. Decide which you prefer most-- ideal weather or off-season bargains. The brochure should explain what is and what isn't included. You'll usually find this information on the back page of a travel brochure.

PACKAGE TOURS--If you are taking a package tour, find out if there is a tour director on your tour; if so, does he/she stay with you from start to finish? Is he/she employed specially by your company? If so, such a person will have your interests at heart and will try to please you. It's the tour director's job to see that you are well cared for. Find out if the tour has been "checked out." How much does the tour operator really know about your accommodations? Has someone from the tour company or travel agency been there recently? Things can change drastically, and comforts may be promises, not facts.

Ask yourself, and then ask the tour company, what some words really mean. An "air-cooled" sightseeing bus may mean you

can open the windows and let the air flow through. "Average temperature 70 degrees" may mean it's 90 in the summer and 50 in the winter. Phrases like "you may want to cruise this glorious isle" or "perhaps take in the glamorous nightlife" may mean these are additional travel treats for which you must pay extra. If in doubt, ask to speak to a traveler who has already taken the tour.

Check the cancellation and refund policy. Know exactly what happens if you change your mind. Cancellation penalties vary, and some are more severe than others.

> See the article on packaged tours, page 196, for some more travel tips.

PASSPORTS--Make sure your passport is current. Some countries will not permit you to enter or give you a visa if your passport's remaining validity is less than 6 months. If you don't have a passport, get one way earlier than your departure date. You'll need proof of U.S. citizenship (a birth certificate), proof of identity (a driver's license), two recent two-inch by two-inch photographs of a good likeness, and a completed official passport form. Although fees have gone up, passports are now valid for 10 years. If your town doesn't have a State Department Passport Agency, get your passport application from the federal or state courthouse or from the post office. Allow at least two to four weeks for processing. After you receive your passport be sure

to sign it and fill in the personal notification data page. Your previous passport will be returned to you with your new passport.

If your passport is lost or stolen, report the loss immediately to the nearest embassy or consulate and to local police. If you can provide a photocopy to the consular officer it will help in issuance of a new passport. Your passport is a valuable document and should be carefully safeguarded.

VISAS--Some countries require visas. A visa is an endorsement made in and on a passport allowing entry into the country you're visiting, testifying that your passport was examined and found in order. It permits you to visit that country for a specified purpose and usually for a limited time; for example, a 3-month tourist visa. Apply directly to the embassies or consulates of the country you plan to visit. Passport agencies cannot help you obtain visas.

You can obtain a copy of Foreign Visa Requirements, publication M-264, for $.50 from the Consumer Information Center, Dept. 438T, Pueblo, CO 81009. It lists the entry requirements for U.S. citizens traveling to most foreign countries and where to apply for visas and tourist cards. You will need to fill out an application form and give your passport to an official of each foreign embassy or consulate. Some visas require a fee. The process may take several weeks for each visa, so apply well in advance.

> You know more of a road by having
> traveled it than by all the conjectures
> and descriptions in the world.
> -William Hazlitt

TOURIST CARD--If the country you plan to visit requires a tourist card, you can obtain one from that country's embassy or consulate, from an airline serving the country, or at the port of entry. For some tourist cards, a fee is required. Check entry requirements while you are planning your trip.

PROOF OF CITIZENSHIP--Some countries require only proof of U.S. citizenship to enter and depart the country. Check with the appropriate embassy or consulate for exact requirements before departure.

> ## Don't take anything you can't afford to lose!

WHAT TO TAKE?--Leave at home all unnecessary credit cards, expensive jewelry, or irreplaceable family objects. Don't pack too much or your bag will be too heavy to manage. Read the Travel Health articles in this book, pages 202 through 204, for what to take for your health needs.

Make photocopies of your airline ticket, passport identification page, driver's license, and the credit cards you take with you. Leave one set at home and keep another with you in a place separate from these valuables. Leave a copy of the serial numbers of your traveler's checks at home; take another with you, separate from the checks themselves and, as you cash in the checks, keep a tally of which ones remain unredeemed.

Have your affairs at home in order: Leave an up-to-date will, insurance documents, and a power of attorney with your family, so you can feel secure about traveling and are prepared for any emergency that may occur while you are away. Before departing, provide your family or friends with a copy of your proposed itinerary and keep them informed of your travel plans should they change or in case they need to contact you in an emergency.

Carry with you appropriate photo identification and the name of a family member or friend to contact in case of an emergency.

Find out whether you own insurance which will cover you for loss or theft abroad in case of accident or illness.

LUGGAGE--Limit your baggage and make sure it is lightweight as there may be times when you might have to carry it yourself. Be sure your baggage is clearly labeled. Remove old destination labels and paste your name, address, and tour group (if appropriate) in a prominent place on the outside and inside of each piece of luggage. The outside tag should show only your name and tour group; print your address on the reverse (concealed) side. Enclose a copy of your itinerary in each bag. Keep your luggage locked even when left empty in your room. Someone could use your luggage to cart off your belongings.

PACKING--Pack and repack articles in the same order each time. During short stays, you can then reach into your bags and find what you want without unpacking everything. Coordinate your wardrobe around a single color; this will automatically eliminate many items of clothing. Don't pack too much. Lay out everything you'll need for the trip. Now pack half the items and return the balance to your closet. You'll still probably take lots of things you'll never get to use! If you are still not convinced, pack everything and walk around with your bags for a few minutes. If they feel too heavy, take out the unnecessary items.

Use every spare inch of the luggage space. Stuff hosiery into your shoes. Roll up sweaters and underwear to fit into the corners. Place heavy items on the bottom. Button shirts and dresses and fold close to the waist and seams. Don't pack liquids in glass containers; transfer them to plastic ones. Don't take anything fragile or perishable--carry them if you must. Carry medicines in your hand baggage.

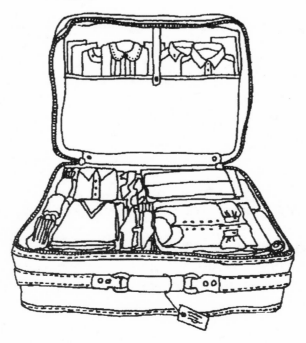

A PACKING CHECK LIST

* A pair of comfortable walking shoes with nonskid soles.
* Electric (with converter-adapter) or battery operated appliances.
* A small flashlight, extra batteries, and nightlight.
* Bottle opener, corkscrew.
* A knife for room snacks. Don't carry the knife on your person.
* Face cloth.
* Extra set of luggage keys (not kept with your regular keys).
* Plenty of film (it's cheaper at home).
* A spare set of batteries for your camera.
* Travel alarm clock.
* Sewing kit.
* Moist towelettes in packages for quick freshening up en route.
* Nail polish remover pads not bottles.
* Plastic or string bags for shopping and dirty clothes.
* Diary or logbook to record your trip.
* Address Book for home and new addresses.
* Language dictionary and phrase book.
* Medicine kit, medical records, and prescriptions (see travel health precautions, pages 202 and 203).

PHOTOGRAPHIC EQUIPMENT--You may be tempted to take three or four lenses, tripods, several camera bodies--don't unless you are a serious photographer. You'll only regret being encumbered. If you carry valuable equipment of foreign manufacture, make sure you register it with the U.S. customs before leaving so that you are not charged duty on it when you return. Take plenty of film and extra camera batteries. If you don't have a film shield bag, don't let your film go through the X-ray machine at airports; hand it to the guard for manual inspection.

DRIVER'S LICENSES--Most countries will accept an international driver's license. You can obtain one before you depart at your local office of an automobile agency.

Tips on travel packages

A travel package is a prearranged vacation. Some package vacations include only basic travel services (for example, transportation, accommodations), while others may include a complete travel plan (for example, meals, sightseeing, transfers, etc.). Usually these packages are assembled by an independent tour operator and are sold to you through travel agents.

Purchasing a travel package has the advantage of convenience and, in many cases, value. However, because of the vast array of travel packages, you can be confused unless you shop wisely and read the fine print in advertisements and brochures.

This article is intended to provide you with an understanding of the terminology used in the travel industry and to advise you of the steps you can take to avoid problems.

Glossary of Travel Terminology

General Terms

Brochure–A printed folder describing a tour or a package and specifying the conditions of the offering.

Carrier--Any organization that deals in transporting passengers or goods.

Certified Travel Counselor (CTC)--A degree attesting to professional competence of a course of study by the Institute of Certified Travel Agents. The Certified Travel Associate Degree is awarded to non-agent personnel who have completed the course (see Travel Agent).

Commission--The amount paid by the supplier (carrier, hotel, tour operator, etc.) to the travel agent for selling transportation, accommodations, or other services.

Conditions--The section or clause of a transportation or tour contract (often the last page of a brochure) that specifies what is offered to the purchaser. A condition clause often specifies what is not offered and may spell out the circumstances under which all or part of the contract may be invalidated. (Also referred to as the participants' agreement, terms and conditions, or responsibility clause.)

Confirmed Reservation--An oral or written confirmation by a supplier that it has received and will honor a reservation.

Escort--A person who accompanies a tour from departure to return, as guide, trouble shooter, etc., or a person who performs such factions only at the destination (also known as a "host").

Escorted Tour--Prearranged travel program, usually for a group, with escort service or sightseeing program conducted by a guide.

Escrow Account--Deposit account in a bank maintained by the charter operator that protects passenger funds until services are performed.

Extension--A fully arranged subtour offered optionally at extra cost to buyers of a tour or cruise. Extensions may occur before, during, or after the basic travel package.

Foreign Independent Tour (FIT)--An international prepaid tour, usually unescorted, although guide service is often offered on some segments. An FIT is designed to the specifications of an individual client or clients.

Gateway--City, airport, or area from which a flight or tour departs.

Group Inclusive Tour (GIT)--A prepaid tour of specified minimum group size, components, and value.

Guaranteed Tour--A travel program guaranteed to operate unless cancelled before an established cutoff date (see Conditions).

Institute of Certified Travel Agents--An organization concerned with developing and administering educational programs for travel agents (see Certified Travel Counselor).

No Show--A passenger or guest who fails to use or cancel his or her reservation.

Overbooking--The practice by a supplier of confirming reservations beyond capacity in expectation of cancellations or no shows; or, the same result due to error. Many carriers have admitted that they intentionally overbook their flights because of the high number of passengers who are no shows.

Package or Package Tour--Any advertised tour. Often a tour to a single destination that includes prepaid transportation, accommodations, and some combination of other tour features--meals, transfers, sight-seeing, car rental, etc.

Tour--Any prearranged (but not necessarily prepaid) journey to one or more places and back to the point of origin.

Tour Operator--A company that creates a package tour and/or performs tour services. Most tour operators sell both through travel agents and directly to clients.

Travel Agent--A person or company that promotes and sells transportation and related services, including travel packages.

Air Transportation Terms

United States Department of Transportation--The federal agency that regulates air transportation to and from the United States as well as within the United States.

Charter Operator--A company that makes all the arrangements to permit individuals to participate on a single itinerary in a public charter and that is directly responsible to the charter participants (see Public Charter).

Direct Flight--Air transportation on which the passenger does not have to change planes. Not necessarily nonstop.

OW--One-way airfare.

Public Charter--Air transportation alone, or air transportation together with hotel and other land arrangements, organized by a charter operator and generally priced below regularly scheduled air service.

RT--Round-trip airfare.

Standby--A conditional status. The holder of a standby ticket is not eligible to board his or her flight until all passengers who have or

As a member of an escorted tour,
you don't even have to know that
the Matterhorn isn't a tuba.
- Temple Fielding

TRAVEL
(page 2 of 3) PACKAGE TOURS 197

want confirmed reservations have been accommodated.

Land Terms

Land Terms--includes those services available to a traveler after he or she has reached his or her destination.

American Plan (AP)--Hotel rate that includes a bed and three meals (see also Modified American Plan).

Bed and Breakfast--Overnight accommodations usually in a private home or boarding house with breakfast included in the rate.

Continental Plan (CP)--Hotel rate that includes bed and continental breakfast (usually at least a beverage and rolls or toast, sometimes juice).

Double--Any hotel plan for two persons; more specifically, a room with a double bed.

Double Room Rate--The full price of a room for two people. (Be careful: Some say double and mean double occupancy.)

European Plan--Hotel rate with bed only; meals extra.

Family Plan--A discount schedule offered by some hotels and resorts to second and successive members of families who travel together.

Guaranteed Payment Reservation--A hotel reservation secured by the guest's agreement to pay for his room whether he uses it or not. Payment is usually guaranteed by a company, travel agent, or tour wholesaler who has an established credit rating with the hotel, or by use of a credit card as a guarantee.

Hotel Classifications

The following are generally understood throughout Europe, and to an extent, the world, but it is sometimes difficult to know whether a hotel is being described by a reliable source. There is neither an official nor generally accepted rating system for U.S. hotels.

European Hotel Ratings

Deluxe--Top-grade hotel; all rooms have private bath; all the usual public rooms and services provided; high standard of decor and services maintained.

1st Class--Medium-range hotel; at least some rooms with private bath; most of the usual public rooms and services are provided.

Tourist (Economy or 2nd Class)--Budget operations; few or no private baths; services may be very limited.

The Official Hotel & Resort Guide (OHRG), which is often referred to by travel agents, further subdivides these three categories into three groups: superior, average, and moderate. Thus, a deluxe/superior hotel rates with the best in the world and a 1st class/average hotel is about midrange.

OHRG says that hotels below its tourist/superior rating should be used with caution by Westerners.

In addition, many governments rate their hotels according to the international five-star system under which a five-star hotel is best. Some countries are meticulous and generally current in their ratings; many are not. In general, three-star and better hotels (and a few two-star properties) are believed to be suitable for Western travelers.

Modified American Plan (MAP)/Demi-Pension (DP)--Hotel rate including bed, breakfast, and either lunch or dinner.

Per Person Double Occupancy Rate--The price per person for a room to be shared with another person; the rate most frequently quoted in tour brochures (often abbreviated: pp. dbl. occ.).

Single Supplement--An extra charge assessed to a tour purchased for single accommodations.

Transfer--Local transportation and baggage handling service, as from one carrier terminal to another, from a terminal to a hotel or from a hotel to a theater. The conditions of a tour contract should specify whether transfers are private car or motorcoach and whether escort service is provided.

How to Avoid Problems

Make every effort to determine if the tour operator you're thinking of doing business with is reliable. Ask your travel agent if he or she has ever used the tour operator in the past. If so, were their clients satisfied with the service? Recommendations from friends and relatives are added evidence, but no assurance, that your travel experience will be a satisfactory one.

Also, before you arrange your trip, check with the Better Business Bureau in the city where the company is located. Give the BBB the complete name of the firm in either a phone call or a postcard and ask the BBB for the customer experience record.

A Buyer's Checklist

When reading travel advertisements and/or brochures, pay particular attention to the following:

1. **Small Print or Asterisks**--Make sure that asterisks or small print are not used as a means of altering the meaning of any advertising statement. Asterisks are commonly used to indicate restrictions--required length of stay, particular days and/or time of departure, or additional charges.

2. **Availability**--Make sure that the travel services are currently available at advertised prices. If the travel service at the advertised price is not immediately effective, availability should be stated in the advertisement.

More tips on package tours

3. **Extra Charges**--Any extra charges such as port taxes, service charges, or single supplement charges should be clearly and conspicuously disclosed.

4. **Features**--If the brochure/advertisement states, for example, you can play golf or you will be able to visit an amusement park, it does not necessarily mean that these attractions will be included in the travel program for the advertised price. Make sure to look for the following:
    a. What features are included in the package price:
       *airfare
       *hotel
       *transfers
       *sightseeing
       *gratuities
       *baggage handling
       *meals
       *mileage charges (where a car rental is involved)
    b. The total number of nights in each city and hotel, as well as the amount of free time you will have on the tour.
    c. The daily itinerary/schedule of events.
    d. The name of each hotel and the type (grade) of accommodations offered by each.
    e. Whether the tour is escorted and, if so, to what degree.

5. **Conditions**--You should pay special attention to the contents of the "conditions" clause, usually found in fine print on the last page of the brochure.
    a. How firm is the price (i.e., does the tour operator have the right to increase the fare)?
    b. What are the cancellation penalties? What is considered a valid reason for either you or the tour operator to cancel the trip?
    c. What are the "major changes" under which a tour operator will give you a full refund?

> Reprinted with permission from the Council of Better Business Bureaus, Inc., 4200 Wilson Blvd., Arlington, VA 22203. To receive copies of the publication, send your request, and check or money order for $1.00 (per booklet), payable to Council of Better Business Bureaus, Inc., Dept. 023, Washington, D.C. 20042-0023. Enclose a SASE.

6. **Abbreviations**--Common abbreviations used in travel ads and brochures include (see glossary of travel terminology for definitions, page 196 to 198):
    *AP--American plan
    *CP--Continental plan
    *dep.--departure date
    *FIT--foreign independent travel
    *GIT--group inclusive tour
    *MAP--modified American plan
    *OW--one-way
    *pp.dbl.occ.--per person double occupancy
    *RT--round-trip
    *single supp.--single supplement

When booking reservations, either through a travel agency or with a tour operator directly, obtain the following information:

1. If you book your vacation through a travel agency, what is the name and address of the tour operator?

2. Has the advertised price changed? Do the charges you pay match the charges you expected?

3. How far in advance is full payment required?

4. How much deposit is required?

5. Is there an escrow account? To whom is payment made? (If you have to sign a contract, make sure it specifies that you pay directly to the escrow account at a bank. Also, ask to know the name of the bank in which the escrow account is maintained.)

6. What is the confirmation procedure? (Warning: Confirmations have limitations--for example, a hotel is not obligated to honor a reservation if the guest arrives after 6 P.M., unless late arrival is specified. However, if the reservation is guaranteed, then that hotel is obligated to honor it.)

Remember--Purchasing a travel package has the advantage of convenience and, in many cases, value--but you must do your homework. Use the Glossary of Travel Terminology and Buyer's Checklist to help you understand what the various packages have to offer, and whether they are right for you. Bon voyage!

Traveling by air--

People face special problems when they have pets and wish to travel. The ideal arrangement is for the animal to stay at home and have a neighbor, friend, or relative go by your house once or twice a day to feed, water, and take care of your pet. Alternatives are a boarding kennel, a professional pet sitter, or assistance from Pets Are Inn. This organization will help place your pet in a private home in your area. For more information for this service call or write: Pets Are Inn, 12 S. 6th Street, Suite 950, Minneapolis, MN 55402, or call (800) 248-7387 or (612) 339-6255.

If you want to have your pet travel with you or you are moving to a new location here are some travel tips:

❑ If the pet travels with you, it will retain a sense of identity. However, pets can become frightened and bolt away from you out of open doors and windows. Keep your pet on a leash when outside your car or hotel.

❑ Whether your pet travels with you or by another means it should wear a special identification tag in addition to its regular one. Write the pet's name, your name, the person to contact at the destination, their phone number, a destination address, or that of a friend or relative, in case you want to be reached.

❑ Except for seeing eye dogs accompanying blind persons, pets are not permitted on buses and trains. Notify the airline, bus, or train company that a seeing eye dog is accompanying you.

❑ Consult with your veterinarian concerning mild sedation of your pet during the trip.

Air Travel Checklist

❑ If you decide to ship your pet by air, make reservations and arrangements ahead of time regarding delivery to and pickup from the airports. Carefully schedule boarding and shipping arrangements for your pet to assure that the pet is well cared for until you are able to receive it at your destination. Boarding may be necessary. Follow airline instructions.

❑ Check the airline's requirements to see if your pet can travel in a carrier that can be kept under a seat in the cabin or must traveling by air freight.

❑ Consider sending smaller pets such as

--or by car with your loving animals

birds, hamsters, gerbils, and tropical fish by air express. Airline freight departments, pet stores, or department stores can supply shipping containers. Tropical fish should be packed by a local pet shop specializing in tropical fish.

❑ Obtain a shipping container a week or two in advance. Familiarize your pet with it by placing the pet in it for a few minutes each day. Gradually lengthen the time until the pet seems to be at ease with it.

❑ Feed the pet no less than five or six hours before flight time. Give the pet a drink of water no less than two hours before flight.

❑ Get the pet to the air terminal in time. Get there 45 minutes in advance if the pet is accompanying you. If shipping the pet, get to the flight terminal two hours in advance of your flight.

❑ Be certain that names, addresses, and telephone numbers of the persons responsible for the pet at origination and destination are clearly marked on the container and on the pet's identification tag. Label your pet's flight kennel with the same information. Add "Live Animal" in big letters and information about any special care requirements.

❑ Notify the person receiving the pet that it is on the way. Give them the flight and waybill number.

❑ Pets can usually be picked up within 90 minutes of flight arrival. The air waybill number is useful when inquiring.

Travel By Car Checklist

❑ If your dog or cat is not used to traveling by car, make short trips with the pet a week or two in advance of the trip to accustom it to motion and to teach it how to behave.

❑ Dogs should be taught to lie quietly, keep their heads inside, and not annoy the driver or passengers. Don't let your dog stick his head in the wind. It can irritate eyes and cause problems.

❑ Cats are often frightened by car travel, but some cats adjust quickly. Some persons allow the cat to find its own place in the car; others feel it is best to confine a cat to its carrier.

❑ Folding kennels or crates especially designed for station wagons can be most useful for dogs and cats.

❑ Accustom your pet to being on a leash and harness. Always use the leash when traveling. Even better is a pet harness (available at most pet stores) that connects to the car's seatbelt; it allows the pet some movement while keeping it safely restrained. Your pets can bolt into traffic or become lost in a strange place if not properly restrained.

❑ If stopping overnight, check in advance to find a motel that will permit your pet to spend the night.

❑ Be sure that your pet is properly tagged and its rabies tag firmly attached.

❑ Pet travel kit: pet food, food and water dishes, can opener (if needed), a few treats, a favorite toy, a blanket, comb or brush.

❑ Also, to be on the safe side: a sedative (if prescribed by your veterinarian), paper towels, spray room deodorant if you will be staying overnight at a hotel or motel, a scooper and plastic bag to clean up after your pet.

When the pet has arrived at its new destination, you will find that your pet has the same problems adjusting as you do. It must learn the way around the house and neighborhood. The pet must meet new neighbors, both animals and humans. It must adjust to new water and climate, and must learn where it can and cannot go.

It is advisable to keep the pet within the home until it realizes that this is a HOME and not a temporary residence (even though it may be your vacation destination). It may wander off and try to find the former residence. This is especially true of cats; they should be confined for several weeks.

Make the animal feel at home by using familiar dishes, blanket, toys, and other items. Check with your neighbors to determine any special problems your pet might encounter, for example, the neighborhood grouch. Also, make a particular effort to keep your dog inside on garbage collection day. There are better ways to meet your neighbors than over a garbage can upset by your dog.

If you carefully plan your vacation with your pet, you may make a smooth transition from your old to new destination But be prepared for the unexpected; it can and probably will happen.

Fur that flies!

Entry Requirements

❑ If your destination is across state lines, nearly every state has laws on the entry of animals, with the exception of tropical fish. For information, call or write to the State Veterinarian, State Department of Animal Husbandry, or other appropriate authority.

❑ Interstate health certificates must accompany dogs and horses entering nearly all states. About half have the same requirements for other pets. In some cases, this certificate must be in the hands of the state regulatory agency in advance of the entry.

❑ All but four states require an up-to-date rabies inoculation for dogs and many require it for cats. The rabies tag must be securely attached to the pet's collar. Hawaii requires that cats and dogs be quarantined for 120 days.

❑ Some pets must have an entry permit issued by the destination state's regulatory agency. Receipt of the interstate health certificate may be required before the permit can be issued. Some states limit the time during which the entry permit is valid.

❑ A few states have border inspections of all animals being transported; others have random inspection by highway patrol officers. State agriculture representatives are usually present at airports to inspect pets arriving by air.

Local Laws

❑ Local communities have pet control and licensing ordinances. In some cases, the number of dogs and cats per residence is limited. Large animals, such as ponies and horses, may be prohibited. Be sure to check with the city clerk or town hall for specific information.

TRAVEL --ideas for the second 50 years

Many psychologists tell us that a vacation should be an experience that represents a complete change from our daily lives. They call it discontinuity. Such a vacation tends to put behind you the strains and cares of your daily life so that your body and mind deal with entirely different concerns. When you add to this discontinuity the exotic, the foreign, and the idyllic, the change and the benefit for you increases significantly.

As we become older, we have new travel needs and interests. The trips we take must be within our physical limitations, and should appeal to mature interests. In this article we write about two good travel organizations. Elsewhere, on page 173 you can read about Elderhostel and the kind of travel experience that organization provides for seniors.

SAGA HOLIDAYS

A travel organization that is devoted to senior needs is Saga Holidays. Saga was founded in England shortly after World War II. They attempted to tailor their travel arrangements to the needs of people over 60 years old. They expanded and eventually opened offices in Boston to serve mature travelers from the United States.

Advantages--You can be sure that any package sold by Saga will not require excessively robust physical activity. Comprehensive travel insurance is provided as a part of the holiday cost. Flight insurance on all tickets they provide for you is also included. Saga insurance protection provides coverage that is secondary to your primary medical insurance and common carrier protection.

Solo Travel--Because Saga recognizes that older persons may still wish to travel in spite of the loss of a spouse, they welcome single travelers. They even publish short biographies of older persons seeking traveling companions, and provide the means of establishing contact with each other. Extensions of trips are easy to arrange directly with them, so you can maximize the opportunities associated with passing through places like London, Paris, or Hong Kong.

Designations--while you can travel almost anywhere in the world with Saga, it also has numerous trips to locations in the United States and Canada. Garden tours are a specialty, and you also may select a variety of cruises if that is your cup of tea.

Requirements--for a Saga trip is being 60 or over, or anyone 50-59 who is traveling with someone who is 60 or older. Two categories of Saga tours are open to persons of any age: White Flower Farm Tours and Smithsonian Odyssey Tours.

For Information--write Saga International Holidays, Ltd., 120 Boylston Street, Boston, MA 02116-9719, or call 1-800-343-0273.

CLUB MEDITERANEE

Forty years ago, with a tiny beginning, the French travel organization Club Med opened its first locations. The idea was to provide an exotic setting and all the ordinary needs of a vacationing person in one package. Thus, for instance, you would be transported to Tahiti where you would have simple, comfortable quarters, delicious meals (including wine), recreational opportunities and equipment, and entertainment. Nothing is compulsory. Only a few things cost extra such as drinks, horseback riding, and other types of specialized recreation.

Gentils Organisateurs (GO's)--The activities in the Club Med villages were built around young people called GO's. They conduct activities, lead expeditions, give lessons, take care of the grandchildren (if you brought them along), and in the evening, entertain you and your fellow vacationers. If you want to snorkel, sail, fish, scuba dive, water ski, play tennis, or take a hike, these young people are there to lead the activity.

The Program--Different villages offer different special features. You can't snorkel in the Alps, but skiing is provided at several Club Med locations. Snorkeling is available at several dozen villages, along with other water sports and activities. Tennis, volleyball, bocce ball, archery, aerobics, basketball, and other sports are available. Another special offering in some locations is golf. Ping pong, arts and crafts, and circus workshops are offered at several locations.

Breakfast is served to those who wish it on a buffet basis. Lunch is also a buffet meal with an incredible display of food and variety that suits the most adventurous palate. Red, white, and rose wines are waiting for the diner at the table. Dinner is served family style with a set menu. Wine is again provided. This meal especially is one where you tend to meet new people and begin to take advantage of the diverse backgrounds of the participants.

Days are spent pursuing the kind of sports or other activities that are provided. Side trips, hikes, picnics, cruises, and other planned activities are available simply by signing up to attend. You can opt for completely passive activity, loafing on the beach, or reading that novel you have been wanting to get into.

Evenings always have some sort of entertainment that highlights the splendid showmanship that is a part of the Club Med concept. The GO's often take part in these productions with a resident music group, dancing, and other production numbers. Vacationers sometimes get into the act, but the highlight of the week is generally an evening devoted to the arts and entertainment of the country you are visiting. The evening meal features food and dining style of the country with entertainment during and after dinner. It can range from an evening of Polynesian dancing to snake charmers, belly dancers, and fantastic acrobatic displays. A highlight might be a group of Arab horsemen in full regalia galloping on the scene with their long rifles blazing away.

Locations--In the beginning only a few villages were available in French locations. Now Club Med has expanded into the Americas with many installations in the Caribbean, Mexico, and farther south. At this writing, there are 110 villages in more than 30 countries. Club Med has the reputation for being a place for singles. That is very true for many of the villages. However, there are lots of installations that are geared for families, and in most of those locations vacationers who are on the second 50 years would be comfortable and thoroughly enjoy the experience.

Club Med offers a unique opportunity to play with people from many countries and backgrounds. It exposes the vacationer to other cultures in a way that is difficult to duplicate. Finally, if you should find yourself in a Club Med village on July 14, you are in for the special experience of their celebration of Bastille Day. You should be so lucky. Any travel agent can provide information about Club Med.

> **Money, it turned out, was exactly like sex:
> You thought of nothing else if you didn't have
> it and thought of other things if you did.**
>
> - James Baldwin

TRAVELING MONEY--take along a combination of cash, traveler's checks, personal checks, and at least two major credit cards. If traveling to foreign countries take international credit cards and leave local ones home. Before departing the United States, purchase small amounts of foreign currency to use for buses, taxis, phone calls, tips, and other incidentals when you arrive.

Some countries regulate the amount of local currency you can bring in and take out of the country; others require that you exchange a minimum amount of currency. If you leave the U.S. with more than $10,000 you must file customs form 4790 at the time of entry or departure. For current information, check with a bank, foreign exchange firm, the embassy or consulate of the countries you plan to visit, or a travel agent before you leave.

TRAVELER'S CHECKS--Take most of your money in traveler's checks. Do not carry large amounts of cash. These are safer than cash since you're the only person who can use them and because you can get a refund or replacement if they're lost or stolen.

To save money, buy traveler's checks where you don't pay a fee. They are available in denominations of $20, $50, $100, $500, and $1,000 checks. The smaller ones are easier to cash. For safety, sign the checks on the signature line as soon as you buy them. When you want to cash a check you will countersign (sign it again) in the presence of one who is cashing it. Don't countersign the check until you know it will be accepted. Always bring adequate identification with you. If you're out of the U.S. a passport is all you need; otherwise be prepared to show a driver's license and credit cards.

To minimize your potential of total loss keep some of your traveler's checks in your luggage, purse, wallet, or handbag. If traveling with a friend, split the checks between yourselves.

Keep a record, at home as well as with you, of traveler's check serial numbers, denominations, the date and location of the issuing bank or agency where you purchased them. Do the same with credit card numbers and keep this information in a safe place separate from your traveler's checks so you can quickly get a replacement. Have the phone number to call in case of lost checks.

When you return home, cash in your unused traveler's checks as soon as you can. You can hold them indefinitely but you lose interest on your money tied up in these checks.

CREDIT CARDS--Carry at least two major credit cards in case you have seriously underestimated the cost of your trip. Visa, MasterCard, Diners Club, and American Express have many bank cash machines (ATM's) and allow you to charge merchandise and travel expenses all over the world. Acceptance of certain cards can vary from country to country. Check with your issuing bank for the countries where the card is accepted. Don't take with you any unnecessary credit cards.

Check the expiration date to make sure it will be valid the whole time of your trip. Also make sure you know how much credit you have available. To avoid having your credit unexpectedly cut off, keep a running total of your charges. Travelers have been arrested overseas for mistakenly exceeding their credit limit. If you are going away for more than a few weeks make arrangements with your card issuer for payment.

Most hotels require a credit card to guarantee the payment of the bill, even though you plan on paying with traveler's checks. This also "freezes" a certain amount of your credit limit that you need to plan for. Be sure your credit card is returned to you after each transaction.

In case of lost or stolen cards, have the telephone numbers to call to get a replacement.

CREDIT CARD ADVANTAGES--The Discover card (issued by Sears) gives a 5% rebate on all eligible travel arrangements. Visa will replace lost or stolen airline tickets purchased with their card. Diners Club members can book a suite at the Hilton for about the price of a single room and can be picked up at the airport. MasterCard holders can get pretrip information, emergency cash, and message transmissions all over the world.

American Express's Global Assist offers cardholders a 24-hour medical and legal referral service around the world. They will also send a prescription to people at no cost

if they forgot their's. Many provide automatic travel accident insurance for personal accidents, some up to $1 million plus coverage for lost or stolen luggage. Some of the gold cards assume responsibility for loss or damage when you use their cards to rent a car. Benefits change so ask in advance. Many gold cards offer many benefits that you may not know exist--check them out.

Credit cards can also be used to obtain cash advances or additional traveler's checks in case you run out of money--up to your credit limit. Some credit cards can be used at selected ATM's (automatic teller machines) in many places around the world for cash advances. Before you can use a credit card at an ATM you must have a specific PIN (personal identification number) given to you by your bank. Keep the PIN separate from your credit cards.

If your credit card is lost or stolen, report the loss immediately. Until you report the loss you may be liable for each unauthorized transaction up to $50.

Keep careful tabs on your travel tickets--they're as good as cash. Carry them in an inside pocket, not protruding from a jacket or bag.

Deal only with authorized agents when you exchange money, or buy tickets.

Never exchange more money than you're sure you'll be able to use. If you don't use the money you will be paying for two exchange premiums.

Don't rely on having money wired from home if you run out. It can take days. Instead, bring your checkbook; some hotels will let you cash $50 or $100 at the front desk if you are a guest. In the U.S. someone can send you money using Western Union, Citicorp, or American Express.

Get your shots early

MEDICAL PRECAUTIONS--Good health is essential for successful travel. Nothing can spoil it more than becoming ill. Take preventive measures before you leave home. Study the area that you plan to visit--its climate, elevation, humidity, native or epidemic diseases, the quality of its water, the availability of medical services--to ensure you will have a good trip. Ask your travel agent or local consulate what vaccinations you need for the places you plan to visit and get them well in advance in case of a reaction.

The booklet "Health Information for International Travel" is published annually by the U.S. government. It specifies the vaccinations required by different countries and includes information on measures for travelers to take to protect their health and facilitate their travel. International travelers should contact their local health department physician at least 4 weeks before departure to obtain the current health information on countries they plan to visit. You can obtain the booklet by sending $5 (ask for booklet 017-023-00184-1 latest edition; delivery is about 6 weeks) to: U.S. Government Printing Office, Superintendent of Documents, Washington, DC 20402-9329.

PRESCRIPTION DRUGS--Take along a copy of the prescriptions for necessary medicines. Ask your doctor to include the generic name as some trade name prescriptions are not available in foreign countries. Keep medicines in their original labeled container. If you need to take medications containing habit-forming or narcotic drugs with you, carry a doctor's certificate attesting to that fact. These precautions will make customs processing easier, although a doctor's certificate may not suffice as authorization to transport drugs to all foreign countries. Travelers have been arrested for drug violations for possessing items not considered narcotics in the U.S. but illegal in other countries. To ensure you do not violate the laws of the countries you visit, consult the embassy or consulate of those countries for precise information before leaving.

Do not buy medications "over the counter" (OTC) unless you are familiar with the product. Protection against some potentially hazardous drugs is nonexistent in some countries.

MEDICAL ALERT--Signing up with a medical data service can make traveling less worrisome. If you have allergies, reactions to certain medicines, or other unique medical problems, like diabetes or heart trouble, consider wearing a medical alert bracelet or carrying a medical alert card in your wallet or purse. It's a compact card available at most pharmacies stating any special medical conditions, allergies, and your blood type. For more information see page 255, or contact Medic Alert 800-432-5378 or MedFax 213-821-1984 (see page 255).

Leave a copy of your medical and dental records with your family or other contact person.

JET LAG--Most travelers can only manage three time zone changes without feeling jet lag. It's best to get plenty of rest before departure and sleep as much as you can on the plane or rest with your eyes closed. For a few days before departure, if you are traveling west, go to bed a few hours later than you normally would. If you are traveling east, go to bed a few hours earlier. Eat lightly on departure day, drink plenty of fluids, and avoid alcohol. Avoid fat-laden airline fare. Order plenty of fluids but avoid coffee. Try to get some exercise before the flight. Walk around the airport. Avoid sitting down while waiting to board.

Some travelers swear if you diet for four days beforehand, it helps. The first day, have three high-protein meals. On the second day, have only liquids, fruit, and salad. Day three, again the three high-protein meals. Day four, the day of departure, back to the liquids, fruit, and salad but eating lightly.

ALTITUDE SICKNESS--If you live at a low altitude and travel to one that is higher by more than 5,000 feet, you can expect to take 10 to 14 days to adjust to an altitude change. You may tire easily, so reduce physical activity until you become accustomed. Avoid alcohol as it will have more pronounced effects. Altitude sickness symptoms include headache, nausea, fatigue, shortness of breath, and insomnia. Altitude sickness is generally cured by descending to a lower altitude, and if needed, getting oxygen. Severe cases can become life threatening. At the first signs of fatigue, take a break.

TRAVELERS' MEDICINE KIT

antacids	antiseptic spray and wipes
aspirin or Tylenol	bowel regulators for diarrhea
adhesive bandage	condoms, diaphragms, spermicide
Chapstick	cough and cold remedies
eye ointment	fiber supplements or laxatives for constipation
insect repellent	Halozone--water purifying pills
spray anesthetic	motion sickness medicine
sunburn lotion	sun block with SPF 15 or higher
vitamins	anything else you think you need

A suntan is no longer considered healthy

SIGHT SAVING TIPS--Take an extra set of eyeglasses in case the first is lost or broken. If you cannot afford a second pair take along an older pair. Take along enough cleaning solutions for contact lenses and spare lenses. Even if you wear contacts, it is imperative that you take along a pair of conventional glasses. Take eye ointment and a good decongestant eye drop, sunglasses, extra batteries for hearing aids, and other health-related items. Carry these and any medicines you need in your carry-on luggage.

SUNBURN-- Americans are having a hard time letting go of the idea of a "healthy tan." A suntan is not healthy. Exposure to the sun is the primary cause of skin cancer. It also causes long-term skin damage and premature wrinkles. You should stay out of the sun during the middle of the day between 10 A.M. and 3 P.M. or wear protective clothing or a sun block with SPF 15 or higher. It also should be waterproof if you plan to swim. Get one that protects you from different kinds of ultraviolet (UV) rays. Make sure your sunglasses protect your eyes from UV; otherwise you might increase your risk of developing cataracts and retinal damage. See the article on sunscreens, page 374.

DRESSING FOR TRAVEL--The International Association for Medical Assistance to Travelers (IAMAT) puts out a climate chart for major cities around the world. It lists high and low temperatures, altitude, days of rain, and information about food to eat and avoid. It is published monthly and is free, but they will ask for donations to help with their work. For a copy write: IAMAT, 736 Center St., Lewiston, NY 14092.

When you know the climate you will know how to dress. For the hottest, you should wear pure cotton and the clothes should be loose-fitting. Light-colored clothes reflect rather than absorb light. Clothes made of cotton/synthetic blends won't crease, are easily washed, and are good for tropical climates. Watch how the natives dress. If

they carry an umbrella you can expect rain. In cold areas take long johns, a sweater, and wool ski pants. Wool socks are best. Wear a windbreaker and long-sleeve shirts. Wear a wool cap that extends down over your ears and wear gloves. Consider the wind-chill factor and altitude as the wind combined with cold makes the body feel it is much colder. Limit the amount of clothing you pack, but make sure it is adequate for the climate.

SEXUALLY TRANSMITTED DISEASES-- HIV and AIDS and antibiotic-resistant STD's are high risks in some areas of the world. The latter, especially strains of gonorrhea (PPNG), are of concern in the Philippines, Korea, Singapore, Thailand, Cote d'Ivoire, Ghana, Kenya, Nigeria, and of increasing concern in the Caribbean and many countries in Central and South America.

To reduce the risk of STD's, travelers should avoid anonymous partners, prostitutes, and other persons who have multiple sex partners. Avoid anyone who has a genital discharge, warts, herpes lesions or any other suspicious genital lesions, AIDS, or evidence of HIV infection; avoid anal contact and genital contact with oral "cold sores." Males should use condoms. Females should use diaphragms and spermicide but also insist male partners use condoms. If any symptoms of STD develop see a physician immediately to receive appropriate treatment. For more information on venereal disease and contraceptives see the article on pages 401 through 404.

FINDING MEDICAL HELP--Should you become ill while traveling abroad, contact the nearest U.S. embassy or consulate for a list of local doctors, dentists, medical specialists, or hospitals. Consular offices cannot supply you with medication. The International Association of Medical Assistance to Travelers (IAMAT) can provide a valuable service in the unlikely event you become ill while traveling. The group coordinates medical treatment (with set fees) by English-speaking physicians trained in North America or Europe, whenever possible. Membership is free although a donation helps support their work. Membership entitles you to a directory of physicians with their overseas locations, phone numbers, and fees. For information, contact IAMAT, 736 Center Street, Lewiston, NY 14092.

If you have a handicap or disability, there is an information service to help you plan trips in the U.S. and abroad. Contact: Travel Information Service, Moss Rehabilitation Hospital, 12th St. and Tabor Rd., Philadelphia, PA 19141; (215-329-5715).

Medicare does not pay for hospital or medical services outside the United States!

HEALTH INSURANCE--For travelers who become seriously ill or injured on a trip abroad, getting medical care in foreign hospitals can be costly. Make sure your medical insurance policy provides adequate protection for you and your family while out of the United States. If you wish to get supplemental medical coverage, consult your health insurance company or contact your state insurance association for information on available protection for travelers.

Travel-specific policies written by major insurers like Blue Cross/Blue Shield and Traveler's are available through most travel agencies. Health Insurance Association of America should cover office visits, hospitalization, and outpatient care costs occurring outside the United States. Air ambulance coverage is a plus in case you need medical assistance to return home from overseas. For a 2-week stay, you'll pay from $50 for a single person to $200 for a family. Be sure to ask about maximum payouts, age restrictions, and which services aren't covered. Many international insurance companies offer trip cancellation, and travel accident insurance.

AFTER YOU'RE HOME--If you become ill after you return home, tell your physician where you have been. Most persons who get viral, bacterial, or parasitic infections abroad become ill within 6 weeks after returning. Some diseases may not manifest themselves immediately, such as malaria, so it is advisable to tell your physician where you have been to aid in the correct diagnosis if you become ill.

Here are two experiences you can do without

MOTION SICKNESS--Some travelers like to tell their ailing shipmates "It's all in your mind." You probably already know if you are prone to get it. No one is immune to motion sickness no matter how strong their intestinal fortitude. Given strong enough stimulus, everyone with a normal sense of balance will succumb. The process by which motion sickness occurs centers on the function of the inner ear, an organ that helps us keep our balance. Most modern cruise ships are equipped with stabilizers to minimize that rolling motion, and most avoid stormy seasons in various regions.

Generally, the first symptom is unusual paleness of the skin. This may be followed by yawning, restlessness, and a cold sweat. As the symptoms progress, malaise and drowsiness may set in, sometimes accompanied by a slightly upset stomach, or "gastric awareness." Then follows excessive salivation, nausea, and vomiting. Vomiting brings relief, if only for a short time.

While motion sickness can ruin one's pride, one's suit, or an entire vacation, it seldom causes severe health complications. In extreme cases, though, prolonged vomiting can cause severe headache, prostration, dehydration, and disturbed mineral balance.

> ## Prevention is easier than treating motion sickness once it has begun.

PREVENTION
* In a car, sit in the front seat, looking ahead.
* In an airplane, choose a seat over the wing.
* On a ship, remain amidships (preferably on deck), rather than below.
* Lie on your back, in a semireclined position, and keep your head as still as possible.
* Look ahead, at the distant horizon. If that's not possible, it may be better to close your eyes rather than focus on fast-moving scenery or waves. Focus attention on something other than the motion of the vehicle.
* Overindulgence in food or drink can predispose you to nausea and promote the onset of other motion-sickness symptoms.
* Tobacco smoke and other odors, particularly from food, should be avoided.

NONPRESCRIPTION DRUGS--There are currently three nonprescription drugs for preventing motion sickness. They are cyclizine hyrochloride (trade name Marezine), meclizine hydrochloride (Bonine), and dimenhydrinate (Dramamine). They are antihistamines. Take 30 minutes to an hour before traveling. These can cause drowsiness so you shouldn't be driving. Beware if you have glaucoma or prostate problems.

You may need a prescription drug called scopolamine if the others don't work for you; contact your doctor.

TRAVELER'S DIARRHEA--TD, as it is known, affects 20% to 50% of travelers. In addition to frequent bowel evacuations, its symptoms include abdominal cramps, nausea, bloating, fever, and feeling lousy. High-risk areas include most of the developing countries of Latin America, Africa, the Middle East, Asia, and USSR. Intermediate-risk areas include southern Europe and a few Caribbean islands. Low-risk areas include Canada, northern Europe, Australia, and New Zealand.

The onset of TD is usually within the first week, but may occur at any time during the visit, and even after returning home. You get TD through ingestion of food or water that contains bacteria.

Before leaving home, do not take any antibiotics as preventive measures, since they can foster the growth of antibiotic-resistant bacteria in your body.

> ## NEVER drink tap water or any drink with ice in it in certain countries.

AVOIDING DIARRHEA--To avoid diarrhea and other internal distresses common to travelers, stay away from fresh vegetable salads, which can't be disinfected, and food that has been left out in the sun. In certain countries--but not all--you must never drink tap water or any drink with ice in it. Boil the water before drinking it or using it--even to brush your teeth. Better yet, stick to bottled water. Avoid uncooked vegetables, unpasteurized milk and milk products such as cheese, and eat only cooked food that is still hot, or fruit that you have peeled. Avoid undercooked and raw meat, fish, and shellfish. Safe beverages include bottled carbonated beverages (especially flavored beverages), beer, wine, hot coffee or tea, or water boiled or properly treated water. The eating place is important with private homes, restaurants, and street vendors listed in order of increasing risk.

IF YOU GET TRAVELER'S DIARRHEA--one or two unformed stools within eight hours accompanied by cramps, nausea, and malaise; do not succumb to the temptation to immediately swallow some medicine to stop it. Fortunately, most cases of TD are usually short-term. You will need to replace fluids and salts lost. To treat, prepare one glass (8 oz.) of juice and one of water. Drink alternately from each until thirst is quenched. The first glass should contain orange, apple, or other fruit juice with 1/2 teaspoon of honey or corn syrup plus a pinch of salt. The second glass should contain boiled or carbonated water and 1/4 teaspoon of baking soda. You also can use carbonated beverages or tea made with boiled or carbonated beverages. Avoid solid foods and milk. Pepto-Bismol tablets taken during your travels may help prevent the problem.

Consult a physician, rather than attempt self-medication, if the TD is severe or does not lessen within several days; if there is blood or mucus in the stool; if fever occurs with shaking chills; or if there is dehydration with persistent diarrhea.

Tips on shopping, sight-seeing, tipping, and phoning

SHOPPING--Do some preliminary shopping research before you leave home. Make a list of items you most want to buy, especially those that are area specialties. Make a gift list. Identify whom you need gifts for and how much you want to spend, then pick up the items along the way.

Tuck plastic or string bags into your carryall or purse when you go shopping. In many places customers are expected to provide their own bags. Pack an extra flat fabric bag in the bottom of your suitcase. On your homebound trip, put all of your purchases in it. It will ease your way through customs.

Keep a log of all your purchases and include what you paid in foreign currency and the equivalent in U.S dollars. This will make it easier to fill out your customs forms. Take along a pocket calculator for shopping and calculating exchange rates. If you pay by credit card, you're taking a gamble. You will be billed at the exchange rate on the day the charge clears in the U.S., not the rate at the time of purchase.

The $400 per person duty-free allowance only applies to items you carry home with you. All items mailed home are subject to duty, unless the package is marked "unsolicited gift" and is less than $50 in value. Any small items purchased abroad should be mailed personally to your home address or carried in your luggage. This will limit the number of misaddressed packages, nonreceipt of merchandise, or receipt of wrong merchandise. If you do mail a purchase, be sure to ask about insurance. Mailing forms are available at foreign post offices.

SIGHT-SEEING--Planning reduces your chances of becoming the victim of a crime. Select tour guides carefully. Make up lists beforehand of things you'd like to see. Check museum and shopping hours. Ask for directions at the hotel/motel to those attractions you want to visit. Allow time for exploring and adventure. Don't feel you have to see everything to get your money's worth.

Ask if any areas in town should be avoided. Stick to well-lighted main streets and public areas. Avoid dangerous areas. Don't use short cuts or narrow alleys. Try not to travel alone at night. Let someone know when you expect to return, especially if out late at night.

Keep a low profile. Dress and behave conservatively, avoiding flashy dress, jewelry, luggage, rental cars, or conspicuous behavior that would draw attention to you as a tourist or a foreigner. Be polite and low-key. Avoid loud conversations and arguments. Looking lost may make you look like an easy target for crime. If you do get lost, find an open business and ask for directions.

Don't give your room number to persons you don't know well. Meet visitors in the lobby. Only carry with you the cash you will need, and carry only small denominations.

Accept the customs of the country. In some countries everything stops in the middle of the day for siesta, and dinner is very late. Don't skip meals. Sight-seeing takes energy! You can still economize by buying, say, bread, cheese, and fruit and enjoying a picnic in a park instead of going to a restaurant.

TIPPING--Don't worry about whom to tip. If someone performs a service you really appreciate, go ahead and tip. If someone is not deserving of a thank you, don't tip. Always ask if service has been included in the bill. If it has been included leave only about 3% extra at a hotel or restaurant and by no means leave a regular tip. The rule of thumb is the same all over--tip 15% to 20% if not included.

Tipping for luggage handling, for local guides and bus drivers, etc., is covered on some tours, but not on others. Check your tour brochure for included features. It is customary to tip the tour director at the end of your tour. Depending on the person's performance, $2.50 per day is sufficient.

Get plenty of small bills and change for tipping purposes as soon as you enter the country. Take 25 to 30 one-dollar bills in U.S. currency for emergency use. Bellmen and chambermaids in hotels that have a foreign exchange will accept American bills (but not coins) as tips.

PRECAUTIONS--Coat pockets, handbags, and hip pockets are particularly susceptible to theft. Carry your belongings in a secure manner. Women should carry shoulder bags tucked under the arm and held securely by the strap. Men should put their wallets in their front trouser pockets or use money belts or money socks instead of hip pockets. A wallet wrapped in rubberbands is more difficult to remove undetected. Be especially cautious in a large crowd--in the subway, marketplace, at a festival, or if surrounded by groups of children. Do not make it easy for thieves to pick your pocket!

TRAVELER'S ADVISORY

Never stand when you can sit!

Never sit when you can lie down!

Never pass up a chance to use a bathroom!

COMMUNICATING--in a foreign country. Study your phrase book--be prepared. Practical phrases for anywhere you travel include: *Please speak slowly; I don't understand; and I'll see if I can find it in this book.* If the language is familiar, you may need only a good bilingual dictionary. A phrase book can help you use the right words in the right places.

PHONING--Find out when discount phone rates apply. You will not only save money, but you'll also find it's easier to get through at those times. Before calling long distance from your hotel, find out the hotel's fees for calls. Sometimes these are very high. It may be much cheaper to call collect or to use a telephone credit card; but even on these calls your hotel will collect a modest fee for putting the call through. Better still, place your call from the local post office and avoid the surcharge altogether.

♪and away we go! ♪

The following general information is for your travel by air. It is important to realize specific rules may differ from airline to airline. For domestic travel, an airline may provide all its contract terms on or with your ticket. Some may elect to "incorporate terms by reference." This means your ticket does not explain all the terms. Airlines must make available to you the full text of their contract of carriage if you ask. They will mail you a copy free.

For international travel, the detailed requirements for disclosing contract terms do not apply. Airlines file "tariff rules" with the government and passengers are generally bound by these rules. Airline agents must answer your questions about information in the tariff, or if necessary help you locate specific tariff rules. You have a right to know about domestic or international terms of the contract of carriage and you should not be afraid to ask questions.

AIRLINE PASSENGER TIPS--When making a reservation, always ask about fees or penalties for changing or canceling a reservation or a paid ticket. There may be a variety of ticket prices with varying penalties and conditions. Choose the one that best fits your needs.

If a flight is cancelled, ask the airline representative to seat you on the next available flight. Always check the ticket options available on the flight you choose and the options available on alternate flights.

Read the disclosure statement on the back of your ticket. It explains your rights and responsibilities as a passenger, as well as the airline's liability for overbooking seats and for losing or damaging luggage.

When flights are overbooked, airline representatives are required to ask for volunteers to give up their reservations in exchange for payment of the airline's choosing. If you volunteer, be sure to get any compensation arrangements in writing.

If you are "bumped" or involuntarily reassigned to a later flight, the airline must provide you with a written statement of your rights and entitled compensation. The company rules for compensation are available at all airport ticket counters and boarding locations.

If your luggage is lost or damaged in flight, you are entitled to the fair market value of your belongings--up to $1,250 per passenger for checked and $400 for unchecked baggage.

Many airlines offer "excessive value" insurance for luggage above the $1,250 limit. Read the contract terms carefully to figure out exactly what is covered and under what circumstances you are eligible for compensation.

AIRFARE DISCOUNTS--Nearly 90% fly on discounted airfares--why not you? Instead of calling one airline, check with a computerized travel agency; they have fares and destinations for all airlines. These computers make flight schedules and fares immediately available to travel agents and show the highest to the lowest fares between any two locations. You also should be aware of the different types of discounts offered to minimize your flying costs.

■ Off-peak flight discount fares: Monday noon to noon Thursday, and noon Saturday to noon Sunday.

■ Off-season airfares: subject to the location you wish to go and whether it's peak tourist season or not. Airlines limit the number of discounted seats on flights but increase the number during off-season. For example, after April 15 you can look for bargain fares to the Caribbean and Florida. Check with your travel agent.

■ Early-bird discounts: You'll get the lowest fares if you buy your tickets in advance, typically either 7 days or 2 weeks--each offers different discounts. The departure and return dates and times are fixed--you can't change your mind; if you do you could lose 50% to 100% of the ticket price. Once you have purchased tickets, you can't turn them in for a refund.

■ Fly-charter: The number of charter flights has decreased since airlines started offering discount fares. There are still some super bargains, especially in Europe.

SENIOR CITIZEN DISCOUNT AIRFARES--Always ask for a senior citizen discount. You may get a straight 10% discount off most airfares. Or you could qualify for one of the airline senior citizen clubs that offers fare discounts. Continental's Golden Travelers Club and United's Silver Wings Plus (call 1-800-628-2868) are open to travelers 60 and older. If 62 or older, benefits include a 10% discount on all published fares including discount ones. You can get these discounts even with other airlines, such as European carriers, associated with these clubs. Some clubs charge a small fee.

AFRAID TO FLY?--Remember that flying, according to statistics, is 20 times safer than driving in a car. You can reduce risks and your concern if you schedule nonstop flights as 80% of all accidents occur during takeoffs and landings. Schedule your flights so they avoid peak traffic hours at airports. Fly early in the day as you may get a fresh crew. Choose a major carrier over smaller commuter airlines. Avoid airlines that have the lowest-priced tickets as they may be cost cutting. Choose the safest seat, an aisle seat near an emergency exit, over a wing or in the rear of the plane. Don't wear high heels. Wear cotton or wool clothing and not synthetics. Avoid traveling during thunderstorms or during snowy or icy conditions.

When you are in the air, read the safety briefing card at your seat. Study the diagram of how the oxygen mask works. Wear your seat belt at all times. Keep carry-on baggage to a minimum. Avoid caffeine, sugar, and alcohol before and during the flight. Meet the crew, if you can, and ask questions--even silly ones. Walk around the cabin and talk to other flyers. Think positive thoughts. Take deep breaths, lean back, relax, and avoid upsetting ideas.

Keep repeating the
three magic words
from Sai Baba
Not to worry!

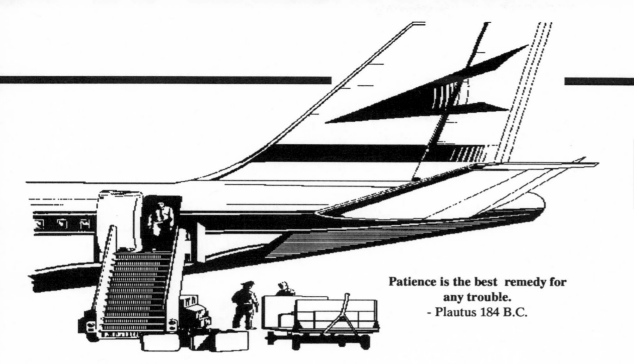

Patience is the best remedy for any trouble.
- Plautus 184 B.C.

To qualify for compensation, you must have a confirmed reservation, meet the deadline for buying your ticket, and meet the ticketing or check-in deadline for that particular airline. If you miss the ticketing or check-in deadline, you may have lost your reservation and your right to compensation particularly if the flight is oversold.

AIRLINE DELAYS--Delays occur because of bad weather, "bunched" flights, limited airport capacities, not enough air-traffic controllers, and mechanical failure. Airlines are under no obligation to get ticketed passengers to their destinations at any scheduled time. Neither do they need to compensate you for missed cruises, tours, and connections.

ON-TIME RATINGS--The largest U.S. airlines now must rate each flight's on-time arrival record. On time is defined as within 14 minutes of the scheduled time. The rating is from 0 to 9. This number stands for the percentage of on-time arrivals, for example, 8 means 80% of that flight's arrivals are on time; 2 signifies 20 percent. This number appears next to the flight number on the computer screens of airline and travel agents. You have a right to know the number.

DEALING WITH DELAYS
❑ Use the on-time rating system to select airlines and flights.
❑ Before you leave for the airport, call to see if the flight is on time.
❑ Allow an hour to make a domestic connecting flight and more time in cities with congested airports.
❑ If your flight is cancelled or seriously delayed and you have an emergency such as a family illness, cruise ship departures, etc., tell the airline's counter representative, who will try to help.
❑ When a flight is cancelled or going to be delayed for several hours, ask the airline to place you on the next available flight. They may put you on a competitor's flight if they have nothing scheduled. Ask the airline to endorse your ticket to the new carrier; this could save you a fare increase.
❑ Check with airline staff to find out what services they will provide. Ask about meals and phone calls. Request a meal voucher if a delay extends through a mealtime. If the

delay extends past 1 A.M. request a hotel voucher. Airlines will not provide meal or hotel vouchers at the origin of a flight.
❑ Avoid traveling at peak times.
❑ Be prepared for delays--they will occur. Stay calm. Getting upset doesn't help.

OVERBOOKING--Most airlines overbook their scheduled flights to a certain extent and sometimes require passengers to be "bumped"--left behind. Airlines ask for volunteers to give up their seats and they receive compensation for doing so. If you are not in a rush you can sell back your seat. Before you do, find out what airline can confirm your seat, and what amenities such as free meals, hotel rooms, telegrams, or transportation will be provided. Airlines may bargain with you.

> **Most airlines bump
> the last people
> to arrive
> at the boarding gate!**

INVOLUNTARY BUMPING--If you are bumped, ask for a written statement of your rights. Frequently, you are entitled to an on-the-spot payment of denied boarding compensation. If the airline can get you to your destination by any means within an hour of your expected arrival time, there is no compensation. If they get you there within 2 hours (4 hours on international flights) they must pay you equal to the one-way fare, with a maximum of $200. The compensation doubles (200% of the fare, $400 maximum) if greater than 2 hours (4 hours international).

The compensation rules do not apply to charter flights, flights of less than 60 passengers, inbound international flights, or flying between two foreign cities.

BAGGAGE--Between the time you check your luggage in and the time you claim it at your destination, it may have passed through a maze of conveyor belts, baggage carts, and forklifts. Once airborne, baggage may tumble around in the cargo compartment if the plane hits rough air. Relatively few bags are damaged or lost.

You can reduce the possibility that yours is the one that gets lost by placing labels inside and out. Lock your bags to prevent pilferage. If they do arrive with broken locks or torn sides, check inside immediately. If something is missing notify the airline right away.

Never put money, jewelry, cameras, medicine, liquids, glass, or any other things that are valuable, irreplaceable, delicate, or have sentimental value in your check-in bag. If you are taking these items with you put them in your carry-on bag. Fragile items should be packed in containers specially designed to survive rough handling--preferably a factory-sealed carton or a padded hard-shell case.

BAGGAGE TAGS--The airline puts destination tags on your bags and gives you the stubs as claim checks. Each tag has a three-letter code and flight number showing the plane and final airport designation. Double-check the tag. Don't lose your claim checks.

If your bags are delayed, lost, or damaged on a domestic flight, the airline may invoke a $1,250 ceiling of total value. If you think what you are taking is worth more, purchase "excess valuation." Airlines may refuse to sell excess valuation on some valuable or breakable items. On international flights, unless you buy excess valuation, the liability limits are 250 French gold francs for each kilo (approximately $10 per pound--dependent upon the exchange rate).

Luggage, baggage claims, and airline safety

CARRY-ON LUGGAGE--Your carry-on luggage should have overall dimensions of no more than 40 inches (20 inches long by 15 inches high by 9 inches wide). It should not weigh more than 40 pounds. The size and weight can vary with plane size and carrier so check with your airline. Put your name and address on all carry-on luggage, including camera bags and binocular cases. Sew a name tag in topcoats, raincoats, etc. The airlines provide no insurance coverage for carry-on items you left on the plane or lost. If identified, you might find them at the airline's lost and found department.

DAMAGED BAGS--If your luggage arrives smashed or torn, the airline will usually pay for repairs or negotiate a settlement if it can't be repaired. Report external damage before you leave the airport. Insist on filling out a form. Airlines may refuse to pay for damage to fragile items in your bags, or where there is no evidence of external damage.

When you check in, airline personnel should let you know if they think your bags or packages may not survive the trip intact. They may ask you to sign a waiver so they are not at risk--except they may pay for damages caused by their negligence shown by external injury.

DELAYED BAGS--If your bags don't arrive when you do, don't panic. The airlines have means to track down 98% of misplaced bags and return them to you. Fill out a form describing your loss before you leave the airport and keep a copy. Some airlines will provide you with money for emergency purchases while they look for your bags.

The amount depends upon if you are away from home and how long it takes to track down your bags. If you do get cash, purchase only necessities and keep all receipts. If airlines misplace sporting equipment, they sometimes will pay rental fees.

TRAVEL TIP

If you are traveling with someone else, wear the same bright-colored clothes. Then, it will be easy to spot each other in crowds.

LOST LUGGAGE--Once declared officially lost, you may have to submit a claim unless the airline uses the form you completed when your bag was considered simply missing; check on this. Your claim, including the value of your bags and contents, is then subject to negotiations between you and the airlines. They often ask for sales receipts to back your claim. Airlines don't automatically pay the full amount of the claim. Claims take 6 weeks to 3 months.

HAZARDOUS ITEMS--It is illegal and extremely dangerous to carry on board or to check in your luggage the following items:

Aerosols–polishes, waxes, degreasers, cleaners, etc.
Corrosives--acids, cleaners, wet cell batteries, etc.
Flammables--paints, thinners, lighter fluid, liquid reservoir lighters, cleaners, adhesives, etc.
Explosives--fireworks, flares, signal devices, loaded firearms, etc. (Small arms ammunition for personal use may be transported in checked luggage securely packed in fiberboard, wood, or metal boxes. These may not be placed in carry-on bags.)
Radioactives--betascopes, radiopharmaceuticals, uninstalled pacemakers, etc.
Compressed gases--Tear gas or protective-type sprays, oxygen cylinders, divers' tanks (unless they are empty), etc.
Loose book matches or safety matches--may be carried only on your person.

If you must travel with any of these items check with the airline's freight department to see if arrangements can be made. Otherwise carrying hazardous items carries a civil penalty of up to $10,000, or a criminal one of up to $25,000 and up to 5 years in jail.

AIRLINE SAFETY--Every time you board a plane:

❑ Make sure all your carry-on luggage will fit under the seat in front of you.
❑ Be careful about what you put into the storage bins over your seat. Their doors may pop open during an accident or even a hard landing. Bins are intended to hold coats, blankets, pillows, not hard suitcases or packages.
❑ Always keep your seat belt fastened and know how it works.
❑ Pay attention to the safety briefing explaining how to use the emergency procedures.
❑ Review the safety information on the plastic card in the seat pocket.
❑ Look for the closest emergency exit and have a second in mind.
❑ Stay in your seat with your seat belt buckled until the plane comes to a complete halt at the departure gate.

IF YOU ARE IN AN ACCIDENT
❑ Stay calm.
❑ Listen to crew members and do exactly what they say.
❑ Before you try to open any emergency exit yourself, look outside the window. If you see a fire, don't open it or the fire may spread into the cabin. Try to use your alternate escape route.
❑ Remember, smoke rises, so try to stay down if there is smoke in the cabin. If you have a cloth, put it over your nose and mouth.

GOT COMPLAINTS?--First, talk to the airline's Customer Service Representative at the airport. If you can't resolve the problem and want to file a complaint, it's best to write the airline's consumer office. Include your daytime phone number, flight numbers, dates, and times. State what happened and who was involved. Send copies of all tickets, stubs, or other receipts. State what you expect from the carrier to make amends. Be reasonable. The airlines will probably treat your complaint seriously.

If you need assistance or want to put your complaint about an airline on record, call or write:

Office of Community and
Consumer Affairs
U.S. Department of Transportation
400 7th Street, S.W., Room 10405
Washington, D.C. 20590

♪ on the road again! ♪

SECURITY ON THE ROAD

If driving, plan your route carefully, travel on main roads, and use maps. Map two routes for each auto trip. One should be the quickest route, the other the most scenic. Rand McNally and AAA are good sources. Avoid traveling during night hours.

Have your car serviced and tires checked before leaving. Keep car doors locked at all times. Wear seat belts. Don't drive too long.

Never pick up hitchhikers. Do not stop to offer help to a stranded motorist. Go to a telephone booth and call for assistance.

Don't get out of the car if there are suspicious individuals nearby. Drive away. If you suspect someone is following you, drive to the nearest service station, restaurant, or business and call the police or sheriff's department. If you believe it is unsafe to get out of your car, honk your horn and flash your lights to draw attention.

CAR SECURITY

Never leave your car unlocked. Always lock valuables out of sight, preferably in the trunk. Always carry wallets, checkbooks, and purses with you. Do not advertise that you are a tourist. Place maps and travel brochures in the glove compartment.

If you stop overnight, remove bags and other valuables from the car and take them inside. Don't park your car on the street overnight if the hotel has a garage or secure area. If you must park on the street, select a well-lit area. Check the back seat before getting in. Mark your car radio and other removable car equipment with your driver's license number.

BE PREPARED ON THE ROAD
Carry these safety items:

flashlight and fresh batteries
fire extinguisher
gloves
spare tire, jack, and lug nut wrench
tool kit
first aid kit
jumper cables
flares/warning triangles
blanket

IN CASE OF A BREAKDOWN--If your car breaks down, get the vehicle as far off the road as possible. Raise the hood and attach a white cloth to the car antenna as an emergency signal. Get passengers out of the vehicle and away from traffic. Set up flares or warning triangles at least 250 feet behind the vehicle. Stand on the shoulder at least 100 feet behind the vehicle to signal for help. Ask anyone who stops to call the police or a garage. Don't attempt to fix a flat in busy traffic--wait for roadside assistance. If you must remain inside the vehicle while waiting for help, keep your seat belt fastened. If you must abandon your car, keep all passengers together.

> # Don't advertise your travel plans to strangers!

TRAVELING IN FOREIGN COUNTRIES
Find out about the international driver's license beforehand. Some countries will not allow people over 70 to rent cars. There may be other restrictions. Memorize the international road signs. Check out the auto insurance requirements before you enter each country. Learn the words for police officer and doctor. Know the location of the nearest U.S. consulate. If you rent a vehicle, don't insist on an American model if there are not many in use. Make sure a rental car is in good repair.

HOTEL AND MOTEL SECURITY

When you first check in, get a map of the city with your hotel or motel location clearly marked. Get a map of the bus and subway lines. Ask an English-speaking hotel employee to explain the local public transportation system. Find out the proper charges for taxis, and if there is a surcharge for night or holiday trips.

If possible, book a room between the second and the seventh floor--above ground level to prevent easy entrance from outside and low enough for fire equipment to reach. Keep your hotel/motel door locked at all times. Use all auxiliary locking devices on doors and windows. Use the door viewer to identify anyone requesting entry. Open the door only if you are certain the person has a legitimate reason to enter your room. If in doubt, call the office. Be observant. Report any suspicious movements in the corridors or rooms to the management.

Determine the most direct route to and from your room to the fire escapes, elevators, and nearest telephone. Know how to use the room phone or where a pay phone is located. Make a note of emergency numbers you may need: police, fire, your hotel, the nearest U.S Embassy or consulate. Know how to use the pay phone and have the proper change on hand.

Learn a few phrases in the local language so you can signal your need for help, the police, or a doctor.

Unpack and place belongings in the closet and dresser. Arrange your things so you will know if anything is missing. Inventory your belongings daily. Consider locking any electrical appliances in your luggage. Suitcases should always be locked so they cannot be used to carry your property out of your room.

Never leave money, checks, credit cards, or car keys in the room. Always take them with you. Use the hotel/motel safe to store extra cash, expensive jewelry, or other valuables. Report any lost or stolen items to the management and the police.

Cruising at its best--seniors at sea

navigate in narrow passages large cruise vessels cannot reach. Nature is a common focus, and your cruise line may feature naturalists on board who'll present slide shows, conduct lectures, and guide shore expeditions. Other themes may be archeology, marine wildlife, or astronomy.

Theme cruises are offered on vessels both large and small. Topics can range from health (with well-known physicians aboard to conduct lectures and workshops) to big band music (with well-known musicians and celebrities aboard to set the rhythm!) to bridge tournaments. There are even murder mystery cruises where you can play sleuth.

Yacht cruises offer the ultimate in luxury. Personal service, gourmet dining, elegant surroundings, and access to intimate ports are part of the allure. **River cruises** may be aboard barges, steamers, ferries, even one-time Mississippi paddleboats. Every day brings another port, and though the activities and amenities are not as luxurious as those offered on ocean liners, you'll still enjoy fine service.

Many of us remember when taking a trip on a cruise ship was only for the wealthy. Because we do remember, it is hard to break stereotypes and change impressions. Obviously times have changed, and now those who can afford a modest vacation can manage to find a cruise that will fit their needs and means.

TWO VIEWS OF CRUISING

There are many approaches to cruising that vary according to need and desire. However, there are two basic approaches that may help you to think about what you might choose to do.

1. A cruise can be viewed as a large and luxurious resort with many amenities that happens to go to interesting and/or exotic places.

2. A ship can be seen as a floating hotel room that offers ports of call and the attendant adventure of those places.

Obviously you look for very different accommodations if you desire number one rather than number two. In the cruise industry today there are all gradations between these two extremes. With the new launching or remodeling of each cruise ship luxury and pampering have been refined to new heights. Large ships have also permitted the addition of such amenities as big-name entertainers.

At the other end of the scale, some small ships have been added to the array of choices. They often offer less plush accommodations but permit the option of special experiences such as sailing up a river or pulling up to the shoreline where you can explore, shop, or snorkel without elaborate and difficult debarking activities. Another more specialized sort of trip is offered by sailing ships that cruise. These can be as a pampered passenger or as one who takes a turn at hoisting sail or taking the helm.

CHOOSE THE RIGHT TYPE OF CRUISE FOR YOU

If you're interested in doing in-depth sightseeing, inquire whether your cruise offers pre- or post-cruise extensions. These packages usually include a few nights at a hotel in your port of embarkation or debarkation. It's a great way to make the most of your sight-seeing time, and your package often includes some touring, meals, or special event. For more in-depth land exploration, a cruise tour fits the bill. Part of your intinerary will be spent cruising (with several port stops), and then you'll disembark for a land tour (with overnight stays in hotels). Alaska is one kind of popular destination for this kind of cruise, which really offers the best of both worlds.

If your goal is to enjoy a relaxing getaway where you can simply pamper yourself, consider a transoceanic crossing or a cruise to nowhere. These let you take full advantage of the "resort at sea" your ship really is.

Expedition cruises focus less on luxury (though amenities are at your disposal), and more on adventure, education, and exploring. Your destinations may be more exotic, rugged, out-of-way places. Generally, your vessel will be smaller in order to

SPECIAL CRUISES

Sometimes we can be enticed to get on a cruise ship for other reasons than the destination. Thus there are a number of different special categories that may beckon. Among the most popular:

* Alumni Cruises (most universities sponsor them)
* Celebrity Cruises (travel with your favorite entertainer or sports figure)
* Conference Cruises (financial seminars--write it off)
* Fitness or Calorie Cruises
* Freighter Travel
* Senior Cruises
* Singles Cruises (young or old)

CHOOSE THE RIGHT-SIZE SHIP FOR YOU

Ships come in four basic sizes: **intimate,** up to 10,000 gross registered tonnage (grt, the weight of a ship in the water); **small** (between 10,000 and 20,000 grt); **medium** (between 20,000 and 30,000 grt); and **large** (30,000 grt and over). The larger the ship, the more passengers it holds, which will affect your possibilities for socializing, service, convenience (waiting in lines for events, excursions, etc.), and general atmosphere.

Remember that larger ships often cannot dock right in the port. In these cases, your ship will anchor at sea and you will be ferried to shore by tender. These small craft make frequent round trips, so you can get back aboard ship at various times. Just ask a crew member for the schedule. The inconvenience of tendering ashore may be offset by the other advantages of a large ship.

FIND OUT ABOUT YOUR CRUISE LINE
They vary in many ways besides price. Atmosphere is a critical distinguishing factor. Ask your travel agent or tour company about the general style of the ship: elegant? casual? oriented toward mature travelers, young singles, or families? These issues can have a big impact on your overall enjoyment of the cruise.

DESTINATIONS
The multiplication of cruise vessels has led to the concomitant growth in cruise destinations. Here are the most popular:
* Alaska
* Australia/New Zealand
* Black Sea/Turkey
* The Caribbean
* The Danube
* Eastern Canada
* Greek Islands
* Hawaiian Islands
* Mediterranean
* Mexican Riviera
* The Mississippi
* The Nile
* Panama Canal
* Scandinavian Fjords
* South America
* Southeast Asia

Of course there are many more, but we could all find one or more places we would like to go from that list, especially if we could travel in the comfort of a cruise ship with haute cuisine.

ADVENTURE DESTINATIONS
There are literally hundreds of special destinations that would be tempting for even the armchair traveler, but just to whet your appetite here are just five that should get your imagination working:
* Antarctica
* The Amazon
* Easter Island
* The Galapagos
* Tahiti

QUESTIONS AND ANSWERS
Are you ready to pack your bags? I'm sure you still have some questions such as what to pack or about getting seasick. Indeed, two of the most persistent questions about cruising are dressing for dinner and tipping. Happily, on most cruises you don't need formal wear for the dressy occasions. You will feel more comfortable at the captain's dinner if you wear a dark business suit rather than tennis togs. There will be some tuxedos and more, but some people like to dress up. Some ships will expect a jacket and tie for evening events. Others will not. On the other hand, if you choose a 14-day cruise in a $10,000 cabin you can be certain that dinner will be formal.

What else you pack depends somewhat on your destination and the program aboard ship. Sportswear, shorts, swimsuits, and good shoes for walking and play aboard ship will be needed. If you are going to Alaska or somewhere else where it can be rainy and cold, pack rain gear and a very warm jacket.

Sailing is also more possible for more people now from the standpoint of seasickness. There are two major reasons. Modern ships are now more stable, so that some of the most unpleasant motion is minimized. The other large change is the medication that is now available. Without going into great detail, Dramamine and other drugs have made a trip on a ship possible for millions who formerly would have found only misery at sea. Talk to your doctor about your best bet. One of the most convenient applications is dispensed from a stick-on bandage. Remember also that you will undoubtedly have the service of a doctor on board for this and any other medical problems that might arise. As with medical care at home, specific information about medical conditions and medications you take will help. Be sure to bring an adequate supply of any prescription medications you must take.

Can you take the kids or grandchildren? In general, yes. However, it is best to check on the nature of a given ship and its facilities for entertaining and care of children. Obviously some destinations will be more interesting to children than others.

Tipping is a subject we all feel concern about. Most cruise lines and travel books will suggest what is appropriate. You will feel much more at ease if you check this out

before you leave and budget generously for it. Then, when you find that certain service is not up to expectations, you tip less or not at all and come home with money in your pocket.

GETTING INFORMATION ABOUT CRUISES
There are many sources and some of the best are friends and family who have taken particular cruises or ships. Remember that it should be recent because all kinds of things change very rapidly in the cruise industry these days. One only has to trace the history of an older vessel through different owners and staff to see that up-to-date information is a must. If you have a good travel agent you trust, ask him/her for advice. There are many books on the subject. Haunt your library to find the best for your purposes. Most travel publications have sections on cruises. *Cruise Travel Magazine* is devoted totally to cruising on the latest new or refurbished vessels and schedules of departures. Other annual publications such as Frommer's give you information about all destinations and ships available for the traveler.

SAVING MONEY ON YOUR CRUISE BOOKING
There are many ways to save money on the cruise you plan. The two things that help most are to plan early and to be flexible. Put some research into your planning and compare prices. Here are some suggestions:
1. Select a cruise line that is less expensive than others.
2. Go during the off-season. Tropical cruises are cheaper in the summer.
3. Wait until the last moment and bargain with the cruise line. They may be willing to cut the price to avoid vacancies.
4. Deal with an organization that specializes in selling short-notice travel. Three of them are: Stand Buys, Spur of the Moment, and Grand Circle's Last Minute cruise club.
5. Decide early so you can get early booking discounts and will have the cheaper accommodations available to you.
6. Some large travel organizations obtain discounted fares because of their huge buying power.
7. If you live in Seattle and the ship sails from Miami, look for sea-air packages. This can cut the cost of your airfare because of the early booking of low cost space by the cruise companies.
Bon Voyage!

Portions of this article are taken from the brochure "Going Abroad: 101 Tips for Mature Travelers" by Grand Circle Travel, 347 Congress St., Boston, MA 02210; call 1-800-221-2610 for free travel advice.

Unlimited 1st-class travel in 17 countrie.

Probably most Americans have never ridden on an inter-city train. Train travel began to suffer losses when air travel became so much faster and then eventually more economical. So, in spite of the rebirth and interest in rail travel in the United States, most have not used it.

Many Americans have had their interest in rail travel rekindled because of their positive experiences in using trains in Europe or Japan. There one finds rail travel is fast, convenient, frequent, comfortable, and economical. For the person who is touring Europe, rail travel is a great way to go, because you see so much more as you travel, and you can leave from the center of the city rather than miles and miles from the city center at an airport.

Plan Ahead

The Eurailpass is a prime example of why it is important to plan ahead if you are going to travel. Besides, that is half the fun--anticipating what to expect and discovering how best to use your precious vacation time. The Eurailpass and all separate country passes must be purchased before you leave home. They are not available in Europe. Therefore, you must decide before you leave home whether a pass will save you money and be a convenience. If touring is your plan, then some sort of rail pass makes real sense.

What You Get

Eurailpass gives you unlimited travel in first class on the trains of 17 different countries for a given period of time. It is important to understand that Britain is not one of these countries.

You buy an open pass and then, when you are ready to use it, you take it to any ticket counter to have it validated before board-

ing the train. Now you are in business. You must still make reservations, especially for the crack trains, and Spain even requires a boarding pass for its trains. However, making a reservation is a small price to pay for assuring space to travel. The following 17 different countries will give you plenty to choose from:

Austria	Ireland
Belgium	Italy
Denmark	Luxembourg
Finland	Norway
France	Portugal
Germany	Spain
Greece	Sweden
Holland	Switzerland
Hungary	

The cost of a first-class 15-day Eurailpass is approximately $350. The cost of a 21-day pass is approximately $450. Longer periods up to 6 months are also available. The passes also get you free or reduced rates on many buses, ferries, and steamers. Traveling with a group of three or more people (two in off season) can qualify for a Eurail Saverpass and is considerably less expensive. There are no senior discounts.

Other Eurailpasses

There are group passes that provide special rates. A Youthpass that provides second-class travel for persons under 26 years of age is also available. This gives one month of unlimited travel for about $380. There are also combination rail/drive passes now that provide so many days of rail travel and so many of car rental, depending upon the combination you select. The so-called Flexpass gives the holder a given number of days of travel within a longer period, such as 5 days of rail travel during a period of 15 days.

Country Passes

Almost every country has its own pass arrangement so that if you are limiting your travel to that area you can obtain a pass for less than the cost of the Eurailpass. Perhaps the best known of these is the Britrail Pass. They even have a combination BritFrance Pass that allows travel in both countries. These too must be purchased before you leave the United States.

Where to Buy These Passes

Your travel agent can facilitate your purchase of these rail passes, or you may buy them direct from the agency representa-

tives in the United States. One American company that can sell you all of the different passes offered in Europe and Britain is The Forsyth Travel Library, 9154 West 57th Street, P.O. Box 2975, Shawnee Mission, KS 66201-1375. Forsyth has brochures that describe all of these passes in the same document so that your choices are clear. They also have a complete collection of travel books from Fodor, Frommer, and Michelin, as well as maps of all countries and cities you may wish to visit.

If you do decide on a rail pass, you definitely will want to purchase a copy of Thomas Cook's European Timetable. It is published monthly and costs $19.95 plus freight and handling.

Each year new features are added to these rail passes. For example, 1991 is the first year that the eastern part of Germany has been included in Eurailpass. Travel experts are predicting that eventually Britain will be included in the Eurailpass. When the channel tunnel is completed between Britain and France, new packages will be forthcoming to speed your travels. Therefore, be sure to get the latest information when you plan your trip. For information on Eurailpasses call your travel agent or write to Eurailpass, Box 325, Greenwich, CT 06870.

To emphasize the fact that there are numerous choices available, we list here the different passes that are enumerated in the Forsyth Library brochure:

Britrail/Drive Pass
Britrail Flexipass
Britrail Pass
BritFrance Railpass
Eurailpass
Eurail Flexpass
Eurail Saverpass
France Fly Rail & Drive Pass
France Railpass
France Rail & Drive Pass
German Rail Pass
Hertz Eurail Drive Pass
Holland Leisure Card
Italian Rail Pass
London Visitor's Travel Card
Scanrailpass
Spain Rail Pass
Swiss Card
Swiss Flexpass
Swiss Pass
Swiss Rail & Drive Pass

The overwhelming characteristic of Alaska is its size. One recalls the story about the Texan who annoyed an Alaskan so much with his bragging that the Alaskan threatened to cut his state in half and make Texas number three in area. The other geographical reality is that there are several Alaskas.

Beginning in the far north is the Arctic and Western Section. With almost no population and few visitors, it is remote wilderness, consisting mainly of treeless tundra. The exceptions are the small settlements of Point Barrow, Nome, Katzebu, and Prudhoe Bay. Central or Interior Alaska, while largely wilderness, does have the city of Fairbanks, and one of the most sought-out sights in Alaska--Mt. McKinley and Denali National Parks.

Southwest Alaska and the Aleutians point out into the Bering Sea toward Asia. Best known to many of us because of the activities there during World War II, there are the population centers of Kodiak, Dutch Harbor, Bethel, and Dillingham. This area is also famous for the Pribilof Islands with the huge seal populations.

South-central Alaska is relatively more populated with Anchorage, Seward, Homer, Valdez, Whittier, and Cordoba. By most standards, these cities are small and the wilderness and natural wonders that abound in the area make it a marvelous place to visit.

Southeast Alaska is the part that is closest to the lower 48, and the most populated part of the state. Juneau, the capital, Ketchikan, Wrangel, Petersburg, Sitka, Haines, and Skagway are all found here. It consists of an incredible network of islands, bays, peninsulas, and waterways that make the sea an integral part of the state.

GETTING THERE
The most popular way of getting to Alaska today is by air. The major airlines that serve the state are: Alaska, Delta, Northwest, TWA, United, and Hawaiian. Almost every major international airline also serves Alaska, mostly as a stopover point on the way to Asia or Europe. The major terminal is Anchorage.

You can drive to Alaska, and although it is a much easier trip than before the Alcan Highway opened, it is still a long hard drive of about 2,000 miles from Seattle to Anchorage. Another route is to drive north to Prince Rupert, British Columbia, and take Alaska Ferry Service from there. There is a regular ferry service from Seattle to Southeastern Alaska with accommodations for automobiles.

CRUISE SHIPS
In recent years, cruising to Alaska has become one of the most common means of touring the 49th state. There is no shortage of choices of cruise lines. As of this writing, the following companies serve Alaska:

Chandris Celebrity Cruises
Clipper Cruise Line
Costa Cruises
Cunard Line
Holland America/Westours
P & O--Princess Line
Regency Cruises
Royal Caribbean Cruise Line
Royal Viking Line
Windstar Sail Cruises
World Explorer Cruises

Most of these offer the conventional cruises on large ships with all the trimmings. Clipper Line, however, has ships that carry only about 100 passengers. Windstar Line's Wind Spirit is a computerized sailing ship that carries only 148 passengers for a very special experience. Its 13-foot draft allows this vessel to go into areas that the large ships cannot.

One other unusual cruise ship is The Universe of World Explorer Cruises. This ship leads the double life of being a floating campus for the University of Pittsburgh during the winter and an Alaskan cruise ship in the summer. It has an 11,000-volume library and all sorts of academic professionals aboard to offer instruction or enrichment in flora, fauna, history, etc., for passengers on a two-week cruise. Even the cultural arts are represented.

GETTING AROUND ALASKA
The Alaska Railroad is state-owned, and while it has limited routes, it does provide a spectacular ride. It begins in Anchorage and goes 350 miles to Fairbanks. On the way it passes through Mt. McKinley and Denali National Parks. There is also a line from Anchorage to Whittier and one to Seward. Whittier offers access to the exquisite Prince William Sound.

Two major but separate ferry lines connect many points in South Central Alaska and Southeastern Alaska. Both lines have feeder routes that go to smaller communities. The South Central system connects Kodiak and Dutch Harbor, among other destinations. One unique feature of these lines is that in spring, winter, and fall senior citizens have free fare, although they are charged for accommodations such as staterooms.

WHAT TO DO IN ALASKA
If you tour Alaska independently, you need to spend considerable time planning where you want to go and what you want to see. This state is far too complex to wait until you get there to make these decisions. A few dollars spent on books and maps before you go can pay off in many ways, both in terms of enhanced pleasure and money saved. Alaska offers incredible beauty and a lot more. It is a feast for the eyes. Everywhere you go spectacular beauty awaits you. If you have the time, hiking, camping, river-running, and mountain climbing are available.

One of the most exciting things about visiting Alaska is the ever-present sense of history. Remnants of the gold rush remind us of that exciting phase of the past. Place names like the Yukon, Skagway, Dawson, and Chilkoot Pass help us to recall the past. There are also reminders of the Russians and their tenure in Alaska.

Exposure to Indian and Eskimo arts and culture is also a high point of a trip to Alaska. You will want to bring back a permanent reminder of your trip in the form of stone carvings, a totem pole, or similar purchase. These objects are simple and elegant at the same time.

Finally, sportsmen find Alaska a paradise. Hunting and fishing are unparalleled anywhere. Lakes, rivers, and the sea offer an experience for the Isaac Walton in you that will never be forgotten.

Haven't you put off that trip to Alaska too long?

Caribbean--a most memorable travel experience

All the popular notions about Caribbean travel are true. There are palm trees, sandy beaches, calypso music, cruise ships, and trade winds. But there is much more. Certainly in the New World there is no place where so many different cultures are in such juxtaposition.

The Caribbean, especially if you add the Bahamas, is a huge area. It literally stretches from North to South America. It is 1500 miles long and 700 miles wide. For the most part, these islands separate the Atlantic Ocean from the Caribbean. Thus the Atlantic side of the islands tends to be the most stormy and the leeward side offers the best beaches and leisure areas.

The western reaches of the Caribbean wash the coasts of the Cancun Peninsula in Mexico, Guatemala, Honduras, Costa Rica, Panama, Colombia, and Venezuela. History has left a rich heritage in many of these places. You can begin with the ancient ruins on the Yucatan Peninsula, move through the islands where Columbus and other explorers sailed and left their mark, and then see the remnants of the colonial era in the presence of the English, Spanish, French, Dutch, and Danes.

THE SPANISH
The most predominant European culture to be enjoyed is the Spanish. Between Cuba, Puerto Rico, Dominican Republic, and numerous other islands, the Spanish language, culture, and religion remains, even though Spain itself is no longer present. In these areas you find cathedrals and many other remnants of transplanted Spanish culture. Spanish music remains also, but

with a very distinctive Caribbean flavor that has been added. Some of the more ancient buildings are being restored. One of the most handsome is the house of Diego Columbus in Santo Domingo.

THE BRITISH
The presence of the English is also felt in many areas of the Caribbean and the Bahamas, Jamaica, the Virgin Islands, and Barbados. One of the favorite activities in these places is shopping. Local products are supplemented by all of the typical British goods such as china. Here especially one hears the distinctive treatment of the English language by local cultures, both in spoken language and music.

THE FRENCH
Martinique and Guadeloupe are the largest French islands in the Caribbean. There you can experience both French culture and government and the influence of the indigenous people. One half of the small island of St. Martin is also French. In spite of their half being only 21 square miles, it is distinctively French.

THE DUTCH
The Dutch own the other half of the island, but they spell it Sint Maarten. This is the smallest area in the world where two distinct countries coexist and maintain their language and culture so successfully.

Other popular Dutch destinations are in the Netherlands Antilles. The best known are Aruba and Curacao. These islands allow you to enjoy Dutch architecture, language, and food in a benign climate.

HOW TO GET THERE
There are many direct flights from the population centers of the north and northeast United States. West coast residents will probably fly through Miami, but an enterprising travel agent may be able to arrange a stopover in New York for very little additional fare. Many Caribbean cruises leave from Miami and provide wonderful samplers of Caribbean life as they go from port to port.

CRUISING
There are many cruise ships that serve the Caribbean. They tend to be limited to short stays at the islands they visit, so they are not usually a way to get to a destination for a

longer visit. Cruising is a topic in itself and provides a marvelous sampler of these islands.

SAILING
The Caribbean is one of the greatest areas of the world for sailing. Trade winds tend to make it always satisfying and exciting for those who enjoy this pastime. There are large sailing vessels that provide cruises for those who wish. There are numerous places in the Caribbean where charters are available for either powerboats or sailboats. They are available in a variety of sizes and with or without crew. Friends often share the cost of such a charter by going together. Boats can also be chartered with or without provisions.

TRAVEL DOCUMENTS
Tourists have been known to travel all through the Caribbean on a driver's license or voting card. However, it is much better to have a valid passport to avoid any problem with customs or immigration. This is especially true if you plan to stop at several islands.

Some areas require the use of local currency, but many accept American money and prefer it.

There are no special health requirements to travel in the Caribbean, but it always pays to check with your local health department or clinic where they stay up to date on local hazards. Be sure to obtain timely information about political conditions for the area you wish to visit. For example, Haiti has had many troubles and violent episodes. Be sure that conditions are suitable for tourist travel before going to such a destination.

It's time to stop putting it off and plan a trip to the Caribbean. It will be one of your most memorable travel experiences, no matter which areas you visit. If you are not sure where you want to go, take a cruise and then return to the places you liked best. Then you can spend some time to really enjoy those areas as they should be enjoyed.

> The world is a great book,
> of which those who never
> stir from home
> read only a page.
> - Augustine (354-430 A.D.)

Because we share a 4,000-mile border with Canada and think of its citizens as being "like us," you may not think of Canada as a good place to travel or vacation. Nothing could be more wrong. Of course, Canadians are North Americans as we are, but there is a difference, and it is especially true in French Canada and in the Maritime Provinces. What west-coast Canadians may lack in exotic quality they make up for in their warm and open hospitality.

Perhaps the most salient feature of our northern neighbor is its vastness. There are ten provinces and two territories comprising 3,851,809 square miles, almost 16,000 square miles larger than the U.S. With its small population, there are not many people per square mile. As everyone knows, the vast majority of Canadians live close to the U.S. border.

To be realistic, with the exception of the west coast, Canada is not comfortable for the traveler except in the summer and short periods in the spring and fall. On the other hand, if winter sport is your thing, it is great year-round.

Railroad Travel
After World War II when U.S. rail travel began its decline with the accompanying growth of airlines, many of our citizens discovered the joys of transcontinental travel through Canada. In those days it was the Canadian Pacific and the Canadian National Railways. In 1977, the two systems merged and became VIA Rail Canada.

The most spectacular part of that trip is from Vancouver, British Columbia, to Calgary, Alberta, through the Canadian Rockies. However, the rest of the trip to Halifax, Nova Scotia, is well worthwhile and the whole trip takes about four days.

Canrail passes, sometimes with senior discounts, are available for unlimited travel at certain times each year. For more information write VIA Rail, 2 Place Ville Marie, Suite 400, Montreal, Quebec H3G, or call (514) 871-1331. Amtrak connects Washington, D.C., and New York with Montreal.

Every province has a tourist office with information about visiting that part of Canada. Tourist offices are available in the Canadian embassy in Washington, D.C., and consulates in Atlanta, Dallas, Los Angeles, and San Francisco.

Incidentally, it is possible to travel in much of Canada without a passport. They require a proof of citizenship and of residence, and naturalized U.S. citizens should carry proof of their naturalization. However, the passport solves all such problems, so it is best to carry one if you have it. Now let's talk about what there is to see in Canada.

Maritime Provinces
If you look at the map of eastern Canada you see quickly why Nova Scotia, New Brunswick, Prince Edward Island, and Newfoundland (including Labrador) are called the Maritime Provinces. They face the wild North Atlantic, and give way to the Gulf of St. Lawrence and connecting waterways. The most important cities and ports are Halifax, Nova Scotia, St. John's, Newfoundland, and Saint John, New Brunswick. A popular way of visiting is by cruise ship from U.S. east coast ports.

These areas have rich historical pasts that are evident in monuments, museums, and the backgrounds of the residents. Today's population is a mixture of French, English, Scotch, German, Indian, those related to runaway slaves from the War of 1812, and others from the United States.

Shipping and fishing have been the major commercial activities of the region, although military activity must be a close rival because of the strategic locations of major ports and settlements.

Quebec
The province of Quebec was, of course, part of a French colony in the 1700s. The Treaty of Paris (1763) finalized diplomatically what had been settled in 1759 on the battlefield, and Quebec became part of the British colony of Canada. Through years of conflict Quebec was given more and more independence in language, laws, and culture, but it remained part of Canada. As we learn in the news reports, this question is not settled for all time. Some in Quebec still crave total independence.

What is clear is that this largest province of Canada is fiercely independent and continues to be a fascinating place to visit. Best known, next to Montreal, is Quebec City. It is one of the most beautiful cities in North America. Montreal is several times larger (one of the largest French-speaking cities in the world).

Both cities lie on the St. Lawrence River, one of the busiest trade routes of the world. Skiing is big in Quebec. There are countless resorts that cater to winter sports. In the summer, the many parks and resorts provide delights for campers and tourists.

Montreal
Recent years have resulted in great growth and modernization of this French Canadian city. The world's fair Expo' 67 and the summer Olympics of 1976 brought world attention to Montreal. It is a truly cosmopolitan city with two-thirds French, and a marvelous mix of other cultures and backgrounds. As some point out, Montreal is like having a European city only a few miles away from the U.S., and with no jet lag.

As in other Canadian cities, some modern developments are underground. Shopping malls, hotels, banks, office buildings, and railway stations have all become available from these areas, sheltered from the cruel winter climate. Indeed, there are now six underground complexes in Montreal.

Ottawa and Toronto
Moving west into Ontario, you come into an area that is dominated by the Great Lakes on its southern border. Ottawa is, of course, the capital of Canada. Toronto has a metropolitan population of 3.5 million. Residents pride themselves on living in a dynamic city. Seventy percent of the population is nonwhite. Eighty nationalities speaking sixteen languages make it anything but an English city. It is an industrial center that is bursting with vitality.

The Prairies
Moving west from Ontario you cross the provinces that provide the bread basket of Canada. Settlers came to Manitoba, Saskatchewan, and Alberta to farm large parcels of land. Cow-towns like Calgary became oil towns in a latter day and eventually it became an internationally recognized city as the Winter Olympics of 1988 confirmed. Winnipeg, Saskatoon, and Edmonton have all prospered and become destinations for the traveler.

The most spectacular sight of all in this region is not prairie, but the Rocky Mountains. The small city of Banff has become a destination for world travelers who want to see the glaciers and turquoise lakes of Banff and Jasper National Parks. Lake Louise has often been singled out as one of the world's greatest beauty spots.

Vancouver
As you reach the Pacific Coast of Canada, you come to one of the most dynamic parts of the country. Anyone who has observed the growth of Vancouver, British Columbia, over the last 25 years has seen what some have called the Hong Kong of North America. The city enjoys an incomparable setting of bays and mountains.

All sorts of outdoor activities can be enjoyed from Vancouver. Skiing is available at Grouse Mountain within a few minutes drive of the city center. Sports fishing and camping are just a few miles out of town. West from Vancouver on Vancouver Island is Victoria. This small city has preserved much of its English character. This area enjoys the mild west coast marine climate that keeps things green year-round.

Clearly, there is much to enjoy
on a trip to Canada.
The problem you face is to select
which Canada you want to visit
first.

KAUAI

NIIHAU

OAHU

Pearl Harbor

Honolulu

The palmy paradise in the Pacific Ocean

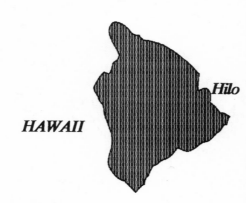

MOLOKAI

MAUI

LANAI

Hilo

HAWAII

The Hawaiian Islands

Hawaii might be compared to the proverbial candy store. We all tend to be children when it comes to the attractions of this state. The first candy case is usually Oahu, and you can barely begin to take in all it has to offer when you discover that there are six other cases that have similar goodies in them but each has some unique ones.

There are seven inhabited islands in the chain. Reading from left to right on a map they are: Niihau (privately owned), Kauai, Oahu, Molokai, Lanai, Maui, and Hawaii. All of them are tropical paradises in the classic sense, and each of them has a unique quality that wins its converts to favor that island. As Americans, one of the very best things about the Hawaiian Islands is that they are ours! We can travel there without passports or visas, and can experience an entirely different order of scenery and lifestyle that refreshes and renews.

HISTORY
The Hawaiian Islands were settled first by immigrants from the Marquesas around 500 A.D. Later, around 1000 A.D., more new settlers came from Tahiti. Captain James Cook discovered the Islands in 1778 and named them for the Earl of Sandwich. Cook was eventually killed in the Islands. Waves of immigrants from China, Portugal, Japan, and the Philippines from 1850 on contributed to the rich racial mix one finds there. There are very few pure Hawaiians

left, thanks to western diseases and the intermixture of other peoples. The missionaries arrived in the 1820s and exerted much influence in the modern development of Hawaii. They were annexed by the United States in 1898 and became a state in 1959.

GETTING THERE
Almost all of the major airlines operate between the mainland and Hawaii. While most flights land in Oahu, three other islands do enjoy direct connections. There are also available several inter-island and charter airlines. There are a few inter-island boats that provide a limited service to some destinations. Cruising is also one way of seeing the islands with the luxury of modern cruise ships taking you from island to island. If you are traveling on to other destinations, there are foreign airlines and steamship companies that stop over in Hawaii.

CLIMATE
The general climate of the Hawaiian Islands is tropical, but it is moderated by trade winds that make life pleasant and free of extremes. Rainfall is extremely variable with some isolated areas receiving over 400 inches a year and some that approach arid conditions. Several of the islands have living areas where the tropical climate is moderated by altitude, making them more temperate and comfortable.

INDUSTRY
Tourism is the largest and most important industry in the Islands. However, agriculture is a major contributor to the local economy. The important crops are: pineapples, sugar cane, macadamia nuts, avocados, and papayas. One that may surprise the visitor is cattle raising. Here the obvious advantage of having year-round growth of grass serves the cattle raising well. Another industry that may surprise you is that of clothing manufacturing. After all, Hawaii has had a significant influence on the leisure-time garb of all Americans.

OAHU
Oahu is the most populated of the Islands and the most famous from a history point of view. Pearl Harbor is in the American mind almost as firmly as Plymouth Rock or Manhattan Island. The first-time visitor will want to see these areas so important in the events of World War II. Most will want to see the Arizona Memorial at Pearl Harbor in order to clarify some of those momentous events.

There are many other historical sites such as the palace and government buildings in Honolulu. But inevitably one is drawn to Waikiki and Diamond Head for their romantic values praised so often in song and story. Happily you don't have to look very hard to find programs that share the distinctive dances and culture of Hawaii that every visitor wants to see.

While Oahu is the major population center, it has all of the classic Hawaiian qualities as well. Volcanic mountains, tropical forests, beautiful botanical gardens, and sandy beaches are all available. Car rental is relatively cheap, so that it is possible to explore the Island at your leisure. One of the interesting and informative experiences is the Polynesian Cultural Center where distinctions in Pacific island cultures are shown in model villages. Native customs and dances are also demonstrated in an elaborate program.

It used to be a good hotel, but that proves nothing--I used to be a good boy.
Mark Twain

The sooner you are there, the sooner you
will find out how long you will be delayed.

Shelley Berman

TRAVEL

HAWAII 217

KAUAI

Kauai is 72 miles northwest of Oahu. It is 550 square miles and most of the island is very rugged. The roads hug the coast for the most part. Occasional access to the interior is available such as Waimea Canyon State Park. Tropical gardens in such places as Pacific Tropical Botanical Garden, Allerton Estate Garden, and the Fern Grotto of Smith's Tropical Paradise are all special experiences.

The Na Pali Coast State Parks provide opportunities for camping, hiking, and trips into the interior. Kokee State Park adjoins Waimea Canyon State Park, where spectacular views of Waimea Canyon rival the Grand Canyon in splendor if not in size.

MAUI

Maui is the second largest island in the chain with 729 square miles. Its highest point is the dormant volcano, Mt. Haleakala, at 10,023 feet above sea level. Clearly, this is the favorite island in the fiftieth state for many people who return year after year to enjoy the beauty and comfort of Maui.

Direct access by air is available from the mainland. The main airport is at Kahului. Best loved spots are hard to select because there are so many. Certainly the trip to the crater of Mt. Haleakala is not to be missed. It is often favored for sunrises because they are so beautiful and clouds tend to accumulate in the afternoon. Be sure to bring warm clothes for that trip because you travel to a different climate. Hana Town is another special treat as is the area around it. Lahaina is favored for its historic importance.

There are lots of resorts and other accommodations on Maui. They tend to be concentrated in Lahaina and Kaanapali, Napili, and Kapalua, and from Kihei south to Wailea. There are luxury hotels and lots of condominiums. Beautiful beaches are a specialty.

MOLOKAI

Molokai is the island closest to Oahu. Its main historic fame was the leper colony and its heroic Father Damien who fought for decent care and eventually developed lep-

rosy himself. The old leper colony is now a national historic park. The hospital continues to exist. Visitors are welcome, although you will need a permit that is easily obtained.

Molokai is shaped like a shoe and is the fifth largest of the islands. There is less activity there than on most of the other islands. While tourism is growing, there are only a few hotels and some condominiums, with more to come. There are all of the conventional sights associated with the islands and one historical vestige that will interest many. Hawaiians constructed fish ponds in shallow shoreline areas where they could raise and fatten native fish. The fish could swim in them when small, but could not leave after they grew larger. A number of these ponds have been preserved and are still used to supply fish for local markets.

LANAI

Lanai is a small island with a small population, settled mostly in Lanai City, near the center of the island. It is only 17 miles by 13 miles and is largely devoted to agriculture. There is only one hotel, appropriately named the Hotel Lanai. In many respects, the story of Lanai is the story of agriculture in Hawaii.

James D. Dole, a Harvard graduate, came to Hawaii in 1899. His uncle, Sanford B. Dole, was president of the Republic of Hawaii at that time. The younger man became involved in the development of agriculture in Hawaii and soon had a thriving business. Dole is largely responsible for the modern pineapple and its successful culture in the Islands. In 1922, after a disastrous sugar cane failure, Dole bought Molokai, and it became the pineapple center it is today. The cannery is located in Honolulu on Oahu and you may find it interesting.

HAWAII--THE BIG ISLAND

Hawaii is larger than all the other islands put together, with 4,034 square miles. It is 200 miles east of Oahu. It is often said that Hawaii has the highest mountain in the 50 United States, because Mauna Loa and Mauna Kea rise more than 30,000 feet from the seafloor. Mauna Loa is 13,697 feet

above sea level. Happily, they are both dormant at the present time, although Mouna Loa has had small eruptions twice since 1950. Real volcanic activity is more than supplied by Kilauea,which continues to destroy houses and countryside even as this is written. No visit to the island of Hawaii would be complete without including Volcanoes National Park.

A substantial part of Hawaii is volcanic wasteland, which is a sight in itself. In the arable areas there is no pineapple culture, but the island is the biggest producer of sugar cane, papayas, avocados, macadamia nuts, anthuriums, vegetables, beef, and most unexpected of all, Christmas trees. This island is also responsible for the propagation of the famous Kona coffee, the only coffee grown in the United States.

Hawaii does not have the best natural beaches in the islands, but local operators have remedied that by trucking in sand where it is needed for beach enjoyment. There are lots of swimming pools. There are many accommodations at all levels and plenty of condominiums. They are concentrated in the Hilo and Kona areas. There are spectacular state parks, some of which have cabins for rent. Aloha.

ON TRAVEL

We are all naturally seekers of wonders. We travel far to see the majesty of old ruins, the venerable forms of the hoary mountains, great waterfalls, and galleries of art. And yet the world wonder is all around us; the wonder of the setting sun, and evening stars, of the magic spring-time, the blossoming of the trees, the strange transformations of the moth ...

Albert Pike (1809-1891)

Good company in a journey makes the way seem shorter.

Izaak Walton (1593-1683)

When you're safe at home you wish you were having an adventure; when you're having an adventure you wish you were safe at home.

Thornton Wilder (1897-1'975)

Mexico--an interesting neighbor

If you have trouble settling on travel destinations, Mexico is the wrong place to go. Once you have made the decision about the country, you face the problem of which Mexico. Is it the Mexico of the sophisticated city, with its cultural and other attractions, or is it the country of tropical seashore? That is only the beginning, because there are several other Mexico's to choose from.

Most travel advisors would divide the country into about seven major categories:

1. North and East Mexico
2. Yucatán
3. Southern Mexico
4. Mexico City
5. Colonial Circle
6. West Coast--Mexican Riviera
7. Baja

Northeast Mexico

This area borders the boundary with Texas and the Gulf of Mexico. Highway 45 out of El Paso is the major route into this area of Mexico, heading south all the way to Mexico City. Other major roads head off to the east to some of the main attractions. Among the cities to be seen are Chihuahua with its contrasts of old and new. Because it was used as the backdrop of many movies, Durango is perhaps the best known city to Americans. Their annual film festival may be of interest.

There are almost countless interesting towns and spectacular sights as you wend your way south. The ideal way to see this area is by automobile, so side trips beckon wherever you go. One of those side trips on Highway 57 takes you to San Luis Potosi, interesting both for its historical offerings because it is an industrial city with American factories. The romantic city of Monterey, also an important industrial site, is another attraction. One of the major industries of Monterey is beer production. The last of the major cities before Mexico City is Tampico on the Gulf of Mexico. It is an important seaport with large oil installations including a refinery. This is a good place to fish on the East Coast for all those tropical fish you have dreamed about.

Finally, this section provides the gateway to one of Mexico's most important tourist attractions--Copper Canyon. This spectacular area is best seen by train. The Chihuahua-Pacific Railway runs southwest from Chihuahua, passing through this huge park area, ending up at Los Mochis on the west coast. There are several kinds of rail service through the Sierra Madre, including sleeper service. Best enjoyment is obtained by stopping over along the way such as at Ojinaga.

Yucatán

Ruins of ancient civilizations exist in many parts of Mexico, but among the most spectacular and significant are those in Yucatán. The Yucatán Peninsula separates the Gulf of Mexico and the Caribbean Sea. In this jungle land, the ruins of Mayan civilization have fascinated anthropologists as they will you. Sites such as Kabah, Labna, Xlabpak, Sayil, Chichen Itza, and Uxmal can spark your interest for an hour or a lifetime.

You can operate from the capital city, Merida, founded by the Spanish on the site of a Mayan settlement in 1542. It can be reached by highway, rail, or airline. From there it is easy to get to any of the ruins or to the brand new phenomenon of Cancun. This ultra-modern luxury resort attracts thousands of visitors each year. You can do a great deal worse than adding your name to that group.

Southern Mexico

This section of Mexico certainly has its share of ruins too. There is a distinctive character of the country that can be attributed to the Indians. Only Veracruz on the Gulf Coast and Oaxaca in the interior are of any real size. Founded in 1519, Veracruz is an important port of entry for Mexico. The United States, France, and Spain all invaded this city at one time or another. Other towns and cities that have much to offer are Cordoba, Jalapa, Villahermosa, and the jungle ruins at Palenque.

Founded in 1522, Oaxaca lies at an elevation of more than 5,000 feet, thus providing a mild and pleasant climate. It has a rich colonial past and some of its massive buildings have been able to survive the many earthquakes of the area. Local handicrafts are distinctive and are easy to find in the shops and from street vendors. Some of the most spectacular ruins in Mexico are only a few miles away in Monte Alban. A civilization existed there from 700 B.C. to 1000 A.D. and covered 64 square miles. Other ruins are also available near the little town of Mitla.

Mexico City

Mexico City has to be considered in a class by itself. Much of our recent awareness of the city was associated with their terrible earthquake of 1985. It remains a very special place that must be visited on at least one of your trips to Mexico. In the first place it is a metropolis of more than 17 million people. It has a moderate climate because its elevation is more than 7,000 feet. All Mexican highways radiate like spokes from the hub of the city. It makes an excellent base from which to visit many of the outlying areas we have described earlier.

Two major attractions that most tourists take in are the Ballet Folklorico and the local jai-alai pavilion with its betting activity. Of course you must visit the Zocalo and the church and government buildings around it. While crowded, the city subway, with its rubber-tired trains, is worth a visit and is useful for getting around. One of the most well-known places to visit is the Archeol-

What brings gringos south? The great beauty of the sun-splashed Mexican land, the stunning historical sites, the warm welcome of the smiling Mexican people.

TRAVEL

(page 2 of 4) MEXICO   219

ogical Museum and Chapultepec Park. It is one of the great museums of the world. If you are a shopper, Mexico City has much to offer. Of course there are markets, but the most seductive area is the Pink Zone. Located in the heart of the city, the Pink Zone is about 24 square blocks of hotels, restaurants, shops, and other attractions that are special indeed. It would be easy to spend weeks in Mexico City alone to see what is offered there and in the surrounding countryside. For example, it is not far to San Jose Purua, a Shangri-la-like spa that sits in a tropical canyon. There is Cuernavaca and Taxco that should be visited as you make your way to the coast.

The Colonial Circle

Much of the Revolution of Independence of 1810 took place in the area called the Colonial Circle. At the heart of it is Guadalajara. It is a wonderful base for the exploration of the colonial past and the important sites associated with independence. It is the second largest city of Mexico. It is a city that combines the new with the old. The cathedral was begun in 1571, but has undergone many changes since that time. There are museums, government buildings, and the Degellado Theater. Shopping includes modern shops, a market, and an enormous flea market (every Sunday) that should satisfy anyone.

The other major city of this area is Morelia. Between Guadalajara and Morelia are a number of special treats such as Lake Chapala, Guanajuato, a silver city, and Leon, famous for shoes and other leather goods. Especially important as symbols of the Revolution are the village of Dolores Hidalgo, and San Miguel de Allende, a monument to independence.

West Coast--Mexican Riviera

Most famous of the resorts along the west coast of Mexico is Acapulco. From the luxury hotels to the cliff divers, Acapulco lives up to its reputation as a marvelous place in the sun. Best known of the other resort areas on the coast are Mazatlan and Puerto Vallarta. They have grown enormously as Americans have discovered all they have to offer as a change from their winter weather. Cruise ships have discovered these areas too, calling at these ports for brief forays of shopping and beach enjoyment as they bring their passengers from Los Angeles and San Diego.

As these more famous places have grown, other names have begun to come to the front as they are discovered and developed. Guaymas, San Blas, Manzanillo, and Ixtapa are just a few of them. The latter includes one of the west coast locations of Club Med, the other being Playa Blanca.

Baja California

Baja is the long peninsula that extends south from the U.S. border to the Tropic of Cancer. Best known to Americans as the site of the torture tests of four-wheel drive vehicles, it has grown in popularity as a vacation location for people with other interests. Fishermen find it to be a marvelous place to go for deep-sea angling. The major city of La Paz has been joined by many locations that have become favorite vacation spots, on both the Sea of Cortez and the Pacific side. You can drive all the way, but air service and ferries from the mainland give you a choice about how to get there.

> ### REMEMBER
>
> Mexico remains one of the most economical vacation spots available to residents of the United States. The exchange rate is usually very favorable, and its proximity to the U.S. makes it one of the smartest choices you can make. Besides that, Mexico offers an exotic environment in regard to language and culture that enhances the quality of your precious vacation time.

> **All travel has its advantages. If the traveler visits better countries, he may learn to improve his own; and if fortune carries him to worse, he may learn to enjoy his own.**
> Johnson (1709-1784)

SHOPPING IN MEXICO--For most travelers, shopping for souvenirs or for items that are particularly unique to that country is one of the great attractions of leaving home in the first place. Mexico is one of the special countries when it comes to shopping. For one thing, their products are distinctive. Most of us can identify Mexican goods without any difficulty. The second attractive thing about their products is that they are usually handmade. The third factor that appeals to the real shopper is the act of bargaining. Once the initial reluctance of most Americans is overcome, bargaining becomes half the fun. If it is your first time, practice on some item that is not too important to you. Don't be afraid to bid too low. They don't have to sell anything to you, so start lower than you are willing to pay for the item. Bid in a good-spirited way and avoid anger. When you are close to the price you might pay, start to walk away and you will test the limits of the vendor.

Of course, not every store has variable prices. The more established places and the city stores are likely to have rigid prices that will not be reduced by bargaining.

Reading about Mexico before you travel can inform you about special areas that have distinctive products of high quality. For example, you know that when you go to Taxco there will be a special opportunity to buy silver products. You will find distinctive pottery in Puebla (Talavera Ware) and Guadalajara. Oaxaca and Saltillo are famous for their sarape weaving. Other areas specialize in basket making and leather goods. Roam through the markets and watch the artisans plying their skills. When you do see something, don't put off your purchase on the hope of paying a few less pesos because you may not see that item again, and you will regret it later.

One drawback of purchasing items is that they have to be carried home. Large items can be shipped home. You will want to carry your smaller items in order to bring them home with you, to avoid customs hassles, and to safeguard them. One ideal solution is to purchase an appropriate-sized basket to carry your purchases. That keeps them together for easy accounting during customs. It also gives you one more neat souvenir to remind you of that great trip to Mexico!

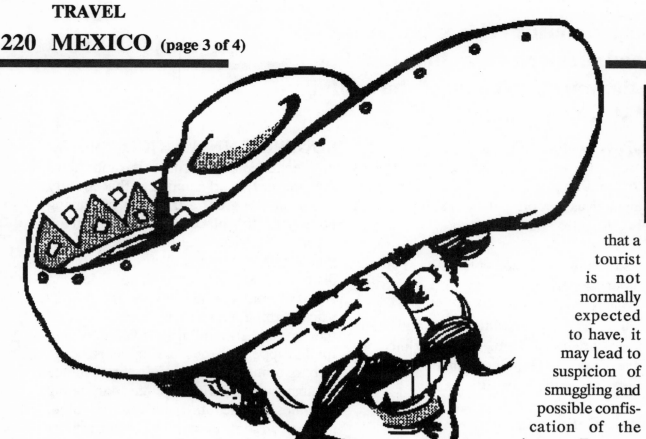

Mexico's proximity to the United States makes it a popular vacation place for Americans to visit. Mexicans are proud of their rich history and unique culture and are eager to share it with tourists. Approximately 4 million U.S. citizens visit Mexico annually. The majority experience few or no problems. However, if you plan to visit Mexico you should be aware of their regulations.

BEFORE YOU GO--provide your family or friends with a copy of your proposed itinerary and keep them informed of your travel plans so they can find you in an emergency. Carry with you appropriate photo identification and who to contact in the event of an emergency.

ENTRY AND EXIT REQUIREMENTS--If you plan to visit for no more than 72 hours and remain within 20 kilometers of the Mexican border, no permit is required. You will need a tourist card (FMT in Spanish) to visit longer. These are free and can be obtained from Mexican consulates, Mexican tourism offices, Mexican immigration officers at port of entry, and most airline services to Mexico. To get them, you will need a U.S. passport or birth certificate plus driver's license. These tourist cards are issued for a maximum stay of 180 days. You must present your tourist card upon leaving Mexico.

CUSTOMS REGULATIONS--You should enter Mexico with only the items needed for your trip. If you enter with a large quantity of expensive items, like TV's and stereos, that a tourist is not normally expected to have, it may lead to suspicion of smuggling and possible confiscation of the items. Do not bring in firearms without a permit. If you are traveling in an RV or equivalent, you sometimes can be subject to a second inspection inside Mexico, about 25 miles from the border. Unlawful items may be seized and travelers prosecuted even though you passed the initial customs inspection.

CURRENCY--You can freely change U.S. currency for pesos at the free market rate. The exchange rate is subject to change, sometimes on a daily basis. Take traveler's checks with you since personal checks are not accepted. Major credit cards are accepted in many places. You get a better exchange rate at exchange offices.

HEALTH--No vaccinations are required to enter Mexico. If you plan to travel in rural areas, there is some risk of malaria, and you should ask your doctor about taking chloroquine. Take along insect repellant and other protective measures against mosquitoes.

Due to heavy air pollution, elderly travelers and those persons with respiratory or cardiac problems, high blood pressure, or anemia may face increased risk to their health in Mexico City's high altitude or during trips to Ciudad Juarez in the winter. Consult your doctor.

See Travel--Health Precautions, pages 202 through 204 for problems with "Montezuma's Revenge" and altitude sickness and for recommendations for medicines and first-aid kits for travelers. If you are traveling by motor vehicle to remote areas you may find few medical facilities.

BRINGING PETS--Visitors may bring a dog, a cat, or up to four canaries if they have a pet health certificate from a registered vet that has not been issued more than 72 hours before entering. You'll need a vaccination certificate showing the animal has been treated for rabies, hepatitis, pip, and leptospirosis. There is a permit fee charged at the entry.

SAFETY TIPS WHILE TRAVELING--Mexico is a foreign country with its own laws, customs, and standards of behavior. Visitors can become victims of crime just as in the U.S. Take precautions against assault, robbery, or pickpockets. If you become a victim, immediately call the U.S. Embassy in Mexico City or the nearest U.S. consulate and the local police. File a formal complaint.

Some Americans have been harassed, mistreated, and gouged by persons representing themselves as Mexican police or local officials. The Mexican authorities are concerned about these events and cooperate in investigating them. The "officer's" name, badge number, and patrol card number are necessary to pursue the complaint.

Driving in Mexico at any time of the day is dangerous in most of the country, especially alone. Never sleep in vehicles alongside the road. Caution should be exercised on all roads especially remote ones. Never pick up hitchhikers. If your vehicle breaks down, stay with it and wait for police or in the province of Chihuahua the "green angels." Be very cautious on Hwy 15 in the state of Sinaloa and Hwy. 40 between the city of Durango and the Pacific coast. You may wish to check with local authorities, a U.S. embassy, or consulate for an update on potential danger places.

Highway construction and services such as gas stations, restaurants, motels, and auto repair facilities are not the same as in the U.S. Watch for loose animals and heavy bus and truck traffic on some routes. In Mexico a blinking left turn signal can mean three things: It is clear ahead, they want you to pass, or they are making a left turn. If you're not sure, don't pass.

Mexico has fabulous archeological treasures, picturesque volcanoes, quaint Indian villages, fiestas, and is a shopper's paradise! (An ideal place for my wife!)

TRAVEL

(page 4 of 4) MEXICO 221

> ## DO NOT
>
> **Drink the water or drinks with ice.**
>
> **Eat raw vegetables, meats, seafood or salads, milk or dairy products and fruit you haven't peeled yourself.**

Safety regulations and enforcement are not up to U.S. standards. Some newer resorts lack complete medical facilities. You should be more cautious in risk areas such as swimming pools and beaches.

ASSISTANCE IN MEXICO--If you find yourself in any serious legal, medical, or financial difficulty, contact the U.S. Embassy or consulate. They can provide you with lists of local attorneys and inform you of your rights under Mexican laws. If you become seriously ill, they can help you find a doctor. They also may help arrange for funds to be transferred to you should you need them. The U.S. Embassy and consulates are restricted by Mexican laws on what legal assistance they can provide for you, so take precautions.

JUDICIAL SYSTEM--When in Mexico, you are subject to Mexican laws and subject to full prosecution under their judicial system. If detained, American consular officers can monitor your status to see you're treated fairly but cannot act as your legal counsel. If arrested, ask to notify a consular officer-- you have this right under our agreement with Mexico.

Mexican law does not presume you to be innocent until proven guilty. Trial takes a long time and is based largely on documents examined in the court at a fixed date. There is no trial by jury. Bail exists but usually is not granted to visitors as they might just go home, skipping bail. Under Mexican law you have certain rights subject to interpretation. Nonpayment of hotel bills or failure to pay for other services is considered fraud.

DRUGS--Mexico rigorously prosecutes those possessing heroin, marijuana, amphetamines, or any narcotic. Even a token amount is subject to a sentence of 7 years. You could be detained for 1 year before a verdict is reached. If you are required to take medications containing narcotics, carry a valid doctor's certificate for them.

TAKING YOUR VEHICLE--You will need a temporary vehicle import permit issued at border entry points. You must remove your vehicle from Mexico before the permit expires or it may be confiscated. You may not sell, transfer, or otherwise dispose of a vehicle brought in. You may not leave without the vehicle. In case of an emergency, or following an accident where the vehicle cannot be removed, you may request from the Mexican Customs Office in Mexico City to depart. Do not allow anyone else to drive your vehicle unless you are a passenger.

VEHICLE RENTAL--Many U.S. rental companies prohibit traveling out of the U.S. Mexico police, without authority to do so, sometimes impound cars if you drive them to Mexico. If you rent a car in the U.S., make sure it's okay to drive in Mexico.

VEHICLE INSURANCE--is sold in most towns on both sides of the border. If possible, obtain insurance when you cross the border, because your U.S. liability, collision, and comprehensive coverage are not valid in Mexico. If you are under the influence of alcohol or drugs your insurance becomes invalid. If you are involved in an accident that causes injury, even to your passengers, you will be taken into custody until it can be determined who is liable.

CB RADIO--You will need a permit that allows only personal communications and emergency road assistance using only channels 9, 10, or 11, max. 5 watts. CB's can't be used near radio installations. Permits can't be obtained at the port of entry, only from a Mexican consulate or a Mexican tourism office.

RETURNING TO THE U.S.--You can bring back $400 worth of merchandise and 1 quart of alcohol duty-free. The next $1000 worth is subject to a 10% duty. If returning by motor vehicle, you'll need your certificate of vehicle registration handy when you cross the border.

Products made from sea turtles, black coral jewelry, items made from the fur of endangered cat species, crocodile leather, stuffed birds, Mexican birds such as parrots, parakeets, or birds of prey cannot be brought in.

USEFUL ADDRESSES AND PHONE NUMBERS

U.S. Embassy, Mexico City
Paseo de la Reforma 305
Mexico 5, D.F.
Local tel: 211-0042
U.S. tel: 011-52-5-211-0042

U.S. Trade Center
31 Liverpool
Mexico 6, D.F.
Local tel: 591-0155
U.S. tel: 011-52-5-591-0155

Consulates (C) and Consulates General (CG)
Ciudad Juarez (CG), Chihuahua
Avenue Lopez Mateos 924-N
Local tel: 134048 day
U.S. tel: 011-52-16-134048 day
U.S. tel: 916-525-6066 night

Guadalajara (CG), Jalisco
Progreso 175
Local tel: 252998
U.S. tel: 011-52-36-252998

Hermosillo (C), Sonora
Calle Monterrey 141, Poniente
Local tel: 72375
U.S. tel: 011-52-621-72375

Matamoros (C), Tamaulipas
Ave. Primera No. 2002
Local tel: 25251
U.S. tel: 011-52-891-25251

Mazatlan (C), Sinaloa
Circunvalacion No.120 Centro
Local tel: 12685
U.S. tel: 011-52-678-12685

Merida (C), Yucatán
Paseo Montejo 453
Local tel: 55409
U.S. tel: 011-52-992-55409

Monterrey (CG), Nuevo Leon
Avenida Constitucion 411 Poniente
Local tel: 452120
U.S. tel: 011-52-83-452120

Nuevo Laredo (C), Tamaulipas
Avenida Allende 3330, Col Jardin
Local tel: 40512
U.S. tel: 011-52-871-40512

Tijuana (CG), Baja California
Tapachula 96
Local tel: 817700
U.S. tel: 011-51-66-817700

CONSULAR AGENTS
Acapulco, Guerrero (748) 5-5596
Cancun, Quintana Roo (4-24-11)
Durango, Durango (181)1-22-17
Mulege, Baja Calif. Sur (685) 3-0111
Oaxaca, Oaxaca (951) 606-54
Puerto Vallarta, Jalisco (322) 2-0069
San Luis Potosi, San Luis Potosi (481) 7-25-01
San Miguel de Allende, Guanajuato (465-22357)
Tampico, Tamaulipas (121) 3-2364
Vera Cruz, Vera Cruz (29) 31-0142

Observations on life...quotations from history

We are sinful not merely because we have eaten of the tree of knowledge, but also because we have not eaten from the tree of life. - Franz Kafka

❀

Do not be anxious about tomorrow, for tomorrow will be anxious for itself. Let the day's own trouble be sufficient for the day.

- Jesus

❀

It matters not how strait the gate,
How charged with punishments the scroll,
I am the master of my fate:
I am the captain of my soul.
- William Henley (1842-1903)

❀

There are three periods in life: youth, middle age, and "how well you look."
- Nelson A. Rockefeller

❀

Tradition does not mean that the living are dead, it means that the dead are living.
- Harold MacMillan

❀

It is better to live rich than to die rich.
- Samuel Johnson

❀

The secret of health for both mind and body is not to mourn for the past, not to worry about the future, or not to anticipate troubles, but to live in the present moment wisely and earnestly. - Buddha

❀

The courage of life is often a less dramatic spectacle than the courage of a final moment; but it is no less a magnificent mixture of triumph and tragedy. - John F. Kennedy

❀

To live long, it is necessary to live slowly.
- Cicero (106-43 B.C.)

❀

No matter what looms ahead, if you can eat, enjoy today, enjoy the sunlight today, mix good cheer with friends today, enjoy it and bless God for it. Do not look back on happiness--or dream of it in the future. You are only sure of today; do not let yourself be cheated out of it. - Beecher (1813-1878)

❀

Happiness is not a station you arrive at, but a manner of traveling. - Runbeck

Life is real! Life is earnest!
And the grave is not its goal;
Dust thou art, to dust returnest,
Was not spoken of the soul.
- Longfellow (1819-1892)

❀

"On with the dance, let the joy be unconfined" is my motto, whether there's any dance to dance or any joy to unconfine.
- Mark Twain

❀

The only real failure in life is not to be true to the best one knows.
- Farrar (1831-1903)

❀

Life's but a walking shadow, a poor player, that struts and frets his hour upon the stage and then is heard no more. It is a tale told by an idiot, full of sound and fury, signifying nothing. - William Shakespeare

❀

I gave my life to learning how to live. Now that I have organized it all its just about over. - Sandra Hochman

❀

We do not live an equal life, but one of contrasts and patchwork, now a little joy, then a sorrow, now a sin, and then a generous or brave action.
- Ralph Waldo Emerson

❀

All say, "How hard it is that we have to die" --a strange complaint to come from the mouths of people who have yet to live.
- Mark Twain

❀

Life is a language in which certain truths are conveyed to us; if we could learn them in some other way, we should not live.
- Schopenhauer (1788-1860)

❀

Give me the luxuries of life and I will willingly do without the necessities.
- Frank Lloyd Wright

❀

That man lives happy and in command of himself who from day to day can say, I have lived. Whether clouds obscure, or the sun illuminates the following day, that which is past is beyond recall. - Horace

❀

All you need in this life is ignorance and confidence, and then success is sure.
- Mark Twain

❀

When I hear somebody sigh that "Life is hard," I am always tempted to ask, "Compared to what?" - Sidney Harris

Lost, yesterday, somewhere between sunrise and sunset, two golden hours, each set with sixty diamond minutes. No reward is offered, for they are gone forever.
- Horace Mann

❀

Half our life is spent trying to find something to do with the time we have rushed through life trying to save. - Will Rogers

❀

You are young, my son, and, as the years go by, time will change and even reverse many of your present opinions. Refrain, therefore, awhile from setting yourself up as a judge of the highest matters. - Plato

❀

There are two things to aim at in life: first, to get what you want; and, after that to enjoy it. Only the wisest of mankind achieve the second. - Logan Pearsall

❀

Hurried and worried until we're buried, and there's no curtain call, life's a very funny proposition after all.
- George M. Cohan

❀

Life does not cease to be funny when people die any more than it ceases to be serious when people laugh. - George Bernard Shaw

❀

All the animals excepting man know that the principal business of life is to enjoy it.
- Samuel Butler

❀

I object to people running down the future. I'm going to live all the rest of my life there.
- Charles F. Kettering

❀

Life is a progress and not a station.
- Emerson (1803-1882)

❀

No life that breathes with human breath
Has ever truly longed for death.
- Alfred Tennyson (1809-1892)

❀

Enter by the narrow gate; for the gate is wide and the way is easy, that leads to destruction, and those who enter by it are many. For the gate is narrow and the way is hard, that leads to life, and those who find it are few. - Jesus

❀

Learn to live well, that thou may'st die so too: To live and die is all we have to do.
- John Denham (1615-1668)

❀

One life--a little gleam of time between two eternities. - Carlyle (1795-1881)

Help for a person to die in their own home

The hospice movement began in Britain. Its purpose was to provide a service that would enable the terminally ill to die with dignity, sensitive care, and minimum pain. Now hospice services have become very widespread in the United States, organized on a local basis in cities and counties. Whereas the British approach was to provide special-care facilities, in the U.S. the tendency has been for organizations to provide outreach services to whoever is giving the care to the patient.

Most people agree that when it is possible, a person should be able to die in the comfort and familiarity of his or her own home. Hospice services often can make that possible with minimum stress for the family.

In general, hospices provide assistance in three areas: medical service and advice, social services, and emotional support.

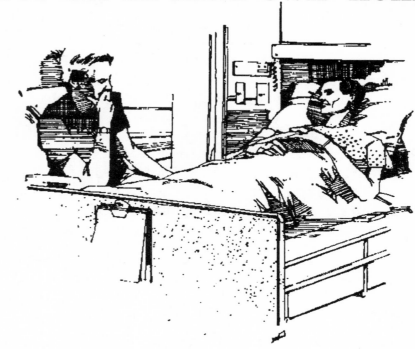

MEDICAL SERVICE AND ADVICE

1 One of the classic problems of providing pain relief for the terminally ill has been the understandable caution concerning the use of drugs. Hospices help the doctor to differentiate between drug dependence and addiction. They give advice about appropriate dosage and about the most effective medication.

2 Some hospices provide a visiting nurse service at regular intervals, as needed, or assist the family to obtain such help through existing agencies.

3 Nurses and other caregivers consult with family members to provide tips on terminal patient care for the greater comfort of the patient. They can help the family obtain medical supplies for home care and arrange for rental of needed special equipment such as a hospital bed.

4 Medical personnel help the family and the patient make important decisions on the nature of the care the patient is to receive. For example, they help to decide whether heroic measures are to be used in the event of a medical crisis.

SOCIAL SERVICES--Many problems and decisions face the family
as the patient nears death. Social workers or trained volunteers are able to answer many questions because they deal with them all the time. Several categories of problems illustrate the point:

■ Social workers know what medical services are available to the patient. They are generally informed about Medicare and Medicaid regulations and can direct the family to information sources to deal with their specific problems.

■ Family members often have questions about insurance, funeral plans, who must be informed, death certificates, etc. Social workers can relieve many of these anxieties. They can also remind the family that certain areas need their attention.

■ Social workers can help the family plan ahead. Are services desired? If they are, do they wish to have a conventional funeral or a memorial service? Do they prefer cremation or burial? Where should services be held? All of these matters are easier to discuss when an informed person is available to answer questions and initiate contacts.

EMOTIONAL SUPPORT--is provided through all the activities mentioned. They help the family deal with the reality of impending death and they have the assurance that the patient is receiving the best care possible. Other activities are directly intended to help family members get through the ordeal of a terminal illness. Referrals to grief counseling and support groups can usually be made. Much of the strength of the support of hospice results from the feeling that develops among family members that they are not alone in this most difficult of times.

MEDICARE COVERAGE--If a person is eligible for Medicare (Part A), and is terminally ill, they can choose between standard Medicare benefits or hospice care. Medicare pays 100% (except medications) of hospice services. The patient's doctor and the hospice medical director must certify the patient is terminally ill. Then there is no time limit for coverage if the patient is certified as terminally ill each 210 days. The services include: doctor's and nursing services, medical equipment, drugs for pain relief, home health aide, homemaker services, therapies, medical social services, and short periods of inpatient care. Services include counseling for the patient and family members.

Your local hospice service can generally be located by looking in the white pages of your telephone book, calling United Way offices, or your local health department.

Don't hesitate,
ask for help!

Planning for the eventual tomorrow

The Importance of Preplanning

It is important that family members discuss future funeral arrangements. Preplanning can provide opportunities for everyone to discuss personal preferences, feelings, and desires. In the event of death, the family will be comforted by knowing that they are carrying out their loved one's wishes. This is especially significant if someone desires a simple, inexpensive funeral or no funeral at all. In the grief-laden period following the death of a loved one, many emotions are experienced and consumers can easily over-extend themselves financially on funeral arrangements. If they know the deceased definitely wanted a simple funeral then the family will not feel guilty about spending less. Thus, a choice for simplicity will not be mistaken for a lack of respect.

Taking time to collect information on varying costs and calmly choosing funeral arrangements ahead of time can protect the family from any possible sales pressure, intended or not, at the time of extreme emotional crisis. In this way, you can carefully choose the specific items you want and need and can compare prices offered by one or more funeral providers. By considering all the options available now, the family eliminates the possibility of making hasty, often expensive, decisions later.

Preplanning can place the funeral provider and the funeral consumer on a more equal footing. The inexperienced consumer who makes arrangements at the time of need can be extremely vulnerable. Prior knowledge helps the consumer decline certain services and purchase only what is wanted. The consumer can decide the type and cost of the funeral or other disposition rather than someone else.

If death occurs unexpectedly, it is a good idea to have a non-family member or clergy accompany the family when making funeral arrangements to provide emotional support and to help the family make decisions more clearly.

What Are Your Choices?

Funerals can be simple or lavish. Many Americans are beginning to question the value or need of a traditional funeral. Actually, the modern American funeral only dates back to the Civil War, when a Brooklyn doctor invented the idea of embalming bodies of soldiers so that they could be shipped home. Embalming is essential to the modern or traditional funeral. A traditional funeral generally includes the following costs: moving the body to the funeral home, using the funeral home facilities, embalming, providing cosmetology and restoration, dressing the body, purchasing the coffin, using the hearse, arranging for pallbearers, caring for flowers, and providing guest register and acknowledgment cards. It also includes professional service fees, burial and transit permit, newspaper death notices, extension of credit, and completion of filing of the death certificate.

All of the above goods and services have generally been included in a package-priced traditional funeral. The following costs are usually additional depending on the type of service selected: clergy's honorarium, music, extra limousines, flowers, burial clothes, cremation service charges, urn, marker or monument, crypt, cemetery charges for opening and closing grave, burial plot, long-distance telephone calls or telegrams, distance and other additional transportation items, cemetery perpetual-care charges, burial vault or grave liner, and taxes. Many of these items and services may be handled by and billed to the funeral provider, becoming cash-advance items that are then reimbursed by the family. Consumers should know that they may decline or even provide many of these services themselves.

Direct Disposition

Consumers may wish to choose direct disposition because they do not wish to delay interment, and/or it is less expensive than a traditional funeral. With direct disposition, the body is usually taken from the place of death directly to the cemetery. A graveside service may be conducted at a later time, if desired. The cost of direct disposition is related to the degree to which funeral goods and services are used. The expenses of a direct disposition service primarily involve removal of the body from the place of death, shelter of the body prior to disposition, a suitable container to transfer the body, transportation to the cemetery, and filing of the necessary legal documents.

Cremation

Generally less expensive than either traditional funeral or direct disposition, cremation is a process in which the body is placed in an inexpensive container and taken to the crematory where it is placed in a retort, exposed to intense heat, and reduced to ashes. The ashes (or cremains) may then be stored in an urn or other receptacle or disposed of by the survivors.

State and local laws should be checked before disposing of the ashes. Some states and localities have regulations restricting the process of scattering cremated remains over land or water. The costs may include the cremation itself, transportation of the body and cremated remains, an urn or other container for the ashes, burial in a niche in a columbarium (a special building designed to hold cremation urns) or in a burial plot, a memorialization plaque, and scattering of the ashes (unless done personally). In addition, a suitable container such as cardboard, knock-down-wood, pressboard, fiberboard, or composition container is usually all that is required by law. Thus, such alternative suitable containers eliminate the need to purchase a casket.

Direct cremation and scattering of the ashes would probably be the least expensive alternative if cremation is the chosen method of disposition.

Memorial Service

Usually a memorial service is held after a direct cremation or burial. This option may be less expensive than a traditional funeral depending on the extent to which the funeral home becomes involved. The service may be similar to a traditional funeral service or may be modified to reflect uniquely personal values and/or traditions.

There may be an extra charge for use of the chapel on the crematory premises to hold a memorial service and for any goods or services provided by the funeral home.

Do-It-Yourself

This alternative is possible in some localities, but practically impossible in others. In some states, the law stipulates that only licensed undertakers can transport bodies from one place to another. Also, most states have fairly stringent burial site restrictions. If consumers wish to choose this alternative, it is important that they plan carefully in advance, and check the pertinent laws in their locality. Crematories and cemeteries should also be questioned about their practices.

If there is a memorial society in the area, it may be knowledgeable about legal considerations. The State Board of Undertakers and Embalmers can also provide information about state rules and regulations, as can the Office of the Attorney General.

Body/Organ Donation

Body donation is considered by many to be a valuable service to medical research, as well as a less expensive method of disposition. Consumers should investigate this option carefully beforehand, and alternative arrangements should be made in case the body is not accepted at the time of death.

In the case of organ donation, the donee institution may return the body to the survivors for disposition following removal of the donated organ(s). The family also may be required to pay transportation costs to the donee medical institution.

Such a donation can be made legally binding on the survivors by properly completing a wallet-sized Uniform Donor Card. However, some medical schools and physicians will not accept bodies or organs unless the consent of the nearest of kin is also given. Many states now have donor forms on the back of drivers' licenses, which should be used in addition to the wallet card. A free Uniform Donor Card can be ordered from Continental Association of Funeral Memorial Societies, Inc., 2001 S Street, N.W., Suite 530, Washington, D.C. 20009; (202) 745-0634.

Memorial Societies

There are over 200 memorial societies throughout the United States and Canada. Volunteer-run, these nonprofit organizations are advocates of preplanning and freedom of choice in funeral arrangements.

Memorial societies generally do not provide merchandise or funeral services directly; rather they seek contracts or arrangements with cooperating funeral providers to take care of the needs of their membership.

Membership in a memorial society is obtained by paying a one-time membership fee of usually between $15 and $25. If a member dies while away from his/her society's area, the memorial society at or close to the place of death can provide assistance. Membership may be transferred at little or no cost if a member moves.

Consumers should not confuse profit-making businesses with memorial societies since many businesses use the word "memorial" or "society" in their names. Authentic nonprofit societies do not normally sell services or merchandise directly, or charge high membership fees. Most belong to the Continental Association of Funeral and Memorial Societies (see address under Body/Organ donation) or the Memorial Society Association of Canada.

Prepayment

Prearrangement does not necessarily have to be accompanied by prepayment of funeral goods and services. The following is a brief outline of the potential arguments for and against prepayment.

Pro:
* Allows for an increasing feeling of security that prearrangements will be carried out because they have already been paid for.
* Provides peace of mind to those who have no reliable survivor, relative, or other person to handle funeral arrangements.
* Protects survivors from making uncomfortable or irrational decisions under the stress of bereavement.
* Allows for comparison shopping among competing funeral providers.
* Reduces the risk that survivors will have heavy funeral expenses at the time of need.

The advantages listed seem attractive; however, they may not necessarily hold true for all pre-need plans. Even where they do,

a pre-need plan may not be the best way to secure a given advantage.

Con:
* If the consumer dies before completing payments on a pre-need plan and does not have credit life insurance, the agreement may not be honored unless survivors pay the amount outstanding.
* There is no guarantee that the seller of today's services will be in business at the time of need.
* If consumers move, they may not be able to shift their arrangements to another location or receive a refund.
* In many states, money deposited in a pre-need plan receives little or no accrued interest because such interest may be withdrawn annually by the seller to cover administration costs.
* In some states, money paid does not have to be placed in trust, in which case the recipient of the funds may be free to spend them and the consumer runs the risk of having nothing at the time of death.
* If payment is made in installments and not paid when due, there may be penalties assessed. If payments are stopped altogether, any refund may be substantially less than the amount paid into the plan.
* Survivors may not even be aware the funeral expenses have been pre-paid.

Possible Alternatives
As an alternative to prepayment, consumers may wish to consider setting up a specific interest-bearing bank account to pay for services at the time of need rather than paying in advance for services with the funeral provider. In this manner they will be able to benefit from the interest it will accrue, and protect themselves if the funeral home goes out of business. A "Totten" trust is an example of a special type of savings account to which the depositor adds the name of a beneficiary. The beneficiary can be a funeral home, friend, or relative who is trusted to use the funds as the depositor directs.

The advantage of a "Totten" trust is that the funds stay in control of the depositor and can be withdrawn in an emergency or transferred if the consumer should move to a new area. It is revocable during the depositor's lifetime, but, in most states, becomes

Some words about cemeteries and death benefits

irrevocable at the time of death. The disadvantage of such an arrangement is that, as with any other savings account, the depositor may be tempted to use the funds for other purposes.

Burial Insurance

Like a special savings account, a standard life insurance (or burial insurance) policy can be taken out to cover anticipated funeral expenses. Upon death, the policy can provide the funds needed to cover funeral expenses.

Other Considerations

In general, prepayment of funerals should be considered only if the funds are adequately safeguarded (placed in trust), if the seller has a sound reputation, if the consumers are certain that they will want to use services of a particular funeral home, and if the price is guaranteed. Also, the consumer should consult an attorney before signing any agreement.

A Separate Word About Cemeteries

Funeral arrangements are only part of the expense if the consumer selects burial in a cemetery or entombment in a mausoleum.

Still the most common form of disposition, earth burial, can be an expensive part of funeral arrangements. Expenses may include the following:

* a burial plot;
* opening and closing the grave (which can be more expensive on weekends);
* a vault or a less expensive grave liner (although not required by law, one of these may be required by individual cemeteries to prevent subsequent collapse of the grave); and
* a grave marker.

Earth burial can be without ceremony. In addition, it may be preceded by a funeral or graveside service, or followed by a memorial service.

Burial in an aboveground tomb or mausoleum is generally more expensive than a cemetery plot. Services may or may not be conducted as described for an earth burial. However, if the consumer wishes an earth burial, a cemetery plot will have to be selected and paid for (note: most all cemeter-

ies require that a plot be paid for in full before it is used).

There are almost as many things to keep in mind when buying a cemetery plot as when making funeral arrangements. Each cemetery has its own requirements, which should be ascertained in advance of purchase. Consumers should make certain that they read the cemetery's rules and regulations. Cemetery costs usually cover three or four separate items:

❶ the plot of ground or the crypt;
❷ the coffin enclosure for ground burial (a grave liner or vault);
❸ the opening and closing of the grave or entombment; and
❹ the memorial (marker, monument, or plaque).

The consumer should take note that the location of the plot and the use of materials for markers or stones has a direct affect on the cost.

Many cemeteries also charge for installing or settling the monument or marker at the grave site. Although some cemeteries charge an extra fee for perpetual care of the grave site or mausoleum crypt, others consider perpetual care to be part of the price of the lot or crypt and a certain percentage of the price is set aside in a trust fund for this purpose. Some states require such funding by law. The consumer should try to visit various cemeteries to compare prices and see how well they are maintained.

Purchasing a grave plot or mausoleum crypt on a pre-need basis should be approached with caution, and, generally speaking, should be done only if the consumers are relatively certain that this will be their final choice. A purchase in advance of need could result in additional costs at the time of death. These additional costs can occur due to the high rate of mobility in American society. A good idea for the consumer would be to check to determine if the cemetery belongs to a lot exchange program.

As is the case with pre-need funeral arrangements, another aspect to consider as well is that the family's money remains in someone else's possession. Consumers should at least make certain that the money is put in an interest-bearing escrow account. They may also wish to consider setting up

their own interest-bearing account, as previously discussed (see paragraph on Possible Alternatives).

Pre-need plans involving prepayment of burial expenses, however, may offer a reasonable price advantage. Remember, whenever cemetery lots or mausoleum crypts are bought in advance of need, just as in the case of any pre-need funeral purchase, family members should be informed about all the particulars of the sale.

Death Benefits

As soon as possible after death occurs, survivors should take steps to determine the availability of death benefits. Almost all benefits must be applied for and are not provided automatically. Among the benefits survivors may be entitled to are highlighted below.

Social Security Death Benefits

The Social Security Administration provides assistance to eligible survivors of an eligible beneficiary by way of a "lump sum death benefit" (currently $255). This death benefit is payable only to a spouse or minor dependent children of the deceased. The surviving spouse and minor children can also be entitled to monthly benefit checks. Consumers should contact their local Social Security office for any information and assistance.

Veterans Administration Death Benefits

The Veterans Benefits Counselor at the nearest VA regional office or a local veterans service organization representative should be contacted regarding survivor benefits and to secure a burial flag and/or burial in a national cemetery. If requested to do so, the funeral provider can alert the VA insurance division so that an insurance claim form is sent to the veteran's beneficiary without inquiry on the beneficiary's part. Veteran's mortuary benefits are available only if the veteran was:

✓ receiving a pension or compensation for military service,
✓ in a veterans hospital at the time of death,
✓ indigent at the time of death.

Three hundred dollars is available to an eligible surviving spouse or children. One hundred fifty dollars is available for a plot allowance and can be claimed by the family, funeral provider, or cemetery. If the death was a direct result of injuries received while in service, the veteran's survivors can be eligible to receive up to $1,100.

Other Death Benefits

* Life or casualty insurance--If death results from a motor vehicle accident, benefits might be provided under no-fault insurance provisions.
* Employer's payments--These could include severance pay and/or vacation time.
* Credit unions, trade unions, and fraternal organizations.
* Federal Government Railroad Retirement Board insurance--Providers to survivors of railroad employees, either active or retired, but depending on length of service.
* State victims of crime statutes--Some states provide benefits to survivors of a crime victim.
* Federal, state, or local government employees' benefit programs.
* State or local welfare allowances.

A Word of Caution

Remember, whether negotiating funeral or cemetery arrangements, it is the consumers' decision and right to choose only those services they desire. Prior to signing, it is important that the consumer read and understand any contract to determine exactly what services and costs they are agreeing to pay. It would be wise for the consumer to consult an attorney before signing any agreement.

The consumer should be wary of any high-pressure promotions for prearrangement, and should have all oral promises put in writing. Also, the consumer should be aware that any contract signed in the home over $25, and away from the merchant's place of business, may be cancelled in writing within three business days.

> Heavy hearts, like heavy clouds
> in the sky, are best relieved by
> the letting of a little water.
>
> Antoine Rivarol

RECORDING YOUR WISHES

It is important to list names, addresses, and phone numbers of people to be contacted immediately in the event of death (e.g., clergy, lawyer, employer, immediate family, funeral director). Decisions should be put in writing and left where the document can be easily found by family, a friend, or lawyer--not in a safe deposit box or in a will. It is also important to include the location of any safe deposit box (state number) and safe deposit key.

The following is a form which, when completed, can supply the family and others with information needed after an individual's death.

IMPORTANT INFORMATION IN THE EVENT OF MY DEATH

My name is _____
      first   middle/maiden   last

When I die, please contact _____
                              name   relationship

My important papers are located at _____

INFORMATION FOR DEATH CERTIFICATE AND FILING FOR BENEFITS

My street address _____

City_____ County_____ State_____ Zip code_____

Citizen of_____ Race_____

Birthplace_____ Date of Birth_____

Social Security Number_____

Occupation/type of business_____

If veteran: rank_____ branch of service_____ serial no._____

date and place entered service_____ date discharged____

I have ___never married, ___married, ___been widowed, ___separated, ___divorced, ___remarried.

Spouse's full (maiden) name_____

Name of next of kin (other than spouse)_____

Relationship_____ Address_____

Father's full name and birthplace_____

Mother's maiden name and birthplace_____

PLEASE NOTE: AFTER DEATH I PREFER

To donate these organs_____

That my body be:

____donated: arrangements made on (date)_____

  with: medical school_____

I prefer: ___simple arrangements, ___no embalming, ___no public viewing,
  ___the least expensive burial or cremation container, ___immediate disposition
    ___a nice funeral
  ___cremated and the ashes ___scattered or ___buried
    in _____
    or disposed of as follows_____
    buried: at location_____

The following services: ___memorial (after disposition) ___funeral (before disposition)
    ___graveside

  Services to be held at: ___my church ___mortuary ___other_____

    Memorial gifts to _____; omit flowers_____

I have made prearrangements with (mortuary)_____

Signature_____ Date_____

Your protection against unscrupulous providers

Most decisions about purchasing funeral goods and services are made by people when they are grieving and under time constraints. Thinking ahead may help you make informed and thoughtful decisions about funeral arrangements. In this way, you can carefully choose the specific items you want and need and can compare prices offered by one or more funeral providers.

Each year, Americans arrange more than 2 million funerals for family or friends. When arranging a funeral, consumers may not be initially concerned about costs. Still, many customers may spend more for a funeral than for almost anything else they buy. In fact, at an average cost of $2,400, a funeral may be the third most expensive consumer purchase after a home and a car.

The Federal Trade Commission (FTC) developed a trade regulation rule concerning funeral industry practices, which went into effect on April 30, 1984. It is called the Funeral Rule, and its purpose is to enable consumers to obtain information about funeral arrangements.

In general, the rule makes it easier for you to select only those goods and services you want or need and to pay for only those you select. Now, for example, you can find out the cost of individual items over the telephone. Also, when you inquire in person about funeral arrangements, the funeral home will give you a written price list of the goods and services available. When arranging a funeral, you can purchase individual items or buy an entire package of goods and services. If you want to purchase a casket, the funeral provider will supply a list that describes all the available selections and their prices. Thus, as described in greater detail in the following sections, the FTC's Funeral Rule helps you obtain information about the cost and availability of individual funeral goods and services.

Telephone Price Disclosures

When you call a funeral provider and ask about terms, conditions, or prices of funeral goods or services, the funeral provider will:

* tell you that price information is available over the telephone.
* give you prices and other information from the price lists to reasonably answer your questions.
* give you any other information about prices or offerings that is readily available and reasonably answer your questions.

By using the telephone, you can compare prices among funeral providers. Getting price information over the telephone may thus help you select a funeral home and the arrangements you want.

General Price List

If you inquire in person about funeral arrangements, the funeral provider will give you a general price list. This list, which you

> **See the example of a typical Funeral General Price List in the following pages. Please Note: This is only an example to show you what is offered. Prices vary for services and goods in various parts of the country. Out-of-town transportation is additional.**

can keep, contains the cost of each individual funeral item and services offered. As with telephone inquiries, you can use this information to help select the funeral provider and funeral items you want, need, and are able to afford.

The price list also discloses important legal rights and requirements regarding funeral arrangements. It must include information on embalming, cash advance sales (such as newspaper notices or flowers), caskets for cremation, and required purchases.

Embalming Information

The Federal Rule requires funeral providers to give consumers information about embalming that can help them decide whether to purchase this service. Under the Rule, a funeral provider:

* may not falsely state that embalming is required by law.
* must disclose in writing that, except in certain special cases, embalming is not required by law.
* may not charge a fee for unauthorized embalming unless it is required by state law.
* will disclose in writing that you usually have the right to choose a disposition such as direct cremation or immediate burial if you do not want embalming.
* will disclose to you in writing that certain funeral arrangements, such as a funeral with a viewing, may make embalming a practical necessity and, thus, a required purchase.

Cash Advance Sales

The Funeral Rule requires funeral providers to disclose to you in writing if they charge a fee for buying cash advance items. Cash advance items are goods or services that are paid for by the funeral provider on your behalf. Some examples of cash advance items are flowers, obituary notices, pallbearers, and clergy honoraria. Some funeral providers charge you their cost for these items. Others add a service fee to their cost.

The Federal Rule requires the funeral provider to inform you when a service fee is added to the price of cash advance items, or it the provider gets a refund, discount, or rebate from the supplier of any cash advance item.

Caskets for Cremation

Some consumers may want to select direct cremation, which is cremation of the deceased without a viewing or other ceremony at which the body is present. If you choose a direct cremation, the funeral provider will offer you either an inexpensive alternative container or an unfinished wood box. An alternative container is a non-metal enclosure used to hold the deceased. These containers may be made of pressboard, cardboard, or canvas.

Because any container you buy will be destroyed during the cremation, you may wish to use an alternative container or an unfinished wood box for a direct cremation. These could lower your funeral cost since they are less expensive than traditional burial caskets.

Under the Funeral Rule, funeral directors who offer direct cremations

✳ may not tell you that state or local laws require a casket.
✳ must disclose in writing your right to buy an unfinished wood box (a type of casket) or an alternative container.
✳ must make an unfinished wood box or alternative container available.

Required Purchase

You do not have to purchase unwanted goods or services as a condition of obtaining those you do want unless you are required to do so by state law. Under the Funeral Rule:

✳ You have the right to choose only the funeral goods and services you want, with some disclosed exceptions.

✳ The funeral provider must disclose this right in writing on the general price list.

✳ The funeral provider must disclose on the statement of goods and services selected the specific law that requires you to purchase any particular item.

Statement of Funeral Goods and Services Selected

The funeral provider will give you an itemized statement with the total cost of the funeral goods and services you select. This statement also will disclose any legal, cemetery, or crematory requirements that compel you to purchase any specific funeral goods or services.

The funeral provider must give you this statement after you select the funeral goods and services that you would like. The statement combines in one place the prices of the individual items you are considering for purchase, as well as the total price. Thus, you can decide whether to add or to subtract items to get what you want. If the cost of cash advance items is not known at the time, the funeral provider must write down a "good faith estimate" of their costs. The Rule does not require any specific form for this information. Therefore, funeral providers may include this information in any documentation they give you at the end of your discussion about funeral arrangements.

Preservative and Protective Claims

Under the Funeral Rule, funeral providers are prohibited from telling you a particular funeral item or service can indefinitely preserve the body of the deceased in the grave. The information gathered during the FTC's investigation indicated these claims are not true. For example, funeral providers may not claim embalming or a particular type of casket will indefinitely preserve the deceased's body.

The Rule also prohibits funeral providers from making claims that funeral goods, such as caskets or vaults, will keep out water, dirt, and other grave site substances when that is not true.

Other Considerations

If you decide to make advance plans about funeral arrangements either for yourself or a loved one, you can choose among several types of dispositions and ceremonies. The type of disposition you choose may affect the cost. Some people prefer a ceremonial service, religious or secular, with the body present. Another service is cremation, which may be performed either directly or after a ceremony. In addition, the deceased body may be donated (either directly or after a ceremony) to a medical or educational institution. To help ensure that your wishes are carried out, you may want to tell relatives and other responsible persons what you have decided.

For More Information

Most states have a licensing board that regulates the funeral industry. You may contact the licensing board in your state for information or help. You may also contact the Conference of Funeral Service Examining Boards, 520 E. Van Trees Street, P.O. Box 497, Washington, IN 47501; (812) 254-7887. This association, which represents the licensing boards of 47 states, will provide information on the laws of the various states and will accept and respond to consumer inquiries of complaints about funeral providers.

For Further Help

If you have problems concerning funeral matters, first attempt to resolve them with your funeral director. If you are dissatisfied, contact your federal, state, or local consumer protection agencies or the Conference of Funeral Service Examining Boards.

> **Why is it that we rejoice at birth and grieve at a funeral? It is because we are not the person involved.**
>
> Mark Twain

An example of funeral costs--costs vary by location

GENERAL PRICE LIST OF SERVICES

The goods and services shown below are those we can provide to our customers. You may choose only the items you desire. If legal or other requirements mean you must buy any items you did not specifically ask for, we will explain the reason in writing on the statement we provide describing the funeral goods and services you selected.

This list does not include prices for certain items that you may ask us to buy for you, such as cemetery or crematory services, flowers, and newspaper notices. The prices for those items will be shown on your bill or the statement describing the funeral goods and services you selected.

	Cost of services or goods	Your selections and costs

SERVICES OF FUNERAL DIRECTOR AND STAFF

		Cost	Selection
1	Removal from place of death (vehicle, personnel, equipment)	$ 185	
2	Basic Care and Handling	$ 490	
	Includes filing death certificate, obtaining permits, arrangement conference, claims-notifications-benefits assistance, temporary care of remains (first 24 hours)		
3	Embalming	$ 260	

THE FOLLOWING DISCLOSURE IS REQUIRED BY THE FEDERAL TRADE COMMISSION

Except in certain special cases, embalming is not required by law. Embalming may be necessary, however, if you select certain funeral arrangements, such as a funeral with viewing. If you do not want embalming, you usually have the right to choose an arrangement which does not require you to pay for it, such as direct cremation or immediate burial.

		Cost	Selection
4	**Other Preparation**		
	Autopsy Repair	$ 185	
	Modified Preparation for Limited Viewing (includes refrigeration)	$ 210	
	Dressing and Placement in Container	$ 175	
5	**Funeral Director and Staff for:**		
	Funeral Services in Mortuary Chapel or Church	$ 220	
	Graveside Funeral Service Only	$ 220	
	Memorial-Type Service in Mortuary Chapel	$ 195	
	Memorial-Type Service in Church	$ 150	

FACILITIES CHARGES

		Cost	Selection
1	Use of Facilities for Funeral or Memorial Ceremony	$ 195	
2	Use of Facilities for Viewing Only (until 5:00 P.M.)	$ 90	
3	Use of Facilities for Evening Viewing	$ 120	
4	Use of Refrigeration Facilities	$ 40	
5	Use of Hospitality Room	$	

AUTOMOTIVE EQUIPMENT

		Cost	Selection
1	Hearse/Funeral Coach	$ 120	
2	Sedan/Limousine Service	$ 130	
3	Alternate Delivery Vehicle	$ 85	
4	Motor Escorts	$	
5	Mileage Outside Local Service Area ($1.35/Loaded Mile)	$	

SUPPLEMENTAL GOODS AND SERVICES

		Cost	Selection
1	Acknowledgment Cards (per box)	$ 12	
2	Memorial Folders (per 100)	$ 50	
3	Guest Registry	$ 18	
4	Cremation (Includes minimum cremation container)	$ 285	
5	Newspaper Fees for Obituary Notices	$	

6	Flowers	$ _____	_____
7	Estate Claim Service Fee	$ 150	_____
8	_____	$ _____	_____
9	_____	$ _____	_____

CONTAINERS

Caskets and body containers are available at prices from $ 85 to $5,126 .... $ [▒▒▒▒▒] _____

A complete price list will be provided at the funeral home.

1	Casket/Container Description _____	$ _____	_____
2	Urn Description _____	$ _____	_____
3	Casket Rental Fee	$ _____	_____
4	Viewing Dais Fee	$ 65	_____
5	Transport Container	$ 120	_____
6	Outer Burial Container Description _____	$ [▒▒▒▒▒]	_____

Outer Burial Containers are available from $ 340 to $9,995.

A complete price list will be provided at the funeral home.

CASH ADVANCE ITEMS

1	Clergy Honorarium	$ _____	_____
2	Musician Honorarium	$ _____	_____
3	Vocalist Honorarium	$ _____	_____
4	Certified Copies of Death Certificate	$ _____	_____
5	Common Carrier Transport Charges	$ _____	_____
6	Permit Fees	$ _____	_____

DIRECT CREMATION

A "direct cremation" is a disposition of human remains by cremation, without formal viewing, visitation, or ceremony with the body present. Our direct cremation includes removal of the remains to the mortuary and transportation to the crematory.

Direct Cremation (purchaser provides body container)	$ 775	_____
Direct Cremation (minimum body container)	$ 775	_____
Direct Cremation (minimum casket)	$ 1,097	_____

THE FOLLOWING DISCLOSURE IS REQUIRED BY THE FEDERAL TRADE COMMISSION

If you want to arrange a direct cremation, you can use an unfinished box or an alternative container. Alternative containers can be made of material like heavy cardboard or composition materials (with or without outside covering) or pouches of canvas.

IMMEDIATE BURIAL

An "immediate burial" is a disposition of human remains by burial, without formal viewing, visitation, or ceremony with the body present. Our immediate burial includes removal of remains to mortuary, basic care, graveside service, alternate delivery vehicle.

Immediate Burial (purchaser provides body container)	$ 980	_____
Immediate Burial (minimum body container)	$ 1,065	_____
Immediate Burial (minimum casket)	$ 1,302	_____

FORWARDING REMAINS TO ANOTHER FUNERAL HOME .... $ 1,195 _____

Includes removal from place of death, basic care and handling, embalming, dressing, placement in container, alternate delivery vehicle (container not included).

RECEIVING REMAINS FROM ANOTHER FUNERAL HOME .... $ 270 _____

Includes staff and vehicle for local removal to mortuary and alternate delivery vehicle for delivery to local place of disposition.

[▒▒▒▒▒] indicates a potential high-cost item.

YOUR TOTAL COST [ ]

How to cope with being widowed by Wm. J. Diehm

If I should die and leave you here awhile,
Be not like others, soon undone, who keep
Long vigil by the silent dust and weep.
For my sake turn again to life and smile,
Nerving thy heart and trembling hand to do
Something to comfort weaker hearts than thine.
Complete those dear unfinished tasks of mine,
And I, perchance, may therein comfort you.

Anonymous

Almost every Sunday for the past four years my wife and I have sat behind Jim and Mayple in church--what a lovely couple. Although Mayple was in a state of gradually losing it, Jim took such tender care. They were obviously very much in love, and then Jim called to announce that Mayple had died. How could he stand the pain?

During the funeral procession I looked at my wife and said, "I hope I go first." How could I cope with being a widower after 50 years of marriage? My wife looked at me and softly said, "I don't know how people endure the loss that makes them alone. I don't want to be a widow either." Then we began to discuss the various people who had recently gone through this experience and how they learned to cope.

Harry became a widower about a year ago. He joined a club of widows and widowers. Now he has remarried and seems very happy. George became a widower about two years ago--basically he dropped out of society. He appears to be still in the state of mourning, and also seems to be very unhappy. Sarah became a widow about three years ago. She has found herself in service to the community. Jane lost her husband about two years ago. She is still wearing black and acts very unhappy. As my wife and I thought over the people who had lost a mate, some simple truths became apparent.

YOU ARE NOT ALONE

First of all, multitudes have gone through a similar experience. There are 175,000 new widows each year, 10 million widows in the United States. It is almost impossible to find a person of any age who has not lost a loved one. And eventually, everyone who is married will lose their mate. Small comfort, but true. When you say, "What shall I do?" most people will understand, and many of them can give words of comfort. When your visceral turns over and ties in a knot of despair, almost everyone around you can empathize, sympathize, and give solace.

It is not too popular in our secular world to speak about God, faith, and religion. The fantasy land of Mickey Mouse does not deal with such subjects--only good, clean family fun. But, in the real world, sorrow, separation, loneliness, and death are a part of living. Some who do not believe in God may solve their grief in other ways, but believers lean heavily on a God who cares and promises eternal life. The sun has set in the world of the widowed, but in the other world, on the other side, the sun is rising. In this thought, you are not alone.

YOU HAVE PERMISSION TO REACT

I remember how hard Jim held back his tears of grief at the funeral. His whole body wracked with pain, and yet he refused to let go. The shortest verse in the New Testament is "Jesus Wept." So did Abraham, so did Moses, so did David, so did Mohammed, so did Buddha, and so does everyone

> Tears are the softening showers
> which cause the seed of heaven to
> spring up in the human heart.
> - Walter Scott (1771-1832)

who ever loved someone and had that loved one taken away from them. Those who bottle the grief up inside are doomed to have the grief burst out another way. Tears of grief are nature's way of reducing the tension caused by a loss. If we don't use the natural way, we may have to deal with the unnatural, which can be ominous indeed.

Anger is a normal response when our life partner is taken. We ask "Why me?" And, it makes us angry and frustrated--as if we had lost a winning lottery ticket. It is particularly true that we will be angry if the loved one is lost through an accident or an act of violence. Then, if we are not careful, bitterness and hostility will drive away those who try to comfort us.

To feel guilty about the death of a spouse can be very painful. Yet, it is a common experience and normal. Who doesn't think of something he or she could have done differently. Often our partner has had a long period of sickness and suffering. Who can say and do everything perfectly at such a time. After he or she is gone, it is the most natural thing in the world to remember something we neglected. Guilt can be deadly and destroy peace of mind. We must absolve guilt, even if we are guilty. We must talk to a professional, a friend, or our God and get the guilt taken care of in order to have a satisfying life.

Ruth and John had a marital disagreement. Ruth screamed at John and told him she hated him. John took a shower, reached over to pick up a bar of soap, and dropped dead of a massive stroke. Now Ruth is trying to recover, but she is blocked with terrible feelings of guilt. She can't even remember what they quarreled about. If only....

Believe it or not, such circumstances are very common. Half the time in grief counseling the person left behind can point to some circumstance that they interpret as being the cause of death. A person can get over this kind of insidious guilt, but it takes a lot of help. Keep reminding yourself that words don't cause heart attacks or strokes. Remember that quarrels are inevitable between people who truly love each other. If your loved one could come back and speak to you, he or she would not blame you and would surely forgive you. Sometimes I think there is no substitute for a belief in a loving God who can pronounce the fiat of forgiveness to those who hurt from either false guilt or actual guilt.

Loneliness is another basic emotion that we must conquer. First of all, consider: "Why wouldn't I feel lonely? I just lost a companion that has been with me for X number of years." In the first days of our loss, lots of people call and express sympathy. Then again, we are so busy with notifying friends and taking care of the details of a death that we do not have time to feel lonely. Now, a couple of weeks have gone by, people have stopped calling, the relatives have gone home, and we are left in an empty house with an empty bed. One woman said, "When my husband was alive, I hated his snoring and made him go to the doctor to get cured. Now, I would give anything I have to get that snoring man back in bed with me." Yes, becoming a widow or widower makes us lonely. What can we do about it?

1 Keep busy. Fill your days with worthwhile stuff. Get involved in community affairs, volunteer to do charitable work, take a trip, associate with your family and friends, set goals and keep them.

2 Don't spend too much time daydreaming, thinking of the past, or regurgitating the bad events of yesteryear. Fill your mind with worthwhile stuff and order your life to live for today, plan for the future, and forget the past. If your mind does take a stroll down memory lane, force it to remember those beautiful moments. Linger on lovely things; do not embrace those traumas that hurt you. Most bad things have already taken their pound of flesh; don't give them any more. Fill your mind with thoughts of happiness, contentment, good health, and bright hope.

3 Count your blessings, not your troubles. Instead of saying, "I miss him or her so much," say, "I had him or her for X number of years. Most of the time, it was heaven on earth--how lucky can I get." Again I find a religious response helpful; "My husband or wife is in heaven, where life is more beautiful than life on earth; when my time comes, I will go to the eternal world and meet him or her. Until that time, I will try to live my life as if I were already in the heavenly condition."

4 Create happiness for others. Laugh, sing, joke, encourage others, be positive. Make yourself a joy to be around because you are lifting the other people to a higher level. Involve yourself in the task of making other people happy and lo and behold you have made yourself happy, useful, and contented.

THE TIME OF ACCEPTANCE

Our reaction to separation goes through various phases of grief starting with shock, numbness, and a sense of disbelief. Many times we give to other people the appearance of holding up well and being quite accepting of our loss. However, phases of grief are natural and acceptance takes a long time for most people. The initial intense numbness will turn to feelings of pain and longing. Our home and all our surroundings seem full of painful reminders. Sometimes the bereaved feels like the dead partner has been literally torn out of his or her body. Unconsciously, we search for our lost mate everywhere we go.

When the full impact of the death sets in, we begin to realize that our lost mate will not return. Despair, depression, and guilt make us feel irrational and sometimes irritable. The tendency is to shun offers of comfort and support, to focus on memories of our lost spouse, or, to become angry at being left. All this and more is the process of learning to live with our loss. This process of grief will continue on a diminishing scale until we gradually come to the time of acceptance. Bereavement takes time and effort to heal. If we don't put some effort into the healing process, we may lengthen the time of grief and suffering until the possibility of permanent damage to our system will loom above us.

We seek for the time of acceptance and the beginnings of a new life. It can't be rushed, but neither can it be delayed too long. At this time of grief leading to acceptance, alcohol may represent a special risk. If you are emotionally upset or tired, a couple of drinks will make matters worse, not better. Here is also the time when many people find themselves looking forward to the next pill. It is quite easy to become hooked on prescription drugs, and it is not easy to undo the damage.

HOW TO KEEP FROM GOING CRAZY

The feelings we suffer during grief gradually disappear, but sometimes they get so severe, it is common to think we are going crazy. It has been said that when we think we are going crazy, we are not. Mentally ill people often do not realize they are mentally ill. We must remember that there is a big difference between intense emotions that make us feel crazy and actual mental illness.

Another common thing for men and women who have lost their marriage partner is to continue to see, feel, and sometimes touch the one who has died. To see ghosts and sometimes talking to them is a very scary experience. When it happens (and it often does) it is easy to believe that we are going crazy. It is the opinion of many who have studied the field that the dead whom we have loved do not really leave us. In some fashion, to some people, the dead continue as faithful companions, sustaining and inspiring us. We often meet them in some familiar place, perhaps as a reminder of the coming resurrection. It is a part of the daily mystery, beauty, and excitement of life. There is no need to have fear of the ghost of a loved one--he or she did not hurt you during life and he or she won't hurt you during death.

It is quite normal to harbor some very angry feelings about the death of a wife or husband. Of course, anger will turn to guilt and the guilt will make us think we have gone crazy. It is especially true that anger and guilt will possess a person if the spouse committed suicide. In fact, a person may become so overwhelmed that he or she may require professional intervention. This is particularly true if we start harboring suicidal thoughts or impulses.

There comes a time when we all must say goodbye

In the book *Survival Handbook for Widows* by Ruth Jean Loewinsohn, she says that a time comes when we must say goodbye. She suggests that we make a list of ten virtues of the husband or wife who has gone before. Then make a list of ten things you disliked or did not respect. It may be hard, but you will soon recognize that your spouse was a real person with real faults and real virtues, who is now dead. And, you must go on--sanely.

DEALING WITH SEX

Of all the human emotions, sensuality is the most varied. The sex need to some people is romance, companionship, and closeness--often the need for actual sex is quite minimal. In other people the need is quite strong. When we lose our spouse, we lose our sexual partner and our feelings can be anything from the desire to shun sex for the rest of our lives to powerful needs, and anything in-between. Sexual feelings after being widowed are quite common and the feelings should not make us feel guilty.

My wife's mother died when she was 96. She had lived for 20 years without her husband. One time she complained that she had dreamed that someone had tried to rape her. She was such a virtuous woman that she could not express the sexual need for her husband, and so it came out in her dream world. Often for a widowed person there can be a conflict between societal taboos and his or her personal needs. If you are thinking about getting another partner, you may want to consider just where sex fits into the picture.

HOW TO STAY HEALTHY

Dr. Hans Selye, a famous stress specialist, lists the loss of a life partner as the number one stress factor. Stress and grief can have an extremely adverse effect on the health of our body and mind. It is not uncommon for a widow or widower to sicken and die shortly after their loss--the stress of grief can do serious damage to the immune system.

Some brief rules following your grief:

- ❤ Get proper nutrition whether you feel like it or not.

- ❤ Get some form of regular exercise.

- ❤ Get out and around and associate with people.

- ❤ Go back to work or to doing something useful as soon as possible.

- ❤ Report your physical complaints to your doctor. Remember to be very careful--your body is suffering trauma, which makes it vulnerable to accidents.

Acute grief is like a serious illness; it has a series of symptoms:

- ❤ Your sleep patterns are disturbed; you may find yourself up all night and down all day.

- ❤ You are gripped with a chronic fatigue syndrome and a loss of energy.

- ❤ You may have a loss of appetite and cooking will lose its appeal.

Beginning a new life--

The best time to show respect and love for one's spouse is while that spouse is living.

I have had a more rewarding and fruitful life than I probably deserve, for which I am grateful. But the day I die, my last thought will be regret that I shall leave you alone.

If three days, or three months after I've gone, you find someone who will love you and cherish you for a few years as I have for so many--go for it.

"Mac" in Oregon

- ❤ Stomachaches and intestinal pain and vague feelings of illness may permeate your body.

- ❤ Sometimes the widow or widower may so identify with the lost partner that he may take on the symptoms of the illness that killed his spouse.

During the time of mourning the temptation to drink too much, smoke more cigarettes than usual, and overuse tranquilizers, pain pills, sleeping pills, and other medication can be very common. Many people who use prescription drugs and artificial relief during their grief discover that the drugs only delay the time it takes to come to acceptance of their pain.

Usually it is not recommended that a person spend much time alone when he or she is suffering grief. Swap chores with friends, neighbors, and relatives and keep yourself involved with people. Long hours alone will simply aggravate the tendency to be ill with grief.

THE FUNERAL ARRANGEMENTS

It seems unfair and cruel for a person to be forced to make funeral arrangements when he or she is suffering the loss of a spouse. However, after a short time of intense grief, the best thing to do is to take care of the urgent details that death requires:

- ■ Notify all the relatives and friends or have someone do it for you. You won't be able to speak to the first few loved ones in a coherent way; but, by the time you have spoken to 10 people about your spouse's death, you will be able to talk about it--which is good.

- ■ Make the funeral arrangements that are best for you and your family. You don't need a costly funeral to show your respect and love for your mate. Almost immediately it will be necessary to decide how much you will pay for a casket (which usually includes the cost of the

> **Nothing can prepare you for the shock and grief of widowhood. One of the myths of mourning is that is has an ending point. That if you just wait long enough, it suddenly stops hurting. It doesn't. It requires working through the various phases of grief and eventually it gets better when one recognizes grief but no longer is paralyzed by it. However, there are those who have a spiritual outlook that lets them see the loss in a way that they can accept: part of life's plan or some greater purpose.**

funeral). Believe it or not, you will find yourself wandering in a large room full of caskets, shopping for one, much like you buy a new car. Prices usually range from $1200 to $10,000, with $2500 as a common medium.

- You must immediately look over insurance policies, the will, deeds, bank books, stock certificates, and other important papers. Do not let your grief jeopardize your future.

- Notify the bank, the insurance company, your lawyer, social security, pension funds. Advise all creditors, including issuers of credit cards, that your spouse has died. Some of your loans or perhaps the house may be paid for. Be sure to get an ample supply of death certificates. Be sure you discuss fees before you engage any legal help. You may not feel like it now, but money does matter now and for your future.

> Be still, sad heart! and cease repining;
> Behind the clouds is the sun still shining;
> Thy fate is the common fate of all,
> Into each life some rain must fall,
> Some days must be dark and dreary.
> - Longfellow (1819-1892)

- The reaction of family and friends can be both troubling and comforting. Let them help you, but be sure you are in on all major decisions. They will soon go back to what they were doing, and you will be, often, left alone to live with the decisions. Make all decisions that must be made and put off making any decision you can until you feel better. If any of the decisions involve legal matters, be sure to consult your lawyer, and again, be sure to ask how much it will cost.

- Family and friends are seldom able to give all the comfort and support that you will need at this time. They will also have their expectancies of your role; and, you probably won't be able to live up to it. It may help to try to remember how you treated widowed friends and relatives before you had experienced widowhood yourself. Again, I personally stress the "invisible" means of support--now is the time for your "faith" to come to your rescue.

SOME BUSINESS MATTERS

Now, the funeral is over. The relatives and friends have gone home and you are left with a new lifestyle. If you have been in charge of the business matters, then things should flow quite smoothly. But, if the spouse has always handled banking, taxes, and investments, then whether you like it or not, you have some important work to do.

- ☐ Contact Social Security to apply for widowed persons benefits and ask for details on eligibility for Medicare.

- ☐ If your spouse was a veteran, there may be some benefits, so contact the Veterans Administration.

- ☐ You are lucky if your spouse has clued you in concerning all benefits. If not, search again among the important papers and consult your spouse's lawyer, banker, employer, insurance com-

pany, and investment broker. If you feel there is reason to, look under every business stone.

- ☐ Don't make important life decisions too quickly; your grief is likely to lead you to make terrible financial mistakes. Consider carefully and sanely before you sell your house, quit your job, move to another town, move in with your family, give away large sums of money, or retire from your former lifestyle. Make tentative decisions--for example, move in with your family for two weeks to see if you can stand it before you decide on a permanent move.

SUGGESTIONS

- ❤ Make sure you have plenty of green plants and fresh flowers in the house. Living things, especially pets, force you to think of life.

- ❤ Dress in bright, cheerful colors and do so every day.

- ❤ Plan each day so you have lots of things to do and fewer blocks of time with nothing to do.

- ❤ Exercise each day or take walks.

- ❤ Don't stay in bed in the mornings or during the day.

- ❤ Plan to have visitors during the supper hours if you can.

- ❤ Get out of the house at least once a day.

- ❤ Get help by contacting AARP's Widowed Persons Service and ask for a local chapter (see the article on Widowed Persons Service, page 243).

> A booklet, *On Being Alone*, written for the newly widowed, is available free from AARP. For an English version ask for stock number D150. For a Spanish version ask for stock number D13949. Write:
> AARP
> 601 E Street, N.W.
> Washington, D.C. 20049

Dealing with loneliness by Wm. J. Diehm

It's funny when you're lonely,
How your mind will always stray;
To the sentimental memories,
That you've had another day.

You think about the nice things,
And happiness you've met;
It hurts to remember,
But it hurts more to forget.

Anon

The elderly population is large and growing. In 1987, 8.5 million elderly lived alone; by 2020, 13.3 million elderly will live alone. More than 6.5 million, or 77%, of all elderly living alone are women. The percentage of older women living alone exceeds that of men in each age group, but women become progressively more likely than men to live alone with age. Among those over 85, 52% of women live alone compared to 29% for men. Widowhood is by far the most common situation for older women who live alone. Between the ages of 65 and 74, 77% of women living alone are widows, as are 88% of those over 75. Men who live alone are far more likely to be divorced or never to have married. This phenomenon occurs because women tend to marry men older than themselves, and because women live longer than men.

Although not the only cause, by far the loneliest American adults are those who are divorced, widowed, or separated and those who live alone.

I will never forget the time that I walked into a hospital and heard the unhappy cry of an old man, "Nurse, I'm lonely." Over and over again he expressed his need in heart-rending sobs that touched my soul in a unforgettable way. I asked the nurse on duty, "What's wrong with the old man?" She replied, "He has outlived all his relatives and no one comes to see him anymore; and I can't spend all day holding his hand."

Over the years, I have visited hundreds of retirement homes. Some are very well-run, caring organizations, handling older people effectively who are in every state of functioning. Other convalescent hospitals are snake pits from hell--the range of hospital and retirement homes extends from awesome to awful. We who are advanced in years must take the time to consider where we will live, if we live too long to take care of ourselves.

If we wisely prepare in advance, we can select a home that does have some people who can take the time to hold our hand. When my Aunt Evelyn was just 60 years old, her husband, Lee, died unexpectedly. My aunt soon sold her property and moved to an American Baptist life-care retirement home in Seattle, Washington. Our whole family was aghast that Auntie would retire so early in life.

However, the life-care facility furnished Auntie with a nice room where she could do her own cooking; or, she could eat in the cafeteria whenever she wanted to. In addition, she could travel and come and go as she desired, which she did extensively. For years, Auntie spent very little time at the home. Now, at the age of 90, she is infirm and in a wheelchair. She needs around-the-clock care-- and she gets it. The family, what is left of us, are scattered all over the country; and Auntie seldom gets visitors. But whenever one of us does call, we find a happy, contented, well-cared-for senior citizen who never calls out, "Nurse, I'm lonely."

When I first started visiting retirement and full-care homes, I considered them to be awful places and one day I said to a son: "Son, before you put me in one of these homes, shoot me." Of course I was kidding; but, you can see how terrible I thought the homes were. Since that time, I have seen dozens of beautiful caring places. Recently, I toured the Alzheimer's facilities run by my cousin Tom Sharon in Tacoma, Washington. No one wants Alzheimer's, but this terrible condition has been minimized by these thoughtful, happy facilities.

Loneliness comes to people who do not prepare for a good retirement. I have met young people who said they were never going to retire; but when the time comes, almost everyone has to drop the old loads and pick up new ones. We must all carry some type of burden or occupy ourselves with something of interest. The saddest tale ever told concerns the person who never made any provision to retire or change occupations.

So, if you find a care facility that cares, you will not need to worry about the frightening conditions of loneliness. Today, social services, churches, lodges, schools, and institutions are dedicated to the proposition that many people need to be cared for. If you are one of those people, relax and let other people cure their loneliness by curing yours.

Another type of lonely person has come to my attention: people who have retired and find themselves at a loss as to what to do. Here are eight sure-fired cures for such loneliness:

1. Keep busy.
2. Involve yourself.
3. Help others.
4. Avoid escapes.
5. Choose to be happy.
6. Collect good thoughts.
7. Join a social group.
8. Go to church.

Don't wallow in your feelings of loneliness --do something about it!

1 **Keep busy**--If you are lonely, do with eagerness whatever is in front of you to do: write letters, visit people, fix something that needs to be fixed, take up a hobby, start collecting something of value, become amazed and fascinated by everything around you. Keep busily involved in everything that gets your attention--every little thing and every middle-sized thing can soon grow into big significant projects. The happiest person I ever met and the busiest person I ever met are one and the same. Cure loneliness by keeping busy.

2 **Involve yourself**--If you are lonely, involve yourself in community affairs. Many times when people retire they find themselves in a burned-out condition. Some folks have told me, all I want to do is just sit in a chair, pet my dog, stare out the window, or watch TV. This kind of mental attitude sets a person up to be lonely. And, if a person continues to be a hermit, there will come a time when an incurable loneliness will be the order of the day.

3 **Help others**--If you are lonely, look for and strive to cure the loneliness of someone else--it will cure your own. How about holding the hand of some of those people who made no provisions for old age. There are myriads of people who need help--find them and help them.

4 **Avoid escapes**--If you are lonely, avoid day dreaming, sleeping too much, and watching too much TV. When you do dream dreams, make them possible, obtainable, and something you can work on. Dream magnificent goals for the future and start to bring them about. TV can be a life-saver on occasions; but to mesmerize your brain in a constant dose of radiation from the idiot box is a sure-fire way of becoming depressed and lonely. Too much sleep can be a powerful escape mechanism. We can find ourselves fleeing from guilt, responsibility, failure, and hopelessness. To run away through sleep is just like running away with alchohol--it only makes matters worse. Fight the tendency to sleep too much as if it were a demon from hell--it is.

5 **Choose to be happy**--If you are lonely, you are probably depressed and unhappy. Fight unhappiness with a direct attack of the will--choose to be happy in spite of the circumstances. Ask yourself the question, "How does my unhappiness change my situation?" The answer will be, "It doesn't, it just makes it worse." So make things better for yourself by choosing to be happy. Fight depression by talking out your problems. If alcoholics can join a group and get control of their drinking, you can join a group and get control of your depression. Talk to friends, a counselor, or your pastor, and keep talking until you find yourself maintaining an attitude of optimism. See our article on depression (page 346) to find methods of dealing with it.

6 **Collect good thoughts**--If you are lonely, collect inspirational thoughts, good jokes, meaningful poems, and literary masterpieces. Read lots of good books, if you can; if you can't, have someone read to you. Make a list of good things that you read about and then try to memorize some inspirational quotation and share it with whoever comes your way. Collect good thoughts to share with those people who come your way, and soon others will search for your companionship like the proverbial guru of the mountain.

7 **Join a social group**--If you are lonely, join one of the many social groups in your community. See that you visit the Senior Center regularly and meet new people. You will find many individuals there that are involved in social gatherings of various types. Commit yourself to one or more groups that you find of interest.

8 **Go to church**--If you are lonely, go to church. How do I have the nerve to tell people to go to church when I am writing a secular work? I do for the following reason: There is a lot of criticism of the church, but no substitute for it. Most churches care for their people and treat everyone who attends like family. If we cut the church out of the community there would be tens of thousands of more lonely people. I have heard some people say, I went to church and the people were unfriendly. If we are friendly, the church will be friendly. If we are unfriendly, more than 75% of the time, the church will still be friendly.

You are not alone; feelings of loneliness strike over one-third of all Americans at least sometime.

Loneliness is often caused by wanting people to do something for us. When we do things for other people, we are never lonely. Self-referenced thinking often leads to a barrenness of spirit that breeds discontent and loneliness. Think up, think out, toward people, think around, toward all the exciting things of life; and avoid thinking too much about yourself, and the problem of loneliness will disappear.

Loneliness generally occurs at specific times of the day or during specific days such as holidays, birthdays, and anniversaries. Planning ahead for these times so that you are active and busy with other things helps provide a very effective means of dealing with loneliness.

Courage is the price that life extracts for granting peace.
The soul that knows it not, knows no release.
From little things;
Knows not the livid loneliness of fear,
Nor mountain heights where bitter joy can hear
The sound of wings.

Amelia Earhart (1898-1937)

Men living alone--here's a chance to spruce up your lif

**Older men:
an overlooked
minority!**

Men are a distinct minority of Americans over 65. Older women outnumber older men three to two, and this disparity becomes even greater in the older-old. In 1985, there were only two men for every five women 85 and older. Women have a longer life expectancy, outliving men by an average of seven to eight years.

Today's generation of older men age differently than today's older women, having had lifestyles that place them at higher risk for today's leading causes of death. It is worth noting that this can be expected to change if successive generations of women take up smoking and other harmful practices that place them at equal risk for diseases such as lung cancer and heart disease. In addition, certain diseases/conditions affect men only. Some of the specific health issues facing today's older men are:

- ❑ **Coronary heart disease.** CHD is the number one cause of death in men over 40 and is responsible for half of all deaths among older people. Control of blood cholesterol, blood pressure, and weight, and smoking cessation can help reduce an older man's risk for CHD.
- ❑ **Stroke.** Strokes affect 1.5 times as many men as women and are a major cause of disability as well as death. The same risk factors as those mentioned for CHD increase a man's risk for stroke.
- ❑ **Lung disease.** Many lung diseases are more prevalent among men than women. For example, lung cancer kills four times

as many men than women. More men die from emphysema and pneumonia, too. The major causes are occupational hazards and smoking. While smoking rates have gone down considerably for the general population, one-third of men over 65 still smoke. Quitting at any age benefits the pulmonary system, and some damage may even be reversed.

- ❑ **Digestive system cancers.** Cancer of the colon and rectum is a major cause of death among older men. The incidence of colorectal cancer is increasing for white men and even more dramatically for black men. When detected early, this type of cancer can often be arrested with surgery.
- ❑ **Osteoporosis.** While generally thought of as a women's disease, 20% of the 24 million Americans with osteoporosis are men. Men are largely unaware of the positive measures that can be taken in the area of diet and exercise.
- ❑ **Prostate disease.** As many as 80% of men over age 50 experience some problem with their prostate gland. The problem may just be enlargement, or it could be cancer. Prostate cancer is the second most common form of cancer in both white and black males and has caused 30,000 deaths in 1990 alone. Early detection is critical to effective treatment and survival.
- ❑ **Sexual function.** While changes in sexual function, including changes in erection and orgasm, occur in the older man, most older men can lead a satisfying sex life. Problems may be caused by disease, medications, or other physical conditions that can be successfully treated.

Under these physical changes and conditions are issues that arise from the particular life experiences and social roles of this generation that affect use of healthcare services or involvement in programs for older adults.

- ❑ Older men come from a generation in which much of their self-worth was derived from work. They may have prepared for retirement with a focus on financial planning but with little atten-

tion to knowledge or skills for coping with life after work.
- ❑ Some older men may resist showing emotions, talking about their feelings, or asking for help. This may make adjusting to losses more difficult, as studies have shown the grief process may actually be intensified by the inability to talk about or show feeling.
- ❑ Older men have not typically spent a lot of time and energy developing support systems outside of work and family that could help them with adjustments in later life.
- ❑ Older men see themselves as being self-reliant. Yet they may lack skills in self-care, such as cooking, shopping, and doing laundry.
- ❑ While most caregiving is provided by women, some older men find themselves in this role and are unprepared for the demands and stress.
- ❑ Many older men lack information about available services and programs or perceive the services and programs as being irrelevant to them.

Mental Health Issues for Older Men
Mental health problems are often overlooked or misinterpreted with older people, and mental health services are underutilized. This may be even more true for men than for women. Older men may have trouble acknowledging and seeking help for emotional or psychological problems.

Suicide is a serious problem among older men. The suicide rate among older white men is higher than it is for any other age group, and is significantly higher than for women. For example, the rate for men age 75 to 84 is eight times higher than the rate for women of the same age. Depression, illness, and changes in marital status may contribute to the increased risk of suicide for older men.

There are many issues that place older men at risk:

- ❤ **Living alone.** It is estimated that there are 1.8 million older men living alone. Men who are widowed or divorced at this time of their lives often lack self-care skills and become socially isolated, increasing the burdens of loneliness. The death rate among widowers is much higher than that of their married peers: four times as high from suicide, three times as high from auto accidents, ten times as high from strokes, and six times as high from heart disease.

❤ **Bereavement.** AARP's Widowed Persons Service, a community-based self-help program across the country, found that only one widower out of every ten widowed persons will seek help in coping with bereavement. In fact, studies have shown that in the first four months after the death of a wife, a man is vulnerable to both physical and emotional problems. The assumption that men experience different feelings following a loss is simply not true. But WPS research found men do not view themselves differently and are less likely to seek help. Often it's a shock to the widowed man himself that he is not as strong and self-sufficient as he thought. Men may have little understanding of how support groups work and worry about being embarrassed, outnumbered by women, or pressured into disclosing feelings. Any efforts at developing support or self-help groups for older men must take these fears and characteristics into consideration.

❤ **Retirement.** This is a major change in a man's life. Again, a man may be surprised that once retired he encounters feelings of loss--loss of authority, purpose, and self-worth. Changes in a man's relationship with his spouse and other family members can occur when he retires and can cause stress. As many as 90% of retirees may experience a health crisis requiring a hospital stay in the first year of retirement. More is needed than standard retirement planning that deals with finances, insurance, and housing. Men need to develop interests, friendships, and a sense of self-worth beyond work.

Programs That Help
For many of the above reasons, older men are less likely to ask for help, attend programs, or seek support services than women. Yet, each and every male can benefit greatly from health promotion programs offered by the health and aging professionals that are trying to help. Some programs include teaching food shopping, food preparation, and what you can do to keep healthy. In addition, the classes create a social and support network among individuals in the class. If you or someone you know needs help you can find out more about programs in your area by contacting:

National Resource Center on Health Promotion and Aging:

AARP
601 E Street, N.W.
Washington, D.C. 20049
(202) 434-2277
or

Area Agency on Aging (see the Older American Act pages 24 and 25 for State Agencies. They will provide local addresses. Area Agencies will also be found in your telephone directory.)

A Chance to Volunteer
You don't have to wait for a health professional to start a program in your area. You can get help to start a program by contacting your local manager of the Area Agency on Aging or AARP's area office. For example, in Eureka, California, the Gent's Kitchen Survival Class is offered by the Area I Agency on Aging and Humbolt Senior Citizens council. A staff dietician led the first six lessons, and then the participants were able to take over the class and carry it on. The class continues to meet without professional leadership. In many other programs, in addition to leading the meeting, the peer leader makes calls to participants, announces the topics, and arranges for a snack.

Many find retirement boring but here's a chance to spruce up your life, meet new friends, and do something worthwhile for yourself and others. If you do decide to start a program here are some tips:

✔ Recruit other male volunteers and have them find other men to participate.
✔ Conduct "men-only" programs that are specific to men's needs and interests, addressing some of the topics and issues in this article.

✔ Establish ongoing, focused outreach efforts to reach men. Consider using a visible older male spokesperson or celebrity from the community.
✔ Stress comradeship; begin with social activities like card parties or sports events. Go on to develop the idea and group framework for mutual support.
✔ Discussion groups can integrate health issues and other topics of interest to men, such as politics, current events, sports, or local history.
✔ Teach household management skills to all "men-only" groups to ensure individual comfort. Include how to do laundry, cooking, shopping, and mending.
✔ Sponsor programs at places where men regularly get together, such as veterans' associations or sports clubs.
✔ Make information about potential services widely available to organizations that men belong to such as veterans' or fraternal groups.
✔ Address "life adjustments" rather than "mental health." Include activities that may help men socialize with each other and express emotion.

> **We can learn more from our peers than from professionals.**

When I was young I was amazed at Plutarch's statement that the elder Cato began at the age of 80 to learn Greek. I am amazed no longer. Old age is ready to undertake tasks that youth shirked because they would take too long.
W. Somerset Maugham

Widowed Persons Service (WPS) is a national AARP program of self-help for widowed persons (see page 243); for more information about programs and materials, contact:

WPS AARP
601 E Street, N.W.
Washington, D.C. 20049

Women--going it alone

The elderly population is large and growing. The phenomena of the graying of America also could be called the feminization of America; for as our population ages, it also will become more predominantly female. Today, there are 68 men for every 100 women over the age of 65. With age, the ratio of men to women decreases steadily. There are 83 men for every 100 women between the ages of 65 and 69, and only 40 men for every 100 women among those 85 and older. This trend is expected to grow into the next century. This disparity in numbers of men verses women results in significant numbers of older women living alone.

Of all the older persons living alone, more than 6.5 million--77%--are women. By the year 2020, this total will be 13.3 million and 85% of those will be women. The percentage of older women living alone exceeds that of men in each age group, but women become progressively more likely than men to live alone with age.

Widowhood is by far the most common situation for older women who live alone. Between the ages of 65 and 74, 77% of women living alone are widows, as are 88% of those over 75. Men who live alone are far more likely to be divorced or never to have married. This phenomenon occurs both because women tend to marry men older than themselves, and because women live longer than men.

For women who live alone, poverty is a development in their golden years.

Quality of Life Constraints

Income

Poverty affects women disproportionately throughout their lives, but particularly in their later years. Income is a particularly critical issue for older women who live alone. Forty-five percent of older women living alone are poor or near-poor. While some of these women are from low-income families, many face poverty for the first time, after divorce or death of a spouse.

Poverty plagues older women for several interrelated reasons. Women tend to have limited or intermittent stays in the paid work force, largely because our society leaves to women the care of the young, sick, and old family members. The work history patterns common among women make it difficult to accrue adequate private pensions, or to become eligible for pensions at all. A woman's Social Security retirement benefits reflect any reduction in hours or absences from the paid work force. Yet, one-third of older single women rely on Social Security benefits for at least 90% of their income with the average monthly benefit of $412.

Many widows rely on the Social Security spousal benefits. Yet there are many widows who forfeit their spousal Social Security benefits if they divorce after having been married for less than ten years. They also frequently lose their spouse's private pensions regardless of the length of marriage.

Widows are likely to experience a sharp drop in income and benefits upon the death of their spouse. Once a man is out of her life a woman often finds herself in reduced financial circumstances. One study revealed that within three years, widows found their income reduced by 44%.

Poverty and living alone make all other elements of well-being more difficult to attain. Housing, food, clothing, medical care, health, and assistance with chores are all affected to a greater or lesser extent by the amount of income one has and by the availability of routine or emergency care from others or a family member.

The Supplemental Security Income (SSI) program is intended to provide an income safety net for older persons, but it falls short of this goal. The program provides a monthly benefit to low-income older persons but brings poor women to only 76% of the federal poverty level. Still, many elderly poor are ineligible for the program because their assets exceed the asset limit of $1,900 for individuals. Another problem is that a large group of older women do not receive benefits they are eligible for either because they do not know about them or how to get them, or because they are too proud to accept this assistance. Others, especially those for whom English is a second language, may not understand the complicated paperwork necessary to initiate payments. Thus, only half of elderly persons eligible for Supplemental Security Income actually receive benefits. (See the article on SSI on page 61.)

There are many mid-life women or older women who start their own business or establish a new career and who have proved--in more ways than one--that you can start over, you can succeed, you can beat the odds.

Employment

Employment is critical for many older women to avoid poverty. Yet when widowed or divorced women try to find jobs, if they have been a housewife for most of their adult life, they find that all there is available are poorly paid jobs such as salesperson, file clerk, or receptionist. Many women past 50 encounter the great prejudice that exists against hiring older women. Those older women who do find work are more likely to work in jobs that are less secure and lower paying than younger or male workers. For all workers, a woman makes 68 cents to a man's dollar, but a woman over 45 makes only 61 cents for every dollar a man her age makes, and a woman over 65 makes only 57 cents for his dollar.

Housing

Adequate housing options are critical for the well-being of older women, but particularly so for those older women who live alone. While most older people own their own homes, older women are less likely to do so than are older men. Since the incomes of older women are smaller than those of older men, housing consumes a larger part of their income. Older women may be forced to choose between safe, adequate housing and other necessities. Public housing units are in short supply and frequently fail to meet even minimum standards of health and safety.

The high cost of housing is a particularly difficult burden for older women who live alone. Financial strains often mean that the woman has to sell her house and move to cheaper quarters. (For more information on housing options see pages 78 through 84.)

Health

Older women have healthcare needs that are quite distinct from those of older men. The illnesses, appropriate treatment, availability of unpaid caregivers, and financial resources of older women are very different from those of older men. Treatments, research, medical insurance, and government health programs fail to address the needs of older women because older men are treated as the norm for the elderly. In addition, although women of different ethnic and racial backgrounds have different health needs, the situation of white elderly is treated as the norm.

Older women are more likely to suffer from long-term, chronic illness and disabilities and are less likely to have acute illnesses than older men. The institutional bias of Medicare and Medicaid, therefore, has a negative impact on women. Frequently,

home healthcare and home-making assistance are more appropriate and effective services for persons with chronic health problems than are hospital or nursing home stays. Women are much more likely to live alone, and therefore, to lack in-home, unpaid assistance.

Healthcare Costs

Healthcare costs also have a disproportionate impact on older women. In 1986, Medicare paid for 48% of the total healthcare expenditures of an unmarried man over 65, but only 33% of unmarried older women. Since the income of a woman alone is far less than that of either a couple or a man living alone, every dollar spent on healthcare is a greater percentage of a woman's income than it is of a man's. In addition, since most women outlive their husbands, they are more likely to pay for the cost of a spouse's medical care, particularly for nursing home care, and are less likely to have someone to help pay for their own care. The income requirements for nursing home coverage under Medicaid require that a couple "spend down" to poverty level to obtain care for one spouse. While recent legislation has increased the amount the spouse in the community may retain to live on, the assault on the dignity and the resources of the couples affected remains. (See the article on spousal asset protection, page 100.)

Women as Caregivers

Women are more likely to carry the burden of being primary caregivers themselves. Approximately 75% of home care for disabled elderly was unpaid and generally provided by a female relative. Caregiving represents an additional financial, emotional, and physical burden to women in mid- and late life. The average age of caregivers is 57. Support services, such as respite care, are rarely available to these caregivers.

Safety and Security

Safety in the home is a special problem for older women living alone. While there is some disagreement about whether elderly women are victims of crime at rates greater than the general population, there is no doubt that the fear of crime causes tremendous isolation and anxiety for older women. For those who live alone, the consequences

of accidents can be considerably more serious than for older people who have someone continually available to monitor their safety. In particular, hip fractures and their complications are a major factor in institutionalization for older women. (See the articles on home safety and preventing accidents on pages 176 through 179.)

Don't treat being alone like it was the end of the world.

Divorce

One of the most emotional experiences a woman now living alone must overcome is a divorce. Many women after many years of marriage joined a growing number of other women who, on their path to the golden years, made a pit stop in the courtroom. Women who believed in "til death do us part" find that many older couples are getting divorced more than their counterparts of 10 or 20 years ago. Today, there are 1.3 million divorced Americans 65 and older, a group that, since 1980, has increased more than twice as fast as the population of older Americans as a whole.

Marriages run into different challenges upon retirement and can end in divorce. You have heard of the old saying "For better or for worse, but not for lunch." All of a sudden with all that time with one another you come to realize that you have not worked at the relationship. Dividing up friends after a long-term marriage often is as stressful as dividing up the property. The most serious consequences of a divorce for women in their later years may be the economic impact. The men usually have pensions; the women may not.

Loneliness

It is safe to say that loneliness is one of the greatest problems of living alone for women as well as for men. However, women in general have more friends and acquaintances than men who they can call upon to talk about their troubles or to get together

Living solo--and meeting the challenges of single life

with just for company. Fortunately, any individual has the opportunity to become more comfortable with this problem by doing something about it. (See the article on loneliness, page 236.)

What You Can Do To Make Living Alone Rewarding

This article would not be complete if we didn't write about all the advantages that are available for those living alone. Even though you may be lonely at times, you can live your life now as a free agent. Too many older people regard time as their biggest enemy--make it your most valuable asset. You are in command of your "second 50 years." If you want to go shopping and then on the spur of the moment are invited to lunch or dinner or for that matter an ocean trip, it is up to you. Here are some positive steps you can take:

❑ **Make friends.** Visit the senior center in your area regularly. Join some afternoon card games. Go to church. Ask others to accompany you to lunch or dinner. Here are some other possibilities for meeting people:

> Museums, theaters, operas, ball games
> Jogging or dog walking
> Playgrounds and parks--Grandchildren are an excellent "decoy," or conversation opener
> High school or college reunions
> Auctions
> Libraries
> Stores and shops--particularly book stores or video and record shops
> Exercise clubs

❑ **Get involved with yourself and others.** There are many volunteer opportunities to help those less fortunate that need your help (see pages 160 through 168). You meet new friends and learn of new opportunities. Take some classes at a local school or opportunities like Elderhostel (see page 173). Find others to share your hobbies.

❑ **Maintain your self-respect.** Often being alone is the time to lose some weight,

try new hairstyles, new makeup, or to spruce up your wardrobe. Above all maintain cleanliness in yourself and your surroundings. A sense of self-confidence will build the strength that is necessary to make it through the hard times--and make the most of the good times. If you can feel good about yourself, you can feel good about living alone.

❑ **Learn to enjoy your independence.** Look upon being alone not as a curse but as an opportunity to become more independent, more self-sufficient, and, hopefully, an even more interesting person.

❑ **Take care of your health.** Older women need to know about the positive effects of healthy behaviors such as proper diet and regular exercise. Locate through others or your local area office on aging the available resources that can help you become more informed, wiser, and an assertive healthcare consumer.

❑ **Find out what opportunities and support is available.** If you need help, don't be afraid to ask for it. There are many community and government programs that are available to provide assistance to those who need it. (See the articles on the Older American Act, pages 20 through 25.)

❑ **Get a job.** If you need to supplement your income and are physically able, look for work--even part-time employment if it will help with your income needs and you can make new friends.

❑ **Rent out a room or add an apartment to your home.** The room rent could add to your income; the apartment, considerably more, depending on the local rental market. The arrangement can also provide companionship and an exchange of services. If you do take in a boarder, be sure to draw up a home-sharing agreement that clearly spells out the ground rules concerning shared living spaces, pets, guests, smoking, drinking, parking, and other details.

❑ **Invite friends to dinner.** If you find a man whose company you like don't be afraid to invite him out to dinner. Don't feel offended if you are rejected. There

are no rules about who should initiate a date anymore. Make sharing of food a gift of love.

❑ **Travel near and far.** Unattached women do not have to find traveling alone a lonely, frightening experience. Often it is not the fear of loneliness that keeps singles from traveling; it is the anxiety about details connected with the trip. (Read the articles on travel, pages 194 through 221.) Nowadays, there are many travel opportunities that cater to single persons.

If you are thinking about taking a vacation by yourself here are some organizations to contact (or contact your travel agent) about trips: Gramercy's Singleworld, 444 Madison Ave., New York, NY 10022; 1-800-223-6490. Mature Travel Mates (a new solo traveler's match-making club), P.O. Box 26833, Tamarac, FL 33320. For Jewish singles past 50, American Jewish Congress Travel Department runs special tours to Israel. They can be contacted at 15 E. 84th Street, New York, NY 10028, 1-800-221-4694.

❑ **Get involved in politics.** There are many local, state, and federal opportunities and problems that could use your input. There's a veritable gold mine of interesting and stimulating people already there. Meet new friends and cast your ballot. To learn how to write to your congressman see page 172.

❑ **Use your imagination.** Think of things to do you'd never have dreamed of when you were not alone. Then, get out and do them!

The American Association of Retired Persons (AARP) and the Commonwealth Fund Commission on Elderly People Living Alone are expanding their efforts to inform low income older persons about public benefits to which they may be entitled. AARP outreach programs focus on Medicaid, Food Stamps, and Low Income Energy Assistance, along with their Supplemental Security Income Outreach Program. For more information contact:

AARP, Consumer Affairs,
601 E. Street, N.W., Washington, D.C.
20049; (202) 434-2277

Help for the newly widowed

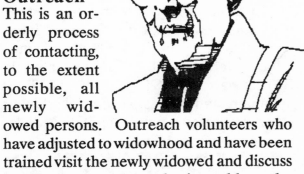

After the funeral, newly widowed persons are often left alone in altered life circumstances for which there has been virtually no preparation. For those who have not had to work their way out of grief it is easy to assume that the church or social service agencies, mental health programs, or the medical and legal professions offer all the assistance necessary and that Social Security or government assistance programs, insurance, or pension provisions protect the interest of the widowed.

Yet, no more than 40% of our population today claim church affiliation and only 3% of the newly widowed look upon their church or clergy as a source of help after the week of the funeral. Also, when the diagnosis is grief, the staffs in social service, mental health, medical and legal groups seldom come up with a response. Financially, the newly widowed must then deal with a "blackout" period in the Social Security program and the realization that most pension programs do not protect the interest of the survivor. Add to that the fact that most individuals shy away from the newly widowed because of their own fears and insecurities.

Our society's value system, in general, rewards people who are young, married, self-sufficient, socially aggressive, and contain their emotions. When one is widowed, one's status in this married social system is disrupted. Even with years of life experiences, widows and widowers often are not prepared to cope with the immediate adjustments needed in housing, family relations, finances, legal requirements, and social demands. Many newly widowed are unable to release the emotional tension, the fear and apprehension, the feelings of guilt, anger, or resentment that well up inside. Often they are overwhelmed by the magnitude of their loss, their loneliness, and their isolation.

What About Family and Friends?
In today's mobile, often impersonal, competitive society, for many, much of their family and supportive social structure is stripped away, leaving them very much alone in times of personal stress. The unfortunate fact is that public attitudes, and our social, legal, health, and governmental structures tend to deal with death and survivors in abrasive, thoughtless ways. This posture drives the newly widowed toward even greater isolation, remorse, and fear than is necessary.

AARP's Program
Experience over a number of years has demonstrated that widowed persons who have made a satisfactory life adjustment can provide a unique opportunity to help the newly bereaved. To this end, the American Association of Retired Persons (AARP) established the Widowed Persons Service Program (WPS).

WPS is based on the concept that significant help can come from those who have survived a similar experience and are willing to share the trauma with others. Widowed persons, men and women of all ages, who have adjusted to being widowed, help newly widowed persons. Experienced volunteers bring from their own life experiences new perspectives, hope, and understanding. Help is provided through outreach volunteers and mutual help groups.

AARP's Widowed Persons Service programs bring together the resources of local religious organizations, educational institutions, social service agencies, professional associations, fraternal and service clubs, health and mental health facilities, and AARP groups in a coordinated effort. The national WPS provides organizational, consultative recruitment and training assistance, as well as published materials for local programs and for the public. Each WPS program functions locally under the umbrella of the national WPS.

Not all communities follow the same operational pattern, but generally the goal in each community is to provide:
- ❤ outreach;
- ❤ telephone service;
- ❤ mutual help group sessions;
- ❤ public education; and
- ❤ a referral service.

The heart of Widowed Persons Service lies in:
- ✳ the development of an organizational structure that can support the volunteers; and
- ✳ the recruitment and training of volunteers who are willing to give their time and effort to participate in one or more of the services of the program.

Outreach-- This is an orderly process of contacting, to the extent possible, all newly widowed persons. Outreach volunteers who have adjusted to widowhood and have been trained visit the newly widowed and discuss openly, on a one-to-one basis, problems the newly widowed face.

Telephone Service-- A local telephone number is widely publicized so that the community will know about the program and people can call for program information, or to request service from WPS.

Mutual Help Group Sessions-- Based on the needs of the community and availability of qualified leadership, mutual help meetings are held. The purpose is to provide an environment where people with a common bond can discuss issues, learn how to help each other, and initiate social and personal contacts. To learn more about how these groups function refer to the article on mutual help under the Assistance to Senior section, page 17.

Referral Service-- Through local organizations, public service agencies, workshops, and the media, the Widowed Persons Service program and the needs of widowed persons are brought to the attention of the community. Each community has organizations and professional personnel to whom widowed persons can turn. The local Widowed Persons Service program then develops a directory or manual to provide easy reference to local services and appropriate agencies or personnel.

For more information: Refer to your local telephone directory in the yellow pages under the heading "Senior Citizen's Service Organizations" or contact:
Widowed Persons Service
AARP
601 E. Street, N.W.
Washington, D.C. 20049
(202) 434-2260

This is a list of telephone numbers that provide health-related information. They do not diagnose or recommend treatment for any disease; only your physician may do that. Some numbers offer recorded information; others provide personalized counseling, referrals, and/or written materials. EST is eastern, CST is central, MST is mountain, and PST is pacific time. Unless otherwise stated numbers operate Monday through Friday (M-F).

Guide:
- ◆ Plan ahead before you dial.
- ◆ Draw up a list of questions and be as specific as you can.
- ◆ Call early in the day if you can when phone lines are less apt to be busy.
- ◆ If you have questions that fall outside the hotline's territory, be sure to ask where else you can call.
- ◆ Be patient--some numbers are very busy. You may have to keep calling.
- ◆ Have a pen and paper ready.

GENERAL 1-800-336-4797
(301) 565-4167 in MD
ODPHP National Health Information Center. Provides a central source of information and referral for health questions. No diagnosis made or treatment recommended. Spanish-speaking staff available. Hours: 9 am-5 pm EST, M-F.

AIDS 1-800-342-2437
(800) 342-7437 in Spanish
U.S. Public Health Service AIDS Information Hotline. Recorded message explains symptoms, means of transmission, and high-risk categories; gives addresses for brochure "Facts about AIDS" and other publications. 24 hours, 7 days a week.

AIDS 1-800-458-5231
National AIDS Information Clearinghouse. Distributes publications on AIDS. Refers callers to local information numbers for specific information on AIDS and treatment sources. Hours: 9 am-7 pm EST, M-F.

ALCOHOLISM 1-800-622-2255
National Council on Alcoholism. Refers to local facilities and provides written information on alcoholism. Hours: 24 hours, 7 days a week.

ALCOHOLISM 1-800-382-4357
Alcoholism and Drug Addiction Treatment Center. Provides referrals to local facilities where adults can seek help. Hours: 8 am-9:30 pm PST, M-F.

ALCOHOLISM 1-800-356-9996
(212) 245-3151 in NY
AL-Anon Family Group Headquarters. Provides printed materials on alcoholism specifically aimed at helping families dealing with the problem of alcoholism. Hours: 24 hours, 7 days a week.

ALZHEIMER'S 1-800-621-0379
(800) 572-6037 in IL
Alzheimer's Disease and Related Disorders Association. Offers publications and refers callers to local chapters. Hours: 9 am-5 pm CST, M-F.

ARTHRITIS 1-800-327-3027
Arthritis Medical Center. Sends information on the Holistic Approach to the treatment of Arthritis. Hours: 9 am-3 pm EST, M-F.

ASTHMA & ALLERGIES 1-800-822-2762
American Academy of Allergy and Immunology. Provides booklets, information, and physician referral. 24 hours, 7 days a week.

Note:
Only 800 numbers are toll-free. All others may result in long-distance charges.

ASTHMA-LUNG DISEASE 1-800-222-5864
(303) 355-5864 in Denver
Answers questions about asthma, emphysema, chronic bronchitis, tuberculosis, and environmental lung diseases. Sponsor: National Jewish Center for Immunology and Respiratory Medicine. Hours: 8 am - 5 pm MST, M-F.

BREAST CANCER 1-800-221-2141
(312) 799-8228 in IL
Y-ME Breast Cancer Support Group. Provides breast cancer patients with presurgery counseling, treatment information, and patient literature; also makes referrals according to guidelines from its medical advisory board. Hours: 9 am-5 pm CST, M-F; In IL: 24 hours, 7 days a week.

CANCER 1-800-422-6237
Cancer Information Service (CIS). Answers cancer-related questions. No diagnosis is made or treatment recommended. Hours: 9 am-10 pm EST, M-F; 10 am-6 pm Saturday.

CANCER 1-800-525-3777
(303) 233-6501 in CO
AMC Cancer Information. Provides information on causes of cancer, prevention, methods of detection and diagnosis, treatment and treatment facilities, rehabilitation, and counseling services. A service of AMC Cancer Research Center. Denver, CO. Hours: 8:30 am-5 pm MST, M-F.

COCAINE 1-800-262-2463
Answers questions on the health risks of cocaine for cocaine users, their friends, and family. Provides referrals to drug rehabilitation centers. A service of the Psychiatric Institute of America. 24 hours, 7 days a week.

DEPRESSION 1-800-248-4344
National Foundation for Depressive Illness. Provides a recorded message describing symptoms of depression and gives an address for more information and physician referral. Hours: 24 hours, 7 days a week.

DIABETES 1-800-232-3472
(703) 549-1500 in VA and DC
American Diabetes Association. Answers questions, provides fact sheets, pamphlets, and newsletter. Callers will be referred to one of 62 affiliates, which will provide names of local doctors, dietitians, and hospitals. Hours: 8:30 am-5 pm EST, M-F.

EYE CARE 1-800-222-3937
National Eye Care Project Hotline. Offers information and referral service for free eye examinations for the financially disadvantaged who are at least 65 years old and who have not seen an ophthalmologist in 3 years. Hours: 8 am-4 pm PST, M-F.

800 toll-free

FITNESS 1-800-233-4886
Aerobics and Fitness Foundation. Answers questions regarding safe and effective exercise programs and practices. Hours: 10 am-5 pm PST, M-F.

HEADACHE 1-800-843-2256
(800) 523-8858 in IL
Headache Foundation. Provides information on possible causes, treatments, and prevention of all types of headaches; makes referrals to local physicians. Hours: 8 am-5 pm CST, M-F.

HEARING 1-800-424-8576
Better Hearing Institute provides information on better hearing and the prevention of deafness, and a list of doctors upon request. Provides information on hearing aids and assistance, and distributes a directory of certified hearing-aid specialists. Consumer kit on hearing aids available upon request 1-800-521-5247. Hours: 9 am-5 pm EST, M-F.

HEARING 1-800-222-3277
(800) 345-3277 in PA
Dial-a-hearing screening test. Tells where to call in your area for a free screening test. Offers numbers for self-help groups. Hours: 9 am-6 pm EST, M-F.

HOSPICE 1-800-331-1620
Hospice-Link/Hospice Education Institute. Provides a directory of hospices and local referral, answers general questions on principles and practices of the group, and lends a sympathetic ear. Hours: 9 am-5 pm EST, M-F.

HOSPITAL 1-800-638-0742
(800) 492-0359 in MD
Hill-Burton Free Hospital Care. Sponsor: Dept. of Health. Sends information about free care in hospitals and other health facilities in caller's area that participate in the program. This is primarily for low-income people without Medicare or Medicaid. Hours: 9:30 am-5:30 pm EST, M-F.

INCONTINENCE 1-800-237-4666
Simon Foundation. Provides a recorded message on incontinence and ordering information for a quarterly newsletter and other publications. Hours: 24 hours, 7 days a week.

IMPOTENCE 1-800-835-7667
(313) 966-3219 in MI
Recovery of Male Potency. Sponsored by Grace Hospital of Detroit. Provides information and referrals for self-help support groups. Hours: 9 am-5 pm EST, M-F.

KIDNEY 1-800-638-8299
(800) 492-8361 in MD
American Kidney Fund. Grants financial assistance to kidney patients who are unable to pay treatment-related costs; provides information on kidney-related diseases. Hours: 8 am-5 pm EST, M-F.

LIVER 1-800-223-0179
American Liver Foundation. Provides literature on liver diseases and physician referrals; membership and fund-raising for liver research. Hours: 8:30 am-4:30 pm EST, M-F.

LUNG DISEASE 1-800-222-5864
See listing: Asthma-Lung Disease hotline.

MEDICAL DEVICES 1-800-638-6725
(301) 881-0256 in MD
U.S. Pharmacopeia, problem reporting program. Distributes information concerning medical devices; consumer dissatisfied with medical self-help products may contact this number. Hours: 9 am-4:30 pm EST, M-F. Taped and monitored at other times.

MEDICARE 1-800-368-5779
(301) 597-0724 in MD
U.S. Dept. of Health, Inspector General's Office. Handles complaints on evidence of fraud or abuse in Medicare and Medicaid programs; answers questions about Medicare coverage. Hours: 24 hours, 7 days a week.

PARKINSON'S 1-800-223-2732
American Parkinson's Disease Association. Sends brochures, offers information on medicines combating Parkinson's disease, and provides referrals. Hours: 8:30 am-5 pm EST, M-F.

PESTICIDES 1-800-858-7378
(512) 399-5352 in AK and HI
National Pesticides Information Clearinghouse. Answers questions about effects on health of pesticides, herbicides, fungicides,

and safety precautions. Hours: 24 hours, 7 days a week.

PLASTIC SURGERY 1-800-635-0635
American Society of Plastic and Reconstructive Surgeons. Provides referrals to board-certified plastic surgeons. Offers pamphlets describing preoperative conditions, surgical procedures, and postoperative recovery. Hours: 24 hours, 7 days a week.

PREVENTATIVE MEDICINE 1-800-345-2476
American Institute for Preventative Medicine. Provides information about programs to stop smoking, reduce stress, control weight, and other issues of health education. Hours: 8 am-4:30 pm EST, M-F.

SURGERY 2nd Opinion 1-800-638-6833
(800) 492-6603 in MD
Health Care Financing Administration provides help in locating a specialist nearby for a second opinion on nonemergency surgery. Hours: 8 am-midnight EST, 7 days a week.

TRAUMA 1-800-556-7890
(301) 925-8811 in MD
American Trauma Society (ATS). Offers information and answers questions about trauma and medical emergencies. Hours: 9 am-5 pm EST, M-F.

VENEREAL DISEASE 1-800-227-8922
VD Hotline (Operation Venus). Provides information on sexually transmitted diseases and confidential referrals for diagnosis and treatment. A service of the American Social Health Association and the United Way. Hours: 8 am-8 pm PST, M-F.

Your family doctor is always the first source of information-- ask, you pay his bills!

Organizations that want to help you

If you have a health problem, one of the most important things you can do is to inform yourself about the disease. The United States government has useful information on nearly every health problem. They want to share this data with the public. Most publications are free of charge in single copies if they come from a public agency and many private associations. Other publications are provided at minimum fees. Here's what to do:

❶ If you know what subject is of interest to you, check this list of information sources to determine if one has a specialty regarding your needs.

❷ If you are uncertain where to go for help you can contact the National Health Information Center (ODPHP) and ask for assistance.

❸ It may be best to write the organization requesting a list of publications regarding your subject. Keep in mind that some organizations' general list of publications may be too extensive and they may not offer such a list, so be as specific as possible with your request.

❹ Some organizations require four to six weeks before you will receive information so you might want to call them.

❺ When you receive a list of publications select the ones appropriate for your needs and request them.

❻ Keep in mind that most government personnel are very helpful and courteous and it helps if you act in the same manner.

National Health Information Center ODPHP P.O. Box 1133, Washington, D.C. 20013-1133; (800) 336-4797; (301) 565-4167 in Maryland only. Helps the public locate health information and refers questions to appropriate resources. Distributes publications and directories on health promotion and disease prevention topics.

Al-Anon Family Group Headquarters, 1372 Broadway, New York, NY 10018-0862; (800) 356-9996; (212) 245-3151 in NY. Helps spouses and family members of alcoholics cope with the problems at home through information, group support, and publications. Cooperates with alcoholism treatment programs by support to patients and families.

Alzheimer's Disease and Related Disorders Association, 70 East Lake Street, Suite 600, Chicago, IL 60601-5997; (800) 621-0379; (800) 572-6037 in IL. Provides practical information on caring for the patient at home and describes community healthcare services that assist caregivers, such as respite care, services for the family of the patient, and long-term residential care. The national office will refer callers to local chapters and resources.

American Cancer Society, National Office, Attn: Cancer Response Systems, 1599 Clifton Road N.E., Atlanta, GA 30329; (800) 227-2345. List of publications is not available. Provides information on the topics you have questions about. Can provide address of local affiliates.

American Diabetes Association, 1660 Duke St., Alexandria, VA 22314; (800) 232-3472; (703) 549-1500 in VA. Publishes materials on food and nutrition for diabetics.

American Heart Association, National Office, 7320 Greenville Avenue, Dallas, TX 75231; (214) 373-6300. Provides information on topics relating to prevention and control of cardiovascular diseases, high blood pressure, and varicose veins. You can also contact a local affiliate.

American Parkinson's Disease Association, 116 John Street, Suite 417, New York, NY 10038; (800) 233-2732. Provides pamphlets on Parkinson's disease, home exercise programs, and aids for daily living.

Asthma and Allergy Foundation of America, 1717 Massachusetts Avenue, N.W., Suite 305, Washington, D.C. 20036; (202) 265-0265. Provides information on resource materials and support services.

Cancer Information Service, National Cancer Institute, Office of Cancer Communication, Building 31, Room 10A24, 9000 Rockville Pike, Bethesda, MD 20892; toll-free (800) 422-6237; (301) 496-5583 in Maryland. Answers questions, provides information and NCI publications free of charge about cancer, cancer prevention, and related resources. Information is available on all types of cancer, breast exams, breast biopsy, Pap exams, treatment options, prevention, and coping with catastrophic illness.

Center for Medical Consumers and Health Care Information, Inc. 237 Thompson Street, New York, NY 10012; (212) 674-7105. A nonprofit organization that encourages people to make a critical evaluation of all information received from health professionals to use medical services more selectively and to understand the limitations of modern medicine.

Consumer Information Center, Pueblo, CO 81009. Distributes consumer publications on topics such as food and nutrition, health, exercise, money management, federal benefits, and weight control. Write for a free Consumer Information Catalog.

Digestive Diseases Information Clearinghouse, P.O. Box NDDIC, Bethesda, MD 20892; (301) 468-2162. Provides patients and their families with information on digestive diseases.

Food and Drug Administration (FDA), Office of Consumer Affairs, 5600 Fisher Lane, HFE-88, Rockville, MD 20857; (301) 443-3170. Answers inquiries from the public and serves as a source for the FDA's consumer publications.

Nar-Anon Family Groups Inc., P.O. Box 2562, Palos Verdes, CA 90274-0119; (213) 547-5800. Patterned on the Al-Anon model, local groups offer education, information, and support for relatives and friends concerned about drug abuse by a family member or friend.

National Aids Information Clearinghouse, P.O. Box 6003, Rockville, MD 20850; (301) 762-5111. Provides referral and information on AIDS-related organizations and their services, as well as educational materials.

National Arthritis and Musculoskeletal and Skin Information Clearinghouse, P.O. Box AMS, Bethesda, MD 20892; (301) 468-3235. Provides information on arthritis and musculoskeletal and skin diseases.

National Cholesterol Education Program Information Center, 4733 Bethesda Avenue, Room 530, Bethesda, MD 20814; (301) 951-3260. Provides information on cholesterol and how you can keep it under control.

National Chronic Pain Outreach Association, Inc., 8222 Wycliffe Court, Manassas, VA 22110; (703) 368-7357. Is a network of self-help groups offering emotional support for those with chronic pain conditions.

National Clearinghouse for Alcohol and Drug Information (NCADI), P.O. Box 2345, Rockville, MD 20852; (301) 468-2600. The Office for Substance Abuse Prevention (OSAP) provides information on prevention and treatment for substance abuse including alcohol and the elderly and using medicines wisely.

National Council on Alcoholism, Inc., 12 W. 21st St., New York, NY 10010; (800) 622-2255; (212) 206-6770 in NY. Combats the disease alcoholism through efforts in prevention, education, community service programs, and programs for women.

National Council on the Aging (NCOA), 600 Maryland Avenue, S.W., West Wing 100, Washington, D.C. 20024; (202) 479-1200. Acts as central national resource for research, planning, training, technical assistance, information, and publications relating to older persons.

National Diabetes Information Clearinghouse, Box NDIC, Bethesda, MD 20892; (301) 468-2162. Provides information on diabetes and its complications including cookbooks, diabetes and aging, diet and nutrition, foot care, dental tips, sports and exercise for the diabetic, facts about insulin and non-insulin-dependent diabetes, and self-blood glucose monitoring. Most publications are free in single copies.

National Eye Institute, Information Office, Building 31, Room 6A32, 9000 Rockville Pike, Bethesda, MD 20892; (301) 469-5248.

National Heart, Lung, and Blood Institute, Information Office, NIH, Building 31, Room 4A-21, 9000 Rockville Pike, Bethesda, MD 20892; (301) 496-4236. Responsible for scientific investigations of heart, blood vessel, lung, and blood diseases. Publishes information including a Healthy Heart Handbook for women.

National High Blood Pressure Education Program Information Center, 4733 Bethesda Avenue, Room 530, Bethesda, MD 20814; (301) 951-3260. Provides information on the detection, diagnosis, and management of high blood pressure.

National Information Center on Deafness, Gallaudet University, 800 Florida Ave., NE, Washington, D.C. 20002; (202) 651-5051. This center is a centralized source of information about hearing loss and deafness. NICD collects information about programs and services for deaf and hard-of-hearing people across the nation and develops resource lists and fact sheets for deaf and hard-of-hearing people, their families, friends, and others.

National Institute on Aging (NIA), Public Information Office, Federal Building, Room 6C12, Bethesda, MD 20892; (301) 496-1752. Promotes and supports biomedical research on issues pertaining to aging.

Distributes a handbook that lists state contacts for community services, such as respite care, that are generally available to caregivers. NIA distributes free "Age Pages" and other consumer information including mental health and wellness that pertains to health issues of older people.

National Institute on Aging Information Center, NIH, Building 31, Room 5C-35, 9000 Rockville Pike, Bethesda, MD 20892; (301) 496-1752. Sponsors study of biomedical, psychological, social, educational, and economic aspects of aging. Its Gerontology Research Center publishes brochures and a series of fact sheets called Age Pages covering a number of subjects including women's health topics.

National Institute of Allergy and Infectious Diseases (NICAD), Office of Communications, NIH, Building 31, Room 7A32, 9000 Rockville Pike, Bethesda, MD 20892; (301) 496-5717. Conducts and supports research on immunology, asthma and allergic diseases, AIDS, vaccine development, antiviral agents, sexually transmitted diseases, and parasitic and fungal diseases.

National Institute of Arthritis, Musculoskeletal, and Skin Diseases, Information Office, NIH, Building 31, Room 9A-04, 9000 Rockville Pike, Bethesda, MD 20892; (301) 496-8188. Conducts and supports research on arthritis, other musculoskeletal diseases, and skin diseases. Produces and distributes a number of publications, including one on cause, prevention, and treatment of osteoporosis.

National Institute of Mental Health (NIMH), Public Inquiries Branch, Office of Scientific Information, Parklawn Building, Room 15C-05, 5600 Fishers Lane, Rockville, MD 20857; (301) 443-4513. Disseminates information on mental health and mental illness and answers requests from the public. Distributes publications on rape prevention for older women; stress; women's alcohol, drug, and mental health issues.

National Kidney and Urologic Diseases Information Clearinghouse, Box NKUDIC, Bethesda, MD 20892; (301) 468-6345. Collects and provides information on kidney and urological diseases.

National Mental Health Association, 1021 Prince Street, Alexandria, VA 22314-2971; (703) 684-7722. Provides emotional support for families and helps them learn how to help mentally ill family members. Publishes pamphlets on all aspects of mental health and mental illness including aging.

National Osteoporosis Foundation, 1625 Eye Street, N.W., Suite 1011, Washington, D.C. 20006; (202) 223-2226. Advocates increased governmental support for research on the prevention and treatment of osteoporosis. Provides information about osteoporosis to patients and their families.

National Parkinson's Foundation, 1501 N.W. 9th Ave., Bob Hope Road, Miami, FL 33136; 1-800-327-4545; In FL 1-800-433-7022.

National Second Surgical Opinion Program; (800) 638-6833; (800) 492-6603 MD only. Provides information for people faced with the possibility of nonemergency surgery. Sponsors a toll-free telephone number to assist the public in locating a surgeon or other specialist.

National Stroke Association, 300 E. Hampden Avenue, Suite 240, Englewood, CO 80110-2622; (303) 762-9922. Provides an information exchange and support network for stroke victims and their families.

Office of Minority Health Resource Center, P.O. Box 37337, Washington, D.C. 20013-7337; (800) 444-6472; (301) 587-1983. Provides information and referrals to appropriate sources on minority health-related topics.

President's Council on Physical Fitness and Sports, 450 5th Street N.W., Suite 7103, Washington, D.C. 20001; (202) 272-3430. Provides informational materials on exercise, sports, and physical fitness for adults and the elderly.

Widowed Persons Service, 1909 K Street N.W., Washington, D.C. 20049; (202) 728-4370. WPS of AARP works to identify community leadership and resources that will help newly widowed persons to recover from the loss and rebuild their lives. WPS cooperates with local organizations to establish a volunteer program in the community. Volunteers, who are themselves widowed, are trained to reach out and offer support to the newly widowed.

Clearinghouse for the Handicapped, Switzer Building, Room 3132, 330 C St., S.W., Washington, D.C. 20202; (202) 732-1244. Responds to inquiries by referral to organizations that supply information to handicapped individuals. Provides information on federal benefits, funding, and legislation for the handicapped.

> It is impossible for a man to learn what he thinks he already knows.
> - Epictatus (50-138 A.D.)

On finding the right physician

Your family doctor (M.D. or D.O.) may help you with your problem or recommend a specialist. Specialists are physicians (M.D.'s or D.O.'s) who elect to practice in a particular field of medicine requiring additional training and certification. You may elect to go to a specialist directly. It is important for you to find the right physician for your problem. However, as medicine becomes more specialized it is increasingly more difficult to know where to turn for help. The yellow pages list different medical specialists in your area. These definitions may be of help:

ALLERGIST/IMMUNOLOGIST--helps manage disorders of the immune system including asthma, eczema, hay fever, hives, food and drug allergies, insect stings, and immune system deficiency conditions.

ANESTHESIOLOGIST--administers anesthesia during surgery.

CARDIOLOGIST--manages abnormalities in your heart and blood vessels and has experience in electrocardiography, cardiac catheterization, and pacemaker management.

DERMATOLOGIST--specializes in the treatment of diseases of the skin, hair, and nails.

EMERGENCY MEDICAL SPECIALIST--treats emergencies with practice limited to the trauma center, especially in ER's.

ENDOCRINOLOGIST--specializes in the management of problems of hormone production or overproduction including disorders of diabetes and thyroid hormone production.

FAMILY PHYSICIAN--specializes in internal medicine, obstetrics, pediatrics, and surgery in a comprehensive care approach to the whole family, M.D. or D.O.

GASTROENTEROLOGIST--treats disorders of the gastrointestinal tract and liver.

GENETICIST--specializes in inherited disorders such as mental retardation, cystic fibrosis, muscular dystrophy, and hemophilia.

GERIATRICS SPECIALIST--specializes in the treatment of the aged.

HEMATOLOGIST--specializes in diseases of the blood and blood-forming organs. Treats anemias as well as malignant blood diseases such as leukemias and lymphomas sometimes with bone marrow transplants.

INFECTIOUS DISEASE SPECIALIST--focus is on organisms that cause human infections including AIDS, how they spread, and medications to treat them.

INTERNIST--Internal medicine encompasses the diagnosis and nonsurgical treatment of disease in adults. An internist spends three to four years in training developing in-depth understanding of the body systems before specializing in one of many subspecialties (a good choice for a family doctor for any senior).

NEUROLOGIST--specializes in the nonsurgical treatment of the diseases of the brain, nerves, and muscles. Neurologists care for victims of stroke, Parkinson's disease, multiple sclerosis, epilepsy, and other disorders of the nervous system and brain.

NEUROSURGEON--evaluates and surgically treats conditions such as brain tumors, abnormalities affecting supply of blood to the brain, disorders of the spinal cord, and trauma involving the nervous system.

OBSTETRICIAN/GYNECOLOGIST--specializes in diseases that affect a woman's reproductive organs.

ONCOLOGIST--specializes in the treatment of cancer.

RHEUMATOLOGIST--focuses on the diseases of the joints and muscles caused by abnormalities in the immune system including rheumatic arthritis.

THORACIC DISEASE SPECIALIST--treats diseases of the lungs including breathing abnormalities, infections, and cancer of the respiratory tract.

OPHTHALMOLOGIST--specializes in the care of the eyes and treats eye disorders such as cataracts, glaucoma, retinal detachment, or obstruction of tear ducts.

ORTHOPEDIC SURGEON--specializes in diagnosing and surgically treating disorders that affect bones and their supportive structures.

OTORHINOLARYNGOLOGIST--specializes in disorders of the ears, nose, throat, and related regions of the neck and base of the skull.

PATHOLOGIST--specializes in the study of body fluids and tissues to determine the cause and status of disease.

PREVENTIVE MEDICINE SPECIALIST--focuses on the prevention or early detection of disease.

PSYCHIATRIST--diagnoses and treats mental, emotional, and behavioral disorders.

PHYSIATRIST--specializes in physical medicine and rehabilitation. Treats all physical disabilities nonsurgically such as strokes, fractures, amputees, back problems, osteoporosis, and sprains.

RADIOLOGIST--specializes in the use of imaging technologies such as X-ray, ultrasound, and magnetic resonance imaging.

SURGEON (GENERAL)--has expertise in the diagnosis and surgical treatment of diseases.

SURGEON (COLON AND RECTAL)--specializes in treating diseases of the large bowel such as inflammatory bowel disease, cancer, ulcerative colitis, as well as hemorrhoids.

SURGEON (PLASTIC)--specializes in cosmetic and reconstructive surgery to enhance physical appearance.

SURGEON (THORACIC AND CARDIOVASCULAR)--specializes in the treatment of structural abnormalities that can affect the heart such as valve dysfunction and blockage, implants, pacemakers, or treats disease of the lungs and esophagus.

SURGEON (TRANSPLANT)--focuses on organ transplants.

SURGEON (VASCULAR)--corrects abnormalities of the arteries other than the coronary arteries.

UROLOGIST--specializes in diagnosing and treating diseases of the urinary and urogenital tracts including prostate, incontinence, and male impotence.

Before nonemergency surgery, get a second opinion!
Call the HOTLINE 800-638-6833; in MD 800-492-6603
8AM-midnight EST--7 days--for free referrals to specialists.

Secrets of the medical vocabulary

Every field of endeavor or "discipline" has special words, phrases, and methods of putting ideas together that are unique. In fact, learning the vocabulary of any specialty goes a long way toward making you an expert in that field. As a discipline, medicine is no exception. Who hasn't been awed and mystified by the big words that doctors use like: adrenomyeloneuropathy, psychoneuroimmunology, osteodystrophy, immunotherapy, and cardiomyopathy.

Prefixes and suffixes run amok in the unspellable, unspeakable language of medicine. Who can understand them? However, in today's world, keeping healthy and being in touch with your doctor is a necessity, so it becomes essential to become familiar with medical jargon to comprehend a possible disease and talk to your doctor.

The first secret to understanding the vocabulary of medicine consists of breaking big words down into manageable parts you can grasp or find in a desktop dictionary. For example, let's take the word psychoneuroimmunology.

> *psycho* = a prefix referring to the mind and its mental function. It is also used in the word "psychology."
> *neuro* = the nervous system. A "neurologist" is a specialist in the nervous system.
> *immune* = the complex system that defends the body from disease.
> *ology* = a branch of learning. It means "the study of."

And so we put the tongue twister together: "psychoneuroimmunology" and it describes the scientific field delving into the mind-body connection, or how what we think and feel affects our health. Reading the word backward, "study of," "immune system," "nervous system," "mind"; or, the study of how the immune system is affected by the nervous system and the mind.

Let's take a word like "immunotherapy."
> *immuno* = the immune system of the body.
> *therapy* = treatment.

When we put the two words together we have a treatment that uses the immune system.

How about a word like "antibody."
anti = a common prefix meaning against or preventing. Link it to the word
body = and we have a molecule that defends the body against bacteria, viruses, and other foreign bodies.

Here's a guide to some medical terms:
hyper = tacked on to the beginning of almost anything means too much or too high as in the word "hypertension."
hypo = at the beginning of a word means not enough or too little as in "hypoglycemia," meaning low blood sugar.
itis = at the end of a word means inflamed or infected as is used in "appendicitis."
osis = at the end of a word means abnormal or diseased as used in "halitosis," or bad breath.
ia = at the end of anything means state or condition as in the word "amnesia," meaning the absence of memory.
scler = in a word means something hardens such as in arteriosclerosis, hardening of the arteries that kills hundreds of thousands of Americans every year.
carcin = refers to cancer, as in "carcinogen," referring to the ability to cause cancer.
oma = on the end of a word means a tumor. But it's not always cancerous. "Neuroma," for example, is a benign tumor made up of nerve cells and fibers.
algia or *dynia* = suffixes that describe pain, such as "myalgia," a word for muscle pain, and "pleurodynia," a painful swelling of muscles between the ribs.
rhage, rhagia, or *rhea* = when attached to a word means bleeding as in "hemorrhage."
hem = blood.
plasia = at the end of a word simply means growing, as in the case of "hypoplasia," meaning not enough growth.
trophy = on the end of a word means developing wrong, as in "muscular dystrophy."
pathy = at the end of a word means diseased, as in "retinopathy," a disease of the retina common in diabetes.
patent = another word for open, as in patent duct.
micro = small.
macro = big.
mal = bad.

pseudo = "phoney," or "other."
tachy = means fast as in the word "tachycardia," used to describe a fast heartbeat.
brady = slow.
plasty = on the end of a word means to reconstruct it, as in the nose job plastic surgeons call "rhinoplasty."
ectomy = to remove, as used in "hysterectomy."

Of course, we can also learn the words:
hyster = the Greek word for womb.
oscopy = to look inside as in the lung examination "bronchoscopy."
ostomy = to make a hole, as in "colostomy," an abdominal opening for evacuating fecal material.
ileum = small intestine.
lysis = to free up, as in "electrolysis," or "lysis of adhesions."
desis = to fuse, as in "spondylosyndesis," the fancy word for a spinal fusion.

Here are some more of the secret words:
derm = skin
arthro = joint
myo or **tendo** = muscle or tendon
adeno = gland
osteo = bone
myel = marrow
angio = vessel
cardio = heart
pulmo = lung
hepato = liver
renal = kidney

Of course, the above is not a complete course in medical terminology, but it should be a step toward the mastery of the lingo. If in doubt, ask your physician to explain unfamiliar words or phrases.

Do-it-yourself medical testing

Medically trained or not, people are testing their eyesight, stool, urine, blood, and blood pressure in search of health clues related to vision problems, gastrointestinal diseases, infection, diabetes, hypertension, and a host of other conditions. In fact, $100 million a year is spent on home medical tests and that market is expected to reach $2.2 billion by 1995.

Several things seem to be promoting the self-testing surge:

- The tests are relatively inexpensive and simple, yet fairly reliable.
- There is a national trend toward preventive medicine.
- People are living longer, so the need to monitor diabetes, high blood pressure, and other chronic health problems is increasing. About 80% of the elderly are said to have at least one chronic condition.
- Medical expenses are high and people are looking for ways to save money.
- We live in a day in which a second opinion is being promoted.
- Do-it-yourself medical testing seems to be a way of verifying (sometimes) what we have been told.

In general, there are three categories of self-testing products:

1. Those that help diagnose a specific condition or disease in people with symptoms--such as a suspected urinary tract infection.
2. Screening tests that identify indications of disease in people without symptoms--as in examining stool for hidden blood.
3. Doctor-recommended monitoring devices that provide ongoing checkups on an existing disease or condition--blood glucose testing by diabetics, for instance.

Self-tests can offer many health benefits. A more accurate picture of blood pressure fluctuation is beneficial information for both doctor and patient. However, remember blood pressure is often lower in "friendly surroundings" than in a doctor's office. Thanks to convenient portable tests, patients with chronic health problems can maintain testing regimens away from home. An example is glucose monitoring, which has long helped diabetics keep their disease under control and live healthier, more normal lives.

Further, fecal occult (hidden) blood test kits are believed to have such potential for detecting early indications of colorectal cancer that the American Cancer Society has been distributing free kits. The society says that early detection and prompt treatment could save the lives of three out of four patients with that type of cancer and recommends, therefore, that people over 50 have their stool tested every year.

Many health professionals believe that properly administered self-tests show great promise for improving the public health, provided the tests are performed in conjunction with medical guidance.

There are certain dangers and problems that can occur when a person tests himself or herself without consideration of the medical doctor:

- Lay users might translate their use of "self-test" as "self-diagnosis." However, considering the results of one test to be a diagnosis is risky.
- The user may perform the test incorrectly, causing hidden blood in the stools to go undetected.
- A positive test result doesn't always signify colon or rectal cancer. It can also reflect such factors as bleeding gums or last night's t-bone steak.
- A diagnosis by a physician involves an evaluation of the patient's medical history, a physical examination, other tests, and sometimes consultation with other medical experts.
- When used as directed, self-tests are often reliable, but not up to the standards of professional laboratories that use proper lighting, chemical storage requirements, instrument maintenance, sanitary conditions, and supervisory review of results.

- Technicians have training, experience, and expertise in conducting tests not found in home users.
- The inexperienced, untrained user may misinterpret results, a mistake that can be compounded by the fact that no test is 100% accurate even under the best conditions and that results can differ from brand to brand.

When the physician can say, "Here's your condition. I want you to go home and test yourself periodically and report the results back to me," that can be of benefit. And when the results of an off-the-shelf test prompt someone to get needed medical care earlier than would have occurred without the test, that's a significant benefit, too.

To promote safe and effective self-testing, here are some general precautions:

- ✔ For test kits that contain chemicals, note the expiration date. Chemicals may lose potency, which affects results.
- ✔ Follow storage direction, considering whether the product needs protection from heat or cold--so don't leave it in the car trunk or by a sunny window.
- ✔ Read and study the instructions until you understand each step.
- ✔ If something isn't clear, don't guess; consult your physician.
- ✔ Learn what the test is intended to do and what its limitations are. Remember that tests are not 100% accurate.
- ✔ Have someone help you if you can't discern colors (10% of males are color blind).
- ✔ Note special precautions, such as avoiding physical activity or certain foods and drugs before testing.
- ✔ Follow instructions exactly; sequence is important. Don't skip a step.
- ✔ When a step is timed, be precise. Use a stopwatch or at least a watch with a second hand.
- ✔ Note what you should do if the results are positive, negative, or unclear.
- ✔ Keep accurate records of results.
- ✔ Keep testkits out of reach of children.

The pharmacy has many medical self-test kits. Just remember to follow the instructions provided with the test kits and share the results with your doctor.

Every human being is the author
of his own health or disease.
- Sivananda (born 1887)

ADVICE AND HELP
SELF-TEST PRODUCTS 251

BLOOD PRESSURE MONITORING

Function--Measures blood pressure, which is the pressure of blood on the walls of the arteries. The measurement consists of two numbers: The first (the higher number) is the systolic blood pressure--when the heart is in contraction. The second is diastolic pressure--when the heart is in relaxation.

How It Works--Most kits include a cuff (air bladder), a monitoring device (sphygmomanometer), and a listening device (stethoscope or microphone). The center of the cuff--or the microphone--is placed directly on the pulse point of the artery in the upper arm. The cuff is wrapped around the arm just above the elbow and is inflated rapidly until it stops the blood flow. The stethoscope user or the microphone listens for sounds in the artery to detect systolic and diastolic blood pressures and records the readings. Instructions vary with the instrument's degree of automation. Blood pressure is usually lower in the morning and increases from the afternoon on, so test daily at about the same time. The standard-size cuff fits arms up to 13 inches in diameter. People with larger arms should order a larger cuff.

The newer finger-cuff blood pressure monitors are as effective as arm-cuff devices, unless a person has poor blood circulation to the hands. The finger should be slipped all the way into the cuff but kept level with the heart; in other words, the user should sit rather than lie down and should not hold the device higher or lower than the heart. Follow the manufacturer's instructions carefully.

Time for Results--2 to 5 minutes.

Comments--In people 18 to 45, normal systolic pressure is about 120 millimeters of mercury (mm Hg); normal diastolic pressure is near 80 mm Hg. That's generally expressed as 120 over 80. In older people, somewhat higher pressures are normal. If repeated readings show that systolic pressure is over 140 and diastolic pressure is over 90, consult a physician promptly.

The body should be at normal temperature, neither too hot nor too cold. A room colder than 60 degrees F, for instance, is too cold for taking a blood pressure reading. This is especially true for finger-cuff monitors; cold fingers may give low readings or no readings at all.

Inaccurate readings can be caused by extraneous noises affecting the listening device, anxiety, movement during measurement, or an incorrectly placed or incorrectly deflated (too fast, too slow) cuff. Eating, drinking, smoking, or exercises before testing can also affect results. An average of three readings, 5 to 10 minutes apart, is more accurate than a single reading. The device should be checked for accuracy against a physician's blood pressure monitor. Regardless of results, people should never stop taking or change medications without consulting a physician.

BLOOD GLUCOSE MONITORING

Function--Measures the level of glucose (a type of sugar) in blood. The tests are not intended to diagnose diabetes. Glucose self-monitoring should be done under a physician's guidance. Glucose concentration in blood indicates the body's ability to metabolize carbohydrates. Because diabetics can't use carbohydrates normally, they monitor their glucose levels so they can adjust diet or medication to normalize their carbohydrate processing. (For more information about glucose self-monitoring, contact a local chapter of the American Diabetic Association (see also article on Diabetes, page 301).

How It Works--After a thorough handwashing, the user pricks a finger or earlobe to obtain a drop of blood. The specimen is placed on a chemically treated test strip, where the chemical reacts with glucose in the blood to produce a color. After a specified time (this varies from brand to brand), the blood is blotted or wiped off the strip. After another time period, the color of the strip is matched to a color guide. Color intensity varies according to the specimen's glucose concentration. Test strips are also available for use with an electronic monitor, which times the steps automatically and displays the blood glucose value numerically. Skill in testing should increase with practice. Urine glucose tests are also available, but they're not as accurate as blood tests.

Time for Results--1 to 2 minutes.

Comments--If results seem inconsistent with other symptoms, test again and, if results still seem questionable, consult a physician.

URINARY TRACT INFECTIONS

Function--Detects nitrite in urine. Urine normally contains small amounts of nitrate. The bacteria that causes nearly all urinary tract infections changes nitrate in urine to nitrite.

How It Works--On three consecutive mornings, a chemically treated test strip is dipped in a urine specimen. If nitrites are detected, there will be a uniform color change on the strip--not just color in spots or around the edge. (Another dipstick test identifies urinary tract infections by detecting white blood cells in urine.)

Time for Results--30 to 40 seconds.

Comments--If results are positive, consult a physician promptly. But since 1 in 10 infections may be caused by bacteria that won't react with the test's reagent, a false negative can occur. So if results are negative but other symptoms--such as frequent, painful urination or pus-like discharge--are present, consult a physician promptly.

HIDDEN FECAL BLOOD

Function--Detects hidden (occult) blood in stools. This test is intended to screen people without symptoms. It does not replace a regular checkup by a physician. Someone who has already observed blood in stools should consult a physician.

How It Works--A stool specimen is brought into contact with peroxide and guaiac, a chemical sensitive to blood. (The specimen-collecting process varies from brand to brand.) If hidden blood is present, a color change will appear. Since bleeding may be intermittent, the American Cancer Society recommends taking specimens from three separate bowel movements. There are diet restrictions that should be followed before testing, but a specific diet or a prescription drug regimen shouldn't be changed without consulting a physician. Toilet deodorizers and cleaners could affect results in some tests, so follow any instructions about removing them. Don't use rectal ointments just before or during the testing time. Don't test if you're already bleeding, as from hemorrhoids, menstruation, or cuts.

Time for Results--1 to 16 min.

Comments--Blood may appear in the stools from such causes as bleeding gums, hemorrhoids, ulcers, diverticulitis, colitis, polyps, or colon or rectal cancer. If results are positive, consult a physician promptly. The earlier a gastrointestinal problem is detected, the easier it is to treat. False positive results may be caused by many factors, including the intake of dietary supplements and red meat; certain raw fruits and vegetables, such as melons, turnips, broccoli, cauliflower, red radishes or horseradish; and drugs such as aspirin, indomethacin, corticosteroids, reserpine, or phenylbutazone. False negative results may be caused by high intake of vitamin C (over 250 milligrams a day) or laxatives with mineral oil.

Despite repeated negative results, consult a physician promptly if you have symptoms--for example, unexplained weight loss or any change in bowel habits such as diarrhea or constipation lasting longer than one week.

Are you considering surgery?

Sometimes surgery is done on an emergency basis, because any delay could be life-threatening. But much surgery is not an emergency. You have the time to choose when you want to have it, and even if you will have it. Some operations that are usually not emergencies are tonsillectomies, gallbladder operations, hysterectomies, hernia repairs, and some cataract operations.

Deciding whether or not to have an operation is difficult for anyone, but especially for the elderly. Normal changes that occur with age and diseases that are more common in later life, particularly heart ailments, may make surgery more risky for older people. If you think you need an operation, the process is as follows:

✔ Begin by seeing your family doctor to find out about your illness and treatment choices.

✔ Consult a surgeon once you and your doctor have decided that surgery is a promising method of treatment. Here are some qualifications to look for:

❶ A good sign of a surgeon's competence is having board certification that is approved by the American Board of Medical Specialties.

❷ The letters F.A.C.S. (Fellow of the American College of Surgeons) after a surgeon's name are an indication to the patient that the surgeon has passed a thorough evaluation of both professional competence and ethical fitness.

❸ Your surgeon will arrange for your operation to be performed in a hospital and it is a good idea to make sure that the hospital is accredited by the Joint Commission on Accreditation of Healthcare Organizations (JCAHO).

❹ Try to choose an experienced surgeon who operates on a regular basis (several times a week).

If you are unsure of a surgeon's qualifications, don't hesitate to ask him or her about them, or direct your inquiries to your local or state medical society, to the hospital where your operation will be performed, to the surgical department of the nearest medical school, or to your family physician.

Before you agree to the operation you should discuss the following questions with your surgeon:

■ What are the indications for surgery?
■ What alternative forms of treatment are available?
■ What will happen if you don't have the operation?
■ What are the risks?
■ How is the operation expected to benefit you?
■ Are there likely to be residual effects from surgery?

Getting a second opinion is a common medical practice that most doctors and insurance companies encourage or require. Don't be afraid to tell your surgeon that you want another opinion and would like your medical records forwarded to the second doctor.

Giving your informed consent is your legal right. Patients should understand the indications for the operation, the risk involved, and the results that are hoped for. Remember, the final decision will be yours. It's a decision that should be made with all the facts, so don't hesitate to discuss with your surgeon any questions or concerns that you have.

UNNECESSARY MEDICAL TREATMENT AND SURGERY

An operation is obviously necessary when no other treatment can save life or limb. Operation also is called for to relieve a condition that makes life unbearable or miserable for the patient. The necessity for a particular operation may depend on how much a patient wishes to prolong life or to improve the quality of life. Every year, thousands of elderly individuals choose to undergo operations to repair faulty heart valves, remove cataracts, or replace painful hip joints. These operations help to improve their quality of life, enhance their mobility, and allow them to maintain an independent lifestyle.

Unfortunately, unnecessary surgery with an attendant hospital stay does occur. Sometimes the determining factor is not the doctor or the hospital, but the patient. It is possible to become so self-centered and so preoccupied with physical ailments that we force the people around us to give attention where no attention is needed. An aggressive hypochondriac can force a physician into unnecessary surgery. After all, doctors are people and it is difficult for them to determine if the constant complaining comes from the body or the mind.

Medical records show that patients undergoing surgery run three times the risk of developing an infection than nonsurgical patients do. The most significant correctable determinant of the risk of surgical-wound infections is the surgeon's technique. Studies now reveal that if surgeons are shown their own surgical infection rates, these rates drop by half. Doctors themselves are sometimes responsible for unnecessary or even incompetent surgery often involving one of the following: surgeons being too quick to operate, too confident of their skills, or too concerned with performing a currently fashionable procedure. Thank God, it doesn't happen often; but, be aware, it does happen.

"Nosocomial" means hospital-acquired illness. The most common nosocomial illness is an adverse reaction to a drug, which accounts for about half of all iatrogenic (doctor-aquired) complications. Of all the medical hazards a patient may encounter in a hospital, however, infections are most frequent. On the average, nosocomial infection will increase the length of a hospital stay by about one week. These infections are responsible for more deaths than any other single iatrogenic illness--more than 300,000 each year. Bacteria, viruses, and parasites can be acquired from a hospital stay.

Hospital-acquired pneumonias are also often deadly. Operations are the most common cause of pneumonia in hospitals. These infections may often be prevented by giving the patients preoperative breathing instructions. Improper breathing can cause parts of the lungs to become stagnant and provide an area for germ growth.

Poor hospital design and engineering may also be contributing to the risk of infection in hospitals. Wide-open intensive-care units will allow hospital personnel to go from one patient to another without washing their hands at a convenient sink. This can play a direct role in the transmission of disease.

A happy word: During the past decade a major infection-control movement has emerged in our hospitals. Hospitals now recommend a host of preventive measures, including a change in intravenous needles every three days, closed systems of urinary drainage, preoperative breathing instructions, and a change of the breathing circuits of respirators every 24 hours. Although hospitalization still has some hazards, most people would argue that the benefits far exceed the risks. Nowadays, the medical community is making a concerted effort to develop further monitoring mechanisms to assess and reduce all the hazards of hospitalization and patient care. Luckily for us, they have already come a long way.

The final decision regarding your health is up to you. After all, it's your body. Isn't your body worth a second opinion?

ADVICE AND HELP
2ND OPINION 253

Do I really need an operation?

Think about it.
When your doctor recommends surgery for the treatment of a nonemergency medical problem, you owe it to yourself to understand all the facts involved.

Most of the 9 million surgical procedures performed in the United States each year result in desired outcomes of better health, the repair of undesirable conditions, or the control of disease. But not all surgery is necessary. Some operations may even be unwarranted. Some can be deferred. And many conditions may be treated just as effectively without surgery.

While physicians usually agree on whether surgery is actually unwarranted, they may not always come to the same conclusion as to whether elective surgery is the best course of action for a particular patient. In some cases the choice in a situation may weigh equally, and the preference of you, the patient, may tilt the decision toward or against surgery. In all cases you are entitled to know the range of choices open to you, to have those choices objectively considered by professionals, and to have your own preferences considered before undergoing a surgical procedure.

If your physician recommends surgery, and it is not an emergency, you may want to be sure that the recommendation is the best choice for you. You may want to get a second opinion from another physician. Medicare, as well as many private health insurance plans, encourage second opinions. Medicare will help pay for a second opinion in the same way it pays for other services of a physician.

QUESTIONS YOU SHOULD ASK
Before agreeing to any nonemergency surgery, you should know the answers to these questions:

1. What does the doctor say is the matter with you?
2. What is the operation the doctor plans to do?
3. What are the likely benefits of the operation to you?
4. What are the risks of the surgery and how likely are they to occur?
5. How long would the recovery period be and what is involved?
6. What are the costs of the operation?
7. What will happen if you don't have the operation?
8. Are there other ways to treat your condition that could be tried first?

Ask these and any other questions to get a full understanding about your surgery or treatment. Your decisions may be better for it.

WHEN YOU SHOULD GET A SECOND OPINION
Sometimes surgery is done on an emergency basis, because any delay could be life-threatening. Cases of acute appendicitis or injuries from an accident are considered emergencies. Second opinions are seldom possible for this kind of surgery because it must be done right away or within a few days.

But much surgery is not an emergency. You have the time to choose when you want to have it, and even if you want to have it. Some operations that are usually not emergencies are tonsillectomies, gallbladder operations, hysterectomies, hernia repairs, and some cataract operations.

Getting a second opinion is standard medical practice. Most doctors want their patients to be as informed as possible about their condition.

HOW TO FIND A SPECIALIST TO GIVE YOU A SECOND OPINION
If your doctor recommends nonemergency surgery, there are several ways to find a surgeon or another specialist in the treatment of your medical problem:

- Ask your doctor to give you the name of another doctor to see. Do not hesitate to ask; most physicians will encourage you to seek the second opinion.
- If you would rather find another doctor on your own:
  - You can contact a local medical society or medical school in your area for the names of doctors that specialize in the field of your illness.
  - You can call Medicare's toll-free number, 800-638-6833. In Maryland, call 800-492-6603, to find out how to locate a specialist near you.
  - If you're covered by Medicare, you can call your local Social Security Office (listed in your telephone directory under Health and Human Services).
  - If you're eligible for Medicaid, you can call your local welfare office.

GETTING A SECOND OPINION
Some people do not feel comfortable letting their doctor know they want a second opinion. However, if you tell your doctor, you can also ask that your records be sent to the second doctor. In this way, you may be able to avoid the time, costs, and discomfort of having to repeat tests that have already been done.

When getting a second opinion, you should tell the second doctor:
* the name of the surgical procedure recommended, and
* any test you know you have had.

If the second doctor agrees that surgery is the best way to treat your problem, he or she will usually send you back to the first doctor to do the surgery.

If the second doctor disagrees with the first, most people find that they have the facts they need to make their own decision. If you are confused by different opinions, you may wish to go back to the first doctor to further discuss your case. Or you may wish to talk to a third physician.

PAYING FOR A SECOND OPINION
Medicare will pay for the second opinion at the same rate it pays for other services. Always ask your doctors, therapists, or other medical suppliers if they will accept assignment of Medicare benefits as full payment.

Many private insurance companies pay for second opinions. You can contact your health insurance representatives for details. Most state Medicaid programs will also pay for second opinions.

KEY POINTS TO REMEMBER
You can get a second opinion whenever nonemergency surgery is recommended. Most doctors approve of patients getting a second opinion and will assist you in doing so.

Second opinions are a way for you to get additional expert advice from another doctor who knows a lot about treating medical problems like yours.

Second opinions can reassure you and your doctor that the decision to have the surgery is the correct one.

Second opinions are your right as a patient. They can help you make a better informed decision about nonemergency surgery.

Medicare will pay 80% of reasonable charges for beneficiaries enrolled in Medicare Part B who seek a second opinion. A third opinion, if necessary, will be covered in the same way.

Patients may call a Health Care Financing Administration toll-free number, 800-638-6833, to locate the name of a nearby second-opinion health specialist.

Tips to make your hospital visit less stressful

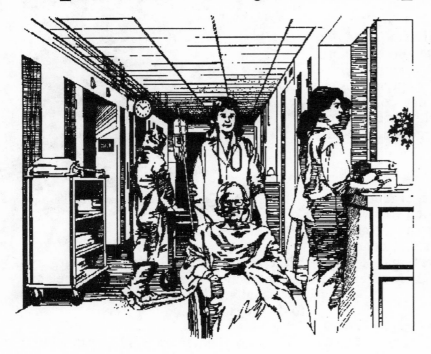

WHAT NOT TO BRING--Leave cash, jewelry (including wedding rings, earrings, and watches), credit cards, and checkbooks at home or have a family member or friend keep them. If you must bring valuables, ask if they can be kept in the hospital safe during your stay. Leave electric razors, hair dryers, and curling irons at home since they may not be grounded properly and could be unsafe.

- **Respiratory therapists** prevent and treat breathing problems.
- **Technicians** conduct a variety of laboratory tests such as blood and urine tests and X-rays.
- **Dieticians** teach you how to plan a well-balanced diet.
- **Pharmacists** know the chemical make-up and the correct use of drugs. They prepare the medicines you will use.
- **Social workers** offer support to patients and their families. They can provide details about how to obtain healthcare and social services after leaving the hospital and know about financial aid programs, support groups, and home-care services.

Going to the hospital is somewhat like traveling to a foreign country--the sights are not familiar, the language sounds strange, and the people are all new. No matter what the reason for the trip--whether it's an overnight visit for a few tests or a longer stay for medical treatment or major surgery--nearly everyone worries about entering the hospital.

If you go to the hospital by choice or because of an emergency, the following information may make the trip less stressful. Relatives and friends of patients also may find this information useful.

WHAT TO BRING--It's best to pack as little as you can and put your name on all personal items. However, bring the following items:

- a few nightclothes, a bathrobe, and sturdy slippers (put your name on all personal items)
- comfortable clothes to wear home
- a toothbrush, toothpaste, shampoo, comb and brush, deodorant, shaving cream, and razor
- a list of all the medicines you take, including prescription and nonprescription drugs
- details of past illnesses, surgeries, and any allergies
- your health insurance card
- a list of names and telephone numbers (home and business) of family members to contact in case of an emergency
- $20 or less for newspapers, magazines, or any other items you may wish to buy in the hospital gift shop

ADMISSION--The first stop in the hospital is the admitting office. Here, the patient or a family member signs forms allowing the hospital staff to provide treatment and to release medical information to the insurance company. Those who don't have private health insurance can talk with an admissions counselor about other payment methods and sources of financial aid such as Medicaid and Medicare.

HOSPITAL STAFF--After getting settled in your room, you begin to meet the members of your healthcare team.

- **Doctors** attend to each patient and are in charge of your overall care. It may be your regular doctor, one of the hospital staff, or a specialist. In hospitals where doctors are trained, in addition to the attending physician, medical students, interns, and residents (doctors training in a specialty) also may see you.
- **Nurses** of many types including registered nurses, nurse practitioners, licensed practical nurses, nurses aides, and nursing students provide patient-care services.
- **Physical therapists** teach patients to build muscles and improve coordination. They may use exercise, heat, cold, or water therapy to help patients whose ability to move is limited.
- **Occupational therapists** work with patients to restore, maintain, or increase ability to perform daily tasks such as cooking, eating, bathing, and dressing.
- **Speech therapists** work with stroke patients or those recovering from throat surgery, also neurosurgery.

GERIATRIC ASSESSMENT--Some older people have many complex problems that may threaten their ability to live independently after they go home from the hospital. In some hospitals, a team including a doctor, a nurse, social worker, specialists, and therapists perform a geriatric assessment. It is an exam to learn about a patient's physical and mental health, family life, income, living arrangements, access to community services, and ability to perform daily tasks. The team develops a plan to help older patients get the healthcare and social services they need.

HOSPITAL GEOGRAPHY--Hospitals have many patient-care areas. You may be placed in a private room (one bed) or a semiprivate (two-bed) room. The intensive care unit (ICU) has special equipment and staff to care for very ill patients. Coronary care units (CCU's) give intensive medical care to patients with severe heart disease. In both the ICU and CCU, visiting hours are strictly limited and only family members are allowed to see patients. Surgery is done in the operating room (OR). After an operation, patients spend time in a recovery room.

In the emergency room (ER), trained staff treat life-threatening injuries or illnesses. Patients who are badly hurt or very sick are seen first. Because the ER is so busy, some patients may have to wait before they are seen by an emergency medical technician (paramedic), nurse, or doctor.

If you're seriously injured or sick call 911

SAFETY TIPS--Because medical equipment is not familiar and medications can make you feel tired or weak, it's good to take a few extra safety steps while in the hospital:

* Use the call bell when you need help.
* Use the controls to lower the bed before getting in or out.
* Be careful not to trip over the many wires and tubes that may be around the bed.
* Try to keep the things you need within easy reach.
* Take only the medicines prescribed for you.
* If you brought your own medicines, tell your nurse or doctor, and take them only with your doctor's permission.
* Be careful getting in and out of the bathtub or shower. Hold on to the grab bars for support. Ask for assistance.
* Use handrails on stairways and in hallways.
* Smoke only where allowed, and never smoke around oxygen.

QUESTIONS--During your hospital stay, you may have many questions about your care. Always feel free to ask your doctor these questions. Your nurse or social worker also may be able to answer many of your questions or get the information you need. You may find it useful to write down your questions as you think of them. Examples are:

* What will this test tell you? Why is it needed?
* What treatment is needed, and how long will it last?
* What are the benefits and risks of treatment?
* When can I go home?
* When I do go home, will I have to change my regular activities?
* How often will I need checkups?
* Is any other follow-up care needed?
* Will I need physical therapy or occupational therapy?

DISCHARGE--Before going home, you must have discharge orders from your doctor and a release form from the hospital's business office. Discharge planning before leaving the hospital can help you prepare for your health and home-care needs after you go home. This planning service is often provided by a registered nurse, social worker, or discharge planner. The discharge planner also knows about senior centers, nursing homes, and other long-term-care services.

IN CASE OF EMERGENCY

In the event of serious illness or accident, it's vital to seek medical help right away. In many areas, you can reach emergency help by calling 911 or the telephone operator. Be sure to tell the operator the type of emergency and your location.

If you have a minor injury or your symptoms aren't severe, call your family doctor or a nearby clinic before going to the emergency room (ER) or a hospital. Sometimes a visit to the ER isn't needed.

If your doctor thinks you should go to the ER, he or she can make things easier for you by calling the hospital to let them know you are coming. Your doctor also may arrange to meet you there.

If there is time, try to take the following items with you to the ER:

* your health insurance card or policy number
* your doctor's name and telephone number
* a list of medicines you take, including prescription and nonprescription drugs
* details of other medical problems
* the names and phone numbers of close family members

You may want to write all of this information on a note card that you can carry in your wallet or purse. Persons with medical problems (such as diabetes, epilepsy, and allergies) should wear or carry identification (an ID card or bracelet) to let medical persons know about these hidden conditions.

If possible, ask a relative or friend to go to the hospital with you for support.

Medic Alert

Medic Alert is an internationally recognized emergency medical system that provides busy emergency personnel with vital patient information quickly, accurately, in one place, and on time. The international Medic Alert Foundation provides protection to members anywhere in the world 24 hours a day via the telephone emergency hotline.

Here's how the Medic Alert system works:

1. Enrollment in the system provides you with a bracelet (or neck chain) engraved with your primary medical condition, personal identification number, and Medic Alert's 24-hour hotline phone number.
2. A hotline call from a medical professional starts the information retrieval process.
3. Within seconds, Medic Alert's emergency operator responds with your computerized medical information.
4. Your vital data relayed back to the emergency room staff help medical personnel provide appropriate diagnosis and care, and could save your life.
5. A one-time membership provides a lifetime service.

Engraving space on the bracelet is limited to 60 spaces. You might consider using this service if you have any one of the following primary medical problems: diabetes, asthma, emphysema, epilepsy, glaucoma, heart valve implant, hypertension, pacemaker, angina, Alzheimer's disease, coronary artery bypass, allergy to insect stings, allergy to penicillin, multi-drug allergies, cataracts, malignant hyperthermia, take anticoagulants, allergy to codeine, take steroids, allergy to Demerol, take betablocker, hypoglycemia, wear contact lenses, hemophilia, allergy to sulfa, take Dilantin, renal failure/hemodialysis, or organ donor.

To enroll contact:
Medic Alert Foundation International, Turlock, CA 95381-1009; 1-800-ID-ALERT.

In Case of Emergency

You're awakened in the middle of the night by severe chest pains. You notice a lump in your right breast during your morning shower. You've had a fever and a persistent cough for the last three days. If faced with one of these or other health problems, what would you do? Should you go immediately to the emergency room? Or should you just wait and see? How you perceive symptoms strongly influences whether you'll seek emergency care for problems that aren't serious--or whether you'll delay seeking treatment for conditions that could threaten your life. Take this quiz to discover which symptoms represent medical emergencies.

IS THIS AN EMERGENCY?

Assign 1, 2, or 3 to each of these 10 medical symptoms.
Key 1: Seek emergency care.
     2: Call your doctor or clinic for advice or an appointment.
     3: Wait and see.

1 ❑ Chest pain or upper abdominal pain or pressure.
2 ❑ Sudden, severe headache with no prior history.
3 ❑ Unexplained weight loss.
4 ❑ Dizziness, sudden weakness, or sudden change of vision.
5 ❑ Vomited once in six hours; no fever, pain, or other symptoms.
6 ❑ Lump in your breast.
7 ❑ Suicidal or homicidal feelings.
8 ❑ Blood in your urine.
9 ❑ Abdominal cramps lasting two weeks.
10 ❑ Difficult breathing or shortness of breath.

ANSWERS

1 (#1) Seek Emergency Care--Chest pains are among the most difficult symptoms to interpret. Each year, thousands of people die because they fail to get emergency help when experiencing this type of pain. Intense, prolonged chest pain, often described as a feeling of pressure or heaviness, may be a sign that you're having a heart attack. The pain of the heart may spread to your left shoulder, left arm, both arms, your back, or even your teeth. Sometimes the pain occurs in the upper abdomen and is confused with severe indigestion. You may also experience nausea, vomiting, shortness of breath, intense sweating, weakness, restlessness, or anxiety.

2 (#1) Seek Emergency Care--Minor headaches are minor, and usually temporary. But a headache can also signal a more serious medical problem, especially if you typically don't have headaches, or if the type of headache is new. For example, a severe headache that is accompanied by fever, vomiting, confusion, drowsiness and, perhaps, a stiff neck may indicate meningitis (infection or inflammation of the lining that surrounds your brain). Such a headache may also signal a cerebral hemorrhage (bleeding in the brain).

3 (#2) Call Your Doctor--If you unintentionally lose weight (typically about 10 pounds or more in a couple of months), call your doctor. Unexplained weight loss, especially when it accompanies a loss of appetite, can signal a serious illness such as cancer. Poor appetite could also be a symptom of depression, kidney or liver disease, or simply a side effect of medication.

4 (#1) Seek Emergency Care--Dizziness, sudden weakness, or deterioration of vision, speech, or sensation within minutes to hours could be symptoms of a stroke. This occurs when blood flow in the brain is blocked. Partial or complete paralysis in one limb or in an arm and leg, with or without involvement of the face, also can signal a stroke.

5 (#3) Wait and See--A single episode of vomiting with no other symptoms is most likely due to minor gastrointestinal viral infection. If you vomit repeatedly over several hours, call your doctor.

What would you do

6 (#2) Call Your Doctor--A breast lump can be the first sign of breast cancer. Even though only 2 out of 10 lumps are cancerous, it's important to determine early if a lump represents breast cancer.

7 (#1) Seek Emergency Care--If a friend or relative talks of suicide or of plans to hurt someone else, believe the person. Watch closely to prevent him or her from finding the opportunity to carry out the plan. Get professional help immediately from your local suicide hotline, emergency room, or a psychiatrist. If the person appears ready to carry out the threat, call 911 or your local emergency telephone number.

8 (#2) Call Your Doctor--Even a small amount of fresh blood may make the toilet bowl appear full of blood. Chances are that you may have lost only a small amount of blood. But because bloody urine can signal a tumor, infection, kidney disease, or another serious medical problem, call your doctor for advice.

9 (#2) Call Your Doctor--It's uncommon for abdominal cramps due to a minor illness, such as a viral infection, to last two weeks. After this period of time this symptom may indicate a serious gastrointestinal problem.

10 (#1) Seek Emergency Care--These breathing problems may signal a heart or lung problem. A heart attack can bring on these symptoms. A pulmonary embolism--the passage of a blood clot from somewhere in the body, through the veins, to the lungs--is another condition that can cause these symptoms.

Many variables, such as your age and past medical history, can change what is a "wait and see" situation for you into an emergency for someone else. It's always best not to interpret new symptoms yourself. If you think your symptoms represent an emergency, they do. **Don't worry if you're not absolutely sure that you need emergency care. And don't delay getting medical advice just because your symptoms seem to have gone away.** The earlier in the course of an illness that your doctor evaluates you, the better your chances are for a favorable outcome.

URGENCY VS. EMERGENCY

Medical centers across the country are designed to treat your symptoms as timely and efficiently as possible. Many medical centers now have urgent care centers. When does your condition warrant urgent care rather than emergency care?

If you need medical assistance within days to weeks for an acute condition, you need urgent care. Typical urgent conditions are upper respiratory infections and flu. Both illnesses are usually not serious enough to warrant a visit to the emergency room, yet often too serious to wait weeks or, perhaps, months for an appointment with your doctor. Urgent care centers also treat certain forms of minor trauma such as scrapes, cuts, and burns.

EMERGENCY WARNING SIGNS

Minor trauma and life-threatening conditions such as heart attack and stroke are emergencies. The American College of Emergency Physicians offers these seven warning signs that indicate a medical emergency:

❶ Chest pain or upper abdominal pain or pressure.
❷ Difficulty in breathing or shortness of breath.
❸ Fainting or feeling faint.
❹ Dizziness, sudden weakness, or a sudden change in vision.
❺ Sudden severe pain anywhere in your body.
❻ Severe or persistent vomiting.
❼ Suicidal or homicidal feeling.

Choosing to be happy in the second 50 years

Abraham Lincoln is purported to have said, "A man is about as happy as he makes up his mind to be." There is a lot of truth in the idea that happiness is a choice. But then, it becomes a little more difficult when we ask, "How do we make that choice?"

No philosopher worth his salt would dare to say that happiness had anything to do with money. Some wag put it, "I've had money, and I have been without it--it's definitely better to have it." Most research shows that as far as money is concerned the people in the middle are the happiest--not too wealthy, and not too poverty stricken, just enough to get by. Anyhow, this article is about acquiring happiness, no matter how much or how little money you have.

Besides money, we often connect happiness with health. In my experience, people with excellent health never realize that they have it, and so they find other reasons to be unhappy. Personally, I spent seven years of my life in a hospital and I found that people with horrible crippling diseases, often in great pain, and sometimes terminal, can be happier than the most healthy athlete. I will never forget Frieda May Clayville, a terminal patient at Ada County Hospital in Boise, Idaho. She was dying of an incurable blood disease, bleeding through her pores, in excruciating pain, and yet she was so radiantly happy that people visited her just to get cheered up.

There is no doubt you can be happy in bad health and unhappy with good health. Happiness is dependent upon factors other than wealth or health.

It is not necessary to say that fame does not bring happiness. In fact, pain and fame are notoriously connected. If we can have a reasonable amount of health and the things of this world, do some fulfilling work or hobby, feel useful, have a good reputation, love and be loved, and I will add, feel some connection with the future and eternity-- well then, we sure ought to be happy. Ought to be happy and being happy are two different things. Lots of people who ought to be happy commit suicide.

If health, wealth, and fame do not add up to happiness, and choosing happiness requires explanation, what then are the factors of happiness?

First we must look at the factors that block happiness, ugly constructs that are incompatible with happiness--certain mental conditions that drive happiness right out of our lives:

I. The factor of ANGER with its cousins BITTERNESS, RESENTMENT, and HATE will block happiness.

Can you tell me how anyone can be happy when they are full of anger, bitterness, resentment, and hate? These critters are an antithesis to happiness. They can't exist side by side in the same person. Just suppose you are willing to admit that you are filled with anger and it has driven away your happiness. How can you drive these burning demons from your hearth?

A. Ask yourself some questions: What are you angry at? Is it circumstances, other people, or yourself? Does the anger do you any good? Does it change anything? Does it solve any problems? Does it make things easier for you or harder?

If your anger is making things better for you, then cultivate it. If your anger is destroying your happiness, then use your cerebral cortex to do away with your anger in order to preserve your happiness. If your anger is directed at a worthy cause, it can be quite motivating. If your anger is introverted or directed at yourself, it can be quite destructive.

B. Decide to get rid of self-destructive, energy-burning anger. You acquired it--you can get rid of it. When you bring anger out into the light of reason, it often disappears. A person can be quite clever at making up excuses for being angry, but in the clear light of reason the excuses are seldom viable.

"A man is about as happy as he makes up his mind to be."

Abe Lincoln

C. Turn anger around by cultivating direct opposites. For example, love, joy, and peace are opposites--cultivate them. Find someone to love, something to feel joyous about, and work on yourself until you can feel a sense of peace. Look for something to laugh about. Sing, whether you feel like it or not. Dance with fun-loving people. Talk to the happy souls. Play games, and deliberately try to enjoy yourself.

D. Practice the art of prayer or meditation to bring peace of mind and tranquility of soul. Anger will burn you up; peace will grow you up. Relax, let the sweet wind of peace blow out your fire. To some people, the meditation and relaxation exercises that go with a biofeedback machine help to bring peace. To others, an old-fashioned chapel does the trick.

E. Count your blessings, not your curses. Try to see the good in people, not just the bad. When something is wrong, the pain makes it easy to express. When something is right, we must fall back on an intelligent choice of will to recognize it. Usually ten things are right for every one that is wrong. People get angry when they don't recognize that fact.

F. Put things in a proper perspective-- bring the good things up close to your awareness; hold the bad things at a distance. A very small thing can block our vision, if it is too close to our eyes. Don't let a mean little thing that is very close to you ruin your vision. Don't waste your energy getting angry at mean little things; it only makes them grow.

Thus, happiness depends as nature shows, less on ...

Someone could say, that's a lot of trouble and energy to get rid of anger. Yes, but nowhere near as much energy as anger takes to maintain itself; and it is inclined to burn down the home, not heat it. Anger, bitterness, resentment, and hate are going to burn down your house of happiness; so, it is imperative to fight back.

II. The factor of FEAR with its cousins WORRY, ANXIETY, and INSECURITY will destroy happiness.

Is there any emotion more terrorizing than fear? How can happiness maintain itself struggling in the jaws of fear? And then when worry and anxiety join the attack, they can easily turn our world into an insecure place and our personality into an inferior paranoid, and we've got "Trouble at River City."

No matter how much we claim that anxiety and worry are factors of love and caring, it isn't so. Anxiety and worry come from faithless suspicion and sick fear. Honest concern and thoughtful action spring from the heart of love and caring. When we allow our concern to grow into worry and anxiety, we doom ourselves to an impotent position --fear introverts and destroys our ability to be happily activated.

Fear, anxiety, worry, and inferiority take maximum energy to sustain--there is no power left for problem solving, planning, or maintaining a modicum of happiness. When we support fear, it consumes our being. So, what can we do about it?

A. Choose to have faith in someone or something. It may be a loved one, it may be an idea, it may be your God, or it may be a future goal. It may be anything that you care for more than yourself. Just suppose your faith is misplaced or wrong--well, nothing can be more misplaced than to try to exist with fear; any type of faith is an improvement. Fear will destroy you, and faith will save you, so choose faith.

B. Face your fears. Ask yourself what is the worst thing that can happen? Prepare to accept the worst, then try to improve on it. Fear is a ghostly shadow on a darkening evening; when you look at it carefully, you discover a friendly tree that will shelter you, not harm you. Facing your fears means to

admit them. When you say, "I'm afraid of the dark," it goes a long way toward eliminating that fear, or at least moderating it. Tell others of your fears and people will help you.

C. Pain creates fear, and of course, fear grows pain. So, learn to handle pain with distraction, substitution, physical activity, or pills. If the pills are too debilitating, deliberately fight pain with mental, spiritual, and physical energy. Pain is usually a warning that something is wrong; so, if you can fix it, then fix it. If you indulge yourself in a bittersweet, attention-gathering pain, that's your reward. If you choose not to, then defeat pain with the power of your will to do so. Big words, but I have done it, and I have seen it done. Everyone needs an occasional pain pill, but when the pain pills wear thin, nothing is left but the will to fight back.

III. NEGATIVISM accompanied by PESSIMISM, HOPELESSNESS, and DISCOURAGEMENT lead to a depression that drives happiness away.

No matter what happens, some people only see the negative side. They count their curses, not their blessings. Nothing turns out right for them because they interpret it that way. They are so jaded that when a drop of dirt falls on their pile of gold they scream to high heaven. Like an owl who only sees at night, they can only see the dark side of life. They drive happiness from their side by gripping, complaining, criticizing, nagging, and accentuating the negative. It has become a serious life habit.

The direct result of being negative is to adopt a pessimistic attitude that makes the most benign situation a hopeless one, so we become discouraged and depressed. Happiness is smothered out of existence by the negative person.

If we find ourselves making happiness impossible with a pessimistic negative mental attitude, we need to search for a method of changing. Here are a few suggestions:

A. Start using as many positive uplifting words as you can. If the word "awful" has become a favorite, make a concentrated effort to change to a word like "awesome." Train your tongue to speak in a positive way. Some people start with the thought proc-

esses and try to make them positive. I find it easier to start with words--they gradually convert the thoughts.

B. Be complimentary. Find something right about every person you meet and tell them about it.

If you can't find something good in the worst person you meet, you are not looking.

In order to exist, everyone must have something of value. To overcome negative thinking, look for something of value and tell the person that you have found it.

C. Change your atmosphere and you will change your feelings. Try singing cheerful tunes and telling funny stories.

D. Anytime you express the fact that something is wrong try looking for two things that are right and express them. Of course, things go wrong. The plumber just informed us that it will cost almost $1,000 to fix our furnace. How awful, we don't have the money, but we do have good credit--that's a plus. It will be nice to have the furnace back. That's two pluses for the one negative breakdown.

IV. The fourth emotional factor that preys on and gobbles up happiness is GUILT. People who feel guilty just can't let happiness break through.

There are two types of guilt and they both cause the same pain--false guilt and true guilt. True guilt is a feeling of remorse and regret because we violated our conscience or moral code or rules of proper interpersonal relationships. Some people do not have a highly developed sense of right or wrong, but we all live in a society that has adopted proper standards of conduct. True guilt follows the violation of our standards or the standards of the society in which we live.

... external things than most suppose.

— William Cowper (1731-1800)

False guilt involves a number of dimensions:

(1) We maintain a feeling of guilt about minor social infractions (belching in public).

(2) We maintain a feeling of guilt about some lack of good fortune (we didn't get a raise or win a lottery).

(3) We get forgiveness for an infraction, but we don't forgive ourselves.

(4) We maintain a feeling of guilt based on our feeling of inadequacy.

(5) We use a feeling of guilt to punish ourselves for imagined shortcomings.

(6) We feel guilty about our temptations rather than our acting out.

Whatever causes the guilt, and whether it is false or true, we must learn to handle it effectively or suffer the consequences of an unhappy life. Here are some ways to cope with guilt:

A. Think over your life and make a list of the people with whom you are angry, resentful, or bitter. Decide that if they did something against you, you will forgive them and blot out any grudge you may have. You eliminate guilt through forgiveness. If you don't forgive people for the harm they caused you, you cannot expect forgiveness for the harm you caused others.

B. Think of anyone you have harmed and put it to rest. If you can make restitution without harming yourself or the other person, then do so. Otherwise, plan to forgive and forget the things you have done that would make you feel guilty.

C. Don't dig up anything that is past and buried. You can't relive the past; everyone makes mistakes. Forgive yourself and come to peace with your past. If the devil reminds you of your past, you remind him of his future.

D. Don't speak evil of your past enemies. My mother used to say, "Never speak evil of the dead." I'm not sure why, but it works to your disadvantage. Do not speak evil of a buried issue.

So we have dealt sparsely with four major blocks to happiness: ANGER, FEAR, NEGATIVISM, AND GUILT. Perhaps there are other demons that block the door to happiness. But if you learn to handle the above, nothing else should be too hard.

We have opened the door that blocks happiness, but it doesn't automatically come in. Here are a number of suggestions that help us to build a life rooted and grounded in the tree of happiness:

❤ Live life in the present moment. The past is gone; the future may never come. Live well in the time you have.

❤ Face your problems. Often they will go away when they are recognized. If you can, do something about your problems; if you can't, then accept them--maybe they belong to you.

❤ Keep active, keep busy, and never stop until the Big Man in the sky gives you that final tap on the shoulder.

❤ Don't fuss about trifles; allow little things to happen without them disturbing your equilibrium.

❤ Remember the good in your past, and come to peace with transgressions. Collect good memories.

❤ Never try to get even with your enemies. Let your Creator bring things to final justice.

❤ Be yourself; don't imitate other people. How dull it would be if all flowers were roses; being a little different brings beauty and charm to life.

❤ You are never too old to learn, so learn from your mistakes. If you need to, change and become a better person.

❤ Create happiness for other people; it is the best way to be happy yourself.

❤ Treat criticism as a disguised compliment. No one ever kicks a dead dog, so you must be worth quite a lot for someone to take the time to criticize. If the critic is right, then change. If the critic is wrong, thank him for his interest.

❤ When you retire, you will not know how to participate in life unless you learn how to enjoy something except your work. So, take up hobbies and become interested in many things.

❤ Continue your love life. Make your mate a partner and learn how to enjoy life with him or her. In the second 50 years, it is time to solve all marital problems.

❤ Fill your mind with worthwhile stuff; don't daydream or occupy yourself with useless regrets or preoccupation with problems that have no solution.

❤ Learn how to rest, learn how to relax, and particularly learn how to enjoy yourself.

❤ Be thankful for every good thing that happens to you and that very spirit will draw fortune to you.

❤ Don't become sloppy. Organize your life, fill it with good things, and keep yourself clean and groomed and occupied.

❤ Be of good cheer--it's much easier than bad cheer. Smile--it helps your face and the faces of the people around you.

❤ Set as your life goal that you will "finish your course with joy."

Three grand essentials to happiness in this life are something to do, something to love, and something to hope for.
Joseph Addison (1672-1719)

The foolish man sees happiness in the distance;
The wise man grows it under his feet.
James Oppenheim (1882-1932)

The most happy man is he who knows how to bring into relation the end and beginning of his life.
J. Goethe (1749-1832)

It is not how much we have, but how much we enjoy, that makes happiness.
Charles Spurgeon (1834-1892)

Aging
Aging
Aging
Aging
Aging

Why should the human body give out after 70, 80, or even 120 years? Why are older people more susceptible to disease, more inclined to have impaired vision and hearing, and likely to lose some of the physical and mental capacity they once enjoyed?

There are no fully satisfactory answers to these questions. Although we are mortal, it is entirely possible that one day humans could live much longer. The present potential life span for humans is said to be 115 years and today thousands of people live to be over 100. United States citizens now expect to live an average of 74.7 years. Women have a life expectancy of 78.3 years and men 71.1 years. Yet these figures have very little to do with potential life expectancy, because most people have their life altered and cut short from disease and disability, not from aging.

It is still true that approximately 70% of all deaths in the United States are from heart disease, strokes, and cancer. Other diseases, accidents, and violence account for the rest--but not age. These same diseases and Alzheimer's disease account for much of the disability attributed to aging. As these diseases are conquered, far more people will live to their full potential life span and remain active and healthy for life.

A lot is known about the diseases that affect people and cause death. Much less is known about real aging because it involves fundamental cell processes that are quite complex. However, this mystery of life is being unraveled and will offer opportunities in the future that were once considered to be only possible in science fiction. It is hard to improve on the advice given by Seneca (4 B.C. -65 A.D.) to eat moderate amounts of well-balanced foods, get plenty of fresh air, exercise, and live a stress-free life-style.

Your life literally depends upon the ability of your cells to regenerate. They do this in a manner similar to one-cell organisms that simply divide and go on living as two "daughter" one-cell organisms. Before your cells can divide to reproduce themselves, they must first produce a duplicate copy of the genes. One of the most important examples of replication is of your blood cells. Your red blood cells live only an average 110 days, and they must be constantly replaced. Without replacement, you would soon develop serious anemia. The lining of your small intestine is completely replaced every three days. Your skin is constantly regenerated with the new cells formed in the deeper layers, while the old cells move to the top and are shed. It is this constant state of regeneration that enables the body to be young. It also enables healing to take place, as occurs after an injury.

> **No one is so old as to think he cannot live one more year.**
> - Cicero (106-43 B.C.)

WHY DOESN'T THE BODY JUST CONTINUE TO RENEW ITSELF INDEFINITELY SO THAT WE DON'T GROW OLD?

There are a number of theories for this big question:

1 The regeneration process is under the control of a genetic script that determines when certain events should occur in your life. It controls when speech will begin, when teeth will erupt, the onset of puberty, the onset of menopause, and other changes in the stages of life. The nature of this script, sometimes called the biological clock, is not determined, but it is suspected that it is part of the brain's function.

Organs and tissues often undergo changes because the cells used to form them no longer function in the same manner that they once did when young, or in the first years of duplication. For example, ovaries are not activated until puberty arrives. What activates them? Then the ovaries begin to sputter to a stop. What stops ovarian function? The timing of these events depends on the genetic script a person inherits at birth.

2 Some investigators believe the immune system is responsible for aging. As people get older, two things happen related to this. The body produces more autoimmune antibodies. Sometimes these antibodies attack the body's own tissues as if they were foreign substances or bacteria. In extreme states they cause many diseases, called autoimmune diseases. Other changes occur when the body's immune defenses decrease. The thymus gland, which prepares white blood cells (the T-cells) to carry out their defense actions to protect the body, deteriorates. The decrease in immunity can cause a person to be more susceptible to diseases, like pneumonia, for example. In other words, the body just stops functioning, maybe because it accurately reads an unconscious signal from the brain that this person is discouraged and depressed and no longer wants to live.

3 There are other theories like the "free-radical theory" and the "cross-linked theory" that tells us what happens but does not tell us why. In fact, no theory really explains why the body ages.

To be happy,
we must be true to nature
and carry our age along with us.
- William Hazlitt (1778-1830)

AGING AND LIFE EXTENSION
(page 2 of 5) **AGING 261**

SENILE DEMENTIA

A major concern of many people is the possibility that they will lose their mental abilities as they grow old. The extreme of this is senile dementia, which can result in a person being totally incapacitated and no longer in touch with reality. Medical science now recognizes that this is not aging at all, but the result of disease. The problem to solve here is not to unravel the mystery of aging, but to find ways of preventing and treating the diseases responsible for senile dementia. The complex interrelation of nerve cells and brain chemistry is one of the most important frontiers of medicine, and there is no doubt that within this field lie many of the answers to the questions about the biological clock that may determine the phases of life and aging.

THE AGING BRAIN

Often it is not aging but disuse that results in decreased mental functions with increasing age. Maintaining the ability to concentrate, continuing to stimulate your memory with memory tasks, and problem solving all help to maintain those functions. The brain may continue to regulate your blood pressure and heart rate and affect whether you sweat or not, because these functions are exercised, but if you don't use your brain for mental tasks, its ability to remember does decrease, not from age but from disuse.

SEXUAL FUNCTION

Sexual interest does not disappear in women after menopause, but the loss of estrogen definitely influences a woman's interest in sex. Estrogen will maintain her organs in a state of sexual readiness. Estrogen replacement helps to prevent the loss of sexual interest and function.

The healthy older male continues to produce high levels of testosterone for life. The testicles clearly have a different age cycle from the ovaries. The failure of sexual performance in most older males is not related to lower testosterone levels. The failure to have an erection is usually related to poor circulation because of disease, changes in nerve fibers that control erection because of diabetes and other illness, or to medicines as used in the control of high blood pressure. The decrease in sexual activity in healthy older men seems to be related to opportunity and attitudes rather than hormone levels or real aging.

THE SENSE ORGANS

The special senses, such as hearing, seeing, and tasting, are extensions of the nervous system. The progressive loss of taste, smell, and hearing may represent aging of the end cells of the system, such as the taste bud cells or the cells in the nose to detect smell. You can compare them to the ovaries, which have a limited interval for normal function and then disappear. But these same end organ cells can also be affected by disease. The maintenance of these functions at optimal levels may depend on both preventing or curing disease and also preventing aging of specialized sensory cells.

THE HEART

Very little is known about aging of the heart. Coronary heart disease that results in heart attacks is not caused by aging at all. It is a disease of the arteries that supply the heart muscle. There are genetic factors that influence the level of cholesterol, which in turn may increase fatty-cholesterol blockage of coronary arteries. Many older people have a decreased capacity for physical activity because the heart has not been exercised adequately.

THE MUSCLES AND SKELETON

The changes in the muscles and skeleton are another area where disease is confused with age. A major portion of the decrease in muscle size and strength, seen as people get older, is from disuse. There is some loss of muscle fibers because some of the nerve cells in the spinal cord that control them degenerate with increasing age. But proper exercise can maintain, strengthen, and enlarge the remaining muscle fibers. The skeleton does begin to decrease in size after about age 30. The bones undergo constant changes with remodeling of the bone architecture. This is a regeneration process. After age 30, there is not as much new bone formed as is lost, resulting in a gradual decrease in skeletal size and strength.

PREVENTING AGING

Body weight is a factor in many of the diseases associated with increasing age. People who are lean, because of limiting their calories, exercising more, and perhaps from inherited factors, do live longer than their heavier age counterparts.

Body weight is undoubtedly affected by the genetic script. Some people are programmed to get heavier as they get older. This is often the real reason for the middle-aged spread. Others have a script that does not call for increased obesity at that phase of life. That inherited script has a lot to do with how successful people are with weight control programs of diet and exercise. It is probably true that individuals who overly restrict their diet, in an effort to be leaner than their genetic script intended, are not in an optimal state of health. But like the research with the starved rats, they may actually live longer.

CONTROVERSIAL ANTI-AGING FACTORS:

■ **Vitamins,** particularly vitamins A, C, and E. These are "antioxidants," meaning they are claimed to prevent superoxide radicals from inducing aging effects. Some scientists say, "There is no evidence that any vitamins retard aging." Other scientists, like Linus Pauling, disagree.

■ **SOD, superoxide dismutase.** This enzyme enables the rapid removal of superoxide radicals from the cells, and long-lived animals do have higher tissue levels of SOD than short-lived animals. But, according to the medical field, taking SOD will not do anything to extend your life span or make you younger.

■ **Gerovital-H3 and H7** has been promoted as a youth pill for more than 30 years. It is really procaine hydrochloric acid, which is the basic chemical used as an anesthetic for dental work. According to the medical community, it has no anti-aging effects at all. Some doctors say that the benefits originally reported by Ana Aslan of Hungary were actually not because of the procaine. Older people did do better, because someone took an interest in them, their diet was improved, and they exercised. Gerovital-H7 is now being advertised as an improvement on the old formula.

■ **Removal of the pituitary gland** has been used to try to prolong the life span. This was done on the belief that there is a "death hormone" and that it comes from the pituitary. Animals tested in this way did live longer, but they also lost weight. Regardless of which of these procedures is tried, most of the apparent beneficial results come back to the common factor--weight loss.

■ **Cell therapy.** This consists of injecting young and immature cells of various organs taken from sheep fetuses. The theory is that injecting these young cells into an old body will rejuvenate the old cells. Dr. Paul Niehans of Switzerland used this technique on Pope Pius XII, and it became quite popular in Europe. This procedure can have complications because the body may react to the injected cells. This form of cell therapy is outlawed in the United States. Our scientists do not think it will achieve what it claims.

■ **DHEA-S,** dehydroepiandrosterone sulfate is a weak steroid formed by the adrenal gland. It is present in high concentrations in young adults, then declines drastically with increasing age. The men with the lowest levels of DHEA-S were the ones with the highest rate of death from any cause. Whether DHEA-S has a real role in preventing aging, or has actions that prevent disease, or both, will require further study.

■ **Aminoguanidine** is a chemical that prevents cross-linking of protein. Rockefeller Foundation scientists think it will help to prevent many of the changes noted in diabetics and perhaps prevent changes from aging. It needs further study.

LIFE EXTENSION LIFESTYLE

As far as science is concerned, the methods for extending our life span will be found in genetic engineering and we have not yet discovered the secrets. It helps to be born into a family where people have a long life span. Since people rarely die of old age, it would, of course, pay to keep ourselves free from disease, poisonous substances, and risk of fatal accident. Any other suggestions can quite simply be summed up in the advice of Seneca on page 264.

As far as human wisdom and anecdotal evidence is concerned, there are many suggestions, some of which may have validity:

❤ **Drink alcohol in moderation.** Heavy drinking can cut down a lifespan by years. Do not use street drugs.

❤ **Stop smoking.** Smoking two packs a day cuts seven years from the normal life span.

❤ **Eat nutritiously.** Don't eat too much sugar, fat, and highly processed foods. Eat a low-fat diet consisting of high fiber, fresh vegetables, fruits, beans, nuts, seeds, and whole grains. The famous Framingham Heart Study concluded "When we eat a diet sparse in meats, fats, and sugar, we do a lot better."

> **Surveys show that almost every healthy, long-lived person has been a traditionally light eater. They never overeat. They quit eating before they are full, and they always leave the table feeling slightly hungry.**

❤ **Exercise, exercise, and exercise.** The one word that most life-extending experts agree upon is exercise, and they all recommend walking. (See physical fitness, page 140.)

Until the 1930s, exercise was a way of life for most Americans. We had to walk everywhere, maintain large vegetable gardens, chop wood, and keep house without appliances. These activities maintained most older people at an acceptable level of fitness. By the mid-1950s, the American lifestyle had become so sedentary that heart disease was epidemic. Physiologists have found that genuine fitness could be produced only by aerobic-type exercise. Those safe for older people include: walking, swimming, bicycling, and any type of rhythmic exercise performed at a moderate pace, but check with your doctor before starting any exercise program.

❤ **Maintain your weight at the normal level.** Based on the Metropolitan Life Insurance Company's height-weight charts, 33% of American women and 45% of American men are currently overweight. Research confirms that almost every healthy long-lived person has been lean and wiry and few have been overweight. Diets that lose weight only to gain it again are not considered healthy. The way to lose weight is to exercise and gradually cut out fats, sugars, and too much food. In other words, "change your lifestyle."

❤ **Get a good night's sleep.** If you can't sleep, find methods to relax, increase your exercise time, and get involved in interesting activities--not television.

❤ **Ignore your chronological age.** Age is not the number of birthdays that have passed. It is an attitude, an awareness, a feeling. The ability to have the self-image of a younger person is characteristic of most long-livers. Youthfulness is focused on activity. So keep active and maintain a youthful attitude. Remember, "You're only as old as you feel."

> **To know how to grow old
> is the master work of wisdom,
> and one of the most difficult
> chapters in the great art of living.**
>
> - Henri Frédéric Amiel (1821-1881)

❤ **Learn to relax.** Here are some suggestions:

♥ Deliberately slow the pace of your life.
♥ Live fully in the present moment.
♥ Do only one thing at a time.
♥ Don't be too concerned about saying "no"; turn down demands on your time that stress you out.
♥ Learn to accept that if you cannot complete a job today that it's acceptable to finish it later.
♥ Spend some time alone each day.
♥ To enjoy life to the fullest, learn to see, smell, touch, and feel everything around you right now.

❤ **Develop a powerful will to live,** and never give up. What most distinguishes long-livers from the rest of us is their indestructible capacity to rebound from misfortune and adversity.

❤ **Make important goals.** As soon as you achieve any goal, replace it with another immediately. Choose only goals that you can succeed in achieving. Otherwise, you are defining dreams, not goals.

❤ **Be a success.** Success is an essential component in creating a powerful will to live. We can readily experience the exuberance of success by making a list of small successes, each of which can be attained within 15 minutes, like cleaning your bicycle or the interior of your car. Achieving several small successes can fortify your will to live and make it easier to attain more important goals that can leave you flushed with the inspiration of success.

❤ **Create a newer and stronger self-image.** Think about your strengths and let yourself be forgiven for your weaknesses. Walk tall and erect with a quick step. Let yourself feel confident and optimistic about the future. Adopt a positive mental attitude; feel good about yourself and you will feel good about other people and life.

❤ **Minimize stress in your life.** Most stress is due to change, so it pays to subject ourselves to as few changes as possible. Live a systematic life in harmony with the rhythms of nature. People who live long usually rise and retire at the same time and have an orderly, somewhat routine, life. However, whenever physical changes are necessary, greet them with a flexible, accepting attitude.

❤ **Eliminate harmful mental attitudes;** turn to the good thoughts of life and forget the bad:

Fear, anxiety, and worry are deadly killers that make it easier to get all kinds of disease and effectively destroy the quality of life we might have. The opposite of fear and worry is faith and trust. Take time to develop a belief in yourself, in life, and in the fellow travelers that come your way. People with an honest faith are not cheated anywhere near as often as those who are afraid. An ancient homily says: "The things we fear are sure to come to pass."

Anger, bitterness, hostility, and resentment will drive happiness from our life and leave us with a profound depression. The opposite of anger and resentment is love and forgiveness. Start by forgiving, now and forevermore, anyone you believe may have caused you harm of any kind. Refuse to have any part of being unforgiving. People who are hostile have cardiovascular disease five times more often than those who are loving. So treat yourself to happiness and adopt a loving attitude. Don't try to compete with other people. Keeping up with the Joneses is a continual drain on our emotions and energy. Compete only with your own excellence. Learn to excel at something, then attempt to beat your own best performance. And be willing to share your expertise with others. Nobody can win unless we all win.

❤ **Lead a fun life; laugh a lot.** Investigations by Norman Cousins and others have demonstrated the therapeutic benefits of fun and laughter in promoting health and long life. Few long-livers take themselves too seriously. They laugh often at themselves and their mistakes. They maintain a youthful enthusiasm for anything new and different. And they possess an almost childlike enthusiasm for spontaneous fun and play.

❤ **Be a loving, generous person.** Researchers who have observed groups of longevous people report that virtually every long-liver is generous, kind, loving, and unselfish. Dr. Solomonovich, a Russian gerontologist who spent long periods living in close proximity with the long-lived Abkhasian people in the Caucuses, reported that he had never heard any long-lived person use a harsh word.

To be a loving person means that we accept other people the way they are without criticizing or judging them or trying to manipulate or change them. To achieve this level of unconditional love we must first let go of any artificiality or pretension, which so often separates us from others. This liberates us to tell the exact truth at all times and to reveal our deepest inner feelings. Through revealing our innermost feelings we immediately become closer to others. Loving people are emotionally transparent, with nothing to hide.

❤ **Avoid living alone.** People live healthier and longer lives in the presence of close and loving relationships. Studies from around the world show that loneliness is a major threat to health and long life. Virtually every gerontologist agrees that we can extend life significantly by creating a compatible and stable marriage with accompanying family life, and by cultivating many friends and being active in a number of social organizations.

❤ **Maintain monogamous sexual activity** regularly through life. Regular sexual activity with one permanent partner has been estimated to extend life expectancy by at least two years. Almost all healthy long-lived people stay married and enjoy regular lovemaking until the end of their days. Those who are unable to have sex past 50 usually are not well or are engaging in antihealth habits.

No Spring nor Summer Beauty has such grace
As I have seen in one Autumnal face.

- John Donne (1572-1632)

❤ **Keep growing.** Long-lived people are an independent and adventuresome lot who are not afraid to take an occasional prudent risk to succeed. But they see no reason to endanger their lives and health by exposing themselves to unnecessary risks. We become old on the day we stop growing and we stop growing on the day we become unwilling to take a prudent risk. People stop growing by dropping out of the mainstream of life, thoughts, and ideas, and by seeking safety in the status quo. Numerous studies have shown that ceasing to grow is synonymous with physical atrophy and mental withdrawal.

❤ **Stay mentally active throughout life.** A series of studies show that an active mind is man's greatest resource against aging. People live longer when they use their intelligence and education to acquire and practice wisdom. At all socioeconomic levels, intelligent people tend to use their minds actively and constantly all their lives. Although the mind ages more slowly than any other organ, without constant use it can atrophy and our memory can begin to lapse.

❤ **Believe in and rely on a higher power.** Investigations are showing that all forms of spiritual belief and faith exert a powerful benefit on health and long life. In a study of 1,000 long-lived Americans, the Committee for an Extended Lifespan found that almost without exception, every single longevous person has strong spiritual beliefs. The same study found that over 50% of all long-livers turn their problems over to a higher power and they rely on this same power to guide them toward the best possible solution. While their faith safeguards them from stress, they are able to relax and enjoy living.

❤ **Continue to work** at a satisfying job for as long as possible. When the National Institute of Health made an 11-year investigation of 600 possible variables that contribute to longevity, they found that the degree to which a person derives satisfaction from his or her job is the greatest single factor affecting longevity. Work makes us who and what we are. Work is life and life is work. To not work can be totally destructive. No one can live healthfully knowing their talents are not needed. Many people who retire at the age of 65, die within a few months unless they are able to pick up some meaningful hobbies, or volunteer work, or change occupations.

Scientists who have studied work response at all levels have concluded that only by working at a job with the following qualities can we expect to enjoy optimum health and long life.

♥ We should be free to make all or most of our own decisions. We should be under no one's authority or supervision. The closer we are to being our own boss, the better.

♥ The job should make maximum use of our abilities, skills, and talents. An underutilized person is invariably frustrated.

♥ The job should allow us to reach a position of eminence in our chosen field. We should be able to rise through promotion to a position of authority and responsibility.

♥ We should be able to work at our own pace free of all deadlines and pressures.

♥ Successful work leaves no stress scars. Enjoyable and satisfying work cannot be distinguished from play.

♥ The job should allow us to do our very best work and to take pride in the work we do. It should encourage us to reach out for high achievement by being ready to tackle challenging new tasks that we have never done before and that, in the process, provide a feeling of success and accomplishment.

♥ We should be able to continue to work without any pressure to retire for as long as we wish.

There may be a hundred more life-extenders, but the above are sufficient to give us an idea of what it takes to live to be 100. In fact, the secret to longevity can be wrapped up in "living the good life." Happiness and longevity are a choice. If we choose to live well and live happy, we have chosen to live long.

REFLECTIONS ON AGING

Remember, old folks are worth a fortune, with silver in their hair, gold in their teeth, stones in their kidneys, lead in their feet, and gas in their stomachs.

Some people, no matter how old they get,
never lose their beauty--they merely
move it from their faces into their hearts.

I have become a little older now and a few changes have come into my life. Frankly, I have become quite a frivolous old gal. I am seeing five gentlemen every day. As soon as I wake up, WILL POWER helps me get out of bed. Then I go down the hall and see JOHN. Next, CHARLIE HORSE comes along and takes a lot of my time and attention. When he leaves ARTHUR RITIS shows up and stays the rest of the day. He doesn't like to stay in one place very long, so he takes me from joint to joint. After a busy day, I'm really tired and glad to relax with BEN GAY.

As for old age, embrace and love it. It abounds with pleasure if you know how to use it. The gradually declining years are among the sweetest in a man's life, and I maintain that, even when they have reached the extreme limit, they have their pleasures still. - Seneca (3 B.C.-65 A.D.)

How beautifully leaves grow old, How full of light and color are their last days. - John Burroughs (1837-1921)

What is Your Aging I.Q. ?

TRUE OR FALSE	ANSWERS

TRUE OR FALSE

1. Everyone becomes "senile" sooner or later, if he or she lives long enough.

2. American families have by and large abandoned their older members.

3. Depression is a serious problem for older people.

4. The numbers of older people are growing.

5. The vast majority of older people are self-sufficient.

6. Mental confusion is an inevitable, incurable consequence of old age.

7. Intelligence declines with age.

8. Sexual urges and activity normally cease around age 55-60.

9. If a person has been smoking for 30 or 40 years, it does no good to quit.

10. Older people should stop exercising and rest.

11. As you grow older, you need more vitamins and minerals to stay healthy.

12. Only children need to be concerned about calcium for strong bones and teeth.

13. Extremes of heat and cold can be particularly dangerous to older people.

14. Many older people are hurt in accidents that could have been prevented.

15. More men than women survive to old age.

16. Deaths from strokes and heart disease are declining.

17. Older people on the average take more medications than younger people.

18. Snake oil salesmen are as common today as they were on the frontier.

19. Personality changes with age, just like hair color and skin texture.

20. Sight declines with age.

ANSWERS

1. **False**   Even among those who live to be 80 or older, only 20% to 25% develop Alzheimer's disease or some other incurable form of brain disease. "Senility" is a meaningless term that should be discarded.

2. **False** The American family is still the number one caretaker of older Americans. Most older people live close to their children and see them often; many live with their spouses. In all, 8 out of 10 men and 6 out of 10 women live in family settings.

3. **True** Depression, loss of self-esteem, loneliness, and anxiety can become more common as older people face retirement, the deaths of relatives and friends, and other such crises--often at the same time. Fortunately, depression is treatable.

4. **True** Today, 12% of the U.S. population are 65 or older. By the year 2030, one in five people will be over 65 years of age.

5. **True** Only 5% of the older population live in nursing homes; the rest are basically healthy and self-sufficient.

6. **False**   Mental confusion and serious forgetfulness in old age can be caused by Alzheimer's disease or other conditions that cause incurable damage to the brain, but some 100 other problems can cause the same symptoms. A minor head injury, a high fever, poor nutrition, adverse drug reactions, and depression can all be treated and the confusion will be cured.

7. **False** Intelligence per se does not decline without reason. Most people maintain their intellect or improve as they grow older.

8. **False** Most older people can lead an active, satisfying sex life.

9. **False** Stopping smoking at any age not only reduces the risk of cancer and heart disease, but also leads to healthier lungs.

10. **False** Many older people enjoy and benefit from exercises such as walking, swimming, and bicycle riding. Exercise at any age can help strengthen the heart and lungs, and lower blood pressure. See your physician before beginning a new exercise program.

11. **False** Although certain requirements, such as that for "sunshine" vitamin D, may increase slightly with age, older people need the same amounts of vitamins and minerals as younger people. Older people in particular should eat nutritious food and cut down on sweets, salty snack foods, high-calorie drinks, and alcohol.

12. **False**   Older people require fewer calories, but adequate intake of calcium for strong bones can become more important as you grow older. This is particularly true for women, whose risk of osteoporosis increases after menopause. Milk and cheese are rich in calcium as are cooked dried beans, collards, and broccoli. Some people need calcium supplements as well.

13. **True** The body's thermostat tends to function less efficiently with age and the older person's body may be less able to adapt to heat or cold.

14. **True** Falls are the most common cause of injuries among the elderly. Good safety habits, including proper lighting, nonskid carpets, and keeping living areas free of obstacles, can help prevent serious accidents.

15. **False** Women tend to outlive men by an average of 8 years. There are 150 women for every 100 men over age 65, and nearly 250 women for every 100 men over 85.

16. **True** Fewer men and women are dying of stroke or heart disease. This has been a major factor in the increase in life expectancy.

17. **True** The elderly consume 25% of all medications and, as a result, have many more problems with adverse drug reactions.

18. **True** Medical quackery is a $10 billion business in the United States. People of all ages are commonly duped into "quick cures" for aging, arthritis, and cancer.

19. **False**   Personality doesn't change with age. Therefore, all old people can't be described as rigid and cantankerous. You are what you are for as long as you live. But you can change what you do to help yourself to good health.

20. **False** Although changes in vision become more common with age, any change in vision, regardless of age, is related to a specific disease. If you are having problems with your vision, see your doctor.

Source: National Institute on Aging

Coping with old age   by Wm. J. Diehm

A few years ago I attended the fiftieth anniversary of my high school graduating class in Pasco, Washington. As we gathered for the opening ceremonies, I looked around and said to my wife, "What are we doing here with all these old people?" My wife looked surprised and responded, "It's your class, they are the same age as you are." "True, but I don't feel as old as these people look." With a twinkle in her eye, my wife said, "Maybe they think the same about you." I inquired from various old-time friends. It was true, they thought I looked old too.

Old age creeps up on a person like a thief in the night. Toward the end, just before it grabs you, there are certain tiny signs: hard breathing over little exercise, slight trembling of the hands, certain little twitches, flabby muscles, slight aches and pains, increased trips to the doctor, wrinkles, gray hair, slight impairment of short-term memory, generalized weakness, less latitude in eating and sleeping habits, decreased interest in sex, less adventuresome, and on and on. May I repeat, these symptoms and others like them gradually creep on us without our noticing that we are growing old.

Many people are sensitive about old age. They say, "A person is as old as he feels," or "I don't have birthdays anymore." They don't reveal their age, hoping the process will go away. Other people do not even admit that old age exists. And others spend a fortune trying to cover it up by camouflaging wrinkles, dying their hair, surgically lifting their face, and taking all kinds of potions to keep themselves looking youthful. We have all seen people that don't look their age--some who are 50 years old and look like they are 90, and others who are 90 and look like they are 50. Ahem! Some folks say I hold my age of 70 as if I were much younger--it makes me feel good to think that it might be true.

We have hardly recovered from the shock of realizing that we are getting old when we receive more bad news. The thing we thought would never happen--we are going to retire or be retired from the job we have held for 40 years or more. Like others, I have said, "I'm never going to retire." And then, chagrin of chagrins, I did. It is so difficult to retire that a small percentage of people appear to shrivel up and die shortly after retirement. Most people who successfully face old age and retirement claim that they do not retire; they only change what they do.

When I think of coping with old age a number of cliches come to mind: "Act your age," but I don't want to act old. In fact, it comes to me that I don't even want to admit that I am old. "Ignore old age" is my motto. Then some of the aches and pains of arthritis catch up to me and old age cannot be ignored. The "march of time" is inexorable--everyone who doesn't die young is doomed to get old and die, but there are certain things we can do to delay old age and make it more livable.

I. TAKE GOOD CARE OF YOUR BODY

That ancient book of wisdom, the Bible, declares, "The body is the Temple of the Holy Spirit . . . which you have from God." We are expected to take good care of this extraordinary house that contains our Spirit, mind, and soul.

❶ Keep yourself clean. The old saying by Benjamin Franklin, "Cleanliness is next to Godliness" gets truer as the years go by. When suffering, sickness, and mental deterioration come upon older people it is more difficult for them to keep clean. But, it is a necessity, even if we must hire someone to help. To be unkempt is the surest way to hasten the problems of old age.

❷ Exercise regularly and moderately. Older people often are sedentary and have problems with exercise and activity; but to stay alive exercise isn't a choice; it's a necessity. I can remember how pleased I was to get my electric wheelchair, only to discover that I quickly lost body strength when I stopped pushing myself around. Now my electric wheelchair is in a semiretired condition and I am getting better.

I remember Betty Johnson, a patient at the Riverside Convalescent Home. She was just 35 years old, but she got tired of life and refused to move. It only took her a year to wither and die without exercise. I used every argument I knew trying to get her to move her body. She had chosen this vindictive form of vengeance against her family--the slow suicide of not moving her body. A sedentary life-style can be a form of suicide. We must persuade ourselves and others to keep moving as old age approaches.

❸ Eat a little less, but be sure the food is well balanced and nutritious. Growing a garden is a neat idea. There is nothing better than fresh vegetables. It seems to me that some warning needs to be made about fad diets and peculiar eating habits. If a person has reached retirement age, probably they need to go slow in radically changing their mode of eating. The older we get, the less we eat for pleasure and the more we eat for survival. We eat, not so much to satisfy our appetites, but to satisfy our nutritional needs.

One 90 year-old lady said to me, "I don't feel like eating any more, so I won't." I said to her, "You can't fool God that way; your choice is slow miserable suicide, and you are just as guilty of taking your life as the person who chooses a gun." She was a wise and mature spiritual lady so she said, "I never thought of that before. You are right! I will start eating again." She did, and the next 5 years were quite beautiful.

❹ Take a sensible approach to dieting. Many people who reach retirement age are overweight. Now is the time to do something about it. The magic formula is simple: Eat a little less and exercise a little more. Don't go on a crash diet. Fast weight loss only means fast weight gain. Gradually cut down on fat, sugar, and the amount you eat and increase the amount of exercise. Gradual weight loss by changing your life-style of eating and exercising is the only way.

However, I knew a man by the name of W. A. Moore who lived to be 105, worked every day, and weighed over 300 pounds. Research tells us that when you get to be a certain age (probably over 70), weight no longer is a factor in longevity. But, don't count on it. If you are overweight, reduce it a little, if you can. Sometimes the worry over weight is more serious than the weight itself. So, try to reduce; but, don't kill yourself trying.

Unfortunately, many times weight loss is based on depression or some other serious condition. It is possible to be very slender because of a mental disorder known as anorexia nervosa or bulimia in which a person forces vomiting after each meal. Preoccupation with slenderness can often be more debilitating than plain ol' fat.

❺ Eliminate bad habits. It's never too late to stop smoking, boozing, or kicking any addictive condition. In my psychological practice I have treated people of every age who have quit "cold turkey" every addictive practice known, no matter how severe. I treated a 70 year-old man who had been addicted to alcohol all his life. He stopped short one day, by choice, and never drank again. He died at the age of 82. I treated another man, age 52, heavily addicted to heroin. He threw away the needle and with a prayer "God Help Me" never went back to his addiction. I have seen it happen in my prison work a thousand times. A true religious faith is stronger than any addiction. With the help of God and our faithful friends, the world of booze and narcotics can be conquered.

❻ Fight back at sickness and disease. In our day of Social Security and Medicare there is little excuse for older people to let health conditions slip up on them. With little expense, we senior citizens can get regular checkups; and if something is coming, we can take preventive steps. If you have a medical problem find out as much as you can about it. The government has free booklets on every health subject imaginable. The booklets are easy to read and contain the latest information on every item of health. Examine the health information source listings, pages 246 and 247 and write for a list of publications relating to the subject you would like information on. This way you can stay up on the latest information about good health.

The rules for good body health are so simple that they are taught early in grade-school years to children. However, those simple rules are often so neglected and so costly to health that the U.S. Department of Health estimates that 25% of our senior citizens die needlessly of simple neglect years before their time.

The body is a marvelous machine; but, like all machines, it will eventually wear out. However, we know that with a little care a machine may go for 100,000 miles or more before it gives up; but, with a little neglect the best of machines can be brought to an untimely end. A major rule in coping with old age consists of taking care of our machine--our body.

II. MAINTAIN A GOOD MENTAL OUTLOOK

Obviously the mind and body can't be separated, so what you do for one, you do for the other. One of the saddest sights the world has ever known is Alzheimer's disease. Of course, we do not at present know the cause or the cure. How terrible it is when an older person loses his or her memory and the ability to think. Believe it or not, more people do it by default than do it by catching the disease.

We need to keep our minds vigorous and active up until the end of our body. Here are some things that help to preserve the mind until the end:

■ **Do useful work for the fun of it and sometimes for pay.** Retirement really does mean changing occupations. Don't let yourself sit around and stare into space. Get occupied. Be careful for people who can and will take advantage of you; but, usually we have friends, family, or church that can advise and keep us from being hurt.

My wife does beautiful handwork that she will enter in the county fair. I write and have the pleasure of seeing some of it bring in a little income. My wife sews and I fool around with the computer--we both take classes at the local community college. We are as busy and more happy than we ever were in occupational land.

■ **Go places, if possible.** See the world. Travel to faraway places and gasp in amazement at the beauty, the glory, the majesty, and the wonder of life. Some people can't travel because of physical conditions. Then travel with brochures, magazines, TV programs, and your imagination. I knew a man who lay on his lawn and studied the myriads of tiny life forms with a pocket magnifying glass. He said, "I am astounded at the amount of travel a person can do in an area the size of a postage stamp."

Sometimes travel is limited because of bathroom conditions. My wife and I go everywhere and I still must urinate at least once an hour and I can't use most public toilets because they are not equipped for wheelchairs. Believe it or not, there are devices you can wear that work beautifully and equipment that you can carry inconspicuously everywhere you go. I find it impossible to get in and out of showers and bathtubs that are not specially equipped. We have discovered that a wonderfully refreshing bath can be taken in any sink with liquid baby soap and a sponge to rinse off. If you really want to travel, it can be done with comfort.

I know a man who is confined to his wheelchair. He took a year and all alone went around the world. Everyone he met, even primitive natives of Africa, were eager to help him. He tells a few wild stories, but he had the time of his life.

■ **Write letters to relatives and friends.** An old song goes, "Make new friends, but keep the old, one is silver and the other gold." Don't lose track of your relatives--call them, write to them, talk to them, share their joys and sorrows, and they will do the same for you. Never go to a gathering and say the people aren't friendly. What you really mean is that you didn't go out of your way to be friendly with them. Often people can pick up our coldness and they avoid us. I went to a church one time that was full of "God's frozen people." Instead of resolving that I would never go back to that church, I resolved to go back and break the "ice." I walked up to the frozen people, stuck out my hand, and said, "I am trying to be a warm and friendly Christian; will you help me?" They did, with laughter.

■ **Maintain your hobbies and get some new ones.** Hobbies are fun things to do. If you don't have a hobby, arbitrarily choose one and stick with it long enough for it to grow on you. Or, if it is not for you, you can honestly reject it. Then, choose another hobby and stick with it long enough to gain some expertise. Keep choosing hobbies, until one becomes so fascinating you can go for broke. Hobbies do not necessarily cost a lot of money. Most reputable hobbies have clubs of interested people. Join the club, read their literature, and get involved in having fun.

■ **Read good books.** If you can't read, go back to school and learn, or join Frank C. Laubach's program of "Each One Teach One," and get someone to be your tutor. If your eyes are too bad to read, then get some tape-recorded books and listen to them. If you can't hear or see, then get some help from the government, take some braille courses, and have the <u>Reader's Digest</u> send to you their books in braille. Radio and television have some interesting educational channels that on occasion can substitute for good reading.

■ **Go to community and school activities.** Get yourself involved with the programs of your area. My wife and I live in Lake Shastina, a community of approximately 1200 people. Last night we journeyed to a nearby community (8 miles away) and listened to the 105-piece San Francisco Philharmonic Orchestra. We go to the monthly clubhouse programs, the grade-school festivals, the county fair, the high school ball games, etc. In fact, we are busier in this small community than we were when we lived in Los Angeles. Go to community functions and talk to people. When you get involved you won't be bored, and better than that, senility slows to a halt.

■ **Play games and enjoy sports.** Learn how to play the parlor games that kept the families of yesteryear together. Checkers, chess, backgammon--there are a thousand games that are fun and will keep your mind alert. T.V. often will not. Every evening when the day's work is done, my wife and I get out one of the many games we have collected and have fun. It keeps us young.

Seldom can we afford to go to a big league or professional game. But, we can afford to go to the local high school and grade-school sports. When you get acquainted with some people, it becomes even more exciting, particularly if one of the participants is a grandchild.

■ **Avoid negative daydreaming about the past.** The past is over and done with. Whenever you think about it, remember the pleasant and good times, but don't even dwell on them. Provide for yourself some new pleasant good times. Do not end your days with regrets on how you lived--good or bad. End your days like Moses, full of life, energy, and exciting happenings.

■ **Go back to school and take some courses and find out what our kids are doing and learning.** We have a community college just 8 miles away from our area. How I love to go back to school and take courses I didn't have time for when I was a young man. On occasion it is a little embarrassing to sit in a class full of people younger than my grandchildren. Even my teachers are children to me, some barely out of college with a fresh B.A.; and me with my awesome Ph.D. Forget all that--I want to learn things and keep my mind alert; so, it's back to school for me.

■ **Monitor your attitudes by keeping a daily journal.** There are certain mental attitudes that are destructive to the happy life of anyone and particularly to senior citizens.

❂ **Avoid crankiness and bad temper.** Record your slips. Give yourself a daily grade on temperament and strive to improve through daily monitoring.

❂ **Avoid seeing only the negative side of things** by counting your blessings, not your curses. It is so easy to become negative. Older people have lots of aches and pains and sometimes severe financial worries. We older people must fight hard to keep a positive attitude and maintain our faith.

❂ **Check yourself against the fruits of the spirit.** The good Book tells us to grow the fruits of the spirit, which are "love, joy, peace, patience, kindness, goodness, faithfulness, gentleness and self-control." As a person begins to deteriorate physically and mentally, it is easy to let the spiritual life ebb away, by developing a strong self-righteous, complaining (ain't it awful) attitude. Check that the fruits of the spirit are growing.

❂ **Fill your mind with positive words:**

+---+
| **Like** |
| |
| **YES, YES, I CAN**; rather than no, I can't |
| |
| **FINE, WONDERFUL, SPLENDID**; rather than terrible |
| |
| **HOW NICE, THANK YOU**; rather than ugh, I don't like it |
| |
| **I'M GETTING BETTER**; rather than I'm getting worse |
+---+

III. KEEP YOUR SPIRITUAL LIFE INTACT

Sadly, I have seen too many devoutly religious people work hard for the good most of their lives and then as they approach the end of their journey give up, waste away, and lose their faith. Here are some suggestions:

❤ **Keep practicing your faith.** Not so long ago in a big city area a famous bishop of a great denomination approached old age, developed a severely painful case of arthritis, cursed a God that could visit such agony on one of his servants, publicly proclaimed he had given up his faith, became a snarling skeptic, and died a bitter old man. What a sad thing for a quarterback to give up just before the touchdown.

❤ **Get in touch with nature.** Spend some time each day outside in nature. If that is not possible, get some plants in your room and grow something. Get your fingers in the dirt, lift your head toward the sky, watch the stars, the clouds, the changing heavens, and then turn your eyes upon the beautiful growing things and exult in the glory of life.

❤ **Speak a good word, or do a good deed, or think a good thought** about the positive nature of things. The other day I was feeling a little tired after a long trip to Sacramento. I stopped in a gas station and a young man waited on me. When I paid the bill and started up my car to leave, the young man said, "God go with you on your journey. May you be safe and happy." Maybe he was a religious gook, I don't know. But, I do know that he cheered me up and made me realize the value of a good word to a passing stranger.

❤ **Never give up your hopes for the future.** Death is only a step away for those who lose hope and eternal life is available to those who keep up their hope. The great master was crucified between two thieves: one who lost hope and scoffed and sneered; one who still thought life contained some answers and cried out for the master to remember him. When I approach the end of my days, even if I am suffering the tortures of the cross, I want to hear the Golden One say to me, "Today you will be with me in Paradise." How important it is not to give up hope.

❤ **Don't let yourself get bitter or mean.** On occasions when people get difficult, a friend will say, "I'm going to move to the middle of the Alaska tundra, a thousand miles from my nearest neighbor." My son John heard my friend make that statement and replied, "Then, you will be involved in a deeper problem, that of raw survival with the elements." A person can't get away from problems. "Life consists of solving problems, and the good life consists of solving them without becoming bitter."

If people are not tactful and hurt your feelings, show them how to be tactful. E. Stanley Jones, a missionary to India, once said, "I never allow people to hurt my feelings or insult me. No matter what they say, I never take offense; because, the deeper my offense, the shallower my faith." Most of us might find that policy a bit too much, but it works.

I keep asking myself the question, "How does my bitterness help me to solve this problem?" The answer always is, "It doesn't. Bitterness only makes it more difficult."

❤ **Fight off death to the very end.** You believe in life, not death. Show by your eagerness, vitality, and enthusiastic living that you want to live forever. Fill yourself with love of life and keep yourself alive as long as you can and death will be for you a magnificent graduation ceremony.

Now if we have old people who have disciplined their lives and keep the advice given in the article "Coping with Old Age" and have learned how to live pleasantly in their old age--well then, anyone can get along with them. But, in case you haven't noticed, older people are not perfect either; and also the people who deal with them sometimes lack understanding, patience, and tolerance. The problem of coping with old people is not just found in their poor health, bad mental attitude, and a philosophy of life that runs against the grain. The people who deal with senior citizens must also have some knowledge of the problems of older people and some ability to deal with these problems.

The ten years we took care of my elderly mother were some of the best years of our lives, because my mother was a jewel. Every night I could hear her say her prayers: "Dear Heavenly Father, help me to be a good person and not to be a burden on my son and his wife. Let me carry myself so that I will not make life hard for my loved ones." Mother made it easy for us even when she was desperately ill and unable to take care of the simple functions of life.

Here are some suggestions for dealing with senior citizens that I have gleaned from working with my mother, my Aunt Dorothy, my Aunt Agnes, and innumerable ladies and gentlemen from the church and life who are older than I am:

■ **Do not expect old people to be much different from any other age.** Some old people can become very childish; but, some young people are very childish also. I do not believe that people change much by getting old. A stubborn young person becomes a cantankerous old one. A lifetime of evil character does not suddenly become sweet and innocent with age. People can change at any age, if they want to; but they don't automatically change for the better just because they grow old.

One day I pondered this problem: "Why is it that people who have been driving for 50 years are often worse than someone who has been driving for a few months. Doesn't practice make perfect?" No! Practice does not make perfect, because we often practice our errors, and without proper feedback we cannot correct them. A person who has been driving for 50 years can be a lousy driver if he or she continues to perpetuate bad driving skills.

Just because a person has lived long, don't expect to find a saint or a perfect person. Accept people, even old ones, like they are.

■ **Give honor and respect to those who are old.** Of course I feel that everyone in existence deserves honor and respect. I make it a practice to not despise any of God's creatures, no matter how small or deformed or worn out.

One day I watched a nurse delighting in the experience of changing the diapers of a baby. The baby giggled as the nurse cooed, and extolled the virtues of the potty. Then she kissed the infant on her stomach and the bottoms of her feet as she carefully washed, wiped, oiled, and powdered her. She wrapped the baby in a blanket and with a little squeeze exclaimed, "There, you little precious one, that will make you feel better."

As it happened, I stood outside the room as the same nurse changed the bed of an old lady who had messed in it. The nurse called her every name in the book, jerked her around, and said such things as: "You make me puke, you dirty old bag. If I had my way, I'd let you lay in it." The nurse had no compassion or understanding in her care of an injured older person.

Frankly, an old person who is incontinent does not deserve any less respect than a baby who is not yet potty trained. We need to show respect for those who have lived long on the face of this earth. If we do, when we get in that condition, people will be more likely to show respect for us.

■ **Learn to love older people.** Anyone can love the young and beautiful, particularly when the hormones flow. Young love does exist but it is often confused with passion. To love an older person comes closer to true love. Of course, it is a pleasure to deal with an old person who is sweet, lovely, intelligent, and self-sufficient. Anyone can do that. It takes real character to love those who don't love us, and especially to

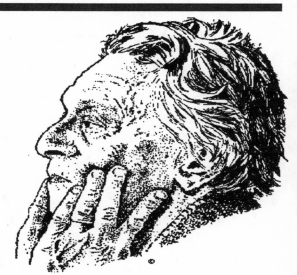

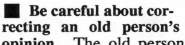
by Wm. J. Diehm

love those who aren't lovable. So, if the person you are dealing with is an impossible old man or old woman, rise to the occasion and be challenged to treat them especially well.

■ **Be careful about correcting an old person's opinion.** The old person may be wrong; but again, you may be wrong. He or she has lived a long time and his or her opinion is worth the consideration of age. Many times, when my mother was in her eighties, she would give me advice. Usually, sorry to say, I would argue with her and tell her why I couldn't do this or that. As I look back on it, she was right. Every single time she was right. I just did not have the good sense or the flexibility to accept her counsel. Here is one of the times I would like to live life over and listen carefully to an old person who loves me.

■ **Treat old people just like you want to be treated when you get old.** When I was growing up we had a special friend in the family who had little consideration for her parents. She abandoned her parents and dumped them into a poor house (we no longer use that terminology). As a grown man, I watched her children do the same thing to her. They put her away in an indecent, poorly cared-for institution. Now that I am old, I am watching the third generation do to the second generation what the second generation did to the first. If you want to perpetuate cruelty to the second and third generation, then treat your old folks cruelly. Your children will treat you like you treated your parents, and on and on it goes.

■ **Old folks love to laugh.** I learned that older people have a priceless sense of humor when I taught a senior citizens class at First Christian Church in Santa Ana some years ago. The teachers who came before me interpreted the older look as the serious look--it is not true. More than any other age, older people have a sense of humor. As I write these lines George Burns is an old man of 93, people love to laugh with him, and he loves to laugh. Perhaps that is why he has lived so long.

■ **Visit the old people.** One day I was walking down the corridors of a hospital and I heard an old man crying out, "Nurse, nurse, I'm lonely. Oh nurse, I am so lonely." His cry haunts me to this day. So, whenever I have a chance, I visit my old friends and try to alleviate their loneliness.

At another time I was visiting old friends in a nursing home when I heard the quiet sobs of a little old lady in a corner bed. She had outlived all her relatives. She was blind and very emaciated. Her bony fingers clawed feebly at the air as she moaned for a husband who wasn't there. I walked over to her bed, sat down, took her hand, and held it for two hours. She knew I wasn't her husband and since she couldn't see or hear she didn't know who I was. But, she did know that someone cared as she walked alone down the scary path to death.

The Bible very clearly tell us, "Honor your father and mother" (older people), which is the first commandment with promise "that it may be well with you and you may live long on the earth." This principle of honor is the major way of dealing with our senior citizens--not just because I am one, but because it is the best way of dealing with older people.

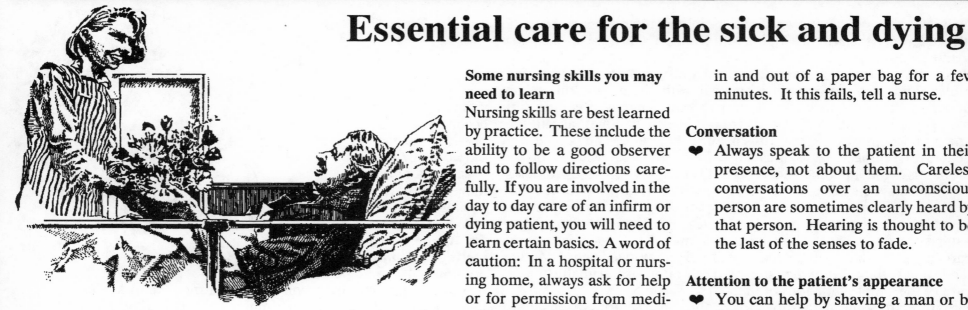

Essential care for the sick and dying

Combatting loneliness and despair

Volunteer visitors, relatives, and friends bring their own special abilities to the sick and dying. Above all, the sick and dying need company. You are an essential part of the healthcare team.

A natural reaction for those not accustomed to helping the dying is to withdraw and leave the dying person alone. Thus, dying people are often lonely and depressed. They feel abandoned and hopeless and may become resentful or withdrawn.

Sometimes there is nothing for you to do but hold the patient's hand. At other times they may wish to talk or they may want you to talk to them. Talk about shared experiences, their life, your life, what's going on in the world. Take cues from the patient. If they want to talk about dying, listen and respond appropriately and honestly. If you do not know how to respond, simply assure them that you care.

Praying with a patient often can be comfortable for both of you and "break the ice" so to speak. It can be either spontaneous prayer or formal prayer. I have found that the Lord's Prayer is the most universally known among Christians and is very comforting. Likewise, the Twenty-Third Psalm.

A dying person who feels abandoned--now that is real suffering! And you have the ability to relieve that suffering, even if all you can do is simply sit by their bedside and comfort them with your presence.

Some nursing skills you may need to learn

Nursing skills are best learned by practice. These include the ability to be a good observer and to follow directions carefully. If you are involved in the day to day care of an infirm or dying patient, you will need to learn certain basics. A word of caution: In a hospital or nursing home, always ask for help or for permission from medical personnel before assisting a patient for the first time. The simplest thing, like giving a patient a drink of water, may require special skills or knowledge of the patient's condition. A word of encouragement: Do not let your natural hesitancy or discomfort deter you. Remember, if one person is to receive comfort, someone else has to give it.

Recognizing pain and assisting in relief of pain

❤ You can tell if a person is in pain simply by being observant. A grimace, a wrinkled brow, tense fingers, cautious breathing, moans, etc., are all telltale signs. Even in an unresponsive person, these signs tell us they are in pain.

❤ Report signs of pain to medical personnel. Most pain can be effectively relieved with medical intervention.

❤ Excitement, anxiety, and depression can contribute to pain. After all, not all pain is physical. Also, the more bright and alert a patient remains, the more enjoyable and frequent their company, and the more they are kept interested in life, the less they will suffer.

❤ Sometimes a gentle back rub or leg rub or a change in the person's position can relieve restlessness, tension, and discomfort that may be perceived as pain.

Vomiting

❤ Usually there is a basin for this purpose close at hand. Turn the patient on their side so they will not choke or aspirate the vomitus into their lungs. Hold the basin against their cheek and under their chin. Call for help. Antiemetic drugs can control vomiting.

Hiccups

❤ Hiccups usually stop if carbon dioxide is inhaled, so help the patient to breathe in and out of a paper bag for a few minutes. It this fails, tell a nurse.

Conversation

❤ Always speak to the patient in their presence, not about them. Careless conversations over an unconscious person are sometimes clearly heard by that person. Hearing is thought to be the last of the senses to fade.

Attention to the patient's appearance

❤ You can help by shaving a man or by fixing a woman's hair and makeup. These small tasks boost morale, help the patient to feel more "normal" and to be more comfortable, and improve the general atmosphere in the hospital or nursing home.

Feeding a patient

❤ Make certain the patient is sitting up in a comfortable position before beginning the meal. Take a real interest in helping the patient to enjoy his meal. Be patient and always be mindful of the patient's dignity. Try to keep the food warm. If feeding takes a long time, ask for an extra plate. Put small amounts of food on it and keep the rest covered until needed. Give the patient the feeling that there is nothing you'd rather be doing at the moment. Give them your undivided attention throughout the meal.

❤ Know about special difficulties the patient may have. Is swallowing difficult? Give small amounts of food and frequent sips of water or other liquids. They may choke. Don't panic. If they are unable to cough the food up, call a nurse. Is chewing difficult? Cut food into very small pieces. You may observe that dentures do not fit well or that food gets caught under dentures. If so, remove the dentures and rinse them and rinse the patient's mouth before replacing them. This will make eating more comfortable and enjoyable.

❤ Does the patient drool or does food run out of one side of their mouth? These are frequent problems. Simply place a napkin on the patient's chest, wipe their chin as necessary, and give them small amounts of food. Feed them slowly. With a stroke patient, turning their head slightly to the unaffected side may help. Always help the patient with oral hygiene after eating.

Helping care for a bedridden patient

❤ Patients confined to bed require extra nursing care. They must be turned frequently (approximately every two hours), washed and perhaps fed, and always treated gently. The patient, as well as busy medical personnel, will appreciate your help if you are willing and able to be taught the correct way to do these things. Lifting and turning a patient requires training and practice and two people. Never change a patient's position without help from the medical staff unless you have been given permission to do so.

❤ The primary reasons for frequent changes in position are to prevent bedsores and to increase the patient's comfort. Frequent turning from side to side is essential to avoid bedsores. You must be careful to lift the patient when turning them so that the sheet does not rub against their skin. Sometimes ripple mattresses or sheepskins are used to help spread the patient's weight.

❤ All lumps and wrinkles should be smoothed out of the bedding under the patient.

❤ Bedsores are not necessarily a sign of bad nursing care--they are sometimes inevitable. Then one must try to heal them or render them painless. There are many forms of treatment for bedsores--too many to list here. If you are caring for a bedridden person at home, you will need special training and advice. Talk with the person's doctor about proper care and have a nurse show you what to do.

❤ The places to watch for bedsores are the base of the spine (tailbone), heels, hips, and other places where bones are close to the skin. It is important to notice areas that are red. These may be the beginning of bedsores. A visitor should be observant and report any changes in skin condition to the medical staff.

Care of the incontinent patient

❤ Many patients have catheters to drain urine from the bladder. Infection is a constant concern for a person with a catheter. If it is necessary for you to empty the catheter bag, observe the color (yellow, white, greenish, bloody) and appearance (cloudy or clear) of the urine, any unusual odor, and the amount. Report this to the patient's nurse.

❤ If the patient has a bowel movement, it is important that they be cleaned up promptly for comfort and hygiene to avoid embarrassment to the patient.

Mouth care

❤ Adequate care of the mouth is essential. Dentures should fit properly. If they do not, they will cause a sore mouth and difficulty eating. A visit from a dentist is in order if dentures bother the patient.

❤ When a patient is debilitated, frequent mouthwashes are important. Their mouth may drop open and become dry. Water should be given in frequent small quantities if the patient can swallow. The patient should be on their side so that fluid doesn't trickle down their windpipe, making them cough.

❤ Brushing the teeth and tongue with a soft-bristled brush and a small amount of a mild toothpaste and rinsing is helpful.

Abdominal distention and constipation

❤ The observant visitor may notice that the patient's abdomen is distended or the patient may complain of constipation to a friend or family member who has the time to listen to their woes. These are common problems when pain-killing drugs are used or when the patient is immobile and they are an additional cause of discomfort and distress. They can usually be relieved with medication or medical interventions. Report these problems.

Labored breathing

❤ The patient who is having difficulty breathing may find relief by being turned slightly on their side with their head propped up on pillows. Sometimes opening a window may also help.

Profuse sweating

❤ Patients with high fevers and often patients who are close to death will perspire profusely. Give the patient frequent sponge baths and change bedding as needed.

Conclusions

There are many more things that you can learn to do for the severely debilitated patient if you are a frequent visitor. It is my hope that this article will help you to realize that there is much you can do to help patients to live with dignity until the moment of death.

It is essential for you to believe that whatever you do in loving service for the sick and dying you are contributing to their comfort and happiness. You are not helpless in the face of illness and death, regardless of how much or how little you are able to do. What counts is your presence, not your activity.

Touch the patient, hold their hand, reassure them. Whatever we do outwardly, it is our concern and respect for the suffering person that matters.

Reproduced by permission of author:

Julie A. Grimstad, Executive Director
The Center for the Rights of the
Terminally Ill, Inc.
2319 18th Avenue South
Fargo, North Dakota 58103

Some wisdom of the ages.

It is in sickness that we most feel the need of that sympathy which shows how much we are dependent upon one another for our comfort, and even necessities. Thus disease, opening our eyes to the realities of life, is an indirect blessing.
    Hosea Ballou (1771-1852)

To wish to be well
is a part of becoming well.
    Seneca (B.C. 3-65 A. D.)

Health is a gift,
but you have to work to keep it.
    Elbert Hubbard (1859-1915)

Men fear death, as if unquestionably the greatest evil, and yet no man knows that it may not be the greatest good.
    Milton (1744-1827)

Dealing with people who are sick by Wm. J. Diehm

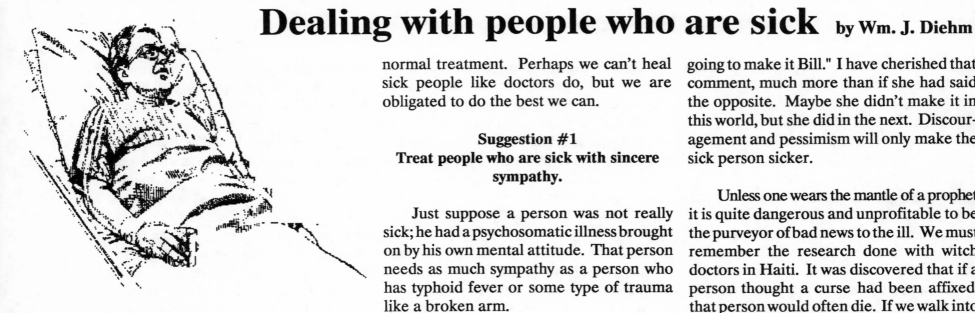

When people are healthy, happy, and doing well, it is not always easy to cope with them. But when we add bad health and illness to all the other contingencies, it is a wonder that people get along at all. I don't suppose people who are sick or who have a handicap or who are somehow disadvantaged or damaged like to think of themselves as "difficult" to cope with. Nevertheless, bad health is not only hard on the people who have it but on the people who must deal with it. We are expected to help the sick, those with a handicap, and the disadvantaged by relating to them to the best of our ability.

Usually a disease is caused by viruses or germs. However, it is extremely difficult to separate categories of illness. They blend together even as they differentiate. Psychosomatic illness can imitate the symptoms caused by germs and viruses so accurately that the best of doctors can be fooled. I knew a man who had a tricky tropical disease. Doctors kept telling him the symptoms were all in his head, but the autopsy proved it wasn't so. And, I have known some people who wasted their lives trying to find out what was wrong when it truly was all in their head.

Today's society often thinks that medicine is 100% accurate and scientific--not so. A lot of medical diagnosis is still an art; and furthermore, those who have faith in the doctor are much more likely to get healed than those who believe that the practitioner is a quack.

Sick people deserve special treatment; and often, those who are taking care of the sick are not prepared to give them even normal treatment. Perhaps we can't heal sick people like doctors do, but we are obligated to do the best we can.

Suggestion #1
Treat people who are sick with sincere sympathy.

Just suppose a person was not really sick; he had a psychosomatic illness brought on by his own mental attitude. That person needs as much sympathy as a person who has typhoid fever or some type of trauma like a broken arm.

People who are sick need sympathy, even if they caused the illness. Why not just say, "I'm sorry you are ill," and leave it at that. Never say, "I told you so" or "You had it coming." If a person has a disease like AIDS and you personally think it was because of an evil life-style, do not attempt to be the judge, jury, and executioner--that person does not need our punishment. In fact, like a medical doctor, it is not our job to punish sick people, but to help them. Helping a person is not a signal of approval of life-style. If we have no sympathy for the plight of the ill, who will have sympathy for the consequence of our judgment? Be kind, gentle, and sympathetic with those who are sick.

Suggestion #2
Conform to the limitations of the sick.

For example, do not offer candy to a diabetic; do not sit on or jostle the bed of a person who has just had surgery; do not talk too long or too loud to the ill; do not tire the sick with too much visiting; do not announce to a person recovering from surgery what a burden his sickness is causing.

A hundred specific rules could be expressed according to particular circumstances; but, being alert to special conditions and trying to help the sick recover is the general principle. Treat people who are sick in the way you like to be treated when you are sick.

Suggestion #3
Be encouraging and optimistic.

When my sister was dying of cancer, all I could do was cry. She taught me a valuable lesson. Just before she died, she said, "I'm going to make it Bill." I have cherished that comment, much more than if she had said the opposite. Maybe she didn't make it in this world, but she did in the next. Discouragement and pessimism will only make the sick person sicker.

Unless one wears the mantle of a prophet it is quite dangerous and unprofitable to be the purveyor of bad news to the ill. We must remember the research done with witch doctors in Haiti. It was discovered that if a person thought a curse had been affixed, that person would often die. If we walk into a hospital room and announce to a loved one that he is going to die of his illness, there is a strong chance that it will happen. When we deal with sick people it is important to be enthusiastic about their treatment and positive about their future.

Suggestion #4
Don't "catch" another person's illness.

Mother Teresa massages the sores of lepers--that seems to me a little dangerous. However, she does not massage in order to catch the disease, but to do what she can with the sick person.

Sometimes, when a loved one is very ill, those who care for him or her find themselves catching a psychological disease like depression. Remember that the greatest doctors have compassion for the sick but they do not lose their integrity by becoming mentally, psychologically, or physically ill themselves. Ask yourself, "How does my illness help my loved one recover from his?" The answer will be, it doesn't, it won't, it can't. So, when treating the sick, keep yourself well.

Suggestion #5
Pray for people who are sick.

Never fall into the trap of only emphasizing either prayer or treatment. It is not either-or, but both-and. Pray as if prayer were the only answer and give medical treatment as if it were the only answer. Those who only pray and don't use medical treatment are as disobedient to God's principles as those who only use medical treatment and do not pray.

There are no magical absolutes. People do get sick and people do die, and nothing that any doctor or any religious healer can do will stop the inevitable. Our best bet is to pray hard, take medical treatment, delay death as long as possible, and accept it without fear when the time comes.

Suggestion #6
Fight sickness by working for wellness.

Sickness is an enemy.

- Don't treat it like a friend.
- Don't cultivate sickness; it's like cultivating weeds.
- Don't make yourself sick in order to manipulate anyone--it isn't worth it.
- Don't talk about sickness or be abnormally interested in it--sickness does not need to be encouraged.
- Don't pretend like you are sick when you are not--it might truly happen.

It is normal to be well--be grateful for it and encourage it. It is not normal to be sick--fight it. A good person does not fight evil with evil, but rather he or she fights evil with good. Bitterness, hatred, anger, hostility, or a mean spirit will not help a person to get well. A person is more inclined to get well when he or she allows good thoughts to rule the disposition: thoughts of love, joy, peace, patience, kindness, goodness, faithfulness, gentleness, and self-control.

A good mental attitude can be the most effective way to help the doctor with his treatment. The rule of a good mental attitude applies not only to the person who is sick, but those people who must deal with the sick.

Suggestion #7
Pay attention to the rules of good health.

Here are the basic rules:

- ✔ proper nutrition
- ✔ adequate exercise
- ✔ fresh air
- ✔ a positive spirit
- ✔ a fulfilling occupation
- ✔ satisfying interpersonal relationships
- ✔ a good disposition
- ✔ service to others
- ✔ a friendly relationship to life
- ✔ freedom from harmful habits

The body is a temple, and it must be treated with respect. If we are abusing our body, we can't expect it to respond without complaint. We are to keep ourselves well and help others (as much as possible) to keep themselves well also. However, when dealing with sick people do not lecture down to them the rules of good health. It never helps sick people to fight a disease if we put them down by telling them what they should have done.

Suggestion #8
Sometimes it is necessary to tell sick people the hard truth--kindly, but firmly.

There are three occasions in which this is necessary:

1 When we are dealing with a sick loved one who is making life a hell for those who care. As a child when I was recovering from surgery, I was in severe pain. I was bawling and caterwauling up a storm and making life difficult for the nurses. A nurse came up and slapped me hard and exclaimed, "Billy Diehm, you stop that screaming and take your pain like a man." I stopped, the pain got less, and I learned a valuable lesson. I am not suggesting that we slap crying sick people, but I am suggesting that sickness is no excuse for bad manners or self-indulgent behavior. Sometimes we must at least say so.

2 When dealing with a sick person whose harmful habits brought on the illness. My brother-in-law Earl was visiting his brother who was very ill from cirrhosis of the liver brought on by too much drinking. Earl said to his brother, "Bill, you've got to cut down on your drinking." His brother replied, "Mind your own business; you're not my keeper." Earl was rebuked and ceased trying to help his brother. Two years later Bill died of acute alcoholism. Earl said, "I wish I could have helped him." Personally, I thought my brother-in-law was discouraged too easily. I know from long years of experience that sometimes a person must get tough with a loved one who is destroying himself.

3 When dealing with a sick person who is depressed to the point of suicide. Everywhere that Barry went he carried a Smith and Wesson .357 Magnum revolver. Barry was ill with a deteriorating disease called

multiple sclerosis. He was determined that he would take his life when the disease progressed to a certain state. There is no way to deal softly with such a situation.

When working with the suicide prevention clinic in Los Angeles, I saved many lives by a tough, caring, but no-nonsense approach. One day a man pointed a gun at me and said, "I'm going to kill you and then I'm going to kill myself." I responded, "You are not going to do anything of the kind. Put that gun down. I am going to give you a bath, you stink." I led him to the bathroom, helped him undress, gave him a bath, helped him dress, took him to our home, fed him, and kept him for three days. He got well and went back to work.

Dealing with people who are sick can be very difficult, but the rules for coping are similar to dealing with the well, except for the need for strong doses of compassion, empathy, and caring. Perhaps our efforts will not be able to heal every sick person we meet, but we can do what we can to help.

Once a disease
has entered the body, all parts which
are healthy must fight it:
not one alone, but all.
Because a disease might mean their
common death. Nature knows this;
and Nature attacks the disease with
whatever help she can muster.

Paracelsus (1493-1541)

The feeling of health
is acquired
only through sickness.

Georg Lichtenburg (1742-1799)

I have learned much
from disease
which life could never have
taught me anywhere else.

Goethe (1749-1832)

Dealing with people who have a handicap by Wm. J. Diehm

In 1924, when I was 5 years old, I contracted a disease known as poliomyelitis or infantile paralysis. The hospitals in that day would not accept a contagious disease while the fever raged. The only place that my father could find in the town was some rabbit hutches that he rebuilt. There we fought for my life.

When the fever abated I was sent to Children's Orthopedic Hospital in Spokane, Washington. For 7 years, off and on, I had treatment at this place. The hospital was a dumping ground for all types of crippled children: mentally retarded, including Down's syndrome and other types of genetic damage; mentally ill, including those with childhood schizophrenia and autism; emotionally disturbed, including those who were hyperactive and suffering from psychological trauma; brain damaged; and all forms of physical deformity. The only ones they didn't accept were those who had a contagious disease.

When I was 13 years old I got out of the hospital and went to high school as a freshman in Pasco, Washington. I wore braces on both legs and was moderately impaired in both arms. I have lived my life in a paraplegic condition, and now have additional limitations due to a postpolio condition.

I earned my Ph.D. from U.C.L.A., specializing in Special Education and Psychology. I could be considered an expert in the field of people with a handicap--both from education and personal experience. My suggestions for coping with these people have grown out of my own involvement, my education, my religion, and my knowledge of life.

❶ **Don't use demeaning terminology in dealing with those who have a handicap.** The word "handicapped" is today's buzzword to label those who have a physical disability. The word came from the Old English "cap in hand," as referring to the beggars and disabled who would sit on the city streets and beg with their cap in hand. Some people think that calling a person "handicapped" is softer and more acceptable than calling a person "crippled." I fail to see the difference.

I object to defining a person by their disability. Words like "cripple," derived from the Old English "to creep," will perpetuate false ideas. The same is true of "invalid," which means "not valid," or obvious ugly words like "abnormal" or "deformed." Some other words like disabled, lame, limping, gimpy, disabled, or even special bring to mind stereotyped images and often make people who have a disability seem less than human. Such words play upon pity and stimulate illusions of inadequacy.

I have heard people say: he is schizophrenic, he is mentally ill, he is sociopathic, or he is a cripple. Would we say he is measles, he is mumps, or he is chicken pox? We don't define people by their diseases; neither is it right to define people by their handicaps. A person may "have" a handicap but that doesn't make him a handicap. "He is handicapped" defines a person by his disability; while saying "He has a handicap" allows him to be more than "crippled."

Some people are sensitive about their handicap; others do not mind being called "crippled." Some people are so sensitive that they back away from the current labels with one euphemism after another. One man said to me, "I am not handicapped, I am handicapable." Another person said, "Everyone has some handicap; mine is physical and a little more evident." Most people with a handicap have some level of

sensitivity about it, particularly when the handicap becomes the center of attention and other obvious virtues are ignored.

I am opting for saying, "He or she has a handicap" (whenever possible) rather than "He or she is handicapped." I know it is a little thing and that I don't do it myself, but it is a step in the right direction. Don't label people by their deficiencies.

However, calling people demeaning names is a matter of the attitude and the heart rather than verbiage. One person can say "crippled" with a sincere attitude that would not bring offense; and another person can correctly address "that person with a handicap" and make you feel like a worm.

❷ **Do not help people with a handicap in a deferential manner.** When you look down on a person that you choose to help, it doesn't set well, whether that person has a disability or not. Most of the time when people help me on account of my handicap, they are gracious and friendly. Sometimes I get that "you poor thing" attitude, and I find it not uplifting.

An example of the difference between being deferential and helpful can be found in war when soldiers give special care as they bandage their own wounded--care that the enemy doesn't receive. Or, when we bury the enemy, it is often a common grave without the special services we give our own. That difference is called "empathy." Don't treat a person with a handicap as any less valuable than a person without one. The "I am glad to do it" attitude will set well; but the "why are you in my way" posture can cause offense.

❸ **Treat people with a handicap in a normal way.** People with a disability like to think of themselves as mainly normal. So just because you look like Quasimodo, the Hunchback of Notre Dame, doesn't mean you want to be confined to a tower ringing bells. If a person is mainly normal, he or she likes to be treated normally--like anyone else.

One time I was horrified by a man who had no legs, no arms, and was blind. Then I heard him read by passing his lips over raised Braille words. That man did more to change my attitude than any well person.

When you meet a handicapped person you can be grateful you don't have to bear that burden--not a gratitude that makes you condescending or aloof, but one that brings you to a realization that some people are called upon to bear burdens that we wouldn't want.

❹ **Let people with a handicap do things for themselves.** People with a disability usually like to do things for themselves, if they can. There may be some exceptions to this rule, but not from me. If I need help, I ask for it: "Could you please reach that shelf for me?" And then I say, "Thank you so much for helping." Sometimes a person rushes over when I am doing something and offers to help me. I usually say, "Thank you very much, but I can do it." On occasions I let them help me when I could do it, just to make them feel better.

The quickest way to make a handicap worse is to be pushed around in a wheelchair and waited on hand and foot. Usually a person needs the exercise of pushing himself and the stretch of reaching for things. Do not take away the independence of people with a handicap. If it is at all possible, let them do it themselves.

❺ **Don't lecture people with a handicap on how they ought to be unless you really know how they are.** People with a handicap sometimes experience quite a bit of pain; I know I do. Pain makes you cross and sometimes creates a frown on your face. I have a prejudice: I don't like it when people say to me, "Smile, it can't be all that bad." What do they know. On occasions, it is all that bad. Of course, I smile and say, "Thank you for reminding me." Inside I say, "I wonder if you would be smiling if you were in my condition?"

Softly and gently I need to warn zealous, dedicated people that not everyone who has a crippling condition can be healed by their prayers. I could write a book on the subject, but sufficient for the time being are these words: "Don't throw someone else into the deep water, unless you are walking on it."

❻ **Put your evaluation priorities on something higher than a physical disability.**

♥ A person's personality, character, spiritual acumen, and mental ability are all of more importance than physical prowess.

♥ A person with a handicap is first of all a "person" and needs to be defined that way rather than by a deficiency. However, it seems to me that people have overemphasized physical handicaps and underemphasized mental, emotional, and personality-type handicaps. I would much rather worry with a physical handicap than be all fouled up with a bad mental attitude, constant emotional distress, or scrambled brain circuitry.

❼ **Some buttons to press when you find you are stressed out from dealing with sickness or a handicap are:**
Button

1 Accept people and life as they are, not as you think they should be.
2 Count your blessings, not your curses.
3 Live according to what you have, not according to what you lack.
4 Don't establish blame. What difference does it make whose fault it is?
5 Get excited about playing the game of life. Enjoy being blocked, hit, tackled, and knocked down. That's a part of the game.
6 Recognize your limitations. When a person is running as hard as he can and gets a little push, he won't run faster-- he'll only fall down. Don't try more than you can do.
7 Don't forget the "fun button" to recharge your batteries. Everyone needs rest, diversion, change of pace, and recreation.
8 Think about good things, things that are true, honest, just, pure, lovely, and of good report.
9 Remember life on earth is temporary-- no matter how difficult the situation, this too shall pass away.
10 Turn impossible problems over to the Creator and leave them there.

Dealing with people who are profoundly injured   by Wm. J. Diehm

I have seen unbelievable deformities and incredible deficiencies in the state institutions like Fairview State Hospital in Costa Mesa, California. I also worked as a psychologist at the Arnold Homes for Disturbed Children in Anaheim. Some of the children could not talk or even control their bowels at the age of 16. Some would stare into space in a withdrawn autistic fashion for endless hours.

No matter how graphically I could describe the condition of certain people, it would be unbelievable. Those who work at such places are dismayed at the few answers to heavy problems; but there are some answers.

1st: **No matter how intense the disability there is no substitute for love and hands-on care.**

Jack and Judy had a little baby boy who was born with the shunt tube to his brain plugged. This condition did not allow the water to drain from the brain. Therefore, as he grew older the head enlarged and the brain was crushed by the accumulation of water. Hydrocephalus allows the child to have an enormous head, an infinitesimal brain, and terrible limitations with gross deformities.

Jack and Judy took loving care of their highly damaged child until he was 5 years old. At that time they put him in a state institution. Soon he died. Not to say anything against state institutions--they do the best they can. But, to say something powerful for love and care, there is no substitute for love in dealing with any profoundly injured child or adult.

2nd: **Look for the positive blessings in any profoundly injured person.**

My little grandson, Dan, was injured at birth and as a consequence has been left with a condition called cerebral palsy. He is now 19 years old and he can't walk, or talk, or feed himself, except with extreme difficulty. He has very little control over his bathroom functions. Sometimes he can notify, but certainly he can't take care of himself and must wear diapers.

Dealing with the profoundly injured by Wm. J. Diehm

His spastic muscles curl parts of his body into terrible deformities. For example, his foot will twist until the bone sticks out of the flesh. I have cried in despair when I have watched this little boy suffer through the years.

HOWEVER (notice the word is capitalized), Dan will stretch out his deformed hand to touch you and bow his head to pray for you if he sees that you are sad. Of course, no one but God can understand the guttural words he uses. But, he does pray for those who are sad or suffering.

During a recent Christmas cantata at Dan's church, someone wheeled him to the front to sing with the children. Dan looks like he is about 6 years old. He sang in a loud, off-key, unintelligible voice that jarred on the singing of the sweet children. I cried unabashedly for my grandson. At the end of the Christmas program a medical doctor who had been invited to the service came forward to accept the faith. He turned to the audience and said, "I have been an atheist most of my life. No one could convert me. Tonight I listened to the little boy in the wheelchair sing and I was affected in such a way that I could no longer deny the existence of God. If that little boy can sing in his condition, then I can too."

Dan has a terribly deformed body, but there is something about him that draws people. Often he cures my tendency to become depressed. I often think, "God can wield a mighty powerful blow with an awful crooked stick."

3rd: **When you feel totally helpless, do something: pray, smile, lend a hand, encourage, etc.**

Despair at a time of despair only adds to the problem. Despair plus despair equals a catastrophic disaster; while despair plus encouragement can be the beginning of a possibility.

At Pacific State Hospital in Pomona, I entered a room full of grossly deformed abandoned children. I began to cry and felt nauseous. A Spanish lady attendant said to me, "I know how you feel, but it doesn't help my children for you to cry. If you must cry, go elsewhere. If you want to help, we have 69 children who need to be changed, fed, and loved." That day I learned what love meant.

4th: **Encourage legislature to fund research and give special care to those who need it.**

The flies were so bad at Pacific State Hospital that they resembled a black blanket covering the bodies of the helpless. The state would not spend money on these forgotten places of hopeless suffering until a ward attendant invited large groups of college kids and public-spirited people to see what was happening. After many complaints, at last the money came, and fly traps were installed at the doors and windows. The disadvantaged couldn't thank anyone, but God recorded it.

5th: **Have the attitude, "What can I do to help?"**

Many of the severely retarded and deformed got that way when their parents used drugs, alcohol, and sometimes cigarettes. Other damage was caused by the children being cruelly treated or abused. Some were victims of disease and others of accidents and trauma. Psychological and emotional rejection accounts for others and genetic errors also takes its toll. Anyone can be damaged. Let us be grateful when we are not.

Some people see the damaged and get very negative. They say such things as: "How can anyone who cares let such things happen?" I don't know all the answers to such rhetorical questions, but I do know that such questions are often used as an excuse to do nothing. The proper attitude toward heavily damaged people is to say, "I am grateful that I don't have such a condition." And, "What can I do to help?"

6th: **Count the little miracles.**

We all want great miracles to happen; we want to wave a magic wand or say the right prayer and have all illness, all handicaps, and all damage healed immediately, on the spot. Sometimes it does happen that way, and I am ecstatic with joy! But, when the stupendous, spontaneous, glorious miracle does not happen--**How about counting the little miracles?**

- ❤ a brace for a crippled limb
- ❤ a home for an abused child
- ❤ eyeglasses and laser surgery for impaired vision
- ❤ hearing aids for weak ears
- ❤ false teeth for those who haven't any
- ❤ drugs for the epileptic and hyperactive
- ❤ training for the mentally retarded
- ❤ care for the emotionally disturbed
- ❤ medical research for the profoundly injured
- ❤ people who care about those who need help
- ❤ etc. and etc. and etc.

7th: **When dealing with the disadvantaged, put your priorities on optimistic things.**

Deformities can be terrible, but some types of criminal behavior are even worse. The greatest comfort and the greatest power in this world is faith. Happy is the person who realizes how temporary is the body and how permanent is the spirit and they choose not to be damaged by living without faith.

If I were to sum up the meaning of this article on coping with the sick, those with a handicap, and the damaged ones, I would say:

- ■ Do what you can to help those who are disadvantaged, and
- ■ Look for the meaning and the blessing behind every disadvantage.

As I see it there are many methods for healing the sick:

- ✳ Medical doctors through medicine and surgery
- ✳ Good food and scientific nutrition
- ✳ Changing climate and moving from allergic situations
- ✳ A good positive, happy mental attitude
- ✳ Deliverance from underlying psychological problems
- ✳ Elimination of bad habits: drugs, smoking, drinking
- ✳ A program of exercise and physical therapy
- ✳ A challenging job that brings purpose to living
- ✳ A happy family and supportive relationships
- ✳ A harmonious relationship to life
- ✳ The direct action of healing by the Spirit
- ✳ Some things are left to the next life

Whenever we are involved in any of the above activities even a little bit, we shall receive our reward.

Learning to cope with chronic illnesses

Chronic illness may involve repeated episodes of deterioration in which the patient confronts and adjusts to the losses imposed. Example of these losses can include mobility, balance, sexuality, and cognitive function. After working through the normal response to loss, many people are able to find meaning despite being in a physical condition which, prior to the onset of their illness, they would have deemed intolerable and unacceptable. Such patients handle the burden of chronic illness with amazing fortitude and are able to find meaning and value even when extremely disabled.

Individuals who are able to successfully cope with chronic illness share certain characteristics. They generally have good self-esteem and a realistic understanding of their own strengths and weaknesses. They retain an ability to define personal goals and to find gratification in their accomplishments. They retain some sense of control over their own destiny--a belief that they can still influence their world, including the course or symptoms of their illness. They are able to maintain hope.

With chronic illness, hope shifts from cure to coping. If we are chronically ill, besides a cure, we can hope for:
- a reasonable quality of life,
- diminished discomfort,
- maintenance of dignity and a sense of self-worth, and
- retention and enrichment of our loving relationships.

Those who cope successfully typically have strong support from family or "significant others;" they have open communication with those who care and confidence in their healthcare personnel.

SUGGESTIONS FOR PATIENTS

❶ Assume responsibility for your own healthcare. Get as much information from as many sources as you can. Learn enough about your condition so that you know something about its treatment, and what you can and can't do to help yourself. Learn about your medications and recognize the side effects you experience. Try to be as compliant as possible but accept that despite the best of intentions some minor deviations can occur.

❷ Try to define what you have lost. As you do this, you may be able to develop alternate ways to regain, or achieve, at least some of what you have lost. For example, if you have difficulty with balance, work with your physiotherapist to find a walking aid to help you compensate for the loss of balance.

❸ Recognize that behavior that is appropriate for acute illness may not be adaptive when one is chronically ill. Avoid being overly passive or dependent on others as you might be with an acute illness.

❹ Deal with the emotional realities. Chronic illness is unfair. It is sad to lose any amount of freedom, our confidence in our health and future, or our physical abilities. It is natural to weep, feel angry, wonder "why me?" and feel anxiety about an uncertain future. These are painful but normal emotions that generally will fade over time. They may be experienced a number of times, as new symptoms develop, or as the illness deprives us of some valued ability. Most people will, after a period of time, come to terms with their new reality and will not become depressed. If necessary, however, seek help in dealing with these emotions and go forward with your life.

❺ If chronically ill, monitor your thinking. Try to minimize negative or anxiety-producing thinking. Some chronically ill individuals can develop interpretations of events that are unduly negative or anxiety provoking, such as "I can't do it... It's hopeless... I'm defeated" (depressive thoughts), or "I can't stand it... I never know what's happening... I'm hopeless" (anxiety-producing thoughts). Such automatic thoughts only increase the burden under which we function. Find a balance of coping styles.

❻ Identify and avoid vicious cycles. For example, chronic fatigue may make a person feel discouraged and being discouraged may contribute to feelings of uselessness. These, in turn, can contribute to a sense of fatigue, which then increases the feelings of being useless and unhappy. This is a classic vicious cycle.

❼ Try to accept the way things are with you at this moment in time. This does not require an admission that you prefer to be ill, but is simply an acknowledgment of your current situation. With such acceptance comes an ability to plan realistically. Do not electively take on additional burdens or responsibilities without carefully considering the options.

❽ Be positive. Focus on what you can do rather than on what you can't do. Remember that you are a competent individual with many talents and attributes that are inherently yours and will be yours forever. Allow them to flourish.

SUGGESTIONS FOR SIGNIFICANT OTHERS

❶ Recognize that you cannot control or be responsible for the behavior of anyone but yourself. Your task is to try to maximize the likelihood that the patient will behave in an adaptive, realistic manner.

❷ Remember that we don't know anyone else's internal reality. We only know their verbal and nonverbal behaviors. We need to avoid negative self-fulfilling prophesies about the patient. Check your assumptions. Are you sure they can't bathe themselves, do simple housework, go outside for a walk, take a vacation, or hold you close?

❸ As with the patient, it is important to become an expert on the disease and its treatment. The more you know, the more you can help the patient make the right decisions about his/her care, and the more you can monitor your own expectations.

❹ An important aspect of living with someone with a chronic illness is understanding and accepting your own limitations. Even the most loving and attentive people need time for themselves, whether it's to rest, to take care of personal needs, or to be pampered. Give yourself permission to continue to live your life.

❺ Support realistic efforts by the patient to be more independent. Give the person permission to try, even if they fail. Active coping inevitably involves some attempts that don't succeed. However, "errors of commission," which is to say, trying and failing, are much healthier for the chronically ill than "errors of omission," or making no effort at all.

❻ Try not to inflict guilt, rejection, or frustration onto the patient. The illness imposes considerable frustration on both the patient and their loved ones. Recognize this, and try to deal with it in ways that do not increase it.

❼ Monitor your own grief. As your loved one experiences losses (of independence, health, future) you will experience some normal bereavement. You, too, are losing something of value and will grieve. Recognize that this is normal and try not to let it unduly influence your relationship with your loved one.

We hope that these pointers are helpful with the enormous challenge that you and your loved one face. We do want to emphasize that it is important to view chronic illness holistically with the understanding that emotional and psychological support can be just as important as medical treatment.

Material for this article was obtained with permission from the authors of an article entitled Coping with Parkinson's Disease: Cheryl H. Waters, M.D., and William G. Crary, Ph.D., University of Southern California, National Parkinson Foundation Clinic, 1510 San Pablo, Suite 615, Los Angeles, CA 90004.

Older jokes for older folks!

Aged husband and wife sitting on the front porch.
Wife: "I certainly would appreciate a vanilla ice cream cone."
Husband: "I'll hobble right down to the drugstore and get you one, dear."
Wife: "Now, remember, I want vanilla. You always get chocolate. Write it down. Vanilla."
Husband: "I can certainly remember vanilla. The store is only two blocks away."
Husband comes back with a hamburger and hands it to his wife. She looks at it disgustedly. "I knew you'd forget the mustard," she says.

An old man sees a friend sitting on a park bench weeping. "How have things been with you, Bob," he asks his older friend.
"Great. I just married a beautiful young woman."
"Wonderful! But then why are you crying?"
"I can't remember where I live."

An old golfer whose eyesight is failing him fears he will have to give up golf. He can't see where the ball lands. Nonsense, says his friend. Just get an old partner with 20/20 vision. He can tell you where your ball lands. The golfer with poor eyesight is delighted with the suggestion. The next time his friend sees him he asks how the scheme worked. "Well, I found an old friend with excellent eyesight; he had no trouble following the flight of the ball, but by the time we got up the fairway, he's forgotten where it landed."

Anyone who calls a rose by any other name is probably pruning.

A dedicated aging golfer discusses with his minister the desirability of going to Heaven. He asks his minister to communicate with Saint Peter to find out if there is golf in Heaven. The minister agrees. He will let him know as soon as he has heard from Saint Peter. On Sunday the minister draws the golfer aside: "There's good news and bad news. The good news is that there is golf in Heaven. The bad news is that they've got you down for a round next Wednesday."

When George follows his wife to Heaven, he discovers that transportation there is allocated on the basis of marital fidelity. Those departed souls who were most faithful to their spouses are assigned Mercedes and Cadillacs. Those more fallible to Fords and Hondas and even more modest forms of transportation. Still weaker sisters and brothers to bicycles. George, who was unwaveringly faithful to his marriage vows, is given a Cadillac, but the next day a friend sees him sitting in the Cadillac weeping bitterly. "What's wrong, George?" the friend asks. "Your fidelity has been rewarded with the top-of-the-line transportation." "I just saw my wife go by on a bicycle," George says, choking back sobs.

A grandson asks his grandmother a series of impudent questions. "How old are you, grandmother?" "How much do you weigh?" "Why did grandfather leave you?" His grandmother rebuked him, "It is rude to ask such personal questions, you should know better."

Several days later the grandson declares that he has found the answer to all his questions on his grandmother's driver's license. She is 72, weighs 160, and grandfather left her because she got an F in Sex.

An older woman who was sitting by the pool saw an attractive man nearby. She went over and asked, "Why are you so pale? Did you just arrive?"
"I've been in jail for over 30 years," the man replied.
"For what?" she asked.
"Killing my wife," he replied.
"Good. That means you're single?"

Shake any family tree and a few nuts will fall.

Definition of a good salesman:
This salesman sold the farmer two milking machines when the farmer had only one cow. Then he took the cow as a down payment.

The difference between education and experience is really quite simple: Education is what you get from reading the fine print. Experience is what you get from not reading it.

Statistics tell us that one out of four people is mentally unbalanced. If you don't believe it, just think of three of your best friends.

A busload of tourists was passing Arlington Cemetery. One eager passenger who had been firing questions nonstop since the tour began asked," How many are buried here?" An annoyed fellow passenger quickly answered, "All of them."

I read in the newspaper that a couple of California raisins died, and they suspect a cereal killer.

Adam was talking to God and God told him to go over to Eve and give her a big hug. Adam asked, "What's a hug?" On his return God asked Adam how it was and he said, "It was pretty nice." Then God told Adam to give Eve a kiss. On his return he told God that was even better. Then God told Adam he should have sex with Eve to procreate. On his return Adam asked God, "What's a headache?"

We have an older friend that is an excellent judge of other older women, and a fine jury, and a good executioner.

If you find a road map as your placement mat, it could mean two things: it's time to travel or it's time for you to travel.

I guess we are lucky that preachers are not travel agents. As they tell it, Heaven would cause everyone to be clamoring to be on the next boatload.

> He who has a thousand friends
> has not a friend to spare.
> and he who has an enemy
> will meet him everywhere.
> **Ali Ibn-abi-Talib (c. 601-661)**

and older persons

Most older adults are tired of the constant stream of information being distributed about AIDS (acquired immunodeficiency syndrome). Secretly we think that the hullabaloo about AIDS doesn't apply to us--it's those young homosexuals that started it and keep it going.

Unfortunately, the facts are that as many as 10% of all AIDS cases reported have involved people aged 50 and over. And many more older people are believed to be infected, although not yet experiencing symptoms.

Older People Are Vulnerable

With increased age there tends to be a decline in immune system functions, making older people more susceptible to a variety of illnesses such as infections and cancers. Because of these changes in immune function, AIDS may affect older people differently than it does the young. Data from the Centers for Disease Control suggest that most older persons infected with the AIDS virus have developed disease symptoms more quickly than younger patients.

The older population also receives the highest rate of blood transfusions during routine medical care. As a result, the second most common cause of AIDS in people over 50 (after homosexual and bisexual activity) has been exposure to contaminated blood transfusions received before 1985 when the public blood supply was not being screened for the virus. Blood banks now offer the assurance of cleaner blood products; however, the number of older persons who received contaminated blood and who may now be unintentionally infecting spouses or other sexual partners remains unknown.

A further complication is that older AIDS patients who have early symptoms are likely to go undiagnosed. Because early symptoms of AIDS (such as fatigue, loss of appetite, and swollen glands) are similar to other more common illnesses, many people--including health professionals--may dismiss these as symptoms of a minor ailment.

What Is AIDS?

The virus now known as HIV (human immunodeficiency virus) was first isolated in 1983. Two years later in the U.S. the disease caused by the virus was described as AIDS (Acquired Immune Deficiency Syndrome). The disease is so new that no one knows what proportion of people infected with the virus called HIV will go on to develop the disease AIDS. Some estimates suggest that about 50% of HIV--infected people will develop AIDS within 10 years of becoming infected, although many doctors believe that most people infected with the virus will eventually develop AIDS. A recent study from San Francisco put the average incubation period, from the time of the development in the blood of antibodies to HIV to the diagnosis of AIDS, at 9.8 years.

No other disease in history has descended upon the world so suddenly and spread so silently, striking people down in their most productive years. Even if transmission of the human immunodeficiency virus (HIV), which causes AIDS, were to stop tomorrow, there would probably be at least one million new cases of AIDS over the next 5 years.

AIDS is spread from one person to another mainly by exchange of body fluids (blood, semen, saliva, sweat, fecal matter, etc.) during contacts. It is also spread by sharing the use of contaminated needles during the injection of drugs into the bloodstream. For a while, the donation of contaminated blood to blood banks by an infected person was a source. That is now a rarity. More recently, some transmission by heterosexual contacts has occurred and babies are being born with AIDS.

However, AIDS is not easy to catch. It is not spread by mosquito bites, using a public telephone or restroom, being coughed or sneezed on by an infected person, or touching someone with the disease. There has been a slight scare that AIDS can be transmitted by an infected professional such as a careless dentist. Some dentists, reportedly, do not use the sterilization method that kills the virus. Most doctors use stringent cleansing methods and rubber gloves if it is necessary to invade the body of a patient.

At the moment, the strategies for controlling AIDS depend mainly on education and information. But the task of trying to change human behavior, particularly sexual behavior, is a monumental one. That is why scientists are racing to develop a vaccine to protect uninfected people from the virus. Researchers are also trying to design drugs that, if they do not cure AIDS, could at least keep the virus in abeyance in the body, preventing or delaying the onset of severe immunodeficiency.

It is possible that before this article is published some striking discovery will lessen the threat of AIDS. Researchers today seem to be quietly confident that before long they will be able to develop a range of drugs that would treat AIDS and prevent people infected with HIV from developing immunodeficiency. Today, treatment for AIDS usually involves some form of drug therapy, such as AZT (azidothymidine), which has been used to prolong life. But we must remember that at the present time we are dealing with a terminal illness.

In the meantime, the responsibility for preventing the spread of AIDS rests on each individual's behavior (for example, making the choice to use condoms when sexually involved with someone other than a mutually faithful, uninfected partner).

People with AIDS should stay in touch with a doctor who is well-informed about the latest AIDS research. For help in finding the name of an expert, call a local university medical school's department of infectious disease or call the National AIDS hotline (1-800-342-AIDS). Other referral sources that offer information on transmission, prevention, testing, and a variety of written materials are:

American Red Cross
AIDS Public Information Office
1730 E. Street, N.W.
Washington, D.C. 20006

National AIDS Information Clearinghouse
P.O. Box 6003
Rockville, MD 20850
1-800-458-5231

National Institute of Allergy & Infectious Diseases
Office of Communications
Building 31, Room 7A32
Bethesda, MD 20892

National Institute on Aging
Public Information Office
Federal Building, Room 6C12
Bethesda, MD 20892
(301) 496-1752

The common crippler of elderly people

Sometimes people use the word *arthritis* to describe an ache or pain or anything that hurts. But in medicine *arthritis* means *inflammation of the joint*. It is taken from the Greek word *arthron* for joint and *itis* for inflammation.

What a simple word for a condition called the nation's primary crippler. More than 37 million Americans--one in every seven--suffer from arthritis. It is one of the oldest diseases known to man. It belongs to the rheumatic group that differentiates into 100 various kinds and forms of arthritic and rheumatic diseases ranging from rheumatoid's ravaging condition to osteoarthritis, **the common crippler of elderly people,** to tendinitis, the scourge of weekend athletes. While the term *rheumatism* generally refers to the painful inflammatory conditions in the various parts of the body--like lumbago, sciatica, neuritis, etc.--the term *arthritis* refers specifically to inflammation of the joints.

The most common symptom of arthritis is that the joints at first become painful. The pain can have many degrees of intensity and it can come and go. Sometimes it disappears for months, even years, then it returns again. At first the pain could be a feeling of numbness and stiffness. Sometimes a creaking and cracking of the joints is felt. Often the joints become swollen and inflamed. Pain can be dull but also very severe, occurring mostly at night and in the morning.

A second symptom of arthritis is inflammation, which is marked by four signs: swelling, redness, heat, and pain. The inflammation is in a joint, which is a junction where two bones meet. There are 68 joints in the body composed of cartilage, space, capsule, synovium, and ligaments. To avoid friction and strain during movements, the ends of the bones are covered with a smooth, white, glistening, very tough, slippery, elastic tissue called cartilage. Between the bones is a space and a capsule, which is a bag of soft tissue filled with synovium fluid to cushion pressure and lubricate the joint. The bones are held together and aligned by rope-like structures called ligaments. Most arthritis can be a minor problem; but sometimes joint inflammation can cause major pain.

> When we are well, we all have good advice for those who are ill.
> - Terence

A third symptom is impairment. With the onset of arthritis the normal functions of the joints are impaired. They become inflamed, enlarged, and swollen; or they may shrivel up and dry. The cartilages can lose their elasticity and become dry and brittle. The secretions of the synovial membrane may diminish and with progression of the disease cease completely. The joints thus will dry out, become congested, rough, and stiff. Also the ligaments and the muscles, which surround the joint, become affected, inflamed, and progressively lose their tone and flexibility.

These symptoms are followed by profound and destructive changes in the joints. Due to faulty metabolism, excessive amounts of calcium and other minerals are deposited in the joints. Sometimes osteoporosis, or leaching of the calcium and other minerals from the bones, can cause severe destruction of bones and joints.

All these changes are usually accompanied by swelling and increased pain during motion. Eventually the pain becomes so unbearable that the patient will be unable to move the affected parts of his body.

ARTHRITIS CAN APPEAR IN MORE THAN 100 FORMS. SOME EXAMPLES:

OSTEOARTHRITIS
Symptoms: A wearing-out of the joints; aches, swelling, stiffness, especially in hips, knees, spine, fingers.
Prevalence: 16 million mostly aging Americans; almost 3 times as many women as men.

OA, also called degenerative joint disease, involves a fraying of bone and cartilage, which then becomes inflamed. Traditionally, scientists attributed the phenomenon to simple wear and tear on joints--an inevitable consequence of aging. But that conventional wisdom is changing, too. As joints are used, they release enzymes that digest cartilage; at the same time, cells within the cartilage busily repair the loss. Scientists now think that osteoarthritis may develop when the breakdown races ahead of the repairs, either because too much enzyme is released, or the repair process is slowed, or both, and believe that if they could block the enzyme, or stimulate cartilage, they could attack the disease itself.

There are 16 million osteoarthritis sufferers, in which walking across a room, turning a doorknob, or making a cup of coffee can require a supreme effort of will. The pain is not necessarily visible, so employers and loved ones often don't sympathize.

Divorce is three times more common in couples where one spouse has the disease. Depression is rampant; so is anger, anxiety, loss of self-esteem; and the inability to enjoy life, either due to immobility or the debilitating side effects of medications.

RHEUMATOID ARTHRITIS
Symptoms: Inflammation of joints; acute pain; fatigue; weight loss.
Prevalence: 2.1 million; more than twice as many women as men. RA usually affects up to 15 or 20 joints at one time.

RA can produce such general symptoms as weakness, fatigue, and loss of appetite. Many other tissues may be involved including the lungs, spleen, skin, and sometimes the heart. **However, the major problems of most patients involve joint destruction and pain**. The condition is characterized by alternating periods of remission, during which symptoms disappear, and then reappear. The primary target of rheumatoid arthritis is the synovium, the joint lining that becomes inflamed, rough, granulated, and swollen, causing pain in the joints. It is assumed that a virus may trigger an immune reaction that causes pain and swelling and results in synovial destruction. Stiffness is a major complaint, and as the condition progresses, deformities may appear.

GOUT
Symptoms: Swelling of large toe, spreading to other joints, attacks of sudden acute pain.
Prevalence: 1 million, four times as many men as women.

Gout is an acutely painful condition that usually attacks middle-aged men, although it can occur in women after menopause. It was historically blamed on rich food and too much wine; but now we know it is caused by excessive uric acid. In an attack of gout, excess uric acid in the blood forms needle-like crystals that irritate and inflame one or more joints in the body, particularly the big toe. It can be controlled by medication.

ANKYLOSING SPONDYLITIS
Symptoms: Loss of movement in back legs, collarbone; abnormal curvature of spine; lung and heart problems.
Prevalence: 318,000 Americans, two and a half times as many men as women.

Ankylosing spondylitis is an inflammatory disease of the spine. It is a hereditary ailment that usually afflicts men in young adulthood. Small joints of the spine and sacroiliac are attacked first, making pain in the lower back and legs an early symptom. Other joints, especially the hips and shoulders, also may become involved. Without treatment, the spine may become progressively stiffer until it is completely rigid. Curvature of the spine may develop, forcing the victim into a stooped position.

PSORIATIC ARTHRITIS
Symptoms: Inflammation, stiffness in both of the symmetrical small joints, hands, elbows, hips; fever; pleurisy.
Prevalence: 160,000 Americans; strikes small percentage of people suffering from psoriasis.

SYSTEMIC LUPUS
Symptoms: High fever; rash; anemia; hair loss; kidney dysfunction.
Prevalence: 131,000 Americans; eight times as many women as men.

LYME DISEASE
Symptoms: Rash in tick-bite area; fatigue; shooting pains; stiffness in joints; visual and memory disturbances.
Prevalence: 14,000 cases since 1980.

TREATMENT--Many victims of arthritis consult a gamut of rheumatologists, physiatrists, neurologists, orthopedists, podiatrists, surgeons, and chiropractors, only to hear conflicting advice or patronizing platitudes because science has no cure for most forms of the condition. Arthritis sufferers spend more than $1 billion a year on dubious cures--sadly, $25 for every $1 devoted to legitimate research. One million new cases are diagnosed every year. Together, the related illnesses account for 27 million lost workdays annually, and cost the U.S. economy an estimated $8.6 billion a year, including $4.4 billion in hospital and nursing home services.

QUACKS--Arthritis, next to cancer, is the disease most susceptible to quackery, probably because of its custom of going into remission. The treatments are often frustratingly slow or ineffective, so people get desperate. Some quack treatments have included rubbing the household solvent WD40 on elbows and knees--*people figure it will do the same for their joints as it does for door hinges.*

MEDICATION AND EXERCISE--Doctors usually prescribe analgesics to fight the pain and inflammation, and specific exercise to preserve the "range of motion" in afflicted joints and to strengthen the muscles that support them. An imbalance may occur with a misalignment in the body that places excess stress on joints. Specially designed programs of exercise and physical therapy are bringing relief to some patients. Massage, heat, cold, and biofeedback can also bring temporary relief.

DRUGS--They are the current acceptable treatment program for arthritis and new ones are constantly hitting the market. In 1988 the FDA approved methotrexate, an anticancer drug, for use in cases of rheumatoid arthritis. In 1989 another new drug, Cytotec, went on sale, promising to relieve the common stomach irritation caused by aspirin and other nonsteroidal anti-inflammatory drugs.

SURGERY--The perfection of actual joint replacement, including computer-designed custom prostheses, has brought many victims the first mobility and relief they have had in years. When all else fails, reconstructive surgery can help redirect musculoskeletal forces and clean out debris from afflicted joints. Innovations in joint-replacement surgery represent a quantum leap in the ability to help people who have significant damage.

COUNSELING--Physical and emotional stress, fatigue, pain, stiffness, and disfigurement caused by arthritis and related musculoskeletal diseases all can interfere with sexual functioning. Education or counseling of patients with disabilities often can solve sexual difficulties, enhance the patient's self-image, and lead to enriched interpersonal relationships.

RESEARCH--Research holds the best hope for the future. For example, scientists suspect that rheumatoid arthritis is actually a disorder of the immune system, in which the body's natural defenses mistakenly seem to turn on bone and cartilage as if they were foreign invaders. It may be that bacteria and viruses produce proteins so similar to joint tissue that they trick the body's immune defenses into attacking healthy joints as well as the invading organism. If theories like this are true, then the cure is not far behind.

FUTURE--The outlook for the future is optimistic for the cure of arthritis.

For more information on arthritis write:

Public Affairs Officer
NIH
Building 31, Room 5C-35
9000 Rockville Pike
Bethesda, MD 20892

Drugs used in the treatment of arthritis

Most forms of arthritis cannot be prevented or cured, so the goals of treatment are to relieve pain and maintain or restore the function of the arthritic joint. A treatment program may include rest, weight control, heat therapy, exercise, and drug therapy. Appropriate treatment depends on the type of arthritis, the stage of the disease, and the general health of the patient.

Nonsteroidal Anti-Inflammatory Drugs (NSAIDs)
NSAIDs are commonly used to relieve arthritis pain. These drugs block the production of prostaglandins, chemicals in the body that cause pain and inflammation, which is the stiffness, swelling, and warmth felt by people with arthritis. Although some NSAIDs are available without a prescription, most are prescription drugs. It often takes a few days to a week before NSAIDs start to work and 2 to 3 weeks before the full benefits of treatment are felt.

Some of the most frequently used NSAIDs are listed in the table. These drugs are divided into two groups: salicylates and nonsalicylates. Although both groups of drugs have similar pain-relieving effects, they may have somewhat different side effects.

Frequently Used NSAIDs

Salicylates

Generic Name	Sample Brand Names
Aspirin	Bayer, Bufferin, Easprin, Ecotrin
Choline magnesium trisalicylate	Trilisate
Choline salicylate	Arthropan
Diflunisal	Dolobid
Magnesium salicylate	Magan
Salicylsalicylic acid	Disalcid, Mono-Gesic

Nonsalicylates

Generic Name	Sample Brand Names
Diclofenac	Voltaren
Fenoprofen	Nalfon
Flurbiprofen	Ansaid
Ibuprofen	Motrin, Rufen, and over-the-counter brands such as Advil, Nuprin, Medipren
Indomethacin	Indocin
Ketoprofen	Orudis
Meclofenamate	Meclomen
Mefenamic acid	Ponstel
Naproxen	Naprosyn
Naproxen sodium	Anaprox
Prioxicam	Feldene
Sulindac	Clinoril
Tolmetin	Tolectin

Side Effects of NSAIDs--Along with much-needed pain relief, NSAIDs may cause unwanted side effects in some people. However, side effects do not occur in everyone. They are listed here so that you will know they are possible and so that you can recognize them early and report them to your doctor. In some cases, it may be necessary to adjust treatment to keep side effects to a minimum.

NSAIDs can cause stomach ulcers. Because ulcers sometimes don't cause symptoms, it's important for people taking NSAIDs to see their doctor for regular checkups. Other stomach problems caused by these drugs include heartburn, nausea, stomach pain, vomiting, diarrhea, and occasionally gastrointestinal (GI) bleeding. GI bleeding, which can be especially serious in older people, is signaled by black or very dark stools or blood in the stool. NSAIDs also can cause headaches, dizziness, and blurred vision.

Coated aspirin tablets and long-acting aspirin products may lessen stomach irritation. NSAIDs should be taken with a full glass of water (or milk), food, or antacids to reduce stomach upset. In addition, an antiulcer drug--misoprostol (brand name Cytotec)--is approved for preventing stomach ulcers that can be brought on by NSAIDs in people at high risk of ulcer complications (for example, older people or those who have had ulcers in the past). Ulcers and other serious stomach problems are more common in smokers and people who drink alcohol while taking these drugs. People who have stomach problems should see their doctor as soon as possible.

Corticosteroids
Corticosteroids also may reduce arthritis inflammation. These drugs closely resemble cortisone, a natural hormone produced by the body. They can be taken by mouth or by injection directly into a stiff, swollen joint.

Although corticosteroids rapidly relieve the pain, swelling, and redness caused by arthritis, long-term use of these powerful drugs has serious side effects. Lowered resistance to infection, indigestion, weight gain, loss of muscle mass and strength, mood changes, blurred vision, cataracts, diabetes, thinning of bones (osteoporosis), and increased blood pressure can be caused by this treatment. Other side effects may develop and should be discussed with your doctor. Also, serious stomach problems may occur in people who take corticosteroids along with NSAIDs.

Commonly Prescribed Corticosteroids

Generic Name	Sample Brand Names
Betamethasone	Celestone
Cortisone	Cortone
Dexamethasone	Decadron
Hydrocortisone	Hydrocortone
Methylprednisolone	Medrol
Prednisolone	Hydeltrasol
Prednisone	Deltasone
Triamcinolone	Aristocort

> I am interested in physical medicine because my father was. I am interested in medical research because I believe in it. I am interested in arthritis because I have it.
>
> — Bernard Baruch

Disease-Modifying Drugs

Researchers believe that disease-modifying, antirheumatic agents slow the progress of rheumatoid arthritis, but these drugs are not used for osteoarthritis. These prescription drugs include gold compounds, D-penicillamine, and antimalarial medications.

Gold compounds can help people with mild to moderate rheumatoid arthritis. Auranofin (Ridaura) is taken by mouth. Aurothioglucose (Solganol) and gold sodium thiomalate (Myochrysine) are available in injection form. It may be 2 to 6 months before relief is felt. Possible side effects are blood in the urine, easy bruising, sores in the mouth, skin rash, and numbness in the hands and feet. Diarrhea often occurs in those who take gold by mouth, and many people receiving injectable gold notice a metallic taste.

Penicillamine (Depen and Cuprimine) is also used to treat rheumatoid arthritis. This drug may take 2 to 6 months to work. Side effects include blood in the urine, fever, joint pain, skin rash, sores in the mouth, easy bruising, weight gain, and rarely muscle weakness. People taking gold compounds or penicillamine should be checked regularly by their doctor.

Hydroxychloroquine (Plaquenil) and other drugs originally developed to treat malaria can be used to relieve swelling, stiffness, and joint pain caused by rheumatoid arthritis. People taking these drugs should have regular eye exams because these medicines can permanently damage the retina (the light-sensitive tissue at the back of the eye). Diarrhea, headaches, loss of appetite, skin rash, and stomach pain are other possible side effects. Liver problems may develop in people who drink alcohol while taking antimalarial drugs.

Immunosuppressants

The immune system normally protects the body against foreign invaders such as viruses. Some researchers believe that rheumatoid arthritis is an autoimmune disease, a disease in which the immune system reacts against the body's own tissues. Immunosuppressants, drugs that suppress the immune system, can ease the symptoms of rheumatoid arthritis. Azathioprine (Imuran) and methotrexate are immunosuppressants used to treat this form of arthritis. Side effects, which include mouth sores, infection, fever, chills, sore throat, nausea, diarrhea, and unusual tiredness, should be reported to your doctor.

Gout Medications

Uric acid is the normal waste product found in the body. When uric levels become extremely high, crystals form in and around joints, causing gout. The pain and swelling caused by this form of arthritis is treated with two types of drugs: one to reduce inflammation and the other to lower uric acid levels. For example, colchicine blocks inflammation. Allopurinol (Zyloprim and Lopurin) reduces uric acid production. Sulfinpyrazone (Anturane) and probenecid (Benemid) increase uric acid elimination. Allopurinol, sulfinpyrazone, and probenecid can help prevent gout attacks, but they must be taken for several months to work effectively. (In fact, allopurinol can actually make gout worse if this drug is started during an attack.) Common side effects may include diarrhea, nausea, vomiting, stomach pain, and a rash.

A warning about NSAIDs

Over-the-Counter Drugs

Over-the-counter (OTC) products such as aspirin and ibuprofen (e.g., Advil, Nuprin, and Medipren) temporarily relieve minor arthritis pain. "Extra strength" and "arthritis formula" aspirin products contain more aspirin in each tablet than regular aspirin. As with prescription drugs, these drugs can cause side effects, particularly when directions are not followed carefully. For example, long-term, high-dose use of ibuprofen or aspirin may cause liver or kidney damage. Do not take OTC products for long periods without consulting a doctor. Combinations of OTC products, or OTC products and prescription drugs, should never be taken without checking with your doctor first.

In addition, some OTC ointments offer short-term relief of minor arthritis pain. However, these ointments, which are rubbed over painful joints, do not reduce swelling and should not be used for long periods of time.

Taking Arthritis Drugs Safely

Because arthritis drugs may interact with other types of medicine, it is important to let your doctor know if you are taking any other prescription or over-the-counter medications. Be sure to follow your doctor's instructions exactly when taking your medicine—take only the amount specified, ask what to do if you miss a dose, and do not suddenly stop taking your medicine without consulting your doctor. It is also important to keep all appointments with your doctor so that your progress can be checked regularly.

The latest news reports claim there are nearly 68 million prescriptions a year written for NSAIDs in the United States alone and over 2 million (15% of the elderly) take NSAIDs. The prescription NSAID Motrin, whose generic name is ibuprofen, is available over-the-counter (without a prescription) as Advil, Nuprin, Motrin IB, and Medipren. These OTC forms of NSAID are limited to 200-milligram tablets and carry instructions to take no more than six tablets a day.

NSAIDs are said to be capable of damaging the stomach by first breaking down the protective inner lining of the stomach. And second, they may suppress body chemicals that protect the lining. The FDA warning in March 1990 read, "Serious gastrointestinal toxicity such as bleeding, ulceration, and perforations can occur at any time, with or without warning symptoms, in patients treated chronically with NSAID therapy."

The FDA suggests that as many as 10,000 to 20,000 people a year die of NSAID complications and 200,000 are hospitalized. A new drug called Cytotec was approved by the FDA for the specific purpose of reducing the risk of bleeding from NSAIDs. Some claim Cytotec should only be taken by those who already have a bleeding problem. To date, only limited studies have been done as to the side effects of Cytotec.

The conclusion: First, follow the exact instructions of your doctor. Second, if taking over-the-counter NSAIDs, scientists claim they are safe IF taken as directed. If you have questions or concerns it's always best to consult with your doctor.

Without a cure--pain seeks relief--or only a promise

Every year, at least 1 million people in the United States learn that they have arthritis. Virtually everyone who lives long enough will know the pain of arthritis. Some 97% of those past the age of 60 will have arthritis severe enough to be seen on an X-ray.

Why Do Unproven Remedies Flourish?
With so little being spent on legitimate arthritis research, it is ironic that so much is spent on unproven arthritic remedies ($3 billion). Some unproven remedies are an outright fraud. Others hang on to a scintilla of credibility that requires neutrality at least until they are once and for all proved either to be effective or ineffective. According to the Arthritis Foundation quackery succeeds because:

➤ There is widespread lack of understanding about arthritis.

➤ There is no cure at present.

➤ There is tremendous pain associated with the disease.

➤ There are so many people suffering that promoters have a huge market.

➤ The symptoms of arthritis come and go like the tide, allowing people to connect a disappearance with a phony remedy they have just been taking.

Another reason that should be added is the so-called placebo effect. This is the power of the mind over the body. People who want to get better and have faith that they will get better often do get better--temporarily. The placebo effect is a scientifically proven phenomenon. People often improve in controlled tests getting "sugar pills" instead of the real medicine. So, the placebo effect clouds the picture of what does and does not help arthritics.

Still another reason for the success of unproven remedies is that there is very little by way of policing the problem. Penalties for selling unproven remedies are small. There is little by way of enforcement going on at either the state or the national level. The chances of being caught and prosecuted are slim. In short, there is little risk and a tremendous amount of money to be made in selling hope to the desperate. The Arthritis Foundation offers these guidelines for spotting the unscrupulous promoters:

✔ They may offer a "special" or "secret" formula or device for "curing" arthritis.

✔ They advertise "case histories" and testimonials from satisfied patients.

✔ They promise (or imply) a quick and easy cure.

✔ They claim to know the cause of arthritis and talk about "cleansing" your body of "poisons" and "pepping up" your health, or claim surgery, X-rays, and drugs prescribed by a physician are unnecessary.

✔ They accuse the medical establishment of deliberately thwarting progress, or of persecuting them, but they don't allow their method to be tested in tried and proven ways.

Questionable Drugs Said to Cure Arthritis
There are millions of chemical preparations that have been offered for use in alleviating arthritis pain or the underlying causes of arthritis. There are some that have been proven to work. Unfortunately, their relief is temporary. None of the products is a "cure." Equally unfortunate, the products sometimes have serious side effects. The sad part of the story is that the products that are helpful are outnumbered by a ratio of 10,000 to 1 by the products that are not.

Some of the drugs that had been pushed as arthritis remedies over the past 20 years and were found to be unhelpful, sometimes even dangerous, are:

✱ **Cocaine**--Although hard to believe, a California physician up until 1980, when authorities intervened, was offering cocaine as a remedy for arthritis. Few doubt the pain-killing effects of the drug.

✱ **Defencin**--This drug was sold for the relief of arthritis. It contained aspirin along with phenyltoloxamine dihydrogen citrate, an antihistamine, and glyceryl guaicolate. Again, this was a case where the extra ingredients added little to the relief but a great deal to the cost.

✱ **DMSO** (dimethyl sulfoxide)--It is an industrial solvent that acts as an analgesic when rubbed on the skin. There is little doubt but that it kills pain to some extent. The drug is also useful as a carrier in that it penetrates the skin and finds its way rapidly into the bloodstream. Some evidence indicates the drug may be useful in the treatment of arthritis, particularly osteoarthritis, which is not accompanied by inflammation. The Arthritis Foundation takes the position that DMSO is another unproven remedy. However, it has supported scientific studies to determine the drug's effectiveness. The House Committee on Aging reported that there is little doubt that the drug is safe. The FDA points out that because of its unique quality as a carrier it could cause

problems. They say an individual who had insecticide on his hands, and who then applies DMSO, might soon have the poison in his bloodstream. The FDA is also concerned about the purity.

✱ **Doxyhydren**--This product was advertised with the statement "Guaranteed Help for Arthritis and Rheumatism." The ingredients analyzed chemically revealed water, sodium, and dihydroxyethylglycinate. Medical opinion stated the product cannot have any pharmacologic value at all. Texas officials took it off the market.

✱ **DPA**--D-phenylalanine or DPA is a synthetic modification of a naturally occurring amino acid that some people allege empowers the body's own pain-reducing system. The Arthritis Foundation emphasizes that this is an unproven remedy and there is no scientific evidence that the drug is effective.

✱ **Mericin**--In the early 1960s this drug, which was a combination of salicylamide and gebtustic acid, was sold. It was found to be less effective than aspirin, but sold at five times the cost.

✱ **Norkon**--Norkon was a drug promoted with ads saying "Relieves Pain Faster with No Aftereffects." The FTC filed a suit claiming false advertising since the active ingredient was only aspirin.

✱ **Procaine (Novocaine)**--Gerovital H-3 is an old-age and arthritis "remedy" that has been a matter of controversy for many years. The drug is procaine and there is no scientific evidence it is effective in treating arthritis.

✱ **Tetracycline**--Tetracycline is an effective drug approved for use by the FDA to fight bacteria. It is an antibiotic. The drug has been used in a controversial way to treat arthritis. A physician who is a well-respected member of the medical profession and who specializes in arthritis, began using this drug and enjoyed some success in caring for an arthritic gorilla. After a series of injections the gorilla did improve. The Arthritis Foundation remains skeptical, stating approval of this therapy for humans should await proof of effectiveness in scientific studies.

Hormone Cures and Therapy
Hormones are substances produced by various glands in the body. Perhaps best known are estrogen, the female sex hormone, and progesterone, its male counterpart. Not surprisingly, there have been attempts to prescribe one or more hormones individually or in combination as a cure for arthritis. Some research suggested that hormones may have benefit. Unfortunately, the research

was blown out of proportion. The Arthritis Foundation takes the position that this and other hormone cures have been shown to be worthless and dangerous. One Foundation report emphasized that estrogen has been publicized as a possible cancer-causing agent. Following are examples of these kinds of products:

✳ **Specifex**--A Federal District Court banned the sale of the so-called adrenal hormone cream saying that its curative powers were unproven and that false and misleading claims were made about it.

✳ **Rheuma-Cream**--The active ingredient was epinephrine hydrochloride. It is similar to Specifex.

✳ **Liefcort**--It is the name of a highly controversial remedy developed by Dr. Robert Liefmann in the early 1960s in Montreal. Patients lined up to take the cure, which was a combination of cortisone (prednisone) with estradiol and testosterone (female and male sex hormones). There has been a protracted legal battle concerning this drug, which is being distributed in clinics in various parts of the country. It has been sold under the name of Rheumatril as well as the Leifmann Balanced Hormone method. The FDA said that Liefcort was an irrational mixture of potent ingredients and that it was dangerous to a person who uses it even when under medical supervision. The drug has been banned in the U.S. and Canada.

Questionable Dietary Cures for Arthritis
The subject of diet has attracted more claims of sure-fire cures for arthritis than any other category of unproven remedies. It is one of the oldest claims. Folk medicine from almost every culture has offered recipes for preventing and curing arthritis.

Today, arthritis is attributed to various causes including deficiency (vitamins or minerals), excess (fats), toxins or poisons (acid foods or animal products), pollutants (food additives), allergy (vegetables of the nightshade family), and improper habits (drinking water with meals). Some diets contradict others. One source claims, for example, citrus fruits are bad for arthritis, while another promotes citrus fruits for relieving symptoms.

As the Arthritis Foundation notes, people insist on believing that special diets or exotic diets are helpful in arthritis. "If there was a relationship between diet and arthritis, it would have been discovered long ago. The simple fact is, there is no scientific evidence that any food or vitamin deficiency has anything to do with causing arthritis and no evidence that any food or vitamin is effective in 'curing' it."

According to experts, more people are susceptible to false promotion of foods than any other product in the health field. Frederick Stare, M.D., professor of nutrition at Harvard University, describes the four great myths in nutrition as follows:

❶ That all diseases stem from a faulty diet;

❷ That soil depletion causes malnutrition and disease;

❸ That our food is worthless and overprocessed; and

❹ That subclinical deficiency diseases abound in our population.

Following is a list of some of the foods either implicated falsely as causing arthritis or falsely promised to cure the disease. The one exception to the rule is gouty arthritis. Certain foods can increase the uric acid levels in the body and cause gout, which is classified as a form of arthritis; such food should be avoided.

✳ **Dessicated Liver Tablets**--In response to an ad (along with a check) you receive a typewritten diet. Postal authorities stopped it as it made false claims in promising a cure for arthritis.

✳ **Devitamized Foods**--The promoter claimed that arthritis was caused by eating concentrated carbohydrates in excess. He recommended a diet, daily enema, and you purchase a stainless steel juicer for $167.95.

✳ **Elimination Diets** (food allergies)--There are many proponents including some reputable physicians who assert that allergy is the cause of arthritis. Their research is directed not only at foods but at drugs, chemicals, inhalants, and other products of the environment such as fluorescent lights and gases generated by a new carpet. One course of treatment in certain clinics is highly controversial. It involves taking the patient off of all the foods and drugs for a period of 7-10 days. After this time foods are slowly reintroduced until an allergic reaction is discovered. The patient is then told to avoid that food. Of course, the cure can take months and the cost of treatment can run anywhere up to $5,000. According to some people, "nightshade" foods are the definite cause of arthritis. These foods include the tomato, the white potato, peppers, eggplant, and tobacco. The theory holds that the elimination of these foods will "cure" arthritis. Comments the Arthritis Foundation: "There is no shred of evidence for the effectiveness of the no nightshade diet." Another says the problem is food additives. Still another says flour and

flour products including spaghetti and pasta are the problem. Another says processed sugar is the culprit. Coffee, tea, wine, beer, and soft drinks are also on the suspect list. The Arthritis Foundation says of this allergy theory and the clinic's treatment of it: "It is not quackery but falls into the category of unproven methods of treatment of arthritis. (We are) not aware of any clinical tests demonstrating that allergic food elimination diets are effective in arthritis."

✳ **Fasting**--not a recommended therapy for any type of arthritis.

✳ **Green Lipped Mussel Extract**--sold under various names such as Seatone, Freedon, and Aquatone.

✳ **Honegar**--A national best-seller called *Folk Medicine: A Vermont Doctor's Guide to Good Health*, advocated honey and vinegar as a cure. Sale of the book was soon prohibited.

✳ **Honey Al-Fa Tea**--The AMA says "(N)either alfalfa nor honey, nor apple cider vinegar, either singly or in combination, is known to have any effect on diseases which affect bodily joints."

✳ **Low-fat Diets**--have no benefit for arthritis.

✳ **Macrobiotic Diet** (Zen Macrobiotics)--claims that by eating a proper balance of yin and yang foods restores the balance of the body. Diets are not anti-arthritic.

✳ **Natural and Organic Foods**--claims that organically grown foods have more nutrients to promote health because they lack harmful chemicals. They are of no benefit for arthritis.

✳ **Raw (Unpasteurized) Milk**--no special benefit for arthritis.

✳ **The Arthritis Cookbook**--In this book Dr. Collin Dong revealed how he conquered his own arthritis by eliminating fat and chemical additives from his diet. Under his diet certain foods are prohibited. The Arthritis Foundation found in a double-blind study with arthritis patients that neither Dr. Dong's diet or a more standard one showed any changes in the disease.

✳ **Vegetarian Diets**--controlled studies have not shown these diets benefit those with arthritis, although they have other benefits.

✳ **Vis Vitae Powder or VVP**--made of steer liver, steer muscle, and natural herbs in soybean meal. The Arthritis Foundation says VVP would not have any medical value for an arthritis sufferer.

More information on ineffective cures for arthritis

Nutritional Supplements

Vitamins are organic molecules that for the most part are not made by the human body but are required to sustain normal metabolism. Minerals such as iron, zinc, copper, and aluminum play a similar role. Humans obtain vitamins and minerals through what they eat. Therefore, there is no need for vitamin or mineral supplements if an individual is eating a well-balanced diet. By and large, the American diet is fairly balanced.

In the literature of the questionable practitioners, a shortage of vitamin A, vitamin B3 (niacin), vitamin B12, vitamin B6 (pyridoxine), vitamin C, vitamin E, and sometimes a combination of all of the above (or several of them) constitute the cause of arthritis. Similarly, the ads of promoters insist a shortage of copper, zinc, iron, lead, nickel, tin, manganese, molybdenum, manganese, or cesium is the cause of arthritis. There is no medical evidence to suggest that the absence of any of these or other vitamins and minerals is the cause of arthritis. A classic example of this quackery calls for using copper bracelets--one of the oldest medical swindles. Some common nutritional supplements claimed to help arthritics include:

* **Amino Acids**--Histidine, glutothione, and cysteine are said to reduce the symptoms of arthritis. They have no benefit for arthritis.
* **Anti-oxidants**--promoted for the treatment of arthritis and other diseases, they have no real benefit for arthritis.
* **Cod Liver Oil**--no scientific evidence that it helps arthritis.
* **Coenzyme Q-10**--said to reduce inflammation in arthritis (promoted as an antioxidant). There is no evidence as a benefit for arthritis.
* **Evening Primrose Oil**--has not been shown to benefit arthritic patients.
* **Fish Oil**--mild effect against arthritis symptoms, requires 15-20 tablets per day. It is best to add fish to the diet.
* **Germanium** (also name GE-132)--a trace mineral, with no evidence that it has any benefit for arthritis.
* **Megavitamin Therapy**--studies failed to support claims of benefit for arthritic patients--potential of overdose and serious illness.
* **Propolis, Royal Jelly, Bee Pollen**--no benefit for arthritis.
* **Selenium** (promoted as an anti-oxidant)--no help for arthritis.
* **Superoxide Dismutase** (SOS; Oregotein)--no value for arthritis.
* **Vitamin A and Beta-carotene** (Retinol)--Megadoses claim to boost the immune system and help treat arthritis; no known benefit for arthritis.
* **Vitamin B Complex**--promoted as an antidote to "stress," promoted for arthritis including pyroxidine, niacin, folic acid, pantothenic acid, and riboflavin. Scientific studies show no benefit in either reducing pain or improving joint functioning.
* **Vitamin C** (Ascorbic acid)--megadoses used, no benefit for arthritis.
* **Vitamin D**--not useful for arthritis patients.
* **Vitamin E**--no benefit for arthritis.
* **Zinc**--not useful for arthritis.

NOTE: Any OTC vitamins (especially A, B complex, C, D) can be toxic in megadoses. Take recommended doses on bottle and no more, unless instructed by a physician.

Herbal Remedies

Herbs have been an important part of traditional folk medicine in all cultures. When modern medical treatment fails to cure a disorder, the disillusioned person may turn to a remedy in the belief that an herb was successfully used for centuries.

There are literally millions of plant varieties in existence. Many plants have medicinal value and at one time all drugs came from natural origins. Among these are digitalis, a heart medicine obtained from the foxglove plant; resperine, a tranquilizer and blood pressure-lowering agent from the snakeroot plant; quinine, an antimalarial drug from the bark of the cinchona shrub; atropine, which is obtained from the deadly belladonna plant; and ephedrine, a nasal decongestant and central nervous system stimulant obtained from the ephedra shrub.

While it is true that common substances found in plants do have a medicinal effect, the effect is not always predictable. Herbal compounds taken innocently can result in serious injury or even death. Great care, therefore, has to be used in the selection of "herbal teas," some of which will counter the effects of drugs taken by the elderly and sometimes interact with them to produce toxic side effects.

The simple fact is that no plant, herb, or spice is a cure for arthritis either by itself or in combination with other ingredients. Many of these concoctions, either in the form of tea, pills, or ointments, are harmless. They do, however, sometimes have positive medical applications for particular problems. They can also have serious side effects. The list of herbs and plants said to have curative powers in arthritis is long and includes: allspice, basil leaves, bitterroot, burdock, caraway seed, cayenne pepper, dill, licorice, nutmeg, pine bark, ragweed, rose hips, wintergreen, and wormwood. Here are a few samples of products falsely billed as cures:

* **Alfalfa or Alfalfa Seed Cures**--no benefit.
* **Aloe Vera**--unproven remedy.
* **Arnica**--contained in ointment form, no evidence that it helps arthritis; poisonous to the heart if taken internally.
* **Chaparral Tea**--neither a cancer nor arthritis cure.
* **Chuifong Toukwan**--very dangerous product; side effects can result in death.
* **Coix Combination** (Ma-huang contains it)--promoted for arthritis, is said to relieve symptoms of stiffness and swelling in the knees and ankles, purity questionable, possible severe side effects.
* **Devil's Claw**--available by itself and as an ingredient in some arthritis formulas sold in health food stores, has no benefit for arthritis.
* **Feverfew** (chrysanthemum parthenium)--may reduce inflammation, and may help headaches, no evidence showing benefit for arthritis.
* **Foxglove**--potential for erratic heart rhythm and death.
* **Garlic**--garlic oil may reduce high blood cholesterol; no studies have been done on the effects of garlic on arthritis.
* **Ginseng**--no limit to false claims, use not recommended.
* **Gotu Kola**--contains massive amounts of caffeine.
* **Kelp**--no benefit for arthritis.
* **Indian Squaw Tea**--ineffective.
* **Pau D'arco**--poisonous, severe side effects, ineffective against arthritis.
* **Poke Root**--poisonous.
* **Rattlebox**--contains a toxic chemical capable of causing a rapid rise in blood pressure.
* **Sassafras**--a tea, may cause cancer, no benefit for arthritis.
* **Toneka**--eucalyptus oil, menthol, peppermint oil, thymol, and camphor; ineffective for arthritis.
* **Wolf Herb** (Gordolobos)--contains a toxic substance.
* **Yelsrap** (parsley spelled backward)--claims false.
* **Yucca**--an herbal extract, safe, does not appear to help arthritis.

And the list goes on.

At the present time medical science has shown increased interest in Chinese herbal medicine. Chinese and American doctors are working together to learn whether these ancient remedies have any real value in the treatment of disease. Results are mixed.

Venom

For centuries mankind has been fascinated by the notion that venom from poisonous snakes, ants, and bees might have curative powers. Reports of these methods are found in the earliest medical writings. The ques-

Note: If you are allergic to bee, wasp, ant, or other hymenoptera insects, stings could cause anaphylaxis and immediate death.

tion at this point is: Is there any scientific evidence that such venoms are effective in curing arthritis?

✹ **Bee venom**--*The AMA Journal* reports that bee venom contains a substance similar to snake venom. It notes that "the procedure employed of bringing about the stinging of the patient by live bees is somewhat hazardous," and that other procedures had been developed to extract the toxin and allow its injection under the skin. The report says: "Untoward reactions to bee venom therapy are fairly common and usually take the form of painful local swelling at the site of the injection." The report adds that these swellings have sometimes hemorrhaged and that moderately severe general reactions have been observed. It continues: "On the basis of the evidence available at this time, bee venom therapy cannot be recommended." Interestingly, the Arthritis Foundation notes that this remedy has been in the folklore for a number of years but that a number of arthritis specialists would like to see it tested in properly controlled trials. Such trials have yet to be conducted. Says the Foundation: "Bee venom should not be given the quackery label. But because it has been in that category in the past, it is difficult today to break down the resistance, and researchers have to worry about the threat of malpractice suits."

✹ **Ant venom**--There are reports that a magic cure for arthritis called Rhuvax is available in the Bahamas. This is alleged to be an extract made from the venom of a South American ant called pseudomyrmex. It is said the ant is cinnamon-colored and lives in a tree called "palo diablo"--tree of the devil. The ant's bite has been described as being "like a blow from a hot poker." The ant's venom is said to be unique, made of 12 kinds of protein, a complex sugar molecule, and other ingredients. To date there is no evidence that ant venom can cure arthritis. Legitimate research, however, is reported underway at the University of Miami. The official position of the Arthritis Foundation is as follows: The ant venom being tested as a remedy for arthritis is only one of several promising new drugs that today are undergoing their very early-stage scientific trials.

✹ **Snake venom**--Venom from several species of snakes, including the cobra, pit viper, water moccasin, and copperhead, have been employed by various workers in the treatment of arthritis and rheumatism disorders. Their virtues have not been impressive according to physicians, although laymen have long favored ointments of snake oil and stings of bees in the treatment of rheumatism. Many people across the country have been using a snake venom product called PROven even though there is no evidence it

is either safe or effective. The FDA blocked the interstate sale of it. Like bee and ant venom, with snake venom there is no evidence that it can be considered a cure.

Radiation Cures
Radiation, such as X-rays, is used as therapy in some kinds of arthritis such as ankylosing spondylitis. However, relatively large doses must be given to be effective and great care must be used to protect the body against side effects. Unfortunately, there is no end to con artists who seize on something that has legitimate therapeutic value and warp it to their own nefarious ends.

For example, promoters offered a product called the Rado Pad for sale claiming its effectiveness as a cure for arthritis and rheumatism. It purportedly contained a significant amount of healing uranium that emitted radioactive particles that speed up the healing process. It contained worthless pea gravel. There are several variations on this same theme including "health slippers" and "health mittens."

One of the longest-running myths that continues to the present day is that sitting in a uranium mine will somehow cure or improve a sufferer's arthritis. Despite all the publicity attendant to the FTC crackdown on uranium mine cures, the Arthritis Foundation reports that, pushed by pain, some arthritis sufferers are still paying money to sit in damp mines.

Other Questionable Cures for Arthritis
One of the most prominent themes in the mythology is that water is a cure for arthritis and/or other diseases. This applies to water consumed by mouth, taken by injection, sprayed with a nozzle on part of the body, or water in which the joints are to be immersed. There is virtually no limit to the permutations. It can be hot water, lukewarm water, cold water, ice cold water, solid water in the form of ice, salt water, mineral water, distilled water, spring water--the list is endless. Examples include:
✱ **Miraculous Water from Lourdes**--actually water from a spring in California.
✱ **Healing with Water**--a book that claimed water cured virtually every major health problem by spray with the coldest water.
✱ **Freezer Exercise**--a cold therapy.
✱ **Catalyst Altered Water** (CAW)--water spiced by caster oil and three kinds of salts.

Other so-called remedies include:
✱ **Vaccines**--ineffective according to the Arthritis Foundation.
✱ **Light**--some con men claim that the right color light will return the energy needed by the body.

✱ **Manure**--a Pennsylvanian claimed to have stumbled into this "cure."
✱ **Sex** (assuming proper techniques are employed)--several times a day is purported as a cure for arthritis.
✱ **Mud Cures**--can temporarily relieve pain only.
✱ **Bath Water Additives**--can temporarily relieve pain only.
✱ **Acupuncture and Acupressure**--the Chinese remedy for arthritis. The Arthritis Foundation finds the beneficial effects are only on the symptoms of arthritis and not the disease itself.
✱ **Blood Treatments**--popular myths as cures (transfusion from a pregnant woman) and blood washing (removing plasma).
✱ **Tonics and Elixirs**--many reported "cures" such as: Muscletone, Triwanda, cod liver oil and orange juice, Kamee, Nue-ovo, WD-40, Sacred Anointment Oil, Pain Stop, Mr. Arthur, Eden, Rel-EEZE, and many more.
✱ **Colonic Flushing**--no help, dangerous.
✱ **Laser Therapy**--Legitimate research is underway but claims are premature and misleading as a cure for arthritis.
✱ **Voodoo and Psychic Healing**--Faith healers sometimes help people.
✱ **Moon Dust**--plain quackery.

Conclusion
At present, most forms of arthritis cannot be prevented or cured as the cause is unknown, so the goals of treatment are to relieve pain and maintain or restore the function of the arthritic joint. You can help in two ways:
❶ Write your congressmen and demand that more funding be approved for research on arthritis.
❷ Remember the Arthritis Foundation in your will. Write: P.O. Box 19000, Atlanta, GA 30326; (404) 872-7100.

Commentary
An enemy injures 37 million and kills over 6,000 Americans each year. If it were a foreign enemy attacking our shores we would mobilize every resource we had in order to combat that killer. We know the enemy--it is arthritis. In 1981, the U.S. House Select Committee on Aging did propose a "War on Arthritis." We aren't winning that war--in fact, we have mobilized little resources. We are our own worst enemy as we allow funding of far-out, enormously expensive, nearly useless science projects in place of research that might relieve some pain. You have met the real enemy and it is us.

Cancer--a dread disease by Wm. J. Diehm

Lots of people I have known and loved have died of CANCER. What a dread disease! A million people a year get cancer and one-half of them die from it. All told, about 76 million Americans who are alive today will eventually encounter cancer.

Experts say that three out of every four families will be affected by one form of the disease or another. It's the price we pay for living in a society that smokes, drinks, lies out in the sun, eats a lot of fatty foods, and works with hazardous substances that are incompatible with human life. We are making some progress; many people are being cured, but still too many people die from cancer.

My sister developed cancer of the breast. The surgeon removed both breasts (a double mastectomy), also the lymph nodes, and some chest and arm muscle. In spite of that, the cancer metastasized (moved) to the lungs. Besides the major surgery, our doctors used radiation therapy, cobalt treatments, and various drugs (chemotherapy), but the cancer raged on. Our family decided to search for an unconventional cancer cure. We toured the world and found no hope. I read every book I could find on the subject of cancer, took courses, and researched the UCLA medical library. Then, we spent a year in Mexico at two different cancer clinics that used extreme dietary measures and the now discredited laetrile.

We spent six weeks in Texas at Dr. O. Carl Simonton's Cancer Clinic. He taught us visualization techniques to fight cancer--a type of meditation. For example, after deep relaxation, you picture the cancer cells (my sister imagined cancer as little black spider-like creatures), and then imagine the lovable strong white cells surrounding the cancer cells and destroying them. This was an attempt by mental control to turn on the immunization system to fight the cancer. After all our efforts, I watched my sister die an excruciating and deteriorating death. What a noble fighter to lose a terrible battle.

After my sister's death, I aligned myself to a Dr. Glenn Justice, distinguished oncologist at Fountain Valley Community Hospital Cancer Clinic. He tried all the latest cancer treatments, plus allowing me to try some of the "on the edge" stuff such as visualization, biofeedback, group therapy, positive think-ing, and psychotherapy with my patients. I watched dozens of people die, and dozens get well--we often did not know why. I am certain the magic bullet that will home in to kill cancer has not yet been found. But, here are some things we ought to know.

Understanding Cancer

Cancer begins, grows, and multiplies in the cells, so in order to understand cancer, let's begin with a cell. In the beginning, the half-cell (sperm) of a man unites with the half-cell (egg) of a woman. Each half-cell contains 23 chromosomes that combine into a cell of 46 chromosomes; each chromosome has thousands of genes and other material attached to it that determine the structure of the human body.

The cell is the basic unit of all living matter. In the microscopic package of the cell nature has enclosed all the parts and processes necessary to the survival of life. In fact, there is no life without a cell. In a remarkable miniaturization of life's functions, the cell moves, grows, reacts, protects itself, and even reproduces. To sustain this varied existence, it utilizes a tightly organized system of parts that is much like a tiny industrial complex. It has a central control point, power plants, internal communications, construction and manufacturing elements. Some cells live alone, as free-moving, independent creatures; some belong to loosely organized communities that move from place to place; some spend their lifetime in fixed immobility as part of the tissue of a larger organism.

Cells in a body can be compared to the people in a city. Each person has a task or position and sometimes people band together to make up a police force or health department. So, each cell has a position and collectively cells band together to make the parts of the human body that are assigned a function such as the heart or liver.

Cancer is a disease or dysfunction of the cells caused by an injury to some part, probably the DNA code that instructs the cell on how to properly grow, reproduce, and function.

When the cell divides or reproduces to make more cells and to replace the naturally dying ones, the injury causes the cell to pass on damage from cell to cell, like genetic defects are passed from mother to child, until it forms a large mass called a tumor.

If a cell were magnified to be as big as a human, it would be just as complicated. Like the paramecium and amoeba (one-celled animals), a human cell is a tiny completely functioning life form. A cell contains thousands of parts like chromosomes, genes, DNA, RNA, proteins, enzymes, molecules, atoms, protons, electrons, neutrons, quarks, and many other interacting bits of life that combine to make up the endless variations of cells that band together to formulate different life forms. Cells have a seat of power (mitochondrion), a brain (nucleus), a way to ingest and digest nutrients, a way to dispose of waste, to protect itself, to perform useful work, and to reproduce.

Cancer is any of a group of more than 100 related diseases characterized by the uncontrolled multiplication of abnormal cells in the body. Although each disease differs from the others in many ways, every cancer is a disease of some of the body's cells. Healthy cells that make up the body's tissues grow, divide, and replace themselves in an orderly manner. This process keeps the body in good repair. Cells and tissues are said to be cancerous when, for reasons not clearly understood, they lose the ability to limit and direct their growth. They divide too rapidly and grow without any order. They assume abnormal shapes and sizes, and cease functioning in a normal manner. The rapid abnormal growth causes too much tissue to be produced, and tumors begin to form.

Tumors can be benign or malignant. Benign tumors are not cancer. They do not spread to other parts of the body and are seldom a threat to life. Sometimes, however, benign tumors must be removed by surgery. Once removed, these tumors are not likely to return. Cancer can be primary or metastatic. Primary indicates that the cancer stays and grows in the tissue where it started; metastatic means the cancer has moved from the primary position through the bloodstream or the lymphatic pathways to a secondary site.

> **Cancer is a mass of tissue cells possessed of potentially unlimited growth that serves no useful function in the body. The cancer robs the body or host of nutrients necessary for survival. Unless this growing, spreading involvement of a vital organ by cancer can be recognized early and removed, it may lead to death.**

There are two major types of cancers: carcinoma and sarcoma. Carcinomas occur in the skin and linings of inner cavities. Sarcomas develop in connective tissues, fat, muscle, blood, vessels, bone, and cartilage.

Everyone has cancer or at least the potential for it. The body gets diseases and suffers traumas; so does that miniature form of life called the cell. When any cell in the body gets sick and starts to grow and divide in an abnormal manner, we have cancer. **Because the sick cancer cell belongs to the body, the immunization system does not conventionally recognize it as an enemy, so it lets it go wild.**

As far as we know, a number of different villains can injure a cell and start the cancer process:

- Traumas, blows, pressures, abnormal friction, or irritation to parts of the body until an irreparable injury is created in that part of the cell that controls the reproduction or division of the cell.

- Toxics, poisons, and various carcinogens that inhabit the air, earth, or water. Chemicals such as asbestos, polycyclic hydrocarbons, and cigarette smoke can injure the cell.

- Radiation from such sources as X-rays, radioactive fallout, and ultraviolet light are carcinogenic and can burn cells. Even sunlight in large doses contains enough radiation to injure cells. Our atmosphere is bombarded with all sorts of measurable radioactive energy waves.

- Some viruses cause cancer. Viruses are tiny bits of nonlife material that sometimes invade cells and take over their function, turning the normal cell into a dysfunctional one. Genes called oncogenes are equivalent to those in viruses known to cause cancer.

- Depression, severe mental illness, emotional traumas, stress, and other debilitating psychological problems can reduce the body's ability to function normally. It is my observation that most people can identify an emotional trauma (like a death in the family) that took place before the onset of cancer.

- Cancer itself causes cancer. Cells are injured by the destructive work of the cancer, which is passed on from cell to cell like the plague.

- Our own immune system by its failure to recognize a dysfunctioning cell allows the cancer to grow and kill.

Undoubtedly there are at least seven other causes, and it is possible that one of the above does not cause cancer. Cancer is usually considered to be due to a combination of carcinogens and predisposing factors such as heredity, age, trauma, or chronic irritation. Wouldn't it be wonderful if we knew the causes and the proper cures. We still do not know the whole story.

Now comes a major question: **Why doesn't the immune system (which consists of free flowing cells in the blood assigned to the task of destroying invaders) kill the cancer?** Well, it does most of the time. Since carcinogens (things that poison cells) everywhere; we all get cancer (injured cells) all the time. When a white cell sees an injured cell, it removes it; if not, then we have cancer, or growing injured cells. We do not have the answer to the question as to why the white cells that are so close to the cancer cells do not spot them and remove them. Cancer can be compared to an army of revolutionaries who take over a city before the citizens know what is happening.

Let's go to a fundamental conundrum of philosophy: "Evil exists, why don't the good guys eliminate the bad guys." Well, sometimes they do, and sometimes they can't spot them, and sometimes the bad guys are too clever, and sometimes...

The History of Cancer

Cancer is older than man; stalking dinosaurs long before the earliest written records document its ravages among humans. Cancer was described by the ancient Egyptians. Hieroglyphic inscriptions and papyri manuscripts distinguish between benign and malignant tumors, and reveal that surface tumors were removed surgically. For cancers of the stomach and the uterus, compounds of barley, pigs' ears, and other ingredients were ordered.

Cancers were identified by the Greeks and Romans. Galen and Hippocrates warned against treatment of the more severe forms. In the medieval times cancer was explained as the result of an excess of black bile, curable only in its earliest stages. Ambroise Pare, surgeon of the Renaissance, recommended surgery for cancer only if the cancer could be totally removed. A wide variety of pastes containing arsenic were compounded to treat its manifestations.

The foundations of modern science were laid in the 17th century. Galileo's telescope and Newton's laws of gravitation advanced understanding of the physical universe, and William Harvey described the continuous circulation of the blood. A renowned German surgeon, Fabricius Hildanus, removed enlarged lymph nodes in breast cancer operations. Johann Scultetus performed total mastectomies. Lymphatic drainage became the key factor in developing more extensive surgical removal of cancer.

The systematic study of Cancer

Modern pathology was established in the 18th century and physical diagnosis became common. With the first systematic experiments in cancer, oncology was born as a medical discipline. Two French scientists, physician Jean Astruc and chemist Bernard Peyrilhe, conducted experiments to confirm or disprove hypotheses related to cancer. Their efforts, however absurd they seem in retrospect, established experimental oncology, the science of seeking better diagnoses, treatments, and understanding of the causes of cancer.

A series of remarkable discoveries in the closing years of the 19th century set the stage for 20th century research in oncology and biomedical sciences. Cancer research accelerated as Roentgen described X-rays, the Curies isolated radium, and Muller observed abnormalities of cancer cells. Study of cancer tissues and tumors revealed that cancer cells were markedly different in appearance than cells of surrounding tissue.

Early in this century it was found that X-rays selectively damaged cancer cells, causing less harm to other tissues. In 1913 was the publication of the first known article on cancer's warning signs in a popular women's magazine, and formation of a nationwide organization dedicated to public education on cancer.

Theory became fact in 1915 when experiments confirmed that cancer could be induced by chemicals. In 1937 Congress made the conquest of cancer a national goal with a unanimous vote to pass the National Cancer Institute Act, authorizing annual funding.

Molecular biology--the study of living systems at the molecular level--revolutionized both medicine and cancer research. In 1953 James Watson and Francis Crick unveiled their model of the structure of DNA (de-oxyribonucleic acid), the cellular material carrying genetic information.

As microscopes improved, viruses became visible and their structure was revealed to be tiny particles of either ribonucleic acid or deoxyribonucleic acid that were wrapped in a sheath of protein--DNA and RNA were discovered.

In 1971 the National Cancer Act was created and a National Cancer Program administered by the National Cancer Institute.

1971 -- War Declared on Cancer

The new biotechnologies of the early 1970s--recombinant DNA technology, genetic engineering, and hybridoma technology--have spawned a biomedical revolution and a whole new industry. With the capacity to cut, splice, sequence, and recombine DNA, the basic material of life, it has become possible to isolate, identify, manipulate, study, and modify the action of individual genes--the process of genetic engineering. Two major discoveries in molecular biology were important to the development of recombinant technology. One was restriction enzymes--the "scissors" of genetic engineering with the ability to cut DNA at known points. The other was reverse transcriptase, which allowed sections of DNA to be copied from RNA.

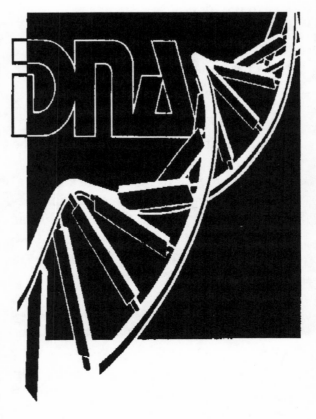

In 1975 biomedical science and oncology took a giant step forward with the introduction by Cesar Milstein and George Kohler of hybridoma technology, in which an earlier cell fusion technique was used to create and mass-produce a special kind of antibody. This antibody, named a "monoclonal antibody," would have an enormous impact on cancer diagnosis and treatment.

Researchers now realize that the body itself has a system that could be, and often is, used to fight cancer. Hybridoma technology enables the immune system to be manipulated and enhanced. We may possibly begin using antigens to promote immunity. Unlike drugs used primarily to poison cancer cells in conventional chemotherapy, biologicals harness the body's defenses. Some, such as monoclonal antibodies, are among the most promising. As antigens of specific cancers are identified, monoclonal antibodies can be used alone to "tag" such cells for destruction by the immune system.

It now appears that certain proteins, called cytokines, can enhance the immune system's effectiveness through a variety of means. One of the first cytokines to be discovered was interferon. By the early 1980s scientists had identified more than 20 cytokines, and located the genes that coded for many of them. Cytokines, proteins that stimulate the immune system, became feasible as treatments when genetic engineering made their mass production possible. Two of the most promising cytokines are interferon and interleukin-2.

Most of the progress made against cancer in the past 5,000 years has occurred in the last decade and a half. When "war on cancer" was declared in 1971, cancer was still basically a mystery. Today it is a more solvable problem, with known questions and the tools to ultimately answer them. We now have the knowledge to substantially reduce deaths caused by cancer.

It is wonderful to know that the body itself has a system that can be used to fight cancer. Let us hope that the new biotechnology, hybridoma, will enable the immune system to be manipulated and enhanced to more effectively fight cancer.

The various types of Cancer

Cancer of the Lungs

The lungs, a major part of the respiratory system, are a pair of cone-shaped organs made up of pinkish-gray spongy tissue. They occupy most of the chest cavity and are separated from each other by the mediastinum, which is an area in the chest containing the heart, trachea (windpipe), esophagus, and lymph nodes. The right lung has three sections, called lobes, and is a little larger than the left lung, which has only two lobes. The lungs exchange gases between the body and the air. They remove carbon dioxide, a waste product of the body's cells, and take in oxygen, which is necessary for cells to live and carry out normal activities.

Lung cancers are generally divided into two types: small cell lung cancer and nonsmall cell lung cancer. Small cell lung cancer is sometimes called oat cell cancer because the cancer cells look like oats when they are viewed under a microscope. This type of lung cancer makes up about 20% to 25% of all cases. It is a rapidly growing cancer that spreads very early to other organs. It is generally found in people who are heavy smokers.

There are three main kinds of nonsmall cell lung cancer:

1. *Epidermoid carcinoma,* which is also called squamous cell carcinoma, makes up about 33% of all lung cancer cases. Carcinoma is a cancer that begins in the lining or covering tissues of an organ.

2. *Adenocarcinoma* accounts for about 25% of all lung cancers. It often grows along the outer edges of the lungs and under the tissue lining the bronchi.

3. *Large cell carcinomas* make up about 16% of all lung cancer cases. These cancers are found most often in the smaller bronchi.

Lung cancer may cause a number of symptoms. A cough is one of the more common symptoms and is likely to occur when a tumor grows and blocks an air passage. Another symptom is chest pain, which feels like a constant ache that may or may not be related to coughing. Other symptoms may include shortness of breath, repeated pneumonia or bronchitis, coughing up blood, hoarseness, or swelling of the neck and face. When the lung cancer spreads, symptoms can include headache, weakness, pain, bone fractures, bleeding, or blood clots.

If lung cancer is suspected, a patient undergoes a series of tests to confirm whether cancer is present, such as chest X-ray, CAT scan and bronchoscopy, that permits the doctor to see the breathing passages through a thin, hollow, lighted tube.

There are three basic ways to treat lung cancer: surgery, radiation therapy, and chemotherapy. An operation that removes only a small part of the lung is called a wedge resection. When an entire lobe of the lung is removed, the procedure is called a lobectomy. Pneumonectomy is the removal of the entire lung.

Today, there do exist some cancers that with proper medicine can be beaten. Unfortunately, many major forms are still incurable, and we can only hope that someday new research will let us defeat them.

The Kidneys

The kidneys are a matched pair of vital organs located below the liver and stomach and near the backbone on either side. Shaped like a "kidney bean" with a slight indentation in one side, the adult kidney is 4 to 5 inches long, 2 to 3 inches wide, and weighs about half a pound.

The kidneys help remove wastes from the body by making urine. They do this by filtering urea, salt, and other substances from the blood as it flows through the kidneys. The kidneys are also glands that manufacture and secrete a variety of hormones.

Kidney cancer, like other cancers, is a disease of the body's cells. Cells normally grow in an orderly, controlled pattern. When cell division is not orderly, abnormal growth takes place. Masses of tissue called tumors build up. Tumors may be benign or malignant. Benign tumors remain localized and usually do not spread or threaten one's life. They can be removed completely by surgery and are not likely to recur. Malignant tumors are cancers. They can invade and destroy nearby tissues and organs or spread to other parts of the body by way of the bloodstream or lymphatic system.

The most common symptom of kidney cancer is visible blood in the urine. The blood may be present one day and absent the next. Blood in the urine can be the sign of a number of disorders other than cancer. Other common symptoms of kidney cancer are the presence of a lump or mass in the abdomen, and pain in the side. The mass will probably feel smooth, hard, and "fixed." Like all cancers, kidney cancer can cause fatigue, loss of appetite, weight loss, and anemia.

Diagnostic radiology is always used to confirm a suspected diagnosis of kidney cancer. More than 8 out of 10 kidney cancers are renal adenocarcinomas, which start in one of the cells that form the lining of a renal tubule.

Surgery is the treatment for most cases of adult kidney cancers that have not spread to distant areas of the body. Radiation therapy may be used as a supplement to surgery. If you have widespread kidney cancer, your doctor may recommend chemotherapy. Anticancer drugs kill cancer cells, but can act on normal cells as well, so your doctor must maintain a delicate balance of enough drugs to kill cancer cells without destroying too many healthy cells.

The Larynx

The larynx, or voice box, is composed of the epiglottis, false cords, and true cords. The air you breathe enters the nose or mouth. From there, it goes through the oropharynx, the epiglottis, and into the trachea to the lungs. The epiglottis closes during swallowing and prevents food from entering the larynx. The true vocal cords produce sound when air passes through the larynx, causing the vocal cords to vibrate.

Cancer of the larynx, like all cancers, is an irregular and abnormal growth of cells that can build up into masses of tissue, or tumors. One of the most common early symptoms of laryngeal cancer is a prolonged

Pancreas and Skin Cancer

hoarseness, change in voice pitch, lump in the throat, coughing, difficulty and pain in breathing or swallowing, or even an earache.

Your doctor will examine your larynx using a laryngeal mirror. This device resembles a dentist's mirror with a long handle. Your physician can detect most tumors of the larynx by using this mirror. In addition, a thorough examination of the lymph nodes in the neck is important. Your doctor will examine your lymph nodes by feeling them. If your doctor finds a tumor he will arrange for a biopsy. If a diagnosis of cancer is confirmed, it is best to begin treatment in a hospital that has an expert staff and resources. Radiation therapy is probably the best treatment for early, localized laryngeal cancer, and successful radiation therapy often produces a minimum of aftereffects. Surgery and radiation is generally used for larger laryngeal cancers.

The Pancreas

The pancreas is a thin, lumpy gland about six inches long that lies behind the stomach. It releases insulin into the bloodstream, which regulates the amount of sugar in the blood. It releases pancreatic juice into the small intestine, which aids in the digestion of food.

> **There is an emotional strain in dealing with all cancer.**
> **It is best to discuss freely all aspects with loved ones, the doctor, and sometimes with a counselor.**

Cancer of the pancreas, like other cancers, is a disease of the body's cells, and usually begins in the cells of the duct system. The symptoms are usually a vague pain that develops in the upper abdomen and sometimes spreads to the back. The pain gradually becomes persistent. Nausea, loss of appetite, weight loss, and a general feeling of weakness also may occur. If the cancer develops in the head of the pancreas, it may block the common bile duct, which will cause the skin and whites of the eyes to become yellow and the urine to become darker.

Three tests have been excellent aids in diagnosing pancreatic cancer:

1. retrograde pancreaticoduodenography,
2. ultrasound scanning, and
3. CAT scanning.

Treatment at this time usually involves:

- Surgery, removal of the diseased part of the pancreas, a part of the stomach, and the entire duodenum.

- Radiation therapy that uses X-rays, cobalt, or other sources of ionizing radiation to kill cancer cells.

- Chemotherapy (treatment with anti-cancer drugs). Doctors plan the doses carefully in order to kill cancer cells without destroying too many healthy cells.

Skin Cancer

Skin cancer is the most common type of cancer in the United States. According to present estimates, 40% to 50% of Americans who live to age 65 will have skin cancer at least once.

The most common warning sign of skin cancer is a change on the skin, especially a new growth or a sore that doesn't heal. Skin cancer has many different appearances. For example, it may start as a small, smooth, shiny, pale, or waxy lump. Or, the cancer can appear as a firm red lump. Sometimes, the lump bleeds or develops a crust. Skin cancer can also start as a flat, red spot that is rough, dry, or scaly. Pain is not a sign of skin cancer.

> **The cure rate for skin cancer could be 100% if all skin cancers were brought to a doctor's attention before they had a chance to spread.**

Doctors generally divide skin cancer into two stages: local (affecting only the skin), or metastatic (spreading beyond the skin). Because skin cancer rarely spreads, a biopsy often is the only test needed to determine the stage.

Treatment for skin cancer may involve surgery, radiation therapy, or cryosurgery. Sometimes, a combination of these methods is used. Most skin cancers can be removed quickly and easily by curettage surgery. The area is generally treated by electrodesiccation (an electric current to control bleeding and kill cancer cells remaining around the edge of the wound).

Cryosurgery or extreme cold may be used to treat precancerous skin conditions, such as actinic keratosis, as well as skin cancers. In cryosurgery, liquid nitrogen is applied to the growth to freeze and kill the abnormal cells. After the area thaws, the dead tissue falls off.

Skin cancer responds well to radiation therapy (also called X-ray therapy, radiotherapy, or irradiation), which uses high-energy rays to kill cancer cells. This treatment is used for cancers that occur in areas that are hard to treat with surgery. For example, radiation therapy might be used to treat skin cancers of the eyelid, the tip of the nose, and the ear.

For additional helpful information on sunscreens and skin care, see the article on "Appearance and Skin Care" on pages 372 through 375.

Cancer in Women

Cancer of the Ovary

Among women in the United States, cancer of the ovary is the eighth most common cancer and the fifth most frequent cause of death from cancer. It accounts for about 27% of all cancers affecting the female reproductive organs. One out of every 70 American women (1.4%) will develop this disease at some time during her life. The incidence of ovarian cancer increases steadily with age, with most cases found in women 55 to 75 years old.

The ovaries are the female reproductive organs in which the ova, or eggs, are formed. During each menstrual cycle, an egg is discharged from one of the ovaries. The egg travels through a fallopian tube to the uterus, and if fertilized by a male sperm, develops there into an unborn child.

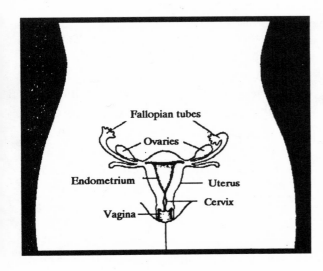

The ovaries also release the female hormone, estrogen, as part of the monthly cycle. A gradual decline in this periodic release of estrogen normally takes place in a woman between the ages of 48 and 52. At the same time, the production of eggs and the menstrual periods become irregular and then stop completely. This is called menopause.

Ovarian cancer usually occurs after menopause. Cancer of the ovary, like other cancers, is a disease of the body's cells. When cell division is not orderly, abnormal growth occurs. Masses of tissue called tumors build up. Some tumors are benign. Though they may interfere with body functions and require removal, they do not invade neighboring tissue. But cancerous or malignant tumors compress, invade, and destroy surrounding normal tissues. Cancer cells can break away from the tumor and spread (metastasize) through the bloodstream or lymphatic system to distant parts of the body, where they form new cancers.

Pelvic examinations each year are the best way to guard against undetected development and spread of ovarian cancer. The Pap test, a microscopic examination of cells shed into the vagina from the uterus, also is an important part of a pelvic examination.

The most frequent symptom associated with ovarian cancer is enlargement of the abdomen; this is generally due to an accumulation of fluid in the abdomen incident to the presence of the cancer, or it may be the tumor itself. Abnormal vaginal bleeding is another sign associated with cancer of the ovary.

If a doctor feels a mass or sees signs of a tumor in the ultrasound images or X-rays, laparoscopy may be performed to determine the nature and extent of the disease. Laparoscopy involves cutting a tiny peephole in the abdomen and then examining the ovary with a special lighted instrument. Instead of laparoscopy, the doctor may arrange for an operation called a laparotomy, which involves making an incision in the abdomen to reach the ovaries. A biopsy is performed; if cancer is discovered the entire growth can be removed immediately. In some cases, only one ovary is removed. But more often, both ovaries, the fallopian tubes, and uterus are removed as a precautionary measure or because the cancer has spread. After surgery, radiation therapy or chemotherapy may be given to treat any remaining cancer.

Cancer of the Cervix

The uterus (womb) is a hollow, pear-shaped organ located in a woman's lower abdomen between the bladder and the rectum. The narrow, lower portion of the uterus is called the cervix. Cancer that develops in the cervix is called cervical cancer and is one of the most common cancers. Six percent of all cancers in women are cervical cancers.

When cervical cancer spreads, it usually travels through the lymphatic system. Early cervical cancer seldom causes symptoms. It can only be detected by a pelvic exam and a Pap test. Symptoms generally do not appear until cervical cancer becomes invasive. The most common symptom of cancer of the cervix is abnormal bleeding.

In some women, the cells in the cervix may go through a series of changes. Normal, healthy cells may become abnormal (a condition known as dysplasia). Dysplasia is not cancer, although it may develop into very early cancer of the cervix. Very early cancer of the cervix (also called carcinoma in situ) involves only the top layer of cervical cells and does not invade deeper layers of cervical tissue for many months, perhaps years. Invasive cervical cancer is cancer that has spread deeper into the cervix and/or to nearby tissues or organs. **Most cases of invasive cervical cancer could be prevented if all women had pelvic exams and Pap tests regularly.**

Cancer of the Uterus

In women of childbearing age, the inner layer of the uterus (endometrium) goes through a series of monthly changes known as the menstrual cycle. Each month, endometrial tissue grows and thickens in preparation to receive a fertilized egg. Because most uterine cancer develops in the endometrium, cancer of the uterus also is called endometrial cancer.

> The treatments used against cancer must be very powerful. It is rarely possible to limit the effects of treatment so that only cancer cells are destroyed. Normal, healthy cells may be damaged at the same time. That's why cancer treatment often causes side effects.

Cancer in Women

Abnormal bleeding after menopause is the most common symptom of cancer of the uterus. Cancer of the uterus does not often occur before menopause, but it does occur around the time menopause begins.

Fibroids are benign tumors in the uterus that are found most often in women over 35 years of age. While single fibroid tumors occur, multiple tumors are more common.

Endometriosis is a benign condition in which tissue that looks and acts like endometrial tissue begins to spread to unusual places, such as on the surface of the ovaries, on the outside of the uterus, and in other tissues in the abdomen.

Hyperplasia is an increase in the number of normal cells lining the uterus. It may develop into cancer and so usually requires treatment.

When symptoms suggest uterine cancer, the doctor will ask a woman about her medical history and will usually perform one of the following exams:

- ■ *Pelvic exam.* The doctor thoroughly examines the uterus, vagina, ovaries, bladder, and rectum for any abnormality in their shape or size.

- ■ *Biopsy.* Surgical removal of a small amount of suspicious-looking uterine tissue, which is examined under a microscope by a pathologist.

- ■ *D and C.* The doctor dilates (widens) the cervix and inserts a curette (a small spoon-shaped instrument) to remove pieces of the lining of the uterus to be examined for evidence of cancer.

- ■ *Pap test.* The Pap test is usually used for detection of cancer of the cervix.

If cancer cells are found, other tests are used to find out whether the disease has spread from the uterus to other parts of the body. Blood test, X-ray, CAT scan, and ultrasound are used to view organs inside the body.

As this article is written, the usual methods of treating uterine cancer are surgery, radiation therapy, hormone therapy, and chemotherapy.

Cancer of the Breast

Breast cancer kills about 50,000 women per year in the United States. More than half of all breast cancer deaths occur in women 65 or older. Knowledge about breast cancer--symptoms, detection and treatment procedures--is imperative to the health of women. We do not know exactly why breast cancer develops, but the disease is not caused by bumping, bruising, or caressing the breast. We must also remember that cancer is not contagious. Any woman can develop breast cancer, but some are more at risk than others. A woman has a higher-than-average risk of developing breast cancer if:

- ❑ she is over 50 years old, or
- ❑ her mother or sister has had breast cancer, or
- ❑ she has had breast cancer before.

The earlier breast cancer is detected, the better the chances of survival and successful treatment. The warning signs:

- ❑ a lump or thickening in the breast, or
- ❑ a change in breast shape, or
- ❑ discharge from the nipple.

Monthly breast self-examination is an important key to early diagnosis. It is important for you to be familiar with your own breasts. After you learn how your normal breast tissue feels, you will be able to recognize a change if one occurs. Follow the instructions on the opposite page.

If you are age 50 or older, you should have a mammogram yearly. A mammogram is the most reliable method for detecting breast cancer while a tumor is very small, before it can be felt.

When a lump is detected, sometimes a biopsy is done with a needle that withdraws fluid or tissue from the lump. The specimen is then analyzed in a laboratory to determine whether cancer cells are present.

The treatment of breast cancer today encompasses several options:

- ■ *Mastectomy,* the surgical removal of the breast, is a common treatment for breast cancer.

- ■ *Lumpectomy* followed by radiation therapy is a technique for women who have early-stage breast cancer.

- ■ *Radiation therapy* can sometimes be as effective as the traditional surgical approach.

- ■ *Chemotherapy,* the use of drugs to destroy cancer cells, is another treatment often used in addition to either surgery or radiation therapy if the cancer has spread beyond the breast.

- ■ *Hormone therapy* is used to discourage the growth of a tumor.

- ■ *Genetic engineering* has produced a number of substances, not yet proven. For example, the protein, mammastatin, is produced by a gene that the researchers hope to clone using genetic engineering techniques. It has been shown to halt the growth of breast cancer cells.

We are making progress every day in cancer research. You can take advantage of it. If a woman is considering treatment for breast cancer she may obtain the opinion of a second physician, if she wants another point of view. It is best to avoid nonmedical treatment for any cancer. Quackery abounds in the field, and it can be expensive and dangerous.

> There is a saying that goes:
>
> **If you haven't had your yearly mammogram, you need more than your breasts examined!**

Breast Self-Examination

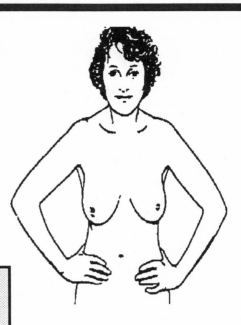

Breast self-examination should be done once a month so you become familiar with the usual appearance and feel of your breasts. Familiarity makes it easier to notice any changes in the breast from one month to another. Early discovery of a change from what is "normal" is the main idea behind BSE. The outlook is much better if you detect cancer in an early stage.

If you menstruate, the best time to do BSE is 2 or 3 days after your period ends, when your breasts are least likely to be tender or swollen. If you no longer menstruate, pick a day such as the first day of the month, to remind yourself it is time to do BSE.

Here is one way to do BSE:

3 Next, press your hands firmly on your hips and bow slightly toward your mirror as you pull your shoulders and elbows forward.

Some women do the next part of the exam in the shower because fingers glide over soapy skin, making it easier to concentrate on the texture underneath.

1 Stand before a mirror. Inspect both breasts for anything unusual such as any discharge from the nipples or puckering, dimpling, or scaling of the skin.

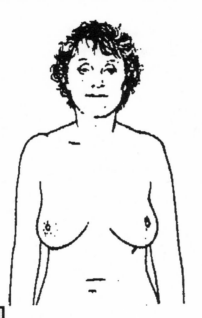

The next steps are designed to emphasize any change in the shape or contour of your breasts. As you do them, you should be able to feel your chest muscles tighten.

4 Raise your left arm. Use three or four fingers of your right hand to explore your left breast firmly, carefully, and thoroughly. Beginning at the outer edge, press the flat part of your fingers in small circles, moving the circles slowly around the breast. Gradually work toward the nipple. Be sure to cover the entire breast. Pay special attention to the area between the breast and the underarm itself. Feel for any unusual hump or mass under the skin.

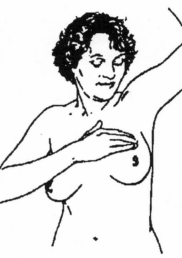

5 Gently squeeze the nipple and look for a discharge. (If you have any discharge during the month-- whether or not it is during BSE--see your doctor.) Repeat steps 4 and 5 on your right breast.

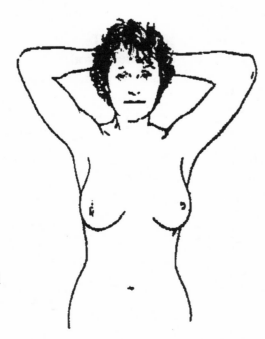

2 Watching closely in the mirror clasp your hands behind your head and press your hands forward.

6 Steps 4 and 5 should be repeated lying down. Lie flat on your back with your left arm over your head and a pillow or folded towel under your left shoulder. This position flattens the breast and makes it easier to examine. Use the same circular motion described earlier. Repeat the exam on your right breast.

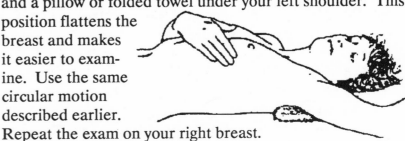

Cancers men need to know about

Men 50 years of age and older need a number of medical tests periodically to help in finding cancer early while it can be cured or controlled. Your medical history and the medical histories of your close blood relatives are used to find out the tests you need. Your doctor can advise you about how often the tests should be done. Even if you have no cancer warning signs, you should have a checkup every year. The recommended exams include:

- Colon and rectum
- Lungs
- Skin
- Prostate gland
- Testicular self-examination

Colon and Rectum

Check each of the following items that applies to you and advise your doctor that:

- ☐ Someone in my family has had intestinal polyps or colon cancer.
- ☐ I have had intestinal polyps, ulcerative colitis, or colon or rectal cancer.
- ☐ I have rectal bleeding.
- ☐ Change in bowel habits.

If any of these items apply to you, your doctor probably will advise you to have:

- ✳ **Digital rectal examination**--lets the doctor feel the rectum for lumps or sores. Using a gloved, lubricated finger, the doctor will check the lower 4 inches of the rectum.
- ✳ **Stool-blood tests**--tells the doctor if there are any unseen traces of blood in the stool.
- ✳ **Proctoscopic examination**--Proctosigmoidoscopy ("procto") lets the doctor examine the inside of the lower colon with a tubelike instrument.
- ✳ **Barium enema**--fills the large intestine with a barium solution so the doctor can see the colon clearly on X-ray film.

Lungs

If any of the following items of your medical history apply to you, your doctor may suggest a chest X-ray:

- ☐ I have smoked a pack of cigarettes or more daily for at least 20 years.
- ☐ I have been exposed to asbestos, BCME, or uranium at work. Some chemical workers are exposed to BCME (also called bis-CME or bis-chloro-methyl ether).
- ☐ My spouse or other members of my household have been exposed to asbestos at work.
- ☐ I have a nagging cough or persistent hoarseness.

If you are a smoker, you will lower your risk of lung cancer and many other diseases if you quit. This is true no matter how long or how much you have smoked.

Skin

Most men over 50 notice changes in their skin. Usually, these are normal changes and are due to aging. But the risk of skin cancer increases with age. If found, skin cancer is almost always curable. If any of the following items apply to you, you will need frequent examinations.

- ☐ I have fair skin that sunburns easily.
- ☐ I have been exposed to the sun a lot during work or leisure.
- ☐ I have had a skin cancer removed.

Skin examination. Check your skin monthly and look for unusual changes in the color or texture (that is, feel) of the skin or in the size, shape, or height of a mole. Check for any new moles that look different from the others. Report any unusual skin changes to your doctor quickly. Also have a yearly skin exam done by your doctor.

**REMEMBER:
Know your skin and
be alert to changes.
Be careful when out in
the sun. Use a sunscreen
that blocks out the sun's
harmful rays.**

Prostate Gland

More than half the men over 50 have some prostate problems. Most of these are not cancer. But the risk of prostate cancer increases with age. Rates are also higher among black men. If found, many prostate cancers can be cured or controlled. Chances of cure are best when the disease is found early.

Testicular Cancer

Testicular cancer is the most common type of cancer in younger men; however, it can occur at any time and even in older men. Yet, because it accounts for only about 1% of all cancers in men, many people have never heard of this type of cancer. White men are four times more likely to develop testicular cancer than black men.

Two groups of men have a greater risk of developing testicular cancer--those whose testicles have not descended into the scrotum and those whose testicles descended after age 6. Testicular cancer is 3 to 17 times more likely to develop in these men.

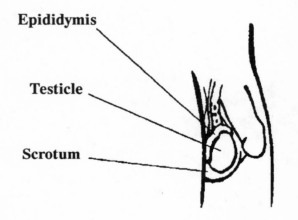

Epididymis

Testicle

Scrotum

Testicles are male reproductive organs. They produce and store sperm. They also produce testosterone, a hormone that causes such male traits as facial hair and lower voice pitch. Testicles are smooth, oval-shaped, and somewhat firm to the touch. They are below the penis in a sac of skin called the scrotum. The testicles normally descend into the scrotum before birth.

Fifteen years ago, testicular cancer was often fatal because it spread quickly to vital organs such as the lungs. Today, due to advances in treatment, testicular cancer is one of the most curable cancers, especially if detected and treated promptly.

Symptoms

The most common symptoms of testicular cancer are a small, painless lump in a testicle or a slightly enlarged testicle. It is important for men to become familiar with the size and feeling of their normal testicles, so that they can detect changes if they occur.

Other possible symptoms include a feeling of heaviness in the scrotum, a dull ache in the lower stomach or groin, a change in the way a testicle feels, or a sudden accumulation of blood or fluid in the scrotum. These symptoms can also be caused by infections or other conditions that are not cancer. A doctor can tell you if you have cancer and what the proper treatment should be.

How to Do TSE

A simple procedure called testicular self-exam (TSE) can increase the chances of finding a tumor early.

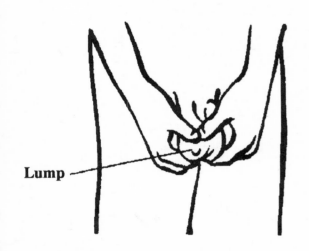

Lump

Men should preform TSE once a month--after a warm bath or shower. The heat causes the scrotal skin to relax, making it easier to find anything unusual. TSE is simple and only takes a few minutes:

■ Examine each testicle gently with both hands. The index and middle finger should be placed underneath the testicle while the thumbs are placed on the top. Roll the testicle gently between the thumbs and fingers. One testicle may be larger than the other. This is normal.

■ The epididymis is a cord-like structure on the top and back of the testicle that stores and transports the sperm. Do not confuse the epididymis with an abnormal lump.

■ Feel for any abnormal lumps--about the size of a pea--on the front or the side of the testicle. These lumps are usually painless.

If you do find a lump, you should contact your doctor right away. The lump may be due to an infection, and a doctor can decide the proper treatment. If the lump is not an infection, it is likely to be cancer. Remember that testicular cancer is highly curable, especially when detected and treated early. Testicular cancer almost always occurs in only one testicle, and the other testicle is all that is needed for full sexual function.

Routine testicular self-exams are important, but they cannot substitute for a doctor's examination.

Your doctor should examine your testicles when you have a physical exam. You also can ask your doctor to check the way you do TSE. Call your doctor right away if you find any of these changes in your body:

■ Unusual bleeding

■ Lumps that are unusual

■ Changes in elimination (bowel or bladder habits)

■ Change in size or color of a wart or mole

■ Indigestion lasting more than two weeks

■ Sore that does not heal

■ Hoarseness lasting more than two weeks

See a doctor every year even when you're feeling fine. That way, you'll be more certain you are cancer-free.

Although it's usually best to call your physician with health questions, you may want to consult additional sources to add to your knowledge. Here are places where you can get more information:

Cancer Response System
1-800-227-2345

They can provide information on the signs and symptoms of cancers and treatment options by American Cancer Society information specialists. Offers referrals to ACS chapters; literature available. Call between 5:30 A.M. and 2 P.M. (eastern time) weekdays except holidays.

Office of Cancer Communications
National Cancer Institute
Bethesda, MD 20892
Or call 1-800-4-CANCER

According to a medical report in the *New England Journal of Medicine*, a simple blood test appears to detect prostate cancer. A study conducted by doctors at the Washington University School of Medicine suggests the blood test is faster than ultrasound or a rectal examination. More studies are being conducted.

The blood test, manufactured by Hybritech Inc. of San Diego, looks for a chemical made by the prostrate called PSA. The PSA test reportedly detects prostate cancer earlier than ultrasound or a rectal examination, making it a potent weapon in the early detection of one of the leading killers of older men, according to new research.

Some 122,000 men develop prostate cancer each year, and some 32,000 die. In two-thirds of the fatal cases, the tumor is not detected until it has spread.

In 1988, doctors reported 152,000 new cases of colon cancer and 139,000 deaths from the disease in the United States. A new study in the *Journal of the National Cancer Institute* reports the per person rate in the U.S. is four to seven times that of China. The authors of the study concluded that it is the "best evidence yet" that a diet high in animal fats increases the risk of colon cancer.

Symptoms, suggested medical tests, and treatments

Before the Onset of Cancer

Why do some people get cancer and others do not? The answer is a complex mix of diet, environment, lifestyle, genetics and exposure to carcinogens. Scientists are trying to sort it out. It's estimated that 66% of all cancers could be prevented by avoiding cigarette smoke and making some simple dietary changes.

The American Cancer Society presently recommends:
* reduce intake of fat in calories to 30% of your total diet--others say 10%
* eat more fiber (vegetables, fruits, whole grains)
* eat daily vitamin A/Beta-carotene foods
* eat daily vitamin C foods
* include in diet cauliflower, cabbage, broccoli, turnips, and other cruciferous vegetables
* minimize charred or smoked foods
* use alcohol in moderation
* no smoking
* minimize nitrites (cured/preserved foods)
* avoid obesity

Cancer occurs more often in people 50 or older, so it is important as senior citizens to safeguard our health by learning the warning signs of cancer, have regular checkups, eat good low-fat food, exercise, reduce stress, and keep a good mental attitude.

Some Symptoms to Watch For

❑ Lung--Cough that won't go away; coughing up blood; shortness of breath.

❑ Breast--Lump or thickness in the breast; change in breast shape; discharge from the nipple.

❑ Colon and Rectum--Changes in bowel habits; bleeding from the rectum; blood in the bowel movement, which may make the stool appear bright red or black.

❑ Prostate (men)--Difficulty or pain while urinating; the need to urinate often, especially at night.

❑ Uterus, Ovary, and Cervix (women)-- Bleeding after menopause; unusual vaginal discharge; enlargement of the abdomen; pain during intercourse.

❑ Skin--Sore that does not heal; change in shape, size, or color of a wart or mole; sudden appearance of a mole.

Some Suggested Medical Tests for People Over 50

■ *Guaiac Test*--examine stool for traces of blood; it can be a symptom of colon or rectal cancer.

■ *Rectal Exam*--doctor's gloved finger can detect prostate tumors in men, and rectal tumors in men or women.

■ *Sigmoidoscopy or "Procto"*--an examination of the rectum and part of the colon with a lighted instrument to detect tumors and other abnormalities.

■ *Pelvic Examination and Pap Test*--The physician, using a gloved finger, checks the vagina, uterus, and ovaries for any sign of a problem. A Pap smear involves removing cells from the cervix and examining them through a microscope to see if they are cancerous or precancerous (see hysterectomy, page 431).

■ *Breast Examination and Mammography*-- Breasts are examined for changes such as a lump or thickening. A mammogram (X-ray of the breasts) can reveal tumors even before they can be felt. Women should learn how to do a BSE, (Breast Self-Examination) monthly to detect lumps or other changes.

After the Detection of Cancer

The American Cancer Society estimates that 49% of those with cancer are still alive five years after the disease is diagnosed-- that means 51% do not make it.

Questions to ask the doctor if you have a tumor:
❑ Is the tumor benign or malignant?
❑ If it is benign, can it be cured?
❑ If it is cancer, what kind is it?
❑ If it is cancer, has it spread?
❑ Can you predict how successful an operation, radiation treatment, or drug treatment would be?
❑ What are the risks?
❑ Should I get an opinion from another doctor?
❑ If an operation is done, will I need other treatment?
❑ How helpful will this be in resuming normal activities afterward?
❑ If I take anticancer drugs, what will the side effects be?
❑ How often will I need medical check-ups?
❑ What should I tell my relatives and friends?

The Treatment of Cancer Can Be Quite Harsh, But Life-saving

1. **Chemotherapy**--the use of drugs and hormones. Drugs are designed to attack the genetic material--the DNA--of the tumor cells in an effort to stop them from multiplying and spreading the tumor. But these drugs are not specific and can also kill normal healthy cells.

2. **Radiation therapy**--Radiation directed at the cancer may destroy normal tissue in adjacent areas. Improvements in equipment and radiation source have been able to reduce this risk.

3. **Surgery**--If the tumor is confined to a distinct area, such as a portion of the colon or lung, it may be possible to remove it surgically, but the malignant cells must be completely removed in order to reduce significantly the risk of developing metastases through the migration of cancer cells.

4. **Transplantation of bone marrow cells**-- is reducing the death toll from childhood leukemias.

5. **Hybridoma**--creation of substance to enhance the immunization system through genetic engineering; it has some exciting promise.

Unconventional Cancer Treatments

There are a hundred types of cancer and it is not the domain of this article to cover them all. The treatments are so similar that it is not necessary to be too redundant. However, each year thousands of U.S. cancer patients use treatments that fall outside the generally understood bounds of mainstream medicine. It seems to me that people reach for unconventional cancer treatments for at least six reasons:

1 Effective treatments are lacking for many cancers, especially in the advanced stages. The message is "You are going to die," and so in desperation the search begins for alternatives.

2 Mainstream treatments entail considerable toxicity, pain, and side effects. Treatments are sometimes considered to be worse than the cancer, so some people seek nontoxic cancer control by unconventional means.

3 The survival rate for mainstream medical approach is less than 50%. Many unconventional treatments claim a higher percentage of cure.

4 Sometimes humane, caring, and psychological support from caregivers is missing in mainstream treatment. Unconventional treatment people can be very personable, caring, and interested.

5 Although words like quackery and greed are used concerning unconventional treatments, mainstream treatment is even more expensive than the quacks, and the pain and death rate is quite profound. The unconventionals give lots of hope to people who have none; **however, they conveniently do not let you see their failures.**

6 Sometimes that which was quackery yesterday becomes the treatment of choice for today. The unconventionals keep reminding their patients that they are on the cutting edge, while medicine is stuck in the old-fashioned traditions of the past.

Here are a few of the unconventional cancer treatments that on occasion have registered claims of tumor regression.

* **Mental imagery**--O. Carl Simonton, M.D.

* **Gerson regimen**--low-salt, high-potassium, vegetarian diet and coffee enemas--Max Gerson, M.D., Tijuana, Mexico

* **Kelley regimen**--vitamin and enzyme supplements and metabolic typing--Nicholas Gonzalez, M.D.

* **Macrobiotic diet**--cooked vegetables and whole grains.

* **Holistic medicine**--includes conventional cancer treatment, stress reduction, exercise, and psychological support--Keith Block, M.D.

* **Herbal substances**
    * Hoxsey treatment of mixed herbs offered in Tijuana;
    * Iscador, made from European mistletoe;
    * An herbal tea, developed by Rene Caisse, R.N., offered in Canada;
    * Chaparral tea, prepared from the leaflets of the creosote bush;
    * Pau d'Arco, a substance derived from the inner bark of trees native to Brazil and sold in health food stores;
    * Jason Winters herbal tea.

* Virginia Livingston, M.D., clinic in San Diego uses a vaccine designed to treat and prevent infection with the microbe that she believes to be a cause of cancer. Also tries to boost immune response, uses antibiotics, vitamin and mineral supplement with a special diet.

* Stanislaw Burzynski, M.D., Ph.D., at his clinic in Houston uses what he calls **"antineoplastons,"** substances described as peptides or amino acid derivatives isolated from urine or synthesized in the laboratory.

* Emanuel Revici, M.D., of New York uses **"biologically guided chemotherapy"** reported to consist of a variety of minerals, lipids, and lipid-based substances.

* **"Eumetabolic"** is a treatment offered by Hans Nieper, M.D., in Hannover, Germany. It is a combination of drugs, vitamins, minerals, and animal and plant extracts plus a special diet and avoidance of certain foods and physical locations.

* **"Immuno-augmentative therapy,"** offered by Lawrence Burton, Ph.D., at his clinics in the Grand Bahamas, Germany, and Mexico, consists of daily injections of dilute serum fractions made from pooled blood samples.

* **Laetrile**, a substance from apricot pits, widely popular in the 1970s and currently offered in several clinics in Mexico.

* **Vitamin C**, whose most prominent advocate for use in cancer treatment is the biochemist Linus Pauling, Ph.D.

* **Dimethyl sulfoxide** (DMSO), an industrial solvent often used in combination with laetrile and vitamin C.

* **Cellular treatment**, processed tissue obtained from animal embryos or fetuses given orally or by injection.

* **Hydrogen peroxide and ozone**, substances containing oxygen and taken orally, rectally, or via blood infusion.

* **Hydrazine sulfate**, a substance that, from 1975 to 1982 was on the American Cancer Society's Unproven Methods List. It was taken off when clinical trials under an investigational new drug exemption were started. Supporters of unconventional treatments often point to hydrazine sulfate as a treatment that was unfairly branded by the mainstream but is actually effective.

There are many other unconventional cancer treatments; some may prove to be effective and some may not. One of the problems is the happy but unpredictable habit of cancer, for some unknown reason, going into remission. Of course, whatever treatment is being used at the time may seem to be the right one. Another problem is that sometimes placebos (a neutral substance) will be more effective than actual drugs. We don't know why--perhaps cancer in remission has some psychological overtones. While working in Mexico, I observed cancer apparently being cured by the power of psychological suggestion.

Finally, we must bear testimony to various forms of religious healing, faith healing, laying on of hands, and prayer. People from all over the world have traveled to the famous religious shrine at Lourdes, France, to pray for miraculous cures. The Lourdes medical board has examined thousands of cases claiming cures--some have no other explanation. My philosophy is both prayer and medicine: *to pray as if everything depended upon prayer and to take medical treatment as if everything depended upon medical treatment.*

In the fight for life against the ravages of cancer, we may find it necessary to try one or more of the hopeful solutions found in unconventional cancer treatments. If we do, I recommend that we continue with our physician and the conventional mainstream medical treatment. Doctors are not in a conspiracy; they die of cancer, too.

CFS--not just an everyday experience

In everyday life we all respond to physical and emotional stress by getting tired. Sometimes we get tired and depressed for no particular reason. But the enigma known as chronic fatigue syndrome (CFS) is not just an everyday experience.

Chronic fatigue syndrome, formerly known as chronic Epstein-Barr virus, comes on suddenly and stays relentlessly, causing debilitating tiredness and easy fatigability for no apparent reason. It is similar to the mind fog of a serious hangover. It does not go away with a few good nights of sleep, but instead slyly steals a person's vigor over months and years. The hallmark of the illness is fatigue. Conservatively, as many as 1.5 million Americans with chronic fatigue syndrome have been identified--many more are undiagnosed. Some physicians are treating hundreds of patients with all the symptoms, and many patients are so devastated by it that they are completely disabled.

SYMPTOMS--consist of a sudden onset of headache, sore throat, low-grade fever, fatigue and weakness, tender lymph gland, muscle and joint aches, and inability to concentrate. It often mimics the symptoms of flu. Flu symptoms usually go away in a few days, but chronic fatigue syndrome symptoms persist or recur frequently for more than a year. For some people CFS begins after an acute infectious illness such as the flu, bronchitis, hepatitis, or gastrointestinal illness. For others it follows a bout of mononucleosis. Sometimes it develops gradually and seemingly with no apparent cause.

HISTORY--Clinical portraits of diseases similar to chronic fatigue syndrome have appeared under different guises in the medical literature for more than a century. In the 1860s Dr. George Beard named the syndrome neurasthenia, believing it to be a neurosis characterized by weakness and fatigue. Succeeding generations have agreed but not proved different explanations--iron poor blood (anemia), low blood sugar (hypoglycemia), environmental allergy, or a bodywide yeast infection (candidiasis).

Some scientists have considered the Epstein-Barr virus (EBV) as a possible cause of chronic fatigue syndrome. It may also be caused in people who never recovered from mononucleosis, or in whom the virus has somehow been reactivated.

Medical researchers at the University of Connecticut found that chronic fatigue syndrome, or chronic Epstein-Barr virus syndrome, is rare if it exists at all. They say that exhaustion, fever, swollen glands, disturbed sleep, and fogged thinking, all occurring or recurring for months or years, are due to treatable psychiatric disorders, particularly depression. Some have even called it the new "yuppie disease." These findings have fueled a heated debate from those who think CFS is caused by an unidentified virus.

Dr. Paul Cheney, senior staff physician at the Noile Clinic in Charlotte, NC, says he has seen 1,000 patients with chronic fatigue in the past three years. Cheney says of the majority of his patients, "They have objective abnormalities that they could not manufacture through psychic means."

Physicians sometimes misdiagnose chronic fatigue syndrome as depression, and vice versa, because the two illnesses share many symptoms: fatigue, malaise, sleep disorders, low-grade fever, and memory and concentration problems. Yet other chronic fatigue syndrome symptoms--including persistent sore throat, tender lymph glands, muscle and joint aches, and feelings of feverishness--do not fit the typical clinical picture of depression.

Research is underway using standard psychiatric interviews and some correlation has been detected. Other National Institute of Health scientists are probing the more subtle molecular interactions between the brain and the immune system. Brain scans are being used to help locate possible areas of brain dysfunction. Scientists have observed several immune system abnormalities in people with chronic fatigue syndrome. Many patients have relatively high antibody levels to virtually any virus measured. Several research groups have seen abnormal "natural killer" cell function in many patients. However these and other findings are inconsistent and not highly reproducible. Research continues on this condition.

TREATMENT--Currently, no proven effective treatment for chronic fatigue syndrome exists. Physicians have reported some small success with a wide range of treatments including antiviral, antidepressant, and immunomodulating drugs and psychiatric treatment.

In a current study, doctors at four hospitals tested Ampligen, an experimental antiviral drug. Ampligen dramatically relieved the extreme tiredness, memory loss, and other debilitating miseries of people severely afflicted with chronic fatigue syndrome.

Dr. Anthony Komaroff of Brigham and Women's Hospital in Boston, an authority on CFS, cautioned that the use of Ampligen does not settle several important issues, such as whether benefits last when treatment is stopped and whether there are unwanted side effects of long-term use of Ampligen.

The lack of any proven effective treatment is frustrating to both patients and their physicians. Experts recommend that people with chronic fatigue syndrome try to maintain a healthy lifestyle by eating a balanced diet and getting adequate rest. Physical conditioning should be preserved by exercising regularly as much as can be tolerated short of causing more fatigue. It is important that people with this condition learn to pace themselves--physically, emotionally, and intellectually--since too much stress can exacerbate the symptoms. Counseling may help some people cope with the uncertain prognosis and ups and downs of the illness.

The limited use of Ampligen with promising results clearly implies that there is an immunological or viral cause to this illness. It seems to support the idea that chronic fatigue syndrome is not a psychological disorder.

Additional information and help can be received from the following organizations:

Chronic Fatigue and Immune Dysfunction Syndrome Association
P.O. Box 220398
Charlotte, NC 28222
(704) 362-CFID
Marc Iverson, President

National Chronic Fatigue Syndrome Association
919 Scott Avenue
Kansas City, KS 66105
(913) 321-2278
Janet Bohanon and Orvalene Prewitt, Co-Directors

THE WARNING SIGNS OF DIABETES

TYPE I
CHILDREN AND YOUNG ADULTS
Symptoms usually develop rapidly
Frequent urination (bet-wetting)
Excessive thirst
Sudden weight loss
Weakness and fatigue
Irritability
Nausea and vomiting

NO CURE, but:
Type I can be controlled with insulin.
Type II can be controlled by diet,
exercise, and medications.

TYPE II
ADULT-ONSET
Symptoms usually develop gradually
Frequent urination
Excessive thirst
Sudden weight loss
Weakness and fatigue
Irritability
Nausea and vomiting
Blurred vision or any change in sight
Tingling or numbness in legs, feet, or fingers
Slow healing of cuts (especially on the feet)
Frequent skin infections or itchy skin
Drowsiness

The "sweet pea" disease

Diabetes is one of our leading causes of death in America. Each year diabetes and its complications will kill 150,000 people. Diabetes also plays a major role in blindness, heart attacks, strokes, kidney failure, amputation, and impotence. With such a deadly rampant killer it is surprising that almost half the 11 million Americans afflicted with diabetes do not know they have it. Even among those who have been diagnosed, only a small percent are aware of the latest findings and treatment.

Such a dangerous enemy to your longevity needs to be met with some knowledge and understanding of its nature, cause, and control. Your doctor is the best source of treatment of the disease, but we all need a little information written down for our consideration.

The diabetic condition was known to the ancient Egyptians. The early Greeks and Romans called it "diabetes mellitus," meaning the "honey-urine disease." The major symptom of diabetes is high levels of glucose (sugar) found in the blood and the urine. The early doctors detected diabetes by tasting the urine; if it was sweet, you had it. It was known on the sly as the "sweet pea disease."

ITS NATURE--Diabetes is a disease in which the body has problems changing food into energy. When sugars and starches are eaten and digested in the stomach and intestines, most of it is turned into a specific sugar called glucose. This glucose moves through the walls of the intestines and into the bloodstream, which carries it to all the millions of cells in the body as "fuel." An organ called the pancreas, which is located behind the stomach, releases a substance called insulin into the blood to control the amount of glucose in the blood. If your glucose level

goes too high you can go into a coma. If it goes too low it can lead to unconsciousness. Either condition damages body organs. Insulin also acts like a messenger that tells your millions of cells to take in the sugar and start using it for energy.

ITS CAUSE--One in 20 people have diabetes because:
Their pancreas stopped making insulin, or is not making enough,
Or because the insulin produced fails to regulate the blood glucose level,
Or because the cells in their bodies do not receive the insulin message properly to use the sugar,
Or because there is too much fatty tissue for the available amount of insulin.

If the cells can't use sugar, too much of it begins to build up in the blood where it can damage the system. So, another source of energy has to be sought--the body reaches for the stored fat. When fat breaks down too quickly in the blood we get a condition known as ketosis. It is this accumulation of ketones of fat that can lead to nausea, vomiting, diabetic coma, all sorts of immune system breakdowns, and death.

There are two types of diabetes and they are different diseases. This distinction is not always clear in news reports and magazine articles on diabetes. The causes, short-term effects, and treatment for the two diseases are different but both can cause the same long-term health problems.

CHILDREN AND YOUNG ADULT TYPE--
Type I diabetes occurs when cells in the pancreas that manufacture insulin stop producing it. In 1921, insulin, a hormone that regulates the glucose level in blood, was discovered. Daily insulin injections permitted the diabetic to metabolize sugars

and starches and convert them into heat and energy. The type I disease is called insulin-dependent diabetes. Those with type I (500,000 diabetic Americans--10% of the diabetic population) must have daily insulin injections and carefully balance energy input (diet) and output (exercise or work) to control body chemistry. Injections do not cure the disease, but help to control it.

ADULT-ONSET DIABETES--With type II diabetes, the pancreas usually continues to produce insulin, but the insulin fails to limit the level of blood glucose or properly activate the cells to take in glucose. Scientists don't know why. Most people with this type of diabetes do not need insulin injections; therefore, type II is known as noninsulin-dependent diabetes. This is the common form of diabetes among older people and this type accounts for over 85% of cases.

Type II may take several years to develop. Obesity is a very important factor. Eighty percent of people who find out they have diabetes are overweight. Other factors such as family history of diabetes increases your chances of having the disease. Type II can often be controlled with diet and exercise, although some people also need oral medications such as glipizide (Glucotrol) and glyburide (DiaBeta, Micronase). The symptoms are the same as Type I, although type II may have others in addition.

No one knows for sure
exactly what causes diabetes.

IF YOU HAVE DIABETIC SYMPTOMS

* See your doctor, of course.
* Keep your blood sugar at normal levels. (You can buy kits at the drugstore for testing urine or the blood.)
* If you are overweight, lose weight.
* Get a diabetes diet from the doctor and go on it.
* Adopt a program of moderate but consistent exercise.
* Remember, diabetes cannot be cured, but it can be controlled. If you don't control it, well...150,000 people die that way, every year.

For further information about Diabetes and a free newsletter "Diabetes" containing the latest findings, write: American Diabetes Association, Inc., 1660 Duke Street, Alexandria, VA 22314.

The Digestion Works--operation, care, malfunctions

Disorders of the digestive tract cause more hospital admissions than any other group of diseases. They occur most often in people who are middle-aged or older.

The digestive system performs the amazing task of breaking down the food we eat into the nutrients our bodies need. Most of the time this system stays remarkably free of trouble. As we grow older, however, our body begins to work less efficiently in some ways and our lifestyle may change. As a result, we may occasionally have a digestive problem.

HOW THE DIGESTIVE SYSTEM WORKS

The digestive system is a series of hollow organs joined in a long, twisting tube from the mouth to the anus. Inside this tube is a lining called the "mucosa." The mucosa contains tiny glands that produce juices to help digest food. There are also two solid digestive organs, the liver and the pancreas, which produce juices that reach the intestine through small tubes. Parts of other organ systems, for instance, nerves and blood also play a major role in the digestive system.

Digestion begins in the mouth. As we chew our food, tiny glands give off a fluid, saliva, which lubricates food so that it can be swallowed easily. Saliva also contains an enzyme that begins to change carbohydrates--like vegetables and breads--into a form the body can absorb. Once the food is swallowed, peristaltic (wave-like) motions push it through the esophagus and into the stomach. Stomach muscles crush and mix the food with enzymes and acids, creating a mixture called chyme. The stomach allows small amounts of the chyme to enter the duodenum, the first part of the small intestine. The stomach holds the rest of the chyme until the duodenum is ready to receive it. It is in the duodenum that most digestion takes place. There, juices from the liver and pancreas break down fats, protein, and carbohydrates. As the digested food passes into the last two-thirds of the small intestine, nutrients are absorbed into the blood. The remaining material is pushed into the colon, part of the large intestine. This material includes water and waste--the part of food that is not digested, such as fiber from fruits, vegetables, and grains. The lining of the colon absorbs water from the material and, when the waste is solid enough, nerves in the wall of the large intestine signal the urge for a bowel movement.

During the chemical process of digestion, food is broken down into pieces tiny enough to be taken into the blood. The blood, in turn, carries these food elements to cells in all parts of the body where they are changed into energy or used to form new structures.

When food or liquid is swallowed it becomes involuntary and proceeds under the control of the nerves. The esophagus is the organ into which the swallowed food is pushed. It connects the throat above with the stomach below. A ring-like valve closes the passage between the two organs. When the food enters the stomach it has three mechanical tasks to do:

1. First, the stomach must store the swallowed food and liquid (the upper part of the stomach relaxes to accept large volumes of swallowed material).
2. Second, the lower part of the stomach mixes the swallowed material by its muscle action.
3. Third, the stomach empties its contents slowly into the small intestine.

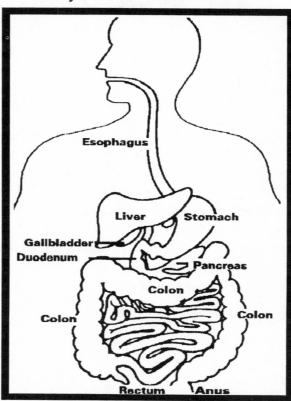

DIGESTIVE JUICES: The glands of the digestive system produce the juices that break down the food and the hormones that help to control the process:

1. The saliva glands in the mouth produce an enzyme that begins to digest the starch from food into smaller molecules.
2. Digestive glands in the stomach lining produce acid and an enzyme that digests protein. The stomach mucosa is able to resist this acid or else it would dissolve the stomach itself.

3. The small intestine enzymes come from the walls of the intestine.
4. The pancreas produces enzymes to break down carbohydrates, fat, and protein in our food.
5. The liver produces bile that is stored in the gallbladder and squeezed into the intestine to mix with the fat in our food. The bile acids dissolve the fat into the watery contents of the intestine, much like detergents in dishwater that dissolve grease from a frying pan.

Changes in lifestyle can interfere with the workings of the digestive system. Such lifestyle changes include increased use of medicines, reduced exercise, and changes in eating habits.

TAKING CARE OF THE SYSTEM
* Eat a well-balanced diet that includes a variety of fresh fruits, vegetables, and whole grain breads, cereals, and other grain products.
* Eat slowly and, whenever possible, try to relax for 30 minutes after each meal.
* Exercise regularly.
* If you drink alcohol, do it in moderation.
* Avoid large amounts of caffeine.
* Follow your doctor's directions exactly when taking prescribed medication; and, use caution when taking over-the-counter drugs.

KNOWING WHEN SOMETHING IS WRONG
No matter how well we treat our digestive system, there are times when things go wrong. Often the problem will take care of itself. Sometimes, however, symptoms can be a signal that something more serious is wrong. Some important warning signs that should send you to a doctor are:

→ Stomach pains that are severe, last a long time, are recurring, or come with shaking, chills, and cold, clammy skin.
→ Blood in vomit or recurrent vomiting.
→ A sudden change in bowel habits and consistency of stools lasting more than a few days. For example, diarrhea for more than three days or the sudden onset of constipation.
→ Blood in stools or coal-black stools.
→ Jaundice, which is a yellowing of the skin and the whites of the eyes.
→ Dark, tea-colored urine.
→ Pain or difficulty in swallowing food.
→ Continuing loss of appetite or unexpected weight loss.
→ Diarrhea that wakes you up at night.

Common digestive disorders affecting older people

Some of the digestive disorders that most commonly cause problems for older people are:

CONSTIPATION is a decrease in the number of bowel movements, along with prolonged or hard passage of stools. Older people report this problem much more often than younger ones do. "Regularity" does not necessarily mean one bowel movement every day. Normal bowel habits can range from three movements each day to one each week. A poor diet, drinking too few liquids, inactivity, some prescription medications, or misusing laxatives can lead to constipation. Regularity is usually improved by eating foods high in fiber (see page 125), increasing liquids, avoiding laxatives (see page 307), and staying physically active (see also constipation, page 306).

CROHN'S DISEASE is an inflammation that extends into the deeper layers of the intestinal wall. The disease either is limited to one or more segments of the small intestine or involves both the ileum and the colon. Sometimes, inflammation may also affect the mouth, esophagus, stomach, duodenum, appendix, or anus.

DIARRHEA is a condition in which body wastes are discharged from the bowels more often than usual and in a more or less liquid state. There are many possible causes, but many cases are related to infection. Treatment of the underlying disorder is needed, along with replacement of lost fluids.

DIVERTICULOSIS--In diverticulosis, which is common in older people (more than half of all Americans have it by the time they reach 60), small grape-like sacs form on the wall of the large intestine, caused when the lining of the intestine is forced out through the gut's muscular wall. Although they usually cause no symptoms, occasionally there is pain in the lower left side of the abdomen. Treatment includes a diet high in fiber and liquids.

DIVERTICULITIS--Sometimes the sacs become inflamed, causing fever. The condition is then known as diverticulitis. Treatment consists of bed rest and antibiotics (see article on Diverticulosis and Diverticulitis, page 304).

FUNCTIONAL DISORDER is when the intestinal tract fails to work properly. Sometimes symptoms such as pain, diarrhea, constipation, bloating, and gas are caused by a "functional" disorder such as irritable bowel syndrome. A functional disorder may cause discomfort, but it is unlikely to lead to a serious disease. A doctor may prescribe medication to relieve symptoms. Because diet and stress are thought to trigger functional disorders, the same guidelines that help to keep your system running smoothly help control the symptoms.

GALLBLADDER DISEASE is when stones (usually composed of cholesterol) form in the gallbladder. The stones are often "silent," that is, they cause no symptoms or discomfort, but sometimes they cause problems requiring drug treatment or surgery. Severe pain in the upper abdomen may mean that a gallstone has lodged in one of the tubes leading from the gallbladder. You can also have gallbladder disease without having gallstones (cholecystitis; also see article on page 308).

GAS is normally present in the digestive tract. It is usually caused by swallowing air or eating foods such as cauliflower, brussel sprouts, brown beans, broccoli, bran, and cabbage. The body rids itself of gas by means of belching and flatulence (passing gas through the rectum). However, if it collects in some portion of the digestive tract, it can lead to pain and bloating. A change in dietary habits will often relieve extra gas (see also page 305).

GASTRITIS is an inflammation of the stomach. Gastritis is a symptom, not a disorder, and can be caused by many different digestive ailments. Treatment is aimed at correcting the condition that is causing the gastritis.

HEARTBURN is a burning pain felt behind the breastbone that occurs after meals and may last for many minutes to several hours. It is often caused by eating foods such as tomato products, chocolate, fried food, or peppermint, and smoking cigarettes. It is relieved by a change in diet, taking an antacid, sleeping with the head of the bed raised 6 inches, or stopping cigarette smoking.

HEMORRHOIDS is a condition in which veins in and around the rectum and anus have become weakened and enlarged. It is caused by pressure in the rectal veins due to constipation, pregnancy, obesity, or other conditions. The veins may become inflamed, develop blood clots, and bleed. Hemorrhoids are treated with frequent warm baths, creams, or suppositories, and if necessary, by injections or surgery.

HIATAL HERNIA is a condition in which part of the stomach slides up through the diaphragm (a thin muscle that separates the abdominal cavity from the chest cavity). Hiatal hernias are common after middle age and rarely cause symptoms. Contrary to popular myth, hiatal hernias do not cause heartburn, although they are sometimes associated with it. Usually, they do not need surgical or drug treatment.

INDIGESTION is a common condition involving painful, difficult, or disturbed digestion. Doctors often call it dyspepsia. The symptoms may include nausea, regurgitation, vomiting, heartburn, abdominal fullness or bloating after a meal, and stomach discomfort or pain. Overeating or eating the wrong foods can cause symptoms, but they may also be related to other digestive problems, such as peptic ulcer, gallbladder disease, or gastritis. Indigestion usually can be controlled through diet or by treating the specific disorder.

INFLAMMATORY BOWEL DISEASE (IBD) is a group of chronic disorders that cause inflammation and/or ulceration in the lining of the bowel; most common types are ulcerative colitis and Crohn's disease. The symptoms are diarrhea, abdominal pain, rectal bleeding, fever, weight loss, and inflammation and ulceration of bowel lining. Surgery is required for about one-third of ulcerative colitis patients and two-thirds of Crohn's disease patients. Most persons with IBD hold productive jobs, marry, raise families, and function successfully at home and in society.

IRRITABLE BOWEL SYNDROME is characterized by muscular spasms of the intestinal tract that may be brought on by a poor diet, emotional upset, or stress. Reducing stress may help relieve IBS. Eating more bran and roughage such as whole-grain breads, cereals, and vegetables may also help. The fiber in these foods keeps the colon stretched, which will help prevent spasms.

MILK INTOLERANCE is the inability to properly digest milk and milk products due to a deficiency of lactase, the intestinal enzyme that digests the sugar found in milk. Some people develop this problem as they grow older. The symptoms, which include cramps, gas, bloating, and diarrhea, appear 15 minutes to several hours after consuming milk or a milk product. Most people can manage the problem by eating fewer dairy products, taking smaller servings more frequently, or adding a nonprescription preparation Lactaid to milk that makes it easy to digest. Lactaid is

More disorders

available OTC in pill form (to take before eating milk products) and in liquid form to add to regular milk. It is also available in the dairy case with regular milk (already mixed) in whole and skim milk form. If fewer dairy products are eaten, other foods that have calcium (such as dark green leafy vegetables, salmon, and bean curd) should be substituted to help keep the bones strong. Many people can eat yogurt without having discomfort.

PEPTIC ULCER is a sore on the lining of the stomach or duodenum (the small intestine just below the stomach). An ulcer occurs when the lining is unable to resist the damaging effects of acid and pepsin that are produced by the stomach to digest foods. Antacids, which neutralize acid in the stomach, and drugs that decrease the production of acid or coat the ulcer are very useful in treating peptic ulcer.

ULCERATIVE COLITIS is a chronic disorder in which parts of the large intestine become inflamed, causing abdominal cramps and often rectal bleeding. Joint pain and skin rashes may also develop. The symptoms are usually controlled with drugs such as sulfasalazine. Cortisone-like drugs called steroids may be administered for a short while, but they have serious side effects. Some patients eventually need surgical removal of the colon, called a colectomy, or the removal of both the colon and rectum, called a proctocolectomy. After these procedures are performed, waste matter is drained through an opening in the abdominal wall into a contoured plastic pouch strapped to the patient's abdomen, which is emptied up to six times a day.

For more information on digestive diseases, write:
National Digestive Diseases
Information Clearinghouse
1255 23rd Street, N.W., Suite 275
Washington, D.C. 20037
Phone: (202) 296-1138

> **Give me a good digestion, Lord**
> **And also something to digest.**
> **Anonymous**
> **Pilgrim's Grace**

What is diverticulosis?

Diverticulosis is a condition in which pouches, know as diverticula, about the size of large peas, form in the walls of the intestines. They form in weakened areas of the bowels, most often in the lower part of the colon. A more serious condition known as diverticulitis occurs when these pouches become infected and inflamed.

Diverticulosis is very common in older persons with 10% over 40 having it, and nearly 50% of those over 60. Among those who have it only 20% develop the more serious condition, diverticulitis, and only a small number of those have very serious or life-threatening complications.

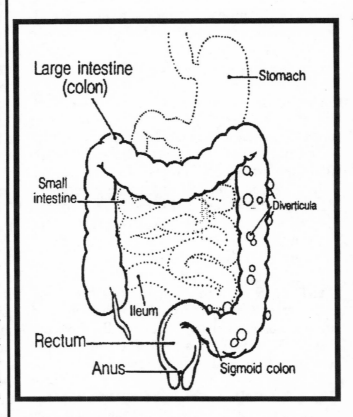

THE CAUSE--No one knows why the pouches form. Scientists think the sacs might form when increased pressure, muscle spasms, or straining acts on soft spots along the bowel wall, especially if a person has constipation problems or uses laxatives too often.

SYMPTOMS--Some people have no symptoms. Some feel tenderness over the affected area or muscle spasms in the abdomen, disturbed bowel function, and fever. Pains may be felt on the lower left side of the abdomen or, less often, in the middle or on the right side. Bleeding is uncommon and usually not severe.

With infection or inflammation--diverticulitis--there may be fever, an increase in white blood cell count, and acute abdominal pain, resulting in large abscesses (infected areas of pus), bowel blockage, or breaks and leaks through the bowel wall.

HOW SERIOUS?--For most, diverticulosis is not a problem. Diverticulitis is a problem, sometimes a serious one. If the infection remains localized it may go away in a few days. In rare cases the infection spreads and breaks through the wall of the colon, causing peritonitis (infection of the abdominal cavity) or abscesses in the abdomen. Such infections are very serious and can lead to death unless treated without delay.

DIAGNOSIS--Often diverticulosis is unsuspected and discovered by an X-ray, a barium enema-type X-ray using a flexible tube (colonoscope) inserted through the anus, or from an intestinal examination done for an unrelated reason.

If rectal bleeding occurs, the doctor may take a special X-ray (angiography). Dye is injected into an artery that goes to the colon so that the site of the bleeding can be located.

TREATMENT--If you have diverticulosis with no symptoms, no treatment is necessary. Some doctors advise eating a high fiber diet and avoiding certain foods. Laxatives and enemas should not be used regularly. Those with diverticulitis may be hospitalized and treated with bed rest, pain relievers, antibiotics, fluids given by vein, and watchful care.

SURGERY--The vast majority of patients recover from diverticulitis without surgery. Some need surgery to drain an abscess resulting from a ruptured pouch and to remove that portion of the colon. Surgery is reserved for patients with very severe or multiple attacks. Get a second opinion! In those cases, the involved segment of colon can be removed and the colon rejoined. Sometimes more than one operation is required.

WHAT ABOUT DIET? -- If you have diverticulosis with no symptoms, you probably don't need treatment, but it is a good idea to watch your diet. Eat more foods high in fiber! Fiber-rich foods include whole-grain cereals and breads, fruits, and vegetables. Remember, diverticulosis usually causes you no problems but you should be checked regularly to make sure that if you have the disease it does not progress--which it can.

The discomfort caused by gas

Excessive gas is a common complaint of older persons. Though the subject is not one that most of us talk about, the truth is that all of us have gas in our intestinal tract and must get rid of it some way. Flatulence, the passage of gas through the rectum, and belching are normal and necessary functions that allow the body to rid itself of gas.

Causes of Gas

The most common cause of intestinal gas is swallowing air. Indeed, most of the gas inside us is composed of oxygen and nitrogen. Swallowing air is hard to avoid--a little goes down with each mouthful of food. Eating too fast can increase air intake. Poor-fitting dentures and chewing gum are other sources of air swallowing. In addition, drinking carbonated beverages such as soda and beer may increase the amount of gas in the stomach.

Other intestinal gases include hydrogen, carbon dioxide, and methane. They are produced in the large intestine when undigested food, mainly incompletely absorbed carbohydrates, is fermented by bacteria that live in the colon. This is known as colonic fermentation. It's normal to incompletely absorb a variety of carbohydrate-rich foods. Beans are well known for their gas-forming ability. The sugars in such foods as baked beans, lima beans, and lentils resist breakdown by the enzymes in your small intestine. Some people differ in their abilities to absorb lactose, the dominant sugar in milk and milk products. Lactose-intolerant people lack sufficient lactase, an intestinal enzyme needed to digest and absorb it. Bacteria ferment these sugars in your large intestine and cause gas.

Those five gasses previously mentioned are odorless and constitute about 99% of all intestinal gas. The unpleasant odor associated with flatus comes from trace amounts of other chemicals and gasses, such as hydrogen sulfide, ammonia, indole, and skatole, that result from the fermentation process. Some of these trace gases can be detected by smell in concentrations as low as one part per 100 million.

The Amount of Gas

The amount of gas a person takes in and produces varies from individual to individual (from about 400 to 2,400 cubic centimeters a day). The amounts differ because people are different: Some swallow more air than others, and some produce more gas than others. It is reported that most healthy people have an average of 14 flatus incidents daily and this is considered normal. About half the gas passed as flatus represents swallowed air. But if you tend to produce more gas or often eat gas-forming foods you could find it necessary to relieve yourself of gas as often as 50 to 100 times daily. However, it may not be the amount of gas that causes stomach and social discomfort but the movement of gas.

Growls and Gurgles

Researchers have found that the complaint of "too much gas" often results from slow transit time through the digestive tract, rather than excessive volume. The growls and gurgles you sometimes hear (technically, borborygmi) usually stem from the digestive process as food and air squeeze their way out of the stomach and through the long, narrow, twisting tubes of your intestines.

Bloating

Occasionally, gas collects in some portion of the digestive tract, a situation that can lead to pain and bloating. Bloating is a feeling of fullness in the mid-abdominal region often occurring after meals.

Abdominal Pain and Distention

Some people experience upper abdominal pressure and pain after eating. Usually, this can be relieved by belching. Some people deliberately swallow more air to make themselves belch. Such a practice is not recommended, however. It only adds to the amount of gas already in the stomach without reducing the discomfort.

Gas can collect anywhere in the colon. When gas accumulates on the right side of the colon, the pain can be similar to that caused by gallbladder disease.

Gas in the upper left portion of the colon can result in a condition called *splenic flexure syndrome*. The pain associated with this condition can spread to the left side of the chest and be confused with heart disease.

Limiting Gas

The most common cause of intestinal gas is swallowing air. To reduce belching and bloating: eat and drink slowly; limit foods and beverages that contain air, such as baked goods, whipped cream, souffles, and carbonated beverages; eat fewer rich foods; and don't smoke or chew gum.

Internal production of gas is probably best limited by diet. Don't eat foods that you find are the worst offenders (see table). Everyone's tolerance is different. Don't use excessive amounts of dietetic foods or sugar-free candies and gums that contain sorbitol or mannitol. Lactose-intolerant people, for example, need to avoid milk and most milk products in order to escape discomfort and embarrassment. In one study, the number of flatus episodes in one lactose-intolerent individual increased from 34 to 141 a day with a pure milk diet.

Some people find relief with products containing simethicone such as Mylanta, Riopan Plus, Mylicon-80, Gas-X, or Phazyme 95. Simethicone breaks up gas bubbles by reducing surface tension.

These foods can give you gas

Researchers have found that certain foods tend to increase colonic fermentation activity, which produces gas. While not all people are susceptible to the same foods, here is a list of foods that are generally regarded as flatus producers (flatulogenics, as the experts say).

Extremely gassy		Normal to moderately gassy
dried beans	prunes and prune juice	pastries
dried peas	raisins	eggplant
baked beans	whole-wheat bread	potatoes
soybeans	bran cereals	apples
lima beans	bran muffins	citrus fruits
lentils	pretzels	broccoli
cabbage	wheat germ	cauliflower
radishes	milk and cream	cucumbers
onions	ice cream and ice milk	tomatoes
brussels sprouts	sorbitol and mannitol	kohlrabi
sauerkraut	contained in some	rutabaga
apricots	dietetic and sugar-free	
bananas	foods	

Because all these foods are important to your health, don't avoid any of them unnecessarily. Minimize gas production from high-fiber foods by gradually adding more fiber to your diet during a period of several weeks. See article on fiber, page 125.

Information to help avoid "irregularity"

Older people are five times more likely than younger people to report problems with constipation. Poor diet, insufficient intake of fluids, lack of exercise, the use of certain drugs to treat other conditions, and poor bowel habits can all result in constipation. Experts agree, however, that too often older people become overly concerned with having a bowel movement and that constipation is frequently an imaginary ailment.

Who Has Constipation?
Some doctors suggest asking yourself these questions to decide if you are really constipated:

- ❑ Do you often have fewer than two bowel movements each week?
- ❑ Do you have difficulty passing stools?
- ❑ Is there pain?
- ❑ Are there other problems such as bleeding?

Unless these are regular symptoms for you, if you are constipated, there are steps you can take to improve your condition without resulting to harsh drug treatments.

What Causes Constipation?
Doctors do not always know what causes constipation. But an older person who eats a poor diet, drinks too few fluids, or misuses laxatives can easily become constipated. Drugs given for other conditions (for example, certain antidepressants, antacids containing aluminum or calcium, antihistamines, diuretics, and antiparkinsonism drugs) can produce constipation in some people, as can lack of exercise.

The Role of Diet
A shift in dietary habits away from high-fiber foods (vegetables, fruits, and whole grains) to foods that are high in animal fats (meats, dairy products, and eggs) and refined sugars (rich desserts and other sweets) and low in fiber can contribute to constipation. Fiber is the nondigestible portion of plant foods. It retains water as it passes through the system, adding bulk to stools. Some studies have suggested that high-fiber diets result in larger stools, more frequent bowel movements, and therefore less constipation (see the article on fiber, page 125).

Lack of interest in eating--a common problem for many people who live alone--may lead to heavy use of convenience foods, which tend to be low in fiber. In addition, loss of teeth may force older people to choose soft, processed foods that also contain little, if any, fiber.

Older people sometimes cut back on liquids in their diet, especially if they are not eating regular or balanced meals. Water and other fluids add bulk to stools, making bowel movements easier.

Other Causes of Constipation
Lengthy bedrest, for example after an accident or illness, and lack of exercise may contribute to constipation. For patients who stay in bed and who suffer from chronic constipation, drug therapy may be the best solution. But simply being more active is a better idea for individuals who are not bedfast.

Ignoring the natural urge to defecate (have a bowel movement) can result in constipation. Some people prefer to have their bowel movements only at home, but holding a bowel movement can cause ill effects if the delay is too long.

In some people, constipation may be caused by abnormalities or blockage of the digestive system. These disorders may affect either the muscles or nerves responsible for normal defecation. A doctor can perform a series of tests to determine if constipation is the symptom of an underlying (and often treatable) disorder.

Treatment
If you become constipated, you should first see your doctor to rule out a more serious problem. If the results show that no intestinal disease or abnormality exists, and your doctor approves, try these remedies:

- ■ **Eat more fresh fruits and vegetables,** either cooked or raw, and more whole grain cereals and breads. Dried fruits such as apricots, prunes, and figs are especially high in fiber. Try to cut back on highly processed foods (such as sweets) and foods high in fat.
- ■ **Drink plenty of liquids especially water** (1 to 2 quarts daily) unless you have heart, circulatory, or kidney problems. But be aware that drinking large quantities of milk may be constipating for some.
- ■ Some doctors recommend **adding small amounts of unprocessed bran** ("millers bran") to baked goods, cereals, and fruits as a way of increasing the fiber content of the diet. Millers bran is unprocessed bran and is sold in health food stores or in the health food section of supermarkets. It should not be confused with the packaged cereals that contain large amounts of bran or bran flakes.

If your diet is well-balanced and contains a variety of foods high in fiber, it is usually not necessary to add bran to other foods. But if you do use unprocessed bran, remember that some people suffer from bloating and gas for several weeks after adding bran to their diet. All changes in the diet should be made slowly, to allow the digestive system to adapt.

- ■ **Stay active.** Even taking a brisk walk after dinner can help tone your muscles.
- ■ **Try to develop a regular bowel habit.** If you have had problems with constipation, attempt to have a bowel movement shortly after breakfast or dinner.
- ■ **Limit your intake of antacids**, as some can cause constipation as well as other health problems.
- ■ **Avoid taking laxatives** if at all possible. Although they will usually relieve the constipation, you can quickly come to depend on them and the natural muscle actions required for defecation will be impaired.

Laxatives
For persons in relatively good health, laxatives should be a last resort. Persons suffering from heart disease, high blood pressure, hemorrhoids, hernia, and stroke-related conditions may take laxatives according to a physician's instructions to reduce straining. In addition, bedridden constipated patients, surgery patients, and patients preparing for rectal or intestinal exams may take laxatives under a physician's supervision. Bedridden patients should avoid taking mineral oil orally; it can cause pneumonia if accidently inhaled. Kidney patients should steer clear of saline laxatives containing potassium, magnesium, or phosphates.

Laxatives are intended for relief of occasional constipation (irregularity). They should not be used for more than one week except on the advice of a physician. If the recommended dose of the laxative has had no effect after one week, if rectal bleeding develops, or if a sudden change of bowel habits lasts two weeks or more, it's really important to see your doctor. Later, if you do take laxatives, make sure you follow instructions carefully and don't overuse them. With overuse, the body begins to rely on the laxatives to bring on bowel movements and, over time, the natural "emptying" mechanisms fail to work without the help of these drugs. If you reach for a laxative every time your bowels refuse to move, you could be headed for trouble. Laxatives are, after all, drugs. And, like other drugs, they pose the risk of side effects and habituation. Moreover, the use of a laxative at the onset of constipation could delay treatment for serious underlying problems that cause the irregularity.

Prolonged laxative use can also deplete the body of fluids, salts, and essential vitamins and minerals and inhibit the absorption or effectiveness of other drugs. Furthermore, it can cause dizziness, confusion, fatigue, skin irritation, diarrhea, irregular heartbeat, belching, and a range of other side effects, depending on the laxative used. Laxatives should not be used in the presence of abdominal pain, nausea, vomiting, or fever unless directed by a doctor.

Laxative Types

Laxatives now available over-the-counter (OTC) come in liquid, tablet, gum, powder, granule, suppository, and enema dosage forms. They work in different ways to promote stool evacuation.

Stimulant laxatives agitate or excite intestinal walls, causing waves of muscular contractions that expel fecal matter. Product names include Carter's Little Pills, Castor Oil, Dulcolax, Ex-Lax, Feen-A-Mint, Fletcher's Castoria, and Modane. The FDA has banned the following stimulant-laxative ingredients: calomel, colocynth, elaterin resin, gamboge, ipomea, jalap, podophyllum resin, aloin, bile salts, bile acids, calcium pantothenate, frangual, oxbile, prune concentrate, prune powder, rhubarb-Chinese, and sodium oleate.

Lubricant laxatives "grease" stools, facilitating excretion. Mineral oil and mineral-oil emulsions are the most common forms of lubricants. Among them are Agoral Plain and Fleet Mineral Oil Enema. Overuse of mineral oil may reduce the absorption of certain vitamins (A, D, E, and K). Mineral oil may also interact with drugs such as anticoagulants (given to prevent blood clots) and other laxatives, causing undesirable side effects.

Saline laxatives act like a sponge to draw water into the bowel, thereby promoting easier passage for stools. Loss of body salts is a key risk of long-term use of these products. Among laxatives in this group are Milk of Magnesia, Citrate of Magnesia, and Epsom Salts. The recent ban by the FDA forbids the use of tartaric acid as a saline-laxative ingredient.

Stool softeners, or emollients, soften hard stools by enabling them to absorb more liquids. They are often given to patients recovering from surgery. Brands include Colace, Dialose, Regutol, and Surfak. Stool softeners should never be taken within two hours of a mineral-oil dose because the combination can result in excessive buildup of mineral oil in body tissues. Polaxamer 188 is now banned as a stool-softener ingredient.

Hyperosmotic laxatives mimic the action of saline laxatives but pose less risk of salt depletion. Over-the-counter hyperosmotics such as glycerin are available for rectal use only. Oral hyperosmotics must be prescribed by a physician. Overuse of hyperosmotics can cause continuing diarrhea.

Carbon-dioxide-releasing suppositories produce carbon dioxide in the bowels. The gas pushes stubborn stools toward excretion. The suppositories are available OTC under the brand name of Ceo-Two.

Bulk-forming laxatives absorb water in the intestine and swell the stool into an easily passing soft mass. Each dose should be taken with an eight-ounce glass of liquid. Although bulk agents are generally regarded as the safest form of laxative, users should be aware that the products can interfere with the absorption of certain drugs, including aspirin, digitalis, antibiotics, and anticoagulants. People with a genetic disorder should not take any sugar-free bulk laxative containing phenylalanine, because it can damage their brain tissue.

Bulk laxatives include FiberCon, Metamucil, and Serutan. Although bran is considered a bulk agent, the FDA has said that bran cereals marketed solely as food products will not be subject to laxative regulations. However, any bran product marketed as a laxative will be regarded as a drug, and, therefore, must conform with FDA rules.

The following bulk-laxative ingredients are now banned: carrageenan (degraded), agar, carrageenan (native), and guar gum. Many bulk-laxative products contain water-soluble gums as their active ingredients--for example, karaya, methylcellulose, plantago seed, psyllium, and polycarbophil. Water-soluble gums taken without adequate water can cause problems. The FDA has proposed these products have the following warning on their labels:

Warning: Take or mix this product with at least 8 ounces (a full glass) of water or other fluid. **Taking this product without adequate fluid may cause it to swell and block your throat or esophagus and may cause choking. Do not take this product if you have ever had difficulty in swallowing or have any throat problems. If you experience chest pain, vomiting, or difficulty in swallowing or breathing after taking this product, seek immediate medical attention.**

Combination laxatives and bowel cleansing systems. Some products contain a combination of laxatives that act together to promote evacuation. These drugs may carry a higher risk of side effects. A combination laxative drug with more than two active ingredients will be permitted by the FDA only if it can be shown that the combination is equal to or better than each of the active ingredients used alone at its therapeutic dose and presents no additional safety risk.

Although bowel-cleansing systems contain a number of ingredients, these ingredients are used sequentially at specified intervals and are not true combination drug products. Bowel-cleansing systems are used to evacuate the bowel before surgery or diagnostic exams. But such products are not intended for general laxative use and are labeled for use only as directed by a doctor.

Conclusion

The FDA found that overuse of laxatives was common. Many people are under the impression that serious health-endangering consequences will occur if the bowel is not evacuated daily. In fact, the normal range varies from as many as three bowel movements a day to as few as three a week. "Regularity" differs from person to person.

**If your bowel movements
are usually painless and
occur regularly
(whether the pattern is three times a day
or two times each week),
then you are probably not
constipated.**

Even when constipation does develop, sufferers can usually relieve their symptoms by increasing their fiber and fluid intake, or simply by altering their daily routines to allow more time on the commode to relax and let nature take its course.

Gallstones--a source of excruciating pain

THE GALLBLADDER

The gallbladder is a small, pear-shaped organ that lies on the underside of the liver, in the right upper portion of the abdomen. It is about three to four inches long and about one inch wide. It is connected by ducts (or tubes) with the liver and the upper portion of the small intestine (duodenum). Gall is another word for bile.

The liver produces bile (a substance that is essential for digesting fats) and secretes it into the gallbladder where it is concentrated

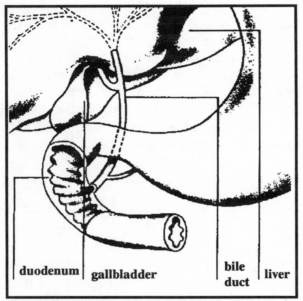

Gallbladder, situated underneath the right lobe of the liver; secretes bile into the duodenum.

and stored. The bile emulsifies fats and neutralizes acids in partly digested food. When food is eaten, especially fatty or greasy foods, the gallbladder contracts and forces bile out of the ducts leading into the intestine. When the gallbladder is removed, this function is taken over by the liver and its ducts.

In some individuals, a problem exists in the function of the gallbladder as it does not empty bile into the intestine as it should. The exact causes of these conditions are not known, but they are frequently associated with diets that are high in fatty and greasy foods. Anyone can develop gallbladder disease, but it is more common in people who are overweight, and between the ages of 36 and 55. Women are more likely to suffer from it than men, a factor that appears to be associated with metabolic changes that take place during pregnancy.

GALLSTONES

Frequently, the gallbladder contains stones or develops an infection that can interfere with its role in the digestive process. A gallstone is a mass of concentrated bile, resembling a stone, that forms in the gallbladder, or sometimes in the common bile duct. Medically, a gallstone is a type of calculus. It is usually a mixture of cholesterol, bilirubin (a bile pigment), and protein. The size of a gallstone can vary from a tiny crystal to a lump the size of a small egg. Usually, more than one gallstone is formed.

Some 20 million people in the United States have gallstones. About 1 million new cases of the malady develop each year. Autopsy studies show that 20% of all women and 8% of all men have gallstones when they die. The older you are, the more likely you are to have gallstones. Up to one in five elderly people are estimated to have them.

> **Gallstones are not always a benign condition but can in fact cause serious and even life-threatening complications. Therefore, treatment of gallstones should not be indefinitely deferred.**

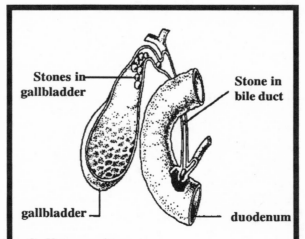

Gallstone sites:
Gallstones may remain in the gallbladder or pass through the bile duct into the duodenum. In either case you will probably have no symptoms. Problems arise if the gallstones are trapped in the bile duct.

GALLBLADDER DISEASE SYMPTOMS

Sometimes, persons with gallbladder disease have few or no symptoms. Most, however, will eventually develop one or more of the following symptoms:

* **Frequent bouts of indigestion**, especially after eating fatty or greasy foods, or certain vegetables such as cabbage, radishes, or pickles.
* **Nausea, heartburn, and bloating.**
* **Attacks of sharp pains** in the upper right part of the abdomen. This pain occurs when a gallstone becomes lodged in the duct from the gallbladder to the intestine.
* **Jaundice** (yellowing of the skin) may occur if a gallstone becomes stuck in the common bile duct that leads into the intestine, blocking the entire flow of bile from both the gallbladder and the liver. This is a serious complication and usually requires an immediate emergency operation.

DIAGNOSIS

Gallbladder disease is frequently diagnosed with X-rays. The patient is given a special dye, either in a pill or an injection, which causes the gallbladder to be visible on the X-ray film. If the gallbladder does not appear on the X-ray, it may indicate that a stone is blocking the bile ducts. Another method that may be used for diagnosing gallbladder disease is ultrasound, a safe and painless technique that uses high-frequency sound waves to project an image of the gallbladder onto a special screen.

If a person experiences gallbladder symptoms but does not have gallstones, consultations with physicians or surgeons should be continued until a solution to the problem is found since not all people who have gallbladder pain necessarily have stones. Many general internists, gastroenterologists, and surgeons are becoming more aware of this phenomenon and the use of nuclear medicine tests in studying gallbladder emptying.

> **It is better to have old secondhand diamonds than none at all.**
> - Mark Twain (1835-1910)

News Item: A new oral medication, Actigall, is reported to dissolve some stones. Check with your doctor.

DISEASES AND DISORDERS
GALLBLADDER AND GALLSTONES 309

TREATMENT

Some patients, such as those who have a functional problem of the gallbladder with no stones or infection, may be successfully treated with medications and a special diet. It is recommended that people eat sensibly, particularly not overeating any foods that bring on pain or indigestion. However, when stones are present and causing symptoms, or when the gallbladder is infected and inflamed, removal of the organ is usually necessary.

GALLBLADDER REMOVAL, THE OPERATION, CHOLECYSTECTOMY

■ Removal of the gallbladder is one of the most frequently performed of all operations; it is not considered a dangerous or risky procedure in otherwise healthy individuals. The incision for the operation is made either longitudinally (up and down) in the upper portion of the abdomen, or obliquely (at a slant) beneath the ribs on the right side.

When the gallbladder is removed, the surgeon also examines the bile ducts, sometimes with X-rays, and removes any stones that may be lodged there. The ducts are not removed, so that the liver can continue to secrete bile into the intestine after the gallbladder has been removed. During the operation, drains may be inserted into the wound. These will be removed while the patient is still in the hospital.

In many instances, the surgeon may also remove the appendix. This is a preventive measure to avoid a possible future operation for appendicitis.

RECOVERY

In uncomplicated situations, the hospital stay following gallbladder surgery is approximately one week. Most patients can get out of bed the day following the operation, and can return to normal activity within four to eight weeks. The great majority of patients experience no further symptoms once the gallbladder has been removed. However, mild residual symptoms are not uncommon. These can usually be controlled with a special diet and medication.

■ **Laparoscopic cholecystectomy** is a new technique for removing the gallbladder. With laparoscopic surgery, four small holes are poked into the belly, and the finger-sized gallbadder is removed up a thin tube. Two types of laser beams are used: one for cutting the tissue and one for cauterizing the wound. Both beams can be delivered down the same fiber-optic cord. Doctors performing laparoscopy observe their work on a video screen as they manipulate the long slender tools.

Laparoscopic cholecystectomy minimizes the size of the incision needed for gall bladder surgery, and greatly reduces the patient's pain, hospital stay, and recovery time, according to reports.

GALLSTONE REMOVAL

Throughout history, gallstones have been a cause of excruciating pain. Until recently, surgical removal of the gallbladder was the only way to remove these rock-like deposits. Today, treatment alternatives are being developed to remove gallstones without surgery.

Among these advances is a new technique that uses a chemical called methyl tertbutyl ether (MTBE) to dissolve gallstones. Originally developed as an industrial solvent and octane-enhancer for gasoline, it has low levels of toxicity and is similar in makeup to the ether used in anesthesia. MTBE, however, is a liquid rather than a gas. In this experimental procedure, MTBE is injected directly into the gallbladder.

MTBE dissolves the most common forms of stones within several hours to a few days. Used alone or in conjunction with other treatments, this procedure can benefit many people who experience gallbladder attacks but are not candidates for surgery.

After a local anesthetic and intravenous pain medications are administered, the physician inserts a fine needle containing a guide wire through the skin of the right side of the upper abdomen and into the gallbladder. Next, a catheter about the diameter of a strand of spaghetti is threaded over the guide wire. MTBE is then pumped into and out of the gallbladder four to six times per minute. This process may be repeated for up to three days.

MTBE is as effective on clusters of small gallstones as it is on a single, large stone. After a stone dissolves, a muddy-looking residue may remain, but can be suctioned out of the gallbladder. Most people who have undergone MTBE treatment have had their gallstones completely or almost completely (95%) dissolved. When MTBE treatment is successful, gallstones dissolve in much the same way as a sugar cube does in a cup of coffee. To date, the treatment has been most successful in treating stones composed primarily of cholesterol.

In addition to alleviating the need for surgery, MTBE treatment permits a shorter hospital stay. Return to normal activity usually is possible within a few days. By contrast, gallbladder surgery requires general anesthesia, a longer hospital stay, and usually a month or more for full recovery.

About 50% of persons whose gallstones are removed ultimately develop new ones. Younger people, therefore, may benefit from surgical removal of the gallbladder, which eliminates the risk of gallstones forming in the future.

"In my experience of approximately 150 patients with gallbladder pain who do not have stones, most of these are in the relatively young age group; however, I have seen two patients over the age of 70 whose symptoms were so disabling that they considered conventional gallbladder surgery even at that point in life. When the pain has been proven to be of gallbladder origin, removal of the organ results in more than a 90% cure rate."--H. T. Servis, M.D.

I like work; it fascinates me.
I can sit and look at it for hours
I love to keep it by me;
the idea of getting rid of it,
nearly breaks my heart.

- Jerome K. Jerome (1859-1927)

The heart and circulatory system

Every year about 1,500,000 Americans suffer a heart attack. Of that number, 500,000 die within one year; 100,000 die before they can be hospitalized. We need to know something about heart attacks and what we can do to prevent them.

HOW THE HEART WORKS AS A PUMP: To understand how to deal with disorders of the heart, it helps to learn the basic mechanisms of how the heart works. The heart is a pump. It pumps by contracting and relaxing, forcing blood on its journey to deliver oxygen and nutrients to the far reaches of the body. The pumping action occurs some 100,000 times a day.

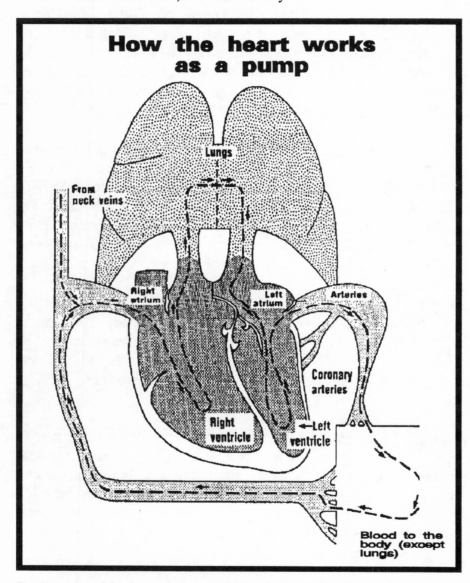

Let's start with the oxygenated blood returning from the lungs to the heart. The blood flows into the upper chamber of the left side of the heart (left atrium). After it collects there it passes into the next chamber, the left ventricle. This chamber does the most work. It has to pump oxygenated blood out of the arteries and to all parts of the body (brain, kidneys, liver, muscles, skin) except the lungs. When the heart muscle (the left ventricle) is too weak to pump enough blood into the arteries, a left heart failure occurs and all parts of the body will be affected.

Continuing the journey, the blood passes through the innumerable small vessels called capillaries and enters into the smallest veins. The blood in the veins supplies oxygen to the various tissues and takes on carbon dioxide. It flows back to the larger veins, and finally returns to the right side of the heart. Here it enters the upper right

chamber, the right atrium. It collects there and then empties into the lower right chamber, the right ventricle. The ventricle then pumps the blood to the lungs to release carbon dioxide and take on oxygen. Then the process starts over as the oxygenated blood returns again to the left atrium.

It is the muscle in the wall of the heart that does the pumping. That muscle, known as the myocardium, is like other living tissue in that it needs oxygen to function. When part of the muscle is denied oxygen, it dies. A piece of the heart is damaged and no longer contracts; or, the pump works less efficiently. This condition is called a "myocardial infarction" or simply an "infarct" or, even more simply, an "MI."

HEART ATTACKS: Heart attack is the largest single cause of death in the United States. Heart attacks may cause death almost instantaneously, or they may leave a person severely impaired. Sudden death occurs in about one-fourth of heart attack cases. Most deaths occur within two hours of the attack.

Some heart attacks are disguised. They are silent attacks, showing no symptoms. These silent attacks nevertheless leave damage and evidence that something is wrong. Electrocardiograms (EKGs) can reveal if a silent heart attack has occurred. In an EKG, the heart's electrical impulses are recorded. Variations in the impulse patterns can reveal damaged areas of the heart.

For other than silent heart attacks, the usual symptoms are tightening of the chest or chest pain (often radiating to the shoulder, arm, neck, or jaw), nausea, cold sweat, and shortness of breath.

ANGINA: For more than 2.4 million Americans, running to catch a bus or disagreeing with a spouse doesn't just leave them out of breath or angry; such physical exertion or emotional stress can trigger an attack of severe chest pains. It is a condition called angina or angina pectoris. It is a symptom of a condition known as myocardial ischemia, an inadequate blood flow to a part of the heart muscle. Angina occurs when the heart muscle gets enough blood for normal heart needs, but not enough to accommodate the heart when it is under moderate stress such as during exercise or emotional upset. Angina is not a heart attack. It is a temporary reduction in blood flow to the heart muscle. Heart attack is caused by permanent blockage of blood flow through a coronary artery to the heart muscle. Angina in itself can be a warning sign that a person is at risk of having a heart attack.

Angina is often felt as pain, like a sharp squeezing in the chest. In some people, this pain is quite intense, while in others it is a dull sensation similar to indigestion or heartburn. This pain can occur:
* During or after vigorous activity
* While you're lying in bed
* After a meal
* When you're under emotional stress
* In response to cold temperatures

Another characteristic of angina is that the pain often comes at about the same time each day.

Risk factors--including HIGH blood pressure

FIBRILLATION: The heart can sometimes--through injury, accident, or disease--falter and slip into a meaningless flutter called "fibrillation." Or it may stop abruptly. Cardiac arrest has occurred. No blood moves through the body. Respiration ceases, the pupils dilate, and the pulse disappears. Organs and tissue will die within minutes, beginning with the brain.

When the heart muscle doesn't get enough blood (and oxygen), it is usually because one of the arteries supplying blood has become sealed off. Such a blockage is known in medical terms as coronary occlusion or thrombosis. Coronary refers to the heart arteries; occlusion means blockage; thrombosis is another name for a clot.

Arteries become blocked, narrowed, or clotted because the inner walls are thickened or made irregular by deposits of fatty substances. Deposits usually form where artery walls are weakened. The deposits may become hardened with calcium, the rough edges becoming places for more substances in the blood to collect. These deposits, or plaques, gradually narrow the artery and thereby allow less blood to pass through. The plaque may also serve as a place for clots to form. The process represents a degeneration, or "hardening," of the arteries. It's a process that goes on throughout life and in arteries throughout the body but, of course, when it occurs in a severe form in the heart, life is threatened.

The eminent heart specialist Paul Dudley White, M.D., said, "Heart disease before 80 is our own fault, not God's or Nature's will." How we live and what we eat largely determine our susceptibility to heart attack and other heart disease.

THE RISK FACTORS: The big three risk factors are cigarette smoking, high blood pressure, and high levels of cholesterol and triglycerides in the blood. A person with those three risk factors is eight times more likely to have a heart attack than a person with none of them. Other risk factors for heart disease are diabetes, a family history of heart disease, obesity, lack of exercise, and stress.

❶ **Cigarette smoking--**The link between smoking and heart attack and other heart diseases is established beyond a doubt. Smokers face two to four times the risk of sudden cardiac death as nonsmokers.

Smoking makes me sick!

❷ **High blood pressure--**When the pressure is high, the heart has to work harder to pump blood. High pressure indicates that the arteries are either narrow or tightened. Eating habits and exercise can affect blood pressure. Overweight people run a greater risk of high blood pressure. Regular exercise is linked with lower blood pressure. Up to 58 million Americans have high blood pressure. Since high blood pressure may eventually lead to a heart attack, stroke, or kidney disease, taking steps to control it will pay off with a longer life.

Blood pressure is measured using the familiar inflatable cuff and the stethoscope. The reading is reported in two numbers such as 120/80. The top number is the systolic blood pressure, which is the pressure exerted against the artery walls when the heart contracts. The bottom number is the diastolic blood pressure, which is the lowest pressure remaining in the arteries between heartbeats when the heart is at rest. A systolic reading of 140 or more, or a diastolic reading of 90 or more, or both, on repeated occasions indicates high blood pressure.

It is very important to lower elevated blood pressure to normal levels. Often this can be accomplished by changes in lifestyle. Weight reduction for the overweight individual is often very effective in lowering blood pressure. Other means such as avoiding salt and starting a regular exercise program are steps that can be taken to lower blood pressure. However, if these lifestyle alterations are not successful in lowering blood pressure, the doctor will prescribe medication for the condition.

Advancing age does not inevitably lead to hypertension, but the disease does become more common at later ages (Afro-Americans are especially vulnerable to high blood pressure). Indeed, one third of the population over 65 has high blood pressure. As with the young, high blood pressure raises the risk of cardiovascular damage in the elderly. However, some of the older medications for blood pressure have also reduced the quality of life. Because people become increasingly vulnerable to the complications of drugs as they age, care must be taken to protect them from side effects.

HIGH BLOOD PRESSURE MAY CAUSE:
❶ The heart to get larger;
❷ Little baloons (aneurysms) in the brain blood vessels;
❸ Progressive narrowing of the kidney blood vessels;
❹ Narrowing and speedup of hardening of the arteries all over the body, especially in the heart, brain, and kidneys.

Today, more people are keeping their hypertension under control and it has contributed substantially to a dramatic reduction in deaths from stroke and coronary artery disease.

> More information on high blood pressure
> can be obtained by writing to:
> The National High Blood Pressure Information Center
> 120/80
> Bethesda, MD 20205

Symptoms that can break your heart!

A tightness in my chest...
A worrying kind of indigestion...
Heaviness and an unusual sensation in my left arm...
A pain in my neck, sometimes even in my jaw or teeth...
A shortness of breath.

Only you can spot the warning signs and report them to your physician.

RISK FACTORS (Con't)

❸ **Cholesterol and Triglycerides**--Generally, these two substances are associated with fatty foods, such as meat, milk products, and eggs. The National Cancer Institute found that one-third comes from egg yokes (270 milligrams). Other leading sources were: beef, whole milk, hot dogs, processed meats, pork, doughnuts, cookies, cake, butter. These substances become the fatty deposits that cling to the walls of the arteries, eventually narrowing or blocking them.

If people have high cholesterol levels in the blood, it increases their chances of having a heart attack. High levels are due largely to too many calories from too much saturated fat in the diet. (Saturated fat, usually hard at room temperature, is found more often in animal products such as meat, milk, and egg yolks.) Blood cholesterol levels tend to rise with age in this country, perhaps because of the large amounts of saturated fats we consume. Any blood count below 200 milligrams is considered safe; and persons 40 years and older with blood cholesterol above 260 are at high risk and should be treated.

The National Institute of Health, as long ago as 1984, reported that "elevated blood cholesterol level is a major cause of coronary artery disease" and proper dietary changes could reduce blood cholesterol levels. The NIH recommends that Americans change their diets to reduce the level of blood cholesterol. They urge everyone except children under 2 to reduce fat intake from the current level of about 40% of total calories to no more than 30%. Americans should reduce their intake of saturated fat from the current 16% to 18% of total calories to less than 10%. Polyunsaturated fats should be increased from the current 5% to 8%, but to no more than 10% of total calories. Cholesterol intake should amount to no more than 250 to 300 milligrams a day.

Cholesterol and triglyceride levels can sometimes be controlled by drugs. However, the American Medical Association recommends diet therapy be tried first, saying it is more effective and safer. Today most of us consume about 40% of our calories in fat. The experts want us to reduce that intake to 30% fat and to decrease the amount coming from saturated fat.

Men usually have higher cholesterol counts than women. Women have more of a desirable type of cholesterol called HDL (high-density lipoproteins) before menopause, as opposed to the villainous LDL (low-density lipoproteins), the kind associated with heart problems.

❹ **Diabetes**--Blood vessels are damaged by diabetes, and damaged blood vessels are susceptible to hardening and subsequent narrowing. Diabetes can also lead to hypertension.

❺ **Family History**--We are all subject to the genes passed along to us, and a history of heart attacks in the immediate family can be a risk factor.

❻ **Obesity**--Usually among adults, the more weight, the higher the blood pressure and cholesterol levels.

❼ **Exercise**--Regular exercise is good for the heart and helps to maintain proper weight, lower blood pressure, and may cut down on cholesterol levels. Some good exercises for cardiac health are: walking, jogging, swimming, cycling, rowing, cross-country skiing, tennis, golf, gardening, dancing, and softball. The rule is: exercise vigorously at least three times a week for one-half hour. Always check with your doctor before starting any exercise program.

❽ **Stress**--The body reacts to stress with a complicated fight/flight syndrome. The body gets ready for action, pumping adrenaline and speeding up the heart, sending more blood to the brain and muscles; as blood pressure rises, the liver dumps cholesterol into the bloodstream.

Unpredictable chest pain?

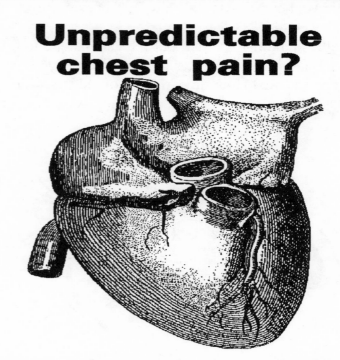

Don't take it lightly!

Two things are bad for the heart--running uphill
and running down people.
- Bernard Gimbel

DISEASES AND DISORDERS
HEART PROBLEMS 313

Dealing with heart disease--the techniques used

FIGHTING AGAINST HEART DISEASE: Pumping contractions of the heart depend on tiny electric currents generated within the heart. Cardiac arrest occurs when these currents are disrupted. The pulsing rhythm disappears and the blood no longer moves. Most often the cause is a heart attack (myocardial infarction) from clogged or narrowed arteries leading to or within the heart. But arrest can also result from suffocation, near drowning, drug overdose, stroke, anesthesia, electrical accidents, head injury, and other causes. Regardless of the cause, the person will die unless the heartbeat and circulation are quickly restored.

In the past a sharp blow to the chest might start the heart up again. If medical aid was available, adrenaline could be injected directly into the heart, or the chest could be opened and the heart physically massaged. These efforts did not work too often.

❤ **Drug therapy** can be effective for many persons with cardiac arrhythmias--interruptions in the heart's normal rhythm--that can lead to cardiac arrest. There are 1.2 million people in the United States who take medications like flecainide acetate to control fibrillation and tachycardia, a wildly rapid heartbeat.

❤ **Taking an aspirin tablet** every other day reduces the risk of a heart attack for healthy men ages 50 and over, regardless of their cholesterol levels, reported the *New England Journal of Medicine* in late July 1989. These findings are from a major medical study of 22,071 male physicians who took a standard 325-milligram tablet of aspirin, or a placebo, every other day. The heart attack rate was 44% lower for the physicians taking the aspirin.

Aspirin inhibits the formation of blood clots and can be used as a form of prevention in the incidence of heart attacks. Doctors warn, however, that it is not a "cure-all" and that other preventive steps need to be taken such as quitting smoking, making healthy food choices, and exercising. Doctors also warn about taking aspirin without consulting one's physician because some people have difficulties with its possible side effects, including stomach upset or bleeding.

❤ **Defibrillator.** Some 400,000 persons susceptible to fibrillation or tachycardia cannot be helped by medication. They use an implantable defibrillator, an electric pulse generator that monitors heart action. It can sense interruptions of the normal heartbeat and shock the heart back into proper rhythm. Generally, a single shock is sufficient. If not, up to three additional shocks can be given. With the heart back in rhythm, the generator stops sending impulses, recycles, and settles down to monitoring the heart again. The defibrillator is intended for persons who have suffered cardiac arrest or episodes of tachycardia or fibrillation that cannot be reversed or controlled by medication or surgery. It is not suitable for those who have frequent or recurring episodes that would soon deplete the batteries. Also, it should not be implanted in persons who already have cardiac pacemakers since the two may interact.

❤ **Pacemakers** are different from the implantable defibrillator in that they help the heart maintain a proper rate of beating. They cannot control tachycardia or jolt a stopped or fibrillating heart back into action.

❤ **CPR.** In 1950, Johns Hopkins researchers discovered that blood could be moved through the body of victims of cardiac arrest by pressing firmly and forcefully on the chest. This discovery went on to become cardiopulmonary resuscitation, now used and taught throughout the world as CPR. The Red Cross provides a free training course--sign up!

CPR must be administered within minutes of a person's being stricken. First, check for pulse and breathing, to be certain the person has not simply fainted. Next, call for help but do not wait for it to arrive. Position the victim on his back, tilt back the head, check that the airway is open, and begin CPR. Until help arrives, CPR can be done by one rescuer kneeling by the victim's side, pressing down quickly and firmly on the lower chest to push blood out of the heart, then letting up so that the heart can refill. After every fifteen compressions the rescuer pauses to breathe twice in the victim's lungs. A second rescuer kneeling on the other side can take over the ventilation breathing, giving one full breath into the victim's lungs after every five compressions by the first rescuer. The second rescuer also checks for spontaneous pulse and breathing. Rescuers can trade places as desired, since doing the compression part of CPR is tiring.

❤ **Coronary bypass surgery.** In this procedure, as most commonly performed, a large vein called the saphenous vein is removed from the leg. One end of the vein is implanted into the aorta and the other end is connected to a coronary vessel beyond its obstruction. The coronary bypass operation supplies blood to an area of the heart with deficient blood supply, thereby relieving chest pain. Patients who were once incapacitated now have improved function of the left ventricle, which makes the heart pump better. Also, chest pain is relieved.

❤ **PTCA.** A small percentage of patients who are candidates for bypass surgery may qualify for a simpler procedure, performed under local anesthetic, called PTCA (percutaneous transluminal coronary angioplasty) or the balloon catheter. For this procedure, the doctor inserts a balloon-tipped catheter into an artery through a small incision in the groin. The tip of the catheter is fed through the arterial system and positioned in the coronary artery at the site of the blockage. The small sausage-shaped balloon on the tip of the catheter is then inflated briefly to press the blockage against the walls of the artery and open up the narrowed artery. The doctors follow the progress of the procedure on an image intensifier so they can see when the channel of the artery has been opened. Once the opening has been enlarged, the balloon catheter is removed.

❤ **The atherectomy catheter,** a stainless steel cylinder with a cutting device inside, is an effective alternative to balloon angioplasty. It is used when arterial plaque must be removed, due to recurring blockage. Another device has a rotating blade, similar to a Roto rooter, to slice away the plaque that is then sucked out by a vacuum attachment. In laser angioplasty doctors insert a catheter with a laser tip that burns or breaks down the plaque. The difficulty, however, is to do that without damaging blood vessels.

❤ **Heart transplant**--The final and most dramatic method of dealing with heart attacks is the heart transplant. This method has become increasingly effective, and many people are alive today using the heart of someone else. The future may find many more people using transplants or a form of an artificial heart; but let us hope that tomorrow will find more people eating and living in such a way that their own hearts will last through their life.

Your personal warriors--fight for your life everyday

In the microscopic world, the body is surrounded by a number of lethal enemies called bacteria, viruses, yeasts, fungi, and parasites. Just outside our skin and mucous membranes swarms a horde of countless tiny creatures that would like to turn our bodies into a microbe housing project. They don't look like much; you can't even see them without the aid of a microscope. But, when they do get inside of us, their collective presence is called an infection, if they get out of control.

Since our warm bodies are engorged with a continual supply of water and life-giving nutrients, we may think it's okay to let the infections in to raise their families and share our plenty. First, consider the names of these infections: tuberculosis, leprosy, malaria, the common cold, plague, influenza; in fact, all the ills to which the human species is heir.

More than a million of these invaders swarm on every square inch of our freshly washed skin. We carry them by the legions to our mouth with every fork full of food, and with every breath of air we breathe in multitudes of these virulent enemies. However, the body has a defensive system against the hordes of invaders that wish to live in us. It is called the immune system.

PUBLIC ENEMY
No. 1
Mr. Iam Virus

The human immune system is probably the most awesome fighting force on earth. Without being consciously aware of it, you produce billions of warrior cells that patrol your body looking for signs of trouble. These foot soldiers of your immune system nip diseases in the bud. They eliminate cancerous cells before they ever grow into life-threatening malignancies. And if you do get sick, they mobilize to wipe out infection and restore you to health.

The human immune system is an efficient war machine that never negotiates a treaty. It strikes no bargains with the enemy. It takes no prisoners. Microbes that dare contemplate taking up residence inside your nice warm body encounter a standing army of trained warrior cells, willing to martyr themselves in defense of the cause--your health and well-being. Invading bacteria, viruses, fungi, and parasites are exploded, dissolved, digested to death, and carried out of your body until the very last enemy is eliminated. Peace finally returns to your sinews and tissues, but even then your immune system is not finished. It prepares a resume on the enemy so that if any more of them show up, they will be recognized and dissipated even more quickly the next time. That's how you became immune to diseases like mumps or chickenpox.

The immune system is not like any of the body's other major mechanisms. Circulation is like a plumbing setup; the nervous system can be compared to an electronic switching network; and digestion is similar to a freight-handling agency. However, the best way to understand the immune system is not to think of a mechanical device, but to imagine instead a highly mobile, thoroughly disciplined military organization. Like a well-run army, it includes training and support bases, crack units of specialized troops, a sophisticated communications network, and an extremely effective intelligence service. Like an army on the march, its vital components don't stay put, but instead move freely through the body, invading both fluids and tissues. It works in the blood, in the lymph, and even inside the organs of other systems.

Surveillance units on constant alert comprise the body's first line of defense. Like vigilant border guards or rooftop plane spotters, specialized cells constantly search for and identify unwelcome aliens. Using highly specific signals, they then summon fighters who are expert in just the type of combat required to overcome the particular foe. Meanwhile, other troops join in the fray or supply needed equipment. And, finally, effective disposal units move in to mop up.

A modern defense establishment includes frogmen, paratroopers, commandos, ski troops, artillery, infantry, tank battalions, anti-aircraft batteries, and other specialists in searching out and destroying many kinds of enemies. Similarly, the immune system has components equipped to find and kill such varied attackers as bacteria, viruses, foreign chemicals, and even the body's own cells undergoing threatening changes.

The foot soldiers of the immune system are white blood cells, or lymphocytes; large numbers of them man bases in the lymph nodes and spleen and also circulate throughout the body. They arise as immature, undifferentiated stem cells in the bone marrow, but later grow into specialized cells with particular functions. Like raw army recruits, new lymphocytes report to "training bases" where they mature and acquire their special features. Those that attend boot camp in the thymus gland are called T-cells (thymus-mediated) or T-lymphocytes. They include killers that fight the enemy directly; helpers that aid in the recognition and attack; and suppressors that turn off the immune response when the battle is won. T-cells serve a variety of regulating, communicating, and combat functions.

The training group for B-cells, or B-lymphocytes, has not yet been definitely located, but researchers suspect that they mature in the tonsils, the lymph nodes, and lymph tissue in the gut. The main function of B-cells is to produce antibodies that attack specific antigens (a general term for anything that triggers an immune response).

Although the two main classes of lymphocytes differ in many respects, they share two features that make the immune response possible. They can recognize and become activated by specific molecules, and in their active

The greatest secret of doctors, known only to their wives, but still hidden from the public, is that most things get better by themselves; most things, in fact, are better in the morning.

- Lewis Thomas

mode they can rapidly reproduce copies of themselves. Thus, unlike a volunteer army, which must entice recruits into joining up, embattled lymphocytes can simply clone battalions of reinforcements, as needed, on the spot.

The crucial ability of lymphocytes to identify other entities arises from receptors that dot their outer surfaces. Each receptor is, in effect, a molecular lock capable of accepting only a single key. When a lymphocyte encounters its target molecule--which may be a part of an invading organism, or may be on the surface of another cell, or may be moving freely through the body fluids--a receptor locks onto it, and the lymphocytes become "activated." The activated cell is then ready to carry out its designated function of fighting, signaling, coordinating, or helping. Receptors also play an important part in the immune system's internal communications. Cells signal one another by emitting appropriate molecules that are then recognized by other receptive cells. T-cells, in particular, produce a number of different signaling and control chemicals known as lymphokines.

The body does not have a set of genes serving as blueprints for each of these sentries, called B cells. Instead, it has a small library of DNA (deoxyribonucleic acid) fragments that are constantly being chopped up, shuffled, and recombined to produce millions of different B cells during the course of a lifetime.

The immune army includes numerous other components. Natural killer cells, for example, are lymphocytes specially designed to eliminate tumor cells. Macrophages-- lymphocytes whose Greek name "big eaters" indicates both their size and one of their main functions--can digest unwanted organisms and materials. They also help coordinate other immune system functions. Antibodies--large, complex protein molecules produced by B-cells--bind to particular antigens, puncture their membranes, and kill them by allowing their contents to drain out. Still other proteins, called the complement, enhance the antibodies' ability to destroy cells. Bringing all these forces to bear against an enemy requires both a grand strategy and ingenious tactics.

Invading Bacteria

Suppose, for example, that Salmonella bacteria have hitched a ride on your dinner. As the invaders make their way into the body, they scatter bits of themselves--antigens that can be recognized as foreign by the right lymphocyte. On their scavenging rounds, macrophages pick up these pieces of molecular debris and carry them about, rather like banners.

If you are resistant to this infection, the macrophage will soon, literally, bump into a T-cell that recognizes this antigen. The T-cell raises the alarm, emitting a shower of signaling chemicals, and the antibody response swings into action. The appropriate B-cells, alerted by the signal, start churning out antibodies which make their way through the bloodstream to the enemy. Suitable T-cells gather to coordinate operations and give the B-cells needed help. Complement molecules also converge and, in so doing, call in the macrophage cleanup squad. The antibody tackles the invaders, trying to pierce their outer membranes and disperse their fluids. The macrophages, spurred on by the complement, attempt to gobble the enemies up. Once the combined defensive forces have the intruders on the run, suppressor T-cells give the all-clear, the immune response slows, and the system returns to its customary state of watchful readiness.

All of these immune cells we're talking about have to be born someplace. That place is in the bone marrow. The bone marrow is just a great big nursery ward with little babies in it. Every day our bone marrow nursery pours out millions of new red and white blood cells. The red cells carry oxygen and food for us and the white cells constitute our standing army against disease. Let's watch what happens during a localized infection.

Suppose you have just hauled in some wood for the fireplace and got a splinter in your hand. A number of bacteria rode in on that splinter, and they think they have gone to microbe heaven. They are cavorting about in the spaces between your muscle cells and slurping up food. They have found so much liquid nourishment that they are multiply-

ing. Bacteria multiply so that 2 become 4, 4 become 8, 8 become 16, and so on. If they are allowed to carry on their dining and reproductive activities unmolested, they can become a big problem, fast.

However, unknown to this unsavory multitude of microbes, their doom is already sealed. When the splinter broke the skin, a silent chemical alarm went off. The blood in the immediate area started getting "sticky."

PUBLIC ENEMY
No. 2
Mr. Ibe Bacteria

Blood cells started hanging up on the capillary vessel walls and slowing down. Blood cells keep arriving, making the area slightly swollen and tender. The increased blood flow and tenderness in the area is known as the inflammatory response. In a few moments, white blood cells start to crawl right through the capillary walls. They actually leave the blood vessels and head right for the splinter. Now the bacteria are really in for it. There are several different kinds of white blood cells that are likely to get involved in the ensuing battle.

First on the scene are the neutrophils. The shock troops of the immune system, these cells are numerous, constituting 60% to 75% of our white blood cells. The neutrophils are the ones that get really excited when an infection comes--they rush there

More about the internal wars that protect your life

like mad and gather around the splinter to destroy it. Some of them die in the process. That's how we get pus--it is a mass of dead neutrophils. Neutrophils ooze over bacterium and kill it by digestion.

Behind the neutrophil comes the macrophage cells. They move in like some primeval tank corps. This big, cell-eating monster views all those bacteria as so many orders of hamburgers and french fries. The more they eat, the faster they move, seemingly delighted with the microbial banquet. Some macrophages live a life devoted solely to clean-up duties. They digest everything around a wound and eventually leave it antiseptically clean. They even live in your lungs and carry off stray bits of dust, pollens, and pollutants that sneak past the filtering system in your nostrils. If you happen to be a smoker, they turn black in their efforts to eat up all the tar and carbon deposits that reach your lungs.

The Virus Invader

Viruses are much smaller than bacteria. If you think of a common *Escherichia coli* bacteria as the size of a football field, then a polio virus would be the size of the football. Viruses are shaped like minuscule jewels or tiny rocket ships; they are only partly alive. In order to produce offspring, they need to slip inside the very cells of our body and snatch the DNA, the genetic stuff of life that we have bound up inside the nucleus of every cell. They turn the DNA into a little factory that manufactures more viruses. When the cell finally dies, thousands of new viruses can spew out, all looking to snatch other body cells to turn into new virus factories.

Macrophages and neutrophils can't do too much against a viral attack. This is a job for a specialist--the T-cell. They circulate throughout our bodies looking for a viral intruder. In order to slip inside a cell, a virus has to remove its protein coat, which it leaves outside on the cell membrane. The viral coat hanging outside signals the passing T-cell that viral hanky-panky is going on inside the cell. The T-cell bumps against the body cell with the virus inside and perforates it. That quick destruction shuts down the virus assembly line.

A T-cell can kill only one sick cell at a time. What happens when one of those viral factories has already delivered up its first load of thousands of viruses? Once a T-cell is onto an invasion, it pulls off the same trick as the plasma cell. The T-cell clones itself. These duplicates, primed to respond to that particular enemy virus, also scurry about killing virus-infected cells.

Besides the killer T-cells, there are also helper and suppressor T-cells. Helper T-cells check out the action and let the other components of the immune system know how big a defense to mount, how many antibodies are needed, and how many clones to make. Suppressor T-cells watch the progress of the battle and call things to a halt when the final microbial corpse is carried from the field and the final virus is dead. A few lymphocytes that remember what the enemy looks like continue to circulate in your blood just in case it shows up again. When you have some of these experienced old warrior cells on patrol for you, you are immune to the particular disease that they remember.

Identifying Your Own Cells

The immune system's cellular troops have your entire body under constant surveillance, yet they don't have eyes with which to see, or ears to hear. How can they tell an invading virus from a piece of your pancreas, or a bacterium from a brain cell? They know because every single cell in your body is issued a badge of identification. The badge is actually a special arrangement of protein molecules as unique to you as your fingerprints. It says that you are you. Patrolling immune cells give everything that comes past them a little chemical feel. When a passing cell or pollen grain comes along and it's not wearing this badge of identification, its game is up.

Similarly, when one of your own cells goes bad and becomes a tumor cell, something on its surface is apparently not quite right. It is unclear just how a natural killer cell spots a tumor cell, but it seems there is some sort of a surface marker that betrays it.

Cancer

When a cold virus enters your body, the immune system's task is to find and destroy "self" cells gone haywire. The same holds for the cells that have become cancerous--that have become a subversive force bent on overrunning the body's normal cells. The defending immune system must recognize both these types of turncoat cells by antibodies carried on their outer surfaces. Two classes of troops undertake the attack: natural killer cells, lone hunters that roam the body on search-and-destroy missions; and killer cells, T-cells turned into killers under orders of a lymphokine, interleukin.

AIDS

Given the crucial position of the T-cells in both sounding the alarm and organizing the battle, a person without a proper T-cell defense is clearly open to all kinds of dangerous diseases. And that is precisely what happens in AIDS (acquired immune deficiency syndrome). The AIDS virus kills T4 lymphocytes, which play a central role in initiating and coordinating the immune

PUBLIC ENEMY
No. 3
Mr. Itchy Fungi

response. In ways not yet fully understood, the virus apparently also disables macrophages, leaving the body defenseless against the cancers and infectious diseases that eventually prove fatal to those with AIDS. (see page 279 for more information on AIDS).

Allergies

Not all malfunctions of the immune system involve infectious agents. Sometimes the white cells overdo their vigilance and mount an attack against substances that are harmless, or even beneficial. An allergy is a case of mistaken identity. The body mistakes such innocuous items as eggs or ragweed pollen for harmful invaders and calls out powerful chemical defenses, including histamine and leukotrienes. These substances help in the fight against real enemies by making the blood vessels more permeable-- easier for the relatively large white cells to pass through on the way to battle. But, in this case, they are simply nuisances that bring on the rashes, sneezing, and wheezing so familiar to allergy sufferers.

Autoimmune Diseases

Sometimes the immune system gets a little confused about who is who. It mistakes components of your own body for the enemy. In this case, the immune mechanism can turn dangerous. In autoimmune diseases--rheumatoid arthritis, lupus, rheumatic fever--the immune system falsely identifies certain of the body's own tissues as foreign, and moves in for the kill. This immune system confusion is behind a whole host of diseases, from rheumatoid arthritis to multiple sclerosis.

Organ Transplants

Sometimes the foreign matter the immune system attacks is not threatening but beneficial, as in the case of life-saving organ transplants. A major challenge to physicians is keeping the body from attacking a transplanted liver, kidney, or heart. The drug cyclosporine has been useful in preventing organ rejection. Cyclosporine apparently blocks production of interleukin, a signaling chemical needed to turn T-cells into killers

and launch the immune attack. Using this drug, doctors can deliberately suppress the immune response that would ordinarily protect the transplant recipient against foreign tissues. Although this keeps the patient from rejecting the new organ, it also reduces protection against ordinary invaders. The same goes for many chemotherapies used against cancer, which temporarily suppress the marrow's ability to produce lymphocytes.

During a lifetime, a human encounters tens of thousands of different infectious bacteria, viruses, fungi, and parasites. Most of the time, the encounters are benign because of the remarkable immune mechanism that, at any given time, posts more than 100,000 unique sentries to identify invaders and sound the warning call for their destruction.

Scientific Advances

Scientific understanding of the immune system has exploded since AIDS (acquired immune deficiency syndrome) burst onto the public health scene in 1981. Cancer research and organ transplants have added their own impetus to the worldwide effort to understand our bodies' defenses. Nearly every week brings new findings on what has become medical science's fastest-moving frontier. For example, biologists have long puzzled over how the body could generate the large number of individual antibody-secreting cells that are known to exist in the immune system. Immunologist Susumu Tponegawa of Japan solved that in the early 1980s by demonstrating that a small genetic library could be constantly reshuffled and recombined to produce the necessary number of antibodies--a feat for which he won the 1989 Nobel Prize for Medicine.

Molecular biologists from the Massachusetts Institute of Technology say they have isolated and identified the "master builder" gene that controls the disease-fighting process, marshaling its forces like a general preparing to repel an enemy invasion.

The immune system's immense power to combat disease holds great promise for better health as medical science learns to harness the body's own defenses for the war against

major killers. Already, doctors have developed methods of producing immune substances outside the body and then using them to step up the natural attack against disease. As researchers understand more about the immune system, hope grows that some of humankind's deadliest enemies may come under medical control.

In the past few years an idea has been presented. When the immune system is not working against cancer, the person involved tries to take conscious control of the immune system through meditation in which he pictures in his imagination the white cells eating the cancer cells. An oncologist claims to have success in turning the killer T-cells to their task of fighting cancer. Perhaps this idea has merit; in any case, the mysteries of the immune system are fast being revealed to the inquiring mind of people.

Remember, when things go right, as they usually do, your immune system keeps you healthy. If you don't like the idea of a military regime marching around inside you and making war without your conscious approval, you might take heart in the thought that your own internal army is purely defensive. It doesn't go out looking for trouble. It responds only when attacked. The violence of your immune system keeps you alive to think thoughts of peace.

Incontinence is not an inevitable result of aging

Incontinence, or the loss of bladder control and the associated involuntary loss of urine, is a symptom or malady and not a disease itself. At least one in ten persons aged 65 or older has a problem of this nature and as many as one third of women over age 60 suffers from this condition.

> **Incontinence is the second most common reason for institutionalizing older people.**

Incontinence can range from the discomfort of slight losses of urine to the disability and shame of severe, frequent wetting. Persons who are incontinent often withdraw from social life and try to hide the problem from their family, friends, and even their doctors. Sad to say, only one in 12 people with incontinence seeks medical help--a fact perhaps due to embarrassment, isolation, or the mistaken notion that incontinence is normal with aging. This is unfortunate, because in many cases incontinence can be treated and controlled, if not cured.

Incontinence is not an inevitable result of aging. It is caused by specific changes in body function that often result from diseases or use of medications. Even in cases where incontinence cannot be completely eliminated, modern products can ease the discomfort and inconvenience it causes.

Many older people with normal urine control may have difficulty reaching a toilet in time because of arthritis or other crippling disorders. A person who is not always able to reach a toilet in time to avoid wetting should not be considered incontinent. Instead, every effort should be made to make reaching the toilet easier.

INCONTINENCE TYPES

❶ *Incontinence* may be brought on by an illness that is accompanied by fatigue, confusion, or hospital admission. Incontinence is sometimes the first and only symptom of a urinary tract infection. Curing the illness will usually relieve or clear up the incontinence.

❷ *Stress incontinence* describes the leakage of urine during exercise, coughing, sneezing, laughing, or other body movements that put pressure on the bladder. It occurs most often in women of all ages.

❸ *Urge incontinence* refers to the inability to hold urine long enough to reach a toilet. It is often associated with conditions such as stroke, senile dementia, Parkinson's disease, and multiple sclerosis, but it can occur in otherwise normal elderly persons.

❹ *Overflow incontinence* describes the leakage of small amounts of urine from a constantly filled bladder. A common cause in older men is blockage or urine outflow from the bladder by an enlarged prostate gland. Another cause is loss of normal contraction of the bladder in some people with diabetes.

TREATMENT

◆ Medication can be used but these drugs may cause side effects and must be carefully supervised by a doctor. Hormonal treatments and bladder-relaxing medications are commonly prescribed.

◆ Behavioral management techniques, including biofeedback and "bladder retraining," have proven helpful in the control of urination.

◆ Exercises can be used to strengthen the muscle that helps close the bladder outlet. The Kegel exercises consist of squeezing and relaxing the urethra, vagina, and anal openings to strengthen the PC muscle.

◆ Several types of surgery can improve or even cure incontinence if it is related to a structural problem.

◆ Prosthetic devices, some requiring surgical implantation, can be used to aid the muscles that control urine flow. For example, an artificial sphincter is an inflatable cuff encircling the urethra. When the cuff is inflated, it applies external pressure to the urethra and prevents loss of urine.

◆ Sometimes incontinence is treated by inserting a flexible tube (catheter) into the urethra and collecting the urine into a container. Long-term use of a catheter can cause infections. In men, an alternative to the indwelling catheter is an external collecting device, called a Texas catheter. This is fitted over the male genitalia, like a condom, and connected via a tube to a drainage bag worn on the body.

◆ Specially designed absorbent underclothing is available. Many of these garments are no more bulky than normal underwear, can be worn easily under everyday clothing, and free a person from the discomfort and embarrassment of incontinence.

Of those affected by urinary incontinence, 80% can be cured. Because it is a symptom, not a disease, the method of treatment depends on diagnostic results. Diagnosis includes a medical history and a thorough physical examination. Tests such as X-rays, cystoscopic examinations, blood chemistries, urine analysis, vaginal smears, and special tests to determine bladder capacity, tone, and sphincter condition, urethral pressure, and the amount of urine left in the bladder after voiding may also be required.

Oftentimes simple changes in diet and medication, or the use of a combination of medicine, biofeedback, exercise, collection devices, and absorbent products is effective in controlling incontinence. Some individuals benefit from surgery.

> **Since only one out of every 12 people affected with incontinence seeks help, many are sent to a nursing home needlessly. In fact, of the 1.2 million people in nursing homes, an estimated 50% are incontinent.**

How to Get Help

Two national organizations offer information and support for incontinence sufferers and their families. Send a self-addressed, stamped, business-size envelope to:

Help for Incontinent People (HIP)
P.O. Box 544, Union, SC 29379
or
The Simon Foundation
P.O. Box 835, Wilmette, IL 60091
1-800-23-SIMON

A problem that has plagued mankind for a long time

The kidneys are large bean-shaped organs located below the ribs toward the middle of the back. Urine is formed when the kidneys remove waste products from the blood that passes through. The blood flows through the kidneys at the rate of 18 gallons an hour. The urine produced equals a little over 2 quarts every 24 hours. Some-

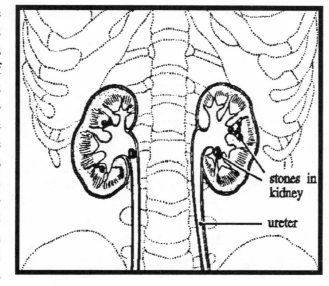

stones in kidney

ureter

times the urine contains substances that form a small hard stone.

A kidney stone is usually a hard mass that builds up gradually when various salt or mineral crystals are deposited on the inner surfaces of the kidney. This can be a very painful disorder. The problem has plagued mankind for a long time. Scientists have discovered kidney stones in Egyptian mummies from 5,000 B.C. In the past 20 years much progress has been made in the treatment and prevention of stones.

Kidney stones that remain in the kidney or that break loose from the lining of the kidney and move to other parts of the urinary system are sometimes referred to as "urinary stones." Sometimes smaller stones pass through the ureters and lodge in the bladder where they enlarge, or stones may originate in the bladder. In either case, these are referred to as "bladder stones." When stones grow so large that they cannot be passed out of the body easily, they obstruct the normal flow of urine, causing pain and possibly infection or kidney damage. Some small stones can pass out of the bladder.

CAUSES OF STONES--Age, genetic disorders, occupation, climate, metabolic disturbances, presence of infection, dietary patterns, and the amount of water consumed can cause kidney stones. Heredity may play an important role in the tendency to form stones. About three males are afflicted for every female. Seventy percent of the people who get the hereditary disease "renal tubular acidosis" also get stones. Another genetic defect that causes stones is "hyperoxaluria," which is the over-production of oxalate and salt into the urinary tract, also known as gout. Stones are composed of substances such as calcium oxalate, calcium phosphate, and uric acid. Calcium stones are the most common. A urinary stone may consist entirely of one compound, but most stones are a combination of salts.

Drinking too little fluid can result in dehydration, decreasing the amount of urine and increasing the concentration of the elements that accumulate to form stones. In some cases, a person may habitually eat too much food that is high in calcium, resulting in excessive calcium being passed through the kidneys.

Other causes of stone formation are hyperuricosuria (a disorder of uric acid metabolism), overactivity of the parathyroid glands, excessive consumption of vitamin D, urinary tract infection, and blockage of the urinary tract.

SYMPTOMS--Excruciating pain is usually the first symptom of a kidney stone. The pain often begins suddenly when a stone moves from the kidney into the ureter, causing irritation or obstruction. Typically, the patient experiences pain in the back and side in the vicinity of the kidney or in the lower abdomen. Later, the pain may radiate to the groin.

If the stone is too large to pass easily, the severe, constant pain continues as the muscles in the walls of the tiny ureter try to squeeze the stone along into the bladder. Sometimes the patient will find blood in the urine, and may experience a burning sensation during urination, or frequency of urination. Other symptoms may include the presence of urinary infection accompanied by fever, vomiting, nausea, loss of appetite, and chills. The patient may find that his kidney and abdomen in the region of the stone are very tender to the touch.

DIAGNOSIS AND TREATMENT--X-ray examination can be used to verify the presence of a stone. The physician will also perform analyses of the blood and urine to help determine the cause of the episode, and to enable him to plan the proper course of treatment. Some stones, for example uric acid stones, don't show up on X-ray.

"Silent" stones--those that are not causing any problem for the patient--normally do not require treatment. Acute attacks, on the other hand, usually require hospitalization, because the pain is so severe. In most cases, the stone is small and the patient needs only pain relief and instructions concerning recovery of the stone after it is passed. About 90% of stones pass spontaneously through the urinary system.

In some cases, the doctor must attempt removal by passing a cystoscope (a hollow tubular instrument) up into the bladder, trying to grasp and withdraw the stone with a basket-like device. Sometimes stones that are stuck in the bladder can be crushed using a tiny instrument inserted with a catheter. Some stones (those composed of uric acid) may be dissolved by medical treatment. In other cases, surgery may be necessary to extract stones stuck in the urinary system.

When the stones are in the kidney and upper ureter, in some instances, a needle and probe can be inserted through the skin, creating a channel straight to the area of the stone. The doctor can insert an ultrasonic probe through the channel, placing it against the stone and gradually disintegrating it. There is also a new therapy developed in West Germany that uses high-energy acoustic shock waves to pulverize kidney stones. It is called lithotrypsy.

Today scientific progress has brought greater understanding of the causes and mechanisms of stone formation and far more effective clinical management of stone disease.

> May I govern my passions with absolute sway,
> And grow wiser and better, as strength wears away,
> Without gout or stone, by a gentle decay.
>
> The Old Man's Wish, Walter Pope (1685)

Osteoporosis--the silent epidemic in women

Osteoporosis is a major predisposing cause of bone fracture and an important health problem in women after age 50. In spite of appropriate treatment of hip fractures, rehabilitation is often unsuccessful among elderly people. At least half of those ambulatory before a hip fracture cannot walk again after it occurs. Thus, the ability of such persons to get about and care for themselves is considerably limited and their quality of life is seriously impaired. One out of eight elderly persons who suffers a hip fracture will die of complications within the first four months.

In addition to hip fractures, breaks in the wrist bones and compression ("crush") fractures of the spinal vertebrae add greatly to the toll of pain and disability and to the economic burden of this condition. It has been estimated that 1 million fractures of the hip, wrist, and spine each year in the United States are caused by osteoporosis.

WHAT IS OSTEOPOROSIS?

Osteo = bone; and porosis = increased pores. The interior structure of many bones normally resembles a sponge. Osteoporotic bone is like a sponge in which the holes are enlarged with resulting weakness and fragility (see illustration). In osteoporosis progressive thinning of the bones may leave the skeleton too fragile to withstand even minimal mechanical stress. The bones gradually weaken and become prone to factures.

WHO IS AT GREATEST RISK FOR OSTEOPOROSIS?

Women after menopause are by far the largest group of people who develop osteoporosis that leads to fractures. Elderly men also may have osteoporosis but less commonly and less severely than women. Caucasians are affected much more frequently than blacks. Cigarette smoking and alcohol consumption also appear to be risk factors, but the reasons are not well understood.

Slender women who exercise little are more likely to develop the condition than those of heavier build who are more physically active. Prolonged inactivity, especially bed rest, is also a predisposing factor.

WHAT CAUSES OSTEOPOROSIS?

The loss of bone mineral may arise from a great variety of causes. The major factor in postmenopausal women is deficiency of estrogen--the main female sex hormone. At the time of naturally occurring menopause, a loss of bone mineral occurs. This decrease is considerably greater than in men of similar age.

Normal bone undergoes continuous remodeling, as do most body tissues. The amount of mineralized bone at any time is a balance between these breakdown and rebuilding processes. In those with osteoporosis, the rate of bone loss ("resorption") exceeds the rate of new bone formation ("accretion"). Estrogen deficiency is a major factor in causing this negative balance.

WHAT ROLE DOES CALCIUM PLAY IN OSTEOPOROSIS?

Since the mineral content of bone is continually being renewed, insufficient amounts of calcium in the diet play a major role in development of osteoporosis. In the United States, dairy products are the major dietary source of calcium. Milk, cheese, yogurt, and buttermilk are all good sources of calcium. Others sources include green, leafy vegetables, salmon, and sardines (see calcium, page 123).

The adult Recommended Daily Allowance (RDA) of calcium is 800 mg per day. Surveys indicate that the diets of many adult women contain considerably less than this amount. Some authorities now believe the current RDA is too low, especially in postmenopausal women. They suggest up to

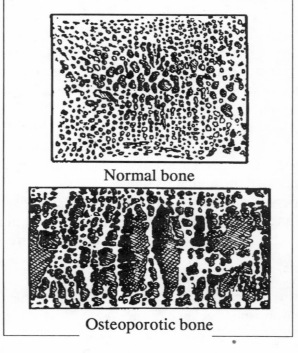

Normal bone

Osteoporotic bone

1500 mg per day for women after menopause. A higher intake for postmenopausal women is necessary because estrogen deficiency may impair calcium absorption from the intestine. Those whose diet has a relatively high protein content and those who eat a diet high in fiber also may require extra dietary calcium.

Calcium has been called the forgotten nutrient of Western society. Lactose intolerance rises with increasing age so many people stop drinking milk and reduce intake of other calcium-rich dairy products after adolescence. Life-long dietary habits (typically characterized by a low calcium intake) are difficult to change. If it is not feasible to increase dietary intake of calcium, it may be necessary for you to take special calcium supplements.

Some physicians believe that ensuring adequate calcium content earlier in life might increase bone density. Thus, even though a reduction in bone mineral content develops later in life, the bones might still be strong enough to prevent some of the fractures now suffered by older women with osteoporosis. Some studies suggest that a high calcium intake over a period of years might retard bone loss enough to reduce susceptibility to fractures.

WHAT ARE THE SYMPTOMS OF OSTEOPOROSIS?

There are no early warnings. The diagnosis is frequently not made until after a disabling bone fracture. Due to progressive vertebral compression, women often note a gradual loss of height, starting after menopause. This is frequently accompanied by forward bending of the upper spine (doctors call this dorsal kyphosis) with a protuberance known as "dowager's hump." The compression fractures of the vertebrae commonly cause pain in the back.

Insufficient amounts of calcium in the diet and deficiency of estrogen play major roles in development of osteoporosis. The loss of height also results in a prominence of the abdomen--"pot belly." This frequently is puzzling to women, since their weight does not increase and there are usually no other areas of apparent obesity in the body.

For additional information see articles on: calcium (page 123), preventing falls (page 176), and hip fractures (page 323).

The morbidity and mortality of osteoporosis is far greater than that of hormone replacement!

DISEASES AND DISORDERS

(page 2 of 3) OSTEOPOROSIS 321

HOW IS THE DIAGNOSIS MADE?

Your physician will do appropriate studies to be sure there is not another medical condition present that may mimic postmenopausal osteoporosis.

As noted earlier, the diagnosis may not be suspected until a fracture prompts a person to seek medical attention. Ordinary X-ray films do not reveal osteoporosis until marked loss of bone mineral has already occurred. Sophisticated instruments to measure bone density and specialized chemical determinations of blood and urine are available in research centers to detect the early development of osteoporosis. These tests are expensive and are not yet available for screening the vast majority of older women. Thus, all women after the menopause should be regarded as being potentially at risk for this condition. Careful measurement of your height each year is one of the simplest ways to detect osteoporosis affecting the spine.

HOW IS OSTEOPOROSIS TREATED?

Preventive treatment is best. An adequate dietary calcium intake throughout life, with extra calcium supplements if necessary, is important. Regular physical exercise is one of the best ways for women to help maintain strong bones. Women whose ovaries must be surgically removed early in life usually are given estrogen to prevent premature menopause symptoms.

Until recently, many physicians were reluctant to prescribe estrogen over prolonged periods for women after the normal menopause. There is a increased risk of developing cancer of the lining of the uterus (endometrium) from prolonged estrogen use. This hazard must be balanced against the pain and disability of wrist and spine fractures and the risk of death following hip fracture in women who develop osteoporosis as a result of estrogen deficiency. Use of progesterone tablets (another female sex hormone) during part of the monthly cyclic administration of estrogen may reduce the risk of cancer. Your physician should discuss these matters with you before a decision is reached about prolonged treatment with hormones.

For those with osteoporosis affecting the vertebrae, improving muscular support of the spine by proper strengthening exercises may be helpful. This exercise program may not be possible in those with painful crush fractures and should be prescribed individually. A firm mattress with a plywood board underneath improves spinal support during sleep. A thin pillow against the back of the chair gives support to the lower back while sitting. A properly fitting back support with shoulder straps often relieves back pain and improves posture. Avoiding heavy lifting and bending activities helps to prevent further vertebral damage.

IS FLUORIDE TREATMENT HELPFUL?

Fluoride (in the form of sodium fluoride tablets) treatment for osteoporosis is under long-term study at the Mayo Clinic and other medical centers. It is still regarded as experimental and is not yet approved by the U. S. Food and Drug Administration for general use in the treatment of this disorder.

The use of calcium supplements and estrogen may help stop continuing loss of bone but does not replace bone mineral already gone. Fluoride stimulates new bone growth and has the potential to reverse the process. The effect of fluoride on increasing bone density was initially noted in people whose drinking water contained high amounts of fluoride.

Unfortunately, fluoride treatment also may have troublesome side effects, including stomach upset and rheumatic symptoms in the legs and feet. These problems are relieved when fluoride is stopped. Researchers are trying to find a dose level that will be effective in strengthening bone without causing the undesirable effects.

WHAT ABOUT FUTURE DEVELOPMENTS?

Studies of the most effective treatment of established osteoporosis are underway. The combined use of estrogen, supplementary calcium, and fluoride looks promising. Treatment with these three agents can't be expected to improve bone strength rapidly, but studies show that by the second year of use the risk of bone fractures is considerably reduced.

In the long run, prevention of this disorder is the most cost-effective approach. Research now in progress may define a group of postmenopausal women most susceptible to fractures due to osteoporosis. Identification of these individuals will allow a more concentrated effort to prevent the disease and its disabling complications.

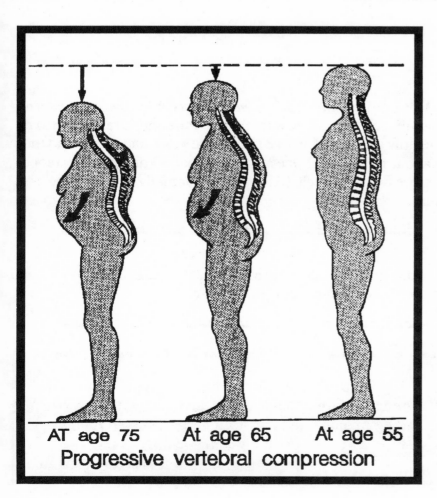

AT age 75   At age 65   At age 55
Progressive vertebral compression

Progressive vertebral compression, caused by osteoporosis, results in a gradual loss of height in women and often is accompanied by a forward bending of the upper spine, which leads to a condition known as **"dowager's hump."** Insufficient amounts of calcium in the diet and deficiency of estrogen play major roles in development of osteoporosis.

Reprinted from August 1984 *Mayo Clinic Health Letter* with permission of Mayo Foundation for Medical Education and Research, Rochester, MN 55905.

Old people
have fewer diseases than the young,
but their diseases never leave them.

Hippocrates (460-370 B.C.)

ESTROGEN--should you take it?

Estrogen loss is the leading cause of bone loss in older women. A lowered estrogen level increases the calcium lost from bone; in some women lack of estrogen contributes to osteoporosis. During menopause a decline in the amount of estrogen, a female hormone, can cause a number of troublesome symptoms, such as vaginal dryness and hot flashes (a sudden flush or warmth followed by sweating). Although approximately 75% of women have little or no difficulty with these symptoms, some have severe discomfort.

Some women take estrogen (usually in pill form) to replace the natural estrogen lost during and after menopause. Estrogen is given to women at high risk of developing osteoporosis and to those with severe symptoms of menopause. The Food and Drug Administration announced that it now considers estrogen "to be effective for the treatment of postmenopausal osteoporosis," although this does not mean that estrogen is necessarily recommended for menopausal or postmenopausal women.

FORMS OF ESTROGEN: Estrogen is available in several forms: pills or tablets, vaginal creams, injections, and skin patch. The form of estrogen prescribed by the doctor depends on the patient's symptoms--for example, topical creams are used for severe vaginal symptoms while pills or patches are used both to prevent bone loss and to reduce other generalized effects of menopause.

SIDE EFFECTS: Many authorities believe the benefits of estrogen outweigh the dangers. However:

❶ Studies show that about 10% of women who take estrogen have side effects such as headaches, nausea, vaginal discharge, fluid retention, swollen breasts, or weight gain.

❷ Endometrial cancer has been found to occur more often in women who use estrogen.

❸ Heart disease studies show contradictory findings. A Harvard Medical School report indicates that estrogen may actually reduce risk of heart disease, while the Framingham Heart Study reports that heart attack and stroke are more common in persons using estrogen.

❹ Women treated with estrogen are also more likely than untreated women to have abnormal vaginal bleeding.

Thus, persons who have a low risk of developing serious bone loss or have no major menopausal symptoms may prefer to avoid using a hormone replacement therapy.

WARNING: Conditions that may warrant caution in the use of estrogen therapy are obesity, high blood pressure, diabetes, liver disease, blood clots, seizure disorders, migraine headaches, gallbladder disease, and a history of cancer. Your doctor knows best.

ALTERNATIVES: For women who cannot or choose not to take estrogen, there are other ways to deal with the symptoms of menopause. Also, certain health habits can help produce strong bones, particularly when started early in life. Even as an adult, taking additional calcium may be helpful. However, there are different types of calcium and some types are better absorbed than others. Often it is necessary to take additional amounts of some vitamins for calcium to be absorbed; ask your doctor.

LATEST NEWS

As reported in the July 12, 1990 issue of the *New England Journal of Medicine,* a large national study raises hope that a drug can stop or even reverse disfiguring and sometimes crippling bone loss affecting millions of older American women. Doctors at seven United States medical centers found that bones in the spine became denser and vertebral fractures fell by more than half during the two-year treatment with a drug called etidronate (Didronel).

Etidronate is reported to have fewer side effects than other antiresorptive drugs such as calcitonin. The doctors gave the women in the study the etidronate for two weeks straight, followed by more than two months with no drug, repeating the cycle eight times through the two-year study period. The drug cannot be given continuously because to permanently shut off turnover of bone minerals could block mechanisms that keep bone tissue healthy.

On average, spinal bone density went up from 4% to 5% in treated women, and spinal fractures fell from a calculated rate of 62.9 fractures per 1,000 patients per year to 29.5. The fracture risk fell the most in women who had the weakest bones to start with. The improvement was greatest in women in whom the disease was the worst.

The Food and Drug Administration now approves etidronate for Paget's disease. Medical experts say wide approval for use in cases of osteoporosis is now probable, and there is no practical way to stop doctors from prescribing it for osteoporosis. It is best to ask your doctor about etidronate.

Dr. Dean Edell's *Medical Journal* reports that osteoporosis isn't just a women's disease. Researchers in Portland, Oregon, followed 86 healthy men, aged 30 to 87, for three years and found that they lost about 1% of their bone mass each year. Women with osteoporosis lose twice as much. (Alcohol and/or malignancy are the keys to male bone loss.)

According to the experts, the most reliable thing you can do to keep your bones from thinning is to exercise.

> In human life there is constant change of fortune: and it is unreasonable to expect an exemption from the common fate. Life itself decays, and all things are daily changing.
>
> **Plutarch (46-120 A.D.)**

Bone loss and dangerous falls--both can be prevented

Over 200,000 hip fractures occur every year in the United States. Almost 50% occur in persons who are 80 or older. Increasing numbers of older people will incur these injuries as our society steadily grays. We now have the ability to survive until our bones give out. Women account for 75% to 80% of all hip fractures, mainly because of the bone-weakening effects of osteoporosis, a disfiguring, often crippling condition that strikes women far more than men due to hormone changes that occur after menopause.

Fractures of the hip are associated with more deaths, disability, and medical costs than all other fractures. Out of 112,000 people in nursing homes because of fractures last year, more than half--62,200--had suffered hip fractures. One out of five of those who do not recover normal function after a hip fracture will die within a year. Of the people who survive hip fractures, 15% to 25% must remain in nursing homes for at least one year after the fracture.

BONE LOSS AND GAIN--During childhood and adolescence, bone mass increases rapidly. A process called mineralization gradually deposits calcium and phosphorus into a protein framework made by the bone-forming cells. The body's total bone mass continues increasing this way until the skeleton reaches maturity in a person's mid-30s. After a short period when the loss and gain of bone tissue is equal, bone loss will begin to win out. While the mid-30s are the starting point for a gradual increase in bone loss in both sexes, the first few years after natural or surgical menopause can result in very rapid bone loss--and osteoporosis--for some women.

Some decrease in bone density, or "osteopenia," is believed to be normal, with aging inevitable for everyone. But it's not necessarily inevitable for so much bone tissue to be lost that the fractures of osteoporosis occur. Most fractures are in the vertebrae, the wrist bones, and hip bones. The hip may also be involved in rheumatoid arthritis or osteoarthritis, or it may become infected, causing pyogenic arthritis.

The widest part of the pelvis, including the underlying bone, is the hip. The hip bone at the top of the leg is a ball-and-socket joint in which a ball at the end of the thigh bone (femur) fits into a socket in the pelvis, making it capable of movement in many directions. The hip joint is supported by strong ligaments and is extremely secure. However, fractures of the neck of the femur occur commonly in the elderly. Surgical procedures either pin the bones together, or replace the head of the femur with an artificial one that fits into the hip joint. These devices are made of metal, such as stainless steel, or alloys of cobalt, chrome, and titanium.

HIP REPLACEMENT--The older person who has advanced stages of osteoarthritis, with all three elements of the hip damaged, usually will follow the trend toward total hip replacement. Total replacement will allow them to walk well without waiting for a fracture to heal. Replacement devices renew the shaft of the femur (thigh bone), the head of the femur, and the acetabular cup (the socket)--see illustration.

Replacing the fractured hip bone has become so commonplace that steady improvements are being made in the field. At one time the bone cement would let go and new hip replacements were needed every 7 to 10 years. Today, a porous-coated prosthetic hip is being used without cement to make a more stable prosthesis.

LEARNING TO WALK AGAIN--If there are no complications from the surgery, patients are encouraged to sit up on the side of the bed the day after the operation. By day two, they should try to stand. How much standing they should do and how much weight should be put on the leg depends on the type of prosthesis. With cemented hip replacements, patients can put the amount of weight on the leg that feels comfortable to them whenever they want. This is because the cement fixes the prosthesis in place immediately.

With noncemented hip replacements, however, bone growth is desired to hold the prosthesis in place, so patients must limit the amount of weight they put on their hips until the support is firm Usually, therapy begins with six weeks on crutches or a walker, followed by one crutch for four weeks, and two weeks with a cane. Patients with cemented hips may need to use crutches, too, but usually they're walking sooner than those with noncemented prostheses.

PREVENTION--The best solution is to prevent hip fractures in the first place. The simplest form of prevention is to remove physical hazards from the home and to have properly fitted glasses and adequate podiatric (foot) care to reduce the risk of falls. Women should wear properly fitted shoes with low heels to prevent falls (see article on preventing home accidents and falls, page 176).

Pelvis

typical fracture location

Socket cemented into pelvis

Shaft (metal) cemented into the thighbone

thighbone (femur)

hip ball & socket replacement

One out of every four women by the age of 70 develops an osteoporotic fracture.

The shaking palsy--

Parkinson's disease is a chronic central nervous system disorder characterized by slowness and poverty of purposeful movement, muscular rigidity, and tremor. It affects between 500,000 and 1 million Americans, virtually all of whom are over 50. The symptoms were first described by Dr. James Parkinson, a London physician, in his "Essay on the Shaking Palsy" in 1817.

Parkinson's disease does not come on suddenly; in fact, it is so insidious that victims often don't realize anything is wrong, although family and friends may notice subtle changes.

SYMPTOMS: The early symptoms, such as a little shakiness or a general sense of slowing down, may be dismissed as part of growing old. (The average age of a patient at diagnosis is 65.) A slight tremor then appears, often in the form of a "pill rolling" movement involving the fingers and thumb of one hand. Classically, the tremor is most pronounced at rest and is less severe when the affected limb is in motion.

Another characteristic symptom is rigidity of the arms and legs. Muscles remain tight, instead of relaxing. If another person tries to move a patient's arm, the movements will be short and jerky, as though the arm is being moved by a gear.

A third, and very definite, sign of Parkinson's disease is a slowness of movement, known medically as "bradykinesia." There is a loss of facial expression, the patient's voice becomes low and monotonous, and eye blinking decreases. Handwriting that gets smaller and more cramped after the first few words is another telltale sign.

As the disease progresses, the patient finds it hard to start walking and, once movement is started, takes short steps with a shuffling gait. Another characteristic is a slight forward lean, which causes the patient to take a series of quick, small steps forward to "catch up" with a changed center of gravity. At times the patient may actually fall down when confronted with an obstacle, for stopping can be as hard as starting.

A backward lean also may develop in advanced cases. This may make the patient step backward when starting to walk or when bumped from the front. Patients often have difficulty maintaining a stable posture.

As time goes on, the loss of spontaneous movements may worsen. There may be times when the person can't move at all. This "frozen" state affects walking most dramatically and may be triggered by an open doorway or a line drawn on the floor.

Other late symptoms include an overproduction of normal skin oils and drooling due to decreased function of the throat muscles. Most patients continue to think clearly, though late in the course of the illness some may suffer loss of mental skills. Parkinson's patients may also feel depressed.

The symptoms of Parkinson's themselves are not fatal. Death most often results from some other illness acquired during the later stages of the disease.

CAUSES: Studies of the brains of Parkinson's patients have found diminished concentrations of dopamine, a chemical messenger that transmits signals from one nerve cell to another. Dopamine is produced by nerve cells in the substantia nigra, located in the brain stem. Without a constant supply of dopamine, movement fails. As people grow older, the supply of dopamine dwindles, apparently because of a loss of producer cells in the substantia nigra. Even so, most people can continue to function. However, if more than 80% of the dopamine-producing cells are lost, Parkinson's symptoms begin to appear.

TREATMENT: There is hardly a drug that hasn't been tried in the treatment of Parkinson's disease. Today there are four basic categories of anti-parkinsonism drugs:

1 Anticholinergics. Normally, there is a fine balance between the activity of dopamine and that of acetylcholine, another chemical that transmits nerve impulses. When the inhibiting effect of dopamine is lost, as the dopamine-producing cells degenerate, the functioning of acetylcholine-releasing cells becomes overactive, causing parkinsonian symptoms. This hyperactivity can be blocked with anticholinergic drugs.

Patients on anticholinergic drugs may experience occasional gingivitis, constipation, mild dizziness, nausea, nervousness, and slight blurring of vision. More serious side effects include confusion, urinary retention, and psychosis.

2 Levodopa-containing Compounds. Since the cause of Parkinson's is a loss of dopamine, the logical treatment is to put dopamine back into the brain. Dopamine can't be carried in the blood to the brain, but levodopa, its immediate precursor, can. Once in the brain, levodopa (L-dopa) is transformed into dopamine. L-dopa reduces all the primary symptoms of Parkinson's disease. Unfortunately, many patients find that L-dopa's effectiveness early in the course of treatment may not persist beyond several years.

Side effects associated with L-dopa include nausea, involuntary movements, mental changes, cardiac irregularities, and urinary retention. One particularly troubling problem that develops after three to five years of treatment is called the "on-off" reaction. The patient rapidly shifts from a state of uncontrolled movement to one of total lack of movement. Another problem is "end-of-dose akinesia"--the return of the Parkinson's symptoms three to four hours after taking medication.

3 Dopamine Agonist. The one drug in this class, bromocriptine (Parlodel), stimulates dopamine receptors in the brain. Clinical studies have shown that bromocriptine, used in conjunction with L-dopa, reduces the end-of-dose phenomenon in many patients and occasionally benefits those with the "on-off" response.

Patients should not take this drug if they have a history of coronary or peripheral vascular disease, gastrointestinal ulcers, or psychosis. Side effects include hypertension, confusion, nasal stuffiness, blurred vision, liver problems, and swelling of the feet.

4 Deprenyl. Last year the Food and Drug Administration approved Deprenyl for use in the United States to treat patients with severe Parkinson's disease. For years, physicians in Europe have prescribed the drug in conjunction with the conventional medication Sinemet, a compound that raises levels of dopamine in the brain. Now, a preliminary study by James W. Tetrud and J. William Langston, neurologists at the California Parkinson's Foundation, suggests that Deprenyl retards the rate of the disease's progress. Deprenyl acts directly on the neurons in the brain's substantia nigra, where depletion of dopamine is known to cause parkinsonism.

Dr. Langston says, "Right now we cannot halt the disease, only slow its progression. But this raises questions. If we go a step further, can we stop the disease entirely? That would be a tremendous advance in treatment, since most patients have very mild symptoms when they first observe the disease. Those people could go on to live a normal life."

For more information call or write: National Parkinson Foundation, Inc., 1501 N.W. 9th Ave. /Bob Hope Road, Miami, FL 33136; 1-800-327-4545; 1-800-433-7022 (in Florida); 305-547-6666 (in Miami); 1-800-544-4882 (in California).

More good reasons to exercise

Pulmonary embolism is the medical term for a blood clot that plugs the arteries supplying blood to the lungs. Each year there are about 630,000 cases of pulmonary embolism in the United States, and approximately 70,000 people die within an hour of their first symptoms. Of the 560,000 patients who survive longer than one hour, approximately 70% or about 400,000, are misdiagnosed. Since about a third of this group dies, it is estimated that correct diagnosis and therapy could save more than 100,000 lives each year.

A blood clot in the lung is not formed there, but elsewhere in the body. About 95% of the time, clots that end up in the lungs develop in the large vein deep inside the muscles of the leg and pelvis. Only about 1% to 2% originate in the upper extremities, and that is usually in young, healthy men following strenuous exercise or activity. A deep vein clot of pulmonary embolism is not the same as blood clots that form in arteries and block the flow of blood to the brain, causing a stroke, or those that block the flow to the heart, causing a heart attack.

Causes of Pulmonary Embolism

Three underlying conditions in the body contribute to the formation of a deep vein clot, usually in the leg:

1 The first condition is injury to a vein wall, which can be caused by inflamed valves in the deep leg veins, an indwelling catheter, an injection, an accident, or other problems. When a blood vessel is injured, a clot (thrombus) forms at the injured site to prevent further blood loss. Over a period of days or weeks, the blood vessel heals itself and the clot gradually dissolves. If the blood clot doesn't stick to the damaged vein wall, but breaks away (embolus), or fragments of it break away, it is carried to the lungs via the bloodstream, which causes pulmonary embolism.

2 The second condition is sluggish blood flow. The circulatory system needs some help to get the venous blood back up to the heart against the force of gravity. To keep the blood flowing in one direction, most leg veins are equipped with valves that prevent blood from flowing backward. Breathing in and out creates a partial vacuum that also helps send the blood upward. The muscles of the legs, especially calf muscles, pump blood toward the heart by squeezing the deep veins in the leg during exercise and activity.

When the body is inactive, blood may stagnate in the veins. Thickening and slowing of the blood flow tends to make the blood clot more readily. This condition may occur when people are bedridden because of a heart attack or congestive heart failure, are immobilized in a cast, or are recuperating from burns or surgery, especially orthopedic or prostate surgery. Stroke victims run as high as a 75% risk of developing deep vein clots in a paralyzed leg.

3 The third condition that causes pulmonary embolism is when blood becomes hypercoagulable (prone to clot excessively). Normally, circulating blood stays fluid through a kind of balancing act between clotting promoters and clotting inhibitors. If the clotting promoter increases, or the activity of the clotting inhibitors decreases, the result may be blood that clots too readily.

People especially vulnerable to this hypercoagulable state are those who have cancer, blood diseases such as polycythemia vera (characterized by an increase in red blood cells), some inherited diseases, and chronic ulcerative colitis. Women who use oral contraceptives, especially those who smoke, are also more likely to develop this condition. A rise in hormone levels may cause blood to coagulate more readily in pregnant women, who are five times more likely to develop deep vein clots than nonpregnant women in the same age group. Women who have just given birth are at increased risk if they are obese or have varicose veins,

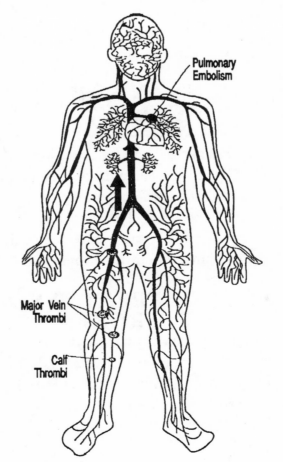

Pulmonary Embolism

Major Vein Thrombi

Calf Thrombi

or if they've had deep vein clots or pulmonary embolism in the past.

Prevention

The best way of keeping deep vein clots from forming is exercise. The body requires activity to keep itself in good condition. People in sedentary jobs need to ambulate as well as eat during lunch hour. Devoted TV fans should make a habit of moving about during commercials and other dull spots.

Healthy, active people don't usually have to worry about pulmonary embolism. However, when traveling and sitting nearly immobile for long periods, some danger is involved. Doctors advise air travelers not to smoke, as smoking thickens the blood; and they recommend drinking plenty of nonalcoholic liquids to counteract the dehydrating effects of low humidity in air cabins. Frequent walks around the plane will keep blood from pooling in leg veins and feet from swelling.

Other exercises that can be done in place are moving the feet up and down, toe-wiggling, and extending the lower legs. Contracting the muscles in the stomach and buttocks encourages blood flow in the pelvic veins, while deep breathing increases the flow of blood to the upper part of the body. Though the risk of blood pooling is slight in the upper extremities, people whose hands swell should do reaching exercises, or open and close the fingers occasionally.

The same goes for long trips in other vehicles. Walking up and down the train, or stopping the car occasionally to stretch the legs, helps the circulation. Wearing restrictive clothing in general is not sensible, but it is especially important to forego tight girdles or pantyhose on the road, as they may act as tourniquets to the upper legs.

People at High Risk for Pulmonary Embolism

1 People immobilized for long periods due to illness or accidents.
2 Congestive heart failure patients.
3 Those with tumors, especially certain cancers of the GI tract.
4 Postsurgical patients.
5 Women over the age of 30 using oral contraceptives.
6 Patients with intrinsic vein disease.
7 Chronic obstructive lung disease patients.
8 The obese.

STROKE

A condition requiring immediate attention

Stroke is the third leading cause of death in this country, behind heart disease and cancer. Each year, about 400,000 Americans suffer a stroke. About 150,000 die immediately or shortly after the stroke's onset. Of every 100 who survive the acute illness, about 10 will be able to return to work virtually without impairment, 40 will be slightly disabled, 40 will be more seriously disabled and require special services, and 10 will need institutional care. Only about 16% of the 1.8 million Americans today who have survived stroke are completely independent. The good news is that the death rate from stroke has declined since records on the disorder were first kept in 1910 and the advances in the specialty of rehabilitation medicine maximize residual abilities and minimize disabilities.

WHAT CAUSES A STROKE?

The brain represents 2% of the body's weight, but it commands 25% of the body's oxygen supply and 70% of the glucose consumed by the body, and 15% of the blood pumped by the heart through the arteries. The brain, unlike other organs, cannot store the energy that it makes from glucose and oxygen in the blood. Brain cells can live only for a few minutes if their blood supply stops. A stroke occurs when an area of brain tissue dies because its blood supply has been cut off or decreased.

As brain cells die, the functions they control-- speech, muscle movement, understanding--die with them, or are impaired. Once they die, they cannot be regenerated.

About two-thirds of all strokes occur because of blockages that gradually form in the arteries that feed the brain. Strokes from such blockages are called *ischemic strokes* or infarctions. The blockages are caused by a clot, called a *thrombus* (artery in the head or neck) or *embolus* (a clot breaking away from a diseased artery in another part of the body, ending up in the brain). This clogging is usually caused by atherosclerosis, also known as hardening of the arteries. Through the years, plaque (consisting of fat-containing material and calcium) builds up on the inner linings of blood vessels, much as mineral deposits build up within a water pipe. The plaque may get so thick it shuts off the blood supply. Or clots may form on the rough surface of the plaque, plugging up the arteries.

WHEN CAN STROKES OCCUR?

A major stroke can occur quickly, just like a bolt of lightning. The old word for stroke, "apoplexy," conjures up an image of a person felled like a tree. However, the factors leading to a stroke usually have been building up within the body for a long time.

THE DIFFERENT TYPES OF STROKES

There are four basic types of strokes:
1. Transient ischemic attacks (TIA's)
2. Thrombotic
3. Embolus
4. Hemorrhagic

■ **Transient Ischemic Attacks** (TIA's)--Eleven percent of all strokes are of this type. A TIA is a kind of mini-stroke that signals the blood flow to the brain has been temporarily interrupted (ischemia)--in most cases from tiny clots (emboli) that have broken loose from plaque in heart or neck arteries. Depending on the part of the brain affected, a TIA can cause blindness in one eye, difficulty in speaking or writing, or numbness or weakness of the face, arm, or leg on one side of the body. An attack usually lasts less than 30 minutes, with complete return to normal. A TIA is a strong predictor of a major stroke–about one-third of those who have had a mini-stroke can expect to have a major stroke within five years.

When someone has many TIA's, a test called an arterial angiogram can be performed in the hospital to locate the narrowed blood vessel. A long, thin, flexible tube is inserted into an artery in the arm or leg and is threaded up into a neck artery. In cases where the blockage looks severe, the doctor may recommend an endarterectomy, in which a surgeon opens the artery and cleans out the blockage.

■ **Thrombotic Strokes**--In major thrombotic strokes, symptoms often progress by steps. It may take minutes or even hours for the full damage to be felt. Typically, a victim may experience clumsiness upon getting up in the morning, soon followed by a headache. At breakfast, the right half of the field of vision in both eyes may disappear. Then, suddenly, the victim may find it difficult or impossible to speak, and ultimately may develop weakness or complete paralysis on the right side of the body. The peak age for thrombotic stroke is 70.

■ **Embolus**--An embolus, in contrast, plugging one of the brain arteries at random, produces all its damage within a matter of seconds. There is usually no warning or pain. It can happen at any time, but it comes more frequently during sleep than other strokes.

■ **Hemorrhagic Stroke**--A hemorrhagic stroke occurs when a blood vessel ruptures (aneurysm) in or around the brain. Hemorrhagic strokes are more dangerous than those caused by blockages because not only does the part of the brain served by the blood vessel die, but blood may spurt out so forcefully that surrounding brain tissue is damaged. Hemorrhages tend to come on abruptly, preceded in half of the victims by a headache. In most cases, the blood pressure is extremely high. Nausea and vomiting are also common. Since hemorrhagic strokes generally occur during the day when a person is active, victims may be alert when the stroke begins and quite aware that something terrible is happening to them. This type of stroke is fatal in about four of five cases. Those who survive are left with major disabilities.

WHAT TO DO?

A stroke is a medical condition that requires immediate care. An early diagnosis is made by evaluating symptoms, reviewing the patient's medical history, and performing routine tests. Tests that may be given include an electrocardiogram (measuring the electrical activity of the heart), an electroencephalogram (measuring nerve cell activity in the brain), a computerized tomography (CT) scan (a painless technique that can assess brain damage), or a magnetic resonance imaging (MRI) of the brain.

Treatment begins as soon as the stroke is diagnosed to ensure that no further damage to brain cells occurs. Strong drugs, called anticoagulants, may be prescribed to prevent blood clots from becoming larger; or, in the case of a hemorrhagic stroke, drugs may be prescribed to lower the blood pressure, which is usually high.

FIGHTING BACK AGAINST STROKES

The risk factors or conditions that lead to stroke include high blood pressure, atherosclerosis (fat forming on the inner walls of blood vessels), heart disease, diabetes, smoking, and being overweight. You can help prevent stroke by taking these steps:

❤ **Control your blood pressure.** Have your blood pressure checked regularly, and if it is high follow your doctor's advice on how to lower it.

❤ **Stop smoking.**

❤ **Eat a healthy diet** that includes protein sources low in cholesterol such as chicken, turkey, fish, and beans, skimmed milk, fruits, and vegetables.

❤ **Exercise regularly.** There is evidence that exercise strengthens the heart and improves circulation. It will also help in weight control; being overweight increases the chance of developing high blood pressure, heart disease, and atherosclerosis. Check with your doctor about what is an appropriate weight for your height and age.

❤ **Control diabetes.** If untreated, diabetes can cause destructive changes in the blood vessels throughout the body.

❤ **Promptly report warning signs** to your doctor.

Transient ischemic attacks (TIA's) are the clearest warning that a stroke may occur; they produce temporary stroke-like symptoms such as numbness or weakness in an arm or leg, difficulty with speech, unexplained headaches, dizziness, momentary blindness, and impaired judgment.

> To-morrow I will live, the fool does say;
> Today itself's too late;
> The wise man lived yesterday.
> **Martial (43-104 A.D.)**

REHABILITATION

Rehabilitation should begin as soon as possible after the patient's condition is stable. A physiatrist, the physician who specializes in physical medicine and rehabilitation, leads the rehabilitation team. It consists of various types of therapy: *physical therapy* helps strengthen muscles and improves balance and coordination (patients may learn to use mechanical aids such as a walker, crutches, a cane or braces); *speech and language therapy* helps those whose speech has been damaged; *occupational therapy* helps improve eye-hand coordination and strengthens skills needed to wash and dress, use tools, or prepare food.

Rehabilitation usually begins while the patient is still in the hospital and, for most, continues at home. Healthcare experts (physicians, physical and occupational therapists, nurses, social workers, and speech and language specialists) work together as a team to coordinate activities that will help the patient as well as the patient's family. Progress in rehabilitation varies from person to person. For some, recovery is completed within weeks following a stroke; for others, it may take many months or years.

Where to Get Help

For information on treatment or rehabilitation services, call a university teaching hospital in your area or write to:

The American Heart Association
7320 Greenville Ave., Dallas, TX 75231

For information about research on stroke and stroke prevention, write to:

National Institute of Neurological and Communicative Disorders and Stroke
Office of Scientific and Health Reports
Building 31, Room 8A06
Bethesda, MD 20892

For information concerning federal benefits and services on rehabilitation, write to:

The Clearinghouse on the Handicapped
Switzer Building, Room 3132
330 C St., S.W., Washington, D.C. 20202

The latest on ulcers

One out of every 10 Americans will have an ulcer sometime in their lives (about 20% of the men and 10% of the women). The incidence of ulcers is declining among younger people, but it is rising among those over 50.

What Is an Ulcer?--A gastric ulcer is a sore in the lining of the stomach. A duodenal ulcer is a sore just below the stomach, at the beginning of the lining of the small intestine. Ulcers are usually confined to the lining but, in rare instances, they will break through, resulting in so-called perforated ulcers.

The stomach crushes and mixes food with the digestive juices, hydrochloric acid, and pepsin. If there is any injury in the lining of the stomach or duodenum, the acid and pepsin (hence the name peptic ulcer) try to digest that injured spot, creating a crater-like sore from one-fourth to an inch or two in diameter.

What Causes Ulcers?--In the past we have blamed bad diets, spicy foods, coffee, and a Type A stressful lifestyle. Today, we have less evidence that these are the culprits. Now we are looking at two factors:

> **First:** too much acid and pepsin can damage the lining of the stomach or duodenal and cause an ulcer.
>
> **Second:** the damage comes from some other cause, making the lining susceptible to the gastric acid.

Principal Causes of Damage to the Lining

■ A *bacteria* called *Helicobacter pylori*. You may be able to "catch" an ulcer from someone else who has one, just as you can catch a cold. Children in the same family tend to infect one another with the germ *Helicobacter pylori*. Eliminating the bacteria leads to the prolonged healing of ulcers.

■ *Nonsteroidal anti-inflammatory drugs* (NSAIDs) such as aspirin, ibuprofen (Motrin, Advil, Nuprin), naproxen (Naprosyn, Anaprox), or piroxicam (Feldene). This is why older people who often take NSAIDs for arthritis and other problems are especially susceptible to ulcers.

■ *Smoking* will double the chances of getting ulcers; it will also slow the healing of ulcers and make them recur.

■ *Heavy drinking* has been shown to delay the healing of ulcers, and alcoholic cirrhosis has been linked to an increased risk of ulcers. However, moderate drinking seems to have little effect on the production of ulcers.

■ *Stress* and ulcers have been linked in some studies. But the difficulty of measuring stress or of gauging an individual's response to stress have made it hard to reach a conclusion.

What Are the Symptoms of Ulcers?--The most common symptom of ulcers is a gnawing or burning pain in the upper abdomen--often between meals, or during the night--that can last a few minutes or a few hours.

Sometimes ulcers do not cause pain; this is particularly true in older people. These "silent" ulcers are detected by X-ray or when the ulcer has progressed to the point that it causes bleeding and anemia.

The Results of an Ulcer--An ulcer can narrow or block the duodenum, preventing food from leaving the stomach and causing vomiting and severe illness. An ulcer can erode into a blood vessel and, depending on the size of the vessel, cause gradual, slow loss of blood, or a sudden hemorrhage, in which case a person may vomit blood and suddenly collapse. This is a life-threatening emergency.

If an ulcer penetrates through the wall of the stomach or the duodenum, partially digested food, digestive juices, and bacteria empty into the abdominal cavity, causing peritonitis.

If a person becomes suddenly dizzy, weak, or pale; passes black, foul-smelling stools; feels severe pain in the stomach or back; has prolonged nausea, vomiting, or a regurgitation of acid material or partially digested food into the mouth; or if blood or material that looks like coffee grounds is vomited, then a doctor-hospital emergency has arisen.

Detecting an Ulcer--The doctor will usually order an upper GI (gastrointestinal) series that consists of an X-ray of the esophagus, stomach, and duodenum. You will swallow a chalky liquid that contains barium, which makes the ulcer visible on the X-ray. The doctor may also order a gastroscopy, in which a flexible tube-shaped device with a light will be put down your throat to enable the doctor to see the ulcer and obtain tissue samples for microscopic examination to determine if the ulcer is cancerous.

How Are Ulcers Treated?--For anyone whose ulcers have been caused by NSAIDs, ceasing to take them may be enough to heal the ulcer. If aspirin is used to relieve arthritis pain, perhaps lower doses will help without causing gastric disturbances.

Some physicians hope that eliminating the bacteria *Helicobacter pylori* with bismuth and antibiotics will become the treatment for ulcers, making all other medications obsolete--but that hope remains to be realized. Some of the drugs used in the treatment are:

◆ Antacids, which neutralize the hydrochloric acid. They are available over the counter and may be sufficient to relieve mild ulcers. Large doses may cause diarrhea or constipation.

◆ H2 receptor antagonists, which reduce the secretion of stomach acid, are currently the most widely used treatment for ulcers. Tagamet, Zantac, and Pepcid are the best-selling prescription drugs in America.

◆ Sucralfate (Carafate) does not reduce the amount of acid in the stomach but seems to act directly on the site of the ulcer by increasing the production of a prostaglandin, a natural substance that protects the area from further damage and gives it time to heal.

◆ Misoprostol (Cytotec) is especially effective against NSAID-induced gastric ulcers and is often prescribed for those who must continue to take NSAIDs. It causes diarrhea in some.

◆ Omeprazole (Losec) is a powerful drug that completely inhibits acid secretion and heals ulcers quickly. It is reserved for short-term therapy of serious ulcers because it does induce cancer in animals if used for a long time.

◆ Bismuth and antibiotics, bismuth salts as found in Pepto-Bismol, and such antibiotics as amoxicillin and tetracycline in combination have been used to attack the bacteria *Helicobacter pylori*. This treatment could result in the development of a resistance of other bacteria to the medication.

If drugs don't work, and you experience obstruction, perforation, or serious bleeding, you may be a candidate for surgery. Or, the preferred treatment for serious, bleeding ulcers has been to seal them off with electrocoagulation, a heater probe, or even a laser. A doudenal ulcer is almost always benign; a gastric (stomach) ulcer is considered malignant until proven otherwise.

The urinary system

The urinary system consists of:

two kidneys, located below the ribs toward the middle of the back;

two drainage tubes called **ureters,** which connect the kidneys to the bladder in the lower abdomen;

the **bladder,** which stores urine ready for discharge;

and the **urethra,** the tube through which urine flows from the bladder to outside the body.

The purpose of the urinary tract system is to extract and dispose of the body's liquid waste products and to help maintain a stable balance of salts and other dissolved substances in the blood. The average adult passes about a quart and a half of urine each day and one half that much at night. Normal urine is sterile. It contains fluids, salts, and waste products, but it is free of microorganisms such as bacteria, viruses, or fungi. In fact, several centuries ago urine was used as an antiseptic to cleanse wounds. At one time, doctors would drop urine in the eyes of newborn babes to prevent eye infections. Thankfully, today we have better methods.

Infections of the urinary tract are among the most common in the human body--so common that only respiratory infections occur more often. Each year, patients with symptoms of a urinary tract infection account for 5 million visits to a doctor's office. It is estimated that up to 20% of women develop a urinary tract infection sometime in their lives.

An infection of the urinary tract occurs when microorganisms, usually bacteria from the digestive tract, adhere to the opening of the urethra and begin to multiply. Most infections can be traced to one type of colon bacteria, called *Escherichia coli.* As they reproduce, bacteria colonize the urethra. An infection that is limited to the urethra is called *urethritis.* Often the bacteria migrate from the urethra to the bladder, causing a bladder infection, *cystitis.* It is important to treat the infection promptly, before bacteria that invade the lower urinary tract have a chance to travel upward, causing a kidney infection *(pyelonephritis)* and possibly kidney damage.

Other microorganisms called "chlamydia" and "mycoplasma" have been found to cause urinary tract infections in both men and women. These infections tend to remain limited to the urethra and genital system. The infections caused by these two microbes are sexually transmitted. They are not detected by standard culturing methods, and require treatment of both sexual partners.

The urinary system is structured in a way that helps guard against infection. For instance, the ureters normally prevent the backup of urine toward the kidneys, and the flow of urine from the bladder helps wash harmful bacteria out of the body. In men, the prostate gland produces secretions that kill or inhibit infection-causing bacteria. In both sexes, various immune defenses also play a role in keeping infection at bay. Despite these and other safeguards, infections still occur.

Infections

SYMPTOMS OF URINARY TRACT INFECTION--Not everyone with infection has symptoms, but most people get at least some. Symptoms include a frequent urge to urinate and a painful, burning feeling during urination. It is not unusual to feel bad all over--tired, shaky, washed out--and to feel pain even when not urinating. Often women feel an uncomfortable pressure above the pubic bone, and some men experience a fullness in the rectum. It is common for a person with a urinary infection to complain that, despite the urge to urinate, only a small amount of urine is passed. The urine itself may appear milky or cloudy--even reddish if blood is present. A fever may indicate that the infection has reached the kidneys. Other symptoms of a kidney infection include pain in the back or side below the ribs, nausea, or vomiting.

DIAGNOSIS--A urinary infection can easily be diagnosed by testing a sample of urine for the presence of pus and bacteria. The urine will be examined for white and red blood cells and bacteria in a test called urinalysis. The bacteria will be grown in a culture and tested against various antibiotics to determine which drug most effectively destroys the bacteria. If the patient has a persistent infection, the doctor will order an intravenous pyelogram (IVP). This examination gives X-ray images of the bladder, kidneys, and ureters. Another test that may be useful for patients with recurring infections is a cystoscopy. A cystoscope is an instrument made of a hollow tube with several lenses and a light source, which allows the doctor to see the inside of the bladder.

TREATMENT--Urinary tract infections are treated with antibacterial drugs. The choice of drug and length of treatment depends on the patient's history and the urine tests that identify the offending bacteria. Uncomplicated infections can be cured in 1 or 2 days of treatment. However, many physicians prefer to have their patients take antibiotics for a longer period (7 to 14 days). Lengthier treatment is needed by patients with infections caused by "mycoplasma" or "chlamydia." These sexually transmitted microorganisms are treated with tetracycline, doxycycline, or trimethoprim/ sulfamethoxazole. In case of kidney infections, severely ill patients may be hospitalized until they are able to take fluids and drugs on their own. Kidney infections rarely lead to kidney damage or kidney failure unless they go untreated.

MEN AND URINARY TRACT INFECTIONS--Urinary tract infections are unusual in men. When they do occur, it is likely that the patient has some kind of obstruction like a urinary stone or enlarged prostate, or recently had a medical procedure involving a catheter. The first step is to identify the infecting organism and the drugs to which it is sensitive. Usually, doctors recommend lengthier therapy in men than in women, in part to prevent infection of the prostate gland. When infection does involve the prostate (prostatitis), it is harder to cure because antibacterial drugs are unable to penetrate prostatic tissue very well. For this reason, men with prostatitis often need long-term treatment with a carefully selected antibiotic.

Further information on urinary and kidney problems may be obtained from:

National Kidney and Urologic Diseases Information Clearinghouse, Box NKUDIC Bethesda, MD 20892 (301) 468-6345

Getting a leg up on varicose veins

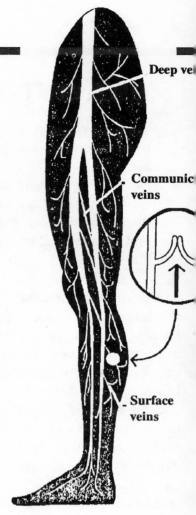

Deep vein

Communicating veins

Surface veins

The illustration shows a cross-section of a vein showing the cup-like structure called a valve. Valves open to let blood flow upward toward the heart and close to keep blood from dropping backward toward the feet. The arrow indicates the direction of flow.

VARICOSE VEINS: A weakened valve that doesn't close properly permits blood to flow the wrong way--from the deep veins to the surface veins instead of the other way. This extra weight of blood presses on the surface vein walls, stretching them. Valves in this stretched area may be pulled apart one by one by pressure from above, causing blood to fall backward and pool in the veins. More pressure is put on the remaining healthy valves and the vein wall, which must now support a longer column of blood. This pressure eventually causes some of the surface vein walls to balloon out into varicose veins.

It is estimated that 25% of adult women and 10% of adult men in this country have varicose veins. For some people, this condition is a minor inconvenience. They are reluctant to wear clothes that show too much leg. Other people can find varicose veins very painful or even disabling. People with unsightly veins may have no discomfort, while others with minor varicosities suffer torment. Many experience aching, tired legs, especially after being on their feet a long time. Other common symptoms are a feeling of fullness or a burning sensation. Others may have swollen or itchy ankles, leg cramps at night, stabbing pains that become worse at the end of the day, tenderness along the veins, ankle discoloration, or ulcers.

Aging can be a factor in varicose veins. Just as skin becomes less elastic with age, veins also lose elasticity and muscles weaken. Varicose veins are not common in people under 25, except for women who have had lots of pregnancies. They most often develop in men between the ages of 70 and 79 and women between 40 and 49. Some people are born with valves that have a tendency to weaken, so heredity is a factor. Varicose veins are more common in men and women who are not physically active.

Varicose veins may lead to chronically swollen legs and skin ulcers that are difficult to heal; or, they may become inflamed, a condition known as phlebitis; or, when a blood clot forms, a more serious disease called thrombophlebitis is the result. Varicose veins can also hemorrhage, although it doesn't happen very often.

The word "varicose" actually means unnaturally dilated or twisted. Varicose may occur anywhere in the body, for example, hemorrhoids. Straining during bowel movements transmits increased abdominal pressure to the veins in the anal area. Some doctors theorize that the strain of constipation causes hemorrhoids and also causes varicose veins in the leg.

Varicose veins are usually bluish and distended, barely visible in some people who have lots of skin fat, and resembling bulging, knotty ropes or a bunch of grapes in others. Small groups of tiny blue or red veins under the skin called spiderbursts often accompany varicose veins.

HOW VEINS ARE CONSTRUCTED: Veins are thin-walled, hollow tubes with only a small amount of elastic and muscle tissue. The arteries have thick, muscular walls and throb with every heartbeat, conveying oxygenated blood under pressure to every cell in the body. The veins operate at a more leisurely pace, carrying blood containing carbon dioxide back to the heart, where it will be pumped to the lungs for reoxygenation.

Blood pressure, though lower in the veins than the arteries, is still the main driving force in circulation. But in the areas farthest from the heart--the feet and legs--venous blood needs assistance in returning uphill against the force of gravity. The veins have tiny valves spaced at irregular intervals in their inner walls, which open when blood flows upward, but close if blood from above falls back, thus ensuring a one-way flow. Blood also gets a boost upward by the actions of leg muscles, which squeeze the deep veins in the leg during exercise, pumping blood toward the heart. Another factor that assists in returning blood to the heart is the act of inhaling, which creates a negative pressure in the chest that draws the blood upward.

TREATMENT: If varicose veins cause no problems, and the deep vein system is healthy, nothing needs to be done. When legs ache slightly, elevating them to drain pooled venous blood may give all the relief that is needed.

✳ **Elastic stocking**--Sometimes an elastic stocking is used that exerts the greatest pressure at the ankle, with gradually lessening pressure as it goes up the leg. Elastic stockings put pressure on vein walls, forcing blood from the superficial veins back into the deep veins and squeezing valves closer together. When combined with regular leg elevation and exercise such as walking or swimming, elastic stockings may be a good choice for people who must be on their feet all day long and for those with mild varicosities. It is probably the best treatment for older people.

✳ **Sclerotherapy**--Another treatment is sclerotherapy, or injection therapy. Sodium tetradecyl sulfate is injected into the vein. The solution irritates the inner vein walls so that scar tissue forms and closes it off. The shrunken vein remains in the leg, and blood flow is routed to other veins. The procedure sometimes causes a brown discoloration of the skin that may not fade. Sclerotherapy is never used on people who have many incompetent valves or deep vein disease.

✳ **Stripping**--Sometimes varicose vein surgery is used in a procedure called "stripping." The saphenous vein is removed with a device called a vein stripper that actually pulls the vein out of the body. With the diseased vein gone, the blood is forced to find new channels to the deep vein system and circulation is improved. When deep veins are blocked or have been damaged by accidents or diseases, such as phlebitis or thrombophlebitis, they cannot pump blood to the heart efficiently enough to compensate for the removal of superficial veins, so the varicose veins will not be removed.

WHAT CAN YOU DO?

Some people are predisposed to varicose veins, but they can help ease the pain.

✳ Avoid long periods of sitting or standing that cause blood to accumulate in the lower legs. Stretch and walk frequently.

✳ Walk, run, or swim regularly to get the leg muscles pumping and blood moving up the vein.

✳ Obesity can be a factor. Overweight people have a higher proportion of fat to muscle, which means less muscular support for the veins and less muscle to do the pumping.

✳ Don't wear tight constricting clothing that can slow down the circulation in the legs.

✳ Elevate the legs when sitting.

✳ Wear elastic stockings if your doctor has prescribed them.

✳ Eat more fiber. Low-fiber diets can cause constipation, which in turn leads to abdominal straining that may damage vein valves in the leg.

They go together like a horse and carriage

Married men are horribly tedious when they are good husbands, and abominably conceited when they are not. - Oscar Wilde

❤

To keep your marriage brimming.
With love in the loving cup.
Whenever you're wrong admit it;
Whenever you're right shut up.
- Ogden Nash

❤

Ishtar was some woman, goddess of both love and war, but of course if you're married you know that the two are closely related.

❤

One woman confiding to another: "I don't want a perfect man. Just one with faults I like."

❤

Marriage is the most natural state of man, and...the state in which you will find solid happiness.   - Franklin (1706-1790)

❤

Familiarity breeds contempt--and children   - Mark Twain

❤

It's a funny thing that when a man hasn't anything on earth to worry about, he goes off and gets married.   - Robert Frost

❤

When you see a married couple coming down the street, the one who is two or three steps ahead is the one that's mad.
- Helen Rowland

❤

Before marriage, a man will lie awake all night thinking about something you said; after marriage, he'll fall asleep before you finish saying it.   - Helen Rowland

❤

It takes a man a lifetime to find out about one particular woman; but if he puts in, say ten years, industrious and curious, he can acquire the general rudiments of sex.
- O Henry

❤

The way my wife finds fault with me, you'd think there was a reward.   - Jack Lemmon

❤

A man may be a fool and not know it, but not if he is married.   - H. L. Mencken

❤

In marriage, being the right person is as important as finding the right person.
- W.D. Gough

❤

Love as a relation between man and woman was ruined by the desire to make sure of the legitimacy of children.   - Bertrand Russell

Eve: Do you really love me?
Adam: There's no one but you.

❤

What's so remarkable about love at first sight? It's when people have been looking at each other for years that it becomes remarkable!

❤

The love we give away is the only love we keep.   - Elbert Hubbard

❤

If two people love each other, there can be no happy end to it.   - Ernest Hemingway

❤

Lovers' quarrels are the renewal of love.
- Terence (185-159 B.C.)

❤

He who for love hath undergone
The worst that can befall,
Is happier thousandfold than one
Who never loved at all.
- Richard Milnes (1809-1885)

❤

'Tis better to have loved and lost than never to have loved at all.
- Alfred Tennyson (1809-1892)

❤

I love thee, I love but thee,
With a love that shall not die
Till the sun grows cold,
And the leaves of the Judgement Book
unfold!   - Bayard Taylor (1825-1878)

❤

Wine comes in at the mouth
And love comes in at the eye;
That's all we shall know for truth
Before we grow old and die.
- Yeats (1865-1939)

❤

Love is all we have, the only way that each can help the other.   - Euripides

❤

He who does not love wine, women, and song, remains a fool his whole life long.
- Martin Luther

❤

A successful marriage requires falling in love many times, always with the same person.
- Mignon McLaughlin

❤

Men always want to be a woman's first love --Women like to be a man's last romance.
- Oscar Wilde (1856-1900)

❤

Marriage--a community consisting of a master, a mistress, and two slaves--making in all two.
- Ambrose Bierce (1842-1914?)

If I had a single flower for every time I think about you, I could walk forever in my garden.
- Claudia Grandi

❤

A man who marries a woman to educate her falls into the same fallacy as the woman who marries a man to reform him.
- Elbert Hubbard (1859-1915)

❤

The calmest husbands make the stormiest wives.   - Thomas Dekker (1577-1632)

❤

Marriage has many pains, but celibacy has no pleasures.   - Johnson (1709-1784)

❤

First get an absolute conquest over thyself, and then thou wilt easily govern thy wife.
- Thomas Fuller (1608-1661)

❤

Let there be spaces in your togetherness.
- Kahlil Gibran (1883-1931)

❤

Don't marry for money, you can borrow it cheaper.   - Scottish Proverb

❤

And on her lover's arm she leant,
And round her waist she felt it fold,
And far across the hills they went
In that new world which is the old.
- Alfred Tennyson (1809-1892)

❤

The light has a thousand eyes, And the day but one;
Yet the light of the bright world dies, With the dying sun.
The mind has a thousand eyes, And the heart but one;
Yet the light of a whole life dies, When love is done.
- Bourdillon (1852-1921)

❤

If you love something set it free
If it returns, you haven't lost it
If it disappears and never comes back,
Then it wasn't truly yours to begin with.

And if it just sits there watching television,
Unaware that it's been set free,
You probably already married it.
- Shoebox Greetings

Alcohol abuse and consequences for older people

The general public and even health professionals have been inclined to ignore the problem of excessive drinking in the elderly. Chronic problem drinkers often die before old age; and those who live are often retired or have fewer social contacts. Older people are often able to hide drinking problems. The families that notice the problem seem to think that the elderly have a limited time left and therefore should be allowed to "enjoy" themselves.

In old age, problem drinkers seem to be one of two types: First, chronic abusers who have used alcohol heavily throughout life--most die by middle age, although some survive into old age. Second, late onset drinkers, those who begin excessive drinking late in life, often in response to situational factors--retirement, lowered income, declining health, and the deaths of friends and loved ones. Alcohol is first used for relief, but later on it becomes a problem.

The National Institute on Alcohol Abuse and Alcoholism estimates that approximately 10% of the elderly male population and 2% of the elderly female population are heavy or problem drinkers--over three million elderly.

Not everyone who drinks regularly or heavily is an alcohol abuser, but the following symptoms frequently indicate a problem:

- ❑ drinking alone with increasing frequency;
- ❑ drinking to calm nerves, forget worries, or reduce depression;
- ❑ lying about drinking habits;
- ❑ gulping drinks and drinking too fast;
- ❑ loss of interest in food;
- ❑ injuring oneself, or someone else, while intoxicated;
- ❑ needing to drink increasing amounts of alcohol to get the desired effect;
- ❑ getting drunk more than three times in the past year;
- ❑ frequently acting irritable, resentful, or unreasonable during nondrinking periods; and
- ❑ having medical, social, or financial problems that are caused by drinking.

There are many signs of possible alcohol abuse; here are a few to look for: poor balance, trouble walking, insomnia, fatigue, grief and depression, withdrawn behavior, anxiety, memory lapses, confusion, falls, anemia, malnutrition, weight loss, inability to care for oneself.

Alcohol abuse among the elderly has been linked to adverse health effects greater than those experienced by younger people. The physical effects of alcohol on the aging often take away "joy" and leave a considerable amount of "pain." Alcohol slows down brain activity, impairs mental alertness, damages judgment, diminishes physical coordination and worsens reaction time-- increasing the risk of falls and accidents. Alcohol commonly causes sleep disturbances, insomnia, restlessness, and terrorizing nightmares among the elderly. It also negatively affects the ability to handle stress. The central nervous system in the elderly is especially vulnerable to the effects of alcohol and drugs.

Heavy drinking can cause permanent damage to the brain and central nervous system, as well as to the liver, heart, kidneys, and stomach. The effects of alcohol on the cardiovascular system can mask pain, which may otherwise serve as a warning sign of a heart attack. Alcoholism can also produce symptoms similar to those of dementia-- forgetfulness, reduced attention, and confusion. If incorrectly identified, such symptoms may lead to unnecessary institutionalization.

Alcohol and Drugs

It is dangerous, sometimes fatal, to drink alcohol while taking certain medications. Alcohol, itself a drug, mixes unfavorably with many other drugs. Drugs often intensify the older person's reaction to alcohol, leading to more rapid intoxication.

The liver is the body's cleaning system for getting rid of chemicals. It cannot efficiently handle both alcohol and a drug. The liver will slow down and both the drug and alcohol will accumulate to toxic levels. On other occasions, alcohol can interfere with the effectiveness of a drug. An overworking liver can clear a prescription drug too fast; then it doesn't have enough time to do its job and that can have serious consequences.

Drugs that don't mix with alcohol:

- ✳ **"Minor" tranquilizers** such as Valium (diazepam), Librium (chlordiazepoxide), and Miltown or Equanile (meprobamate) combined with alcohol result in excessive sedation and serious depression of vital brain functions that will reduce driving skills.
- ✳ **"Major" tranquilizers** such as Thorazine (chlorpromazine), Mellaril (thioridazine), and others with alcohol will produce blurred vision, excessive sedation, and reduced driving skills.
- ✳ **Barbiturates** such as Luminal or Amytal (phenobarbital), and others, with alcohol will impair functions and can be fatal.
- ✳ **Antidepressants** such as Elavil (amitriptyline) and monoamine-oxidase inhibitors (MAOI) are mood elevators that when combined with alcohol greatly increase its depressant effect, can cause high blood pressure, and can be fatal.
- ✳ **Painkillers** such as Tylenol (acetaminophen) with alcohol can cause liver disorders; aspirin with alcohol can increase stomach irritation; Darvon (propoxyphene) or Demerol (meperidine) with alcohol can cause excessive sedation and depressed respiration.
- ✳ **Antihistamines** (both prescription and over-the-counter forms found in cold remedies) combined with alcohol can cause the drugs to be metabolized more readily, producing exaggerated responses. Such drugs also include anticonvulsants such as Dilantin, anticoagulants such as Coumadin, and antidiabetes drugs such as Orinase.

Finding Help

One encouraging aspect of the concern about problem drinking among older persons is that treatment can be very effective and outcomes can be very successful. Self-help, preretirement planning, and counseling are the best preventive approaches to the problem. Support groups can be very effective and work best when all the participants are in the same age group. Group members are more likely to have similar experiences, reactions, and problems. Recognizing this dynamic, Alcoholics Anonymous has created special Golden Years groups.

Prevention and education efforts should be targeted at the late-onset or reactive drinker. Prevention efforts that focus on preparing the elderly individual for some of the stresses that may accompany older age seem very successful. Another effective prevention approach has been to involve older persons in activities that nurture feelings of worth-- volunteer or part-time work, community activism, or consumerism. Local chapters of Alcoholics Anonymous (AA) are listed in the phone book in the white pages or under "Alcoholism Treatment Centers" in the yellow pages.

Time for a second cup of java?

Mention the word caffeine and most people will think you are talking about coffee. Coffee has been around for centuries. For years it has been America's most popular beverage and the largest single source of caffeine in the human diet. Today, the soft drink industry is the biggest user of caffeine and it is now the favorite beverage of Americans.

Coffee consumption reached its peak in the United States in 1962, when nearly three out of four Americans were consuming the beverage; now, slightly more than half the population drinks coffee. Today, nearly six out of every ten persons include soft drinks in their daily diet. Although at least some consumers are concerned about their caffeine intake, it is ironic that soft drinks with caffeine are today's biggest sellers.

Caffeine is a drug that stimulates the central nervous system. It can cause nervousness, irritability, anxiety, insomnia, and disturbances in heart rate and rhythm. It also seems to influence blood pressure, coronary circulation, and the secretion of gastric acids.

Its effects on individuals vary. Some people can consume substantial amounts without apparent ill effects. Others are quite sensitive to it. That's one reason why there will always be some uncertainty over the health effects of caffeine. No one knows for sure what the long-term effect may be on at least some segments of the population. Also, much of what is known about caffeine today is based mostly on animal studies.

Since the early 1960s researchers have found that coffee is no good for you only to turn around and proclaim it is not harmful. The research is in conflict, for example: The researchers found that people who drink four or more cups a day increase their risk of a heart attack by 40%. But, the next year, the same group performed a similar study and found no adverse risks associated with coffee.

At the present time a summation of the research reports reveals the following data:

1 **Elderly coffee drinkers are more sexually active than non-coffee drinkers.** A study of 800 Michigan residents age 60 and older found that 62% of regular coffee drinkers still enjoyed an active sex life compared with 37% of the non-coffee drinkers. The study also found that older, male coffee drinkers were less likely to be impotent.

2 **Drinking a cup of coffee in the morning really does make you feel better and more alert.** Research found that among two groups of young men that received a good night's sleep those consuming a capsule of caffeine equivalent to the amount in two cups of coffee said that they were in a better mood and more alert than those receiving a placebo.

Swiss researchers also found that coffee can increase work efficiency by improving the brain's capacity to process information. Results on coffee and brain power are mixed. Other studies have shown that while coffee consumption can speed performance of some mental tasks, it does not necessarily improve the quality or outcome of those tasks.

3 **Coffee, particularly boiled coffee, increases blood cholesterol levels.** The way you prepare coffee may have something to do with whether it raises your cholesterol. The method that most Americans use--electric drip machines or stove-top filter pots--appears safe. People who drank boiled coffee experienced a 10% increase in cholesterol levels while those who drank filtered experienced no changes in cholesterol levels. Another study found decaffeinated coffee increases cholesterol levels although not enough to warrant a change in habits.

4 **Coffee may protect against cancer of the colon and rectum.** A study found a 40% lower risk of colon and rectal cancer among people who consumed five or more cups a day. But the World Health Organizations also reported that coffee may increase the risk of bladder cancer. Some studies suggest an association between caffeine and a benign breast ailment, fibrocystic disease, which can lead to breast cancer, while other studies have dismissed the connection between caffeine and breast cancer. Dietitians often advise women at high risk for breast cancer to avoid excessive doses of caffeine--such as ten cups a day--from sources such as coffee, colas, and chocolate.

Studies have examined whether coffee increases the risk of cancer of the bladder, urinary tract, kidney, and breasts; most have been inconclusive. One study tying caffeine to pancreatic cancer was later retracted.

5 **Coffee seems to have little effect on stomach disorders.** It can cause heartburn and seems to aggravate ulcers, but researchers say it does not cause ulcers. Coffee is something of a laxative and in some sensitive individuals can cause diarrhea.

6 **Coffee can magnify the effects of stress.** Researchers found that coffee combined with the cardiovascular stress of exercise can elevate blood pressure, especially among people already at high risk. The scientists suspect that caffeine increases the body's production of the natural brain stimulant epinephrine, which makes the heart beat faster.

7 **Coffee can sometimes increase the risk of heart attack.** The new study by Kaiser researchers raises doubts about the safety of excessive coffee consumption, especially among people at high risk for heart disease. But, in general, experts largely agree that moderate coffee consumption-- less than four cups a day--is safe. According to a long-running study on heart disease and lifestyle risk factors called the Framingham Heart Study, coffee intake does not influence cardiovascular disease.

8 **Coffee has very little nutritional benefits and does not provide any vitamins or minerals.** It does speed up the excretion of calcium from the body. However, this deficit can be overcome by adding a couple of teaspoons of milk to the coffee. A cup of black coffee has no calories; with a teaspoon of sugar and a tablespoon of heavy cream, one cup has about 150 calories.

9 **Heavy coffee drinking can lead to a kind of dependency.** Coffee is not crack, but among heavy drinkers, five or more cups a day, it can lead to caffeine dependency. When heavy coffee drinkers quit cold turkey they experience nervousness, irritability, and the inability to concentrate. Many also suffer a severe headache. But studies show that coffee drinkers can kick the caffeine habit in only a few days after stopping.

For all the interest in coffee and health-- more than 500 scientific studies in the last 40 years--the drink consumed in moderation appears to be relatively benign. But, pour yourself a cup and judge for yourself. There must be some reason why 53% of all American adults drink at least one cup of coffee in the morning.

Food and Drug Interactions

Food is essential for life; drugs are important, too, when used to treat or prevent illness. Mixed together, however, food and drugs can interact in ways that can diminish the effectiveness of a drug or deprive the body of the nutrients it is receiving. In some instances, certain drug-food combinations can produce serious illness, even death.

While food and drug interactions can occur in people of any age, they pose particular problems for the elderly, who are major users of prescription and over-the-counter drugs. The 30 million Americans over 65 take 25% of all prescription drugs used in this country. More than half take at least one medication daily and many take six or more a day. What is more significant, they are less likely than younger patients to be well-informed about how and when to take these drugs. And that includes being forewarned of potential side effects that can occur when certain drugs and foods are taken together.

Nutrition experts stress that the elderly, who have to take drugs regularly, should be made aware of possible food-drug interactions. They claim the elderly are at increased risk of complications from drug therapy for two main reasons:

1. They often have multiple medical problems requiring multiple drugs.

2. With age there are changes in physiology that sometimes lead to changes in the ways drugs affect the body.

The extent of interaction between foods and drugs may depend on a variety of factors, including the drug dosage and the individual's age, size, and specific medical condition. In general, though, the presence of food in the stomach and intestines can influence a drug's effectiveness by slowing down or speeding up the time it takes the medicine to go through the gastrointestinal tract to the site in the body where it is needed.

Foods also contain natural and added chemicals that can react with certain drugs in ways that make the drug virtually useless. Some reactions can be downright dangerous, triggering a medical crisis or, in rare instances, even death.

It is because of these interactions that your doctor tells you to take some medications on an empty stomach, some just before meals, and some with meals.

A major way foods affect drugs is by enhancing or impeding absorption of the drug into the bloodstream. There are a few cases in which foods speed up absorption. For example, blood levels of griseofulvin, a substance that combats fungus infections such as ringworm, rise markedly if the patient eats fatty food before taking the drug.

More commonly, though, foods and beverages interfere with absorption. A classic interaction is the one between tetracycline compounds and dairy products. The calcium in milk, cheese, and yogurt impairs absorption of tetracycline. On the other hand, taking some iron supplements with citrus fruits or juices that contain ascorbic acid (vitamin C) enhances absorption of the iron.

In general, it is unwise to take drugs with soda pop or acidic fruit or vegetables. Check with your doctor first. These beverages can result in excessive acidity that may cause some drugs to dissolve quickly in the stomach instead of in the intestines where they can be more readily absorbed into the bloodstream.

To avoid possible complications from drug-nutrient interactions, experts stress that it is essential that patients be advised of the importance of strictly following label directions regarding the time when drugs may be taken in relation to mealtime as well as what foods may not be taken at the same time as the drugs.

Food has been found to have both short- and long-term effects on the way drugs behave in the body. It can speed up or slow down the absorption of the drug, influence the time it takes for the drug to pass through the gastrointestinal tract, and alter the way in which it is metabolized for use in the body. (There are some times, however, when drugs have to be taken with food or a beverage to help prevent gastrointestinal upset.) The kinds of interactions that can occur are too numerous to list but some examples will illustrate the point.

The calcium in dairy products can impair absorption of the antibiotic tetracycline, making it less effective. The effectiveness of anticoagulants (which are prescribed to prevent blood clots) can be adversely affected when liver, leafy green vegetables, and other foods high in vitamin K--which promotes the clotting of blood--are eaten in excess.

Alcohol and Drugs

Alcohol is often considered a drug, but it also is classified as a food--i.e., a beverage. Whatever it is called, alcohol can both interact with other drugs and, in excess, play havoc with human health. Intoxication may occur much more rapidly when alcohol and certain medications are taken together. Consumed with drugs that have a depressant effect on the central nervous system--tranquilizers, barbiturates, painkillers, and antihistamines--alcohol can compound that depressant effect. Performance skills, judgment, and alertness can be slowed dangerously.

Alcohol can cause other drugs--anticonvulsants and anticoagulants, for example--to be metabolized more rapidly, producing exaggerated responses. Alcohol also can raise blood sugar levels and interfere with medications prescribed for diabetes, a common disease of the elderly. With MAO (monoamine oxidase) inhibitors, alcohol can spark sharp increases in blood pressure levels. With diuretics, it can reduce blood pressure, causing dizziness. With antibiotics, it can produce nausea, vomiting, headaches, and stomach cramps. Alcohol may also destroy the coating of time-release capsules, causing more rapid absorption of a drug. The advice is obvious: Don't drink while taking drugs unless a doctor gives specific approval.

Alcohol consumption by the elderly is of particular concern to many healthcare professionals, and the problem may be more serious than many realize. The chronic drinker who has been consuming alcohol over many years, as well as those who drink excessively in later life, often lose interest in food, leading to potential nutritional deficiencies and a breakdown in health. Alcohol consumption can increase the body's requirement for such nutrients as folic acid, thiamine, vitamin B-6 zinc, and magnesium.

Even if not taken with drugs, heavy alcohol consumption impairs mental alertness, judgment, physical coordination, and reaction time and increases the risk of falls and accidents. Chronic drinkers also can consume enough to cause permanent damage to the brain, liver, heart, kidney, stomach, and the central nervous system. Further, alcohol can mask the symptoms of other medical problems.

Over-the-counter Drugs

Among the over-the-counter (OTC) drugs that may promote deficiencies are antacids, analgesics, and laxatives. Although stomach acidity generally decreases as one gets older, many elderly people are regular consumers of these antacids. Some contain aluminum hydroxide, which can contribute to phosphate deficiency because dietary phosphate reacts with the aluminum to form aluminum phosphate, which is passed in the stool. As a result, blood phosphate may be at a normal level but only at the expense of extracting phosphorus from the bone.

How to Prevent Undesirable Food-Drug Interactions

Here are a few suggestions:

✳ **Read the labels** on the over-the-counter remedies and package inserts that may come with prescription drugs.

✳ **Follow your doctor's orders** about when to take drugs and what foods or beverages to avoid while taking medication.

✳ **Don't be afraid to ask** how drugs might interact with your favorite edibles, especially if you consume large amounts of certain foods and beverages. Be sure to tell your doctor about any unusual symptoms that develop after eating particular foods.

✳ **Eat a nutritionally well-balanced diet** from a wide variety of foods. Any medication taken, even on a long-term basis, is not likely to cause depletion of vitamins and minerals if your overall nutritional status is good.

Drug labeling and informed health professionals can be helpful to you, but your doctor and pharmacist cannot follow you to the dinner table or the snack bar. Remember that warnings about food-drug interactions are only as good as the patient's willingness to heed them.

Physicians and pharmacists recognize that some food and drugs, when taken during the same period of time, can alter the body's ability to utilize a particular food or drug, or cause serious side effects. The following information is provided to help you decide if your diet should be changed in any way to adjust to the effects of medicine you are using. It covers the interactions--that is, what can occur between foods and drugs--of the more commonly used medications, both prescription and nonprescription (or over-the-counter).

This information should not be used in place of advice from a family physician or family pharmacist. Make sure your doctor knows about every drug you are taking, including drugs you obtain without a prescription. **If you have any problems related to medication, call your physician or pharmacist immediately. One drug may react with another, in some cases creating serious medical problems. This information does not cover the interaction of one medicine with another. Interactions will vary according to the dosage, your age, sex, and your overall health.**

The generic (nonproprietary) name for each drug is stated first. Brand names are capitalized and represent only some examples.

Allergies, Asthma, Colds, and Coughs

Antihistamines--are used to relieve or prevent the symptoms of colds and hay fever and other types of allergies. They act to limit or block histamine that is released by the body when we are exposed to substances that cause allergic reactions. Some commonly used antihistamines: brompheniramine/Dimetane, Bromphen; chlorpheniramine/Chlor-Trimeton, Teldrin; diphenhydramine/Benadryl, Benaphen.

Interaction--Avoid taking with alcoholic beverages because antihistamines combined with alcohol may cause drowsiness and slowed reactions. Dangerous in the presence of glaucoma or hypertension.

Bronchodilators--are used to treat the symptoms of bronchial asthma, chronic bronchitis, and emphysema. These medicines relieve wheezing, shortness of breath, and troubled breathing. They work by opening the air passages of the lungs. Some commonly used bronchodilators: aminophylline/Phyllocontin, Somophyllin; theophylline/Slo-Phyllin, Theo-Dur.

Interaction--Avoid eating or drinking large amounts of foods or beverages that contain caffeine because both bronchodilators and caffeine stimulate the central nervous system.

More food and drug interactions you should know abo

Arthritis and Gout

Aspirin--reduces pain, fever, and inflammation. Aspirin is available in many brands.

Interaction--Because aspirin can cause stomach irritation, avoid alcohol. To avoid stomach upset, take with food. Do not take with fruit juice.

Aspirin is one of the nonprescription drugs most often consumed by the elderly, and it is the primary drug used to treat arthritis. Many elderly suffering from arthritis take aspirin regularly, and many are such long-time users that their aspirin intake can range from one to three grams a day. Aspirin can cause bleeding in the gastrointestinal tract. Alcohol also can irritate the stomach and aggravate its bleeding. Bleeding can lead to iron depletion. A person taking lots of aspirin may have to follow a diet high in iron.

Some studies suggest that aspirin competes with folic acid for a place in the protein molecule in blood that transports this vitamin to the tissues. Studies also suggest aspirin may increase the rate of folic acid loss in urine. Long-time users may need diets high in folic acid as well. Chronic aspirin users also may need additional vitamin C. Ask your doctor.

Corticosteroids--Cortisone-like drugs are used to provide relief to inflamed areas of the body. They lessen swelling, redness, itching, and allergic reactions. Some commonly used steroids are: betamethasone, dexamethasone, hydrocortisone, methylprednisolone, prednisone, triamcinolone.

Interaction--Avoid alcohol because both alcohol and corticosteroids can cause stomach irritation. Also avoid foods high in sodium (salt). Check labels on food packages for sodium. Take with food to avoid stomach upset.

Ibuprofen and Other Anti-Inflammatory Agents--relieve pain and reduce inflammation and fever. Some commonly used anti-inflammatory agents are: ibuprofen/Advil, Haltran, Medipren, Motrin, Nuprin; naproxen/Naprosyn, Indovin, Feldene, etc.

Interaction--These drugs should be taken with food or milk because they can irritate the stomach. Avoid taking the medication with those foods or alcoholic beverages that tend to bother your stomach.

Heart and Circulatory Diseases

Diuretics--increase the elimination of water, sodium and chloride from the body. Some commonly used diuretics are: furosemide/Lasix; triamterene/Dyrenium; hydrochlorthiazide (HCTZ)/Esidrix, Hydrodiuril.

Interaction--Long-term use of diuretics, or "water pills," to treat high blood pressure and chronic heart disease in which fluid accumulates, a condition called edema, can lead to serious potassium depletion. If the potassium loss is not corrected in heart patients taking digitalis, the heart may become more sensitive to the effects of the drug. People taking diuretics regularly may require potassium supplements or should eat foods that are good sources of potassium. These include tomatoes and tomato juice, oranges and orange juice, dried apricots, cantaloupes, figs, raisins, bananas, prunes, potatoes, sweet potatoes, and winter squash. Some diuretics also can cause increases in calcium excretion and depletion of other minerals. Thus, it is obvious that anyone taking diuretics should follow doctors' orders carefully, including dietary recommendations. Your doctor may prescribe a potassium supplement.

Vasodilators--are used to relax veins and/or arteries to reduce work of the heart. Some commonly used vasodilators are: nitroglycerine/Nitrogard, Nitrostat.

Interaction--Use of sodium (salt) should be restricted for medication to be effective. Check labels on food packages for sodium.

Anti-hypertensives--relax blood vessels, increase the supply of blood and oxygen to the heart, and lessen its work load. They also regulate the heartbeat. Some commonly used antihypertensives are: atenolol/Tenormin; captopril/Capoten; hydralazine/Apresoline; methyldopa/Aldomet; metoprolol/Lopressor.

Interaction--Use of sodium (salt) should be restricted for medication to be effective. Check labels on food packages for sodium.

Anticoagulants--are used to reduce clotting of the blood. A commonly used anticoagulant: warfarin/Coumadin, Panwarfin.

Interaction--Moderation in consumption of foods high in vitamin K is recommended because vitamin K produces blood-clotting substances. Such foods include spinach, cauliflower, brussels sprouts, potatoes, vegetable oil, and egg yolks. Do not take aspirin or NSAIDs with anticoagulants.

Infections

Erythromycin--is an antibiotic used to treat a wide variety of infections, including those of the throat, ears, and skin. Some commonly used products are: erythromycin/E-Mycin; erythromycin estolate/Ilosone; erythromycin ethylsuccinate/E.E.S., E-Mycin E.

Interaction--Erythromycins vary in their reactions with food; consult your doctor or pharmacist for instructions.

Methenamine--is used to treat urinary tract infections. Some commonly used brand names are: Mandelamine, Urex.

Interaction--Cranberries, plums, prunes, and their juices help the action of the drug. Avoid citrus fruits and citrus juices. Eat foods with protein, but avoid dairy products.

Metronidazole--This agent is an antiinfective that is used to treat intestinal and genital infections due to bacteria and parasites. Commonly used brand name: Flagyl.

Interaction--Do not take alcohol while using this drug, because it may cause stomach pain, nausea, vomiting, headache, flushing, or redness of the face.

Penicillins--are antibiotics used for treatment for a wide variety of infections. Some commonly used ones are: amoxicillin, ampicillin, bacampicillin, penicillin G, and penicillin V.

Interaction--Amoxicillin and bacampicillin may be taken with food; however, absorption of other types of penicillins is reduced when taken with food.

Sulfa Drugs--are antiinfectives that are used to treat stomach and urinary infections. Some commonly used sulfa drugs are: co-trimoxazole/Bactrim, Septra; sulfisoxazole/Gantrisin.

Interaction--Avoid alcohol, as the combination may cause nausea.

Tetracyclines--are antibiotics that are used to treat a wide variety of infections. Some commonly used brand names: tetracycline hydrochloride/Achromycin, Sumycin, Panmycin.

Interaction--These drugs should not be taken within two hours of eating dairy products such as milk, yogurt, or cheese, or taking calcium or iron supplements.

Pain

Aspirin (see aspirin under Arthritis and Gout)

Codeine--is a narcotic that is contained in many cough and pain relief medicines. Codeine suppresses coughs and relieves pain, and is often combined with aspirin or acetaminophen in medications. Some commonly used names: Aspirin with Codeine, Tylenol with Codeine.

Interaction--Do not drink alcohol with this medication because it could increase sedative effect of the medication. Take with meals, small snacks, or milk because this medication may cause stomach upset. Can cause constipation.

Other Narcotic Analgesics--Narcotics are used for the relief of pain. Some commonly used narcotic analgesics: meperidine, morphine, oxycodone, pentazocine, propoxyphene.

Interaction--Do not drink alcohol because it increases sedative effect of the medications. Take these medications with food, because they can upset the stomach. Can cause constipation.

Ibuprofen and Other Antiinflammatory Agents (see Ibuprofen under Arthritis and Gout)

Stomach and Intestinal Problems

Cimetidine, Famotidine, Ranitidine--These medications are prescribed to treat ulcers. They work by reducing the amount of acid in the stomach. Some commonly used brand names: cimetidine/Tagamet; famotidine/Pepcid; ranitidine/Zantac.

Interaction--Follow the diet your doctor orders.

Laxatives--Some laxatives stimulate the action of the muscles lining the large intestine. Other types of laxatives soften the stool, or add bulk or fluid to help food pass through the system.

Interaction--Constipation is a chronic complaint of the elderly, and many older people seek relief with laxatives, for which Americans spend about $250 million a year. Doctors do not always know what causes constipation, but poor diet, inadequate consumption of fluids, misuse of laxatives, and lack of exercise may contribute to it. Certain drugs--like antidepressants, antacids containing aluminum or calcium, and diuretics--also may cause it.

Laxatives can adversely affect nutrient intake. Some can affect vitamin D absorption, which in turn can make a poor calcium balance even worse. If a laxative has mercury, this can result in depletion of phosphorus from the bones. Mineral oil, a widely used constipation remedy, can interfere with the absorption of vitamins A, D, E, and K, and it can interact with such drugs as anticoagulants (given to prevent blood clots). Most laxatives are available without prescription. Excessive use of laxatives can cause loss of essential vitamins and minerals and may require replenishment of potassium, sodium, and other nutrients through diet. Discuss the use of laxatives with your doctor or pharmacist.

Emotional Problems

Most medications for psychiatric or emotional disturbances interact with alcohol in a dangerous manner.

Lithium Carbonate--Lithium regulates changes in hormone levels in the brain, balancing excitement with depression.

Interaction--Follow the dietary and fluid intake instructions of your physician to avoid very serious toxic reactions.

MAO Inhibitors--are used primarily to treat depression. Some commonly used MAO inhibitors: isocarboxazid/Marplan; phenelzine/Nardil; tranylcypromine/Parnate.

Interaction--A very dangerous, potentially fatal, food-drug interaction can occur between monoamine oxidase (MAO) inhibitors--which are prescribed for depression and high blood pressure--and foods containing tryamine. Patients taking MAO inhibitors should avoid aged and fermented foods, such as pickled herring; fermented sausages (salami and pepperoni); and a variety of other foods, including sharp and aged cheeses, yogurt, sour cream, bananas, avocados, soy sauce, active yeast preparations, raisins, beef and chicken livers, and meat prepared with tenderizers. Beer, Chianti wine, sherry, cola beverages, coffee, and chocolate should be taken in moderation. MAO inhibitors react with tryamine in these foods and can send blood pressure soaring. Severe headaches, brain hemorrhage, and sometimes death are some of the consequences. Be sure to follow physician's instructions.

Sleep Disturbances

Do not use alcohol with any sleep medications. See the article on Sleep and sleep disorders, page 406.

Before you take it, talk about it

My mother came to live with us when she was 78 years old. She was very sick, and she took half of a cup of pills per day. We took her to the doctor and he said, "she is taking so many different pills from so many different sources that they are probably working against each other. Let's take her off of all pills; we will closely monitor her and see what it is she really needs."

We did what the doctor ordered and a miracle happened–within three days my mother was better than I had seen her in ten years. When she was finally regulated, all she needed was a heart pill, a diuretic, and some added potassium. We threw in a multiple vitamin, and that added up to four pills a day.

The minor and major disorders of old age need treatment in the form of tablets, pills, and liquid medicine, but sometimes it is overdone. In one U.S. study, the average number of prescription drugs taken by residents in an urban dwelling for senior citizens was 4.5 per person; in addition they took 3.4 nonprescription drugs--that equals 7.9 medications per day, and that's average.

Some older people take too many drugs, and sometimes plead for more. They get confused, shaky, and sick, and feel like they're going crazy.

A U.S. government report went so far as to call "mismedication of the elderly" one of the country's most pressing health concerns. One of the most arresting statistics in the report was that 51% of the deaths from drug reactions in the U.S. involve people 60 and older.

The greatest epidemic of drug abuse in American society is among our older people.

The Arizona *Republic* estimated drug reactions kill 73,000 U.S. senior citizens annually, said reporter Chuck Cook. That calculation was based on American Hospital Association and Food and Drug Administration statistics. "That could very well be in the right ballpark," said Richard Kusserow, inspector general of the U.S. Department of Health and Human Services. In a report this year, Kusserow estimated that at least 200,000 elderly Americans are hospitalized each year because of adverse drug reactions.

"The greatest epidemic of drug abuse in American society is among our older people," who suffer 9 million adverse reactions to medicine a year, says Sidney M. Wolfe, M.D. author of *Worst Pills, Best Pills.* Side effects include depression, hallucinations, confusion, memory loss, delirium, impaired thinking, shaking and twitching, nausea, vomiting, appetite loss, stomach pain and bleeding, constipation, diarrhea, difficulty urinating and controlling urination, dizziness, and falls that result in hip fractures.

It is very easy to become confused about which medicine to take, how often, how much, and how long to continue. Elderly patients often have several doctors. To avoid drug misuse, older patients should "get a brown paper bag, put everything they're taking in it, and go review it with their primary doctor," said Dr. T. Franklin Williams, director of the National Institute on Aging. In addition, pharmacists should do a better job monitoring patients' drug use to prevent harmful interactions.

Certain drugs don't "mix," and can lead to adverse reactions when taken in combination. Also, normal age-linked changes in the body make drugs react in a different way.

According to the Food and Drug Administration, when a prescription drug isn't working properly, the top five reasons for failure are:

1 failure to have the prescription re-filled;

2 taking too much or too little of the drug;

3 taking the medication at intervals other than what the doctor ordered;

4 forgetting a dose or two; and

5 stopping the medication too soon.

Studies have established that older people are quite likely to misuse medication. Here are some suggestions to help you avoid this practice:

❑ Use memory aids to help you remember dose times. Write down a checklist of all the drugs you are taking, and update the list whenever there are changes. Make your list in the form of a calendar so that you can mark off each dose of each drug as you take it. Another aid is to use an egg carton and put each required dose of medication in a separate section.

❑ Ask your physician to give you a drug in the easiest possible form to take--liquid, tablet, or pill form. Also, you can request an easy-to-open container if child-proof containers are difficult for you. Making it easy to take your prescription will lower frustration and make errors less frequent.

❑ Make sure that all containers are clearly labeled with their contents and when they should be taken. If you have trouble reading a label, ask to have it rewritten in larger, clearer characters.

❑ Be sure to inform every physician who treats you about all the drugs you are taking. Show them your checklist if you can, or bring in the containers for the drugs you are taking. This will help prevent double treatment or dangerous interactions of drugs.

❑ Don't be a drug hoarder, or permit unused pills to accumulate in your medicine cabinet. Keep drugs that you are currently using, and those you use occasionally such as antihistamines or aspirin, and discard partially used supplies of all others.

❏ Never start taking a drug again after a long interval without consulting your physician. Your present symptoms may be due to an entirely different disorder from the one for which last year's drug was prescribed. Moreover, some drug that you may now be taking could interact dangerously with that old one. Also, many drugs have a limited "shelf life," after which they become less effective or even harmful.

❏ Don't keep containers of pills on your bedside table unless it is absolutely necessary. There is too much risk of taking either the wrong medicine or an overdose of the right one when you are sleepy. This can happen especially if instead of switching on the light you trust your sense of touch.

❏ Don't leave similar-looking drug containers grouped together. To avoid confusion, ask your pharmacist to change the packaging of a drug, if necessary. You yourself should not transfer the contents of one container to another without making absolutely sure that the new container is correctly and clearly labeled.

❏ Always ask your doctor specific questions about a new drug, such as what it is supposed to do, how long you should take it, and whether you should stop drinking alcohol or stop driving while taking it. Also ask in advance about possible side effects.

❏ Always report any symptoms--aches, pains, dizziness, confusion--to your doctor. Don't assume it's "just old age."

❏ Always use the same pharmacy if possible. It should have a computer system that profiles all the medications you're taking and alerts the pharmacist to a possible adverse reaction.

❏ Look up information about prescription drugs and become knowledgeable about their use and abuse.

Remember, the more you know about the medicines you take, the better off you will be.

Remember when there was time to talk with your doctors and pharmacists? And remember how your relationship with them seemed more personal? Today, it can be the same way--if you speak up. Even though things may seem more rushed and impersonal, your doctors, pharmacists, and nurses want to take time to talk about the things you should talk about most--your medicines. As you grow older, it's more likely that you'll be treated by more than one doctor and be prescribed more than one medicine to take at a time. And as you age, your body may react in different ways to the medicine you take. Learn about the drugs you take.

Drug Reference Books

The Complete Drug Reference, by the U.S. Pharmacopeial Convention Inc., Consumer Reports Books, 1991, $39.95. Includes nonprescription drugs.

The Essential Guide to Prescription Drugs, by James W. Long, Harper Collins, 1991, $14.95.

The Pill Book, Bantam Books, 1990, $5.95.

Worst Pills, Best Pills, The Public Citizen Health Research Group, 1988, $12.

Prescription Drugs, by the editors of Consumer Guide, Beekman House, 1990, $6.95.

Complete Guide to Prescription and Nonprescription Drugs, by H. Winter Griffith, The Body Press, 1991, $15.95.

The ABC's of Prescription Drugs, by Edward Edelson, Ivy Books, 1987, $4.95. Organization by medical condition.

Prescription Drugs and Their Side Effects, by Edward L. Stern, Perigee Books, 1991, $9.95.

Graedons' Best Medicine, by Joe and Teresa Graedon, Bantam Books, 1991, $14.95.

AARP Pharmacy Service Prescription Drug Handbook, Little, Brown and Company, 1988, 940 pages. Comprehensive guide to prescription medicines most frequently used by persons 50 and older.

Prescription Drugs: An Indispensable Guide for People Over 50, by Brian S. Katcher, Pharm.D. Avon Books, $4.95. Answers 5 important questions about 94 of the most popularly prescribed drugs.

The Physician's Desk Reference, Medical Economics Company, 1991, $49.95. An awesome, technical book, difficult to read, but comprehensive and upgraded every year. A professional book about prescription drugs that you can find in almost any public library. If you want to take the time, everything that is known about a prescription drug is printed in sophisticated medical language.

Deciphering Prescriptions

Your prescriptions from your physician may contain some medical "shorthand" that looks like a secret code. Actually they are Latin abbreviations that can be "decoded" as follows:

ac (ante cibum): before meals
bid (bis in die): twice a day
c (cum): with
daw: dispense as written, generic substitution illegal
dis: dispense
gtt (guttae): drops
hs (hora somni): at bedtime
mg: milligrams
non rep (non repetatur): no refill
pc (post cibum): after meals
po (per os): by mouth
prn (pro re nata): as needed
qh (quaque hora): every hour
qid (quater in die): four times a day
rep (repetatur): refill
s (sine): without
Sig (signetur): label; directions
tab: tablet
tid (ter in die): three times a day

"Nicorette," a nicotine gum, has been found by some people to ease the inevitable and unpleasant withdrawal from smoking.

If you want to quit smoking, here's some help

It's never too late to stop smoking, and if you want to, you can. "Not another article against smoking-- nag, nag, nag. Why are you doing this to me?" Because . . .

The National Centers for Disease Control reported in 1991 that 434,175 Americans died from smoking in 1988, and over 400,000 for each year since then. It's as if 3-1/2 fully loaded 747s were crashing every day in the U.S. Smokers are 22 times more likely than nonsmokers to die of lung cancer and 10 times more likely to die from bronchitis or emphysema. Also note that 3,825 Americans died from lung cancer caused by others' smoking, or passive smoke.

Heavy smokers can still improve their chances if they kick the habit. They may be able to avoid lung cancer, mouth cancer, pancreatic cancer, cardiovascular diseases, and a host of others. You have very little chance of being well and smoking. After a smoker quits, the risk of smoking-related cancer begins to decline and within a decade the risk is reduced to that of the nonsmoker.

There are many ways to stop smoking. No single method works for everyone, so each person must try to find what works best for him. Most people stop on their own, but others need help from doctors, clinics, or organized groups. Older people who take part in programs to stop smoking have higher success rates than younger ones do. Here are some suggestions:

■ "Cigarette smoking is the chief single avoidable cause of death in our society and the most important public health issue of our time."
    --Surgeon General C. Everett Koop

■ Read everything you can about smoking; it will scare you into stopping. Not everyone who smokes dies of a smoking-related illness, but many do. Not every one of the 130,000 Americans who will die of lung cancer this year smokes, but 92% do. Not all of the 150,000 Americans who will die of emphysema and chronic obstructive lung disease this year smoke cigarettes, but 95% do. Not all of the nearly 500,000 Americans who will die this year from cardiovascular diseases, including heart attacks, are smokers, but most of them are.

■ Determine that you can quit and start formulating your plans to do so. An estimated 40 million former cigarette smokers in the United States are living proof that it can be done.

■ Seek help and investigate quit-smoking programs. For example, Smokenders offers a six-week program (phone 1-800-828-4357). Try to find the program that will be best for you. Organizations, doctors, and clinics offering stop-smoking programs are listed in telephone books under "Smokers' Treatment and Information Center."

■ Make a list of all the reasons you want to stop smoking. Develop some strong personal reasons in addition to your health. Ask some friends and knowledgeable nonsmokers for their reasons. Keep reading your list.

■ Get ready for quitting by conditioning yourself physically. Start a modest exercise program, drink more fluids, get plenty of rest, and avoid fatigue.

■ Set a target date for quitting. Make the date sacred, and don't let anything change it. The day of quitting could be a birthday, anniversary, or some special day to you.

■ Involve someone else. Bet a friend you can quit on your target date. Ask your spouse or a friend to quit with you. Tell your family and friends that you're quitting and when. They can be an important source of support.

■ Make some strong commitments on your quitting day.
    ▶ Throw away all your cigarettes and matches. Hide your lighters and ashtrays.
    ▶ If you can, visit the dentist and have your teeth cleaned to get rid of tobacco stains.
    ▶ Make a list of things you'd like to buy for yourself or someone else with the money you save from not buying cigarettes.
    ▶ Keep very busy on the big day. Go to the movies, exercise, take long walks, or go bike riding. It's a special day, so do as many special things as you can.
    ▶ Remind your family and friends that this is your quit date, and ask them to help you over the rough spots of the first couple of days and weeks.

■ Practice the things that help when temptation comes. Here are some suggestions:
    ▶ Spend as much free time as possible in places where smoking isn't allowed.
    ▶ Drink large quantities of water and fruit juice (avoid sodas that contain caffeine).
    ▶ Avoid alcohol, coffee, and other beverages that you associate with cigarette smoking.
    ▶ Instead of smoking, strike up a con-

versation with someone and keep your mouth busy talking.
    ▶ If you smoked after meals, now get up from the table and brush your teeth or go for a walk.
    ▶ At first avoid situations you strongly associate with the pleasurable aspects of smoking.
    ▶ If you must be in a situation where you'll be tempted to smoke, try to associate with the nonsmokers.
    ▶ When your desire for a cigarette is intense, distract yourself--wash your hands, do the dishes, anything that requires you to use your hands.
    ▶ Keep yourself in condition, looking sharp.
    ▶ Keep yourself busy.
    ▶ Never allow yourself to think that one cigarette won't hurt--it will.
    ▶ Keep oral substitutes handy--try carrots, pickles, sunflower seeds, apples, celery, raisins, sugarless gum, or hard candy instead of a cigarette.
    ▶ Learn to relax quickly and deeply.
    ▶ Reward yourself for not smoking. Congratulations are in order each time you get through the day without smoking. After a week, give yourself a pat on the back and a reward of some kind.
    ▶ Mobilize the power of positive thinking! Putting yourself down and trying to hold out through willpower alone are not effective coping techniques.

■ If you fail and smoke one cigarette, let that one inspire you to increase your determination to quit. A small setback does not make you a smoker again. Think about what tripped you up, and develop a strategy for it. Quitting isn't easy, but it's not impossible either. More than 3 million Americans quit every year.

Some strong behavior modification techniques are available for those who want this assistance. Biofeedback and relaxation have been effective for some as have psychotherapy, group therapy, acupuncture, and hypnosis. Quitting smoking is an individual matter--many people simply go "cold turkey"; throw away the cigarettes and stop smoking. Choose the best method for you and stop smoking; you will never regret it and you will be healthier, and live from two to ten years longer.

Reflections on growing old...historic quotes

I heard the old, old men say,
"All that's beautiful drifts away;
like the waters."
- William Butler Yeats (1865-1939)
♥ ♥ ♥

Old age, especially an honoured old age, has so great authority, that this is of more value than all the pleasures of youth.
- Cicero (106-43 B.C.)
♥ ♥ ♥

The first forty years of life give us the text; the next thirty supply the commentary on it.
- Schopenhauer (1788-1860)
♥ ♥ ♥

A graceful and honorable old age is the childhood of immortality.
♥ ♥ ♥

No one is so old as to think he cannot live one more year.
- Cicero (106-43 B.C.)
♥ ♥ ♥

I will never be an old man. To me, old age is always fifteen years older than I am.
- Bernard Baruch
♥ ♥ ♥

The greatest thing about getting older is that you don't lose all the other ages you've been.   - Madeleine L'Engle
♥ ♥ ♥

Few persons know how to be old.
- La Rochefoucauld (1613-1680)
♥ ♥ ♥

Babies haven't any hair; Old men's heads are just as bare; Between the cradle and the grave, lies a haircut and a shave.
- Samuel Hoffenstein
♥ ♥ ♥

God will not look you over for medals, degrees or diplomas, but for scars.
- Elbert Hubbard
♥ ♥ ♥

I love everything that's old: old friends, old times, old manners, old books, old wine.
- Oliver Goldsmith
♥ ♥ ♥

You know you're getting old when the candles cost more than the cake.   - Bob Hope
♥ ♥ ♥

I have everything now I had 20 years ago-- except now it's all lower.
- Gypsy Rose Lee
♥ ♥ ♥

We laugh and laugh. Then cry and cry--then feebler laugh, then die.
- Mark Twain
♥ ♥ ♥

No wise man ever wished to be younger.
- Swift (1667-1745)

We are all here for a spell, get all the good laughs you can.
- Will Rogers
♥ ♥ ♥

If you don't learn to laugh at trouble, you won't have anything to laugh at when you grow old.   - Edgar Watson Howe
♥ ♥ ♥

If wrinkles must be written upon your brows, let them not be written upon the heart. The spirit should not grow old.
- James Garfield (1831-1881)
♥ ♥ ♥

Fun is like insurance: the older you get the more it costs.
- Kin Hubbard
♥ ♥ ♥

I've always thought that the stereotype of the dirty old man is really the creation of a dirty young man who wants the field to himself.
- Hugh Downs
♥ ♥ ♥

I was young and foolish then; now I am old and foolisher.
- Mark Twain
♥ ♥ ♥

Old men like to give good advice in order to console themselves for not being any longer able to set bad examples.
- La Rochefoucauld (1613-1680)
♥ ♥ ♥

Grow old along with me!
The best is yet to be,
The last of life,
For which the first was made:
Our times are in his hand who saith
"A whole I planned, youth shows but half;
Trust God: see all nor be afraid."
- Robert Browning
♥ ♥ ♥

To keep the heart unwrinkled, to be hopeful, kindly, cheerful, reverent--that is to triumph over old age.
- Thomas Bailey Aldrich
♥ ♥ ♥

Whatever a man's age, he can reduce it several years by putting a bright colored flower in his buttonhole.
- Mark Twain
♥ ♥ ♥

As soon as a man acquires fairly good sense, it is said he is an old fogey.
- Edgar Watson Howe
♥ ♥ ♥

You must become an old man in good time if you wish to be an old man long.
- Cicero (106-43 B.C.)

Age is a high price to pay for maturity.
Who soweth good seed shall surely reap; the year grows rich as it groweth old, and life's latest sands are the sands of gold!
- Julia Ripley Door (1825-1913)
♥ ♥ ♥

What makes old age hard to bear is not the failing of one's faculties, mental and physical, but the burden of one's memories.
- Somerset Maugham (1874-1965)
♥ ♥ ♥

On Getting Older
There is nothing the matter with me,
I'm healthy as I can be.
I have arthritis in both knees
And when I talk, I talk with a wheeze.
My pulse is weak, and my blood is thin
But I'm awfully well for the shape I'm in.

Arch supports I have for my feet,
Or I wouldn't be able to be on the street.
Sleep is denied me night after night,
But every morning I find I'm all right.
My memory is failing, my head's in a spin
But I'm awfully well for the shape I'm in.

The moral is this as my tale I unfold--
That for you and me who are getting old
It's better to say "I'm Fine" with a grin,
Than to let folks know the shape we are in.
-Anon
♥ ♥ ♥

God made wrinkles to show where smiles have been.
♥ ♥ ♥

Years may wrinkle the skin, but to give up interest wrinkles the soul.
- Douglas MacArthur
♥ ♥ ♥

You really know you're getting old when you bend over to tie your shoes, and you wonder what else you can do while you're down there.
♥ ♥ ♥

To be seventy years young is sometimes far more cheerful and hopeful than to be forty years old.
- Oliver Wendell Holmes
♥ ♥ ♥

Old age has a great sense of calm and freedom. When the passions have relaxed their hold and have escaped, not from one master, but from many.
- Plato
♥ ♥ ♥

Forty is the old age of youth; fifty is the youth of old age.
- Victor Hugo (1802-1885)

FOR ONLY

THE PROSTATE GLAND

THE PROSTATE GLAND--is a walnut-size organ that is a part of the male urinogenital system. It is not one single gland, but a cluster of small glands that surround the urethra at the point where it leaves the bladder. The glands are tubular, and have muscles that squeeze their secretions into the urethra. The addition of prostatic secretion to the seminal fluid stimulates active movement of the sperm.

The main disorders that can affect the prostate are infections and growths. In elderly men, cancer of the prostate is relatively common. Because the prostate gland encircles the urethra, any kind of prostate disorder may hamper the free flow of urine, an uncomfortable and sometimes dangerous problem.

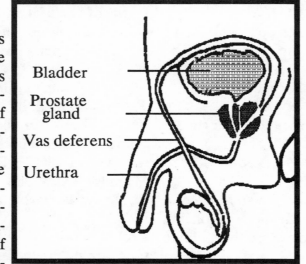

Bladder

Prostate gland

Vas deferens

Urethra

—— PROBLEMS ——

1. **ENLARGED PROSTATE** (benign prostatic hypertrophy)--Routine tests show that by age 50, 20% of all men have an enlarged prostate; by age 70, at least half have; and by 80 it is more than 80%. Harmless overgrowths of normal prostate tissue are a natural result of the aging process. Small gristly nodules gradually develop, and as they accumulate the size of the gland changes. The size of a harmless enlargement matters less than the consistency of the tissue. In some men the prostate gland becomes stiff and inflexible, which can constrict the urethra. The muscles of the bladder tend to compensate by becoming more powerful. This extra strength is often enough to keep the urethra open. Serious problems occur only when the bladder muscles are unable to overcome resistance caused by the rigid prostate, and the flow of urine is severely obstructed.

SYMPTOMS--A common symptom of an enlarged prostate is a weak urinary stream. The patient will have a frequent urge to urinate, and yet only pass a dribble, leaving with a feeling that the bladder is not empty. No matter how strong the urge, it is difficult to start the sluggish stream. There is almost never any pain, but there may be blood in the urine on occasion. The patient may have to urinate several times a night. Sometimes the patient cannot pass urine at all. The backflow of excess urine can lead to kidney failure. Any form of urinary retention needs urgent medical treatment.

RISKS--Prostate enlargement is extremely common and not dangerous in itself, but there are three main risks:

(1) If the bladder is never entirely emptied, pools of stagnant urine within it can cause infection.

(2) When the outflow of urine is blocked, pressure within the bladder increases and the kidneys and the ureters may be affected.

ONLY

(3) If severe enlargement of the prostate remains untreated, the muscles of your bladder may not be able to overcome the resistance to urine flow and may suddenly or gradually fail to function.

WHAT SHOULD BE DONE--If you have symptoms of an enlarged prostate, consult your physician, who will examine the gland by inserting a gloved finger into the rectum. You may also be given an intravenous pyelogram (IVP) to find out if your symptoms are due to a urinary-tract disease rather than to an enlarged prostate.

WHAT IS THE TREATMENT--Often the symptoms clear up without treatment. But if the problem does not go away, if it worsens, or if tests show a serious obstruction to the outflow of urine, the tissue that is causing the enlargement of the prostate must be removed.

The operation is called a prostatectomy. It can be done by traditional surgery or by a method known as transurethral resection (TUR). A thin tube is passed up the penis to the prostate. In the tip of the tube is an electric cutting loop that can be guided with the help of a miniature telescope.

Regardless of the technique, most prostatectomies are successful. Sometimes a patient will become impotent after the operation. Others may still be able to have an erection but become sterile because their semen is expelled backward into the bladder instead of being ejaculated. Seminal fluid in the bladder is not harmful. It is simply eliminated in the urine.

2. **PROSTATITIS**--is inflammation of the prostate gland and is usually the result of a urinary tract infection that has spread to the prostate. It may occur as the result of a venereal disease, nonspecific urethritis, or infection spreading from the intestine, or it may develop after an examination of the inside of the bladder. As with infection and inflammation anywhere in the body, prostatitis may improve of its own accord, may fester and form pus, or may linger indefinitely and become chronic.

SYMPTOMS--An acute attack of prostatitis usually begins suddenly and can make one feel ill, with a high fever, chills, and pain in and around the base of the penis. Later, as the prostate gland becomes increasingly swollen and tender it may become difficult and painful to urinate, because the prostate surrounds the urethra and the swelling of the gland narrows the passageway and blocks the flow of urine. Chronic prostatitis often appears slowly with some minor pain. It can be difficult to treat. The symptoms can last a long time.

RISKS--Elderly men with enlarged prostates are most susceptible, and the disease tends to recur once an initial attack occurs. If prostatitis is not treated, or if, as sometimes happens, treatment with drugs is unsuccessful, the gland may fester, become pus-filled, burst open, and release blood and pus into the urethra. This is quite painful.

TREATMENT--The physician will probably prescribe antibiotics. If that doesn't work, sometimes massage is used. The physician may recommend an operation to drain the pus and infection.

The subject of impotence

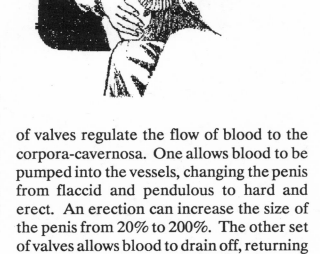

Regular checkups that include a careful prostate examination are the best protection against prostate cancer!

3. CANCER OF THE PROSTATE--is the third most common cause of cancer death among middle-aged and older men in the United States, with about 100,000 new cases and 20,000 deaths each year. In the early stages of prostate cancer the disease stays localized and does not endanger life. But without treatment the cancer can spread to other tissues and eventually cause death. Prostate cancer usually progresses very slowly.

Regular physical checkups that include a rectal exam increase the chances of detecting prostate cancer in its early, most curable stage before symptoms appear. When symptoms do appear, they are usually similar to those caused by an enlarged prostate.

If a suspicious area is found in the prostate, the urologist may recommend a biopsy (a simple surgical procedure in which a tiny piece of prostate tissue is removed with a needle and examined under a microscope).

TREATMENT–Prostate surgery is often done to treat enlarged prostate and prostate cancer. (Chemotherapy and radiation play important roles.) Such surgery is generally safe and patients usually recover rapidly.

During surgery for prostate cancer the entire prostate and adjacent structures may be removed. This is called a radical prostatectomy. Many patients are impotent after this surgery, but new surgical techniques are being developed to overcome this condition.

Then there was this man
that went to a doctor
for a prostate examination.
The doctor said, "Should I use two fingers?"
And the man asked "What for?"
The doctor said "I thought
you might want
a second opinion."

Sex researchers have found that while sexual prowess gradually diminishes with age, men should expect to be able to enjoy sex well into their later years. All men experience temporary periods of impotence at some time in their lives, and these need not cause alarm. A large number of men (10 million) suffer from more long-lasting impotence.

Impotence is a man's inability to produce, or maintain, a penile erection. For this reason, an impotent man cannot have sexual intercourse. Medical specialists define impotence as the persistent inability to achieve an erection of the penis. Masters and Johnson (sex therapists) have formulated a more precise definition: the inability to achieve or maintain enough of an erection for sexual intercourse--sufficient to penetrate the vagina--at least once in four attempts.

DIAGNOSIS--Impotence is a common problem. Surveys show that it occurs in at least 2% of American men under age 35, 10% of those age 55, and 50% of those age 75 and older. A few decades ago physicians and sex therapists believed that impotence was mostly an emotional or psychological problem in 90% of the males. Now, with recent research the sex specialist believes that 50% to 60% of impotence has a physical basis, which is a sign of a medical problem.

During a single night, most normal men will experience several periods of erection lasting for a total of one to three hours. When investigators checked impotent men during sleep, they were surprised to find that half of them experienced erections. The occurrence of erections during sleep was almost always evidence that a man's physical erectile capacity was intact. When an impotent male did not have erections during sleep, in all likelihood his impotence had some physical cause.

HOW THE SYSTEM WORKS--The physical mechanism that makes an erection possible includes the corpora-cavernosa, two unique blood vessels that are filled with spongy matter. These cigar-shaped vessels flank the underside of the penis. They begin just behind the pubic bone, where the penis is attached to the trunk, and run along the length of the shaft to the head. Two sets

of valves regulate the flow of blood to the corpora-cavernosa. One allows blood to be pumped into the vessels, changing the penis from flaccid and pendulous to hard and erect. An erection can increase the size of the penis from 20% to 200%. The other set of valves allows blood to drain off, returning the penis to its pre-aroused state.

Also important in the erectile process is the corpus spongiosum tissue surrounding the urethra (the tube that runs from the bladder through the center of the penis to its end). The male hormone testosterone also is essential to normal sexual functioning. It acts not only on the penis, but also on the prostate gland, the testicles, and the sex centers of the brain.

PSYCHOLOGICAL CAUSES OF IMPOTENCE--A man who has normal erectile responses during masturbation, or who regularly awakens with an erection, is likely to have a psychological basis for impotence.

The brain can help bring about an erection and it can prevent one. The upper portion of the brain known as the cerebral cortex can be involved in blocking the reflex action that causes an erection. By this means, thoughts or emotions can inhibit the erectile mechanism and cause so-called psychogenic impotence. Psychogenic impotence seems to feed on itself because its number one cause is fear of the possibility of failure to perform. Other factors in psychological impotence are guilt, depression, and boredom with the subject of sex stimulation.

PHYSICAL CAUSES OF IMPOTENCE--Some of the physical factors that lead to impotence are:

MORE FOR ONLY

Diabetes--It ranks high on the list of physical problems that cause impotence. Half of the men who suffer from diabetes are impotent because the disease damages the nerve controlling the valves of the corpora-cavernosa.

Medications--Some of the drugs currently being used to treat high blood pressure and heart disease produce this unwanted side effect in many men.

Clinical, locked-in depression.

Alcoholism.

Deficiencies of testosterone or thyroid hormones.

Elevated level of prolactin, another hormone involved in sexual function.

Hardening of the arteries.

Physical deformities of the penis.

Spinal cord injuries.

Brain damage.

Endocrine abnormalities--Impotence is often the first important sign of a hypothalamic-pituitary abnormality.

Damage of the vital nerves that control erection and ejaculation.

Poor circulation--Increased incidence of impotence with age is because of the increasing degree of fatty-cholesterol deposits blocking the circulation to the penis.

Weight problems--Controlling weight may lower blood pressure and make high blood pressure medicine unnecessary, or decrease the amount to the point that impotence is no longer a problem. It must be added that excessive weight loss or fad diets can also be a cause of impotence.

WHAT CAN BE DONE--The first step in correcting impotence is to identify the cause. If it is psychological, counseling is the right approach. Reassurance and confidence building are important aspects of psychological treatment. Training in giving and receiving affection is often needed. Often, the key is found in having a loving, intimate relationship without sex. A sexual partner's attitude is very important. She should be supportive. Some men are impotent because their wives are not interested in sex. Others have basic conflicts with their wives. When the basic relationship is not good, it usually is not good in the bedroom, either.

In the mature, experienced male, correcting an underlying medical problem may be the answer. That includes correcting a thyroid disorder, or other causes. If tests show an excess of prolactin, bromocriptine is the treatment of choice. When diabetes is present, tight control of the blood glucose levels may help. When medicines such as antihypertensive medications or antidepressants are the cause, changing the medications may be all that is required. Zantac can be substituted for Tagamet for those impotent patients with peptic ulcer problems. Eliminating alcohol can cause a significant improvement in testosterone levels and may correct impotence. The abuse of other drugs may also be a factor in causing impotence.

A man's lifestyle is important to both preventing and correcting impotence. That includes controlling all the factors related to developing fatty-cholesterol deposits that cause heart attacks and strokes. Not smoking, getting adequate exercise, avoiding obesity, and following a proper diet low in fat, low in saturated fat, and low in cholesterol all help to protect the arterial system that supplies the penis.

Testosterone may be given to men who have low testosterone levels. One of the newer methods of treating impotence consists of injecting medicine into the base of the penis that dilates the arteries and allows more blood to flow into the penis; papaverine and phentolamine have been most successful. These drugs cause an erection that lasts for 30 to 45 minutes.

Nerve damage is a common cause of impotence in men who have had spinal cord injuries. Now, with the use of an electric probe, there is a method of producing erection and ejaculation in men with this problem.

To men who cannot be adequately treated with medical and psychological modes, the answer is often a penile prosthesis--a mechanical device to support erection. The prosthesis will not increase sexual desire that is blocked by psychological factors. The oldest prosthesis is two silicone rods implanted directly into the cylinders of the shaft of the penis. There is also an inflatable penile prosthesis.

WHERE TO GET HELP?

Many men with impotence due to physical causes can be restored to normal sexual function. Heart patients often can be switched to other medications. Hormonal deficiencies can be made up with medications. Alcoholism can be treated. Many physical deformities can be corrected with surgery. For some, penile prostheses provide an artificial means to make a flaccid, impotent penis rigid. Often penile prostheses can enable sexually impaired men to recapture the intimacy that goes with a shared sexual experience, pleasing their sex partner and restoring their self-confidence.

Impotent men are understandably sensitive about their affliction, and so are reluctant to try to get help.

There is some good help available:
Impotents Anonymous
National Headquarters
5119 Bradley Blvd.
Chevy Chase, MD 20815

Depending on the nature of the problem, impotent men can also seek help from physicians, clergymen, family counselors, and sex therapists. There is a professional organization that accredits sex therapists:

American Association of Sex Educators
Counselors and Therapists
1 East Wacker Dr., Suite 2700
Chicago, IL 60601

Dr. Leon Lome, co-director of the Center for Sexual Dysfunction at Michael Reese Hospital in Chicago, says delays in getting treatment are unfortunate "because nearly every case of impotence can be treated successfully." For a free booklet on the subject, write to The Impotence Information Center, Dept. NC, P.O. Box 9, Minneapolis, MN 55440, or call 1-800-843-4315.

Note: Severe, untreated depression in the elderly can closely mimic Alzheimer's disease.

MENTAL HEALTH
ALZHEIMER'S 345

The tragedy of Alzheimer's disease

Alzheimer's disease, the memory-stealing mental disorder, is now the fourth major cause of death among the aged. In its most severe form, it affects some 3 million Americans, and accounts for most nursing-home admissions. The developing brain disorder strikes 5% of the population that reaches 65, and more than 20% of people over 85. The risk for Alzheimer's increases about 1% for each year over 65.

Alzheimer's disease is a degenerative illness of the brain and nervous system with no known cause, no cure, and no effective treatment, save for medication to treat the depression that sometimes accompanies it. The disease is usually fatal within 5 to 10 years. Its first symptom is typically loss of recent memory, followed by speech difficulties and severe disorientation.

Alzheimer's causes memory lapses, confusion, loss of ability to function, and eventually death, and often goes undiagnosed for two to three years because people wrongly blame its early symptoms on the normal effects of aging. Alzheimer's eventually robs people of their ability to care for themselves, as well as exaggerating personality traits such as hot-temperedness or passivity. In advanced stages, it confines victims to bed and renders them unable to respond to their environment. Death usually comes after complications from bed sores, feeding problems, and pneumonia.

This disease has been around for centuries. Written descriptions date back to the ancient Greeks. But, it was not until 1906 that Alois Alzheimer first saw the characteristic plaques and nerve tangles in autopsy tissue from people who had suffered from dementia. Then he described it in medical journals in 1907, and the disease was named after him. Almost a century later, its causes and cures are still unknown. Medical professionals still struggle with ways to arrest or reverse the ugly progression from simple forgetfulness to death.

In Alzheimer's there's a loss of nerve cells called cholinergic cells. They're located in an area of the brain called the nucleus basilis and send connections into the cerebral cortex. The cortex is responsible for thought, memory, movement, and sensation. This cell death results in a corresponding decrease in the cortex of a neurotransmitter called acetylcholine.

For a time, scientists thought that replacing acetylcholine in Alzheimer's patients would alleviate the symptoms of dementia. A number of approaches have been tried, but there is hope for developing an effective therapy.

A new computer-enhanced X-ray technique called SPECT provides a relatively inexpensive and safe way of helping diagnose Alzheimer's. In SPECT, an acronym for single photon emission computed tomography, patients are injected with a radio-pharmaceutical, a chemical compound that emits a small amount of radiation. The chemical travels to the brain, where it settles into the tissues in direct proportion to the amount of blood flow in that area of the brain. Alzheimer's is characterized by abnormalities in brain blood flow. Early in the disease, brain cells begin to die, and this reduces the flow of blood in that portion of the brain. These areas show up very well with SPECT.

All of our physical actions as well as our thought processes are accomplished through the work of brain chemicals (neurotransmitters) that maintain the brain's organization and integrate its numerous activities. Incoming information is transformed into biochemical units by these neurotransmitters, which then direct nerve cells to either store information (memory) or initiate some action, such as speech.

In Alzheimer's disease there is a loss of nerve cells in specific areas of the brain, disrupting communication within. Alzheimer's patients then begin to show typical deficits in behavior and reasoning. Usually, cells in the outer layer or cortex of the brain die first, followed by more significant cell loss in deeper brain structures.

Early symptoms of Alzheimer's disease include:

* forgetting words and going to long, wordy efforts to replace them;
* losing objects like the car in the parking lot and the checkbook in the desk and the newspaper in the living room; and
* showing personality changes.

Advances in research hold out hope for effective treatment within five years for Alzheimer's disease. Tests may be available for diagnosing it in its early stage and new drug therapies will be able to prevent the progressive loss of critical brain cells.

Key Advances in Alzheimer's Research

■ Studies on animals that show a newly discovered brain chemical prevents the death of the specific kind of brain cells destroyed in Alzheimer's patients. This chemical, a member of a newly discovered class of brain chemicals called nerve growth factors, perks up the cells, which produce a vital chemical that transmits signals between brain cells and is involved in memory.

■ The announcement by Swedish scientists of the first successful transplant of fetal tissue brain cells into a Parkinson's patient, producing a dramatic improvement in his symptoms. The fetal cells produce L-dopa, the neurotransmitter whose absence causes tremors and rigidity.

■ Identification of specific chemical changes in skin cells that may lead to early diagnostic tests for Alzheimer's.

■ Clinical trials of 16 experimental drugs designed to ease the symptoms of Alzheimer's, which could reach the market in the 1990s. These drugs attempt to replace missing brain chemicals or prevent their destruction.

The turning point in Alzheimer's research came when scientists discovered the gene that leads to the production of the crucial nerve growth factor. This factor nurtures the kind of cells that Alzheimer's destroys, called cholinergic brain cells. It makes sure they develop properly and then maintains them in good working order. Growth factors are like vitamins for brain cells, and the goal of present research is to find these vitamins so that we can help sick brain cells get better. This is the most promising approach for the first effective treatment for Alzheimer's disease.

Instead of trying to replace missing neurotransmitters, which is the purpose of current pharmacology, we are trying to use nerve growth factor to save brain cells that would otherwise disappear.

Alzheimer's disease is marked by a progressive loss of memory that parallels the gradual destruction of the cholinergic brain cells. The cause of the disease is unknown. The idea of nerve growth therapy is to prolong the lives of these cells that are threatened by disease and to keep them functioning in a normal way, thereby preventing memory loss.

Alzheimer's is not the forgetfulness that sometimes accompanies aging, but it is instead a severe, irreversible impairment of the brain's ability to function properly.

The most common caregivers are family members. Help is available. The nearest chapter of the Alzheimer's Association may be a source of information. For more information call (800) 621-0379.

Coping with depression by Wm. J. Diehm

My mother suffered from profound depression. She refused to retire as a real estate broker until she became ill at the age of 78; then she came to live with us, and died when she was 88. During that time, my wife and I learned a lot about geriatrics and the aging process. We also learned a lot about depression. Although I had been a clinical psychologist for 20 years and had treated many people for acute depression, I was not prepared to deal with a loved one.

When my mother fell and broke her hip, we provided a warm atmosphere with round-the-clock care at home. But, when mother became depressed and said such things as, "I wish I would die" or "Why don't you just take a gun and shoot me so I won't bother you anymore?" then we had a hard time coping.

A few months after my mother died, a postpolio syndrome came upon me and I decided to retire. At the age of 68 my mind still wanted to do many things, but my body would not cooperate. Soon I found myself locked into a depressed state, feeling awful and saying some of the same things my mother had said. Now at the age of 72, I know from personal experience how to cope with a depressed person and also how to cope with being that person.

Depressed people typically have a negative view of themselves as worthless, inadequate, unlovable, and deficient. They also picture their surroundings as overwhelming, presenting insurmountable obstacles that cannot be overcome, and as continually resulting in failure or loss. Moreover, they imagine the future as hopeless. This negative perception often leads to suicidal ideation and actual attempts.

I know from the study of psychology that more rapid responses to curing depression come from people who are:

★ appropriately introspective
★ abstract thinkers
★ well organized
★ good planners
★ conscientious about carrying out responsibilities
★ successfully employed
★ not excessively angry, either at self or other people
★ less dogmatic and rigid in their thinking
★ able to identify a clear precipitating event for the depression
★ able to have close relationships with others

I also know from experience that people with the above ten characteristics seldom get depressed; but neither do people who love life, have goals, and make the right choices. Depressed people consistently distort their interpretation of events so that they can maintain a negative impression of themselves, their environment, and their future. Depressed people use inconsistent reasoning, all-or-nothing thinking, selective examples, overgeneralization, and magnification of adverse situations to keep their depression alive.

As a counselor I found it a challenge to deal with depressed people; but, when the mental disease hit a member of my family, I needed all the wisdom I had, and then some. The most difficult time of all came to me when I was the suffering one.

As a psychologist, I am familiar with the nomenclature and the processes recommended for therapy to depressed people. The standard procedures condensed from the *Handbook of Clinical Psychology* consist of:

◆ a guided discovery process
◆ counteracting the effect of maladaptive assumptions
◆ giving regular positive feedback
◆ correcting underlying destructive assumptions
◆ eliciting automatic rewarding thoughts
◆ giving them encouraging homework
◆ fighting depression, not the person who has it
◆ giving depressed people a reason to live

◆ keeping them physically active
◆ encouraging them to be well groomed
◆ verbalizing a positive future
◆ normalizing sleeping habits
◆ exploring the past but emphasizing present and future
◆ treating them as if they were a person not a disease
◆ teaching them proper exercise and nutrition
◆ helping them avoid negative verbalizations
◆ using optimistic visualization and meditation
◆ practicing principles of stress reduction
◆ involvement in other-centered thinking
◆ utilizing the uplifting aspects of religion
◆ letting them catch your positive spirit

Along with my experience and expertise, I want to use the above psychological principles to deal with all three major aspects of depression:

PART ONE:
CONSISTS OF SUGGESTIONS TO DEAL WITH PEOPLE WE MEET IN EVERYDAY LIFE WHO ARE OBVIOUSLY IN DEPRESSION

We may meet these people anywhere, from a hospital to a successful business. We will find them teaching, preaching, doing business, working or not working in any field. We can also meet them socially as one of our peer group. They are depressed, unhappy, gloomy, melancholic, excessively pessimistic, despondent, glum, and negativistic. Nothing can spoil a day more than meeting a person who communicates such a depressed unhappy state of being.

First: Run, if necessary, but don't allow yourself to catch the mind disease of depression from anyone. This is my first suggestion in dealing with casual acquaintances or strangers who are depressed.

Depression is contagious and we must be very careful that even a friend does not pass on to us this terrible oppressive, luckless, disagreeable lifestyle. In fact, it is often the prelude to every disease known to mankind.

Depressed people think they have a strong reason for their miserable mind set. They have the ugly habit of trying to drag other people down to their level with some remark, often a rude one, with elements of

There is tide in the affairs of men, which, taken at the flood, leads on to fortune; omitted, all the voyages of their life is bound in shallows and in miseries; on such a full sea we are now afloat; and we must take the current when it serves, or lose our ventures.

- Shakespeare (1564-1616)

truth in it. Don't bite into that poisonous apple. What other people do or say need not decide how you are choosing to design yourself.

If you can deal with the unhappy person in a cheerful fashion without jeopardizing your happiness, then do so. However, being jovial yourself has a higher priority than any good business deal.

Second: Let them catch your positive spirit. If your own spirit of happiness is secure, and you think you can help the depressed one, and you feel called upon to do so, then put on your rubber gloves and jump into the arena.

If a person challenges your good humor, then drop your exuberant affect and assume a sober demeanor, but keep your cheerful feeling. You can still be pleasant and polite, but you do not want to appear as if you are laughing at a person. Depressed people become very hostile if they think you are putting them down. It very well may be that they truly have had a rough time. Seriously and cheerfully wish them well and go your way. Start whistling a merry tune as soon as the unhappy one is out of sight.

Third: Make an attempt to persuade the depressed person that depression only makes it more difficult to change the things that bother him or her. If the depressed person wants to talk and share and you can or want to listen, then listen, but not too long. If that person tells you why they are so unhappy, listen to his or her tale of woe and then try to persuade them that choosing depression will not help them solve their problems.

Make a contribution from your own experience. Say something like, "One time I shared my troubles with a very wise man. He said to me, 'Yes, I hear your problems, but how does your unhappiness solve that problem? If you would start being and feeling happy, you would have more strength to solve your difficulties. Being unhappy is a choice, you know.'"

Fourth: Communicate the idea that if you could you would help that person solve his or her problems.

Fifth: Give a depressed person your understanding by speaking positive words of encouragement. Sometimes they will resist you vigorously to your face and then later, while thinking it over, will receive your acceptance and believe your words. Finish by giving the person a warm hug and telling him or her, "I'm for you." It is a sad world when a depressed person has no well-wishers. Do not join in with the negative verbalization depressed people are prone to use. If you want to help them, use uplifting words and don't repeat their Cassandrite sayings.

A word of warning: Unfortunately there are many unhappy people who are like professional panhandlers. They carry a negative affect to attract attention, to get sympathy, to extract financial aid--or other forms of seduction. Hard luck and unhappiness is a game to sociopathic types and they are not content until they have used someone. Don't be sucked into their trap, but do wish them well. We are told to beware of casting our pearls before swine and giving that which is holy to the dogs. So, watch out for the professional user.

Sixth: Don't always give money--give what you can. When an Apostle passed by the beautiful gate on the way to the Temple in Jerusalem, a crippled beggar called out for alms. He said, "Silver and gold have I none, but such as I have I give to thee." There are several points to be made, but I take just one: A sincerely unhappy person may be made well with a smile, a prayer, or a blessing. But nothing will please the professional user (the swine and dogs)--they are looking for an excuse to hurt you or use you. Significant help is not limited to money.

Seventh: Check up on the results of your gift. After you have given your help, or whatever it is that you are led to give, at a later time contact that person and ask him how he is doing. Specifically, ask him about the problem that he shared with you. Let the unhappy person know that someone cares for him.

Good people will act in a responsible way to other people's needs. If you cross paths with a depressed, unhappy person, stop and help him and later check on how he is doing. Help doesn't always mean money--most of the time the best help is a good word. In any case, check up on the results of your gift.

There are many other practical suggestions for dealing with depressed people whom you meet in everyday life. The above seven suggestions basically tell us to love and care for people who hurt but don't fall into their trap.

PART TWO:
LEARN TO DEAL WITH A LOVED ONE WHO HAS PLUNGED INTO THE GRIPS OF DEPRESSION.

I recommend that they be put under professional psychological care, if you can. My personal choice would be a licensed, experienced, competent therapist who uses cognitive-type therapy. If the person is in danger of suicide or approaching a comatose state, then I recommend hospitalization and antidepressant drugs. Some doctors use these drugs too frequently and some doctors don't use them at all. Drugs are tricky and dangerous and need to be monitored more closely than many doctors can do.

Cognitive therapy is mind choice therapy. The therapist tries to persuade depressed people that they can make up their mind to change depression to happiness. Abraham Lincoln said, "A man is about as happy as he makes up his mind to be." Cognitive therapy says that you can make up your mind to change and do it.

To me, cognitive-type therapy makes a command and then expects us to use the power of choice, the power of our mind, the power of our will to obey the command.

In fact, cognitive-type therapy is similar to biblical commands; however, I have also found that when a loved one is depressed and you whack them over the head with the Bible or a direct command, it only makes it worse. Often, the loved one will reply, "I know you are right, but I just can't do it. I'm a hopeless case." We are to use the soft powerful words of the Bible as a guide, not as a judgment. Scripture is best expounded as personal testimony rather than a preachy barb.

> ## The pain in the mind is worse than the pain in the body.
>
> - Publilius Syrus (42 B.C.)

Hints to combat depression

It helps to think of the mechanism of depression as a seven-step circular negative reasoning process that works as follows:

Step One: Depression starts with feelings of inferiority--a sense of being rejected, inadequate, unloved, and useless.

Step Two: Out of the basic attitude of inferiority will grow severe feelings of anxiety and frustration--or fear and anger.

Step Three: Anxiety and frustration (fear and anger) will in turn create a deep sense of unrequited guilt.

Step Four: Unresolved guilt, both conscious and unconscious, demands punishment.

Step Five: Guilty people volunteer to punish themselves by accepting hard luck and rejection as their deserved lot.

Step Six: Furthermore, guilty people punish themselves by creating deep feelings of unhappiness and depression to revel in.

Step Seven: We are now back to step one in which people who choose depression automatically feel inadequate, rejected, inferior, and unloved.

In one sentence the seven steps can be stated thusly: When people feel unacceptable they become frustrated and anxious, which makes them experience guilt so they need punishment and they volunteer to punish themselves by choosing depression, which of course makes them feel unacceptable again. Any place one can interrupt the circular negative thinking process will prevent the person from going deeper into depression.

The process of circular negative thinking repeats itself over and over again, drilling its miserable steps deeper into the impossible black hole of depression and hopelessness. Once depression becomes firmly entrenched in the psyche, I believe a person has to have help to get it out.

If the depressed person is a loved one and you must deal with him, here are some simple suggestions from cognitive therapy that help:

First: Listen patiently to the depressed loved one describe his or her reactions and interpretations. Suspend your own personal assumptions. One of the best things for a depressed person is to be able to "talk it out." We are to be "swift to hear and slow to speak." Sometimes the person will find the answer for themselves if given a chance to ventilate a position.

When you encourage people to talk about the troubles that lead to their depression, you will find them speaking in a negative, repetitious, and hopeless way. No matter how boring or how long it takes, let them talk until they start coming up with some answers.

Hundreds of times I have concluded a counseling session and had the patient say, "Thanks for not talking or giving advice; all I really wanted was just a chance to talk it out." So, listen.

Second: Communicate warmth, genuineness, sincerity, and openness. Let the loved one know that you love him or her. Do not let yourself be sucked into the negative spirit of the depressed or get involved into an "ain't it awful" conversation. Let every part of you communicate compassion and love. Good people are even instructed to "love their enemies." But, do not get caught up in the problems of people even if they are close relatives. If you do, you will likely join them in depression.

You could say something like, "it makes me sad to see you so unhappy, but I don't think it would be profitable for me to give up my happiness because of your troubles. Rather, I am going to bring you up to my level of joy."

Third: Empathize, which means to see events from the other person's perspective. We are told to, "Rejoice with them that rejoice, and weep with them that weep." When you listen long enough to a depressed person, you will soon realize that he or she has done something to contribute to his or her feelings of anxiety, frustration, and guilt. Depressed people have judged themselves guilty and refuse to forgive themselves. It is not our job to increase a person's guilt, but to lead him or her to the healing waters of forgiveness.

Use the words "I know how you feel" or "I wish I could help you" or "I understand" or "I'm with you, my friend" or anything that will establish empathy with how the person you love feels.

Fourth: Listen carefully to detect his or her fallacious thinking and correct it. Subtle flaws in the other person's reasoning are not too difficult to spot. For example: Some depressed people will latch onto the idea that they have committed the unforgivable sin. You can immediately detect the erroneous reasoning. The unforgivable sin is unforgivable mainly because the person does not want forgiveness. If he wants forgiveness, he's got it.

Often the depressed person will use "all-or-nothing" type reasoning, "Everything always goes wrong with me, I can never do anything right; there is absolutely no hope." You know that everything couldn't be wrong. These depressed people are merely exaggerating the negative and eliminating the positive.

Do not brood over your past mistakes and failures as this will only fill your mind with grief, regret and depression. Do not repeat them in the future.

- Sivananda 1887

Elicit a more convincing interpretation of the same event. Correct all-or-nothing thinking by saying, "You don't mean everything is wrong. You are still alive, you are still breathing, you can still eat, etc." A little sense of humor will help. Do not let a depressed person get away with fallacious thinking. Correct them. Point out the truth. Be positive. Debate the issues.

Several years ago I worked for the Suicide Prevention Clinic in Los Angeles County. We were on 24-hour call. One night I rushed to the home of a young couple. The husband was holding his wife and she was fighting hard to get loose to commit suicide. She yelled and screamed and cursed and swore and used every argument in the book to rationalize suicide. I talked to her from 10:00 P.M. until 6:00 A.M. when finally she said, "You win. I'll never try to do this again." Several years later I met the couple and she exclaimed to me, "I'm glad you won the debate. It's nice to be alive." I have discovered that when people are depressed they can be, in fact they want to be, reasoned out of their dilemma.

Fifth: Make the future look bright. Take the lead--provide structure and direction to the therapy process. Plan strategies several steps ahead, anticipating the desired outcome. Be optimistic about the future, you may surely bring it to pass.

One of the greatest errors I made in dealing with my mother's depression was in trying to be negatively truthful. Mother would often say, "Son, will I be able to get well and go back to work?" In my pessimistic honesty I would say, "No mother, just be content in living with us." I personally feel that my negative honesty took ten years off her life. Who was I to take away her hope of a future? But, what about honesty. In all honesty, neither I nor anyone else knows the possibilities of the future. Negative honesty looks on the ugly side; positive honesty looks on the bright side. Who is right? Who knows? So why not use positive honesty, which usually ends in a positive future.

Sixth: Get the loved one involved in other-centered thinking. The best thing you can do is to get them doing something for you or someone else. No matter how disabled your depressed loved one seems to be, you must remember that life's most depressing event, the start of circular negative thinking, is to feel useless. Tell your loved one that you need him or her. Get them involved, if pos-

sible, in any project that lifts their minds from themselves to others.

Every week, we encouraged my mother to fold the bulletins for church, to do the dishes for my wife, to pass on her wisdom to me, to visit with the guests in our home; in short, to feel useful to others. However, I wish we had done a better job.

Seventh: If a loved one is a religious person, help them out of depression by the utilization of the uplifting aspects of religion. That's what the prophets came to do, to tell us that God loves us and He has saved us by His grace, and even if we die, He has a place for us. It is one thing to "preach" the Gospel; it is another to "live" it. Saying that "God is love" and acting as if "the devil rules" will not help anyone cure depression.

The behavior that the prophets opposed more than any other was hypocrisy (saying one thing and doing another). When we emphasize biblical truths we must live by them. Depressed people will not be able to hear our words if our actions are inconsistent.

Of course we must remember to pray earnestly, each day of our life for the loved one who is suffering from depression. It is a very serious problem, the preliminary to suicide or a gradual deterioration of the joy of living. It makes people very ill. A person may say, "Well, I can't do all the things you suggest." My answer is, "Can you do even one of them?" The loved one needs professional help--but if for any reason you can't get a professional, then take the above seven steps, and with God's help, you can help.

PART THREE:
WHAT TO DO WHEN YOU ARE THE DEPRESSED ONE.

As I have said before, shortly after my mother's death I entered into a period of depression. According to my rationaliza-

Depression:
is self-constructed unhappiness!

tion it was brought on by my knowledge of what I thought was a terminal illness--post-polio syndrome. I experienced the horrible circular negative reasoning that leads from a feeling of uselessness, to anxiety and frustration, to guilt, to the need for punishment, to my doing the punishing by manufacturing depression to punish the guilty one--me.

I wallowed in the deep, dark, slimy, miserable pit of self-constructed unhappiness and I thought there was no way out. However, I was not dying from post-polio syndrome, but from a common mental illness called "give-up-i-tus." Both my daydreams and night dreams were filled with despair and terminal desperate melancholy. One day I slept for 23 hours and felt even worse, if that were possible. Down in the midst of that black, bleak, dejected, despondent, pessimistic, pit of hellish depression, a tiny voice spoke to me, like the voice of Tinker Bell: "You told a thousand people to avoid this useless pit, what are you doing here?"

A light in my mind turned on and I asked myself, "What was the first thing I told people to do when they were enveloped with depression?"

First: Ask for help. Immediately, I began to cry aloud to God, "Help me, I don't want to die this way." I continued to ask until I felt the curtain to the window in heaven part slightly and the eye of God observe my plight and beam some help. So many times I had told people who were in the pit of depression to pray to God for help, and I had warned them against negative prayer that often remains unanswered. When I asked for help, I violated every rule for prayer and still got an answer.

My answer to prayer came from a longtime friend who angrily told me off for allowing myself to deteriorate into a useless depression. No rationalizations were allowed, no cognitive dissonance, just plain spoken facts--"This sickness is coming from you and you can stop it if you want to."

Asking for help is actually a decision that all is not hopeless--something can be done. So, the minute a person decides that he or she wants to do something about depression, and asks for help, help is on the way.

Second: Take stock of your resources. One of the major reasons people slip into the slew of despondency is that they have se-

More about coping with depression

cretly been taking stock of their deficiencies. Anyone who consistently counts his or her failures will end up being one. Instead, count your blessings, count your skills, count your friends, count your assets. Do not compare yourself to anyone. People who compare have the tendency to contrast themselves to the lifestyle of the rich and famous. And, of course, we know nothing of their aches and pains. If you must compare, compare yourself to a starving child on the Ethiopian trail. I've known some people who were so negative they thought those dying children were more fortunate than themselves.

Force yourself to enumerate your assets by writing them down and sharing with a friend. If the friend does not approve, write some more, until you have honestly and positively listed your resources.

Third: Keep yourself physically active and busy. Depression comes from thinking too many negative thoughts and doing too little in the way of activity. Force yourself to walk, exercise, and do manual labor. Don't stop for one second to contemplate the hard work of cleaning the garage--do it. Seldom are depressed people busy people. A depressed person will feel totally tired, as if a bull elephant seal were resting on his shoulders. But we don't get depressed from physical tiredness. If you are still tired after sleeping for twelve hours, you can know that the tiredness is caused by depression.

**Depression
is a sickness
that is coming
from you
and
only you
can stop it
if you want to.**

If you are depressed, move your body: swim, row, walk, run, jog, exercise, dance, jump rope, play ball, etc. Unless you have some disability that medically prevents the exercise, do it. When the doctors discovered the post-polio syndrome, I was advised not to exercise. I will tell you a secret if you promise not to tell--"they were wrong, I almost died from lack of exercise." I have now developed a program of physical activity that keeps the blues away.

Fourth: Involve yourself in a good health program:

❋ Repeat: Keep yourself physically active.

❋ Keep yourself well groomed--shave, bath; brush your teeth, comb your hair, keep your nails nice, dress your best, even shine your shoes.

❋ Practice good nutrition along with proper exercise.

❋ Normalize sleeping habits.

❋ Keep a good mental attitude.

❋ Laugh a lot and keep a sense of humor.

There can be no substitute for good health. Often bad health causes depression. The reverse is also true--depression causes bad health. Which comes first the chicken or the egg--no one really knows, so it behooves us to plan and work out a program for the best health we can get.

If perchance you are one of those people who is desperately ill...I remember Frieda May Clayville, a beautiful, talented 21-year-old girl, who died of a torturing long-term illness. She was the happiest, most cheerful person I have ever met. She had bad health and good disposition--it can be done. But it is very difficult, so keep your health at an optimum level, if possible.

Fifth: Act as if you were the happiest person on earth. Soon you will begin to feel better. Some people think that the feeling comes first. I disagree--the decision comes first. Act happy, and the feeling will follow.

You are now involved in a program to do something about depression, and so your choice is two-fold: to hate the program or to love it. What good does it do to hate it, so arbitrarily choose to love it and to act that

way. Acting for the purpose of changing disposition is not hypocrisy but rather a method of therapy.

Sixth: Talk positively; eliminate negative words. Have a loved one keep track of the kinds of words that come from your mouth, and make sure they are uplifting and positive. If you use bad words, you will have bad results. If you use negative words, you will catch depression. So, use positive words and catch happiness.

I remember the day my sister died. I called her on the telephone and she said, "I'm going to make it, Bill." That day she died, but she did make it.

Seventh: Use optimistic visualization, peaceful meditation, and positive prayer. Whenever you have a daydream or picture the future, make it optimistic. Our visualizations often come to pass, so make them beautiful. If you find yourself involved in a squalid vision, shake your head, bat your eyelashes, slap your hands together, and change the squalid to the splendid. Whenever you sit and contemplate or meditate, let the scene be one of peace, contentment, harmony, and loveliness. Don't allow the ugly to invade; it has a tendency to take over.

Avoid negative meditation, those with thoughts like "what have I done to deserve this," or thoughts of self-pity like "help me, help me, help me, I hurt, oh what pain, I am so miserable." Most important, look for and expect a resolution of your depression.

I believe we can help people who are depressed, even loved ones and even ourselves. The above suggestions should help us to cope with depressed people.

We need to realize that at birth we were given a "sound mind"; when we choose depression we are denying this truth. Choose happiness; it is the only sound thing to do.

Severe depression can cause institutionalization for what looks like organic mental syndrome.

Those severely depressed often need antidepressant medication and psychiatric follow-up.

Fear and older persons by Wm. J. Diehm

A little fear can motivate one to avoid danger, but too much fear can become paranoid feelings that profoundly terrorize the mind and destroy our quality of life. Some older people get into the grips of morbid fear and waste their closing days occupied with goblins of fear that actually don't exist.

There is little in the geriatric literature about the phenomenon of fear and its tendency to become a part of advancing years, but anyone who has worked with the elderly has noticed the paralyzing effect of fear.

I remember standing outside a convalescent facility in Riverside, California, talking to the director. A nurse came running out the front door and exclaimed to us, "You are talking too close to a ward window. The patients can hear faint mumbling words and they are frightened. Please move, you know how paranoid older people can get." Although I had worked extensively with geriatrics, it had not yet occurred to me that getting older and becoming afraid often go together.

My mother lived with us for the last ten years of her life and I watched fear advance as age increased. During her working years my mother often stayed out late at night in unsafe sections of the city--she was unafraid. But there came a time when she would sit in our living room trembling in fear. It was night, the curtains were drawn, she was surrounded by loving relatives, and yet life was ruined because of her fear. Since that time, I have learned many useful ways of reducing fear and increasing the quality of life in senior citizens.

THE RESULTS OF FEAR

Fear is not always bad. When fear is nonexistent, life can be boring, inefficient, and unsatisfying. A moderate amount of fear and anxiety (not too little, not too much) motivates us and adds zest to life. When fear is great, however, we begin to experience crippling physical, psychological, defensive, and spiritual reactions. Abnormal fear destroys our quality of life and makes it difficult to involve ourselves in anything else. We exhaust our energy sources.

(a) **Physical reactions.** It is common knowledge that fear can produce ulcers, headaches, skin rashes, backaches, and a variety of other physical problems. Almost everyone has experienced stomach discomfort ("butterflies"), shortness of breath, an inability to sleep, increased fatigue, loss of appetite, and a frequent desire to urinate during times of anxiety and fear. Less conscious are changes in blood pressure, increased muscle tension, a slowing of digestion, and chemical changes in the blood. If these are temporary they cause little harm. When they persist over time, the body begins to break under the pressure. This is the origin of the psychosomatic (psychologically caused) illness.

(b) **Psychological reactions.** Everyone who has taken an examination knows how anxiety can influence psychological functioning. Research has shown that fear and anxiety reduce one's level of productivity, stifle creativity and originality, hinder the capacity to relate to others smoothly, dull the personality, and interfere with the ability to think or to remember.

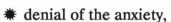

(c) **Defensive reactions.** When fear and anxiety build up, most people unconsciously rely on behavior and thinking that dull the pain of fear and enable them to cope. These defensive reactions, which are well-known and are often seen in counseling, include:

* denial of the anxiety,
* pretending the fear-producing situation does not exist,
* blaming others for a fault that is really their own,
* rationalizing by logically explaining away the symptoms and their causes,
* slipping back into childish ways of reacting,
* escaping through alcohol and drugs,
* a host of hypochondriacal complaints,
* withdrawing into bizarre behavior or mental illness.

(d) **Spiritual reactions.** Anxiety and fear can motivate us to seek divine help where it might be ignored otherwise. But fear can also drive us away from spiritual considerations at a time when they are most needed. Fraught with worry and distracted by pressures, even religious people find that there is a lack of time for prayer, decreased ability to concentrate on spiritual reading, reduced interest in worship, impatience, and sometimes bitterness, with the heavens seemingly silent.

WHERE DOES FEAR COME FROM?

On the top of the spinal cord deeply imbedded in the center of the skull is a mass of fiber four inches long and two inches wide called the brainstem. The top of the brainstem arches like a snake's head poised to strike. In fact, it is sometimes called the reptilian formation. Suspended from the nose of the snake's head is the pituitary gland, master gland of the body's hormonal system. Protruding from the back of the "snake brain" is a small gland looking something like a thumb. It is called the hypothalamus. From this small gland, in cooperation with the reptilian formation, the human body generates four basic emotional forces: fear, anger, sensuality, and appetite. We are dealing with "fear."

How do we know this to be true? When a probe is put into the brain of an animal and electrically stimulated, the animal will act as if it felt fearful, angry, hungry, or sensual according to the area of the probe. The hypothalamus, the brainstem, and the reticular activating system send pulsating signals through the brain via the limbic system. When this team of activators is fired up, it creates an emergency alarm system that generates strength for feeling fear on emergency occasions.

In order to fight fear, you need to know about fear

Yale physiologist Jose Delgado entered a bullring and faced an angry fighting bull with nothing but a small black box. The black box was a radio transmitter connected to an electrical probe embedded in an inhibitory center of the bull's hypothalamus. When the angry bull charged Delgado, he pressed a button and the bull halted in his charge as if he had suddenly run out of steam. Why did the bull freeze in his tracks? Because Delgado stimulated FEAR in the hyothalamus instead of ANGER. The research literature is full of references about the hypothalamus and its ability to stimulate or inhibit fear.

The mass of the brain: The cerebellum, cerebrum, cerebral cortex, and frontal lobes, surround the reptilian formation, perhaps revealing the intent of nature that the higher centers of the brain are to rule the lower. How to control, direct, utilize, and inhibit our fears, angers, sexual feelings, and appetites has long been a major problem. When we learn how the mechanism of the brain works, that knowledge can be useful in devising methods to help us direct and utilize the emotions of the hypothalamus.

When the body hears, sees, or receives some input or stimulus, the input is tossed around in the memory bank of the brain to figure out what to do with it. For instance, if the eye sees a bear and the nose smells him and the ears hear his growl, the memory bank would hold a brief meeting to ascertain if bears were dangerous. The danger signal would be sent from the thalamus to the hypothalamus to the brain stem to the pituitary and in one-eighth of a second the gland would fire and send an electrical charge to all parts of the body, alerting the system, and flooding us with a feeling of fear.

A little fear can motivate one to avoid danger, but too much fear can become paranoid feelings that profoundly terrorize the mind and destroy our quality of life.

In order to fight back, we need to know some facts about the subject of "fear." There are five types of fear:

■ **Normal, natural, or innate fear**

Normal fear comes naturally when there is a real threat or situational danger. Normal fear protects us from harms way. Normal fear is usually proportional to the danger (the greater the threat, the greater the fear). Normal fear can be recognized, managed, and reduced, especially when outward circumstances change. We need normal fear to keep us out of the way of dangerous situations such as steep cliffs and Bengal tigers.

A baby begins life with two basic normal fears: (1) a fear of falling and (2) a fear of loud noises. A small child can learn to fear something else, for example: If you make a loud noise while presenting the child with a toy, the natural fear of loud noises will transfer to the toy and become a false fear. This process is called "conditioning."

Human babies have an inborn tendency to imitate the behavior of other organisms around them. Infants also have an innate tendency to become emotionally attached to the adults who care for them, to adopt their fears, and to become fearful of strangers. Thus, nature protects the little children, but is ominous when adults begin a "second childhood."

A lifetime of remembering negative experiences can build a load of fear in older people.

Natural or normal fear is part of the human gift to preserve and protect our life. But when it attaches itself to unnatural events that we acquire from experience, it can terrorize us with false fears that can render us mentally ill, if carried to its final conclusion. A lifetime of remembering negative experiences can build a load of fear in older people.

To understand how fear operates and to keep it in perspective, we ought to define what we are dealing with. A technical definition of fear is:

> An inner feeling of apprehension, uneasiness, concern, worry, and/or dread that is accompanied by increased physical arousal.

Fear is an emotion genetically designed within our system by nature to protect us from harm. If we had no fear of high places, we would fall much more often. If we had no fear of a dangerous beast like a lion, wolf, or snake, life would be in constant jeopardy. If we had no fear we would be reckless with our life in a dangerous world. However, when we have too much fear, we paralyze our life with worry, anxiety, and phobias that make action and faith difficult.

Fear can be compared to appetite; if we eat too much, we get obese and ill; if we eat too little, we get anemic and sick. Fear is also like anger. Anger is a motivator to action and it is all right to have it as long as we do not let our anger lead us to foolish behavior.

Often a soldier will be afraid before the time of battle, or even during it. But a good soldier does not let his fear lead him to cowardice. It is normal to feel afraid, under fearful circumstances --the problem comes when the fear determines our action.

Too little fear is risky, we may endanger ourselves; and too much fear can become a sickness.

Fear must be brought under control. Fear, like appetite, can be on a gradual continuum; a little fear protects us and too much hurts us. Hopefully, we can recognize that a little normal fear of a scary situation is a protective emotion, sent by nature, to keep us from doing dangerous things.

❷ Neurotic fear, or exaggerated fear, which is normal innate fear turned up too high

Fear can vary in its intensity. Mild to moderate fear can be desirable and healthy. Often it motivates people to avoid dangerous situations and leads to increased efficiency. However, a high degree of fear is quite hazardous to our physical and mental health. Research shows that high fear will:
* shorten one's attention span
* make concentration and thinking difficult
* adversely affect memory
* hinder performance skills
* interfere with problem solving
* block effective communication
* arouse panic
* cause undesirable physical symptoms such as paralysis or intense headaches.

When we start exaggerating our fears and becoming so timid that we bolt at every little scare, then we have too much fear and it starts to interfere with our health.

It can be scary under certain circumstances to ride in an airplane, or a car, or a bicycle, or even to walk around the block at night. But it doesn't behoove us to have so little faith that we are "scaredy-cats." Of course, we must not test God and needlessly jump off the pinnacle of the Temple; but neither must we be so frightened that we can't walk the streets of Jerusalem or travel in a foreign land.

Like "Star Trek" that "Boldly goes where no man has gone before," we elderly must set the standards for bravery as we also take care not to "test" our fate.

Too much fear, or neurotic fear, involves intense exaggerated feelings of helplessness and dread even when the danger is mild or nonexistent. It cannot be faced squarely and dealt with rationally, perhaps because it arises from unconscious inner conflicts.

Too much fear gradually creeps upon us and we must deal with it like the proverbial story of the Arab and the camel. The camel begged to just put his nose into the tent because the night was cold. When the Arab consented, the camel continued to encroach until the morning found the camel in the tent and the Arab on the cold sand. We must not let fear encroach. A little fear is like the camel staked outside the tent--very useful. Too much fear is when we allow it to take over our tent.

❸ False, conditioned, misplaced, unnatural fear

Fear can come in reaction to some specific identifiable danger, or it can come in response to an imaginary or unknown danger. False fear is conditioned fear.

In one of psychology's most famous experiments John B. Watson and his wife Rosalie taught a child named Albert to become afraid of a gentle and placid white rat. At the beginning of the study, Albert was unafraid of the animal and played with it freely. While Albert was doing so one day, Watson deliberately frightened the boy by sounding a terrifying noise behind him. Albert was unpleasantly startled and began to cry. Thereafter, he avoided the rat and cried if it was brought close to him. Once this bond was fixed, the fear response could also be elicited by showing Albert any furry object.

Fear or anxiety also generalizes to any random or accidental stimulus cues that happen to be present when the conditioning takes place. A burnt child not only dreads the fire, but also fears stoves, pots and pans, ovens, pictures of flames, and even stories about the Chicago fire.

Some people get into the grips of morbid fear and waste their closing days occupied with goblins of fear that actually don't exist.

If you were chased by a bull when you were young, you would probably still show some fear response as an adult, especially if you were forced to enter a pen containing a pawing, snorting, long-horned Brahman bull. In fact, you might show some response if you merely read the word "bull," saw a picture of one, or were asked to think about one.

False fear will lead to compulsions and frantic upset. To be excessively afraid of a nonexistent threat can be a debilitating situation. To worry about something that has very little possibility of coming to pass is a destructive waste of energy.

For example, today in Mexico a false fear is clutching the land. Mothers grab their babies in frantic fear of a rich gringo from the North stealing baby parts. People, particularly the peasants, are taking extreme measures to protect their children from a fear that does not exist. The poor people are terrorized by the false fear that

"The only thing we have to fear, is fear itself " - Franklin Roosev

rich Americans are roaming their streets trying to find small children and dig out their eyes to sell to other Americans for their blind children.

Everyone knows that to transplant a part from one person to another takes a team of highly skilled doctors. No one could gouge out the eye of a Mexican child, ship it to America, and then use that eye for a blind American child. Even teams of skilled surgeons in our best hospitals have not been able to transplant eyes. Besides that, pagan though some Americans may be, even if it were possible we haven't yet reached that depth of debauchery.

What a waste to be terrorized by an impossible thought. False fear, being fearful of a nonexistent threat, is a waste, a shame, and a needless terror.

▣ Free-floating, all-pervasive fear

In "free-floating" fear, the person senses that something terrible is going to happen, but he or she does not know what it is or why. The person has been conditioned through adverse life experiences, scary T.V. programs, reading, thinking, or acting in a way that has connected natural fear to strange situations. So, many bonding situations have taken place in which the person becomes fearful and in free-floating fear the fear becomes attached to almost every situation. It is called "panophobia," which means "fear of everything."

Panophobics become so frightened that fear rules their lives, and in a certain sense, as they run from everything, they fall down and worship at the altar of fear. They run when no one pursues.

Sometimes when people grow old and come to the end of their days, the accumulation of life experiences brings about a generalized all-pervasive fear.

It is easier to remember a fearful, negative circumstance because it makes more impact on the central nervous system. For example, if the day is pleasant and contains no traumatic events, we will soon forget it, but if we are attacked by a rabid dog we will never forget that day. So, older people sometimes only remember the traumatic days, and it turns life into a fearful experience with no hope for the future.

To live life
being afraid
of every little squeak or noise
is such a hellish condition
that it often
drives people mad.

▢ Phobic or compulsive fear

The Greek word for fear is "phobia." However, the word "phobia" has come to mean a type of set-in, compulsive fear of some specific thing, for example, claustrophobia is a morbid fear of being confined in enclosed places; kakorrhaphiophobia is a fear of failure; aviophobia is a fear of flying; xenophobia is a fear of strangers; acrophobia is a morbid fear of high places; achluophobia is a fear of darkness or night; phengophobia is a morbid fear of daylight--the list is endless.

These compulsive fears are sometimes very difficult to eradicate. They stick so hard that they become a crippling mental illness. Some people are so afraid of high places (acrophobia) that they can't even climb the steps to their own home, let alone travel by air or go into an elevator.

Medical science has a method called desensitization in which the person is gradually exposed to his phobia and conditioned out of believing in it.

The major thrust of a phobia consists of it being in so much control (a deep-seated problem) that the person cannot choose to heal himself.

Phobias are intense, irrational fears about people, places, things, or situations. Usually these fears are so strong that the person with the phobia cannot control her or his reactions even when the person clearly realizes that the terror is illogical and unreasonable-- "morbid fears." (Morbid comes from the Greek word meaning diseased, gloomy, or unhealthy feelings.) These morbid dreads are often created almost overnight, from a single emotion-charged encounter with the dreaded object or perhaps from a continuing series of highly unpleasant interactions.

In our clinic we once treated an elderly lady who was possessed with a morbid fear of germs that compelled her to spend long hours every day at the sink, compulsively washing her hands, over and over again. She cried out in despair, but she was nailed by her fear to that bathroom basin. Thank God, she was cured. The method: in psychology it is called "conditioning," or "sensitivity training."

We now know that there are five major types of fear to consider.

1. Normal fear, which consists of respect or innate fear that keeps us from harm's way.

2. Neurotic fear, which has allowed normal fear to become excessive and take control of our lives.

3. False fear, which consists of innate fear being conditioned to a subject that is not fearful.

4. Free-floating, all-pervasive fear, comes from fixing our minds on negative, fearful, anxiety-producing experiences.

5. Phobias locked in to a particular subject. They are highly exaggerated fears that lead to compulsive behavior and mental illness.

FACTORS RESPONSIBLE FOR FEAR

1. Threats cause fear, such as a threat to some value that the individual holds essential to his existence as a personality. The threat may be to physical life (the threat of death) or to psychological existence (the loss of freedom, meaninglessness). Or the threat may be to some other value that one identifies with one's existence, like patriotism, or special love of another person who is threatened. Threats can be of different kinds:

a. A threat of danger. Crime, war, violent weather, unexplained illness, even visits to the dentist, can be among those events that threaten individuals and cause fear. Often this fear comes because of our uncertainty and feelings of helplessness.

Before the Desert Storm battle with Iraq there was lots of fear. Saddam Hussein threatened a blood bath to our soldiers. We proceeded anyway, in spite of our fears. Our prayers and the courage of our brave men and women overcame the fear that followed the threats.

b. Threats to our self-esteem. Most people like to look good and to perform competently. When anything comes along to threaten our image or to imply to others or to ourselves that we are not competent, then we feel threatened. Some people avoid taking exams or risking failure because the failure that might come would be too threatening to their self esteem.

Some people don't try because the threat of failure creates a paralyzing fear. Our faith urges us to not let the threat of failure determine our conduct.

c. Threats of separation. It is never easy to be separated from significant other people. It can be confusing to be on our own and painful to realize that an important person in our life has left or rejected us. Individuals often feel threatened and saddened when losses occur through moves, death, divorce, or other separations; some say there is a certain anxiety and fear at separation from the mother's womb.

d. Threats that come from an unconscious influence. When threats and concerns are pushed into the unconscious they may fester away from conscious awareness. Later these unconscious ideas move toward becoming conscious and that can be threatening because we are then forced to face difficult problems that we don't understand or know how to solve.

We are threatened by inner negative voices. These inner threats can take control and turn us into people who follow their fears. If the inner voice does not speak of positive things, it is not good. If the inner threat makes us feel fearful, we need to reject it.

2. Conflict causes fear, such as when a person is influenced by two or more pressures there is a sense of uncertainty that often leads to fear and anxiety. Conflicts come from two tendencies: approach and avoidance. To approach is to have a tendency to do something or to move in a direction that will be pleasurable and satisfying. Avoidance is to resist doing something, perhaps because it will not be pleasurable or satisfying.

a. Approach-approach conflict. Here is a conflict over the tendency to pursue two desirable but incompatible goals. For example, we may greatly desire to make a lot of money, and at the same time desire to be a missionary to a primitive tribe in Africa. We desire two things that are incompatible with each other. Another example is we may greatly desire to marry a certain person, and at the same time desire to please our parents who happen to dislike that person. A conflict caused by two incompatible goals that are both desirable is called approach-approach.

b. Approach-avoidance conflict. Here is a desire both to do something and not to do it, for example, the desire to have extramarital sex (approach) and an equal desire to stay away from it (avoidance); or a desire to drink alcohol (approach) coupled with a desire to keep away from it (avoidance). We want to be good and we want to be bad, both at the same time. This approach-avoidance conflict creates anxiety, worry, fear, and despair.

c. Avoidance-avoidance conflict. Here there are two alternatives, both of which may be unpleasant, like having pain versus having an operation that might in time relieve the pain. You are faced with two choices and you don't want either one and that position creates anxiety and fear.

3. Anxiety and worry causes fear. And the reverse is also true--fear causes anxiety and worry. Fear and anxiety often have the same base. Here are some fears that come from anxiety:

* fear of failure
* fear of the future
* fear of achieving success
* fear of rejection
* fear of intimacy
* fear of conflict
* fear of meaninglessness in life
* fear of sickness
* fear of death
* fear of loneliness

There is a host of other real or imagined possibilities. Sometimes these fears can build up in one's mind and create extreme anxiety, and sometimes these anxieties create a terrorizing fear--often in the absence of any real danger, a fear without foundation that separates us from the power of reason. Anxiety and worry are more than cousins to fear; they are a part of the body, but a part that we do not ordinarily recognize as wrong.

Anxiety and worry are mental manifestations and grow out of morbid fear.

"To conquer fear is the beginning of wisdom" - Bertrand Russell

4. Unmet needs cause fear. For many years wise people have tried to identify the basic needs of human beings. A therapist, Cecil Osborne, for example, has concluded that six needs are fundamental:

1. Survival (the need to have continued existence)
2. Security (economic and emotional)
3. Sex (as an expression of love; as a sexual being)
4. Significance (to amount to something; to be worthwhile)
5. Self-fulfillment (to achieve fulfilling goals)
6. Selfhood (a sense of identity)

If we fail to meet these or other needs, Osborne believes we are anxious, "up in the air," afraid, and often frustrated. Cecil Osborne is a wise man and he has thought about the basic needs of people for a long time, but his list is not sacred. He may have missed a few needs. In any case, people do have some basic needs.

But what if all of these needs are met? Would life be complete and satisfying? Probably not! There still would be questions that transcend life on earth: Where will I go after death? Does existence consist of only a few short years on earth? One writer has lumped these and related questions into something called finite-eschatological anxiety and paired this with the anxiety of failure. We can have no real freedom from fear until we are at peace with life.

> **There is great beauty in going through life without anxiety or fear. Half our fears are baseless, and the other half discreditable.**
>
> - Bover (1820-1904)

5. Individual differences cause fear. People react differently to fear-producing situations. Some people are almost never fearful, some seem highly fearful most of the time, and many are in between. A number of factors contribute to individual differences:

a. Psychology--Most behavior is learned as a result of personal experience or teaching by parents and other significant persons. Each person is unique, and when a unique person is faced with another factor, he or she reacts in a unique way. Here are some psychological reasons for fear that will create a unique reaction in different people:

* when we have failed and must try again,
* when we have been hurt in the past,
* when others have demanded more than we could give,
* when we have seen fear in other people (the child who

learns to be fearful in thunderstorms because his/her mother was always fearful),
* when we have developed the capacity to think of the potential dangers in a situation,
* when our perception of a situation gives us reason to suspect danger.

All of the above are psychological reactions that arouse fear.

b. Personality--It may be that some people are more fearful or high-strung than others. Some are more sensitive, self-centered, hostile, or insecure than others. These personality differences arise from a combination of inherited and learning influences which, in turn, create individual differences in fear.

c. Sociology--The causes of fear may rest in our society: political instability, mobility that disturbs our sense of rootedness, shifting values, changing moral standards and religious beliefs and so on. Our culture and subculture stimulate fear in some people but give others such a secure environment that fear is much less prominent.

Certainly, the people on the Ethiopian trail of starvation and death will have some different fears than those who live in Beverly Hills. Of course, our concerns will shift during times of war and peace; and, when we are uprooted by a job change and uncertain of the future, our fear, worries, and anxieties will match these sociological changes.

d. Physiology--The presence of disease can stimulate fear, but so can dietary imbalance, neurological malfunctioning, and chemical factors within the body. Fear can trigger physiological reactions, but physiology can also contribute to increased fear.

A body that is malfunctioning creates worry and anxiety that results in fear. And fear inhibits the healing of the body. Because fear is the opposite of faith, fear will lessen the effectiveness of faith healing. Fear will also inhibit the power of medicine and surgery. Fear creates a bad mental attitude and a low morale that induces a climate of hopelessness and becomes the number one enemy of the healing process.

e. Theology--Beliefs have a great bearing on one's fear level. If God is seen as all-powerful, loving, good, and in ultimate control of the universe, then there can be trust and security even in the midst of turmoil. If we believe that God forgives when we confess our sin, that He promises life eternal, and that He meets our needs on earth, then there is less cause for fear. It should not be concluded that fear always reflects a lack of faith. The causes of fear are too complex for such a simplistic explanation.

> **Fear always springs from ignorance.**
>
> Ralph Waldo Emerson (1803-1882)

SOME METHODS FOR GETTING RID OF FEAR

We are dealing with a natural phenomenon that has gone wrong...so a methodology to defeat the forces of abnormal fear is not easy to come by. Psychology has found an answer when older folk are deeply captured by fear forces. And as we gradually approach old age and feel ourselves slipping into a life of insecurity and fear, there is plenty we can do to help ourselves.

1. Not using fear or threats to conquer fear

Many of us seem to believe that people would behave in more socially acceptable ways if threatened by someone in authority. In recent years, for instance, nationwide campaigns against venereal disease, the use of hard drugs, cigarette smoking, and the dangers of not wearing seat belts have employed the "hellfire and damnation" approach--that is, the main thrust of the propaganda has been to describe in exquisite detail the terrible consequences of various types of misbehavior.

But are such threats really as effective as we sometimes think them to be? The experimental evidence suggests that the actual effects of the punitive approach are more subtle and complex than we might previously have guessed. Irving Janis and Seymour Feshbach investigated the effects of fear-arousing communications on high school students. These scientists picked as their topic dental hygiene, or the dangers of not taking care of your teeth. They wrote three different 15-minute lectures on tooth decay. The first was a "high fear" lecture that contained 71 references to pain, cancer, paralysis, blindness, mouth infections, inflamed gums, ugly or discolored teeth, and dental drills. The second or "moderate fear" lecture was somewhat less threatening. But the third or "minimal fear" lecture was quite different. It made no mention at all of pain and disease, but rather suggested ways of avoiding cavities and decayed teeth through proper dental hygiene.

Janis and Feshbach presented each of the three appeals to a different group of 50 high school students (a fourth group of students heard no lecture at all and thus served as a control group). Janis and Feshbach found that immediately afterward the subjects exposed to the "high fear" lecture were highly impressed with what they heard. The students also admitted that the lecture got them very worried about the health of their own teeth. A week later, however, only 28% of them had brushed their teeth more often, and 20% of them were actually doing worse.

In marked contrast, the "low fear" students were not particularly impressed with the lecture, but a week later 50% of them were "brushing better" and only 14% were doing a worse job.

The high fear appeal apparently evoked strong emotional responses in the students, many of whom thought that being frightened was somehow "good for them." As one student said, "Some of the pictures of decayed teeth went to extremes, but they probably had an effect on most of the people who wouldn't want their teeth to look like that. I think it is good because it scares people when they see the awful things that can happen."

Despite this student's beliefs, when it came to actually changing behaviors, the high fear message simply didn't work as well as did the minimal fear message. In fact, the high fear propaganda seems to have had exactly the opposite long-term effect than one might have predicted.

In the spring of 1979, a film called *Scared Straight* was shown on many U.S. television stations. The movie shows how inmates at a prison in New Jersey have been using "scare tactics" to frighten troubled young people into avoiding further scrapes with the law. The youths spend several hours in the prison, mostly listening to the convicts describe (in gory detail) the effects of homosexual rape, fights, and prison brutality. The film is highly dramatic, and implies strongly that the *Scared Straight* program has been a great success. The film won an Academy Award in 1979, and after it was televised many state legislatures debated whether or not to make such treatment compulsory for all juvenile offenders.

Unfortunately, the actual data simply do not support the effectiveness either of the program or of the film's fear-arousing message. In the August 1979 issue of *Psychology Today,* Rutgers University professor James O. Finckenauer reports on a detailed study he had made of the juvenile offenders involved in these jail visitations. That the prisoners doing the "scaring" think the program works is without doubt. But Finckenauer discovered that only some 60% of the juveniles were scared straight enough to avoid further arrest. By contrast, some 90% of highly similar offenders in Finckenauer's control group "went straight" without being scared. Worse than this, of 19 youngsters who had no criminal record before they visited the New Jersey prison, 6 later broke the law. The data suggest that the program actually increases the crime rate rather than reducing it.

Why didn't the program work? Pearl West, director of the California Youth Authority, offers one answer: "These kids are yelled at, at home. Yelling at them some more won't do any good." Marian Wright Edelman, director of the Children's Defense Fund, offers another reason: "Having kids visit a jail for a few hours is not going to help them learn to read or deal with unstable family life."

2. Deconditioning treatment

S. H. Kraines reported a young medical student who feared the sight of blood. This young man considered giving up the study of medicine because each time he walked into an operating room he keeled over in a dead faint. Kraines first attempted to determine the causes for this response and tried to change the boy's attitude toward medicine, but he also tried a step-by-step deconditioning treatment. J.M. was told to walk into the operating chamber during an operation and then immediately to walk out. On the second day J.M. went into the room, counted to five, and then walked out. On the third day J.M. was told to stay a full minute before leaving. On subsequent days, J.M. stayed longer and longer.

"The first duty of man is that of subduing fear" - Thomas Carlyle

Two weeks later, when J.M. was supposed to stay 10 minutes, he got so interested in the operation that he stayed until it was completed. Thereafter, Kraines reports, J.M. had no trouble at all--even when called on to assist in operations. His "blood phobia" appeared to be gone for good.

3. Relaxation techniques

Phobic reactions usually involve some form of sensitization to stimuli that elicit autonomic arousal and muscular tension. A major part of desensitization therapy, therefore, consists of teaching the patient to relax voluntarily--the theory being that you can't very well be tense or aroused at the same time that you are physically limp as a wet rag. By alternately tensing and then relaxing your muscles, you can acquire the ability to relax at your own verbal or mental command. Once you have mastered this skill, you can order the muscles in your body to relax even when you are faced with a mildly disturbing situation, such as the least threatening stimulus on a fear hierarchy, if you happen to suffer from a phobia.

4. Desensitization training

Dr. Joseph Wolpe, now at Temple University in Philadelphia, is usually given credit for having popularized desensitization training. Wolpe believes that the secret of its success comes from never over stimulating the patient or letting the phobic reaction get so strong that it cannot be counteracted by voluntary muscular relaxation. Wolpe and his colleagues achieve this goal by always starting with the least-feared item on the hierarchy and working up the scale. They also stop treatment momentarily whenever the client shows the slightest sign of distress.

5. Psychoanalysis

The psychoanalytic view is that the phobia is simply a symptom of an underlying personality problem that cannot be helped or alleviated merely by curing the symptomatic behavior. The expectation is that if one merely cures the symptom without first changing the personality structure that gave rise to the phobic reaction other and perhaps more devastating symptoms are bound to take its place. (There is not much scientific evidence to support this fear of "symptom substitution.") Wolpe holds that what the analysts call the "underlying problem" is typically an attitude or perception that was learned by the same laws of conditioning as was the phobic reaction.

6. Guided imagery--visualization--studious reflection

Two psychologists from the University of Michigan, David Himle and Clayton Shorkey, attempted a form of counterconditioning called desensitization therapy on Anne M., an older woman who was afraid to ride in a car. First they drew up a list of disturbing stimuli arranged in rank order from the least to the most frightening. The act of actually riding in an automobile was the most frightening thing Anne could think of. Getting into a parked automobile was somewhat less disturbing, so sitting in a car ranked lower on the hierarchy than did riding. Walking past a car was even less threatening, but was still more likely to induce panic than

merely seeing a car or truck through a window. Merely imagining what a car looked like evoked very little fear, so this item was at the bottom of the hierarchy.

When Himle and Shorkey began treating Anne M., they first got her to relax as much as possible. Once she was quite comfortable, they asked her to imagine seeing a car out of the window. She soon got to the point where she could tolerate seeing a car "in her mind's eye" without feeling any anxiety at all. Then they asked Anne M. to look out a window briefly, and got her to relax again. Soon Anne M. was able to look at cars out the window whenever she pleased.

At this point in her treatment, Anne M. had been conditioned to handle the lowest item on her fear hierarchy. The stimulus of "seeing a car through the window" now elicited the conditioned response of relaxation rather than the conditioned response of panic.

Next, Himle and Shorkey asked her to imagine walking out the front door of the building and approaching a car. Once she could manage this imagery, they turned thought into action and got her to leave the hospital building and actually touch a parked automobile outside. When she was relaxed enough to handle this real-life problem, they encouraged her to get inside the car and take a short ride.

To help Anne M. imagine what each step in her desensitization would be like, Himle and Shorkey built a scale model of the hospital and its grounds. The model included all the streets and highways in that area. Anne learned to move toy cars around the streets without becoming fearful. Once she had thought through a given journey using the toy cars, she was able to make the same brief trip in a real automobile.

At the end of just 10 training sessions, Anne M. was driven out of the hospital grounds onto a nearby highway on a short excursion--a trip that caused her little or no discomfort. Thereafter, with no further therapy, Anne M. began taking part in more of the social activities on the ward, including short visits to points of interest near the hospital. Once she saw that she could tolerate these brief trips, she spontaneously began visiting friends who lived in nearby towns.

The final test of Anne's desensitization came when she was invited to spend a few days with some relatives who lived several hundred miles away. Anne had to make the trip by bus. When she felt she was relaxed enough to handle this experience--which might well have rated right at the top of her original hierarchy of fears--she packed her bag and caught the bus.

Ironically, the vehicle broke down while on the expressway and Anne and the rest of the passengers had to sit by the side of the road for more than an hour while traffic buzzed furiously past them. However, Anne handled the situation without any panic and reached her destination safely. She no longer had a phobic reaction to moving vehicles.

> Of all passions, fear is most accursed.
> - Shakespeare (1564-1616)

SOME PRACTICAL SUGGESTIONS FOR CONQUERING FEAR

◆ Fight back. Do not let the feeling of fear determine your conduct.

General Toulare was shaving early in the morning before the Battle of Tours. When he nicked his face, an aide heard him say, "Tremblest thou, vile carcass? Thou wouldst tremble even more if thou knewest where I was going to take thee today."

So you are afraid. Be brave and fight back.

◆ When you get old, as much as possible, surround yourself with loving relatives and friends. Do not allow yourself to be lonely--seek companionship.

◆ As much as possible, let your surroundings be familiar. Keep meaningful pictures and memorable artifacts in your room. The new Alzheimer's homes are allowing their clients to dress up their rooms with fond memories of the past.

◆ Keep as busy as possible doing those things that interest you. Do not let your interest lessen or go away. If you do lose a life interest, quickly search for and adopt another one.

◆ Act like you want to feel. The cerebral cortex and the cerebrum surround the hypothalamus. With your mind you can override the source of fear. Act brave and it will smother the fire of fear.

◆ Ask people to help you with your fears. Discuss fear in a group. You will be surprised how many people have the same fear that you do. A group effort helps.

◆ Don't be afraid to use professional services. Psychiatrists, psychologists, social workers, therapists, and counselors have methods to help people with their fears. We have listed some methods that they use: conditioning, relaxation, sensitivity training, guided imagery, and psychoanalysis. They have other methods; and, of course, there is medication such as tranquilizers.

◆ Do the thing you are afraid to do, and the death of fear is certain. Too much fear is patently false, and so when you do the thing that generates false fear, you will quickly discover there is nothing to be afraid of.

◆ Use prayer, meditation, and positive thinking to give you the strength to conquer your fears.

◆ To conquer fear we must have hope--hopelessness brings helplessness. Don't put evil on the future; step into the Kingdom of the Unafraid by renewing and establishing your hope.

◆ Renew your mind and straighten out your thinking. Most people in the kingdom of fear are thinking talking in a hopeless circle. Fill your mind with worthwhile stuff. Talk nice to yourself and to other people, focus your attention on problems and not on solutions, and wrestle with your day dreams and night dreams until they become more friendly. Remind yourself how foolish it is to be afraid of something that does not exist.

◆ This article on "Conquering Fear" is fairly long and comprehensive, but there is other information on the subject. Remember that all ugly emotions, like fear, do not like the light of day. So, face your fears, study them, discuss them, share them, and search for their source. Basically to understand your fear, to expose it to the light of day, and to fight its cause is to conquer it.

WORDS OF WISDOM FROM THE PAST

Do not be anxious about tomorrow, for tomorrow will be anxious for itself. Let the day's own trouble be sufficient for the day.

Jesus

Cowards die many times before their deaths;
The valiant never taste of death but once.
Of all the wonders that I yet have heard,
It seems to me most strange that men should fear;
What will come when it will come.

Shakespeare (1564-1616)

Fear makes men believe the worst.

Curtis-Rufus (f.l. A.D. 100)

They can conquer who believe they can. He has not learned the first lesson of life who does not every day surmount a fear.

Emerson (1803-1882)

What are fears but voices airy?
Whispering harm when harm is not.
And deluding the unwary
Til the fatal bolt is shot!

Wordsworth (1770-1850)

Nothing in the affairs of men is worthy of great anxiety.

Plato (427?-347? B.C.)

Our instinctive emotions are those that we have inherited from a much more dangerous world, and contain, therefore, a larger portion of fear than they should.

Bertrand Russell (1872-1970)

We fear in proportion of our ignorance of them.

Livy (59 B.C.-A.D. 17)

Your memory use it or lose it!

You are not the only one who is forgetful. Having difficulty in recalling things occurs at all ages. Children often have to be reminded not to forget their books, executives need to be reminded of meetings, and geniuses may forget what day it is.

Recent findings seem to debunk the idea that people's ability to remember decreases with age. The new concept is in the absence of disease older people can continue to learn and retain their memory in retirement if they make a concerted effort to stay active and alert.

Fortunately, scientific researchers are paying more attention to aging and memory. With the increase of the 65 + group, you can expect heightened interest in research on this subject. For example, the National Institute of Mental Health reports: "This is the year of memory; we've had more interest in it than any year on record."

The old expression, "if you don't use it, you lose it," holds true for retaining memory. Exercising the mind keeps it fit and youthful, just as physical exercise keeps the body in shape. In brief, give yourself time to remember things, write yourself notes and lists, establish routines, don't become too easily distracted, take part in a few mental games such as crossword puzzles, rehearse information in your head, create a mental picture of what you want to remember, keep physically active, and don't doubt yourself.

Major Types of Memory

Most psychologists agree that there are at least three major kinds of memory:

1. **Episodic** memory, which deals with specific events such as what happened at yesterday's meeting, the name of someone you have just met, or where the keys to the car were left.
2. **Semantic** memory, the overall store of information and experience that people accumulate over a lifetime.
3. **Implicit** memory for skills one exercises automatically, such as speaking grammatically or hitting a golf ball.

New studies show that semantic and implicit memory do not decline with age. The scientific literature shows that episodic memory is stable through the mid-60s, with a slight drop but no real problems for most people. But there is a pronounced drop in episodic memory in the 70s for most people. The drop may be largely due to retirement and the way it changes how you use your memory; people usually don't exercise their mental faculties as much when they are no longer working.

Semantic memory is the seat of wisdom. When you make decisions and judgments, you draw on this store of knowledge. Semantic memory is the most powerful. A report in *Psychology and Aging* used a vocabulary test to compare semantic memory in people from 18 to 34 with that in an older group ranging in age from 57 to 83. Those in the older group scored higher on the vocabulary test. Of 70 possible correct answers, the older group got an average of 60 correct, while the younger group scored just 51 on average. Semantic memory does not decline with age; it grows.

A group of men and women in their 60s were tested on a vocabulary list and then tested again 10 years later. During the intervening decade of life, the men and women improved their scores by an average of six or seven words, which was a substantial increase. It is semantic memory that the elderly rely on for distant memories; plaguing the elderly is a failing episodic memory that interferes with remembering recent events, like where you put your glasses last.

Although most people experience a strong drop in episodic memory in their 70s, other kinds of memory remain robust. For example, among healthy adults there is generally minimal decline with age in implicit memory, which deals with the large variety of mental activities that occur spontaneously without having to make an intentional effort. Implicit memory is at work in situations such as recognizing someone you have met before or knowing how to drive a car.

There are strategies older people can use to compensate for their episodic memory deterioration in some situations. One of the most important is anxiety about memory itself. Unlike young people, older people tend to get upset when their memories fail them. If, rather than fearing for their mental competence, they relax and say to themselves, "I will remember that later," chances are that they will.

The metabolism of the brain--its use of energy--begins to slow in middle age. Sometimes it is further slowed by medication. People who regularly take medication and have memory problems may want to check with their doctors to make some adjustments.

Memory is a use-it-or-lose-it proposition. The older brain often fails to spontaneously organize new information as well as it once did. Older people often lose their will, or get discouraged, or seem too tired to remember. Younger people will try hard to fix something in their memory, while older people seem to give up too easily. When asked to learn a sequence of numbers or words, for example, young people typically keep at it until they hit on a way to do it. Many older people often quickly give up if they don't succeed after a few tries.

The young brain instinctively forms mental images when its attention is called to new information. But we lose much of this tendency with age. We start to depend on pure rote memory, or automatic memory, which didn't work too well when we were young. Visualization, deliberately fixing a subject in memory, repetition, and associating it with a well-known fact are techniques that we seem to give up on when we get older.

For example, we go shopping or to a movie and then can't remember where we parked the car, or we find ourselves misplacing things and forgetting people's names. When parking a car, don't just lock it and walk away; instead, note something nearby that is distinctive (association), pause to register it in your consciousness (fixing), stop to look back so that it will ring a bell when you return (repetition), and picture yourself returning to your car and note what you will see when you do come back (visualization).

Short-term memory doesn't necessarily diminish with age; it just takes longer to function. Most people (90%) past the age of 65 think they have some memory impair-

Iron rusts from disuse; stagnant water
loses its purity and in cold weather becomes frozen;
even so does inaction sap the vigor of the mind.

- Leonardo da Vinci (1452-1519)

ment. And that slowdown is certainly not proof that a brain disease is at work. None of us expects to throw a baseball as hard at age 50 as we did at 20. Brain function is similar. As we get older, our brain--including memory simply can't perform as efficiently as it once could. We don't normally lose it; it just slows down and takes a little more effort to operate.

Here are some suggestions that will help us to live comfortably with the idea of a slight drop in brain efficiency.

◆ Don't worry too much about memory loss; you are probably doing as well as you did when you were younger. Besides that, the brain needs to forget some things just to clear the junk out.

◆ Keep your brain active by having a program of memorization. Deliberately work your brain by memorizing poems, jokes, scripture, and memorable sayings. Impress young people by quoting from your memory. Do crossword puzzles, play games that require mind skill, and keep your brain going by reading, listening, and sharing.

◆ Keep your body in a clean, healthy, exercised state of being as much as possible. Your brain is connected to your body; they are inclined to slip together.

◆ Eliminate depression, anxiety, frustration, and negative thinking from your life. These things clog the brain cells and preoccupy you with hopelessness.

◆ When you want to remember something, use the four rules of memory to help it happen. They are:

❶ **Focusing**--concentrate on the thing you want to remember; give it time to fix in the brain by focusing on the object of memory.
❷ **Repeating**--Repetition will channel a path in the brain. So, say it over and over again until the brain has built a path to that memory.
❸ **Associating**--We remember those things that we place next to what we already know. For example, if you want to remember where you left your keys, don't just set the keys down and go

away. Fix in your mind, I am putting the keys on the table. Focus on it, repeat it, and think keys and table, keys and table. Associate mobile keys with a fixed table. When you put the two together and then look for your keys, you will think of the table.

❹ **Visualization**--Picture in your mind what you want to remember and then put it into some kind of action. For example, if you are trying to remember where you put the keys, visualize the keys on the table and see them crawling across the table top. When you go to recall where your keys are, it will be associated with a table and set in the memory by visualizing movement of the keys.

Another technique that helps in remembering lists is to use memory pegs. First of all, you must memorize a sequence of memory pegs. I use Dale Carnegie's memory pegs. They are: one, run; two, zoo; three, tree; four, door; five, hive; six, sick; seven, heaven; eight, gate; nine, dine; ten, den. The procedure is simple. Any list you want to remember, you simply hang the item on the memory peg and visualize the item and the peg in some kind of action.

For example: My wife might send me to the grocery store to buy ten items like: 1. white flour, 2. brown sugar, 3. sea salt, 4. vinegar, 5. cornflake cereal, 6. rye bread, 7. quart of milk, 8. raisins, 9. frozen fish, and 10. six bananas. I would attach these items to my list of ten memory pegs as follows:

One, "run"--visualize a race horse running around the track with a bag of (1) white flour on his head; some of the flour is spilling out of the bag onto the horse's head.

Two, "zoo"--picture a monkey in a zoo handing a sack of (2) brown sugar to you through his bars. The monkey is jumping up and down and laughing at you.

Three, "tree"--See in your mind's eye a large tree growing near the ocean with (3) sea salt waving from its branches instead of fruit.

Four, "door"--imagine a revolving door in which a bottle of (4) vinegar pops out of it as you barely catch it.

Five, "hive"--envision a beehive in which bees are buzzing out carrying item (5) cornflakes cereal.

Six, "sick"--conceive in your imagination the picture of a sick person in a hospital with the doctor feeding him (6) rye bread.

Seven, "heaven"--formulate in your mind a vision of heaven with the angels coming down a ladder to give you (7) a quart of milk.

Eight, "gate"--put your fancy to work forming the idea of a revolving gate on which item (8) raisins are riding.

Nine, "dine"--conjure up a story in which you imagine yourself dining with a loved person and eating (9) frozen fish.

Ten, "den"--paint a picture in your imagination of Daniel in the lion's den. The lions are eating (10) six bananas instead of Daniel.

These pegs are simple and easy and with a little practice they can assist you in remembering lists of things. Someone might say, "Memory pegs are ridiculous." That's true, but it works--perhaps because it is ridiculous. When I go to recall the ten things my wife asked me to pick up at the grocery store, I succeed because: I have associated the unknown list with the known pegs, I have pictured my association in a colorful way, I have focused my attention on an attempt to remember, and I have repeated the list over again. The memory peg idea uses the rules of memory:

❶ **Focusing**
❷ **Repeating**
❸ **Associating**
❹ **Visualizing**

There are many other techniques for remembering that work as well as the above suggestions. The idea is: **Don't complain that you can't remember things.** Develop a system and try to do it. You will find that old age does not have as much to do with memory loss as one might think.

It is impossible for a man to learn what he thinks he already knows.

Epicetus (50 -138 A.D.)

Stress--a dangerous "opportunity"

Stress is any action or situation that places special physical or psychological demands upon a person--anything that can unbalance his or her individual equilibrium. The physiological responses to such demands are surprisingly uniform.

❋ The heart races and pounds.

❋ The blood pressure soars.

❋ A flood of hormones stimulates some organs and depresses others.

❋ Breathing quickens.

❋ Muscles tense.

❋ The reticular activating system of the brain fires an electrical storm of neurons.

❋ The person experiences a "keyed-up" feeling.

The forms of stress are innumerable. For example, a divorce is stressful, but so is a marriage. Getting dismissed from a job is stressful, but so is a promotion. Sometimes we are not aware that we are being stressed from such common events as the noise of the city or activities like the daily chore of driving a car.

The keyed-up feeling of stress is a part of the fabric of life. It belongs to everyone. It is needed to keep life going. Without positive stress, not much would get done in this world. The athlete needs stress to psych himself up for competition. The singer needs stress to give a performance that brings down the house. Everyone needs some positive tension in order to perform with excellence.

Negative stress, or bad stress, or unnecessary stress, or too much stress can bring a person to the point of distress and depression. Stress can be gauged by changes in the rate of error in carrying out a task, in productivity on the job, or simply in the ability to get along with people. Stress in moderate doses will usually improve performance. Stress in overdoses is devastating. Specialists in the study of psychosomatic medicine find that stress can be a contributing factor in headaches, backaches, ulcers, heart disease, etc. Stress is a principal influence on all human behavior, in illness or in health.

People cannot long tolerate stress overload. However, neither can they tolerate a lack of stress. The external body reacts to lack of stress, paradoxically similar to the symptoms of stress. The absence of stress is in itself a kind of stress. Both planned experiments and practical experience have repeatedly demonstrated the profound emotional changes brought about by the deliberate isolation of men from stresses imposed by society. People who spend long periods alone in a stress-free environment will develop bizarre symptoms--hallucinations, an inability to reason or to judge time and distance, and an impaired emotional response.

CAUSES OF STRESS

What are the causes of stress? The answer can be conceived in an analogy of ten stress bears. Just suppose you are walking in the woods, and you see a bear. The emergency alarm system of the brain will discharge in the following way:

The sight of the bear is recorded on the occipital lobe of the brain. The occipital lobe sends a message to the cerebral cortex (the brain's manager), which searches in the cerebrum (the memory bank) to discover whether or not bears are dangerous. The memory bank has programmed the idea that you consider bears dangerous.

The cerebral cortex orders a reaction and sends a message down through the thalamus (a type of switch board), which shunts the message to the Reticular Activating System (RAS) located on the brainstem. The RAS will give a little electrical throb and discharge a stream of neurons to the hypothalamus, which is an emotional generator about the size of your thumb. The hypothalamus in a mysterious way produces a feeling of fear and directs it toward the pituitary gland and the autonomic nervous system. The pituitary triggers the thyroids and the adrenals, demanding, "More energy, quick." The adrenals release about 32 hormones into the bloodstream almost immediately. The autonomic nervous system activates, via the sympathetic branch, and alerts the rest of the body through an electrical charge to every nerve fiber.

During this process, you experience some changes: You begin to breathe a little faster to get more oxygen into the body. Your heart speeds up in order to pump more blood. The capillaries on the surface of the skin close down so that if you get scratched by the bear, you won't bleed too readily. The veins and arteries expand to give a greater flow of blood to bring oxygen and strength to the muscles. The sweat glands open up so that they can cool the system in this emergency. The digestive system closes down tightly except for the lower colon and bladder, which relaxes (accounting for what sometimes happens in moments of severe fright). The eyes dilate to let in more light and 52 anatomical changes take place in approximately one-eighth of a second to prepare the body and the mind for the emergency confrontation with bear #**1**--a real live dangerous bear.

The Emergency Alarm System (EAS) of the brain has discharged, and you are in a state of readiness to do what you have to do--either fight or flight. The major purpose of the EAS is to prepare us either to run from or to fight life's "bears." Herein is the problem: The board of directors of the brains of people often fires the EAS when no real live dangerous bear is present.

For example, Bear #**2** is our imagination. If we imagine that we see a bear, the system will fire just as it does with a real live dangerous bear. So, when things go bump in the night and we imagine goblins, the brain fires the Emergency Alarm System and stresses us just as if there were real live dangerous goblins.

Bear #**3** is similar to #**2**: We make a mistake. We see a big black friendly dog and mistake it for a big black unfriendly bear. If we make a mistake, the system makes a mistake and we are mistakenly stressed.

Bear #**4** fires up when we go hunting and deliberately seek the adventure of a confrontation with a real live dangerous bear. We anticipate finding a bear and the EAS fires up stress to prepare us for the event.

Bear #**5** consists of remembering an encounter with a bear. The EAS is such a sensitive mechanism that if you think back in your life and just remember a bear or some story about one, the system will prepare you, firing on the provocation of memory.

Bear #**6** is an accumulation of bears. If we have too many bears, too many scary events, the alarm system gets into a perpetual state of firing and can exhaust us into a state of paralysis. Too many bears and the EAS will fire at every little provocation and turn our life into a paranoid hell.

We can now see that most of the stress bears are not real but are manufactured by ourselves. Some other situations will fire the system. They are just a part of the personality of people.

Bear #**7** is resentment. If we allow our personality to be filled with hate, anger, and resentment, any small trigger can pull our "gun" and fire the EAS. A temper tantrum brought on by frustration or a fit of anger can set the system up for an emergency and put us into a state of stress.

Bear #**8** is fear. Anxiety and worry can trigger the system to fire up a state of fear, which will set us up for stress as quickly as if a real live dangerous bear were chewing on our leg. Fear can habituate into phobic reactions at every benign subject.

Bear #**9** is a negative attitude that constantly anticipates bears. This lack of hope and pessimism causes the system to drain its strength. We could speak of the stress bears entitled GUILT, DEPRESSION, HOPELESSNESS, DESPAIR, etc., but the mental attitudes of hate, anxiety, and negativism adequately illustrate how the mind can upset the system and subject us to stress.

Bear #**10** is just a little different from the rest. We have no bears at all in our life, and the system just fires to exercise itself. It sometimes becomes so habituated that people who have absolutely no reason at all for stress are more stressed than anyone else.

Too many uses of the emergency alarm system, too much crying, "**Bear, Bear,**" brings the body to a stage of resistance in which it pulls away from reactions of all kinds and sets the stage for mental illness, a withdrawal from life because we can't cope. If we continue to allow the "stress bears" of life to fire the system, we then finally reach a stage of exhaustion in which the system won't work, and we have no further energy to cope with life's problems. We drop into

a stage of depression and lose our fundamental joy of living. If we do not protect ourselves from the "stress bears" of life, they will literally eat us alive.

STRESS CONSEQUENCES

It is the thesis of a growing number of medical scientists that the basic cause of much 20th-century disease is stress. Stress does not strike all individuals equally. Some people seem to thrive on it. If you spend your life doing something that really matters to you and you do it well, you can withstand a great deal of stress. When the emergency alarm system fires and then overfires, the body is drained of its electrical and chemical nervous energy. Then the terrain of the body is weakened, the immunization system barely functions, and the life force ebb is lowered. In this weakened condition, bacteria love to live, and viruses love to take command.

Stress pioneer Dr. Hans Selye experimented with white rats by continually subjecting them to severe stress--similar to the type many humans experience. Dr. Selye found that the rats' aftermath of stress followed a three-part pattern of response that he called the General Adaptation Syndrome:

1. An *alarm reaction*--The system fires and a "fight or flight" response is made.
2. The *stage of resistance* -- The stressed animal's functions return to normal, and its resistance to further stimuli rises.
3. If severe stress continues, the third and final *stage of exhaustion* may occur-- The symptoms of the reaction reappear, this time irreversibly, and the animal soon dies. It dies because it has been unable to alter its behavior to accommodate the stress.

When the dead animal is dissected, it invariably has three dysfunctions:
1. Enlarged adrenal glands (a cause of depression).
2. Shrunken Lymphatic nodes and thymus (organs that play a vital role in immunity to disease).
3. A stomach covered by bleeding ulcers (ominous news to modern man).

Throughout the day, all humans and animals find themselves involved in stage 1 of the General Adaptation Syndrome (the

alarm reaction), and some degree of stage 2 inevitably follows (the stage of resistance). It is the amount of time that we remain in stage 2 that determines to a large degree our psychological and physiological well-being in life.

The Cardiovascular System
One of the first body systems to be affected by even minor sensations of stress is the cardiovascular system. Dr. Ray Rosenman, a San Francisco cardiologist and researcher, says, "Diet, exercise, family history, and blood cholesterol are important, but the thing that has increased over the years when heart disease has grown so alarmingly is PACE." Pace creates stress.

The "type A" personality was investigated by Dr. Myer Freedman and Dr. Rosenman, two cardiologists. The type A personality was always driving, aggressive, ambitious, competitive, pressured for getting things done, with the habit of pitting himself against the clock. He had significantly more coronary problems.

The Digestive System
Other research has been done in the field of the digestive system in which such things as ulcers, colitis, constipation, diarrhea, and diabetes have been linked to stress. Dr. Stewart Wolf established beyond contradiction that the mucous membrane lining that protects the inside of a person's stomach is clearly affected, not only day to day, but minute to minute by both conscious and unconscious emotions. When life seems harried and the future seems pale, the lining of our stomachs can turn pale, too. When our emotions are upset and we are in a stage of constant agitation, it is quite easy for the stomach to get involved. The medical doctor recognizes this fact when he cuts the vagus nerve, which transmits live from the brain to the stomach, in order to cure ulcers.

The Immunization System
The consequences of stress are widespread. Run-down people get infections easily. That's a known fact. The second is not so commonly known--stress runs people down. If a microbe is in or around us all the time and yet does not cause disease until we are exposed to stress, what then is the cause of our illness--the microbe or the stress? The immunization system protects us against

Rule Number 1 is, don't sweat the small stuff.
Rule Number 2 is, it's all small stuff.
And if you can't flee, flow.

- Robert S. Eliot

infections, allergies, autoimmunity, and cancer. The evidence is mounting that stress uses up the energy forces that produce white cells and antibodies so that a highly stressed person is on his way toward a condition of "illth," not health.

The Musculoskeletal System

Even disorders of the musculoskeletal system are stress related. Dr. Hans Kraus, at a back clinic in Columbia, NY, discovered that 80% of his patients were suffering from muscular deficiency, pure and simple. "Sitting tight" describes the state of the typical patient with chronic functional backache. Some people get a toothache from habitually clenching their jaws. A more common affliction is a tension headache. For years, physicians have been struck by the fact that certain emotional problems seem to make arthritis worse. Even in the typical fracture patient, Dr. Dunbar observed that statistics run much too high to be explained by accident. Accidents are not accidental. Psychogenic forces are at work. In a recent survey, 20% of all fatal car accidents involved drivers who had suffered an upsetting experience within three hours before the crash.

One of the fierce enemies of the human body is stress. It can have profound effects on the cardiovascular, the digestive, the immunity, and the skeletal-muscular systems of the body. Claude Bernard, French physiologist, maintains, "Illness hovers constantly about us, their seeds blown by the wind, but they do not take root in the terrain unless it is ready to receive them." By terrain, Bernard meant the human body. When the human body is subjected to too much stress, it becomes ready for invaders.

Psychosocial Response to Stress

One of the significant experiments in the field of stress was done by Dr. Richter. If a rat is stressed and thrown into a bucket of water, it will sink in two minutes. Nonstressed, it will swim for 20 to 80 hours. Stress exhausts a rat. It will exhaust a human too. Some humans become so worn out from being stressed that they develop various types of mental illness.

Schizophrenia is a complex disease that commonly means "out of touch with reality." People with schizophrenia are sometimes violent, but they typically prefer to withdraw and be left alone. Stress by itself

is not usually said to be a cause of this mental illness. Scientists do not agree on a particular formula that is necessary to produce the disorder. It is a probable result of an interplay of cultural, psychological, biological, and genetic factors. However, there is no doubt that stress can drive schizophrenics into suicidal or psychotic episodes.

Not only is stress quite likely to induce a deeper level of schizophrenia, but the disease itself creates a response of stress, making a vicious circle. Antipsychotic medications are commonly used to help a person with schizophrenia to reduce their response to stress.

Paranoia is a character disorder in which a person is extremely suspicious and has feelings of being persecuted and grandiose ideas. The paranoid is often self-destructive, always expecting the worst from other people and is often belligerent. Often they invent another world and another story and another type of life and another series of voices and actors with which they play out an elaborate script. Most of the time, the real world is not really as fierce as the inventions of the paranoid mind. Why do they invent and believe these wild stories? They invent them because they actually feel that bad about life. They have exhausted their mental and emotional strength through fearful false firings of the Emergency Alarm System. I believe they are not getting enough attention and appreciation from peers.

Today, *depression* is the most prevalent of all the mental illnesses in this country. It is so widespread it has been called the common cold of mental disturbance. Depression is the most common mental consequence of stress. The more depression, the more the stress, and the more the stress, the more the depression--a vicious circle. Any time the dark brown cloud of depression descends upon your emotions, take steps to reduce stress.

Hysterical reactions is another mental illness that often comes from stress. Have you ever hit your thumb with a hammer? Notice how sensitive the bruised thumb can be. Every little touch will bring forth an "ouch." That's what "hysterics" do. They have allowed the stresses of life to bruise them, so that every little event in life calls forth a hysterical reaction.

Entropy is an engineering law that says, "As the heat increases in the machine, so the energy available for work decreases." As it applies to life, when we give our energy to internal problems that heat ourselves up, we have less energy to devote to happiness and joy. The human was built to have strength to solve problems. If our strength has been needlessly exhausted, all we have is anxiety and worry, which creates more stress--a fruitless vicious circle, further dissipating our energies.

Symptomology

Let's look at some of the symptomology of acute short-term stress:

✔ You have vague aches and pains.
✔ You can't sleep at night and you don't know why.
✔ You feel restless, antsy, and generally upset for no apparent reason.
✔ You feel tired, dull, and listless, and you just don't seem to be able to get enough sleep.
✔ You appear cross, cranky and irritable, quick to get angry, quick to cry and to express emotional upset.
✔ You experience nervous ticks and itches. Eyes twitch, muscles cramp, and rash or acne develop.
✔ Minor neurological signs:
  Pupils of eyes unnaturally dilate.
  The tongue trembles and assumes odd positions when protruded.
  Body balance is slightly impaired.
  Hands or feet become cold and clammy.
  Skin becomes sensitive to pain.

Long-term or chronic stress goes past symptomology into function. Heart attacks, phlebitis, stomach ulcers, migraines, etc.-- real live functional illness will develop out of chronic long-term stress.

Short-term stress leads to major long-term stress. So, when you find yourself with the symptoms of acute short-term stress, it is best to start with a preventive program, lest you really get sick. Here is a condensed version of a program that has been useful to handle the hassles of stress.

1 **Start the day right**--Maintain a positive mental attitude filled with optimism and kind thoughts. As you go to sleep at night, put all problems on

On getting unstressed

the shelf to be solved during the daylight hours; set your mind on pleasant dreams. Let yourself go to sleep pleasantly and sweetly with the idea that tomorrow will be a beautiful day, and choose to make it so.

2 **Take time to think pleasant thoughts**--When you hear the whistle of the noisy locomotive of stress and strain coming upon you, take time to relax your mind with a trip to a beautiful meadow. Imagine yourself surrounded by wild flowers next to a swiftly moving mountain stream. In the distance envision a snow-capped mountain surrounded by tall green trees. Picture yourself sitting on a rock by the bank of a lovely stream and survey your meadow: Feel the warm sun; observe the blue sky; experience the fleecy clouds; smell the perfume of the flowers; relax your body and just plain "feel good." This thought trip only takes a few minutes, but it stops the approaching locomotive of stress dead in its tracks.

3 **Exercise**--One of the best ways to dissipate pent-up energy forces is to exercise. If you are laboring under too much stress, turn off the TV and move your body. There are a number of methods to exercise and increase physical activity. None of the suggestions are worth anything unless you do them. It is not so important what type of exercise; it is very important that the body is physically active. Here are some suggestions to improve your level of activity:

❋ Set aside time to be active.
❋ Plan outings that will demand activity.
❋ Seldom use an elevator or escalator.
❋ Don't park close to shopping; park far away.
❋ Get a bike and use it.
❋ Take up an active sport.
❋ Substitute a physical activity for TV.
❋ Do deep breathing and stretching exercises daily.

4 **Practice good nutrition**--If you are dealing with only acute short-term stress, you probably don't have to be too concerned about what you eat. No specific food on its own induces stress (except alcohol). But, if major chronic stress is taking over your life, then what and how much you eat can drastically affect your productivity and your sense of well-being.

Consider such ideas as balanced meals, moderate intake, natural foods, regular meals, roughage, and wholesome eating. Avoid such things as junk food, too much sugar, salt, fat, or meat. Eat light, nutritionally balanced, regular meals.

5 **Appreciate the beauty of little things**--One of the great problems of modern life stares at us; we have become jaded. In order to be entertained, we must be overwhelmed. Beauty is no longer one rose; we must have a gigantic rose garden to make us gasp. We must go to the Grand Canyon on occasion to exult in the overwhelming magnificence of one of the wonders of nature's world, but that is a special occasion. Everyday life usually does not stage itself on the cliffs above the Grand Canyon. We must learn to appreciate the beauty of the little things that are around us. A single flower can be as great a thing of beauty to the appreciator as can a million roses inflaming a grassy hill.

Stress and strain diminish quickly in the presence of beauty, and true beauty is in the eye of the beholder. Everywhere you go, appreciate beauty in the little things of life-- look at a picture, walk in the woods, dig in the soil, carefully observe a blade of grass, or linger over the smell of a flower. Positively cling to every little bit of beauty that comes your way.

6 **Organize your time**--Sometimes stress is caused by bad time management. Poor priorities make the day seem like a waste. Nonproductiveness often makes a person feel depressed. The job pressure cycle can easily be set in motion: poor organization = low productivity = poor self-concept = poor mental attitude = a high "type A" level stress.

Plan your time and household chores so that you do things one step at a time. As each step is accomplished, take pride in checking it off your list. Planning allows you to pace yourself and avoid feeling overwhelmed.

Dr. Barr Taylor of Stanford University suggests that you set priorities for relaxation to avoid stress:

❤ Take breaks from work and use them to relax.
❤ Take five-minute thought trips to

your secret place of beauty each day.
❤ Leave for engagements 15 minutes earlier so that you can drive slower with less stress.
❤ Put notes on your schedule calendar and by your phone to remind you to relax during the day.
❤ Take time off regularly; don't skip your vacations.

7 **Aim for the moon, but be satisfied when you hit the fence**--"Aim for the moon" means to set high goals; "but be satisfied when you hit the fence" means that realistic expectations are enough to create happiness. Actually, all our goals are high and holy. There is no such thing as an insignificant person or an inconsequential purpose. We are to believe in ourselves and believe in our purposes. A high sense of purpose with lofty goals that are satisfied with pragmatic, practical achievement brings little stress.

If you are the tiniest little wheel, remember that tiny wheels run little wheels, that run average wheels, that run large wheels, that run the huge wheel, that runs the factory, that puts people to work, that builds homes, communities, and nations--you are important. If you are the smallest little horseshoe nail in existence, remember that one little horseshoe nail out of place can cost the shoe that disables the horse, that stops the rider, that loses the message that would have saved the kingdom. A little horseshoe nail is very important and so is the tiniest little wheel.

Small achievements are never small. Small achievements often add up to large differences. Robert Browning wrote, "A little more, Oh how much, A little less, What worlds apart."

8 **If your answers are not working, seek new ones**--No one has all the answers. If you are laboring under too much stress, then don't be afraid to change your lifestyle. If the climate is bad for your allergies, consult a doctor and consider moving. If your job is too stressful, consider cutting down on your hours. If your husband or wife is too demanding, have a loving encounter and discuss what's bugging him or her.

When the door is closed and you can't get

More help on getting unstressed

through the way you're going, then choose an alternative route.

9 **Let criticism give you a boost**--The one thing that causes more stress and strain on people than any other factor is another human. We are more responsive and sensitive to the peer group than to any other circumstance. So, when the peer group rejects us with criticism, we are likely to develop a strong case of "the stresses." Pay close attention to the following statement: "Consider criticism as a disguised compliment."

If you are being criticized, you can bet your bottom dollar you must be doing something worthwhile. In this world, the critics are many; the performers are few. Fifty thousand people who can't do as well often critically yell at one pitcher who fails to strike out a batter.

10 **Assume the attitude of gratitude**-- To conquer stress and strain, assume the attitude of gratitude. Be thankful for whatever you've got. That's exactly what the grateful people do with life--they thank God for all their blessings, and when the curses come they are so busy thanking that the curses are ignored. Grateful people are happy people and happy people can handle the hassles of life.

11 **Be yourself and compete with yourself**--In handling the hassles of life, be natural, be normal, and be yourself. If you say one thing and mean another, you create conflict; and stress is born out of conflict. If the inner you wants to go one way and the outer you wants to go another, the conflict will tear you apart, and stress is created. Be yourself, and say what you mean--it's the only way to go.

Competing against someone can be quite exciting and a form of good stress. Constantly competing can become very wearing and stressful. Trying to do better than you did before (competing against yourself) is not stressful. Trying to beat everyone around you is high-order stress. Most of the time, play the game of life for the fun of it-- compete only on special occasions.

12 **Take a holiday**--Doing something entirely different from your usual occupation is an excellent way of getting

your mind off your problems and reducing stress. A two-week vacation every year is a must--more if possible. Ideally, a change of scenery is called for, but a complete break from work even if you stay at home is better than no break at all.

Take mini-vacations, a few minutes every hour, a few hours every day, at least a day every week. Take time away from the daily routine. It will make the handling of hassles much easier.

Stop and smell the flowers!

13 **Cultivate a hobby**--Cultivating a hobby or an interesting pastime prevents obsessive preoccupation with minor personal problems. Give your brain a rest from what you have to do and spend some time doing what you want to do. Develop interests other than work. When people break this rule, and then retire, it devastates them.

14 **Learn to say "NO"**--We all have our limits, and it's important to recognize them. Don't get labeled as the too willing volunteer of whom everybody can take advantage. You can easily learn to resent your friends and even hate yourself for not having the nerve to say "No." Do what you can do, but do not do more than you can do.

15 **Talk out your problems**--Talking things out will help to relieve stress and strain and will put things in perspective. It can even lead to a plan of action. Dr. Earl Carter of Mayo Clinic says, "The stress of holding in your worries and anxieties can eventually make you sick, but if you can confide in a close friend or loved one, half of your problems will evaporate."

16 **Accept the inevitable**--Refuse to worry or get upset about any inevitable happening. If you can't do anything about it, then accept it. Some things are as

inevitable as the rising of the sun. To fight against such things is to fight against God. People cannot throw mud at the sun--they can only get their own head dirty. Accept what you cannot change.

17 **Trust life**--If your security is all wrapped up in your possessions, your job, or your status quo, you are a prime target for the stress syndrome. Trust God, trust life, trust people, and trust yourself. Then it is much more powerful, fulfilling, and easier to live stress-free.

18 **Don't fight against stress; use it**-- Stress is an energy source, a power. Instead of saying, "I'm nervous" (which is bad stress), say, "I'm excited" (which is good stress). It's the same emotion, but one is negative and the other is positive. When stress and strain fire up their steam and put you into a high state of agitation, don't fight it; use it. Turn the power generated by the firing of the neurons of the brain and the discharge of the hormones of the glands into a constructive field of endeavor.

Stress and strain are a part of the energy forces put within us to give us extra power to conquer problems and fight the battles of life. Perhaps the most effective method of fighting stress is to grab hold of the feeling of stress and put it to work. If we allow stress to run rampant in our lives, it will burn us down to exhaustion, depression, sickness, and death. But if we use the power of stress to light the lamp of life, we will be winners. Then we can handle our hassles.

CONCLUSION

The Chinese word for danger means, **Opportunity.** Stress is a dangerous opportunity. It is dangerous because it debilitates the body, lowers the resistance, and creates a milieu in the "terrain" that is receptive to pathology. Stress is an opportunity, because without its extra strength, push, and drive, the athlete could not achieve, the businessman could not succeed, and the artist would not be endowed with creativity. Stress can be dangerous if misused or over used. Stress can also be an opportunity if the force, in cooperation with the body powers, is directed toward accomplishment, fulfillment, and achievement of life goals.

Some reflections on death...famous quotations

To-morrow, and to-morrow, and to-morrow, creep in this petty pace from day to day; to the last syllable of recorded time; and all our yesterdays have lighted fools the way to dusty death.   - Shakespeare

Let no man fear to die, we love to sleep all, And death is but the sounder sleep.
                    - Francis Beaumont

I refuse to attend his funeral. But I wrote a very nice letter explaining that I approved of it.   - Mark Twain

Two out of three deaths are premature; they are related to a loafer's heart, smoker's lung and drinker's liver. - Thomas J. Bassler

If you don't know how to die, don't worry; Nature will tell you what to do on the spot, fully and adequately. She will do this job perfectly for you; don't bother your head about it.   - Montaigne (1533-1592)

The gods conceal from men the happiness of death, that they may endure life.
                    - Lucan (39-65 A.D.)

Pity is for the living, envy is for the dead.
                    - Mark Twain

Each person is born to one possession which outvalues all his others--his last breath.
                    - Mark Twain

Life is a dream walking
Death is a going home.
                    - Chinese Proverb

This day, which thou fearest as thy last, is the birthday of eternity.
                    - Seneca (3 B.C.-65 A. D.)

In this world, nothing is certain but death and taxes.   - Benjamin Franklin

The goal of all life is death. - Sigmund Freud

You will not die because you are ill, but because you are alive.   - Seneca

Nobody dies prematurely who dies in misery.   - Publilius Syrus (42 B.C.)

And I still onward haste to my last night; Time's fatal wings do ever forward fly; So every day we live, a day we die.
- Thomas Campion (1567-1620)

Death is a release from the impressions of the senses, and from the desires that make us their puppets, and from the vagaries of the mind, and from the hard service of the flesh.   - Marcus Aurelius (121 A.D.)

You die as you've lived. If you were paranoid in life, you'll probably be paranoid when you're dying.   - James Cimino

Death is a cure for all diseases.
                    - Thomas Browne (1605-1682)

At the moment of death there will appear to you, swifter than lightening, the luminous splendor of the colourless light of Emptiness, and that will surround you on all sides. Terrified, you will flee from the radiance. Try to submerge yourself in that light, giving up all belief in a separate self, all attachment to your illusory ego. Recognize that the boundless Light of this true Reality is your own true self, and you shall be saved!
- Tibetan Book of the Dead (c. 780 A.D.)

Do not be frightened or bewildered by the luminous, brilliant, very sharp and clear light of supreme wisdom. Be drawn to it. Take refuge in it. Do not take pleasure in the soft light. Do not be attracted to it or yearn for it. It is an obstacle blocking the path of liberation.
- Tibetan Book of the Dead (c. 780 A.D.)

Your lost friends are not dead, but gone before, advanced a stage or two upon that road which you must travel in the steps they trod.   - Aristophanes (448-380 B.C.)

I don't believe in dying. It's been done. I'm working on a new exit. Besides, I can't die now--I'm booked.   - George Burns

For it is not death or hardship that is a fearful thing, but the fear of death and hardship.   - Epictetus (50-138 A.D.)

Cowards die many times before their deaths; The valiant never taste of death but once. Of all the wonders that I yet have heard, It seems to me most strange that men should fear;
What will come when it will come.
                    - Shakespeare (1564-1616)

I'll tell you thus, my pretty frail, each of us owes God a death and the check is in the mail.   - Charles Embree

Our Lord has written promises of the resurrection, not in books alone, but in every leaf in Springtime. ---
- Martin Luther

I never wanted to see anybody die, but there are a few obituary notices I have read with pleasure.   - Clarence Darrow

For dust thou art, and unto dust shall thou return.   - Genesis

We begin to die as soon as we are born, and the end is linked to the beginning.
                    - Maniliue (100 A.D.)

Death is a golden key that opens the palace to eternity.   - Milton (1608-1674)

It is as natural to die as to be born; and to a little infant, perhaps, the one is as painful as the other.   - Bacon (1561-1626)

Strange--is it not?--that of the myriads who before were passed the door of Darkness through, not one returns to tell us of the road which to discover we must travel too.
                    - Omar Khayyam (1100)

The birds of the air die to sustain thee; the beasts of the field die to nourish thee; the fishes of the sea die to feed thee. Our stomachs are their common sepulcher. Good God! with how many deaths are our poor lives patched up! How full of death is a momentary man!   - Quarles (1592-1644)

Death, so called, is a thing that makes men weep, and yet a third of life is passed in sleep.   - Byron (1788-1824)

Because I could not stop for Death,
He kindly stopped for me;
The carriage held but just ourselves
And Immortality.
                    - Emily Dickinson (1830-1886)

The last words of Thomas Alva Edison, "It's very beautiful over there."

Life is strewn with so many dangers, and be the source of so many misfortunes, that death is not the greatest of them.
                    - Napoleon Bonaparte

I am the most miserable man living. If what I feel were equally distributed to the whole human family, there would not be one cheerful face on Earth. Whether I shall ever be better I cannot tell. I awfully forebode I shall not. To remain as I am is quite impossible. I must die to be better it appears to me. I can write no more.

A person in the deepest despair wrote the above note. He was Abraham Lincoln. He didn't commit suicide but I just wanted you to get the picture that suicide feelings can occur in any family, in any profession, in any occupation, and with any person, no matter how great.

As we all know, suicide is the taking of one's own life. It is a common cause of death between the ages of 20 and 40, second only to accidents. Attempted suicide is responsible for about 20% of all emergency hospital admissions. According to the National Center for Health Statistics, in 1988, the latest year available from the federal government, the suicide rate for all age groups was 12.4 per 100,000 people; but for those ages 65 and older, it was 20.9 per 100,000. In older men the rates are 45 per 100,000--it is a major and devastating public health problem. Suicide is the tenth leading cause of death in adults. A conservative estimate is that there are 200,000 suicide attempts and 30,000 completed suicides in the United States each year; over 600,000 years of productive life are lost each year in this country. In the world, more than 2,000 suicides occur every day--around a million a year. In the past decade, incidence of suicide has dramatically increased in children ages 10 to 14 and in adults over 65.

Today, the greatest proportion of suicides are among the elderly. More than 40% of the suicides involve persons over 55 years of age. We are concerned about the hidden and unspoken problems of despair among the elderly, leading them to take their own lives. Many elderly people feel that their lives are over. Often they are sick and in pain. They routinely feel lonely and abandoned by their families, and they face dwindling financial resources. Our society must see that suicide is not the final answer to the problems of the aging.

"When younger people attempt suicide, they have the resilience to fight to recover," said Betty Davis of the American Association of Retired Persons. "But old people don't have that resilience--and oftentimes they really mean it; it's not a threat or a plea for help."

Today, older people demand a higher quality of life than was the case of their predecessors. The breakup of the family in our decade leaves people who have no children or no living relatives at a point where they don't have to answer to anyone but themselves.

Dr. Daniel A. Plotkin, a geriatric psychiatrist at UCLA, said he believes more attention should be paid to recognizing depression in the elderly, particularly among the terminally ill. In some cases, he said, a sick person contemplating a suicide pact may feel differently after counseling.

Throughout history, suicide has been both condemned and praised by various societies. It is condemned by Islam, Judaism, and Christianity, and attempts are punishable by law in several coun-

tries. The Brahmans of India, however, tolerate suicide, and the theoretically voluntary suicide of an Indian widow (sutte), now outlawed, was highly praised at one time. In ancient Greece, convicted criminals were permitted to take their own lives, but the Roman attitude toward suicide hardened toward the end of the empire as a result of the high incidence among slaves, who thus deprived their owners of valuable property. The Japanese custom of seppuku (hara-kiri), or self-disembowelment, was long practiced as a ceremonial rite; noblemen were granted the privilege of punishing themselves in this way for wrongdoing, and it was also used to escape the humiliation of failure, to shame one's enemies, or to demonstrate loyalty to a dead master or emperor. (Compulsory hara-kiri was outlawed in 1868.) Buddhist monks and nuns have also committed sacrificial suicide by burning themselves alive as a form of social protest.

Since the Middle Ages, society has used first the canonic and later the criminal law to combat suicide. Following the French Revolution of 1789 criminal penalties for attempting to commit suicide were abolished in European countries, England being the last to follow suit in 1961. Many of these countries and numerous U.S. states also adopted laws against helping someone to commit suicide. The change in the legal status of suicide, however, has had no adverse influence on the suicide rate.

Why do people try to commit suicide?

The major reason for suicides is considered to be mental illness. An elderly or chronically ill person may take his or her life in a state of acute depression, misery, and pain. A person with a personality disorder, unable to cope with stress, depression, or a physical disorder, is a typical potential suicide. Three types of mental illness can result in suicide: major depression, manic-depression, and schizophrenia. The remainder are suicides that result from anxiety and panic diseases, substance abuse, and a handful of "impulsive" suicides that may occur after a sudden catastrophic loss or disaster.

Other reasons for suicide are antisocial behavior, delinquency, alcoholism, poor school attendance, poor work record, depression, loneliness, or indications of problems with social relationships. Many persons who attempt suicide do not really want to kill themselves at all. Their attempts are desperate acts to draw attention to their plight.

In the past a typical suicide was a younger mentally ill or depressed person, who in a state of loneliness or hopelessness ended his or her life. Today, suicide has taken a different turn. The papers are full of the new motivations for suicide. As the quality of life diminishes for older people, they make a pact with their mate or a loved one who assists them in a suicide. The law calls it murder, but juries are prone to dismiss charges against the killer in these so-called mercy deaths.

"The question of assisted suicide is so difficult," said Dr. William Gershell, a geriatric psychiatrist with the Mount Sinai School of Medicine in New York. "It raises many ethical and legal questions that society hasn't faced. But we're going to have to come to grips with it."

Sometimes couples who love each other very much make a double suicide pact. One couple left a note saying, "We have lived a long, full and rich life. We don't want to be separated by illness. We have had enough; we are going out together."

Today suicide is presenting new issues such as euthanasia, mercy killing, and disconnecting the life support system. It is common for people to let their doctors know that they do not want the hospital to use artificial means to keep them alive. We still have suicides from mentally ill depressed people, but the news today is of an increasing number of people who terminate life when its quality goes below a certain point.

The greatest gift of life is life itself, but people are also concerned with the quality of life, and the cornerstone of a quality life is good health.

The answer to the problem of euthanasia, mercy killings, double suicides, assisted suicides, and terminating life support systems is not in. My old-fashioned humble opinion is that when God is ready, He will take me. I don't intend to commit suicide. However, I have not spent long helpless hours of excoriating, seemingly hopeless, useless suffering. Who knows how I would feel? I cannot pass judgment on those who think that they have lived long enough and choose to terminate their life. It is wrong to me, akin to murder, but then again, I am not the judge.

The permissiveness of modern society, which implies greater tolerance of deviant behavior, may be partly responsible for the increase in suicidal acts, especially of self-poisoning. Society's attitude toward suicidal behavior has grown less moralistic and punitive. There is now a greater readiness to understand rather than to condemn, but a tendency to conceal suicidal acts still persists.

Among the elderly, unrecognized and untreated affective disorders, the presence of a physical illness, the stresses of aging, bereavement, and isolation are the most powerful predictors of suicide. Bereavement substantially heightens suicide risk.

A fatal suicidal act tends to cause grief reactions and guilt feelings on the part of those who may feel that they could have prevented it by caring and loving more than they did. If the act is nonfatal, it serves as an appeal for help and may give rise to efforts at reparation; it may lead to an improvement in the relationship to the person who attempted suicide. Conscious or unconscious expectation of these responses is one of the factors underlying suicidal acts.

Psychological theories emphasize personality and cognitive factors that cause suicide, while sociological theories stress the influence of social and cultural pressures on the individual. Social factors such as widowhood, childlessness, residence in big cities, a high standard of living, mental disorders, and physical illness were found to be positively correlated with suicide. The decline of the suicide rates in wartime has been related to the turning of aggression toward the common enemy and away from oneself. Social isolation is regarded as the most important causative factor in suicide.

Attitudes That Precede Suicide

Some people who complete suicide are feeling very angry, often at people near to them. This anger may or may not be justified. Others who kill themselves genuinely believe their families will be better off without them, and perceive their deaths as being a benefit. Still others feel abnormally guilty, ashamed, and deserving of punishment. A small number of people who kill themselves are out of touch with reality, and may hear voices telling them to do so. Nonetheless, all suicides are seeking escape from unbearable emotional pain. Some people kill others before killing themselves.

There is a chemical in the brain called serotonin, and low levels of a part of serotonin, called 5-HIAA, are associated with violence. In one study, people who murdered others were found to have lower levels of 5-HIAA than people who do not kill. The same low level was found for people who only killed themselves.

Do some people actually advocate suicide?

Yes. Some claim that people should have the "right" to kill themselves, and that they should be helped if they are unable to do it unassisted. They publish advice on how to kill oneself, and print the names of drugs required. They insist they are humanitarians fighting for the right to a "peaceful death." Their typical candidate for suicide is a person who is painfully dying from cancer. However, these people stress only the extremes--the choice is between peaceful death or unbearable pain. They do not consider the fact that the pain of cancer is relieved by painkilling medicine. Also, there is no evidence that very many terminal cancer patients wish to kill themselves.

We have today the Hemlock Society, an Oregon-based group that believes terminally ill people have the right to end their lives. By monitoring newspaper stories and medical journals, the society counted only 44 cases of assisted suicide in the six decades between 1920 and 1979. But in the 1980s alone, there were 307 such cases.

Some Answers

Early recognition and treatment of mental disorders are important deterrents to suicide. Since the 1950s special centers and organizations for the prevention of suicide have been created in many countries. The majority of times people who have been counseled out of the death wish are extremely grateful to the one who talked them out of it.

Rational and perfectly normal people do not kill themselves. Mood and seemingly insurmountable problems prevent the suicidal person from seeing any alternative but death. Almost always there is a rational alternative.

We must remember that each year about 200,000 people in the United States try to kill themselves. About 30,000 succeed. Those who fail often want to fail; an unsuccessful attempt at suicide may be a lonely, frustrated, or ill person's way to attract attention. You can never be certain, however, that someone who tries to commit suicide and fails will not succeed some day. So if anyone you know seems emotionally disturbed and threatens to commit suicide, try to get him or her to see a physician or counselor. If quick action seems necessary, call your physician, a local crisis "hot line," or a hospital for help. While waiting for help, encourage the suicidal person to talk while you listen patiently without passing judgment. Do not leave such a person alone; wait with them at least until professional help arrives. Disturbed individuals often seek death by taking an overdose of sleeping pills. If you find tablets or a medicine container anywhere near the person, be sure to give them to the hospital staff or the ambulance crew.

Danger Signs of Suicide

- ◆ Making statements about hopelessness
- ◆ Claiming that they are helpless to change things
- ◆ Talking about being worthless
- ◆ Bringing up the subject of suicide
- ◆ Preoccupation with death
- ◆ Loss of interest in things they cared about
- ◆ Setting their affairs in order and calling loved ones
- ◆ Giving prized possessions away

Aaaah...choo!

You are not alone-- an estimated 35 million Americans suffer from an unusual sensitivity to some substance.

An allergy is a condition in which a person reacts with various physical symptoms and unusual sensitivity to certain substances that don't affect most other people. These substances are called antigens and consist of various proteins. When these antigens (protein substances) get into the body, they stimulate the bloodstream to produce antibodies, whose purpose is to weaken or destroy the invading antigens. In some cases, when an antibody reacts with an antigen, the organic compound histamine is released from special body cells called mast cells. It is an excess of histamine that results in allergy symptoms.

Allergic reactions:

✱ Hay fever or allergic rhinitis resulting in a runny nose, nasal itching, congestion, sneezing, watering or itching eyes.

✱ Asthma in the lungs, resulting in shortness of breath, wheezing, and chest tightness.

✱ Conjunctivitis in the eyes, resulting in itching, redness, and tearing.

✱ Eczema (atopic dermatitis) with an itchy rash that often appears on skin creases of the arms, legs, and neck, but also can occur on most other parts of the body.

✱ Contact dermatitis on the skin with an itchy, oozing rash caused by substances such as poison ivy.

✱ Hives (urticaria) with itchy welts of different sizes that often may appear on the skin, lips, and inside the mouth or ears.

✱ Allergies may occur in the digestive tract with stomach cramps, vomiting, and diarrhea. Chronic headaches and fatigue can be symptoms of allergy.

Some people are allergic to certain substances and others are not, partly due to hereditary factors. Some families seem to be more susceptible to allergies than others. Emotional disturbances, too, can set off allergic conditions, and some physicians believe that in asthma an emotional factor may be the main reason for starting an attack.

Early diagnosis and treatment are important

If allergies are detected early and are properly treated, the condition may improve, be kept under control, and the possibility of more serious future complications may be reduced.

A physician gets a detailed history from the patient to find the most likely source of the problem, and may then carry out a skin test. Weak solutions of the substances that are suspected are injected into the skin. A red reaction indicates an allergy to that particular substance.

When the cause of an allergy is known, the patient can undergo desensitization with injections of the allergen known to cause the symptoms. Beginning with a weak solution, the dose is gradually increased over a period of months or years until a strong solution is reached and the patient is immune to its effects.

If the cause of the allergic reaction is not known, or if the reaction is already taking place, a physician may prescribe antihistamine pills or corticosteroid nasal and lung sprays to control the symptoms.

People often think of allergy as only hay fever, with sneezing, runny nose, nasal stuffiness, and itchy, watery eyes. However, allergies can also cause symptoms such as chronic sinus problems, postnasal drip, head congestion, frequent colds, recurring ear infections, chronic cough, asthma, stomach and intestinal problems, and skin rashes.

An allergist is a physician who specializes in treating people with allergies. Some ear, nose, and throat physicians may also treat people with allergies and are known as ENT allergists or otorhinolaryngologists. Diagnosis and treatment of an allergy patient usually involves three stages: medical evaluation, allergy testing, and allergy treatment.

The initial evaluation involves a physical examination and a complete allergy history. The allergy history includes questions about when and where symptoms occur, whether there are family pets, whether other family members also suffer from allergy, etc. These questions are very important because they help guide the physician's choice of allergy tests and treatment.

Based on your physician's preference, testing for your allergies will be done either by a traditional skin test technique called skin endrin titration (SET) or by a laboratory test using a sample of your blood. The most common blood test uses radioactive isotopes to identify the presence of allergy-causing antibodies in your serum, and is called the in vitro test. Usually just one blood sample needs to be drawn, and the test is not affected by most illnesses or by medication.

Inhalant allergies (allergies to substances in the air, such as pollen, mold, or dust) can be treated in several ways. Whenever possible, the patient is told to simply avoid the allergen (the offending substance). Medication such as antihistamines can also offer relief. However, when the allergy is more severe, allergy immunotherapy (allergy injections) is necessary. Allergy injections usually continue for at least two years, and about 70% of allergy patients benefit significantly from them.

Contact dermatitis, an inflammation of the skin, may occur possibly from wearing rubber gloves or touching anything that you are allergic to. A reaction to antibiotics, particularly penicillin, may be in the form of a rash. Allergic reactions to three native plants --poison ivy, poison oak, and poison sumac--have long been a source of misery to people. Recognizing these plants and avoiding them saves lots of misery. If you do get exposed, washing with water within five minutes can be effective in removing the toxic oil urushiol.

The best way to control allergies is to avoid the causes

You should try as much as possible not only to avoid the known causes of your allergy, but also other irritating substances such as cigarette smoke, paint fumes, and strong perfumes that may provoke or worsen your symptoms.

To avoid food allergens...

If you are allergic to certain foods, you should not only avoid the foods themselves, but also other food products that may contain the causative food allergens. For example, if you are allergic to milk allergens, you should avoid other dairy products such as creams and cheeses. Tracking down and treating food allergies may be difficult but it is usually rewarding. A cooperative approach between a patient and his allergist can usually control food allergy problems.

To avoid house dust...

Remove as much dust as possible from your home and eliminate or avoid household items that invite dust to accumulate. If you are allergic to house dust, it is likely you may be allergic to substances in the dust such as lint, house mites, mold spores, food particles, hair, feathers, and animal danders. It is therefore important to eliminate as much as possible these components.

Because house dust enters your body when you inhale, you should try to avoid stirring it up into the air even when you're cleaning. It is especially important to remove as much house dust as possible from the bedroom, family room, and other areas of your home where you spend most of your time. Reducing the amount of dust in a home may require new cleaning techniques and eliminating furnishings that are dust collectors. Wood floors are preferable to carpeting.

Frequent vacuuming is preferable to sweeping. A dust mop or cloth should be dampened with an appropriate cleaner to collect and hold dust. Air conditioners or electrostatic air purifiers can remove a large amount of dust and other airborne allergens. (Be sure to clean them regularly.)

To avoid household molds...

A mold is a fungus that thrives in an environment of moisture, organic matter, warmth, and poor air circulation. Certain food products such as cheese and dried fruit contain or encourage mold growth, and should be avoided.

Basements and crawl spaces are primary sites for mold growth. Some people think they avoid mold allergens by simply avoiding those areas. However, even slight air disturbances cause the dusty mold allergens to become airborne and circulate upward throughout the house. A dehumidifier may help.

To avoid animal allergens...

Animal allergens not only come from tiny scales of skin (dander) normally shed by animals, but also their dried saliva and urine. The major sources of animal allergens are household pets such as gerbils, hamsters, and birds as well as cats and dogs, and barnyard animals such as rabbits, cows, and horses. Like mold allergens, animal allergens circulate throughout the home as part of house dust.

Although it may be emotionally upsetting, successful control of your allergy might mean the removal of a pet from your home as well as the surrounding yard area. If not, the use of air filter masks and protective clothing may be helpful.

To avoid insect allergy...

An insect allergy brings about an overreaction of the immune system in a sensitive person. The salivary secretions of biting insects (such as mosquitoes, flies, lice, and fleas) or the irritating substances left on the skin by some crawling insects may lead to sensitivity, but it is the stinging insects that are generally the most dangerous.

Insect stings can cause a variety of reactions, depending on the type of insect, the amount of venom injected, the presence or absence of a specific type of allergy in the person attacked, and the site of the sting. A serious allergic reaction to a sting should be treated as an emergency. Epinephrine is given by injection as soon as possible. Adrenal steroids may be given in addition.

A person who is prone to allergic reactions from insect stings should always have emergency insect sting treatment at hand, such as epinephrine in a syringe ready for injection, antihistamine tablets, a tourniquet, and alcohol swabs for cleaning the injection site. A physician must prescribe these devices.

To avoid drug allergy...

One of the major public health problems today is drug-induced illness. Between 3% and 5% of medical hospital admissions are due to adverse drug effects, and 10% to 20% of patients hospitalized for other reasons have an adverse reaction to a drug prescribed while they are hospitalized.

The first step in treating drug allergy is identification of the offending drug. The second step is its removal; and the third step is to avoid use of the drug. Often this action is all that is needed. Treatment with several drugs in combination should be avoided if possible. Because the array of drugs available to the physician is growing annually, allergic reaction are an important consideration in the use of drugs.

To avoid pollens and outdoor molds...

The pollens of trees, grasses, and weeds as well as allergens from outdoor molds are virtually impossible to avoid. If you have an allergy to pollen, even a move to an entirely different part of the country may be of little or no help because you will tend to become allergic to outdoor allergens found in the area.

Although no cure for pollen allergy has yet been found, there are three strategies:

❶ Avoidance of the allergen. You should try to stay indoors as much as possible with windows and doors closed, particularly on hot, sunny, windy days. The use of air conditioners and air purifiers can remove a large amount of the airborne allergens that enter from outdoors.

❷ Medication to relieve symptoms such as antihistamines, corticosteroids, and cromolyn sodium. Many effective decongestants are available without a prescription. Ask your doctor.

❸ Immunotherapy, commonly called allergy shots. The aim of this treatment is to increase the patient's tolerance to the particular pollen to which he or she is allergic. Diluted extracts of the pollen are injected under the patient's skin to build up tolerance.

Whether you are allergic to indoor or outdoor allergens, the best way to control your allergy is to avoid the allergens.

Aaaah...choo!

Gesundheit!

Keeping yourself looking good

We senior citizens often think that, "youth is wasted on the young." As age with its vicissitudes descends upon us, there is an inclination to say, "what's the use," and give up the struggle to maintain our health and our looks. The battle is not over until the chief referee blows the final whistle. Until that time we are to play the game and keep ourselves in the best shape possible. How we look is very important. We can't turn back the years, but with a little care we can look better than if we didn't take that care.

Here are some problems that face the elderly and a few things that we can do about them.

SKIN PROBLEMS

Skin, known medically as inteugument, is the largest "organ" in the body, weighing about 7 pounds and covering about 18 square feet in an adult. It is something like a big baggie that keeps your insides from falling on the ground. It is a waterproof covering, a defense against damage and infection, a regulator of body temperature, and a sensory organ. The outer layer of the skin consists of dead cells that break away continually. They are formed as the underlying layer of living cells gradually grows outward to form the protective substance keratin. These two layers are known as the epidermis. Beneath the epidermis is the dermis. It consists of supporting connective tissue surrounding blood and lymph vessels, sweat and sebaceous glands, nerve endings, and hair follicles. Fat storage cells lie beneath the dermis.

This largest organ of the body is essential to immunity. It not only keeps the right things inside, it also keeps the wrong things outside. Very few infectious organisms can penetrate healthy, undamaged skin. That's why treatment of cuts, scrapes, and burns is so important. In addition, the skin produces fatty acids that are poisonous to many infectious agents. In fact, some germs' power to cause disease is related to their ability to survive on the surface of the skin. The skin is also a major factor in our appearance.

Aging skin becomes increasingly thin, more wrinkled, and less flexible. There is a gradual change in the nature of the fibrous and elastic elements that keep your skin supple and smooth. This and other physical changes are irreversible, and as the aging process continues, the skin may also become more susceptible to some skin disorders. In addition, many blotches and oddly pigmented patches tend to appear in old age.

ADULT ACNE can be brought on by sun exposure, which thickens the skin's outer layer and clogs follicles. When sebum stays in the follicles, bacteria breed and you end up with acne. Today's emphasis on keeping the skin smooth and young-looking may lead to overusing cosmetics, creams, and lotions that clog pores and follicles. Changes in estrogen or testosterone level in mid-life can result in pimples.

In women, an increase in estrogen levels will help, but you can't do that to men. Some doctors prescribe topical and oral antibiotics to fight inflammation or they use acne-fighting retinoids like Retin-A, which also reduces wrinkles.

BROKEN BLOOD VESSELS that typically appear on the nose and cheeks are actually tiny new capillaries. Sun exposure often stimulates growth but hormones do too, particularly after menopause. The primary cause is a rise in internal body temperature--from hot drinks, alcohol, smoking, and even hot baths. They're new little blood vessels that form because of the pressure to cool the body. Although removal is possible with an electric needle or laser, prevention is the key. Avoiding alcohol, scalding drinks, and long, steamy baths can help.

DRY ITCHING SKIN is another irritating by-product of old age. Skin itches when it dries out. An estimated 85% of older people develop "winter itch," caused by overheated indoor air that lacks moisture. Another cause of dry skin is the loss of sweat and oil glands with age; anything that dries the skin further (such as overuse of soaps, antiperspirants, perfumes, or hot baths) worsens the condition. Drinking too much coffee, or alcohol, or eating spicy foods, or exercising strenuously may make itching worse, because these things rob the body of moisture.

Severe itching can interfere with sleep and cause irritability. It can also lead to scratching, which can cause long-term skin irritation or infection. Wearing a rough fabric--such as wool--next to the skin can start a cycle of itching and scratching.

The best defense against dry skin is to drink large amounts of water. If you are bothered by constant itching see your physician, who may recommend an ointment or lotion to relieve the itching.

LIVER SPOTS, in spite of their name, have nothing whatsoever to do with the liver; perhaps they get their name from their color. Liver spots or "age spots" are small, flat skin patches that look like freckles and they may come and go and usually are not a cause for concern. Their medical name is "lentigines." They are most common on the back of the hands. These brown spots are caused by the accumulation of melanin pigment. Their color ranges from light brown to black. The cause of liver spots is unknown. There is no pain, no itching, no soreness--no symptoms.

They occur mainly on skin surfaces that have been exposed to the sun over a period of years. If you are 55 years of age or older, you almost certainly have them. They are "little fingerprints of Father Time." With time, oil production slows, elastic fibers weaken, skin thickens or thins, and bumps and discolorations appear. Dermatologists refer to the condition by terms such as "lentigo senilis" or "senile lentigines" meaning "old freckle."

Although liver spots can be unsightly and cosmetically undesirable, they have no medical significance. They do not become cancerous. The blemishes can be cosmetically masked or removed if they are objectionable in appearance.

Cosmetic counters have bleaches such as Esoterica or Porcelana that can lighten the spots. Skin specialists can eliminate them through the use of liquid nitrogen, which destroys the spots with a freezing action, but they can recur. The best way to discourage a recurrence is to minimize exposure to sunlight or use a high protection factor sunscreen.

RUBY DOTS, or moles of the blood vessels, commonly occur after the age of 40. They are usually tiny and flat but sometimes they become nodular, grow to the size of a dime, and proliferate. The only reason to remove them is strictly cosmetic. Early removal, usually with an electric needle, avoids scarring.

SEBORRHEIC KERATOSIS, or mole of the sebaceous glands, is the most common of all benign skin growths. They look like raised warts, range from tan to black, and can grow as large as a silver dollar. Usually they're found on the torso, where friction from clothing can lead to itching, irritation, and infection. They can grow quickly and change color, but they are rarely, if ever, malignant. To play it safe, have them checked by a doctor. They can be removed surgically or by scraping, freezing, electric cutlery, or laser.

SENILE PURPURA is a reddish-brown or purplish area, sometimes as large as 2 inches across. It may appear anywhere on the body. These spots are usually most noticeable on the legs, the forearms, or the back of the hands. These markings are caused by bleeding under the skin. Blood seeps slowly from tiny vessels that have become damaged by loss of elasticity in the skin. Most spots are harmless, but you should see a physician about any unexplained spot because of the possibility of skin cancer.

SKIN CANCER--Sun damage causes not only "premature aging" but skin cancer as well. The chance of developing skin cancer increases with age, especially among persons living in sunny regions of the country. There are over 400,000 new cases of skin cancer a year in the United States.

Common skin cancers are:
1. **Basal cell carcinomas,** which should be removed because they destroy surrounding skin.

2. **Squamous cell carcinomas** are more harmful because they can grow quickly and can spread to other organs.

3. **Malignant melanomas** often look like moles and are dark and irregular in outline. They can spread and kill; thus, **any sudden change in the appearance of a mole requires a visit to a doctor.** There are about 8,400 new cases each year in the United States. About 2,800 of these individuals will die within five years from the disease.

When detected early and treated promptly, most cases of skin cancer can be cured. Thus, the best defense against cancer is learning to notice its warning signs. These include the growth of a new spot or changes in a mole such as a difference in color, size, shape, or surface quality (scaliness, oozing, crusting, or bleeding).

SKIN TAGS are flesh-colored columns of skin protruding from the surface around the neck or eyes, under the arms or breasts, in the groin and elsewhere. Typically they're tiny but they can grow to thumb length. Skin tags are benign, but the sudden appearance of a large number of them calls for a medical exam. They are often related to obesity and diabetes, but some scientists suspect a link between skin tags and malignant internal polyps.

To avoid possible scarring, it's best to remove skin tags when they are tiny. Usually they're just snipped off with scissors; sometimes an electric needle or liquid nitrogen is used. Most tags don't grow back.

WRINKLES--Americans spend millions of dollars each year on wrinkle creams, bleaching products to fade spots, and dry skin lotions to keep the skin looking smooth and healthy. Yet, one-third of all adults work on developing a tan even though most know that sun exposure damages the skin. Exposure to sunlight is the most important single cause of those skin changes we usually call aging: wrinkling, looseness, leathery dryness, blotches, various growths, yellowing, and pebbly texture.

Long-term exposure to ultraviolet (UV) light from the sun weakens the elastic fibers of the skin, causing a loss of collagen. The breakdown of this fibrous network results in skin

that is looser, stretches easily, and loses its ability to snap back after stretching. So, while sun damage goes unnoticed in younger years, it will eventually show decades later. Most people will exceed their tolerance to sun radiation in 12 to 20 minutes of noon exposure in the summer. Others may not reach their tolerance even after 45 minutes of exposure.

Wrinkles are a major medical and psychological problem. The anxieties they create can spoil life. Why does a person get wrinkled? Underneath the skin is a supporting tissue known as the dermis. It contains water, fat, and cells that help produce fibers. The two most important fibers are collagen and elastin. It's these fortifying fibers that give the skin firmness and elasticity and make it bounce back after it's stretched into a smile or a scowl.

As we age, the dermis retains less water and fat, so the skin doesn't look as firm and plump. Fewer supporting fibers are produced, so the skin is less resilient. Less oil is produced, so the skin gets dryer. Cell renewal rate slows, especially in women past menopause. The skin receives less oxygen and nutrients as tiny capillaries beneath it close off. We begin to look old--creases appear, cheeks and neck sag, bags bulge out, spots show up.

Fortunately, there are a few things you can do to ward off wrinkles and guard against looking older than you feel.

* The dermis will definitely improve if you stay in the shade or use a sunscreen.

* Another dread enemy of the skin is dryness. Combat dryness by:
   *wearing a moisturizing night cream while sleeping;
   *in fall and winter hook up a humidifier, especially in the bedroom; and
   *hot water strips away your skin's natural oils, so take fewer, faster, cooler showers and baths.

* Avoid exposure to heat. Heat can penetrate the skin and damage connective tissues and fibers--the stuff that keeps your skin from sagging.

* Good nutrition is important for healthy, young-looking skin that's less likely to

crack, peel, or dry out. And healthy skin is less likely to show wear and tear.

❀ Dermatologists have often seen the connection between stress and all kinds of skin diseases--acne flare-up just before an exam, severe eczema during a divorce. Emotion can play havoc with our skin.

❀ James White, Ph.D., an exercise physiologist at the University of California in San Diego, declares that in his research, "people who exercise for 30 minutes a day will have fewer wrinkles than non-exercisers."

❀ Smoking deprives the skin of normal blood flow and increases the crow's feet and leaves the skin leathery.

MAINTAINING HEALTHY SKIN

■ **Limit your exposure** to the sun beginning early in life. Tanned skin is not necessarily a sign of good health but may be an indication that the skin has been injured. Try to limit sun exposure between the hours of 10 A.M. and 3 P.M., and avoid visiting tanning parlors.

■ **Wear protective clothing** such as hats, long-sleeved shirts, and sunglasses when outdoors.

■ Use a sunscreen when outdoors. These are an important protection against sun exposure since they greatly reduce the amount of ultraviolet light penetrating the skin. Sunscreens should be put on at least an hour before going outside and should be reapplied after swimming or sweating.

■ **Examine your skin regularly** for warning signs of skin cancer. If there are changes in your skin that make you suspicious, call your dermatologist right away. Dermatologists are doctors who specialize in the diagnosis and treatment of skin problems for people of all ages. They provide both surgical and nonsurgical care for conditions such as poison ivy (and other types of contact dermatitis), allergic skin reactions, warts and fungal infections, psoriasis, and skin cancers.

■ **Drink lots of water daily, use a good moisturizing lotion, bathe with soap less often, and raise the humidity in your home.** Also, protect your hands by wearing gloves for dishwashing, gardening, or other chores.

SUNSCREENS

What kind of sunscreen protection do you need?
Most people benefit from sunscreens with high sun protection factor (SPF) numbers, such as 15 or greater. The SPF number gives you some idea of how long you can remain in the sun before burning. If, for example, you would normally burn in 10 minutes without sunscreen, applying a 15 SPF sunscreen will provide you with about 150 minutes in the sun before burning. Swimming and perspiration, however, will reduce actual SPF value for many sunscreens.

Sunscreens with SPF numbers greater than 15 may benefit those who want to minimize their exposure to the sun, especially those who are fair-skinned, live in climates close to the equator or at high altitudes, work or play outdoors, or perspire heavily. Because skin irritations may result from various sunscreen ingredients, you may want to first test a product by applying a small amount to a limited area of your skin.

Do high SPF number sunscreens fully protect you?
Unfortunately, even sunscreens with high SPF numbers offer you less than full protection. Sunlight exposes you to two kinds of ultraviolet light, called UVA and UVB. Both can cause skin damage, including wrinkling and skin cancer.

Although virtually all sunscreens provide some level of protection against UVB rays, no product sunscreens out all UVA rays. SPF sunscreen numbers indicate sunscreen protection from UVB rays only. No rating system yet exists for UVA.

There is no way, then, to tell how much UVA protection you are getting. Some researchers estimate that the level of protection in many products advertising UVA protection, even those with high SPF numbers, is probably equivalent to an SPF 3 or 4. So, even if you use high SPF number sunscreens, you are still vulnerable to skin damage from the sun's UVA rays.

How much sunscreen should you use?
You will not get the full protection offered by the sunscreen unless you apply the recommended liberal amount on your skin. Unfortunately, many people use much less. A sunscreen with an SPF of 15 may give only half that protection if you do not use enough of it.

If you are on the beach, for example, use about an ounce of sunscreen over your whole body for one application. That means you should plan to buy about one 8-ounce container or more of sunscreen per person for each week you are at the beach.

If you frequently go swimming or perspire, use a waterproof product for the best protection. Make sure to reapply the sunscreen as needed during any outdoor activity; otherwise, you are not getting the protection you need from the sun's rays.

When should you use sunscreen?
Skin damage does not occur only on the beach or the ski slopes. Most people who are going to be out in the sun for more than 10 minutes would benefit from daily use of sunscreen on the parts of the body exposed to the sun. Even casual exposure to sunlight--while driving a car, walking to the store, taking an outdoor lunch break--contributes to the cumulative lifetime exposure that may lead to skin damage.

Make sure you apply the sunscreen about one-half hour before going out in the sun to give your skin a chance to fully absorb it.

If you are taking any medications, ask your doctor or pharmacist if these medications will sensitize your skin to the sun and aggravate sunburn or rashes. Common drugs that may do this include: certain antibiotics, diuretics, antihistamines, and antidepressants.

Are all sunscreens basically the same?
Sunscreens contain a variety of ingredients. Although some sunscreens may provide more moisturizers, those with identical SPF numbers give you equivalent sunburn protection from UVB rays. Because of the high cost of buying sunscreen products year-round, you may want to shop for competitively priced brands of sunscreen offering the level of protection you need.

How effective are sunblocks?
Do not be misled by sunscreen products that claim they are sunblocks. Only opaque substances, such as zinc oxide or titanium oxide totally block the sunlight. These products are most practical to use on specific areas of the body most exposed to the sun, such as the nose or lips.

Are indoor tanning devices safe?
Tanning devices, like natural sunlight, emit ultraviolet rays. These UVA or UVB rays, whether from artificial or natural sources, can cause skin damage.

Where can you go for more information?
Your doctor or dermatologist will have additional material on tanning and sunscreens. Further information about the skin can be obtained from:

American Academy of Dermatology
1567 Maple Avenue
Evanston, IL 60201
Phone (312) 869-3954

BALDNESS

About 30 million American men suffer from male pattern baldness to some degree. The hairline recedes from the temples in an ever-expanding u-shape until the top of the head is bare. In extreme cases, only a fringe of hair remains around the ears and nape of the neck.

For several years, Americans have spent over $300 million annually on ineffectual cures for baldness. But now the Food and Drug Administration has banned any lotions or potions that claim to prevent baldness or stimulate hair growth, except minoxidil, which was approved by the FDA in 1988 for use by men and is marketed by Upjohn under the name Rogaine.

In clinical tests half of the men who tried Rogaine saw at least moderate hair growth. There are disadvantages to Rogaine. It must be applied two times a day, forever, or the balding pattern resumes, and the hair that is generated often resembles duck down. It is also expensive.

Transplants for men (moving tiny plugs of hair forward on the head) and scalp reduction (closing up the bald spot) have been around for some time with various degrees of success. Some men can successfully improve their appearance by the use of hair pieces (wigs)--new adhesives have been developed to anchor them in place. Many men can accept baldness with dignity and even turn it into a certain charm like Yul Brynner and Telly Savalas. John Capps, founder of the Bald-Headed Men of America, says,

"We believe that we have found a cure for baldness, and that's to laugh about it and accept it."

Studies show that hair loss tends to be more emotionally devastating for women than for men since society deals with balding men as normal adults, whereas a woman with visible hair loss would not be viewed as normal. When Rogaine was first introduced by the Upjohn Company in 1988 it was approved by the government for use by men only while the company continued testing it on women. In 1991, the FDA granted approval for its use as a hair restorer on women. The Upjohn Company estimates that 20 million women in the United States are affected by androgenetic alopecia, which causes hair loss.

In women, baldness manifests itself with hair thinning over the entire head. Male pattern baldness typically leaves men with a bald spot or receding hairline. In women, as in men, the condition is caused by heredity, age, and the presence of the male hormone testosterone. Clinical trials show Rogaine may be slightly more effective on women than men. While men may expect to fill in an entire bald spot, women are usually just trying to fill in some thinning areas or stop progressive hair loss. Women, therefore, may be more easily satisfied than men with Rogaine's results because their goals are not dramatic.

OTHER FACTORS

There are many other factors in maintaining your looks after the age of 50. Sometimes a bout of illness, like cancer, can create a havoc of both looks and self-esteem. The American Cancer Society has an all-volunteer program called "Look Good ... Feel Better" that provides cancer patients with a chance to at least fight back on the outside while doctors are working on the inside. "Look Good ... Feel Better" provides free wigs, wig cutting and styling, turbans, scarves, makeup lessons, cosmetics, facials, and skin care information from certified cosmetologists and estheticians.

ATTITUDE is also essential to looking your best. Many people spend a lot of time and money to get that well-groomed look, only to spoil it by their facial expressions. Tension, anger, and worry are very aging. An attitude of happiness and appreciation shows on the face better than the best cosmetics.

A MOUTH TO SMILE ABOUT. My wife's sister, at the age of 70, had braces put on her teeth. The power of cosmetic dentistry today is awesome.

Things like beautiful eyes, healthy hair, manicured fingernails, and soft lovely hands are things that wise women have always been aware of. The other day, I was between my 16-year-old granddaughter and my 70-year-old wife. I was holding hands with both of them. My wife works hard in the garden and has arthritis in her hands; and yet, I swear, my wife's hands were softer and more delightful to the touch than my granddaughter's. You see, with a little care, we can maintain lovely features.

CONCLUSION

The rules for looking good are simple and fun to do: Keep yourself clean, keep yourself in shape, exercise, eat moderate amounts of good food, think positive, take time to be well groomed, and be friendly.

Asthma--cause, complications, and treatment

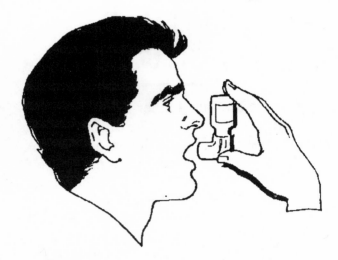

An asthma attack

Shoulders hunched, head thrust forward, chest bellowed out, desperation fills you as you struggle to push air out of your lungs and to acquire new air. Often, within moments, sweat pours from your body, trickles over your scalp. Your back becomes hard as wood. Your chest feels totally constricted. If you are wearing anything close-fitting around your neck... you want to tear it off. You wheeze, gasp, even moan... Friends and relatives watch... terrified....

Many of the estimated 9.6 million American asthmatics don't view asthma as a serious illness. But it is. About 3,000 deaths a year are attributed to this condition.

WHAT IS ASTHMA?--The word asthma from the Greek language means "to breathe hard." Asthma is a disorder in which the patient experiences difficulty in breathing, accompanied by a slight wheezing and a "tight" chest. Additional symptoms can be a dry cough and vomiting. An asthma attack may start suddenly, and the fear and worry that this causes can prolong the attack.

WHAT CAUSES ASTHMA?--Asthmatics are simply born with, or develop, extra sensitive bronchial tissue. There is nothing a person can do to avoid getting asthma. It is not caused by emotions, but emotions can make an attack worse. Asthma usually occurs as an allergy. Many pollens, molds, dusts (especially dust containing the house mite), and animal hair and dander can all cause asthma attacks. Infection in the respiratory system is another cause of asthma.

Exposure to cold, unusual exercise, fatigue, irritating fumes, and certain emotional and psychological states can also trigger an asthma attack; but the notion that asthma is all in the head is not justified, not helpful, and may even be harmful.

WHAT HAPPENS DURING AN ASTHMA ATTACK?--Air passes through the lungs via tubes (called bronchi) and smaller vessels (bronchioles). In an asthma attack the smaller bronchi and bronchioles become swollen and clogged with mucus to protect against substances that the body is allergic to or infected by. The swollen tissue causes the muscles surrounding the bronchioles to contract so that the air that should pass through is unable to do so. The body reacts to the lack of oxygen, and the patient forces more and more air into the lungs. But, because of the blockages, there is difficulty in exhaling it. The wheezing noise is caused by air being forcibly exhaled through the narrowed bronchi.

HOW LONG DOES AN ASTHMA ATTACK LAST?--An attack of asthma may last from a few minutes to several hours. The attack can come on gradually or suddenly. Frequently an attack occurs in the middle of the night. A severe attack called asthmaticus may last for several days. Hospitalization is recommended for asthmaticus, during which a slow injection of adrenaline may stop the attack.

WHAT IS THE TREATMENT FOR ASTHMA?--More severe attacks require that the patient sit upright. A table in front of the patient can be grasped and the arm muscles used to assist breathing. Patients should be encouraged to drink large amounts of liquids, even if they don't feel thirsty. Anti-spasmodic inhalants from aerosol cans may be helpful in relaxing the muscles of the bronchioles. When the cause of asthma is an allergy, antihistamines are used. Other drugs such as terbutaline (Bricanyl) can be taken in tablet form or in an aerosol spray. Aerosol sprays can be overused and cause a heart attack. A new inhalant drug called cromolyn sodium (Intal) has also achieved success in treating asthma. Appropriate medication should be taken prior to events known to trigger an episode.

OTHER REMEDIES FOR ASTHMA--A person with allergic asthma should sleep in a room without carpets or rugs. Blankets and pillows of synthetic fiber reduce the risk of house dust and mites. In dry climates, a humidifier can be used to increase the moisture content of the air in the room. If you know what is triggering the asthma attack, remove it--or yourself--from the area.

When asthma is caused by respiratory infection, breathing exercises can be taught by a physiotherapist.

COMPLICATIONS--Air is held in the lungs during an asthma attack and the air cells (alveoli) can become so stretched that the cell walls may tear, which causes a gradual loss of elasticity and can lead to emphysema. If the person coughs too much the surface of a lung may burst, causing pneumothorax. If the fluids in the lungs do not drain properly a person can get bronchitis and sometimes bronchial pneumonia.

A condition known as cardiac asthma has symptoms similar to asthma (gasping for breath, a "tight" chest), but it is actually a type of heart disease that requires medical attention.

More information about asthma can be obtained from:
The Asthma and Allergy Foundation of America
1302 18th St. N.W.
Washington, D.C. 20036.
Their *Asthma Handbook* can help asthmatics better understand their disease and perhaps breathe a little easier.

Oh, my aching back!

Anyone can get a backache, and 80% of Americans suffer from it at one time or another. On any given day 6.5 million Americans will experience a bout of low back pain that ranges from a dull, annoying ache to absolute agony. After headaches, low back pain is the second most common ailment, topped only by colds and flu in time lost from work. What helps one person cure back pain may have no effect on someone else. Experts often disagree on some of the causes and cures of a pain in the back. So, it is helpful to know a broad range of treatments for an aching back.

WHY DO BACKS "ACHE"?

- The majority of lower back pain is caused by weak or tense muscles and a program that emphasizes relaxation, flexibility, and strengthening eliminates most pain.
- Muscle strain or ligament or joint sprains can cause muscle spasm that results in pain.
- Improper lifting and sports that involve a lot of twisting can lead to ruptured or displaced disks.
- The sponge-like disks in the spine become smaller, less resilient, and more susceptible to damage with age.
- The bones become weaker and more prone to fracture in a condition known as osteoporosis (thinning of the bones).
- The joints in the hips, knees, hands, and back wear out and are more susceptible to arthritis.
- Tumors and infection can cause a backache.
- A herniated disk occurs when a disk flattens out and the gelatin-like material within protrudes and pinches a nerve.
- A worn facet joint may result in misalignment of vertebrae, causing vertebrae to grind against one another.
- Other causes include: rheumatoid arthritis, metabolic disease, circulatory problems, kidney infection, stomach ulcers, viral pneumonia, tipped uterus, infections of ovaries and fallopian tubes, cancer, pancreatitis, aortic aneurysms, and prostate problems.

ELEMENTS THAT INCREASE THE RISK OF BACK PAIN:

- poor muscle tone, so exercise
- a sedentary lifestyle, so move around
- incorrect lifting, so bend knees, not back
- too much driving, so park and walk
- poor posture, so straighten up
- heavy manual labor, so rest and slow down
- being overweight
- emotional stress, so calm down
- smoking may interfere with blood circulation to disks
- high-risk sports such as gymnastics or weightlifting
- weekend athletics

PREVENTING LOW BACK PAIN

- Warm up before exercising so joints are lubricated.
- Exercise. Do thirty minutes of low-impact aerobic exercise three times a week to release endorphins, the body's natural painkillers.
- Sleep on a firm mattress that doesn't sag.
- Don't wear very high heels.
- Lift properly. Bend your knees and lift with both hands.
- Don't strain the spinal column by carrying heavy shoulder bags.
- Use a pillow or "lumbar roll" to protect the curve in the lower spine.
- Stop and stretch every few hours on long car trips.
- Sit correctly, with hips all the way back in the chair, feet flat on the floor, and knees higher than hips.

- Stand straight, ears in line with your shoulders. Try to change your position at least every half hour.
- Keep back limber by doing five back bends several times a day. Place hands on hips and arch backward from the waist.
- Take a twenty-minute back break at least once a day, lying flat on your back with feet elevated.
- Strengthen your abdominal muscles with mild regular exercise.

SOME HOME REMEDIES THAT WORK SOMETIMES

- Bed rest, sometimes for as long as two or three days.
- Take aspirin, Tylenol, or ibuprofen as directed on the bottle for pain and inflammation.
- Have slow, rhythmic massages.
- Sleep on your back on a firm mattress, pillows under knees.
- Ice pack or ice cubes to painful area 15 to 30 minutes every 4 hours.
- Use mind over matter, relax, reduce tension, think pain away.

PEOPLE WHO CAN HELP YOUR ACHING BACK

The **family physician M.D.** or **D.O.** uses bed rest, cold and heat, muscle relaxants, or anti-inflammatory drugs. The D.O. (osteopathic physician) also administers spinal manipulation therapy.

Orthopedic surgeons use traction, epidural injections, a special corset, chemonucleolysis (an injection of papaya extract into a ruptured disk to dissolve it--although very controversial), and surgery (operations on the back should be considered only as a last resort).

Physiatrists, physicians who specialize in physical medicine and rehabilitation, can work out a treatment plan or prescribe physical therapy tailored to your needs.

Physical therapists use light, heat, water, electricity, massage, and mechanical apparatus to relieve back pain upon a doctor's prescription.

Acupuncturists are specially trained and licensed to use pressure as well as needles on certain key points of the body to relieve pain, but they don't change or modify the cause of the pain.

Chiropractors are trained to use spinal manipulation and physical therapy to treat back pain.

Mild flexibility exercises, proper diet, interest in life, and freedom from stress are among the best preventives and cures for back problems. A touch of happy news: Back problems become rarer as people reach their sixties and beyond because the vertebrae stabilize.

To relieve some of the pain try a product called "Mineral Ice" made by the Biopratic Group, Phillipsburg, NJ, or a competitive product with the same formula. It's available in most drugstores. My dear mother, who is 89 years old, swears by it and she knows back pain.

Correcting less-than-perfect parts of one's anatomy

In the quest to look better, millions of Americans are turning to cosmetic surgery. Each year, more consumers elect to have their faces lifted, their stomachs "tucked," or their thighs slimmed.

In response to this growing demand, many doctors now widely advertise their ability to surgically correct the less-than-perfect parts of one's anatomy. The majority of surgeons performing cosmetic surgery are qualified and perform successful operations. However, doctors with insufficient training or experience or questionable credentials are also attracted to this field because of the millions of consumer dollars spent annually on cosmetic surgery.

As with all surgical procedures, cosmetic surgery carries with it certain risks. If performed poorly, it can be disfiguring or even life-threatening. It is essential, therefore, to select a doctor who is well-trained and experienced in performing the specific procedure you desire. The following information may help you if you are considering cosmetic surgery.

How do you choose the right doctor?

Before beginning your search, you may want to learn more about surgical options by reviewing books on cosmetic surgery that can be found in your local library and discussing your plans with your family physician. If you decide to pursue cosmetic surgery, ask your physician for the names of qualified surgeons. You can also obtain names of appropriate physicians by calling your local hospital or consulting the Directory of Medical Specialists, available in most libraries.

Plan to consult with several surgeons who specialize in the type of cosmetic surgery procedure you want. While this may seem a considerable investment of time and money (physicians will charge a consultation fee), remember that if the operation is not performed properly, you could carry the scars for life.

Be wary of physicians who:
* suggest that you have features "fixed" that do not bother you,
* offer a "guarantee,"
* use a hard sell to obtain your business, or
* brush aside your concerns about safety.

In addition, no responsible doctor should mind your asking the following questions.

What is your area of specialty and what training do you have in the specific cosmetic surgery procedure I want?

Make sure the doctor you choose is well-trained to perform the type of surgery you want. Ask: Where did you receive your medical degree? In what specialty did you complete an accredited residency program? Ask for information on how this training relates to the specific procedure you desire, as well as information on any fellowships, workshops, and other education programs the physician has completed that may pertain to your operation.

Finally, find out if the doctor is certified by an appropriate medical board. A board tests the level of physicians' knowledge in specific specialties. Normally, before qualifying to take the exams in a particular specialty, physicians must first complete a formal residency training program in that field. Those who pass the voluntary exams are considered "certified" in that area of expertise. Confirm the physician's credentials and board affiliation with your county medical society or state medical board.

Where do you have hospital privileges?

Even if the surgery you want will be performed in the doctor's office or clinic, you should check to see if the doctor is on staff at a local hospital and has privileges there to perform the procedure you desire. Hospital privileges generally assure that the physician you select has been reviewed by his or her peers.

How many operations like mine have you performed in the past year? During your career?

A doctor may be skilled in facial surgery, but no matter how good the doctor's credentials, he or she may not be the best one to enlarge your breasts or perform liposuction on your thighs. Find one who has experience specifically in the procedure you want.

How many of your patients have needed additional surgery?

Additional surgery is sometimes needed to correct problems arising from the original operation. An ethical surgeon will answer this question. He or she also will answer questions about the likelihood of problems and tell you whether there will be an additional charge in the event that more surgery is required.

How safe is the operation?

Nobody can guarantee an absolutely successful outcome to any surgical procedure-- and you should be suspicious of anyone who does. All surgery involves some risk and unpredictability. Although rare, people have been known to die or suffer from life-limiting disabilities after cosmetic surgery. The surgeon you choose should explain all the possible risks and complications associated with the procedure you want, as well as their degree of probability.

What are the potential side effects of my surgical procedure? How long will they last?

Many doctors agree that patients are often unprepared for the side effects that may occur after cosmetic surgery. These include pain, scarring, swelling, bruising, bleeding, infection--or worse. Some patients may not be able to resume their normal activities for weeks after their operation. Be certain to have the physician you choose explain the potential side effects of your procedure.

What should I expect before, during, and after my operation?

Have your doctor and his or her nursing staff explain in detail what to expect at every stage of the procedure. If they are not willing to spend the time needed to address all of your questions and concerns, then you should probably look elsewhere.

Information materials such as brochures and videotapes should be available for you to read or view. Note also that if your physician uses "computer imaging" to show what changes you can expect from surgery, he or she should also tell you that drawing on a TV screen is very different from working with real flesh and bone. The computerized image you see may not be exactly what you get.

> A much more effective and lasting method of face-lifting than surgical techniques is happy thinking, new interests, and outdoor exercise.
>
> - Dr. Sarah Murray Jordan

The same is true of pre- and post-op photographs of other patients. Before-and-after photos may give you some feel for the surgeon's skill, but every patient's physical characteristics and experience are different.

Will you perform the operation yourself? Who will administer the anesthesia? Where will my operation take place?
Make sure that you talk to the doctor who will perform your surgery and ask who will take care of you after the operation. Find out what type of anesthesia will be used and who will administer it. Be certain the individual is qualified to administer the anesthesia.

Where will your surgery take place?
If your physician suggests his or her office or clinic, ask about the facility's equipment for life-support and other emergencies. If you are having major surgery, you may want to seek extra protection by making sure the facility is approved by one of the three accrediting organizations listed at the end of this article.

What are your fees?
Find out in advance what the procedure and follow-up care will cost. If your surgery will be performed in a hospital or ambulatory surgical center, remember that in addition to your doctor's fee, there will be a charge for the use of the facility and the services of the anesthesiologist.

Although prices range from a few hundred dollars for nonsurgical treatments, such as collagen injections to smooth wrinkles, to more than $10,000 for face-lifts and hair transplants, patients must pay most, if not all, costs themselves.

Insurance usually does not cover costs for elective cosmetic surgery, and many doctors require payment in advance. Therefore, you may want to compare fees. But just because a surgeon charges higher prices does not mean he or she is better than other physicians.

How realistic are my own expectations for this operation?
Most doctors consider the best candidates for elective cosmetic surgery to be those who are well-adjusted and emotionally secure. Ideal patients desire the operation to enhance their own self-esteem--not to influence the opinions of others. Although greater self-confidence may lead to other enhancements in life, consumers who hope cosmetic surgery will help add excitement to their social lives, win back a spouse, or obtain a promotion at work are often disappointed. Discuss with your doctor what you hope to accomplish with surgery and whether your goals are realistic.

Can I contact former patients who have had the same surgical procedure I want?
Talking to former patients who have had the same procedure you desire is one way to learn more about the operation and your doctor. But keep in mind that each patient had different physical characteristics and expectations. Although a physician may have had a good result with one person, that does not guarantee your surgery will turn out the same.

What are some common cosmetic surgery procedures and their potential risks?
Before having any operation, it is important to understand the possible risks and side effects. Following is a brief, simplified overview of some of the potential complications and side effects of common cosmetic surgery procedures. It cannot substitute for a consultation with a properly trained physician.

■ **Face-lift** (rhytidectomy): Although the results of a facelift can last five to ten years, the surgery will not stop the aging process. Following the operation, there may be significant puffiness and bruising for several weeks, and in very few cases, blood that has collected beneath the skin must be surgically drained. Some individuals may feel a temporary numbness or tightness in the face or neck. However, nerve damage that causes permanent loss of sensation or movement in the facial muscles is rare.

The scars resulting from the face-lift are normally in the hairline and folds of the ear, and usually lighten with time until they are barely visible. The kind of scars cannot be predicted with total accuracy, because everyone heals differently.

■ **Nose surgery** (rhinoplasty): Changing the shape of the nose is one of the most complex procedures, even for a skilled surgeon. If too much cartilage or bone is removed, the nose can look misshapen. Additionally, if care is not taken with the internal structure of the nose, you can end up with a nose that does not function correctly. Before the operation make sure you and your doctor thoroughly discuss what kind of changes you would like and how the changes will "fit in" with your other facial features.

It can take several weeks for bruising around the eyes to go away and several months for any swelling that occurs to completely disappear. You may experience some difficulty breathing for some weeks following the procedure.

■ **Eyelid surgery** (blepharoplasty): Performed to remove excess skin and fat above and below the eyes, this procedure usually causes bruising that fades within a week to ten days. However, discoloration can last for several weeks, and some people experience dry eyes. Although rare, the small scars within the lash line can become thickened and may be difficult to repair. In addition, the physician must be very careful not to remove too much skin, which could cause too much "white of the eye" to show.

■ **Breast enlargement or reduction:** Breast enlargement or augmentation has become one of the most popular cosmetic surgery procedures for women. In augmentation, silicone "bags" filled with salt water, silicone gel, or a combination of both are implanted to enlarge the breasts. Implants are sometimes used as well in operations to lift sagging breasts.

Perhaps the most common side effect that can occur is called "capsular contracture," in which the capsule of scar tissue that forms around the implant

Wrinkles should merely indicate where
smiles have been. - Mark Twain

Some believe surgery will help get a mate

contracts tightly inward, making the breast feel unnaturally firm. Some physicians have had success in preventing or alleviating this condition with such techniques as using different types of implants, placing implants under the chest muscle rather than over it, or instructing their patients to massage their breasts regularly. In the case of significant capsular contracture, further surgery may be needed, or in rare cases, the implants may have to be removed.

The presence of implants can make it more difficult to examine the breasts using mammography, but most physicians agree that if special techniques are used by an experienced radiologist, cancer detection should not be inhibited. Discuss this issue thoroughly with your surgeon.

With breast reduction or lift surgery (mastopexy), there will be some degree of scarring and there may be unevenness in breast size. You will want to ask your physician about this and other possible effects, such as a temporary or permanent change in nipple sensation.

■ **"Tummy tuck"** (abdominoplasty): The common nickname for this procedure--which removes excess, sagging skin from the abdomen--belies the fact that it is major surgery normally done under general anesthesia. An incision is made from hip bone to hip bone and, although it is located low along the "bikini line," a significant scar results. Full recovery, as with other major surgery, may take a couple of months or perhaps even a little longer.

■ **Facial wrinkles** may be treated by injecting them with collagen or fat. Neither substance produces permanent results, and collagen carries a small risk of allergic reaction. The longevity of the results depends on the patient's skin and reaction to collagen.

Although some physicians "plump out" wrinkles by using liquid silicone, this substance has not been approved for this purpose by the Food and Drug Administration, except in experimental studies at selected teaching centers.

■ **Liposuction** (suction-assisted lipectomy): To perform this very popular procedure, a doctor inserts a tube into a fatty part of the body and using a special vacuum pump suctions out unwanted fat, leaving a flattened area with little scarring. The growing popularity of the procedure has attracted many physicians with widely varying training and experience. There have been reports of blood clots, fluid loss, infection, and even death following liposuction. Make certain the doctor you choose is well-trained and experienced in performing this procedure.

Contrary to popular belief, liposuction is:

❏ Not a substitute for good routines of diet and exercise. Ideal candidates are close to their ideal weight, but have pockets of resistant fat on their hips, thighs, abdomens, or chin.

❏ Not a cure for cellulite, the popular term for the dimpled skin often found on the thighs.

❏ Not a solution for people with stretched-out inelastic skin that cannot redrape around the body contours.

If you are a good candidate and proceed with the surgery, you will need to wear a girdle or other compression garment until any bruising or swelling disappears.

For more information
If the physician you choose suggests that your operation be performed in his or her office, check with one of the following organizations to see if the facility has passed inspection: the Accreditation Association for Ambulatory Health Care, Inc. (708-676-9610); the American Association for Accreditation of Ambulatory Plastic Surgery Facilities (708-949-6058), or the Joint Commission for the Accreditation of Healthcare Organizations (312-642-6061).

After surgery, if you have a problem that cannot be resolved with the physician, contact your county medical society, state medical board, or your local consumer protection agency.

You may also report any problems to the Federal Trade Commission. Write: Service Industry Practices, FTC, 6th and Pennsylvania Avenue, N.W., Washington, D.C. 20580. Although the FTC does not generally intervene in individual disputes, the information you provide may indicate a pattern of possible law violations requiring action by the Commission or referral to state authorities.

WORDS TO PONDER
The popularity of cosmetic surgery is said to be a by-product of divorce and dieting. While dieting results in sagging skin, divorce demands that people, sometimes later in life, start looking and feeling their best. And what better way to build confidence than with a new head of hair or a new set of breasts?

Some people have no compunction about subjecting themselves to the pain and risk of plastic surgery for purely cosmetic reasons. Not everybody who has had plastic surgery is so enamored with it. According to one psychologist, even when the change is for the better, flatter stomachs and smoother faces do almost nothing to change an individual's relationships with other people.

One Los Angeles psychiatrist believes: "As far as I am concerned I am entitled to a perfect body only after I have a perfect personality. As soon as I am always nice, always patient, always insightful, then maybe it's time to start thinking about letting someone work on my behind and belly with a knife."

All kinds of beauty
do not inspire love;
there is a kind
which only pleases the sight,
but does not captivate the affections.

- Cervantes (1547-1616)

Some light at the end of the tunnel

You may first notice numbness or tingling in one or both of your hands. As time goes by, your condition may become painful, and you may find it more difficult to do simple tasks that involve your fingers and hands. Eventually, the tingling or pain in your hand may awaken you at night.

If you experience these symptoms, you may be one of the thousands of people who suffer from a common hand condition called carpal tunnel syndrome (CTS).

Named after the part of your hand where the disorder originates, carpal tunnel syndrome affects women two to five times more frequently than men. It strikes most often in your dominant hand when you're in your 40s to 60s. In some instances, carpal tunnel syndrome can cause permanent nerve and muscle damage. But even if you have severe symptoms, there is an excellent chance for complete relief.

What Causes the Symptoms?

In carpal tunnel syndrome, your median nerve is compressed at the point where it passes through the "tunnel" made by the carpal bones and ligament in your hand.

The median nerve transmits sensations and controls some movement of your thumb. The compression of this nerve results in the pricking, numbness, tingling, burning, or pain you may experience in your fingers and hand. In most instances, carpal tunnel syndrome affects your thumb, index finger, middle finger, and half of your ring finger. The tingling, numbness, or pain sometimes can radiate upward into your arm or even your shoulder.

People who have carpal tunnel syndrome frequently report that their symptoms are most pronounced in the morning and at night. Weakness and stiffness sometimes occur. If you have these symptoms, you may find temporary relief with self-help treatments such as hanging your arm over the side of the bed at night, rubbing or shaking your hand, or running warm or cold water over your hand.

In some cases, the median nerve can be compressed with the carpal tunnel by a ganglion (a cyst on a tendon), a tumor, or an inflammatory condition such as rheumatoid arthritis.

Carpal tunnel syndrome sometimes is associated with an underactive thyroid, diabetes, a fracture, infection, or rare disease of the pituitary gland called acromegaly (ak'ro-meg'ah-lee).

More typically, however, the condition develops when daily activities keep your wrists in a bent condition for prolonged periods. Tasks that can lead to carpal tunnel syndrome typically are repetitive in nature. Among these are writing, typing, drawing, driving, using power tools, gardening, wringing clothes, playing the piano, knitting, crocheting, or doing needlepoint. You may also develop CTS if you sleep on your hands or in a position in which your wrists are bent.

Diagnosis Is Relatively Easy

If you experience symptoms of carpal tunnel syndrome, one or several of these signs or tests may help make the diagnosis:

1 *Phalen's maneuver*--Your physician will ask you to place your elbow on a table top with your arm and hand in an upright position. He or she will then ask you to flex your hand at your wrist joint and hold it in that position for about one minute. If this test causes your symptoms to appear, it helps to confirm a diagnosis of CTS.

2 *Tinel's sign*--Your physician will tap lightly on your wrist over the median nerve. If the tapping makes your fingers tingle, carpal tunnel syndrome could be the reason.

3 *Electrodiagnostic tests*--These tests, which consist primarily of motor and sensory nerve conduction studies, are most useful for a definite diagnosis. These examinations are preformed in electomyography (e-lek'tro-my-og'rah-fee) laboratories.

Nerve conduction velocity studies measure the nerve's ability to send electrical impulses. They can be uncomfortable. However, these tests can accurately determine if electrical impulses are slowed as they travel through your carpal tunnel. If one of these studies determines that this is true in your case, your physicians will be able to make a diagnosis of carpal tunnel syndrome.

Treatment Options

If you're diagnosed with carpal tunnel syndrome, the first step in treating the condition is for you to stop doing the activities that aggravate your symptoms. Sometimes, you may only need to stop for a brief period of time.

In addition, here are several other methods of managing carpal tunnel syndrome:

■ *Splinting*-- 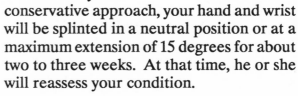 You can find relief from minor symptoms of CTS by wearing a lightweight, molded plastic splint that supports your hand and wrist.

If your physician decides to try this conservative approach, your hand and wrist will be splinted in a neutral position or at a maximum extension of 15 degrees for about two to three weeks. At that time, he or she will reassess your condition.

Some physicians recommend wear the splint at all times. Other doctors find many people achieve satisfactory results from wearing their sprint only at night.

■ *Cortisone (steroid) injections*--Injections of a cortisone-like drug into the carpal tunnel often provides dramatic, but limited, results.

■ *Nonsteroidal anti-inflammatory drugs (NSAIDs)*--This class of medications, which includes drugs such as aspirin and ibuprofen, can decrease inflammation enough to eliminate symptoms for some people.

■ *Surgery*--This treatment involves dividing the transverse carpal ligament so it no longer compresses your median nerve as it passes between the ligament and carpal bones.

For most people with CTS, surgery provides permanent relief without adversely affecting hand function or strength. However, it may take some time for the numbness to resolve completely.

Total recovery of normal hand function may not be possible if you've experienced numbness for several years.

Many people who have carpal tunnel syndrome in both hands elect to have surgery on one of their hands first. If successful, they then have surgery on the other hand.

Reprinted from April 1990 *Mayo Clinic Health Letter* with permission of Mayo Foundation for Medical Education and Research, Rochester, Minnesota 55905.

The anatomy of a headache

Forty-five million Americans experience chronic headaches. Sufferers make more than 50 million visits a year to doctors, children miss more than 1 million days of school, and businesses lose 150 million workdays a year, all because of headaches.

WHAT HURTS--Several areas of the head can hurt, including a network of nerves that extends over the scalp and certain nerves in the face, mouth, and throat; also the muscles of the head and blood vessels found along the surface and at the base of the brain. The bones of the skull and tissues of the brain itself, however, never hurt, because they lack pain-sensitive nerve fibers.

WHEN DO YOU GO TO THE DOCTOR--Not all headaches require medical attention. Some are alleviated with aspirin, over-the-counter drugs, rest, stress reduction, a cold cloth, and other home remedies. Those headaches that require medical attention include:

* Any sudden severe headache
* Headache associated with convulsions
* Headache accompanied by confusion or loss of consciousness
* Headache following a blow on the head
* Headache associated with pain in the eye or ear
* Persistent headache in a person who was previously headache-free
* Recurring headache in children
* Headache associated with fever
* Headache that interferes with normal life

HEADACHE TYPES--There are four major types of headache: vascular, muscle contraction, traction, and inflammatory.

I. VASCULAR includes the well-known migraine. This headache group is thought to involve abnormal expansion and contraction of the brain's blood vessels, thereby causing pain.

   A. Migraines afflict four times as many women as men. The headache is heralded by an aura, a distortion of vision that can be hallucinatory in nature. In both classical and common migraine, the throbbing pain generally attacks only one side of the head; victims often feel nauseated and vomit, and they may be exquisitely sensitive to light and sound. There are two types:

      1. Classic migraine--Ten to 30 minutes before a classic migraine attacks the person an aura is experienced. The person may see flashing lights or zigzag lines, or may temporarily lose vision. A person may have speech difficulty, weakness of an arm or leg, tingling of the face or hands, and confusion. The pain is an intense throbbing or pounding and is felt in the forehead, temple, ear, jaw, or around the eye. Although it starts on one side of the head, it may eventually spread to the other side. An attack can last one to two pain-wracked days.

      2. A common migraine is not preceded by an aura. Some people experience a variety of vague symptoms beforehand, including mental fuzziness, mood changes, fatigue, and unusual retention of fluids. During the headache phase of a common migraine, a person may have diarrhea and increased urination, as well as nausea and vomiting. Common migraine pain can last as long as four days.

WHAT CAUSES MIGRAINE--One theory of the migraine process: (a) A patient's nervous system responds to a trigger such as stress by creating a spasm in the arteries at the base of the brain. The spasm and the release of serotonin reduce blood flow to the brain. Blood-borne oxygen is decreased, causing the "aura" of neurological symptoms; (b) arteries in and around brain tissue then dilate or widen to meet the brain's energy and oxygen needs. Pain-producing chemicals are released and nerve endings on the scalp are stimulated. The patient then feels a throbbing pain in the head.

TREATMENT--During the ninth century in England treatment for migraine headache is said to involve drinking the juice of elderseed, cow's brain, and goat's dung dissolved in vinegar. Today we use: drug therapy, biofeedback training, stress reduction, elimination of certain foods, regular exercise such as swimming and walking, whirlpool baths, and cold packs.

DRUGS
* Ergotamine tartrate, a vasoconstrictor, helps counteract the painful dilation stage of a headache. It can cause nausea and vomiting so it is often combined with antinausea drugs.
* Methysergide maleate counteracts blood vessel constriction.
* Propranolol stops blood vessel dilation.
* Amitriptyline is an antidepressant.
* MAO inhibitors block an enzyme called monoamine oxidase, which blocks pain.
* Papaverine hydrochloride produces blood vessel dilation.
* Cyproheptadine counteracts serotonin.

BIOFEEDBACK AND RELAXATION TRAINING
Biofeedback can give people better control over such body function indicators as blood pressure, heart rate, temperature, muscle tension, and brain waves. Some patients who are able to increase hand temperature can reduce the number and intensity of migraines. Some people can learn to control muscle tension in the face, neck, and shoulders.

National Headache Foundation HOTLINE Mon-Fri CST 9am-5pm 800-843-2256; IL 800-523-8858

THE ANTIMIGRAINE DIET--By experimentation a person can eliminate headache-provoking foods and beverages. Other migraine patients may be helped by a diet to prevent low blood sugar, which can cause dilation of the blood vessels in the head.

OTHER VASCULAR HEADACHES

Cluster headaches are the most devastating. They affect men for the most part, striking with such excruciating severity they can drive the sufferer to violent acts, smashing walls and furniture, or even to suicide. Cluster headaches are named for their repeated occurrence in groups or clusters. They begin with a minor pain around one eye, eventually spreading to that side of the face. Thermographs will show a "cold spot" of reduced blood flow above the eye.

Toxic headaches are produced by fever or foreign chemicals in the body. For example, repeated exposure to nitrite compounds can result in a dull, pounding headache accompanied by a flushed face. Another example: "Chinese restaurant headache" can occur when a susceptible individual eats foods prepared with monosodium glutamate, a staple in oriental kitchens. Common household poisons like insecticides, carbon tetrachloride, and lead can cause headaches. Drugs such as amphetamines can cause headaches as a side effect.

II. MUSCLE CONTRACTION OR TENSION HEADACHE

is a type of headache that seems to involve the tightening or tensing of facial and neck muscles. Tension headache has always been a wastebasket. If it wasn't migraine and it wasn't cluster headache, it must be tension. The pain of this headache is usually more dull than sharp, and it often encircles the head like a cruel hatband. Tense muscles in the scalp and neck are generally blamed for the pain, and most of us get a tension headache at least once in a while.

III. TRACTION HEADACHES

can occur if the pain-sensitive parts of the head are pulled, stretched, or displaced, as, for example, when eye muscles are tensed to compensate for eyestrain.

IV. INFLAMMATION HEADACHES

include those related to meningitis as well as those resulting from diseases of the sinuses, spine, neck, ears, and teeth. Ear and tooth infections and glaucoma can cause headaches.

SOME OTHER TRACTION AND INFLAMMATORY HEADACHES include: brain tumor, stroke, spinal tap, head trauma (a blow to the head), arteritis (an inflammation of arteries).

Tic douloureux is a significant condition that results from a disorder of the trigeminal nerve. This nerve supplies the face, teeth, mouth, and nasal cavity with feeling and also enables the mouth muscles to chew. Headache and intense facial pain come in short, excruciating jabs set off by the slightest touch to trigger points in the face.

Sinus headaches may be caused by an allergy to such irritants as dust, ragweed, animal hair, and smoke or they may be caused by an infection.

The following is what the fine print says on the labels of some of the common over-the-counter headache remedies.
(Follow the manufacturer's instructions as they are subject to change.)

For temporary relief of **minor** headaches. **Severe or recurrent pain or continued fever may be indicative of serious illness:** Under these conditions **always consult a physician.**

ASPIRIN--5 grain tablets--Typical adult dosage 1 to 2 tablets with a glass of water 4 to 6 times a day as necessary, not to exceed 12 tablets in any 24-hour period. Active ingredient--dibasic calcium phosphate.

EXCEDRIN (Extra Strength)--Typical adult dosage 2 tablets every 2 hours as needed. Do not exceed 8 tablets in 24 hours or use more than 10 days unless directed by a physician. If pain persists more than 10 days consult your physician immediately. Do not take without advice of physician if under medical care. Active ingredient--acetaminophen 250 mg, aspirin 250 mg, caffeine 60 mg.

TYLENOL--500-mg tablets--Typical adult dosage 2 tablets 3 or 4 times daily. No more than 8 tablets in any 24-hour period. Active ingredient--acetaminophen 500 mg--contains no aspirin.

IBUPROFEN, ADVIL, NUPRIN, or **MEDIPREN**--200-mg tablets--Typical adult dosage 1 tablet every 4 to 6 hours while symptoms persist. If pain or fever does not respond to 1 tablet, 2 tablets may be used, but not to exceed 6 tablets in 24 hours unless directed by a physician. Active ingredient--ibuprofen 200 mg.

Traction and inflammatory headaches are treated by curing the underlying problem. This may involve surgery, antibiotics, or other drugs.

Some people find that their headaches disappear once they deal with a troubled marriage, solve their problems with finances or children, pass an exam, or resolve some other stressful situation. Stress reduction and the solution to life's problems and a good mental attitude can sometimes help even serious headaches.

More information can be obtained from:
National Migraine Foundation
5252 North Western Avenue
Chicago, IL 60625
Phone: (312) 878-7715

Hearing loss--do you hear as well as you used to?

The ear is the organ of balance as well as hearing. It has three parts: the outer, middle, and inner ear. The outer ear includes both the ear that we see--folds of skin and cartilage known as the pinna--and the outer ear canal, a passage about three-fourths of an inch long that leads from the pinna to the eardrum. The opening of the canal is surrounded by cartilage. This cartilage is covered with skin that contains wax-producing glands and hairs. The deeper part of the canal is lined by a thin membrane and surrounded by bone. The eardrum is a thin membrane stretched across the end of the outer ear canal. It separates the outer ear from the middle ear.

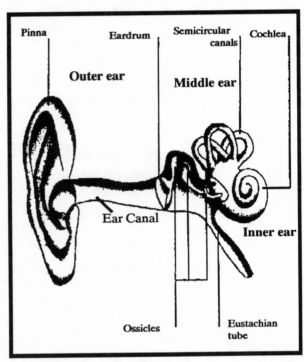

Ear has complex parts, some of which are used for hearing, and others for sensing balance.

The middle ear is a small cavity between the eardrum and the inner ear. It is bridged by three small, connected bones. These bones are named the hammer, anvil, and stirrup because of their shapes. The hammer is attached to the inner lining of the eardrum. The stirrup is attached by a ligament to the oval window, an opening that leads to the inner ear. The anvil lies between the hammer and the stirrup, and is attached to them.

There are various openings in the middle ear. One of these leads into the air spaces in the mastoid region of the temporal bone (the bone that contains all of the internal regions of the ear). Two others lead into the inner ear. One opening, known as the eustachian or auditory tube, leads to the cavity at the back of the nose. The eustachian tube permits equalization of the air pressure in the middle ear with pressure on the outside. Sometimes the tube becomes blocked during a cold. When it becomes clear again, the sudden equalization of pressure makes you feel as if the ear has "popped."

The inner ear consists of two structures that contain membrane-lined chambers filled with fluid: the labyrinth and the cochlea. The labyrinth is the part of the ear used for balance. It consists of the semicircular canals, three connected tubes bent into half circles. The cochlea, which plays a role in hearing, starts on the inner side of the oval window and curls around like a snail's shell. The auditory nerve attaches to the labyrinth and the cochlea, and connects the hearing and balance functions of the inner ear to the appropriate parts of the brain.

HOW YOU HEAR

A sound starts as a disturbance of the air, which produces sound waves. The visible ear helps to channel these waves down the outer ear canal, so that they hit the eardrum and make it vibrate. The vibrations pass through the hammer, anvil, stirrup, and oval window into the fluid in the cochlea. Tiny hairs that line the cochlea change the vibrations in the fluid into nerve impulses, which are transmitted to the brain along the auditory nerve. Most sounds reach you through this route, but this kind of hearing is supplemented by vibrations conducted through the bones of the skull to the inner ear. You hear your own voice mainly through this secondary kind of hearing.

HOW YOU KEEP YOUR BALANCE

Your brain constantly monitors positions and movements of your head and body so that you are able to keep your balance. In each inner ear is a structure called the labyrinth, which monitors the positions and movements of the head by means of three semicircular canals. Each canal is at right angles to the other two, so whichever way you move your head--nod it, shake it, or tilt it--one or more of the semicircular canals detects the movement and relays the information to the brain. The brain coordinates these data with more information from your eyes and from the muscles in your body and limbs to assess your exact positions and the movements you need to keep your balance.

PROBLEMS OF THE EAR

The Outer Ear

■ **Wax blockage**--Glands in the outer ear canal produce wax to protect the canal. The amount produced varies from person to person. The symptoms of wax blockage are a feeling that the ear is plugged, partial hearing loss, ringing in the ear, and sometimes earache. No serious risks are involved. Do not try to remove wax with a stick or swab. It is all too easy to pack ear wax against the eardrum and cause damage. The best way to prevent wax buildup is by wearing ear plugs while swimming or in dusty conditions. The physician may need to flush wax out of the ear.

■ **Infections**--Infections take two forms: a localized infection such as a boil or abscess, or a generalized infection that affects the whole lining of the canal. Ear infections can occur after swimming. Polluted water from lakes and rivers can cause infection by direct contact. Another cause is scratching inside the ear to relieve itching or while attempting to remove wax. The doctor will probably clean your ear with a suction device or probe. He may prescribe any number of drugs or an antibiotic or ear drops. While waiting for the doctor, aspirin or Tylenol may be helpful. Don't try home remedies if you have an ear infection.

■ **Tumors**--They may be either benign (unlikely to spread) or malignant (likely to spread and threaten life). On the visible ear, a benign tumor occurs as a painless wart. In the canal itself, it occurs as a hard growth of underlying bone tissue called an osteoma. With an osteoma, there may be no symptoms at all, or an accumulation of wax, discomfort, and hearing loss. Benign tumors can be removed in a minor surgical procedure. Malignant tumors located on the visible ear require either surgery or radiation therapy.

The Middle Ear

■ **Infections**--Infections are commonly caused by bacteria or viruses that enter the middle ear either through a perforated eardrum or along the eustachian or auditory tube from the back of the nasal cavity. The symptoms are a feeling of fullness in the ear, followed by severe stabbing pain. If the infection is bacterial, there is a danger that the eardrum may rupture or that the infection may spread to a portion of the bone behind the ear called the mastoid, which may result in an operation known as a mastoidectomy. Your physician may prescribe drugs to help unblock the eustachian tube and clear infection.

Chronic infection of the middle ear is far more serious than an acute infection. A chronic infection is slow, relentless, and can cause permanent damage. Pus produced continually from the chronic infection eventually causes a hole to form in the eardrum, and often damages or destroys the small bones of the middle ear.

■ **Otosclerosis**--It is an abnormal growth of spongy bone that can immobilize the base of the stirrup. As a result, the stirrup cannot transmit some or all of the sound waves that enter the ear. This causes conductive hearing loss in that ear. If your hearing deteriorates or you hear ringing in your ears, see your physician. The only treatment that will halt or cure otosclerosis is an operation called a stapedectomy. The surgeon will remove the diseased stirrup, and replace it with a tiny metal substitute. The eardrum heals in two or three weeks.

■ **Barotrauma**--Normally the air pressure in the middle ear is the same as the pressure in the outer ear. If a severe imbalance occurs, the eardrum can be damaged by the resulting pressure. This is called barotrauma. If you have a nose or throat infection and you must travel by air or change altitude quickly, use a decongestant spray or tablets. Suck candy or chew gum to encourage frequent swallowing. These measures will usually keep the eustachian tube open. You can also breathe in, hold your nose, and then try to force air up your eustachian tube by gently blowing out while keeping your mouth closed.

■ **Ruptured eardrum**--There are four common causes for ruptured eardrums: a sharp object put into the ear to relieve itching; an explosion; a severe middle ear infection; and a blow to the ear. A less frequent cause is a fractured skull. Some possible symptoms are pain in the ear, partial loss of hearing, and slight discharge or bleeding from the ear. There is a risk that infection may enter the middle ear through the rup-

ture. Your physician may prescribe an antibiotic and keep checking the ear until it heals naturally in one to two weeks.

■ **Cholesteatoma**--In cholesteatoma the eustachian tube, which leads from the middle ear cavity to the nose and throat, either failed to open properly in infancy or has become blocked due to repeated middle ear infections. As a result, the air in the middle ear cavity becomes isolated. Mild to moderately severe hearing loss is a common symptom. Sometimes pus will seep from the ear. Headache, earache, weakness of facial muscles, and dizziness are also symptoms. If the cholesteatoma is not treated effectively, it can eat away the roof of the middle ear cavity. If the cholesteatoma is small it may be possible to remove it and clean out the middle ear cavity thoroughly in a minor operation. If the cholesteatoma is large then the operation is more complicated, involving an operation to rebuild the hearing structure. If hearing is damaged badly a hearing aid may help.

The Inner Ear

■ **Meniere's disease**--In Meniere's disease there is an increase in the amount of fluid in the labyrinth, the part of the ear that controls balance. This increases pressure and the inner ear distorts and sometimes ruptures the membrane of the labyrinth wall. This disturbs your sense of balance. The main symptom of an attack is vertigo, or dizziness. This is often accompanied by noises in the ear and by muffled or distorted hearing, especially of low tones. In most people, the disorder is mild and clears up spontaneously. However, in a few particularly bad cases complete deafness occurs either in one or in both ears. The physician may prescribe medication to control nausea and vomiting. Drugs to reduce excess body fluid may also be prescribed. You may need surgery. In one possible operation, a surgeon drills a hole through the bone of your middle ear into the labyrinth to release the excess fluid. In about 70% of cases such an operation cures the vertigo and prevents further hearing loss.

■ **Labyrinthitis**--A virus causes an infection and inflames the labyrinth, which totally disrupts its function. The main symptoms are extreme vertigo, or dizziness. In some cases, there is extreme nausea and

vomiting. You will probably have to rest quietly in bed for several days. Most cases clear up completely within one to three weeks.

■ **Occupational hearing loss**--Prolonged exposure to noise at or above 90 decibels, especially if the noise is high-pitched, can damage the sensitive hair cells lining the cochlea, the innermost part of the ear. This may cause partial to severe hearing loss. Some occupations that are particularly hazardous to unprotected ears are heavy construction, driving a tractor, and working around very noisy equipment. Exposure to loud rock music over periods of time also endangers your hearing. Sensorineural hearing loss that is caused by damage to the cochlea is irreversible. Therefore, prevention is crucial. If you are exposed to dangerous levels of noise, you should wear suitable ear protectors. Ear muffs that are designed for the purpose are the most effective.

COSTS

Because hearing impairments have so many causes, it is important to be examined by your doctor as soon as you suspect a problem with your hearing. Too often, people with hearing problems fail to get medical attention until the condition is beyond help. Unfortuately, the high cost of hearing healthcare contributes to this neglect. Medicare will pay for the diagnosis and evaluation of hearing loss if requested by a physician, but it will often not pay for the means to correct it. In some states Medicaid covers some costs of a hearing aid. Before buying an aid you may want to contact one of the organizations listed on page 387. Many local chapters are able to provide information concerning Medicaid coverage of hearing aids.

IF YOU HAVE PROBLEMS HEARING
✳ See your doctor to determine the cause of your hearing problem. Ask if you should see a specialist.
✳ Don't hesitate to ask people to repeat what they have just said.
✳ Try to limit background noise (stereo, television, etc.).
✳ Don't hesitate to tell people that you have a hearing problem and what they can do to make communications easier. Most people are understanding.

Hearing loss--how to recognize it

According to the National Hearing Aid Society, nearly 21 million Americans are deaf or hearing-impaired. Liz White, consumer affairs specialist at the society, says, "Considering that approximately 80% to 85% of these people could possibly be helped by a hearing aid yet only 4 million are wearing one, only a fraction of those Americans with a hearing impairment are getting the help they need."

Many people who have a hearing impairment are afraid to admit it, or are unaware of the sophisticated communication devices available to improve their hearing. Present-day aids have come a long way from the ear trumpets used centuries ago. Today's state-of-the-art hearing aids include miniaturized, hard-to-see instruments tucked in the ear canal that are capable of more than just amplifying sounds. They're able to filter out background noise, change tonal quality, and adjust themselves to various frequencies. For those with a total hearing loss, or who otherwise cannot be helped with a hearing aid, an implantable electronic inner ear device called a cochlear implant may be beneficial.

RECOGNITION OF HEARING IMPAIRMENT

Hearing-impaired older persons, who account for nearly half of all those with a hearing loss, may even be considered confused, unresponsive, or uncooperative if their impairment goes undetected.

A hearing problem may exist if a person needs to:
* shout in conversations
* turn up the television or radio excessively
* ask people to repeat themselves
* favor one ear
* strain to hear

Other signs of hearing impairment include hearing a persistent hissing or ringing background noise, or not hearing such sounds as a dripping faucet or the high notes of a violin.

DIAGNOSIS

Hearing impairment can be related to many medical problems, such as viral infections, heart conditions, strokes, head injuries, certain drugs, tumors, excessive ear wax, or age-related changes in the ear mechanisms, or by a hereditary predisposition. Individuals who suspect they have a hearing loss should consult a physician. This type of physician may be known as an otolaryngologist, otologist, or otorhinolaryngologist and will attempt to establish the cause of a person's hearing loss through ear examination. The doctor may order several medical tests to establish a person's general health. A hearing test by an audiologist, a specialist in evaluating and rehabilitating people with a hearing loss, may also be ordered.

Audiological testing involves simple, painless tests to determine how well the eardrum and middle ear bones function to conduct sound to the inner ear and the brain.

The eardrum is a thin membrane shaped like a drum. When sound "beats" on the eardrum, it vibrates. Behind the eardrum is the middle ear. Though it's no bigger than the size of a large pea, the middle ear contains three "hearing" bones named for their shapes--the hammer (malleus), anvil (incus), and stirrup (stapes). When the eardrum vibrates, the vibrations move through the handle of the hammer bone to the anvil and then to the stirrup. These bones conduct the sounds as they are carried along. Their vibrations shake feathery hair cells in the cochlea, or inner ear, that are tuned to vibrate at different frequencies. These cochlear hairs are the ends of nerve cells that conduct the impulses along the auditory nerve to the brain, where the sounds can be interpreted into meaningful information.

One portion of a complete hearing assessment may consist of tympanometry. A person undergoing this test sits in a soundproof booth where a snug-fitting probe is placed in the external ear canal. By varying the air pressure between the probe tip and the eardrum at the same time that a tone is sounded through the probe tip, the audiologist is able to evaluate the function of the middle ear. The results are printed as a graph--the tympanogram. The same probe can be used to check a person's acoustic reflex to loud noises.

The audiologist may conduct further tests, such as an audiograph, to see how well a patient hears pure tones, speech, or other tones in each ear. As the loudness level is varied, a patient, usually wearing head-phones, indicates to the audiologist when he or she can just barely hear sounds. Through these tests, an audiologist will be able to determine if a hearing loss is conductive, sensorineural, or mixed, terms that reflect the location at which the impairment occurs.

TREATMENT

■ **Conductive hearing loss** can involve the outer or middle ear, where a problem can exist bringing sound vibrations to the inner ear. This type of hearing loss can often be treated medically or surgically. Common causes of conductive hearing loss may be wax in the external ear canal and fluid or pus behind the eardrum. Other causes may be that the eardrum is scarred or ruptured as a result of infection or trauma, or the hearing bones have become fixated.

■ **Sensorineural or nerve hearing loss** results from damage to the auditory nerve and often affects the elderly. Hearing usually cannot be restored through medical or surgical treatment. A hearing aid, however, is often beneficial unless there is a profound hearing loss. An audiologist can recommend a specific type of hearing aid and dispense the hearing aid or refer the patient to another hearing aid dispenser.

WHEN TALKING TO A HEARING IMPAIRED PERSON

❤ Wait until the person can see you before speaking. If necessary, touch the person to get attention.

❤ Never speak directly into a person's ear. This may distort the message and hide your visual clues (i.e., your facial expression).

❤ Try to position yourself about 3 to 6 feet from the person when speaking, not up too close.

❤ Speak slightly louder than normal, but don't shout. Shouting won't make your message any clearer and may distort it.

❤ Speak at your normal rate.

❤ Avoid chewing, eating, or covering your mouth with your hands while speaking.

❤ Do not exaggerate sounds when speaking. This distorts the message and makes it hard to "read" visual cues from your facial expression.

❤ Don't keep repeating the same message.

❤ Keep statements to short sentences.

❤ Treat the hearing impaired with respect. Include the person in all discussions.

Tuning in on hearing aids

Though designs may differ somewhat, most hearing aids work in a similar manner. A hearing aid is a miniature, battery-powered sound amplifier system with a microphone that picks up sound waves and converts them into electrical signals. An amplifier then increases the strength of the signal, and a receiver changes the electrical signals back to sound waves and sends them into the ear canal. A "monaural" system consists of a hearing aid for one ear; a "binaural" system uses two hearing aids.

Hearing aids are designed for different degrees of hearing loss.

◆ **In-the-canal** hearing aids are custom-made to fit directly in the ear canal and have no external wires or tubes. Roughly 75% of all hearing aids sold today are of this type.

◆ **Behind-the-ear** hearing aids are housed in small, curved cases that fit behind the earlobe and carry sound to the ear through a custom ear mold. They are beneficial for essentially all degrees of hearing loss.

◆ **Eyeglass** hearing aids are a version of behind-the-ear aids. They are built into an eyeglass frame.

◆ **Body** hearing aids can often be more powerful than the others and are used primarily for the most severe hearing losses. They have larger microphones, amplifiers, and power supplies, and the aids are enclosed in cases that can be carried in pockets or attached onto clothing and are connected by a wire to an ear receiver that is attached directly to the ear mold.

◆ **Bone-conduction** hearing aids can be used by a person with a deformity of the external ear or other medical condition that interferes with wearing a conventional hearing aid. An external oscillator that transmits sound may be worn behind the ear by attaching it to a headband or eyeglasses. With one version of this device, a small transmitter is surgically implanted in the skull. When activated by a small, external processor, the transmitter sends sound waves directly through the skull to the inner ear.

◆ Another device is a **vibrotactile** or electrotactile hearing aid. The skin is sensitive to stimulation over a range of frequencies. With this type of device, which is worn on the body, a wearer can learn to interpret stimulation as words and sentences.

◆ If a person's cochlear hair cells do not function at all, no hearing aid will help. A **cochlear implant** may improve the quality of life for people with this nerve damage. In the cochlear implant, a tiny audio receiver is implanted in the bone behind the ear. Hairlike platinum wires connect the receiver to a special electrode with either one channel or 22 channels. The wires and electrodes are surgically inserted into the cochlea, or inner ear. The external portion of the system is a microphone and a transmitter on a lightweight headband. These are then connected by wires to a speech processor--a miniature computer--worn in a shoulder pouch or pocket or on a belt.

The microphone picks up sounds and relays them to the speech processor, which is custom-tuned by an audiologist to transmit those sounds that will help the patient interpret speech. The sounds are sent from the speech processor to the external transmitter, which then sends the impulses across the skin to the implanted receiver and on to the inner ear. There, the electrodes assist damaged sensory cells in stimulating the auditory nerve, which relays the signals to the brain, where they are interpreted. There is great variability with results of this implant. Some people are well-pleased and others find it too difficult to adapt to the technique.

One of the greatest benefits of hearing aids today is that they are becoming ever smaller and many are programmable, allowing a user to make fine adjustments instead of replacing them when their hearing changes.

> **Hopes
> are but the dreams
> of those who are awake.**
>
> - Pindar (518?-438 B.C.)

PROBLEMS WITH PRODUCTS

Many problems have come from sellers of mail-order hearing aids. In most states, dispensers of hearing aids are licensed. An FDA regulation of August 25, 1977, requires a seller to obtain a written statement from you signed by a licensed physician stating that your hearing ability has been medically evaluated (within 6 months of the sale) and you need an aid. The seller may ask you to sign a waiver of the medical evaluation requirement but must warn you that the medical evaluation is in your best interest.

Sellers must also advise you to consult a physician promptly if they find any of these conditions: visible or congenital or traumatic deformity of the ear; history of active drainage within the last 90 days; acute or chronic dizziness; hearing loss within the last 90 days of sudden or recent onset; visible evidence of significant accumulation of wax or presence of a foreign body; pain or discomfort in the ear; or audiometric air-bone gap equal to or greater than 15 decibles at 500, 1000, and 2000 hertz. (Hertz is a measure of sound frequency.)

If you have problems with sellers of hearing aids you should report them to the nearest FDA District Office listed in your phone directory. Investigators will visit the seller and audit the sale. Violations of the laws carry a $1,000 fine or 1 year in jail. You can also call your State Attorney General.

WHERE TO GET INFORMATION ON HEARING AND HEARING AIDS

Nat'l. Information Center on Deafness
Gallaudet University
800 Florida Ave. N.E.
Washington, D.C. 20002
(202) 651-5051

Amer. Speech-Language-Hearing Assoc.
10801 Rockville Pike, Dept. AP
Rockville, MD 20852

Nat'l. Assoc for Hearing & Speech Action
1-800-638-8255

Self-Help for Hard of Hearing People
4848 Battery Lane, Dept. E
Bethesda, MD 20814

When you write, state clearly what type of information you would like to receive.

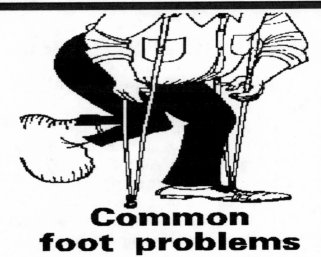

Common foot problems

Many people think it is normal for feet to hurt, but it is not. Foot disorders can be cured before they become severe. Eight out of ten Americans will have a foot problem at some time in their lives serious enough to make walking difficult or impossible. Of course your own doctor or podiatrist is your best bet for foot care, but sometimes it can be done at home with nonprescription supplies from the local drugstore. It is good to know the common foot ailments and what you can do about them.

Most common foot problems may result from disease, long years of wear and tear, ill-fitting or poorly designed shoes, poor circulation to the feet, or toenails that are not properly trimmed. (See also Diabetics, page 301).

ATHLETE'S FOOT: This fungal infection is found primarily between the toes, where the foot is most moist. People whose feet perspire heavily are more susceptible to it than others. It will not go away on its own and, if not cured, can lead to chronic infection that is very difficult to cure. In severe cases, consult your doctor.

Home treatment: To prevent infection keep the feet--especially the area between the toes--clean and dry and expose the feet to sun and air whenever possible. Carefully dry between toes after bathing or removing shoes. Apply a topical antifungal preparation such as Tinactin or Desenex daily. Soak your feet three times a week for 15 minutes in a solution of 2 teaspoons baking soda to 1 quart warm water. Change your socks twice a day, and avoid colored socks because dyes can aggravate the condition.

PLANTAR WARTS: These warts grow inward instead of outward because of the weight of the body. They are skin growths caused by viruses. A doctor may apply medicines, remove the wart surgically, or--using anesthesia--burn or freeze it off.

Are your feet killing you?

Home treatment: Soak the foot for 10 minutes in 2 tablespoons of mild household detergent mixed with one-half gallon of warm water. Then cut out a square of 40% salicylic-acid plaster about the size of the wart. The plaster can be bought over the counter at the pharmacy. Remove tape from the sticky side and apply directly to the wart, and then cover it with adhesive tape or a bandage. Remove the plaster in two days and brush the wart vigorously for one minute twice a day for two days with a toothbrush moistened with soap and water. Repeat the process for two weeks or until the wart is gone.

CORNS: These hard, thickened areas on the toe are round and yellow or sometimes red if inflamed. The more a corn rubs against your shoe, the faster it grows. The larger it gets, the more painful it is. So it's a good idea to get rid of it as soon as you can. A podiatrist or a physician can determine the cause of corns and can recommend treatment, which may include obtaining better-fitting shoes or wearing special pads.

Home treatment: Immediately start wearing shoes looser in the toe. Soak your foot in Epsom salts for 15 minutes a day, and then apply moisturizing cream. Cover the corn with a gauze pad, and then wrap your foot in plastic for 15 minutes. Remove the plastic and pad and rub area in a side-to-side motion with a pumice stone. Repeat this daily until the corn disappears.

SMELLY FEET: This problem is usually caused by bacteria or by a fungus infection. It's especially common among people whose feet perspire excessively.

Home treatment: Thoroughly scrub feet daily using a wash cloth with a solution of warm water and laundry detergent--rinse and dry well (a hair dryer is effective to dry feet). Powder feet liberally with medicated foot powder such as Tinactin or Aftate, taking special care to powder all spaces between toes. If this is ineffective, apply Mitchum's roll-on deodorant to a clean, dry foot bottom and cover with plastic wrap and wear with a sock overnight. Wash in the morning, and repeat nightly for one week, then once or twice a week, as needed.

CALLUSES: These usually develop on the bottom of the foot or bottom of the heel due to extra pressure from obesity or improper walking or standing. They are caused by the friction and pressure from bony areas rubbing against shoes. Layers of compact, dead skin cells build up, and the pressure of this hard mass on sensitive nerves in the skin can be painful. Treating calluses yourself can be harmful if you have diabetes or poor circulation.

Home Treatment: Crush five aspirin tablets into a powder. Mix with 1 teaspoon water and 1 teaspoon lemon juice into a paste. Apply to callus, then wrap a plastic bag around foot for 15 minutes. Remove the plastic and use a pumice stone to slough off dead tissue. Repeat two to three times weekly until callus is gone. If callus is caused by walking or standing problems it may be necessary to seek professional help to prevent recurrence.

INGROWN TOENAILS: This occurs when a piece of the nail pierces the skin and allows bacteria in. Ingrown toenails are caused by improper trimming of the nails, picking at your toenails, cutting the nails at an angle, wearing tight pantyhose or socks, or cutting the cuticles along the side of the nail.

Treatment: Ingrown toenails can usually be avoided by cutting the toenail straight across and level with the top of the toe. Apply an antibacterial cream such as Neosporin on the area until pain goes away and the nail grows out. Of course, avoid tight pantyhose or socks.

THICK TOENAILS: A thick toenail can result from an injury or fungus infection. It may turn dirty-yellow or brown with some blackened areas and be unsightly. It may also have an unpleasant odor.

Home Treatment: Thoroughly clean and dry the foot. Cut nail straight across with nail clippers. Clean under and around nail with the point of a nail file covered with a wisp of cotton. Cut a piece of 40% salicylic-acid plaster the size and shape of the nail. Apply to nail and wrap in an adhesive bandage. Keep toe dry for two days. Remove plaster and brush with a nailbrush or a toothbrush. Cut down as much of the nail as possible. Clean with warm, soapy water and apply an antiseptic solution such as Merthiolate. Repeat this three or four times.

I felt sorry for myself as I had no shoes. Until I met a man who had no feet.

More on feet

BUNIONS: Bunions occur when big toe joints are out of line and become swollen and tender. Bunions may result from ill-fitting shoes pressing on a deformity or from an inherited weakness in the foot. If a bunion is not severe, wearing shoes that are wide at the instep and the toes may provide relief. Protective pads can also be used to cushion the painful area.

Treatment: There are several methods for treating bunions, including the application or injection of certain drugs, or whirlpool baths or surgery. See your doctor about bunions.

HAMMERTOE: This results from a shortening of the tendons that control the movements of the toes. The knuckle of the toe is usually enlarged, and the toe is often drawn back. Over a period of time the joint enlarges and stiffens as it rubs against the shoe. This can cause a loss of balance since the affected toes provide less assistance in standing and walking. Hammertoe is treated by wearing shoes and stockings with plenty of toe room. In advanced cases, surgery is generally recommended.

SPURS: These are calcium growths that develop on bones of the foot. They are caused by strain on the muscles of the foot and are aggravated by prolonged standing, having improperly fitting shoes, or being overweight. Sometimes they are completely painless; at other times the pain can be severe. Treatments for spurs include proper foot support, heel pads, heel cups, drug injections, and occasionally surgery.

Please Note:

DIABETES makes people prone to sores and infections on their feet. Diabetics should be especially careful to avoid extremely hot or cold bath water, keep their feet clean and dry, and to be careful not to cut themselves when trimming toenails. Diabetics should seek immediate medical attention for any cut or injury to the foot, including removal of minor corns and ingrown toenails. Diabetics often have decreased sensation in their feet and can have life-threatening injuries or infections without being aware--diabetics should see a podiatrist every month.

For more information write to:
American Podiatric Medical Association
20 Chevy Chase Circle, N.W.
Washington, D.C. 20015

Standing against leg cramps

Both my mother and my father experienced leg cramps, usually in the middle of the night. I will never forget the moaning and groaning and loud cries of anguish and thumping on the floor that awakened the household. The next day my father would describe the sharp, shooting, excruciating pain in his lower leg that defied his efforts to massage it away. The only way to stop the spasm was to stand up and walk, thumping his foot against the floor. Later in her life my mother carried a bottle of liquid calcium, which she claimed helped her when she was writhing in pain from leg cramps.

Occasional leg cramps afflict millions of Americans, although no one knows exactly how often they occur or why. Cramps may result from overexertion, medical conditions such as diabetes, or reaction to medication.

Leg cramps seem to occur most commonly in athletes and others who exercise strenuously, in people who have reached middle age and beyond, and in those who suffer circulatory problems. They occur most often at night or when resting. Cramps are particularly common among older or "weekend" athletes, who are less active and less likely to warm up first. Leg and foot muscles are not the only ones that cramp. People who write a lot using pen or pencil often get hand cramps, and those who play the cello or violin may get arm cramps.

In order for the body to move, muscles must contract and expand. This involves an impulse signal from the brain to the spinal cord. The signal travels down a nerve and across a short break called a synapse using acetylcholine, a chemical "neurotransmitter." When the signal for contraction reaches the muscles, proteins inside the muscle fibers slide over each other much like a sliding door, and cause a contraction, a shortening and thickening of the muscle. A cramp or spasm occurs when the electrical impulses from the brain occur very rapidly, causing the muscle to contract in a sudden, disorganized and uncontrollable fashion. The contraction is affected by basic minerals inside the muscle fiber, mostly potassium, sodium, and calcium.

CAUSES OF MUSCLE CRAMPS

Poor circulation: When there is not enough blood flow to a muscle, it will cause a person to have a cramp-like pain, usually involving the calf muscles and, in some cases, the foot. The cause is usually from fatty cholesterol deposits in the arteries.

Fatigue: When a muscle is overworked, it responds more readily to contraction stimulation. Irritating chemicals that are normally cleared from the muscles accumulate and affect their function.

Mineral balance: Changes in sodium, potassium, and calcium can all affect muscle contraction and cause cramps. People who work or exercise hard enough to sweat will lose a lot of sodium, and when water is consumed a lot of muscle cramps from lack of sodium will be experienced. Calcium deficiency is also a common underlying factor in muscle cramps.

Cold: Body temperature is an important factor in causing muscle contractions, spasms, and cramps. A swimmer may have more trouble with muscle cramps when he swims in cold water, or when he doesn't swim hard enough to generate body heat.

Nerve pressure: Some cases of leg cramps are caused by compression of spinal nerves. Where the nerve emerges from the spine, a bone spur may compress the nerve. The irritation is likely to stimulate the many fibers inside the nerve, and cause very painful muscle contraction.

Mechanical factors: When the toes are pointed down, it causes the calf muscles to be shortened. In a sense, the calf muscles are already in a semi-contracted state. This invites progression of muscle contraction, or the nocturnal leg cramps.

Local factors: When there is an increased release of acetylcholine at the junction of motor nerve fibers and the cell membrane, the muscle fibers' response to stimulation may increase leg cramps.

Managing "restless" legs

Nerve hyperactivity: Anything that stimulates nerve cells can increase the susceptibility to cramps. A variety of neurological disorders can be responsible. So can taking any medicines that increase nervous activity. A tense individual may have a hyperactive nervous system, which, in turn, tends to send discharges to the motor nerve cells in the spinal cord.

Combinations: Often there is a combination of factors related to frequent leg cramps. Not only are the toes pointed down during sleep, but also the leg cools. Both factors combine to increase a person's susceptibility to nocturnal leg cramps. Changes in mineral balance, plus cooling of the legs at night, work together to increase cramping. Nighttime cooling, combined with an overactive nervous system, may be the right combination to induce leg cramps.

> Note: Not all leg cramps are easily treated. Some result from serious medical conditions and are not helped by home remedies. Check with your doctor to ensure safe treatment.

MANAGING MUSCLE CRAMPS

❶ Usually, the most effective thing you can do for immediate relief is to stretch the cramped muscle. As the muscle is stretched,

> Usually, the most effective thing you can do for immediate relief is to stretch the cramped muscle!

the nerve fibers that transmit the stretch signal to the spinal cord literally inhibit the nerve cells that stimulate contraction. **Almost everyone who has nocturnal leg cramps has learned that getting out of bed and standing on the ball of the foot to stretch the cramped calf muscle can abort the cramps.**

❷ A strong effort to pull the toes up as far as possible can often abort a developing muscle cramp.

❸ Some people seem to have success massaging the area with ice; some find that warming the muscle helps.

❹ Stretching the calf muscles frequently, especially before going to bed, is a big help in preventing leg cramps in many people. Stretch the tendons as much as you can without pain. Do the same exercise with your knees bent. Relax and repeat several times.

❺ Don't sleep with your toes pointed down. Put a board at the foot of your bed. Put it on

its edge, and be sure to use one wide enough to hold up the covers at the foot of the bed. Put a pillow against the board; then you can prop your feet against the pillow to hold your toes up.

❻ One of the most useful, practical things to do to prevent nocturnal leg cramps is to keep your feet and legs warm. Good, warm, wool socks that come up over the calf help many people.

> While some leg cramp attacks are mild, you can often be faced with agonizing pain resulting in the loss of sleep for you and others around you.
>
> If you are one out of the seven people over the age of 45 who experience this problem, you might find help with quinine.
>
> Quinine sulfate (1 grain or 65 mg) tablets are available for leg cramps as a nonprescription drug.

❼ A variety of medicines are helpful in preventing nocturnal cramps. If a person is low in sodium, potassium, or calcium, replacing them will help. Increasing milk intake will usually get enough calcium. Quinine that is used for heart irregularities sometimes decreases the excitability of skeletal muscle, too. Vitamin E has been useful in decreasing leg cramps. Also, any medicines that decrease excessive nerve irritability may help, including tranquilizers. But stretching, keeping your legs warm, and replacing your minerals, such as calcium, are a lot less likely to disturb your physiology than any medicines.

Quinine preparations are available over-the-counter (OTC), but a physician should be consulted to make sure the problem is not a limb-threatening peripheral vascular disease (from smoking, diabetes, etc.).

❽ Surgery does have a place in some cases of leg cramps. When bone spurs are compressing spinal nerves, it may be necessary to remove them or take other surgical measures to remove the pressure. When muscle cramps are related to obstruction of arteries to the legs, the problem can be solved by removing the obstruction.

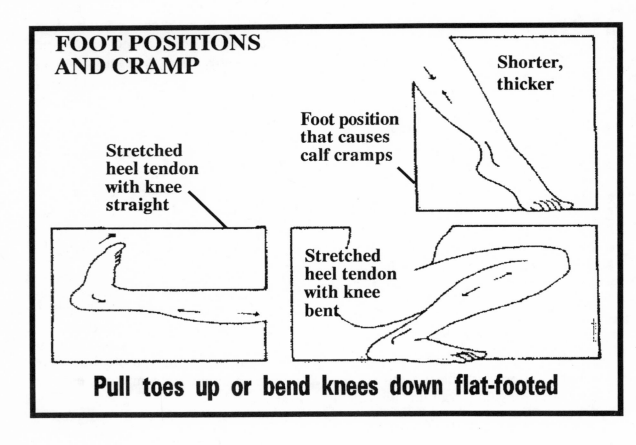

FOOT POSITIONS AND CRAMP

Shorter, thicker

Foot position that causes calf cramps

Stretched heel tendon with knee straight

Stretched heel tendon with knee bent

Pull toes up or bend knees down flat-footed

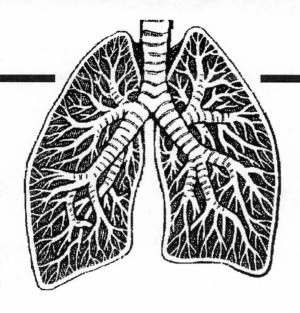

The lungs are part of the respiratory system. They are situated within the chest cavity (thorax). Between the lungs lies the heart and the esophagus.

Air is drawn into the body by the expansion of the diaphragm. It enters through the nose and mouth and passes into the throat. From there it enters the larynx and then the windpipe (trachea), which divides into two tubes (bronchi), each of which leads to a lung.

As the two main bronchi enter the lungs they divide into five narrower bronchi, one for each lobe. There are three lobes in the right lung and two in the left lung. These bronchi then divide and subdivide into narrower and narrower tubes, called bronchioles. The bronchioles terminate in tiny and extremely thin-walled air sacs called alveoli. The oxygen-carbon dioxide exchange takes place through the moist walls of the alveoli into the fine blood vessels (capillaries) surrounding the alveoli. Oxygen in the air breathed in enters the bloodstream; at the same time, carbon dioxide leaves the blood and enters the lungs to be breathed out. The breathing-in-and-out process takes place about 12 to 15 times a minute.

The lungs and the inner surface of the chest cavity (thorax) are covered by a thin membrane called the pleura. A small amount of lubricating fluid on the pleura permits the lungs and rib cage to move against each other without friction.

The bronchi and bronchioles are lined with cells that keep them moist. These cells have small hair-like projections that sweep mucus and debris up toward the trachea, and eventually to the throat.

Two types of cells line the trachea to protect against harmful substances in the air we breathe. The goblet cells line the airways like a blanket and produce mucus. The mucus traps harmful substances that might be inhaled, such as pollutants and dangerous bacteria.

The other cell type is called the ciliated cell, containing finger-like projections that sweep the mucus with a wave-like motion. This moves the mucus up toward the throat where it can be cleared out of the airways into the mouth and unconsciously swallowed.

Macrophages, other cells that defend the body, are found in the alveoli. These scavenger cells are able to destroy harmful objects by swallowing them or by releasing enzymes.

CAUSES OF LUNG DISEASE
* Inhaling harmful substances such as coal dust and silica from mining, cotton dust from mills, talc and asbestos in homes.
* Living matter such as organisms that grow in moldy hay; the condition is known as "farmer's lung." Organisms that grow in air conditioners and humidifiers (Legionnaires' disease), also found in sauna baths.
* Cigarette smoking is the worst thing you can do to your lungs. Lung cancer, emphysema, chronic bronchitis, heart disease, and peripheral vascular disease are all caused by smoking cigarettes.

SOME PULMONARY OR LUNG DISORDERS
* Abscess of the lung fabric.
* Actinomycosis (fungal infection of the lung).
* Alveolitis (inflammation and fibrosis of alveoli).
* Asthma.
* Atelactasis (collapsed lung).
* Bronchiectasis, which is the scarring of the bronchi.
* Bronchitis, which is the inflammation of the bronchi.
* Cancer of the lung fabric.
* Cancer, which is the presence of a malignant tumor in the lung usually in a bronchus (one of the tubes that carries air to and from the lungs).
* Cystic fibrosis, a formation of abnormally sticky mucus.
* Embolism (blockage of an artery).
* Emphysema (destruction and enlargement of lung air sacs).
* Empyema (pus in the pleural fluid).
* Hemothorax (blood in the pleural fluid).
* Pleurisy (infection of the pleura).
* Pneumoconiosis (inflammation of the lung caused by inhaling dust).
* Pneumonia.
* Pneumothorax (air in the pleural cavity).
* Tuberculosis.

LUNG CANCER--is a serious disorder, usually not detected until the disease has spread to other parts of the body, when it is too late for effective treatment. A heavy smoker has a much greater chance of getting lung cancer.

The first symptom of bronchus cancer is usually a cough, with only a little sputum that may be blood-stained (hemoptysis). This may be followed by pneumonia or collapse of a segment of the lung (atelectasis) caused by partial blockage of the bronchus. The later symptoms include weight loss and increasing weakness and lethargy. Breathlessness, caused by a general weakness, is another symptom.

The average survival time for an untreated patient of cancer of the lung is less than a year, and even with treatment only 10% to 20% survive for five years.

HOW CAN YOU TELL IF SOMETHING IS WRONG?
❑ Shortness of breath is a warning signal if it happens during routine activities that have not caused breathing difficulty in the past.
❑ Coughing is a significant symptom of lung disorder. While it is not necessary to worry about a cough accompanying a cold, a chronic cough is not normal and should not be ignored.
❑ Sputum production, even a small amount, particularly in the early morning, is not normal; it is a sign that you should see a physician.
❑ Blood coughed up is a sign of a serious problem that should receive medical attention immediately.
❑ Chest pain can have a number of causes, including chronic lung disorders and infection in the lung. Any chest pain should be attended to immediately by a physician.

HOW TO PROTECT YOUR LUNGS
* First of all, do not smoke.
* Second, work to keep your atmosphere clean; environmental pollutants damage the lungs.
* Third, avoid becoming overweight. The heavier a person is, the more the lungs have to work to supply oxygen and to expel carbon dioxide. Extra weight around the waist can push against the diaphragm and make breathing more difficult.
* Fourth, take action with any symptom of lung disease--cough, sputum, shortness of breath, blood coughed up, or chest pain. In the early stages many lung diseases can be treated to prevent serious lung damage. If you wait it may be too late.

A pain in the neck--

the trouble, and the treatments

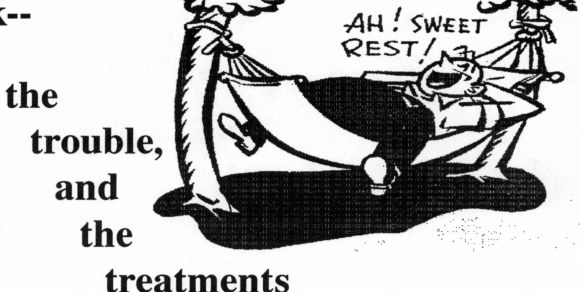

AH! SWEET REST!

The neck is a flexible structure that supports the head and contains major blood vessels and separate tubes for air and food. The seven bones in the neck, called cervical vertebrae, form the upper part of the spine. The top two cervical vertebrae, the atlas and axis, are pivoted so that they allow rotation of the head.

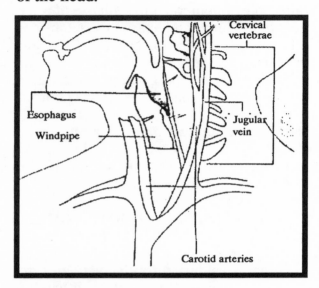

Cervical vertebrae

Esophagus
Windpipe

Jugular vein

Carotid arteries

Strong muscles on each side of the spine partly protect the structures in the front part of the neck. These structures include the esophagus, the trachea (windpipe), and the larynx (voice box). The carotid arteries and jugular veins in the neck carry blood to and from the head and brain. There is also a series of lymph nodes that guard against the entry of infection from the throat. The salivary and parotid glands, below the ears and adjacent to the jaw, produce saliva. The thyroid gland, just below the larynx in front of the trachea, produces hormones that control the body's metabolism.

NECK TROUBLE--The neck gives trouble in three ways: (1) a disease such as arthritis, (2) injury or fracture, and (3) strain, or any combination of the three. The neck is strained more frequently than any other structure in the body. Aside from direct injury, most neck strains occur following unfamiliar exercise or when the neck is maintained in any unnatural position for too long. Conditions such as arthritis or rheumatism can weaken and inflame the neck structures. Also, deficiencies in calcium, proteins, vitamins, and other essential nutrients may produce a fatigue ability, rendering the neck susceptible to strain. Infections, lack of activity, or a period of time in bed weaken the neck structures and strain may follow "unnatural" positions while confined or upon resumption of activities.

PROBLEMS OF THE NECK

1. A **stiff neck** involves either difficulty in moving the neck from its normal position or "torticollis," meaning the neck remains in an unusual position. Stiff neck is usually caused by a twisting or whiplash injury suffered from jerking the neck too hard, as in a car accident or sports injury. It may also occur after sleeping with the neck in an awkward position.

Treatment: Cold, heat, massage, and traction may be used. Sometimes painkilling drugs are prescribed; and, if inflammation is present, antirheumatic drugs are used. Spinal manipulation or neck exercises may help so check with your M.D., D.O., or chiropractor.

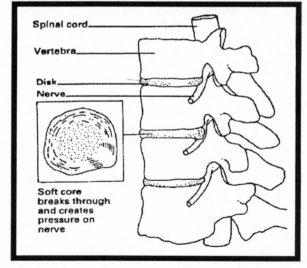

Spinal cord

Vertebra

Disk
Nerve

Soft core breaks through and creates pressure on nerve

2. A **slipped disk,** which is also known as a prolapsed intervertebral disk. The disks between the bones of the neck are composed of gristle-like fibrous tissue with a soft center. A disk can rupture as a result of a twisting injury that develops into a stiff neck. Gradually the pain spreads as the disk presses on the nerves that affect one shoulder and arm. If the disk protrudes deeply into the spinal cord, there may be a loss of sensation in the extremities.

Treatment: A slipped disk in the neck sometimes involves immobilizing the neck with a stiff collar. This helps the patient sleep or drive a car without too much pain. In addition, antiinflammatory drugs, physiotherapy and massage, and, in some cases, hospitalization and traction are necessary.

3. **Cervical spondylosis** is a stiff neck caused by bony outgrowths on the vertebrae accompanied by a misalignment or hardening of the plate-like disks. The nerve pathways are subjected to an abnormal amount of pressure that causes such symptoms as tingling "pins and needles," numbness, and pains in the shoulders or arms. This condition is particularly prevalent among middle-aged and elderly people, perhaps simply because some bones tend to become knobby and irregular as the body ages.

Treatment: Minor symptoms present no serious problems, but if the condition progresses, a physician should be consulted. Also you may be advised to take analgesics, or painkillers. A physician may also prescribe a tranquilizer to relax you and keep your neck muscles from tightening up and causing still more discomfort. Surgery may also be an option for severe neck problems. There are risks so talk them over carefully with your doctor and get a second opinion if you have doubts.

Like most other conditions of the human body, a pain in the neck is usually a sign that we have allowed ourselves to be subjected to unusual stress and strain.

I enjoy convalescence. It is the part that makes the illness worthwhile.
- George Bernard Shaw

Quotations and verses to ease a worried moment

Buy old masters. They fetch a much better price than old mistresses.
- Lord Beaverbrook

★

Hear no evil, speak no evil, and you'll never be invited to a party. - Oscar Wilde

★

One should play fairly when one has the winning cards. - Oscar Wilde

★

Democracy is the art of saying "nice doggie" until you can find a rock. - Will Rogers

★

The things people want to know about are usually none of their business.
- George Bernard Shaw

★

God gave us two ends:
One to sit on and one to think with.
Success depends upon
which one we use most.
Heads we win
tails we lose.

★

Discussion is an exchange of knowledge; argument an exchange of ignorance.
- Robert Quillen

★

The existing phrase books are inadequate. They are well enough as far as they go, but when you fall down and skin your leg they don't tell you what to say. - Mark Twain

★

Nothing is impossible to the man who doesn't have to do it himself.

★

Too bad ninety percent of the politicians give the other ten percent a bad reputation.
- Henry Kissinger

★

A doctor can bury his mistakes, but an architect can only advise his clients to plant vines. - Frank Lloyd Wright

★

When somebody says it's not the money but the principle, it's almost certainly the money.

★

Next to the city the loneliest place in the world when you're broke is among relatives. - Kin Hubbard

★

I don't care what is written about me so long as it isn't true. - Katharine Hepburn

★

The man with the best job in the country is the vice-president's. All he has to do is get up every morning and say "How's the president?" - Will Rogers

To laugh is to risk appearing the fool.
To weep is to risk appearing sentimental.
To reach for another is to risk involvement.
To expose your ideas, your dreams before a crowd is to risk their loss.
To love is to risk not being loved in return.
To live is to risk dying
To believe is to risk failure.
But risks must be taken, because the greatest hazard in life is to risk nothing.
The people who risk nothing, do nothing, have nothing.
They may avoid suffering and sorrow, but they cannot learn, feel, change, grow, love, live.
Chained by their attitudes, they are slaves; they have forfeited their freedom.
Only a person who risks is free.
Anon

★

Problems are only opportunities in work clothes. - Henry J. Kaiser

★

Nobody ever forgets where he buried the hatchet. - Kin Hubbard

★

The wretchedness of being rich is that you live with rich people. - Logan Pearsall Smith

★

The most difficult thing in the world is to know how to do a thing and to watch someone else doing it wrong, without commenting. - T. H. White

★

I don't know what makes him so obnoxious. But whatever it is, it works. - Bob Goddard

★

I'd like to live like a poor man with lots of money. - Pablo Picasso

★

To say the right thing at the right time, keep still most of the time. - John P. Roper

★

When red-headed people are above a certain social grade their hair is auburn.
- Mark Twain

★

Let Wall Street have a nightmare and the whole country has to help get them back in bed again. - Will Rogers

★

When a stupid man is doing something he is ashamed of, he always declares that it is his duty. - George Bernard Shaw

★

What is moral is what you feel good after and what is immoral is what you feel bad after. - Ernest Hemingway

I would rather have my ignorance than another man's knowledge, because I have so much of it. - Mark Twain

★

Judge not a man by his clothes, but by his wife's clothes. - Thomas B. Dewar

★

When choosing between two evils, I always like to take the one I've never tried before.
- Mae West

★

A Psalm of Life

Tell me not, in mournful numbers,
Life is but an empty dream!
For the soul is dead that slumbers
And things are not what they seem.

Life is real! Life is earnest!
And the grave is not its goal;
Dust thou art, to dust returnest,
Was not spoken of the soul.

Not enjoyment, and not sorrow,
Is our destined end or way;
But to act, that each to-morrow,
Finds us farther than to-day.

Art is long, and Time is fleeting,
And our hearts, though stout and brave.
Still, like muffled drums, are beating
Funeral marches to the grave.

In the world's broad field of battle,
In the bivouac of Life,
Be not like dumb, driven cattle!
Be a hero in the strife!

Trust no Future, howe'er pleasant!
Let the dead Past bury its dead!
Act, act in the living Present!
Heart within, and God o'erhead!

Lives of great men all remind us
We can make our lives sublime,
And, departing, leave behind us
Footprints on the sands of time;

Footprints, that perhaps another,
Sailing, o'er life's solemn main,
A forlorn and shipwrecked brother,
Seeing, shall take heart again.

Let us, then, be up and doing,
With a heart for any fate;
Still achieving, still pursuing,
Learn to labor and to wait.
- Henry Wadsworth Longfellow

New hope for controlling chronic pain

Do you remember the last time you felt pain? Perhaps you stubbed your toe on the corner of a door, hit your thumb with a hammer, or burned your finger by touching the top of a steaming pot of coffee.

As in these situations, most of the pain you suffer over the course of your life is intense--but short-lived. This is called acute pain. Through your body's natural healing powers and, in some cases, medical treatment, your pain goes away.

But there is another form of pain that doesn't go away. This is called chronic pain. When it strikes, signals of pain keep firing within your nervous system for weeks, months, or even years. In some cases, chronic pain stems from an injury that occurred years before. At other times, chronic pain appears in the absence of any past injury or bodily damage.

For at least 20 million Americans, chronic pain is a daily torment. There are many types of chronic pain. Some of the most common causes are arthritis, back problems, cancer, headaches, facial pain, nerve damage, spinal cord injury, and burns. Of all types of chronic pain, lower back pain is the most common. And of all age groups, chronic pain most often affects middle-aged to senior adults.

Some experts say chronic pain is America's most costly health problem. The impact of chronic pain in the United States, including direct medical expenses, lost income, lost productivity, compensation payments, and legal charges, is estimated at close to $50 billion annually. Aside from these staggering financial implications, the toll in human suffering is immeasurable. Chronic pain can hold its victims in a savage, demoralizing grasp.

But if you have chronic pain, there is good news. Today, new treatments, combined with a better understanding of how pain impulses originate and travel throughout your body, bring more hope than ever for conquering chronic pain.

HOW PAIN MESSAGES TRAVEL THROUGH YOUR BODY
In the past decade, scientists have learned much about pain. In fact, the more researchers learn about the nature of pain, the more complex they find it to be. This greater knowledge about what causes pain and how pain messages travel through your body is important for developing more effective treatments to combat pain.

What exactly is pain? It is an individual, highly subjective perception. No two people interpret pain signals in the same manner. In 1979, the International Association for the Study of Pain defined pain as "an unpleasant sensory and emotional experience associated with actual or potential tissue damage, or described in terms of such damage." This statement emphasizes the emotional and psychological aspects of pain, in addition to its more widely recognized physical dimension. How, then, does pain originate? And how are pain signals relayed to your brain for interpretation and response?

Acute pain and some forms of chronic pain originate with a noxious (unpleasant) stimulus to nerve endings embedded in your skin, joints, muscles, or internal organs. Your body is supplied with a variety of nerve endings sensitive to touch, pressure, heat, and cold.

In addition to these peripheral nerve endings, many nerve cells with extremely fine nerve fibers are activated only by intense, potentially harmful stimulation. Scientists call these nerve cells *nociceptors* (no'see-cep-tors), derived from the word noxious, which means physically harmful or destructive.

These nerve cells transmit pain stimuli through various nerve fibers called *nociceptive* (pain) pathways to a part of the spinal cord called the *dorsal horn*. Here, synapses send the signals on through the spinal cord in a manner analogous to electrical relay switches. These pathways, called *spinothalamic* <u>tracts</u>, then carry the pain impulses to the *thalamus*, the main relay center in your brain.

From here, the impulses are relayed to the *cerebral cortex*, the conscious area on the surface of the brain. Ultimately, the brain interprets the stimuli as pain and initiates action to halt it. For example, imagine that you've accidentally placed your hand on something hot. Your brain will "read" the pain impulses coming into your central nervous system from the injury site and initiate movement to stop the pain. In this instance, your brain sends a message to your muscles telling them to contract, and you pull back your hand.

Some peripheral nerve fibers that run to the spinal cord and brain transmit pain impulses faster than others. One such pathway acts

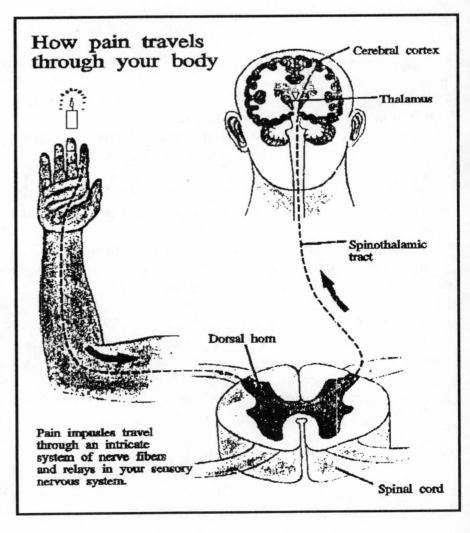

How pain travels through your body

Cerebral cortex

Thalamus

Spinothalamic tract

Dorsal horn

Spinal cord

Pain impulses travel through an intricate system of nerve fibers and relays in your sensory nervous system.

PAIN--your mind's perception of nerve impulses

as a sort of "express route" that reports facts instantaneously: where it hurts; how badly it hurts; and whether the pain is sharp or burning. Neuroscientists call these faster-transmitting pathways *A-delta pain fibers*. Slower-conducting pathways, which make connections with many nerve cells (neurons) en route, are known as *C-pain fibers*. In all instances, these impulses ultimately are relayed to the brain, where information about the location, intensity, and nature of the pain is interpreted.

In addition to tissue injury, infection or inflammation can also activate these pain pathways. Nerve cells damaged by any of these causes release naturally occurring chemicals, called *bradykinin*, *prostaglandin*, and *substance P*. These chemicals enhance the sensitivity of nociceptors. This heightens your sensation of pain.

The impulses relayed through all these pathways together contribute to the emotional impact of pain--whether you feel frightened, anxious, angry, or annoyed. Meanwhile, other branches of these pain pathways alert another division of the nervous system, the *autonomic nervous system*. This system controls your body's vital functions such as breathing, blood flow, pulse rate, digestion, and elimination. For example, pain can sound a general alarm in your autonomic nervous system, causing you to sweat and your pulse rate and blood pressure to increase.

Unfortunately, some chronic pain syndromes don't follow these "traditional" pain pathways. This is why treating chronic pain does not meet with unlimited success.

PAIN: ACUTE VS CHRONIC

The English language is replete with vivid descriptions of pain: throbbing, searing, numbing, sharp. In scientific terms, however, pain falls into two main categories:

■ **ACUTE**--This type of pain often results from disease or tissue damage. It starts suddenly, such as when you cut your hand or break a bone. Usually, you feel acute pain in the area where your body is damaged. This pain can last from a few seconds to several months, but subsides as normal healing occurs.

Physically, you may react to acute pain with an involuntary facial expression, such as a grimace, and body language of sheltering or protecting the injured area. You also may perspire, breathe rapidly, turn pale, and have changes in blood pressure.

■ **CHRONIC**--This form of pain lasts for more than three months, or beyond the time the condition would normally take to heal. Chronic pain may occur without a specific injury or disease; it ranges from mild to disabling.

You won't have involuntary responses such as rapid heartbeat. Rather, physical deterioration--such as loss of muscle strength--is common. Several behavioral changes also can accompany chronic pain: decline in sexual function, social relationships, and job performance. Depression or anxiety may worsen the condition and are common resultants--and the cycle begins.

THE GATE THEORY OF PAIN CONTROL

It's a natural reaction: When you bump your elbow, you rub it to relieve the ache. Researchers now have a theory to explain why this spontaneous action works.

In the 1960s, Canadian and British scientists (Melzack and Wall) formulated the gate theory of pain. According to the theory, pain signals excite a group of small neurons that constitute a pain "pool."

When activity reaches a certain level, a hypothetical "gate" opens to transmit pain impulses upward to your brain. However, large nerve fibers nearby can help regulate activity within the pool and keep the gate closed. Ice, heat, and pressure can stimulate those fibers and suppress the relay of pain messages.

Your brain can also close the gate by activating a descending pathway to block pain messages.

Researchers speculate that brain-based pain control takes place when people act heroically and seem to disregard pain; for example, when an injured athlete keeps playing in a game or when a soldier fights on, despite serious injury.

THE FOUR STAGES OF PAIN

Researchers have proposed various models to help explain the complexities of pain. One model involves four stages:

❶ **Activation or nociception**--The stimulation of nerve endings.
❷ **Pain**--Your mind's perception of nerve impulses.
❸ **Suffering**--Your emotional reaction to pain, such as alarm, anxiety, frustration, or depression. Suffering varies from person to person based on such factors as your sense of self-esteem, memory of past pain, job status--as well as family, social, and cultural factors.
❹ **Pain behavior and psychological changes**--Chronic pain can lead to negative feelings and a lowered sense of self-worth, which can result in significant psychological changes. Some people who suffer from chronic pain cast themselves into what psychiatrists and psychologists called the "invalid role" or "sick role." A person may assume this role to gain additional help from family or medical personnel, or to avoid conflict or responsibility. Sometimes, family, friends, or colleagues unknowingly reinforce this behavior.

Some people who experience chronic pain also engage in certain behaviors to win other benefits from their condition. Examples include trying to win sympathy or attention, and to avoid difficult activities or day-to-day responsibilities. Doctors refer to this as "pain behavior." Many pain specialists recommend psychological or psychiatric counseling for pain behavior.

Here are the common forms of chronic pain

Lower back pain--More people--about 15% of the population--suffer from lower back pain than from any other form of chronic pain. Occasionally, special imaging techniques may reveal a ruptured disk or other source of pressure on the spinal cord or nerve roots. More frequently, osteoarthritis of the spine is the cause. Despite progress in understanding how pain occurs, many questions remain unanswered about the causes of most lower back pain. Deconditioning, obesity, and poor posture play a role (see article on backache, page 377).

Cancer pain--Between 60% and 80% of cancer pain results from the pressure of a growing tumor or the spreading of tumor cells into other organs. Radiation treatment or chemotherapy can also generate pain or palliate the pain depending upon the tumor. Depression and anxiety, common psychiatric conditions in cancer victims, can worsen the pain.

The pain associated with cancer may be mild at first, but can increase as the illness progresses. Cancers that affect the bones, cervix, stomach, lungs, and pancreas are usually the most painful. More than any other form of chronic pain, cancer pain often responds well to drug therapy and radiation. In addition, surgery to remove the cancerous tissue, hypnosis, and self-help

groups may offer relief (see articles on cancer, pages 288 to 299).

Headache pain--The most common form of headache is the so-called tension headache. However, doctors are not certain that this head pain is specifically linked to muscle tension. Often, stressful events and the onset or worsening of this type of headache are not directly related.

The throbbing pain characteristic of a migraine headache may be related to alterations in the blood vessels within your head. Arteritis (inflammation in the arteries) can cause severe headache and is a medical emergency. Genetics, medications, alcohol, certain foods, exertion, and anxiety or depression may provoke a migraine (see article on headaches, page 382).

Arthritis pain--Arthritis is a general description for an affliction of the joints (see article on arthritis, page 280).

Osteoarthritis is a form of arthritis. It typically affects joints in the knees, hands, hips, and backbone. Pain stems from use of the joint and is worse at the end of the day.

Rheumatoid arthritis involves inflammation (swelling, congestion, and thickening) of the soft tissue that surrounds the joint spaces, typically in the areas of the hands and feet. Rheumatoid arthritis results from a disorder of the immune system. Psychological factors do not appear to play a major role in the development of rheumatoid arthritis.

Tension myalgia--This syndrome of generalized aching in most parts of the body has occurred for generations. When the condition lasts for more than three months, it is commonly called *fibromyalgia* (fibromy-al'je-ah). The condition sometimes is associated with poor, nonrestful sleep. Fibromyalgia is only disabling if you allow the pain to rule your life.

An imbalance of neurochemicals may be responsible for the pain of fibromyalgia. Treatment focuses on restoring good sleep, enhancing physical conditioning, and providing reassurance that there are no crippling, deforming, or life-threatening consequences of this pain.

Neuropathic pain--Damage to the peripheral or central nervous system can produce one of the most difficult forms of chronic pain for doctors to treat. *Trigeminal neuralgia* (tri-gem'in-nal nur-al'je-ah) and *postherpetic neuralgia* are two common types of neuropathic pain.

People who have trigeminal neuralgia experience severe, stabbing pain that affects the cheek, lips, gums, or chin on one side of the face. Even though the pain may last at most only a few minutes, it can be debilitating. Because the pain often provokes wincing, the condition is commonly called *tic douloureux* (tik-doo-loo-roo') or "painful twitch." Postherpetic neuralgia is another type of burning, searing pain that follows an attack of herpes zoster (shingles).

Like other types of chronic pain, tic douloureux and postherpetic neuralgia may be associated with emotional upset. Both conditions are more common among senior citizens and are treatable; see your doctor.

Another severely painful neuropathic disorder is "phantom pain." This is a puzzling condition that an estimated 5% to 10% of all amputees experience. Nerves in the stump of the limb may transmit electrochemical messages to the brain, where they are misread as originating in the missing limb.

Somatization disorder--Somatoform pain refers to pain and changes in behavior that cannot be fully explained by physical disease or injury. The problems of the "sick role," pain behavior, and abuse of prescription drugs are frequently the most troublesome parts of this syndrome for the patient, family, and healthcare professional. Psychiatric and/or psychological help are necessary for treatment.

> As my grandmother
> used to say,
> "If you didn't
> experience pain
> you would eat
> your fingers."

Nonmedicinal pain control techniques

FACTORS THAT INFLUENCE HOW YOU PERCEIVE PAIN

You don't experience chronic pain as only physical discomfort. Your perception of pain also is shaped by your own personality, and by the social and cultural environment in which you live.

✷ **Anxiety and depression**--The longer you experience pain, the more irritable and depressed you can become. That, in turn, leads to more pain and anxiety.

✷ **Childhood experiences**--Being deprived of normal nurturing as a child, while receiving undue attention when injured, may teach you to use pain to obtain the same kind of attention as an adult.

✷ **Relationships**--Some people use pain as a way to avoid other problems, such as the fear of intimacy.

✷ **Sense of control**--High self-esteem and a feeling of being in control of your life may help you cope better with pain. On the other hand, a poor self-image can make pain the focus of your identity. This can magnify your sense of pain.

THE ENDORPHINS: YOUR BODY'S OWN PAINKILLERS

Opium and related compounds, such as morphine and heroin, have long been used for the relief of pain. These compounds, called opiates, act by attaching themselves to specific structures, called receptors, on the surface of individual brain cells.

As an outgrowth of these discoveries, scientists learned that certain molecules the brain produces can attach themselves to the same receptors to relieve pain.

Scientists refer to this broad category of molecules with morphine-like characteristics as endorphins (endogenous morphine).

There is growing evidence that endorphins represent the means by which nonmedicinal treatments, such as acupuncture and transcutaneous nerve stimulation (TENS), treat chronic pain. Greater knowledge and understanding of how these receptors work, as well as how to manipulate them, offers hope for more effective relief from many types of chronic pain.

Here are nonmedicinal treatments that physicians, psychologists, and other healthcare professionals use to control various forms of chronic pain:

✔ **Acupuncture**--A growing body of information confirms that this ancient approach, popular in Asia, triggers pain-suppressing chemicals within your body. Needle placement at prescribed locations along nerve pathways can reduce the perception of pain.

✔ **Biofeedback**--The principle, in short, is that by learning to monitor your body's responses, you can modify these responses and reduce the impact of pain. Biofeedback uses an electronic monitor to note physical responses, such as changes in skin temperature, muscle tension, and heart rate, which are part of your body's response to pain.

For example, a sound or light may signal an increase in electrical activity in your muscles. Using these signals, you can learn to modify your body's response to pain. Biofeedback is especially helpful in coping with headaches, back pain, and other forms of chronic pain, particularly when used with other pain control methods, such as distraction, reinterpreting pain, and relaxation.

✔ **Exercise**--If you have arthritis, exercise can increase the range of motion for specific areas (such as the arms, legs, and neck). Exercises that tone both abdominal and back muscles may help relieve and prevent back pain. Exercise also releases endorphins.

✔ **Whirlpool/massage**--Muscle tension increases your awareness of pain. These traditional techniques promote muscle relaxation and general comfort.

✔ **Hypnosis**--Self-hypnosis may lessen your perception of pain. For example, hypnosis may help lessen the pain of childbirth or cancer and enhance recovery from other painful conditions. The technique works particularly well with children.

✔ **Nerve blocks**--An injection of a local anesthetic may play a dual role in the management of chronic pain. Doctors use this technique to localize or exclude a nociceptive stimulus as the cause of a pain problem. The temporary nature of the local anesthetic's effect can be beneficial in facilitating mobilization and rehabilitation for many people with chronic pain.

In many instances, doctors use a cortisone-like preparation to prolong the effect. This is especially true in cases where inflammation is present. In patients with advanced cancer, doctors may inject a chemical that destroys the nerve. Permanent nerve blocks are less desirable for other types of chronic pain, however, because the remaining live nerve may begin to send its own pain messages in a few months. Also, local anesthetics tend to affect more than the target area. (That's why your cheek and tongue feel numb after your dentist injects a local anesthetic.) Research may help pinpoint which nerve fibers should receive the blockage.

✔ **TENS**--This acronym stands for transcutaneous (trans'cu-tane'ee-us, or across the skin) electrical nerve stimulation. The use of electrical current as a means of "healing" dates back to the ancient Romans, who used electric eels and torpedo fish to treat pain. In recent years, doctors have revived the concept of using electrical current to treat pain.

In TENS therapy, electrodes are placed directly on your skin over the painful area, or at key points on the pain nerve pathway. A small battery-powered generator sends pulses of current to the electrodes. The procedure has few side effects and also helps relieve mild, persistent pain, such as sore muscles, tennis elbow, or postoperative discomfort.

✔ **Surgery**--Often, nerve fibers that carry signals about tissue injury are packed together in small bundles called *spinothalamic* (spine'no-thal'mic) *tracts* in the spinal cord. Surgically cutting selected nerve bundles in the spinal cord may reduce the sensation of pain. However, pain often returns within a few weeks or months after this type of surgery. Surgeons reserve this procedure, called a cordotomy, for people in whom all other pain control methods have failed. The operation is most successful for pain that originates on one side of the body. This form of treatment is reserved for terminally ill patients. Certainly, it is a last resort.

Medications that treat chronic pain

Medications can play an important role in treatment of chronic pain. Here are medications your physician can choose from when trying to control your chronic pain:

■ **Nonsterodial anti-inflammatory drugs (NSAIDs)**--This large group of medications brings about pain relief by inhibiting the production of hormones called prostaglandins in your system. These hormones appear to assist nerve fibers that carry pain impulses to your brain. NSAIDs, which include such well-known pain medications as aspirin and ibuprofen, are available over the counter in smaller doses than the prescribed form. Recent evidence indicates that some of the known side effects of NSAIDs, such as worsening of minor degrees of kidney disease, can even occur at these lower doses.

■ **Opiates**--Opiates are the most effective class of analgesic medications for people with pain from cancer, surgery, burns, and kidney stones. Opiate drugs include morphine, methadone, codeine, hydromorphone (Dilaudid) and meperidine (Demerol). Morphine, which gets its name from Morpheus, the Greek god of dreams, is the opiate against which the potency of all others traditionally is measured.

Opiates can cause drowsiness, nausea, constipation, and mood changes. In addition, extended use of opiates can lead to tolerance--the body becomes accustomed to certain amounts of the drug and no longer responds as well to it. Because of the inevitable addiction that accompanies chronic opiate use, their use in treating chronic pain should be extremely limited. An exception to this caveat is in the treatment of people who are terminally ill.

■ **Antidepressants**--These medications can bring relief to some people with chronic pain, even in the absence of depression. For example, these medications may help some persons with peripheral nerve damage (such as in the discomfort of shingles or the "burning foot" sensation of diabetes).

Depression, even when mild in degree, often accompanies chronic pain. Treating this depression may play a role in bringing pain relief. Because antidepressants are not addicting, you can use them for longer periods. But they can have uncomfortable side effects such as fatigue and bladder-emptying problems if taken at high dosages.

■ **Anticonvulsants**--Some medications that treat epilepsy provide relief from some forms of chronic pain. Although chronic pain is not associated with epilepsy, the ability of these medications to stabilize electrical activity within the brain may be the reason they benefit some people with chronic pain.

COMMUNICATING WITH YOUR PHYSICIAN
If you experience chronic pain, work closely with your physician to determine the cause of the pain, if possible, and the most effective form of treatment. Here are some practical tips for talking with your physician:

❋ **Describe your symptoms completely.** Tell your doctor what your pain is like. Is it sharp or dull? When are your symptoms most pronounced? Is your pain worse at night?

❋ **Recount any past injuries.** Chronic pain sometimes is linked to an injury or disease that occurred many years before.

❋ **Follow your physician's instructions to the letter.** No matter what type of treatment your physician decides to try first to manage your pain, follow instructions. Deviations from prescribed treatments can make them ineffective.

❋ **Be patient.** The longer you suffer from chronic pain, the less likely it is that your physician will find a single, treatable disease as the cause. If, after a thorough search, your doctor cannot pinpoint the cause of your pain, don't construe such a report as an accusation by your doctor that you are a hypochondriac or are imagining your symptoms.

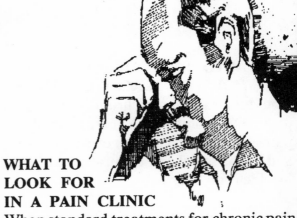

WHAT TO LOOK FOR IN A PAIN CLINIC
When standard treatments for chronic pain have failed, you may learn to cope with your discomfort while achieving a degree of independence from your symptoms through the help of a pain clinic or pain management center. These centers may use one or a combination of the following three treatment approaches:

➊ **Comprehensive**--A thorough physical examination excludes any correctable problem that may be responsible for your pain. Physical and occupational therapy, behavior modification, group interaction, educational experiences, biofeedback, and counseling are the mainstays of this type of program. This treatment approach emphasizes the elimination of medications as well as the initiation of physical activity to gain independence from chronic pain.

➋ **Symptom-oriented**--This treatment approach focuses on a single form of pain, such as headache or backache. These clinics typically offer an array of different treatments that address a specific type of pain.

➌ **Treatment-oriented**--This type of clinic emphasizes specific forms of therapy, such as neurosurgery or nerve blocks, which may be appropriate courses of treatment for several types of pain.

Persistent pain often signals an underlying health problem. So besides simply looking for relief from pain, when pain persists or recurs, it's good common sense to see a doctor to diagnose and treat its cause.

This article was reprinted from June 1990 *Mayo Clinic Health Letter Medical Essay* with permission of Mayo Foundation for Medical Education and Research, Rochester, MN 55905.

Pneumonia goes after the ill and elderly

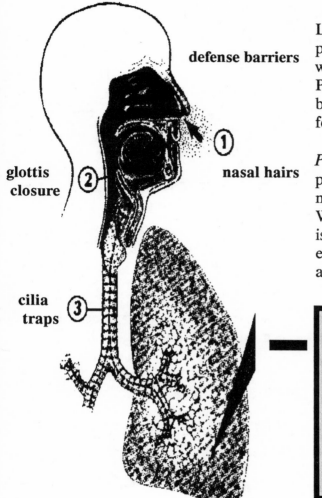

defense barriers

nasal hairs

glottis closure

cilia traps

① ② ③

Legionnaires' disease is a severe form of pneumonia first recognized among elderly war veterans attending a convention in Philadelphia in 1976. It was caused by breathing *Legionella pneumophila* bacteria found in an air-conditioning system.

Pneumocystis carinii caused by a protozoan parasite was labeled when it ravaged malnourished infants in orphanages during World War II. Because it is an "opportunistic" disease, striking people already weakened by another illness, people with AIDS are likely victims.

> **The older you get, the more likely you are to develop this lung condition.**

SYMPTOMS

Cough with an abundance of sputum, fever, chills, and chest pains. In pneumococcus pneumonia the sputum is usually bloody or pink in color, but becomes rust-colored tending toward yellow as the patients get past the worst of the illness.

In other bacterial pneumonia, the patient develops the symptoms of a cold followed by a sudden shivering attack, sputum that is often bloody, and a high fever (104 degrees F) with rapid respiration and pulse rate. The patient feels pain in the side of the chest. Vomiting and diarrhea may occur; confusion is common.

Elderly people with pneumonia often don't run high fevers.

In forms of pneumonia caused by virus or fungus infection, especially among elderly patients, the symptoms develop slowly with clear evidence of bronchitis and a worsening cough, often with blood-stained sputum. Headache, muscle aches, and cyanosis (blue-tinged lips because of poorly oxygenated blood) are common.

DIAGNOSIS

A physician will listen to the chest, have an X-ray taken, and have blood and sputum tests made to identify, if possible, the particular organism causing the disease. Sometimes a white blood cell count may help to determine whether the infection is caused by bacteria or by a virus.

TREATMENT

Antibiotics are used in the treatment of bacterial and fungal infections. Antibiotics are not effective against viruses.

Breathing exercises and percussion to shake the chest wall encourage the patient to cough up sputum. If the sputum is thick and sticky, steam inhalation may also help. Treatment also includes ample bed rest and drinking lots of fluids. A seriously ill patient may need oxygen therapy. Painkilling drugs are prescribed if the patient has pleurisy.

Most patients suffering from mild forms of pneumonia can be treated at home with rest, antibiotics, and breathing exercises. The body encourages coughing, which expels foreign matter. The white blood cells, or phagocytes, in the lung tissue can surround, engulf, neutralize, and help destroy invading microbes that cause pneumonia. The body's immune system also produces antibodies to fight this disease. It is counterproductive to take cough suppressants.

WAYS TO FORTIFY YOUR RESISTANCE

1. Get a yearly influenza vaccination.

2. Check with your doctor to see if you should be immunized against the pneumococcus bacteria.

3. Don't smoke. Smoking damages your lungs' natural defenses against respiratory infections.

The Centers for Disease Control and the American College of Physicians recommend vaccination against pneumococcus for: adults age 65 or older; those with immune-deficiency diseases or chronic illnesses; and people who have had their spleen removed. Side effects from the vaccine are rare, and a single dose once in your lifetime is sufficient.

In spite of all the advances of medical science, pneumonia is still a major public health problem and one of our nation's leading causes of death. Each year 500,000 Americans will contract pneumococcal pneumonia and 25,000 will die from it. Elderly people and those who have other serious diseases are pneumonia's major target. It is the nation's sixth leading cause of death.

Pneumonia is an inflammation of the lungs caused by bacteria, viruses, or fungal infection, infestation by worms, or from toxic or infected inhaled matter that live around us every day. If you inhale a big enough dose of a half-dozen different bacteria, your body's natural protective responses can't eliminate them.

Pneumonia is a general term for a variety of diseases that cause lung inflammation or infection. If infection spreads down the bronchioles, it is known as bronchopneumonia. If only one lobe of the lung is involved, it is called lobar pneumonia.

Pneumococcus pneumonia is caused by the Streptococcus pneumonia bacteria and accounts for 60% to 90% of pneumonia caused by bacteria.

SEX and the second 50 year

The sexual role models that we conventionally see are 18- to 30-year-old people. We seldom have a picture or vision of 60-, 70-, 80-, or 90-year-old people enjoying sex. Society in general and particularly the medical community is guilty of assuming that when you retire from your job, you also retire from your love life and your sexual life.

Young people often act as if they invented sex. However, according to a recent anonymous questionnaire of men and women from ages 80 to 102, sexual activity was so common that perhaps the role model for intimacy should be shifted from young people.

One of the problems with sex is the false image conveyed by our "R"-rated movies that seem to specialize in heavy breathing, thumping bed springs, and sensual, sweating, moaning young bodies that turn intimacy into an athletic performance. Actually, good meaningful sex is less performance-oriented. It can be done very quietly without much hubbub. If sex enhances you as a person and enhances the other person and enhances your togetherness, then it's a good thing. It really doesn't make much difference whether or not you have had an orgasm, or if you did it in 12 different positions, or even if you had an erection or whatever. Sex is a close, intimate, loving relationship between a man and a woman who are unafraid of doing the things that please each other.

WHAT ABOUT SEXUALITY IN LATER LIFE:
Most older people are able to lead an active, satisfying sex life. Older women do not usually lose their physical capacity for orgasm, nor do older men lose their capacity for erection and ejaculation.

However, we can expect a gradual slowing of response in the physical body. When problems occur, they are usually the result of disease, disability, drug reaction, or emotional upset.

Those changes that do occur in women (shape, flexibility, and lubrication of the vagina) can be traced directly to lowered levels of the hormone estrogen during and after menopause.

Older men may take somewhat longer to attain an erection than when young. The erection may not be quite as firm or as large as in earlier years. There can be a shorter ejaculation sensation, the loss of erection following orgasm may be more rapid, and a longer period of time passes before an erection is again possible.

EFFECTS OF ILLNESS OR DISABILITY:
Even the most serious diseases rarely warrant stopping sexual activity. Here are some that are used as an excuse:

* **HEART DISEASE,** especially if a heart attack has occurred, leads many older people to give up sex for fear of causing another attack. The risk is low; in fact, an active sex life may decrease the risk of a future attack.

* **DIABETES** is one of the few diseases that can cause impotence. Once diabetes is diagnosed and controlled, however, potency in most cases may be restored.

* **STROKE** rarely damages physical aspects of sexual function, and it is unlikely that sexual exertion will cause another stroke. Using different positions or medical devices that assist body functions can help make up for any weakness or paralysis that may have occurred.

* **ARTHRITIS** can produce pain that limits sexual activity. Surgery and drugs can relieve these problems, but in some cases the medicines used can decrease sexual desire. Exercise, rest, warm baths, and changes in position and timing of sexual activity (such as avoiding evening and early-morning hours of pain) can be helpful.

* **HYSTERECTOMY,** if performed correctly, does not harm sexual functioning. Those women who believe that they have been damaged by a hysterectomy, or men who consider their partners "less feminine" after this surgery, should seek counseling. The same is true of mastectomy.

* **PROSTATECTOMY** rarely affects potency. Except for a lack of seminal fluid, sexual capacity and enjoyment after a prostatectomy should return to the presurgery level.

* **ALCOHOL** reduces potency in men and delays orgasm in women. It is the most widespread drug-related cause of sexual problems. Tranquilizers, antidepressants, and certain high blood pressure drugs can cause impotence; other drugs can lead to failure to ejaculate in men and reduced sexual desire in women.

* **EMOTIONAL** problems. Remember, all men are impotent at times due to tiredness, tension, illness, or alcohol. Usually, potency returns by itself, but if a man is too worried he may continue to be impotent due to his fear alone.

GOOD SEX FOR SENIOR CITIZENS (those over 55): As the body changes with age, sexual response changes, too. In other words, if you expect to react like newlyweds in the bodies of 50- to 90-year-olds, you may become frustrated and unhappy. But, if you learn to go with the flow and adjust and adapt to the changes in your body, sex can be fulfilling. Sex in the young is fast and furious. **But older people need to grow in sexual sophistication and find new vistas of sexual satisfaction.** Sex can be expanded to a richer experience that will compensate for the deficits of older people. The message is clear:

> **For willing learners who make the effort, sex for senior citizens can be better than ever.**

ACCEPT THE CHANGES: An older man can still be athletic, but he no longer expects to break Olympic records. The sexual adjustment is really no different from the overall adjustment that we all have to make to the fact that time has a certain impact on our bodies.

- With age, the circulatory flow lessens; the muscles relax. Men have more difficulty attaining and maintaining an erection. Erections may be softer and at a less upright angle. A little more time for stimulation may cure this problem.

- A woman usually has reduced vaginal lubrication after menopause, which may cause irritation during intercourse. Estrogen and/or the use of lubricating gels can prevent this problem.

- Changes in attractiveness such as weight gain, wrinkles, loss of muscle tone, and physical disabilities often make arousal more difficult. A change of focus from physical to mental and spiritual will help. Also a longer period devoted to a prelude of lovemaking and loving words helps.

CHANGE THE ROUTINE: When the children are gone and the couple is alone in the home, why must sex be postponed until the eleventh hour of the night. Why not early mornings? Why not weekend afternoons?

- **Innovations**--for some, sex in a different surrounding is stimulating and highly desirable. Why not read a good book on techniques and positions and try some. We recommend *Fundamentals of Human Sexuality* by Dr. Herant Katchadourian.

- **Fantasy**--making up stories costs nothing if it doesn't disrupt the relationship. If the partner perceives the fantasy as a hidden wish--today you talk about it, tomorrow you do it--it can become threatening and unacceptable. But if a fantasy helps, use it.

- **Change roles**--If the man has always been the sexual aggressor, try a shift in roles. The goal is to please each other; talk it over and make your plans.

USE IT OR LOSE IT: The most important factor in keeping sexually active is keeping sexually active. You do this by doing it. If we stop eating, the desire for food may go away; it will come back when we start eating, whether we like it or not.

- Keep the body in the best shape possible. Good nutritious food and physical exercise--whether you feel like it or not--will keep the body active.

- Keep your mind alert and well. Read and study on a regular basis and report to someone what you have read; it will keep your mind in good shape.

- Maintain your habits of worship and do things for other people. When my wife's mother was 92 years old she opened a thrift shop to sell things to help the old folks. Helping people is a key, believe it or not, to a fulfilling sex life in the elderly.

THE BOTTOM LINE: Sexual preference is as variable as culture and food habits. One man's poison is another man's food. The bottom-line suggestion is to please each other. If you are not pleasing each other, then talk about sex, read and study it, take some counsel from a licensed sex therapist, adapt and change a little until both partners are pleased. Sometimes a partner complains about the other person as an excuse to find another contact. Don't let this happen--take care of each other's needs.

Discoveries About Sex

According to a study reported in the latest issue of the *Archives of Internal Medicine*, there's a numerical correlation between "coffee drinking and a higher rate of sexual activity in elderly women and a decreased prevalence of impotency among elderly men."

Ananais Diokno of the William Beaumont Hospital in Royal Oak, Mich., said that the reason may be that coffee is a powerful stimulant of the central nervous system and relaxant of the smooth muscles. Then again, "Coffee users may be more liberal in their sexual behavior."

Then again, maybe they just can't fall asleep.

According to the "experts," marital ardor declines as couples age, both for biological reasons and because society frowns on Grandma and Grandpa having sex. Of course, we have found that most of these "experts" haven't reached the age of real maturity.

According to sex surveys:
Adults have sex 57 times a year, or about once a week.
Under 40 years of age--78 times a year.
Over 70 years of age--8 times.
Married people--67 times.
Separated people--66 times.
Divorced and never married people--55 times
Widowed people--6 times.

Married people who say they are the happiest have the most sex. Whether happy people have more sex, or more sex makes you happy, researchers don't know. Among all people, married or not, happy people are having sex 64.5 times per year compared with 55.5 for those who are "pretty happy" and 49.5 for those that are "unhappy."

Some other surveys report that men on the average have sex 66.4 times during the year, and women reported having intercourse 50.6 times. Something is amiss, don't you think?

Information on venereal disease and contraceptives

Generally, if you confine your sexual activity to a mutually faithful partner there is no need for you to read this article on sexually transmitted diseases because you will never get one. And, if you are a male over 50, you don't need the information about contraception, unless your wife has not gone through the menopause and may get pregnant, and you do not want a baby.

Most people don't want the following information, but statistics tells us that men and women over 50 and even into the 80s and 90s can be quite sexually active with multiple partners and do get venereal diseases. Both men and women can get a sexually transmitted disease at any age--nobody is immune. At least 20 sexually transmitted diseases (STD's) have now been identified, and they affect more than 10 million men and women in this country each year.

Sexually transmitted diseases (venereal diseases) frequently have no symptoms, so millions of people won't know they're infected until serious and often permanent damage has occurred.

Many people do have symptoms of sexually transmitted diseases (STD's) or venereal diseases. If you or your partner has any of the following signs in the genital area, see a doctor right away: abnormal or smelly discharges from the vagina, penis, or rectum; bleeding, blisters, boils, chancres, growths, irritations, itches, pains, pus, rashes, sores, swelling, tenderness, ulcers, or warts.

There are other symptoms of venereal diseases, not caused exclusively by sexual activity, but they are serious and indicate that something is wrong with your health: arthritic pain, bowel problems, chills, coatings of the mouth and throat, constipation, coughs, diarrhea, discolored skin, fatigue, feeling run down, fevers, growths, hair loss, headaches, jaundice, lack of appetite, lightheadedness, mental disorders, menstrual problems, nausea, night sweats, constant or rapid unexplained weight loss, swollen glands, urine changes, vision loss, or vomiting. Again, if you have one of the above symptoms, see your doctor, particularly if you have been sexually active with a partner you aren't sure about.

Chlamydia (kla-mid-ee-uh)--is the most prevalent sexually transmitted disease. It strikes between 3 and 4 million Americans each year. If left untreated the infection can spread throughout the reproductive system. Sixty-five percent of infected women have no symptoms. In others, the first symptoms appear within 14 days, and are a watery, white discharge that causes discomfort during urination. Men can have inflammation of the urethra and the epididymis, the long cord behind the testicles that transports sperm. Women may have irregular bleeding and men may develop prostatitis. It's the leading cause of pelvic inflammatory disease in women, and it can lead to male and female sterility.

The treatment of chlamydia is antibiotics--tetracycline, erythromycin, or doxycycline, taken orally. The cure rate is 95% effective; but, we must remember that the disease sometimes has no symptoms and can be passed on without a person knowing that he or she has it.

Gonorrhea--is caused by the gonococcus, a bacterium that grows and multiplies quickly in moist, warm areas of the body such as the cervix, urinary tract, mouth, or rectum. Two to eight days after infection, a man will get a yellowish discharge from a reddened urethra and experience frequent, painful urination. Women's symptoms may include lower abdominal pain, a whitish vaginal discharge, abnormal uterine bleeding, and painful urination. But 10% to 30% of infected men and 70% to 90% of infected women don't have any symptoms.

Gonorrhea can spread and cause complications. Some infected women will develop pelvic inflammatory disease and inflammation of the fallopian tubes, which can cause ectopic pregnancy and permanent sterility. Sterility also can develop in men, and the infection can extend to the prostate and the rectum.

Doctors blast the disease with a minimum one-time dose of 4.8 million units of penicillin. Ampicillin or amoxicillin are sometimes used. The ingenious gonococci have mutated their chromosomes so that antibiotics do not have as much effect. There is increasing concern about the emergence of penicillin-resistant gonorrhea in this country. Fortunately, spectinomycin or ceftriaxone can be used to treat resistant strains.

Because gonorrhea is highly contagious and yet may cause no symptoms, all men and women who have sexual contact with more than one partner should be tested regularly for the disease. Using condoms during sexual intercourse is very effective in preventing the spread of infection.

Syphilis--is a sexually transmitted disease caused by a spirochete and passed on by direct contact with infectious sores, rashes, or mucous patches. The first symptoms appear from 10 to 90 days (usually 3 weeks) after being infected as a chancre (pronounced "shan-ker"), which is a painless pimple, blister, or sore that usually appears on the penis or around or in the vagina.

If untreated, syphilis may go on to more advanced stages; the full course of the disease can take years and be fatal. Penicillin remains the drug most commonly used to treat syphilis.

Genital warts (also called venereal warts, or condylomata acuminata)--are caused by a virus related to the virus that causes common skin warts. Genital warts usually first appear as small, hard, painless bumps in the vaginal area, on the penis, or around the anus; if untreated, they may grow and develop a fleshy, cauliflower-like appearance.

Genital warts infect up to 3 million Americans each year. Scientists believe that the virus causing genital warts also causes several types of cancer. Genital warts are generally treated with a topical drug (applied to the skin), or by freezing. If the warts are very large, they may be removed by surgery.

Genital herpes--is a recurrent viral disease that affects an estimated 30 million Americans. Approximately 500,000 new cases of this incurable infection develop annually. The major symptoms of herpes infection are painful blisters or open sores in the genital area. These may be preceded by a tingling or burning sensation in the legs, buttocks, or genital region.

The herpes sore usually disappears within two to three weeks, but the virus remains in the body and the lesions may recur from time to time. The recurring episodes are usually not as severe as the first episode. Genital herpes is now treated with acyclovir (trade name Zovirax), an antiviral drug available by prescription; it helps control the symptoms but does not eliminate the herpes virus from the body.

Acquired Immunodeficiency Syndrome (AIDS)--was first reported in the U.S. in 1981. It is caused by a virus that destroys the body's ability to fight off infection. People who have AIDS are therefore very susceptible to many diseases, called opportunistic infections, and to certain forms of cancer.

The virus is present in body fluids such as blood, semen, and vaginal secretions. It also has been found in saliva and tears. Transmission of the virus primarily occurs by intimate contact with semen during sexual activity and by sharing of needles used to inject intravenous drugs. The virus is fatal.

AIDS may be prevented by using condoms during sexual intercourse (although not 100% effective) with an infected person and by not sharing needles to inject intravenous drugs. The U.S. Public Health Service has a toll-free hotline number for persons with questions about AIDS: 1-800-342-2437 (see also page 279).

Prevention and Treatment

The best way to avoid getting a sexually transmitted disease is to not have sex. No sex, no transmission. Among those who are monogamous, there is no need to refrain from sex. The chances of getting a sexually transmitted disease are slight. If you are not monogamous, experts recommend that you select your partners very carefully, and that you make full use of condoms, spermicides, and diaphragms.

Most sexually transmitted diseases are readily treated, and the earlier a person seeks treatment and warns sex partners about the disease, the less likely that the disease will do irreparable physical damage, be spread to others or, in the case of a woman, be passed on to a newborn baby.

The American Social Health Association (ASHA) provides free information and keeps lists of clinics and private doctors who provide treatment for people with sexually transmitted diseases. ASHA has a national toll-free telephone number, 1-800-227-8922. Callers can get information from the ASHA hotline without leaving their names.

Suggestions for a safe sex life:
* Confine sex to a mutually faithful partner.

* Be selective when you choose a sex partner. Beware of smooth talkers; have sex only with a partner who will make you feel secure about health concerns; and know the name and phone number of your partner.

* Limit your number of sex partners. It is safest to have sex with only one person who is also only having sex with you. Be certain that your partner is mutually

faithful, does not use IV drugs, and is not at risk for sexually transmitted diseases, including AIDS.

* If you do have sex with more than one person or if your partner does, protect yourself. Always use a latex condom along with spermicide to give yourself the highest degree of protection.

* Talk with your partner about sex before the heat of passion. Don't let your partner remain silent. Find out about your partner's health and sexual history. Make conversations about health a natural part of your sexual relationship. Again, watch out for the smooth talker.

* Keep medically fit. If you have sex with more than one person, or if your partner does, have regular physical check-ups and blood tests.

* Sex with too much alcohol or mood-altering drugs can be dangerous as it may lessen your ability to make responsible choices.

* If you have been exposed to someone with a sexually transmitted disease, go to your doctor, clinic, or health department for testing and treatment. Urge your partner to be treated at the same time. Do not have sex until you and your partner have been tested and are considered disease-free.

Contraceptives

We are fully aware that the subject of contraceptives is controversial--many people do not believe in any contraception except abstinence or Fertility Awareness Methods (FAMs), sometimes called the "rhythm method." Then again, people over 50 do not normally need contraceptives for birth control.

However, statistics tell us that people over 50 can be quite sexually active, often with younger partners who do need birth control. And sexually active people of any age can get sexually transmitted diseases.

Scientists have been hard at work to develop "methods of choice" to avoid unwanted pregnancies, and at the same time, to find a way to avoid venereal disease (STD's). The drug RU-486, that induces early abortions is in the midst of political controversies.

Another new contraceptive is on the way. It is a unique new vaccine made from sperm cells. It would involve a pill or an injection that a woman could use to signal her immune system to develop antibodies to the protein in the head of the male sperm. The antibodies would then bind to the sperm cells and destroy their ability to fertilize the woman's eggs. Its effects would wear off in two to five years and leave women with the option of conceiving if they wished. It is not yet on the market.

Condoms--are easy to get, easy to carry, easy to use, and are the most common method of birth control. They also help protect against sexually transmitted diseases. Condoms are sheaths of thin rubber or animal tissue that fit over the erect penis during intercourse.

Condoms catch semen before, during, and after ejaculation, thereby preventing sperm from entering the uterus. Latex condoms are believed to offer better protection than animal tissue condoms. The use of condoms is sometimes faulted for interfering with the spontaneity of sex, and some say, for decreasing sensation.

Condoms are highly effective if used properly. Condom breakage is usually due to improper use. Condoms are to be used only once and then thrown away. Using a substance like Vaseline to lubricate the condom can contribute to its breakage. KY jelly is a proper lubricant. Condoms are easily obtained at most drugstores and are reasonable in price, usually 25 cents apiece.

Birth control pills--are available only by prescription and are the most effective temporary method of birth control. Birth control pills consist of one or both of two compounds similar to the natural hormones that regulate the menstrual cycle. Women on pills have more regular periods, fewer ectopic (tubal) pregnancies, and less cramping, blood loss, iron-deficiency anemia, and pelvic inflammatory disease. The pill appears to offer some protection from ovarian and endometrial cancer, noncancerous breast tumors, and ovarian cysts. However, there are some long-term risks. Ask your doctor.

Birth control pill users may experience minor reactions, including breast tenderness, nausea, vomiting, weight gain or loss, and spotting between periods, which often clear up after two or three months. Serious problems are rare. But as a woman gets older the possibility of blood clots, stroke, heart attack, or liver tumors may increase, particu-

More information on contraceptives

larly if the woman smokes, has high blood pressure, high cholesterol levels, or diabetes. A woman on the pill should immediately report to her doctor unusual swelling or pain in the legs; yellowing of skin or eyes; pain in the abdomen, chest, or arms; shortness of breath; severe headache; severe depression; or eye problems such as blurred or double vision.

People over 50 can be quite sexually active, often with younger partners who do need birth control. And sexually active people of any age can get sexually transmitted diseases.

Intrauterine devices (IUDs)--are small pieces of shaped plastic (usually containing copper and/or hormones) that are inserted into the uterus. IUD threads coming through the cervix into the vagina help check placement. IUDs generally create a condition in the fallopian tubes and uterus that hinders a pregnancy from occurring. Some types can remain in place for a long time, if there are no problems. Others have to be replaced periodically.

A complete pelvic examination will indicate whether an IUD is appropriate and what kind may be used. The user may experience some pain during the brief time of insertion, especially if the user has never been pregnant. Some users report cramps, heavier menstrual bleeding, and spotting. Most adjust in a few months, but some may require removal for pain, bleeding, or infection. Sometimes the uterus pushes out an IUD, and in rare cases, a dangerous infection may occur.

A woman is cautioned to never try to remove an IUD herself and to have regular checkups. The IUD may be inserted by a private doctor or a clinic. IUDs are very effective but expensive initially.

Diaphragms and cervical caps--are rubber barriers that fit securely in the vagina and cover the cervix. Both devices block the sperm from the entrance to the uterus. They must always be used with contraceptive cream or jelly to keep sperm from getting past the barrier.

Properly fitted, the diaphragm or cervical cap should not be felt by either partner during sexual intercourse. There are no side effects except in rare instances of allergic reaction to the material the device is made from or to the spermicide used. Contraceptive creams and jellies used with diaphragms and cervical caps may offer some protection against certain sexually transmitted diseases. A checkup for size is needed every year, or if weight is gained or lost, or following pregnancy.

A diaphragm can be inserted up to 6 hours before intercourse and may be left in place for 24 hours. Each time sex is repeated, more jelly, cream, or foam must be inserted in the vagina. A diaphragm fits against vaginal walls and may not fit if the woman gains or loses say 10 pounds. A cervical cap is a suction cup that fits directly over the cervix. The cap doesn't require additional spermicide if sex is repeated, the diaphragm does. Just put some in the cup before insertion. The diaphragm may become dislodged in the woman-superior position, or in women with relaxed vaginas (that may result from childbirth).

A cervical cap can be inserted anytime before intercourse and can be left in place for 48 hours. It can be used by women who cannot hold a diaphragm because it fits like a suction cup over the cervix and doesn't depend on the pelvic muscles to hold it in place. Because the cap may become dislodged before or during intercourse, it should be checked occasionally to see if it is properly positioned. A prescription is needed for the purchase of both diaphragms and cervical caps.

Over-the-counter spermicides--consist of contraceptive sponges, foams, creams, jellies, and suppositories that are inserted deep into the vagina to stop or kill the sperm. Sponges are doughnut-shaped, 2 inches in diameter, and made of soft, synthetic material impregnated with spermicide. They fit over the cervix, a polyester loop allows easy removal. Sponges come in one size; there is no need for a fitting. The sponge absorbs sperm and provides a physical barrier to prevent sperm from entering the uterus. All spermicides spread into the crevices of the vagina, forming barriers that paralyze and block sperm from entering the uterus.

Fertility Awareness Methods (FAMs)--are systems designed to help a woman estimate the time in her menstrual cycle when an egg is most likely to be produced and she is fertile. In women whose periods are regular, an egg is released about 14 days before the start of her next expected period. A woman may be fertile five days before the egg is released (ovulation), during ovulation, and up to three days after ovulation. During those days it is unsafe to have unprotected intercourse without risking pregnancy.

Fertility awareness techniques can be used to prevent or to plan a pregnancy and are acceptable to couples with religious concerns about birth control. The method requires keeping a daily chart of body changes and it needs expert instruction for successful use. A fertility awareness method with abstinence requires the self-control of both partners. Even with correct use, failure may be more likely than with other methods. Frustration can result from long periods of abstinence.

In the basal body temperature method, abstinence must last from menstruation until after ovulation. Body temperature is taken each morning before getting out of bed. A small but significant rise of less than one degree occurs when the egg is released. After three days of the higher level, the unsafe period is past.

The vaginal mucus system associates changes in a woman's vaginal moisture with phases of her menstrual cycle. Normally cloudy, tacky mucus will become clear and slippery and will stretch between the fingers when the egg is released. When slippery mucus appears, abstinence becomes necessary and must continue until four days after the final day that the slippery mucus is observed.

Each fertility awareness method can be used alone, but it is better to combine awareness with the basal body temperature method and the vaginal mucus system. All three methods used together have a fairly high degree of reliability. Charts are carried by family planning clinics. Temperature kits can be bought at drugstores.

Conclusion

As we have said before, older couples seldom have to worry about the above information. But, life being as it is, with all sorts of exceptions and an unpredictable future, who knows what could happen.

When the head aches, all the members
partake of the pain.

-Miguel de Cervantes (1547-1616)

Having a sinus attack?

The sinuses are hollow air spaces in the human body. The term usually refers to the cavities in the bone behind the nose. These sinuses reduce the weight of the skull, and act as resonant chambers for the voice. When people say they are having a sinus attack (sinusitis) they are referring to one or more of four groups of cavities known as paranasal sinuses. They are located within the skull or bones of the head surrounding the nose. They usually come in pairs, one on each side of the head, and are individually identified by their location.

Frontal sinuses are located over the eyes in the brow area while the maxillary sinuses are inside each cheekbone. Just behind the bridge of the nose are the ethmoids and, behind them, in the upper region of the nose are the sphenoid sinuses.

Each sinus has an opening into the nose for the free exchange of air and mucus and each is joined with the nasal passages by a continuous mucous membrane lining. Therefore, anything that causes a swelling in the nose--be it a viral or bacterial infection or an allergic reaction--can similarly affect the sinuses. Air trapped within an obstructed sinus, along with pus or other secretions, may cause pressure on the sinus wall. The result is the intense pain of a sinus attack. When air is prevented from entering a paranasal sinus by a swollen membrane at the opening, a vacuum can be created, causing pain.

The combination of allergic and infectious sinusitis has long been considered the most difficult form of sinus disease to treat. The patient with uncontrolled nasal allergies frequently experiences a high degree of congestion, swelling, excess secretions, and discomfort in the sinus areas.

An allergic individual is one who is highly sensitive to certain substances with which he comes in contact. These substances are known as allergens. Inhaled allergens, such as dust, molds, animal hairs, or the pollens of trees, grasses, and weeds, often set off the allergic reaction that, in turn, contributes to a sinusitis attack. As body cells react against these foreign substances, chemical compounds, such as histamine, are liberated at the mucosal surface. This, in turn, produces swelling and blockage of the nasal passages and sinuses.

ACUTE SINUSITIS
MAY BE CAUSED BY

* A nasal infection (rhinitis)--sinuses become blocked
* The common cold
* Any feverish respiratory illness, such as influenza
* A dental abscess (in rare cases)
* A fracture of a bone in the face
* Sudden pressure changes, such as jumping or diving during swimming or pressure changes during air travel

CHRONIC SINUSITIS
MAY BE CAUSED BY

* An allergy, such as hay fever
* Repeated attacks of acute sinusitis
* Inadequate treatment of acute sinusitis
* Nasal obstruction, as may occur with a polyp
* A deviated nasal septum
* Chronic dental infections

SYMPTOMS OF SINUSITIS--The symptoms of acute sinusitis are very much like those of a bad cold. The area over the affected sinus may be painful and tender, and there is usually a severe headache. The nose may be blocked on the affected side, causing the patient to breathe through the mouth. The patient may also have a fever, chills, and a sore throat. Headache upon awakening in the morning is characteristic of sinus involvement.

* Inflammation of the frontal sinuses causes a pain when the forehead is touched.
* Infection in the maxillary sinuses can cause the upper jaw and teeth to ache, and the cheeks become tender to the touch.
* Inflammation of the ethmoids causes swelling of the eyelids and tissues around the eyes, pain between the eyes and tenderness when the sides of the nose are touched, a loss of smell, and a stuffy nose.
* Infection in the sphenoid sinuses can result in earaches, neck pain, and deep aching at the top of the head.
* Another symptom of sinusitis is the drainage of mucus behind the nose and down the back of the throat. This postnasal drip can lead to irritation of the throat or membranes lining the larynx or upper windpipe.

TREATMENT of sinusitis is aimed at reestablishing drainage of the nasal passages, controlling or eliminating the source of the inflammation, and relieving the pain. A physician may prescribe medication to reduce the congestion, antibiotics to control a bacterial infection, and painkillers to relieve the discomfort.

Painkilling drugs, such as aspirin or acetaminophen, may help. Inhaled steam may open the sinuses, and help to promote drainage of mucus that has accumulated within the affected sinus. In severe cases, surgery may be necessary.

PREVENTIVE MEASURES

■ Appropriate amounts of rest, a well-balanced diet, and exercise can help the body function at its most efficient level and maintain resistance to infections.

■ When the room is dry, humidifiers can give partial relief. Air conditioners help to provide an even temperature and electrostatic filters are valuable in removing dust and pollen from the air.

■ Cigarette smoke and other air pollutants should be avoided by a person susceptible to sinus disorders. Since alcohol causes a swelling of the nasal sinus membranes, its ingestion should be curtailed.

■ Sinusitis-prone individuals may be uncomfortable in swimming pools treated with chlorine, since this substance is irritating to the lining of the nose and sinuses.

■ Air travel, too, poses a problem for the individual suffering from acute upper respiratory disease, chronic sinusitis, or allergic rhinitis. A bubble of air trapped within the body expands as air pressure in a plane is reduced. This expansion causes pressure on surrounding tissues and can result in a blockage of the sinuses or eustachian tubes.

■ If a person suspects that his sinus inflammation may be related to an allergic reaction to dust, mold, food, or pollen, or any of the hundreds of allergens that can trigger a reaction, he would be wise to seek his physician's referral to an allergist.

■ Adults who have had allergic and infectious conditions over the years sometimes develop polyps (small growths) on the mucous membrane lining of the sinuses that interfere with proper drainage. Removal of these polyps to ensure an open airway often provides considerable improvement.

■ Drink plenty of water.

To sleep; perchance to dream; ay, there's the rub;

A good night's sleep can make a big difference in the way we feel, live, and respond to our daytime life. Many older people find that bedtime is the hardest part of the day, and nothing can be more miserable than endless hours of disturbed sleep. In America more than 50 million people complain about the quality of their sleep--sleep problems that profoundly disturb both sleeping and waking life.

Sleep is one good thing you can't get too much of, claims psychologist and sleep researcher Timothy Roehrs, Ph.D., of the Sleep Disorder Center in Detroit. Even folks who don't complain of daytime sleepiness benefit from extra rest.

Dr. Roehrs studied a group of healthy men who reported that they slept well and didn't need any more rest than they were getting. A standard test of sleepiness showed otherwise. When given a comfortable place to rest, some of the men dozed off in 6 minutes or less. These men usually slept about 7 hours a night. A group that took 16 minutes or more to drift off averaged 8 hours of sleep a night. Everyone in the study benefited when extra nighttime sleep was added to their schedule. The sleepiest group improved their alertness the most, but the nonsleepy group also improved. In an ideal world, says Dr. Roehrs, we would simply sleep until we awoke naturally. Barring that, he recommends that most of us sack out earlier.

The scientific study of sleep began in the 1930s when investigators, using the electroencephalograph (EEG), measured the brain's rhythm and activity during sleep. Instead of being a quiet and peaceful period of rest and recuperation, as most of us think of it, sleep is a very complex, dynamic activity. Your body may be the picture of tranquility while you sleep; but, in fact, numerous biochemical, physiological, and psychological events are constantly taking place.

Normal sleep consists of four stages, characterized by alpha rhythms from an EEG recording. A state of being awake records ten alpha rhythm cycles per second slowing down to deep sleep in stages 3 and 4 of two cycles per second. Deep sleep is known as slow-wave sleep because during it there is reduced electrical activity in the brain. It is also known as non-REM sleep, because the eyes do not move rapidly during this phase. In slow-wave sleep, there is a decrease in the basal metabolic rate, blood pressure, and respiratory rate so that the person lies still and is totally relaxed. Without the deep slow-wave sleep, daily wakefulness may be impaired.

The first two stages of sleep are known as REM sleep, because of the rapid eye movements that take place behind the closed eyelids. Also during this phase, dreaming takes place, the heartbeat and respiration become irregular, and there may be limb movement. Sleep alternates between periods of slow-wave and REM sleep lasting 10 to 20 minutes and occurring every hour and a half until the person awakes. Dreaming is a necessary part of normal sleep, and is also probably necessary for the well-being of the mind.

HOW LONG TO SLEEP

No one really knows how much sleep we need. Sleep duration varies widely. A newborn infant may sleep 16 hours a day or more, an adolescent may sleep very deeply for 9 or 10 hours straight, while an elderly person may take daytime naps and then sleep only 5 hours a night. Most adults sleep between 7 and 8 hours. A natural "short sleeper" may sleep for only 3 or 4 hours; a "long sleeper" may need more than 10 hours. "Variable sleepers" seem to need more sleep at times of stress and less during peaceful times. People are sleeping as much as they need if, during their waking hours, they are alert and have a sense of well-being.

To find out how much sleep you need, try to determine your own sleep pattern. You should feel sleepy about the same time every evening provided you get up at the same time each morning. If you frequently have trouble staying awake in the daytime, you may not be sleeping long enough. Or perhaps you are not sleeping well enough. Both the quantity and quality of sleep and wakefulness are important.

INSOMNIA

The most common sleep complaint is insomnia, which is the habitual difficulty of falling asleep when it is time to go to bed. It is often accompanied by constantly awaking during your time in bed. Insomnia is a feeling that you have not slept well or long enough. It occurs in many different forms. Most often it is characterized by difficulty in falling asleep (taking more than 30 to 45 minutes), awakening frequently during the night, or waking up early and being unable to get back to sleep.

According to data gathered on almost 8,000 people by the National Institute of Mental Health researchers, the chances are good that people who sleep too much or too little also have depression or severe anxiety. Anxious people may be plagued by unpleasant or obsessive thoughts that prevent them from sleeping. Depressed people may have similar problems, complicated by feelings of helplessness and hopelessness that they cannot escape. Treatment of the anxiety or depression usually results in improved sleep.

Some researchers claim that one's requirement for sleep lessens with age; others say that it stays the same. While a newborn may spend 18 hours a day sleeping, an elderly person may or may not do very well on 4 1/2 to 6 hours. Basing a complaint of insomnia on number of hours slept is not valid. Only when chronic insomnia results in chronic fatigue, irritability, and diminished mental performance does a problem exist.

CAUSES OF INSOMNIA

With rare exceptions, insomnia is a symptom of a problem, and not the problem itself. Good sleep is a sign of health. Poor sleep is often a sign of some malfunctioning and may signal either minor or serious medical or psychiatric disorders. Insomnia can begin at any age. And, it can last for a few days (transient insomnia), a few weeks (short-term insomnia), or longer (long-term insomnia).

Transient insomnia may be triggered by stress--say, a hospitalization for surgery, a final exam, a cold, headache, toothache, bruised muscles, backache, indigestion, or itchy rash. It can also be caused by jet travel that involves rapid time-zone change.

Providence has given us hope and
sleep as a compensation for the many
cares of life.

- Voltaire

PHYSICAL AILMENTS

(page 2 of 3) SLEEP DISORDERS 407

Short-term insomnia, lasting up to three weeks, may result from anxiety, nervousness, and physical or mental tension. Typical are worries about money, the death of a loved one, marital problems, divorce, looking for or losing a job, weight loss, excessive concern about health, plain boredom, social isolation, or physical confinement.

Long-lasting distress over lack of sleep is sometimes caused by the environment, such as living near an airport or on a noisy street. Working a night shift can also cause problems: Sleeping during the day may be difficult on weekdays, especially when the person sleeps at night on weekends.

But more often, long-term insomnia stems from such medical conditions as heart disease, arthritis, diabetes, asthma, chronic sinusitis, epilepsy, or ulcers. Long-term impaired sleep can also be brought on by chronic drug or alcohol use, as well as by excessive use of beverages containing caffeine and abuse of sleeping pills.

Sometimes long-term sleep difficulty can result from sleep apnea, nocturnal myoclonus, or "restless legs" syndrome. Many patients with long-term insomnia may be suffering from an underlying psychiatric condition, such as depression or schizophrenia. Depression, in particular, is often accompanied by sleep problems (which usually disappear when the depression is treated). People with phobias, anxiety, obsessions, or compulsions are often awakened by their fears, worries, nightmares, feelings of sadness, conflict, and guilt.

Causes of insomnia may be medical, psychological, or behavioral. Arthritis pain, nocturnal asthma, angina pectoris, congestive heart failure, or peptic disease all may result in increased symptoms at night with resulting insomnia. Primary sleep disorders such as sleep apnea in which the sleeper frequently stops breathing, snores, snorts, and occasionally wakes is a relatively common cause of insomnia. Frequently this disorder is associated with obesity and hypertension.

Behavioral causes of insomnia are multiple; perhaps the biggest problem in this area is alcohol. While in the short term alcohol may make one feel sleepy, within a few hours after ingestion of an alcoholic drink a kind of withdrawal begins. This disrupts sleep and results in a night of tossing and turning. Beverages containing caffeine taken in the afternoon or evening are also a frequent cause of insomnia if you are not a regular coffee drinker.

Anyone troubled by insomnia should review his or her sleep hygiene: Make sure the bedroom is appropriate for sleep--light, temperature, ventilation, and humidity all must be taken into account. Noise level is also important. For city dwellers or others in noisy environments, ear plugs may be necessary. The bed should be comfortable and of appropriate size. Individual preferences obviously make a big difference. People with orthopedic problems or esophageal reflux should modify their beds accordingly. Bedtime should be fixed, as should wake-up time. Routinization of sleep behavior can be very helpful in alleviating insomnia.

SLEEPING PILLS

Prescription sleeping pills should be avoided except at times of emotional or physical stress, that is, following the death of a loved one, or while traveling to combat jet lag. Sleeping pills quickly lose their effectiveness if used on a nightly basis. More than that, they can become addictive. Sleeping pills may also cause a "hangover" of some type that may impair mental and physical performance the following day.

Older people have a slower metabolism, so sleeping pills take longer to work and may stay in the person's system for many hours. The elderly fall enough as it is without having to deal with drowsiness. When sedative and hypnotic drugs are used in the treatment of insomnia, the length and number of periods of REM sleep are reduced. This can cause mild depression. When the drugs are stopped, sleep may be disturbed for ten to fourteen days. REM sleep increases, and the person feels that the insomnia is worse than before. After using sleeping pills, it takes about two weeks for natural sleep patterns to return.

Another problem with sleep-inducing drugs is the slight daytime sedation that may occur and reduce a person's speed of reaction. This is particularly relevant when driving an automobile, using machinery or, most important of all, taking alcohol. Alcohol in combination with barbiturates is dangerous and can be fatal. Contact your doctor if any adverse effects occur when using sleeping pills.

Nonprescription sleeping medications employ antihistamines as their active ingredient. These medications cause drowsiness, which may result in sleep. They are most effective in people who don't use antihistamines on a regular basis. L-tryptophan is marketed as a "natural" sleeping aid. It is an amino acid precursor to serotonin, a brain chemical active in the sleep process. It must be taken in a dose of 500 to 1000 mg to be effective and its long-term safety has not been established.

TIPS FOR A GREAT NIGHT'S SLEEP

Sleepless nights plague everyone once in a while, but there are steps you can take to ensure refreshing slumber. All tips do not work for everyone, so do a little experimenting.

* Make sure you are physically tired before going to bed, says sleep expert Gregor Bolland of Los Angeles. Use your time to read a book, write a letter, or catch up on your housework. Exercise is good for some people.
* Sleep comes easier if your bedroom is a comfortable temperature. If you don't like the bulk of too many blankets on top of you, invest in a good electric blanket to keep you warm at night. Likewise, a room that is too stuffy is often difficult to sleep in. Crack a nearby window for a breath of fresh air.
* Soundproof your bedroom or wear earplugs if outside noise keeps you awake at night.
* Stay away from coffee, tea, or colas immediately before bedtime. They are full of caffeine, which stimulates the body. Alcohol and tobacco can have a similar sleep-wrecking effect.
* Try to go to bed without any worries. Write down your problems before you hit the sack and resolve to take care of them the following day.
* Make sure your pillow is comfortable and offers proper support to your head and neck.
* Don't go to bed hungry--but don't eat a heavy snack immediately before bedtime. It can keep you awake. Eat lightly.
* A warm bath half an hour before you go to bed will help relax your muscles.

It is a delicious moment, certainly,
that of being well nestled in bed,
and feeling that you shall drop gently to
sleep. The good is to come, not past...

- Leith Hunt (1784-1859)

* Soak your feet in hot water for 10 minutes before you go to bed. The medico that suggests it claims it's almost, but not quite as good a sleep inducer, as a 10-minute stroll in the fresh air. Both tease blood away from the brain.
* Regular exercise tends to benefit sleep, but not right at bedtime. A brief period of vigorous exercise in the late afternoon or early evening may help in falling asleep later in the evening. A brisk walk or comfortable jog also helps relax the body and the mind.
* Don't try too hard. If you go to bed when you feel sleepy but find that you can't fall asleep, don't stay in bed brooding about being awake. Get out of bed, leave the bedroom, and do something else, like read a book.
* Laboratory tests have shown that daytime naps disrupt normal nighttime sleep. However, many older people do sleep better at night when they take daytime naps.
* The effect of alcohol is deceiving. It may induce sleep, but it will be fragmented sleep. The sleeper will probably wake up in the middle of the night when the alcohol's relaxing effect wears off.
* The best way to sleep better is to keep a regular schedule for sleeping. Go to bed at about the same time every night, but only when you are tired. Set your alarm clock to awaken you about the same time every morning--including weekends and regardless of the amount of sleep you have had. If you have a poor night's sleep, don't linger in bed or oversleep the next day. If you awaken before it is time to rise, get out of bed and start your day. Most insomniacs stay in bed too long and get up too late in the morning. By establishing a regular wakeup time, you help solidify the biological rhythms that establish your periods of peak efficiency during the 24-hour day.

OTHER SLEEP DISORDERS

■ **Snoring.** Snoring is a sign of impaired breathing during sleep. The older you get, the more apt you are to snore. Almost 60% of males and 45% of females in their 60s are habitual snorers--in all, 1 in 8 Americans. Light snoring may be no more than a nuisance. But snoring that is loud, disruptive, and accompanied by extreme daytime sleepiness or sleep attacks should be taken very seriously. Such snoring may be a sign of sleep apnea.

■ **Sleep Apnea.** Sleep apnea is believed to affect at least 1 out of every 200 Americans--70% to 90% of them men, mostly middle-aged, and usually overweight. But the condition can afflict both men and women at any age. People with this disorder actually may stop breathing while asleep--even hundreds of times--without being aware of the problem.

During an apnea attack, the snorer may seem to hold his breath or gasp for breath. Air stops flowing through the nose and mouth, but throat and abdominal breathing efforts are uninterrupted. Typically, the individual will wake up, emit a vigorous snort or grunt while gasping for air, then immediately fall back to sleep, only to repeat the cycle. The person is deprived of oxygen, the deep stages of sleep are severely interrupted, and the person may be at risk for death or at least narcolepsy or chronic fatigue syndrome. Doctors can reliably diagnose this disorder in a sleep clinic only by monitoring oxygen intake, breathing, and other physical functions in the sleeping patient.

■ **Narcolepsy.** A sleepy feeling during the day could be caused by insufficient, inadequate, or fragmented sleep, by insomnia, or by boredom, social isolation, physical confinement, or depression. But, if you continually experience excessive daytime sleepiness--sometimes expressed as tiredness, lack of energy, and/or irresistible sleepiness--you could be suffering from another chronic sleep disorder called narcolepsy.

Narcolepsy, believed to be caused by a defect in the central nervous system, has no known cure. However, after proper diagnosis, the disorder can be effectively managed with drugs.

■ **Nocturnal Myoclonus** (unusual movement during sleep). Just before some people fall asleep, they experience an uncomfortable, but not always painful, sensation deep in the thigh, calf, or feet. They usually find that vigorous movement eases the discomfort enough to fall asleep, but they complain of sleepiness and fatigue during the day. These people are generally not aware that such episodes of repetitive leg muscle jerks or muscle twitches--nocturnal myoclonus--are followed through the night by hundreds of related awakenings. People with nocturnal myoclonus may have involuntary movement in their legs, in addition to twitches, while trying to relax. This condition is known as "restless leg syndrome." Upon awakening, some people with nocturnal myoclonus complain of an itching-crawling sensation in their legs, like "current going through them."

In some cases, nocturnal myoclonus has been associated with too little vitamin E, iron, or calcium, and vitamin and mineral supplements have been used as treatment. In other cases, drugs have been found effective, and, in still other, less severe cases, relief has come from leg exercises.

■ **Sleepwalking** or somnambulism is fairly common, especially among children. Sleepwalkers don't always make their rounds in safety. They sometimes hurt themselves, stumbling against furniture and losing their balance, going through windows, or falling down stairs. In adults, sleep walking could indicate a personality disturbance. Preventive measures can be used, and sometimes in severe cases, drugs are effective.

■ **Nightmares** can be very threatening to small children and to older feeble adults. These frightening dream experiences tend to occur at times of insecurity, emotional turmoil, depression, or guilt. It can be best handled by someone who will give love, care, and reassurance. Incubus or suffocating nightmares often go with sleep apnea and can be both terrifying and dangerous.

TREATMENT

Today, sleep clinics are diagnosing and treating sleep disorders in very effective ways. Patients are typically seen as outpatients. They are interviewed thoroughly, given a battery of psychological tests and, if indicated, have their sleep patterns recorded in the laboratory for one night to determine the cause of the sleep disturbance. For a complete roster of accredited and provisional sleep disorder centers and clinics, write to:

The American Narcolepsy Association
P.O. Box 5846
Stanford, CA 94305

The American Narcolepsy Association is an independent, not-for-profit corporation that was established in 1975 to help solve the many problems associated with narcolepsy and related sleep disorders.

or

Association of Professional
Sleep Societies
604 2nd Street, S.W.
Rochester, MN 55902

After age 60--smelling ability declines

More than 10 million Americans have smell and taste disorders. Each year 200,000 persons visit a physician for a smell or taste difficulty. The predominant problem is a natural decline in smelling ability that typically occurs after age 60.

The complicated processes of smelling and tasting begin when tiny molecules released by the substances around us stimulate special cells in the nose, mouth, or throat. These special nerve cells transmit messages to the brain where specific smells or tastes are identified. Taste and smell cells are the only cells in the nervous system that are replaced when they wear out or become damaged.

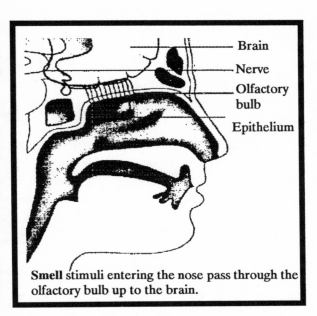

Smell stimuli entering the nose pass through the olfactory bulb up to the brain.

THE SENSE OF SMELL--is the ability to detect odors. The organ of smell consists of a group of sensitive cells situated in the upper part of the nasal cavity, which is connected to the brain by the olfactory nerve. The sense of smell is not well developed in humans. It is limited to the sensation of seven basic odors and their combinations. It is, however, an important contributory factor to the sense of taste. And, like the sense of taste, it becomes less acute as a person becomes older or in persons who smoke.

TASTE--is the sensation that is obtained when specialized sensory nerve endings (the taste buds) detect soluble substances. The taste buds can register four fundamental tastes, either singly or in combination: sweet, bitter, sour, and salty. Taste buds are sensory nerve endings on the surface of the tongue, mouth, and throat. When they detect tastes, they send impulses to the brain, where the perception of taste occurs.

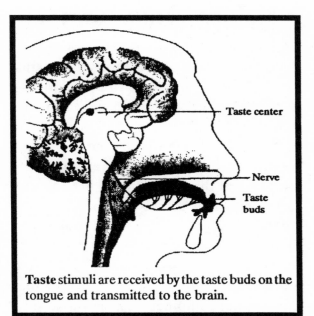

Taste stimuli are received by the taste buds on the tongue and transmitted to the brain.

CHEMOSENSORY--A third chemosensory mechanism contributes to our sense of smell and taste in our system. Thousands of free nerve endings, especially on the moist surfaces of the eyes, nose, mouth, and throat, give rise to sensations like the sting of ammonia, the coolness of menthol, and the "heat" of chili peppers.

Certain combinations of the four basic taste sensations--sweet, sour, bitter, and salty--along with texture, temperature, odor, and the sensations from the common chemical sense produce a flavor. It is the flavor that lets us know whether we are eating peanuts or caviar.

SMELL AND TASTE DISORDERS
* **Hyposmia:** a reduced ability to detect odors
* **Hypoqeusia:** a reduced ability to taste sweet, sour, bitter, or salty substances
* **Anosmia:** inability to detect odors
* **Aqeusia:** inability to taste

WHAT CAUSES DISORDERS
1. Genetics--people are sometimes born that way
2. Upper respiratory infections
3. Injuries to the head, particularly a fracture
4. Polyps in the nasal or sinus cavities
5. Hormonal disturbances
6. Dental problems
7. Prolonged exposure to toxic chemicals or some medications

ARE SMELL AND TASTE DISORDERS
SERIOUS?--A person with faulty chemosenses is deprived of an early warning system that most of us take for granted. Smell and taste alert us to fires, poisonous fumes, leaking gas, and spoiled food. Chemosensory problems may also be a sign of sinus disease, growths in the nasal passages, or, in rare circumstances, brain tumors. Because taste triggers many digestive processes, a malfunction of this sense may upset normal digestion. Smell and taste losses can also lead to depression.

CAN SMELL AND TASTE DISORDERS BE TREATED?--If a certain medication is the cause of a smell or taste disorder, stopping or changing the medicine may help eliminate the problem. Some patients--notably those with serious respiratory infections or seasonal allergies--regain their smell or taste simply by waiting for their illness to run its course. In many cases, nasal obstructions such as polyps can be removed to restore airflow to the receptor area. When there is a more serious cause for the disorder--a brain tumor, for example--correcting the larger medical problem can also correct the loss of smell and taste. Occasionally, chemosenses return to normal just as spontaneously as they disappeared.

Marcel Proust

1871-1922

When from a long-distant past nothing subsists, after the people are dead, after the things are broken and scattered, still, alone, more fragile, but with more vitality, more unsubstantial, more persistent, more faithful, the smell and taste of things remain poised a long time, like souls, ready to remind us, waiting and hoping for their moment, amid the ruins of all the rest, and bear unfaltering, in the tiny and almost impalpable drop of their essence, the vast structure of recollection.

Remembrance of Things Past (1913-1926) Swanns's Way

TMJ--Temporomandibular Joint Disorder

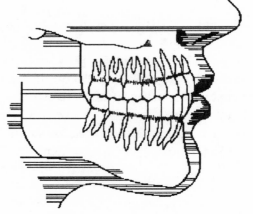

Flaws in the jaws!

Temporomandibular (**TMJ**) refers to the temporal bones and the mandible, or jawbone, which form the hinges that allow the jaw to move.

Jaw motion maladies may afflict as many as 60 million Americans, says the American Dental Association. Women between 15 and 44 appear to be the most susceptible, though reported cases have included both sexes in all age groups. About 5% of patients have severe, even disabling, symptoms that require extended care and, infrequently, highly specialized surgery.

SYMPTOMS

Pain is the most frequently reported complaint with a TMJ disorder. The pain is a dull ache, usually following eating or yawning. Most patients feel pain on only one side--usually in the temple, cheek, and front of the ear. Some patients also have pain in the neck or shoulder muscles. The pain is often continuous or at least once a day.

Limited jaw movement often is a result of a TMJ disorder. Also commonly reported are various joint noises, which can come from other sources.

> Young people tell what they are doing, old people what they have done, and fools what they wish to do.
>
> French Proverb

CONFIGURATION OF THE JAW

A complex network of bones, ligaments, joints, and muscles makes up the specialized system by which we chew, yawn, and move the jaw. The temporal bones join the jawbone at the sides of the head via fibrous tissue called ligaments, which form a capsule around the joint. Inside the capsule, firmly attached to the jawbone and the capsule, is a thin, cartilage-like, pliable oval disk. This disk separates the bones and forms compartments between itself and the bones; one compartment is on its temporal bone side and another on its jawbone side. Within each compartment is a fluid-filled membrane or sac. The disk and membranes absorb shocks and lubricate the joint.

Opening and closing the mouth and moving the jaws forward, backward, and side to side require different types of motions in different joint compartments with different sets of muscles. Anything that interferes with the proper functioning of any part of this complex system of structures could result in a TMJ disorder.

CAUSES

❋ Do you grind your teeth? Nonchewing gnashing, a common sign of stress, tires the muscles to set the stage for a spasm-pain-spasm cycle that can result in a TMJ disorder in which facial pain may spread to nearby muscles.

❋ Disk displacement due to stretching or tearing of the fibrous tissue attaching it to the joint capsule.

❋ Problems due to injury. For example a jawbone dislocation from a car accident.

❋ Degenerative joint disease such as osteoarthritis.

❋ The membranes on the sides of the disk can become inflamed due to rheumatoid arthritis.

❋ Fibrous ankylosis, in which fibrous tissue forms in the joint to reduce jaw move-

ment. Untreated, it can eventually freeze the jaw shut.

❋ The jawbone may continue to enlarge after growth should have stopped. This causes the bite and joint movements to become abnormal.

TREATMENTS

Most cases of TMJ disorders will improve or go away with little or no treatment within three or four weeks. If it doesn't go away it will be necessary to seek professional help and get a proper diagnosis of the cause. Dentists, physicians, oral surgeons, psychologists, and chiropractors have treated TMJ. Whenever possible, TMJ disorder therapies should be conservative and reversible. Eighty percent of the patients can be treated successfully with mild methods:

❋ Over-the-counter aspirin, ibuprofen, or acetaminophen may be given for pain.

❋ A muscle relaxant can be prescribed.

❋ Moist heat, massage, and a temporary soft diet have proved helpful.

❋ When grinding causes the spasms, a bite appliance can be used to help the patient hold the upper and lower teeth apart.

❋ If chewing patterns become altered from damage caused by the grinding, the bite may become out of line. A dentist can restore alignment.

❋ Counseling, relaxation training, or biofeedback may help if stress is a problem.

❋ Surgery is an appropriate treatment when a tumor must be removed or when there is severe jaw immobility.

Ten years ago TMJ disorders were rarely heard of, but today they are a very common facet of dentistry. People often overrespond to new conditions and it is not uncommon for TMJ disorders to be overtreated with unproven therapies.

Tender or bleeding gums?--see your dentist

Most of us have learned the basic elements of good dental health, but we all need to be reminded on occasion. Our teeth were intended to last a lifetime--and they can, if cared for properly. Preventive dental care dates back to the 1950s, so many people over 65 did not grow up with the idea. Good oral health will give us a pretty smile at any age, even if we wear dentures.

TOOTH DECAY--or cavities are caused by bacteria that normally live in the mouth. The bacteria stick to the teeth and form a sticky, colorless film called dental plaque. The bacteria in plaque produce decay-causing acids that dissolve minerals in the tooth surface. The bacteria in plaque lives on sugar and must be brushed off daily.

PERIODONTAL (GUM) DISEASE--is caused by buildup of plaque. If plaque is not removed from the teeth every day it may harden into tartar, which must be removed by a dentist. Bacteria in plaque irritate the gums, which become inflamed and bleed, becoming painful and causing bad breath. If left untreated, the disease gets worse as pockets of infection form between the teeth and gums, causing the gums to recede and teeth to loosen. At some point in life, about three out of four adults will be affected by this disease.

GINGIVITIS--More than half of all adults over age 18 have an early stage of periodontal disease called "gingivitis" in which only the soft gum tissue has been affected. Although it is common, it can easily be prevented with proper daily care by brushing and flossing.

PERIDONTITIS--is the later stage of periodontal disease in which the gums, bone, and other structures that support the teeth have been seriously damaged. Then the infection spreads toward the roots of the teeth and, eventually, teeth become loose and fall out. Periodontal disease is the major cause of tooth loss in adults.

TREATMENT OF PERIODONTAL DISEASE--is done by general dentists; in more advanced cases the patient may be referred to a periodontist. In the early stages of periodontal disease, professional cleaning may be all the treatment that is necessary. The teeth are scaled (scraped free of plaque and calculus). If inflamed tissue is present in pockets, it is also scraped away (curettage). Finally, the root surfaces are planed to make them completely smooth. Some patients need a systemic or topical (locally applied) antibiotic to bring the infection under control. When the pocket depths of the infection exceed about five millimeters, surgery may be necessary to remove the diseased tissue. When the disease has progressed to the bone, a flap of gum tissue is laid back to allow access, and calculus, plaque, and diseased tissue are removed. The bone may need to be reshaped or replaced with transplanted natural bone. Periodontal surgery is generally an office procedure.

PROPER CARE OF TEETH AND GUMS

- Adding fluoride to the water supply is the best and least costly way to prevent tooth decay.
- Brush your teeth thoroughly at least once a day with a fluoride toothpaste. This will remove plaque from the outer, inner, and chewing surfaces of the teeth.
- Floss thoroughly every day. This removes plaque from the areas along the gum line and between the teeth, where a toothbrush can't reach. Be careful not to let the floss cut the gum tissue. Flossing will reverse the early stages of periodontal disease.
- Use a disclosing solution that will stain any remaining plaque and show you those areas you have missed. Just brush and floss these areas more carefully.
- Rinse the mouth thoroughly. An antimicrobial mouthrinse may be helpful to control harmful bacteria in your mouth.
- Eat a "balanced" diet so that your body gets the nutrients needed for good health.
- Schedule regular dental visits to get your teeth professionally cleaned and any dental problem taken care of.

FACTORS IN PERIODONTAL DISEASE

- Physical and chemical irritants in the mouth
- Impacted food between the teeth
- Improper flossing and brushing
- Smoking or chewing tobacco
- Malocclusion (badly aligned teeth)
- Sloppy fillings that impair cleaning
- Improperly fitted crowns, bridges, or partial dentures
- Nail biting or bruxism (clenching or grinding the teeth)
- Poor diet
- Systemic diseases such as diabetes and others that can lower resistance to infection
- Medications such as steroids and cancer therapy
- Stress

The above factors contribute to the severity of periodontal disease, but they do not cause it. Practice plaque control and oral hygiene.

DENTURES--If you have dentures, you should keep them clean and free from food deposits that can cause permanent staining, bad breath, and gum irritation.

- Once a day, brush all surfaces of the dentures with a denture-care product.
- Rinse your mouth well to free it of food particles in the morning, after meals, and at bedtime.
- Dentures need to be replaced or readjusted to the changes in the tissues of the mouth that may have occurred over time.
- Do not try to repair dentures at home.
- Have regular dental checkups.
- Partial dentures should be cared for similar to full dentures. Because bacteria tend to collect under the clasps of partial dentures, it is especially important that this area be cleaned thoroughly.

A METHOD FOR CLEANING TEETH

1. Use only a soft brush and buy a new one as soon as it wears out! It will take about three minutes of brushing to make your teeth really clean.
2. Place the head of the toothbrush beside your teeth, with the bristle tips at a 45-degree angle to the gums.
3. Move the brush back and forth in short strokes, using a gentle scrubbing motion to loosen plaque below the gum line.
4. Brush the outside surfaces of the teeth, the inside surfaces, then the chewing surfaces using any motion that works for you.
5. Tilt the brush vertically to clean the inside surfaces of the front teeth.
6. Brush your tongue to freshen your breath (bacteria live there, too).

DENTAL HEALTH SPECIALISTS

Dental assistants--help dentists and dental hygienists.

Dental hygienists (R.D.H.)--examine, clean, and polish the teeth, take X-rays, and teach patients about proper dental care.

Dentists (D.D.S. or D.M.D.)--treat oral conditions such as gum disease and tooth decay. They also do regular checkups, give routine dental and preventive care, fill cavities, remove teeth, provide dentures, and check for cancers in the mouth.

Endodontists--focus on treating diseased tooth pulp.

Oral surgeons--do difficult tooth removals and surgery on the jaw.

Orthodonists--specialize in correcting misaligned teeth.

Periodontist--specialist in gum diseases.

Prosthodonists--specialize in replacing missing teeth.

The second 50 years of sight!

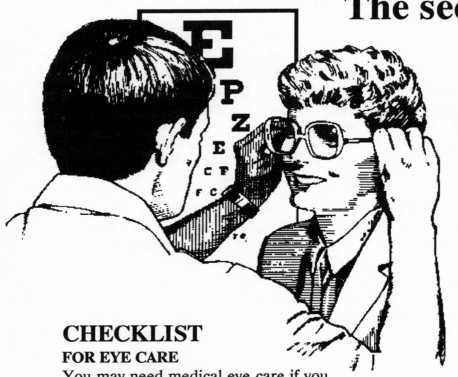

CHECKLIST

FOR EYE CARE

You may need medical eye care if you have any of the following symptoms:

Blurry vision uncorrectable by lenses

Double vision

Dimming of vision that comes and goes

Sudden loss of vision

Red eye

Eye pain

Loss of side vision

Haloes (colored rays or circles around lights)

Crossed, turned, or wandering eye

Twitching or shaking eye

Flashes or streaks of light

New floaters (spots, strings, or shadows)

Discharge, crusting, or excessive tearing

Swelling of any part of the eye

Bulging of one or both eyes

Difference in the size of the eyes

Diabetes

WHO TAKES CARE OF YOUR EYES?

An **OPHTHALMOLOGIST** is a doctor (M.D. or D.O.) licensed to practice medicine and surgery. They specialize in all aspects of eye and vision care.

An **OPTOMETRIST** is a doctor (O.D.) licensed to practice optometry and specializes in determining the need for glasses and screens the patient for abnormalities.

An **OPTICIAN** is licensed to fit, adjust, and dispense glasses and other optical devices on the written prescription of a licensed physician or optometrist.

SOME BACKGROUND ON YOUR EYES--The eye is an almost perfect sphere about one inch in diameter. The front part of the eye between the cornea and the lens is filled with a clear, watery fluid called aqueous humor. Behind the lens the eye is filled with a transparent, colorless mass of soft, gelatinous material called the vitreous body that helps to maintain its shape. The inside of the lids and the white of the eye are covered with a mucous membrane called conjunctiva.

The sclera is the eye's white outer surface, a tough covering that forms the external protective coat of the eye. The transparent area in the front called the cornea transmits light to the retina. The middle covering of the eyeball lines the sclera. It contains veins and arteries that furnish nourishment to the eye, especially the retina, and is called the choroid. The front edge of the choroid is called the ciliary body. The iris is the colored disk in front of the lens. The retina is a layer of millions of light-sensitive nerve cells that overlies the choroid. There are two types of nerve cells in the retina: rods and cones. The individual nerve fibers from these cells join to form the optic nerve.

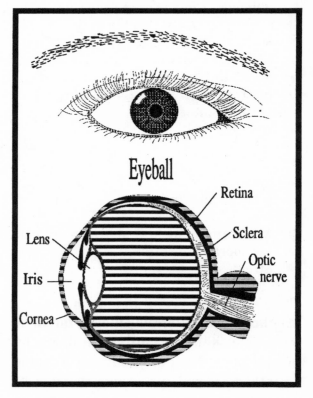

Eyeball

Lens — Iris — Cornea — Retina — Sclera — Optic nerve

The amount of light entering the eye is controlled by the iris, which contains circular muscles and radial muscles. When the circular muscles contract, the pupil gets smaller. When the radial muscles contract, the pupil gets larger. These muscles are controlled by the autonomic nervous system.

Light is focused by the cornea and the lens. The cornea is the major focusing component; the lens performs fine focusing. The lens can change its shape so that near and far objects can be focused; this is called accommodation.

Light is focused mainly on one area of the retina called the macula lutea. In the center of the macula lutea is the fovea, the region that gives the greatest visual acuity. Visual acuity depends upon the number and density of the rods and cones, since each cell can record only the presence of light and, in cones, its color. There are about 10 million cones and 100 million rods in each eye.

When light falls on a rod or cone, the cell sends impulses along the optic nerve to the brain, which interprets them into a representation of the image. Each of the three types of cone cells are sensitive to either red, green, or blue light. These colors stimulate particular cone cells so that color is perceived.

VISUAL ACUITY--You are considered to have normal 20/20 vision if you can read letters that are 3/8 of an inch high on a chart when you are 20 feet from it. If you can only read letters that are 1/2 inch in height your vision is recorded as 20/30. If the letters must be 3/4 of an inch high before you can read them 20 feet away, your vision acuity is recorded as 20/40. If the only letters you can read at 20 feet are 3 1/2 inches high your visual acuity is recorded as 20/200. The legal definition of blindness is 20/200 or worse with the most efficient corrective lens.

You can obtain a noncommercial driver's license if your vision is 20/40 with or without glasses.

Normally an individual who can see clearly at 20 feet also can read tiny print at a distance of 14 inches.

Vision problems and tips on eye care

SOME COMMON VISION PROBLEMS THAT OLDER ADULTS EXPERIENCE

PRESBYOPIA--the blurring of near vision, usually beginning at the age of 40 to 45. Reading may become difficult. Reading glasses, contact lenses, or multifocal lenses will help.

SPOTS AND FLOATERS--We frequently see spots or floating particles as we grow older. It is often harmless, but should be evaluated.

DRY EYES--occur when the tear glands produce too few tears. The result is itching, burning, or even reduced vision. An eye specialist can prescribe special eyedrop solutions to correct the problem.

EXCESSIVE TEARS--may be a sign of increased sensitivity to light, wind, or temperature changes. Protective measures such as sunglasses may solve the problem. Tearing may also indicate an eye infection or a blocked tear duct, which can be treated.

GLAUCOMA--One of every eight blind Americans is a victim of glaucoma. This condition occurs when fluid pressure inside the eye rises above normal, causing loss of side vision or blindness. If detected in time, it can usually be controlled by medication. Surgery is sometimes used to help fluid escape from the eye, and thus reduce pressure. Regular eye examinations, especially for older people, are important because they are more prone to this condition.

CATARACTS--As people grow older, they may begin to develop cataracts, which is an opaque film or cloudiness in your eye's lens. Symptoms often include blurred or hazy vision, spots before the eyes, and double vision in the early stages. If left untreated, cataracts can progress, causing severe visual impairment. The surgery can involve removing the eye's natural lens and repairing it with laser surgery or replacing it with various types of lenses or a lens implant. For more information on cataracts, see page 418.

DIABETIC RETINOPATHY--a serious disease of the eye's retina, often affecting the eye fluid as well. It is a leading cause of new blindness among adults. It is caused by the deterioration of the blood vessels nourishing the retina at the back of the eye. When leaking blood or fluid damages or scars the retina, the image sent to the brain becomes blurred. Laser treatment welds the leaking or bleeding vessels and the fragile or torn retinal tissue.

MACULAR DEGENERATION--Among older people, macular degeneration is a major problem. The macula is the small area of the retina that is responsible for fine or distinct vision, such as is required for reading. Degeneration of the macula usually results in gradual loss of central vision caused by damage to the light-sensitive cells and pigment cells in the retina. A number of these patients can be treated effectively with laser photocoagulation to seal the leaking blood vessels and prevent further loss of vision.

ADENOMA--Loss of vision due to pressure on optic nerve by a tumor.

DACRYOCYSTITIS--Inflammation of tear sac.

DETACHED RETINA--Flashes of light, followed later by sensation of curtain drawn over the eye.

HYPERTENSION--Degeneration of retina as result of high blood pressure.

KERATITIS--Blurred vision due to inflammation of cornea.

FARSIGHTEDNESS--Hyperopia, diminished ability to see things at close range.

MYOPIA--Nearsightedness; objects can be seen distinctly only when close to eyes.

NIGHT BLINDNESS--Absence of or defective vision in the dark.

SARCOMA--Tumor, causing pain and blurred vision.

STROKE--Blind spots, actual blindness, or temporary loss of vision due to interruption of blood supply to brain.

STYE--Infection of one or more of the small glands of the eyelid.

MIGRAINE--Blurred vision and flashes of light due to intense headache.

RETINAL DISORDERS--Other visual problems have a greater chance of developing in older adults due to the natural aging process. Modern medical advances make it easy to treat most visual problems.

METHODS OF EYE CARE

Eyeglasses may help a person with faulty vision, but they must be correctly prescribed and fitted to the individual or they will be of little value. Prescription eyeglasses should not be borrowed or loaned to others. (See vision aids, page 414.)

Contact lenses offer advantages for some eye problems and, indeed, are the only solution for a few. Not everybody can or should wear them. Contrary to claims that may be made by some, they are not entirely without hazards such as eye damage, and some persons never feel comfortable wearing them.

Proper lighting. When reading, writing, sewing, or doing other close work, take a position comfortable for the task at hand. Be sure there is sufficient illumination on the work being done. Light should be evenly diffused over the area to eliminate glare. To avoid shadows on the work, sit so the light comes over the left shoulder if right-handed, or over the right shoulder, if left-handed. Take a rest now and then. Shift position; look into the distance or close eyes momentarily.

Sunglasses should be worn to block glare and invisible, potentially harmful ultraviolet (sunburn) rays. And, they should be of optical-quality glass or plastic. Plastic lenses are generally more impact-resistant than glass but they can scratch easier. Even when wearing sunglasses, never look directly at the sun. The glasses should fit well enough that light and glare do not enter the eye over and around the lens.

Sunglasses should not be worn indoors or while driving after dark. They will reduce your ability to see and may cause you to miss road signs and signals that could cost a life.

Eye safety. The dangers to eye safety are sharp objects, hazardous materials, and foreign objects. Accidents take the sight of a tragic number of adults. If the activity is at all hazardous, eye protectors should be worn. Remember--there's no second chance at seeing.

Eye examinations are recommended every one to three years depending upon each individual's needs since many eye diseases have no early noticeable symptoms. The examination should include a vision and glasses evaluation, eye muscle check, check for glaucoma, and thorough internal and external eye health exam.

More information can be obtained from: National Society to Prevent Blindness 79 Madison Avenue New York, NY 10016

Pursuing 20/20 at 50 plus--combatting presbyopia

Although few of us care to admit to it, as we grow older not only do we encounter gray hair and wrinkles but our vision blurs when doing close work, such as reading.

This particular vision impairment goes by the name of presbyopia. Most people first notice signs of presbyopia when they are in their 40s, and virtually everyone older than 50 has the condition. It gets its start, however, at about age 10 when the eyeball stops growing. Because the eye's lens still continues to churn out new cells after this age, its cells become so crowded together that the lens gradually loses its flexibility. Consequently, the eye's muscles cannot bend or focus the lens for the sharp, clear vision needed for near objects. A person who is farsighted may experience the symptoms of presbyopia earlier than average, whereas nearsightedness can sometimes delay the condition by a few years.

The most common sign of presbyopia is blurred vision at a normal reading distance, with a tendency to hold reading materials further away in order to see them better. Eye fatigue and headaches commonly result from doing close work. Sometimes a person with the beginnings of presbyopia finds that he or she can read without blurriness in the morning, but has hampered close vision by the end of the day. This "now you see it, now you don't" phenomenon occurs because eye muscles are fatigued from trying to focus the eye lens throughout the day for close vision, so that by evening the muscles don't have the strength to focus the eye sufficiently for near sight.

> **The soul would have no rainbow had the eyes no tears.**
> - John Vance Cheney (1848-1922)

Conditions other than presbyopia, such as farsightedness and cataracts, can also cause blurred vision close up, however. Only a thorough eye exam by an optometrist or ophthalmologist testing the eye's ability to change focus can determine which eye condition is causing the problem.

Research has not yet provided us with any clues to preventing presbyopia. But the wide range of bifocal, trifocal, reading, and progressive addition eyeglasses, as well as specialized contact lenses now available, can provide crisp near vision to people who lack it. All of these are regulated by the Food and Drug Administration.

READING GLASSES

First used in the late 13th century by middle-aged scholars, reading glasses improve near vision only. Since they tend to blur objects in the distance, reading glasses can be worn only for close work.

Reading glasses may be inconvenient when shopping or doing anything requiring good vision at more than one seeing distance. Reading glasses in half-frame can sometimes relieve that inconvenience for people who have no vision problems besides presbyopia. These eyeglasses are particularly useful when doing office work, cooking, or pursuing such hobbies as playing cards or knitting.

The continual putting on and taking off of reading glasses calls for sturdy frames. A typical pair of prescription reading glasses costs anywhere from $20 to $200 depending on the type of frame purchased and where it is bought.

Although nonprescription reading glasses are available for less than $20 a pair, these mass-produced eyeglasses may not accurately correct vision. While the correction of both lenses often is the same in these glasses, almost everyone needs a different lens prescription for each eye. Commercial reading glasses also can cause headaches, tired eyes, and other symptoms of eyestrain if the wearer's line of sight doesn't coincide with the optical center of the lens. Ask your doctor before buying these glasses if they will work for you.

BIFOCALS

Many older adults wear bifocals or trifocals because they need different lens prescriptions to see clearly at different distances, and find it inconvenient to continually switch between reading glasses and regular glasses.

Some people who have presbyopia but who also have normal distance vision may also wear bifocals with a nonprescription (technically called "plano") segment on top to avoid the inconvenience of taking off reading glasses to see something far off.

Generally, an upper portion of a bifocal lens is used for seeing far distances and the lower portion for seeing near. To read, a person looks down through the lower portion.

Bifocals come in a variety of types to meet specific vision needs. A person who works at a large desk, for example, and needs to see things near over a wide range often opts for bifocals in which the entire bottom half of the lens can be used for near vision. A casual reader, however, can get by with a near vision segment that is a small circle or half-sphere at the bottom of the lens. Electricians, in contrast, who work close overhead when connecting wires, may need bifocals that have the prescription for near vision in the upper portion of the lens.

Bifocals are much more expensive than reading glasses, and most people take more time adjusting to them because eye and head movements must be used in order to take best advantage of the lenses. For example, you would gaze downward when reading, and tilt your head down when walking down a flight of stairs. Ask your eye practitioner for instructions on how to adjust to bifocals.

Some people adjust to bifocals after wearing them for just a few minutes, but other people never feel comfortable with them. A person who feels that bifocals make them look old and are opposed to wearing them may have a hard time adjusting to them. A person who must see both near and far objects, however, will often adjust rapidly to bifocals because they relieve the inconvenience of continually switching from one set of glasses to another.

Of all the portions of life it is in the two twilights, childhood and age, that tears fall with the most frequency; like dew at dawn and eve.
- William R. Alger (1822-1905)

PHYSICAL AILMENTS
VISION AIDS 415

TRIFOCALS

Generally, presbyopia worsens with age. People older than 50 often find that though they can see well close up with the bottom part of their bifocals and can see objects clearly in the distance with the top part, there's a range of vision between 16 and 24 inches that becomes blurry. Clear vision at that range may be critical when using a computer, for example, or playing cards.

If bifocals don't meet all vision needs, trifocals may be the answer. These glasses have a bottom portion of the lens for near viewing, a top portion for far viewing, and a middle section with power in between the other two segments so that the wearer can see things clearly at mid-distance range. Because three different prescriptions are crammed into one lens, however, the field of vision for each distance is limited. This makes it more difficult to adjust to trifocals than bifocals. They are also more expensive than conventional bifocals.

PROGRESSIVE ADDITION LENSES

Bifocal and trifocal wearers who are bothered by the telltale lines on these glasses may want to consider getting what are known as progressive addition lenses. These eyeglasses give a gradual invisible change in lens power from the top of the lens to the bottom. To get clear vision from far to near distance, you move your eyes up or down.

Progressive addition lenses are much more expensive than bifocals, and adjustment to them is more difficult. The main problem these lenses pose is distortion in the peripheral areas of the lenses. If wearers have to look through the edges of their lenses in order to see someone beside them, for example, the person may appear blurred. The amount of blurring experienced can be limited, however, by turning the head rather than the eyes to look at something not directly in front.

The distortion on the periphery of progressive addition lenses may be spatially disorienting. People who use these glasses for the first time may feel they are moving uphill or downhill when in fact they are on level ground. The distortion on the sides may increase the more complex the prescription is for other vision problems besides presbyopia, such as astigmatism or nearsightedness.

CONTACT LENSES

Those who prefer contact lenses to glasses may not have to give them up when presbyopia strikes. Many people find they can continue to wear their regular contacts for long-distance vision and put on reading glasses for close work. Because the prescription for these glasses is determined, in part, by the prescription for the contact lenses, the reading glasses alone cannot provide good close vision.

Hard, gas-permeable, and soft contact lenses are all available with bifocal corrections. Bifocal contacts come in a variety of designs. Working with an eye-care professional, consumers can decide which option will work best for them based on individual vision needs, eye shape, and other factors.

It is harder to adjust to multifocal contact lenses than to multifocal eyeglasses. Fewer than one in three people using bifocal contacts, for example, is able to adjust to them, whereas most people can adjust to bifocal eyeglasses. Because of this difficulty, most practitioners usually recommend bifocal contacts only to people who have successfully worn contacts in the past.

Multifocal contacts can be double or triple the price of multifocal eyeglasses. A much less costly contact lens alternative is to fit one eye with a contact lens for near vision and, if needed, the other eye with a lens for distant vision. They cost about the same as regular contacts and are easier to replace or change. However, contacts worn in this manner may hamper depth perception and peripheral vision. Monovision contact lenses work more successfully in people whose normal vision lacks fusion--that is, their eyes do not work together properly.

The greater distance there is between prescriptions for far and near vision, the harder it is to adjust to this manner of wearing contact lenses.

New on the market are "diffractive" contact lenses. The surface of these lenses has invisible ridges molded into concentric circles. The space between the circles gets smaller as the distance increases from the center of the lens, which is used for distance vision. The ridges bend the light in such a way that the wearer is able to see things both close and far alternatively. Consequently, a person using diffractive contacts doesn't have a narrowed area on the lens in which to look to see far or near, as with bifocal lenses. Wearers must learn to adjust to diffractive contacts, however, and since they are relatively new, it's too early to tell how successful these contact lenses will be. They are more expensive than bifocal contacts.

Whether opting for reading glasses, multifocal lenses, or contacts, wearers usually need new ones every 12 to 18 months to correct for worsening presbyopia.

ADJUSTMENT TIPS

To get the best results with your bifocals or trifocal eyeglasses, let your eye doctor know all the various tasks you do that require clear vision. This information will help in the correct placement of the various lens prescriptions. Improperly placed lens segments can make seeing difficult and cause accidents, particularly when walking, using stairs, or driving.

The American Optometric Association offers these suggestions to new bifocal and trifocal wearers:

- ❏ Don't look at your feet when walking.
- ❏ Hold reading material closer to your body and lower your eyes, not your head, so that you are reading out of the lowest part of the lens.
- ❏ Fold the newspaper in half or quarters and move it, rather than your head, to read comfortably.
- ❏ Make sure that eyeglass frames are always adjusted for your face so that the lenses are properly positioned.

Let us be thankful for the fools,
But for them the rest of us
could never succeed.
- Mark Twain (1835-1910)

A fool always finds some greater fool to admire him.
- Nicolas Boileau (1636-1711)

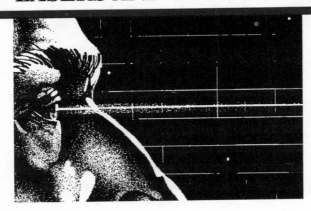

Lasers help solve vision problems

A laser is a simple device that generates an intense and narrow beam of a single type of light, such as infrared or ultraviolet. The word "laser" is an acronym for "light amplification by stimulated emission of radiation." Sunlight, in contrast, is composed of a jumble of different colors, spread out in different directions. The laser beam is generated using electricity, a series of mirrors, and a special crystal or gas.

The laser's usefulness in ophthalmology stems from the precision and ease with which it can be used to reach tissues deep within the eye. Unlike the smallest scalpel used in surgery, which makes cuts as wide as the tip of a pin and crushes neighboring tissue, a "laser scalpel" can slice as thin as the width of a cell without damaging the surrounding cells. This precision allows eye doctors to target diseased blood vessels, for example, while sparing healthy ones, and fosters a speedy recovery with little resulting scar tissue.

Even minor amounts of scar tissue can pose major impediments to sight by blocking the pathway of light entering the eye. That pathway is what makes the laser so useful in treating patients with eye disorders: The pupil acts as a natural window through which laser beams can enter to mend tissues deep within the eye. Because the ophthalmologist doesn't have to cut open the eye during laser surgery, there are fewer risks of infection and less pain than with standard surgery. Laser surgery can be done in an ophthalmologist's office or hospital outpatient department, so it is also less expensive.

Posterior Capsulotomy
A cataract is a clouding of the normally clear and transparent lens of the eye. During cataract surgery, an ophthalmologist often replaces the natural lens with an artificial one. Several months later, however, the membrane in the back of the eye, which surrounds and supports the lens, may become cloudy, impairing vision.

Ophthalmologists counter this problem by using an intense infrared light of a neodymium: yttrium aluminum garnet (Nd:YAG) laser to create an opening in the membrane. During this procedure, called a posterior capsulotomy, each flash of the laser causes a microscopic explosion in the membrane. It may take about a dozen one-billionth-of-a-second blasts. The miniexplosion is thought to vaporize cells.

Although the laser beam travels through other eye tissue before it reaches the membrane, it doesn't harm these tissues because only the highly focused tip of the beam has enough energy to cause a miniexplosion. This tip touches only the membrane in the back of the eye, which has no nerve endings. Posterior capsulotomies consequently are painless. This quick procedure rarely has any serious complications.

Glaucoma
An Nd:YAG laser is also used to treat some cases of glaucoma. This disease, which affects at least 2 out of every 100 Americans over 35, is one of the leading causes of blindness in this country.

The hallmark of glaucoma is an excessive buildup of fluid pressure in the eye. The unhealthy pressure is caused by a blockage of the canals through which the clear inner eye fluid continuously flows. If left untreated, glaucoma eventually damages the sight (optic) nerve.

An Nd:YAG laser can relieve the fluid pressure by creating an opening, allowing the eye fluid to drain properly. Although a slight risk of bleeding accompanies this type of laser surgery, it rarely causes serious problems.

Macular Degeneration
A different type of laser--the argon laser--is used to treat some patients with the more severe form of an eye disorder called macular degeneration. Although this disease doesn't cause total blindness, it is a leading cause of loss of both central and reading vision. Macular degeneration is particularly common in people over 65.

The macula is the portion of the light-sensing retina that light rays strike to provide the sharp, straight-ahead vision needed for driving and reading small print. In the less common but more severe form of macular degeneration, for no known reason, new blood vessels grow beneath the macula. These abnormal vessels leak fluid and blood, destroying nearby macula cells. If the leakage and bleeding continue, much of the macula may be damaged irreparably within a few weeks or months. The resulting dense scar tissue blocks out central vision, much like an opaque smudge does in the center of one's glasses.

With early detection, severe vision loss from this type of macular degeneration can usually be prevented with argon laser treatment. This relatively low-energy laser heats, rather than vaporizes, tissues, acting essentially like a welder. A study conducted by the National Eye Institute showed that argon laser treatment can slash by more than half the chances of experiencing severe vision loss from macular degeneration.

The green beams of the argon laser are only absorbed by red objects, so it selectively heats up and seals blood vessels (because they contain red blood cells) and leaves most other parts of the eye undisturbed. The narrowness of the beam enhances laser precision, allowing the ophthalmologist to target only the diseased blood vessels.

This type of surgery generally takes only a few minutes and may be done with the aid of a local anesthetic to prevent discomfort. Soon afterward the patient is able to return home and resume normal daily activities.

A fungal disease called ocular histoplasmosis can cause faulty blood vessels to grow and damage the macula. This is a significant cause of vision loss in the southeastern and midwestern United States, where this particular fungus is prevalent. Experts estimate that laser treatment of the abnormal vessels can prevent up to 2,000 cases of serious vision loss due to the disease each year if treatment is given early, before extensive damage has occurred.

Diabetic Retinopathy
Ophthalmologists use a similar procedure to seal off leaky blood vessels or destroy diseased tissue in the retinas of patients with diabetic retinopathy, another leading cause

of blindness. The hallmark of this disease is faulty blood vessels on or within the retina. These vessels bleed, scarring the retina. According to the National Eye Institute, nearly half of all diabetics have at least mild diabetic retinopathy. If used in early stages of the disease, laser treatment often halts the patient's loss of vision and sometimes even reverses it. The procedure is usually painless and without complications.

Retinal Tears

An argon or another type of tissue-heating laser called a krypton laser is also used to spot-weld retinal tears. These horseshoe-shaped holes in the retina may open small blood vessels and cause bleeding into the central cavity of the eye. Often caused by a blow to the head, retinal tears can cause flashes of color or black spots to appear in one's line of sight.

Laser Sculpting

Still experimental is the use of the laser on the eye's surface to treat people with nearsightedness, farsightedness, or astigmatism.

When light rays enter the normal eye, they are bent by the transparent front covering of the eye (cornea) and the lens so that they are brought to a single, sharp focus on the retina. But in the nearly one-third of Americans who are nearsighted (having trouble seeing distant objects), the light rays bouncing off faraway objects come to focus in front of--instead of directly on--the retina. This happens because either the curve of the lens or cornea is too steep or the eye is too long. In farsightedness (trouble seeing objects close up), the eye is too short or the curve of the cornea or lens is not steep enough. The rays, consequently, merge in back of the retina. The end result of both conditions is blurred vision.

To counter these vision flaws, most nearsighted or farsighted individuals wear glasses or contact lenses shaped to bend the light rays so that they properly reach the retina. By precisely reshaping the cornea with the laser, ophthalmologists hope to achieve the same effect. Theoretically, once the laser surgery is done, the person could throw away the no-longer-needed glasses.

Nearsightedness

Corneal surgery to cure nearsightedness has been attempted with traditional surgical tools, but without reliable results. In this procedure, called a radial keratotomy, an ophthalmologist uses a scalpel to cut several small slits in the cornea. These slits slightly flatten the cornea by changing the pressure in the eye and weakening the cornea's structure.

But nearly half of all the eyes treated with this procedure are either undercorrected or overcorrected, according to a study. Apparently, the surgery often fails because the depth and shape of cuts made by the hand-held scalpel are inconsistent, or because scar tissue alters the desired contour of the cornea.

When an ultraviolet excimer laser is used, however, preliminary studies show that exact uniform tissue removal cuts can be accomplished with minimum scarring. The high energy of this laser beam ejects cell-sized fragments from the surface of the cornea. Such precision has enabled several research groups to directly remove minute quantities of tissue from the center of the cornea to flatten it, thus restoring sharp vision. Investigators hope to use the excimer laser on farsighted individuals, in whom the curve of the cornea is steepened rather than flattened.

Researchers speculate that because the excimer laser damages such small amounts of tissue, it "fools the eye into not knowing its been traumatized." Once the body knows its been invaded, it tries to heal itself. That healing process can alter the desired recontouring of the eye.

The total sculpting procedure with the excimer laser takes less than a minute to complete, although about 20 minutes are needed beforehand to train patients to keep their eyes steady. The cornea may ache for about a day following surgery, and patients need to wear an eye patch for one or two days.

Initial results of laser sculpting by researchers are encouraging. Investigators were able to improve one patient's 20/300 eyesight to 20/40 eight weeks after treatment. More extensive and longer-term testing will have to be done, however, to ensure the safety and effectiveness of laser sculpting for nearsightedness.

Astigmatism

The excimer laser is also being used experimentally to correct astigmatism. This blurred vision is caused by bumps and pits on the corneal surface that prevent light rays entering the eye from merging into a single, sharp focus. Preliminary tests on more than 50 patients in Berlin, Germany, indicate that a series of T-shaped incisions made by the laser may be effective in smoothing out corneal irregularities.

The Future of Laser Sculpting

If more extensive tests show laser sculpting is a safe and effective method of correcting near- or farsightedness or astigmatism, and it becomes an accepted practice, various laser companies estimate the procedure will probably cost between $1,000 and $2,000 per eye.

The surgery to reshape the cornea has been tested on about 300 patients in the United States and about 1,800 worldwide. There is little data available on how long the effect of the surgery lasts. Even if laser sculpting continues to show promise in clinical trials, however, it will be several years before a patient will be able to enter the ophthalmologist's office wearing glasses, get a few zaps of laser light, and achieve perfect vision after a few weeks.

> The major portion of this article was written by Margie Patlak and appeared in the July-August 1990 issue of *FDA Consumer*.

Cataract Surgery

Cataract surgery removes the clouded lens of your eye. With the new technology only the front of the lens capsule is removed to hold the replacement lens. Leaving the back of the capsule reduces bleeding and the risk of a detached retina. Ophthalmologists are using ultrasound to break up the clouded lens. The pieces are then sucked out through a small incision and replaced with a permanent plastic lens. Improved antiseptic solutions are reducing the risk of infection. Most patients have good vision within three to eight weeks.

For more information on cataracts, see the article on page 418.

Cataracts--what they are and how they are treated

My widowed sister-in-law, Erma Hiser, 82, lives alone (well, with a dog and two cats) in an apartment complex for senior citizens in Lincoln, California. Recently she called, greatly distressed: "The doctor told me I had cataracts and that I had to have surgery on my eyes. I've been going blind for some time, but I didn't think it would come to this."

Knowing I was in for a long session, I replied, "Erma, I heard of an Oriental man who recently came to the United States. He went to an ophthalmologist. During the examination, the eye doctor said, 'Do you have a cataract?' With limited English, the man replied, 'No, I drive a rincoln.'"

"That's not funny, Bill. I'm going blind and you joke about Cadillacs and Lincolns."

"Erma, I'm joking because I have good news for you. Today, the doctors have perfected cataract surgery until it is almost fool-proof. Don't be afraid. Cataract surgery is almost always successful."

A couple of months later, Erma called back. "I can see better than I ever could, and it hardly hurt at all." It is so wonderful that technology can give us relief from an ancient scourge--blindness from cataracts.

What Are Cataracts?

Cataracts form in the lens of the eye. The lens of the eye is located just behind the pupil opening and the colored iris in the direct center of both the eyes. Its function is to keep your eyes in focus. Unless your mother had rubella measles during pregnancy, you are born with two crystal clear lenses. As you grow older, chemical changes in the lens make it change color and lose its clearness--this cloudy condition is called a cataract.

Cataracts alter the vision of at least 3.5 million Americans. A cataract is an opaque (cloudy) area in the normally clear lens of the eye. Over a period of years, the cataract blocks or distorts light that is entering the eye and progressively reduces vision. A cataract causes a gradual, painless deterioration of sight, beginning with an inability to see detail clearly, and distortion of sight in the presence of bright lights.

Except in some advanced cases, cataracts cannot easily be seen by an observer. In advanced cases, the lens may become white, opaque, and quite readily visible through the pupil. A very advanced cataract may produce painful inflammation and pressure within the eye. Cataracts are fairly common, and you are more likely to have them as you get older. The disorder may lead to severe deterioration of vision, but this can usually be rectified by surgery.

What Are the Symptoms?

Cataract formation is generally not associated with "signals" such as pain, redness, or tearing. The symptoms of a cataract all revolve around interference with vision: blurred vision, double vision, spots, ghost images, the impression of a "skim" over the eyes; problems with light, such as finding lights not bright enough for reading or near work, or being "dazzled" by intense light. The need for frequent changes of eyeglass prescriptions--which may not help--is another symptom. As a cataract develops it may be noticeable to others as a milky or yellowish spot in the normally black pupil.

When the area of clouding is small and away from the center of the lens, there may be little interference with vision, except for the annoyance of corresponding loss of detail in the visual image. If such a cataract progresses a great deal, however, or if the cataract began in the center of the lens, visual difficulty may be marked and may interfere with everyday activities. When this point of "life interference" is reached, the eye physician usually advises surgery.

A cataract is not an infection nor is it contagious. It is not a "skim" growing over the eye. It will not be made worse by using the eyes; nor can it be made better by medicines. Other than surgical removal of the cataracts, there are no proven treatments, eye drops, or other medications that will dissolve a cataract or slow down its progression. A cataract may develop rapidly over a period of a few months, or it may progress very slowly over a period of years. In other instances it may progress so far and then stay the same--and many people never experience visual difficulty to the point that the ophthalmologist will advise surgery.

What Causes Cataracts?

Cataracts often develop in elderly persons as a result of degeneration of the tissue of the lens. Cataracts may be present at birth (congenital) and the most common reason for this is thought to be rubella infection (German measles) in the mother during early pregnancy. Injury to the eye later in life may also cause cataracts, or they may accompany a disease, particularly diabetes.

There are many reasons why a lens may gradually lose its transparency:

1. Ultraviolet sun rays speed up discoloration.

2. Deprivation of nutrients may hasten cataracts.

3. Lack of vitamins A, E, C, or zinc may make the lens of the eye opaque.

4. A high concentration of sugars as in diabetes may cloud a lens and keep the light from coming through.

5. Infrared heat rays as from a blast furnace or a glass blower can make a lens cloud faster.

6. Radiation that comes from such sources as X-rays or an atomic bomb at Hiroshima causes lenses to be opaque.

7. Some medications such as tranquilizers, steroids, tetracycline, or psoralens for psoriasis may interfere with cell structure and cause the lens to be stained.

8. By age 60 the lens only transmits 38% of light back to the retina, it becomes thicker, less transparent, and much harder, so vision begins to become fuzzy.

9. By age 70, 50% of all lenses have imperfections, and this increases to 90% for people over age 80.

> To keep the heart
> unwrinkled, to be
> hopeful, kindly, cheerful, reverent--that
> is to triumph over old age.
> - Thomas B. Aldrich

How Are Cataracts Treated?

Cataracts are removed in patients of all ages, usually with excellent results. In fact, this operation is one of the most common surgical procedures performed. Frequently cataracts are removed on an outpatient basis, and even when patients are admitted to the hospital for cataract surgery, the stay is usually short. Most patients are up and about on the day of surgery.

When the lens of an eye becomes cloudy and impairs vision (below 20/40) a surgeon removes the lens so you can see clearly again and usually replaces it with an intraocular lens implant (IOL), contact lenses, or special cataract glasses.

Ten years ago, you would not have had cataract surgery unless you were legally blind--that is, less than 20/100 vision. Today 1.25 million cataract operations are performed annually in the United States, many times on people with vision just below 20/40, the minimum level required to pass the driver's license eye test.

With the old method of surgery used 40 years ago, the lens and the capsule that holds the lens were completely removed. But stitches couldn't be used because they were not thin enough for the eye, so the incision had to heal by itself. Patients often had to lie in dark rooms for six weeks with their head movements restricted by sandbags to ensure proper healing. Two-week hospital stays were common even 20 years ago, partly because of the high risk of developing an infection. After surgery, patients had to wear glasses with thick lenses to help the lensless eye to focus. Those glasses were cumbersome and often distorted vision.

Now, only the front of the lens capsule is removed. Some surgeons use ultrasound to break up the clouded lens. The pieces are suctioned out through a very small incision. This leaves the back of the capsule intact and reduces bleeding and the risk of a detached retina. An artificial replacement lens reduces the need for special cataract glasses.

Technological advances in cataract surgery have reduced the risk of infection by the improved antiseptic solutions. Fine nylon sutures close the incision, speeding recovery. Surgery is often done on an outpatient basis. About 90% of patients have good vision in three to eight weeks after surgery.

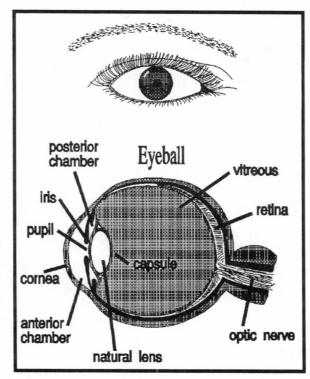

Eyeball — posterior chamber, vitreous, iris, retina, pupil, capsule, cornea, anterior chamber, natural lens, optic nerve

What Happens After Surgery?

Most people who undergo cataract surgery are treated as outpatients and can go home the same day. For others, a stay in the hospital of one to three days may be required. In either case, during the early stages of recovery, patients need to take special care to avoid strenuous physical activity.

Sometimes people whose cataract surgery was performed by the extracapsular method develop a problem called "after-cataract." After the operation, the back part of the lens capsule left in the eye may become cloudy and interfere with passage of light to the retina.

The cloudy material must be cleared away, if possible, so that full vision can be restored. Ophthalmologists often treat after-cataract with an ophthalmic laser called the neodymium-YAG or "cold" laser. When this procedure is successful, the patient's vision is restored without additional eye surgery.

For more information:
See articles on "vision problems and eye care," page 412, "vision aids," page 414, and "eye surgery and lasers," page 416.

What Can Be Done to Prevent Cataracts?

Some research indicates that drugs including simple aspirin may help prevent or delay the development of cataracts. Research conducted at the University of Western Ontario by Drs. John Trevithick and James Robertson suggests that taking supplements of vitamin E alone or vitamins E and C together can significantly reduce a person's risk of developing cataracts. Also, research on animals conducted at Tufts University has shown that vitamin C may protect the lenses of the eyes from the constant bombardment and damage by light and oxygen that makes them vulnerable to cataracts.

Dr. Hugh Taylor, an ophthalmologist at Johns Hopkins University in Baltimore, MD, linked smoking to the risk of developing cataracts. Another study by Taylor found prolonged exposure to the sun's ultraviolet light can triple a person's risk of developing cataracts. Taylor suggested wearing a brimmed hat and using UV-screening sunglasses when you are outside to reduce the risk.

Other suggestions to help protect your eyes in old age:

1. Have regular health checkups to detect such treatable diseases as high blood pressure and diabetes, both of which may cause eye problems.

2. Have a complete eye examination every two or three years since many eye diseases do not have early noticeable symptoms. The examination should include a vision (and glasses) evaluation, eye muscle check, check for glaucoma, and thorough internal and external eye health exams.

3. Seek more frequent eye health care if you have diabetes or a family history of eye disease. Make arrangements for care immediately if you experience signs such as loss or dimness in vision, eye pain, excessive discharge from the eye, double vision, or redness or swelling of the eye or eyelid.

Signs that need attention

Who has not been worried sick about some symptom of illness and then gone to the doctor and had him exclaim, "Oh, that's nothing." And on the other hand, who has not heard of someone that had the news, "Why didn't you come to me sooner?" It is far better to have a doctor proclaim that what we thought to be cancer is "Just a flea bite" than to have a doctor exclaim "It's too late, that's not a flea bite--that's cancer." We mere humans are often caught between the doctor's suspicious frown that we are hypochondriacs and the fatal glare that informs us we are too late.

Here are some critical signs of illness that may help us to improve our reaction time. We are not trying to cover every symptom of every minor or major illness. **These are a few of the critical symptoms that require you to consult your physician without delay.**

THE SYMPTOMS	THE POSSIBILITIES
ABDOMEN PROBLEMS	
severe pain, vomiting, tender or swollen abdomen, constipation and intestinal obstruction, temperature over 100 ° F.	appendicitis or dangerous intestinal obstruction--an emergency--get help
pain with diarrhea	possible food poisoning
pain in small of back and move to groin	kidney stones
above with temperature	kidney infection
pain below the ribs and on the right	gallbladder disorder
pain with burning skin	nerve infection
pain following heavy drinking or eating	gastritis
pain relieved by antacid	inflamed stomach or peptic ulcer
pain in waves mainly in the upper right side, temperature 100 ° F or above.	inflamed gallbladder
recurrent upper abdominal pain with loss of appetite or weight	may be cancer, see doctor
recurrent lower abdominal pain with change in bowel habits	may be cancer of intestine
lower pain, diarrhea, feeling ill, temperature up	diverticulitis
above with blood or mucus in bowels	may have ulcerative colitis

THE SYMPTOMS	THE POSSIBILITIES
ANXIETY (A feeling of tension, apprehension, or edginess that may be accompanied by symptoms such as heart palpitations or diarrhea)	
anxious only in certain situations such as when in enclosed places	phobia
loss of weight and eyes bulging	overactive thyroid gland
BACKACHE	
sudden onset, loss of bladder or bowel control, difficulty moving limbs, numbness or tingling	damage to your spinal cord
after several weeks in bed or wheelchair a sharp pain in one place in your spine	bone damage--osteoporosis
BREATHING DIFFICULTIES	
with crushing chest pain radiating from the center of the chest to the jaw, neck, or arms.	may be a heart attack
pain made worse by breathing in	blood clot or collapsed lung
cough up thick, gray or greenish-yellow phlegm and puffy ankles	congestive heart failure
severe difficulty in breathing with bluish tinge around lips	medical emergency
CHEST PAIN	
crushing pain from chest to arms	may be a heart attack
short of breath with recent operation	may have a blood clot
CONFUSION	
suffered head injury followed by sudden confusion	brain injury
heart or lung disease or diabetes	confusion indicates worsening of condition
confusion with dizziness, weakness, numbness, blurred vision, and speech	stroke
confusion in elderly appearing over several weeks following a fall	may be bleeding inside skull
confusion in elderly with fever, cough, lack of bladder control	many types of physical illness
confusion in elderly with change in personality, decline in personal appearance or cleanliness, and impaired memory of recent events	senile dementia or depression

THE SYMPTOMS	THE POSSIBILITIES
CONSTIPATION	
prolonged attacks after years of regularity	may be cancer of large intestine
with lower abdominal pain	may have growth--diverticulitis
COUGHING	
a dry cough with no other symptoms	inflammation of the windpipe
coughing with temperature 100 ° F, breathless	may be pneumonia
a cough for several weeks or months and getting more severe	tuberculosis or lung cancer
cough up blood, phlegm pink and frothy	pulmonary edema or embolism
coughing up blood	may be sign of lung cancer
DEPRESSION (A feeling of sadness, futility, unworthiness, and/or despair that may make you feel unable to cope with normal life)	
feel life is not worthwhile and have talked of or contemplated suicide	danger of suicide
DIARRHEA	
persistent diarrhea	loss of body fluid
blood in bowel movements	ulcerative colitis
DISTURBING THOUGHTS	
feel that life is worthless and futile	depression
feel apprehensive, tense, on edge	anxiety
seriously worried about your health even though your physician assures you that nothing is wrong	hypochondriasis
DIZZINESS	
dizziness with weakness, numbness, blurred vision, slurred speech	may have had a stroke
dizziness with recurrent headaches accompanied by nausea or vomiting	may be brain tumor or hemorrhage
EAR ACHE	
pain worse when pull at earlobe	infection of the outer ear canal
blocked-up feeling in ear	damage to middle ear
sticky greenish-yellow discharge	infection of middle ear

THE SYMPTOMS	THE POSSIBILITIES
FEELING FAINT AND FAINTING	
faintness with numbness and/or tingling in body, blurred vision, confusion, difficulty in speaking, loss of movement in arms or legs	mild stroke or transient ischemic attack
if you have any form of heart disease and noticed heart slowing down or speeding up, with loss of consciousness	disorder of heart rhythm
FEELING UNDER THE WEATHER	
unusually tired with discomfort in chest or arms	occasionally a sign of impending heart trouble
FEVER	
100 ° F or above with cough and short of breath	possibility of pneumonia
coughing up grayish-yellow phlegm	acute bronchitis
headache and/or aching joints or bones	influenza
pain when bending the head forward, nausea or vomiting, dislike bright light, drowsiness or confusion	meningitis
very high fever, 104 ° F or above	dangerous
FEVER WITH RASH	
red spots, runny nose, sore red eyes, dry cough	measles
raised red itchy spots that turn into blisters	chicken pox
rash of purple spots with vomiting, headache, dislike strong light, pain trying to bend head forward	meningitis
HALLUCINATIONS	
with general confusion about times, places, or events with agitated behavior and signs of illness	may be delirium
HEADACHE	
pain in head, temperature 100 ° F, injured your head, feeling drowsy and nauseated	possibility of brain hemorrhage
HOARSENESS OR LOSS OF VOICE	
with feeling the cold, dry skin, weight increase, tiredness	may have an underactive thyroid
hoarseness lasting more than a week with several attacks	may be growth on the larynx

THE SYMPTOMS	THE POSSIBILITIES
INCONTINENCE with PROBLEMS	
cloudy urine and strong smell	urinary tract infection
constipated for more than week	pressure on the bladder
difficulty in controlling the bowels and lack of bladder control	disorder of the brain and nervous system such as a stroke
IMPAIRED MEMORY	
unable to remember events immediately before or after head injury	may be brain injury, needs medical attention
unable to cope, personality change, lack of cleanliness, difficulty in following instructions	onset of senile dementia or depression
IMPAIRED VISION	
with recent head injury	bleeding inside skull
suddenly lost field of vision in one or both eyes	may be retinal artery occlusion
vision blurred, eye painful	retinal detachment, glaucoma
flashing lights and/or floating spots	retinal detachment
ITCHING, NO RASH	
itching around anus, severe at night	may have pinworms
bleeding from anus and painful bowel movements	hemorrhoids
NIGHTMARES	
occasionally	normal
feeling unusually tense or worried	probably due to anxiety
sleeping pills, drugs, or alcohol	sleeping patterns disturbed
NUMBNESS and/or TINGLING	
difficulty in speaking, blurred vision, confusion, dizziness, weakness in arms or legs	stroke
PAIN in the FACE	
severe pain radiating from one bloodshot eye	acute glaucoma
continuous, throbbing pain on one side of face, worse when you touch tooth	tooth abscess
severe throbbing pain in one or both temples, scalp sensitive to touch	inflammation of the arteries in your head
severe stabbing pain on one side of the face, brought on by touching or chewing	damaged nerve

THE SYMPTOMS	THE POSSIBILITIES
PAINFUL ANKLES	
recent severe pain, hard to move	strained ligament, broken bone
pain with redness and swelling, other joints affected with temperature and feeling ill	rheumatic fever, arthritis
one ankle and calf swollen	blood clot in vein
both ankles swollen and breathless	may be congestive heart failure
PAINFUL ARM or HAND	
severe pain following injury, arm	may be broken or fractured
feeling ill, temperature	rheumatic fever
PAINFUL/ENLARGED TESTICLE	
with injury to genital area	internal damage
painful swelling in one or both	infection of the glands
one of testicles enlarged	harmless cyst or cancer
a painless swelling of one testicle	may be a sign of cancer
PAINFUL EYE	
injured with visible damage	requires urgent medical attention
pain from behind eye with headache drowsiness, dislike of bright light, pain when you bend head forward	may be hemorrhage or meningitis
PAINFUL KNEE	
injured, misshapen, or unable to move	dislocation
other joints affected, temperature and feeling ill	infectious arthritis
PAINFUL LEG	
pain following injury	broken leg or fracture
persistent pain, temperature, and feeling ill	bone infection
pain in swollen and tender calf	may have a blood clot
one of your veins red and inflamed	may be thrombophlebitis
PAINFUL NECK and/or STIFF	
recent pain, severe headache, nausea, confusion or drowsiness, and dislike of bright lights	brain hemorrhage or meningitis
violent jolt or whiplash with difficulty controlling muscles	may be damage to spinal cord

THE SYMPTOMS	THE POSSIBILITIES
PAINFUL SHOULDER recent injury, hard to move and seems misshapen	dislocation or fracture
sudden pain, temperature, feeling ill	rheumatic fever, bursitis
PALPITATIONS with a history of heart disease and feeling ill	disorder of heart rate
SKIN PROBLEMS a new mole, or change in appearance of one you have had, an open sore that has not healed, a slowly growing lump, a dark lump or patch appearing on your face	may be skin cancer
SLEEPING DIFFICULTY you often wake up feeling breathless	heart or lung disorders can make you breathless when lying down
SORE MOUTH and/or TONGUE any sore area in the mouth or on the tongue that fails to heal in 3 weeks	may indicate cancer
SPEAKING DIFFICULTY with dizziness, weakness in arms or legs, numbness and tingling, and blurred vision	you may have had a stroke
words pronounced normally, but content confused, deterioration in coping, appearance, and ability to follow instructions	onset of senile dementia
STRANGE BEHAVIOR (Any behavior, whether it develops suddenly or gradually, that seems out of keeping with previous behavior patterns can indicate a mental problem)	depression
increasingly preoccupied with a single idea or activity	compulsive disorder
SWALLOWING DIFFICULTIES gradually getting worse with loss of weight	cancer of the esophagus
SWEATING, EXCESSIVE sweating at night, persistent cough, and/or loss of weight	tuberculosis or cancer
SWELLING under the SKIN lumps in neck, armpit, or groin	infection or cancer of lymphatic system

THE SYMPTOMS	THE POSSIBILITIES
swellings with temperature 100° F, sore throat	infectious mononucleosis
lump in the breast	may be a harmless cyst but may also be cancerous
TWITCHING and TREMBLING taking prescribed medicines	some drugs can cause it
trembling or shaking in one part of body when body is at rest	Parkinson's disease
URINATION PROBLEMS passing pink, red, or smoky-brown urine	may have kidney or bladder cancer
painful urination with ache in small of back	kidney infection
painful urination with discharge from penis	sexually transmitted disease
painful urination with heavy ache between legs	infection of the prostate gland
VOMITING with abdominal pain	may be appendicitis
with red or black blood in vomit	acute abdominal condition
with a head injury within 24 hours	may be brain injury
persistent vomiting with blood	emergency
WEIGHT GAIN (OVERWEIGHT) weight gain	as you grow older may be a result of decline in exercise and changes in metabolism rate
WEIGHT LOSS weight loss, loss of appetite, bouts of diarrhea or constipation with blood in bowel movements	inflammation of small intestine or cancer of large intestine
recurrent attacks of upper abdominal pain	stomach ulcer, or may be cancer of the stomach
sweating at night, recurrent fever, tiredness, ill health, persistent cough, blood in phlegm	chronic infection such as tuberculosis
WHEEZING wheezing just started, coughing up frothy, pink or white phlegm	may have a buildup of fluid in lungs, pulmonary edema
breathing so difficult that you feel you are suffocating	severe attack of asthma
WOMEN: PAIN or LUMPS in BREAST see or feel one or more lumps in the breast	may be a harmless cyst but may also be cancerous

Common truths about the common cold

Almost everyone has had colds, and almost everyone has his or her favorite theories about them. That's why they are called "common." We need a quick review of the cold--its nature, symptoms, causes, and cures--in order to be sure that our common knowledge is correct.

The common cold is medically known as "coryza." It is a contagious virus disease of the respiratory tract. It is a droplet infection, that is, people catch a cold by inhaling airborne water droplets, sneezed or coughed out by a patient with the disorder. Symptoms appear about 48 hours after exposure to the virus, which may be any one of (or a combination of) more than 100 different types. Often, transmission is from hand to eye or other mucous membranes.

Early symptoms of a cold include a runny nose, watering eyes, a headache, and a sore throat. Later, there may be a stuffy nose, a slight cough, and aching muscles. The patient may also have a chill and a slight fever.

A cold, although extremely annoying, is seldom serious. But babies and young children and patients with asthma, bronchitis, heart disorders, or kidney disease who have symptoms of a cold may be at risk and should have medical advice.

There is no cure for a cold. Home treatment to relieve the symptoms includes regular doses of a mild painkiller such as aspirin or acetaminophen, an antihistamine or a decongestant drug to help clear a stuffy nose, cough medicine, and throat lozenges for the sore throat. Contrary to popular belief, antibiotics do not cure a cold (or any other virus infection). The patient should drink plenty of fluids and avoid contact with others to prevent spreading the infection.

Recent research has indicated that people are twice as likely to catch a cold if their resistance is lowered due to stress.

The above is basic knowledge about colds, but because colds are so common, some folktales have arisen that distort the truth. At the risk of becoming redundant, here are some folktales about colds followed by the hard facts:

Folktale: *Doctors don't know much about colds.*

Fact: Experts know a great deal. Colds are caused by viruses, tiny particles visible only through an electron microscope. There are more than 100 different types of cold viruses that can result in upper respiratory infections. Once you've had a cold, you're immune for life to that particular virus but not to the others. Eventually, if we have enough colds we will develop an immunity to all of them. Children may average six to eight colds per year, and young adults half that number. Because of immunity to the different types, by middle age we can look forward to only an occasional cold. Doctors can also treat the complications of colds.

Folktale: *Colds are caused by cold weather.*

Fact: A cold is a contagious illness. You catch it from another person. Thirty years ago an experiment was performed in which volunteers were stripped, dunked in ice water, and sat for hours in the cold air. They caught no more colds and were no more susceptible than subjects who weren't exposed to those harsh conditions.

Folktale: *Being around people with a cold dooms you to one.*

Fact: Most cold victims touch infectious secretions, then rub their eyes, touch their nose, or put their fingers in their mouth, thus placing the virus where it can enter the body. The best way to avoid infection is to wash your hands frequently when around infection. Doctors see a half-dozen patients with colds a day and seldom get a cold. A cold is hard to catch and those who have one put in considerable effort to get it.

Colds are often mistaken for some other sickness such as:

Bronchitis ... is a cold with a bad cough and not to be confused with chronic bronchitis, a disease of middle-aged smokers with emphysema and damaged lungs.

Strep throat... is a bacterial infection and typically produces a high fever and severe sore throat without coughing or stuffiness. It is treated with antibiotics. Viruses cause sore throats accompanied by colds.

Sinusitis ... produces agonizing pain over a single sinus area (such as one cheek), sometimes accompanied by a discharge from one nostril. Uncomfortable aching over both cheeks and around the eyes is caused by the stuffiness of a cold, and the treatment is a decongestant. But check with your doctor before taking anything, especially if you have high blood pressure.

Measles and chicken pox ... act like a cold until the telltale body rash appears. Whooping cough and meningitis may begin with cold symptoms that soon get worse. The former is characterized by a severe cough and the latter by high fever and a stiff neck. These conditions usually do not affect older persons.

Allergies ... especially those we call "hay fever," can act like colds with their runny noses, sneezing, and general miserable feeling. Allergies are typically caused by dust, mold, fungus spores, and pollen from trees, grasses, and other plants. They differ from colds by their persistence, particularly when pollen counts are high in spring and summer.

> A bad cold wouldn't be so annoying if
> it weren't for the advice of our friends.
> - Kin Hubbard

Research may someday lead to better ways of preventing and treating colds. Briefly, here are some things that may help:

■ Wash your hands more frequently when you are around people with colds. Avoid putting your fingers near your nose and eyes. Stay away from people with colds who are sneezing and coughing, if possible.

■ Don't smoke. Smokers have more colds than nonsmokers.

■ If you get a cold, keep warm and eat wisely. Drink plenty of fluids, especially water, hot drinks, and chicken soup, to help alleviate the symptoms of colds.

■ Use a humidifier to help relieve a dry, hacking cough. Keep the humidifier clean.

■ Gargle frequently with saltwater, a half-teaspoon in eight ounces of lukewarm water unless you have high blood pressure.

■ Don't use cough suppressant medicines for "moist" coughs. Such coughs actually help clear mucus from the body.

■ Those with high blood pressure should avoid over-the-counter cold remedies unless prescribed by their doctor.

■ Make yourself as comfortable as possible by resting and treat the symptoms of the cold with medication, but remember: "Treat a cold and it will last two weeks; don't treat a cold and you will be over it in fourteen days." There is some truth in that.

Americans spend $700 million a year on cold remedies. Not a single remedy (according to the FDA) will prevent, cure, or even shorten the course of the common cold.

Many people are convinced that taking large quantities of ascorbic acid (vitamin C) will prevent colds or relieve symptoms. To date, most studies do not show that large doses of vitamin C will prevent colds. There is some indication that the vitamin may reduce the severity or duration of symptoms, but conclusive evidence is still lacking.

Differences Between a Cold and the Flu

Symptoms	Cold	Flu
fever	rare	usually
headache	rare	usually
general aches & pains	slight	usually, severe
fatigue & weakness	quite mild	extreme
down in bed	seldom	prominent
runny, stuffy nose	common	sometimes
sneezing	usual	sometimes
sore throat	common	sometimes
chest discomfort, cough	mild to moderate	common, severe

Source: National Institute of Allergy and Infectious Diseases

A TALK ABOUT INFLUENZA

Influenza, usually called flu, is caused by a virus that spreads from one person to another in the spray from coughs and sneezes. The virus enters the upper part of the respiratory tract through the nose or mouth, and it may also invade the rest of the tract, including the lungs.

Flu can be fatal, particularly to those most vulnerable to its complications: infants, the elderly (even some without obvious underlying health problems), and people plagued with chronic heart and lung ailments.

At the end of World War I in 1918, "Spanish flu" infected one-fifth of the people in the world, killing more than 20 million, almost twice as many as perished in the war. A primitive vaccine proved useless as that outbreak and its milder 1919 variant attacked 28% of Americans and carried off 500,000, one-half of 1% of the U.S. population. No outbreak since has approached such dire proportions, yet influenza can still be deadly. Every year 10,000 to 20,000 Americans die from its complications, with up to 40,000 mortalities in years when new influenza strains appear.

We're not likely to see a return of the viral strain that caused the 1918 epidemic because influenza changes over time. As humans develop antibodies to fight the virus, its outer surface changes to elude resistance. To anticipate such changes, scientists the world over share information every year to predict what flu strains will emerge. Their prediction must be completed months in advance of flu season to allow time for a vaccine appropriate for the dominant strains to be perfected and mass produced. Their recommendations about who should be immunized deserve to be heeded.

Epidemics of influenza occur at unpredictable intervals. Sometimes there are as many as five or six successive winters without one, but at other times there are two or three epidemics in the same community in a single year. In a severe outbreak, most people in an affected area will have at least a mild attack of the disease.

Epidemics die out when everyone who has been infected by a particular strain or type of flu virus becomes immune to further attack by that strain. There are several strains of influenza virus, however, and new strains are constantly developing. These new viruses are often named according to their assumed place of origin. That is why you may hear about Hong Kong flu one year and Russian flu the next. Immunity from one strain does not protect you from other flu viruses, and immunity is only temporary.

SYMPTOMS OF INFLUENZA

After an incubation period of about two days there is a sudden onset of shivering, sometimes with a chill; headache; weakness and fatigue; aching in the muscles and joints; a sore throat; running nose; and a dry, painful cough. At the beginning of the illness there may also be vomiting and an aversion to light and noise. Initially, the body temperature may rise to about 104 degrees Fahrenheit, dropping to between 102 and 103 degrees for two or three days,

Flu shots--do you need one?

then settling at between 100 and 102 degrees. As the illness progresses, the cough may become less dry and painful because of the production of sputum. If no complications develop, the fever generally lasts for about five days. Recovery is usually rapid and with no relapse, although it may be accompanied by some weakness and depression. BEWARE: Seniors often don't (or can't) run high fevers.

COMPLICATIONS

Influenza lowers the body's resistance to infection. This makes the patient vulnerable to invasion by other organisms that may cause secondary infections, especially of the throat, sinuses, and ears, such as laryngitis, sinusitis, and otitis media. With such relatively minor complications, the original symptoms of influenza are intensified, and may be accompanied by bronchitis and a persistent cough. Pneumonia may also occur.

TREATMENT

Influenza should be treated as any other fever. The patient should go to bed in a warm, well-ventilated room as soon as symptoms appear, and should remain there until a complete recovery has been made. The patient should drink plenty of fluids, especially while there is a fever. Water tends to dilute mucus, making it easier to expel. Aspirin and other over-the-counter remedies that work best for you may help to relieve muscle and joint pains, and to reduce fever. A cool mist vaporizer may help soothe the inflamed linings of the respiratory tract. The patient should be isolated, both to prevent the spread of infection and to reduce the risk of secondary infections. A physician should be consulted especially if you have high blood pressure, asthma, diabetes, or any other chronic disease.

Amantadine can be given as an alternative to vaccination. It may also be useful in reducing the severity of the disease caused by the influenza A virus. Since amantadine is available only by prescription, your physician can judge when it is appropriate. If any complications develop, a physician should be consulted. Antibiotics are often prescribed, but these are of no value against influenza itself-- they may be useful for treating secondary infections.

HOW EFFECTIVE IS VACCINATION?

Vaccine is compounded from egg-grown, inactivated, highly purified particles of the two influenza A and one influenza B viruses expected to be most prevalent. People with severe egg allergies should not be vaccinated at all, but if you can eat eggs, you can take flu vaccine. Vaccine side effects can include soreness at the location of the injection, muscle aches, or fever. All, however, are less severe and don't last as long as the effects caused by the influenza infection itself.

Some people shy away from getting shots of any kind. Other people use arguments that flu vaccine is based on guesswork, that adverse reactions to the vaccine are common, or that the shots are only 70% effective anyway. There's no denying that this is a major, intramuscular injection (for adults generally administered through the deltoid muscle of the shoulder), and that some folks are simply afraid of needles. Still, the choice is between taking the vaccine or risking the flu. Lots of people will trump up any number of reasons to avoid the needle. My mother had a severe reaction to a flu shot. My wife found the same shot quite effective with no side effects. After reading everything we could find on the subject, we recommend the U.S. government health policy on controlling the spread of influenza among those groups most likely to suffer severely from its complications, including:

- Persons aged 65 or older
- Nursing-home or long-term-care residents with chronic medical conditions
- Anyone with chronic pulmonary or cardiovascular disorders
- Anyone who needed regular medical follow-up or hospitalization during the previous year for chronic metabolic diseases (including diabetes mellitus), kidney function problems, immunosuppression, or certain blood abnormalities known as hemoglobinopathies

> **It is especially important that people in the above high-risk groups be protected against the flu.**
>
> **They can be infected by contact with anyone carrying the influenza virus, even if the carrier has just a few mild symptoms, or even none at all.**

However, we must remember that flu shots are not 100% effective and on occasion there are some side effects. Some people should not be vaccinated: (1) those with strong egg allergies, (2) those with high fevers at the time the injection is to be given, and (3) anyone with a previous severe adverse reaction to influenza vaccine. The choice and risk is ours to make and take.

Influenza is a miserable experience. All things considered, for most people, the best bet for avoiding the flu remains yearly vaccination. Moreover, a highly immunized population is our country's best defense against a debilitating epidemic.

A free booklet called FLU is available from the National Institute of Allergy and Infectious Diseases, 9000 Rockville Pike, Bethesda, MD 20892, or call (301) 496-5717.

Too hot = Hyperthermia

Regardless of weather conditions, the healthy human body keeps a steady temperature of 98.6 degrees Fahrenheit. In hot weather, or during vigorous activity, the body perspires. As this perspiration evaporates from the skin, the body is cooled off. If the body endures long periods of intense heat it may lose its ability to respond efficiently. When this occurs, a person can experience hyperthermia and the body temperature goes to 100 degrees or more.

Hyperthermia (too hot) can take the form of heat exhaustion or heat stroke. Heat stroke is especially dangerous and requires immediate medical attention. A person with heat stroke has a body temperature above 104 degrees Fahrenheit. Other symptoms may include confusion, combativeness, bizarre behavior, faintness, staggering, strong rapid pulse, dry flushed skin, lack of sweating, possible delirium, or coma.

> **Heat stroke can be life-threatening. Victims of heat stroke almost always die so immediate medical attention is essential when the problem first begins. Many people die of heat stroke each year; most are over 50 years of age.**

FACTORS THAT INCREASE RISK OF HYPERTHERMIA
1. Poor circulation, inefficient sweat glands.
2. Heart, lung, and kidney diseases.
3. Any illness that causes general weakness or fever.
4. High blood pressure.
5. People on salt-restricted diets.
6. The inability to perspire, caused by medications including diuretics, sedatives, and tranquilizers.
7. Taking several drugs for various conditions.
8. Being substantially overweight or underweight.
9. Drinking alcoholic beverages.
10. Unbearably hot living quarters.
11. No fans or air conditioning.
12. Older people sometimes may not feel the heat and so they wear too much clothing.
13. Visiting hot overcrowded places.
14. Not understanding weather conditions.
15. Not drinking enough water to compensate for sweating.

PREVENTING HYPERTHERMIA
✳ Drink plenty of liquids, even if not thirsty.
✳ Dress in lightweight, light-colored, loose-fitting clothing.
✳ Avoid the mid-day heat and do not engage in vigorous activity during the hottest part of the day.
✳ Wear a hat or use an umbrella for shade.
✳ Use air conditioners or try to visit air-conditioned places such as shopping malls (even an electric fan will help).
✳ Get accustomed to heat slowly.
✳ Avoid hot, heavy meals. Do a minimum of cooking and use an oven only when necessary.
✳ Ask your physician whether or not you are at risk because of medication.

TREATMENT FOR HYPERTHERMIA
❶ Get the victim out of the sun and into a cool place--preferably one that is air-conditioned.
❷ Offer fluids but avoid alcohol and caffeine. Water and fruit and vegetable juices are best; so is Gatorade.
❸ Encourage the individual to shower or bathe, or sponge off with cool water.
❹ Urge the person to lie down and rest, preferably in a cool place.
❺ **Call a physician immediately, especially if there is sleepiness, confusion, or any other changes in mental status.**

Too cold = Hypothermia

Hypothermia is a condition marked by an abnormally low internal body temperature--below 96 degrees Fahrenheit. If body temperature does not drop below 90, chances for complete recovery are good. If temperature has fallen to between 80 and 90, most victims will recover, but some sort of lasting damage is likely. If the temperature goes under 80, most victims will not survive.

According to the National Institute on Aging, hypothermia may kill 25,000 people each year. The risk is five times greater for people over 75 than for younger population groups.

OTHER SIGNS TO CHECK FOR ARE
✔ Confusion, disorientation, or drowsiness.
✔ Slow or irregular heartbeat; slurred speech; shallow, very slow breathing.
✔ Weak pulse; low blood pressure.
✔ A change in appearance or behavior during cold weather.
✔ Uncontrollable shivering, lack of shivering, or stiff muscles.
✔ Low indoor temperatures and other signs that the victim has been in an unusually cold environment.
✔ Lack of coordination; sluggishness.

Older people are particularly at risk of hypothermia because their bodies have difficulty producing needed body heat. Some other factors are:
1. People who live in homes without adequate insulation risk getting accidental hypothermia when the weather is cold.
2. Those with low income and little savings are at risk because they often find it difficult to pay high heating bills.
3. It is important to dress warmly in cold weather. Keeping dry is also important.
4. An understanding of weather conditions may eliminate risk. Brisk winds will cause more rapid heat loss.
5. A person who lives alone and receives few visitors has a greater chance of lengthy exposure to the cold in case of an accident or illness.

Certain medical conditions place a person at risk of hypothermia because they interfere with the body's response to cold:
✳ Disorders of the body's hormone system, especially slow thyroid and diabetes.
✳ Conditions that cause paralysis or reduce awareness such as stroke or spinal cord injury.
✳ Illnesses that limit activity such as severe arthritis and Parkinson's disease.
✳ Any condition that severely impairs the normal constriction of blood vessels.
✳ Medications, such as chlorpromazine and related drugs, given to treat anxiety, depression, and nausea.
✳ Alcoholic beverages lower the body's ability to retain heat.
✳ An elderly person may often seem to be unaware of the cold. While others shiver and put on sweaters, an older individual may not shiver and may insist that he or she is comfortable.

TREATMENT FOR HYPOTHERMIA
❶ The most important step in treating hypothermia is to make the person warm and dry. Prevent further heat loss by wrapping the victim in a warm blanket.
❷ You can use your own body heat to help keep the victim warm. Lie close to the person, being careful not to handle him or her too roughly. Rubbing the person's limbs can worsen the condition.
❸ If you suspect that a person has hypothermia, take his or her temperature. If it is below 96 degrees Fahrenheit (35.5 degrees Centigrade), call a doctor or ambulance or take the victim directly to a hospital. **Hypothermia is a dangerous condition and requires emergency medical care.**

Our life and death struggle against 5 enemies of man

Yucky-Muck Germ

All infectious diseases derive from five major sources:

1. bacteria
2. viruses
3. parasites
4. rickettsiae organisms
5. fungi

These five take a terrific toll of life. In fact, the life expectancy of humans is no more than 30 years in countries where modern medical aid is not available.

> # The control of infectious diseases has allowed people to survive into middle and old age.

Certainly, our survival today is based largely on our ability to conquer and control these five enemies.

BACTERIA

Bacteria, commonly called "germs," exist almost everywhere on our planet. They are one-cell organisms, a form of plant life, that can be seen only through a microscope. Some of them can cause disease in humans.

Most bacteria coexist peacefully with mankind. For example, certain bacteria in the soil convert dead matter such as leaves into humus, or convert organic material into nitrates enriching the soil that is essential for plant growth. Some other bacteria take nitrogen from the air and convert it to nutrients usable by plants. Other helpful bacteria exist in human intestines, feeding on other organisms that might be harmful to us.

Bacteria are classified into three basic groups according to their shapes:

1. rod-shaped, called bacilli

2. spiral-shaped, called spirilla

3. dot-shaped, called cocci
   cocci in pairs--diplococci
   cocci in chains like a necklace--streptococci
   cocci in clusters like grapes--staphylococci

Most disease-producing bacteria, called "pathogenic," that invade the body produce toxic poisonous substances that cause disease. The body's defenses will fight back against the invaders by rushing leukocytes (white blood cells) and antitoxins to the area of infection.

Some of the leukocytes engulf the bacteria while the antitoxins neutralize the poisons. If they win the battle, we live; if not, we die. An infected place will often look red because of the extra supply of blood sent to that spot to fight infection.

Sneezy Germ

Among diseases caused by bacteria are staphylococci (staph) infection, streptococci (strep) throat infection, rheumatic fever, and scarlet fever. Pneumonia, meningitis, and gonorrhea are produced by different types of diplococci. Cholera and syphilis are caused by spirilla. Bacilli are responsible for many serious diseases such as diphtheria, tuberculosis, typhoid fever, tetanus, and plague. Antibiotics and sulfa drugs usually are effective against bacterial diseases.

VIRUSES

Viruses are smaller than bacteria and can only be seen with an electron microscope. They reproduce only in living cells. Viruses cause such diseases as the common cold, influenza, mumps, German measles (rubella), mononucleosis, chicken pox, polio, shingles, fever blisters and cold sores, warts, encephalitis (sleeping sickness), rabies (hydrophobia), and yellow fever.

Viruses can cause cancer in animals, but there is still no proof that they can cause cancer in man. A variety of medications have become available for specific viral diseases, and vaccines often are effective preventives. Poliomyelitis and several other diseases mentioned above are examples of viral diseases that are prevented by proper vaccines.

PARASITES

Parasites are any organism that lives at the expense of another (host) organism. Ectoparasites, such as lice, fleas, ticks, and mites, live on the outside of their hosts. Endoparasites, such as flukes and intestinal worms, live within their hosts. Some parasites carry, or themselves cause, diseases. *Entamoeba histolytica* is a species of amoeba that infects the intestine of human beings. It is the cause of amebic dysentery and amebic abscess.

Worms are primitive animals, many species of which cause parasitic infections. Worms are classified into three main groups: tapeworms (Cestoda); roundworms (Nematoda); and flatworms like flukes (Trematoda).

Let's take flukes as an example: They can cause various parasitic infections in human beings. The life cycle of a fluke is complex:

Icky-Sticky Germ

A small organism (miracidium) hatches from an egg, invades a snail, and develops there. When it changes into a small cystlike structure (cercaria), it is excreted by the snail and finds its home in plants, crabs, or fish. If human beings or animals drink water containing the cysts, flukes that evolve from the cysts invade the tissues and, in human beings, produce clinical symptoms of sickness. Flukes mate in the intestines of their hosts, and eggs excreted in the feces begin the life cycle again. Other parasites are similar.

RICKETTSIAE ORGANISMS

Rickettsiae organisms are small rod-shaped microorganisms found in tissue cells of lice, fleas, ticks, and mites, and are transmitted to humans by the bites of these parasites. They have characteristics of both bacteria and viruses. Rickettsia cause many diseases (like Typhus), which tend to be of sudden onset and produce various symptoms--usually the result of blockage of the blood vessels by the rickettsia.

For example, Rocky Mountain spotted fever is an infectious rickettsial disease caused by the microorganism that is transmitted by ticks. It develops after an incubation period of about a week. There is the sudden onset of a severe headache, muscle pains, and a high fever. Within four days, a rash appears on the arms and legs, and spreads rapidly to the rest of the body. Areas of the rash may coalesce and ulcerate. A dry, unproductive cough also may develop. In severe cases,

the patient becomes delirious or comatose. The fever lasts between two and three weeks. If untreated, various complications may develop, such as pneumonia, brain damage, and heart damage. Immediate treatment with antibiotics, such as tetracycline, usually produces a rapid improvement. Hospitalization may be necessary in severe cases. A vaccine against Rocky Mountain spotted fever is available, but it is necessary only for those who frequently encounter ticks. Prevention of rickettsia diseases depends upon controlling the rat and insect population.

FUNGI

Fungi are vegetable organisms present in soil, air, and water. Only a few species can cause diseases in people. Fungal disorders may be caused by microscopic fungi or their spores. Many of these disorders are difficult to treat because the fungi resist most bactericidal agents (although there are medications available for certain specific diseases).

Some examples of fungal diseases (mycoses) are:

❶ **Actinomycosis**--Fibrous masses about the mouth or tongue that burst and become sinuses or ulcers; also abscesses in the lungs.

❷ **Aspergillosis**--Lumps in the skin, ears, sinuses and, especially, the lungs.

❸ **Athlete's foot**--Skin eruptions on the foot, usually between the toes.

❹ **Blastomycosis**--Lesions all over the body but, especially, infection of the lungs.

❺ **Histoplasmosis**--Infection of the lungs, ulcers in the gastrointestinal tract, and skin lesions.

❻ **Madura foot**--Swollen feet with ulcers.
❼ **Moniliasis** (thrush)--White patches in-

side the mouth that later become shallow ulcers; may also occur in the vagina.

❽ **Ringworm**--Raised, round sores of the skin, scalp, or nails.

Fungal diseases rarely are fatal.

Immunizations and proper sanitary conditions can be effective in preventing and controlling the spread of many infectious diseases. The human immune system produces in the bone marrow millions of white cells that act like warriors in a disease-fighting army. There is no substitute for good food, exercise, and a healthy mental attitude to keep the body's immunization system in condition to fight its five mortal enemies.

When infectious diseases are brought under proper control, the life expectancy of persons all over the world may be increased, and people worldwide can live in better health.

Antibiotics work only for bacterial infections, and colds are caused by viruses. Yet many doctors prescribe antibiotics anyway. They reason that people laid low by viruses may be more likely to catch bacterial infections.

No one knows whether this approach really works. But using antibiotics for any length of time is definitely not smart. Antibiotics suppress the healthy bacterial population and chronic usage invites intestinal and vaginal problems.

Icky-Gooie Germs

The "Change of Life"

Menopause or "change of life" is the time in a woman's life when menstruation stops and the body no longer produces the monthly ovum or egg from which a baby could be formed. It usually occurs at about age 50, although it can occur as early as 45 or as late as 55. Menopause is usually considered finished when a woman has not menstruated for a year. Completion of menopause marks the end of the childbearing years.

Menopause is natural and takes place smoothly for most women. It is part of a gradual process sometimes called the climacteric, which begins about 5 years before menopause and may last about 10 years. During the climacteric a woman's body produces decreasing amounts of the hormones estrogen and progesterone. This reduction in hormone production causes menstrual periods to stop.

The menstrual periods may stop suddenly or become irregular, with a lighter or heavier flow and with longer intervals between periods, until they eventually stop. About 80% of women experience mild or no signs of menopause; the other 20% report symptoms severe enough to seek medical attention.

Two signs associated with menopause are hot flashes (which are often accompanied by sweating) and vaginal dryness. The fatigue, heart palpitations, or depression reported by some women during this time may be symptoms of menopause in some cases, but there is wide disagreement about this.

There is no specific mental disorder associated with menopause, and research shows that women experience no more depression during these years than at other times during life. Tension or depression can occur at any stage, but when these states occur during menopause, there is a tendency to blame the menopause process.

Most women have a healthy outlook throughout the menopause process and afterward feel "in their prime," glad to no longer be menstruating.

CHANGES: With age the walls of the vagina become thinner, less elastic, and drier. The vagina is then more vulnerable to infection. Also, these changes sometimes result in uncomfortable or painful sexual intercourse, although continuing regular sexual activity will reduce the possibility of problems developing.

As body tissues change with age some women experience urinary stress incontinence, which is the loss of a small quantity of urine when exercising, coughing, laughing, or performing other movements that put pressure on the bladder. Lack of physical exercise may also contribute to the condition. While incontinence can be embarrassing, it is common and treatable--for example, certain exercises can strengthen the affected muscles or sometimes surgery is performed to cure it.

Some women are prone to urinary tract infections. These tend to recur but are easily treated with antibiotics or other measures. Preventive techniques include urinating after intercourse, not keeping the bladder over-full for long periods, drinking adequate amounts of fluids, and keeping the genital area very clean. It is important to see a doctor as soon as any symptoms appear, such as painful or frequent urination (see Women's Urinary Tract Infections, page 432).

> We must all obey the great law of change.
> It is the most powerful law of nature.
>
> - Burke (1729-1797)

POSTMENOPAUSAL OSTEOPOROSIS is closely associated with menopause since it is caused in part by the decrease in estrogen that occurs with menopause. It is a major cause of bone fractures in older women. In women with this condition bone mass slowly decreases over the years to produce thinner, more porous bone. Osteoporotic bone is weaker than normal bone and fractures more easily. Common sites for fractures are the spine, wrists, forearms, and hips. The risk of osteoporosis is highest in white women after menopause--particularly in individuals who have an early or surgical menopause (see osteoporosis, page 320).

DOES MENOPAUSE NEED TREATMENT?: Menopause is a natural part of aging and does not necessarily require treatment. However, some women experience great discomfort at this time, and there is some help.

1 Estrogen Replacement Therapy (ERT) is used for hot flashes, vaginal changes, and to prevent osteoporosis. Estrogen has side effects with some women (see estrogen, page 322).

2 Several drugs are available to reduce hot flashes or to relieve other menopausal symptoms for women who cannot use estrogen.

3 Vitamins may be successful in reducing hot flashes or stress. Large doses of some vitamins can have serious side effects. Vitamins depend on one another to be utilized in the body, so taking one without its counterparts may be useless.

4 Tranquilizers are sometimes prescribed particularly for women who are tense, irritable, or nervous, but they are not recommended for symptoms specifically related to menopause. Tranquilizers, like other drugs, can have side effects and should be used with care.

5 Improved diet, exercise, and relaxation techniques have been effective.

6 Developing positive attitudes toward menopause and aging is an important part of adjusting to life changes.

7 Supportive friends and satisfying activities help ease any transition or crisis. Various types of support groups exist that can provide opportunities for women to talk to others who are going through similar experiences.

SEXUALITY AND MENOPAUSE: An active and fulfilling sex life can continue throughout menopause. While some physical responses slow with age, the capacity and need for sexual expression continues into old age. Some women report that sex is even more enjoyable after menopause, possibly because pregnancy is no longer a concern and there is more time and privacy when children are gone from home.

Physical changes do take place during menopause that occasionally cause sexual problems. As the body grows older the walls of the vagina become smooth, drier, and less elastic. This may cause tiny sores on the vaginal wall, a burning or itching sensation, and intercourse may be uncomfortable. These physical changes can be treated successfully through a number of methods including vaginal lubricants and, to those who can tolerate it, estrogen creams.

LOOKING TO THE FUTURE: More and more older women are moving in positive, new directions and assuming new roles in society. It is common to find mid-life and older women in college classes, professional schools, and other types of educational programs. Women are training for and holding jobs in many areas once reserved for men. Older women are now beginning to receive the love, respect, and equality that they have always richly deserved.

A hysterectomy is the surgical removal of a woman's uterus. Each year 650,000 American women undergo a hysterectomy; one-fourth of these women are over the age of 50. About 50% of the women have their ovaries removed at the same time, even if the ovaries are not diseased.

The removal of the uterus may be necessary in cases of cancer of the cervix, uterus, or ovaries, uncontrollable bleeding, tumors, or severe infection. In most other cases, surgery should be avoided if possible. It never hurts to get a second opinion when surgery is suggested (see page 253). Any surgical procedure carries risks, so be sure you need it.

Many people believe the only function of a woman's uterus is to nurture unborn children and that ovaries become useless at menopause. Research, however, indicates that the uterus may help maintain cardiovascular health by secreting prostacyclin, a substance that helps regulate blood pressure. It also may play an important role in the enjoyment of sex. During intercourse, you may derive pleasure from stimulation of the cervix; and during orgasm, the muscles of the uterus contract along with those of the vagina.

Ovaries, too, play an important role even after the childbearing years. They produce estrogens for many years after menopause. They also secrete androgens, some of which are converted into estrogens, some of which are useful as is, and all of which help preserve the health of your bones, heart, blood vessels, and skin.

SOME CONDITIONS THAT MAY NECESSITATE HYSTERECTOMY

- **Uterine prolapse.** In prolapse, the muscles and ligaments that support the uterus relax and allow it to slide downward in the pelvis. In severe prolapse, the uterus actually hangs out of the vagina. You can do Kegel exercises to strengthen the muscles supporting the uterus; you can try a pessary, a device that holds the uterus in place; or surgery can be performed to reposition the uterus. If the above are unsuccessful, hysterectomy is necessary.

- **Fibroids.** Fibroids are tumors of the muscle wall of the uterus. They are rarely cancerous but sometimes cause heavy bleeding. Fibroids usually shrink after you reach menopause, unless you're taking estrogen. Taking progesterone will often control the bleeding. If that doesn't work, myomectomy--the surgical removal of fibroids that leaves the uterus intact--may be an alternative to a hysterectomy.

- **Endometrial hyperplasia.** The endometrium is the lining of the uterus; endometrial hyperplasia is an overgrowth of that lining. It is usually caused by estrogen that is not sufficiently balanced by progesterone. Many hyperplasias don't need any treatment except close follow-up. They reverse spontaneously, sometimes following a diagnostic D & C (dilation and curettage).

- **Abnormal uterine bleeding.** Irregular, heavy, or constant bleeding from the uterus is a symptom, not a disease. It can be caused by cancer, fibroids or other growths, hyperplasia, hormone imbalances, or unknown causes. Even if no cause can be found, hormone therapy is sometimes helpful. If not, a new laser procedure, endometrial ablation surgery, may work by burning away the lining where the bleeding occurs.

- **Carcinoma in-situ.** Despite its frightening name, this is not truly cancer. Cells of the outermost layer of the cervix have characteristics of invasive cancer cells but haven't grown beyond the surface of the cervix or spread elsewhere in the body. The condition can be treated by removing all the abnormal cells with traditional cryosurgery or laser surgery.

Dr. Walter C. Willett of the Harvard School of Public Health released the results of the largest study ever to examine the effects of birth control pills. The study offers reassuring evidence that older women who did not first take the pill until the age of 25 face no unusual risk of breast cancer.

Past use of oral contraceptives does not appear to increase the risk of breast cancer for women in the mid-40s and 50s. While the research is good news for older women, it does not dispel worries that younger women who took the pill throughout their teens and early 20s may have an increased risk of breast cancer.

Dr. Samuel Shapiro of Boston University's Sloan Epidemiology Unit found in studying younger pill users who took oral contraceptives for 10 years or more that the risk of breast cancer was increased four times. Other studies verify these results.

The amount and ratio of sex hormones in birth control pills have changed since their introduction in the early 1960s, and this might make the pill less hazardous today.

Breast cancer follows lung cancer as the leading cancer killer of American women. The American Cancer Society estimates it will cause 43,300 deaths this year.

THE PAP TEST--is a simple, painless test developed by and named after Dr. George Papanicolaou. During a regular pelvic exam, a sample of cells is collected from the cervix using a Pap sampling stick. Cells are then smeared onto one or more slides and sent to a clinical laboratory for microscopic evaluation.

The test is an invaluable tool used to detect cervical dysplasia-- cell abnormalities that can lead to cervical cancer. This detection usually occurs before visible symptoms, such as bleeding or discharge, are present. Vaginal infections and some sexually transmitted diseases are also detected by the Pap test.

Cervical cancers are the third leading cause of cancer among women in the United States. Fifty thousand women will develop an early form of cervical cancer each year. Thirteen thousand will develop invasive cervical cancer--the kind that spreads to other organs. Six thousand women will die from cervical cancer. Many of these deaths can be prevented by proper testing.

If it is detected in its earliest, preinvasive stages, cancer of the cervix is nearly 100% curable. The Pap test is the most reliable way to determine whether cancerous or precancerous conditions exist. Precancerous lesions of the cervix, if discovered early and treated aggressively, can prevent cervical cancer.

Regular and complete gynecological exams are essential for good health. An annual Pap test is important because some cervical cancers develop rapidly. The results of a Pap test can be positive, negative, or indeterminate. In recent years some women have lost confidence in the Pap test due to reports of inaccurate results; but recently Congress has passed some laws to enhance quality assurance standards, which should help improve testing throughout the country.

> The Pap test is the most effective means of early diagnosis of cervical cancer or precancer for women of every age. Make a Pap test part of your annual healthcare routine. Call your doctor today for an appointment if you have not had your yearly Pap test.

Symptoms, causes, and treatment

Urinary tract infections are probably the most common infections that women have other than the common cold. In women, the urethra is very short, and that makes infections easy to get. An infection involving the urethra is called urethritis. If the bladder is involved it is called cystitis, and if the kidneys are involved, it is called nephritis or pyelonephritis.

SYMPTOMS--About 20% of women experience symptoms from urinary tract infections each year. Symptoms are:

❑ The bladder is irritated and there is a frequent urge to urinate.
❑ The act of urination may be painful or difficult.
❑ The urine may have a strong odor, or it may be cloudy, and in some cases have a tinge of blood in it.
❑ Fever is common, but may not be present.
❑ There may be tenderness in the back, over the lower ribs, or in the side of the abdomen.
❑ There is pain during sexual intercourse.

You cannot tell from the symptoms alone whether a woman has urethritis, cystitis, nephritis, or pyelonephritis. It is also important to realize that other conditions, like kidney stones and bladder tumors, will cause many of these same symptoms. Many women with urinary tract infections may have no symptoms. Sometimes without treatment, the urinary tract may clear spontaneously. It should be remembered that normal urine is a sterile solution. It is nothing more than a solution filtered from the blood itself. Since blood is free of bacteria, it follows that urine is free from bacteria, unless an infection is present.

CAUSES OF INFECTION
■ Migration of bacteria into the urethra and the bladder from the vagina.
■ Any mechanical factor that irritates the bladder or the urethra may contribute to the development of a bacterial infection. This includes the use of contraceptive diaphragms, pessaries, or in some instances, a long retention of a tampon.
■ A woman who has not been sexually active and then becomes involved in frequent sexual intercourse may have trauma of the lower bladder.
■ Putting a catheter into the bladder to

drain it results in a high incidence of urinary tract infections. Also mechanical instrumentation to look into the bladder (cystoscopy) can introduce bacteria into the system and cause an infection.
■ Both gonorrhea and chlamydia infections involve the urethra and may cause urinary tract symptoms.
■ The most common bacteria to cause urinary tract infections is *Escherichia coli*, the normal inhabitant of the colon.

WHAT CAN YOU DO?
❑ Maintain good hygiene. Poor hygiene is probably the most common cause of cystitis in women. It is important to keep the area near the urethra as clean as possible, particularly to avoid fecal contamination of the area. Always wipe front to rear.

❑ Drink lots of fluids and make it a habit to urinate frequently. Even if there is no urge, a regular schedule of emptying the bladder is advisable.

❑ Do not wear tight pants or tight underwear (avoid panty girdles). Tight clothing may rub against the urethral area and contact the urethral opening. Because of the short length of the urethra, the bacteria then gain access to the bladder. It is better to wear loose-fitting cotton underwear and avoid synthetics.

❑ Avoid tub baths if you are subject to urinary tract infection. During a tub bath, it is very easy for bacteria to enter the urethra and ascend into the bladder. Also sitting around in a wet bathing suit for long periods of time is not a good idea.

❑ Keep urine slightly acid. That is where cranberry juice has a role. Citrus fruits or taking vitamin C don't help as they don't actually raise the pH, making the urine more basic and less acidic.

❑ The wall between the vaginal vault and the back of the bladder is rather thin, and vigorous thrusting during sex can irritate the bladder. Some changes in sexual technique may help. Make sure there is sufficient lubrication during intercourse (use a lubricant if you have to--

not vaseline, but KY jelly). Also, it is generally agreed that a woman can decrease her risk of urinary tract infections by urinating immediately after intercourse.

MEDICAL TREATMENT--Once an infection has occurred, medical treatment is the best approach. Call your doctor at the first signs of an infection or discomfort. If left untreated it will only get worse--infections cause fevers, etc.--you could get really sick.

Some urinary tract infections can be effectively treated with a single dose of antibiotics. If a kidney is also involved, treatment may be as short as 7 or as long as 14 days. It is important to take all the antibiotics even though your symptoms may have disappeared. Always take every last pill--taking antibiotics on your own discretion could be dangerous to your health.

Follow your doctor's orders to the letter. A follow-up culture may be necessary to be sure the infection is gone.

Recurrent urinary tract infections are more difficult to treat. If a woman has two or more documented urinary tract infections in six months, she may need maintenance therapy for six months. Many older women are particularly susceptible to recurrent urinary tract infections. Hormone replacement that restores the normal acidity of the vagina and improves the cell lining of the urethra and outlet of the bladder is often very helpful.

When medical treatment does not control recurrent infections, or an infection persists in spite of treatment, then most physicians recommend an X-ray or cystoscopic study of the urinary tract.

Despite the discomfort they cause, most urinary tract infections are uncomplicated problems that do respond to proper personal hygiene and medical management. Complications may result if one is diabetic, obese, or has internal anatomical problems such as dropped bladder, narrow urethra, torn urethra (as a result of giving birth), or a prolapsed uterus.

> **It is important to treat urinary tract infections promptly, before bacteria has a chance to travel upward, causing kidney infection.**

YEAST

INFECTIONS

One of the common complaints that sends women to doctors is vaginitis--irritation and inflammation of the vagina. The main symptoms are vaginal discharge, often accompanied by vaginal soreness, and a burning feeling, especially when urinating and having intercourse. Many women also experience an unbearable itch in the vulva.

Vulvar itch has many contributing factors such as diabetes, leukemia, skin diseases, allergies, pubic lice, ringworm, scabies, and irritation due to contraceptive devices, obesity, clothing, or dyes. However, when vaginal discharge, pain, and itching occur together, in most cases, the diagnosis will be vaginitis, caused by infection with the microorganisms *Trichomonas vaginalis, Candida albicans,* or *Gardnerella vaginalis.*

1 Trichomonas vaginalis is a protozoan (one-cell organism) responsible for about 3 million cases of vaginal infection each year. It can cause itching, pain, and a watery, bubbly, greenish or yellowish discharge, sometimes with an odor. It can also produce no symptoms at all, and can only be identified by a doctor during a routine gynecological exam or on the Pap smear. This form of vaginitis is known as trichomoniasis.

Trichomoniasis can be sexually transmitted. For some reason, trichomoniasis is more common among heavy smokers. In women who are very active sexually, it is often paired with gonorrhea. The body never builds up protective antibodies against trichomoniasis, so it's easy to get one infection after another.

Metronidazole taken by mouth is an effective medication. But women who are pregnant should not take it. Metronidazole has been found to cause cancer in rats. Doctors advocate treating the sex partners of women who have trichomoniasis even when the males show no symptoms. Alcohol cannot be consumed when taking metronidazole (Flaggl).

2 Candida albicans, a yeast-like fungus that likes to grow in warm, moist places, causes a vaginitis known specifically as candidiasis, though most women are more familiar with the term yeast infection.

The symptoms are similar to those of trichomoniasis. First comes an itch, which can be maddening, followed by painful urination, soreness of the vulva, and irritation. The vagina may become bright red rather than its normal pink. A yeast infection can be caused by taking antibiotics, which kill off the "good bacteria" that control yeast naturally as well as the bad. If a doctor prescribes an antibiotic for you, ask if there is a chance that it will cause a yeast infection. If it can, you can start taking a preventive treatment while taking the antibiotic. There may be a discharge, usually a white, creamy, or curd-like substance with no odor. But a yeast infection can be cleared up with proper medication in about a week.

Many women have occasional attacks of vaginal candidiasis that respond well to medication. Some women, however, get yeast infections regularly no matter what. These women are often driven to desperate measures that include douching with yogurt or following diets low in refined sugars and fruits, which are thought to aid the growth of fungi. While this practice does no harm, there is no evidence that it does much good, either. In a recent conference on diseases of the vulva and vagina given at the Baylor College of Medicine, some doctors agreed that chronic, recurrent candidiasis may be due to transient immune deficiency. Miconazole or clotrimazole in creams applied topically to the vulva and in vaginal suppositories are effective against the fungus.

A woman's sex partner should be treated when he has a moist, white scaling rash on his penis or an itch or inflammation under his foreskin, or when the woman continually has yeast infections.

3 Gardnerella vaginitis is usually suspected when trichomoniasis and candidiasis have been ruled out. The symptoms are a heavy clear to grayish discharge with a fishy odor and a milk-like consistency. The discharge coats the vagina, but the tissues are not inflamed.

This is yet one more disease that men seem to transmit without showing any symptoms of it themselves. Symptomless males should be treated if they continually reinfect their female partners. Like other forms of vaginitis, Gardnerella can also occur without sexual contact.

Metronidazole may be effective in treating Gardnerella. Ampicillin, an antibiotic, may also be effective and is prescribed for pregnant women who cannot use metronidazole.

When estrogen levels are low, as in postmenopausal women, the lining of the vagina becomes thin and dry and can become infected with bacteria that normally would not affect a vagina with an adequate estrogen supply. **Older women who have the usual symptoms of vaginitis plus a bloody discharge should check with their doctors to rule out other causative factors.** Often, all that is needed is the topical application of an estrogen-containing cream, or estrogen taken by mouth.

Vaginitis can also be caused by allergies to vaginal sprays, bubble baths, and deodorants. Discontinuing their use will usually clear up the irritation. **When symptoms of vaginitis--itching, irritation, and abnormal discharge--persist for more than two days, it is wise to seek medical help.** If yeast infections are allowed to continue too long untreated, swelling and discomfort can actually interfere with walking and urinating.

PREVENTING YEAST INFECTIONS

* Discontinue use of tampons while under treatment. Also, since underwear and pantyhose made from synthetic fibers often increase heat and moisture in the vulval area, switch to cotton underwear and pantyhose with cotton crotches if you are prone to frequent infections. For the same reason, don't wear skin-tight pants.

* Avoid sexual intercourse while undergoing treatment. Have your sex partner checked by the doctor if you get repeated infections. He may need too be treated, too!

* Practice good feminine hygiene. Wash the vulval and anal areas with mild soap and water at least once daily, and after each bowel movement, if possible. Always wipe from front to back, away from the vagina. The bowels harbor bacteria and fungi that can travel to the vulval area.

* Don't douche unless the doctor says to. By disturbing the normal acidity of vaginal secretions, douching may create more problems than it cures.

* Make it a rule that anything that goes into the vagina--pessaries, diaphragms, and other contraceptive devices, for example--should be scrupulously clean.

* Take the medication for as long as the doctor prescribes. Some women stop the medication when they feel better, but that's an invitation to recurrent infections.

foreign travel advisories, 194
glasses, extra, 203
glossary, 196-97
grandparent-grandchild, 71
health insurance, 203
home security, 178
illness after returning home, 203
jet lag, 202
luggage, 195, 207, 208
medical alert bracelet, 202
medical help during, 203
medical precautions, 202, 203
medicine kit, 202
money, 201
motion sickness, 204
package tours, 194, 196, 198
packing, 195
passports, 194
with pets, 198-99
photographic equipment, 195
preparations for foreign, 194-95
prescription drugs, 202
proof of citizenship, 195
security, 205, 209
sexually transmitted diseases, 203
shopping, 205
sight-seeing tips, 205
sunburn, 203
sunglasses, 203
telephoning, 205
theft, precautions against, 205
tipping, 205
tourist card, 195
train, 212
traveler's diarrhea, 204
visas, 194
Traveler's Bookstore, 194
Traveler's checks, 201
Traveler's diarrhea, 204
Treasury bills (T-bills), 65
Trifocals, 415
Trigeminal neuralgia, 396
Triglycerides, 119, 312
Trimethoprim, 329
Trusts, 113-14
Medicaid, 101
revocable living, 113-14
Totten, 225-26
Truth in Lending Act, 189
"Tummy tuck," 380
Tylenol, 383
Tympanometry, 386

U

Ulcerative colitis, 304
Ulcers, 328
peptic, 303
Ultimate concerns, 223-31
U. S. Government securities, 65
U. S. House of Representatives Select
Committee on Aging, 1
United Way, 165
Unordered merchandise scams, 154

Unwed Parents Anonymous, 67
Urethra, 329
Urethritis, 329
Urinary system, 329
Urinary tract infections, 329, 432
menopause and, 430
self-testing, 251
Uterine cancer, 293-94, 298
Uterine prolapse, 431

V

Vacations, See also Travel
fraudulent real estate deals, 151
Vaginal changes during menopause, 430
Varicose veins, 330
Vasodilators, 336
Vegetables, 117
Veins, varicose, 330
Venereal disease, See Sexually
transmitted diseases
Venom as arthritis cure, 286-87
Very low-density lipoproteins, 126
Veterans Administration death benefits,
226-27
Viruses, 428
immune system's handling of, 316
Visas, travel, 194
Vision, See Eyesight
Visitation rights of grandparents, 70
Visiting
nursing home, 90-91
senior citizens, 269
sick and dying, 270-71
Visualization, 358, 361
Vital Connections--The Grandparenting
Newsletter, 67
Vitamin D, 121, 123
Vitamins, 117, 120-21
aging and, 261
arthritis and, 286
cholesterol-lowering, 138
food sources, 121
menopausal symptoms and, 430
U.S. Recommended Daily
Allowances, 120-21
Voluntary Income Tax Assistance, 62
Volunteerism, 55, 239
code of responsibility, 163
legislation supporting, 162
reasons for, 162
suggestions, 162-67
Volunteers in Service to America, 164
Vomiting, 270, 423

W

Walking, 142, 143
Water, 117, 126, 374
as arthritis treatment, 287
Wax blockage of the ear, 384
Weight
aging and, 261, 262

average, 137
instant weight loss schemes, 156
loss of, as symptom, 423
Whirlpool, 397
White, Dr. Paul Dudley, 311
Widowed Persons Service, 19, 235, 239,
243, 247
Widowhood, 232-43, See also Funerals
business matters, 235
funeral arrangements, 234-35
grief, dealing with, 232-34
loneliness, dealing with, 233, 237-38
men's needs, 238-39
self-help groups, 243
sexuality, 234
staying healthy, 234
suggestions, 235
time of acceptance, 233
Widowed Persons Service, 19, 235,
239, 243
women living alone, 240-42
Wife abuse, 180, 184-85
Wills, 112
living, 110-11
Women
birth control pills and cancer, 431
cancer in, 294-95
hysterectomy, 400, 431
living alone, 240-42
menopause, See Menopause
osteoporosis and, See Osteoporosis
urinary tract infections, 430, 432
widowhood, See Widowhood
yeast infections, 433
Wood stoves, 179
Working, 267
age discrimination law, 54
alternatives if you have to work, 55
creative retirement, 160
decision to retire or continue, 55
longevity and, 264
problems of older women, 240-41
selecting type of work, 55
Social Security and earned income,
55
volunteering, 55
work-at-home scams, 154
Wrinkles, 373-74
collagen injections, 380
Retin-A for, 156
Writing
learning to write, 174-75
to representatives, 172

Y

Yeast infections, 433
Young Grandparents Club, 68

Z

Zantac, 328
Zinc, 122